Houghton Mifflin Unified Mathematics, Book 3

Comprehensive content coverage shows the interrelationship of logic, algebra, geometry, probability, and statistics with special attention to problem solving skills and concepts. (Table of Contents, pp. iii–vii)

Special end-of-chapter features include an enrichment page, Vocabulary Review, and Mixed Review Exercises. These pages accompany Computer Exercises, Chapter Review, Chapter Test, and periodic Cumulative Review pages. (pp. 159–167, 338–343)

The **Preparing for Regents Examinations** appendix helps students prepare for the exams and includes topic checklists and sample exam questions. (pp. 663–676)

Algebra Review Exercises and **Extra Practice** appendices contain additional exercises on algebra and other important topics. (pp. 645–651, 630–644)

Applications of the computer to lesson concepts can be found at the end of each chapter in **Computer Exercises** and in the new **Programming in BASIC** appendix. (pp. 36–38, 500–502, 652–662)

The **Summary of Transformations** appendix includes new exercises in addition to the summary proper.

Appendix 1: Using a Graphing Calculator includes a general discussion of some of the important features of graphing calculators, followed by exploratory activities suitable for a graphing calculator and keyed to the student textbook.

Supplementary materials include a **Teacher's Manual with Solutions** and a **Resource Book** that contains permission-to-copy blackline master pages of tests (quizzes, chapter tests, and cumulative tests), practice exercises, enrichment activities, and diagrams.

Houghton Mifflin

Book **3**

Unified Mathematics

COORDINATING AUTHOR

Gerald R. Rising

John A. Graham
John G. Balzano
Janet M. Burt
Alice M. King

HOUGHTON MIFFLIN COMPANY / BOSTON
Atlanta   Dallas   Geneva, Ill.   Palo Alto   Princeton   Toronto

AUTHORS

Coordinating Author

Gerald R. Rising, Professor, Department of Instruction
State University of New York at Buffalo, Buffalo, N.Y.

John A. Graham, Mathematics Teacher
Buckingham Browne and Nichols School, Cambridge, Mass.

John G. Balzano, Mathematics Department Leader
Martha Brown Junior High School, Fairport, N.Y.

Janet M. Burt, Mathematics Department Chairman
Clinton Central School, Clinton, N.Y.

Alice M. King, Director of Entry Level Mathematics Project
California State Polytechnic University, Pomona, Cal.

EDITORIAL ADVISERS

Andrew M. Gleason, Hollis Professor of Mathematics and Natural Philosophy
Harvard University, Cambridge, Mass.

Nicholas J. Sterling, Associate Professor of Mathematics
State University of New York at Binghamton, Binghamton, N.Y.

TEACHER CONSULTANTS

James Burke, Sayville High School, Sayville, N.Y.

Valerie A. Elswick, Roy C. Ketcham Senior High School, Wappingers Falls, N.Y.

John G. Marmillo, Roy C. Ketcham Senior High School, Wappingers Falls, N.Y.

Oystein Ostebo, East High School, Corning, N.Y.

Printed in U.S.A.

ISBN: 0-395-55069-6

ABCDEFGHIJ-D-99876543210

Table of Contents

7   INTRODUCTION TO TRIGONOMETRY

8   TRIGONOMETRIC FUNCTIONS, IDENTITIES, AND EQUATIONS

9   EXPONENTS AND LOGARITHMS

10   TRIANGLE TRIGONOMETRY

11   TRIGONOMETRIC FORMULAS AND INVERSE FUNCTIONS

12   PROBABILITY

ACKNOWLEDGMENTS

Cover concept by Richard Hannus
Biographical portraits by Gary Torrisi (pages 41, 129, 217, 341, and 425)

Photographs
page x: © Jon Wrice 1975 / PHOTO RESEARCHERS
page 44:   © Gordon S. Smith / PHOTO RESEARCHERS
page 89:   © Lou Jones 1982
page 92:   Barbara Marshall
page 132: © Peter Gerba / JEROBOAM, INC.
page 165: Rick Browne / TIME MAGAZINE
page 168: © Clem Haagner / PHOTO RESEARCHERS
page 220: Barbara Marshall
page 271: Bill Gallery / STOCK BOSTON
page 274: Leonard Lee Rule III / THE IMAGE BANK
page 311: courtesy of The Boeing Corporation
page 314: Christopher S. Johnson / STOCK BOSTON
page 388: © Johnnie Walker / THE PICTURE CUBE
page 428: Barbara Marshall
page 474: Jonathan Goell / THE PICTURE CUBE
page 516: Marion Bernstein
page 553: © Freda Leinwand / Monkmeyer Press Photo Service
page 556: Ken Yuszkus / TAURUS PHOTOS
page 589: Cary Wolinsky / STOCK BOSTON
page 592: Barbara Marshall

SYMBOLS

$\{1; 2\}$	the set containing 1 and 2	p. 2	$\approx$	equals approximately	p. 221
$\cup$	the union of	p. 2	$\overleftrightarrow{UO}$	line UO	p. 222
Z	the set of integers	p. 2	$\overrightarrow{TR}$	ray TR	p. 222
$\in$	is an element of, or member of	p. 2	$\overparen{PQ}$	arc PQ	p. 223
$0.1\overline{6}$	bar indicates repetend	p. 3	$m\,\overparen{AB}$	measure of $\overparen{AB}$	p. 224
$\mathcal{R}$	the set of real numbers	p. 4	$\perp$	is perpendicular to	p. 232
$\emptyset$	the null, or empty, set	p. 11	$\parallel$	is parallel to	p. 237
$\angle$	angle	p. 20	$1°2'3''$	1 degree, 2 minutes, 3 seconds	p. 289
$\triangle$	triangle	p. 20	$\log_b x$	the logarithm of x to the base b	p. 353
$\cap$	the intersection of	p. 25			
$\overline{AC}$	line segment AC	p. 29	e	approximately 2.718; the base of natural logarithms	p. 376
$\|x\|$	the absolute value of x	p. 32			
$\sim$	is similar to	p. 79	$\ln x$	$\log x$, or the natural logarithm of x	p. 376
$\cong$	is congruent to	p. 79			
i	imaginary unit ($\sqrt{-1}$)	p. 105	$\vec{u}$	the vector u	p. 416
$\longrightarrow$	maps onto	p. 134	$\|\vec{w}\|$	magnitude of vector $\vec{w}$	p. 416
$f(x)$	"f of x"; the image of the number x under the function f	p. 142	N	the metric unit Newton	p. 418
$h \circ g$	"h following g"; composite function	p. 150	$P(E)$	the probability of an event E	p. 477
f^{-1}	inverse of function f	p. 154	A'	the complement of A	p. 478
A'	"A prime"; the image of point A under a transformation	p. 170	$P(B\|A)$	the probability of B given A	p. 486
A''	"A double prime"; the image of point A'	p. 170	$n!$	n factorial	p. 493
I	the identity transformation	p. 172	$_nP_r$	the number of permutations of n things taken r at a time	p. 494
r_l	reflection over line l	p. 175	$_nC_r$ or $\binom{n}{r}$	"n choose r"; the number of combinations of n things taken r at a time	p. 494, p. 504
$T_{a, b}$	translation of a horizontal units and b vertical units	p. 193			
$R_{P, \theta}$	rotation with center P through θ degrees	p. 198	$\displaystyle\sum_{i=1}^{n} x_i$	the sum of x_i for $i = 1$ to n	p. 523
$\odot$	circle	p. 200			
$D_{C, k}$	dilation with center C and scale factor k	p. 209	$\overline{x}$	the mean	p. 527

Greek letters: $\alpha, \beta, \theta, \pi$ alpha, beta, theta, pi

The ability to solve verbal problems is an important mathematical skill. Organizing the data in a problem in a chart is often an effective problem-solving strategy. This strategy is particularly useful with uniform motion problems, such as Exercise 34, page 21, concerning cyclists in an endurance race.

The Real Numbers 1

For over 2000 years, mathematicians have been refining mathematical notation. One of the most important developments was the creation of *positional notation*, which enabled mathematicians to express integers in a concise, workable form. Positional notation was first used by the Babylonians. It was later incorporated into the Hindu-Arabic system, which was fully developed by the seventh century and which became the basis for the decimal notation we use today.

In positional notation, the relative position of a numerical symbol determines its value. Positional notation differs fundamentally from, say, the notation used in writing Roman numerals. Consider the number 21. Using Roman numerals, 21 is written:

XXI

Each X has a value of 10 units, even though one X is in the leftmost position and the other is in the middle position. In Arabic notation, on the other hand, the "2" in the numeral 21 stands for 20 units, not 2 units, because it is in the tens' position, not the units' position.

Positional notation also provided the means for expressing a fraction as a decimal. Thus, the fraction $\frac{3}{4}$ could be expressed in positional notation as 0.75. In 1585, Simon Stevin, a Dutch scientist, wrote a set of rules for decimal fractions describing their use in arithmetic operations. It was not until the beginning of the eighteenth century, however, that the concept of a decimal point was universally adopted. Even today, what is written as 0.75 in the United States is written as 0·75 in England and as 0,75 in Germany and France.

Section 1-1 THE REAL NUMBER SYSTEM

Throughout your earlier courses you have worked exclusively with the set of real numbers and its subsets. In Chapter 3 of this book you will be introduced to the set of *complex numbers*, of which the real numbers are themselves a subset. But first you will review in this section:
- some subsets of the set of real numbers
- equivalent forms of real numbers

The first set of numbers that you used long ago was the set of *natural numbers* (or *counting numbers*), often denoted by N:

$$N = \{1, 2, 3, \ldots\}$$

Then the usefulness and importance of the number 0 led you to use the larger set, the *whole numbers*, denoted by W:

$$W = N \cup \{0\} \quad \text{or} \quad W = \{0, 1, 2, 3, \ldots\}$$

If a and b are any whole numbers, then both $a + b$ and $a \cdot b$ are also whole numbers. Thus, the whole-number system is said to be *closed* under the operations of addition and multiplication. However, the whole numbers are not closed under the operations of subtraction $(a - b)$ and division $\left(\frac{a}{b}, b \neq 0\right)$. For unless b is less than a, $a - b$ is not a whole number. Similarly, unless b is a factor of a, $\frac{a}{b}$ is not a whole number.

If you consider the set of *integers*, denoted by Z, that consists of all the whole numbers and their additive inverses, then the system will be closed under subtraction. Recall that the *additive inverse*, or *opposite*, of a whole number a is defined as the unique number, denoted $-a$, such that

$$a + (-a) = 0 = (-a) + a.$$

Thus the integers are defined by:

$$Z = W \cup \{-a \colon a \in W\} \quad \text{or} \quad Z = \{\ldots, -3, -2, -1, 0, 1, 2, 3, \ldots\}$$

Subtraction is defined as addition of an additive inverse:

$$c - d = c + (-d)$$

Together with the operations of addition and multiplication, the integers form a number system that is closed under subtraction. However, this system is still not closed under division, so we consider Q, the set of *rational numbers*:

$$Q = \left\{\frac{a}{b} \colon a, b \in Z \text{ and } b \neq 0\right\}$$

If c and d are any rational numbers and $d \neq 0$, then

$$c \div d = c\left(\frac{1}{d}\right),$$

where $\frac{1}{d}$ is the *multiplicative inverse*, or *reciprocal*, of d. Thus, together with the operations of addition and multiplication, the rationals form a number system that is also closed under both subtraction and division (except for division by zero).

A significant characteristic of all rational numbers is the following:

> Every rational number can be expressed as either a terminating or a repeating decimal.

Recall that to find the decimal representation of a rational number, you divide the numerator by the denominator.

EXAMPLE   Express as a terminating decimal: **a.** $\dfrac{7}{20}$ **b.** $-3\dfrac{3}{5}$

SOLUTION   **a.** $\dfrac{0.35}{20\overline{)7.00}}$ **b.** $-3\dfrac{3}{5} = \dfrac{-18}{5}$ $\dfrac{-3.6}{5\overline{)-18.0}}$

$\dfrac{7}{20} = 0.35$ $-3\dfrac{3}{5} = -3.6$

A block of digits that repeat is called a *repetend* and can be indicated with a bar, as shown in the solution of the example below.

EXAMPLE   Express as a repeating decimal: **a.** $\dfrac{1}{6}$ **b.** $5\dfrac{3}{11}$

SOLUTION   **a.** $\dfrac{0.1666\ldots}{6\overline{)1.0000}}$ **b.** $5\dfrac{3}{11} = \dfrac{58}{11}$ $\dfrac{5.2727\ldots}{11\overline{)58.0000}}$

$\dfrac{1}{6} = 0.1\overline{6}$ $5\dfrac{3}{11} = 5.\overline{27}$

The converse of the boxed statement on page 2 is also true:

> Every terminating or repeating decimal can be expressed as the quotient of two integers.

A terminating decimal can be changed to a fraction whose denominator is a power of 10. It is customary to reduce the fraction to lowest terms.

EXAMPLE   Express as a quotient of integers in lowest terms: **a.** 0.12   **b.** -3.1625

SOLUTION   **a.** $0.12 = \dfrac{12}{100} = \dfrac{3}{25}$ **b.** $-3.1625 = -\dfrac{31625}{10000} = -\dfrac{253}{80}$

One commonly used method of converting a repeating decimal to a fraction is illustrated in the following examples.

EXAMPLE   Express $0.\overline{147}$ as a quotient of integers in lowest terms.

METHOD	SOLUTION
1. Let x equal the decimal.	1. $x = 0.\overline{147}$
2. Multiply both sides by that power of 10 whose exponent is the number of digits in the repetend.	2. Since there are 3 digits in the repetend (147), the multiplier is 10^3, or 1000. $1000x = 147.\overline{147}$
3. Subtract the first equation from the second.	3. $\begin{aligned} 1000x &= 147.\overline{147} \\ x &= 0.\overline{147} \\ \hline 999x &= 147 \end{aligned}$
4. Solve for x.	4. $x = \dfrac{147}{999} = \dfrac{49}{333}$

EXAMPLE   Express $1.41\overline{6}$ as a quotient of integers.

SOLUTION   Let $x = 1.41\overline{6}$.

Then: $\begin{aligned} 10x &= 14.16\overline{6} \\ \underline{x} &= \underline{1.41\overline{6}} \\ 9x &= 12.75 \end{aligned}$

Multiplying both sides by 100, we have:

$$900x = 1275$$
$$x = \frac{1275}{900} = \frac{17}{12}$$

A number is rational if and only if it can be expressed as a repeating or terminating decimal. In fact, all *real numbers* can be expressed as decimal numbers, and all decimal numbers are real numbers. But not all real numbers can be written as repeating or terminating decimals. Some real numbers whose decimal representations are nonrepeating and nonterminating are shown below.

$0.010010001\ldots$

$\pi = 3.14159\ldots$ (pi)   (The ratio of the circumference of a circle to its diameter)

$\sqrt{2} = 1.41421\ldots$

$\sqrt{13} = 3.605551\ldots$

$0.6180339\ldots$ $\left(\text{The golden mean, } \dfrac{\sqrt{5}-1}{2}\right)$

Numbers such as these are called *irrational* numbers. The set of *real numbers*, denoted by $\mathcal{R}$, consists of all rational and irrational numbers. You will review the properties of the set of real numbers in the next section.

ORAL EXERCISES

Name all of the following sets that contain the given number: N, W, Z, Q, $\mathcal{R}$, the irrationals.

1. $6\dfrac{1}{8}$ 2. $-7.\overline{6}$ 3. $-\dfrac{9}{10}$ 4. -5

5. 0.25 6. $\sqrt{23}$ 7. $2.151155111555\ldots$ 8. 0

Give an example of the following.

9. A real number that is not a rational number

10. A rational number that is not an integer

11. An integer that is not a whole number

12. A whole number that is not a natural number

Under which of the four operations (addition, subtraction, multiplication, and division) is the given set closed? (Ignore division by zero.)

13. The whole numbers   14. The integers   15. The rationals   16. The real numbers

WRITTEN EXERCISES

Express each number as a quotient of two integers.

A 1. 5   2. 1   3. 0   4. −3

5. $2\frac{1}{4}$ 6. $-4\frac{1}{3}$ 7. 0.3   8. −3.7

Express each number as a decimal.

9. $\frac{7}{10}$ 10. $\frac{4}{25}$ 11. $-\frac{2}{5}$ 12. $-\frac{3}{4}$

13. $\frac{9}{15}$ 14. $-\frac{14}{56}$ 15. $-\frac{7}{8}$ 16. $\frac{18}{48}$

17. $1\frac{9}{50}$ 18. $-3\frac{17}{20}$ 19. $-\frac{6}{5}$ 20. $\frac{11}{4}$

21. $\frac{5}{6}$ 22. $\frac{4}{11}$ 23. $-\frac{8}{9}$ 24. $-\frac{1}{18}$

Express each number as a quotient of two integers in lowest terms.

25. 0.4   26. −3.6   27. −2.57   28. 0.85

29. 1.195   30. −4.125   31. 0.0625   32. 0.00375

B 33. $0.\overline{3}$ 34. $0.\overline{5}$ 35. $0.\overline{18}$ 36. $0.\overline{54}$

37. $0.\overline{312}$ 38. $0.\overline{561}$ 39. $5.\overline{64}$ 40. $2.\overline{68}$

41. $0.1\overline{6}$ 42. $0.8\overline{3}$ 43. $3.2\overline{6}$ 44. $4.1\overline{7}$

45. $0.0\overline{27}$ 46. $0.0\overline{42}$ 47. $1.3\overline{81}$ 48. $2.4\overline{72}$

For what values of x is each of the following expressions equal to
a. a rational number?   b. an integer?

49. $\frac{3}{x}$ 50. $\frac{x}{3}$

C 51. $\frac{5x}{x+1}$ $\left(Hint:\ \text{In (b), let}\ \frac{5x}{x+1} = n \text{ and solve for } x.\right)$ 52. $\frac{8-x}{8+x}$

53. Using the method illustrated on page 3, show that $0.\overline{9} = 1$.

54. Using the facts that $\frac{1}{6} = 0.1\overline{6}$ and $0.\overline{9} = 1$, find the decimal equivalent for $\frac{5}{6}$.
$\left(Hint:\ \frac{5}{6} = 1 - \frac{1}{6}\right)$

55. Using the fact that $\frac{1}{12} = 0.083\overline{3}$, find the decimal equivalent for $\frac{11}{12}$.

56. Using the fact that $\frac{1}{12} = 0.083\overline{3}$, find the decimal equivalent for $\frac{5}{12}$.

Section 1-2 SOME PROPERTIES OF THE REAL NUMBERS

In this section you will review:
- some properties of the real number system
- the order of operations

Properties may be proved or accepted as true without proof. Proven properties are called *theorems*, while those accepted without proof are called *postulates* or *axioms*. The following properties, in which *a*, *b*, and *c* represent real numbers, will be accepted without proof.

Properties of Addition

Closure Property	$a + b$ is a unique real number.
Commutative Property	$a + b = b + a$
Associative Property	$a + (b + c) = (a + b) + c$
Identity Property	$\Re$ contains a unique element 0, called the *identity element for addition*, such that for any *a*, $$a + 0 = a \quad \text{and} \quad 0 + a = a.$$
Inverse Property	For every $a \in \Re$, there is a unique real number, $-a$, called the *additive inverse* of *a*, such that $$a + (-a) = 0 \quad \text{and} \quad (-a) + a = 0.$$

The additive inverse of *a* is sometimes called the *opposite* of *a*.

Properties of Multiplication

Closure Property	ab is a unique real number.
Commutative Property	$ab = ba$
Associative Property	$a(bc) = (ab)c$
Identity Property	$\Re$ contains a unique element 1, called the *identity element for multiplication*, such that for any *a*, $$a \cdot 1 = a \quad \text{and} \quad 1 \cdot a = a.$$
Inverse Property	For every nonzero $a \in \Re$, there is a unique real number, $\dfrac{1}{a}$, called the *multiplicative inverse* of *a*, such that $$a \cdot \frac{1}{a} = 1 \quad \text{and} \quad \frac{1}{a} \cdot a = 1.$$

The multiplicative inverse of *a* is sometimes called the *reciprocal* of *a*.
The following property combines multiplication and addition.

Distributive Property

$$a(b + c) = ab + ac \text{ and } (b + c)a = ba + ca$$

In terms of multiplication and subtraction, the distributive property is:

$$a(b - c) = ab - ac \text{ and } (b - c)a = ba - ca.$$

The following properties can be proved from the properties of the real number system that we are assuming.

Multiplicative Property of 0

$$a \cdot 0 = 0 \text{ and } 0 \cdot a = 0$$

Multiplicative Property of −1

$$a(-1) = -a \text{ and } (-1)a = -a$$

You can use the properties of real numbers to simplify algebraic and numerical expressions. Evaluation of numerical expressions is also governed by the following order of operations.

1. Perform operations within parentheses, including powers.
2. Simplify expressions involving powers.
3. Do all multiplications and divisions, working from left to right.
4. Do all additions and subtractions, working from left to right.

EXAMPLE Simplify.

    a. $6 + 3^2 \cdot 4 - 7$ **b.** $(6 + 3^2) \cdot 4 - 7$ **c.** $(6 + 3)^2 \cdot 4 - 7$

SOLUTION   **a.** $6 + 3^2 \cdot 4 - 7 = 6 + 9 \cdot 4 - 7 = 6 + 36 - 7 = 42 - 7 = 35$

            b. $(6 + 3^2) \cdot 4 - 7 = (6 + 9) \cdot 4 - 7 = 15 \cdot 4 - 7 = 60 - 7 = 53$

            c. $(6 + 3)^2 \cdot 4 - 7 = 9^2 \cdot 4 - 7 = 81 \cdot 4 - 7 = 324 - 7 = 317$

EXAMPLE Simplify: $\dfrac{4 + 6 \cdot 10}{8}$

SOLUTION The fraction bar acts as a grouping symbol, and we treat the numerator as if it were written within parentheses.

$$(4 + 6 \cdot 10) \div 8 = (4 + 60) \div 8 = 64 \div 8 = 8$$

EXAMPLE Evaluate the following when $x = 3$, $y = -4$, and $z = -1$.

    a. $x^2 - 3xz + 6z^2$ **b.** $\dfrac{x + yz}{xy + 2z}$

(The solution is on the following page.)

SOLUTION   **a.** $x^2 - 3xz + 6z^2 = (3)^2 - 3(3)(-1) + 6(-1)^2$
$$= 9 - (-9) + 6(1)$$
$$= 9 + 9 + 6 = 24$$

b. $\dfrac{x + yz}{xy + 2z} = \dfrac{3 + (-4)(-1)}{(3)(-4) + 2(-1)} = \dfrac{3 + 4}{-12 + (-2)} = \dfrac{7}{-14} = -\dfrac{1}{2}$

ORAL EXERCISES

In Exercises 1–10, **(a)** state a value of x that makes the statement true, and **(b)** state the property that justifies your answer.

1. $6(3 - x) = 6 \cdot 3 - 6 \cdot 2$ 2. $8 + 5 = 5 + x$

3. $15x = 15$ 4. $(5 + x) + 2 = 5 + (6 + 2)$

5. $7 + x = 0$ 6. $\dfrac{1}{4}x = 1$

7. $6 + x = 6$ 8. $2(3x) = (2 \cdot 3)7$

9. $8x = -8$ 10. $7x + 4x = (7 + 4)3$

State whether the two expressions always have the same value.

11. $5x + 1$ and $1 + 5x$ 12. $2x - 1$ and $1 - 2x$

13. $3 + (4 + x)$ and $7 + x$ 14. $3(4 + x)$ and $12 + x$

15. $3(4x)$ and $12x$ 16. $4(x - 9)$ and $4x - 36$

17. **a.** Simplify $5 - (3 - 1)$ and $(5 - 3) - 1$.
    b. Is subtraction of real numbers associative?

18. **a.** Simplify $3 - 2$ and $2 - 3$.
    b. Is subtraction of real numbers commutative?

19. **a.** Simplify $4 \div 2$ and $2 \div 4$.
    b. What does part (a) show about division of real numbers?

20. **a.** Simplify $8 \div (4 \div 2)$ and $(8 \div 4) \div 2$.
    b. What does part (a) show about division of real numbers?

WRITTEN EXERCISES

Simplify.

A   1. $5(6 - 4)^3 - 5$ 2. $6 \cdot 2^2 - 5 \cdot 3 + 6$ 3. $(-2)^3 \cdot 3 - 7 + 9 \cdot 2$

     4. $(8 - 5)^3 + 9 - 4 \cdot 2$ 5. $6^2 - 4 \cdot 6 \div 3$ 6. $(8 + 8 \cdot 7) \div (24 - 2^3)$

     7. $8 \cdot 4 \div 16 \div 4 \cdot 7 - (6 + 2 \cdot 1)$ 8. $24 \div (6 - 2^2)^3 + 7 \cdot 3$

     9. $\dfrac{6 + 7 \cdot 6}{(5 + 3^3) \div (12 - 5 \cdot 2)}$ 10. $\dfrac{12 \cdot 3 - 4 \cdot 8 + 5 \cdot 4}{(6 - 3 \cdot 2)^2 + 2^3}$

    11. $\dfrac{(6 + 7) \cdot 6}{(3 \cdot 6 - 8 \div 2) - 12}$ 12. $\dfrac{5^2 - 2^3 \cdot 3}{(2^3 + 3 \cdot 2^2) \div (2^2 \cdot 5)}$

8   *CHAPTER 1*

Evaluate the following when $a = 8$, $b = 4$, and $c = 1$.

13. $a(b - c)$

14. $3ab(a + c)$

15. $(a + b)(a - c)$

16. $\dfrac{4a - 5b}{3b + a}$

17. $\dfrac{(a + b)^2}{a^2 + b^2}$

18. $b^2 - \dfrac{b}{c}$

Evaluate the following when $x = -10$, $y = 5$, and $z = -2$.

19. $6z^2 + y$

20. $5x + y(x + z)$

21. $x + y(y - z)$

22. $\dfrac{x^2 - 3x + 5}{xyz + x}$

23. $\dfrac{3x + yz}{x - z}$

24. $\dfrac{3x^2yz}{xy^2}$

Find **(a)** the additive inverse and **(b)** the multiplicative inverse.

25. 2

26. 6

27. -3

28. -1

29. $\dfrac{7}{8}$

30. $-\dfrac{3}{5}$

31. $-2\dfrac{1}{4}$

32. $1\dfrac{5}{6}$

Find **(a)** the additive inverse and **(b)** the multiplicative inverse. (*Hint*: Change to a fraction first.)

B **33.** 1.4

34. -0.15

35. -0.625

36. 0.025

37. $0.\overline{6}$

38. $-0.\overline{18}$

39. $-0.\overline{312}$

40. $0.4\overline{72}$

State the property that justifies each step.

41. $(x + 6) + (-6) = x + (6 + (-6))$
$= x + 0$
$= x$

42. $\left(\dfrac{1}{2}x\right)2 = 2\left(\dfrac{1}{2}x\right)$
$= \left(2 \cdot \dfrac{1}{2}\right)x$
$= 1 \cdot x$
$= x$

Simplify, and state the property or definition that justifies each step.

43. $(4x + 4)\dfrac{1}{4}$

44. $7 + x - 7$

45. $6(x + 1) - 6$

46. $\dfrac{1}{3}(3 + 3x) - x$

Find the reciprocal of each of the following. Identify those values of x (if any) for which there is no reciprocal.

47. $x + 3$

48. $3 - x$

49. $\dfrac{x + 1}{x - 1}$

50. $\dfrac{6}{x}$

51. $\dfrac{x}{6}$

52. $\dfrac{x^2 - 1}{x + 1}$

Place parentheses appropriately in each of the following in order to make a true statement.

C **53.** $8 + 7 \cdot 6 \div 3 + 2^2 = 2$

54. $8 + 7 \cdot 6 \div 3 + 2^2 = 14$

55. $8 + 7 \cdot 6 \div 3 + 2^2 = 34$

56. $6 + 4 \cdot 3 \div 2^3 - 2 \cdot 3 = 9$

57. $6 + 4 \cdot 3 \div 2^3 - 2 \cdot 3 = 12$

58. $6 + 4 \cdot 3 \div 2^3 - 2 \cdot 3 = 15$

59. $6 + 4 \cdot 3 \div 2^3 - 2 \cdot 3 = 216$

1. Name four subsets of the set of real numbers. Section 1-1

Express each number as a decimal.

2. $\dfrac{3}{8}$ 3. $-\dfrac{30}{25}$ 4. $-\dfrac{5}{12}$ 5. $1\dfrac{1}{11}$

Express each number as a quotient of two integers in lowest terms.

6. -0.18 7. 3.0042 8. $0.\overline{7}$ 9. $2.08\overline{3}$

Simplify.

10. $6(5) - 3(8) \div 2$ 11. $8(14 - 3 \cdot 5)^2$ 12. $\dfrac{2^3 + 3(4)^2}{(6-4)^2 + 2(5)}$ Section 1-2

Evaluate when $x = 3$, $y = -5$, and $z = -1$.

13. $xy - xz$ 14. $y + x(x - z)$ 15. $\dfrac{(x+y)^3}{x^2 + z^2}$

Find the additive inverse and the multiplicative inverse.

16. 8 17. $-2\dfrac{1}{3}$ 18. -0.05

Section 1-3 SOLVING LINEAR EQUATIONS

Solving equations is one of the most basic mathematical skills. In this section you will review:
- equations
- domains and solution sets
- properties of equality
- solving linear equations

An *equation* is a mathematical sentence stating that two expressions are equal.

EXAMPLES OF NUMERICAL EQUATIONS

$$6 + 5 \cdot 4 = 26 \qquad 6 + 5 \cdot 4 = 44 \qquad 2^3 + 8 = 4^2$$
$$\text{(true)} \qquad\qquad \text{(false)} \qquad\qquad \text{(true)}$$

Note that the truth or falsity of numerical equations is based in part on the rules of numerical operations discussed in the previous section.

EXAMPLES OF ALGEBRAIC EQUATIONS

$$3x + 6 = 18 \qquad \frac{x}{6} + \frac{x}{4} = 8 \qquad 4(x + 6) = 3x + 8$$

Note that the truth or falsity of algebraic equations depends on what replacement is made for the *variable*. Unless otherwise indicated, the replacement set, or *domain*, for the variable will be the set of real numbers. The subset of the domain for which an open sentence is true is called the *solution set* of the equation. Each element of the solution set is called a *root* or *solution* of the equation.

Some equations have only one solution, as in the following:

$$4x + 5 = 5 \qquad 4y - 3 = 9$$

Note that the only replacements that will make these equations true are $x = 0$ and $y = 3$. The solution sets are $\{0\}$ and $\{3\}$ respectively.

Other equations have more than one solution:

$$w^2 - 3w + 2 = 0 \qquad 3(z + 2) = 3z + 6$$

As you will review in Chapter 2, the solution set of $w^2 - 3w + 2 = 0$ is $\{1, 2\}$. Since $3(z + 2) = 3z + 6$ is true no matter what real number is chosen as a replacement for z, its solution set is $\mathcal{R}$. Such an equation is called an *identity*. You will study some important identities in Chapters 8 and 11.

It is even possible for an equation to have no solution in the set of real numbers. Consider, for example:

$$x = x + 1 \qquad y^2 + 16 = 0$$

Each of these equations has as solution set the *null*, or *empty*, set, $\emptyset$.

Determining the solution set for an equation generally involves transforming the given equation into a series of *equivalent equations* with the same domain and solution set until you arrive at an equation such as $x = -2$ whose solution set can be determined by inspection. The following properties can be applied in this process.

Properties of Equality

Let $a, b, c,$ and d represent real numbers.

Addition	If $a = c$ and $b = d$, then $a + b = c + d$.
Subtraction	If $a = c$ and $b = d$, then $a - b = c - d$.
Multiplication	If $a = c$ and $b = d$, then $ab = cd$.
Division	If $a = c$ and $b = d$ ($b \neq 0$ and $d \neq 0$), then $\dfrac{a}{b} = \dfrac{c}{d}$.

You will also use the following property frequently when simplifying.

Substitution Property

If $a = b$, you can replace a by b in any expression without changing the truth value of the expression.

The following examples illustrate how the properties of this section and the previous one can be used to solve *linear equations in one variable*, in which the variable is raised only to the first power. When solving equations, you generally will not have to justify each step in the process, as we do below. However, be sure to show enough steps so that you can retrace your work to spot any possible errors. You can often identify an error by substituting your answer in the original equation.

EXAMPLE Solve: $\frac{3}{4}x + 6 = 18$

SOLUTION $\frac{3}{4}x + 6 - 6 = 18 - 6$ Subtraction Property of Equality

$\frac{3}{4}x = 12$ Inverse Property of Addition and Identity Property of Addition

$\frac{4}{3} \cdot \frac{3}{4}x = \frac{4}{3} \cdot 12$ Multiplication Property of Equality

$x = 16$ Inverse Property of Multiplication and Identity Property of Multiplication

Check $\frac{3}{4}(16) + 6 \overset{?}{=} 18$

$12 + 6 \overset{?}{=} 18$

$18 = 18$

Therefore $\{16\}$ is the solution set of $\frac{3}{4}x + 6 = 18$.

EXAMPLE Solve: $2x + 1 = 3(7 - x)$

SOLUTION $2x + 1 = 3 \cdot 7 - 3 \cdot x$ Distributive Property
$2x + 1 = 21 - 3x$ Substitution Property
$3x + 2x + 1 = 21 - 3x + 3x$ Addition Property of Equality
$5x + 1 = 21$ Distributive Property, Inverse Property of Addition, and Identity Property of Addition
$5x + 1 - 1 = 21 - 1$ Subtraction Property of Equality
$5x = 20$ Substitution Property
$\frac{5x}{5} = \frac{20}{5}$ Division Property of Equality
$x = 4$ Substitution Property

Check $2(4) + 1 \overset{?}{=} 3(7 - 4)$
$8 + 1 \overset{?}{=} 3(3)$
$9 = 9$

The solution set is $\{4\}$.

The following example illustrates a streamlined solution.

EXAMPLE Solve: $\frac{x - 6}{3} = \frac{x - 2}{2} - 4$

SOLUTION   Multiplying both sides of the equation by 6, the least common denominator of 3 and 2, will transform the given equation into an equivalent one without any denominators.

$$6\left(\frac{x-6}{3}\right) = 6\left(\frac{x-2}{2}\right) - 6 \cdot 4$$
$$2(x-6) = 3(x-2) - 24$$
$$2x - 12 = 3x - 30$$
$$18 = x$$

Check
$$\frac{18-6}{3} \overset{?}{=} \frac{18-2}{2} - 4$$
$$4 \overset{?}{=} 8 - 4$$
$$4 = 4$$

The solution set is $\{18\}$.

EXAMPLE   Solve: $1.2x - 0.15 = 0.85 + 0.7x$

SOLUTION
$$1.2x - 0.7x = 0.85 + 0.15$$
$$0.5x = 1.00$$
$$x = 2$$

Check $1.2(2) - 0.15 \overset{?}{=} 0.85 + 0.7(2)$
$$2.4 - 0.15 \overset{?}{=} 0.85 + 1.4$$
$$2.25 = 2.25$$

The solution set is $\{2\}$.

ORAL EXERCISES

Describe a sequence of operations that can be performed to solve each of the following.

1. $2x + 5 = 7$
2. $2(x + 5) = 7$
3. $10 - 3x = 2$
4. $6 - (x + 8) = 12$
5. $5 + 2x = 5x + 8$
6. $4x - 3 = 8 - 7x$
7. $\frac{x}{5} - 1 = 8$
8. $\frac{x+4}{3} + 5 = 13$
9. $\frac{x}{3} + \frac{x}{5} = 24$

State whether the equation is *always, sometimes,* or *never* true when the domain of x is $\mathcal{R}$.

10. $x + 5 = x$
11. $x + 5 = 5$
12. $x + 5 = 5 + x$
13. $x + 5 = 5 - x$
14. $3(x + 5) = 3x + 15$
15. $3x + 5 = -3x + 5$
16. $3x + 5 = -(3x + 5)$
17. $6 - (x + 4) = 2 - x$
18. $6 - (x + 4) = x - 2$

WRITTEN EXERCISES

Solve and check.

A 1. $18x + 2 = -1$
2. $10 - x = -4$
3. $8 = 50 - 7n$
4. $5 - 8y = 29$
5. $8 + \frac{z}{2} = -1$
6. $-6 = 3 - \frac{x}{7}$
7. $\frac{2}{5}z + 7 = -13$
8. $\frac{3b}{4} - 9 = 12$

Solve and check.

9. $11c - 0.34 = 0.21$ 10. $0.3 - w = 0.13$ 11. $40 - 0.5z = 5$

12. $10d - 0.8 - 3d = 4.1$ 13. $8x = 2x - 30$ 14. $5n = 40 - 3n$

15. $4v + 5 = 5v - 30$ 16. $10 + 3r = 2r - 20$ 17. $2y - 1.7 = 3y + 1.4$

18. $12d - 5 = 3.28 + 9d$ 19. $\dfrac{8}{7}k + 9 = \dfrac{3}{7}k + 14$ 20. $17 + m = 9 - \dfrac{1}{2}m$

21. $4(x + 1) = -20$ 22. $42 = 7(2x - 1)$ 23. $6(y - 3) = 7y$

24. $8x = 2(x - 15)$ 25. $6 - (x + 5) = -3$ 26. $10 = 4 - (6 - 4x)$

27. $4(x - 2) = 8x - 12$ 28. $12y - 3 = 5(2y + 1)$ 29. $30 - 2(y - 1) = 38$

30. $20 + 8(2 - c) = 44$ 31. $6(k + 2) = 3(2k - 5)$ 32. $2(n - 5) = 4 - 2(7 - n)$

B 33. $\dfrac{x}{2} - \dfrac{x}{3} = 7$ 34. $\dfrac{x}{5} + \dfrac{x}{6} = 11$ 35. $\dfrac{x}{2} = 12 - \dfrac{x}{4}$

36. $10 + \dfrac{c}{6} = \dfrac{c}{3} - 4$ 37. $\dfrac{2x}{3} - \dfrac{3x}{4} = \dfrac{3}{4}$ 38. $\dfrac{5y}{2} - \dfrac{2y}{3} = \dfrac{-11}{6}$

39. $\dfrac{x}{2} = \dfrac{3x}{7} - 5$ 40. $\dfrac{c}{10} = \dfrac{c}{6} - 2$ 41. $\dfrac{2c + 4}{12} = \dfrac{c + 4}{7}$

42. $\dfrac{6d + 3}{11} = \dfrac{3d}{5}$ 43. $\dfrac{w - 2}{4} - \dfrac{w + 4}{3} = \dfrac{-5}{6}$ 44. $3 - \dfrac{3x}{2} = \dfrac{8 - 4x}{7}$

45. $2(z + 1) - 3(4z - 2) = 2(4 - 5z)$ 46. $6(3x - 2) = -7(8 + x) - 5(2 - 5x)$

47. $0.5a - 3.5 = 0.75$ 48. $0.2x + 0.32 = 8.1$

49. $0.4x + 2 = 1.2x - 6$ 50. $4 - 1.6x = 3x + 1.7$

51. $0.8 = 0.02(x - 35)$ 52. $50 - 0.05(x - 100) = 20$

C 53. $\dfrac{1}{6}(2r + 8) + \dfrac{1}{4}(r - 3) = \dfrac{7}{6}$ 54. $\dfrac{1}{4}(4 - 3m) - \dfrac{4}{5}(3 - m) = 7$

55. $1 - \dfrac{2m - 5}{3} = \dfrac{m + 3}{2}$ 56. $\dfrac{1}{2}(4x - 6) - 7 = 5 + \dfrac{2}{3}(3x + 4)$

A *formula*, such as $A = \pi r^2$, is an equation that shows the relationship between two or more quantities represented by variables. When solving problems involving formulas, it is often convenient to transform the formula to an equivalent one representing the desired variable in terms of the others.

EXAMPLE   The area of a trapezoid is given in terms of the lengths of its two bases (b_1 and b_2) and its height (h) as follows:

$$A = \frac{(b_1 + b_2)h}{2}$$

Write an equation that can be used to find the length b_1 in terms of the other variables.

SOLUTION   Solving for b_1 in terms of the other variables, we have:

$$2A = (b_1 + b_2)h$$

$$\frac{2A}{h} = b_1 + b_2$$

$$\frac{2A}{h} - b_2 = b_1$$

Solve for the indicated variable.

57. $d = r \cdot t$; t

58. $P = 2(l + w)$; l

59. $l = a + (n-1)d$; n

60. $F = \frac{9}{5}C + 32$; C

61. $s = \frac{1}{2}at^2$; a

62. $V = \frac{1}{3}Bh$; B

Section 1-4 USING LINEAR EQUATIONS TO SOLVE PROBLEMS

Of all the skills you will acquire, one of the most important is that of problem solving. While it is impossible to list every technique and strategy necessary for successful problem solving, the list below specifies a basic framework for solving problems.

Step 1   Choose a variable and state what the variable represents.

Step 2   Write an equation (or inequality) that represents the facts of the problem.

Step 3   Solve the equation (or inequality).

Step 4   Check your answer to see that it satisfies the facts of the problem. Then write your answer, labeling with appropriate units where necessary.

In this section we will review this technique and focus on several specific problem-solving strategies such as:

• translating words into algebraic expressions
• interpreting and organizing data on sketches or charts
• solving and interpreting results
• checking your answer

An important skill in analyzing and solving problems is translating the words of a problem into an equation (or inequality). As you know, certain key words indicate the particular operations that will successfully solve a problem. A list of frequently occurring words and their algebraic translations appears below.

Addition			*Subtraction*	
the *sum* of x and 7	$x + 7$		the *difference* x minus 3	$x - 3$
7 *more than* x	$x + 7$		3 *less than* x	$x - 3$
x *increased* by 7	$x + 7$		x *decreased* by 3	$x - 3$
exceeds x by 7	$x + 7$		x *diminished* by 3	$x - 3$

Multiplication			*Division*	
the *product* of x and 8	$8x$		the *quotient* x divided by 5	$\dfrac{x}{5}$
half of x	$\dfrac{1}{2}x$			
twice as much as x	$2x$		the *average* of x and 5	$\dfrac{x+5}{2}$

EXAMPLE   The sum of three integers is 38. The greatest is twice the least integer, and the remaining integer exceeds the least by 6. Find the integers.

SOLUTION   Let x = the least integer.
Then $2x$ = the greatest integer.
And $x + 6$ = the remaining integer.
Each side of the following equation represents the sum of the three integers:
$$x + 2x + (x + 6) = 38$$
Solving:
$$4x + 6 = 38$$
$$4x = 32$$
$$x = 8; \quad 2x = 16; \quad x + 6 = 14$$

Check   The sum of 8, 14, and 16 is 38. The greatest integer (16) is twice the least integer (8). Also, 14 exceeds 8 by 6.

The three integers are 8, 14, and 16.

A carefully drawn sketch or a well-organized chart that interprets and structures the facts of a problem often aids in its solution.

EXAMPLE   The dimensions of a rectangle are in the ratio $5:8$. If the perimeter is 78 cm, find the dimensions of the rectangle.

SOLUTION   The ratio $5:8$ indicates that for some real number x the dimensions are $5x$ and $8x$. Using the formula for the perimeter of a rectangle:
$$P = 2(l + w)$$
$$78 = 2(8x + 5x)$$
$$78 = 26x$$
$$3 = x$$

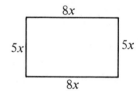

Thus the dimensions are $5 \cdot 3$, or 15 cm, and $8 \cdot 3$, or 24 cm.

Check   The perimeter is 78 cm and the ratio of the sides is $15:24$, or $5:8$.

EXAMPLE   Syrup worth 90¢ per liter is to be mixed with syrup valued at 50¢ per liter to produce 40 L of a blended syrup to be sold at 66¢ per liter. How many liters of each syrup should be used to make the blended syrup?

SOLUTION   This mixture problem involves:
(1) Price per liter of the three syrups
(2) Number of liters of each kind of syrup
(3) Total value of each kind of syrup
We use the relationship:
$$\text{Price per liter} \times \text{Number of liters} = \text{Total value}$$
Note also that the total value of the blended syrup is equal to the sum of the total values of each component syrup.

Let x = the number of liters of 90¢ syrup used.
Then $40 - x$ = the number of liters of 50¢ syrup used.

Make a chart.

Price per liter	Number of liters	Total value
90	x	$90x$
50	$40 - x$	$50(40 - x)$
66	40	$66(40)$

Then:

$$66(40) = 90x + 50(40 - x)$$
$$2640 = 90x + 2000 - 50x$$
$$640 = 40x$$
$$16 = x; \quad 40 - x = 24$$

Check   16 L of syrup at 90¢ per liter is worth $14.40.
24 L of syrup at 50¢ per liter is worth $12.00.
40 L of syrup at 66¢ per liter is worth $26.40.

Blend 16 L of the 90¢ per liter syrup with 24 L of the 50¢ per liter syrup.

EXAMPLE   A local commuter train and an express train each leave the same station for the same destination. The local train leaves at 7:00 A.M. and averages 80 km/h. The express leaves at 7:30 A.M. and averages 100 km/h. If the two trains arrive at the same time, how far do they travel?

SOLUTION   Let t = the number of hours the local train travels.

Then $t - \dfrac{1}{2}$ = the number of hours the express train travels.

To solve a *uniform motion problem*, the data can be organized according to the formula:

	Rate	X	Time	=	Distance
Local	80		t		$80t$
Express	100		$t - \dfrac{1}{2}$		$100\left(t - \dfrac{1}{2}\right)$

Since both trains travel the same distance:

$$80t = 100\left(t - \frac{1}{2}\right)$$
$$80t = 100t - 50$$
$$50 = 20t$$
$$2\frac{1}{2} = t$$

Since the local train took $2\dfrac{1}{2}$ h at 80 km/h, we have:

$$\text{Distance} = 80\left(2\frac{1}{2}\right) = 200$$

The train traveled 200 km.   The check is left for you.

The following example illustrates the importance of checking your solution with the conditions of the problem, since the solution of your equation may not satisfy the requirements of the problem.

EXAMPLE   Find four consecutive odd integers whose average is 43.

SOLUTION   Let x = the first odd integer.
Then $x + 2$, $x + 4$, and $x + 6$ are the next consecutive odd integers.

$$\frac{x + (x + 2) + (x + 4) + (x + 6)}{4} = 43$$

$$x + (x + 2) + (x + 4) + (x + 6) = 172$$

$$4x + 12 = 172$$

$$4x = 160$$

$$x = 40 \quad x + 2 = 42 \quad x + 4 = 44 \quad x + 6 = 46$$

Check   Since 40, 42, 44, and 46 are not *odd* integers, this problem has no solution.

ORAL EXERCISES

Express algebraically.

1. Three more than half a certain number

2. Six times the sum of eight and a certain number

3. The quotient of five times a number and three times the number

4. Half the sum of eight and twice a certain number

Translate into an equation.

5. Six less than eight times a certain number is twelve.

6. The product of ten and a certain number exceeds the number by twenty.

7. The product of three and a certain number is eight less than twice the number.

8. When seven is subtracted from a certain number, the difference is half the number.

9. The sum of two consecutive integers is eleven less than their product.

10. Six increased by half a number equals ten.

11. Twice the sum of eight and a certain number is sixteen.

12. When eight times a certain number is diminished by twenty, the remainder is twelve.

Complete.

13. If n is a multiple of 8, then the next multiple of 8 is __?__ .

14. The area of a square is $16n^2$ square units. The perimeter is __?__ .

15. A rectangle is 12 units long and n units wide. Perimeter = __?__ .

16. Dan is three times as old as Bill. If b is Bill's age now, then Dan's age in 4 years = __?__ .

17. If the first of three consecutive even integers is n, then their sum is __?__ .

18. Eight items costing n cents each are purchased. Change from \$5.00 = __?__ .

19. A team won three times as many games as it lost. If l is the number of games lost, then the total number of games played = __?__ .

20. One number is six more than twice another. Their average = __?__ .

21. The measure of $\angle A$ is $4k$. The measure of its complement is __?__ and the measure of its supplement is __?__ .

22. The ratio of the measures of two angles of a triangle is $1:3$. If $\angle A$ is the smaller of these two angles, then the measure of the third angle = __?__ .

WRITTEN EXERCISES

A 1. Twelve less than five times a number equals ten more than three times the number. Find the number.

2. If six is added to twice a certain number, the result is four less than three times the number. Find the number.

3. One number is three times another number. Their sum is eight more than twice the smaller one. Find the numbers.

4. The sum of two numbers is 20 and their difference is 11. Find the numbers.

5. Find three consecutive integers whose sum is −39.

6. Find three consecutive odd integers such that the sum of the first and second is 19 less than three times the third.

7. Two positive numbers are in the ratio $7:4$ and their difference is 39. Find the numbers.

8. Two positive numbers are in the ratio $5:4$. If twice the smaller one is six more than the larger one, find the numbers.

9. Two angles are complementary and the measure of one is 10 less than three times the other. Find the measures of the angles.

10. Two angles are supplementary and the ratio of their measures is $7:8$. Find the measures of the angles.

11. The length of a rectangle is 8 cm more than twice its width. If the perimeter is 52 cm, what are the dimensions of the rectangle?

12. Two sides of a triangle are each 6 cm shorter than twice the length of the third side. If the perimeter is 23 cm, what are the dimensions of the triangle?

13. The lengths of the sides of a right triangle are in the ratio $3:4:5$. Find the area of the triangle if its perimeter is 24 cm. (*Hint*: Use the converse of the Pythagorean Theorem.)

14. The sides of one square are each 9 cm longer than the sides of another square. Find the dimensions of the two squares if the sum of their perimeters is 100 cm.

Not all problems have solutions. For Exercises 15–22, try to solve the problem and then explain why there is no reasonable answer.

15. Find two integers whose sum is 20 and whose difference is 9.

16. Find four consecutive integers such that the sum of the second and fourth is 57.

17. Find three consecutive even integers such that five times the sum of the first and third equals 18 more than eight times the second.

18. Find two integers whose ratio is $3:2$ and whose sum is 32.

19. Two angles of a triangle are complementary and the measure of the third angle is three times that of the larger of the complementary angles. Find the measures of the three angles.

20. The measure of a supplement of $\angle A$ is 70 less than one-fourth the measure of $\angle A$. Find the measure of $\angle A$ and of its supplement.

B 21. A local commuter train and an express train serve two cities that are 30 km apart. The local train leaves the station daily at 5:00 P.M. traveling at 90 km/h. Fifteen minutes later the express leaves the same station traveling at 120 km/h. When will the express pass the other train?

22. How much water must be added to a liter of 90% acid solution to make 1.5 L of a 70% acid solution?

Solve.

23. The area of an isosceles triangle is 120 cm². Its base is 1 cm shorter than each of the other two sides. If its height is 15 cm, what is its perimeter?

24. The measure of $\angle A$ of $\triangle ABC$ is 9 less than twice the measure of $\angle B$. If the measure of $\angle C$ is 18 more than twice the sum of the measures of $\angle A$ and $\angle B$, find the measures of the angles.

25. A money bag contains 120 nickels and dimes with a total value of $10.00. How many dimes are in the bag?

26. Karen bought 37 stamps consisting of 20¢ and 13¢ stamps. If they cost a total of $5.72, how many of each kind did she buy?

27. A cocoa merchant blended cocoa worth $7.50 per kilogram with cocoa worth $9.50 per kilogram to make a mixture of 12 kg of cocoa to be priced at $8.00 per kilogram. How many kilograms of each cocoa were used to make the mixture?

28. At a carnival, the number of adults' tickets sold was four more than three times the number of children's tickets. The total sales amounted to $57.90. How many tickets of each kind were sold if adults' tickets cost 45¢ and children's cost 30¢?

29. Mary Chai invested two sums of money, the first at 10% and the second at 12%. The ratio of the amounts invested was $8:5$. What was the amount of each investment if the interest on the first investment was $200 per year more than the interest on the second investment?

30. Brian Daniels invested a total of $5600. On one investment he earned 10% and on the other he lost 4%. How large was each investment if the losses equalled the earnings?

31. Joe was born on his father's thirtieth birthday. Now his father is 6 years more than three times Joe's age. How old are Joe and his father now?

32. The sum of the present ages of Kris and her mother is 38 years. Next year her mother will be four times as old as Kris will be. How old are Kris and her mother now?

33. Two cars started at the same time from towns that are 615 km apart and met in 5 hours. What was the average speed of each car if one car went 15 km/h faster than the other?

34. During a five-hour endurance race, one cyclist rode 40 km less than twice as far as another cyclist. If their combined distance was 290 km, find the average speed of each cyclist.

Section 1-5 SOLVING LINEAR INEQUALITIES

In this section you will review:
- linear inequalities
- properties of inequalities
- solving and graphing linear inequalities

An *inequality* is a mathematical sentence that contains a symbol such as $<$, $>$, $\leqslant$, $\geqslant$, or $\neq$. Some inequalities are shown below together with their graphs.

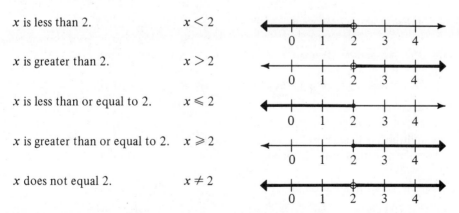

x is less than 2.	$x < 2$	
x is greater than 2.	$x > 2$	
x is less than or equal to 2.	$x \leqslant 2$	
x is greater than or equal to 2.	$x \geqslant 2$	
x does not equal 2.	$x \neq 2$	

Notice that an open dot indicates that 2 is not included in the solution set of the inequality. A solid dot indicates that 2 is included.

We are able to compare any two real numbers because of the Comparison Property stated below. In Chapter 3 you will learn about a system of numbers in which there is no Comparison Property.

Properties of Order

Let a, b, and c represent real numbers.

Comparison Property   Exactly one of the following is true: $a > b$, $a = b$, $a < b$

Transitive Property   If $a > b$ and $b > c$, then $a > c$.

A *linear inequality in one variable* is an inequality in which the variable is raised only to the first power. To solve an inequality, you transform it into a simpler *equivalent inequality* with the same domain and solution set. You may use the following properties.

Properties of Inequality

Let a, b, and c represent real numbers.

Addition   If $a > b$, then $a + c > b + c$.
           If $a < b$, then $a + c < b + c$.

Subtraction   If $a > b$, then $a - c > b - c$.
           If $a < b$, then $a - c < b - c$.

Multiplication   If $a > b$ and $c > 0$, then $ac > bc$.
           If $a < b$ and $c > 0$, then $ac < bc$.
           If $a > b$ and $c < 0$, then $ac < bc$.
           If $a < b$ and $c < 0$, then $ac > bc$.

Division   If $a > b$ and $c > 0$, then $\dfrac{a}{c} > \dfrac{b}{c}$.

           If $a < b$ and $c > 0$, then $\dfrac{a}{c} < \dfrac{b}{c}$.

           If $a > b$ and $c < 0$, then $\dfrac{a}{c} < \dfrac{b}{c}$.

           If $a < b$ and $c < 0$, then $\dfrac{a}{c} > \dfrac{b}{c}$.

Notice that if you multiply or divide both sides of an inequality by a negative number, you must reverse the direction of the inequality sign.

EXAMPLE   Find and graph the solution set.

     a. $2x + 10 > 4$ b. $\dfrac{x}{4} - \dfrac{x}{3} \leqslant \dfrac{1}{6}$

SOLUTION **a.** $2x + 10 - 10 > 4 - 10$
$$2x > -6$$
$$x > -3$$
The solution set is $\{x: x > -3\}$.

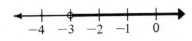

b. $12\left(\dfrac{x}{4} - \dfrac{x}{3}\right) \leqslant 12 \cdot \dfrac{1}{6}$
$$3x - 4x \leqslant 2$$
$$-x \leqslant 2$$
$$x \geqslant -2$$
The solution set is $\{x: x \geqslant -2\}$.

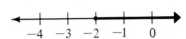

ORAL EXERCISES

Classify as *true* or *false*.

1. $5 < 7$
2. $-5 < -7$
3. $4 - 8 > 12 - 10$
4. $9(-1) < (-9)(-1)$
5. $3(-4) > 2(-6)$
6. $2^3 < 3^2$

State an inequality whose graph is shown.

7.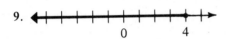

8.

9.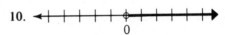

10.

State the solution set.

11. $y - 3 < 8$
12. $5 + z > -3$
13. $-4c \leqslant -12$
14. $\dfrac{d}{6} \geqslant -2$
15. $-\dfrac{2}{5}x > 1$
16. $k < k - 2$

WRITTEN EXERCISES

Find and graph the solution set of each inequality.

A
1. $2x - 1 > 5$
2. $4c - 3 \geqslant 17$
3. $-5 \leqslant 3y - 2$
4. $4 < 2y + 10$
5. $2 - 8y > 6$
6. $3 - 4x \geqslant -21$
7. $\dfrac{c}{2} + 3 \leqslant 0$
8. $-3 > \dfrac{x}{3} - 2$
9. $6 - \dfrac{2}{3}z \geqslant -4$
10. $3 \leqslant \dfrac{4}{5}x - 1$
11. $0.4x + 0.08 \leqslant 4.48$
12. $0.03d - 1.2 > 8.7$
13. $0.8 \geqslant 1.6 - 0.4x$
14. $-0.3x + 2.6 \geqslant -1.6$
15. $5x - 4 + 3x > 4$
16. $29 > 3y - 1 - 8y$
17. $5x + 4 \leqslant 11 - 2x$
18. $m + 3 > 2m + 3$

Solve.

19. $7x + 3 \geqslant 4 + 7x$	**20.** $2x - 3 < 12 + 7x$	**21.** $1 + 3x > 2x + 7$
22. $6 - 7y \geqslant 9 + 2y$	**23.** $4 - 3x > x + 16$	**24.** $3w + 7 < 15 - w$
25. $0.08c - 0.9 < 0.02c$	**26.** $1.5y - 1.69 \geqslant 0.2y$	**27.** $4(x - 1) > 16$
28. $3(4 - z) \geqslant 12$	**29.** $8 \leqslant 2(6n - 8)$	**30.** $4(3 + 5d) < -8$
31. $15 > 3(7 + 3x)$	**32.** $2(7 - x) < 16$	**33.** $8x < 5(2x + 4)$
34. $8m \geqslant -2(2m + 3)$	**35.** $2r - (3r - 5) > 3$	**36.** $3x - 6(x + 1) \leqslant 15$

B **37.** $7 + 2x \geqslant 8 - (6 - 2x)$ **38.** $4x + 5 < 2 + 4(x - 1)$

39. $5x \leqslant 10 + 2(3x - 4)$ **40.** $4(8 - 2c) - 4 > 6c$

41. $\dfrac{5y - 30}{7} \leqslant y$ **42.** $\dfrac{x}{4} - \dfrac{5}{8} > \dfrac{x}{8}$ **43.** $\dfrac{y}{6} \geqslant \dfrac{y + 1}{12}$

44. $\dfrac{5}{6} + \dfrac{2}{3}x \geqslant \dfrac{x}{4}$ **45.** $\dfrac{k}{10} \leqslant 4 + \dfrac{k}{5}$ **46.** $\dfrac{a}{3} - 1 \leqslant \dfrac{a}{2} + 3$

47. $-3(4x - 8) > 2(3 + 2x)$ **48.** $4 - 5(y - 2) \leqslant -2(-9 + 2y)$

C **49.** $\dfrac{8c + 1}{4} < \dfrac{7c}{12} + \dfrac{5}{3}$ **50.** $\dfrac{6x - 3}{2} > \dfrac{37}{10} + \dfrac{x + 2}{5}$

51. $\dfrac{3k - 4}{3} \geqslant \dfrac{2k + 4}{6} + \dfrac{5k - 1}{9}$ **52.** $\dfrac{2r - 3}{5} - \dfrac{r - 3}{3} \leqslant 2$

53. $3(4 - x) - 7(x - 2) \geqslant 9x + 7$ **54.** $2(c - 12) \leqslant 6(2c + 1) + 5(6 - 3c)$

SELF-TEST 2

1. What is the solution set of $8x - 4 = 7$ if the domain is the set of integers?   Section 1-3

Solve and check.

2. $4y + 5 = 35 - y$ **3.** $1.4x - 7 = 5 - 0.6x$

4. $2(x + 3) - 5 = 17 - (4x - 2)$

Complete.

5. If n is the first of three consecutive integers, their average is ___?___ .   Section 1-4

6. The value of $(2n + 3)$ nickels is ___?___ .

7. At 7 A.M. Sara left home traveling 60 km/h. At 8 A.M. her brother Matt started after her on the same road traveling 80 km/h. At what time did Matt overtake Sara?

8. How many kilograms of nuts worth $4.50 per kilogram must be mixed with 20 kg of nuts worth $6 per kilogram to make a mixture that can be sold for $5 per kilogram?

9. Bill is 3 times as old as Frank. Ten years from now, Bill's age will exceed twice Frank's age by 1 year. Find the present age of each.

Find and graph the solution set of each inequality.

10. $6 - 5y \leqslant 2y + 20$ **11.** $3(x + 4) > x - (6 - 2x)$ Section 1-5

Solve.

12. $w - 2 < 3(w - 5)$ **13.** $\dfrac{3x}{2} \leqslant \dfrac{3x - 6}{4}$

Section 1-6 COMPOUND INEQUALITIES

Inequalities can be used to express the range of values for which a variable is defined. Often a combination of inequalities is necessary to express this range. In this section you will review two types of combined inequalities:

- conjunctive inequalities
- disjunctive inequalities

Recall from your study of logic that a *conjunction* is a sentence formed by combining two clauses with the word *and*. A conjunction is true if and only if both clauses are true. A *conjunctive inequality* is a mathematical sentence formed by combining two inequalities with the word *and*. The conjunctive inequality

$$a < x \text{ and } x < b$$

is often written as

$$a < x < b.$$

The solution set of a conjunctive inequality is the intersection of the solution sets of the two inequalities.

$$\{x: a < x < b\} = \{x: a < x\} \cap \{x: x < b\}$$

EXAMPLE   Graph the solution set of $-2 < x \leqslant 2$.

SOLUTION $\{x: -2 < x \leqslant 2\} = \{x: -2 < x\} \cap \{x: x \leqslant 2\}$

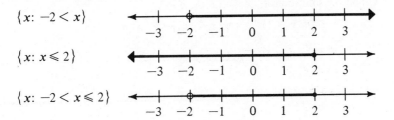

The example on the following page illustrates two methods of solving a conjunctive inequality. In the first method, we solve the inequalities separately and then find the intersection of their solution sets. In the second method, we solve the inequalities simultaneously.

EXAMPLE   Solve and graph the solution set: $-24 < 4(2-x) \leqslant 16$

SOLUTION

Method 1

$-24 < 4(2-x)$	and	$4(2-x) \leqslant 16$
$-24 < 8-4x$	and	$8-4x \leqslant 16$
$-32 < -4x$	and	$-4x \leqslant 8$
$8 > x$	and	$x \geqslant -2$

Method 2

$-24 < 4(2-x) \leqslant 16$
$-24 < 8-4x \leqslant 16$
$-32 < -4x \leqslant 8$
$8 > x \geqslant -2$

Thus, using either method, the solution set is:

$$\{x: -2 \leqslant x < 8\}$$

Its graph is: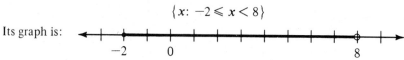

Notice that you can't use the second method in the next example.

EXAMPLE   Determine the solution set:

$$0 < -4-4x \quad \text{and} \quad 3x+7 > 13$$

SOLUTION   Using Method 1, we have:

$$4x < -4 \quad \text{and} \quad 3x > 6$$
$$x < -1 \quad \text{and} \quad x > 2$$

Since no value of x can satisfy both conditions, the solution set is $\emptyset$.

Also recall from your study of logic that a *disjunction* is a sentence formed by combining two clauses with the word *or*. A disjunction is true if and only if at least one of the clauses is true. A *disjunctive inequality* is a mathematical sentence formed by combining two inequalities with the word *or*. The solution set of a disjunctive inequality such as

$$x < a \text{ or } x > b$$

is the union of the solution sets of the two inequalities.

$$\{x: x < a \text{ or } x > b\} = \{x: x < a\} \cup \{x: x > b\}$$

EXAMPLE   Graph the solution set: $x < -2$ or $x \geqslant 2$

SOLUTION $\{x: x < -2 \text{ or } x \geqslant 2\} = \{x: x < -2\} \cup \{x: x \geqslant 2\}$

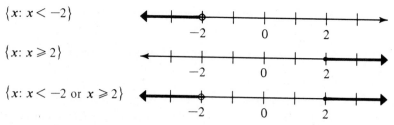

To solve disjunctive inequalities, solve the inequalities separately and then find the union of their solution sets.

EXAMPLE   Solve and graph the solution set:

$$2x - 8 \leqslant -12 \quad \text{or} \quad 8 - x \leqslant 2$$

SOLUTION

$$2x \leqslant -4 \quad \text{or} \quad -x \leqslant -6$$
$$x \leqslant -2 \quad \text{or} \quad x \geqslant 6$$

Thus the solution set is:

$$\{x: x \leqslant -2 \text{ or } x \geqslant 6\}$$

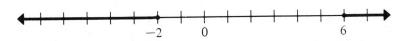

Other examples of conjunctive and disjunctive inequalities will be discussed in Section 1-8.

ORAL EXERCISES

Determine whether or not each solution set is $\emptyset$.

1. $\{x: 3 < x < -2\}$
2. $\{x: 1 < x < 5\}$
3. $\{x: x > 5 \text{ or } x < -3\}$
4. $\{x: x \leqslant 2 \text{ and } x > -1\}$
5. $\{x: x < -4 \text{ and } x > -1\}$
6. $\{x: x < 0 \text{ or } x \leqslant 8\}$
7. $\{x: 2 > x > -4\}$
8. $\{x: 1 > x > 6\}$

Name a member of each set.

9. $\{x: -4 < x < -1\}$
10. $\{x: 0 < x \text{ and } x \leqslant 3\}$
11. $\{x: x \leqslant -3 \text{ or } x > 8\}$
12. $\{x: x \geqslant -2 \text{ or } x < -5\}$
13. $\{x: -6 < 3x - 6 \leqslant 0\}$
14. $\{x: 4 \geqslant 5x - 1 \text{ or } -4 \geqslant 1 - 5x\}$

Match each set with its graph.

15. $\{x: -2 < x \leqslant 3\}$
16. $\{x: x < 3 \text{ and } x > -2\}$
17. $\{x: x > 3 \text{ or } -x \geqslant 2\}$
18. $\{x: 3 < x \text{ or } x < -2\}$
19. $\{x: 0 \leqslant x + 2 < 5\}$
20. $\{x: 2x < -4 \text{ or } 3 + x \geqslant 6\}$

a.
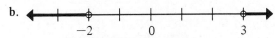

b.

c.

d.

e.

f.
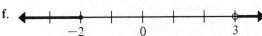

WRITTEN EXERCISES

Solve each inequality and graph any solution set that is not empty.

A
1. $-3 \leqslant 5 + x < 1$
2. $6 \geqslant x - 5 \geqslant -3$
3. $-4 < 7 - x \leqslant -2$
4. $-1 \geqslant 3 - x > 4$
5. $1 \geqslant 3x + 4 > -2$
6. $-7 < 5x - 2 < 3$
7. $-7 \geqslant 1 - 4x \geqslant 1$
8. $-4 < 2 - 6x \leqslant 2$
9. $z - 5 > 2$ or $4 + z < 2$
10. $y + 3 \leqslant 2$ or $2y + 3 > 5$
11. $6 \leqslant 8c - 2$ or $9 \leqslant 1 - 4c$
12. $3 - 3d > 12$ or $9 - 2d < 5$
13. $5 > 1 - 2r$ and $3r < 2r + 1$
14. $6w < 4 + 7w$ and $2 - 3w \geqslant -1$
15. $-4 < 4(x - 1) \leqslant 12$
16. $0 \leqslant 2(6n - 8) < 8$
17. $-6 < 3(4 - z) \leqslant 0$
18. $-8 \leqslant 2(7 - x) \leqslant -2$

Solve.

B
19. $6 > 3(4 + 5d) > -3$
20. $15 \geqslant 3(7 + 3x) > 6$
21. $-5 + 3w < -2$ and $12 + 4w \geqslant 4$
22. $3z + 6 < -12$ and $4 > 10 + 2z$
23. $4 - 3d \geqslant 16 + d$ or $13 - d > 3d + 7$
24. $3x + 4 > 9 + 2x$ or $4x - 3 \leqslant 3x - 4$
25. $6(x + 1) < 3x$ or $6x > 3(x - 1)$
26. $3x < 2(x - 4)$ or $3(2x - 1) > 5x$
27. $3(x - 1) < 4x < 3x - 1$
28. $2x + 1 < 3x < 2(x + 3)$

29. $3x - 1 < 2(x + 4)$ or $7x - 3 \geqslant 2(x + 1)$
30. $8x < 3(2x + 4)$ or $4x - (2x + 3) > 0$
31. $6(z + 1) \leqslant 3(z - 5)$ or $2(3z + 2) > 4(8 - 2z)$
32. $2y - (3y - 5) > 3$ or $5y \leqslant 10 + 2(3y - 4)$

C
33. $3(w - 2) < 4w - 5 < 3(w - 1)$
34. $5d - 1 < 3(2d + 1) < 5d + 3$
35. $\frac{3}{2}(v - 9) < 6v \leqslant \frac{3}{2}(v + 6)$
36. $\frac{2}{3}(2 - x) < \frac{4 - x}{3} < \frac{2}{3}(3 - x)$

Section 1-7 USING LINEAR INEQUALITIES TO SOLVE PROBLEMS

A problem whose solution involves inequalities is translated, solved, and checked in a way similar to that described in Section 1-4. The following key words or phrases are characteristic of problems involving inequalities.

Phrase	Translation
is less than	$<$
is greater than; is more than	$>$
is no more than; is at most	$\leqslant$
is no less than; is at least	$\geqslant$

EXAMPLE At most how many 20¢ stamps can be purchased with a ten-dollar bill after mailing a package whose postage was $4.32?

SOLUTION Let x = number of stamps purchased.

Then: $0.20x + 4.32 \leqslant 10.00$
$$0.20x \leqslant 5.68$$
$$x \leqslant 28.4$$

The greatest integer less than or equal to 28.4 is 28.

Check $28 \cdot 0.20 = 5.60$
$10.00 - (5.60 + 4.32) = 10.00 - 9.92 = 0.08$

Since 8¢ is not enough to buy another stamp, at most 28 stamps can be purchased.

EXAMPLE Kim earns $425 per week. Lee earns $8.50 per hour for the first 40 h worked in a week, and is paid at a time-and-one-half rate for overtime. How many full hours must Lee work in a week in order to earn as much as Kim?

SOLUTION Since $8.50 times 40 hours equals $340, Lee must work overtime to earn at least as much as Kim. A time-and-one-half rate is $1\frac{1}{2}$ times the normal rate.

Let x = number of overtime hours worked.

Then: $8.50(40 + 1.5x) \geqslant 425.00$
$$340.00 + 12.75x \geqslant 425.00$$
$$12.75x \geqslant 85.00$$
$$x \geqslant 6.\overline{6}$$

The least integer greater than or equal to $6.\overline{6}$ is 7.

Check For working 47 hours, Lee would earn:
$$\$8.50(40) + \$12.75(7), \text{ or } \$429.25$$
For working 46 hours, Lee would earn:
$$\$8.50(40) + \$12.75(6), \text{ or } \$416.50$$

Thus, Lee must work at least 47 hours to earn as much as Kim in a week.

As the following examples show, a problem may lead to a compound inequality.

EXAMPLE In $\triangle ABC$, $AB = 6$ and $BC = 9$. What do you know about the length of $\overline{AC}$?

SOLUTION In *Book 2* you learned the Triangle Inequality: The sum of the lengths of any two sides of a triangle is greater than the length of the third side.

$$AB + BC > AC \quad \text{and} \quad AC + BC > AB \quad \text{and} \quad AB + AC > BC$$
$$6 + 9 > AC \quad \text{and} \quad AC + 9 > 6 \quad \text{and} \quad 6 + AC > 9$$
$$15 > AC \quad \text{and} \quad AC > -3 \quad \text{and} \quad AC > 3$$

Therefore $15 > AC > 3$. (Notice that if $AC > 3$, then $AC > -3$ also.)

Check It is difficult to check an infinite number of solutions. However, you can see that reversing the sequence of inequalities above shows that if $15 > AC > 3$, then the sum of the lengths of any two sides of $\triangle ABC$ is greater than the third side. Also, if $AC = 15$, then $AB + BC = AC$. If $AC = 3$, then $AB + AC = BC$.

EXAMPLE Find all sets of four consecutive odd integers whose average is greater than half the first integer and less than half the greatest of the four integers.

SOLUTION Let $x =$ the first odd integer.

Then $x + 2$, $x + 4$, and $x + 6$ are the next odd integers.

$$\frac{1}{2}x < \frac{x + (x + 2) + (x + 4) + (x + 6)}{4} < \frac{1}{2}(x + 6)$$

$$\frac{1}{2}x < \frac{4x + 12}{4} < \frac{1}{2}(x + 6)$$

$$\frac{1}{2}x < x + 3 < \frac{1}{2}(x + 6)$$

$$x < 2x + 6 < x + 6$$
$$0 < x + 6 < 6$$
$$-6 < x < 0$$

The possible choices for x are -5, -3, and -1. The sets of consecutive odd integers that fit the conditions of the problem are $\{-5, -3, -1, 1\}$, $\{-3, -1, 1, 3\}$, and $\{-1, 1, 3, 5\}$.

The check is left to you. Notice that to determine whether these are the only solutions, you must also check that $\{-7, -5, -3, -1\}$ and $\{1, 3, 5, 7\}$ do *not* fit the conditions of the problem.

ORAL EXERCISES

Translate each of the following into an inequality.

1. Three less than half a certain number is greater than 13.

2. When a certain number is subtracted from 70, twice the difference is less than 17.

3. Half a certain number is no less than the quotient when twice the number is divided by 18.

4. The product of eight and a certain number is at most 100.

5. Twelve is more than half the sum of 8 and a certain number.

6. Diane's salary is at least $20,000.

7. To box as a middleweight, Bob must weigh no more than 72.5 kg.

8. The greatest possible bowling score is 300.

9. The least possible passing grade is 65.

10. A flight attendant should be between 150 cm and 180 cm tall, inclusive.

WRITTEN EXERCISES

A 1. George would like to lose at least 0.5 kg and no more than 0.6 kg for each of six consecutive weeks. Write an inequality that will represent his total weight loss (w) if he achieves this goal.

2. Julie can win a car on *Guess the Price* if her guess is no more than $100 from the actual price of the car. Julie guessed $8359. Write an inequality that represents the cost (*c*) of the car if
   a. Julie won the car.
   b. Julie did not win the car.

3. Find the three greatest consecutive integers whose sum is no more than 26.

4. Find the three smallest integers whose sum is no less than 40, if the first is three times the second and the third is 4 less than the first.

5. The sum of three integers is at most 36. One integer is 5 more than the least integer, and the third one is 1 less than twice the least integer. Find the greatest possible values of the three integers.

6. The lengths of two sides of a triangle are 10 and 12. What do you know about the length of the third side?

7. Jeremy has $6.00 in his wallet. If he spends $2.39 for a circuit board, how many transistors at 47¢ each can he buy?

8. Seventy-eight $5 tickets were sold in advance for the Back Bay Garden Tour. How many $6 tickets must be sold on the day of the tour to have receipts of at least $1000?

9. Daryl's scores on his first five tests were 75, 52, 64, 60, and 86. What will need to be true of his next test score for his average to be at least 70?

10. A hurricane is 200 km east of Key Fargo, moving west at 18 km/h. Key Fargo must be evacuated before the hurricane is within 50 km of the town. When should Key Fargo be evacuated?

11. $\angle A$ and $\angle B$ are complementary, and the measure of $\angle A$ is greater than 63. What do you know about the measure of $\angle B$?

12. $\angle C$ and $\angle D$ are supplementary, and the measure of $\angle C$ is no more than 47. What do you know about the measure of $\angle D$?

13. The charge for a certain long-distance call from a pay telephone is $1.85 for the first three minutes and $.30 for each additional minute (or fraction of a minute). If Luis has only enough change to pay for any charge up to $4.00, what is the greatest number of minutes that he can talk?

14. Ellen's age is 7 years less than half her mother's age. If the sum of their ages is at least 61 years, then how old are they now?

B 15. The sum of three negative numbers is at least −21. One number is twice the first, and the third is four times the first.
   a. Find all sets of integers that satisfy the given conditions.
   b. If the three numbers are not necessarily integers, write a compound inequality that gives the possible values of the least number.
   c. What are the possible values of the greatest of the three numbers?

16. Hibiscus National Bank charges $4 a month plus 6¢ a check. Magnolia Federal charges $2 a month plus 10¢ a check. Under what conditions is it cheaper to bank at Hibiscus National Bank?

17. The telephone company offers two types of service. For $12.30 you can make an unlimited number of local calls each month. Or you could pay $4.50 monthly, plus 8¢ for each minute you use the telephone after the first 40 minutes a month. On the average, how many minutes would you need to use the telephone each month in order to make the flat rate a better buy?

18. Vera scored 92, 84, 97, and 75 on her first four quizzes. What score on the fifth quiz will give her an average in the 80's?

19. You would like to rent a car for 6 days. Classy Car Rental offers you two options. Plan A costs $80, plus 13¢ for each kilometer driven after the first 200 km, which are free. Plan B costs $12.95 each day, plus 10¢ for each kilometer. Under what conditions would you choose Plan B?

20. The ratio of the lengths of the sides of two squares is $3:2$. If the sum of the perimeters can range from 80 cm to 120 cm, what are the dimensions of the smaller square?

21. Oil and gas are mixed in a ratio of $3:8$. If the oil costs 73¢ per liter and the gas costs 35¢ per liter, how many full liters of the mixture can be made for $20?

C 22. Corresponding sides of two similar triangles are in the ratio $5:4$. The sum of the perimeters is at least 180 cm. If the ratio of the three sides in each triangle is $4:5:7$, what are the dimensions of the smaller triangle?

23. Your car averages 9 km/L in the city and 12 km/L on the highway. You use about twice as much gas in city driving as you do on the highway. If you drove fewer than 1500 km this month, about how many kilometers did you drive on the highway?

Section 1-8 ABSOLUTE VALUE

As you shop for clothes, have you ever noticed how two "identical" items sometimes fit a little differently? When products are mass-produced, variations in size will often occur. Manufacturers allow for a certain margin of error, or tolerance, in their quality control on assembly lines. For example, a bolt that is intended to be 3 cm long might have a margin of tolerance either way of 0.02 cm, so that bolts as long as 3.02 cm and as short as 2.98 cm are acceptable. Here the positive number 0.02 represents the permissible difference between the intended measurement and the actual measurement.

Mathematicians often deal with situations such as this, where the primary concern is the magnitude of the deviation from the intended measurement. The positive number that represents this deviation is referred to as an *absolute value*.

In this section you will study:
• absolute value
• equations involving absolute values
• inequalities involving absolute values

The *absolute value* of a real number x, denoted $|x|$, is the measure of its distance from 0 on a number line.

EXAMPLES

$|3| = 3$

← 3 units →

number line from −3 to 3, point at 3

$\left|-2\frac{1}{2}\right| = 2\frac{1}{2}$

←2$\frac{1}{2}$ units→

number line from −3 to 3, point at −2½

$|0| = 0$

number line from −3 to 3, point at 0

More formally, we define the *absolute value* of x as:

$$|x| = x \quad \text{if } x \geqslant 0$$
$$|x| = -x \text{ if } x < 0$$

EXAMPLE Solve: a. $|x| = 5$ b. $|4x + 6| = 2$ c. $|4x + 6| = -2$

SOLUTION a. $|x| = 5$ implies that x can be any real number that is exactly 5 units from 0 on a number line. The solutions are 5 and −5. Thus, the solution set of $|x| = 5$ is $\{-5, 5\}$.

b. Either $4x + 6 = 2$ or $4x + 6 = -2$
    Solving: $4x = -4$ or $4x = -8$
       $x = -1$ or $x = -2$

Thus, the solution set of $|4x + 6| = 2$ is $\{-1, -2\}$.

Check: $|4(-1) + 6| = |-4 + 6| = |2| = 2$
     $|4(-2) + 6| = |-8 + 6| = |-2| = 2$

c. This equation specifies that the absolute value must be equal to a negative number, which is impossible. Thus, the solution set of $|4x + 6| = -2$ is $\emptyset$.

Absolute values also occur quite frequently in inequalities. For any positive real number a, $|x| < a$ means that on a number line x is less than a units from 0 on either the positive or the negative side of 0.

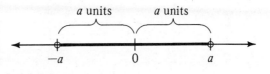

The solution set for $|x| < a$ is $\{x: -a < x < a\}$.
Similarly, the solution set for $|x| \leqslant a$ is $\{x: -a \leqslant x \leqslant a\}$.
Notice that $|x| < a$ and $|x| \leqslant a$ are both examples of conjunctive inequalities.

A corresponding relationship can be established for the inequality $|x| > a$, when a is any positive number. $|x| > a$ means that on a number line the real number x is farther than a units from 0 on either the positive or the negative side of 0.

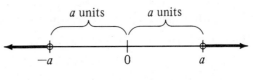

The solution set for $|x| > a$ is $\{x: x < -a \text{ or } x > a\}$.
Similarly, the solution set for $|x| \geqslant a$ is $\{x: x \leqslant -a \text{ or } x \geqslant a\}$.
Notice that $|x| > a$ and $|x| \geqslant a$ are both examples of disjunctive inequalities.

THE REAL NUMBERS **33**

EXAMPLE   Solve and graph the solution set: **a.** $|x| < 5$ **b.** $|2x - 5| \geqslant 3$

SOLUTION   **a.** $|x| < 5$ means that x is any real number less than 5 units from 0.
Therefore the solution set is $\{x: -5 < x < 5\}$.

b. $|2x - 5| \geqslant 3$ means that $(2x - 5)$ is *at least* 3 units from 0.
Therefore $|2x - 5| \geqslant 3$ is equivalent to the disjunctive inequality:

$$2x - 5 \leqslant -3 \quad \text{or} \quad 2x - 5 \geqslant 3$$

Solving: $$2x \leqslant 2 \quad \text{or} \quad 2x \geqslant 8$$
$$x \leqslant 1 \quad \text{or} \quad x \geqslant 4$$

Therefore the solution set is $\{x: x \leqslant 1 \text{ or } x \geqslant 4\}$.

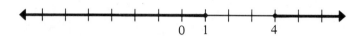

ORAL EXERCISES

Give the value of each of the following.

1. $|7|$ **2.** $|-3|$ **3.** $\left|\dfrac{1}{2}\right|$ **4.** $\left|-3\dfrac{1}{4}\right|$ **5.** $|-1.06|$

6. $|0.065|$ **7.** $|\sqrt{2}|$ **8.** $|-\sqrt{5}|$ **9.** $-|-11|$ **10.** $-|18|$

Match each item in the left column with the graph of its solution set.

11. $|x| = 5$
12. $|x| < 5$
13. $|x| > 5$
14. $|x| \leqslant 5$
15. $|x| \geqslant 5$

a.
b.
c.
d.
e.

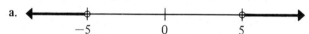

Match each item in the left column with its solution set.

16. $|x| = 2$ **a.** $\{x: -2 < x < 2\}$

17. $|x| < 2$ **b.** $\{x: -2 \leqslant x \leqslant 2\}$

18. $|x| > 2$ **c.** $\{x: x < -2 \text{ or } x > 2\}$

19. $|x| \leqslant 2$ **d.** $\{x: x \leqslant -2 \text{ or } x \geqslant 2\}$

20. $|x| \geqslant 2$ **e.** $\{-2, 2\}$

WRITTEN EXERCISES

Simplify.

A 1. $|2-7|$

2. $|-2|-|3|$

3. $|3|-|-2|$

4. $|7|+|-7|$

5. $|8-5|+2|4-4|$

6. $|7-1|-5|3-1|-2$

7. $\dfrac{2|5-2|-5|2-6|}{-|-7|}$

8. $\dfrac{3|5-11|-5|1+3|}{|-2|}$

Solve.

9. $|x+2|=5$

10. $|y-3|=7$

11. $|x+4|-1=0$

12. $|w-7|=2$

13. $|z+5|=-2$

14. $|x-4|+3=0$

15. $|2y+5|=13$

16. $|3z-4|=5$

17. $|7+4w|=15$

18. $|5-3x|=8$

19. $|9-6y|=0$

20. $|8z-5|=0$

21. $4|w+2|=12$

22. $6|y-3|=30$

23. $\dfrac{2}{3}|4-y|=6$

24. $\dfrac{5}{8}|5z-4|=10$

25. $\left|\dfrac{3x+1}{4}\right|=7$

26. $\left|\dfrac{2y-7}{5}\right|=1$

Solve and graph each solution set that is not empty.

27. $|x|<3$

28. $|y|>7$

29. $|z|<-2$

30. $|w|>-6$

31. $|y|\geqslant 8$

32. $|x|\leqslant 5$

33. $|-y|>3$

34. $|-x|<2$

35. $|x|<0$

36. $|x|>0$

37. $|7w|\geqslant 14$

38. $|3x|<9$

39. $|8z|\leqslant 24$

40. $|6y|>18$

41. $|z+2|<5$

42. $|w-2|<3$

43. $|7+z|>1$

44. $|y-3|>4$

45. $|3-z|>5$

46. $|7-y|\leqslant 8$

Solve.

B 47. $|2w-7|<17$

48. $|3y+6|\leqslant 15$

49. $|4x+5|>19$

50. $|11y-3|\geqslant 8$

51. $|4-2z|<6$

52. $|8-5w|>1$

53. $|6-7x|\geqslant 7$

54. $|4-4x|\leqslant 20$

55. $|2(z+3)|<18$

56. $|3+2(x-4)|>5$

57. $|5-3(2x+1)|\geqslant 2$

58. $|4(6-x)+2|\leqslant 8$

59. $\left|\dfrac{2y+1}{3}\right|<4$

60. $\left|\dfrac{3z-2}{4}\right|\leqslant 5$

61. $3|x-2|\geqslant 6$

62. $-3|2+z|\leqslant -2$

63. $\dfrac{1}{2}|4-2y|>4$

64. $-\dfrac{2}{5}|5-2m|<-4$

C 65. Show that $|a+b|\leqslant|a|+|b|$.
   (*Hint:* Consider the fact that $-|a|\leqslant a\leqslant|a|$ and $-|b|\leqslant b\leqslant|b|$. Now add these two as a system and simplify.)

66. Show that $|a|-|b|\leqslant|a-b|$.
   (*Hint:* Substitute $a-b$ for a in the result proved in Exercise 65.)

Solve and graph the solution set.

1. $6 < 2a + 4 \leqslant 8$

2. $12 > 3(3 - z) > 0$

Section 1-6

3. $5 - 2w > 7$ or $4w \geqslant w + 9$

4. The sum of Rita's age and Dean's age is 44, and Rita is more than 27 years old. What do you know about Dean's age?

Section 1-7

5. The lengths of the sides of a triangle are consecutive odd integers. Its perimeter is at least 50, but no more than 60. What are the possible lengths of the sides?

Solve and graph the solution set.

6. $|x + 5| = 5$

7. $|5w - 10| = 15$

Section 1-8

8. $|x| \geqslant 4$

9. $|8x + 4| < 12$

Computer Exercises

REVIEW OF STATEMENTS IN BASIC

The letters A and B are variables.

PRINT "HELLO";	This prints the material between the quotation marks. The semi-colon causes the next item being printed to continue, in the same line, where this statement leaves off.
PRINT A	This prints the value of A.
INPUT A	This prints a question mark. The computer waits for the value of A to be typed.
INPUT A, B	This prints *one* question mark, but the computer waits to be given *two* values, separated by a comma.
FOR J = M TO N STEP S 　　[Body of loop] NEXT J	This arrangement causes the body of the loop to be performed for the values of J from M to N in increments of S. "FOR J = 3 TO 11 STEP 2" gives the values 　　　　3, 5, 7, 9, 11. If S = 1, then "STEP S" may be omitted.
Subscripted variables A(1), A(2), . . . , A(I)	These are used to handle lists of values.
IF (a) THEN (x)	If the statement (a) is true, then the computer goes to line (x). Otherwise, it goes to the next line in sequence.
END	Many computers require this as the final statement of a BASIC program.

The program below can be used to graph the inequalities

$$2x - 3 \leqslant 9 \qquad 11 - 3x < 17$$

on the same number line. The domain in this program is the set $\{-9, -8, -7, \ldots, 7, 8, 9\}$. The computer prints a * for each solution of the first inequality and a + for each solution of the second inequality.

To graph other pairs of inequalities, change lines 130 and 200, using the new inequalities.

```
10    FOR N=0 TO 18
20    IF N/3=INT(N/3) THEN 40
30    GOTO 60
40    PRINT TAB(2*N); N−9;
50    REM***TAB(2*N+2) FOR APPLE
60    NEXT N
70    PRINT
80    FOR N=0 TO 18
90    PRINT "−"; "+";
100   NEXT N
110   PRINT
120   FOR X=−9 TO 9
130   IF 2*X−3<=9 THEN 150
140   GOTO 170
150   PRINT TAB(19+2*X); "*";
160   REM***TAB(20+2*X) FOR APPLE
170   NEXT X
180   PRINT
190   FOR X=−9 TO 9
200   IF 11−3*X<17 THEN 220
210   GOTO 240
220   PRINT TAB(19+2*X); "+";
230   REM***TAB(20+2*X) FOR APPLE
240   NEXT X
250   PRINT
260   END
```

Type in and RUN the program to solve each compound inequality. For each exercise, enter the inequalities in lines 130 and 200. Use ABS(. . .) for absolute-value expressions.

1. $2x - 3 \leqslant 9$ and $11 - 3x < 17$

2. $-3x - 5 \geqslant 1$ or $x - 4 < -5$

3. $2x + 5 \geqslant -1$ and $-4x - 5 \geqslant 7$

4. $3 - x < -1$ and $2(x - 3) < -8$

5. $|x - 1| < 4$ and $|x + 3| < 3$

6. $|x - 1| < 4$ or $|x + 3| < 3$

7. $|x + 1| \leqslant 2$ and $|x - 1| \leqslant 2$

8. $|x + 1| \leqslant 2$ or $|x - 1| \leqslant 2$

Change the program so that it will graph three inequalities on the same number line. Have the computer print an X for each solution of the third inequality. RUN the program and solve each of the following compound inequalities.

9. $3x - 5 > -8$ and $6 - x < 4$ and $9 - 2x > -3$

10. $|x + 1| \leqslant 4$ and $|x - 1| \leqslant 4$ and $|x| \geqslant 2$

CHAPTER REVIEW

Express as a decimal.

1. $1\dfrac{7}{8}$

2. $-\dfrac{7}{15}$

Section 1-1

Express as a quotient of two integers in lowest terms.

3. -6.024

4. $0.\overline{19}$

Simplify.

5. $(5^2 + 11) \div 3^2$

6. $\dfrac{21 - 2(3) + 7^2}{2^4 - 2^3}$

Section 1-2

Evaluate when $a = -2$, $b = 5$, and $c = -3$.

7. $-a^2 + 4b - 3c$

8. $b(a + c^2) - a^2$

Find (a) the additive inverse and (b) the multiplicative inverse.

9. -5

10. $1\dfrac{1}{4}$

Solve and check.

11. $10x + 4 - 15x = -11$

12. $7 - 8(2 + 3x) = 15$

Section 1-3

13. $\dfrac{3w}{5} - \dfrac{4w}{7} = \dfrac{2}{7}$

14. $0.6z + 10 = 1.8z - 2$

15. The measures of the angles of a triangle are in the ratio $2:3:4$. Find these measures.

Section 1-4

16. A jar contains 45 coins, consisting of nickels and dimes. If the value of the coins is $3.50, how many of each type of coin are in the jar?

Solve and graph the solution set.

17. $4k - 2 < 18$

18. $x - 4 \geqslant -14 - 4x$

Section 1-5

Solve.

19. $2(z - 3) - 5 \leqslant 11$

20. $6 - (4 + 3w) < 20$

Solve and graph the solution set.

21. $-5 > 2x + 1 \geqslant -13$

22. $0 < 6 - \dfrac{2}{3}x < 12$
Section 1-6

23. $7 + 2y < 3$ or $1 - 5y > 6$

24. $6 > -3k$ and $3k < 3(2 - k)$

25. The Gilberts are planning their budget for the following year. They know they will spend at least \$1200 each month and no more than \$1500 each month. Write an inequality that will represent their total expenses (e) for the year.
Section 1-7

26. The lengths of two sides of a triangle are 6 and 16. What do you know about the length of the third side?

Solve.

27. $|3 + 4x| = 9$

28. $|2(3 - 5x)| = 21$
Section 1-8

Solve and graph the solution set.

29. $|5(x - 3)| > 10$

30. $\left| \dfrac{2x + 6}{3} \right| \leqslant 4$

CHAPTER TEST

Express as a decimal.

1. $-2\dfrac{17}{25}$

2. $\dfrac{8}{11}$

Express as a quotient of two integers in lowest terms.

3. -3.0072

4. $0.03\overline{1}$

Simplify.

5. $5(2^2) - 2(3 + 5)^2$

6. $(5 \cdot 2)^2 - 2(3 + 5^2)$

Evaluate when $x = -1$, $y = 2$, and $z = -3$.

7. $x^2 - 2y^2 + 3xz$

8. $\dfrac{x + yz}{2xy + z}$

Find **(a)** the additive inverse and **(b)** the multiplicative inverse.

9. $-2\dfrac{1}{2}$

10. 0.4

State the property illustrated.

11. $6(y + 2) = 6y + 12$

12. $5 + (-5) = 0$

Solve.

13. $-4x + 19 = x + 4$

14. $2 - 5(y - 3) = 2y - 7$

Solve.

15. $\frac{1}{5}w = 3w - 28$ 16. $0.3(z - 3) - 0.2(z - 2) = 0.7$

17. $|6x + 12| = 90$ 18. $|-3(x - 4)| = 18$

Solve and graph the solution set.

19. $8 - (3x + 6) \geqslant -1$ 20. $\frac{3}{4}w - 5 \leqslant 16$

21. $8 \geqslant -4(1 + k) > 0$ 22. $5y + 4 > 18 - 2y$ or $4 - 3y < -4y$

23. $|28 - 4x| \geqslant 12$ 24. $\left| \dfrac{3x - 12}{-4} \right| < 3$

25. The width of a rectangle is 5 less than two thirds of its length. If the perimeter is 80, find the dimensions of the rectangle.

26. Kristina is twice as old as her brother. In 4 years, the sum of their ages will be 32. How old is Kristina now?

27. Karen's scores on her first four tests were 84, 69, 71, and 100. What will need to be true of her next test score for her average to be at least 80?

28. The sum of three consecutive even integers is more than 75 and at most 100.
    a. Write a combined inequality that represents these facts.
    b. Find all sets of integers that satisfy the given conditions.

Biographical Note

Carl Friedrich Gauss (1777–1855) used to say facetiously that he could count before he could talk. This precocious son of a German workingman had conceived of almost all his outstanding mathematical discoveries before he was out of his teens.

Although Gauss is now regarded as one of the greatest mathematicians of all time, such recognition was slow in coming. Gauss disliked controversy and hesitated to publicize his discoveries. Many of them, recorded only in his journals, were not published until long after his death.

The year that Gauss entered the Collegium Carolinum in Brunswick, Germany, he began to question the traditional concepts of geometry. Although he did not publish his work, he was a pioneer in non-Euclidean geometry. During these student years he also did brilliant work in number theory. In 1794 he developed the powerful method of least squares. His classic work on the theory of numbers, *Disquisitiones arithmeticae*, appeared in 1801, after he had finished studying at the University of Göttingen.

By this time Gauss had become deeply interested in astronomy. This interest was increased by Giuseppe Piazzi's discovery of Ceres, the first planetoid. Gauss began to work on formulas for the calculation of planetary orbits, and he made many remarkable contributions. His work resulted in the Gaussian law of error, used in probability and statistics.

In 1807 Gauss was appointed director of the University of Göttingen observatory and professor of mathematics, a position that he held for the rest of his life. His students held him in high regard; many of them later became well known for their own achievements. In the 1830's Gauss collaborated with a young physicist, Wilhelm Weber, in studies of electricity and magnetism.

A geodetic survey of the kingdom of Hanover that Gauss began in 1818 inspired him to study the problems of surveying in hilly country. As a result he invented a new surveying instrument and made some important contributions to the theory of surfaces.

Be sure that you understand the meaning of these terms:

natural (counting) numbers, p. 2
whole numbers, p. 2
integers, p. 2
rational numbers, p. 2
real numbers, p. 4
irrational numbers, p. 4
equation, p. 10
variable, p. 11
solution set, p. 11

identity, p. 11
null (empty) set, p. 11
linear equations in one variable, p. 11
inequality, p. 21
linear inequality in one variable, p. 22
conjunctive inequality, p. 25
disjunctive inequality, p. 26
absolute value, p. 32

MIXED REVIEW

1. Find the four greatest consecutive integers whose sum is less than 45.

Solve and graph the solution set.

2. $19 - 4x > 7(1 - x)$

3. $3x - 5 \leqslant 4$ and $x \leqslant 2(x + 4)$

Express as a quotient of integers in lowest terms.

4. $0.1\overline{45}$

5. 1000

6. 0.795

7. $7.\overline{7}$

8. Two cars left Milton at 9:00 A.M., one traveling north and the other traveling south. By 11:30 A.M. the cars were 420 km apart. If one car traveled 8 km/h faster than the other, find the average speed of each.

Solve.

9. $|-r| > 7$

10. $\dfrac{2y - 1}{3} - \dfrac{4y}{5} = 29$

11. $|2m - 5| = 1$

12. $0.085(x - 150) = 0.08x$

13. $|-3(m - 2)| < 15$

14. $5(1 - z) = 7(1 + z)$

15. State the property that justifies each step.
   a. $x(-1) + x = x(-1) + x \cdot 1$
   b. $ = x(-1 + 1)$
   c. $ = x \cdot 0$
   d. $ = 0$

16. The lengths of two sides of a triangle are 5 and 8. What can you conclude about the perimeter of the triangle?

Solve.

17. $-2 \geqslant 5g + 3 \geqslant -17$

18. $k + 4 > -1$ or $3(k + 8) < 0$

Evaluate when $r = -3$, $s = -4$, and $t = 6$.

19. $4r^2 + st$

20. $\dfrac{r(s - 2t)}{s(r + t)}$

21. $\dfrac{5rst^2}{s - t}$

Is the equation or inequality *always, sometimes,* or *never* true when the domain of x is $\mathcal{R}$?

22. $x - 3 = 3 - x$
23. $3(x \cdot 5) = 15x$
24. $2(x + 4) < 2x - 8$

25. Find the measures of two supplementary angles if the measures are in the ratio 7:3.

Solve.

26. $\dfrac{x}{5} + 7 > 1$
27. $-0.04t \leqslant 5$
28. $2h - 1 - h < h$

Find **(a)** the additive inverse and **(b)** the multiplicative inverse.

29. $-5\dfrac{3}{4}$
30. 0.005
31. $0.\overline{3}$

32. A coin bank contains 80 dimes and quarters worth $11.90 in all. How many quarters are in the bank?

Solve and graph each solution set.

33. $|v - 4| < 3$
34. $8d + 15 < 2 - 5d$ and $18 > 6 - 3d$

Simplify.

35. $5^2 - 2 \cdot 18 \div 4$
36. $(5^2 - 2) \cdot (18 \div 4)$
37. $\dfrac{5^2 - 3^3 + 2^2}{(3^2 + 2^4) \div 5}$

Express as a decimal.

38. $1\dfrac{22}{45}$
39. $\dfrac{123}{125}$
40. $-\dfrac{28}{48}$

The path of an object that is thrown vertically upward or that falls freely from a given height can be described by a quadratic expression. Solving problems concerning such objects involves solving quadratic equations. Exercise 51, page 63, about a gull gliding over the water, is a problem of this type.

Quadratic Equations

2

A ball is thrown vertically upward with a speed of 14.4 m/s from a height of 0.9 m, as shown in the diagram at the right. The following expression gives the ball's height t seconds after being thrown:

$$0.9 + 14.4t - 4.9t^2$$

To determine the number of seconds it will take the ball to land, we can solve the following quadratic equation:

$$0.9 + 14.4t - 4.9t^2 = 0$$

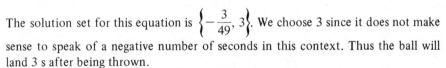

0.9 m

The solution set for this equation is $\left\{-\dfrac{3}{49}, 3\right\}$. We choose 3 since it does not make sense to speak of a negative number of seconds in this context. Thus the ball will land 3 s after being thrown.

In this chapter you will study methods for solving quadratic equations and inequalities. In Section 2-4 you will solve free-fall problems similar to the one just presented.

Section 2-1 LAWS OF EXPONENTS

In this section you will review the laws of exponents and extend your knowledge of exponents to include:
- zero exponents
- negative exponents

We define x^n, where x is the *base* and n is the *exponent*, as follows:

$$x^n = \underbrace{x \cdot x \cdots x}$$

n factors

Recall that x^2 and x^3 are often referred to as "x squared" and "x cubed."

We can use exponents to write the *powers* of a number. The first three powers of 5 are shown below:

$$\text{First power:} \quad 5^1 = 5$$
$$\text{Second power:} \quad 5^2 = 5 \cdot 5 = 25$$
$$\text{Third power:} \quad 5^3 = 5 \cdot 5 \cdot 5 = 125$$

We can develop laws for exponents by applying the definition. Consider the rth power of the product xy.

$(xy)^r = \underbrace{(xy)(xy) \cdots (xy)}_{r \text{ factors}}$ Definition of a power

$\quad = \underbrace{(x \cdot x \cdots x)}_{r \text{ factors}} \underbrace{(y \cdot y \cdots y)}_{r \text{ factors}}$ Associative and Commutative Properties of Multiplication

$\quad = x^r \cdot y^r$ Definition of a power

This result is shown below as the third law of exponents. Similar justifications of the other laws are left as Exercises 41–44.

Laws of Exponents

If x and y are real numbers, r and s are positive integers, and no denominator is 0:

1. $x^r \cdot x^s = x^{r+s}$

2. $(x^r)^s = x^{rs}$

3. $(xy)^r = x^r \cdot y^r$

4. $\left(\dfrac{x}{y}\right)^r = \dfrac{x^r}{y^r}$

5. a. If $r > s$, then $\dfrac{x^r}{x^s} = x^{r-s}$.

   b. If $r < s$, then $\dfrac{x^r}{x^s} = \dfrac{1}{x^{s-r}}$.

   c. If $r = s$, then $\dfrac{x^r}{x^s} = 1$.

EXAMPLES

$$k^4 \cdot k^5 = k^{4+5} = k^9 \qquad \text{(Law 1)}$$
$$(a^7)^8 = a^{7 \cdot 8} = a^{56} \qquad \text{(Law 2)}$$
$$(3b)^4 = 3^4 \cdot b^4 = 81b^4 \qquad \text{(Law 3)}$$
$$\left(\frac{2}{3}\right)^2 = \frac{2^2}{3^2} = \frac{4}{9} \qquad \text{(Law 4)}$$
$$\frac{y^5}{y^9} = \frac{1}{y^{9-5}} = \frac{1}{y^4} \quad (y \neq 0) \qquad \text{(Law 5(b))}$$

When you simplify expressions containing exponents, combine exponents that apply to the same base. Apply Law 2 to simplify "powers of powers."

EXAMPLES

$$(3x^4)(5x^2) = 15x^{4+2} = 15x^6$$
$$(y^6)^3 = y^{18}$$
$$(2hj)^5 = 2^5 h^5 j^5 = 32h^5 j^5$$
$$(7a^4 b)^2 = 7^2(a^4)^2 b^2 = 49a^8 b^2$$
$$\left(\frac{2r}{t}\right)^4 = \frac{(2r)^4}{t^4} = \frac{2^4 r^4}{t^4} = \frac{16r^4}{t^4} \quad (t \neq 0)$$

When you simplify expressions, use Law 5 to make sure that the same base does not appear in both the numerator and the denominator of an expression.

EXAMPLES

$$\frac{7x^{12}}{x^8} = 7x^{12-8} = 7x^4 \quad (x \neq 0)$$

$$\frac{24z^2}{6z^7} = \frac{4}{z^{7-2}} = \frac{4}{z^5} \quad (z \neq 0)$$

Negative and zero exponents are used extensively in higher mathematics. These exponents are defined in such a way that the laws of exponents continue to apply.

EXAMPLE   If $x \neq 0$: $x^3 \cdot x^0 = x^{3+0} = x^3$

This example suggests that x^0 be defined as 1. The next example suggests a definition for x^{-5}.

EXAMPLE   If $x \neq 0$: $x^5 \cdot x^{-5} = x^{5+(-5)} = x^0 = 1$

This example suggests that x^{-5} be defined as $\frac{1}{x^5}$.

Examples such as these suggest the following definition: If x is a nonzero real number and n is a positive integer,

$$x^{-n} = \frac{1}{x^n} \quad \text{and} \quad x^0 = 1.$$

EXAMPLE   Evaluate: **a.** 4^{-2} **b.** 8^0

SOLUTION   **a.** $4^{-2} = \frac{1}{4^2} = \frac{1}{16}$ **b.** $8^0 = 1$

The definition of a negative exponent enables us to express Law 5 of exponents as stated at the top of the next page.

Law 5 of Exponents

If x is a nonzero real number and r and s are positive integers:

$$\frac{x^r}{x^s} = x^{r-s} = \frac{1}{x^{s-r}}$$

When you simplify an expression with negative exponents, use Law 5 to find an equivalent expression with positive exponents. *In the rest of this book we will assume that no variable written with a negative exponent equals zero, and that no variable takes on a value that causes a denominator to be zero.*

EXAMPLES

$$2^2 \cdot 2^{-5} = 2^{-3} = \frac{1}{2^3} = \frac{1}{8}$$

$$(5x^{-5})(2x^2)^2 = 5x^{-5}(4x^4) = 20x^{-1} = \frac{20}{x}$$

$$\frac{(a^{-2}b)^3}{a^{-8}} = \frac{(a^{-2})^3 b^3}{a^{-8}} = \frac{a^{-6}b^3}{a^{-8}} = a^{-6+8}b^3 = a^2 b^3$$

It can be proved (Exercises 45 and 46) that each of the following equations is an identity; that is, each statement is true for all permissible values of the variables. If x and y are nonzero real numbers and n is a positive integer:

$$\frac{1}{x^{-n}} = x^n \qquad\qquad \left(\frac{x}{y}\right)^{-n} = \left(\frac{y}{x}\right)^n$$

EXAMPLES

$$\frac{4x^2 y}{x^{-3}y^5} = \frac{4x^2 \cdot x^3}{y^4} = \frac{4x^5}{y^4}$$

$$\left(\frac{2a^2}{b^3}\right)^{-2} = \left(\frac{b^3}{2a^2}\right)^2 = \frac{b^6}{4a^4}$$

ORAL EXERCISES

Evaluate.

1. 6^3

2. 7^{-2}

3. 9^0

4. $(4^2)^2$

5. $\dfrac{1}{10^{-1}}$

6. $\dfrac{4^3}{4^5}$

7. $(3 \cdot 5)^2$

8. $\left(\dfrac{3}{4}\right)^3$

Simplify.

9. $(2m)^3$

10. $x^5 \cdot x^3$

11. $(-4a)^3$

12. $(z^5)^2$

13. $y^{15} \cdot y^4$

14. $\left(\dfrac{2}{m}\right)^3$

15. $\dfrac{y^8}{y^3}$

16. $\dfrac{v^4}{v^7}$

48 *CHAPTER 2*

17. $\dfrac{r^8}{r^8}$ **18.** $\left(\dfrac{-2t}{v}\right)^2$ **19.** $x^0 y^2$ **20.** $\dfrac{1}{x^{-5}}$

21. $\dfrac{4k^{-2}}{k^4}$ **22.** $(2x^3)(4x^8)$ **23.** $\dfrac{18y^2}{3y^5}$ **24.** $\dfrac{2r^{-5}}{8rs}$

WRITTEN EXERCISES

Simplify.

A **1.** $(2k^4 m)(3k^2 m^3)$ **2.** $(4x^5 y)(7xy^8)$ **3.** $(-3a^5)(ax^2)$

  4. $(-6km)^3$ **5.** $(2a^2 x)^4$ **6.** $(5b^5 z^2)^3 (bz)$

  7. $\left(\dfrac{2tu}{3}\right)^3$ **8.** $\left(\dfrac{4t^2 w}{w^4}\right)^3$ **9.** $\left(-\dfrac{4}{5n^3}\right)^4$

  10. $\dfrac{4k^2 m^3}{2km}$ **11.** $\dfrac{(6xy)(2x^2)}{(-3x^2 y^3)^2}$ **12.** $\dfrac{(4x^2 y^2)^2}{8x^3 y}$

  13. $\dfrac{4m^{-2} n}{36n}$ **14.** $\dfrac{5k^{-2} x}{35kx^{-4}}$ **15.** $\dfrac{42x}{3x^{-4} y^{-2}}$

  16. $\left(\dfrac{3}{5x^2}\right)^{-2}$ **17.** $\left(\dfrac{4x^5}{5y^2 x}\right)^{-3}$ **18.** $\left(\dfrac{6ab^2}{2ab^3}\right)^{-3}$

Write as a single power of 3.

EXAMPLE $\left(\dfrac{1}{27}\right)^2$

SOLUTION $\left(\dfrac{1}{27}\right)^2 = \left(\dfrac{1}{3^3}\right)^2 = (3^{-3})^2 = 3^{-6}$

19. 81 **20.** $(9)^3$ **21.** 1 **22.** $\dfrac{1}{9}$

23. $(3 \cdot 27)^2$ **24.** $\left(\dfrac{9}{27}\right)^5$ **25.** $\left(\dfrac{1}{81}\right)(3^7)$ **26.** $3^2 \cdot 9^5$

Write as an expression without a denominator. Each base should appear only once, and there should be no powers of powers.

EXAMPLE $\dfrac{a^2 b^{-2}}{4a^{-3} b}$

SOLUTION $\dfrac{a^2 b^{-2}}{4a^{-3} b} = 4^{-1} a^{2+3} b^{-2-1} = 4^{-1} a^5 b^{-3}$

B **27.** $\dfrac{x^3 y}{x^2 y^4}$ **28.** $\dfrac{k^5 m^{-2}}{3m^2}$ **29.** $\dfrac{12h^2 z}{4hz^3}$ **30.** $\dfrac{(-5ab^2)^2}{50a^5 b}$

  31. $\dfrac{(3n^2 k)^4}{(-nk)^3}$ **32.** $\dfrac{7x^0 y}{(-x^{-2} y)^3}$ **33.** $\dfrac{(4k)^0}{(n^{-1} k)^2}$ **34.** $\left(\dfrac{r}{s}\right)^{-4}$

Simplify.

35. $\dfrac{x^7 y^{-2} z^0}{x^{-2} y^{-4} z^3}$

36. $\dfrac{2^3 a^{-4} b^6 c^8}{6^3 b^{-3} c}$

37. $\dfrac{2x^{-1} w^0 z^4}{x^2 (wz)^{-4}}$

38. $\left(\dfrac{4m^{-5} p^{-8}}{12m^{-8} q^7}\right)^3$

39. $\left(\dfrac{42a^{-3} b^2}{28a^{-3} c^{-4}}\right)^{-1}$

40. $\left(\dfrac{8^4 h^2 (4k)^0}{(4^2 \cdot h)(2^2 \cdot k^5)}\right)^{-2}$

41. Give a justification of Law 1 of exponents.

42. Give a justification of Law 2 of exponents.

43. Give a justification of Law 4 of exponents.

44. Give a justification of Law 5 of exponents.

Justify the following identities: If x and y are nonzero real numbers and n is a positive integer:

C 45. $\dfrac{1}{x^{-n}} = x^n$

46. $\left(\dfrac{x}{y}\right)^{-n} = \left(\dfrac{y}{x}\right)^n$

Section 2-2 OPERATIONS WITH POLYNOMIALS

In this section you will review the definitions of monomials and polynomials. You will also review:
- polynomial addition
- polynomial subtraction
- polynomial multiplication

A *monomial* is a number, a variable, a variable raised to a positive power, or a product of such factors. The numerical factor is called the *coefficient* of the monomial. The *degree* of the monomial is the sum of the powers of the variables. A *constant monomial*, or *constant*, such as 7, has degree 0. The monomial 0 has no degree.

EXAMPLES	Monomial	Coefficient	Degree
	$3x^2 y^8$	3	10
	$-d^7 f$	-1	8

An expression with a variable in the denominator, such as $\dfrac{8}{y}$, is not a monomial.

Two monomials are said to be *like*, or *similar*, monomials if they are equal or differ only in their coefficients. For example, $-8x^2 y^3$ and $3x^2 y^3$ are like monomials, but $4k^3 n^2$ and $4k^2 n^3$ are not.

A *polynomial* is a monomial or a sum of monomials, called the *terms* of the polynomial. We usually write a polynomial such as $7x^2 + (-3x) + (-4)$ as $7x^2 - 3x - 4$. A polynomial with two terms is called a *binomial*; a polynomial with three terms is called a *trinomial*. A polynomial is in simplest form if it has no like terms. The *degree* of a polynomial is the greatest of the degrees of its terms when it is expressed in simplest form.

EXAMPLES

Polynomial	Terms	Degree
$4x^2 - 3x + 2$	$4x^2, -3x, 2$	2
$4x^3 - 2x^2 + 3xy^2 + 2$	$4x^3, -2x^2, 3xy^2, 2$	3
$a^5b^2 - 2$	$a^5b^2, -2$	7

To add polynomials, we combine like terms.

EXAMPLE $(3a - 2b + c) + (7a - 4b - 8c) = 3a + 7a - 2b - 4b + c - 8c$
$$= 10a - 6b - 7c$$

Sometimes it is convenient to add polynomials using vertical form.

EXAMPLE Simplify: $(3x^2y + 2xy^2 + 4) + (7 - 3x^2y) + (-4xy^2 - 9)$

SOLUTION Write similar terms under one another.

$$
\begin{array}{r}
3x^2y + 2xy^2 + 4 \\
-3x^2y \qquad\quad + 7 \\
-4xy^2 - 9 \\
\hline
-2xy^2 + 2
\end{array}
$$

When we subtract one polynomial from another, we use the principle that subtracting a number is the same as adding its opposite. In general, the opposite of a polynomial is the sum of the opposites of its terms. Thus we can think of subtracting a polynomial as changing the signs of its terms and adding.

EXAMPLE $(7m - 3n + 4) - (11m + 2n - 8) = 7m - 3n + 4 - 11m - 2n + 8$
$$= 7m - 11m - 3n - 2n + 4 + 8$$
$$= -4m - 5n + 12$$

EXAMPLE
$$
\begin{array}{l}
8w^2 + 5w - 10 \\
-(5w^2 - 7w + \ \ 3)
\end{array}
$$

SOLUTION Change the signs of the terms of the second polynomial and add.

$$
\begin{array}{r}
8w^2 + \ 5w - 10 \\
+ \quad -5w^2 + \ 7w - \ \ 3 \\
\hline
3w^2 + 12w - 13
\end{array}
$$

The distributive property is used to multiply polynomials.

EXAMPLE $2hk(h^2 + 4hk^3 - 2k) = (2hk)h^2 + (2hk)(4hk^3) + (2hk)(-2k)$
$$= 2h^3k + 8h^2k^4 - 4hk^2$$

EXAMPLE $(2x - 3y)(4xy - 3y) = 2x(4xy - 3y) - 3y(4xy - 3y)$
$$= 8x^2y - 6xy - 12xy^2 + 9y^2$$

We can use the **FOIL** method to multiply two binomials whose respective first and second terms are similar.

EXAMPLE Simplify: $(2a - 3)(4a + 1)$

SOLUTION Multiply the First terms:

F $(2a - 3)(4a + 1)$ $2a \cdot 4a = 8a^2$

Multiply the Outer terms:

O $(2a - 3)(4a + 1)$ $2a \cdot 1 = 2a$ $\left.\begin{array}{l} \\ \\ \\ \\ \end{array}\right\}$ Add the outer and inner products:

Multiply the Inner terms: $2a - 12a = -10a$

I $(2a - 3)(4a + 1)$ $-3 \cdot 4a = -12a$

Multiply the Last terms:

L $(2a - 3)(4a + 1)$ $-3 \cdot 1 = -3$

$(2a - 3)(4a + 1) = 8a^2 - 10a - 3$

The following multiplication patterns are often useful.

Pattern	*Example*
$(a + b)(a - b) = a^2 - b^2$	$(4x + 3y)(4x - 3y) = 16x^2 - 9y^2$
$(a + b)^2 = a^2 + 2ab + b^2$	$(4k + 7n)^2 = 16k^2 + 56kn + 49n^2$
$(a - b)^2 = a^2 - 2ab + b^2$	$(3z - 5n)^2 = 9z^2 - 30zn + 25n^2$

When you multiply polynomials in a vertical format, it can be helpful to arrange the terms in decreasing degree of one variable.

EXAMPLE Multiply: $(x^2 + 2y^2 + 2xy)(xy + x^2 - y^2)$

SOLUTION
$$
\begin{array}{r}
x^2 + 2xy + 2y^2 \\
x^2 + xy - y^2 \\
\hline
x^4 + 2x^3y + 2x^2y^2 \\
x^3y + 2x^2y^2 + 2xy^3 \\
-\ x^2y^2 - 2xy^3 - 2y^4 \\
\hline
x^4 + 3x^3y + 3x^2y^2 \qquad\quad - 2y^4
\end{array}
$$

ORAL EXERCISES

For each polynomial state:
a. the degree of the second term
b. the degree of the third term
c. the degree of the polynomial
d. the coefficient of the second term
e. the term, if any, that is similar to $17x$

1. $4x^2 - 5xy + y^2$

2. $4x^2y^3 - 3xy^3 + 5xy - 15x + 8$

3. $4a^2x + a^2x^2 - 3x^3$

4. $5wx^2 - wx + 19x + w^4$

Simplify.

5. $(3x + 2z) + (4x - 5z)$

6. $(x + 7)(x - 4)$

7. $(x - 4)(x - 5)$

8. $(3a + 2b) - (2a + b)$

9. $3r(2rs - r^3)$

10. $(5k - 2n) - (2k - 3n)$

WRITTEN EXERCISES

Simplify.

A 1. $(3x - 8y) + (14x + 6y)$

2. $(12f + 3fg - 9g) + (6f - 5fg)$

3. $11a^2 + 5a + (7a^2 - 6a)$

4. $-3b - 4c - (8c - 2b)$

5. $4x^2y - 5xy^2 - (6x^2 + 8xy^2)$

6. $0.4y^2 - 0.5y - 2.6y^2 - 1.4y$

7. $(8a - 6b + 2c) + (-10a + 7b - 5c)$

8. $(12f - 17g - 9h) + (13f - 43g + 15h)$

9. $(15p - 9q - 7r) - (8p + 7q - 3r)$

10. $(6b + 21c + 8d) - (-14b - 4c + 15d)$

11. $(4x^2 + 9xy - 7y^2) + (-2x^2 + 6y^2) - (7x^2 - 17xy)$

12. $(x^2 - 13 - 4x) - (x^3 - 5x) + (3x - 2x^3 + 7)$

Use the FOIL method or a familiar multiplication pattern to simplify each product.

13. $(k - 3m)(k + m)$

14. $(x + 2y)(x + 2y)$

15. $(c - 8d)(c - 8d)$

16. $(9h + j)(9h - j)$

17. $(3w - 7z)(w - 4z)$

18. $(6p + 5r)(3p + 4r)$

19. $(8a - 5b)(3a + 4b)$

20. $(9x + 2y)(11x - 3y)$

21. $(4z - 11)(4z + 11)$

22. $(5k - 12n)^2$

23. $(3z + 13)^2$

24. $(4x - 15y)(4x + 15y)$

Simplify.

25. $3m(4m^2 - 8m + 7)$

26. $pr(2p^2 + 7pq - 8q^2)$

27. $7b^2d(6b^2 - 8bd + 4d^2)$

28. $8g^3(7f + 4g - 12h)$

29. $(8x^2 - 3x + 5)(x - 2)$

30. $(7x^2 + 4xy - y^2)(3x + y)$

31. $(3a - 2)(3a^2 + 2a - 1)$

32. $(2t - 1)(4t^2 + 2t + 1)$

33. $(4x - y)(3x^2 - xy + 4)$

34. $(z - w)(2w^2 - 5wz + 4)$

35. $3(w - 3u) - 7(2w + u)$

36. $2(3 - 12e) + 4(8 + 3e)$

B 37. $(s + 3)(s^3 - 2s^2 + s - 4)$

38. $(a^2 - 3ab - b^2)(2a^2 + 3ab - b^2)$

39. $(2x - 5y)(x^3 - 4x^2y + y^3)$

40. $(w^2 - 3)(w^3 + 6 - w + 3w^2)$

41. $y[x(x + y) - x^2] - xy^2$

42. $5h - \left(\frac{1}{3}[15 - 3(h + 4)] + h\right)$

43. $2[c - 3(c + 4)] - 7[3c - (2c - 3)]$

44. $3 - (2y - [1 - (6y - 1)])$

45. $3[2(m - 8) - 6(m + 4)] - (3m - 11)$

46. $(-7a - 2[4(a - 3) - 6a])(a + 1)$

Express the area of each figure as a polynomial in simplest form.

47.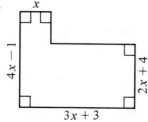

48.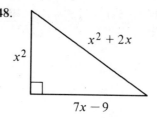

49.

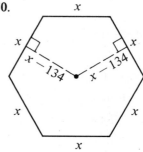

50.

(*Hint*: Divide the polygon into triangles.)

51. If the perimeter of the figure in Exercise 47 is 52, find the value of x.

52. If the perimeter of the figure in Exercise 48 is 36, find the value of x.

Solve for x.

C **53.** $(x + 8)(x + 9) - (3x + 14) = (2x - 3)(x - 2) - (x + 7)(x - 12)$

54. $(5x + 12)(x - 2) - (3x - 4)(x + 2) = (x - 2)(x + 7) + (x - 3)(x + 2)$

55. a. Multiply: $(a - 1)(a^4 + a^3 + a^2 + a + 1)$
 b. Multiply: $(x - y)(x^3 + x^2 y + xy^2 + y^3)$
 c. Using the results of parts (a) and (b), write a formula for finding the product:
$$(a - b)(a^n + a^{n-1} b + a^{n-2} b^2 + \cdots + ab^{n-1} + b^n)$$
 d. Test your conjecture from part (c) by finding the product of $(a - b)$ and $(a^6 + a^5 b + a^4 b^2 + a^3 b^3 + a^2 b^4 + ab^5 + b^6)$.
 e. Use your formula from part (c) to find $(y^8 - x^8) \div (y - x)$.

Section 2-3 FACTORING POLYNOMIALS

In this section you will review factoring polynomials. You will see many similarities between factoring polynomials and factoring integers. We will concentrate on factoring polynomials with integral coefficients.

When you write a polynomial as a product of other polynomials, you are factoring the polynomial. For example:

$$3x + 24 = 3(x + 8)$$

A polynomial with integral coefficients that has no factors other than itself, its opposite, 1, and −1 is called a *prime polynomial*. The factorization of a polynomial is *complete* when the polynomial has been expressed as a product of a monomial and one or more prime polynomials.

The monomial with the greatest coefficient and greatest degree that is a factor of the terms of a polynomial is called the *greatest monomial factor* of the polynomial. The first step in factoring a polynomial is to factor out the greatest monomial factor of the polynomial.

EXAMPLES

$$56x^3 - 28x^2 + 7x = 7x(8x^2 - 4x + 1)$$
$$-2a^3b^2 + 3a^2b^3 - ab^4 = -ab^2(2a^2 - 3ab + b^2)$$
$$13h^2 + 26hj + 39j^2 = 13(h^2 + 2hj + 3j^2)$$

Notice that the greatest monomial factor of a polynomial can be found by forming the product of the greatest common factor of the coefficients and the least power of each variable that appears in every term. When the first term of a polynomial has a negative coefficient, we usually write the greatest monomial factor with a minus sign, as in the second of the three preceding examples.

A polynomial of the form

$$ax^2 + bx + c$$

is called a *quadratic polynomial* when $a \neq 0$. The term ax^2 is called the *quadratic term*, the term bx is called the *linear term*, and the term c is called the *constant term*. Frequently we can factor a polynomial of this type as the product of two binomials.

EXAMPLE $x^2 - 2x - 3 = (x - 3)(x + 1)$

When the coefficient of the quadratic term is 1, as in the preceding example, the factors will be of the form $(x + r)(x + s)$. You must find integers r and s such that rs is the constant term and $(r + s)$ is the coefficient of the linear term. If you cannot determine the values of r and s immediately, try all the pairs of factors of the constant term.

EXAMPLE   Factor: $y^2 - 10y + 21$

SOLUTION   The ways to factor 21 are: 1 and 21; 3 and 7; −1 and −21; −3 and −7. Their sums are as follows:

$$1 + 21 = 22 \qquad\qquad 3 + 7 = 10$$
$$-1 + (-21) = -22 \qquad -3 + (-7) = -10$$

The factors −3 and −7 give the desired sum of −10. Therefore:

$$y^2 - 10y + 21 = (y - 3)(y - 7)$$

When the coefficient of the quadratic term of a trinomial is not 1, you look for a factorization of the form $(ax + b)(cx + d)$. In the next example notice that we must consider the ways to factor the quadratic coefficient.

EXAMPLE   Factor: $6x^2 + 7x - 5$

SOLUTION   The quadratic term, $6x^2$, can be factored as $(6x)(x)$ or $(2x)(3x)$. The constant term, -5, can be factored as $(5)(-1)$ or $(-5)(1)$. Thus, we consider the following possibilities.

$$(6x + 5)(x - 1) \qquad (2x + 5)(3x - 1)$$
$$(6x - 1)(x + 5) \qquad (2x - 1)(3x + 5)$$
$$(6x - 5)(x + 1) \qquad (2x - 5)(3x + 1)$$
$$(6x + 1)(x - 5) \qquad (2x + 1)(3x - 5)$$

By testing the possible factorizations, we find:

$$6x^2 + 7x - 5 = (2x - 1)(3x + 5)$$

The next example presents an alternative method for factoring trinomials.

EXAMPLE   Factor: $10x^2 - 23x + 12$

SOLUTION   1. Find the product of the coefficient of the quadratic term and the constant term.

$$(10)(12) = 120$$

2. Find the factors of this product (120) whose sum is the coefficient of the linear term (-23).

$$(-8)(-15) = 120 \quad \text{and} \quad (-8) + (-15) = -23$$

3. Express the linear term as the sum determined in the previous step.

$$10x^2 - 23x + 12 = 10x^2 - 8x - 15x + 12$$
$$= 2x(5x - 4) - 3(5x - 4)$$
$$= (2x - 3)(5x - 4)$$

It is helpful to be able to recognize the following factoring patterns.

Trinomial Squares: $a^2 + 2ab + b^2 = (a + b)^2$
$a^2 - 2ab + b^2 = (a - b)^2$

EXAMPLES $c^2 + 22c + 121 = (c + 11)^2$
$25k^2 - 30kz + 9z^2 = (5k - 3z)^2$

Difference of Two Squares: $a^2 - b^2 = (a + b)(a - b)$

EXAMPLE $r^2 - 4t^2 = (r + 2t)(r - 2t)$

Sum of Two Cubes: $a^3 + b^3 = (a + b)(a^2 - ab + b^2)$

EXAMPLE $k^3 + 1 = (k + 1)(k^2 - k + 1)$

Difference of Two Cubes: $a^3 - b^3 = (a - b)(a^2 + ab + b^2)$

EXAMPLE $27t^6 - 8 = (3t^2 - 2)(9t^4 + 6t^2 + 4)$

When you factor a polynomial, make sure that each of the polynomial factors is a prime polynomial.

EXAMPLE   Factor: $x^8 - 1$

SOLUTION $x^8 - 1 = (x^4 + 1)(x^4 - 1)$
$$= (x^4 + 1)(x^2 + 1)(x^2 - 1)$$
$$= (x^4 + 1)(x^2 + 1)(x + 1)(x - 1)$$

EXAMPLE   Factor: $4x^2 + x + 19$

SOLUTION $4x^2 + x + 19$ is a prime polynomial because none of the possibilities work.

EXAMPLE   Factor: $-2k^5 + 36k^3 - 162k$

SOLUTION $-2k^5 + 36k^3 - 162k = -2k(k^4 - 18k^2 + 81)$
$$= -2k(k^2 - 9)^2$$
$$= -2k[(k + 3)(k - 3)]^2$$
$$= -2k(k + 3)^2(k - 3)^2$$

ORAL EXERCISES

State the greatest monomial factor of the polynomial.

1. $12m - 18n$
2. $9xy^2 + 15x^3$
3. $33m + 40p$
4. $20a^2bc^3 + 20ab^2$
5. $2x^3 + x^2 + 5x$
6. $4np^2 - 5p^3 + 2p$

Factor completely.

7. $w^2 + 4w + 3$
8. $d^2 + 3d - 4$
9. $y^2 + 6y + 9$
10. $v^2 - 14v + 49$
11. $z^2 - 100$
12. $64x^2 - 25$

WRITTEN EXERCISES

Factor completely. If the polynomial is prime, so state.

A
1. $12pq^2 - 3p^2$
2. $63x^2w + 28xw^2$
3. $32b^5 - 12b^4 + 48b^3$
4. $8a^2 - 6a^3 + 12a^4$
5. $x^2 + 5x + 6$
6. $a^2 + 3a - 4$
7. $c^2 - 4c - 12$
8. $u^2 - 20u + 51$
9. $h^2 - hk - 2k^2$
10. $m^2 - 4jm + 3j^2$
11. $6y^2 + y - 1$
12. $18k^2 - 9k + 1$
13. $8x^2 - 14x + 3$
14. $12t^2 + 5t - 2$
15. $12v^2 - v - 35$
16. $12u^2 + 47u + 40$
17. $28z^2 - 5z - 3$
18. $2n^2 - 13n + 5$
19. $16y^2 + 8yz - 3z^2$
20. $6g^2 - 23gh + 15h^2$
21. $p^2 - 18p + 81$
22. $b^2 + 12b + 36$
23. $4y^2 + 20y + 25$
24. $81z^2 - 36z + 4$
25. $k^2 - 64$
26. $9n^2 - 121$
27. $u^2 + 4$
28. $25x^2 - 100y^2$
29. $y^3 - 27$
30. $a^3 + 8$

B
31. $27v^3 + 125$
32. $8r^3 - 64k^3$
33. $16n^4 - 1$
34. $16u^4 - 200u^2 + 625$
35. $4x^3 + 24x^2 - 64x$
36. $3a^5 - 300a^3$

Factor completely. If the polynomial is prime, so state.

37. $n^4 - 2n^2 + 1$

38. $21j^2 - 57jk - 18k^2$

39. $16b^3 + 62b^2 - 72b$

40. $x^4 - 13x^2 + 36$

41. $16z^3 - 250$

42. $56x^3y - 70x^2y^2 + 21xy^3$

43. $5x^2 + 180$

44. $9x^3y + 12x^2y^2 + 4xy^3$

45. $-243x^3 + 216x^2 - 48x$

EXAMPLE   Factor: $yz + 2z^2 - 7y - 14z$

SOLUTION   This polynomial does not fit any type of factorization previously examined in this section. Polynomials such as this can sometimes be factored by *grouping*.

Group terms with common factors: $(yz + 2z^2) + (-7y - 14z)$

Factor: $z(y + 2z) - 7(y + 2z)$

                                $(z - 7)(y + 2z)$

Factor by grouping.

46. $x^2 - 3x + xy - 3y$

47. $12a^2 - 4ab - 9a + 3b$

48. $12st + 56r - 96rt - 7s$

49. $63h^2 + 4k + 36h + 7hk$

C 50. $p^2 - 4r^2 + 4p^3 + 8p^2r$

51. $d^2 - 1 - 7d^2f - 7df$

Factor completely.

52. $6c^{2x} + 8c^x - 64$

53. $(a^3 + 2)^2 - 100$

54. $(s^2 - 2st)^2 - 2t^2(s^2 - 2st) - 3t^4$

55. $2x^{k+4}w^4 - 8x^{k+2}w^4 - 10x^kw^4$

56. $u^{18} - m^{18}$

57. $2a^{2m} - a^mb^k - b^{2k}$

Section 2-4 SOLVING QUADRATIC EQUATIONS

A quadratic equation in x is any equation that can be written in the *standard form*:

$$ax^2 + bx + c = 0 \quad a, b, c \in \mathbb{R}, a \neq 0$$

EXAMPLES   *Quadratic Equation*   *Standard Form of the Equation*

$y^2 - 4y - 8 = 0$ $y^2 - 4y - 8 = 0$

$x^2 = 8x - 19$ $x^2 - 8x + 19 = 0$

$\dfrac{k^2}{5} = \dfrac{k}{3} + \dfrac{9}{10}$ $\dfrac{1}{5}k^2 - \dfrac{1}{3}k - \dfrac{9}{10} = 0$

$v^2 = 17$ $v^2 - 17 = 0$

Certain quadratic equations may be solved easily by factoring. To do so, we apply the following property:

Zero-Product Property

For all real numbers r and s, $rs = 0$ if and only if $r = 0$ or $s = 0$.

EXAMPLE Solve: $x^2 - 4x - 12 = 0$

SOLUTION 1. Factor the left side of the equation: $(x - 6)(x + 2) = 0$

2. According to the Zero-Product Property, the product $(x - 6)(x + 2)$ equals 0 if and only if the following is true:

$$x - 6 = 0 \quad \text{or} \quad x + 2 = 0$$
$$x = 6 \quad \text{or} \quad x = -2$$

3. Check the roots by substituting them in the original equation.

$$6^2 - 4 \cdot 6 - 12 \overset{?}{=} 0 \qquad (-2)^2 - 4(-2) - 12 \overset{?}{=} 0$$
$$36 - 24 - 12 = 0 \qquad 4 + 8 - 12 = 0$$

Therefore, the solution set is $\{-2, 6\}$.

Before attempting to solve a quadratic equation by factoring, make sure that the equation is in standard form.

EXAMPLE Solve: $2d(d + 5) = 6(21 + d)$

SOLUTION

$$2d^2 + 10d = 126 + 6d$$
$$2d^2 + 4d - 126 = 0$$
$$d^2 + 2d - 63 = 0$$
$$(d + 9)(d - 7) = 0$$
$$d + 9 = 0 \quad \text{or} \quad d - 7 = 0$$
$$d = -9 \quad \text{or} \quad d = 7$$

Checking the roots in the original equation is left for you.
The solution set is $\{-9, 7\}$.

When we solve a quadratic equation, we usually try the method of factoring, but it is not always effective in solving quadratic equations. The *quadratic formula* shown below, however, can be used to solve any quadratic equation.

The Quadratic Formula

The solutions of $ax^2 + bx + c = 0$ $(a \neq 0)$ are given by the equation:

$$x = \frac{-b \pm \sqrt{b^2 - 4ac}}{2a}$$

EXAMPLE Solve: $8x^2 - 2x - 15 = 0$

SOLUTION Apply the quadratic formula: $a = 8; b = -2; c = -15$.

$$x = \frac{-(-2) \pm \sqrt{(-2)^2 - 4(8)(-15)}}{2(8)} = \frac{2 \pm \sqrt{484}}{16} = \frac{2 \pm 22}{16} = \frac{1 \pm 11}{8}$$

Thus, $x = \frac{-10}{8} = -1\frac{1}{4}$ or $x = \frac{12}{8} = 1\frac{1}{2}$.

The check is left for you. The solution set is $\left\{-1\frac{1}{4}, 1\frac{1}{2}\right\}$.

EXAMPLE   Solve: $x^2 - 1 = -3x$

SOLUTION   Write the equation in standard form and then apply the quadratic formula.

$$x^2 + 3x - 1 = 0 \qquad a = 1; \; b = 3; \; c = -1$$

$$x = \frac{-3 \pm \sqrt{3^2 - 4(1)(-1)}}{2(1)} = \frac{-3 \pm \sqrt{13}}{2}$$

The check is left for you. The solution set is $\left\{ \dfrac{-3 - \sqrt{13}}{2}, \; \dfrac{-3 + \sqrt{13}}{2} \right\}$.

ORAL EXERCISES

State the roots of the quadratic equation.

1. $(x - 3)(x + 8) = 0$
2. $(2y - 5)(y - 7) = 0$
3. $(3k - 15)(k + 2) = 0$
4. $v^2 - 7v + 12 = 0$
5. $r^2 - r - 20 = 0$
6. $q^2 + 2q - 24 = 0$
7. $n^2 - 2n = 15$
8. $a^2 + 10 = 7a$
9. $u^2 = u + 42$

10. What is wrong with the following attempted solution? Explain.

$$x^2 - 3x = 4$$
$$x(x - 3) = 4$$
$$x = 4 \quad \text{or} \quad x - 3 = 4$$
$$x = 4 \quad \text{or} \quad x = 7$$

The solution set is $\{4, 7\}$.

WRITTEN EXERCISES

Solve.

A
1. $w^2 + 2w - 8 = 0$
2. $a^2 + 9a + 20 = 0$
3. $z^2 - 16z + 39 = 0$
4. $48 + 2y - y^2 = 0$
5. $x^2 - 81 = 0$
6. $v^2 - 3v = 0$
7. $4p^2 + 3p = 0$
8. $9x^2 - 64 = 0$
9. $16f^2 - 25 = 0$
10. $2k^2 - 9k + 4 = 0$
11. $35m^2 + 24m + 4 = 0$
12. $3q^2 - 17q + 10 = 0$
13. $32 + 17t - 15t^2 = 0$
14. $12z^2 - 13z - 4 = 0$
15. $6m^2 + 5m = 4$
16. $14s^2 + 66 = -89s$
17. $24s^2 = 8s + 10$
18. $10r^2 = r + 24$

19. $w^2 - 5 = 15w - 5$
20. $x^2 - 12x = 2x - 45$
21. $-48 - 3m^2 = 8m - 4m^2$
22. $4x^2 - 10x = x^2 + 10x + 7$
23. $r^2 - 10r + 25 = 9r - 35$
24. $a(a - 4) = 4a$
25. $3t(t + 7) = 16 - t$
26. $y^2 + 2y + 20(y + 2) = 0$

27. $q^2 + 11 = 15(q - 3)$

28. $2r(r + 1) = 7r - 2$

29. $7(x^2 + x) = x^2 - 10(x + 1)$

30. $12p(4p - 1) + p^2 = 12(12 - p)$

Solve by using the quadratic formula.

B 31. $x^2 - 3x + 1 = 0$

32. $2x^2 + 5x + 1 = 0$

33. $x^2 + 3x - 7 = 0$

34. $2x^2 - 5x - 2 = 0$

35. $7x^2 + 1 = 9x$

36. $3x^2 = 7x + 1$

37. The sum of 3 times a positive integer and the square of the integer is 154. What is the integer?

38. If 8 times a positive integer is subtracted from the square of the integer, the difference is 105. What is the integer?

39. The sum of the squares of two positive, consecutive, odd integers is 202. What are the integers?

40. The sum of the squares of three consecutive positive integers is 245. What are the integers?

41. The area of the triangle is 24 square units.
   a. Find the value of x.
   b. Find the lengths of the altitude and base that are shown.

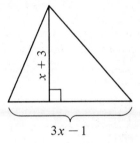

$x + 3$

$3x - 1$

42. The area of the shaded region between the squares is 40 square units. State the length of a side of each square.

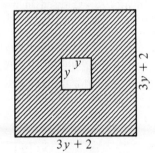

y

$3y + 2$

$3y + 2$

In Exercises 43 and 44 you are given the areas (A) of the figures. Sketch each figure and label each side with its length.

43. $A = 133$ square units

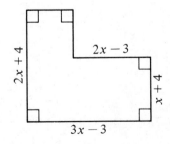

$2x + 4$

$2x - 3$

$x + 4$

$3x - 3$

44. $A = 136$ square units

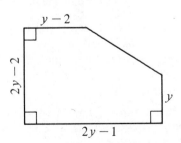

$y - 2$

$2y - 2$

y

$2y - 1$

EXAMPLE   Solve: $24z^3 - 10z^2 - 4z = 0$

SOLUTION $24z^3 - 10z^2 - 4z = 0$

$2z(12z^2 - 5z - 2) = 0$

$2z(3z - 2)(4z + 1) = 0$

$2z = 0$ or $3z - 2 = 0$ or $4z + 1 = 0$

$z = 0$ or $z = \dfrac{2}{3}$ or $z = -\dfrac{1}{4}$

The solution set is $\left\{-\dfrac{1}{4}, 0, \dfrac{2}{3}\right\}$.

Solve.

45. $2z^3 + 5z^2 - 3z = 0$

46. $5p^3 - 33p^2 + 18p = 0$

47. $14y^3 + 20y^2 = 5y - 13y^2$

48. $6x^2(x + 8) + 5x(x + 8) = 0$

Exercises 49–52 concern freely falling objects. Study the formula and example below before doing the exercises.

When an object is propelled upward with a vertical speed (v) from a height (k), then the height (h) of the body after t seconds have elapsed is given by the following formula:

$$h = k + vt - 4.9t^2$$

Both h and k are expressed in meters; v is expressed in meters per second (m/s).

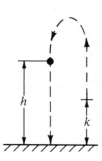

EXAMPLE   A ball is tossed upward with a vertical speed of 14.7 m/s from a cliff 60 m above the ground. After how many seconds will the ball be 11 m above the ground?

SOLUTION   Use the formula, assigning values to the known variables as follows: $v = 14.7$, $k = 60$, $h = 11$

$11 = 60 + 14.7t - 4.9t^2$

$0 = 49 + 14.7t - 4.9t^2$

$0 = 490 + 147t - 49t^2$

$0 = 10 + 3t - t^2$

$0 = (5 - t)(2 + t)$

$5 - t = 0$ or $2 + t = 0$

$5 = t$ or $t = -2$

After 5 s the ball will be 11 m above the ground.

49. A dog accidentally tossed a rubber bone over the balcony railing of its owner's apartment. The bone landed on the roof of a taxicab waiting below. If the bone began its fall from a height of 100 m with a vertical speed of 4.9 m/s, and the roof of the cab was 2 m above the ground, how long did it take the bone to land?

50. A pebble is thrown upward with a vertical speed of 19.6 m/s from a bridge 156.8 m above a river. How many seconds after being thrown will the pebble hit the surface of the river?

51. A gull gliding at a constant height of 50.1 m above the surface of the water folds its wings and falls freely toward the surface of the water. After how many seconds will the gull be 6 m above the surface of the water?

52. A tennis ball is hit upward with a vertical speed of 34.3 m/s by being struck with a racket 1.2 m from the ground. How many seconds after being struck will the ball be 60 m above the ground? Why are there two answers to this question?

EXAMPLE   Solve: $a^4 - 3a^2 - 4 = 0$

SOLUTION   Although this equation is not a quadratic equation, it is quadratic in form.

$$a^4 - 3a^2 - 4 = 0$$
$$(a^2)^2 - 3a^2 - 4 = 0$$
$$(a^2 - 4)(a^2 + 1) = 0$$
$$(a + 2)(a - 2)(a^2 + 1) = 0$$

$$a + 2 = 0 \quad \text{or} \quad a - 2 = 0 \quad \text{or} \quad a^2 + 1 = 0$$
$$a = -2 \quad \text{or} \quad a = 2$$

Notice that there are no solutions to $a^2 + 1 = 0$ since the square of any real number is nonnegative. Therefore, the solution set is $\{-2, 2\}$.

Solve.

53. $y^4 - 13y^2 + 36 = 0$

54. $m^4 - 20m^2 + 64 = 0$

55. $z^4 + 100 = 29z^2$

56. $b^4 - 4b^2 = 4b^2 - 16$

57. $4a^4 + 11a^2 = 36(a^2 - 1)$

58. $9t^2(t^2 - 2) = 7t^2 - 16$

59. $61r^2 - 4 = 225r^4$

60. $200x^4 - 25 = 171x^2 + 4x^4$

SELF-TEST 1

Simplify.

1. $(4x^2y)(5xy^3)$ **2.** $\dfrac{7z^3w}{14w^4z}$ **3.** $\left(\dfrac{3x^2}{y}\right)^3$ Section 2-1

4. $(5x^2 - x + 2) + (3x^2 - 3x + 1)$ **5.** $(4b^2 + b - 5) - (b^2 - 3b + 7)$ Section 2-2

6. $(8n + 2)(3n - 5)$ **7.** $(4a - 3b)(4a + 3b)$

Factor completely.

8. $v^2 - 9v + 20$ **9.** $6x^2 - 11x - 10$ Section 2-3

10. $49k^2 - 28k + 4$ **11.** $3u^3 - 12u$

Solve.

12. $y^2 - 11y + 24 = 0$ **13.** $6k^2 - 13k - 28 = 0$ Section 2-4

14. $20u^2 + 13u = 21$ **15.** $6v^2 = 7v + 5$

16. The sum of the squares of the first two of three consecutive positive integers equals the square of the third. What are the integers?

Section 2-5 DIVISION OF POLYNOMIALS

In this section you will review the division of polynomials and study:
- the Remainder Theorem
- the Factor Theorem

To divide a polynomial by a monomial, you use the Distributive Property.

EXAMPLE Express as a sum in simplest form: $\dfrac{4x^4y^3 + 8x^3y^2 - 2x^2y + 4xy^2}{4x^2y}$

SOLUTION $\dfrac{4x^4y^3 + 8x^3y^2 - 2x^2y + 4xy^2}{4x^2y} = \dfrac{4x^4y^3}{4x^2y} + \dfrac{8x^3y^2}{4x^2y} - \dfrac{2x^2y}{4x^2y} + \dfrac{4xy^2}{4x^2y}$

$$= x^2y^2 + 2xy - \frac{1}{2} + \frac{y}{x}$$

To divide a polynomial by a polynomial with two or more terms, you can use an algorithm similar to the division algorithm of arithmetic.

EXAMPLE Divide $(2x^3 - 14x^2 + 21x - 3)$ by $(x - 5)$.

SOLUTION

$$
\begin{array}{r}
2x^2 - 4x + 1 \\
x-5\overline{)2x^3 - 14x^2 + 21x - 3} \\
\underline{2x^3 - 10x^2} \\
-4x^2 + 21x - 3 \\
\underline{-4x^2 + 20x} \\
x - 3 \\
\underline{x - 5} \\
2
\end{array}
$$

The result can be written as follows:

$$\frac{2x^3 - 14x^2 + 21x - 3}{x - 5} = 2x^2 - 4x + 1 + \frac{2}{x - 5}$$

The method of writing the answer just shown is an example of the relationship:

$$\frac{\text{Dividend}}{\text{Divisor}} = \text{Quotient} + \frac{\text{Remainder}}{\text{Divisor}}$$

The following form of the preceding equation is often used, especially for checking answers:

$$\text{Dividend} = \text{Quotient} \times \text{Divisor} + \text{Remainder}$$

Thus, to check the answer to the preceding example, note that the dividend is $2x^3 - 14x^2 + 21x - 3$, the quotient is $2x^2 - 4x + 1$, the divisor is $x - 5$, and the remainder is 2.

$$
\begin{aligned}
2x^3 - 14x^2 + 21x - 3 &\stackrel{?}{=} (2x^2 - 4x + 1)(x - 5) + 2 \\
&\stackrel{?}{=} (2x^2 - 4x + 1)x + (2x^2 - 4x + 1)(-5) + 2 \\
&\stackrel{?}{=} 2x^3 - 4x^2 + x - 10x^2 + 20x - 5 + 2 \\
2x^3 - 14x^2 + 21x - 3 &= 2x^3 - 14x^2 + 21x - 3
\end{aligned}
$$

When you divide polynomials, arrange the terms of the dividend and divisor in decreasing powers of a variable. Write in missing powers, using a coefficient of 0.

EXAMPLE   Divide $4p^3 - 12 + 5p$ by $2p - 3$.

SOLUTION   Rewrite the dividend in decreasing powers of p and write in the term $0p^2$.

$$
\begin{array}{r}
2p^2 + 3p + 7 \\
2p - 3 \overline{\smash{)}4p^3 + 0p^2 + 5p - 12} \\
\underline{4p^3 - 6p^2} \\
6p^2 + 5p - 12 \\
\underline{6p^2 - 9p} \\
14p - 12 \\
\underline{14p - 21} \\
9
\end{array}
$$

$$\frac{4p^3 - 12 + 5p}{2p - 3} = 2p^2 + 3p + 7 + \frac{9}{2p - 3}$$

The check is left for you.

Earlier in this section we showed that when $2x^3 - 14x^2 + 21x - 3$ is divided by $x - 5$, the quotient is $2x^2 - 4x + 1$ and the remainder is 2. Thus:

$$2x^3 - 14x^2 + 21x - 3 = (x - 5)(2x^2 - 4x + 1) + 2$$

Let us substitute 5 for x in this equation:

$$
\begin{aligned}
2 \cdot 5^3 - 14 \cdot 5^2 + 21 \cdot 5 - 3 &= (5 - 5)(2 \cdot 5^2 - 4 \cdot 5 + 1) + 2 \\
&= 0(2 \cdot 5^2 - 4 \cdot 5 + 1) + 2 \\
&= 0 + 2 \\
&= 2
\end{aligned}
$$

Notice that the value of the polynomial $2x^3 - 14x^2 + 21x - 3$ when $x = 5$ is equal to the remainder when the polynomial is divided by $x - 5$. This result is an example of the *Remainder Theorem*:

Theorem 2-1   Let $c_n x^n + c_{n-1} x^{n-1} + \cdots + c_0$ be a polynomial, which we will refer to as P, such that the coefficients $c_0, c_1, \ldots, c_n$ are real numbers. The value of P when $x = a$ is equal to the remainder when P is divided by $(x - a)$. (The Remainder Theorem)

The proof of this theorem, which may be found in more advanced texts, uses many of the steps presented in the discussion above.

An equation that can be written with 0 as one side and a polynomial as the other side is called a *polynomial equation*. The *Factor Theorem*, which follows directly (Exercise 31) from the Remainder Theorem, is often useful in finding the roots of a polynomial equation. Notice that the theorem refers to factoring a polynomial with real coefficients as a product of polynomials with real coefficients.

Theorem 2-2 Let $c_n x^n + c_{n-1} x^{n-1} + \cdots + c_0$ be a polynomial, which we will refer to as P, such that the coefficients $c_0, c_1, \ldots, c_n$ are real numbers. A real number r is a root of the equation

$$c_n x^n + c_{n-1} x^{n-1} + \cdots + c_0 = 0$$

if and only if $(x - r)$ is a factor of P. (The Factor Theorem)

EXAMPLE Given that 2 is a root of the equation $x^3 - 4x^2 + x + 6 = 0$, find the complete solution set.

SOLUTION Since 2 is a root of the equation, we know by the Factor Theorem that $x - 2$ is a factor of $x^3 - 4x^2 + x + 6$.

$$
\begin{array}{r}
x^2 - 2x - 3 \\
x - 2 \overline{)x^3 - 4x^2 + x + 6} \\
\underline{x^3 - 2x^2} \\
-2x^2 + x + 6 \\
\underline{-2x^2 + 4x} \\
-3x + 6 \\
\underline{-3x + 6}
\end{array}
$$

Since $x^3 - 4x^2 + x + 6 = (x - 2)(x^2 - 2x - 3)$, the original equation is equivalent to the following:

$$(x - 2)(x^2 - 2x - 3) = 0$$

Applying the Zero-Product Property, we can solve for the remaining roots by finding the values of x for which the quotient, $x^2 - 2x - 3$, is 0.

$$x^2 - 2x - 3 = 0$$
$$(x - 3)(x + 1) = 0$$
$$x - 3 = 0 \quad \text{or} \quad x + 1 = 0$$
$$x = 3 \quad \text{or} \quad x = -1$$

The solution set is $\{-1, 2, 3\}$. The check is left for you.

ORAL EXERCISES

State the quotient as a sum in simplest form.

1. $\dfrac{2x^2 + 4xy}{2x}$

2. $\dfrac{8a^2 + ab}{4a}$

3. $\dfrac{3x^2 + 9xy}{3x^2}$

4. $\dfrac{5p^2 + 2p}{5p + 2}$

5. $\dfrac{x^4 + 3x^3}{x + 3}$

6. $\dfrac{2k^3 - 14k^2}{k - 7}$

In Exercises 7-10 we will refer to the polynomial

$$2x^3 + 7x^2 - 46x + 21$$

as P.

7. Given that -27 is the remainder when P is divided by $x - 2$, what is the value of P when $x = 2$?

8. Given that 168 is the value of P when $x = -3$, what is the remainder when P is divided by $x + 3$?

9. Given that $(x + 7)$ is a factor of P, name a solution of the equation:

$$2x^3 + 7x^2 - 46x + 21 = 0$$

10. Given that 3 is a root of the equation $2x^3 + 7x^2 - 46x + 21 = 0$, name a factor of P (other than $x + 7$).

WRITTEN EXERCISES

Express as a sum in simplest form.

A   **1.** $\dfrac{42a^3b - 12a^2b^3 + 18ab^2 - 42a^2b}{6ab}$ **2.** $\dfrac{12x^2y + xy^2 - 7x^2 - x}{xy}$

3. $\dfrac{20k^2m^3 - 10m^2k^2 - 7mk + 2m^2}{5m^2k}$ **4.** $\dfrac{7v + 21u^2 - 28u^3v^2 + 49u^2v^3}{7u^2v}$

Divide the first polynomial by the second; express the result in the form:

$$\frac{\text{Dividend}}{\text{Divisor}} = \text{Quotient} + \frac{\text{Remainder}}{\text{Divisor}}$$

5. $p^3 + p^2 - p - 1; \; p - 1$ **6.** $2a^3 + 3a^2 - a + 2; \; a + 2$

7. $q^3 - 7q^2 + 10q + 8; \; q - 4$ **8.** $3r^3 + 7r^2 - 18r + 8; \; 3r - 2$

9. $b^2 - 6b + b^3 + 24; \; b + 4$ **10.** $11y^2 - 1 + 6y^3 + 2y; \; 2y + 1$

11. $6z^2 - 4 + 4z^3; \; z + 2$ **12.** $6w^3 + 11w^2 + 2; \; 2w + 1$

13. $16 - m + 4m^3; \; 2m + 3$ **14.** $n^2 + 4n + n^4 - 3n^3; \; n^2 - 1$

15. $6c^3 - 9c^2d - 4cd^2 + d^3; \; 2c + d$ **16.** $4h^3 - 6h^2p + 4hp^2 - 2p^3; \; h - p$

In each exercise the value of r is a root of the given equation. Find the complete solution set.

B   **17.** $r = 2; \; x^3 - 4x^2 + x + 6 = 0$ **18.** $r = -1; \; y^3 - 3y^2 + 4 = 0$

19. $r = -2; \; 3d^3 - d^2 - 12d + 4 = 0$ **20.** $r = 3; \; 6a^3 - 17a^2 - 5a + 6 = 0$

21. $r = -4; \; 4x^3 + 11x^2 - 19x + 4 = 0$ **22.** $r = 2; \; 2s^3 + s^2 - 13s + 6 = 0$

23. $r = -3; \; 12m^3 + 31m^2 - 17m - 6 = 0$ **24.** $r = 1; \; 24d^3 - 17d^2 - 13d + 6 = 0$

The following theorem, which is proved in more advanced courses, is a useful one. Use it as shown in the example on the next page to find the rational roots of the equations in Exercises 25-30, also on the next page.

Theorem 2-3   Consider the equation

$$c_n x^n + c_n x^{n-1} + \cdots + c_0 = 0$$

where $c_0, c_1 \ldots, c_n$ are integers, $c_n \neq 0$, and n is a positive integer. If the equation has the root $\dfrac{p}{q}$, where p and q are integers and $\dfrac{p}{q}$ is in lowest terms, then p must be a factor of c_0 and q must be a factor of c_n. (Rational Root Theorem)

EXAMPLE   Find the rational roots of the equation: $2x^3 + 3x^2 - 8x + 3 = 0$

SOLUTION   According to the Rational Root Theorem, if $\dfrac{p}{q}$ is a rational root, then p is a factor of 3 and q is a factor of 2.

Factors of 3: $\pm 1, \pm 3$ Factors of 2: $\pm 1, \pm 2$

Possible rational roots: $\pm 1, \pm 3, \pm\dfrac{1}{2}, \pm\dfrac{3}{2}$

We can now test each of these possibilities. Since
$$2(1)^3 + 3(1)^2 - 8(1) + 3 = 2 + 3 - 8 + 3 = 0,$$
1 is a root of the equation. You can continue to test the remaining roots, or you can factor $x - 1$ from the left side of the equation and proceed as in earlier examples. Completing the solution by either method, you will find that the set of rational roots is $\left\{1, -3, \dfrac{1}{2}\right\}$.

25. $x^3 - 6x^2 + 11x - 6 = 0$ 26. $k^3 + 4k^2 - k - 4 = 0$

27. $4u^3 - 8u^2 - u + 2 = 0$ 28. $2z^3 + z^2 - 13z + 6 = 0$

29. $24n^3 - 14n^2 - n + 1 = 0$ 30. $6y^3 + 7y^2 - 63y + 20 = 0$

C 31. Explain how the Factor Theorem follows from the Remainder Theorem.

Section 2-6 MULTIPLICATION AND DIVISION OF RATIONAL EXPRESSIONS

A *rational expression* is the quotient of two polynomials. In this section you will review:
- multiplication of rational expressions
- division of rational expressions

Some rational expressions are given in the following examples.

EXAMPLES $\dfrac{m^2 n}{3mn^3}$ $\dfrac{x^2 + x - 24}{x^2 + 10x + 24}$

It is easy to see in the first example that m and n are restricted to values other than 0. Notice that in the second example the variable x cannot equal -4 or -6, since these values would cause the denominator to be 0.

A rational expression is *simplified* (or is in *lowest terms*) when the greatest common factor of the numerator and denominator is 1. You simplify a rational expression by factoring the numerator and denominator and then dividing them by their greatest common factor.

EXAMPLE   Simplify: $\dfrac{3r^2 s^2 - 2rs^3}{3r^2 s + rs^2}$

SOLUTION   Factor the numerator and denominator:

$$\frac{rs^2(3r - 2s)}{rs(3r + s)}$$

Dividing the numerator and denominator by their greatest common factor, rs, you obtain:

$$\frac{s(3r - 2s)}{3r + s}, \quad \text{or} \quad \frac{3rs - 2s^2}{3r + s}$$

When you simplify a rational expression, look for factors of the numerator and denominator that are negatives of one another. Such factors may be eliminated using the method shown in the following example.

EXAMPLE
$$\begin{aligned}
\frac{6hg - 3h^2}{3h^2 - 13hg + 14g^2} &= \frac{3h(2g - h)}{(3h - 7g)(h - 2g)} \\
&= \frac{3h(-1)(h - 2g)}{(3h - 7g)(h - 2g)} \\
&= \frac{-3h}{3h - 7g}
\end{aligned}$$

To multiply rational expressions, we use the familiar rule:

$$\frac{p}{q} \cdot \frac{r}{s} = \frac{pr}{qs}$$

We usually write the product in its simplest form.

EXAMPLE
$$\frac{4k^2}{7z^2} \cdot \frac{21z^3}{20k^4} = \frac{84k^2z^3}{140k^4z^2} = \frac{3z}{5k^2}$$

When you multiply rational expressions, you can divide out any factor that is found in both a numerator and a denominator. This process usually makes the computation more efficient.

EXAMPLE
$$\begin{aligned}
\frac{2y^2 - y - 15}{3y^2 - y - 10} \cdot \frac{9y^2 - 25}{y^2 - 10y + 21} &= \frac{(y - 3)(2y + 5)}{(3y + 5)(y - 2)} \cdot \frac{(3y + 5)(3y - 5)}{(y - 7)(y - 3)} \\
&= \frac{(2y + 5)(3y - 5)}{(y - 2)(y - 7)} \\
&= \frac{6y^2 + 5y - 25}{y^2 - 9y + 14}
\end{aligned}$$

Sometimes we find it convenient to leave the product in factored form, as shown in the second line of the previous example.

To divide by a rational expression, you multiply by its reciprocal according to the definition of division. It is relatively easy to determine the reciprocal (or multiplicative inverse) of a rational expression. Suppose that P and Q are polynomials and that the variables involved are restricted so that neither P nor Q is equal to zero. Then the reciprocal of the rational expression $\frac{P}{Q}$ will be $\frac{Q}{P}$ for the following reason:

$$\frac{P}{Q} \cdot \frac{Q}{P} = \frac{PQ}{QP} = 1$$

The definition of division and this method for finding the reciprocal of a rational expression are applied in the next example.

EXAMPLE $\dfrac{6b^3 - 3b^2c}{21bc + 7c^2} \div \dfrac{6b^2 + 24bc}{6bc + 2c^2} = \dfrac{6b^3 - 3b^2c}{21bc + 7c^2} \cdot \dfrac{6bc + 2c^2}{6b^2 + 24bc}$

$$= \frac{3b^{\not2}(2b - c)}{7\not c(3b + c)} \cdot \frac{2\not c(3b + c)}{6\not b(b + 4c)}$$

$$= \frac{b(2b - c)}{7(b + 4c)}$$

When you simplify an expression involving division, you can think of the process of multiplying by the reciprocal as "invert and multiply."

EXAMPLE $\dfrac{2a - 1}{4a - 3} \div \dfrac{3a - 5}{6a^2 - 7a - 5} \cdot \dfrac{12a - 9}{4a^2 - 1} = \dfrac{2a - 1}{4a - 3} \cdot \dfrac{6a^2 - 7a - 5}{3a - 5} \cdot \dfrac{12a - 9}{4a^2 - 1}$

$$= \frac{2a - 1}{4a - 3} \cdot \frac{(2a + 1)(3a - 5)}{3a - 5} \cdot \frac{3(4a - 3)}{(2a + 1)(2a - 1)}$$

$$= 3$$

ORAL EXERCISES

Simplify.

1. $\dfrac{16m^2k}{20mk^3}$ 2. $\dfrac{x^2yz}{xyz^2}$ 3. $\dfrac{9(y - 1)}{18(y - 1)}$

4. $\dfrac{2x^5(x + 1)}{2x^2(x - 1)}$ 5. $\dfrac{(2 + d)(4 - d)}{2d(4 - d)}$ 6. $\dfrac{(t - 3)(t + 4)}{(t + 4)(t + 1)}$

7. $\dfrac{12a}{5b} \cdot \dfrac{b^2}{a}$ 8. $\dfrac{(r + s)}{2} \cdot \dfrac{4}{s(r + s)}$ 9. $\dfrac{y + z}{4} \cdot \dfrac{8z}{(y + z)}$

10. $\dfrac{4}{t^3} \div \dfrac{2}{t}$ 11. $\dfrac{x^2}{y} \div \dfrac{x}{4}$ 12. $\dfrac{u(u + r)}{4r} \div \dfrac{2(u + r)}{r^2}$

WRITTEN EXERCISES

Simplify. Write the answer as a polynomial or a quotient of polynomials.

A 1. $\dfrac{a^2b}{ab^3}$ 2. $\dfrac{4j^2k^4}{8j^3k^7}$ 3. $\dfrac{4h^2}{h^2 - h}$

4. $\dfrac{3n^2}{2n^2 + 3n}$ 5. $\dfrac{x^2 - 3x}{4x - 12}$ 6. $\dfrac{2yz - y^2}{2yz - 6y^2}$

7. $\dfrac{8a^2 - 8ab}{16a^3 - 16a^2b}$

8. $\dfrac{8 + 4x}{x^3 + 2x^2}$

9. $\dfrac{k^2 + 6k + 8}{-5k^2 - 20k}$

10. $\dfrac{9 - y^2}{15y - 5y^2}$

11. $\dfrac{3r^2 - 8r - 3}{3r^2 + 7r + 2}$

12. $\dfrac{2s^2 - 5st + 2t^2}{s^2 + st - 6t^2}$

13. $\dfrac{4h^2 + 7hk - 2k^2}{4h^2k + 8hk^2}$

14. $\dfrac{6k^2 - 30k}{15 + 7k - 2k^2}$

15. $\dfrac{6x^2 + 6x + 3}{8x^2 + 8x + 4}$

16. $\dfrac{3a}{10} \cdot \dfrac{5a - 5b}{a^2 + 4ab}$

17. $\dfrac{uv^2}{u^2v} \cdot \dfrac{u^2 - 2u}{uv + 3v}$

18. $\dfrac{14x - 28}{3x + 27} \cdot \dfrac{6x^2 + 54x}{4x^2 - 8x}$

19. $\dfrac{e^2f + ef^2}{e^3 - 4e^2f} \cdot \dfrac{ef - 4f^2}{ef^2 + 2f^3}$

20. $\dfrac{8z - 3z^2}{4} \cdot \dfrac{8 + 3z}{3z^2 - 5z - 8}$

21. $\dfrac{k^2 + 4k}{k^2 + 6k + 9} \cdot \dfrac{-k - 3}{8k + 32}$

22. $\dfrac{c^3 - c^2d}{d^3 - cd^2} \cdot \dfrac{cd + d}{cd + c^2}$

23. $\dfrac{t^2 - 7t + 10}{t^2 - t - 2} \cdot \dfrac{t^2 + 5t + 4}{t^2 - 2t - 15}$

24. $\dfrac{w^2 + 5w - 24}{w^2 - 16} \cdot \dfrac{w^2 + 6w - 40}{w^2 + 4w - 21}$

25. $\dfrac{ab}{3c} \div \dfrac{a^2b}{6c^2}$

26. $\dfrac{11x}{4y} \div \dfrac{33x}{6y^2}$

27. $\dfrac{27p}{36q} \div \dfrac{p^2 + pq}{2p - 2q}$

28. $\dfrac{r^2s}{t^3} \div \dfrac{2r^2s - rs}{2rt^2 - t^2}$

29. $\dfrac{4x - 8}{x^3 + 3x^2} \div \dfrac{6x - 12}{x^2 + 3x}$

30. $\dfrac{a^2 - ab}{ab + 2b^2} \div \dfrac{a^2 + ab}{ab + b^2}$

B 31. $\dfrac{21k^2 + 10k + 1}{16k^2 + 8k - 15} \div \dfrac{21k^2 - 11k - 2}{20k^2 + k - 12}$

32. $\dfrac{54w^2 + 3w - 2}{56w^2 - 3w - 20} \div \dfrac{72w^2 - 30w + 3}{32w^2 - 28w + 5}$

Simplify. You may leave the answer in factored form.

33. $\dfrac{8a^2 + 2ab - 15b^2}{12a^2 - 7ab - 10b^2} \cdot \dfrac{36a^2 - b^2}{12a^2 + 20ab + 3b^2}$

34. $\dfrac{8x^2 - 15xy - 2y^2}{4x^2 - 5xy - 6y^2} \cdot \dfrac{4x^2 - 17xy - 15y^2}{7x^2 - 36xy + 5y^2}$

35. $\dfrac{4q^2 - r^2}{2q^2 + 9qr - 5r^2} \div \dfrac{2q^2 - qr - r^2}{q^2 - 25r^2}$

36. $\dfrac{x^2 - 3x + 2}{7x - 7x^2} \div \dfrac{8 - 6x + x^2}{14x^3 - 56x^2}$

37. $\dfrac{4y^2 - 21y - 18}{3y^2 + 31y + 56} \cdot \dfrac{3y^2 - 5y - 28}{2y^2 - 15y + 18} \div \dfrac{3y^2 - 17y + 20}{2y^2 + 13y - 24}$

38. $\dfrac{6a^3 - 3ab}{4a^2 - 31ab + 42b^2} \div \dfrac{18a^2b - 60ab^3}{12a^2 - 49ab + 49b^2} \div \dfrac{20a^7 - 10a^5b}{8ab^3 - 48b^4}$

Simplify. (*Hint*: Factor the polynomial in the denominator. Then use the Factor Theorem to see whether or not any factor of the denominator is also a factor of the numerator.)

C 39. $\dfrac{x^3 + 2x^2 - 11x - 12}{x^2 - 4x - 5}$

40. $\dfrac{6a^3 - 7a^2 - 14a + 15}{a^2 - 8a + 7}$

41. $\dfrac{y^3 - 7y - 6}{y^2 - y - 6}$

42. $\dfrac{p^4 - 15p^2 - 10p + 24}{p^3 - p^2 - 12p}$

Section 2-7 ADDITION AND SUBTRACTION OF RATIONAL EXPRESSIONS

In this section you will learn about least common multiples of two or more polynomials and extend your knowledge of rational expressions to include:
- addition of rational expressions
- subtraction of rational expressions
- least common denominators of two or more rational expressions

To add and subtract rational expressions, we use the two familiar rules:

$$\frac{a}{c} + \frac{b}{c} = \frac{a+b}{c} \qquad \frac{a}{c} - \frac{b}{c} = \frac{a-b}{c}$$

EXAMPLES

$$\frac{k^2}{k^2+1} + \frac{3}{k^2+1} = \frac{k^2+3}{k^2+1}$$

$$\frac{5}{3x^2+1} - \frac{x-2}{3x^2+1} = \frac{5-(x-2)}{3x^2+1}$$

$$= \frac{7-x}{3x^2+1}$$

When you add or subtract two or more rational expressions with different denominators, you must first rewrite the expressions as equivalent expressions with a common denominator.

EXAMPLE   Simplify: $\dfrac{1}{5} + \dfrac{2}{w}$

SOLUTION   Rewrite each addend as an equivalent expression with the denominator $5w$:

$$\frac{1}{5} + \frac{2}{w} = \frac{1}{5} \cdot \frac{w}{w} + \frac{2}{w} \cdot \frac{5}{5}$$

$$= \frac{w}{5w} + \frac{10}{5w} = \frac{w+10}{5w}$$

In arithmetic, when you add two or more fractions, you usually use their least common denominator, which is equal to the least common multiple of the denominators of the fractions. This procedure is also used when adding rational expressions.

The *least common multiple* (LCM) of two or more polynomials is the common multiple of the polynomials having the least degree and the least possible constant factor.

EXAMPLE   Find the LCM of $x^3 + 4x^2$ and $x^2 + 8x + 16$.

SOLUTION   Factor the polynomials and then form the product of the highest powers of all the factors that appear.

$$x^3 + 4x^2 = x^2(x+4) \qquad x^2 + 8x + 16 = (x+4)^2$$

The LCM of $x^3 + 4x^2$ and $x^2 + 8x + 16$ is $x^2(x+4)^2$, or $x^4 + 8x^3 + 16x^2$.

The LCM of the denominators of two or more rational expressions is the *least common denominator* (LCD) of the rational expressions. We usually find it convenient to work with the LCD in factored form.

EXAMPLE Simplify: $\dfrac{y-3}{y^2+3y-4} + \dfrac{2y+1}{y^2+6y+8}$

SOLUTION Factor each denominator.

$$\frac{y-3}{y^2+3y-4} + \frac{2y+1}{y^2+6y+8} = \frac{y-3}{(y-1)(y+4)} + \frac{2y+1}{(y+4)(y+2)}$$

The LCD is $(y-1)(y+4)(y+2)$.

$$= \frac{y-3}{(y-1)(y+4)}\left(\frac{y+2}{y+2}\right) + \frac{2y+1}{(y+4)(y+2)}\left(\frac{y-1}{y-1}\right)$$

$$= \frac{(y-3)(y+2)+(2y+1)(y-1)}{(y-1)(y+4)(y+2)}$$

$$= \frac{y^2-y-6+2y^2-y-1}{(y-1)(y+4)(y+2)} = \frac{3y^2-2y-7}{(y-1)(y+4)(y+2)}$$

Notice in the previous example that the denominator was left in factored form. You may leave denominators of sums and differences in factored form unless otherwise instructed. Regardless of how the answer is written, be sure to divide through by any factor of the denominator that is also a factor of the numerator.

EXAMPLE Simplify: $\dfrac{a}{a+2} - \dfrac{2}{3-a} - \dfrac{3a+1}{a^2-a-6}$

SOLUTION Factor denominators:

$$\frac{a}{a+2} - \frac{2}{3-a} - \frac{3a+1}{a^2-a-6} = \frac{a}{a+2} - \frac{2}{3-a} - \frac{3a+1}{(a+2)(a-3)}$$

Notice that $-(3-a) = a-3$. Thus, it is possible to replace the denominator of the second term by its negative and change the sign of the term.

$$= \frac{a}{a+2} + \frac{2}{a-3} - \frac{3a+1}{(a+2)(a-3)}$$

$$= \frac{a}{a+2}\left(\frac{a-3}{a-3}\right) + \frac{2}{a-3}\left(\frac{a+2}{a+2}\right) - \frac{3a+1}{(a+2)(a-3)}$$

$$= \frac{a(a-3)+2(a+2)-(3a+1)}{(a+2)(a-3)}$$

$$= \frac{a^2-3a+2a+4-3a-1}{(a+2)(a-3)}$$

$$= \frac{a^2-4a+3}{(a+2)(a-3)}$$

$$= \frac{(a-1)(a-3)}{(a+2)(a-3)}$$

$$= \frac{a-1}{a+2}$$

ORAL EXERCISES

State the LCD of the fractions.

1. $\dfrac{3}{4z}, \dfrac{2}{3z}$

2. $\dfrac{3}{5x}, \dfrac{1}{5y}$

3. $\dfrac{1}{4g^2}, \dfrac{5}{2g}$

4. $\dfrac{1}{b^2c}, \dfrac{2}{bc^2}$

5. $\dfrac{k}{j(j-k)}, \dfrac{j}{2(j-k)}$

6. $\dfrac{2}{x-3}, \dfrac{2}{x+3}$

Simplify.

7. $\dfrac{2}{m} - \dfrac{3}{m^2}$

8. $\dfrac{3}{pq} - \dfrac{2}{p}$

9. $\dfrac{4h}{h+3} - \dfrac{1}{h}$

WRITTEN EXERCISES

Simplify.

A 1. $\dfrac{1}{5z} + \dfrac{3}{15z}$

2. $\dfrac{7}{m^2} + \dfrac{5}{2m}$

3. $\dfrac{1}{2z} - \dfrac{3}{14z}$

4. $\dfrac{7}{2x} - \dfrac{3}{x^2}$

5. $\dfrac{2}{x} - \dfrac{1}{x^2} + \dfrac{3}{2x}$

6. $\dfrac{3}{7y} + \dfrac{5}{2y} + \dfrac{2}{y^2}$

7. $\dfrac{x}{x+3} - \dfrac{2}{x}$

8. $\dfrac{5}{z} + \dfrac{3}{z-6}$

9. $2 - \dfrac{3}{n-4}$

10. $\dfrac{t}{3} - \dfrac{1}{2} - \dfrac{4}{t+3}$

11. $\dfrac{7}{y} + \dfrac{3}{4} - \dfrac{2}{y+4}$

12. $3x + \dfrac{x-2}{x+1}$

13. $\dfrac{3}{x-2} - \dfrac{4}{x+4}$

14. $\dfrac{3h}{h-1} - \dfrac{4}{h-2}$

15. $\dfrac{4a}{2a-1} + \dfrac{a}{a-3}$

16. $\dfrac{y-2}{y+4} + \dfrac{y-3}{2y-1}$

17. $\dfrac{3z}{z^2+2z} - \dfrac{1}{2z}$

18. $\dfrac{4}{f^2} + \dfrac{1}{f^2-4f}$

19. $\dfrac{x}{x-4} + \dfrac{2}{x} + \dfrac{2x+8}{x^2-4x}$

20. $\dfrac{1}{3y} + \dfrac{y^2+1}{y^2-4y} - \dfrac{y-2}{9y-36}$

21. $\dfrac{4}{r^2-3r} - \dfrac{3}{2r-6} - \dfrac{1}{2r}$

22. $\dfrac{3}{x^2-2x} - \dfrac{8}{x^2+2x-8}$

B 23. $\dfrac{2v}{v^2-2v-15} + \dfrac{3}{4v^2+12v}$

24. $\dfrac{1}{k^2-k-2} + \dfrac{1}{k^2+2k+1}$

25. $\dfrac{2}{u^2-4} + \dfrac{3}{u^2+4u+4}$

26. $\dfrac{2}{v^2-5v+6} - \dfrac{5}{v^2+2v-15}$

27. $\dfrac{y}{y^2-9y+18} - \dfrac{y-2}{y^2-10y+24}$

28. $\dfrac{x-7}{x^2+4x-5} - \dfrac{x-9}{x^2+3x-10}$

29. $\dfrac{3}{9m^2-48m+64} - \dfrac{m}{64-9m^2}$

30. $\dfrac{8z}{25-4z^2} - \dfrac{2}{2z-5} + \dfrac{z}{6z+15}$

31. $\dfrac{3}{2z^2-9z-5} + \dfrac{2z}{4z^2-1}$

32. $\dfrac{4}{y^2+y-6} - \dfrac{6}{2+5y-3y^2}$

74   *CHAPTER 2*

33. $\dfrac{2}{a-2b} - \dfrac{a-b}{a^2-b^2} - \dfrac{6b}{a^2-ab-2b^2}$ **34.** $\dfrac{p}{2p^2+3pq-2q^2} - \dfrac{3q}{4p^2-4pq+q^2}$

C 35. $\dfrac{x-3y}{x^2-y^2} + \dfrac{x-2y}{x^2+xy-2y^2} - \dfrac{3y}{x^2+3xy+2y^2}$

36. $\dfrac{2h-t}{h^2-2ht-15t^2} + \dfrac{h+3t}{h^2-3ht-10t^2} + \dfrac{4h-t}{h^2+5ht+6t^2}$

37. $\dfrac{3(3x+2)}{6x^2-x-1} + \dfrac{28(x+3)}{3x^2+7x+2} - \dfrac{7(x-2)}{2x^2+3x-2}$

38. $\dfrac{15(a+4)}{a^2+a-2} - \dfrac{36(a-4)}{a^2-4a+3} + \dfrac{50(a+1)}{a^2-a-6}$

SELF-TEST 2

1. Divide $q^3 + q^2 - 2q + 14$ by $q + 3$. Express the result in the form of an equation.   Section 2-5

2. Given that 2 is a solution of the equation
$$x^3 + 5x^2 - 2x - 24 = 0,$$
find the complete solution set.

Simplify.

3. $\dfrac{t^2-2t}{t+4} \cdot \dfrac{t^2+4t}{4t-8}$ 4. $\dfrac{v^2-8v+15}{v^2+2v} \div \dfrac{v^2-3v}{v^2-4}$ Section 2-6

5. $\dfrac{1}{r} + \dfrac{r}{r-3}$ 6. $\dfrac{1}{z^2-2z} - \dfrac{1}{z^2+z-6}$ Section 2-7

Section 2-8 COMPLEX FRACTIONS

In the last several sections you have been working with fractions whose numerators and denominators are polynomials. In this section you will work with fractions whose numerators or denominators contain other fractions. You will learn two methods for simplifying such fractions.

A fraction in which the numerator or denominator contains one or more fractions or negative exponents is called a *complex fraction*.

EXAMPLES $\dfrac{8}{1+\dfrac{1}{x}}$ $\dfrac{\dfrac{3}{4}}{\dfrac{1}{2}}$ $\dfrac{y^{-2}+3}{y^2+1}$

A fraction that is not complex is called a *simple fraction*. Any complex fraction can be expressed as an equivalent simple fraction. The method for doing so that is shown at the top of the next page is based on the definition of division.

Method 1 Divide the numerator of the fraction by the denominator.

EXAMPLE $\dfrac{\frac{3}{8}}{\frac{1}{2}} = \dfrac{3}{8} \div \dfrac{1}{2}$

$$= \dfrac{3}{8} \cdot \dfrac{2}{1}$$

$$= \dfrac{3}{4}$$

Method 2 Multiply the numerator and denominator of the complex fraction by the least common denominator of all the simple fractions involved.

The next example shows both methods of simplifying a complex fraction. As this example shows, Method 2 is usually the more convenient.

EXAMPLE Simplify: $\dfrac{\frac{3}{2} + \frac{3}{x}}{2 + \frac{4}{x}}$

SOLUTION

Method 1

$\dfrac{\frac{3}{2} + \frac{3}{x}}{2 + \frac{4}{x}} = \left(\dfrac{3}{2} + \dfrac{3}{x}\right) \div \left(2 + \dfrac{4}{x}\right)$

$= \left(\dfrac{3}{2} \cdot \dfrac{x}{x} + \dfrac{3}{x} \cdot \dfrac{2}{2}\right) \div \left(2 \cdot \dfrac{x}{x} + \dfrac{4}{x}\right)$

$= \left(\dfrac{3x + 6}{2x}\right) \div \left(\dfrac{2x + 4}{x}\right)$

$= \dfrac{3x + 6}{2x} \cdot \dfrac{x}{2x + 4}$

$= \dfrac{3(x+2)}{2x} \cdot \dfrac{x}{2(x+2)}$

$= \dfrac{3}{4}$

Method 2

$2x$ is the LCD of the simple fractions.

$\dfrac{\frac{3}{2} + \frac{3}{x}}{2 + \frac{4}{x}} = \dfrac{\left(\frac{3}{2} + \frac{3}{x}\right)2x}{\left(2 + \frac{4}{x}\right)2x}$

$= \dfrac{3x + 6}{4x + 8}$

$= \dfrac{3(x+2)}{4(x+2)}$

$= \dfrac{3}{4}$

To simplify a complex fraction containing negative exponents, first rewrite the fraction, using positive exponents.

EXAMPLE Simplify: $\dfrac{xy^{-1} + 1}{2 + x^{-1}}$

SOLUTION $\dfrac{xy^{-1}+1}{2+x^{-1}} = \dfrac{\dfrac{x}{y}+1}{2+\dfrac{1}{x}} = \dfrac{\left(\dfrac{x}{y}+1\right)xy}{\left(2+\dfrac{1}{x}\right)xy} = \dfrac{x^2+xy}{2xy+y}$

WRITTEN EXERCISES

Simplify.

A 1. $\dfrac{\dfrac{4}{7}}{\dfrac{2}{21}}$

2. $\dfrac{\dfrac{5}{36}}{\dfrac{25}{27}}$

3. $\dfrac{\dfrac{3}{4}-\dfrac{5}{8}}{\dfrac{3}{8}}$

4. $\dfrac{\dfrac{5}{8}-\dfrac{1}{4}}{\dfrac{1}{2}+\dfrac{2}{3}}$

5. $\dfrac{\dfrac{r}{2}+\dfrac{s}{3}}{\dfrac{r}{4}-\dfrac{s}{8}}$

6. $\dfrac{\dfrac{3}{x}+\dfrac{1}{xy}}{\dfrac{1}{y}-3}$

7. $\dfrac{\dfrac{1}{2}-\dfrac{1}{x}}{3}$

8. $\dfrac{\dfrac{1}{a}+\dfrac{2}{b}}{a}$

9. $\dfrac{\dfrac{7}{3}+\dfrac{1}{w}}{\dfrac{2}{w}-\dfrac{1}{3}}$

10. $\dfrac{\dfrac{h}{2}+1}{\dfrac{2h}{3}+\dfrac{4}{3}}$

11. $\dfrac{x-\dfrac{1}{x}}{2-\dfrac{2}{x}}$

12. $\dfrac{\dfrac{a}{b}-\dfrac{b}{a}}{\dfrac{2}{b}-\dfrac{2}{a}}$

13. $\dfrac{\dfrac{2}{w}-\dfrac{1}{2z}}{\dfrac{3}{w}-\dfrac{1}{3z}}$

14. $\dfrac{\dfrac{h}{4}+\dfrac{5h}{6}}{\dfrac{2g}{3}-\dfrac{g}{2}}$

15. $\dfrac{x^{-1}+2}{x+1}$

16. $\dfrac{y^{-2}+2}{y^{-1}-1}$

17. $\dfrac{kz^{-1}+1}{z^2+1}$

18. $\dfrac{x^{-1}+1}{x^{-1}+2^{-1}}$

19. $\dfrac{4-a^{-2}}{2a^{-1}-a^{-2}}$

20. $\dfrac{t^{-1}+2^{-1}}{3t^{-1}-3^{-1}}$

B 21. $(x^{-1}+y^{-1})^{-1}$

22. $(u^{-2}+v^{-1})^{-2}$

23. $\dfrac{1-\dfrac{1}{w+2}}{w-1-\dfrac{6}{w-2}}$

24. $\dfrac{\dfrac{1}{z-1}-\dfrac{1}{z+2}}{1+\dfrac{1}{z^2+z-2}}$

25. $\dfrac{4-\dfrac{1}{1-t}}{16+\dfrac{7}{t^2-1}}$

26. $\dfrac{1-\dfrac{6}{y^2+y}}{1-\dfrac{8}{y+1}+\dfrac{10}{y^2+y}}$

Simplify. (*Hint:* Begin by simplifying the least complicated part of the complex fraction.)

C 27. $\dfrac{3}{3+\dfrac{2}{2+\dfrac{1}{4}}}$

28. $\dfrac{1}{1+\dfrac{1}{1+\dfrac{1}{1-x}}}$

Section 2-9 SOLVING FRACTIONAL EQUATIONS

As you know, a convenient first step in solving equations involving fractions with whole-number denominators is to multiply both sides of the equation by the least common denominator of the fractions. In this section you will learn how this method can be applied to solve equations involving fractions with denominators containing variables. You will learn about:

- fractional equations
- proportions
- similar polygons

An equation that has a variable in the denominator of one or more terms is called a *fractional equation*. The first step in solving a fractional equation is to multiply both sides by the LCD of the terms.

EXAMPLE   Solve: $\dfrac{1}{x^2} + \dfrac{1}{2} = \dfrac{11}{6x}$

SOLUTION   The LCD of $\dfrac{1}{x^2}$, $\dfrac{1}{2}$, and $\dfrac{11}{6x}$ is $6x^2$.

$$6x^2\left(\frac{1}{x^2} + \frac{1}{2}\right) = 6x^2\left(\frac{11}{6x}\right)$$
$$6 + 3x^2 = 11x$$
$$3x^2 - 11x + 6 = 0$$
$$(x - 3)(3x - 2) = 0$$
$$x - 3 = 0 \text{ or } 3x - 2 = 0$$
$$x = 3 \text{ or } \quad 3x = 2$$
$$x = 3 \text{ or } \quad x = \frac{2}{3}$$

The check is left for you.

The solution set is $\left\{\dfrac{2}{3}, 3\right\}$.

EXAMPLE   Solve: $1 + \dfrac{30}{y^2 - 9} = \dfrac{5}{y - 3}$

SOLUTION   The LCD is $y^2 - 9$.

$$\left(y^2 - 9\right)\left(1 + \frac{30}{y^2 - 9}\right) = \left(y^2 - 9\right)\left(\frac{5}{y - 3}\right) \quad \text{Note that } y \ne -3 \text{ and } y \ne 3.$$
$$y^2 - 9 + 30 = (y + 3)5$$
$$y^2 + 21 = 5y + 15$$
$$y^2 - 5y + 6 = 0$$
$$(y - 3)(y - 2) = 0$$
$$y = 3 \text{ or } y = 2$$

We must discard 3 as a root because substituting 3 for y in the original equation produces a zero denominator. Checking that 2 is a root is left for you. The solution set is $\{2\}$.

The method used in the last two examples involves transforming an equation by multiplying both sides by a variable expression. The solution set of the transformed equation will contain all the roots of the original equation, but it may contain some additional roots, too. As you saw in the previous example, it is essential to check all apparent roots by substituting them in the *original* equation.

Recall that a *proportion* is an equation stating that two ratios are equal. A proportion can be solved by cross-multiplication, which can be justified as follows. Suppose $a:b = c:d$, $b \neq 0$, and $d \neq 0$:

$$\frac{a}{b} = \frac{c}{d}$$

$$\frac{a}{b}(bd) = \frac{c}{d}(bd)$$

$$ad = cb$$

EXAMPLE   Solve: $\dfrac{2}{3} = \dfrac{4}{x + 1}$

SOLUTION   Use cross-multiplication.

$$2(x + 1) = 4(3)$$
$$2x + 2 = 12$$
$$x = 5$$

The check is left for you. The solution set is $\{5\}$.

A fractional equation sometimes results from problems involving similar polygons. Recall that two convex polygons are *similar* ($\sim$) if their consecutive vertices can be paired so that:

1. Corresponding angles are congruent.

2. The lengths of corresponding sides are proportional (have the same ratio).

You are probably familiar with the following theorem, which was presented in *Book 2*: If two angles of one triangle are congruent to two angles of another triangle, then the triangles are similar. (AA Similarity Theorem)

EXAMPLE   Find the value of x in the figure at the right.

SOLUTION   Notice that $\angle C \cong \angle C$ and $\angle D \cong \angle A$. Therefore, $\triangle CDE \sim \triangle CAB$ by the AA Similarity Theorem.

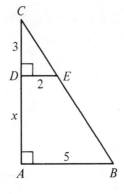

Thus, we can write the following proportion:

$$\frac{CD}{CA} = \frac{DE}{AB}$$

Substitution gives the following:

$$\frac{3}{x + 3} = \frac{2}{5}$$
$$15 = 2(x + 3)$$
$$15 = 2x + 6$$
$$4.5 = x$$

The check is left for you. The value of x is 4.5.

ORAL EXERCISES

Match each equation with the corresponding transformed equation, and state any necessary restrictions on the variable.

1. $\dfrac{1}{z^2} - \dfrac{1}{3z} = \dfrac{1}{6}$

2. $\dfrac{4}{z-1} + \dfrac{4}{z} = \dfrac{3}{z-1}$

3. $\dfrac{1}{z-2} + \dfrac{1}{z+3} = \dfrac{1}{z^2+z-6}$

4. $\dfrac{8}{z^2-4} + \dfrac{1}{z-2} = \dfrac{1}{z+2}$

a. $2z + 1 = 1$

b. $6 - 2z = z^2$

c. $8z - 4 = 3z$

d. $z + 10 = z - 2$

WRITTEN EXERCISES

Solve the following proportions.

A
1. $\dfrac{8}{14} = \dfrac{3}{m}$

2. $\dfrac{10}{b} = 4\dfrac{1}{2}$

3. $\dfrac{x-1}{4} = \dfrac{5}{6}$

4. $\dfrac{x}{4} = \dfrac{16}{x}$

5. $\dfrac{3}{p+2} = \dfrac{7}{8}$

6. $\dfrac{2}{q} = \dfrac{q-1}{3}$

Solve.

7. $\dfrac{4}{m} - \dfrac{1}{m} = 3$

8. $\dfrac{1}{b} - \dfrac{1}{2} = 1$

9. $\dfrac{2}{p} + 1 = \dfrac{1}{4}$

10. $\dfrac{2}{v} - \dfrac{2}{3} = \dfrac{1}{3v}$

11. $\dfrac{1}{3} - \dfrac{2}{z} = \dfrac{1}{12}$

12. $1\dfrac{1}{2} + \dfrac{1}{y} = \dfrac{1}{4}$

13. $\dfrac{1}{x^2} + \dfrac{2}{x} = \dfrac{9}{16}$

14. $\dfrac{4}{u^2} - 10 = \dfrac{3}{u}$

15. $\dfrac{1}{t} - \dfrac{2}{t-1} = \dfrac{2}{t}$

16. $\dfrac{1}{w+2} + \dfrac{1}{w} = \dfrac{3}{w}$

17. $\dfrac{z}{z-2} + \dfrac{z}{z+1} = 2$

18. $\dfrac{2m}{m-2} - \dfrac{m}{m-1} = 1$

19. $\dfrac{x}{2} - \dfrac{5}{2} = 2 - \dfrac{4}{x}$

20. $\dfrac{r}{6} + \dfrac{1}{2} = \dfrac{1}{r} + \dfrac{1}{3}$

21. $\dfrac{a}{4} + \dfrac{5a-20}{4a} = \dfrac{1}{a}$

22. $\dfrac{3y^2}{y-1} + \dfrac{3}{2} = \dfrac{2y-1}{y-1}$

23. $\dfrac{3d^2}{2d-1} + \dfrac{3d-4}{2d-1} = -2$

24. $\dfrac{2n}{n+6} = \dfrac{3}{n-3}$

25. $\dfrac{3x}{x-2} - \dfrac{2x}{x-3} = \dfrac{x+27}{x^2-5x+6}$

26. $\dfrac{m-1}{2m+4} = \dfrac{m}{3m+15} - \dfrac{1}{m^2+7m+10}$

27. $\dfrac{y}{y-2} + \dfrac{y+1}{y+2} = \dfrac{2y-1}{y^2-4}$

28. $\dfrac{b+3}{3-b} + \dfrac{3b+1}{b^2-9} = \dfrac{1-5b}{b+3}$

29. $\dfrac{2z}{z+5} - \dfrac{1}{5-z} = \dfrac{10}{z^2-25}$

30. $\dfrac{x}{x-4} = \dfrac{16}{x^2-16} + \dfrac{2}{x+4}$

80   *CHAPTER 2*

In Exercises 31 and 32 find the value of **x**.

31.

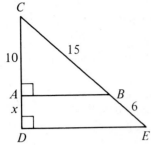

32.

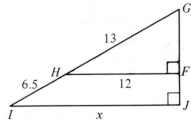

B 33. Find the lengths of $\overline{AC}$, $\overline{ED}$, and $\overline{CB}$.

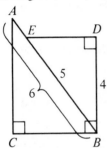

34. In the diagram, $JK = 18$, $MC = 8$, $CK = 4$, and $KL = 24$. If $\overleftrightarrow{AB} \parallel \overleftrightarrow{JL}$, find the lengths of $\overline{KA}$ and $\overline{KB}$.

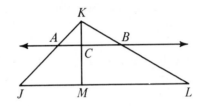

35. Joe drove 20 km at a steady speed to get to the freeway. Once on the freeway, he increased the speed by 40 km/h and traveled another 75 km. If the entire trip was completed in 1 h 14 min, what was his speed on each part of the trip?

36. Marika rowed 4 km upriver and back in 1 h 4 min. If she can row 8 km/h in still water, what is the rate of the river's current?

You can solve work problems using a formula similar to the one you use for motion problems: Rate · Time = Work completed

EXAMPLE   Working together, Mrs. Smith and her young daughter can shovel the snow from their sidewalk in 6 min. Working by herself, the daughter would require 16 min more than her mother to shovel the sidewalk. How long does it take Mrs. Smith to shovel the sidewalk working by herself?

SOLUTION   Let $t = $ the number of minutes it takes Mrs. Smith to shovel the sidewalk. Then $t + 16 = $ the number of minutes required by the daughter. The rates of Mrs. Smith and her daughter are, respectively, $\dfrac{1}{t}$ job per minute and $\dfrac{1}{t + 16}$ job per minute.

(When the entire job is completed, "work completed" must equal 1.)

$$\frac{1}{t} \cdot 6 + \frac{1}{t + 16} \cdot 6 = 1$$

Using the techniques presented in this section, you can find that the solution set of this equation is $\{-12, 8\}$. The solution -12 does not make sense in the context of this problem. Therefore, it takes Mrs. Smith 8 min to shovel the sidewalk by herself. The check is left for you.

37. Working together, Verna and Sam can paint their living room in 2 h. Working alone, it would take Sam 3 h longer than Verna to paint the living room. How long would it take Verna to paint the living room working by herself?

38. One pipe can fill a swimming pool in 15 h; a second pipe requires 18 h. If the first pipe is opened for 7 h and then closed when the second pipe is opened, how long will it take the second to finish filling the pool?

39. Hank can wash and wax the car in 2 h, Sally can do it in 1 h 30 min, and Hank, Sally, and Lena can do it in 40 min working together. How long would it take Lena, working alone, to wash and wax the car?

40. Jason had been putting up wallpaper in his dining room for 2 h when he was joined by his friend Claude, who could put up wallpaper twice as fast as Jason. They completed the job in another 2 h. How long would it have taken Jason to do the entire job working by himself?

C 41. Find the least number such that the sum of the number and twice its reciprocal is $\frac{121}{42}$.

42. Find the greatest number such that the sum of the number and its reciprocal is $-\frac{89}{40}$.

Section 2-10 SOLVING INEQUALITIES BY FACTORING

In Chapter 1 you reviewed solving inequalities in which the variable appears only in the first degree. In this section you will learn to solve inequalities that involve terms of higher degree.

An inequality that involves a variable raised to the second power and that contains no higher power of the variable is called a *quadratic inequality*. To solve quadratic inequalities, we apply certain facts about products of signed numbers. Recall that a product of nonzero factors is negative if there is an odd number of negative factors; otherwise the product is positive.

EXAMPLE Find and graph the solution set of
$$x^2 - x - 2 > 0.$$

SOLUTION Factor the polynomial.
$$(x - 2)(x + 1) > 0$$
The product of the two factors will be positive if both factors are positive or if both factors are negative.

Case 1: Both factors are positive.
$$x - 2 > 0 \quad \text{and} \quad x + 1 > 0$$
$$x > 2 \quad \text{and} \quad x > -1$$
This conjunction is equivalent to the inequality:
$$x > 2$$

Case 2: Both factors are negative.

$$x - 2 < 0 \quad \text{and} \quad x + 1 < 0$$
$$x < 2 \quad \text{and} \quad x < -1$$

This conjunction is equivalent to the inequality:

$$x < -1$$

We use the values of x found in solving the two cases. The solution set is $\{x: x < -1 \text{ or } x > 2\}$, which is graphed below.

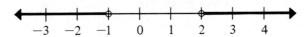

Another method of solving quadratic inequalities is to factor the inequality and then make a *sign graph* as shown in the next example.

EXAMPLE   Find and graph the solution set of

$$4 - 3x - x^2 < 0.$$

SOLUTION   Factor the polynomial.

$$(4 + x)(1 - x) < 0$$

To draw a sign graph:

1. Draw 3 number lines: one for each factor and one for the product.
2. Label the number line for each factor to show where the factor is positive and where it is negative.
3. Label the number line for the product, using the information recorded on the number lines for the factors.

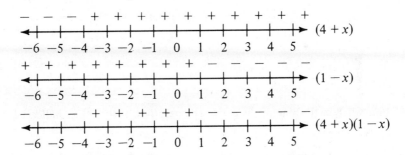

The last number line shows that the solution set is $\{x: x < -4 \text{ or } x > 1\}$, which is graphed below.

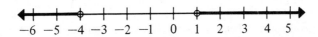

The method of solution just presented can also be applied to inequalities of degree greater than 2, as illustrated by the example on the next page.

EXAMPLE   Find and graph the solution set of

$$4x^3 \geqslant 4x^2 + 24x.$$

SOLUTION   Rewrite the inequality as an equivalent inequality whose right-hand side is 0 and then factor.

$$4x^3 - 4x^2 - 24x \geqslant 0$$
$$4x(x^2 - x - 6) \geqslant 0$$
$$4x(x - 3)(x + 2) \geqslant 0$$

Draw the sign graph for the equivalent inequality:

$$x(x - 3)(x + 2) \geqslant 0$$

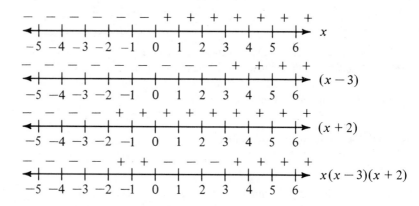

Therefore, the solution set is $\{x: -2 \leqslant x \leqslant 0 \text{ or } x \geqslant 3\}$, which is graphed below.

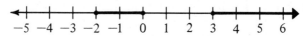

Notice that $-2, 0,$ and 3 are included in the solution set.

ORAL EXERCISES

State whether the binomial is positive or negative for the values indicated.

1. $x - 2;\ x > 2$
2. $x - 2;\ x < 2$
3. $y + 3;\ y > -3$
4. $a - 8;\ a < 0$
5. $m + 5;\ m < -5$
6. $x + 1;\ x < -5$
7. $1 - h;\ h > 1$
8. $2 - k;\ k < -1$
9. $4 + p;\ 1 < p < 3$
10. $t - 6;\ 1 < t < 4$

11. If a is positive and ab is negative, is b positive or negative?

12. If a is positive and ab is positive, is b positive or negative?

13. For what values of x is $x^2 > 0$?
14. For what values of x is $(x - 1)^2 > 0$?
15. For what values of x is $x^2 \leqslant 0$?
16. For what values of x is $(x - 1)^2 \leqslant 0$?

WRITTEN EXERCISES

Find and graph the solution sets.

A 1. $x^2 - 8x + 12 < 0$ 2. $a^2 - a - 12 > 0$ 3. $h^2 - 9h + 8 \geqslant 0$

     4. $r^2 + 6r + 5 \leqslant 0$ 5. $m^2 - 4 > 0$ 6. $w^2 - 7w < 0$

     7. $6 + c - c^2 \leqslant 0$ 8. $12 - 4w - w^2 \geqslant 0$ 9. $d^2 + 4d > 0$

    10. $2t^2 - 8t - 10 < 0$ 11. $s^2 + 9 > 10s$ 12. $a^2 > 6a + 16$

    13. $y^2 - 10y \leqslant 2y - 20$ 14. $r^2 \geqslant 9$

    15. $w^2 + 3w < 2 - w^2$ 16. $31x < 4x^2 + 21$

    17. $3(u^2 - u) \geqslant u^2 + 5$ 18. $13(c + 3) \leqslant 4(c^2 + 1)$

B 19. $z^3 + z^2 - 2z \leqslant 0$ 20. $3k^3 + 18k^2 + 24k > 0$

    21. $v^3 - v^2 \leqslant 20v$ 22. $4u^3 \leqslant 4u$

Find and graph each solution set. (*Hint*: Include a number line for each factor of the numerator and each factor of the denominator in the sign graph. Be sure to exclude from the solution set any value that produces a zero denominator.)

23. $\dfrac{2}{x-1} > 0$ 24. $\dfrac{3}{2+x} < 0$ 25. $\dfrac{z-3}{z-5} > 0$

26. $\dfrac{b-7}{b+2} < 0$ 27. $\dfrac{k}{k+6} < 0$ 28. $\dfrac{c+6}{c+1} > 0$

C 29. $\dfrac{h^2 - 15h + 50}{h} > 0$ 30. $\dfrac{p^2 + 3p - 28}{p-2} < 0$ 31. $\dfrac{4}{b^2 - 4b + 4} > 0$

32. $\dfrac{n}{n^2 - 9} > 0$ 33. $\dfrac{b^2 + 10b + 25}{b+3} < 0$ 34. $\dfrac{x-4}{4x^2 - 12x + 9} > 0$

SELF-TEST 3

Simplify.

1. $\dfrac{\dfrac{5}{2} + \dfrac{4}{x}}{1 + \dfrac{3}{4x}}$ 2. $\dfrac{a^{-1} + b^{-1}}{a - b}$ Section 2-8

Solve.

3. $\dfrac{1}{4} + \dfrac{1}{z} - \dfrac{3}{z^2} = 0$ 4. $\dfrac{1}{u+1} + \dfrac{1}{4} = \dfrac{1}{u-1}$ Section 2-9

Find and graph the solution set of each inequality.

5. $x^2 < 5x + 6$ 6. $y^2 + 3y \geqslant 10$ Section 2-10

Computer Exercises

To find the value of the polynomial

$$2x^3 - 14x^2 + 21x - 3,$$

when $x = 5$, you can divide the polynomial by $x - 5$ and apply the Remainder Theorem, page 65. A short form of such a division is shown on the right below. This condensed form is called *synthetic division*.

Write the value to be substituted. Write the coefficients of the polynomial in order, starting with the term of highest degree. (Write 0 as the coefficient of a missing term.)

$$
\begin{array}{r}
2x^2 - 4x + 1 \\
x-5\overline{)2x^3 - 14x^2 + 21x - 3} \\
\underline{2x^3 - 10x^2} \\
-4x^2 + 21x \\
\underline{-4x^2 + 20x} \\
x - 3 \\
\underline{x - 5} \\
2
\end{array}
$$

$$
\begin{array}{r|rrrr}
5 & 2 & -14 & 21 & -3 \\
  &   & 10 & -20 & 5 \\
\hline
  & 2 & -4 & 1 & 2
\end{array}
$$

The other numbers on the right above were obtained by using the following sequence of steps:

Start with the first coefficient: 2	
Multiply by the value of x: 5	$2 \cdot 5 = 10$
Add the next coefficient: -14	$10 + (-14) = -4$
Multiply by the value of x: 5	$-4 \cdot 5 = -20$
Add the next coefficient: 21	$-20 + 21 = 1$
Multiply by the value of x: 5	$1 \cdot 5 = 5$
Add the next coefficient: -3	$5 + (-3) = 2$

We continue until the last coefficient has been added. The final result, 2, is the remainder. According to the Remainder Theorem, this is also the value of the polynomial when $x = 5$.

A computer program to find the value, y, of a polynomial for a given value of the variable, x, can be outlined as follows:

INPUT the degree, D, the value of X, and the coefficients, C(J), in order, starting with the term of highest degree.
Carry out the computation:

```
LET Y = C(1)          Start with the first coefficient.
FOR J = 2 TO D+1
LET Y = Y*X+C(J)      Multiply by the value of x and add the next
NEXT J                coefficient.
```

PRINT the final value of Y. This is the remainder.

1. Use the outline above to write a program.

2. RUN the program to find the value of the given polynomial at the given value of the variable.

  a. $2x^3 - 14x^2 + 21x - 3; \; x = 5$
  b. $-3x^3 + 17x^2 + 11x - 12; \; x = 6$
  c. $4x^4 + 9x^3 - 7x^2 + 2x - 12; \; x = -3$
  d. $31 + 5x - 12x^2 + x^3 + x^4; \; x = -4$
  e. $3x^3 - 23x^2 + 7; \; x = 8$

3. RUN the program and use the Factor Theorem to determine whether the second polynomial is a factor of the first.

  a. $3x^3 - 14x^2 + 13x - 20; \; x - 4$
  b. $-5x^3 - 41x^2 + 39x + 26; \; x + 9$
  c. $5x^4 + 3x^3 - 49x^2 - 27x + 36; \; x + 3$

CHAPTER REVIEW

Simplify.

1. $\dfrac{21x^5 y^4}{6x^3 y^0}$

2. $\left(\dfrac{k}{2n^2}\right)^3$

Section 2-1

3. $\left(\dfrac{4}{x}\right)^{-2}$

4. $(3a^2 b^{-1})(5b)^2$

5. $(4x^2 - 2) + (3x^2 + 2x + 4)$

6. $(a^2 + 2a) - (a^2 - 3a - 5)$

Section 2-2

7. $(4z - 2)(3z + 8)$

8. $(4x - 5y)^2$

Factor completely.

9. $2x^2 + 17x + 35$

10. $20y^2 + 9y - 18$

Section 2-3

11. $2v^2 - 50$

12. $9k^2 + 24k + 16$

Solve.

13. $4y^2 + 12y + 9 = 0$

14. $18n^2 - 27n + 10 = 0$

Section 2-4

15. Divide $y^3 - 2y - 12$ by $y - 3$. Express the result as an equation.

Section 2-5

16. Given: -1 is a root of $2x^3 - 3x^2 - 8x - 3 = 0$. Find the complete solution set.

Simplify.

17. $\dfrac{4u^2 - 64}{u^3} \cdot \dfrac{3u}{8u + 32}$

18. $\dfrac{x^2 - 6x + 8}{3x + 6} \div \dfrac{x^2 - 16}{9}$

Section 2-6

19. $\dfrac{4}{x - 2} + \dfrac{x}{x + 2}$

20. $\dfrac{3}{v^2 - 3v} - \dfrac{8}{v^2 + 2v - 15}$

Section 2-7

21. $\dfrac{\dfrac{4}{u} + \dfrac{1}{uv}}{\dfrac{1}{v} - 5}$

22. $\dfrac{n^{-1} + 2}{n + 1}$

Section 2-8

Solve.

23. $\dfrac{1}{5} + \dfrac{2}{5n} - \dfrac{3}{n^2} = 0$ **24.** $\dfrac{1}{x+2} - \dfrac{1}{2x} = \dfrac{1}{24}$ Section 2-9

Find and graph the solution set.

25. $y^2 + y - 12 < 0$ **26.** $n^2 + 4 \geqslant 5n$

CHAPTER TEST

Simplify.

1. $\dfrac{7u^4 v^0}{28u^5 v}$ **2.** $\dfrac{5x^{-3}y}{15y^4 y^{-2}}$ **3.** $\left(\dfrac{x^2}{2y}\right)^{-4}$

4. $(2a^2 + 3) - (4a^2 - 5a + 1)$ **5.** $(3z^2 - z) + (4z^2 - 8z)$

6. $(2k + 5)(3k - 4)$ **7.** $(4z + 11k)^2$ **8.** $(3v - 4)(3v + 4)$

Factor completely.

9. $20k^2 - k - 12$ **10.** $70n^3 + 16n^2 - 32n$ **11.** $4u^2 - 144k^2$

Solve.

12. $14z^2 - 41z + 15 = 0$ **13.** $x^3 - 7x^2 + 12x = 0$ **14.** $5 + 14x = 3x^2$

15. Divide $x^3 + 2x^2 + 6$ by $x + 3$. Express the result as an equation.

16. Given that 2 is a root of $x^3 - 3x^2 - 10x + 24 = 0$, find the complete solution set.

Simplify.

17. $\dfrac{3z}{z^2 - 8z + 16} \cdot \dfrac{3z - 12}{z^2}$ **18.** $\dfrac{4u^2 - 100}{u - 2} \div \dfrac{4u - 20}{2u^2 - u - 6}$ **19.** $\dfrac{2}{u^2 - 9} + \dfrac{3}{u^2 + 6u + 9}$

20. $\dfrac{y}{y^2 - 3y - 10} - \dfrac{1}{y^2 + 2y}$ **21.** $\dfrac{\dfrac{1}{2} + \dfrac{1}{3x}}{\dfrac{5}{4x}}$ **22.** $\dfrac{x^{-1} - 1}{x}$

Solve.

23. $\dfrac{1}{k^2} + \dfrac{1}{8} = \dfrac{3}{4k}$ **24.** $\dfrac{x}{x+1} - \dfrac{1}{x-1} = \dfrac{1}{4}$

Find and graph the solution set of each inequality.

25. $u + 2 \geqslant u^2$ **26.** $x^2 + x - 20 > 0$

Careers — Financial Planner

Most large companies either have financial planners on staff or hire outside consultants to assist them. The types of assets and time periods planners work with depend on the industry in which they work. For example, agricultural financial planners help farmers with loans, buying large machinery, and using borrowed money constructively.

Most companies make long-term financial plans. Companies need help allocating their money between new projects and old. Planners also offer them a variety of other services, ranging from setting up employee benefit programs to tax planning.

For banks, finance companies, and insurance companies, money *is* their business. These types of companies often handle billions of dollars, but whether they stay afloat depends on how that money is managed. The task of planners in these companies is to arrange a portfolio of investments that takes into account the company's need for ready cash and the state of the market.

Individuals also need to plan their financial assets. They can turn to consultants, who offer services such as tax shelter strategies, estate planning, retirement planning, and trustee arrangement. Companies whose business is financial strategy also offer the services of planners to individuals. For example, banks, insurance companies, and brokerage houses all offer personalized planning. With this help, individuals can decide among such options as buying treasury bills, stocks, or real estate.

The business curriculum of most universities or business schools includes courses in security markets, security analysis, corporate financial policy, and business cycles. You should also take courses in computer science, statistics, and economics. Many financial companies offer training programs.

Be sure that you understand the meaning of these terms:

like (similar) monomials, p. 50

polynomial, p. 50

binomial, p. 50

trinomial, p. 50

degree of a polynomial, p. 50

complete factorization, p. 55

greatest monomial factor, p. 55

quadratic polynomial, p. 55

standard form of a quadratic equation, p. 58

polynomial equation, p. 65

simplifying a rational expression, p. 68

least common denominator (LCD), p. 73

complex fraction, p. 75

fractional equation, p. 78

proportion, p. 79

similar polygons, p. 79

quadratic inequality, p. 82

MIXED REVIEW

Simplify.

1. $\dfrac{12x^2 + 13x - 4}{12x^2 - 19x + 4}$

2. $\dfrac{r^3 s}{rs^2} \cdot \dfrac{rs + s^2}{2r^3 - 2r^2 s}$

3. $\dfrac{\dfrac{5}{6} - \dfrac{1}{3}}{\dfrac{7}{8} - \dfrac{5}{4}}$

Solve.

4. $5b^2 + 21 = 22b$

5. $\dfrac{9}{4} t + 15 = \dfrac{3}{2}$

6. $-1.52v = 456$

7. $|p - 7| = 0$

8. $n^2 + 4n + 2 = 0$

9. $\dfrac{1}{h} + \dfrac{h}{h - 1} = \dfrac{5}{h^2 - h}$

10. If -4 is a root of $r^3 + 6r^2 + 5r - 12 = 0$, find the complete solution set.

Graph the solution set.

11. $3z - 1 > 4z + 3$

12. $d^2 = d + 20$

13. $5(7 - r) = 2.5r + 5$

14. Su Chun earned $281.50 in interest on $3300 invested partly at $9\frac{1}{2}\%$ and partly at $5\frac{1}{2}\%$. How much was invested at each rate?

Express as a decimal.

15. $\dfrac{58}{101}$

16. $\dfrac{35}{18}$

17. $\dfrac{39}{32}$

18. $\dfrac{53}{24}$

Name the property illustrated.

19. $0.78 \cdot 1 = 0.78$

20. $-9 + 0 = 0 + (-9)$

21. $(-1)(-5) = 5$

Simplify.

22. $\dfrac{\dfrac{1}{x} - \dfrac{y}{x^2}}{\dfrac{1}{y} - \dfrac{x}{y^2}}$

23. $\dfrac{10 \cdot 4 - 18 \div 3 + 4^2}{2^3 - 2}$

24. Use a sign graph to solve $h^3 - 6h^2 > 7h$.

25. The average of the numbers $17, 29, 32,$ and x is at least 24. What do you know about the value of x?

26. If Jennifer jogs 2 km/h faster than her usual rate, she can cover 4 km in 24 min. Find her usual jogging rate.

27. Find the additive inverse and the multiplicative inverse of 0.75. Give your answers in simplest form.

28. Find every pair of consecutive odd integers whose sum is greater than -15 and less than -9.

29. In the figure at the right, if $BC = 9$, $CD = 12$, and $DE = 8$, find AB.

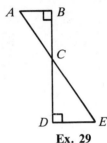

Ex. 29

Simplify.

30. $\dfrac{m^2 - 4}{5m^2 - 10m} \cdot \dfrac{30m^3}{m^2 + 2m}$

31. $\dfrac{3s^3 + 3}{1 - s + s^2} \cdot \dfrac{2s^2 + 2s}{12s^2}$

32. $\left(\dfrac{28x^5yz^{-1}}{7x^3y^{-2}} \right)^{-1}$

33. $4^{-2} + 2^{-3}$

Multiply or divide.

34. $(3x - y)(4x^2 - 5xy + 2y^2)$

35. $\dfrac{99a^5b^2 - 121a^3b^4 + 165b^9}{11a^2b^2}$

Factor.

36. $100p^2 - 140py + 49y^2$

37. $6a^2 + 19a - 20$

38. $z^4 - 81$

39. Show that $1 - 3x < -5 \leqslant -(2x + 7)$ has the empty set for its solution set.

40. Simplify: $\dfrac{a}{a + 3} + \dfrac{1}{2a - 1} - \dfrac{7a}{2a^2 + 5a - 3}$

41. Find and graph the solution set of $\dfrac{x - 4}{x} > 0$.

Solve.

42. $|2a + 4| < 6$

43. $0 \geqslant 9 + 3y$ or $9 + 3y \geqslant 6$

44. Working together, Rhonda and her younger brother Frank can mow the lawn in 2 h. When Frank works alone, it takes him 3 h longer than it takes Rhonda when she works alone. How long does it take Rhonda to mow the lawn by herself?

The water in the fountains above spouts upward in parabolic arcs. In this chapter, you will study parabolas in connection with finding roots of quadratic equations.

92

Radicals and Complex Numbers

3

Time and again in the history of mathematics, concepts (and even whole branches of mathematics) have been created in an effort to solve problems that were previously thought to be unsolvable. Solving the equation

$$x^2 + 1 = 0 \text{ (or } x^2 = -1)$$

was such a problem.

Any solution to this equation must be a number whose square equals -1. Since no real number satisfies this equation, early mathematicians considered the equation to be unsolvable.

As early as the fifteenth century, however, mathematicians began to consider a larger system in which such a number exists. They began to write $\sqrt{-1}$ as a solution of the equation $x^2 + 1 = 0$ and to use the symbol $\sqrt{-1}$ like any other algebraic symbol. René Descartes (1596–1650) introduced the term "imaginary" for any number of the form $\sqrt{-a}$, where a is a positive real number. In 1748, Leonhard Euler first used the symbol i to denote $\sqrt{-1}$.

Imaginary numbers are included in a larger set of numbers called the *complex numbers*, which you will study in this chapter. In his doctoral thesis in 1799, Carl Friedrich Gauss proved that *every* polynomial equation with complex coefficients (including $x^2 + 1 = 0$) has at least one root, and the root is a complex number. This very important fact is known as the Fundamental Theorem of Algebra.

Today, complex numbers are used in advanced mathematics and in a variety of other fields, including map making and electrical engineering. Indeed, they are essential to the development of several important topics in twentieth-century physics, such as quantum mechanics.

Section 3-1 SIMPLIFYING RADICAL EXPRESSIONS

In this section you will learn about:
- square roots, cube roots, and nth roots
- simplifying algebraic expressions containing radicals

As you may recall, the expression $\sqrt{a}$ is called a *radical*. The symbol $\sqrt{}$ is called a *radical sign*, and a is the *radicand*. If $a \geqslant 0$, then $\sqrt{a}$ denotes the unique *nonnegative* number such that

$$\sqrt{a} \cdot \sqrt{a} = a.$$

The equation

$$x^2 = 5,$$

for example, has two roots which we can therefore denote by

$$x = \sqrt{5} \quad \text{and} \quad x = -\sqrt{5}.$$

In this case we can also write

$$x = \pm\sqrt{5},$$

read "x = plus or minus $\sqrt{5}$." Note that the symbol $\sqrt{5}$ denotes only the *positive* number whose square is 5. This positive number is called the *principal square root* of 5.

Since $(-2)^3 = -8$, we say that -2 is a *cube root* of -8. Both 2 and -2 are *fourth roots* of 16, since $2^4 = 16$ and $(-2)^4 = 16$. In general, if $a^n = b$, then a is called an *nth root* of b.

Notice that there is only one real number whose cube is -8. Notice also that 16 has two real fourth roots, and -16 has none. In general, the number of real nth roots a number b has depends on the sign of b and whether n is even or odd, as shown below:

The Real nth Roots of b

	$b > 0$	$b < 0$	$b = 0$
n even	one positive root one negative root	no real roots	one root, 0
n odd	exactly one (positive) root	exactly one (negative) root	one root, 0

The *principal nth root* of b, denoted $\sqrt[n]{b}$, is defined as follows:
1. If n is odd, then $\sqrt[n]{b}$ is the real number whose nth power is b.
2. If n is even and $b \geqslant 0$, then $\sqrt[n]{b}$ is the nonnegative number whose nth power is b.

Thus
$$\left(\sqrt[n]{b}\right)^n = b.$$

The positive integer n is called the *index* of the radical. When the index is 2, we simply write $\sqrt{b}$, of course.

Most of the radicals you will work with in this chapter will be square roots. The following properties are justified for square roots in Exercises 50 and 51.

If $\sqrt[n]{a}$ and $\sqrt[n]{b}$ are real numbers, then:

$$\sqrt[n]{a \cdot b} = \sqrt[n]{a} \cdot \sqrt[n]{b} \qquad\qquad \sqrt[n]{\frac{a}{b}} = \frac{\sqrt[n]{a}}{\sqrt[n]{b}}$$

When you simplify a square root, as in part (a) of the following example, remember to factor out the largest *perfect square* that is a factor of the radicand. To simplify a radical with index n, as in part (b), you factor out each nth power that is a factor of the radicand.

EXAMPLE   Simplify: **a.** $\sqrt{48}$ **b.** $\sqrt[3]{-16}$ **c.** $\sqrt{\dfrac{50}{9}}$ **d.** $\dfrac{\sqrt{60}}{\sqrt{10}}$

SOLUTION   **a.** $\sqrt{48} = \sqrt{16 \cdot 3} = \sqrt{16} \cdot \sqrt{3} = 4\sqrt{3}$

b. $\sqrt[3]{-16} = \sqrt[3]{-8 \cdot 2} = \sqrt[3]{-8} \cdot \sqrt[3]{2} = -2\sqrt[3]{2}$

c. $\sqrt{\dfrac{50}{9}} = \dfrac{\sqrt{50}}{\sqrt{9}} = \dfrac{\sqrt{25 \cdot 2}}{3} = \dfrac{\sqrt{25} \cdot \sqrt{2}}{3} = \dfrac{5\sqrt{2}}{3}$

d. $\dfrac{\sqrt{60}}{\sqrt{10}} = \sqrt{\dfrac{60}{10}} = \sqrt{6}$

An algebraic expression that contains roots of numbers or variables or both is called a *radical expression*. We will say that a radical expression is in *simplified form* (or *simplest radical form*) if it does *not* have:

1. a radicand containing a factor that is an nth power (where n is the index of the radical)
2. a fractional radicand
3. a radical in the denominator of any fraction

You know that $x^5 \cdot x^5 = x^{5+5} = x^{10}$. Thus, if $x \geqslant 0$,

$$\sqrt{x^{10}} = x^5.$$

In general, if k is an integer, then $x^k \cdot x^k = x^{2k}$. Thus, if $x \geqslant 0$,

$$\sqrt{x^{2k}} = x^k.$$

In the following example assume that x and y are positive real numbers.

EXAMPLE   Simplify: **a.** $\sqrt{12x^3y^8}$ **b.** $\sqrt{\dfrac{75x^5y}{x^2y^3}}$

SOLUTION   **a.** $\sqrt{12x^3y^8} = \sqrt{4x^2y^8 \cdot 3x}$

$= \sqrt{4x^2y^8} \cdot \sqrt{3x}$

$= \sqrt{4} \cdot \sqrt{x^2} \cdot \sqrt{y^8} \cdot \sqrt{3x}$

$= 2xy^4\sqrt{3x}$

b. $\sqrt{\dfrac{75x^5y}{x^2y^3}} = \sqrt{\dfrac{75x^3}{y^2}}$

$= \dfrac{\sqrt{75x^3}}{\sqrt{y^2}}$

$= \dfrac{\sqrt{25x^2 \cdot 3x}}{y}$

$= \dfrac{\sqrt{25x^2} \cdot \sqrt{3x}}{y}$

$= \dfrac{5x\sqrt{3x}}{y}$

To simplify a radical expression having more than one term, first simplify each term of the expression using the rules on page 95, and then combine *similar terms* (terms that have the same radical) by applying the distributive property.

EXAMPLE   Simplify: $6\sqrt{80} - 7\sqrt{5} - \sqrt{28}$

SOLUTION $6\sqrt{80} - 7\sqrt{5} - \sqrt{28} = 6\sqrt{16 \cdot 5} - 7\sqrt{5} - \sqrt{4 \cdot 7}$

$$= 6\sqrt{16} \cdot \sqrt{5} - 7\sqrt{5} - \sqrt{4} \cdot \sqrt{7}$$
$$= 6 \cdot 4\sqrt{5} - 7\sqrt{5} - 2\sqrt{7}$$
$$= (24 - 7)\sqrt{5} - 2\sqrt{7}$$
$$= 17\sqrt{5} - 2\sqrt{7}$$

EXAMPLE   Simplify: $\sqrt{\dfrac{30}{6}} + \dfrac{\sqrt{20}}{3} - \sqrt{\dfrac{45}{4}}$

SOLUTION $\sqrt{\dfrac{30}{6}} + \dfrac{\sqrt{20}}{3} - \sqrt{\dfrac{45}{4}} = \sqrt{5} + \dfrac{\sqrt{4 \cdot 5}}{3} - \dfrac{\sqrt{9 \cdot 5}}{\sqrt{4}}$

$$= \sqrt{5} + \dfrac{2\sqrt{5}}{3} - \dfrac{3\sqrt{5}}{2}$$
$$= \dfrac{6\sqrt{5}}{6} + \dfrac{4\sqrt{5}}{6} - \dfrac{9\sqrt{5}}{6}$$
$$= \dfrac{(6 + 4 - 9)\sqrt{5}}{6}$$
$$= \dfrac{\sqrt{5}}{6}$$

ORAL EXERCISES

Simplify.

1. $\sqrt{144}$ 2. $\sqrt{225}$ 3. $\sqrt{9 \cdot 7}$ 4. $\sqrt{25 \cdot 6}$ 5. $\sqrt{11 \cdot 4}$ 6. $\sqrt{3 \cdot 49}$

Name the largest perfect-square factor of the given expression.

7. 48   8. 96   9. 128   10. $50x^6$ 11. $49y^7$ 12. $16x^{17}y^{18}$

For which values of x does the given expression represent a real number?

13. $\sqrt{x}$ 14. $\sqrt{x + 2}$ 15. $\sqrt{4x - 12}$ 16. $\sqrt{3 - x}$

Simplify. If the radical does not represent a real number, so state.

17. $-\sqrt{64}$ 18. $\sqrt{-36}$ 19. $\sqrt[3]{125}$ 20. $\sqrt[3]{-27}$

21. $\sqrt[4]{-16}$ 22. $-\sqrt[4]{81}$ 23. $\sqrt[3]{9 \cdot 8}$ 24. $\sqrt[5]{-100,000}$

State the real roots (if any) of the equation.

25. $x^2 = -4$ 26. $x^3 = -8$ 27. $x^4 = \dfrac{1}{16}$ 28. $x^5 = 32$

WRITTEN EXERCISES

Simplify. Assume that all variables represent positive real numbers.

A 1. $\sqrt{18}$ 2. $\sqrt{20}$ 3. $\sqrt{180}$ 4. $\sqrt{162}$

5. $3\sqrt{44}$ 6. $-5\sqrt{98}$ 7. $-6\sqrt{54}$ 8. $12\sqrt{1200}$

9. $\sqrt{36x^4y^2}$ 10. $\sqrt{81a^{10}b^{18}}$ 11. $\sqrt{24a^5y^6}$ 12. $\sqrt{300xy^8}$

13. $-\sqrt{112k^3m^9}$ 14. $\sqrt{288p^2q^{16}r^{10}}$ 15. $\dfrac{\sqrt{96}}{\sqrt{6}}$ 16. $\sqrt{\dfrac{27}{4}}$

17. $\sqrt{\dfrac{242}{49}}$ 18. $\dfrac{-\sqrt{240}}{\sqrt{12}}$ 19. $\dfrac{3\sqrt{2x^5y^9}}{\sqrt{8x}}$ 20. $\dfrac{\sqrt{75d^9e^8}}{\sqrt{3de}}$

21. $\dfrac{\sqrt{12bc^9}}{2\sqrt{3b^3c^7}}$ 22. $\dfrac{3}{2}\sqrt{\dfrac{20x^6}{9xy^{12}}}$ 23. $2\sqrt{48}-\sqrt{27}$ 24. $6\sqrt{20}+\sqrt{45}$

25. $\sqrt{150}-2\sqrt{96}$ 26. $3\sqrt{135}-2\sqrt{450}$

27. $\sqrt{160}-\sqrt{360}+\sqrt{250}$ 28. $5\sqrt{32}+\sqrt{28}-3\sqrt{128}$

29. $3\sqrt{1440}-2\sqrt{75}-\sqrt{192}$ 30. $-2\sqrt{175}+\sqrt{243}+5\sqrt{63}$

B 31. $\sqrt{\dfrac{24}{3}}+\dfrac{\sqrt{72}}{3}$ 32. $\sqrt{\dfrac{15}{12}}-\sqrt{\dfrac{20}{9}}$

33. $\sqrt{\dfrac{27}{16}}-\sqrt{\dfrac{15}{20}}$ 34. $\dfrac{2\sqrt{28}}{5}+\sqrt{\dfrac{14}{18}}$

35. $\dfrac{\sqrt{108}}{6}+\sqrt{\dfrac{125}{4}}-\dfrac{\sqrt{147}}{3}$ 36. $\dfrac{\sqrt{60}}{4}-\dfrac{\sqrt{1500}}{5}+\sqrt{\dfrac{75}{16}}$

37. $\sqrt[3]{5}+\sqrt[3]{40}$ 38. $\sqrt[3]{108}-\sqrt[3]{32}$ 39. $8\sqrt[3]{-54}-\sqrt[3]{250}$

40. $\sqrt[3]{4000}+\sqrt[3]{-500}$ 41. $\sqrt[4]{32}+\sqrt[4]{1250}$ 42. $\sqrt[4]{20,000}-\sqrt[4]{512}$

43. $\sqrt{2x^5}+3\sqrt{2x^3}$ 44. $7\sqrt{a^9}-5a^2\sqrt{a^3}+\sqrt{a^7}$

45. $\sqrt{\dfrac{3x^3}{25}}-\dfrac{\sqrt{12x^5}}{15}+\dfrac{\sqrt{75x}}{3}$ 46. $\dfrac{y\sqrt{98y^2}}{3}-\dfrac{\sqrt{162y^4}}{7}-\dfrac{y^2\sqrt{50}}{21}$

47. $\dfrac{\sqrt{175n^5}}{2k}+\dfrac{\sqrt{7n}}{k^2}-\sqrt{\dfrac{28n^3}{k^2}}$ 48. $\dfrac{\sqrt{169v^3}}{u^2}-\sqrt{\dfrac{4v^3}{9u^2}}-\dfrac{v\sqrt{100v}}{3u}$

C 49. Complete: a. $\sqrt{(-2)^2}=$ _?_ b. If $x<0$, then $\sqrt{x^2}=$ _?_

50. Show that if $a\geqslant0$ and $b\geqslant0$, then $\sqrt{ab}=\sqrt{a}\cdot\sqrt{b}$. (Hint: If $x^2=y^2$ and x and y are both nonnegative, then $x=y$.)

51. Show that if $a\geqslant0$ and $b>0$, then $\sqrt{\dfrac{a}{b}}=\dfrac{\sqrt{a}}{\sqrt{b}}$. (See the hint for Ex. 50.)

52. Show that if $\sqrt{a+b}=\sqrt{a}+\sqrt{b}$, then a or b must equal zero. (Hint: Square both sides of the given equation.)

Section 3-2 MULTIPLYING AND DIVIDING RADICAL EXPRESSIONS

To simplify a product of two radical expressions, $a\sqrt[n]{b} \cdot c\sqrt[n]{d}$, where $\sqrt[n]{b}$ and $\sqrt[n]{d}$ are real numbers, you use the commutative property of multiplication and the rule for the product of two radicals:

$$a\sqrt[n]{b} \cdot c\sqrt[n]{d} = ac\sqrt[n]{b} \cdot \sqrt[n]{d}$$
$$= ac\sqrt[n]{bd}$$

In the examples of this section, you may assume that all variables represent positive real numbers.

EXAMPLE

$$
\begin{aligned}
5x\sqrt{30xy^2} \cdot 2y\sqrt{6xy} &= 5x \cdot 2y\sqrt{30xy^2 \cdot 6xy} \\
&= 10xy\sqrt{5 \cdot 6 \cdot 6x^2y^3} \\
&= 10xy\sqrt{36x^2y^2 \cdot 5y} \\
&= 10xy \cdot 6xy\sqrt{5y} \\
&= 60x^2y^2\sqrt{5y}
\end{aligned}
$$

Note that in the example above we did not multiply all the numerical factors *under* the radical sign, since it is often easier to recognize perfect-square factors when the numbers are left unmultiplied.

When the expressions to be multiplied are the same, you can find the product by using the laws of exponents.

EXAMPLE

$$(5\sqrt{3})^2 = 5^2(\sqrt{3})^2 = 25 \cdot 3 = 75$$

If $\sqrt[n]{x}$ appears in the denominator of a fraction, you can remove the radical from the denominator by multiplying the fraction by

$$\frac{(\sqrt[n]{x})^{n-1}}{(\sqrt[n]{x})^{n-1}}$$

and using the fact that $(\sqrt[n]{x})^n = x$ when $\sqrt[n]{x}$ is a real number. This is one example of a technique called *rationalizing the denominator*.

EXAMPLES

$$\frac{\sqrt{7}}{\sqrt{5}} = \frac{\sqrt{7}}{\sqrt{5}} \cdot \frac{\sqrt{5}}{\sqrt{5}} = \frac{\sqrt{35}}{5}$$

$$\sqrt{\frac{25}{12}} = \frac{\sqrt{25}}{\sqrt{12}} = \frac{\sqrt{5 \cdot 5}}{\sqrt{4 \cdot 3}} = \frac{5}{2\sqrt{3}} = \frac{5}{2\sqrt{3}} \cdot \frac{\sqrt{3}}{\sqrt{3}} = \frac{5\sqrt{3}}{6}$$

$$\sqrt{\frac{2x}{18y^3}} = \sqrt{\frac{x}{9y^3}} = \frac{\sqrt{x}}{\sqrt{9y^2 \cdot y}} = \frac{\sqrt{x}}{3y\sqrt{y}} = \frac{\sqrt{x}}{3y\sqrt{y}} \cdot \frac{\sqrt{y}}{\sqrt{y}} = \frac{\sqrt{xy}}{3y^2}$$

$$\sqrt[3]{\frac{2}{7}} = \frac{\sqrt[3]{2}}{\sqrt[3]{7}} = \frac{\sqrt[3]{2}}{\sqrt[3]{7}} \cdot \frac{(\sqrt[3]{7})^2}{(\sqrt[3]{7})^2} = \frac{\sqrt[3]{2} \cdot \sqrt[3]{49}}{(\sqrt[3]{7})^3} = \frac{\sqrt[3]{98}}{7}$$

To multiply two radical expressions containing more than one term, you use the Distributive Property.

EXAMPLES

$$3\sqrt{10}(2\sqrt{5} - 4\sqrt{2}) = 6\sqrt{10 \cdot 5} - 12\sqrt{10 \cdot 2}$$
$$= 6\sqrt{2 \cdot 5 \cdot 5} - 12\sqrt{5 \cdot 2 \cdot 2}$$
$$= 6(5\sqrt{2}) - 12(2\sqrt{5})$$
$$= 30\sqrt{2} - 24\sqrt{5}$$

$$(5\sqrt{2} - 3\sqrt{6})(\sqrt{2} + 4\sqrt{6}) = 5\sqrt{2}\sqrt{2} + 5(4)\sqrt{2 \cdot 6} - 3\sqrt{6 \cdot 2} - 3(4)\sqrt{6}\sqrt{6}$$
$$= 5(2) + 20\sqrt{2 \cdot 2 \cdot 3} - 3\sqrt{2 \cdot 2 \cdot 3} - 12(6)$$
$$= 10 + 20(2\sqrt{3}) - 3(2\sqrt{3}) - 72$$
$$= -62 + 34\sqrt{3}$$

$$(7 - 2\sqrt{3})^2 = 7^2 - 2(7)(2\sqrt{3}) + (2\sqrt{3})^2$$
$$= 49 - 28\sqrt{3} + 4(3)$$
$$= 61 - 28\sqrt{3}$$

$$(5\sqrt{3} - 8)(5\sqrt{3} + 8) = (5\sqrt{3})^2 - 8^2$$
$$= 25(3) - 64$$
$$= 11$$

The answer to the last example above is 11, which is a rational number. This suggests a way to rationalize the denominator of a radical expression if the denominator has two terms, one or both of which contain a square root. Recall that expressions of the form

$$a\sqrt{b} + c\sqrt{d} \quad \text{and} \quad a\sqrt{b} - c\sqrt{d}$$

are called *conjugates* of each other. If you multiply the numerator and denominator of a given fraction by the conjugate of the denominator, the resulting denominator will be free of radicals. This technique will be especially important in later sections.

EXAMPLE   Simplify: a. $\dfrac{\sqrt{2}}{\sqrt{5} - 3}$ b. $\dfrac{3}{2\sqrt{2} + \sqrt{5}}$

SOLUTION

a. $\dfrac{\sqrt{2}}{\sqrt{5} - 3} = \dfrac{\sqrt{2}}{\sqrt{5} - 3} \cdot \dfrac{\sqrt{5} + 3}{\sqrt{5} + 3}$

$= \dfrac{\sqrt{10} + 3\sqrt{2}}{(\sqrt{5})^2 - 3^2}$

$= \dfrac{\sqrt{10} + 3\sqrt{2}}{-4}$

$= -\dfrac{\sqrt{10} + 3\sqrt{2}}{4}$

b. $\dfrac{3}{2\sqrt{2} + \sqrt{5}} = \dfrac{3}{2\sqrt{2} + \sqrt{5}} \cdot \dfrac{2\sqrt{2} - \sqrt{5}}{2\sqrt{2} - \sqrt{5}}$

$= \dfrac{6\sqrt{2} - 3\sqrt{5}}{8 - 5}$

$= \dfrac{6\sqrt{2} - 3\sqrt{5}}{3}$

$= 2\sqrt{2} - \sqrt{5}$

ORAL EXERCISES

Simplify. Assume that all variables represent positive real numbers.

1. $\sqrt{2} \cdot 5\sqrt{2}$

2. $(-\sqrt{3})(5\sqrt{10})$

3. $3\sqrt{2} \cdot 5\sqrt{7}$

4. $(-2\sqrt{3})(-9\sqrt{5})$

5. $(2\sqrt{5})^2$

6. $(-3\sqrt{3})^2$

7. $-3(2\sqrt{5} + 4\sqrt{6})$

8. $-\sqrt{2}(\sqrt{2} + \sqrt{3})$

9. $3\sqrt{2}(5 - \sqrt{2})$

10. $\sqrt{x}(\sqrt{x} - \sqrt{y})$

11. $(\sqrt{a} + \sqrt{b})(\sqrt{a} - \sqrt{b})$

12. $(\sqrt{a} + \sqrt{b})^2$

State a number by which you could multiply both the numerator and the denominator of the given fraction in order to rationalize the denominator.

13. $\dfrac{3}{\sqrt{5}}$

14. $\dfrac{\sqrt{2} - 1}{\sqrt{7}}$

15. $\dfrac{8}{3\sqrt{11}}$

16. $\dfrac{-7}{5 + \sqrt{3}}$

17. $\dfrac{9 + \sqrt{3}}{\sqrt{6} - \sqrt{2}}$

18. $\dfrac{5 - \sqrt{7}}{3\sqrt{10} + \sqrt{7}}$

WRITTEN EXERCISES

Simplify. Assume that all variables represent positive real numbers.

A 1. $6\sqrt{2} \cdot 3\sqrt{5}$

2. $-3\sqrt{11} \cdot 7\sqrt{6}$

3. $(3\sqrt{11})^2$

4. $(7\sqrt{2})^2$

5. $5\sqrt{6} \cdot 2\sqrt{3}$

6. $7\sqrt{8} \cdot 3\sqrt{10}$

7. $-5\sqrt{6} \cdot 4\sqrt{15}$

8. $(-3\sqrt{10})(-\sqrt{18})$

9. $\sqrt{x^3 y} \cdot \sqrt{xy^2}$

10. $\sqrt{3ab^3} \cdot \sqrt{30a^3 b^5}$

11. $-5n^2\sqrt{14n} \cdot 2\sqrt{21n^3}$

12. $(-6q\sqrt{20pq^2})(-5\sqrt{35p^5 q})$

13. $\dfrac{\sqrt{3}}{\sqrt{2}}$

14. $\sqrt{\dfrac{2}{15}}$

15. $\dfrac{6\sqrt{5}}{\sqrt{3}}$

16. $\dfrac{4\sqrt{7}}{\sqrt{8}}$

17. $\dfrac{5\sqrt{10}}{\sqrt{6}}$

18. $\dfrac{3}{2}\sqrt{\dfrac{5}{18}}$

19. $\dfrac{\sqrt{y}}{\sqrt{x^3}}$

20. $\dfrac{\sqrt{2a^3 b}}{\sqrt{6a}}$

21. $-\sqrt{3}(\sqrt{5} + \sqrt{7})$

22. $\sqrt{5}(3 - 2\sqrt{13})$

23. $5\sqrt{2}(6\sqrt{2} - 3\sqrt{6})$

24. $-2\sqrt{3}(\sqrt{15} + 4\sqrt{3})$

25. $(\sqrt{5} - 2)(\sqrt{5} + 4)$

26. $(4 - \sqrt{7})(1 - \sqrt{7})$

27. $(\sqrt{2} + \sqrt{3})(\sqrt{2} - \sqrt{3})$

28. $(-\sqrt{5} + 2\sqrt{6})(4\sqrt{5} - \sqrt{6})$

29. $(\sqrt{7} + 2\sqrt{10})^2$

30. $(3\sqrt{6} - 2)(3\sqrt{6} + 2)$

31. $(5 - 4\sqrt{3})(5 + 4\sqrt{3})$

32. $(1 - 6\sqrt{11})^2$

33. $(\sqrt{3} - 8\sqrt{5})^2$

34. $(2\sqrt{6} + \sqrt{5})^2$

35. $(3\sqrt{2} - 6)(3\sqrt{2} + 6)$

36. $(3\sqrt{14} - \sqrt{7})(\sqrt{14} + 2\sqrt{7})$

37. $\dfrac{8}{\sqrt{5} - 2}$

38. $\dfrac{-7}{3 + \sqrt{10}}$

39. $\dfrac{4}{\sqrt{11} + 3}$

40. $\dfrac{\sqrt{2}}{\sqrt{6} - \sqrt{2}}$

41. $\dfrac{6\sqrt{2}}{3\sqrt{2} + 4}$

42. $\dfrac{12}{4\sqrt{5} - 2\sqrt{2}}$

B 43. $\dfrac{2\sqrt{5}+3}{2\sqrt{5}-3}$ 44. $\dfrac{2\sqrt{3}-4}{4\sqrt{3}-6}$ 45. $\dfrac{4\sqrt{6}+2\sqrt{3}}{\sqrt{6}-2\sqrt{3}}$

46. $\dfrac{x-y}{\sqrt{x}-\sqrt{y}},\ x\neq y$ 47. $\dfrac{a\sqrt{3}}{\sqrt{2a}+\sqrt{a}}$ 48. $\dfrac{c}{\sqrt{b+c}-\sqrt{b}}$

49. $\dfrac{e\sqrt{d}}{\sqrt{d+e}+\sqrt{d}}$ 50. $\dfrac{\sqrt{x+y}-\sqrt{x-y}}{\sqrt{x+y}+\sqrt{x-y}},\ x\geqslant y$ 51. $\dfrac{\sqrt{a}+\sqrt{a-b}}{\sqrt{a}-\sqrt{a-b}},\ a\geqslant b$

52. $\sqrt{\dfrac{3}{2}}+\sqrt{\dfrac{2}{3}}$ 53. $\sqrt{\dfrac{1}{8}}+\sqrt{\dfrac{1}{3}}-\sqrt{\dfrac{1}{2}}$ 54. $3\sqrt{\dfrac{2}{5}}-\dfrac{4}{\sqrt{10}}+\sqrt{10}$

55. $\sqrt{\dfrac{1}{5}}+2\sqrt{\dfrac{9}{20}}-\dfrac{\sqrt{15}}{12}$ 56. $\sqrt{\dfrac{a}{b}}+\sqrt{\dfrac{b}{a}}$ 57. $\sqrt{\dfrac{ab}{c}}+\sqrt{\dfrac{bc}{a}}+\sqrt{\dfrac{ac}{b}}$

58. $2\sqrt[3]{9}\cdot5\sqrt[3]{-3}$ 59. $6\sqrt[3]{4}\cdot2\sqrt[3]{6}$ 60. $\sqrt[3]{4}(\sqrt[3]{4}-1)$

61. $\sqrt[3]{100}(\sqrt[3]{10}-\sqrt[3]{4})$ 62. $-2\sqrt[4]{27}\cdot\sqrt[4]{9}$ 63. $\sqrt[4]{25}(\sqrt[4]{125}+\sqrt[4]{25})$

64. $\sqrt[3]{\dfrac{6}{5}}$ 65. $\sqrt[3]{\dfrac{7}{54}}$ 66. $\sqrt[4]{\dfrac{2}{3}}$

67. $(\sqrt{x}+\sqrt{y}-\sqrt{z})(\sqrt{x}+\sqrt{y}+\sqrt{z})$ 68. $(\sqrt{p}-\sqrt{q}+\sqrt{r})(\sqrt{p}+\sqrt{q}-\sqrt{r})$

Solve for x. Leave your answers in simplest radical form.

69. $x\sqrt{3}=5$ 70. $x(\sqrt{2}+3)=-6$ 71. $x\sqrt{6}-2x=4$

72. $x\sqrt{5}+x=3$ 73. $3x=x\sqrt{2}+1$ 74. $x\sqrt{3}=x-2$

Simplify. (*Hint*: Recall the formulas for factoring the sum of two cubes and the difference of two cubes.)

C 75. $\dfrac{1}{1+\sqrt[3]{7}}$ 76. $\dfrac{1}{5-\sqrt[3]{2}}$

Simplify. Assume that all variables represent positive real numbers.

77. $\sqrt{p-q}(\sqrt{p-q}+\sqrt{4p-4q}+\sqrt{p^2-q^2}),\ p\geqslant q$

78. $\dfrac{\dfrac{1}{\sqrt{x}}+\dfrac{1}{\sqrt{y}}}{\dfrac{1}{\sqrt{x}}-\dfrac{1}{\sqrt{y}}},\ x\neq y$ 79. $\dfrac{\sqrt{\dfrac{a}{b}}-2+\sqrt{\dfrac{b}{a}}}{\sqrt{\dfrac{1}{b}}-\sqrt{\dfrac{1}{a}}},\ a\neq b$

80. Let $Q(\sqrt{2})$ be the set of numbers of the form $a+b\sqrt{2}$, where a and b are rational numbers.
   a. Show that $Q(\sqrt{2})$ is closed under multiplication; that is, if x and y are elements of $Q(\sqrt{2})$, then xy is also an element of $Q(\sqrt{2})$.
   b. Show that all nonzero elements of $Q(\sqrt{2})$ have multiplicative inverses; that is, if x is an element of $Q(\sqrt{2})$, $x\neq0$, then $\dfrac{1}{x}$ is an element of $Q(\sqrt{2})$.
   (You may assume that $a^2-2b^2\neq0$ whenever a and b are rational numbers that are not both 0.)

Section 3-3 RADICAL EQUATIONS

An equation containing a variable under a radical sign is called a *radical equation*. In order to solve a radical equation, at some point you have to raise both sides of the equation to the power indicated by the index of the radical. For example, to solve a radical equation containing a square root, you must square both sides. Squaring both sides of an equation preserves the equality of the two sides, but it may introduce apparent solutions that do not satisfy the original equation. Compare, for example, the solutions of the equations

$$x = 3 \quad \text{and} \quad x^2 = 9.$$

The solutions of $x^2 = 9$ are 3 and -3, but only 3 is a solution of $x = 3$. Thus when you square $x = 3$, you introduce the *extraneous* solution -3.

Therefore, after solving a radical equation involving square roots (or any root where the index is even), you must *check* each apparent solution to make sure it satisfies the original equation. If an apparent solution is extraneous, it must be rejected as a solution of the original equation.

EXAMPLE Solve: $\sqrt{2x} = x - 4$

SOLUTION Square both sides.

$$(\sqrt{2x})^2 = (x - 4)^2$$
$$2x = x^2 - 8x + 16$$
$$0 = x^2 - 10x + 16$$
$$0 = (x - 8)(x - 2)$$
$$x - 8 = 0 \text{ or } x - 2 = 0$$

The apparent solutions are 8 and 2.

Check $x = 8$: $\sqrt{2 \cdot 8} \overset{?}{=} 8 - 4$ $x = 2$: $\sqrt{2 \cdot 2} \overset{?}{=} 2 - 4$
$\sqrt{16} \overset{?}{=} 4$ $\sqrt{4} \overset{?}{=} -2$
$4 = 4$ $2 \neq -2$ (reject)

The solution set is $\{8\}$.

If a given radical equation has only one term containing a radical, you should first isolate that term on one side of the equation.

EXAMPLE Solve: $\sqrt{x + 2} + x = 10$

SOLUTION First isolate $\sqrt{x + 2}$ on one side.

$$\sqrt{x + 2} = 10 - x$$

Then square both sides.

$$(\sqrt{x + 2})^2 = (10 - x)^2$$
$$x + 2 = 100 - 20x + x^2$$
$$0 = x^2 - 21x + 98$$
$$0 = (x - 7)(x - 14)$$
$$x = 7 \text{ or } x = 14$$

The apparent solutions are 7 and 14.

Check $x = 7$: $\sqrt{7+2} + 7 \overset{?}{=} 10$ $x = 14$: $\sqrt{14+2} + 14 \overset{?}{=} 10$
                     $\sqrt{9} + 7 \overset{?}{=} 10$ $\sqrt{16} + 14 \overset{?}{=} 10$
                     $3 + 7 = 10$ $4 + 14 \neq 10$ (reject)
          The solution set is $\{7\}$.

Note that in the preceding example, if you square both sides of the original equation, you obtain

$$(x + 2) + 2x\sqrt{x+2} + x^2 = 100.$$

This step is not helpful since it does not eliminate the radical sign.

If a given equation has *two* terms containing square-root radicals, you usually have to square both sides *twice* in the course of the solution. It is often convenient to begin by isolating one of the terms containing a radical on one side of the equation.

EXAMPLE   Solve: $\sqrt{x-2} + \sqrt{7-x} = 3$

SOLUTION   First, isolate one of the terms containing a radical on one side of the equation. For example:

$$\sqrt{x-2} = 3 - \sqrt{7-x}$$

Square both sides.

$$(\sqrt{x-2})^2 = (3 - \sqrt{7-x})^2$$
$$x - 2 = 9 - 6\sqrt{7-x} + (7-x)$$

Now proceed as before, isolating the remaining term containing the radical.

$$2x - 18 = -6\sqrt{7-x}$$
$$x - 9 = -3\sqrt{7-x}$$

Square both sides again.

$$(x - 9)^2 = (-3\sqrt{7-x})^2$$
$$x^2 - 18x + 81 = 9(7-x)$$
$$x^2 - 9x + 18 = 0$$
$$(x - 3)(x - 6) = 0$$
$$x = 3 \text{ or } x = 6$$

The apparent solutions are 3 and 6.

Check $x = 3$: $\sqrt{3-2} + \sqrt{7-3} \overset{?}{=} 3$ $x = 6$: $\sqrt{6-2} + \sqrt{7-6} \overset{?}{=} 3$
                     $\sqrt{1} + \sqrt{4} \overset{?}{=} 3$ $\sqrt{4} + \sqrt{1} \overset{?}{=} 3$
                     $1 + 2 = 3$ $2 + 1 = 3$
          The solution set is $\{3, 6\}$.

ORAL EXERCISES

Describe the first step in solving the given equation.

1. $\sqrt{x-9} = 0$ 2. $5 = 3 + 2\sqrt{x}$ 3. $\sqrt{x+1} + \sqrt{x-4} = 5$

State the number of solutions for the given equation.

4. $\sqrt{x} = 7$ 5. $\sqrt{x} = -3$ 6. $-\sqrt{x} = 5$ 7. $-\sqrt{x} = -13$

Solve the given equation. Check each apparent solution.

8. $\sqrt{x} = 9$ 9. $7 = \sqrt{x} + 1$ 10. $3\sqrt{x} = 12$ 11. $\sqrt{5x} = x$

In Exercises 12-15 the second line is an incorrect step in the solution of the given equation. Tell why it is incorrect and state a correct second line.

12. $\sqrt{x+3} = 16$ (given)
$x + 3 = 4$ (incorrect)

13. $\sqrt{x+2} = x - 4$ (given)
$x + 2 = x^2 + 16$ (incorrect)

14. $\sqrt{3x} + 6 = x$ (given)
$3x + 36 = x^2$ (incorrect)

15. $\sqrt{x+2} = 3 - \sqrt{x-1}$ (given)
$x + 2 = 9 + (x-1)$ (incorrect)

WRITTEN EXERCISES

Solve for x. Check each apparent solution.

A 1. $6\sqrt{x} = 12$
2. $\sqrt{x+4} = 3$
3. $\sqrt{x+2} - 3 = 4$

4. $5 - \sqrt{x-1} = 2$
5. $\sqrt{x^2+8} = 2 - x$
6. $\sqrt{3-x} = 4$

7. $\sqrt{x+1} - 1 = x$
8. $\sqrt{2x+5} - x = 3$
9. $\sqrt{1-2x} = 3$

10. $\sqrt{x^2-9} = x + 1$
11. $3\sqrt{2x} - x = 4$
12. $2x = 3\sqrt{x+3} + 3$

13. $\sqrt{9-2x} = x - 3$
14. $3\sqrt{2x+2} = 2x - 2$
15. $3 - 2\sqrt{4x-3} + x = 0$

16. $\sqrt{1-4x} - x = 5$
17. $\sqrt{x+7} + \dfrac{x}{3} = 1$
18. $\dfrac{\sqrt{5+x}}{2} - x - 2 = 0$

B 19. $\sqrt{x+2} = \sqrt{x+4}$
20. $2\sqrt{x} = \sqrt{4x-3} + 1$

21. $\sqrt{5-x} = \sqrt{x} - 1$
22. $\sqrt{x+6} = \sqrt{x+3} + 1$

23. $\sqrt{x+1} = 3 - \sqrt{4-x}$
24. $2\sqrt{x} = \sqrt{x-1} + 2$

25. $\sqrt{x+2} + \sqrt{3-x} = 3$
26. $\sqrt{x+2} - \sqrt{x-3} = 1$

27. $\sqrt{2x} - \sqrt{x+1} = 1$
28. $\sqrt{7+x} + \sqrt{6-x} = 5$

29. $\sqrt{2x+3} + \sqrt{x+2} = 2$
30. $\sqrt{5-2x} + \sqrt{x-1} = 2$

31. $\sqrt{3x+4} - \sqrt{x+1} = 1$
32. $\sqrt{2x+1} + \sqrt{x-3} = 2$

33. $\sqrt{x^2+3} - \sqrt{x^2+1} = 2$
34. $\sqrt{x^2+5} + \sqrt{5-x^2} = 4$

C 35. $\sqrt[3]{x-2} + 1 = 4$
36. $\sqrt[3]{x-5} + 3 = 0$

37. $\sqrt[4]{x+18} = 2$
38. $\sqrt[4]{2x-8} = \sqrt[4]{6-5x}$

39. $\dfrac{1}{\sqrt{x}} + 2\sqrt{x} = 3$
40. $2\sqrt{x} + 1 = \dfrac{6}{\sqrt{x}}$

41. $\sqrt{4x+5} - \sqrt{x+5} = \sqrt{x-2}$
42. $\sqrt{x+4} + \sqrt{2x-1} = \sqrt{7x+1}$

43. If a, b, and c are any three positive real numbers, show that the equation
$$\sqrt{x+a} + \sqrt{x+b} = c$$
has no real solution if $a > b + c^2$.

Simplify. Assume that all variables represent positive real numbers.

1. $\sqrt{49x^6y^3}$ 2. $\dfrac{\sqrt{88}}{\sqrt{2}}$ 3. $5\sqrt{8} - \sqrt{18}$ 4. $3\sqrt{27} - 4\sqrt{50} + 3\sqrt{75}$ Section 3-1

5. $\sqrt{2a^2b} \cdot \sqrt{16ab^7}$ 6. $\sqrt{2}(\sqrt{2} + 6\sqrt{3})$ Section 3-2

7. $(2 - \sqrt{6})(4 + \sqrt{2})$ 8. $(5 + \sqrt{11})^2$

9. $\sqrt{\dfrac{6}{5}}$ 10. $\dfrac{5}{\sqrt{6} + 2}$

Solve for x. Check each apparent solution.

11. $3\sqrt{x + 4} = 18$ 12. $\sqrt{5x - 1} - 1 = x$ 13. $\sqrt{5x - 4} - \sqrt{x} = 2$ Section 3-3

Section 3-4 THE NUMBER i

For years mathematicians were disturbed by the fact that although the equation

$$x^2 - 1 = 0$$

has two real solutions, the equation

$$x^2 + 1 = 0$$

has no real solutions. They therefore cautiously proposed a new algebraic quantity, later called i, that would be a solution of the latter equation. The number i, called the *imaginary unit*, can thus be defined algebraically as:

$$i = \sqrt{-1}$$

It follows from this definition that:

$$i^2 = (\sqrt{-1})^2 = \sqrt{-1}\,\sqrt{-1} = -1$$

Hence, if you substitute i for x in the equation $x^2 + 1 = 0$, you get:

$$i^2 + 1 = -1 + 1 = 0$$

Note that if the number i is to obey the rules of arithmetic for real numbers, then $-i$ is also a solution of this equation since:

$$(-i)^2 + 1 = i^2 + 1 = -1 + 1 = 0$$

Square roots of negative numbers other than -1 can be expressed in terms of i. Notice that

$$(5i)^2 = 25i^2 = 25(-1) = -25 \quad \text{and} \quad (-5i)^2 = 25i^2 = 25(-1) = -25.$$

In general, if a is a positive number, then there are two numbers whose square is $-a$, namely $i\sqrt{a}$ and $-i\sqrt{a}$. We adopt the convention that

$$\sqrt{-a} = i\sqrt{a}.$$

EXAMPLES

$$\sqrt{-7} = i\sqrt{7} \qquad\qquad -\sqrt{-5} = -i\sqrt{5}$$

$$\sqrt{-9} = i\sqrt{9} = 3i \qquad\qquad \sqrt{-12} = i\sqrt{12} = i \cdot 2\sqrt{3}, \text{ or } 2i\sqrt{3}$$

The numbers $i\sqrt{7}$, $-i\sqrt{5}$, $3i$, and $2i\sqrt{3}$ are all of the form bi, where b is a nonzero real number. Such numbers are called *pure imaginary numbers*.

Notice that $\sqrt{ab} = \sqrt{a} \cdot \sqrt{b}$ is *not* true when a and b are both negative. For example,

$$\sqrt{-1}\,\sqrt{-1} = i \cdot i = i^2 = -1,$$

but

$$\sqrt{(-1)(-1)} = \sqrt{1} = 1.$$

Therefore,

$$\sqrt{-1}\,\sqrt{-1} \neq \sqrt{(-1)(-1)}.$$

This suggests the following guidelines for carrying out algebraic operations on expressions containing negative radicands.

1. Change all expressions of the form $\sqrt{-b}$, $b > 0$, to $i\sqrt{b}$ *before* doing any other operation.

2. Treat i as if it were a variable, but substitute -1 for i^2 whenever it occurs. (Note, however, that the number i is *not* a variable but is always equal to $\sqrt{-1}$, just as π always represents the real number $3.14159\ldots$.)

EXAMPLES   1. $\sqrt{6}\,\sqrt{-18} = \sqrt{6} \cdot i\sqrt{18} = i\sqrt{6 \cdot 6 \cdot 3} = 6i\sqrt{3}$

     2. $\sqrt{-5}\,\sqrt{-10} = i\sqrt{5} \cdot i\sqrt{10} = i^2\sqrt{5 \cdot 5 \cdot 2} = (-1)5\sqrt{2} = -5\sqrt{2}$

     3. $\dfrac{\sqrt{3}}{\sqrt{-4}} = \dfrac{\sqrt{3}}{i\sqrt{4}} = \dfrac{\sqrt{3}}{2i} = \dfrac{\sqrt{3}}{2i} \cdot \dfrac{i}{i} = \dfrac{i\sqrt{3}}{2i^2} = \dfrac{i\sqrt{3}}{2(-1)} = -\dfrac{i\sqrt{3}}{2}$

     4. $\dfrac{-\sqrt{-7}}{\sqrt{-14}} = \dfrac{-i\sqrt{7}}{i\sqrt{14}} = \dfrac{-1}{\sqrt{2}} = \dfrac{-1 \cdot \sqrt{2}}{\sqrt{2} \cdot \sqrt{2}} = -\dfrac{\sqrt{2}}{2}$

Example 3 above illustrates the fact that when you rationalize a denominator containing i, you treat i as you would any radical.

It is useful to extend the laws of exponents (page 46) and the definition of negative exponents (page 47) to apply to expressions with bases containing i. For example,

$$i^{-5} = \frac{1}{i^5}.$$

Expressions like i^{-5}, i^0, and i^{17} are expressions of the form i^n, where n is an integer. See if you can determine the pattern in the simplifications of i^n for $n = 1$ to $n = 8$ that are shown at the top of the next page.

$$i^1 = i \qquad\qquad i^5 = i^4 \cdot i = 1 \cdot i = i$$
$$i^2 = -1 \qquad\qquad i^6 = i^4 \cdot i^2 = 1 \cdot (-1) = -1$$
$$i^3 = i^2 \cdot i = -1 \cdot i = -i \qquad i^7 = i^4 \cdot i^3 = 1 \cdot (-i) = -i$$
$$i^4 = i^3 \cdot i = -i \cdot i = 1 \qquad i^8 = (i^4)^2 = 1^2 = 1$$

As you can see, the pattern involves the four numbers i, -1, $-i$, and 1 and begins to repeat when $n = 5$. Note that when $n \geqslant 5$, you can use the fact that $i^4 = 1$ to simplify a power of i. As illustrated in the following examples, *any* integral power of i can be simplified to i, -1, $-i$, or 1.

EXAMPLE　Simplify:　**a.** i^{60}　　**b.** i^{39}　　**c.** i^{-9}

SOLUTION　**a.** $i^{60} = (i^4)^{15} = 1^{15} = 1$

b. $i^{39} = i^{36} \cdot i^3 = (i^4)^9(-i) = 1^9(-i) = -i$

c. $i^{-9} = \dfrac{1}{i^9} = \dfrac{1}{i^8 \cdot i} = \dfrac{1}{(i^4)^2 \cdot i} = \dfrac{1}{1 \cdot i} = \dfrac{1}{i} = \dfrac{1}{i} \cdot \dfrac{i}{i} = \dfrac{i}{-1} = -i$

ORAL EXERCISES

Simplify.

1. $\sqrt{-9}$　　2. $\sqrt{9}\,\sqrt{-1}$　　3. $\sqrt{-3}\,\sqrt{-3}$　　4. $\sqrt{-3}\,\sqrt{3}$　　5. $(-\sqrt{3})(\sqrt{3})$

6. $-\sqrt{-9}$　　7. $(-\sqrt{3})(-\sqrt{3})$　　8. $(-\sqrt{3})(\sqrt{-3})$　　9. $-\sqrt{9}$　　10. $\sqrt{3}\,\sqrt{3}$

11. Name the two roots of the equation $x^2 + 1 = 0$.

12. Name the two roots of the equation $x^2 + 16 = 0$.

WRITTEN EXERCISES

Simplify.

A　1. $\sqrt{-25}$　　2. $-\sqrt{-36}$　　3. $-\sqrt{-18}$　　4. $\sqrt{-50}$

5. $\sqrt{-175}$　　6. $-\sqrt{-245}$　　7. $\sqrt{20}\,\sqrt{-15}$　　8. $\sqrt{-3}\,\sqrt{-48}$

9. $-\sqrt{10}\,\sqrt{-15}$　　10. $\sqrt{-24}\,\sqrt{12}$　　11. $(-\sqrt{65})(-\sqrt{13})$　　12. $(-\sqrt{27})(-\sqrt{-6})$

13. $\dfrac{\sqrt{-10}}{\sqrt{-5}}$　　14. $\dfrac{\sqrt{-12}}{\sqrt{3}}$　　15. $\dfrac{\sqrt{250}}{\sqrt{-16}}$　　16. $\dfrac{-\sqrt{300}}{\sqrt{-49}}$

17. $\dfrac{\sqrt{-24}}{-\sqrt{3}}$　　18. $\dfrac{\sqrt{60}}{\sqrt{-75}}$　　19. $\dfrac{-\sqrt{8}}{\sqrt{-6}}$　　20. $\dfrac{-\sqrt{-3}}{\sqrt{15}}$

21. $4i\sqrt{3} \cdot i\sqrt{21}$　　22. $(i\sqrt{5})(-2i\sqrt{40})$　　23. $\dfrac{i^3}{i\sqrt{2}}$　　24. $\dfrac{i^2}{i\sqrt{12}}$

25. $\dfrac{\sqrt{64}}{i\sqrt{125}}$　　26. $\dfrac{\sqrt{2}}{-i\sqrt{96}}$　　27. i^{11}　　28. i^6

29. i^{35}　　30. i^{56}　　31. i^{-5}　　32. i^{-11}

33. $i^{14} + i^{15} + i^{16} + i^{17}$　　　　34. $i^{17} - i^{18} + i^{19} - i^{20}$

Solve for x.

35. $x^2 + 25 = 0$ **36.** $x^2 + 64 = 0$ **37.** $x^2 - 12 = 0$

38. $x^2 + 45 = 0$ **39.** $2x^2 + 36 = 0$ **40.** $5x^2 - 100 = 0$

Show that r is a root of the given equation.

B 41. $x^3 - 3x^2 + 4x - 12 = 0$; $r = 2i$ **42.** $x^3 + 5x^2 + x + 5 = 0$; $r = -i$

43. $x^4 - x^3 + 7x^2 - 4x + 12 = 0$; $r = -2i$ **44.** $2x^3 - x^2 + 18x - 9 = 0$; $r = 3i$

Simplify. Assume that n is a positive integer.

45. i^{4n+3} **46.** i^{4n+1} **47.** i^{4n-3} **48.** i^{4n-1}

C 49. Show that $i^{a+4n} = i^a$ for any positive integer n.

Section 3-5 THE COMPLEX NUMBERS

The set of pure imaginary numbers, together with the set of real numbers, generate a new set called the set of *complex numbers*, often denoted as $\mathcal{C}$. In this section you will learn how to:

- add and subtract two complex numbers
- multiply two complex numbers

A number that can be written in the form

$$a + bi, \text{ where } a \text{ and } b \text{ are real numbers,}$$

is called a *complex number*. The number a is called the *real part* of the complex number, and the number b is called the *imaginary part*.

EXAMPLES *Complex Number*	*Real Part*	*Imaginary Part*
$2 + 3i$	2	3
$4 - i\sqrt{7}$	4	$-\sqrt{7}$
$5i$	0	5
-2	-2	0
0	0	0

If $b = 0$, as in the last two examples above, the complex number $a + bi$ is a real number. If $b \neq 0$, as in the first three examples, $a + bi$ is called an *imaginary number*. The set of imaginary numbers and the set of real numbers are subsets of the set of complex numbers. The diagram at the top of the following page shows how some of the sets of numbers you have studied are related.

A complex number written in the form $a + bi$, where a and b are real numbers, is said to be in *standard form*. In this book, when you see a complex number written in the form $a + bi$, you may assume that a and b are real numbers.

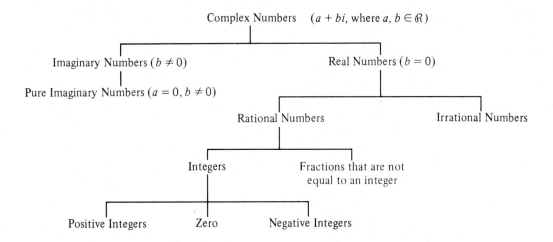

Complex Numbers $(a + bi,$ where $a, b \in \mathcal{R})$

Imaginary Numbers $(b \neq 0)$

Pure Imaginary Numbers $(a = 0, b \neq 0)$

Real Numbers $(b = 0)$

Rational Numbers

Irrational Numbers

Integers

Fractions that are not equal to an integer

Positive Integers   Zero   Negative Integers

EXAMPLE   Express $3 + \dfrac{2}{i}$ in standard form.

SOLUTION $3 + \dfrac{2}{i} = 3 + \dfrac{2}{i} \cdot \dfrac{i}{i} = 3 + \dfrac{2i}{i^2} = 3 + \dfrac{2i}{-1} = 3 - 2i = 3 + (-2)i$

Although technically the standard form for the complex number in the previous example is $3 + (-2)i$, it is convenient to consider $3 - 2i$ as also in standard form. In either case, $a = 3$ and $b = -2$. (We also consider numbers such as 5 and $-2i$ to be in standard form.)

Two complex numbers $a + bi$ and $c + di$ are said to be *equal* if and only if $a = c$ and $b = d$; that is, the real parts of each are equal *and* the imaginary parts of each are equal.

EXAMPLE   Solve for x and y: $(5x + 2) - 3i = 12 + (y + 2)i$

SOLUTION   Equate the real parts and equate the imaginary parts.

$$5x + 2 = 12 \qquad\qquad -3 = y + 2$$
$$5x = 10 \qquad\qquad -5 = y$$
$$x = 2$$

We would like addition and subtraction of complex numbers to obey the rules for adding and subtracting polynomials. Just treat i as you would any variable.

EXAMPLES $(3 + 2i) + (5 - 4i) = (3 + 5) + (2i - 4i) = 8 - 2i$

$(-2 + 5i) - (7 - 3i) = (-2 - 7) + (5i - (-3i)) = -9 + 8i$

These examples suggest the following definitions for addition and subtraction of complex numbers.

For any two complex numbers $a + bi$ and $c + di$:

$$(a + bi) + (c + di) = (a + c) + (b + d)i$$
$$(a + bi) - (c + di) = (a - c) + (b - d)i$$

When multiplying two complex numbers, remember that $i^2 = -1$.

EXAMPLES
$$(2 - 7i)(3 + 4i) = 6 + 8i - 21i - 28i^2$$
$$= 6 - 13i - 28(-1)$$
$$= 34 - 13i$$

$$(a + bi)(c + di) = ac + adi + bci + bdi^2$$
$$= ac + bd(-1) + adi + bci$$
$$= (ac -- bd) + (ad + bc)i$$

The last example suggests the following definition for multiplication of complex numbers.

For any two complex numbers $a + bi$ and $c + di$:

$$(a + bi)(c + di) = (ac - bd) + (ad + bc)i$$

It follows directly from the definitions of addition and multiplication that the set of complex numbers is closed under these operations. In Written Exercises 34–36, you will show that the set of complex numbers shares other properties with the set of real numbers.

ORAL EXERCISES

Name **(a)** the real part and **(b)** the imaginary part of each complex number.

1. $3 + 5i$

2. $2 - 4i$

3. $\dfrac{1}{2} - \dfrac{\sqrt{3}}{2}i$

4. $-\dfrac{\sqrt{2}}{2} + \dfrac{\sqrt{2}}{2}i$

Express each of the following in standard form.

5. $(i + 3i) + 5i$

6. $2(7 - \dfrac{1}{2}i)$

7. $4i$

8. 6

9. $\dfrac{1 + i}{2}$

10. $(1 + i)(1 - i)$

Classify each statement as true or false.

11. Every complex number is a real number.

12. Every real number is a complex number.

13. Every pure imaginary number is an imaginary number.

14. The set of complex numbers is closed under multiplication.

15. $(3 + 2i)^2 = 9 - 4$

16. The number 0 is not a complex number.

17. The product of two complex numbers is never a real number.

18. In the set of complex numbers, what is the additive identity? What is the multiplicative identity?

19. State the additive inverse of the complex number $a + bi$.

WRITTEN EXERCISES

Simplify. Express your answers as complex numbers in standard form.

A 1. $-2i + 7i$

2. $4i - 6i - 7i$

3. $\sqrt{-4} - \sqrt{-9}$

4. $\sqrt{-36} + \sqrt{-16}$

5. $4\sqrt{-27} + 7\sqrt{-12}$

6. $3\sqrt{-5} - \sqrt{-20}$

For each pair of complex numbers give **(a)** the sum, **(b)** the difference (the first minus the second), and **(c)** the product of the two numbers. Express your answers in standard form.

7. $6 + 2i, \; -5i$

8. $3i, \; -1 + 6i$

9. $-5 + 3i, \; 2 + i$

10. $4 - i, \; 7 + 3i$

11. $\dfrac{1}{2} + \dfrac{3}{2}i, \; 4 - 10i$

12. $-3 - 6i, \; \dfrac{2}{3} + \dfrac{4}{3}i$

13. $8 - i\sqrt{5}, \; 8 + i\sqrt{5}$

14. $4\sqrt{2} - 3i, \; 9\sqrt{2} + i$

15. $4 + i\sqrt{6}, \; -3 - 2i\sqrt{6}$

16. $\dfrac{1}{2} + \dfrac{\sqrt{3}}{2}i, \; \dfrac{1}{2} - \dfrac{\sqrt{3}}{2}i$

17. $-\sqrt{3} - 2i\sqrt{2}, \; 2\sqrt{3} - i\sqrt{2}$

18. $2\sqrt{6} - i\sqrt{5}, \; 3\sqrt{6} - 2i\sqrt{5}$

19. $\dfrac{7 - 2i\sqrt{3}}{2}, \; \dfrac{4 + 2i\sqrt{3}}{2}$

20. $\dfrac{5 + 3i\sqrt{10}}{6}, \; \dfrac{5 - 3i\sqrt{10}}{2}$

Solve each equation for x and y. Assume that x and y are real numbers.

B 21. $(2x - 3) + 5i = 7 - (y - 4)i$

22. $3x - 7i = (x + 8) + (5 - y)i$

23. $i(1 - yi) = 4 + 2xi$

24. $6x - 12 + 2yi = 0$

Show that r is a root of the given equation.

25. $x^2 - 4x + 13 = 0; \; r = 2 + 3i$

26. $x^2 + 6x + 10 = 0; \; r = -3 + i$

27. $x^2 + 10x + 29 = 0; \; r = -5 - 2i$

28. $x^2 - 8x + 18 = 0; \; r = 4 - i\sqrt{2}$

29. Let $x = 2 + i$ and $y = \dfrac{2}{5} - \dfrac{1}{5}i$. Show that x and y are multiplicative inverses of each other. (*Hint:* Show that $xy = 1$.)

30. Show that $\dfrac{\sqrt{2}}{2} + \dfrac{\sqrt{2}}{2}i$ is a square root of i. (*Hint:* a is a square root of b if $a^2 = b$.)

C 31. Show that $-\dfrac{1}{2} + \dfrac{\sqrt{3}}{2}i$ is a cube root of 1. (*Hint:* a is a cube root of b if $a^3 = b$.)

32. Show that $\dfrac{\sqrt{3}}{2} + \dfrac{1}{2}i$ is a cube root of i.

33. Show that $\dfrac{1}{2} + \dfrac{\sqrt{3}}{2}i$ is a cube root of -1.

In Exercises 34–36 let $x = a + bi$, $y = c + di$, and $z = e + fi$, where $a, b, c, d, e,$ and f are real numbers. Show that the given property is true in the set of complex numbers.

34. The Commutative Property of Addition. (Show that $x + y = y + x$.)

35. The Associative Property of Addition. (Show that $(x + y) + z = x + (y + z)$.)

36. The Distributive Property. (Show that $x(y + z) = xy + xz$.)

37. If $(a + bi)(3 + 4i) = 1$, find $a + bi$. (*Hint*: Equate the real parts of each side and equate the imaginary parts of each side; then solve the system of equations.)

Section 3-6 COMPLEX CONJUGATES AND DIVISION

In Section 3-2 you learned that the product of conjugates of the form $a\sqrt{b} + c\sqrt{d}$ and $a\sqrt{b} - c\sqrt{d}$ is always free of radicals, and you used that fact to rationalize the denominators of certain fractions. In this section you will use numbers called *complex conjugates* to:
- find the standard form of the multiplicative inverse of a complex number
- divide one complex number by another

Two numbers of the form

$$a + bi \text{ and } a - bi, \text{ where } a \text{ and } b \text{ are real numbers},$$

are called *complex conjugates*.

EXAMPLES OF COMPLEX CONJUGATES

$3 + 4i$ and $3 - 4i$ $-2 - i\sqrt{3}$ and $-2 + i\sqrt{3}$

$6i$ and $-6i$ 7 and 7

Complex conjugates have the property that both their sum and their product are *real* numbers:

$$\text{sum: } (a + bi) + (a - bi) = 2a$$
$$\text{product: } (a + bi)(a - bi) = a^2 - b^2i^2 = a^2 + b^2$$

The second fact above suggests that to express a quotient of the form

$$\frac{a + bi}{c + di}, \quad d \neq 0,$$

in standard form, you multiply the numerator and denominator by the complex conjugate of the denominator.

EXAMPLE Write each quotient as a complex number in standard form.

a. $\dfrac{3}{4-2i}$ b. $\dfrac{3-i\sqrt{5}}{2+i\sqrt{5}}$

SOLUTION   a. $\dfrac{3}{4-2i} \cdot \dfrac{4+2i}{4+2i} = \dfrac{12+6i}{16+4} = \dfrac{12+6i}{20} = \dfrac{3}{5} + \dfrac{3}{10}i$

b. $\dfrac{3-i\sqrt{5}}{2+i\sqrt{5}} \cdot \dfrac{2-i\sqrt{5}}{2-i\sqrt{5}} = \dfrac{(6-5)+(-2\sqrt{5}-3\sqrt{5})i}{4+5}$

$= \dfrac{1-(5\sqrt{5})i}{9}$

$= \dfrac{1}{9} - \dfrac{5\sqrt{5}}{9}i$

You can use the same technique to find the standard form of the multiplicative inverse of a nonzero complex number.

EXAMPLE Write the multiplicative inverse of $3+7i$ in standard form.

SOLUTION $\dfrac{1}{3+7i} = \dfrac{1}{3+7i} \cdot \dfrac{3-7i}{3-7i} = \dfrac{3-7i}{9+49} = \dfrac{3-7i}{58} = \dfrac{3}{58} - \dfrac{7}{58}i$

The multiplicative inverse of $3+7i$ is $\dfrac{3}{58} - \dfrac{7}{58}i.$

Check $(3+7i)\left(\dfrac{3}{58} - \dfrac{7}{58}i\right) = \left(\dfrac{9}{58} + \dfrac{49}{58}\right) + \left(-\dfrac{21}{58} + \dfrac{21}{58}\right)i = 1+0i$

ORAL EXERCISES

Name the complex conjugate of each complex number.

1. $-3+2i$ 2. $\sqrt{3}-5i$ 3. $2i-\sqrt{6}$ 4. $-7i$ 5. 9

State a number by which you could multiply both the numerator and the denominator of the given complex number in order to express the complex number in standard form.

6. $\dfrac{1}{4+3i}$ 7. $\dfrac{1}{4i\sqrt{2}-1}$ 8. $\dfrac{2+i\sqrt{5}}{2-i\sqrt{5}}$ 9. $\dfrac{6-4i\sqrt{3}}{7+2i\sqrt{3}}$

Simplify.

10. $(5-2i)(5+2i)$ 11. $(6+7i)(6-7i)$

12. $\left(\dfrac{2}{3}-\dfrac{1}{3}i\right)\left(\dfrac{2}{3}+\dfrac{1}{3}i\right)$ 13. $(2+i\sqrt{3})(2-i\sqrt{3})$

14. $(3\sqrt{2}+4i)(3\sqrt{2}-4i)$ 15. $(2\sqrt{5}-3i\sqrt{2})(2\sqrt{5}+3i\sqrt{2})$

WRITTEN EXERCISES

Find the standard form of the multiplicative inverse of the given complex number. Check your result by multiplying it by the original number and showing that the product is 1.

A   1. $2 + 4i$ 2. $7 - i$ 3. $\sqrt{3} + i$ 4. $\sqrt{2} + i\sqrt{2}$

Express each quotient in standard form.

5. $\dfrac{5}{2+i}$ 6. $\dfrac{-4}{5-i}$ 7. $\dfrac{-8}{1-i\sqrt{3}}$ 8. $\dfrac{11}{3-i\sqrt{2}}$

9. $\dfrac{\sqrt{2}}{4+2i\sqrt{2}}$ 10. $\dfrac{-\sqrt{5}}{5-2i\sqrt{5}}$ 11. $\dfrac{1-2i}{1-i}$ 12. $\dfrac{-2+i}{3+i}$

13. $\dfrac{7-4i}{2-3i}$ 14. $\dfrac{5+5i}{3-4i}$ 15. $\dfrac{2-4i\sqrt{3}}{3+i\sqrt{3}}$ 16. $\dfrac{-6+7i\sqrt{2}}{1-i\sqrt{2}}$

17. $\dfrac{2+i\sqrt{6}}{2-i\sqrt{6}}$ 18. $\dfrac{6\sqrt{3}-3i}{6\sqrt{3}+3i}$ 19. $\dfrac{3\sqrt{7}-2i}{2\sqrt{7}+i}$ 20. $\dfrac{1+i\sqrt{5}}{1-i\sqrt{5}}$

B   21. $\dfrac{4\sqrt{3}-4i\sqrt{5}}{\sqrt{3}+i\sqrt{5}}$ 22. $\dfrac{3(\sqrt{6}+i\sqrt{3})}{2\sqrt{6}-i\sqrt{3}}$ 23. $\dfrac{-5(\sqrt{3}+2i\sqrt{7})}{2\sqrt{3}-i\sqrt{7}}$ 24. $\dfrac{6\sqrt{2}-5i\sqrt{3}}{60\sqrt{2}+40i\sqrt{3}}$

Express as a single complex number in standard form.

25. $\dfrac{2}{1+3i} + \dfrac{5}{1-3i}$ 26. $\dfrac{5-4i}{5+4i} + \dfrac{5+4i}{5-4i}$ 27. $\dfrac{\sqrt{5}+i}{i\sqrt{5}} - \dfrac{i\sqrt{5}}{\sqrt{5}+i}$

28. Find the standard form of the multiplicative inverse of the nonzero complex number $a + bi$. Check your result by multiplying it by the original number and showing that the product is 1.

C   29. Factor $a^2 + b^2$. (*Hint:* Recall that $a^2 - b^2$ is factored as $(a + b)(a - b)$.)

Use your answer to Exercise 29 to factor the given expression over the set of complex numbers.

30. $x^2 + 25$ 31. $4x^2 + 81$ 32. $1 + 36a^2$

33. $x^4 - 1$ 34. $1 - 16c^4$ 35. $y^8 - 32y^4 + 256$

36. Let $a + bi$ and $x + yi$ be complex numbers. Show that if
  (1) $(a + bi) + (x + yi)$ is a real number, and
  (2) $(a + bi)(x + yi)$ is a real number,
  then $x = a$ and $y = -b$; that is, $x + yi$ is the complex conjugate of $a + bi$.
  (*Hint:* A complex number $p + qi$ is real if and only if $q = 0$.)

37. Let $a + bi$ and $u + vi$ be complex numbers such that $a + b \neq 0$ and $u + v \neq 0$.
  Show that if $(a + bi)(u + vi)$ is a real number, then

$$\frac{u}{v} = -\frac{a}{b}.$$

SELF-TEST 2

Simplify.

1. $\sqrt{-64}$

2. $\sqrt{-4}\,\sqrt{-9}$

3. $\dfrac{\sqrt{-20}}{-\sqrt{5}}$ Section 3-4

4. $i\sqrt{3} \cdot 5i\sqrt{6}$

5. $\dfrac{5}{3i}$

6. i^{21}

7. Solve for x: $x^2 + 36 = 0$

Simplify. Express your answers as complex numbers in standard form.

8. $\sqrt{-81} - \sqrt{-25}$

9. $(-6 + 7i) + (3 - 11i)$ Section 3-5

10. $(5 - i\sqrt{2})(1 - i\sqrt{2})$

11. $\left(\dfrac{7 - 3i}{2}\right)\left(\dfrac{7 + 3i}{2}\right)$

12. Solve for real numbers x and y: $3y + 2i = 4\sqrt{3} - xi$

13. Find the standard form of the multiplicative inverse of $4 - 2i$.   Section 3-6

14. Express the quotient $\dfrac{2 + i\sqrt{5}}{2 - i\sqrt{5}}$ in standard form.

Section 3-7 QUADRATIC EQUATIONS AND THE DISCRIMINANT

In Section 2-4 you reviewed the quadratic formula,

$$x = \frac{-b \pm \sqrt{b^2 - 4ac}}{2a},$$

as a means of solving any quadratic equation in standard form with real coefficients and real roots. In this section you will learn to:

- use the quadratic formula to solve quadratic equations with complex roots
- determine the number and nature of the roots of any quadratic equation

You may recall from previous mathematics courses that if the radicand $b^2 - 4ac$ in the quadratic formula is *negative*, the given equation has no real roots. In the complex number system, however, there are numbers that satisfy such an equation.

EXAMPLE   Solve the equation $3x^2 - 2x = -1$ over the set of complex numbers.

SOLUTION   First put the equation in standard form: $3x^2 - 2x + 1 = 0$. Using the quadratic formula, you obtain:

$$x = \frac{-(-2) \pm \sqrt{(-2)^2 - 4(3)(1)}}{2(3)}$$

$$= \frac{2 \pm \sqrt{-8}}{6} = \frac{2 \pm 2i\sqrt{2}}{6} = \frac{1 \pm i\sqrt{2}}{3}$$

$$= \frac{1}{3} \pm \frac{\sqrt{2}}{3}i$$

The solution set is $\left\{\dfrac{1}{3} + \dfrac{\sqrt{2}}{3}i, \ \dfrac{1}{3} - \dfrac{\sqrt{2}}{3}i\right\}$.

RADICALS AND COMPLEX NUMBERS   **115**

In the preceding example, both roots are imaginary. They are also complex conjugates. This suggests the following theorem, which is justified in Exercises 55-59.

Theorem 3-1   A complex number $a + bi$ is a root of a polynomial equation with real coefficients if and only if its complex conjugate, $a - bi$, is also a root of the equation.

The roots in the previous example are imaginary because the number

$$b^2 - 4ac$$

is negative. This number is called the *discriminant* of the equation

$$ax^2 + bx + c = 0.$$

You can determine the number and nature of the roots from the *sign* of the discriminant:

Let $ax^2 + bx + c = 0$ be a quadratic equation with real coefficients.

1. If $b^2 - 4ac > 0$, the equation has two real roots.
2. If $b^2 - 4ac = 0$, the equation has a real double root.
3. If $b^2 - 4ac < 0$, the equation has two imaginary roots that are complex conjugates.

A quadratic equation is said to have a *double root* (Case 2 above) if the two roots of the equation are equal.

If the coefficients of a quadratic equation are rational numbers, we can be more specific about the nature of the roots in Cases 1 and 2.

If $b^2 - 4ac \geqslant 0$ and a, b, and c are rational numbers, then the roots of the equation $ax^2 + bx + c = 0$ are rational if and only if $b^2 - 4ac$ is the square of a rational number.

If you find that the roots of a quadratic equation are *rational*, you can solve the equation by factoring.

EXAMPLE   Determine the number and nature of the roots of the given equation.

   a. $2x^2 + 13x + 18 = 0$ b. $4x^2 - 20x + 25 = 0$ c. $-x^2 + 3x - 5 = 0$

SOLUTION   a. $b^2 - 4ac = (13)^2 - 4(2)(18) = 25 > 0$. Therefore the equation has *two real roots*. They are *rational* since $25 = 5^2$ and a, b, and c are rational. (The equation can be solved by factoring by writing $(2x + 9)(x + 2) = 0$.)

   b. $b^2 - 4ac = (-20)^2 - 4(4)(25) = 0$. Therefore the equation has *one real double root*. It is *rational* since $0 = 0^2$ and a, b, and c are rational. (The equation can be solved by factoring by writing $(2x - 5)^2 = 0$.)

   c. $b^2 - 4ac = 3^2 - 4(-1)(-5) = -11 < 0$. Therefore the equation has *two imaginary roots* that are complex conjugates.

As you may recall, the graph of an equation of the form

$$y = ax^2 + bx + c$$

is a *parabola* whose *axis of symmetry* is parallel to the y-axis. The roots of the corresponding equation

$$0 = ax^2 + bx + c$$

are the values of x that make $y = 0$ in the first equation. These roots are the x-coordinates of the points where the graph intersects the x-axis and are called the *x-intercepts* of the graph. It follows that the graph will have two, one, or no x-intercepts according as the discriminant of the equation $ax^2 + bx + c = 0$ is positive, zero, or negative. The possibilities are illustrated schematically in the following chart.

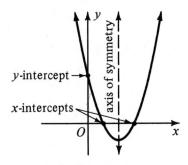

Graph of a Parabola

$y = ax^2 + bx + c$			
Discriminant	$a > 0$	$a < 0$	*Number of x-intercepts*
$b^2 - 4ac > 0$			2
$b^2 - 4ac = 0$			1
$b^2 - 4ac < 0$			0

In order to draw the graph of $y = ax^2 + bx + c$ more accurately, you should also find the y-intercept, the equation of the axis of symmetry, and the coordinates of the *vertex*, or *turning point*, of the parabola.

The *y-intercept* of the graph of $y = ax^2 + bx + c$ is the y-coordinate when $x = 0$. Therefore the y-intercept is $a(0)^2 + b(0) + c$, or c. You may recall from *Book 2* that the equation of the axis of symmetry is $x = -\dfrac{b}{2a}$. Since the vertex lies on the axis of symmetry, the x-coordinate of the vertex is also $-\dfrac{b}{2a}$. You can find the y-coordinate of the vertex by substituting $-\dfrac{b}{2a}$ for x in the original equation.

EXAMPLE   Sketch the graph of the given equation.

a. $y = x^2 - 4x + 3$ b. $y = -\frac{1}{2}x^2 + x - 2$

SOLUTION   a. Since $b^2 - 4ac = (-4)^2 - 4(1)(3) = 4 > 0$, the graph has two x-intercepts. Since the discriminant is the square of a rational number ($4 = 2^2$), the roots of the corresponding equation

$$0 = x^2 - 4x + 3$$

are rational, and the equation can be solved by factoring.

$$(x - 1)(x - 3) = 0$$
$$x = 1 \text{ or } x = 3$$

Therefore, the x-intercepts are 1 and 3.
The y-intercept is the constant term, 3.
The axis of symmetry has equation

$$x = -\frac{-4}{2(1)}, \text{ or } x = 2.$$

By substituting 2 for x in the original equation, you get:

$$y = 2^2 - 4(2) + 3 = -1$$

Therefore, the vertex has coordinates $(2, -1)$.
Since $a > 0$, the parabola opens upward.

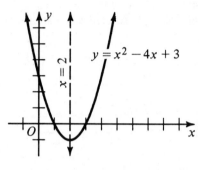

b. Since $b^2 - 4ac = (1)^2 - 4\left(-\frac{1}{2}\right)(-2) = -3 < 0$, the graph has no x-intercepts.

The y-intercept is the constant term, -2.
The axis of symmetry has equation

$$x = -\frac{1}{2\left(-\frac{1}{2}\right)}, \text{ or } x = 1.$$

By substituting 1 for x in the original equation, you find that the vertex has coordinates $\left(1, -\frac{3}{2}\right)$.
Since $a < 0$, the parabola opens downward.

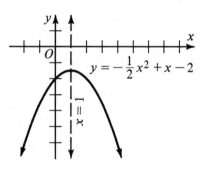

ORAL EXERCISES

Assume that the given number is the discriminant of an equation of the form $ax^2 + bx + c = 0$ and that a, b, and c are integers. State the number and nature of the roots of the equation.

1. -4 2. 13   3. -5 4. 36   5. $12 - 4(-3)(-1)$ 6. $12 - 4(3)(-1)$

Classify the given description of the roots of a quadratic equation with real coefficients as possible or impossible.

7. One real double root

8. One imaginary double root

9. One imaginary root and one real root

10. Two complex roots $a + bi$ and $-a + bi$

11. Two complex roots bi and $-bi$, b a real number

12. Two complex roots $a + bi$ and $c - bi$ with $a \neq c$

State whether the graph of the given equation lies entirely above the x-axis, lies entirely below the x-axis, intersects the x-axis at two distinct points, or intersects the x-axis at only one point.

13. $y = x^2 + 2x + 1$ 14. $y = x^2 - x + 6$ 15. $y = -x^2 - x + 2$

16. $y = x^2 + x + 2$ 17. $y = -x^2 + x - 1$ 18. $y = -x^2 + 6x - 9$

WRITTEN EXERCISES

Find the value of the discriminant of each equation and state the number and nature of the roots.

A   1. $x^2 - 4x + 8 = 0$ 2. $x^2 + 4x - 4 = 0$ 3. $x^2 - 15x + 36 = 0$

4. $x^2 + 28x + 196 = 0$ 5. $3x^2 - 8x + 7 = 0$ 6. $3x^2 - 5x - 12 = 0$

7. $\frac{1}{4}x^2 - 6x + 36 = 0$ 8. $8x^2 - 9x - \frac{1}{2} = 0$ 9. $-2x^2 + 7x = 7$

10. $12 - 3x^2 = 4x$ 11. $x^2 + \sqrt{12}x + 3 = 0$ 12. $\sqrt{6}x^2 - 6x + \sqrt{6} = 0$

Solve for x over the set of complex numbers.

13. $x^2 - 2x + 5 = 0$ 14. $x^2 + 4x + 20 = 0$ 15. $x^2 + 6x + 12 = 0$

16. $x^2 - 4x + 9 = 0$ 17. $2x^2 - 6x + 9 = 0$ 18. $-x^2 + 8x - 8 = 0$

19. $-3x^2 - 6x - 7 = 0$ 20. $-6x = 2x^2 + 5$ 21. $3x - 3x^2 = 1$

22. $3 - x = -4x^2$ 23. $x^2 + \frac{29}{2} = 7x$ 24. $\frac{1}{2}x^2 + \frac{7}{2} = -x$

Sketch the graph of the given equation. State (a) the x-intercepts (if any), (b) the coordinates of the vertex, and (c) the equation of the axis of symmetry.

B 25. $y = x^2 - 1$ 26. $y = x^2 + 1$

27. $y = x^2 - 4x + 4$ 28. $y = -x^2 + 2x + 8$

29. $y = -x^2 + x - 1$ 30. $y = -x^2 - 6x - 9$

31. $y = 2x^2 - 4x$ 32. $y = -2x^2 + x - 1$

In Exercises 33–40:

a. Find the value(s) of k for which the given equation has one real double root.

b. Find the root of the given equation for each value of k you found in part (a).

EXAMPLE $x^2 + kx + 36 = 0$

SOLUTION   a. $b^2 - 4ac = k^2 - 4(1)(36) = k^2 - 144$

The equation has one real double root if and only if the discriminant is 0. Thus,
$$k^2 - 144 = 0, \text{ or } k = \pm 12.$$

b. If $k = 12$, the original equation becomes $x^2 + 12x + 36 = 0$. Solving the equation, you get $x = -6$.

If $k = -12$, the original equation becomes $x^2 - 12x + 36 = 0$. Solving the equation, you get $x = 6$.

33. $2x^2 - 6x + k = 0$

34. $kx^2 + x + 1 = 0$

35. $3x^2 + 12x + k = 0$

36. $(k-1)x^2 + 4x + 3 = 0$

37. $-2x^2 + kx - 18 = 0$

38. $9x^2 + kx + 4 = 0$

C 39. $kx^2 - 3x + k + 4 = 0$

40. $3x^2 - (k+1)x + k - 2 = 0$

41–44. Find the value(s) of k for which the equations in Exercises 33–36 have two real roots. (*Hint:* $b^2 - 4ac > 0$)

45–48. Find the value(s) of k for which the equations in Exercises 33–36 have two imaginary roots.

Solve for x over the set of complex numbers.

49. $x^2 - 2ix + 3 = 0$

50. $x^2 + 3ix + 4 = 0$

51. $x^2 - 2ix - 2 = 0$

52. $x^2 + 3ix + 6 = 0$

53. $ix^2 + 3x - 5i = 0$

54. $2x^2 + (6 - 10i)x - 15i = 0$

Show that when the given number and its complex conjugate are substituted for x in the given expression, the values obtained are complex conjugates.

55. $2 - 5i$; $x^2 - x - 4$

56. $4 - i$; $3x^2 - 9x + 2$

57. $-1 + i\sqrt{3}$; $x^3 - 7$

58. $a + bi$; $cx^2 + dx + e$

59. Assume that if a complex number $a + bi$ is substituted for x in a polynomial with real coefficients, the value obtained is a *real* number r. In light of your results in Exercises 55–58, what value would you expect to get when $a - bi$ is substituted for x? Explain how your answer could be used to justify Theorem 3–1 on page 116.

60. Show that for any nonzero real number k, the discriminant of the equation
$$kax^2 + kbx + kc = 0$$
is positive, zero, or negative according as the discriminant of $ax^2 + bx + c = 0$ is positive, zero, or negative.

Section 3-8 THE SUM AND PRODUCT OF THE ROOTS

In Section 3-7 you learned how to use the coefficients of a quadratic equation to find the roots of the equation. In this section you will learn how to find the coefficients of a quadratic equation whose roots are given. In particular, you will learn the relationship between the coefficients and:

- the sum of the roots
- the product of the roots

Suppose you wish to find a quadratic equation that has roots $\frac{1}{2}$ and $\frac{1}{3}$. According to the Factor Theorem on page 66, $x - \frac{1}{2}$ and $x - \frac{1}{3}$ are factors of the equation. Thus, the factored form of one such equation is

$$\left(x - \frac{1}{2}\right)\left(x - \frac{1}{3}\right) = 0.$$

Multiplying, you have:

$$x^2 - \frac{1}{2}x - \frac{1}{3}x + \frac{1}{6} = 0$$

$$x^2 - \frac{5}{6}x + \frac{1}{6} = 0 \qquad (1)$$

To obtain an equivalent equation with integral coefficients, multiply by the common denominator, 6.

$$6x^2 - 5x + 1 = 0 \qquad (2)$$

Equation (2) is a quadratic equation written in the standard form

$$ax^2 + bx + c = 0,$$

whereas equation (1) is written in the form

$$x^2 + \frac{b}{a}x + \frac{c}{a} = 0.$$

You may have already noticed the following relationships between the roots and the coefficients of equation (1):

$$\frac{1}{2} + \frac{1}{3} = \frac{5}{6} \qquad\qquad \frac{1}{2} \cdot \frac{1}{3} = \frac{1}{6}$$

Thus it appears that when the coefficient of x^2 is 1, the *sum* of the roots is equal to the *opposite of the coefficient of* x and the *product* of the roots is equal to the *constant term*. These facts are summarized in the following theorem, which is justified in Exercise 39.

Theorem 3-2 If r_1 and r_2 are the roots of the quadratic equation

$$ax^2 + bx + c = 0, \quad a \neq 0,$$

then:

$$r_1 + r_2 = -\frac{b}{a} \quad \text{and} \quad r_1 r_2 = \frac{c}{a}$$

You can use Theorem 3-2 to solve a variety of problems.

EXAMPLE Find the sum and product of the roots of the quadratic equation $5x^2 - 7x = -2$.

SOLUTION Write the equation in the form $ax^2 + bx + c = 0$.

$$5x^2 - 7x + 2 = 0$$

Then

$$-\frac{b}{a} = -\frac{-7}{5} = \frac{7}{5} \quad \text{and} \quad \frac{c}{a} = \frac{2}{5}.$$

Therefore, the sum of the roots is $\frac{7}{5}$ and the product of the roots is $\frac{2}{5}$.

EXAMPLE Find a quadratic equation in standard form with integral coefficients whose roots are $1 + \frac{\sqrt{3}}{2}$ and $1 - \frac{\sqrt{3}}{2}$.

SOLUTION The value $-\frac{b}{a}$ equals the sum of the roots of the quadratic equation $ax^2 + bx + c = 0$. Thus:

$$-\frac{b}{a} = r_1 + r_2 = \left(1 + \frac{\sqrt{3}}{2}\right) + \left(1 - \frac{\sqrt{3}}{2}\right) = 2$$

Therefore, $\frac{b}{a} = -2$.

Since $\frac{c}{a}$ equals the product of the roots, you have:

$$\frac{c}{a} = r_1 r_2 = \left(1 + \frac{\sqrt{3}}{2}\right)\left(1 - \frac{\sqrt{3}}{2}\right) = 1 - \frac{3}{4} = \frac{1}{4}$$

It follows that an equation with the given roots is

$$x^2 - 2x + \frac{1}{4} = 0.$$

To obtain an equivalent equation with integral coefficients, multiply both sides by 4:

$$4x^2 - 8x + 1 = 0$$

Therefore, a quadratic equation in standard form with integral coefficients whose roots are $1 + \frac{\sqrt{3}}{2}$ and $1 - \frac{\sqrt{3}}{2}$ is $4x^2 - 8x + 1 = 0$.

Our investigation of the relationship between the coefficients and the roots of a quadratic equation was based on the Factor Theorem. Since the proof of the Factor Theorem does not depend on assuming that the root in question is a real number, we can extend the Factor Theorem to cover imaginary roots. This allows us to apply the concept of sum and product of the roots to quadratic equations with imaginary roots.

EXAMPLE Find a quadratic equation in standard form whose roots are $-2 + 3i$ and $-2 - 3i$.

SOLUTION $\quad -\dfrac{b}{a} = r_1 + r_2 = (-2 + 3i) + (-2 - 3i) = -4$

$\dfrac{c}{a} = r_1 r_2 = (-2 + 3i)(-2 - 3i) = 4 + 9 = 13$

Therefore, a quadratic equation in standard form with roots $-2 + 3i$ and $-2 - 3i$ is $x^2 + 4x + 13 = 0$.

EXAMPLE   Show that $6 - 2i$ is a root of the quadratic equation $x^2 - 12x + 40 = 0$.

SOLUTION   You can use any one of three methods:

1. Use the sum and product of the roots. (By Theorem 3-1, you know that if $6 - 2i$ is a root of the equation, then $6 + 2i$ is also a root.)
2. Show by substitution that $6 - 2i$ is a root of the equation.
3. Solve the equation using the quadratic formula.

We will use method (1).

Since $6 - 2i$ is a root of the equation, you know by Theorem 3-1 that $6 + 2i$ is a root of the equation. Thus:

$$(6 + 2i) + (6 - 2i) = 12$$
$$(6 + 2i)(6 - 2i) = 36 + 4 = 40$$

Since the sum of the roots is 12 and the product of the roots is 40, $6 + 2i$ is a root of the equation $x^2 - 12x + 40 = 0$.

You can also use the sum and product of the roots to find the value of an unknown coefficient in a quadratic equation.

EXAMPLE   One root of the equation $3x^2 + kx - 8 = 0$ is 4. Find the other root and the value of k.

SOLUTION   Let $r_1 = 4$, and let $r_2 =$ the other root of the equation. Then, since $r_1 r_2 = \dfrac{c}{a}$,

$$4r_2 = -\dfrac{8}{3}.$$

Solving for r_2, you obtain

$$r_2 = -\dfrac{2}{3}.$$

Using the fact that $r_1 + r_2 = -\dfrac{b}{a}$, you have:

$$4 + \left(-\dfrac{2}{3}\right) = -\dfrac{k}{3}$$
$$\dfrac{10}{3} = -\dfrac{k}{3}$$
$$k = -10$$

Therefore, the other root is $-\dfrac{2}{3}$ and $k = -10$.

Note that in the preceding example you could also find k by substituting 4 for x in the original equation. You could then factor the equation to find the other root.

ORAL EXERCISES

State (a) the sum and (b) the product of the roots of the given equation.

1. $x^2 - 3x + 2 = 0$
2. $x^2 + 4x - 2 = 0$
3. $x^2 - 5x = 0$
4. $x^2 + 3 = 0$
5. $2x^2 + 3x - 5 = 0$
6. $-3x^2 - 6x + 1 = 0$

State a quadratic equation whose roots are the given numbers.

7. $4, -4$
8. 3 (double root)
9. $2i, -2i$
10. $5, -3$
11. $-2, -7$
12. $0, 6$

13. If the roots of a quadratic equation are $p + qi$ and $p - qi$, where p and q are real numbers, what can you conclude about the coefficients of the equation? Explain.

14. If the roots of a quadratic equation are $p + q\sqrt{2}$ and $p - q\sqrt{2}$, where p and q are *rational* numbers, what can you conclude about the coefficients of the equation? Explain.

WRITTEN EXERCISES

Find a quadratic equation in standard form with integral coefficients and having the given numbers as its roots.

A 1. $5, -7$
2. $-2, -9$
3. -6 (double root)

4. 12 (double root)
5. $-\dfrac{2}{3}, \dfrac{1}{2}$
6. $\dfrac{3}{2}, \dfrac{1}{5}$

7. $\sqrt{3}, -\sqrt{3}$
8. $5 + \sqrt{2}, 5 - \sqrt{2}$
9. $-6 - \sqrt{13}, -6 + \sqrt{13}$
10. $-8 - 4\sqrt{3}, -8 + 4\sqrt{3}$
11. $3 - 2\sqrt{7}, 3 + 2\sqrt{7}$
12. $4i\sqrt{5}, -4i\sqrt{5}$
13. $3 - 4i, 3 + 4i$
14. $2 + 9i, 2 - 9i$
15. $-1 + i\sqrt{2}, -1 - i\sqrt{2}$
16. $2 - i\sqrt{3}, 2 + i\sqrt{3}$
17. $5 - 2i\sqrt{6}, 5 + 2i\sqrt{6}$
18. $-8 + 2i\sqrt{7}, -8 - 2i\sqrt{7}$

Show that the given number is a root of the given equation.

19. $3 + 7i; x^2 - 6x + 58 = 0$
20. $-2 - 6i; x^2 + 4x + 40 = 0$
21. $-1 + i\sqrt{3}; x^2 + 2x + 4 = 0$
22. $5 - 2i\sqrt{5}; x^2 - 10x + 45 = 0$

Find a quadratic equation in standard form with integral coefficients and having the given numbers as roots.

B 23. $\dfrac{-5 - \sqrt{2}}{3}, \dfrac{-5 + \sqrt{2}}{3}$
24. $\dfrac{3 + i\sqrt{11}}{2}, \dfrac{3 - i\sqrt{11}}{2}$

25. $\dfrac{7 + 3i\sqrt{5}}{4}, \dfrac{7 - 3i\sqrt{5}}{4}$ **26.** $\dfrac{5 + 7\sqrt{2}}{6}, \dfrac{5 - 7\sqrt{2}}{6}$

If r_1 is a root of the given equation, find the other root and the value of k.

27. $x^2 + kx - 48 = 0; \; r_1 = 4$ **28.** $x^2 - 3x + k = 0; \; r_1 = 5$

29. $2x^2 + kx - 5 = 0; \; r_1 = -1$ **30.** $3x^2 + x + k = 0; \; r_1 = \dfrac{2}{3}$

31. $2x^2 - 8x + \dfrac{k}{2} = 0; \; r_1 = \dfrac{3}{2}$ **32.** $5x^2 - 3kx + 2 = 0; \; r_1 = -\dfrac{4}{5}$

33. $kx^2 - 6x - k = 0; \; r_1 = 2$ **34.** $kx^2 - kx + 18 = 0; \; r_1 = 4$

C 35. $x^2 - (k - 5)x - k = 0; \; r_1 = 3$ **36.** $x^2 + kx + (k + 3) = 0; \; r_1 = -2$

37. One root of the equation $x^2 + kx + 8 = 0$ is twice the other. Find all possible values of k.

38. One root of the equation $4x^2 + kx + 3 = 0$ is three times the other. Find all possible values of k.

39. Use the fact that $r_1 = \dfrac{-b + \sqrt{b^2 - 4ac}}{2a}$ and $r_2 = \dfrac{-b - \sqrt{b^2 - 4ac}}{2a}$ are the roots of the quadratic equation $ax^2 + bx + c = 0$ to show that Theorem 3-2 is true.

40. Find a quadratic equation whose roots differ by 1 *and* are reciprocals of each other. Find the roots of the equation. (Two answers.)

SELF-TEST 3

Give the value of the discriminant of each equation and state the number and nature of the roots.

1. $x^2 + 3x + 5 = 0$ **2.** $-9x^2 + 12x - 4 = 0$ **3.** $x^2 - 2x = 15$ Section 3-7

4. Solve for x over the set of complex numbers: $3x^2 - 3x + 1 = 0$

5. Sketch the graph of the equation $y = x^2 - x - 6$. State **(a)** the x-intercepts (if any), **(b)** the coordinates of the vertex, and **(c)** the equation of the axis of symmetry.

Find a quadratic equation in standard form with integral coefficients having the given numbers as its roots.

6. $-6, \; 2$ **7.** $1 + \sqrt{6}, \; 1 - \sqrt{6}$ **8.** $5 - 7i, \; 5 + 7i$ Section 3-8

9. Show that $1 + i$ is a root of the equation $x^2 - 2x + 2 = 0$.

10. If 2 is a root of the equation $2x^2 + kx - 22 = 0$, find the other root and the value of k.

Computer Exercises

By analyzing the discriminant of a quadratic equation, you can determine the number and nature of the roots without actually solving the equation.

The program below can be used for equations of the form $ax^2 + bx + c = 0$, where a, b, and c are integers. Observe that the roots of such an equation are rational if and only if the discriminant D is the square of an integer, which is true if and only if $\sqrt{D}$ is an integer. The program will use the INT function to test whether or not $\sqrt{D}$ is an integer.

1. Complete the program by completing lines 30, 90, 130, and 150. Note that the effect of line 80 is to test whether or not S is an integer.

```
10   PRINT "INPUT A, B, C:"
20   INPUT A, B, C
30   LET D = __?__
40   IF D<0 THEN 150
50   IF D=0 THEN 130
60   REM***D IS POSITIVE
70   LET S=SQR(D)
80   IF S−INT(S+.0001)<=.0001 THEN 110
90   PRINT __?__
100  GOTO 160
110  PRINT "TWO RATIONAL ROOTS"
120  GOTO 160
130  PRINT __?__
140  GOTO 160
150  PRINT __?__
160  END
```

2. RUN the program for each of the following equations. State the number and nature of the roots.

   a. $9x^2 + 12x + 4 = 0$
   b. $3x^2 - 8x + 6 = 0$
   c. $22x - 9x^2 = 13$
   d. $19x = 9 + 8x^2$
   e. $64 - 49x^2 = 0$
   f. $64 + 49x^2 = 0$

3. Extend the program to determine whether or not the roots are opposites. Notice that this is not dependent on the value of the discriminant. Complete the new line 160 below.

```
155  GOTO 180
160  IF __?__ THEN 180
170  PRINT "THE ROOTS ARE OPPOSITES"
180  END
```

If the roots are opposites, this will be printed in addition to the other information about the roots.

4. Add the new lines (Exercise 3) to the program and RUN it. Use the equations in Exercise 2. In which equations are the roots opposites?

Simplify. Assume that all variables represent positive real numbers.

1. $\sqrt{63}$ 2. $\sqrt{20a^5b^6}$ 3. $\dfrac{\sqrt{28x}}{\sqrt{7x^3y^2}}$ 4. $3\sqrt{24}+\sqrt{54}$ Section 3-1

5. $2\sqrt{7}(\sqrt{7}-3\sqrt{14})$ 6. $(9+\sqrt{3})(1+\sqrt{3})$ Section 3-2

7. $(7-2\sqrt{3})^2$ 8. $\dfrac{\sqrt{2}}{5-\sqrt{2}}$

Solve for x.

9. $6-\sqrt{x+2}=2$ 10. $\sqrt{x+3}=\sqrt{x}+1$ Section 3-3

Simplify.

11. $\sqrt{-99}$ 12. $-\sqrt{32}\,\sqrt{-28}$ 13. $\dfrac{\sqrt{-16}}{\sqrt{18}}$ Section 3-4

14. $(3i\sqrt{5})(-2i\sqrt{40})$ 15. $\dfrac{5}{i\sqrt{6}}$ 16. i^{32}

17. Solve for x: $x^2+52=0$

Simplify.

18. $5\sqrt{-63}+2\sqrt{-112}$ 19. $(5-i\sqrt{7})-(-3-2i\sqrt{7})$ Section 3-5

20. Solve for real numbers x and y: $x-4yi=2i$

21. Find the standard form of the multiplicative inverse of $3-i\sqrt{6}$. Section 3-6

22. Express the quotient $\dfrac{3-8i}{2+i}$ in standard form.

Give the value of the discriminant of each equation and state the number and nature of the roots.

23. $4x^2+8x+4=0$ 24. $2x^2-6=0$ 25. $5x^2-x=-7$ Section 3-7

26. Solve for x over the set of complex numbers: $x^2-2x+8=0$

27. Find the value of k for which the equation $x^2+5x+k=0$ has one real double root.

Find a quadratic equation in standard form with integral coefficients and having the given numbers as its roots.

28. $-7i,\ 7i$ 29. $3+2\sqrt{5},\ 3-2\sqrt{5}$ Section 3-8

30. Show that $3-5i$ is a root of the equation $x^2-6x+34=0$.

1. State the sum and the product of the roots of the equation $5x^2 - 10x + 1 = 0$.

2. What is the least integral value of x for which $\sqrt{x - 10}$ is a real number?

Simplify. Assume that all variables represent positive real numbers.

3. $\sqrt{44a^9b^2}$ 4. $4\sqrt{3}(2\sqrt{6} + \sqrt{3})$ 5. $\dfrac{1 + \sqrt{7}}{2 + \sqrt{7}}$ 6. $\sqrt{\dfrac{3}{5}} + \sqrt{60}$

7. Solve for real numbers x and y: $3 - xi = 3y + 4i$

Give the value of the discriminant of each equation and state the number and nature of the roots.

8. $x^2 - 3x + 6 = 0$ 9. $1 - x - 12x^2 = 0$ 10. $\dfrac{1}{4}x^2 + x + 1 = 0$

Simplify. Express your answers as complex numbers in standard form.

11. $\sqrt{-12}\sqrt{-5}$ 12. i^{13} 13. $(4 + 3i) - (2 - 7i)$ 14. $(1 + 3i\sqrt{5})(6 - i\sqrt{5})$

15. Solve for x over the set of complex numbers: $2x^2 - 6x + 17 = 0$.

Find a quadratic equation in standard form with integral coefficients having the given numbers as its roots.

16. -4, 9 17. $1 + i\sqrt{5}$, $1 - i\sqrt{5}$

18. Express the quotient $\dfrac{i}{5 - 2i}$ in standard form.

19. Solve for x: $\sqrt{2x - 1} = 8 - x$

20. If $\dfrac{1}{2}$ is a root of the equation $2x^2 + 7x + k = 0$, find the other root and the value of k.

21. Show that $-4 + i$ is a root of the equation $x^2 + 8x + 17 = 0$.

22. Sketch the graph of the equation $y = x^2 + 5x + 4$. State (a) the x-intercepts (if any), (b) the coordinates of the vertex, and (c) the equation of the axis of symmetry.

Biographical Note

The Italian physician and mathematician Girolamo Cardano (1501–1576) wrote more than 200 works on numerous topics including mathematics, medicine, astronomy, physics, philosophy, and music. He also wrote an autobiography that is of interest to historians and literary scholars. He is best known, however, for his contributions to the field of mathematics. His thinking was so far ahead of his time that his ideas were not always welcomed by his contemporaries. Only in later years was their value fully recognized.

Cardano was born in Pavia, Italy. He studied at the universities of Pavia and Padua in northern Italy and in 1526 received his medical degree from the University of Padua. For the next several years he practiced medicine in a small town near Padua. In 1534 he moved to Milan, where he taught mathematics, wrote, and became one of the most famous physicians in Europe. In 1543 Cardano accepted a professorship in medicine at the University of Pavia, and in 1562 he began teaching medicine at the University of Bologna.

In 1545 he published his most famous work, *Ars magna*, a Latin treatise that contributed a great deal to the development of modern algebra. In this work Cardano wrote the first systematic theory of equations. *Ars magna* contained the method for solving reduced cubic equations (third-degree equations that lack a quadratic term) and the method for solving quartic, or fourth-degree, equations (discovered by one of Cardano's students, Ferrari). These solutions had never been published before. Although it was not discovered by Cardano, the solution to the reduced cubic equation is now known as Cardano's formula.

In *Ars magna* Cardano included negative roots of equations, noted several relationships between equations and their roots, gave a method for approximating the roots of an equation of any degree, and performed calculations using imaginary numbers.

Cardano also wrote a book on the games of chance, *Liber de ludo aleae*, in which he expressed the concept of probability as a ratio of favorable to possible cases.

Be sure that you understand the meaning of these terms:

radical, p. 94
principal nth root of b, p. 94
index of a radical, p. 94
radical expression in simplified form, p. 95
rationalizing the denominator, p. 98
conjugates, p. 99
radical equation, p. 102

imaginary unit, p. 105
pure imaginary number, p. 106
standard form of a complex number, p. 108
equal complex numbers, p. 109
complex conjugates, p. 112
discriminant, p. 116
parabola, p. 116

MIXED REVIEW

1. Graph the solution set on a number line: $x^2 + 7x \leqslant 5(x + 3)$

Simplify.

2. $(x^{-2} - y^{-2})^{-1}$

3. $\dfrac{x^2 + \dfrac{1}{x}}{1 + \dfrac{1}{x}}$

4. $\dfrac{2^5 \div 4^2 + 3^2}{6^2 - 5^2 + 1}$

5. The sum of a number and its square is 11. What is the number?

6. Show that $5 - 3i\sqrt{2}$ is a root of $x^2 - 10x + 43 = 0$.

Solve.

7. $0.5x - 3 \geqslant 1.2$ and $-\dfrac{3}{4}x \geqslant -12$

8. $|m - 1| > 0$

9. $\dfrac{x-1}{3} + \dfrac{5}{x+1} = \dfrac{8x-1}{12}$

10. Find the standard form of (a) the additive inverse and (b) the multiplicative inverse of $1 - i$.

Simplify.

11. $\left(\dfrac{100a^{-2}bc^{-3}}{-50ab^3c^{-5}}\right)^{-1}$

12. $\dfrac{3}{u+3} - \dfrac{u-3}{u}$

13. $\dfrac{x^4 - 1}{5 + 5x^2} \div \dfrac{5x^2 - 6x + 1}{5x^2 + 24x - 5}$

14. $\sqrt[3]{\dfrac{9}{40}}$

15. $\dfrac{18}{5\sqrt{3} - 3\sqrt{5}}$

16. $\dfrac{3 - 2i}{i^9}$

17. 3 is a root of $x^3 - x^2 - 13x + 21$. Find the complete solution set.

18. State the sum and the product of the roots of the equation $4x^2 - x - 6 = 0$.

Solve over the set of complex numbers.

19. $\sqrt{3x + 4} - x = -2$

20. $-\dfrac{5}{3}(3t - 7) = -\dfrac{65}{6}$

21. $3g^2 + 4 = 2g$

22. $|3y + 1| = 10$

23. $\dfrac{1}{r-1} - \dfrac{2}{r+3} = \dfrac{4}{r^2 + 2r - 3}$

24. $x^3 = -64$

Simplify. In Exercise 27, express the quotient in standard form.

25. $\sqrt{\dfrac{9}{8}} + 2\sqrt{18} - \sqrt{\dfrac{1}{50}}$ **26.** $(5\sqrt{2} - \sqrt{6})^2$ **27.** $\dfrac{3}{\sqrt{7} + 5}$

Evaluate when $e = -6$, $f = -8$, and $g = 9$.

28. $\dfrac{e^2 + fg}{f - e}$ **29.** $(e + f)(2e + g)$ **30.** $\dfrac{\dfrac{1}{e} + \dfrac{1}{g}}{\dfrac{1}{e + g}}$

31. The length of a rectangle is less than 7 cm and the perimeter is at least 22 cm. What can you say about the width?

32. How much salt must be added to 3 kg of a 25% salt solution to produce a 40% solution?

33. Find the rational roots of $6x^3 + 29x^2 - 7x - 10 = 0$.

Express as a quotient of integers in lowest terms.

34. 12.48   **35.** $0.736\overline{1}$ **36.** $0.\overline{24}$

37. Sketch the graph of $y = -2x^2 + 4x - 4$. Label the vertex and the axis of symmetry. Show algebraically that there are no x-intercepts.

38. Name the property illustrated by the statement $-2x + 2x = 0$.

39. Graph the solution set: $4(7 - 2b) < -12$ or $2b - 7 \leqslant b - 9$

Simplify.

40. $\dfrac{9x^2 - 4}{9x^2 + 9x + 2} \cdot \dfrac{6x^2 + 11x + 3}{6x^2 - 4x}$ **41.** $\dfrac{30y^5 - y^4}{5y^3} - \dfrac{2xy^3 - x^2y^4}{xy^2}$

Solve over the set of complex numbers.

42. $\sqrt{x^2 + 1} = 5\sqrt{2}$ **43.** $x^2 + 100 = 0$ **44.** $\sqrt{7 - 2x^2} = 13$

Express as a complex number in standard form.

45. $\dfrac{15}{1 + 2i} - \dfrac{10}{1 - 2i}$ **46.** $\dfrac{i\sqrt{3}}{4 - 2i\sqrt{3}}$ **47.** $(-6 + 7i)(4 - i)$

48. Find the value of the discriminant of $2x^2 + 2\sqrt{2}x = 1$. State the number and the nature of the roots.

49. If $\dfrac{1}{2}$ is a root of $kx^2 + 2kx - 5 = 0$, find the other root and the value of k.

50. Find the measures of two supplementary angles if the measures have the ratio $7:5$.

51. A canoe traveled 10 km upstream, then turned and returned to its starting point. The entire trip took 3 h 45 min. If the canoe can travel 6 km/h in still water, find the rate of the current.

A function specifies a correspondence between two sets. The correspondence that associates with each of a particular group of high-rise buildings the height in feet of the building is an example. The buildings shown are in San Francisco, California.

Functions

4

When you park your car in a parking lot, the amount of money you must pay when you leave is usually related in a particular way to how long you stayed. For any fixed length of time there is one well-determined amount of money that you will be charged. Such a relationship is called a *function*.

Functions play important roles in our lives, as do the graphs of functions. For example, an electrocardiograph (EKG) is a device that produces a graph of the function relating the electrical impulses produced by a person's heart to moments in time. By examining such a graph, a physician can determine whether or not a person's heart is healthy.

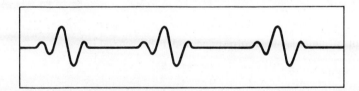

A *polygraph*, sometimes called a lie detector, is a device that draws the graphs of several functions simultaneously. The functions relate the measures of biological quantities, such as breathing rate, perspiration, blood pressure, and heart rate, to time.

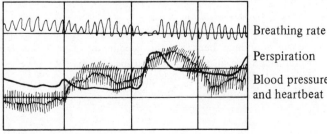

Breathing rate

Perspiration

Blood pressure
and heartbeat

Section 4-1 WHAT IS A FUNCTION?

In this section you will be introduced to an important mathematical concept: the concept of a *function*. You will learn the meaning of the terms:
- function, or mapping
- domain and range
- image and pre-image

A certain type of correspondence between two sets of objects arises often in mathematics, as shown in the following examples.

EXAMPLE   Consider the correspondence between each person in a room and his or her height in centimeters.
In this case, the first set is the set of people in the room. The second set is the set of numbers that represent the heights of the people. Notice that two different people may have the same height, but no person can have two different heights.

Barbara → 165
Keith   → 176
Robert → 165
Maria   → 168

EXAMPLE   Consider the correspondence between $\{1, 2, 3, 4\}$ and $\{0, 5, 6\}$ defined by the scheme shown.

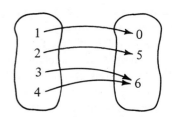

EXAMPLE   Consider the correspondence between the set of real numbers and itself defined symbolically by:

$$x \longrightarrow 2x + 1$$

A few pairs of numbers that correspond under this general rule are:

$$2 \longrightarrow 5$$
$$0 \longrightarrow 1$$
$$-3 \longrightarrow -5$$
$$\frac{1}{2} \longrightarrow 2$$

EXAMPLE   Consider the correspondence between the set of real numbers x and the set of non-negative numbers y defined by the equation $y = x^2$. (This is the same as the correspondence symbolized by $x \longrightarrow x^2$.)

EXAMPLE   Consider the correspondence between the weight of a package in kilograms and the shipping and handling charges given by the table. The entry "1-2," for example, means "greater than 1 and less than or equal to 2."

Weight	Cost
0–1	$2.30
1–2	3.00
2–4	3.90
4–6	4.80
6–10	6.20

In each of the preceding examples, note that whenever an element in the first of the two given sets is specified, an element in the second set is uniquely determined. Such a correspondence is called a *function*. More precisely: A *function* (or *mapping*) is a rule of correspondence between two sets such that exactly one element in the second set corresponds to each element in the first set.

The first set is called the *domain* of the function. Each element of the domain is said to be *mapped onto* the element of the second set that corresponds to it. When 2 is mapped onto 4, for example, then 4 is said to be the *image* of 2, and 2 is a *pre-image* of 4. The set of images of all the elements in the domain of a function is called the *range* of the function.

If no domain is specified for a given function, you should assume that the domain consists of the largest set for which the rule of correspondence is defined. Unless otherwise specified, assume that any variables represent real numbers.

EXAMPLE   Give the domain of the function:

$$x \longrightarrow \sqrt{x + 1}$$

SOLUTION   The function is defined if and only if $x + 1 \geqslant 0$. Otherwise $\sqrt{x + 1}$ would be the square root of a negative number, which is *not* a *real* number. Therefore the domain of the function is the set of all real numbers x such that:

$$x + 1 \geqslant 0$$

or

$$x \geqslant -1$$

You can write this set as

$$\{x : x \geqslant -1\}.$$

One common way of defining a function whose domain and range are both subsets of the set of real numbers is to give an equation, or *formula*, that relates an element x in the domain and its image y in the range. For example, the function

$$x \longrightarrow x^2$$

can be thought of as the function $y = x^2$. We say that $y = x^2$ defines y *as a function of* x.

EXAMPLE   Is y a function of x?

    a. $y = |x|$ **b.** $xy = 2$ **c.** $|y| = x$

SOLUTION   **a.** Yes. For each value of x, there is exactly one value of y. For example, when $x = -2$, $y = |-2| = 2$.

    b. Yes. You can rewrite this equation equivalently as:

$$y = \frac{2}{x}$$

For each nonzero value of x, there is exactly one value of y. For example, when $x = 3$, $y = \frac{2}{3}$. (Note that for $x = 0$ the function is undefined. Thus its domain is $\{x : x \neq 0\}$.)

    c. No. For any given positive real number x, there will be *two* possible values of y. For example, when $x = 3$, $y = 3$ *or* $y = -3$, since $|3| = 3$ and $|-3| = 3$.

In the following example, the domain and range of the function is the set of all points in the coordinate plane.

EXAMPLE Consider the function that maps each point P in a coordinate plane onto the point P' that is 2 units to the right of and 3 units above P.

Find the coordinates of the image of each point.
a. $(0, 0)$ b. $(-2, 0)$ c. $(-1, 4)$

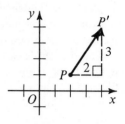

SOLUTION   a.

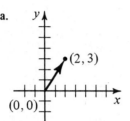

b.

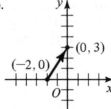

c.

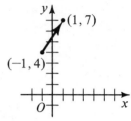

ORAL EXERCISES

State whether or not y is a function of x.

1. $y = x^3$
2. $2y = x$
3. $y = 1 \pm x$
4. $y = \sqrt{|x|}$

State whether or not b is a function of a.

5. $b^2 = 2a$
6. $\dfrac{1}{b} = a$
7. $\dfrac{1}{b^2} = a$
8. $\dfrac{1}{b} = a^2$

A parking lot charges \$1.00 for the first hour or part of an hour and 50¢ for each additional hour or part. How much would you pay if you stayed

9. half an hour?
10. one hour?
11. one hour and five minutes?
12. two hours?
13. two and a half hours?
14. eleven hours?

State the domain of each function.

15. $x \longrightarrow \dfrac{1}{x}$
16. $x \longrightarrow \sqrt{x-1}$

17. If $y = x^2$, state:
   a. The image of 5
   b. The image of 4
   c. The pre-image(s) of 4
   d. The pre-image(s) of 0

18. For the function that maps each point P in a coordinate plane onto the point P' that is 2 units to the right of and 3 units above P, state the coordinates of the pre-image of each point.
   a. $(2, 3)$ b. $(0, 0)$ c. $(0, 2)$ d. $(4, 4)$

19. Suppose a function associates with each real number x the greatest integer y that is less than x. State the image of:

   a. 3   **b.** $4\frac{1}{2}$ **c.** $\sqrt{11}$ **d.** $-\frac{4}{3}$

WRITTEN EXERCISES

Give the domain of each function and find the image of 16.

A **1.** $y = \sqrt{x} - 7$ **2.** $y = \sqrt{x-7}$ **3.** $y = \dfrac{4}{x}$ **4.** $y = \dfrac{1}{x-1}$

    5. $y = \sqrt{x^2 + 1}$ **6.** $y = (x-10)^2$ **7.** $y = x - |x|$ **8.** $y = \sqrt{x} + |x| + 2$

Explain why each statement does *not* define y as a function of x.

    9. $y^2 = x^2$ **10.** $y > x$ **11.** $y = \pm\sqrt{x^2 + 9}$

    12. $y = $ the integer nearest to x on the number line

For each function find the image of **(a)** 12, **(b)** -4, **(c)** 0, and **(d)** $\frac{9}{4}$. If the function is not defined for one or more of these values, so state.

    13. $x \longrightarrow \sqrt{x+4}$ **14.** $x \longrightarrow \dfrac{2}{\sqrt{x+4}}$

    15. $y = \dfrac{1}{\sqrt{x+4}-4}$ **16.** $y = \dfrac{1}{\sqrt{x+4}} - 4$

    17. $y = $ the greatest integer less than x

    18. $y = $ the least integer greater than or equal to x

Find the value of k if the given function associates the two given numbers.

EXAMPLE $y = \dfrac{k}{x}$; $3 \longrightarrow 2$

SOLUTION   Since the function maps 3 onto 2, you know that when $x = 3$, $y = 2$. Thus, substituting these values, you have:

$$2 = \frac{k}{3}$$
$$k = 6$$

B **19.** $y = kx^2$; $2 \longrightarrow 3$ **20.** $y = \dfrac{2k}{x}$; $5 \longrightarrow 3$

    21. $y = \dfrac{\sqrt{x^2+9}}{k}$; $4 \longrightarrow \dfrac{5}{2}$ **22.** $y = \sqrt{kx+1}$; $3 \longrightarrow 4$

    23. $y = \dfrac{k}{x^2}$; $6 \longrightarrow 2$ **24.** $y = \dfrac{k}{\sqrt{x-3}}$; $7 \longrightarrow \dfrac{3}{4}$

Give the domain of each function.

25. $y = \dfrac{|x|}{x}$

26. $y = \dfrac{1}{x^2 + 4}$

27. $b = \dfrac{1}{\sqrt{a} - 2}$

28. $b = \dfrac{1}{\sqrt{a^2 - 9}}$

29. $t = \dfrac{1}{\sqrt{s^2 + 4}}$

30. $t = \dfrac{1}{\sqrt{16 - s^2}}$

31. $y =$ the distance on the number line from x to the nearest integer

32. $y = x -$ (the greatest integer less than x)

For each mapping of the set of points in a coordinate plane onto itself, give the coordinates of the images of the points **(a)** $(1, 0)$, **(b)** $(-2, 2)$, and **(c)** $(3, 4)$.

33. $P \longrightarrow P'$, where P' is 4 units to the left of and 1 unit above P.

34. $Q \longrightarrow Q'$, where Q' is 5 units to the right of and 2 units below Q.

C 35. $R \longrightarrow R'$, where R' is the point on $\overrightarrow{OR}$ such that $OR' = 2(OR)$.

36. $S \longrightarrow S'$, where S and S' are on the same circle with center at the origin, and S' is $90°$ counterclockwise from S.

Section 4-2 THE GRAPH OF A FUNCTION

About 350 years ago the French mathematician René Descartes presented a practical way of interpreting a relationship between two variables geometrically as a set of points in a coordinate plane. You are already familiar with his method of graphing. However, not all graphs represent *functions*. In this section you will:
- interpret the concept of a function as a set of ordered pairs
- learn a geometric test to determine whether a set of points in a coordinate plane is the graph of a function

As you know, each point in the coordinate plane corresponds to an ordered pair of real numbers (x, y). Any subset of the set of all such ordered pairs is called a *relation*. (Two numbers a and b are *related* if the ordered pair (a, b) is in the relation.)

EXAMPLE Graph the relation $\{(1, 3), (5, 4), (1, -1), (3, 2), (2, 0)\}$.

SOLUTION The graph of this relation is a set of five points, as shown.

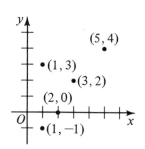

EXAMPLE Graph the relation $\{(x, y): y = x^2\}$.

SOLUTION The graph of this relation is a parabola.

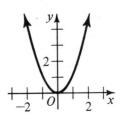

From now on, if a relation can be defined by an equation, as in the example above, we will write "the relation $y = x^2$" to mean "the relation $\{(x, y): y = x^2\}$."

EXAMPLE Graph the relation $x^2 + y^2 = 1$.

SOLUTION The graph of this relation is the circle of radius 1 with center at the origin.

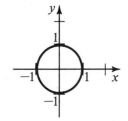

EXAMPLE Graph the relation $y > x$.

SOLUTION The graph of this relation is the region of the coordinate plane above the line $y = x$.

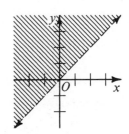

The relation $y = x^2$ is the same as the function

$$x \longrightarrow x^2.$$

Any function whose domain and range are both subsets of the set of real numbers can be thought of as a relation. However, *not* every relation is a function. A relation is a function if and only if each real number that appears as the first coordinate of an ordered pair in the relation appears *only once*. In that case, the set of first coordinates of all the ordered pairs is the domain of the function, and the set of second coordinates is its range.

Note that the relation $\{(1, 3), (5, 4), (1, -1), (3, 2), (2, 0)\}$ is *not* a function, since it contains *two* ordered pairs with first coordinate 1. Geometrically, this means that the line $x = 1$ intersects the graph of the relation twice, as shown.

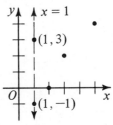

Vertical Line Test

A relation is a function if and only if no vertical line intersects the graph of
the relation more than once.

Thus any nonvertical line is the graph of a function.

EXAMPLE Determine whether each relation is a function. If it is, state its domain and range.

    a. $y = |x|$ **b.** $y^2 = x$

SOLUTION **a.** The graph of this relation is shown. Each vertical line
intersects the graph exactly once. Therefore the rela-
tion is a function with domain $\mathcal{R}$. The range of the
function is $\langle y : y \geqslant 0 \rangle$.

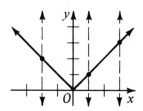

    b. The graph is a parabola that opens to the right. At
least one vertical line intersects the graph twice.
(In fact, there are infinitely many that do so.) Therefore the relation is *not* a function.

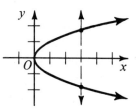

ORAL EXERCISES

State whether or not each relation is a function.

1. $\langle (0, 2), (3, 2), (1, 2), (5, 2), (-1, 2) \rangle$ **2.** $\langle (3, -1), (0, 5), (2, -3), (4, 1), (2, 0) \rangle$

3. $\langle (-2, 3), (-1, 2), (0, 4), (2, 5), (-1, 1) \rangle$ **4.** $\langle (1, 4), (-1, 4), (3, 2), (-3, 2) \rangle$

State whether the graph shown is the graph of a function. State the domain and
range of each function.

5.

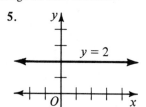

6.

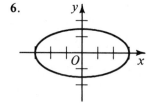

7.

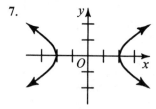

8.

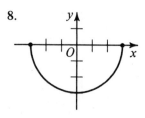

9.

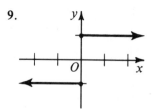

10.

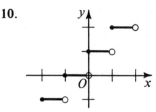

WRITTEN EXERCISES

In Exercises 1-28, sketch the graph of the relation. State whether or not it is a function. If it is, state its domain and range.

A 1. $\{(0, 2), (1, 3), (2, -1), (3, -1), (4, 2)\}$

2. $\{(-1, 2), (0, 1), (0, 3), (1, 4), (2, -3), (3, 1)\}$

3. $\{(1, 3), (2, 0), (1, -1), (3, 4), (1, 2)\}$

4. $\{(-1, 2), (0, 2), (1, 2), (3, 2), (4, -1)\}$

5. $x = 3$
6. $y = 4$
7. $y = -1$
8. $x = -2$

9. $y = 2x - 4$
10. $y = -3x + 1$
11. $x = y - 2$
12. $x = -2y + 6$

13. $y = |x| + 1$
14. $y = \dfrac{|x|}{2}$
15. $|y| = |x|$
16. $y = |x - 2|$

B 17. $y = |x| + x$
18. $y = \sqrt{|x|}$
19. $x^2 + y^2 = 25$
20. $y = \sqrt{9 + x^2}$

21. $y = \sqrt{16 - x^2}$
22. $y = \sqrt{x^2 - 9}$
23. $|y| = x^2$
24. $y^2 = |x|$

25. $y =$ the greatest integer less than x

26. $y =$ the distance on the number line from x to the nearest integer

27. $y = \begin{cases} 1 \text{ if } x \text{ is an integer} \\ 0 \text{ if } x \text{ is not an integer} \end{cases}$

28. $y = x - ($the greatest integer less than $x)$

29. If the postal rate is 20¢ for the first ounce or part of an ounce and 17¢ for each additional ounce or part, sketch the graph of the function that relates the weight of a letter to the cost of mailing it. What are the domain and range of this function?

30. The table below gives an example of a tax schedule (up to $30,000). Sketch the graph of the function relating a person's income to the tax the person pays.

Income	Tax
$0-$10,000	5% of income
$10,000-$20,000	$500 + 10% of excess over $10,000
$20,000-$30,000	$1500 + 20% of excess over $20,000

Section 4-3 PROPERTIES OF FUNCTIONS

Functions having certain important properties recur often in mathematics. If you know that a function possesses one (or more) of these properties, you can draw its graph more easily. In this section you will learn about *functional notation*, which will simplify the discussion of:

- linear functions
- polynomial functions
- odd and even functions

Functions are typically represented by letters such as f, g, and h, and we often write, for example,

$$f: x \longrightarrow x^2$$

to give both the name of the function and the rule of correspondence. The symbol

$$f(x), \quad \text{read "} f \text{ of } x \text{,"}$$

denotes the image of the number x under the function f. (Notice that it does *not* mean "f times x.") Thus a function could be specified in any of the ways shown below.

$$y = x^2 \qquad x \longrightarrow x^2 \qquad f: x \longrightarrow x^2 \qquad f(x) = x^2$$

EXAMPLE If $f(x) = x^2 + 2x - 3$, find $f(4)$, $f(0)$, and $f(-3)$.

SOLUTION
$$f(4) = (4)^2 + 2(4) - 3 = 21$$
$$f(0) = (0)^2 + 2(0) - 3 = -3$$
$$f(-3) = (-3)^2 + 2(-3) - 3 = 0$$

A function f such that

$$f(x) = mx + b,$$

for some constants m and b, is called a *linear function*. As the name suggests, the graph of every linear function is a straight line.

EXAMPLE Find a linear function f such that $f(2) = 3$ and $f(-1) = 4$.

SOLUTION Since you know that the function f is linear, you can write:

$$f(x) = mx + b$$

In order to find the values of m and b, you substitute the given values of x and $f(x)$ in this equation:

$$f(2) = m \cdot 2 + b = 3 \qquad \text{or} \qquad 2m + b = 3$$
$$f(-1) = m \cdot (-1) + b = 4 \qquad \text{or} \qquad -m + b = 4$$

Subtracting, you obtain:

$$3m = -1$$
$$m = -\frac{1}{3}$$

To find b, substitute this value of m in either of the equations $2m + b = 3$ or $-m + b = 4$. Using the second of these, you have:

$$-\left(-\frac{1}{3}\right) + b = 4$$

$$b = \frac{11}{3} \qquad \text{(You should check this value in the other equation.)}$$

The function is: $\qquad\qquad f(x) = -\frac{1}{3}x + \frac{11}{3}$

A linear function is a special kind of *polynomial function*. This is a function that can be defined by an equation of the form shown at the top of the following page.

$$f(x) = ax^n + bx^{n-1} + cx^{n-2} + \cdots + px + q,$$

In the equation above, a, b, c, . . . , q are constants and n is a positive integer. Polynomial functions motivate our next two definitions.

First note that if $f(x) = x^3$, then for every real number x,

$$f(-x) = (-x)^3 = -x^3 = -f(x).$$

More generally, if f is a polynomial function containing only odd-power terms, it is true that $f(-x) = -f(x)$. We therefore call a function f an *odd function* if $-x$ is in the domain of f whenever x is, and

$$f(-x) = -f(x).$$

EXAMPLE   The function $f(x) = x^3 - 6x$ is an odd function, since for every real number x,

$$f(-x) = (-x)^3 - 6(-x) = -x^3 + 6x = -f(x).$$

EXAMPLE   The function $g(x) = x|x|$ is an odd function, since for every real number x,

$$g(-x) = (-x)|-x| = -x|x| = -g(x).$$

A polynomial function f that contains only even-power terms (and possibly a constant term) has the property that for every real number x, $f(-x) = f(x)$. We therefore call a function f an *even function* if $-x$ is in the domain of f whenever x is, and

$$f(-x) = f(x).$$

EXAMPLE   The function $f(x) = x^4 + 3x^2 - 1$ is an even function, since

$$f(-x) = (-x)^4 + 3(-x)^2 - 1 = x^4 + 3x^2 - 1 = f(x).$$

EXAMPLE   The function $g(x) = 3|x|$ is an even function, since

$$g(-x) = 3|-x| = 3|x| = g(x).$$

Examples of graphs of an odd function and an even function are shown below:

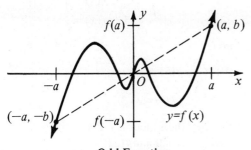

Odd Function

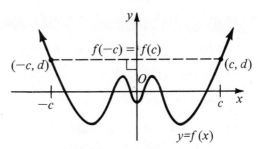

Even Function

Notice that, in the graph of an odd function, if the segment joining any point on the graph and the origin is extended an equal distance beyond the origin, then the other endpoint of the extended segment is another point on the graph. The graph of an odd function is therefore said to be *symmetric with respect to the origin*.

In the graph of an even function, if the perpendicular segment from any point on the graph to the y-axis is extended an equal distance beyond the y-axis, the endpoint of the extended segment is another point on the graph. For this reason the graph of an even function is said to be *symmetric with respect to the y-axis*.

Most functions are *neither* odd nor even. For example, if $f(x) = x + 1$, then $f(2) = 3$ and $f(-2) = -1$. Therefore f is neither odd nor even.

ORAL EXERCISES

State the value of: **a.** $f(2)$ **b.** $f(-2)$ **c.** $f(0)$. If any of these is undefined, so state.

1. $f(x) = |x|$

2. $f(x) = x^2 + x$

3. $f(x) = 3 - 2x$

4. $f(x) = \dfrac{1}{x}$

5. $f(x) = x^2 + 2$

6. $f(x) = x^3 + 2x$

7. $f(x) = \dfrac{|x|}{x}$

8. $f(x) = \dfrac{1}{x^2 - 4}$

9. $f(x) = \sqrt{x}$

10. In which of Exercises 1–9 is the function
   a. a linear function?
   b. a polynomial function?
   c. an odd function?
   d. an even function?

11. Complete: If $f(x) = 3x^2 - 2x$, then $f(r) = \underline{\ ?\ }$ and $f(a) = \underline{\ ?\ }$.

12. Complete: If $g(x) = x - 3$, then $g(2 - k) = \underline{\ ?\ }$.

WRITTEN EXERCISES

Find $f(1)$, $f(3)$, $f(-3)$, and $f(-x)$. Is the function odd, even, or neither?

A **1.** $f(x) = x - |x|$

2. $f(x) = |x| - 2$

3. $f(x) = x^5 + x^3 - x$

4. $f(x) = 1 - x^4$

5. $f(x) = x^2 + \dfrac{1}{x^2}$

6. $f(x) = 2 - \dfrac{1}{x}$

7. $f(x) = |x - 1|$

8. $f(x) = |x^2 - 4|$

9. $f(x) = |x^3|$

10. $f(x) = \sqrt{x^3}$

11. $f(x) = \sqrt{2x^2}$

12. $f(x) = 2^x,\ x \in Z$

Find the linear function that satisfies the given conditions.

13. $f(2) = 1,\ f(0) = -3$

14. $g(0) = \dfrac{3}{2},\ g(5) = -1$

15. $h(4) = 5,\ h(-2) = -4$

16. $k(5) = -3,\ k(-4) = 3$

17. If x is a temperature reading in degrees Fahrenheit, then the function f that associates with x its Celsius reading is linear. Given that $f(32) = 0$ and $f(212) = 100$, find a formula for the function f.

18. If x is a reading on the Kelvin (K) temperature scale, then the function that associates with x its Fahrenheit (F) reading is linear. Given that $273°$K corresponds to $32°$F and $373°$K corresponds to $212°$F, find a formula for this function.

Sketch the part of the graph of each function that corresponds to the values of x such that $x \geqslant 0$. Then use the oddness or evenness of the function to sketch the rest of the graph.

19. $g(x) = x^3 - 4x$

20. $h(x) = \dfrac{x^2}{2}$

B 21. $r(x) = \left| \, |x| - 2 \, \right|$

22. $s(x) = x|x| - x$

23. Show that if a linear function $f(x) = mx + b$ is odd, then $b = 0$.

24. Show that if 0 is in the domain of an odd function f, then $f(0) = 0$. (*Hint*: Consider $f(-0)$.)

In Exercises 25-27 let g be a function with the property that
$$g(a + b) = g(a) + g(b).$$

25. Show that $g(0) = 0$. (*Hint*: $0 = 0 + 0$.)

26. Show that g must be an odd function. (*Hint*: Use the fact proved in Ex. 25, together with the fact that $x + (-x) = 0$.)

27. Show that $g\left(\dfrac{1}{2}\right) = \dfrac{1}{2}g(1)$.

C 28. Let $f(x) = (x - 1)^2 + \dfrac{1}{|x - 1|}$. Show that:

    a. $f(0) = f(2)$ b. $f(-1) = f(3)$ c. $f(-2) = f(4)$

    d. What do the statements (a), (b), and (c) suggest about the graph of f?

29. Let $g(x) = (x - 1)^3$. Show that:

    a. $g(0) = -g(2)$ b. $g(-1) = -g(3)$ c. $g(-2) = -g(4)$

    d. What do the statements (a), (b), and (c) suggest about the graph of g?

30. Let $h(x) = \dfrac{1}{x - 3} + x - 3$. Show that for any nonzero real number k, $h(3 - k) = -h(3 + k)$. What does this tell you about the graph of h?

31. Let $f(x) = \dfrac{1}{(x - 2)^2}$. Show that for any nonzero real number k, $f(2 - k) = f(2 + k)$. What does this tell you about the graph of f?

32. Let p and r be any real numbers and let $q = \dfrac{p + r}{2}$. Show that if f is a linear function, then:
$$f(q) = \dfrac{f(p) + f(r)}{2}$$

33. Let $p < r$. Show that if f is a linear function, then:
$$f(q) = f(p) + \dfrac{q - p}{r - p}(f(r) - f(p))$$

SELF-TEST 1

Give the domain of each function and find the image of -2.

1. $x \longrightarrow |x|$ **2.** $y = \sqrt{x+6}$ **3.** $y = \dfrac{1}{x^2 - 9}$ Section 4-1

Sketch the graph of the relation. State whether or not it is a function. If it is, state its domain and range.

4. $\{(-2, 4), (0, 2), (1, 5), (2, -3), (3, 2)\}$ Section 4-2

5. $x = y + 3$ **6.** $x = |y|$

Find $f(2)$, $f(-2)$, and $f(-x)$. State whether the function is odd, even, or neither.

7. $f(x) = x^3 - \dfrac{1}{x^3}$ **8.** $f(x) = |x^5|$ Section 4-3

9. Find the linear function g such that $g(2) = -1$ and $g(-3) = 2$.

10. Sketch the part of the graph of $h(x) = x^3 - 3x$ that corresponds to the values of x such that $x \geqslant 0$. Then use the oddness or evenness of the function to sketch the rest of the graph.

Section 4-4 LINEAR INTERPOLATION

Most functions that you will encounter in this book have graphs with the property that between any two points $(a, f(a))$ and $(b, f(b))$ that are relatively close together, the graph is almost a line segment. For such a function, you can use a method called *linear interpolation* to approximate $f(c)$, where c is between a and b. This method will be particularly useful in later chapters when you will have tables of values for certain functions and need to compute other values that are not given in the tables.

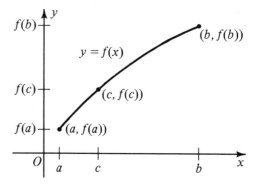

Suppose you know the values $f(a)$ and $f(b)$ and want to find $f(c)$ for $a < c < b$. Let's assume that the graph of the function f is a line segment between $(a, f(a))$ and $(b, f(b))$. Then you can find $f(c)$ if you can find $f(c) - f(a)$, since

$$f(c) = f(a) + (f(c) - f(a)).$$

Using similar triangles, you get:

$$\frac{f(c) - f(a)}{f(b) - f(a)} = \frac{c - a}{b - a}$$

or $f(c) - f(a) = \dfrac{c - a}{b - a}(f(b) - f(a))$

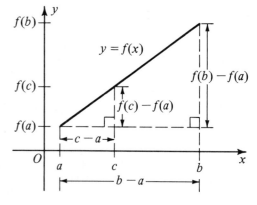

For convenience, we will let $f(c) - f(a) = d$ from now on. Thus:

$$f(c) = f(a) + d \quad \text{and} \quad \frac{d}{f(b) - f(a)} = \frac{c - a}{b - a}$$

It is important to note that when you use linear interpolation the graph is usually *not* a line segment between $(a, f(a))$ and $(b, f(b))$. We will continue to write $f(c) = f(a) + d$, keeping in mind that $f(a) + d$ is usually only an approximation of $f(c)$.

It is particularly easy to find the value of $f(c) - f(a)$, or d, if the function is displayed in a tabular form, as shown below.

$$b - a \left[c - a \left[\begin{array}{cc} x & f(x) \\ a & f(a) \\ c & f(c) \\ b & f(b) \end{array} \right] d \right] f(b) - f(a)$$

EXAMPLE The following table lists two values of a function called the sine of x, or $\sin x$, that you will study later in this book. Find $\sin 0.796$ by interpolating and rounding to four decimal places.

x	$\sin x$
0.79	0.7104
0.80	0.7174

SOLUTION First set up a table.

$$0.01 \left[0.006 \left[\begin{array}{cc} x & \sin x \\ 0.79 & 0.7104 \\ 0.796 & \sin 0.796 \\ 0.80 & 0.7174 \end{array} \right] d \right] 0.0070$$

Thus you have the proportion:

$$\frac{d}{0.0070} = \frac{0.006}{0.01}$$

$$d = 0.0070 \left(\frac{0.006}{0.01} \right) = 0.0042$$

Since $f(c) = f(a) + d$:

$$\sin 0.796 = 0.7104 + d$$
$$= 0.7104 + 0.0042 = 0.7146 \text{ (to four decimal places)}$$

EXAMPLE Interpolate between $\sqrt{4}$ and $\sqrt{9}$ to find the value of $\sqrt{7}$. Round your answer to the nearest tenth.

SOLUTION Here $f(x) = \sqrt{x}$. You interpolate between $\sqrt{4}$ and $\sqrt{9}$ because 4 and 9 are the integers closest to 7 whose function values you know: $f(4) = 2$ and $f(9) = 3$. You can summarize this information in a table, as in the preceding example.

$$5 \left[3 \left[\begin{array}{cc} x & \sqrt{x} \\ 4 & 2 \\ 7 & \sqrt{7} \\ 9 & 3 \end{array} \right] d \right] 1$$

(Solution continues.)

Using the information given in the preceding table, you obtain the proportion:

$$\frac{d}{1} = \frac{3}{5}$$

$$d = \frac{3}{5}, \text{ or } 0.6$$

$$\sqrt{7} = 2 + d = 2 + 0.6 = 2.6 \text{ (to the nearest tenth)}$$

In the examples of this section we have applied linear interpolation to functions that are *increasing* between a and b. It can also be applied to functions that are *decreasing* between a and b.

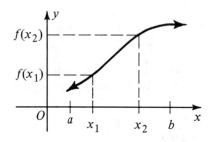
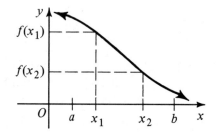

f is *increasing* between a and b if for x_1 and x_2 between a and b such that $x_1 < x_2$,

$$f(x_1) < f(x_2).$$

f is *decreasing* between a and b if for x_1 and x_2 between a and b such that $x_1 < x_2$,

$$f(x_1) > f(x_2).$$

If the function is increasing between a and b, then d is a positive number. If the function is decreasing between a and b, then both d and $f(b) - f(a)$ will be negative.

ORAL EXERCISES

Exercises 1-6 refer to the function $f(x) = \sqrt{x}$, with $a = 4$, $b = 16$, and $c = 9$.

1. What are the values of $f(a)$ and $f(b)$?

2. Referring to the table below and using the values you found in Exercise 1, state a proportion that you could use to find the value of d.

$$12 \begin{bmatrix} 5 \begin{bmatrix} \begin{array}{c|c} x & f(x) \\ \hline 4 & f(a) \\ 9 & f(c) \\ 16 & f(b) \end{array} \end{bmatrix} d \end{bmatrix} ?$$

3. What value of d does this proportion yield?

4. What value of $f(c)$ does this value of d give you?

5. What is the *actual* value of $f(c)$?

6. Explain why the answers to Exercises 4 and 5 are not the same.

State whether each function is increasing, decreasing, or neither between $x = 0$ and $x = 2$.

7. $f(x) = x + 3$

8. $g(x) = x^2 - 2x$

9. $h(x) = |x - 1|$

10. $g(x) = 1 - x^2$

11. $h(x) = x^3 - 1$

12. $f(x) = \dfrac{1}{x - 3}$

WRITTEN EXERCISES

Use linear interpolation between consecutive perfect squares to find an approximation of each value. Round your answer to the nearest tenth.

A 1. $\sqrt{3}$
   2. $\sqrt{8}$
   3. $\sqrt{21}$
   4. $\sqrt{149}$

Use linear interpolation, with $a = 3$ and $b = 4$, to find an approximation of $f(3.2)$. Round your answer to the nearest tenth.

5. $f(x) = x^3$

6. $f(x) = \dfrac{1}{1 - x}$

7. $f(x) = \sqrt{25 - x^2}$

8. $f(x) = \dfrac{3}{\sqrt{24 - 5x}}$

In Exercises 9 and 10, let $f(x) = mx + k$.

9. Show that the approximation of $f(5)$ obtained by interpolating between $a = 4$ and $b = 7$ equals $f(5)$.

10. Show that if $a < c < b$, then the approximation of $f(c)$ obtained by interpolating between a and b is equal to $f(c)$.

Exercises 11–22 refer to the table shown. The table gives the values of a function called $\log x$, which you will study in Chapter 9. Use linear interpolation to find an approximation of each value. (If necessary, round your answer to four decimal places.)

x	$\log x$
7.0	0.8451
7.1	0.8513
7.2	0.8573
7.3	0.8633
7.4	0.8692
7.5	0.8751
7.6	0.8808
7.7	0.8865
7.8	0.8921
7.9	0.8976
8.0	0.9031

11. $\log 7.25$

12. $\log 7.14$

13. $\log 7.38$

14. $\log 7.61$

Use the table to find to the nearest hundredth an approximate value of x for which the given value is $\log x$.

B 15. 0.8531

16. 0.8609

17. 0.8943

18. 0.9020

19. 0.8848

20. 0.8507

21. 0.8735

22. 0.8919

23. Suppose you used linear interpolation to find an approximation of $g(3)$, where $g(x) = x^2$, using $a = 2$ and $b = 4$. Would you expect the interpolated value to be larger or smaller than the true value? Explain.

24. If you used $a = 2$ and $b = 5$ to find an approximation of $g(3)$ in Exercise 23, would you expect a larger or smaller answer than you got in that exercise? Explain.

If $a < b < c$, and you know the values $f(a)$ and $f(b)$, you can use a method called linear *extrapolation* to find an approximate value of $f(c)$. Exercises 25–28 refer to the diagram below.

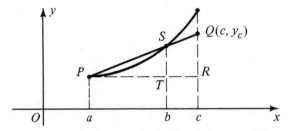

C 25. Use similar triangles PST and PQR to obtain a proportion involving PR, ST, PT, and QR. Rewrite this proportion in terms of a, b, c, $f(a)$, $f(b)$, and y_c, the y-coordinate of the point where $\overleftrightarrow{PQ}$ intersects the line $x = c$.

26. Solve the proportion that you obtained in Exercise 25 for y_c.

27. Use linear extrapolation to find an approximation of $\sqrt{10}$, using $a = 4$ and $b = 9$. Round your answer to the nearest tenth.

28. Use linear extrapolation to find an approximation of $\sqrt{38}$, using $a = 25$ and $b = 36$. Round your answer to the nearest tenth.

Section 4-5 COMPOSITION OF FUNCTIONS

Two given functions can often be combined to form a new function. For example, if $g(x) = x^2 + 9$ and $h(x) = 2x$, then the *composite* function $h \circ g$, read "h following g," can be defined by

$$[h \circ g](x) = h(g(x)).$$

Since $g(4) = 4^2 + 9 = 25$ and $h(g(4)) = h(25) = 2(25) = 50$,

$$[h \circ g](4) = 50.$$

Since $h(g(x)) = h(x^2 + 9) = 2(x^2 + 9) = 2x^2 + 18$,

$$[h \circ g](x) = 2x^2 + 18.$$

If we use this formula to evaluate $[h \circ g](4)$, we will get the same answer as above:

$$[h \circ g](4) = 2 \cdot 4^2 + 18$$
$$= 2 \cdot 16 + 18$$
$$= 50$$

Notice that $h \circ g$ is not the same as $g \circ h$, since

$$[g \circ h](x) = g(h(x)) = g(2x) = (2x)^2 + 9 = 4x^2 + 9.$$

That is, the operation of *composition* is not commutative.

EXAMPLE Let $g(x) = 2x + 5$ and $h(x) = x^2$. Find:

  a. $[g \circ h](3)$ and $[h \circ g](3)$ b. $[g \circ h](x)$ and $[h \circ g](x)$

SOLUTION a. $h(3) = 3^2 = 9$

$$[g \circ h](3) = g(9)$$
$$= 2(9) + 5$$
$$= 23$$

$$g(3) = 2(3) + 5 = 11$$
$$[h \circ g](3) = h(g(3))$$
$$= h(11)$$
$$= 11^2$$
$$= 121$$

b. $[g \circ h](x) = g(h(x))$
$$= g(x^2)$$
$$= 2(x^2) + 5$$
$$= 2x^2 + 5$$

$$[h \circ g](x) = h(g(x))$$
$$= h(2x + 5)$$
$$= (2x + 5)^2$$
$$= 4x^2 + 20x + 25$$

Notice that $[g \circ h](x) = g(h(x))$ is meaningful only for those values of x in the domain of h for which $h(x)$ is in the domain of g. Thus the domain of $g \circ h$ must be a subset of the domain of h (and is often the same as the domain of h). Consider the functions

$$g(x) = \sqrt{x} \quad \text{and} \quad h(x) = 2x.$$

Then

$$[g \circ h](x) = g(h(x)) = g(2x) = \sqrt{2x},$$

and the domain of $g \circ h$ is $\{x: x \geqslant 0\}$, which is not the same as the domain of h, but is a subset of the domain of h. *We will assume that the domain of a composite function is the largest set for which the function is defined.*

ORAL EXERCISES

Let $g(x) = \sqrt{x}$ and $h(x) = 7 + 2x$. Complete.

1. $g(9) = \underline{\ ?\ }$
2. $h(g(9)) = \underline{\ ?\ }$
3. $[h \circ g](9) = \underline{\ ?\ }$
4. $h(9) = \underline{\ ?\ }$
5. $g(h(9)) = \underline{\ ?\ }$
6. $[g \circ h](9) = \underline{\ ?\ }$
7. $g(1) = \underline{\ ?\ }$
8. $h(g(1)) = \underline{\ ?\ }$
9. $[h \circ g](1) = \underline{\ ?\ }$

Let $g(x) = 2x + 3$ and $f(x) = 4x - 1$. Find each value.

10. $[g \circ f](1)$
11. $[f \circ g](1)$
12. $[f \circ g](0)$
13. $[g \circ f](0)$
14. $[g \circ f](-1)$
15. $[f \circ g](-1)$

Find a simplified formula for: a. $[g \circ f](x)$ b. $[f \circ g](x)$

16. $g(x) = \sqrt{x},\ f(x) = 7 + 2x$
17. $g(x) = 2x + 3,\ f(x) = 4x - 1$

Specify two functions, g and h, such that $h(g(x))$ has the given value.

18. $\dfrac{1}{1 - 2x}$
19. $(2x - 5)^4$
20. $8x^3 + (x^3)^2$
21. $\sqrt{\dfrac{x + 3}{2}}$

WRITTEN EXERCISES

Let $f(x) = 2x - 3$, $g(x) = \dfrac{x+1}{2}$, and $h(x) = \sqrt{x}$. Find each value. (In Exercises 9–12 give a simplified formula.)

A   1. $f(g(7))$ 2. $g(f(7))$ 3. $h(g(31))$ 4. $g(h(9))$

    5. $f(h(16))$ 6. $h(f(14))$ 7. $h(g(f(17)))$ 8. $f(h(g(7)))$

    9. $f(g(x))$ 10. $g(f(x))$ 11. $h(f(g(x)))$ 12. $f(g(h(x)))$

Let $f(x) = x^3 + 8$, $g(x) = \sqrt{x}$, and $h(x) = \dfrac{1}{x}$. For each composite function, give a simplified formula.

    13. $f \circ g$ 14. $g \circ f$ 15. $h \circ f$ 16. $f \circ h$

Show that for each pair of functions, g and h,
$$[g \circ h](x) = x \text{ for all } x \text{ in the domain of } g \circ h,$$
and
$$[h \circ g](x) = x \text{ for all } x \text{ in the domain of } h \circ g.$$

B 17. $g(x) = 2x + 3$ $h(x) = \dfrac{1}{2}(x - 3)$

   18. $g(x) = -\dfrac{2}{3}(x + 1)$ $h(x) = -\dfrac{3}{2}x - 1$

   19. $g(x) = \dfrac{1}{x-2}$ $h(x) = \dfrac{1}{x} + 2$

   20. $g(x) = \dfrac{3}{x} - 1$ $h(x) = \dfrac{3}{x+1}$

   21. $g(x) = x^2 + 4,\ x \geqslant 0$ $h(x) = \sqrt{x-4}$

   22. $g(x) = \dfrac{1}{2}\sqrt{x-2}$ $h(x) = 4x^2 + 2,\ x \geqslant 0$

For each function g, find a function h such that $[h \circ g](x) = x$ for all x in the domain of g. For the function that you find, show that $[g \circ h](x) = x$ for all x in the domain of h. (*Hint*: Let $x = g(y)$. Solve for y in terms of x to get a formula for h.)

C 23. $g(x) = 4x - 3$ 24. $g(x) = mx + b$

   25. $g(x) = \dfrac{2}{3-x}$ 26. $g(x) = \dfrac{a}{x+b}$

State the domain of **(a)** $g \circ h$ and **(b)** $h \circ g$.

   27. $g(x) = x + 3$ $h(x) = \dfrac{1}{x}$ 27. $g(x) = x^2,\ x \geqslant 0$ $h(x) = \sqrt{x}$

   29. $g(x) = x^2 + 4,\ x \geqslant 0$ $h(x) = \sqrt{x-4}$ 30. $g(x) = \dfrac{1}{x-2}$ $h(x) = \sqrt{x}$

Section 4-6 THE INVERSE OF A FUNCTION

As you saw in Exercise 17 of the preceding section, the functions $g(x) = 2x + 3$ and $h(x) = \frac{1}{2}(x - 3)$ are such that

$$[g \circ h](x) = x \quad \text{and} \quad [h \circ g](x) = x$$

for all $x \in \mathcal{R}$. Such functions are called *inverse functions*. In this section you will learn about:

- the identity function for a given domain
- inverse functions
- one-to-one functions
- power functions

For any set S, the function

$$x \longrightarrow x, \; x \in S,$$

is called the *identity function* with domain S. Notice that the range is also S.

EXAMPLES $\{(0,0), (1, 1), (2, 2)\}$ is the identity function with domain $\{0, 1, 2\}$.

$\{(x, x) \colon x \in \mathcal{R}\}$, or $x \longrightarrow x$, is the identity function with domain $\mathcal{R}$.

Two functions g and h are *inverse functions* if and only if $g \circ h$ and $h \circ g$ are both the identity function; that is, when

$$[g \circ h](x) = x \quad \text{and} \quad [h \circ g](x) = x.$$

EXAMPLES $g(x) = 3x$ and $h(x) = \dfrac{x}{3}$ are inverse functions because:

$$[g \circ h](x) = g(h(x))$$
$$= g\left(\frac{x}{3}\right)$$
$$= 3\left(\frac{x}{3}\right)$$
$$= x$$

$$[h \circ g](x) = h(g(x))$$
$$= h(3x)$$
$$= \frac{3x}{3}$$
$$= x$$

$g(x) = x + 2$ and $h(x) = x - 2$ are inverse functions because:

$$[g \circ h](x) = g(h(x))$$
$$= g(x - 2)$$
$$= (x - 2) + 2$$
$$= x$$

$$[h \circ g](x) = h(g(x))$$
$$= h(x + 2)$$
$$= (x + 2) - 2$$
$$= x$$

$g(x) = 3x + 2$ and $h(x) = \dfrac{x - 2}{3}$ are inverse functions because:

$$[g \circ h](x) = g(h(x))$$
$$= g\left(\frac{x - 2}{3}\right)$$
$$= 3\left(\frac{x - 2}{3}\right) + 2$$
$$= (x - 2) + 2$$
$$= x$$

$$[h \circ g](x) = h(g(x))$$
$$= h(3x + 2)$$
$$= \frac{(3x + 2) - 2}{3}$$
$$= \frac{3x}{3}$$
$$= x$$

For the function $g(x) = 3x + 2$, notice that if $g(x_1) = g(x_2)$, then

$$3x_1 + 2 = 3x_2 + 2, \quad \text{or} \quad 3x_1 = 3x_2, \quad \text{or} \quad x_1 = x_2.$$

That is, each element in the range of g has *exactly one* pre-image. Such a function is said to be a *one-to-one function*. Only a one-to-one function has an inverse function.

EXAMPLES $\{(1, 0), (2, -3), (3, -5)\}$ is a one-to-one function.

$\{(1, 0), (2, -3), (3, -3)\}$ is not a one-to-one function, because -3 has more than one pre-image.

$\{(1, 0), (2, -3), (2, 4)\}$ is not a one-to-one function, because it is not a function.

$f(x) = x^2$ is not a one-to-one function, because every positive number a has two pre-images, $\sqrt{a}$ and $-\sqrt{a}$.

If a function can be graphed in the coordinate plane, then you can use the following geometric test to see if it is one-to-one:

Horizontal Line Test

A function is one-to-one if and only if no horizontal line intersects the graph more than once.

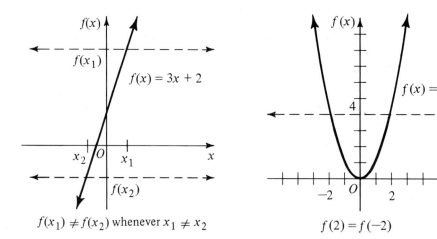

$f(x_1) \neq f(x_2)$ whenever $x_1 \neq x_2$

$f(2) = f(-2)$

If f is a one-to-one function, then its inverse function, denoted f^{-1}, can be defined by

$$f^{-1}: b \longrightarrow a \quad \text{if and only if} \quad f: a \longrightarrow b.$$

Notice that $[f^{-1} \circ f](a) = f^{-1}(f(a)) = f^{-1}(b) = a$ and $[f \circ f^{-1}](b) = f(f^{-1}(b)) = f(a) = b$.

EXAMPLE   Find the inverse of the function $\{(0, 3), (-1, 2), (1, -1), (2, 0)\}$.

SOLUTION   Since the given function can be symbolized by

$$0 \longrightarrow 3 \qquad -1 \longrightarrow 2 \qquad 1 \longrightarrow -1 \qquad 2 \longrightarrow 0$$

its inverse can be symbolized by:

$$3 \longrightarrow 0 \qquad 2 \longrightarrow -1 \qquad -1 \longrightarrow 1 \qquad 0 \longrightarrow 2$$

The inverse is thus the function

$$\{(3, 0), (2, -1), (-1, 1), (0, 2)\}.$$

EXAMPLE   Let $f(x) = 2x - 3$. Find f^{-1}.

SOLUTION   Let $f^{-1}(b) = a$ if and only if $f(a) = b$.

Solve for a in terms of b to get a formula for f^{-1}:

$$f(a) = 2a - 3$$
$$b = 2a - 3$$
$$b + 3 = 2a$$
$$\frac{b + 3}{2} = a$$
$$\frac{b + 3}{2} = f^{-1}(b)$$

Of course, this is the same as $f^{-1}(x) = \dfrac{x + 3}{2}$.

Check

$$[f \circ f^{-1}](x) = f(f^{-1}(x))$$
$$= f\left(\frac{x + 3}{2}\right)$$
$$= 2\left(\frac{x + 3}{2}\right) - 3$$
$$= (x + 3) - 3$$
$$= x$$

$$[f^{-1} \circ f](x) = f^{-1}(f(x))$$
$$= f^{-1}(2x - 3)$$
$$= \frac{(2x - 3) + 3}{2}$$
$$= \frac{2x}{2}$$
$$= x$$

If $f(x) = x^2$, then f is *not* one-to-one, since, for example, $f(2) = f(-2)$. Thus f does not have an inverse function. We can remedy this situation, however, by *restricting the domain* of f. Let

$$g(x) = x^2, \ x \geqslant 0.$$

This new function (different from f because its domain is not the same as that of f) *is* one-to-one. Its inverse is

$$g^{-1}(x) = \sqrt{x}.$$

Functions such as $f(x) = x^n$, $n \in Z$, are called *power functions*. Their inverses involve the nth roots that you studied in Chapter 3. For example, the inverse of $h(x) = x^4$, $x \geqslant 0$, is $h^{-1}(x) = \sqrt[4]{x}$.

EXAMPLE   If $f(x) = x^3 + 1$, find: a. $f^{-1}(x)$ b. $f^{-1}(9)$

SOLUTION   a. If $f(a) = b$, you have:
$$a^3 + 1 = b$$
$$a^3 = b - 1$$
$$a = \sqrt[3]{b - 1}$$
Therefore $f^{-1}(x) = \sqrt[3]{x - 1}$.

b. $f^{-1}(9) = \sqrt[3]{9 - 1}$
$$= \sqrt[3]{8}$$
$$= 2$$

If you know the graph of a function, how can you draw the graph of its inverse? You know that for any real numbers a and b, $f(a) = b$ if and only if $f^{-1}(b) = a$. This tells you that:

> A point (a, b) is on the graph of a function if and only if the point (b, a) is on the graph of the inverse of that function.

This implies that the graphs of a function f and its inverse f^{-1} will always be *reflections* of each other *over the line $y = x$*. (Notice that the line $y = x$ is the graph of the identity function with domain $\mathcal{R}$.)

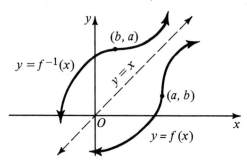

ORAL EXERCISES

State whether or not the function is one-to-one. If it is, state the inverse of the function.

1. $\{(0, 1), (1, -1), (2, 1)\}$ 2. $\{(0, 2), (2, 0)\}$ 3. $\{(-6, 1), (0, 5), (6, -5)\}$

State whether or not the graph is the graph of a one-to-one function.

4.
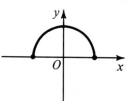

5.
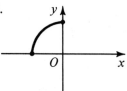

6.
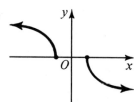

7.
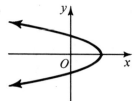

8.
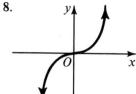

9.
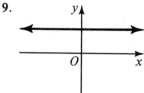

State whether or not each function is one-to-one. If it is not, state a restriction of the domain of the function for which the corresponding function with this domain *is* one-to-one. (There may be more than one correct answer.)

10. $f(x) = x^2 - 1$ **11.** $f(x) = 3x - 1$ **12.** $f(x) = \sqrt{x}$

13. $f(x) = \dfrac{1}{x}$ **14.** $f(x) = |x|$ **15.** $f(x) = (x - 2)^2$

16. If the domain of f is A and the range of f is B, what are the domain and range of f^{-1}?

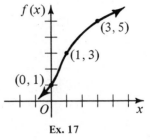

17. State each value for the function f whose graph is shown.

    a. $f^{-1}(3)$ **b.** $f^{-1}(5)$ **c.** $f^{-1}(1)$

Ex. 17

WRITTEN EXERCISES

Find the inverse of the function.

A   **1.** $f(x) = -5x$ **2.** $g(x) = x + 10$ **3.** $h(x) = 5x - 7$

    4. $f(x) = \dfrac{1}{2}(x + 5)$ **5.** $y = \dfrac{1}{4x - 1}$ **6.** $y + 3 = \dfrac{1}{2x}$

    7. $y - 9 = 2x^3$ **8.** $y = \dfrac{x^3 - 1}{5}$ **9.** $f(x) = \sqrt[3]{x - 2}$

    10. $h(x) = 2\sqrt[3]{x} + 6$ **11.** $f(x) = x^4 + 1,\ x \geqslant 0$ **12.** $g(x) = x^6,\ x \geqslant 0$

Show that the function is its own inverse by showing that $f(f(x)) = x$ for all x in the domain of f.

    13. $f(x) = -x$ **14.** $f(x) = \dfrac{1}{x}$

B   **15.** $f(x) = \sqrt[3]{1 - x^3}$ **16.** $f(x) = \sqrt{4 - x^2},\ 0 \leqslant x \leqslant 2$

Find the inverse of the function.

    17. $g(x) = \dfrac{\sqrt{16 + x^2}}{2},\ x \geqslant 0$ **18.** $h(x) = 2\sqrt{4 - x^2},\ 0 \leqslant x \leqslant 2$

On one set of axes, sketch the graph of the given function and its inverse.

    19. $g(x) = 2x - 3$ **20.** $h(x) = x^3$

    21. $f(x) = x^2 + 1,\ x \leqslant 0$ **22.** $g(x) = 4 - x^2,\ x \geqslant 0$

    23. $h(x) = -(x - 1)^2,\ x \geqslant 1$ **24.** $f(x) = (x + 2)^2,\ x \geqslant -2$

On one set of axes, sketch the graph of the given function and its inverse.

(*Hint*: In Exercises 25 and 26 if you square both sides of the equation, then the graph of f will be a *part* of the graph of the resulting equation.)

25. $f(x) = \dfrac{\sqrt{36 + x^2}}{3}$, $x \geqslant 0$ $\qquad$ 26. $f(x) = 2\sqrt{9 - x^2}$, $0 \leqslant x \leqslant 3$

27. Show that if $f(x) = mx + b$, $m \neq 0$, then f is one-to-one.

28. Repeat Exercise 27 for a function of the form $f(x) = \dfrac{a}{x + b}$, $x \neq b$.

29. Sketch the graph of the function
$$f(x) = x^2 - 4x + 3, \ x \geqslant 2,$$
and its inverse on one set of axes. Find an algebraic expression for $f^{-1}(x)$ by letting $f(a) = b$. Solve for a by using the quadratic formula, treating b as part of the *constant term*. Check that $f(f^{-1}(x)) = x$ for all x in the range of f^{-1} and $f^{-1}(f(x)) = x$ for all x in the range of f.

30. Repeat Exercise 29 for the function
$$f(x) = x^2 - 2x - 8, \ x \geqslant 1.$$

C 31. Suppose that the graphs of a function f and its inverse f^{-1} intersect at a point (a, b) with $a \neq b$. Explain how you know that the two graphs will also intersect at the point (b, a).

32. Let $f(x) = 1 - x^2$, $x \geqslant 0$. Find all the points of intersection of the graphs of f and f^{-1}. (*Hint*: $x^4 - 2x^2 + x = x(x - 1)(x^2 + x - 1)$.)

SELF-TEST 2

1. Use linear interpolation between consecutive perfect squares to find an approximation of $\sqrt{40}$. Round your answer to the nearest tenth.   Section 4-4

2. Given that $\log 8.4 = 0.9243$ and $\log 8.5 = 0.9294$, find to the nearest hundredth a value of x for which $\log x = 0.9262$.

For the given functions, find:
a. $[g \circ h](2)$ $\quad$ b. $[h \circ g](2)$ $\quad$ c. $[g \circ h](x)$ $\quad$ d. $[h \circ g](x)$
3. $g(x) = 3x + 1$, $h(x) = 1 - x$ $\qquad$ 4. $g(x) = 4x - 1$, $h(x) = x^2$ Section 4-5

Find the inverse of the function.

5. $f(x) = \dfrac{5}{2 - x}$ $\qquad$ 6. $g(x) = \sqrt[3]{x + 4}$ Section 4-6

7. Show that the function $f(x) = \sqrt{1 - x^2}$, $0 \leqslant x \leqslant 1$, is its own inverse.

Computer Exercises

1. Type in and RUN the following program. The program graphs the function $f(x) = 2 - x^2$, or $y = 2 - x^2$, for values of x in the interval $-2 \leqslant x \leqslant 2$. Notice that the graph is shown sideways, with the x-axis vertical and the y-axis horizontal. (If you are working on a screen rather than a printer, you should make a sketch of the graph of f for reference in later exercises.)

```
10    LET NP = 5
20    REM *** NP IS 3 FOR TRS–80; 5 FOR APPLE AND PET.
30    REM *** FOR OTHERS, EXPERIMENT
40    FOR C = 0 TO 4 * NP
50    LET X = −2 + C/NP
60    LET Y = 2 − X ↑ 2
70    LET YP = 1 + INT (6 * (Y + 3) + .5)
80    REM *** YP IS SCREEN POSITION OF POINT
90    IF C <> 2 * NP THEN 210
100   REM *** X = 0 : PUT IN Y-AXIS
110   FOR T = 1 TO 37 STEP 6
120   READ L $
130   IF (YP > T) OR (YP < = T − 6) OR (YP < 1) THEN 170
140   REM *** NOW PLOT Y
150   PRINT TAB(YP); "*";
160   IF YP = T THEN 180
170   PRINT TAB(T); L $;
180   NEXT T
190   PRINT "Y";
200   GOTO 330
210   IF INT(C/NP) <> C/NP THEN 310
220   REM *** PUT IN X-AXIS
230   READ L $
240   IF (YP > 19) OR (YP < 1) THEN 270
250   PRINT TAB(YP); "*";
260   IF YP = 19 THEN 330
270   PRINT TAB(19); L $;
280   IF (YP < 19) OR (YP > 37) THEN 330
290   PRINT TAB(YP); "*";
300   GOTO 330
310   IF (YP < 1) OR (YP > 37) THEN 330
320   PRINT TAB(YP); "*";
330   PRINT
340   NEXT C
350   PRINT TAB(19); "X"
360   DATA −, −, −, −, −, 0, +, +, +, +, +
370   END
```

2. For the functions $f(x) = 2 - x^2$ and $g(x) = x + 1$, you can graph $g \circ f$ by changing line 60 and adding line 65:

$$60 \quad \text{LET } Z = 2 - X \uparrow 2$$
$$65 \quad \text{LET } Y = Z + 1$$

For each of the following functions, use $f(x) = 2 - x^2$ and the given function g. RUN the program to graph $g \circ f$.

a. $g(x) = x + 1$ b. $g(x) = x - 2$

c. $g(x) = -x$ d. $g(x) = |x|$

3. Choose another function for f.
  a. Repeat Exercise 1, using the new function in line 60.
  b. Repeat Exercise 2, using the new function f and given functions for g.

4. For any function f, describe how the graph of $g \circ f$ is related to the graph of f, when:

a. $g(x) = x + 1$ b. $g(x) = x - 2$

c. $g(x) = -x$ d. $g(x) = |x|$

CHAPTER REVIEW

Give the domain of each function and find the images of -2 and 3.

1. $y = \dfrac{1}{x-1}$ 2. $y = -|x|$ 3. $y = \sqrt{x^2 - 4}$ Section 4-1

4. If $y = \dfrac{k\,|x|}{x^2}$ maps -3 onto -1, find the value of k.

Sketch the graph of the relation. State whether or not it is a function. If it is, give its domain and range.

5. $\{(-2, 1), (0, 4), (3, 2), (1, -1), (2, 1)\}$ Section 4-2

6. $x = -1$ 7. $y = \sqrt{9 - x^2}$

Find $f(3)$, $f(-3)$, and $f(-x)$. State whether the function is odd, even, or neither.

8. $f(x) = 1 + \dfrac{1}{x}$ 9. $f(x) = |x^3 + x|$ Section 4-3

10. Find the linear function g such that $g(-1) = 2$ and $g(2) = -2$.

11. Use linear interpolation between consecutive perfect squares to find an approxi-   Section 4-4
mation of $\sqrt{54}$. Round your answer to the nearest tenth.

12. Given that $\log 5.0 = 0.6990$ and $\log 5.1 = 0.7076$, find to the nearest hundredth a value of x for which $\log x = 0.7060$.

For the given functions, find:
a. $[g \circ h](3)$ b. $[h \circ g](3)$ c. $[g \circ h](x)$ d. $[h \circ g](x)$

13. $g(x) = \sqrt{x}, \ h(x) = x^3 - 1$ 14. $g(x) = 2 + x, \ h(x) = x^2$ Section 4-5

Find the inverse of the function.

15. $\{(1, 2), (3, 4), (-1, 5)\}$ 16. $y = 4x - 5$ 17. $h(x) = \dfrac{x^3 + 2}{4}$ Section 4-6

18. On one set of axes, sketch the graphs of f and f^{-1} if $f(x) = (x + 1)^2$, $x \geqslant 1$.

CHAPTER TEST

State whether or not the relation is a function. If it is, give its domain and range, and state whether it is one-to-one.

1. $\{(0, 5), (5, 0), (1, -1)\}$ 2. $\{(1, 3), (2, 3)\}$ 3. $\{(0, 4), (0, -4)\}$

4. $x + y = 4$ 5. $x = 4$ 6. $y = -4$

7. Graph: $y =$ the greatest integer less than or equal to x

Give the domain of the function.

8. $f(x) = \dfrac{|x|}{x}$ 9. $g(x) = \sqrt{x - 1}$ 10. $h(x) = \dfrac{1}{x + 2}$

Find $f(2)$, $f(-2)$, and $f(-x)$. Is the function odd, even, or neither?

11. $f(x) = 3x^3 - 4x$ 12. $f(x) = \dfrac{x^4 - 3x^2 - 10}{6}$

13. Find the linear function g such that $g(1) = -1$ and $g(-3) = 4$.

For the given functions, find:
a. $[f \circ g](2)$ b. $[g \circ f](2)$ c. $[f \circ g](x)$ d. $[g \circ f](x)$

14. $f(x) = 2x - 3, \ g(x) = x + 1$ 15. $f(x) = \sqrt{x}, \ g(x) = \dfrac{1}{x^2 + 3}$

Find the inverse of the function.
16. $\{(-6, 4), (0, 2), (3, 5)\}$ 17. $y - 5 = 3x$

18. Use linear interpolation between consecutive perfect squares to find an approximation of $\sqrt{87}$. Round your answer to the nearest tenth.

Indicate the best answer by writing the appropriate letter.

1. Simplify: $\dfrac{3 + (10 - 2 \cdot 2)^2}{3 + (5 \cdot 5 - 4 \cdot 6)}$

   a. $\dfrac{39}{4}$ **b.** 36   **c.** $\dfrac{259}{129}$ **d.** $\dfrac{128}{63}$

2. Simplify: $\dfrac{(3xy)^2 x^3 y^{-2}}{18y^2}$

   a. $\dfrac{x^4}{6y^3}$ **b.** $\dfrac{x^5}{6y^2}$ **c.** $\dfrac{x^5}{2y^2}$ **d.** $\dfrac{x^4}{2y^2}$

3. Which of the following represents a function?

   a. 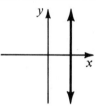   **b.**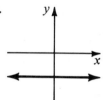

   c. $\{(1, 2), (2, 2), (2, 3)\}$ **d.** $|x + y| = 5$

4. Which of the following is the inverse of the function $\{(1, 2), (3, 4), (5, 6)\}$?

   a. $\{(-1, -2), (-3, -4), (-5, -6)\}$ **b.** $\{(2, 1), (4, 3), (6, 5)\}$

   c. $\left\{\left(1, \frac{1}{2}\right), \left(\frac{1}{3}, \frac{1}{4}\right), \left(\frac{1}{5}, \frac{1}{6}\right)\right\}$ **d.** $\{(-2, -1), (-4, -3), (-6, -5)\}$

5. In which equation is y *not* a function of x?

   a. $y = 1$ **b.** $x = y^2$ **c.** $y = x$ **d.** $|x| = y$

6. Which graph illustrates a function and its inverse?

   a. 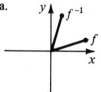   **b.**   **c.** 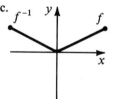   **d.**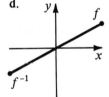

7. The Commutative Property of Multiplication guarantees that $[x + (-x)](-1) = \underline{\ ?\ }$.

   a. 0   **b.** $(-x + x)(-1)$ **c.** $(-1)[x + (-x)]$ **d.** $-[x + (-x)]$

8. Find the solution set of $|5x + 5| = 25$.

   a. $\{4, 6\}$ **b.** $\{-6\}$ **c.** $\{4\}$ **d.** $\{4, -6\}$

9. Solve: $x = \sqrt{5x - 6}$

   a. $\left\{\frac{3}{2}\right\}$ **b.** $\{2, 3\}$ **c.** $\{6\}$ **d.** no solution

10. State the domain (D) and the range (R) of the function $y = \sqrt{4 - x}$.

   a. $D = \{x: x \leqslant 4\}$, $R = \{y: y \geqslant 0\}$ **b.** $D = \{x: x \leqslant 4\}$, $R = \mathcal{R}$

   c. $D = \mathcal{R}$, $R = \mathcal{R}$ **d.** $D = \mathcal{R}$, $R = \{y: y \geqslant 0\}$

11. Simplify: $\dfrac{5}{\sqrt{7}+3}$

　　a. $\dfrac{5\sqrt{7}+15}{58}$　　　**b.** $\dfrac{\sqrt{7}-3}{8}$　　　**c.** $\dfrac{15-5\sqrt{7}}{2}$　　　**d.** $\dfrac{\sqrt{7}}{2}$

12. If $f(x) = |x + |x||$, find $f(-3)$.

　　a. 3　　　　　　　**b.** 0　　　　　　　**c.** 6　　　　　　　**d.** -6

13. Use the discriminant to describe the roots of $x^2 - x + 2 = 0$.

　　a. real, rational, and equal　　　　　**b.** real, rational, and unequal
　　c. real, irrational, and unequal　　　　**d.** imaginary

14. Find the solution set of $3x^2 - 9x + 6 = 0$.

　　a. $\{1, 2\}$　　　　**b.** $\{-1, -2\}$　　　　**c.** $\{3, 6\}$　　　　**d.** $\emptyset$

15. Write $3\sqrt{-81} + 4\sqrt{49} - 6i$ in the form $a + bi$.

　　a. $28 - 33i$　　　**b.** $1 - 6i$　　　**c.** $28 + 21i$　　　**d.** $28 + 3i$

16. Which answer describes the solution set of $-4(x - 5) > 16$?

　　a. 　　　　**b.**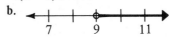

　　c. $\{x : x < 9\}$　　　　　　　　　**d.** $\{x : x < 1\}$

17. Find the solution set of the following inequality: $3x + 1 \geqslant 4$ or $13 > 5 - 4x$

　　a. $\{x : x > -2\}$　　　　　　　　**b.** $\{x : x \geqslant 1 \text{ or } x < -2\}$
　　c. $\{x : x \geqslant 1\}$　　　　　　　　**d.** $\{x : -2 < x \leqslant 1\}$

18. Which of the following is the graph of the solution set of $|4 - z| > 3$?

　　a.

```
 ◄──┼───●───┼───┼───●──►
   −1   1   3   5   7
```

　　b.

```
 ◄──┼───●───┼───┼───●──►
   −1   1   3   5   7
```

　　c.

```
 ◄──┼───┼───┼───┼───┼──►
   −1   1   3   5   7
```

　　d.

```
 ◄──●───┼───┼───●───┼──►
  −7  −5  −3  −1   1
```

19. Find the solution set of $|2x + 5| \leqslant 13$.

　　a. $\{x : x \geqslant -9 \text{ or } x \leqslant 4\}$　　　　**b.** $\{x : -9 \leqslant x \leqslant 4\}$
　　c. $\{x : -4 \leqslant x \leqslant 9\}$　　　　　　**d.** $\{x : -18 \leqslant x \leqslant 8\}$

20. Find the product of $4\sqrt{3} + 2i$ and its complex conjugate.

　　a. 192　　　　**b.** $8\sqrt{3}$　　　　**c.** $44 + 16i\sqrt{3}$　　　　**d.** 52

21. Simplify: $(3 - 5i)(2 + 3i)$

　　a. $21 - i$　　　**b.** $-9 - i$　　　**c.** $21 + 19i$　　　**d.** $21 + i$

22. Solve over the complex numbers: $9x^2 + 5x + 1 = 0$

　　a. $\left\{ \dfrac{5}{18} + \dfrac{\sqrt{11}}{18}, \ \dfrac{5}{18} - \dfrac{\sqrt{11}}{18} \right\}$　　　　**b.** $\left\{ -\dfrac{5}{2} + \dfrac{\sqrt{11}}{2}i, \ -\dfrac{5}{2} - \dfrac{\sqrt{11}}{2}i \right\}$

　　c. $\left\{ -\dfrac{5}{18} + \dfrac{\sqrt{11}}{18}i, \ -\dfrac{5}{18} - \dfrac{\sqrt{11}}{18}i \right\}$　　　　**d.** $\left\{ \dfrac{5}{18} + \dfrac{\sqrt{11}}{18}i, \ \dfrac{5}{18} - \dfrac{\sqrt{11}}{18}i \right\}$

23. Which expression is equivalent to $\dfrac{a^3 + a + 1}{a + 1}$?

    a. $a^2 + a + \dfrac{1}{a + 1}$ **b.** $a^2 - a + 2 - \dfrac{1}{a + 1}$

    c. $a^2 - a + 1$ **d.** $a^2 - a + 2$

24. Simplify: $\dfrac{1}{x} + \dfrac{1+x}{x^2} - \dfrac{5}{3x}$

    a. $\dfrac{x - 3}{3x^2}$ **b.** $\dfrac{3 + x}{3x^2}$ **c.** $\dfrac{1 - 3x}{x^2}$ **d.** $\dfrac{x - 3}{3x^4}$

25. Simplify: $\dfrac{\dfrac{1}{x} - \dfrac{1}{x^2}}{\dfrac{2}{x^2} - \dfrac{2}{x^3}}$

    a. $\dfrac{x}{2}$ **b.** $\dfrac{x^2 - x}{2x - 2}$ **c.** $\dfrac{x - 1}{2x - 2}$ **d.** $\dfrac{1}{2}$

26. Find the solution set of $\dfrac{7}{x^2} - \dfrac{5}{x} = 2$.

    a. $\left\{ -\dfrac{1}{2}, 7 \right\}$ **b.** $\left\{ \dfrac{7}{2}, -1 \right\}$ **c.** $\left\{ \dfrac{1}{2}, -7 \right\}$ **d.** $\left\{ -\dfrac{7}{2}, 1 \right\}$

27. If $f(x) = \dfrac{4}{x^2}$ and $g(x) = \sqrt{x}$, then $g\left(f\left(-\dfrac{1}{2} \right) \right)$ is:

    a. 4   **b.** undefined   **c.** 2   **d.** 1

28. Find the standard form of the multiplicative inverse of $1 - 2i$.

    a. $\dfrac{1}{1 - 2i}$ **b.** $\dfrac{1}{5} + \dfrac{2}{5}i$ **c.** $1 - \dfrac{1}{2}i$ **d.** $\dfrac{1}{5} - \dfrac{2}{5}i$

29. If $f(x) = 4x + 3$, then $f^{-1}(x) = \underline{\quad?\quad}$.

    a. $\dfrac{x - 3}{4}$ **b.** $\dfrac{1}{4x + 3}$ **c.** $\dfrac{1}{4}x + \dfrac{1}{3}$ **d.** $\dfrac{x}{4} - 3$

30. Find a quadratic equation whose roots are $1 + i$ and $1 - i$.

    a. $x^2 - 2x - 2 = 0$ **b.** $x^2 + 2x + 2 = 0$ **c.** $x^2 + 2x - 2 = 0$ **d.** $x^2 - 2x + 2 = 0$

31. Find the solution set of $x^2 + 2x > 0$.

    a. $\{ x : x > 0 \}$ **b.** $\{ x : -2 < x < 0 \}$

    c. $\{ x : x < -2 \text{ or } x > 0 \}$ **d.** $\{ x : x < 0 \text{ or } x > 2 \}$

32. Find the solution set of $x^3 + 5x^2 - 6x \leqslant 0$.

    a. $\{ x : -6 \leqslant x \leqslant 0 \text{ or } x \geqslant 1 \}$ **b.** $\{ x : x \leqslant -6 \text{ or } 0 \leqslant x \leqslant 1 \}$

    c. $\{ x : -6 \leqslant x \leqslant 1 \}$ **d.** $\{ x : x \leqslant -1 \text{ or } 0 \leqslant x \leqslant 6 \}$

33. Translate into an inequality: The sum of three integers is at least 40. The second integer is 5 more than three times the first. The third integer is 3 more than half the second.

    a. $x + (5 + 3x) + \left[3 + \dfrac{1}{2}(5 + 3x) \right] \geqslant 40$ **b.** $x + (5 + 3x) + \left(3 + \dfrac{1}{2}x \right) \geqslant 40$

    c. $x + (5 + 3x) + \left[3 + \dfrac{1}{2}(5 + 3x) \right] > 40$ **d.** $x + (5 + 3x) + \left(3 + \dfrac{1}{2}x \right) \leqslant 40$

Application — Mathematics and Music

Musical instruments produce complicated sound waves that can be represented by mathematical equations. Notice in the diagrams below that different musical instruments, such as (a) the violin, (b) the trumpet, and (c) the clarinet, produce distinctive periodic patterns.

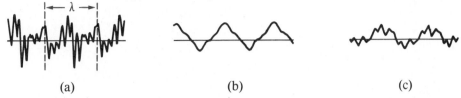

      (a)   (b)   (c)

A musical sound has a definite wavelength, which is measured from a point on the sound wave to the point where the pattern starts to repeat. One wavelength, represented by λ, is indicated on diagram (a) above. For a tone of middle C traveling through air, the wavelength is about 1.2 m. The wavelength of a musical note can be found by dividing the speed of the sound by its frequency. The speed of the sound depends on the medium through which it travels and the temperature of the medium. At 20°C sound travels through air at about 343 m/s. At higher temperatures sound travels more quickly.

The frequency of a musical tone is the number of sound waves occurring per second. Pitch is determined by frequency and is higher when the frequency is higher. Thus, middle C played in air has a frequency of about 261.6 Hz (hertz), while the A above middle C has a frequency of 440.0 Hz. Since a note an octave higher has twice the frequency of the lower note, the C an octave above middle C has a frequency of about 523.2 Hz.

Today computers can be programmed to produce musical sounds made by conventional instruments, as well as sounds that cannot be created by any other means, thus enabling composers to create ensemble effects never before possible. Computers can also be used to reduce the time and effort involved in writing out musical compositions. Composers can create their works by arranging notes and other musical symbols on a staff displayed on a video screen. The computer can even play the composition back, so that the composer

can hear how it sounds! Music can be transposed and measures of music moved to another part of the composition by merely pressing buttons. When the composer is satisfied with the composition, the musical score can be printed.

Be sure that you understand the meaning of these terms:

function (mapping), p. 135
domain of a function, p. 135
image, p. 135
pre-image, p. 135
range of a function, p. 135
relation, p. 138
linear function, p. 142
polynomial function, p. 142

odd function, p. 143
even function, p. 143
composite function, p. 153
identity function, p. 153
inverse functions, p. 153
one-to-one function, p. 154
power functions, p. 155

MIXED REVIEW

1. If $f(x) = \sqrt[3]{x}$, estimate $\sqrt[3]{37}$ to the nearest tenth by interpolating between $\sqrt[3]{27}$ and $\sqrt[3]{64}$.

2. Divide $6x^3 - 11x^2y - 3xy^2 + 2y^3$ by $3x - y$.

Solve for x over the set of complex numbers.

3. $3x^2 - 6x = 1$

4. $x^2 + 4x + 20 = 0$

5. $4x^2 + 100 = 0$

6. If $-\dfrac{1}{3}$ is a root of $3kx^2 - kx - 2 = 0$, find the other root and the value of k.

7. If $f(x) = 1 - x^2$ and $g(x) = \sqrt{x + 3}$, find **(a)** $f(g(1))$, **(b)** $g(f(1))$, and **(c)** a simplified formula for $f(g(x))$.

Solve.

8. $|7 - 2(3x - 1)| \leqslant 3$

9. $\sqrt{5 - t} = \sqrt{8 + t} + 1$

10. $-\dfrac{2}{3}y < 24$ or $2.5y \leqslant 3.1 + 0.02y$

11. Given the relation $y = |2x - 1|$, **(a)** state whether or not it is a function, **(b)** state whether or not it is one-to-one, **(c)** give the domain, **(d)** give the range, **(e)** graph the relation, and **(f)** give the image of -1.

Simplify.

12. $\dfrac{2i}{\sqrt{-6} \cdot \sqrt{-12}}$

13. $\dfrac{1 - i}{1 + i}$

14. $\sqrt{98} - \dfrac{1}{\sqrt{32}}$

15. $\dfrac{\sqrt{20}}{\sqrt{5} - 2}$

16. $\dfrac{1 + \dfrac{2}{x}}{\dfrac{4}{x^2} + \dfrac{2}{x}}$

17. $\left(\dfrac{(-2)^3 \cdot x^{-3}y^0z^2}{4^{-2} \cdot x \cdot z^{-3}} \right)^{-1}$

18. Find and graph the solution set of $x^3 - x^2 > 12x$.

Evaluate when $a = 0.5$, $b = -3$, and $c = 4$.

19. $ac^2 - 3b$

20. $\dfrac{2b + c}{a}$

21. $b^3 + c^2$

22. Two sides of a triangle each have length 8. Between what two values must the perimeter lie?

23. The base of a certain triangle is 3 cm longer than each side of a square. The height of the triangle is 1 cm less than the length of the base of the triangle. If the square and the triangle have equal areas, how long is each side of the square?

Simplify.

24. $\dfrac{5}{b^2 - 3b - 4} + \dfrac{1}{b^2 + 3b + 2}$

25. $\dfrac{2m^2n^2 - mn^3}{m^2 - 4n^2} \cdot \dfrac{m^2 + 4mn + 4n^2}{2m^2 + 3m - 2n^2}$

26. Use the discriminant to determine the number and nature of the roots of $8x - 1 = -2x^2$.

27. Find the sum and the product of $-2 + 7i$ and $3 - 6i$.

28. If $f(x) = \dfrac{1}{2}x^4 + |x|$, find **(a)** $f(4)$, **(b)** $f(-4)$, and **(c)** $f(-x)$, and **(d)** state whether f is odd, even, or neither.

29. Find the inverse of the function $g(x) = \dfrac{1}{x - 3}$. Then show that $[g \circ g^{-1}](x) = [g^{-1} \circ g](x) = x$.

Solve.

30. $|y - 5| = 2$

31. $\dfrac{2}{m} - \dfrac{1}{2m + 1} = \dfrac{m + 1}{2m^2 + m}$

32. $8z^2 + 10z = 63$

33. Two numbers have the ratio $3:4$ and the sum 105. Find the numbers.

34. Find the value of k if $y = kx^2 - 2$ and $4 \to 22$.

35. Show that $-2 - i\sqrt{3}$ is a root of $x^2 + 4x + 7 = 0$. What is the other root?

36. If $g(-2) = -4$ and $g(3) = 26$, use linear interpolation to estimate the value of x when $g(x) = 5$.

37. Graph the relation $x = |y + 2|$ and explain why the relation is not a function.

Transformations are geometric functions that can be used to describe the "motion" of a set of points. The movement of the impala ram shown above from one spot on the plain to another suggests a transformation.

168

Transformations   5

A figure is said to be *symmetric* if it is its own image under a certain kind of *transformation*, or geometric function. Our world is full of examples of symmetry.

In reaction to the force of gravity that pulls everything toward the center of Earth, many living things—for example, people, animals, trees—possess vertical symmetry. Look at yourself in a mirror. There exists an imaginary vertical line (called a *line of symmetry*) that passes through the reflection of your body and divides it into two congruent halves that would match each other if the reflection were folded on this line.

To find natural examples of *rotational symmetry*, try to think of things whose existences are *not* struggles against the vertical pull of gravity. Snowflakes, starfish, and many types of flower blossoms exhibit rotational symmetry. It is generally true that only very small creatures (such as the amoeba) show a complete lack of symmetry.

Objects created by people also exhibit symmetry. Take a close look around you. How many objects can you see that have vertical symmetry? How about your chair? Your desk? Your pencil? In the English alphabet, more letters possess line symmetry (vertical or horizontal) than rotational symmetry or no symmetry. You can even find words that possess symmetry, as shown below.

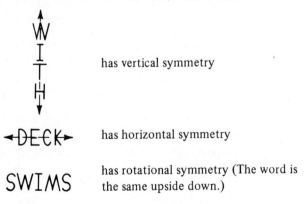

has vertical symmetry

has horizontal symmetry

has rotational symmetry (The word is the same upside down.)

Section 5-1 TRANSFORMATIONS

In Chapter 4 you studied functions and their graphs. In this chapter you will study certain geometric functions called *transformations*. These transformations can be thought of as "motions" of sets of points in a plane. In this section you will learn about:

- transformations
- composites of transformations
- transformations that preserve distances

A *transformation* is a one-to-one mapping whose domain and range are the points of the plane. Every point of the plane has exactly one image and every point has exactly one pre-image. To indicate that transformation T maps A onto A' (read "A prime"), we can write either

$$T: A \longrightarrow A' \quad \text{or} \quad T(A) = A'.$$

Primes are often used to indicate the images of points. For example, the image of A' under a second transformation might be called A'' (read "A double prime").

EXAMPLES OF TRANSFORMATIONS

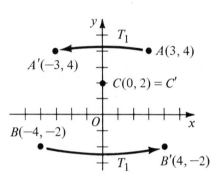

1. The images of three points under the mapping
$$T_1: (x, y) \longrightarrow (-x, y)$$
are shown. Notice that the image of $(0, 2)$ is $(0, 2)$.

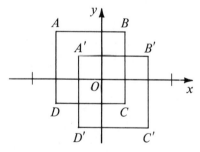

2. The mapping
$$T_2: (x, y) \longrightarrow (x + 1, y - 1)$$
moves points a fixed distance diagonally downward and to the right.

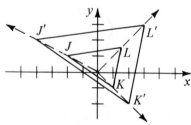

3. The mapping
$$T_3: (x, y) \longrightarrow (2x, 2y)$$
moves each point outward along the ray whose endpoint is the origin and which contains the given point. The image of (x, y) is twice as far from the origin as is (x, y).

4. The mapping

$$T_4:(x, y) \longrightarrow (-y, x)$$

moves a point to its image by rotating it counterclockwise through an angle of $90°$ about the origin. Note that the image of $(0, 0)$ is $(0, 0)$.

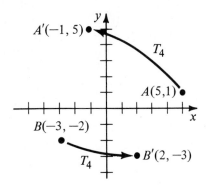

5. Under the mapping $T_5:(x, y) \longrightarrow (x^3, y^3)$, we have:

$$A(-2, 1) \longrightarrow A'(-8, 1)$$
$$B(-2, -2) \longrightarrow B'(-8, -8)$$
$$C(1, 1) \longrightarrow C'(1, 1)$$
$$D\left(\frac{1}{2}, -\frac{1}{2}\right) \longrightarrow D'\left(\frac{1}{8}, -\frac{1}{8}\right)$$

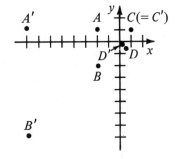

Not all functions that map the plane into itself are transformations. For example, consider the function

$$F:(x, y) \longrightarrow (|x|, |y|).$$

Every point in the plane has a unique image under this absolute value function. However, as the diagram shows, it is not a one-to-one function, and thus cannot be a transformation. Similarly, $G:(x, y) \longrightarrow (x^2, y^2)$ is not a transformation, since, for example:

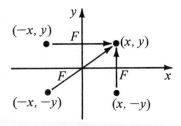

$$G:(0, 2) \longrightarrow (0, 4) \quad \text{and} \quad G:(0, -2) \longrightarrow (0, 4)$$

To verify that a function which maps the plane onto itself is a transformation, you must show that it is one-to-one. That is, you must show that each point has a unique pre-image. Another way to think of this is: If $A'(x_1', y_1') = B'(x_2', y_2')$, then $A(x_1, y_1) = B(x_2, y_2)$.

EXAMPLE Verify that

$$T_1:(x, y) \longrightarrow (-x, y)$$

is one-to-one.

SOLUTION If $(-x_1, y_1) = (-x_2, y_2)$, then

$$-x_1 = -x_2 \quad \text{and} \quad y_1 = y_2.$$

Thus
$$x_1 = x_2 \quad \text{and} \quad y_1 = y_2,$$

or
$$(x_1, y_1) = (x_2, y_2).$$

You will verify that $T_2, T_3, T_4,$ and T_5 are one-to-one in Exercises 27–30.

The special transformation that maps each point of the plane onto itself is called the *identity* transformation, denoted I.

Two transformations can be combined using the operation of composition to form a new transformation. If S and T are transformations such that $T: A \longrightarrow A'$ and $S: A' \longrightarrow A''$, then the composite $S \circ T$ is the transformation that maps A onto A''.

EXAMPLES OF COMPOSITES OF TRANSFORMATIONS

1. If $T_4:(x, y) \longrightarrow (-y, x)$, then
   $T_4:(-y, x) \longrightarrow (-x, -y)$, and

   $$T_4 \circ T_4:(x, y) \longrightarrow (-x, -y).$$

   Thus $T_4 \circ T_4$ rotates points $180°$ counterclockwise about the origin.

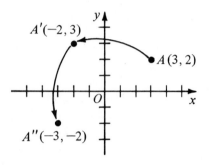

2. If $T_1:(x, y) \longrightarrow (-x, y)$, then $T_1:(-x, y) \longrightarrow (x, y)$, and

   $$T_1 \circ T_1:(x, y) \longrightarrow (x, y).$$

   Hence $T_1 \circ T_1$ is another name for the identity transformation, and T_1 is its own *inverse*. That is, $T_1^{-1} = T_1$.

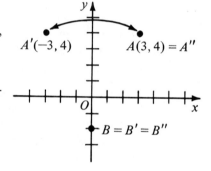

3. If $T_2:(x, y) \longrightarrow (x + 1, y - 1)$ and
   $T_3:(x, y) \longrightarrow (2x, 2y)$, then
   $T_2:(2x, 2y) \longrightarrow (2x + 1, 2y - 1)$, and

   $$T_2 \circ T_3:(x, y) \longrightarrow (2x + 1, 2y - 1).$$

   As you will see in Exercise 20, $T_3 \circ T_2$ is different from $T_2 \circ T_3$.

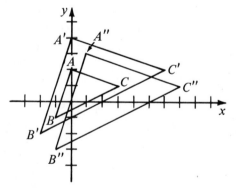

A transformation is called an *isometry* when it preserves distances; that is, when the distance between any two points is the same as the distance between their images. In the exercise set you will show that the transformations T_1, T_2, and T_4 defined earlier are isometries, but that T_3 is not.

172   *CHAPTER 5*

In addition to preserving distances between points, many isometries preserve the *orientation*, or relative position, of points. To determine whether an isometry preserves orientation, we must consider its effect on any three points. Orientation of points is either clockwise or counterclockwise, as illustrated below.

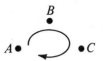

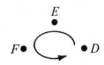

A, B, and *C* are oriented clockwise.   *D, E*, and *F* are oriented counterclockwise.

Those isometries that map points onto points having the same orientation are called *direct* isometries. Those that map points onto points having the opposite orientation are called *nondirect* isometries. Of the transformations discussed in this section, T_2 and T_4 are direct isometries and T_1 is a nondirect isometry.

ORAL EXERCISES

State whether the function is a transformation.

1. $T(x, y) = (y, x)$
2. $T(x, y) = (-y, -x)$
3. $T(x, y) = (-x, -y)$
4. $T(x, y) = (x, -y)$
5. $T(x, y) = (x, 2y)$
6. $T(x, y) = (2x, y)$
7. $T(x, y) = (x^5, y^5)$
8. $T(x, y) = (x^4, y^4)$
9. $T(x, y) = (x + 2, y - 2)$
10. $T(x, y) = (-2x, -2y)$
11. $T(x, y) = (\sqrt{|x|}, \sqrt{|y|})$
12. $T(x, y) = (|x + 1|, |y + 1|)$

Classify as true or false.

13. All transformations are isometries.   14. All functions are transformations.

15. All transformations are functions.

16. All isometries preserve distances between points in the plane.

17. All isometries preserve the orientation of points.

WRITTEN EXERCISES

Find the coordinates of the images of $A(0, 6)$, $B(-4, -2)$, and $C(4, -2)$ under the given transformation.

A 1. $T:(x, y) \longrightarrow (y, x)$
2. $T:(x, y) \longrightarrow (-x, y)$
3. $T:(x, y) \longrightarrow (3x, 3y)$

4. $T:(x, y) \longrightarrow \left(x, \dfrac{y}{2}\right)$
5. $T:(x, y) \longrightarrow (x - 2, y + 2)$
6. $T:(x, y) \longrightarrow (-y, x)$

7. $T:(x, y) \longrightarrow (-x, 2y)$
8. $T:(x, y) \longrightarrow (2x, -y)$
9. $T:(x, y) \longrightarrow (x^3, y)$

10. Which of the transformations in Exercises 1-9
    a. are isometries?   b. are direct isometries?   c. are nondirect isometries?

11-19. Find the coordinates of the pre-image P of the point $P'(-3, 1)$ under each transformation listed in Exercises 1-9.

B 20. If $T_2 : (x, y) \longrightarrow (x + 1, y - 1)$ and $T_3 : (x, y) \longrightarrow (2x, 2y)$, determine:

  a. the coordinates of the images of $A(0, 2)$, $B(-1, -1)$, and $C(3, 1)$ under $T_3 \circ T_2$

  b. a formula for $T_3 \circ T_2$

In Exercises 21–26 determine:

a. the coordinates of the image of $(6, -4)$ under $S \circ T$ **b.** a formula for $S \circ T$

21. $S : (x, y) \longrightarrow (y, x)$

   $T : (x, y) \longrightarrow (x - 2, y + 2)$

22. $S : (x, y) \longrightarrow (x + 5, 2y)$

   $T : (x, y) \longrightarrow \left(\frac{x}{2}, -y\right)$

23. $S : (x, y) \longrightarrow (y, -x)$

   $T : (x, y) \longrightarrow (-y, x)$

24. $S : (x, y) \longrightarrow (-y, x)$

   $T : (x, y) \longrightarrow (y, -x)$

25. $S : (x, y) \longrightarrow (y - 1, x + 1)$

   $T : (x, y) \longrightarrow (x^3, y^3)$

26. $S : (x, y) \longrightarrow (x^3, y^3)$

   $T : (x, y) \longrightarrow (y - 1, x + 1)$

Verify that the given function is one-to-one.

27. $T_2 : (x, y) \longrightarrow (x + 1, y - 1)$

28. $T_3 : (x, y) \longrightarrow (2x, 2y)$

29. $T_4 : (x, y) \longrightarrow (-y, x)$

30. $T_5 : (x, y) \longrightarrow (x^3, y^3)$

Graph $\overline{AB}$ with endpoints $A(2, -1)$ and $B(4, 5)$ and its image $\overline{A'B'}$ under the given transformation. Then describe the relationship between the slopes of $\overline{AB}$ and $\overline{A'B'}$.

31. $T_1 : (x, y) \longrightarrow (-x, y)$

32. $T_2 : (x, y) \longrightarrow (x + 1, y - 1)$

33. $T_3 : (x, y) \longrightarrow (2x, 2y)$

34. $T_4 : (x, y) \longrightarrow (-y, x)$

Use the distance formula

$$AB = \sqrt{(x_1 - x_2)^2 + (y_1 - y_2)^2},$$

where A and B have coordinates (x_1, y_1) and (x_2, y_2), to determine whether the given transformation is an isometry.

C 35. $T_1 : (x, y) \longrightarrow (-x, y)$

37. $T_3 : (x, y) \longrightarrow (2x, 2y)$

36. $T_2 : (x, y) \longrightarrow (x + 1, y - 1)$

38. $T_4 : (x, y) \longrightarrow (-y, x)$

Section 5-2 LINE REFLECTIONS

You are already familiar with the concept of reflection in a flat surface, or plane. Examples of reflective surfaces include a mirror, a calm lake, a clean plate, and the hood of a waxed automobile. In this section you will study a slightly different kind of reflection, a *reflection over a line* such as that created by folding a paper with wet ink. You will learn how to:

- construct the image of a point under a line reflection
- determine the coordinates of an image under a line reflection in a coordinate plane

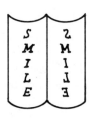

A *reflection over line l* is the transformation that maps:

1. any point A not on l onto the point A' such that l is the perpendicular bisector of $\overline{AA'}$
2. any point B on l onto itself

Line l is called the *reflecting line*, or *mirror line*, of the reflection. We will denote the line reflection over l by r_l. Thus, to show that the reflection of A over line l is A', you could write either

$$r_l(A) = A' \quad \text{or} \quad r_l : A \longrightarrow A'.$$

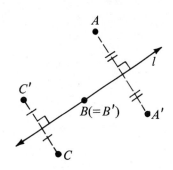

If point A does not lie on line l, you can use a compass and straightedge to construct its image, A', under r_l.

1. With center at A, draw an arc that intersects line l at two points, B and C.
2. With B and C as centers and the *same* radius as in the previous step, construct arcs that intersect at point A'.

Do you see why A' is the image of A under r_l? The justification is left as Oral Exercise 14.

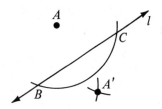

When you construct the image of a point under a line reflection, you can check your construction by folding your paper along the reflecting line. The image and pre-image should then coincide. This suggests the following theorems about line reflections:

Theorem 5-1   If $r_l(A) = A'$, then $r_l(A') = A$.

Corollary 1 $r_l \circ r_l = I$

Corollary 2 $r_l^{-1} = r_l$

As the following examples show, it is fairly easy to determine the coordinates of an image under certain line reflections in the coordinate plane.

EXAMPLE   Find the coordinates of the images of the points

$$A(-1, 1) \quad B(3, 5) \quad C(4, -2) \quad D(5, 0) \quad E(-3, -5) \quad F(0, -3)$$

when the points are reflected over the:

a. *x*-axis   **b.** *y*-axis

SOLUTION   **a.** $r_{x\text{-axis}}$: $A(-1, 1) \longrightarrow A'(-1, -1)$
$r_{x\text{-axis}}$: $B(3, 5) \longrightarrow B'(3, -5)$
$r_{x\text{-axis}}$: $C(4, -2) \longrightarrow C'(4, 2)$
$r_{x\text{-axis}}$: $D(5, 0) \longrightarrow D'(5, 0)$
$r_{x\text{-axis}}$: $E(-3, -5) \longrightarrow E'(-3, 5)$
$r_{x\text{-axis}}$: $F(0, -3) \longrightarrow F'(0, 3)$

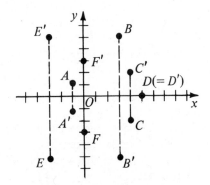

(Solution continued on the next page.)

b. $r_{y\text{-axis}}: A(-1, 1) \longrightarrow A'(1, 1)$
$r_{y\text{-axis}}: B(3, 5) \longrightarrow B'(-3, 5)$
$r_{y\text{-axis}}: C(4, -2) \longrightarrow C'(-4, -2)$
$r_{y\text{-axis}}: D(5, 0) \longrightarrow D'(-5, 0)$
$r_{y\text{-axis}}: E(-3, -5) \longrightarrow E'(3, -5)$
$r_{y\text{-axis}}: F(0, -3) \longrightarrow F'(0, -3)$

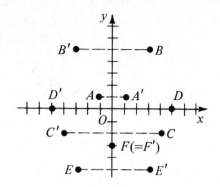

As the preceding example suggests:

$$r_{x\text{-axis}}: (x, y) \longrightarrow (x, -y)$$
$$r_{y\text{-axis}}: (x, y) \longrightarrow (-x, y)$$

The next example uses the fact, which you may recall from a previous course, that two nonvertical lines are perpendicular if and only if the product of their slopes is -1.

EXAMPLE   Find the coordinates of the images of the points

$$A(-1, 1) \quad B(3, 5) \quad C(4, -2) \quad D(5, 0) \quad E(-3, -5) \quad F(0, -3)$$

when the points are reflected over the line k with equation $y = x$.

SOLUTION   The line k with equation $y = x$ has slope 1, so any line segment perpendicular to it has slope -1. To find the image of $A(-1, 1)$, for example, you can count "diagonal units" along the line with equation $y = -x$. The distance from A to line k is 1 "diagonal unit," and $A'(1, -1)$ is the point 1 "diagonal unit" on the other side of k.

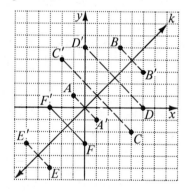

$r_k: A(-1, 1) \longrightarrow A'(1, -1)$
$r_k: B(3, 5) \longrightarrow B'(5, 3)$
$r_k: C(4, -2) \longrightarrow C'(-2, 4)$
$r_k: D(5, 0) \longrightarrow D'(0, 5)$
$r_k: E(-3, -5) \longrightarrow E'(-5, -3)$
$r_k: F(0, -3) \longrightarrow F'(-3, 0)$

As the preceding example suggests, if k is the line with equation $y = x$, then

$$r_k: (x, y) \longrightarrow (y, x).$$

In the exercises you will investigate some other line reflections in the coordinate plane.

The technique used to construct the image of a point under a reflection over a given line is similar to constructions you learned in previous courses. Some of the basic constructions that you will use in this chapter and Chapter 6 are reviewed on the next page.

176   *CHAPTER 5*

1. To construct a line segment congruent to a given line segment

2. To construct an angle congruent to a given angle

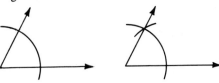

3. To construct the perpendicular bisector of a given line segment

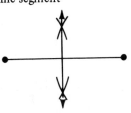

4. To construct the bisector of a given angle

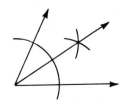

5. Given a line and a point not on the line, to construct the line perpendicular to the given line through the given point

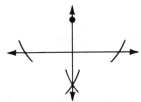

6. Given a line and a point on the line, to construct the line perpendicular to the given line through the given point

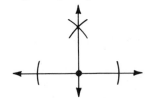

ORAL EXERCISES

State the coordinates of the image of the given point under:

a. $r_{x\text{-axis}}$ b. $r_{y\text{-axis}}$ c. r_k, where k has equation $y = x$

1. A 2. B 3. C
4. D 5. E 6. F

Classify as true or false.

7. A line reflection is a transformation.

8. A line reflection and its inverse have the same reflecting line.

9. If $r_l(P) = Q$ and $P \neq Q$, then $\overline{PQ}$ is parallel to line l.

10. If $r_l(A) = B$, then $r_l(B) = A$.

11. If $r_l(A) = B$ and $A \neq B$, then the midpoint of $\overline{AB}$ lies on line l.

12. If $r_l(A) \neq A$, then A lies on line l.

13. If $r_l(A) = B$, then $r_l^{-1}(A) = B$.

14. Explain why in the construction on page 175 A' is the image of A under r_l.

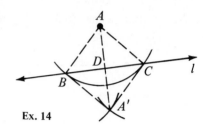

Ex. 14

15. Given two points, P and P', explain how you would construct the reflecting line n so that $r_n: P \longrightarrow P'$.

WRITTEN EXERCISES

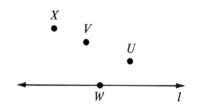

A 1. Draw a figure similar to, but larger than, that shown. Then construct the images of points U, V, W, and X under r_l. (X, V, and U are collinear.)

2. Draw two points, P and P', and then construct the reflecting line for the reflection that maps P onto P'.

Find the coordinates of the image of each point under: a. $r_{\text{x-axis}}$ b. $r_{\text{y-axis}}$

3. $(0, -7)$ 4. $(8, 0)$ 5. $(4, 3)$
6. $(-5, 2)$ 7. $(-6, -1)$ 8. $(3, -4)$

Find the coordinates of the image of each point under the reflection r_k, where k has equation $y = x$.

9. $(-2, 0)$ 10. $(1, 6)$ 11. $(3, -4)$ 12. $(0, 9)$

Graph each point and find the coordinates of the image under the reflection r_n, where n has equation $y = -x$.

13. $(-2, 0)$ 14. $(1, 6)$ 15. $(3, -4)$ 16. $(0, 9)$

17. Complete: If n has equation $y = -x$, then $r_n:(x, y) \longrightarrow$ __?__ .

18. Complete: If n has equation $y = -x$, then $r_n:(-3, 3) \longrightarrow$ __?__ .

Graph the line with the given equation and determine the coordinates of the images when the following points are reflected over the line.

$A(2, 5)$ $B(4, -2)$ $C(-2, -3)$ $D(0, 3)$

19. $y = 3$ 20. $x = 3$ 21. $x = -2$ 22. $y = -2$

Graph the line with the given equation and determine the coordinates of the images when the following points are reflected over the line.

$A(2, 5)$ $B(4, -2)$ $C(-2, -3)$ $D(0, 3)$

B 23. $y = x + 2$ 24. $y = x - 1$ 25. $y = -x + 2$ 26. $y = -x - 3$

Find the coordinates of the image of (x, y) when it is reflected over the given line. (*Hint:* The midpoint of the line segment whose endpoints are (x, y) and its image (x', y') lies on the given line.)

27. $y = 3$ 28. $x = 3$ 29. $x = -2$ 30. $y = -2$

A line reflection maps the first point onto the second point. Graph the two points and determine the equation of the reflecting line.

31. $(2, 0) \longrightarrow (6, 0)$ **32.** $(5, 3) \longrightarrow (5, 5)$

33. $(-2, 1) \longrightarrow (1, -2)$ **34.** $(-3, 4) \longrightarrow (3, 4)$

35. $(2, -7) \longrightarrow (2, 7)$ **36.** $(4, 2) \longrightarrow (-2, -4)$

37. $(2, 1) \longrightarrow (0, 3)$ **38.** $(3, 0) \longrightarrow (1, 2)$

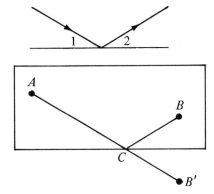

Certain games of skill such as billiards, miniature golf, and many of the new electronic games use reflections to execute *bank shots*. These shots are based on a fundamental principle: the *angle of incidence* ($\angle 1$) equals the *angle of reflection* ($\angle 2$).

For example, to plan a bank shot in billiards from point A to point B, you must aim for B', the image of point B reflected in the closest edge. Assuming the ball will roll freely without picking up any spin, this will allow the ball to hit the edge of the table at point C, where the ball will rebound correctly to point B. Since

$$AB' = AC + CB' = AC + CB,$$

it follows that the path along $\overline{AC}$ and $\overline{CB}$ represents the shortest path from A to B via the edge of the table. This fact enables us to apply the concept of the bank shot to other situations as well.

C **39.** What is the shortest distance from $A(1, 4)$ to $B(9, 2)$ along a path that includes a point on the x-axis? (*Hint*: Reflect point B in the x-axis, and then use the distance formula to find the length of the path from A to C to B.)

40. To what point on the y-axis should a ball be aimed in order to bank the ball from $A(2, 3)$ to $B(4, -9)$?

41. Two antenna towers, 400 m apart, are to be supported by a single cable anchored at a common point between them. One tower is 20 m high, and the other tower is 60 m high. At what point should the anchor be located to use a minimum amount of cable?

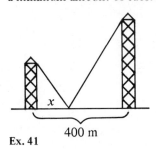

Ex. 41

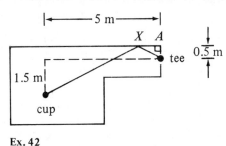

Ex. 42

42. In the diagram of the miniature golf hole shown, X is the point along the upper border where you aim in order to reflect the ball into the cup for a hole in one. What is the distance between X and A?

Section 5-3 LINE SYMMETRY

A figure is said to have *line symmetry* if there exists a line *l* such that the figure and its image under r_l coincide. Such a reflecting line is referred to as a *line of symmetry*, an *axis of symmetry*, or simply a *symmetry line* for the figure, which is *symmetric with respect to* the reflecting line.

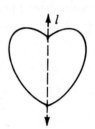

In this section you will learn to:
- recognize and locate lines of symmetry
- classify figures according to their lines of symmetry

EXAMPLES OF LINE SYMMETRIC FIGURES

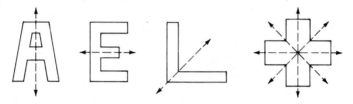

Notice that a figure may have more than one line of symmetry.

Many geometric figures have line symmetry. Can you name each figure shown in the following examples?

EXAMPLES OF GEOMETRIC FIGURES THAT ARE LINE SYMMETRIC

One line of symmetry:

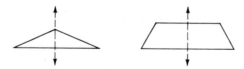

Two lines of symmetry:

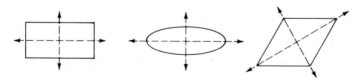

Three lines of symmetry: *Four* lines of symmetry:

EXAMPLE Determine all lines of symmetry for each figure. The figures in (b) and (c) are regular polygons.

a.

b.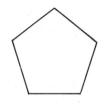

c.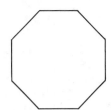

SOLUTION

a.

b.

c.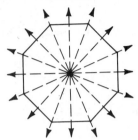

As suggested by parts (b) and (c), a regular n-gon has n lines of symmetry.

The graphs of many relations also have line symmetry. Most noteworthy among them are the graphs of the *conic sections*: circles, ellipses, parabolas, and hyperbolas. Certain other graphs and curves that you have studied also have line symmetry.

EXAMPLE Sketch all lines of symmetry.

a.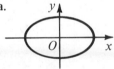

Ellipse
$$\frac{x^2}{25} + \frac{y^2}{9} = 1$$

b.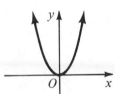

Parabola
$$y = x^2$$

c.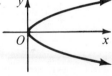

Parabola
$$x = y^2$$

d.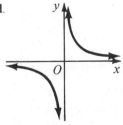

Hyperbola
$$xy = 1$$

e.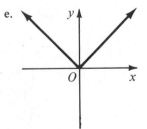

Absolute Value
$$y = |x|$$

f.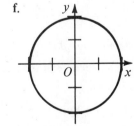

Circle
$$x^2 + y^2 = 4$$

(See next page for solution.)

SOLUTION

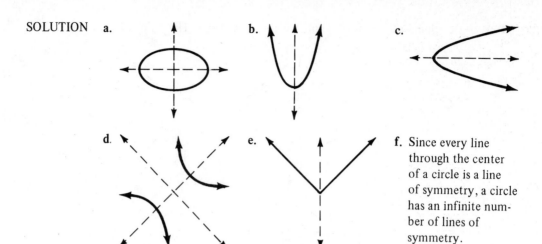

a.

b.

c.

d.

e.

f. Since every line through the center of a circle is a line of symmetry, a circle has an infinite number of lines of symmetry.

In Section 5-8 you will learn about three other kinds of symmetry.

ORAL EXERCISES

Determine the number of lines of symmetry in each of the following. State whether the symmetry lines are vertical, horizontal, or neither.

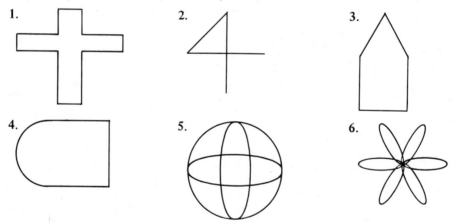

1.

2.

3.

4.

5.

6.

State the *number* of lines of symmetry each figure possesses.

7. an equilateral triangle

8. an isosceles triangle that is not equilateral

9. a square

10. a rectangle that is not a square

11. a rhombus

12. an isosceles trapezoid

13. a regular octagon

14. a regular decagon

15. a circle

16. an ellipse

17. a parabola

18. a hyperbola

WRITTEN EXERCISES

Trace each figure and sketch all lines of symmetry. If none exist, so state.

A 1.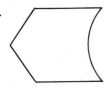

2.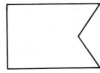

3.

4.

5.

6.

7.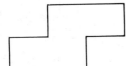

8.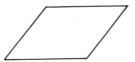

9.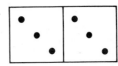

10.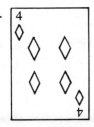

11.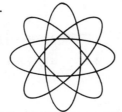

12.

Name a geometric figure that satisfies each description.

13. A triangle with exactly one line of symmetry.

14. A triangle with three lines of symmetry.

15. A quadrilateral with four lines of symmetry.

16. A quadrilateral with two diagonal lines of symmetry.

17. A quadrilateral with only one line of symmetry.

18. A geometric figure with an infinite number of lines of symmetry.

19. A triangle in which a median is a line of symmetry.

20. A triangle in which an angle bisector is a line of symmetry.

21. A triangle in which an altitude is a line of symmetry.

22. A quadrilateral in which an angle bisector is a line of symmetry.

23. Which capital letters of the alphabet have a horizontal line of symmetry?

24. Which capital letters of the alphabet have a vertical line of symmetry?

25. Which capital letters of the alphabet have no lines of symmetry?

26. Which digits (0-9) have at least one line of symmetry?

Use graph paper to sketch the graph and its symmetry line. Then determine the equation of the symmetry line.

EXAMPLE $y = x^2 - 4x - 5$

SOLUTION   1. Sketch the graph.

2. Sketch the symmetry line.

3. Determine the equation of the symmetry line; the slope is undefined and the x-intercept is 2. Thus an equation of the line of symmetry is $x = 2$.

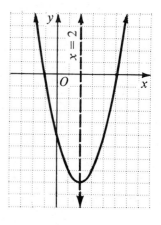

B 27. $y = x^2 + 3$ 28. $y = x^2 - 5$ 29. $x = y^2 + 6$ 30. $x = y^2 - 2$

31. $y = |x + 3|$ 32. $y = |x - 5|$ 33. $x = |y + 6|$ 34. $x = |y - 2|$

35. $y = \pm\sqrt{x + 3}$ 36. $x = \pm\sqrt{y - 1}$ 37. $y = 2x^2 - 6x$ 38. $y = x^2 + 6x + 9$

39. $y = x^2 - 3x - 4$ 40. $y = x^2 + 6x + 8$ 41. $x = y^2 - 4y + 1$ 42. $x = y^2 - 6y + 7$

Section 5-4 PROPERTIES OF LINE REFLECTIONS

Just as the image of a point A reflected over line l can be represented by $r_l(A)$, images of certain sets of points reflected over line l can be represented by notation such as:

$$r_l(\overleftrightarrow{AB}) \qquad r_l(\overline{AB}) \qquad r_l(\overrightarrow{AB}) \qquad r_l(\angle ABC)$$

EXAMPLE   Lines m and n are two of the six lines of symmetry for the regular hexagon $ABCDEF$. Find:

     a. $r_m(A)$ b. $r_n(A)$

     c. $r_m(\overline{AF})$ d. $r_n(\overline{AF})$

     e. $r_m(\angle AFE)$ f. $r_n(\angle AFE)$

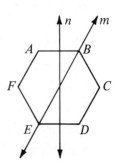

SOLUTION   a. $r_m(A) = C$ b. $r_n(A) = B$

     c. $r_m(\overline{AF}) = \overline{CD}$ d. $r_n(\overline{AF}) = \overline{BC}$

     e. $r_m(\angle AFE) = \angle CDE$ f. $r_n(\angle AFE) = \angle BCD$

EXAMPLE   Given that lines s, k, and l are lines of symmetry for the figure, find:

a. $r_l(\overline{AB})$

b. $r_k(\overline{AB})$

c. $r_k(\overline{EB})$

d. $r_k(\overline{AE})$

e. $r_k(\angle C)$

f. $r_s(\angle C)$

g. $r_l(\overrightarrow{GE})$

h. $r_k(\overleftrightarrow{HF})$

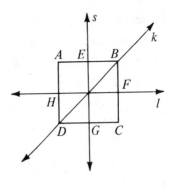

SOLUTION   a. $r_l(\overline{AB}) = \overline{DC}$

b. $r_k(\overline{AB}) = \overline{CB}$

c. $r_k(\overline{EB}) = \overline{FB}$

d. $r_k(\overline{AE}) = \overline{CF}$

e. $r_k(\angle C) = \angle A$

f. $r_s(\angle C) = \angle ADC$

g. $r_l(\overrightarrow{GE}) = \overrightarrow{EG}$

h. $r_k(\overleftrightarrow{HF}) = \overleftrightarrow{GE}$

These examples and your work in preceding sections suggest the following:

Properties of Line Reflections

1. Line reflections preserve collinearity of points.
   (If A, E, and B are collinear, then $r_l(A)$, $r_l(E)$, and $r_l(B)$ are collinear.)

2. Line reflections preserve betweenness.
   (If E is between A and B, then $r_l(E)$ is between $r_l(A)$ and $r_l(B)$.)

3. The image of a line segment under a line reflection is a line segment of the same length. Thus a line reflection preserves distances, and as such is an *isometry*.
   $$(r_l(\overline{AB}) \cong \overline{AB})$$

4. The line reflection of an angle is an angle of the same measure. Thus a line reflection preserves angle measure.
   $$(r_l(\angle C) \cong \angle C)$$

5. Line reflections preserve parallelism and perpendicularity of lines.
   (If $\overleftrightarrow{AD} \parallel \overleftrightarrow{BC}$ and $\overleftrightarrow{AD} \perp \overleftrightarrow{AB}$, then $r_l(\overleftrightarrow{AD}) \parallel r_l(\overleftrightarrow{BC})$ and $r_l(\overleftrightarrow{AD}) \perp r_l(\overleftrightarrow{AB})$.)

6. Under a line reflection, the orientation of points is *not* preserved, but is reversed. Thus a line reflection is a *nondirect isometry*.
   (A, B, and C are oriented counterclockwise if and only if $r_l(A)$, $r_l(B)$, and $r_l(C)$ are oriented clockwise.)

ORAL EXERCISES

Points E, D, and F are the images of A, B, and C, respectively, under r_l.

1. $r_l(\overrightarrow{AB}) = $ __?__

2. $r_l(\overline{BC}) = $ __?__

3. $r_l(\overline{AP}) = $ __?__

4. $r_l(\angle ABC) = $ __?__

5. $\overline{AP}$ is congruent to which segment?

6. $\angle BAC$ is congruent to which angle?

7. $\triangle ABC$ is congruent to which triangle? Why?

8. Describe the orientation of A, B, and C.

9. Describe the orientation of E, D, and F.

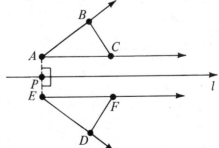

Determine whether each statement is *always, sometimes,* or *never* true.

10. A line reflection preserves the perimeter of a figure.

11. A line reflection preserves the area of a figure.

12. A line reflection preserves the orientation of points.

13. A line reflection preserves the slope of a line.

14. The reflected image of the midpoint of a segment is the midpoint of the image segment.

15. The reflected image of a horizontal line is horizontal.

Classify each statement as true or false.

16. A line reflection is a direct isometry.

17. If line j is perpendicular to line k, then $r_j(k) = j$.

18. If line j is perpendicular to line k, then $r_k(j) = j$.

19. If $r_l(A) = C$ and $r_l(B) = D$, then $AB = CD$.

20. If $r_l(A) = C$ and $r_l(B) = D$, then $AC = BD$.

WRITTEN EXERCISES

Draw a larger version of the figure shown, and use it to construct the image of the figure under r_l.

A   1.
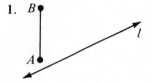

2.
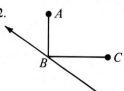

3.
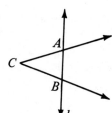

4.
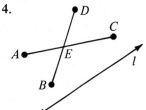

5.
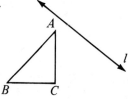

6.
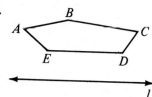

7.
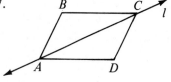

8.
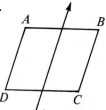

In the figure, $r_l(A) = E$, $r_l(B) = D$, $m\angle GBC = 30$, and $m\angle KAG = 58$. Determine the measure of the given angle.

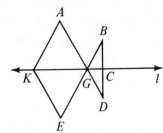

9. $\angle CDG$ 10. $\angle KEG$

11. $\angle BGC$ 12. $\angle AGK$

13. $\angle AKG$ 14. $\angle AKE$

Given that lines p and q are lines of symmetry for square $ABCD$, find:

15. $r_p(A)$ 16. $r_p(C)$

17. $r_q(A)$ 18. $r_q(C)$

19. $r_p(\overline{AB})$ 20. $r_q(\overline{AB})$

21. $r_p(\angle ADC)$ 22. $r_q(\angle ADC)$

23. $r_p(q)$ 24. $r_p(p)$

Given that lines k and m are lines of symmetry for regular pentagon $VWXYZ$, find:

25. $r_k(V)$ 26. $r_m(V)$ 27. $r_k(X)$

28. $r_m(X)$ 29. $r_k(Y)$ 30. $r_m(Y)$

31. $r_k(\overline{VW})$ 32. $r_m(\overline{VW})$ 33. $r_k(\overline{WX})$

34. $r_m(\overline{WX})$ 35. $r_k(\overline{XY})$ 36. $r_m(\overline{XY})$

37. $r_k(\angle ZVW)$ 38. $r_m(\angle ZVW)$ 39. $r_k(\angle W)$

40. $r_m(\angle W)$ 41. $r_k(\angle Z)$ 42. $r_m(\angle Z)$

43. If $P(3, 2)$ and $Q(3, 6)$ are reflected over the x-axis, find the coordinates of the midpoint of $\overline{P'Q'}$.

44. If $P(3, 2)$ and $V(5, 6)$ are reflected over the y-axis, find the coordinates of the midpoint of $\overline{P'V'}$.

B 45. If $P(3, 2)$ and $R(-1, 4)$ are reflected over the line k with equation $y = x$, find the coordinates of the midpoint of $\overline{P'R'}$.

46. If $P(3, 2)$ and $S(-3, 0)$ are reflected over the line n with equation $y = -x$, find the coordinates of the midpoint of $\overline{P'S'}$.

Graph the image of the line w with equation $y = 2x + 3$ under the given reflection, and state the slope of the image. (*Hint:* Find two points of w and their images.)

47. $r_{x\text{-axis}}$ 48. $r_{y\text{-axis}}$

49. r_k, where k has equation $y = x$ 50. r_n, where n has equation $y = -x$

Graph the image of the line z with equation $y = -2x + 3$ under the given reflection and state the slope of the image.

51. $r_{x\text{-axis}}$ 52. $r_{y\text{-axis}}$

53. r_k, where k has equation $y = x$ 54. r_n, where n has equation $y = -x$

On the basis of your investigations in Exercises 47–54, state how the slopes of a line s and its image s' compare when s is reflected over the given line.

55. the x-axis

56. the y-axis

57. the line k with equation $y = x$

58. the line n with equation $y = -x$

Find the slope-intercept form of the equation of the image line when the line whose equation is given first is reflected over the second line.

C 59. $y = 4x + 1$; x-axis

60. $y = -2x + 1$; y-axis

61. $y = 3x + 2$; $y = x$

62. $y = -x + 2$; $y = -x$

63. $y = x + 2$; $y = x$

64. $y = 2x + 4$; $y = -x$

65. a. Express the equation of the image in Exercise 61 in the form $x = my + b$.
  b. Express the equation of the image in Exercise 63 in the form $x = my + b$.
  c. Complete: In Exercises 61 and 63, the original line and its image are graphs of __?__ functions.
  d. Use your result from part (c) to graph the image of the graph of $y = x^2$, $x \geqslant 0$, when it is reflected over the line with equation $y = x$.

SELF-TEST 1

Find the coordinates of the images of $A(2, 0)$, $B(-2, 2)$, and $C(-3, -1)$ under the given transformation if T_2 and T are the transformations:

$$T_2:(x, y) \longrightarrow (x + 1, y - 1) \quad \text{and} \quad T:(x, y) \longrightarrow (-x, 3y)$$

1. T_2

2. T

3. $T_2 \circ T$

Section 5–1

Find the coordinates of the images D' and E' when $D(3, 2)$ and $E(-1, -4)$ are reflected over the given line.

4. x-axis

5. y-axis

Section 5–2

6. the line k with equation $y = x$

7. the line n with equation $y = -x$

State the number of lines of symmetry the figure has.

8.

9.

10.

Section 5–3

11. Draw a larger version of the figure shown, and use it to construct the image of the figure under r_l.

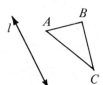

Section 5–4

12. Is the given property preserved under a line reflection?
  a. distance
  b. angle measure
  c. collinearity
  d. betweenness
  e. orientation
  f. parallelism

Section 5-5 COMPOSITION OF LINE REFLECTIONS

The composite $r_m \circ r_n$ of two line reflections r_m and r_n is *not* a line reflection, but it is a transformation. In this section and the following two sections you will learn about:

- composition of line reflections
- properties of these composite transformations

EXAMPLE   Find the coordinates of the image of $A(1, 4)$ under each composite, where line k has equation $y = x$.

a. $r_{x\text{-axis}} \circ r_k$ b. $r_k \circ r_{x\text{-axis}}$ c. $r_{y\text{-axis}} \circ r_k$ d. $r_k \circ r_{y\text{-axis}}$

SOLUTION   a.

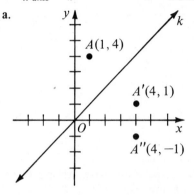

$r_k : (1, 4) \longrightarrow (4, 1)$
$r_{x\text{-axis}} : (4, 1) \longrightarrow (4, -1)$
$r_{x\text{-axis}} \circ r_k : (1, 4) \longrightarrow (4, -1)$

b.

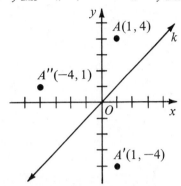

$r_{x\text{-axis}} : (1, 4) \longrightarrow (1, -4)$
$r_k : (1, -4) \longrightarrow (-4, 1)$
$r_k \circ r_{x\text{-axis}} : (1, 4) \longrightarrow (-4, 1)$

c.

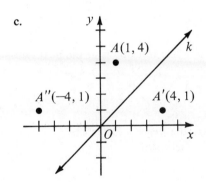

$r_k : (1, 4) \longrightarrow (4, 1)$
$r_{y\text{-axis}} : (4, 1) \longrightarrow (-4, 1)$
$r_{y\text{-axis}} \circ r_k : (1, 4) \longrightarrow (-4, 1)$

d.

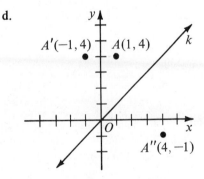

$r_{y\text{-axis}} : (1, 4) \longrightarrow (-1, 4)$
$r_k : (-1, 4) \longrightarrow (4, -1)$
$r_k \circ r_{y\text{-axis}} : (1, 4) \longrightarrow (4, -1)$

This example shows that the composition of line reflections is not commutative. That is, in general:

$$r_m \circ r_n \neq r_n \circ r_m$$

A transformation that is a composite of line reflections possesses many of the same properties that characterize single line reflections. For instance, betweenness, collinearity, distances, angle measures, parallelism, and perpendicularity are all preserved under a composite of line reflections. Since distances are preserved, a composite of line reflections is an isometry.

The diagram below shows the composite of more than two line reflections.

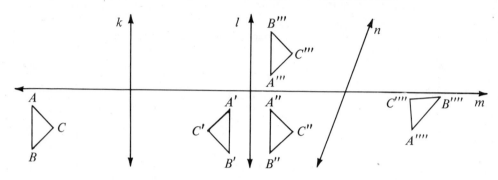

$$r_n \circ r_m \circ r_l \circ r_k \, (\triangle ABC) = \triangle A''''B''''C''''$$

Notice that with each successive reflection, the orientation of points in the triangle changes. After the second and fourth reflections, the images of A, B, and C have the same counterclockwise orientation that A, B, and C have. After the first and third reflections, the images of A, B, and C are oriented clockwise. This pattern continues indefinitely, and in general, we have:

Theorem 5-2   For any positive integer n, a composite of n line reflections is:
1. a direct isometry if n is even
2. a nondirect isometry if n is odd

You will study some special composites of two line reflections in the next two sections.

ORAL EXERCISES

If k, m, and n are lines of symmetry for the regular octagon $ABCDEFGH$, find the image of point C under each of the following composites of line reflections.

1. $r_k \circ r_m$

2. $r_m \circ r_k$

3. $r_k \circ r_n$

4. $r_n \circ r_k$

5. $r_m \circ r_n$

6. $r_n \circ r_m$

7. $r_k \circ r_m \circ r_n$

8. $r_m \circ r_n \circ r_k$

9. $r_n \circ r_k \circ r_m$

10. $r_k \circ r_n \circ r_m$

11. $r_n \circ r_m \circ r_k$

12. $r_m \circ r_k \circ r_n$

Which of the following composites are direct isometries? nondirect isometries?

13. $r_k \circ r_m$

14. $r_k \circ r_m \circ r_n$

15. $r_m \circ r_m$

16. a composite of 60 line reflections

Exs. 1–15

WRITTEN EXERCISES

Trace the diagram. Then sketch the images of the given point under $r_m \circ r_n$ and $r_n \circ r_m$.

A 1.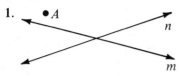

2.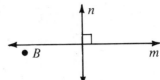

3.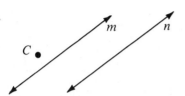

4.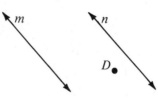

5. In which of Exercises 1–4 was $r_m \circ r_n$ equal to $r_n \circ r_m$?

Trace the diagram. Then sketch the image of the given point under $r_k \circ r_m \circ r_n$.

6.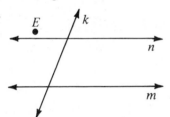

7.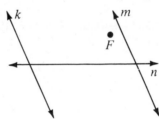

8.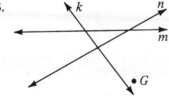

9.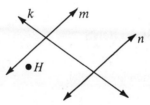

If lines l, m, and n are symmetry lines for the regular pentagon $VWXYZ$, find:

10. $r_n \circ r_l(Z)$

11. $r_l \circ r_n(V)$

12. $r_m \circ r_n(X)$

13. $r_n \circ r_m(W)$

14. $r_n \circ r_m(\overline{ZY})$

15. $r_l \circ r_n(\overline{YX})$

16. $r_n \circ r_l(\angle ZVW)$

17. $r_m \circ r_l(\angle W)$

18. $r_n \circ r_m(\angle ZYX)$

19. $r_m \circ r_l \circ r_n(W)$

20. $r_l \circ r_m \circ r_n(X)$

21. $r_l \circ r_m \circ r_l(V)$

22. $r_m \circ r_n \circ r_m(Y)$

23. $r_l \circ r_m \circ r_n(Z)$

24. $r_m \circ r_l \circ r_n(V)$

Let r_k be the line reflection in the line $y = x$, and let r_n be the line reflection in the line $y = -x$. $\triangle ABC$ has vertices $A(0, 1)$, $B(4, 4)$, and $C(5, 0)$. Graph $\triangle ABC$ and its image, $\triangle A''B''C''$, under the given composite, and state the coordinates of A'', B'', and C''.

25. $r_{\text{x-axis}} \circ r_{\text{y-axis}}$ **26.** $r_{\text{y-axis}} \circ r_{\text{x-axis}}$ **27.** $r_{\text{x-axis}} \circ r_k$

28. $r_n \circ r_{\text{x-axis}}$ **29.** $r_{\text{y-axis}} \circ r_n$ **30.** $r_k \circ r_{\text{y-axis}}$

Let m be the line with equation $x = 4$ and let s be the line with equation $y = -2$. Lines k and n are the same as for Exercises 25–30. Quadrilateral $DEFG$ has vertices $D(1, 3)$, $E(4, 2)$, $F(4, -2)$, and $G(-2, -1)$. Graph $DEFG$ and its image $D''E''F''G''$ under the given composite, and state the coordinates of D'', E'', F'', and G''.

31. $r_{\text{x-axis}} \circ r_s$ **32.** $r_s \circ r_{\text{x-axis}}$ **33.** $r_{\text{y-axis}} \circ r_s$ **34.** $r_s \circ r_{\text{y-axis}}$

35. $r_m \circ r_{\text{y-axis}}$ **36.** $r_{\text{y-axis}} \circ r_m$ **37.** $r_n \circ r_m$ **38.** $r_m \circ r_k$

Let lines k and n and $\triangle ABC$ be the same as for Exercises 25–30. Graph $\triangle ABC$ and its image $\triangle A'''B'''C'''$ under the given composite and state the coordinates of A''', B''', and C'''.

B **39.** $r_{\text{x-axis}} \circ r_{\text{y-axis}} \circ r_k$ **40.** $r_{\text{y-axis}} \circ r_k \circ r_{\text{x-axis}}$ **41.** $r_n \circ r_{\text{x-axis}} \circ r_{\text{y-axis}}$

42. $r_{\text{x-axis}} \circ r_n \circ r_{\text{y-axis}}$ **43.** $r_k \circ r_{\text{y-axis}} \circ r_{\text{x-axis}}$ **44.** $r_{\text{y-axis}} \circ r_{\text{x-axis}} \circ r_k$

Let quadrilateral $DEFG$ and lines k, n, m, and s be the same as for Exercises 31–38. Find the coordinates of D''', E''', F''', and G'''.

45. $r_{\text{y-axis}} \circ r_m \circ r_k$ **46.** $r_m \circ r_{\text{y-axis}} \circ r_k$ **47.** $r_k \circ r_n \circ r_m$ **48.** $r_m \circ r_n \circ r_k$

49. $r_s \circ r_m \circ r_{\text{y-axis}}$ **50.** $r_m \circ r_s \circ r_{\text{x-axis}}$ **51.** $r_s \circ r_{\text{x-axis}} \circ r_m$ **52.** $r_s \circ r_{\text{y-axis}} \circ r_m$

53. $r_m \circ r_{\text{y-axis}} \circ r_s$ **54.** $r_m \circ r_{\text{x-axis}} \circ r_s$ **55.** $r_s \circ r_k \circ r_m$ **56.** $r_m \circ r_k \circ r_s$

Section 5-6 TRANSLATIONS

In this section you will study a special kind of composite of two line reflections, in which the lines of reflection are parallel.

The diagram shows

$$r_n \circ r_m : \triangle ABC \longrightarrow \triangle A''B''C'',$$

where $m \parallel n$. You can think of this as sliding $\triangle ABC$ onto $\triangle A''B''C''$ along lines perpendicular to the parallel reflecting lines. Each point of $\triangle ABC$ slides the same distance onto its image in $\triangle A''B''C''$. As you will see in the exercise set, this distance is equal to twice the distance between the parallel lines of reflection.

This type of transformation that moves every point in the plane the same distance in the same direction is called a *translation*. A *translation* is the composite of two line reflections in which the lines of reflection are either parallel or the same line (in which case the translation is the identity).

EXAMPLE   Line m with equation $x = 4$ is parallel to the y-axis. Find the image of the points $A(-1, 5)$ and $B(2, 3)$ under $r_m \circ r_{y\text{-axis}}$.

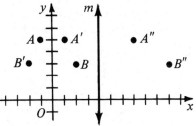

SOLUTION $r_{y\text{-axis}}: A(-1, 5) \longrightarrow A'(1, 5)$
$r_m: A'(1, 5) \longrightarrow A''(7, 5)$
$r_m \circ r_{y\text{-axis}}: A(-1, 5) \longrightarrow A''(7, 5)$
$r_{y\text{-axis}}: B(2, 3) \longrightarrow B'(-2, 3)$
$r_m: B'(-2, 3) \longrightarrow B''(10, 3)$
$r_m \circ r_{y\text{-axis}}: B(2, 3) \longrightarrow B''(10, 3)$

Notice that in the preceding example the distance between the reflecting lines is 4 units, and that each point was translated horizontally a total of 8 units.

EXAMPLE   Given parallel lines k and l with equations $y = x$ and $y = x + 2$, respectively, find the coordinates of the image of the following points under $r_l \circ r_k$:

$$A(6, 0) \qquad B(-3, -2) \qquad C(-1, 3)$$

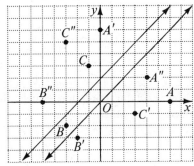

SOLUTION $r_k: A(6, 0) \longrightarrow A'(0, 6)$
$r_l: A'(0, 6) \longrightarrow A''(4, 2)$
$r_l \circ r_k: A(6, 0) \longrightarrow A''(4, 2)$

$r_k: B(-3, -2) \longrightarrow B'(-2, -3)$
$r_l: B'(-2, -3) \longrightarrow B''(-5, 0)$
$r_l \circ r_k: B(-3, -2) \longrightarrow B''(-5, 0)$

$r_k: C(-1, 3) \longrightarrow C'(3, -1)$
$r_l: C'(3, -1) \longrightarrow C''(-3, 5)$
$r_l \circ r_k: C(-1, 3) \longrightarrow C''(-3, 5)$

The preceding example suggests that the translation $r_l \circ r_k$ slides points two units to the left and two units up onto their images. That is:

$$r_l \circ r_k: (x, y) \longrightarrow (x - 2, y + 2)$$

For convenience, we will denote such a translation by $T_{-2, 2}$. That is:

$$T_{-2, 2}: (x, y) \longrightarrow (x - 2, y + 2)$$

Similarly, we will denote the translation that moves each point (x, y) of the coordinate plane a units horizontally and b units vertically as $T_{a, b}$. That is:

$$T_{a, b}: (x, y) \longrightarrow (x + a, y + b)$$

EXAMPLE   Find the coordinates of the image of the point $(-1, 4)$ under each of the following translations: **a.** $T_{3, 2}$ **b.** $T_{-2, 1}$ **c.** $T_{0, -4}$

SOLUTION   **a.** $T_{3, 2}(-1, 4) = (-1 + 3, 4 + 2) = (2, 6)$
b. $T_{-2, 1}(-1, 4) = (-1 - 2, 4 + 1) = (-3, 5)$
c. $T_{0, -4}(-1, 4) = (-1 + 0, 4 - 4) = (-1, 0)$

By Theorem 5-2, translations are direct isometries. Since a translation is the composite of two line reflections, it has all the properties listed on page 185.

ORAL EXERCISES

If n has equation $x = 6$ and m has equation $y = 3$, state the image of the given point under the given composite of reflections.

1. $r_m \circ r_{y\text{-axis}}(A)$

2. $r_{y\text{-axis}} \circ r_n(G)$

3. $r_{x\text{-axis}} \circ r_m(C)$

4. $r_m \circ r_{x\text{-axis}}(I)$

5. $r_n \circ r_{y\text{-axis}}(B)$

6. $r_{y\text{-axis}} \circ r_n(L)$

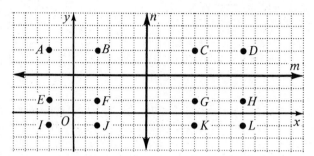

7. **a.** What is the distance between line n and the y-axis?
   b. What is the distance between a point and its image under $r_n \circ r_{y\text{-axis}}$? under $r_{y\text{-axis}} \circ r_n$?

8. **a.** What is the distance between line m and the x-axis?
   b. What is the distance between a point and its image under $r_m \circ r_{x\text{-axis}}$? under $r_{x\text{-axis}} \circ r_m$?

In Exercises 9–11 you may assume that the figure shows congruent equilateral triangles. If the translation T maps the first point onto the second point, find the images of the other points.

9. $T: A \longrightarrow D$
   a. F **b.** L **c.** M **d.** H

10. $T: D \longrightarrow B$
    a. J **b.** N **c.** C **d.** I

11. $T: M \longrightarrow H$
    a. N **b.** O **c.** G **d.** I

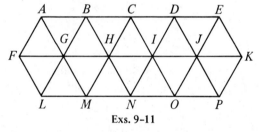

Exs. 9–11

Name the translation in the form $T_{a, b}$.

12. $(x, y) \longrightarrow (x, y + 2)$ 13. $(x, y) \longrightarrow (x - 3, y)$ 14. $(x, y) \longrightarrow (x - 5, y + 1)$

Name the translation, in the form $T_{a, b}$, that maps the first point onto the second point.

15. $(0, 0) \longrightarrow (2, -3)$ 16. $(0, 2) \longrightarrow (3, 5)$ 17. $(1, 0) \longrightarrow (0, 5)$

Given that T is a translation, complete.

18. If $T:(0, 0) \longrightarrow (2, -3)$, then $T:(2, -1) \longrightarrow \underline{\ ?\ }$.

19. If $T:(1, 0) \longrightarrow (3, 4)$, then $T:(1, -2) \longrightarrow \underline{\ ?\ }$.

20. If $T:(2, -3) \longrightarrow (0, 0)$, then $T:(1, 2) \longrightarrow \underline{\ ?\ }$.

21. The distance between $(0, 0)$ and its image under $T_{3, 4}$ is $\underline{\ ?\ }$.

22. The distance between any point and its image under $T_{a, b}$ is $\underline{\ ?\ }$.

WRITTEN EXERCISES

Copy each figure. Then use a ruler to sketch its image under a translation of 3 cm in the indicated direction d.

A 1
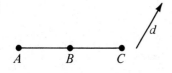

2.
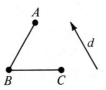

3.
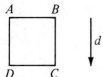

4.
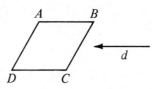

Copy each figure. Then sketch the reflection of the given figure under $r_m \circ r_l$.

5.
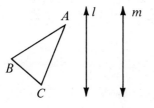

6.
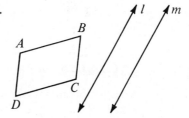

7.
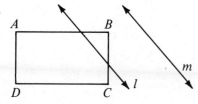

8.
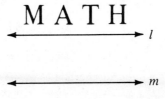

Find the coordinates of the images of $A(1, 3)$, $B(5, 1)$, and $C(1, 1)$ under the given translation.

9. $T_{0, 4}$ 10. $T_{-4, 0}$ 11. $T_{-2, 2}$ 12. $T_{2, -2}$

13. $T_{3, 1}$ 14. $T_{-3, -1}$ 15. $T_{-6, 5}$ 16. $T_{1, -4}$

Find the translation, in the form $T_{a, b}$, for which the second point is the image of the first point.

17. $(2, 2) \longrightarrow (2, 4)$ 18. $(-1, 3) \longrightarrow (2, 3)$ 19. $(1, 1) \longrightarrow (4, -1)$

20. $(1, -4) \longrightarrow (-3, 0)$ 21. $(5, 1) \longrightarrow (-3, 4)$ 22. $(-2, 2) \longrightarrow (1, -1)$

Given that T is a translation, complete.

23. If $T:(0, 0) \longrightarrow (3, 4)$, then $T:(2, -1) \longrightarrow$ __?__ .

24. If $T:(0, 0) \longrightarrow (1, -2)$, then $T:(-2, -3) \longrightarrow$ __?__ .

Given that T is a translation, complete.

25. If $T:(0, 2) \longrightarrow (2, 0)$, then $T:(2, 2) \longrightarrow \underline{}$.
26. If $T:(1, -1) \longrightarrow (4, -2)$, then $T:(-2, 3) \longrightarrow \underline{}$.
27. If $T:(2, 5) \longrightarrow (-1, 1)$, then $T:(1, 0) \longrightarrow \underline{}$.
28. If $T:(-3, 5) \longrightarrow (0, 0)$, then $T:(-1, 3) \longrightarrow \underline{}$.
29. If $T:(1, 1) \longrightarrow (-1, 4)$, then $T:(-3, 6) \longrightarrow \underline{}$.
30. If $T:(3, -2) \longrightarrow (-3, 4)$, then $T:(4, -1) \longrightarrow \underline{}$.

If a translation maps $(0, 0)$ onto $(5, 4)$, find the coordinates of the pre-image of the given point under the same translation.

B 31. $(-1, 4)$ 32. $(5, 0)$ 33. $(6, -1)$ 34. $(-4, -3)$

If a translation maps (x, y) onto $(x - 1, y + 3)$, find the coordinates of the pre-image of the given point under the same translation.

35. $(1, -3)$ 36. $(-2, -1)$ 37. $(0, 5)$ 38. $(4, 3)$

Graph each pair of functions. Then determine a translation that would map the graph of f onto the graph of g. Write your answer in the form $T_{a, b}$.

39. $f(x) = x^2$ $g(x) = x^2 + 3$ 40. $f(x) = x^2$ $g(x) = (x - 1)^2$
41. $f(x) = |x|$ $g(x) = |x| - 2$ 42. $f(x) = |x|$ $g(x) = |x + 2|$

C 43. Find the coordinates of the images of $E(1, 2)$, $F(4, 5)$, and $G(6, 3)$ under each composite if lines k, l, m, and n have the given equations.

$$k: x = 2 \qquad l: x = 4 \qquad m: x = 7 \qquad n: x = 9$$

  a. $r_k \circ r_{y\text{-axis}}$ b. $r_l \circ r_k$ c. $r_n \circ r_m$
  d. $r_{y\text{-axis}} \circ r_k$ e. $r_k \circ r_l$ f. $r_m \circ r_n$
  g. Name each composite in parts (a)–(f) as a translation in the form $T_{a, b}$.

44. Find the equation of the line (l or m) for which the given composite is the translation $T_{-6, 0}$.
  a. $r_{y\text{-axis}} \circ r_l$ b. $r_m \circ r_{y\text{-axis}}$

45. Find the equation of the line (l or m) for which the given composite is the translation $T_{0, 5}$.
  a. $r_{x\text{-axis}} \circ r_l$ b. $r_m \circ r_{x\text{-axis}}$

46. State *two* choices of equations for lines m and n such that $r_m \circ r_n$ is the translation $T_{0, -4}$.

$\triangle ABC$ has vertices $A(1, 4)$, $B(-2, 6)$, and $C(-4, 2)$. Graph $\triangle ABC$, $\triangle A'B'C'$, and $\triangle A''B''C''$, and state the coordinates of A'', B'', and C''.

47. $r_k:\triangle ABC \longrightarrow \triangle A'B'C'$, where k has equation $y = x$
   $T_{-5, 1}:\triangle A'B'C' \longrightarrow A''B''C''$

48. $T_{4, -3}:\triangle ABC \longrightarrow \triangle A'B'C'$
   $r_n:\triangle A'B'C' \longrightarrow \triangle A''B''C''$, where n has equation $y = -x$

Section 5-7 ROTATIONS

In this section you will study the type of transformation that is formed by a composite of two line reflections in intersecting lines.

In the diagram below, lines l and m intersect at point C. Notice that the composite $r_l \circ r_m$ turns, or *rotates*, $\triangle ABC$ about the point C onto $\triangle A''B''C$.

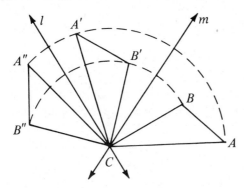

C is a *fixed point* of the transformation $r_l \circ r_m$ because $r_l \circ r_m(C) = C$. Since reflections preserve distances, you know that $CA = CA' = CA''$. That is, the points A, A', and A'' all lie on a circle with center C and radius CA. Similarly, points B, B', and B'' lie on a circle with center C and radius CB.

Each point of $\triangle ABC$ rotates the same number of degrees about point C onto its image in $\triangle A''B''C$. For example,

$$m\angle ACA'' = m\angle BCB''.$$

In the exercise set you will investigate the fact that the number of degrees each point is rotated is equal to twice the measure of the acute or right angle formed by the intersecting lines of reflection.

This type of transformation that rotates each point in the plane the same number of degrees about one fixed point is called a *rotation*. The fixed point is called the *center* of the rotation. A *rotation* is the composite of two line reflections in which the lines of reflection intersect in exactly one point.

EXAMPLE If k has equation $y = x$, find the coordinates of the images of $A(4, 0)$, $B(0, 2)$, and $C(-4, -2)$ under:

    a. $r_{y\text{-axis}} \circ r_k$ **b.** $r_k \circ r_{y\text{-axis}}$

SOLUTION **a.** $r_k: A(4, 0) \longrightarrow A'(0, 4)$
           $r_{y\text{-axis}}: A'(0, 4) \longrightarrow A''(0, 4)$
           $r_{y\text{-axis}} \circ r_k: A(4, 0) \longrightarrow A''(0, 4)$

           $r_k: B(0, 2) \longrightarrow B'(2, 0)$
           $r_{y\text{-axis}}: B'(2, 0) \longrightarrow B''(-2, 0)$
           $r_{y\text{-axis}} \circ r_k: B(0, 2) \longrightarrow B''(-2, 0)$

           $r_k: C(-4, -2) \longrightarrow C'(-2, -4)$
           $r_{y\text{-axis}}: C'(-2, -4) \longrightarrow C''(2, -4)$
           $r_{y\text{-axis}} \circ r_k: C(-4, -2) \longrightarrow C''(2, -4)$

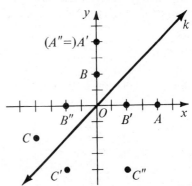

b. $r_{y\text{-axis}}: A(4, 0) \longrightarrow A'(-4, 0)$
$r_k: A'(-4, 0) \longrightarrow A''(0, -4)$
$r_k \circ r_{y\text{-axis}}: A(4, 0) \longrightarrow A''(0, -4)$

$r_{y\text{-axis}}: B(0, 2) \longrightarrow B'(0, 2)$
$r_k: B'(0, 2) \longrightarrow B''(2, 0)$
$r_k \circ r_{y\text{-axis}}: B(0, 2) \longrightarrow B''(2, 0)$

$r_{y\text{-axis}}: C(-4, -2) \longrightarrow C'(4, -2)$
$r_k: C'(4, -2) \longrightarrow C''(-2, 4)$
$r_k \circ r_{y\text{-axis}}: C(-4, -2) \longrightarrow C''(-2, 4)$

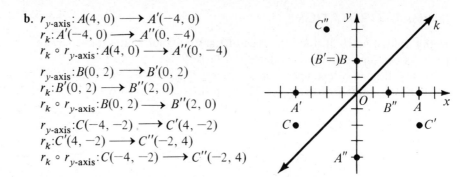

Although the reflecting lines are the same in parts (a) and (b) of the preceding example, the rotations are different. The composite $r_{y\text{-axis}} \circ r_k$ rotates points 90° counterclockwise about the origin.

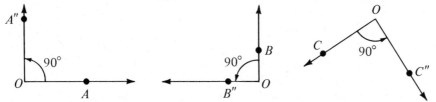

The composite $r_k \circ r_{y\text{-axis}}$ rotates points 90° clockwise about the origin, which we will call a rotation of −90°.

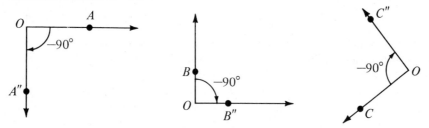

These rotations are denoted by

$$R_{90} \text{ and } R_{-90}$$

respectively. A clockwise rotation of 45° with center P that is not the origin of the coordinate plane is denoted by:

$$R_{P, -45}$$

Notice that a rotation of 180° is equivalent to a rotation of −180°. Every rotation can be expressed either as a clockwise rotation or as an equivalent counterclockwise rotation, as the figures show.

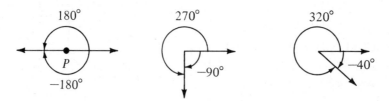

EXAMPLE If P is the point where the diagonals of square $WXYZ$ intersect, find:

    a. $R_{P,\,90}(W)$ **b.** $R_{P,\,180}(Z)$

    c. $R_{P,\,270}(W)$ **d.** $R_{P,\,-90}(W)$

SOLUTION   **a.** $R_{P,\,90}(W)=Z$ **b.** $R_{P,\,180}(Z)=X$

              c. $R_{P,\,270}(W)=X$ **d.** $R_{P,\,-90}(W)=X$

Parts (c) and (d) illustrate the equivalence of $R_{P,\,270}$ and $R_{P,\,-90}$.

EXAMPLE Find the coordinates of the images of (x, y) and $(-3, 5)$ under:

    a. R_{90} **b.** R_{270} **c.** R_{180}

SOLUTION   **a.** As we have already seen, R_{90} is equivalent to $r_{y\text{-axis}} \circ r_k$, where k has equation $y = x$. Since

$$r_k\!:(x, y) \longrightarrow (y, x) \text{ and } r_{y\text{-axis}}\!:(y, x) \longrightarrow (-y, x),$$
$$R_{90}\!:(x, y) \longrightarrow (-y, x) \text{ and } R_{90}\!:(-3, 5) \longrightarrow (-5, -3).$$

    b. R_{270} is equivalent to R_{-90}, or $r_k \circ r_{y\text{-axis}}$.

$$r_{y\text{-axis}}\!:(x, y) \longrightarrow (-x, y) \text{ and } r_k\!:(-x, y) \longrightarrow (y, -x)$$
$$R_{270}\!:(x, y) \longrightarrow (y, -x) \text{ and } R_{270}\!:(-3, 5) \longrightarrow (5, 3)$$

    c. R_{180} is equivalent to a composite of reflections over lines that intersect to form a $90°$ angle, such as the x-axis and y-axis.

$$r_{x\text{-axis}}\!:(x, y) \longrightarrow (x, -y) \text{ and } r_{y\text{-axis}}\!:(x, -y) \longrightarrow (-x, -y)$$
$$\text{Thus } R_{180}\!:(x, y) \longrightarrow (-x, -y) \text{ and } R_{180}\!:(-3, 5) \longrightarrow (3, -5)$$

By Theorem 5-2, rotations are direct isometries. Since a rotation is the composite of two line reflections, it has all the properties listed on page 185.

ORAL EXERCISES

State another name, in the form $R_{P,\,\theta}$ or R_{θ}, for each rotation listed below.

  1. $R_{P,\,300}$ **2.** R_{275} **3.** $R_{P,\,-30}$ **4.** R_{-75}

The points shown are equally spaced around $\odot P$. Determine each image under the given rotation.

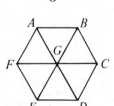

  5. $R_{P,\,45}(C)$ **6.** $R_{P,\,90}(F)$

  7. $R_{P,\,-90}(H)$ **8.** $R_{P,\,-45}(B)$

  9. $R_{P,\,135}(G)$ **10.** $R_{P,\,225}(E)$

  11. $R_{P,\,270}(E)$ **12.** $R_{P,\,-180}(D)$

The diagram shows congruent equilateral triangles. Determine each image.

  13. $R_{G,\,60}(A)$ **14.** $R_{G,\,-60}(D)$

  15. $R_{G,\,120}(C)$ **16.** $R_{G,\,-120}(E)$

  17. $R_{C,\,60}(C)$ **18.** $R_{E,\,60}(G)$

  19. $R_{E,\,-60}(G)$ **20.** $R_{F,\,120}(E)$

WRITTEN EXERCISES

Complete.

A 1. $R_{90}:(3, 2) \longrightarrow$ ___?___

2. $R_{90}:(-6, 4) \longrightarrow$ ___?___

3. $R_{180}:(6, 5) \longrightarrow$ ___?___

4. $R_{180}:(-5, -2) \longrightarrow$ ___?___

5. $R_{270}:(5, -4) \longrightarrow$ ___?___

6. $R_{-90}:(-2, 1) \longrightarrow$ ___?___

Trace the diagram. Then sketch the images of the figure under r_l and $r_m \circ r_l$.

7.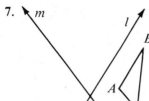

8.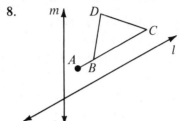

9.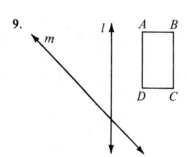

10.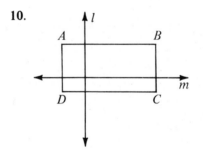

The points shown are equally spaced around $\odot P$. Complete.

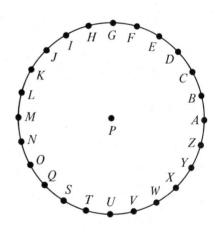

11. If $R_{P, \theta}:D \longrightarrow I$, then $R_{P, \theta}:M \longrightarrow$ ___?___.

12. If $R_{P, \theta}:J \longrightarrow M$, then $R_{P, \theta}:Q \longrightarrow$ ___?___.

13. If $R_{P, \theta}:O \longrightarrow Z$, then $R_{P, \theta}:C \longrightarrow$ ___?___.

14. If $R_{P, \theta}:S \longrightarrow F$, then $R_{P, \theta}:L \longrightarrow$ ___?___.

15. If $R_{P, \theta}:T \longrightarrow N$, then $R_{P, \theta}:H \longrightarrow$ ___?___.

16. If $R_{P, \theta}:E \longrightarrow Y$, then $R_{P, \theta}:A \longrightarrow$ ___?___.

Exs. 11-36

For the given rotation, state two values of θ such that $-360 < \theta \leqslant 360$.

17. $R_{P, \theta}:M \longrightarrow N$

18. $R_{P, \theta}:T \longrightarrow T$

19. $R_{P, \theta}:N \longrightarrow V$

20. $R_{P, \theta}:C \longrightarrow L$

21. $R_{P, \theta}:Z \longrightarrow Q$

22. $R_{P, \theta}:B \longrightarrow W$

Use the diagram on page 200 to determine each image.

23. $R_{P, 75}(E)$ **24.** $R_{P, 105}(L)$ **25.** $R_{P, 165}(S)$ **26.** $R_{P, 285}(U)$

27. $R_{P, -15}(O)$ **28.** $R_{P, -150}(G)$ **29.** $R_{P, 45}(\overline{FG})$ **30.** $R_{P, -90}(\overline{CF})$

31. $R_{P, -135}(\overline{AX})$ **32.** $R_{P, 315}(\overline{NS})$ **33.** $R_{P, 225}(\angle DPE)$ **34.** $R_{P, -75}(\angle MPQ)$

35. $R_{P, -60}$(square $DJQX$) **36.** $R_{P, 120}$(trapezoid $AGKW$)

The diagram shows congruent equilateral triangles. Determine each pre-image.

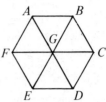

B 37. $R_{G, 60}: \underline{\quad ? \quad} \longrightarrow C$ **38.** $R_{G, -60}: \underline{\quad ? \quad} \longrightarrow F$

39. $R_{G, -120}: \underline{\quad ? \quad} \longrightarrow E$ **40.** $R_{G, 120}: \underline{\quad ? \quad} \longrightarrow E$

41. $R_{E, 60}: \underline{\quad ? \quad} \longrightarrow G$ **42.** $R_{B, -60}: \underline{\quad ? \quad} \longrightarrow G$

Determine the coordinates of the pre-image of the given point under:
 a. R_{90} b. R_{180} c. R_{270}

43. $(-4, 0)$ **44.** $(3, 3)$ **45.** $(2, 4)$ **46.** $(-6, 1)$

Copy the triangle on graph paper. Draw the image under the rotation specified.

47. $R_{A, 90}$ **48.** $R_{B, -90}$ **49.** $R_{C, -90}$ **50.** $R_{D, 90}$

For Exercises 51 and 52, copy the figure.

51. Construct the image of Q under $R_{P, 60}$ by constructing equilateral $\triangle PQQ'$.

52. Construct the pre-image of Q under $R_{P, 60}$.

53. If $r_l \circ r_m: A \longrightarrow A''$ and $m\angle BCD \le 90$, explain why $m\angle ACA'' = 2m\angle BCD$.

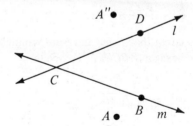

54. a. Graph $P(3, 0)$ and $Q(2, 3)$.
 b. Graph P' and Q', the images of P and Q under R_{90}.
 c. Compare the slopes of $\overleftrightarrow{PQ}$ and $\overleftrightarrow{P'Q'}$. What do you find to be true?

C 55. Copy the figure. Construct the image of $\triangle ABC$ under the rotation with center C that maps A onto a point of $\overrightarrow{CD}$.

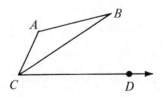

56. Let k and n have equations $y = x$ and $y = -x$, respectively.

    a. Show that $r_{x\text{-axis}} \circ r_n$ is equivalent to $r_{y\text{-axis}} \circ r_k$ by finding the rule for

$$r_{x\text{-axis}} \circ r_n : (x, y) \longrightarrow \underline{\quad ? \quad}.$$

    b. To what rotation is $r_{x\text{-axis}} \circ r_n$ equivalent?

    c. Complete: $R_{-90} = r_n \circ \underline{\quad ? \quad} = \underline{\quad ? \quad} \circ r_n$

57. Copy the figure twice. Construct l', the image of line l under $R_{A, 60}$, in each of the following ways.

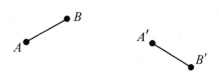

    a. Find the images under $R_{A, 60}$ of any two points of l.

    b. Let B be the point where the perpendicular from A intersects line l. Let B' be its image under $R_{A, 60}$. Then l' is the perpendicular to $\overline{AB'}$ at B'.

For Exercises 58 and 59, copy the given figure.

58. a. Construct the center, C, of the rotation that maps $\overline{AB}$ onto $\overline{A'B'}$. (*Hint:* Recall that a point is equidistant from P and P' if and only if it lies on the perpendicular bisector of $\overline{PP'}$.)

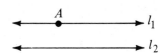

    b. Construct two lines, l and n, such that B lies on n and $r_l \circ r_n : \overline{AB} \longrightarrow \overline{A'B'}$.

59. Draw a diagram like that shown, in which point A lies on line l_1 and $l_1 \parallel l_2 \parallel l_3$. Following the outline below, construct equilateral $\triangle ABC$ so that B lies on line l_2 and C lies on l_3.

    a. Let l_2' be the image of l_2 under $R_{A, 60}$.

    b. Let C be the point where l_2' and l_3 intersect.

    c. Let B be the pre-image of C under $R_{A, 60}$.

    d. Explain why $\triangle ABC$ is the desired triangle.

    e. Does any other triangle satisfy the given conditions? Explain.

SELF-TEST 2

Given that l, m, and n are symmetry lines for regular hexagon $ABCDEF$, complete.

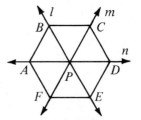

1. $r_l \circ r_n : E \longrightarrow \underline{\quad ? \quad}$

2. $r_l \circ r_m : \overline{AB} \longrightarrow \underline{\quad ? \quad}$

3. $r_l \circ r_m \circ r_l : C \longrightarrow \underline{\quad ? \quad}$

4. $r_{y\text{-axis}} \circ r_{x\text{-axis}} : (3, -4) \longrightarrow \underline{\quad ? \quad}$

5. $T_{2, -1} : (4, 5) \longrightarrow \underline{\quad ? \quad}$

6. If T is a translation and $T : (5, -2) \longrightarrow (0, 3)$, then $T : (-4, 6) \longrightarrow \underline{\quad ? \quad}$.

7. $R_{90} : (2, -1) \longrightarrow \underline{\quad ? \quad}$ **8.** $R_{-180} : \underline{\quad ? \quad} \longrightarrow (-2, 4)$

9. In regular hexagon $ABCDEF$, $R_{P, -120}(C) = \underline{\quad ? \quad}$.

Exs. 1–3, 9

Section 5-5

Section 5-6

Section 5-7

Section 5-8 OTHER SYMMETRIES

In Section 5-3 you learned to recognize line symmetry and to determine lines of reflection. In this section you will learn three other forms of symmetry and how to recognize them. They are:

- rotational symmetry
- point symmetry
- translational symmetry

EXAMPLE Describe the rotations greater than $0°$ and less than $360°$ that map the figure onto itself.

a. equilateral triangle

b. regular pentagon

c. sextile asterisk

d. octile asterisk

SOLUTION a. The lines of symmetry of the equilateral triangle intersect at point C. The rotations $R_{C,\ 120}$ and $R_{C,\ 240}$ map the equilateral triangle onto itself.

b. The lines of symmetry of the regular pentagon intersect at point C. The rotations $R_{C,\ 72}$, $R_{C,\ 144}$, $R_{C,\ 216}$, and $R_{C,\ 288}$ map the pentagon onto itself.

c. Rotations of $60°$, $120°$, $180°$, $240°$, and $300°$ map the asterisk onto itself.

d. Rotations of $45°$, $90°$, $135°$, $180°$, $225°$, $270°$, and $315°$ map the asterisk onto itself.

A figure has *rotational symmetry* when there is a rotation greater than $0°$ and less than $360°$ that maps the figure onto itself. (Every figure is mapped onto itself by a rotation of $0°$.) Thus the four figures in the preceding example all have rotational symmetry.

A rotation of $180°$ is often called a *half-turn*. The diagram shows the images of A, B, and C under the half-turn $R_{P,\ 180}$. Since P is its own image under the half-turn, and all rotations are isometries, you know that $AP = A'P$, $BP = B'P$, and $CP = C'P$. An additional property of a half-turn is that each point is collinear with its image and the center of the half-turn. Thus P is the midpoint of $\overline{AA'}$, $\overline{BB'}$, and $\overline{CC'}$. Point P is referred to as a *point of symmetry*, and we sometimes refer to the half-turn as a *reflection in point P*.

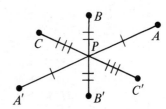

EXAMPLE Find the coordinates of the images of $A(3, 1)$, $B(0, -3)$, and $C(-5, -2)$ when they are reflected in the origin.

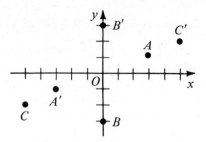

SOLUTION Recall that $R_{180}:(x, y) \longrightarrow (-x, -y)$.
Thus: $R_{180}:(3, 1) \longrightarrow (-3, -1)$
$R_{180}:(0, -3) \longrightarrow (0, 3)$
$R_{180}:(-5, -2) \longrightarrow (5, 2)$

A figure has *point symmetry* when there exists a half-turn rotation for which the figure is its own image.

EXAMPLES OF POINT SYMMETRIC FIGURES

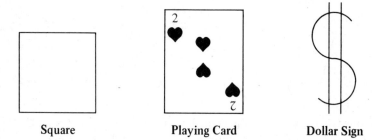

Square   Playing Card   Dollar Sign

The intersection of the diagonals of the square or of the rectangular playing card is the point of symmetry.

Other examples of point symmetry include the pattern of the darkened squares of a typical crossword puzzle, the images in a kaleidoscope, and a pinwheel.

EXAMPLE *ABCDEF* is a regular hexagon whose lines of symmetry intersect at point P.

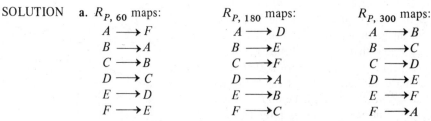

a. Verify that each of the following maps *ABCDEF* onto itself:
$R_{P, 60}$ $\quad R_{P, 180}$ $\quad R_{P, 300}$

b. Find a single transformation that is equivalent to each of the following composites:
$r_n \circ R_{P, 60}$ $\quad R_{P, 60} \circ r_n$ $\quad r_m \circ r_n$

SOLUTION **a.** $R_{P, 60}$ maps: $\qquad R_{P, 180}$ maps: $\qquad R_{P, 300}$ maps:

$R_{P, 60}$	$R_{P, 180}$	$R_{P, 300}$
$A \longrightarrow F$	$A \longrightarrow D$	$A \longrightarrow B$
$B \longrightarrow A$	$B \longrightarrow E$	$B \longrightarrow C$
$C \longrightarrow B$	$C \longrightarrow F$	$C \longrightarrow D$
$D \longrightarrow C$	$D \longrightarrow A$	$D \longrightarrow E$
$E \longrightarrow D$	$E \longrightarrow B$	$E \longrightarrow F$
$F \longrightarrow E$	$F \longrightarrow C$	$F \longrightarrow A$

Each rotation maps *ABCDEF* onto itself, and thus can be considered a symmetry-producing transformation for *ABCDEF*.

b. $r_n \circ R_{P, 60}$ maps:

$A \longrightarrow F \longrightarrow B$
$B \longrightarrow A \longrightarrow A$
$C \longrightarrow B \longrightarrow F$
$D \longrightarrow C \longrightarrow E$
$E \longrightarrow D \longrightarrow D$
$F \longrightarrow E \longrightarrow C$

$R_{P, 60} \circ r_n$ maps:

$A \longrightarrow A \longrightarrow F$
$B \longrightarrow F \longrightarrow E$
$C \longrightarrow E \longrightarrow D$
$D \longrightarrow D \longrightarrow C$
$E \longrightarrow C \longrightarrow B$
$F \longrightarrow B \longrightarrow A$

Thus, $r_n \circ R_{P, 60} = r_k$. Thus $R_{P, 60} \circ r_n = r_m$.

Since the measure of the angle between lines m and n is 30, $r_m \circ r_n = R_{P, 60}$.

Notice that regular hexagon $ABCDEF$ is line symmetric, rotationally symmetric, and point symmetric.

Another form of symmetry often seen on wallpaper and floor tiles is called *translational symmetry*. A figure has *translational symmetry* when there exists a translation that maps the figure onto itself. For example, if the figure on the left below continued without end, it would have translational symmetry.

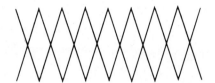 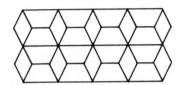

Imagine the figure on the right above repeating indefinitely in all directions so that it covers the plane. Such a pattern is called a *tessellation*.

In Chapter 7 you will study some functions whose graphs have translational symmetry.

ORAL EXERCISES

Name the types of symmetry the figure has.

1.
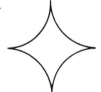

2.

3.

4.

5.

6.

7.

8.

Name at least one polygon that has:

9. only rotational symmetry and point symmetry

10. only line symmetry

11. line, point, and rotational symmetry

Name the capital letters of the alphabet and digits (0–9) that have:

12. point symmetry

13. both point symmetry and line symmetry

Determine whether the statements below are *always, sometimes,* or *never* true.

14. A figure that has rotational symmetry __?__ has point symmetry.

15. A figure that has point symmetry __?__ has rotational symmetry.

16. A figure that has line symmetry __?__ has rotational symmetry.

17. A figure that has rotational symmetry __?__ has line symmetry.

18. A regular polygon __?__ has rotational symmetry.

19. A regular polygon __?__ has point symmetry.

20. A regular polygon __?__ has translational symmetry.

WRITTEN EXERCISES

Describe the types of symmetry each figure has. Include a description of each line of symmetry, point of symmetry, and rotation greater than 0° and less than 360° that maps the figure onto itself.

A **1.** isosceles triangle

2. scalene triangle

3. parallelogram

4. rhombus

5. regular decagon

6. isosceles trapezoid

7. circle

8. ellipse

Find the coordinates of point P if the reflection in point P maps the first point onto the second point.

9. $(2, 6) \longrightarrow (4, 2)$

10. $(-4, -5) \longrightarrow (-2, -1)$

11. $(-6, 1) \longrightarrow (2, -3)$

12. $(5, -7) \longrightarrow (-1, 1)$

Find the coordinates of the image when the point is reflected in the origin.

13. $(5, 2)$ **14.** $(-3, 1)$ **15.** $(-4, -2)$ **16.** $(6, -8)$

Find the coordinates of the image when the point is reflected in the point $(2, 3)$.

17. $(0, 0)$ **18.** $(5, 2)$ **19.** $(3, -2)$ **20.** $(5, 7)$

Copy the figure on graph paper and complete it so that P is a point of symmetry for the figure.

21.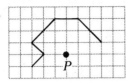

22.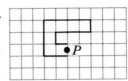

In Exercises 23–30, l and m are lines of symmetry for rectangle $ABCD$. Find the images of A, B, C, and D under the given transformation.

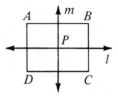

23. r_l **24.** r_m **25.** $R_{P,\,180}$ **26.** $R_{P,\,360}$

Name a single transformation that is equivalent to the given composite.

27. $r_l \circ r_m$ **28.** $r_m \circ r_l$ **29.** $R_{P,\,180} \circ r_l$ **30.** $r_l \circ R_{P,\,180}$

For the square whose vertices are given:
a. Find the coordinates of the point of symmetry.
b. Find the equations of the four lines of symmetry.

B 31. $A(-1, 1)$, $B(5, 1)$, $C(5, -5)$, $D(-1, -5)$ **32.** $W(-1, 2)$, $X(3, -2)$, $Y(-1, -6)$, $Z(-5, -2)$

In Exercises 33–46, lines l, m, and n are lines of symmetry for equilateral triangle ABC.

Find the images of A, B, and C under the given transformation.

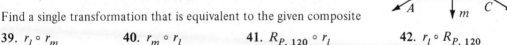

33. r_l **34.** r_m **35.** r_n

36. $R_{P,\,120}$ **37.** $R_{P,\,240}$ **38.** $R_{P,\,360}$

Find a single transformation that is equivalent to the given composite

39. $r_l \circ r_m$ **40.** $r_m \circ r_l$ **41.** $R_{P,\,120} \circ r_l$ **42.** $r_l \circ R_{P,\,120}$

43. $R_{P,\,240} \circ r_l$ **44.** $r_l \circ R_{P,\,240}$ **45.** $R_{P,\,120} \circ R_{P,\,240}$ **46.** $R_{P,\,240} \circ R_{P,\,120}$

In Exercises 47 and 48, A' and B' are the images when $A(x_1, y_1)$ and $B(x_2, y_2)$ are reflected in the origin. Show that the given segments have the same slope.

C 47. $\overline{AB}$ and $\overline{A'B'}$ if $x_1 \neq x_2$ **48.** $\overline{AB'}$ and $\overline{A'B}$

Graph $\triangle ABC$, $\triangle A'B'C'$, $\triangle A''B''C''$, and $\triangle A'''B'''C'''$, and state the coordinates of A''', B''', and C'''.

49. $\triangle ABC$ has vertices $A(1, 4)$, $B(-2, 3)$, and $C(4, -1)$.
$\triangle A'B'C'$ is the image when $\triangle ABC$ is reflected in the origin.
$T_{-3,\,-2} : \triangle A'B'C' \longrightarrow A''B''C''$
$r_n : \triangle A''B''C'' \longrightarrow \triangle A'''B'''C'''$, where n has equation $y = -x$

50. $\triangle ABC$ has vertices $A(2, 1)$, $B(4, 2)$, and $C(3, 5)$.
$\triangle A'B'C'$ is the image when $\triangle ABC$ is reflected in the origin.
$T_{3,\,-1} : \triangle A'B'C' \longrightarrow \triangle A''B''C''$
$R_{90} : \triangle A''B''C'' \longrightarrow \triangle A'''B'''C'''$

Section 5-9 DILATIONS

In earlier sections you studied three kinds of isometries—reflections, translations, and rotations. In this section you will learn about a type of transformation that is *not* an isometry. While an isometry preserves distances and thus is related to congruence, this type of transformation is related to similarity.

In the diagram on the left below, D' is the point on $\overrightarrow{CD}$ such that $CD' = 2 \cdot CD$. The images E' and F' are similarly determined, as is the image of any point P on $\triangle DEF$. Such a transformation of the plane is called an *expansion*.

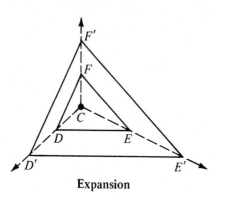

Expansion

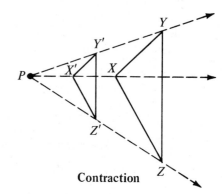

Contraction

In the diagram on the right above, X' is the point on $\overrightarrow{PX}$ such that $PX' = \frac{1}{2} \cdot PX$. The images Y' and Z' are similarly determined. Such a transformation of the plane is called a *contraction*.

The *dilation* with *center C* and *scale factor k* ($k > 0$) is the transformation that maps:

1. C onto itself
2. any other point A onto the unique point A' of $\overrightarrow{CA}$ such that $CA' = k \cdot CA$

Thus an expansion is a dilation such that $k > 1$. A contraction is a dilation such that $0 < k < 1$. (If $k = 1$, then the dilation is the identity transformation.)

The dilation with center C and scale factor k is denoted by $D_{C, k}$. A dilation whose center is the origin of the coordinate plane is denoted by D_k.

EXAMPLE Find the coordinates of the images of $A(-3, 0)$, $B(0, 2)$, and $C(-3, 2)$ under:

      a. D_2 **b.** $D_{\frac{1}{2}}$

SOLUTION   **a.** $D_2:(-3, 0) \longrightarrow (-6, 0)$
              $D_2:(0, 2) \longrightarrow (0, 4)$
              $D_2:(-3, 2) \longrightarrow (-6, 4)$

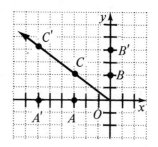

b. $D_{\frac{1}{2}}:(-3, 0) \longrightarrow \left(-\frac{3}{2}, 0\right)$

$D_{\frac{1}{2}}:(0, 2) \longrightarrow (0, 1)$

$D_{\frac{1}{2}}:(-3, 2) \longrightarrow \left(-\frac{3}{2}, 1\right)$

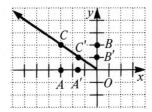

The preceding example illustrates the fact that:

$$D_k:(x, y) \longrightarrow (kx, ky)$$

EXAMPLE   Find the scale factor for the dilation that maps $(-4, 6)$ onto $(-8, 12)$.

SOLUTION   To determine the scale factor k, solve either of the following equations, where (x', y') is the image of (x, y):

$$x' = kx \qquad y' = ky$$

We will use the first of the equations: $-8 = k \cdot (-4)$

$$2 = k$$

Notice that the dilation $D_{C, k}$ maps every line segment onto a parallel line segment that is k times as long, as we show below.

By the definition of a dilation:

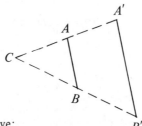

$CA' = k \cdot CA \quad$ and $\quad CB' = k \cdot CB$

$\dfrac{CA'}{CA} = k \qquad$ and $\qquad \dfrac{CB'}{CB} = k$

$$\dfrac{CA'}{CA} = \dfrac{CB'}{CB}$$

Since $\angle C \cong \angle C$, by the SAS Similarity Theorem you have:

$$\triangle CA'B' \sim \triangle CAB$$

Thus: $\dfrac{A'B'}{AB} = k$, or $A'B' = k \cdot AB$

Also: $\angle CAB \cong \angle CA'B'$, which implies that $\overleftrightarrow{AB} \parallel \overleftrightarrow{A'B'}$

While dilations do not preserve distances (unless $k = 1$), they do preserve betweenness, collinearity, angle measure, parallelism and perpendicularity of lines, and orientation of points.

ORAL EXERCISES

Find the scale factor of the dilation with center C if A' is the image of A and B' is the image of B.

1.

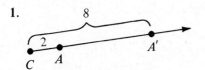

2.

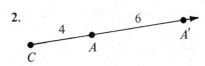

Find the scale factor of the dilation with center C if A' is the image of A and B' is the image of B.

3.

4.

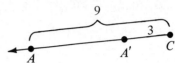

5.

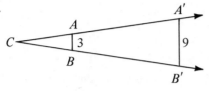

6.

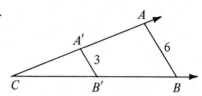

Name the image.

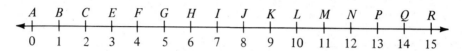

7. $D_{A,\,2}(G)$

8. $D_{A,\,3}(F)$

9. $D_{A,\,\frac{1}{3}}(H)$

10. $D_{A,\,\frac{1}{4}}(J)$

11. $D_{F,\,2}(C)$

12. $D_{F,\,3}(I)$

13. $D_{F,\,\frac{1}{2}}(Q)$

14. $D_{P,\,\frac{1}{4}}(B)$

WRITTEN EXERCISES

Determine the coordinates of the image.

A   1. $D_4(2, 3)$

2. $D_3(-1, 4)$

3. $D_{\frac{2}{3}}(-6, 3)$

4. $D_{\frac{1}{4}}(2, -8)$

If P' is the image of P under the given dilation, state the length of $\overline{CP'}$.

5. $D_{C,\,\frac{1}{4}}$; $CP = 8$

6. $D_{C,\,2}$; $CP = 4$

7. $D_{C,\,4}$; $CP = 5\frac{1}{2}$

8. $D_{C,\,\frac{1}{3}}$; $CP = 15$

If P' is the image of P under a dilation with center C, state the scale factor of the dilation. (You may find it helpful to draw a diagram.)

9. $CP = 2$ and $CP' = 6$

10. $CP = \frac{1}{2}$ and $CP' = 8$

11. $CP = 9$ and $CP' = 3$

12. $CP = 10$ and $CP' = 3$

13. $CP = 3$ and $PP' = 3$

14. $CP = 4$ and $PP' = 2$
(Give all possible values.)

Name, in the form D_k, the dilation with center at the origin that maps the first point onto the second point.

15. $(1, 1) \longrightarrow (4, 4)$

16. $(1, 2) \longrightarrow (3, 6)$

17. $(-1, 3) \longrightarrow (-3, 9)$

18. $(-4, -1) \longrightarrow (-8, -2)$

19. $(4, 6) \longrightarrow (2, 3)$

20. $(-6, 3) \longrightarrow (-2, 1)$

21. If D_k maps $(1, 3)$ onto $(2, 6)$, find $D_k(2, 1)$.

22. If D_k maps $(2, -2)$ onto $(6, -6)$, find $D_k(-2, -1)$.

23. If D_k maps $(4, -2)$ onto $(2, -1)$, find $D_k(-6, 4)$.

24. If D_k maps $(-3, 6)$ onto $(-1, 2)$, find $D_k(9, -9)$.

Copy the figure and construct its image under $D_{C, 2}$.

25. 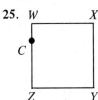 **26.** 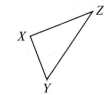 **27.**   **28.**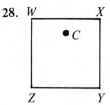

29-32. Refer to Exercises 25-28 and draw a larger version of the appropriate figure. Construct its image under $D_{C, \frac{1}{2}}$.

33. $\triangle ABC$ has vertices $A(1, 1)$, $B(4, -1)$, and $C(5, 1)$. Graph $D_3(\triangle ABC)$ and state the coordinates of its vertices.

34. Quadrilateral $QRST$ has vertices $Q(8, 0)$, $R(0, 4)$, $S(-4, 0)$, and $T(0, -12)$. Graph $D_{\frac{1}{4}}(QRST)$ and state the coordinates of its vertices.

B 35. $\triangle EFG$ has vertices $E(-1, 2)$, $F(3, -2)$, and $G(-1, -5)$. If C has coordinates $(3, -5)$, graph $D_{C, 2}(\triangle EFG)$ and state the coordinates of its vertices.

36. Square $WXYZ$ has vertices $W(-3, 3)$, $X(6, 3)$, $Y(6, -6)$, and $Z(-3, -6)$. If C has coordinates $(0, -3)$, graph $D_{C, \frac{1}{3}}(WXYZ)$ and state the coordinates of its vertices.

Find the center and scale factor of the dilation that maps points A and B onto A' and B' respectively. (*Hint*: Graph the points.)

37. $A(4, 1) \longrightarrow A'(1, 1)$, $B(3, 2) \longrightarrow B'(-3, 5)$

38. $A(1, 3) \longrightarrow A'(7, 4)$, $B(-1, 1) \longrightarrow B'(1, -2)$

Point A' is the image of A under the given dilation. Copy the figure and construct both C and B', the image of B.

39. $D_{C, 2}$ **40.** $D_{C, 3}$ **41.** $D_{C, \frac{1}{2}}$

42. Construct the image of Q under the dilation with center O that maps P onto P'.

Graph the image of the line with the given equation under the given dilation. State an equation of the image line.

43. $y = 2x; D_3$

44. $y = -4x; D_{\frac{1}{2}}$

45. $y = 3; D_{\frac{1}{3}}$

46. $x = -1; D_4$

47. $y = 2x - 3; D_2$

48. $y = -3x + 6; D_{\frac{1}{3}}$

49. Under D_k, what is the equation of the image of the line with the given equation? (c and d are constants.)

a. $y = mx$ b. $y = c$ c. $x = d$

50. What kinds of lines are mapped onto themselves by D_k?

Some textbooks define dilations so that a negative scale factor is permitted. Such a dilation is equivalent to the composite of a half-turn and a dilation with a positive scale factor. For example, the composite $R_{180} \circ D_2$ is equivalent to D_{-2}.

51. $\triangle ABC$ has vertices $A(-2, 0)$, $B(2, 4)$, and $C(6, 2)$. Graph its image under $R_{180} \circ D_{\frac{1}{2}}$, and state the coordinates of the vertices of the image.

52. Parallelogram $KLMN$ has vertices $K(-4, 0)$, $L(-2, 2)$, $M(0, -1)$, and $N(-2, -3)$. Graph its image under $R_{180} \circ D_2$, and state the coordinates of the vertices of the image.

Graph $\triangle ABC$, $\triangle A'B'C'$, $\triangle A''B''C''$, and $\triangle A'''B'''C'''$, and state the coordinates of A''', B''', and C'''.

C 53. $\triangle ABC$ has vertices $A(1, 2)$, $B(4, 1)$, and $C(3, -1)$.
$r_n: \triangle ABC \longrightarrow \triangle A'B'C'$, where n has equation $y = -x$
$T_{-1, 4}: \triangle A'B'C' \longrightarrow \triangle A''B''C''$
$D_2: \triangle A''B''C'' \longrightarrow \triangle A'''B'''C'''$

54. $\triangle ABC$ has vertices $A(0, -4)$, $B(4, -2)$, and $C(3, -5)$.
$\triangle A'B'C'$ is the image when $\triangle ABC$ is reflected in the origin.
$T_{3, -4}: \triangle A'B'C' \longrightarrow \triangle A''B''C''$
$D_3: \triangle A''B''C'' \longrightarrow \triangle A'''B'''C'''$

55. a. Graph the image of the parabola with equation $y = x^2$ under D_3.
b. Graph the image of the parabola with equation $y = -x^2$ under $D_{\frac{1}{2}}$.
c. State the equations of the images in parts (a) and (b).
d. If a is a nonzero constant, what is the equation of the image of the parabola with equation $y = ax^2$ under D_k?

SELF-TEST 3

1. If the diagonals of a square intersect at point P, describe the rotations greater than $0°$ and less than $360°$ that map the square onto itself.

Section 5-8

2. Which of the following letters have point symmetry?

B   H   I   P

3. What are the coordinates of the image when $(2, -5)$ is reflected in the origin?

Complete.

4. $D_4:(2, -1) \longrightarrow \underline{\quad ? \quad}$

5. If $D_k:(-3, 6) \longrightarrow (-1, 2)$, then $D_k:(-6, -12) \longrightarrow \underline{\quad ? \quad}$.

6. Rectangle $RSTW$ has vertices $R(-1, 2)$, $S(7, 2)$, $T(7, -2)$, and $W(-1, -2)$. If C has coordinates $(-3, 2)$, graph $D_{C, \frac{1}{2}}(RSTW)$ and state the coordinates of its vertices.

Computer Exercises

For the line reflection

$$r_l:(c, d) \longrightarrow (c', d')$$

there are formulas expressing the coordinates of an image point in terms of the coordinates of the pre-image and the slope and y-intercept of line l. If l has the equation $y = mx + b$, and (c', d') is the image of a given point (c, d), then:

$$c' = \frac{-2mb + (1 - m^2)c + 2md}{1 + m^2} \quad \text{and} \quad d' = \frac{2b + 2mc - (1 - m^2)d}{1 + m^2}$$

The program below calculates the values of c' and d' when the values of c, d, m, and b are given.

```
10   PRINT "TO FIND COORDINATES OF IMAGE OF (C, D)"
20   PRINT "UNDER REFLECTION IN LINE Y = MX + B"
30   PRINT
40   PRINT "TYPE SLOPE AND Y-INTERCEPT OF MIRROR LINE,"
50   PRINT "SEPARATED BY COMMA:";
60   INPUT M, B
70   LET R = 1 − M*M
80   LET S = 1 + M*M
90   PRINT
100  PRINT "TYPE COORDINATES OF POINT,"
110  PRINT "SEPARATED BY COMMA:";
120  INPUT C, D
130  LET C1 = (−2*M*B + R*C + 2*M*D)/S
140  LET D1 = (2*B + 2*M*C − R*D)/S
150  PRINT "IMAGE IS:    (";C1;", ";D1;")"
160  PRINT
170  PRINT "IS THERE ANOTHER POINT (NO = N, YES = Y)";
180  INPUT U$
190  IF U$ = "Y" THEN 90
200  PRINT "IS THERE ANOTHER LINE (NO = N, YES = Y)";
210  INPUT V$
220  IF V$ = "Y" THEN 30
230  END
```

1. Type in and RUN the program for the line k with equation $y = x$ ($m = 1$, $b = 0$). You know that $r_k:(c, d) \longrightarrow (d, c)$. Choose several points to use as inputs, and check that the program calculates the correct coordinates for the images.

2. RUN the program for the line l with equation $y = 2x + 1$. For each point (c, d) in the first column of the table below, enter its image $r_l(c, d)$ in the second column.

(c, d)	$r_l(c, d)$	$r_n \circ r_l(c, d)$	$r_t \circ r_l(c, d)$
$(0, 0)$	?	?	?
$(2, 5)$	?	?	?
$(-3, 8)$	?	?	?
$(4, 6.1)$	?	?	?

3. **a.** RUN the program again, for the line n with equation $y = 2x - 5$. For each point in the second column of the table, enter its image $r_n \circ r_l(c, d)$ in the third column.
   b. Since lines l and n both have a slope of 2, the lines are parallel. The composite $r_n \circ r_l$ is, therefore, a translation, say $T_{u, v}$. Find the values of u and v.

4. **a.** RUN the program again, for the line t with equation $y = -x + 4$. For each point in the second column of the table, enter its image $r_t \circ r_l(c, d)$ in the last column.
   b. Since lines l and t intersect at $P(1, 3)$, the composite $r_t \circ r_l$ is a rotation $R_{P, \theta}$ for some angle θ. Use the following procedure to find θ.
   Graph each point (c, d) and its image under the rotation. Using a compass, draw arcs with center $P(1, 3)$ that connect each point (c, d) to its image. Use a protractor to measure the angle of rotation, θ, from each point to its image.

CHAPTER REVIEW

Find the coordinates of the images of $A(2, 1)$, $B(-3, 4)$, and $C(-5, -2)$ under the given transformation if T and S are the transformations:

$$S:(x, y) \longrightarrow (y + 1, x - 1) \quad \text{and} \quad T:(x, y) \longrightarrow (x, 2y)$$

1. T 2. $S \circ T$ Section 5-1

Find the coordinates of the image D' when $D(-3, 1)$ is reflected over the given line.

3. x-axis 4. y-axis Section 5-2

5. The line k with equation $y = x$ 6. The line n with equation $y = -x$

7. Which of the following have Section 5-3
   a. a horizontal line of symmetry?
   b. a vertical line of symmetry?

A E H I O Z

Given that l, m, and n are lines of symmetry for the figure, complete.

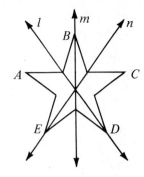

8. $r_l(C) = $ ___?___

Section 5-4

9. $r_m(\angle A) = $ ___?___

10. $r_n \circ r_l : B \longrightarrow $ ___?___

Section 5-5

11. $r_l \circ r_n \circ r_m : E \longrightarrow $ ___?___

12. Complete: $r_{\text{y-axis}} \circ r_n : (-2, 5) \longrightarrow $ ___?___ , where n has equation $y = -x$

13. Name the translation, in the form $T_{a, b}$, that maps $(-2, 4)$ onto $(5, 1)$.

Section 5-6

Complete.

14. If T is a translation and $T : (-2, 3) \longrightarrow (0, 1)$, then $T : (2, 4) \longrightarrow $ ___?___ .

15. If T is a translation and $T : (0, 0) \longrightarrow (-3, 2)$, then $T : $ ___?___ $\longrightarrow (4, 1)$.

16. $R_{-90} : (-3, 4) \longrightarrow $ ___?___   17. $R_{180} : (3, -2) \longrightarrow $ ___?___

Section 5-7

18. Name a counterclockwise rotation that is equivalent to a clockwise rotation of $90°$.

19. Describe the types of symmetry a rectangle has. Include a description of each line of symmetry, point of symmetry, and rotation greater than $0°$ and less than $360°$ that maps the rectangle onto itself.

Section 5-8

20. What are the coordinates of the image when $(-2, 4)$ is reflected in the point $(1, 2)$?

21. Complete: If $D_k : (2, 3) \longrightarrow (6, 9)$, then $D_k : (-2, 4) \longrightarrow $ ___?___

Section 5-9

22. $\triangle ABC$ has vertices $A(-3, 1)$, $B(1, 2)$, and $C(-1, -2)$. If point P has coordinates $(-3, -2)$, graph $D_{P, 2}(\triangle ABC)$ and state the coordinates of its vertices.

23. Name a property of a rotation that is *not* a property of a dilation.

CHAPTER TEST _____

Give the letter corresponding to the *best* name for the *type* of the given transformation.

1. r_l

2. R_{90}

3. $D_{C, 4}$

4. R_{180}

5. $T_{-2, 3}$

6. R_{-180}

7. $r_{\text{x-axis}} \circ r_{\text{y-axis}}$

8. $r_{\text{x-axis}} \circ r_m$, where line m has equation $y = 2$

a. Dilation
b. Half-turn
c. Reflection
d. Rotation
e. Translation

Classify as *always*, *sometimes*, or *never* true.

9. A regular polygon has both line and point symmetry.

10. A figure that has 180° rotational symmetry has point symmetry.

11. A figure that has point symmetry has rotational symmetry.

12. An isosceles trapezoid has point symmetry.

Find the coordinates of the image of $P(-4, 3)$ under the given transformation. The lines k and n have equations $y = x$ and $y = -x$, respectively.

13. $r_{x\text{-axis}}$

14. $r_{y\text{-axis}}$

15. r_k

16. r_n

17. R_{-90}

18. R_{90}

19. R_{180}

20. D_5

21. $r_{x\text{-axis}} \circ r_k$

22. $r_k \circ r_n$

23. $T_{2, -2}$

24. $T:(x, y) \longrightarrow (x, -2y)$

Complete.

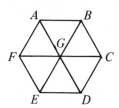

25. $R_{G, 60}: E \longrightarrow \underline{\quad?\quad}$

26. $R_{G, -240}: B \longrightarrow \underline{\quad?\quad}$

27. $R_{B, -60}: G \longrightarrow \underline{\quad?\quad}$

28. $R_{E, 120}: \underline{\quad?\quad} \longrightarrow F$

29. If T is a translation such that $T: A \longrightarrow F$, then
$T: \underline{\quad?\quad} \longrightarrow G$.

30. When $A(-4, 3)$ is reflected in the line with equation $x = 2$, the coordinates of its image are $\underline{\quad?\quad}$.

Exs. 25–29

31. If T is a translation and $T:(-3, 2) \longrightarrow (4, -1)$, then $T:(1, -2) \longrightarrow \underline{\quad?\quad}$.

32. If $D_k:(3, -9) \longrightarrow (1, -3)$, then $D_k:(-12, 6) \longrightarrow \underline{\quad?\quad}$.

33. When $B(-2, 3)$ is reflected through the point $(1, 1)$, the coordinates of its image are $\underline{\quad?\quad}$.

In the figure, lines n, s, and l are symmetry lines for square $ABCD$.

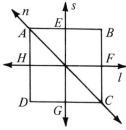

34. $r_s \circ r_n: B \longrightarrow \underline{\quad?\quad}$

35. $r_l \circ r_n: \overline{BF} \longrightarrow \underline{\quad?\quad}$

36. $r_n \circ r_l: \angle GCF \longrightarrow \underline{\quad?\quad}$

37. $r_l \circ r_n \circ r_s: H \longrightarrow \underline{\quad?\quad}$

State whether the letter or group of letters has:
a. point symmetry   **b.** horizontal line symmetry   **c.** vertical line symmetry

38. S

39. O

40. SOS

Biographical Note

Sonya (Corvin-Krukovsky) Kovalevsky

The Russian-born mathematician and novelist Sonya Kovalevsky crowded many achievements into her short life (1850–1891). She was a keen observer and recorder of the life around her and she was also fascinated by the mathematical laws of science.

As a teenager, Kovalevsky showed great mathematical ability. However, since Russian universities did not admit women at that time, she could not continue her studies in her own country. She married and went with her husband to Heidelberg, Germany, where she studied with the physicist Helmholtz and other eminent teachers. A few years later she went to Berlin. There she wanted to study with the great mathematician Weierstrass, but he attempted to discourage her by handing her a set of very difficult problems. Her solutions were so clear and original that Weierstrass accepted her as a private pupil. She studied with him for four years and wrote several important mathematical papers for which the University of Göttingen granted her a doctorate in 1874.

In 1883 Kovalevsky went to Sweden to teach mathematics at the University of Stockholm. Her work became increasingly well known to European mathematicians, and in 1888 her paper on the rotation of a solid body about a fixed point brought her a prestigious award from the French Academy of Science. Because of the excellence of this paper, the usual amount of the award was considerably increased. Further work on the same subject won a prize from the Swedish Academy of Sciences in the following year. In that year, too, Kovalevsky became professor of mathematics at the University of Stockholm and became the first woman to be elected to the Russian Academy of Sciences.

Kovalevsky's greatest contributions to mathematics were made in the theory of differential equations and in mathematical physics. Her best-known novels were stories of Russian life based on her own experience. She also won recognition as an active feminist at a time when women were excluded from many occupations.

VOCABULARY REVIEW

Be sure that you understand the meaning of these terms:

transformation, p. 170
identity transformation, p. 172
inverse transformation, p. 172
isometry, p. 172
direct isometry, p. 173
nondirect isometry, p. 173
reflection over a line, p. 175
line symmetry, p. 180
translation, p. 192

rotation, p. 197
rotational symmetry, p. 203
half-turn, p. 203
point symmetry, p. 204
translational symmetry, p. 205
expansion, p. 208
contraction, p. 208
dilation, p. 208

MIXED REVIEW

1. If $f(x) = \dfrac{1}{2x - 1}$ and $g(x) = \dfrac{1}{2}x^2$, find (a) $[f \circ g](-4)$, (b) $[g \circ f](-4)$, (c) $[f \circ g](x)$, and (d) $[g \circ f](x)$.

2. A report can be copied in 4 h using two copying machines. If one copier is used, 10 h would be needed to produce the copies. How long would the other copier need to do the job alone?

3. A regular octagon is inscribed in a circle with center O. Describe the types of symmetry that the octagon has.

4. Find a quadratic equation in standard form with integral coefficients and with $1 - i\sqrt{5}$ and $1 + i\sqrt{5}$ as roots.

Simplify.

5. $\sqrt[4]{48} + \sqrt[4]{243}$

6. $\dfrac{4}{1 - 3i}$

7. $(\sqrt{3} + 3\sqrt{2})^2$

8. If $f(x) = |x + 2|$ and $g(x) = |x| + 2$, classify each function as odd, even, or neither. Explain.

$ABCD$ is a square and W, X, Y, and Z are the midpoints of the sides. Lines k, l, m, and n are lines of symmetry.

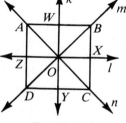

9. $R_{O, 270}: B \longrightarrow$?

10. $r_l \circ r_m \circ r_k: A \longrightarrow$?

11. $r_l \circ r_l: D \longrightarrow$?

12. If $T: W \longrightarrow A$, then $T:$? $\longrightarrow O$.

13. $D_{Z, \frac{1}{2}}: X \longrightarrow$?

14. $R_{B, -90} \circ D_{A, 2}: O \longrightarrow$?

15. Does the square have point symmetry?

Exs. 9-15

Solve and graph the solution set.

16. $|2y - 3| > 5$

17. $m^2 - 4m + 4 \leqslant 0$

18. $11 \geqslant 3.5j - 3 \geqslant -10$

19. Find the rational roots of $18x^3 + 15x^2 - 37x + 10 = 0$.

20. Factor completely: **a.** $24r^5 - 3r^2$ **b.** $8x^2 + 2xy - 15y^2$

21. Given the relation $x^2 + y^2 = 4$, **(a)** give the domain and the range, **(b)** graph the relation, and **(c)** explain why the relation is or is not a function.

Solve over the set of complex numbers.

22. $x^2 + 10x + 27 = 0$ 23. $25y^2 + 9 = 0$ 24. $4z^2 + 7 = 12z$

Find the coordinates of the image of $(4, -2)$ under the given transformation.

25. reflection over the y-axis

26. reflection over the line with equation $y = -x$

27. R_{180} 28. R_{-90} 29. D_3 30. $D_{\frac{5}{2}}$

31. On one set of axes, sketch the graphs of f and f^{-1} if $f(x) = x^3 - 4$.

32. Rae is driving at 90 km/h. She estimates that she has about 8 L of gas left. If Rae's car averages 10.5 km/L, can she drive for another hour without stopping to fill the tank?

33. Use linear interpolation between consecutive perfect squares to estimate the value of $\sqrt{67}$ to the nearest tenth.

Solve.

34. $\dfrac{x}{3x + 2} + \dfrac{5}{8} = 1$ 35. $\dfrac{x + 1}{5x - 1} + \dfrac{2}{x + 1} = 1$ 36. $\sqrt{4x + 1} + 1 = x$

37. If $f(x) = -\dfrac{1}{x}$, find $f(f(x))$. What does your answer show about $f(x)$?

Simplify.

38. $\dfrac{x - x^{-1}}{x - 1}$ 39. $\dfrac{2}{m - 3} - \dfrac{6}{m^2 - 3m}$ 40. $\left(\dfrac{18x^{-2}y}{12xy^{-1}} \right)^{-2}$

41. If $S:(x, y) \longrightarrow (3x, -y)$ and $T:(x, y) \longrightarrow (x - 7, y + 4)$, **(a)** classify each transformation as a direct isometry, a nondirect isometry, or neither, and **(b)** find the image of $(4, -9)$ under $S \circ T$ and under $T \circ S$.

Simplify.

42. $\dfrac{\sqrt{3} - 2}{\sqrt{3} - 1}$ 43. $\sqrt{-50} \cdot \sqrt{-18}$ 44. $(1 - 3 \cdot 4)^2 - 56 \div (-8)$

45. Solve: $-i(4 - 3xi) = \dfrac{1}{2}yi + 9$

The rope shown above has been neatly looped in coils that suggest concentric circles (although the rope is actually in the form of a spiral). In this chapter, you will study geometric properties of circles and figures related to circles, such as chords, tangents, and inscribed angles.

The Geometry of the Circle

6

For thousands of years, mathematicians have known that the ratio of the circumference (C) to the diameter (d) is the same for all circles. In the third century B.C., Archimedes showed that

$$3\frac{10}{71} < \frac{C}{d} < 3\frac{1}{7}.$$

His method involved finding the perimeters of regular polygons inscribed in and circumscribed about a circle.

Consider, for example, regular inscribed and circumscribed hexagons. Using the equilateral triangle shown, you can determine that the length of each side of the inscribed hexagon is $\frac{d}{2}$. Using the 30–60–90 triangle, you can show that the length of each side of the circumscribed hexagon is $\frac{\sqrt{3}d}{3}$. Thus:

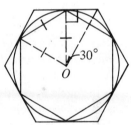

$$6\left(\frac{d}{2}\right) < C < 6\left(\frac{\sqrt{3}d}{3}\right)$$
$$3d < C < 2\sqrt{3}d$$
$$3 < \frac{C}{d} < 2\sqrt{3}$$

As the number of sides of the inscribed and circumscribed polygons increase, the perimeters more closely approximate the circumference of the circle.

Since Archimedes' time, more refined methods have been developed to calculate approximations for the ratio $\frac{C}{d}$. During the eighteenth century this ratio was named π (pi) and was shown to be an irrational number. More recently, with the aid of computers, π has been calculated to over a million decimal places. Rounded to eight decimal places, $\pi \approx 3.14159265$. In Section 6-7 you will use π to calculate the circumference and area of a circle, as well as other measures relating to circles.

Section 6-1 BASIC DEFINITIONS AND RELATIONSHIPS

You are probably already familiar with many of the basic terms used in studying circles. This section reviews the definitions of the following terms:

- circle
- radius, diameter
- interior point, external point
- chord, secant, tangent
- concentric circles
- congruent circles
- central angle, inscribed angle
- inscribed polygon, circumscribed polygon
- semicircle, minor arc, major arc
- intercepted arc

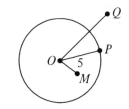

A *circle* is the set of all points in a plane that are a given distance from a given point (the *center* of the circle) in the plane. A *radius* (plural *radii*) of a circle is any segment whose endpoints are the center and a point on the circle. (The length of any such segment is called *the radius* of the circle.)

The radius of ⊙*O* is 5.   *OP* = 5
M lies inside, and is an *interior point* of, ⊙*O*.   *OM* < 5
Q lies outside, and is an *external point* of, ⊙*O*.   *OQ* > 5

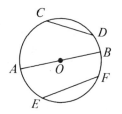

Any segment whose endpoints are two points of a circle is called a *chord* of the circle. A chord that contains the center of the circle is *a diameter* of the circle. (The length of any such segment is called *the diameter* of the circle.)

Chords: $\overline{AB}, \overline{CD}, \overline{EF}$
Diameter: $\overline{AB}$

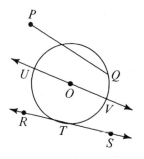

A *secant* is any line (or ray or segment) that has as a subset a chord of the circle. $\overline{PQ}$ and $\overleftrightarrow{UO}$ are secants. A segment such as $\overline{PQ}$ is called a *secant drawn to a circle from an external point.*

A *tangent* to a circle is any line in the plane of the circle that intersects the circle in exactly one point, called the *point of tangency.* $\overleftrightarrow{RS}$ is tangent to ⊙*O* at point *T.* A segment or ray that contains the point of tangency and is part of the tangent line is also called a tangent. Thus, $\overline{TS}, \overline{RS},$ and $\overrightarrow{TR}$ are tangents to ⊙*O.*

Concentric circles are circles in the same plane with the same center but different radii. The diagram at the left below shows concentric circles with centers at *O* and radii of 2, 4, and 5, respectively.

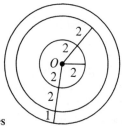

Concentric circles

Congruent circles

Congruent circles are circles with congruent radii. Thus, in the diagram on page 222, if $\overline{OA} \cong \overline{PQ}$, then $\odot O \cong \odot P$.

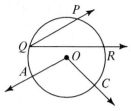

A *central angle* of a circle is an angle whose vertex is the center of the circle. In the diagram, $\angle AOC$ is a central angle.

An *inscribed angle* is an angle whose vertex lies on the circle and whose sides have as subsets chords of the circle. In the diagram, $\angle PQR$ is an inscribed angle.

An *inscribed polygon* is a polygon all of whose vertices lie on the same circle. Quadrilateral *ABCD* is *inscribed in* $\odot O$, and $\odot O$ is *circumscribed about* quadrilateral *ABCD*.

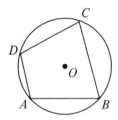

Inscribed polygon

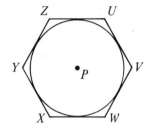

Circumscribed polygon

A *circumscribed polygon* is a polygon all of whose sides are tangent to the same circle. Hexagon *UVWXYZ* is said to be *circumscribed about* $\odot P$, and $\odot P$ is *inscribed in* hexagon *UVWXYZ*.

Three different types of *arcs* are illustrated below.

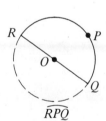

$\overgroup{RPQ}$
Semicircle

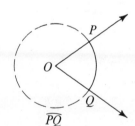

$\overgroup{PQ}$
Minor arc

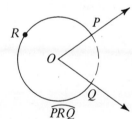

$\overgroup{PRQ}$
Major arc

If *R* and *Q* are endpoints of a diameter of a circle, then *R*, *Q*, and either half of the circle with endpoints *R* and *Q* is called a *semicircle*. If *P* and *Q* are not endpoints of a diameter of $\odot O$, then the arc consisting of *P*, *Q*, and all points in the interior of $\angle POQ$ is called a *minor arc* of $\odot O$ and is denoted $\overgroup{PQ}$. The arc consisting of *P*, *Q*, and all the points on the circle in the *exterior* of $\angle POQ$ is a *major arc*. To name a semicircle or major arc, you must use three letters.

An angle *intercepts* an arc if:

(1) each side of the angle contains an endpoint of the arc
(2) all other points of the arc lie in the interior of the angle

The diagrams at the top of the next page show several angles that intercept arcs.

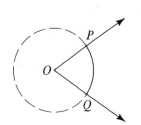

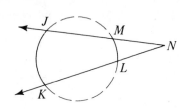

$\angle POQ$ intercepts $\overarc{PQ}$. $\angle DEF$ intercepts $\overarc{DGF}$. $\angle JNK$ intercepts $\overarc{ML}$ and $\overarc{JK}$.

We define the *measure of a minor arc* to be the measure of the central angle that intercepts it. Thus $m\,\overarc{AC} = m\angle AOC$, or $m\,\overarc{AC} = 70$. The *measure of a semicircle* is 180, and the *measure of an entire circle* is 360. The *measure of a major arc* is the difference between 360 and the measure of the corresponding minor arc. Thus, in the figure, $m\,\overarc{CAB} = 180$; $m\,\overarc{AB} = 180 - 70$, or 110; and $m\,\overarc{ABC} = 360 - 70$, or 290.

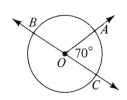

Two arcs of the same circle or congruent circles are *congruent* if they have the same measure.

EXAMPLE   If $m\angle AOB = 120$, find the values of x, y, and z.

SOLUTION $x = m\,\overarc{AB} = m\angle AOB = 120$

$y = m\,\overarc{ACB} = 360 - x = 240$

Since $\overline{OA} \cong \overline{OB}$, $m\angle A = m\angle B$ (by the Isosceles Triangle Theorem, which you studied last year).
Also $m\angle A + m\angle B + m\angle AOB = 180$.
Hence, $z + z + 120 = 180$

$2z = 60$

$z = 30$

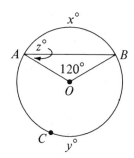

ORAL EXERCISES

1. Refer to the figure and name:
    a. two radii
    b. two tangents
    c. a secant
    d. a diameter
    e. two central angles
    f. two inscribed angles
    g. three minor arcs
    h. two semicircles
    i. two major arcs
    j. an inscribed polygon

2. If $OA = 5$ and $m\,\overarc{AT} = 100$, find:
    a. AB
    b. OT
    c. $m\,\overarc{TB}$
    d. $m\,\overarc{ACB}$
    e. $m\angle TOB$
    f. $m\angle AOT$

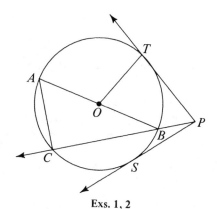

Exs. 1, 2

Classify each statement as true or false.

3. All radii of the same circle are congruent.

4. All chords of the same circle are congruent.

5. A radius of a circle contains two points of the circle.

6. Concentric circles are congruent.

7. If central $\angle AOC$ intercepts $\overset{\frown}{AC}$ on $\odot O$ and $m\overset{\frown}{AC} = 90$, then $\angle AOC$ is a right angle.

8. Each side of a polygon inscribed in a circle is a chord of the circle.

9. A diameter is the longest chord of a circle.

10. Two secants to a circle can intersect inside, outside, or on the circle.

11. A tangent and a chord must intersect at a point on the circle or not at all.

12. Two chords can only intersect inside the circle.

WRITTEN EXERCISES

State the term that best describes each set of points with respect to $\odot O$.

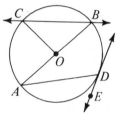

A
1. $\overline{OA}$ **2.** $\overline{AD}$ **3.** $\overline{BC}$

4. $\overleftrightarrow{BC}$ **5.** $\overrightarrow{DE}$ **6.** $\overline{AB}$

7. $\angle BOC$ **8.** $\angle BAD$ **9.** $\overset{\frown}{ACB}$

10. $\overset{\frown}{BC}$ **11.** $\overset{\frown}{BAD}$ **12.** E

13. $\overline{AB}$ and $\overline{CD}$ are diameters of $\odot O$. If $m\angle COB = 105$, find the measure of each minor arc of the circle.

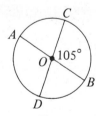

Ex. 13

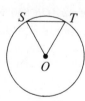

Ex. 14

14. In the figure, $\overline{OS} \cong \overline{ST}$. Find $m\overset{\frown}{ST}$.

15. For $\odot O$, find each of the following:

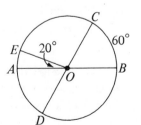

     a. $m\overset{\frown}{AE}$ **b.** $m\angle BOC$ **c.** $m\overset{\frown}{ADB}$

     d. $m\overset{\frown}{AD}$ **e.** $m\overset{\frown}{BD}$ **f.** $m\overset{\frown}{EC}$

     g. $m\overset{\frown}{BDE}$ **h.** $m\overset{\frown}{BDC}$ **i.** $m\overset{\frown}{CDE}$

In Exercises 16–24, O is the center of the circle. Find the values of x, y, and z.

B 16.

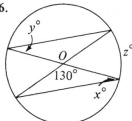

17.

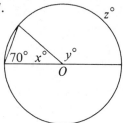

18.

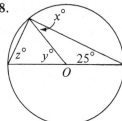

19.

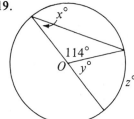

20.

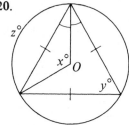

21.

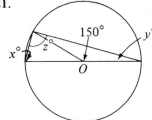

22.

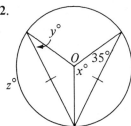

23.

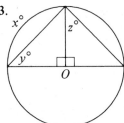

24.

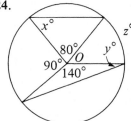

25. In the figure at the right, E is a point on $\odot O$ such that $m\,\widehat{AE} : m\,\widehat{FB} = 2:3$. Find $m\angle AOE$ and $m\angle EOB$.

26. Points C and D on $\odot O$ divide the circle into a major arc and a minor arc. If the measure of the major arc is 15 less than twice the measure of the minor arc, find the measure of each arc.

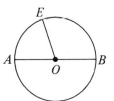

C 27. In the figure, $m\angle YOZ : m\angle XYZ = 3:1$. Find $m\angle XOZ$, $m\angle Y$, and $m\,\widehat{XZ}$. How are $m\angle Y$ and $m\,\widehat{XZ}$ related?

28. Quadrilateral $ABCD$ is inscribed in circle P such that $m\,\widehat{AD} = m\,\widehat{BC}$, $m\,\widehat{CD}$ is 8 less than twice $m\,\widehat{AD}$, and $m\,\widehat{AB}$ is 4 more than three times $m\,\widehat{AD}$. Find the measure of each angle of the quadrilateral. What kind of quadrilateral is $ABCD$?

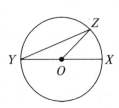

Section 6-2 INSCRIBED ANGLES

In this section you will learn the relationship between the measure of an inscribed angle and the measure of the arc that it intercepts on the circle. To prepare for this and other circle theorems, you need to review the following postulates and theorems from your previous study of geometry.

Angle Addition Postulate	If D is in the interior of $\angle ABC$, then $m\angle ABD + m\angle DBC = m\angle ABC$.
SSS Postulate	If the three sides of one triangle are congruent to the three sides of another triangle, then the two triangles are congruent.
ASA Postulate	If two angles and the included side of one triangle are congruent to two angles and the included side of another triangle, then the two triangles are congruent.
SAS Postulate	If two sides and the included angle of one triangle are congruent to two sides and the included angle of another triangle, then the two triangles are congruent.
HL Postulate	If the hypotenuse and a leg of one right triangle are congruent to the hypotenuse and a leg of another right triangle, then the two triangles are congruent.
AAS Theorem	If two angles and a non-included side of one triangle are congruent to two angles and the corresponding non-included side of another triangle, then the triangles are congruent.
Triangle Angle-Sum Theorem	The sum of the measures of the angles of any triangle is 180.
Exterior Angle Theorem	The measure of an exterior angle of a triangle is equal to the sum of the measures of the two remote interior angles.
AA Similarity Theorem	If two angles of one triangle are congruent to two angles of another triangle, then the two triangles are similar.
Perpendicular Bisector Theorem	A point lies on the perpendicular bisector of a segment if and only if it is equidistant from the endpoints of the segment.

Each of the following two theorems is written as a biconditional, combining a theorem with its converse, which is also true.

Isosceles Triangle Theorem	Two sides of a triangle are congruent if and only if the angles opposite these sides are congruent.
Alternate Interior Angle Theorem	Two lines cut by a transversal are parallel if and only if the alternate interior angles formed are congruent.

Here are some additional facts you should keep in mind.

Corresponding parts of congruent triangles are congruent.

The lengths of corresponding sides of similar triangles are proportional.

Through a given point not on a given line, there is exactly one line perpendicular to the given line.

You should also keep in mind the properties of equality listed on page 11.

The following postulate, which is similar to the Angle Addition Postulate, is useful for solving certain problems involving circles.

Arc Addition Postulate

If the intersection of arcs $\widehat{AX}$ and $\widehat{XB}$ of a circle is a single point X, then $m\,\widehat{AX} + m\,\widehat{XB} = m\,\widehat{AXB}$.

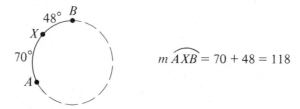

$$m\,\widehat{AXB} = 70 + 48 = 118$$

In the previous section, the measure of a minor arc was defined to be equal to the measure of the central angle that intercepts it. The following theorem states the relationship between the measure of an inscribed angle and the measure of its intercepted arc.

Theorem 6-1   The measure of an inscribed angle is half the measure of its intercepted arc.

There are three cases to consider in the proof of Theorem 6-1, depending on whether the center of the circle is on, inside, or outside the inscribed angle. The three cases are illustrated in the diagrams below.

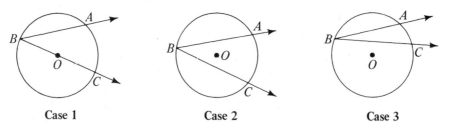

Case 1   Case 2   Case 3

The proof for Case 1 is given below. Cases 2 and 3 will be proved in Exercises 31 and 32.

GIVEN: $\angle ABC$ is inscribed in $\odot O$. O lies on $\overrightarrow{BC}$.

PROVE: $m\angle ABC = \dfrac{1}{2}m\,\widehat{AC}$

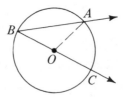

Statements	Reasons
1. Draw $\overline{OA}$.	1. Two points determine a line.
2. $\overline{OA} \cong \overline{OB}$	2. All radii of a circle are $\cong$.
3. $\angle ABC \cong \angle BAO$, or $m\angle ABC = m\angle BAO$	3. If two sides of a $\triangle$ are $\cong$, then the angles opposite these sides are $\cong$.
4. $m\angle ABC + m\angle BAO = m\angle AOC$	4. The measure of an exterior $\angle$ of a $\triangle$ is equal to the sum of the measures of the 2 remote interior $\angle$s of the $\triangle$.
5. $m\angle ABC + m\angle ABC = m\angle AOC$, or $2m\angle ABC = m\angle AOC$	5. Substitution Prop.
6. $m\angle ABC = \frac{1}{2}m\angle AOC$	6. Division Prop. of Equality
7. $m\angle AOC = m\,\widehat{AC}$	7. The measure of a central $\angle$ of a $\odot$ is equal to the measure of its intercepted arc.
8. $m\angle ABC = \frac{1}{2}m\,\widehat{AC}$	8. Substitution Prop.

Several useful corollaries follow from this theorem.

Corollary 1 Inscribed angles that intercept the same arc or congruent arcs of a circle are congruent.

Since $\angle B$, $\angle D$, and $\angle E$ each intercept $\widehat{AC}$, each has measure $\frac{1}{2}m\,\widehat{AC}$.
Therefore, $m\angle B = m\angle D = m\angle E$.

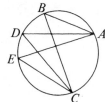

Corollary 2 An angle inscribed in a semicircle is a right angle.

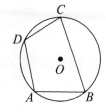

Corollary 3 If a quadrilateral is inscribed in a circle, then opposite angles are supplementary.

The proof of this corollary is left as Exercise 35.

EXAMPLE Find $m\,\widehat{AC}$, $m\,\widehat{BC}$, and $m\,\widehat{AXB}$.

SOLUTION $m\angle A + m\angle B + m\angle C = 180$
$50 + 30 + m\angle C = 180$
$m\angle C = 100$

Since each inscribed angle is half the measure of its intercepted arc, each intercepted arc is twice the measure of the associated angle. Therefore, $m\,\widehat{AC} = 2 \cdot 30 = 60$, $m\,\widehat{BC} = 2 \cdot 50 = 100$, and $m\,\widehat{AXB} = 2 \cdot 100 = 200$.

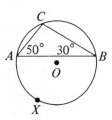

EXAMPLE   Quadrilateral $ABCD$ is inscribed in $\odot O$, $m\angle A = 68$, and $m\angle B = 50$. Find $m\angle C$ and $m\angle D$.

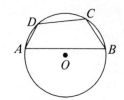

SOLUTION   By Corollary 3 to Theorem 6-1:

$m\angle C = 180 - 68 = 112$

$m\angle D = 180 - 50 = 130$

ORAL EXERCISES

Find the value of x. (Point O is the center of the circle.)

1.
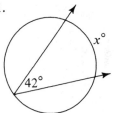

2.
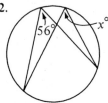

3.
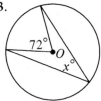

4. Why is it not possible to circumscribe a circle about a quadrilateral whose angles have measures 65, 80, 120, and 95?

5. If $m\,\overset{\frown}{PR} = 140$, and $m\angle R = 32$, find $m\,\overset{\frown}{PS}$ and $m\,\overset{\frown}{RS}$.

6. If $m\,\overset{\frown}{RS} = 170$, and $m\,\overset{\frown}{PR} = 100$, find $m\,\overset{\frown}{PS}$ and $m\angle R$.

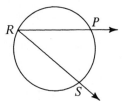

7. Find $m\angle P$ and $m\angle Q$.

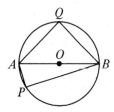

8. Find $m\angle J$ and $m\angle M$.

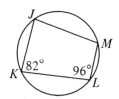

WRITTEN EXERCISES

Find the measure of an inscribed angle that intercepts an arc having the given measure.

A 1. 60   2. 320   3. 45   4. 180   5. $4x$ 6. $a + b$

Find the measure of the arc intercepted by an inscribed angle having the given measure.

7. 16   8. 115   9. 86   10. 45   11. $4x$ 12. $a + b$

In Exercises 13–21, when point O is shown, it is the center of the circle. Find the value of each variable.

13.
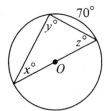
70°
y°
z°
x° O

14.
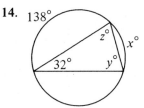
138°
z°
x°
32°
y°

15.
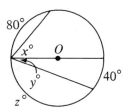
80°
x° O
y°
40°
z°

16.
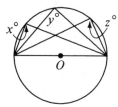
x° y° z°
O

17.
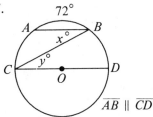
72°
A B
x°
y°
C O D
$\overline{AB} \parallel \overline{CD}$

18.
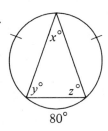
x°
y° z°
80°

19. 150°
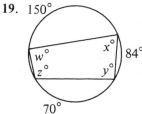
x° 84°
w°
z° y°
70°

20.
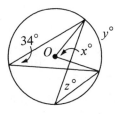
34°
y°
O x°
z°

21. 70°
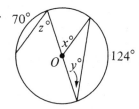
z°
x°
O y° 124°

Exercises 22–24 refer to quadrilateral $ABCD$ inscribed in a circle.

22. If $m\angle A = 95$, find $m\angle C$.

23. If $m\angle B : m\angle D = 1:4$, find $m\angle B$ and $m\angle D$.

24. If $m\,\widehat{AB} = 118$ and $m\,\widehat{BC} = 74$, find $m\angle B$ and $m\angle D$.

B **25.** If an inscribed angle and a central angle intercept the same arc on a circle, what is the ratio of the measure of the inscribed angle to the measure of the central angle?

26. The sum of the measures of an inscribed angle and a central angle intercepting the same arc on a circle is 225. Find the measure of each angle.

Find the value of each variable. (Point O is the center of the circle.)

27.
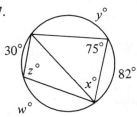
y°
30°
75°
z°
x° 82°
w°

28.
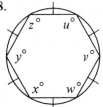
z° u°
y°
v°
x° w°

29.
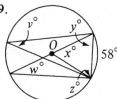
v° y°
O
x° 58°
w°
z°

30. The vertices of an inscribed triangle divide a circle into three arcs whose measures are in the ratio 5:6:7. Find the measure of the largest angle of the triangle.

31. Use the diagram to prove Case 2 of Theorem 6-1, in which the center of the circle is *inside* the angle. (*Hint*: Draw diameter $\overline{BD}$ and use Case 1.)

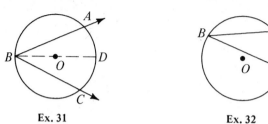

Ex. 31   Ex. 32

32. Use the diagram to prove Case 3 of Theorem 6-1, in which the center of the circle is outside the angle. (*Hint*: See Exercise 31.)

33. Trapezoid *ABCD* with bases $\overline{AB}$ and $\overline{CD}$ is inscribed in $\odot O$. If $m\,\overset{\frown}{BC} = 62$ and $m\,\overset{\frown}{DC} = 48$, find the measure of each angle of the trapezoid.

34. Point *A* lies on minor arc $\overset{\frown}{DE}$ of $\odot O$. If $m\angle DAE = y$, find $m\angle DOE$ in terms of *y*.

35. Prove Corollary 3 of Theorem 6-1: If a quadrilateral is inscribed in a circle, then opposite angles are supplementary.

36. Use Corollary 3 of Theorem 6-1 to prove that a parallelogram inscribed in a circle is a rectangle.

Section 6-3 ANGLES FORMED BY TANGENTS AND CHORDS

You learned in Section 6-1 that the vertex of an inscribed angle lies on the circle. The diagram at the right shows another type of angle whose vertex lies on a circle. $\angle XYZ$ is an angle formed by tangent $\overrightarrow{YZ}$ and chord $\overline{XY}$. $\angle XYZ$ intercepts $\overset{\frown}{XY}$. In this section you will learn the relationship between this type of angle and its intercepted arc.

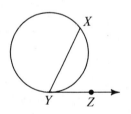

First, consider the angle formed by a tangent to a circle and the radius drawn to the point of tangency. We will use an *indirect proof* to prove that the tangent and the radius are perpendicular.

Theorem 6-2   A tangent to a circle is perpendicular to the radius drawn to the point of tangency.

GIVEN: $\odot O$; tangent $\overleftrightarrow{AP}$, radius $\overline{OA}$
PROVE: $\overline{OA} \perp \overleftrightarrow{AP}$

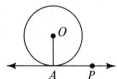

Proof: Through point O (which is not on $\overleftrightarrow{AP}$), there is exactly one line perpendicular to $\overleftrightarrow{AP}$. Assume temporarily that $\overline{OA}$ is *not* perpendicular to $\overleftrightarrow{AP}$. Thus, $\overleftrightarrow{AP}$ contains a point T, other than A, such that $\overline{OT} \perp \overleftrightarrow{AP}$. Then on the ray opposite to $\overrightarrow{TA}$ there is a point B such that $TB = TA$. Since $\overline{OT} \cong \overline{OT}$, $\triangle OTB \cong \triangle OTA$ (SAS). Thus $\overline{OB} \cong \overline{OA}$, which means that tangent $\overleftrightarrow{AP}$ intersects $\odot O$ at both A and B. Since the assumption that $\overline{OA}$ is *not* perpendicular to $\overleftrightarrow{AP}$ leads to this contradiction, that assumption is incorrect. Therefore $\overline{OA} \perp \overleftrightarrow{AP}$.

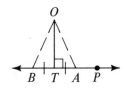

The proof of Theorem 6-3, which is the converse of Theorem 6-2, is left as Exercise 34.

Theorem 6-3 A line that lies in the plane of a circle and is perpendicular to a radius at a point of the circle is tangent to the circle.

Theorem 6-4 The measure of an angle formed by a tangent and a chord is half the measure of the intercepted arc.

Outline of proof: Three cases are shown below.

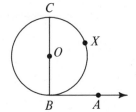 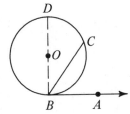 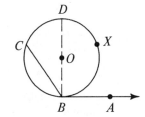

I. O lies on $\angle ABC$.   II. O is outside $\angle ABC$.   III. O is inside $\angle ABC$.

I. When O lies on $\angle ABC$, $\overline{CB} \perp \overrightarrow{BA}$ by Theorem 6-2. Since $m\angle CBA = 90$ and $m\,\overparen{BXC} = 180$, $m\angle CBA = \frac{1}{2}m\,\overparen{BXC}$.

II. When O is outside $\angle ABC$, draw diameter $\overline{BD}$. By Theorem 6-1, $m\angle DBC = \frac{1}{2}m\,\overparen{CD}$.

$$m\angle DBA = m\angle DBC + m\angle CBA \text{ and } m\,\overparen{BCD} = m\,\overparen{BC} + m\,\overparen{CD}$$

By Case I: $$m\angle DBA = \frac{1}{2}m\,\overparen{BCD}$$

$$m\angle DBC + m\angle CBA = \frac{1}{2}(m\,\overparen{BC} + m\,\overparen{CD})$$

$$\frac{1}{2}m\,\overparen{CD} + m\angle CBA = \frac{1}{2}m\,\overparen{BC} + \frac{1}{2}m\,\overparen{CD}$$

$$m\angle CBA = \frac{1}{2}m\,\overparen{BC}$$

III. When O is inside $\angle ABC$, draw diameter $\overline{BD}$ and use an argument similar to that for Case II.

EXAMPLE $\overleftrightarrow{AC}$ is tangent to $\odot O$ at B; $m \widehat{BPD} = 250$
Find $m\angle ABD$.

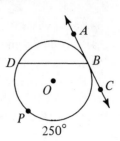

SOLUTION $m\angle CBD = \dfrac{1}{2}m\widehat{BPD} = \dfrac{1}{2}(250) = 125$

Since $\angle ABD$ and $\angle CBD$ are supplementary:
$m\angle ABD = 180 - 125 = 55$

To solve certain problems involving tangents, you will need to review the following relationships between the sides of 45–45–90 and 30–60–90 triangles.

45–45–90 triangle

If length of one leg $= a$, then:
length of other leg $= a$
length of hypotenuse $= a\sqrt{2}$

30–60–90 triangle

If length of *shorter* leg $= a$, then:
length of *longer* leg $= a\sqrt{3}$
length of hypotenuse $= 2a$

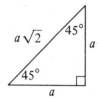

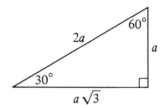

EXAMPLE Find the length of a side of a square with a diagonal of length 6.

SOLUTION Two 45–45–90 triangles are formed.
Let $s =$ the length of a side of the square.
Then $s\sqrt{2} =$ the length of the diagonal.

$$s\sqrt{2} = 6$$
$$s = \frac{6}{\sqrt{2}} = \frac{6}{\sqrt{2}} \cdot \frac{\sqrt{2}}{\sqrt{2}} = \frac{6\sqrt{2}}{2} = 3\sqrt{2}$$

Therefore, a side of the square has length $3\sqrt{2}$.

EXAMPLE $\overline{PQ}$ is tangent to $\odot O$; $OP = 4$; $m\angle OPQ = 30$
Find PQ.

SOLUTION Since $m\angle OPQ = 30$ and radius $\overline{OQ}$ is perpendicular to $\overline{PQ}$, $\triangle OPQ$ is a 30–60–90 triangle.
$\overline{OQ}$ is the shorter leg. Thus if $OQ = a$, $PQ = a\sqrt{3}$, and $OP = 2a$.
Since $2a = 4$, $a = 2$.
Therefore $PQ = 2\sqrt{3}$.

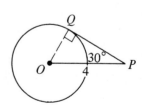

ORAL EXERCISES

Find the measure of each numbered angle. (Point O is the center of the circle.)

1.
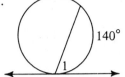
140°

2.
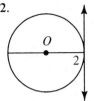
O
2

3.
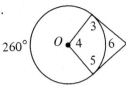
260°

4.
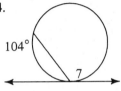
104°
7

5.
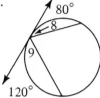
80°
8
9
120°

6.
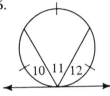
10 11 12

Complete the following table for the lengths of the sides of a 45-45-90 triangle.

	7.	8.	9.	10.
leg	5	?	?	$7\sqrt{3}$
hypotenuse	?	$6\sqrt{2}$	8	?

Complete the following table for the lengths of the sides of a 30-60-90 triangle.

	11.	12.	13.	14.	15.	16.
shorter leg	4	?	?	$5\sqrt{3}$	?	?
longer leg	?	?	$9\sqrt{3}$	?	?	12
hypotenuse	?	14	?	?	$4\sqrt{2}$	?

WRITTEN EXERCISES

Find the value of each variable. (Point O is the center of the circle.)

A 1.
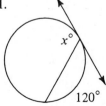
$x°$
120°

2.
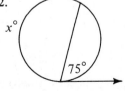
$x°$
75°

3.
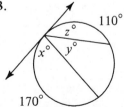
110°
$z°$
$x°$ $y°$
170°

Find the value of each variable. (Point *O* is the center of the circle.)

4.

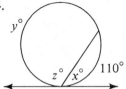

5.

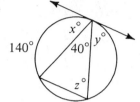

6.

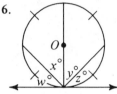

7.

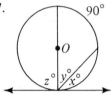

8.

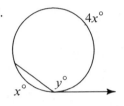

9.

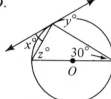

10.

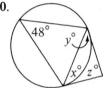

11.

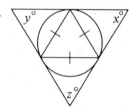

12.

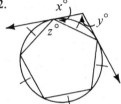

In Exercises 13–16, $\overline{AB}$ is tangent to $\odot O$. Complete.

13. $OA = 5$; $AB = 12$; $OB = \underline{\ ?\ }$

14. $AB = 10$; $OB = 12$; $OA = \underline{\ ?\ }$

15. $OA = 10\sqrt{2}$; $m\angle AOB = 45$; $OB = \underline{\ ?\ }$

16. $AB = 16\sqrt{3}$; $m\angle ABO = 30$; $OA = \underline{\ ?\ }$; $BC = \underline{\ ?\ }$

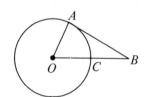

Exs. 13–16

The measure of an angle formed by a tangent and a chord is given. Find the measure of each arc of the circle determined by the endpoints of the chord.

17. 49   **18.** 136

In Exercises 19 and 20, $\overrightarrow{PA}$ and $\overrightarrow{PB}$ are tangent to $\odot O$ at *A* and *B*, respectively.

19. If $m\,\overparen{AXB} = 210$, find $m\angle P$.

20. a. If $m\angle P = 40$, find $m\angle PAB$ and $m\angle PBA$.
     b. How are *PA* and *PB* related?

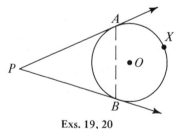

Exs. 19, 20

B 21. Find the measure of the acute angle formed by a tangent and a chord if the ratio of the measures of the two arcs determined by the endpoints of the chord is $4:5$.

236   *CHAPTER 6*

22. In the diagram, $m \widehat{AB} : m \widehat{BC} : m \widehat{CA} = 4:5:11$. Find $m\angle CAP$, $m\angle CAB$, and $m\angle BAQ$.

23. In the diagram, $m \widehat{BCA}$ is 16 more than three times $m \widehat{BA}$. Find $m\angle BAQ$.

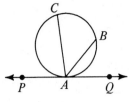

Exs. 22, 23

24. Triangle ABC is inscribed in $\odot O$. $m \widehat{AB} : m \widehat{BC} : m \widehat{CA} = 3:2:1$. Find the measure of the acute angle formed by the intersection of $\overline{BC}$ and the tangent to the circle at B.

25. In the diagram for Exercises 13–16, if $AB = 4$ and $BC = 2$, find the radius of the circle.

26. $\triangle ABC$ is inscribed in $\odot O$. $\overleftrightarrow{RS}$ is tangent to $\odot O$ at C. $\overline{BC} \cong \overline{OB}$
   a. Find $m\angle SCB$.
   b. If $OC = \sqrt{2}$, find AC.

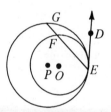

27. $\overrightarrow{ED}$ is tangent to both $\odot O$ and $\odot P$ at E; $m \widehat{EG} = 86$
   Find $m \widehat{EF}$.

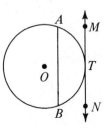

28. Given: Isosceles $\triangle ABC$ is inscribed in $\odot O$; $\overline{AC} \cong \overline{BC}$; $\overleftrightarrow{PQ}$ is tangent to $\odot O$ at C.
   Prove: $\overleftrightarrow{PQ} \parallel \overline{AB}$

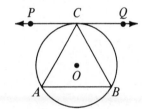

C 29. Quadrilateral $PQRS$ is circumscribed about a circle. $\overline{PQ}$ is tangent to the circle at A, $\overline{QR}$ at B, $\overline{RS}$ at C, and $\overline{PS}$ at D. If $m\angle P = 68$, $m\angle Q = 74$, and $m\angle R = 114$, find the measures of the angles of quadrilateral $ABCD$.

30. Given: $\odot O$; chord $\overline{AB}$; $m \widehat{AT} = m \widehat{BT}$; $\overleftrightarrow{MN}$ is tangent to $\odot O$ at T.
   Prove: $\overleftrightarrow{MN} \parallel \overline{AB}$

31. Given: $\overline{PQ}$ is tangent to $\odot O$ at P; $\overline{NQ} \perp \overline{PQ}$.
   Prove: $\overleftrightarrow{PN}$ bisects $\angle MNQ$.

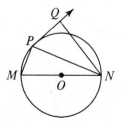

32. Two coplanar circles are *tangent* to each other if they are tangent to the same line at the same point on the line.

Given: ⊙O and ⊙P are tangent to each other at T, as shown in the diagram at the left below.

Prove: OT + TP = OP

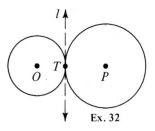

Ex. 32

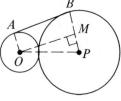

Ex. 33

33. ⊙O and ⊙P are tangent circles, and $\overline{AB}$ is tangent to ⊙O at A and to ⊙P at B. If OA = 4, and PB = 9, find AB, the length of the *common external tangent*. (*Hint:* Draw $\overline{OP}$, and draw $\overline{OM} \perp \overline{PB}$.)

34. Use an indirect proof to prove Theorem 6-3. (*Hint:* Given that $\overleftrightarrow{AB}$ is perpendicular to radius $\overline{OA}$ of ⊙O, assume temporarily that $\overleftrightarrow{AB}$ also intersects the circle at a second point, C.)

SELF-TEST 1

Classify each statement as true or false.

1. All diameters of the same circle intersect in the same point.
   Section 6-1

2. The angles formed by the intersection of any two chords are inscribed angles.

3. Every chord of a circle is longer than the radius.

4. Concentric circles do not intersect.

Find the value of each variable. (Point O is the center of the circle.)

5.
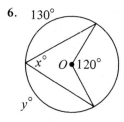

6.
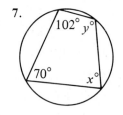

7.
Section 6-2

8.
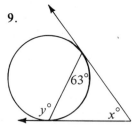

9.

10.
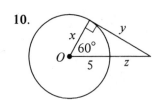
Section 6-3

238   *CHAPTER 6*

Section 6-4 ANGLES WITH VERTICES INSIDE OR OUTSIDE THE CIRCLE

So far you have studied angles with vertices either at the center of the circle or on the circle. In this section, you will learn how to find the measures of angles with vertices either inside or outside the circle; specifically, the measures of angles formed by:

- two chords
- two secants
- a secant and a tangent
- two tangents

As Theorem 6-5 illustrates, the measure of the angle formed in each case listed above depends on the measures of the intercepted arcs.

Theorem 6-5   The measure of an angle formed by two chords intersecting inside a circle is equal to half the sum of the measures of the arcs intercepted by the angle and its vertical angle.

GIVEN: Chords $\overline{AB}$ and $\overline{CD}$, intersecting at R.

PROVE: $m\angle 1 = \dfrac{1}{2}(m\,\widehat{AC} + m\,\widehat{BD})$

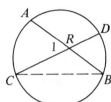

Statements	Reasons
1. Draw $\overline{BC}$.	1. Two points determine a line.
2. $m\angle 1 = m\angle B + m\angle C$	2. The measure of an exterior angle of a triangle is equal to the sum of the measures of the two remote interior angles of the triangle.
3. $m\angle B = \dfrac{1}{2}m\,\widehat{AC}$ $m\angle C = \dfrac{1}{2}m\,\widehat{BD}$	3. The measure of an inscribed angle is half the measure of the intercepted arc.
4. $m\angle 1 = \dfrac{1}{2}m\,\widehat{AC} + \dfrac{1}{2}m\,\widehat{BD}$	4. Substitution Prop.
5. $m\angle 1 = \dfrac{1}{2}(m\,\widehat{AC} + m\,\widehat{BD})$	5. Distributive Prop.

EXAMPLE   In the diagram, $m\angle DEA = 64$ and $m\,\widehat{BC} = 42$. Find $m\,\widehat{AD}$.

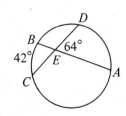

SOLUTION $\dfrac{1}{2}(m\,\widehat{AD} + m\,\widehat{BC}) = m\angle DEA$

$\dfrac{1}{2}(m\,\widehat{AD} + 42) = 64$

$m\,\widehat{AD} = 128 - 42$, or 86

The remaining theorems in this section are concerned with angles whose vertices lie outside a given circle.

Consider the case where two secants, $\overline{AP}$ and $\overline{CP}$, intersect at the external point P as shown in the diagram at the right. If we let $m\angle ABC = x$ and $m\angle BCD = y$, then, by the Exterior Angle Theorem,

$$y + m\angle P = x, \text{ or } m\angle P = x - y.$$

Since $\angle ABC$ and $\angle BCD$ are inscribed angles, you can use Theorem 6-1 to find $m\,\widehat{AC}$ and $m\,\widehat{BD}$ in terms of x and y:

$$m\,\widehat{AC} = 2\,m\angle ABC = 2x \qquad m\,\widehat{BD} = 2\,m\angle BCD = 2y$$

Thus:

$$m\angle P = x - y = \frac{1}{2}(2x - 2y) = \frac{1}{2}(m\,\widehat{AC} - m\,\widehat{BD})$$

This justifies the following theorem for the case involving two secants. The remaining cases will be proved in Written Exercise 35 and Oral Exercise 12.

Theorem 6-6 The measure of an angle formed by two secants, a secant and a tangent, or two tangents drawn from a point outside the circle is equal to half the difference of the measures of the intercepted arcs.

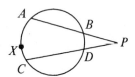

$$m\angle P = \frac{1}{2}(m\,\widehat{AXC} - m\,\widehat{BD})$$

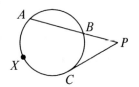

$$m\angle P = \frac{1}{2}(m\,\widehat{AXC} - m\,\widehat{BC})$$

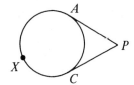

$$m\angle P = \frac{1}{2}(m\,\widehat{AXC} - m\,\widehat{AC})$$

EXAMPLE In the diagram, $m\,\widehat{TW} = 145$ and $m\angle R = 46$. Find $m\,\widehat{SW}$.

SOLUTION Let $m\,\widehat{SW} = x$ and use Theorem 6-6.

$$m\angle R = \frac{1}{2}(m\,\widehat{TW} - m\,\widehat{SW})$$

$$46 = \frac{1}{2}(145 - x)$$

$$92 = 145 - x$$

$$-53 = -x$$

$$53 = x$$

Therefore, $m\,\widehat{SW} = 53$.

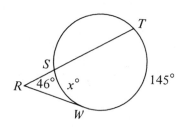

ORAL EXERCISES

Complete.

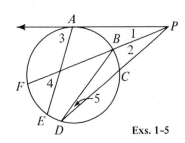

Exs. 1-5

1. $m\angle 1 = \frac{1}{2}(\underline{\quad ? \quad})$ **2.** $m\angle 2 = \frac{1}{2}(\underline{\quad ? \quad})$

3. $m\angle 3 = \frac{1}{2}(\underline{\quad ? \quad})$ **4.** $m\angle 4 = \frac{1}{2}(\underline{\quad ? \quad})$

5. $m\angle 5 = \frac{1}{2}(\underline{\quad ? \quad})$

Find the measure of each numbered angle.

6.
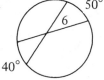

7.
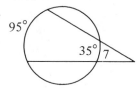

8.
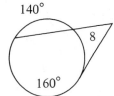

9.

10.
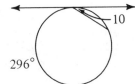

11.
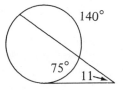

12. State the reasons for each step of the following proof of Theorem 6-6 for the case where the angle is formed by two tangents.

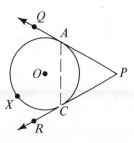

GIVEN: $\overrightarrow{PQ}$ and $\overrightarrow{PR}$ are tangent to $\odot O$ at A and C, respectively.

PROVE: $m\angle P = \frac{1}{2}(m\,\widehat{AXC} - m\,\widehat{AC})$

Statements	Reasons
1. Draw $\overline{AC}$.	1. ___?___
2. $m\angle P + m\angle PAC = m\angle ACR$	2. ___?___
3. $m\angle P = m\angle ACR - m\angle PAC$	3. ___?___
4. $\overrightarrow{PQ}$ and $\overrightarrow{PR}$ are tangent to $\odot O$.	4. ___?___
5. $m\angle ACR = \frac{1}{2}m\,\widehat{AXC}$	5. ___?___
6. $m\angle PAC = \frac{1}{2}m\,\widehat{AC}$	6. ___?___
7. $m\angle P = \frac{1}{2}m\,\widehat{AXC} - \frac{1}{2}m\,\widehat{AC}$	7. ___?___
8. $m\angle P = \frac{1}{2}(m\,\widehat{AXC} - m\,\widehat{AC})$	8. ___?___

THE GEOMETRY OF THE CIRCLE   **241**

WRITTEN EXERCISES

A 1-10. In $\odot O$ at the right, $m\,\overset{\frown}{AE} = 100$, $m\,\overset{\frown}{DE} = 20$, and $m\,\overset{\frown}{BC} = 70$. $\overleftrightarrow{DG}$ is tangent to $\odot O$. Find the measures of the numbered angles.

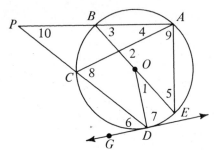

Find the value of x. (Point O is the center of the given circle.)

11.

90° $x°$ 20° O

12.

$x°$ 23° 69° O

13.

O 142° $x°$

14.

134° $x°$

15.

156° $x°$ 48°

16.

35° O $x°$

17.

10° 10° $x°$

18. 165°

40° $x°$

19.

$x°$ 43°

20. Two secants intersect outside a circle to form an angle whose measure is 40. If the measure of the larger intercepted arc is 110, find the measure of the smaller intercepted arc.

21. Two tangents drawn to a circle from an external point are perpendicular. Find the measure of each intercepted arc.

22. Two of the angles formed by two chords intersecting inside a circle have measure 100. Find the sum of the measures of the arcs intercepted by these angles.

23. $\overline{QR}$ and $\overline{QS}$ are tangent to $\odot O$ at R and S respectively. If $m\angle Q = 100$, find $m\angle ROS$.

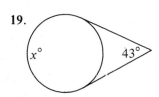

24. Tangent $\overrightarrow{PA}$ and secant $\overrightarrow{PB}$ are drawn to $\odot O$ as shown in the diagram. If $m\,\overset{\frown}{AB} : m\,\overset{\frown}{AC} = 3:2$ and $m\,\overset{\frown}{BC} = 130$, find $m\angle P$.

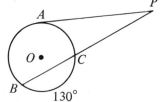

B 25. In the diagram, quadrilateral *ABCD* is circumscribed about ⊙*O*, and $m\stackrel{\frown}{PQ} : m\stackrel{\frown}{QR} : m\stackrel{\frown}{RS} : m\stackrel{\frown}{SP} = 2:1:4:5$. Find the measure of each angle of the quadrilateral.

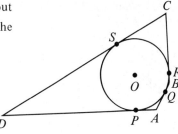

26. In the diagram, $\overline{PA}$ is tangent to ⊙*O* at *A*. If $m\stackrel{\frown}{BC} = 50$, $m\angle BEC = 60$, $m\stackrel{\frown}{BD} = x$, and $m\stackrel{\frown}{AC} = 2x + 30$, find:

a. $m\stackrel{\frown}{AD}$ b. $m\stackrel{\frown}{BD}$

c. $m\angle CPA$ d. $m\angle BAC$

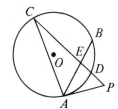

27. In ⊙*O*, $\overline{AE}$ is tangent to ⊙*O*, $m\angle BCF = 112$, and $m\stackrel{\frown}{BE} : m\stackrel{\frown}{DE} = 3:7$. Find:

a. $m\stackrel{\frown}{BE}$ b. $m\angle A$

c. $m\angle DEB$ d. $m\stackrel{\frown}{BF}$

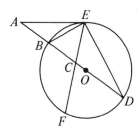

Find the value of *x*.

28.

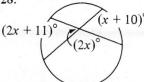

29.

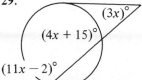

30.

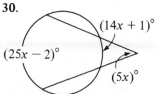

31. Two secants to a circle intersect outside the circle to form an angle whose measure is 29. If the measure of one of the intercepted arcs is 140, find the measure of the other intercepted arc. (*Hint:* There are *two* possible answers.)

32. A tangent and a secant to a circle intersect outside the circle to form an angle whose measure is 26. The measure of one of the intercepted arcs is 80. Find all possible values of the measure of the other intercepted arc.

33. $\overline{LK}$ and $\overline{MK}$ are tangents to ⊙*O* at *L* and *M* respectively.

a. If $m\stackrel{\frown}{LM} = x$, express $m\angle K$ in terms of *x*.

b. Use your result in part (a) to state the relationship between the measure of the angle formed by any two tangents to a circle from an external point and the measure of the intercepted minor arc.

34. Use your result in Exercise 33(b) to find the value of x in the diagram at the left below.

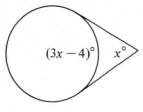

Ex. 34

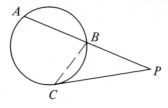

Ex. 35

35. Use the diagram at the right above to prove Theorem 6-6 for the case where the angle outside the circle is formed by a secant and a tangent.

C 36. Find the values of x and y.
(*Hint*: Use a system of equations.)

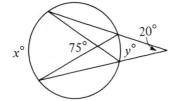

37. $\overline{PQ}$ and $\overline{RQ}$ are tangents to the smaller circle. Express y in terms of x.

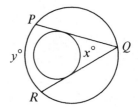

38. Given: $\angle A \cong \angle B$
Prove: $\overset{\frown}{EF} \cong \overset{\frown}{GH}$

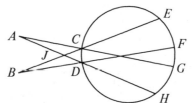

Section 6-5 CHORDS OF CIRCLES

In previous sections of this chapter, you studied the relationship between angles related to circles and the arcs they intercept. In this section you will learn some relationships involving the lengths of chords of a circle.

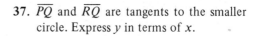

Recall that the measure of a minor arc is equal to the measure of its central angle. Thus, in the diagram $m\angle AOB = m \overset{\frown}{AB}$ and $m\angle XOY = m \overset{\frown}{XY}$. If, in addition, $m\angle AOB = m\angle XOY$, it follows that $m \overset{\frown}{AB} = m \overset{\frown}{XY}$. This justifies the following theorem.

Theorem 6-7 In a circle (or in congruent circles), congruent central angles intercept congruent arcs.

Next we will consider the relationship between a chord and the minor arc with the same endpoints. Since $\overline{PQ}$ in the diagram intercepts $\overparen{PQ}$, we say that $\overparen{PQ}$ *is the arc of chord* $\overline{PQ}$. The next theorem follows from Theorem 6-7.

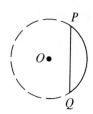

Theorem 6-8   In a circle (or in congruent circles), congruent chords have congruent arcs.

GIVEN: $\odot O$; $\overline{AB} \cong \overline{CD}$

PROVE: $\overparen{AB} \cong \overparen{CD}$

Statements	Reasons
1. $\overline{AB} \cong \overline{CD}$	1. Given
2. Draw radii $\overline{OA}, \overline{OB}, \overline{OC}, \overline{OD}$.	2. Two points determine a line.
3. $\overline{OA} \cong \overline{OC}, \overline{OB} \cong \overline{OD}$	3. Radii of the same $\odot$ are $\cong$.
4. $\triangle AOB \cong \triangle COD$	4. SSS Postulate
5. $\angle AOB \cong \angle COD$	5. Corr. parts of $\cong$ ⬛ are $\cong$.
6. $\overparen{AB} \cong \overparen{CD}$	6. In a $\odot$, $\cong$ central angles intercept $\cong$ arcs.

The converse of Theorem 6-8 is proved similarly, using the SAS Postulate.

In Chapter 5 you learned that a circle is symmetric about every diameter. The diagram at the right shows diameter $\overline{AB}$ and chord $\overline{CD}$ intersecting at E. It appears that $\overline{CD} \perp \overline{AB}$, that E is the midpoint of $\overline{CD}$, and that B is the midpoint of $\overparen{CD}$. The diagram suggests the following three closely related theorems. The proofs of the first two are left as Oral Exercise 1 and Written Exercise 29. You will justify the third theorem in Oral Exercise 2.

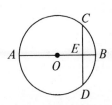

Theorem 6-9   In a circle, a diameter drawn perpendicular to a chord bisects the chord and its major and minor arcs.

Theorem 6-10   In a circle, a diameter drawn through the midpoint of a chord that is not a diameter is perpendicular to the chord.

Theorem 6-11   In a circle, the perpendicular bisector of a chord contains the center of the circle.

Recall that the *distance from a point to a line* is the length of the segment that is perpendicular to the given line and whose endpoints are the given point and a point on the given line. You can use this definition in the following example.

EXAMPLE A chord of length 8 is drawn in a circle of radius 6. Find the distance from the chord to the center of the circle.

SOLUTION Let M be the midpoint of $\overline{PQ}$. By Theorem 6-10, $\overline{OM} \perp \overline{PQ}$. Thus OM is the distance from O to $\overline{PQ}$.

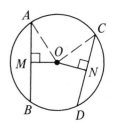

$$(OM)^2 + 4^2 = 6^2$$
$$(OM)^2 + 16 = 36$$
$$(OM)^2 = 20$$
$$OM = \pm 2\sqrt{5} \text{ (reject negative solution)}$$

Therefore, the distance from the center to the chord is $2\sqrt{5}$ units.

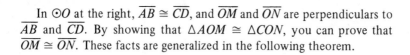

In $\odot O$ at the right, $\overline{AB} \cong \overline{CD}$, and $\overline{OM}$ and $\overline{ON}$ are perpendiculars to $\overline{AB}$ and $\overline{CD}$. By showing that $\triangle AOM \cong \triangle CON$, you can prove that $\overline{OM} \cong \overline{ON}$. These facts are generalized in the following theorem.

Theorem 6-12 In a circle, congruent chords are equidistant from the center.

A somewhat surprising relationship involving the lengths of the segments determined by two intersecting chords is described in our next theorem.

Theorem 6-13 If two chords intersect inside a circle, the product of the lengths of the segments of one chord is equal to the product of the lengths of the segments of the other chord.

GIVEN: Chords $\overline{AB}$ and $\overline{CD}$, intersecting at E
PROVE: $AE \cdot BE = CE \cdot DE$

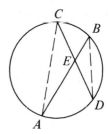

Statements	Reasons
1. Chord $\overline{AB}$ intersects chord $\overline{CD}$ at E.	1. Given
2. Draw chords $\overline{AC}$ and $\overline{BD}$.	2. Two points determine a line.
3. $\angle A \cong \angle D$	3. Inscribed $\angle$s that intercept the same arc are $\cong$.
4. $\angle AEC \cong \angle DEB$	4. Vertical $\angle$s are $\cong$.
5. $\triangle ACE \sim \triangle DBE$	5. AA $\sim$ Theorem
6. $\dfrac{AE}{DE} = \dfrac{CE}{BE}$	6. Lengths of corr. sides of $\sim \triangle$ are proportional.
7. $AE \cdot BE = CE \cdot DE$	7. A property of proportions

EXAMPLE   Given: $CD = 22$; $CE = 4$;
$\qquad\qquad AE : BE = 2 : 1$
$\qquad$ Find AE, BE, and AB.

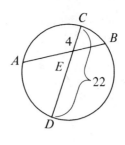

SOLUTION $DE = 22 - 4 = 18$
$\qquad$ Let $BE = x$ and $AE = 2x$.
$\qquad$ By Theorem 6-13:
$$2x(x) = 4(18)$$
$$2x^2 = 72$$
$$x^2 = 36$$
$$x = \pm 6 \text{ (reject negative value)}$$
$\qquad$ Therefore, $AE = 12$, $BE = 6$, and $AB = 18$.

ORAL EXERCISES

1. Supply the missing reasons for the following proof of Theorem 6-9.

$\qquad$ GIVEN: $\odot O$; diameter $\overline{CD} \perp$ chord $\overline{AB}$

$\qquad$ PROVE: $\overline{AE} \cong \overline{BE}$; $\overwidehat{AC} \cong \overwidehat{BC}$;
$\qquad\qquad\quad \overwidehat{AD} \cong \overwidehat{BD}$

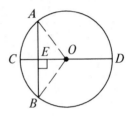

Statements	Reasons
1. Diameter $\overline{CD} \perp$ chord $\overline{AB}$	1. Given
2. $\angle AEO$ and $\angle BEO$ are right $\angle$s.	2. Def. of $\perp$ lines
3. Draw $\overline{AO}$ and $\overline{BO}$.	3. ?
4. $\triangle AEO$ and $\triangle BEO$ are right $\triangle$.	4. ?
5. $\overline{AO} \cong \overline{BO}$	5. ?
6. $\overline{EO} \cong \overline{EO}$	6. ?
7. $\triangle AEO \cong \triangle BEO$	7. ?
8. $\overline{AE} \cong \overline{BE}$ and $\angle AOE \cong \angle BOE$	8. ?
9. $\angle AOE$ and $\angle AOD$ are supplementary; $\angle BOE$ and $\angle BOD$ are supplementary.	9. If the exterior sides of 2 adjacent $\angle$s are opposite rays, the $\angle$s are supp.
10. $\angle AOD \cong \angle BOD$	10. 2 $\angle$s supp. to $\cong$ $\angle$s are $\cong$.
11. $\overwidehat{AC} \cong \overwidehat{BC}$ and $\overwidehat{AD} \cong \overwidehat{BD}$	11. ?

2. Explain why Theorem 6-11 is true.

Find the value of x. (Point O is the center of the circle.)

3.
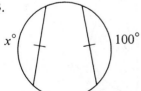

4.
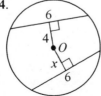

5.

Find the value of *x*. (Point *O* is the center of the circle.)

6.
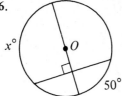

7.
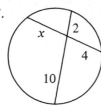

8.
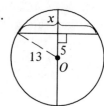

WRITTEN EXERCISES

Find the value of each variable. (Point *O* is the center of the circle.)

A **1.**
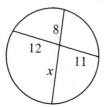

2.
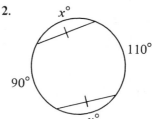

3.
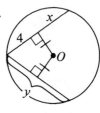

4.
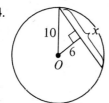

5.
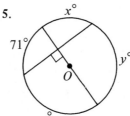

6.
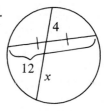

Refer to the diagram. Find all possible values of *x*.

7. $AE = 5$, $AB = 13$, $DE = 10$, $CE = x$

8. $AE = 3$, $BE = 8$, $CE = DE = x$

9. $AE = 3$, $BE = 4x + 1$, $CE = 2x - 1$, $DE = 9$

10. $AB = 14$, $CE = 4$, $DE = 12$, $BE = x$

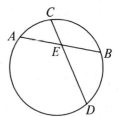

Exercises 11–14 refer to ⊙*O* at the right.

11. $EO = 17$, $OG = 8$, $EF = $ __?__

12. $EF = 12$, $EO = 10$, $OG = $ __?__

13. $EF = 14$, $OG = 3$, $EO = $ __?__

14. $EO = 6$, $OG = 5$, $EF = $ __?__

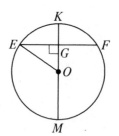

In Exercises 15–18, $HO = 13$, and $FG = 10$. Find the length of the given segment.

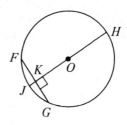

15. $\overline{FK}$ **16.** $\overline{KG}$

17. $\overline{OK}$ **18.** $\overline{KJ}$

19. If a chord 12 cm long is 3 cm from the center of a circle, find the radius of the circle.

20. If a chord 10 cm long is drawn in a circle with radius 13 cm, find the distance from the center to the chord.

21. In a circle of radius 7 cm, a chord is drawn whose distance from the center is 4 cm. Find the length of the chord.

22. Two radii drawn to the endpoints of a chord form an angle whose measure is 120. If the radius of the circle is 8 cm, find the length of the chord.

In Exercises 23–25, O is the center of the circle. Find all possible values of x.

B   **23.**

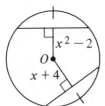

24.

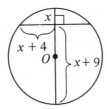

25.

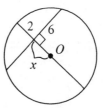

26. If a chord 8 cm long is 3 cm from the center of a circle, how far from the center is a chord 4 cm long?

27. Chords $\overline{PQ}$ and $\overline{RS}$ of a circle intersect at A. If $PA = 12$, $QA = x$, $RA = x + 1$, and $SA = x + 6$, find PQ and RS (two answers).

28. Explain why three noncollinear points determine a unique circle. (*Hint:* See Theorem 6–11.)

29. Prove Theorem 6–10, using the diagram at the right.

    Given: E is the midpoint of chord $\overline{RS}$;
           diameter $\overline{PQ}$ intersects $\overline{RS}$ at E.
    Prove: $\overline{PQ} \perp \overline{RS}$

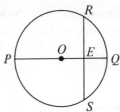

30. Find the values of x and y in the diagram at the right.

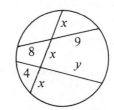

31. In the diagram at the right, chord $\overline{AB}$ is the perpendicular bisector of radius $\overline{OC}$. If $AB = 12$, find OC.

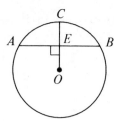

C 32. In a circle, two parallel chords of length 4 and 8 are 6 units apart. Find the distance from each chord to the center of the circle.

In the diagram for Exercises 33 and 34, $\overline{AB}$ is called the *common chord* of $\odot O$ and $\odot P$.

33. Prove that the line segment whose endpoints are the centers of two intersecting circles is the perpendicular bisector of the common chord.

Given: $\odot O$ and $\odot P$ intersect in points A and B.
Prove: $\overline{OP}$ is the perpendicular bisector of $\overline{AB}$.

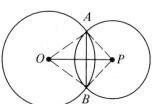

34. If the radius of each circle is 6 and the distance between the centers is 8, find the length of the common chord.

Ex. 33, 34

35. $RY = 6$, $m\angle ROZ = 60$, $XZ = $ __?__
36. $RY = 6$, $m\angle ROZ = 45$, $XZ = $ __?__
37. $RY = 6$, $m\angle ROZ = 30$, $XZ = $ __?__

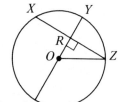

Exs. 35-37

Section 6-6 LENGTHS OF TANGENTS AND SECANTS

In Section 6-4 you learned how the measure of the angle formed by two tangents, a tangent and a secant, or two secants is related to the arcs they intercept on a circle. In this section you will learn how certain *segments* formed by those same pairs of lines are related.

First consider two tangents, $\overline{PA}$ and $\overline{PB}$, drawn to a circle from an external point P. From the diagram it appears that $PA = PB$. This conclusion is generalized in the following theorem, which will be proved in Oral Exercise 4.

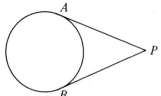

Theorem 6-14   Two tangents drawn to a circle from an external point are congruent.

EXAMPLE $\overline{PQ}$, $\overline{PS}$, and $\overline{ST}$ are tangents to $\odot O$. If $PQ = 4$ and $TS = 6$, find PS.

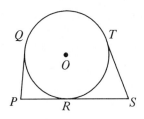

SOLUTION $\overline{PQ} \cong \overline{PR}$ and $\overline{SR} \cong \overline{ST}$.
Thus $PR = 4$ and $RS = 6$.
Hence $PS = 4 + 6 = 10$.

In the diagram for the next theorem, $\overline{PA}$ is called the *external* segment of secant $\overline{PB}$, and $\overline{AB}$ is called the *internal* segment of secant $\overline{PB}$. The relationship between the lengths of the segments determined by two intersecting secants depends on similar triangles.

Theorem 6-15 If two secants are drawn to a circle from an external point, the product of the lengths of one secant and its external segment is equal to the product of the lengths of the other secant and its external segment.

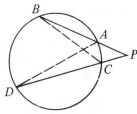

GIVEN: $\overline{PB}$ and $\overline{PD}$ are secants drawn from an external point P.

PROVE: $PB \cdot PA = PD \cdot PC$

Statements	Reasons
1. Draw $\overline{AD}$ and $\overline{BC}$.	1. Two points determine a line.
2. $\angle P \cong \angle P$	2. Reflexive Prop. of $\cong$
3. $\angle PBC \cong \angle PDA$	3. Inscribed $\angle$ that intercept the same arc are $\cong$.
4. $\triangle PBC \sim \triangle PDA$	4. AA $\sim$ Theorem
5. $\dfrac{PB}{PD} = \dfrac{PC}{PA}$	5. Lengths of corr. sides of $\sim$ $\triangle$ are proportional.
6. $PB \cdot PA = PD \cdot PC$	6. A property of proportions

EXAMPLE In the diagram, $ST = 7$, $TU = 1$, and $SK = 4$. Find KM.

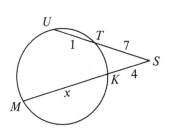

SOLUTION Let $KM = x$. $SU = 7 + 1 = 8$. By Theorem 6-15:
$$ST \cdot SU = SK \cdot SM$$
$$7 \cdot 8 = 4 \cdot (4 + x)$$
$$14 = 4 + x$$
$$10 = x$$

Therefore, $KM = 10$.

If secant $\overline{PB}$ in the diagram at the left below is rotated clockwise about P, A and B get closer together (middle diagram). As the rotation continues, A and B eventually coincide (right-hand diagram). Then $PA = PB$, and $\overline{PB}$ is a tangent to the circle.

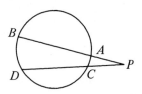 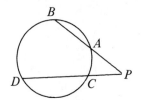 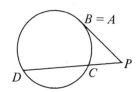

For the case of two secants, we know that $PB \cdot PA = PD \cdot PC$. When A coincides with B, the equation becomes

$$(PA)^2 = PD \cdot PC.$$

Since this is the same as saying that $\dfrac{PD}{PA} = \dfrac{PA}{PC}$, PA is the *geometric mean* between PD and PC. The equation $(PA)^2 = PD \cdot PC$ is an algebraic statement of the following theorem, whose proof is left as Exercise 21.

Theorem 6-16 If a tangent and a secant are drawn to a circle from an external point, the tangent is the geometric mean between the secant and the external segment of the secant.

EXAMPLE $\overline{PQ}$ is tangent to the circle at the right, and $\overline{PS}$ is a secant. If $PQ = 8$ and $RS = 12$, find PR.

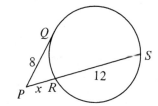

SOLUTION Let $PR = x$. Then:

$$8^2 = x(x + 12)$$
$$64 = x^2 + 12x$$
$$0 = x^2 + 12x - 64$$
$$0 = (x + 16)(x - 4)$$

$x = -16$ or $x = 4$ (reject the negative solution)
Therefore, $PR = 4$.

ORAL EXERCISES

State an equation expressing the relationship of the given variables.

1.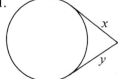

2.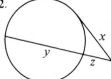

3.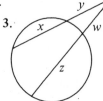

4. Complete the proof of Theorem 6–14.

GIVEN: $\overline{PA}$ and $\overline{PB}$ are tangent to $\odot O$ at A and B, respectively.

PROVE: $\overline{PA} \cong \overline{PB}$

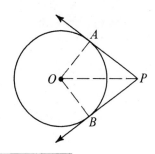

Statements	Reasons
1. Draw $\overline{OP}$ and radii $\overline{OA}$ and $\overline{OB}$.	1. __?__
2. $\overline{PA}$ and $\overline{PB}$ are tangents to $\odot O$.	2. __?__
3. $\overline{OA} \perp \overrightarrow{PA}$, $\overline{OB} \perp \overrightarrow{PB}$	3. __?__
4. $\angle OAP$ and $\angle OBP$ are right $\angle$s.	4. __?__
5. $\triangle OAP$ and $\triangle OBP$ are right $\triangle$.	5. __?__
6. $\overline{OA} \cong \overline{OB}$	6. __?__
7. $\overline{OP} \cong \overline{OP}$	7. __?__
8. $\triangle OAP \cong \triangle OBP$	8. __?__
9. $\overline{PA} \cong \overline{PB}$	9. __?__

Find the value of each variable.

5.

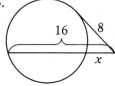

16   8

x

6.

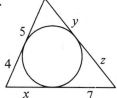

5   y

4

x   7   z

7.

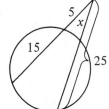

5

x

15

25

8.

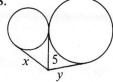

x   5

y

9.

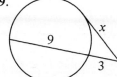

9   x

3

10.

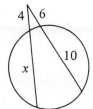

4   6

x   10

WRITTEN EXERCISES

Find the value of each variable.

A 1.

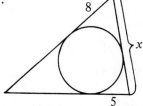

8

x

5

2.

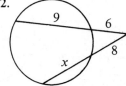

9   6

x   8

3.

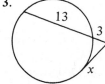

13   3

x

THE GEOMETRY OF THE CIRCLE   **253**

Find the value of each variable. (Point O is the center of the circle.)

4.

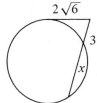

$2\sqrt{6}$

3

x

5.

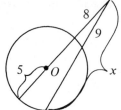

8

9

5

O

x

6.

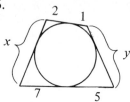

2   1

x

7

5

y

7.

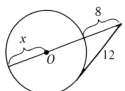

8

x

O

12

8.

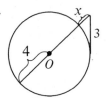

x

3

4

O

9.

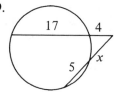

17   4

5   x

10. The lengths of two secants drawn to a circle from an external point are 16 and 20, respectively. If the external segment of the shorter secant has length 5, find the length of the external segment of the longer secant.

11. Two secants are drawn to a circle from an external point. One secant has length 8, and its internal segment has length 5. The length of the internal segment of the other secant is five times the length of its external segment. Find the length of the second secant.

12. A secant and a tangent are drawn to a circle from an external point. The ratio of the length of the external segment of the secant to the length of the internal segment is $1:3$. If the length of the tangent is 12, find the length of the secant.

In the diagram for Exercises 13 and 14, $\overline{PQ}$ is tangent to $\odot O$.

13. If $PA = 9$ and $PQ = 6$, find the radius of $\odot O$.

14. If $\odot O$ has radius 5 and $PQ = 12$, find BP.

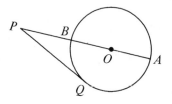

Exs. 13, 14

15. In a circle of radius 4, diameter $\overline{AB}$ is extended its own length outside the circle to point P. From P another secant is drawn to the circle. If the secant's external segment has length 10, find the length of its internal segment.

16. $ABCD$ is a circumscribed quadrilateral; $CR = 2$, $BR = 3$, $AQ = 6$, and $DS = 4$.
   a. Find the perimeter of $ABCD$.
   b. Verify that $AB + CD = AD + BC$.

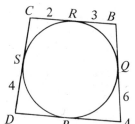

C 2 R 3 B

S

Q

4

6

D P A

The following definition is required for Exercises 17 and 18: The *distance from an external point to a circle* is the length of the external segment of the secant that contains the external point and the center of the circle.

B **17.** A tangent is drawn to a circle of radius 8 cm from an external point 4 cm from the circle. Find the length of the tangent.

18. A tangent of length 4 cm is drawn to a circle of diameter 6 cm from an external point. Find the distance from the external point to the circle.

19. Given: $\overline{PA}$ is a tangent;
$\qquad CF = 4$, $FB = 3$, $BP = 5$;
$\qquad AF : FE = 1 : 3$;
$\qquad DE$ is 7 more than PD.
Find: AF, FE, PA, PD, DE

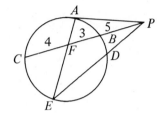

20. Prove that the angle formed by two tangents to a circle from an external point is bisected by the segment whose endpoints are the center of the circle and the external point.
Given: $\odot O$; tangents $\overline{PS}$ and $\overline{PT}$
Prove: $\overline{OP}$ bisects $\angle SPT$.

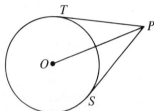

21. Prove Theorem 6–16.
Given: Tangent $\overline{PA}$ and secant $\overline{PD}$
Prove: $(PA)^2 = PC \cdot PD$
(*Hint*: Draw $\overline{AD}$ and $\overline{AC}$. Show that $\triangle PAD \sim \triangle PCA$.)

22. Prove Theorem 6–14 without using congruent triangles.
Given: Tangents $\overline{PA}$ and $\overline{PB}$
Prove: $\overline{PA} \cong \overline{PB}$
(*Hint*: Draw $\overline{AB}$.)

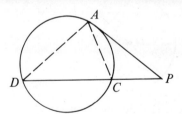

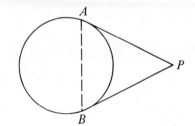

23. Given: $\overline{QS}$ is tangent to $\odot O$;
$\qquad \overline{QT}$ is tangent to $\odot P$.
Prove: $QS = QT$

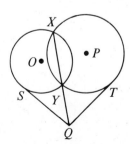

C **24.** Given: *GHJK* is a circumscribed quadrilateral.
   Prove: *GH + JK = GK + HJ*

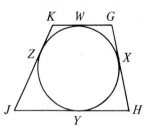

25. Given: △*ABC* is a circumscribed trian-
   gle; *AB* = 7, *BC* = 8, *AC* = 11
   Find: *AR, RB, BS, SC, CT, TA*
   (*Hint*: Let *AR = x*.)

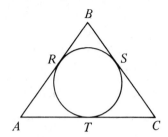

SELF-TEST 2

Find the value of each variable.

1.

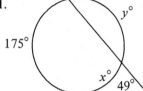

2.

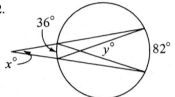

Section 6-4

3. Two tangents drawn to a circle from an external point form an angle of measure 68. Find the measure of each intercepted arc.

Find the value of each variable. (Point *O* is the center of the circle.)

4.

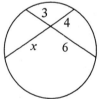

5.

6.

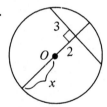

Section 6-5

7. A chord 12 cm long is 8 cm from the center of the circle. Find the radius of the circle.

Complete.

8. *PB* = 3, *PC* = 6, *PD* = 5, *PA* = __?__

9. *PC* = 7, *PD* = 2, *PE* = __?__

10. *AB* = 15, *PE* = 10, *PB* = __?__

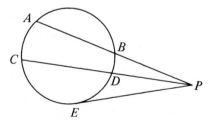

Section 6-6

Section 6-7 CIRCUMFERENCE AND AREA

Many different measurements relating to circles can be made. In previous sections of this chapter, you studied concepts involving the lengths of chords, secants, and tangents and the degree measures of arcs and the angles that intercept them. In this section you will learn about:
- the circumference of a circle
- the length of an arc of a circle
- the area of a circle
- the area of a sector of a circle

As you know, the *circumference* of a circle is the perimeter of the circle, or the distance around the circle.

Using the definition $\pi = \dfrac{C}{d}$, discussed in the introduction to this chapter, you can write a formula for the circumference of a circle.

The circumference C of a circle with diameter d and radius r is given by the formulas

$$C = \pi d \quad \text{and} \quad C = 2\pi r.$$

EXAMPLE Find the radius of a circle of circumference 12.

SOLUTION $C = 2\pi r$

$12 = 2\pi r$

$\dfrac{12}{2\pi} = r$

Therefore, $r = \dfrac{6}{\pi}$.

The measure $\dfrac{6}{\pi}$ is the *exact* value of the radius in the previous example. If a decimal approximation is required, you can use $\pi \approx 3.14$ to obtain:

$$r = \dfrac{6}{\pi}$$
$$\approx \dfrac{6}{3.14}$$
$$\approx 1.91$$

A central angle of concentric circles intercepts arcs that have the same degree measure, but whose *lengths* are different. For example, in the diagram $\overarc{AB}$ and $\overarc{A'B'}$ have the same measure in degrees, namely 54, but the length of $\overarc{A'B'}$ is greater than the length of $\overarc{AB}$.

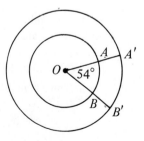

To find the length l of an arc of a circle, you need to know the circumference of the circle and the fractional part of the circle contained in the arc. For example, the length of a 60° arc of any circle is $\frac{60}{360}$ $\left(\text{or } \frac{1}{6}\right)$ of the circumference. If the circle has radius 10, the length of the arc is given by:

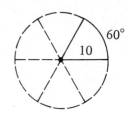

$$l = \frac{60}{360} \cdot C = \frac{1}{6} \cdot 2\pi r = \frac{2\pi(10)}{6} = \frac{10\pi}{3}$$

The length l of an arc of measure n in a circle with diameter d and radius r is given by the formulas

$$l = \frac{n}{360} \cdot \pi d \quad \text{and} \quad l = \frac{n}{360} \cdot 2\pi r.$$

From previous mathematics courses, you are probably familiar with the formula for the area of a circle, $A = \pi r^2$. To justify this formula, consider a regular n-sided polygon with sides of length s, circumscribed about $\odot O$. The area of $\triangle XOY = \frac{1}{2}rs$. Thus the area of the polygon is given by

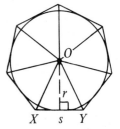

$$\text{area} = n \cdot \frac{1}{2}rs, \quad \text{or} \quad \text{area} = \frac{1}{2}r(ns).$$

But since $ns = P$, where P is the perimeter of the polygon,

$$\text{area} = \frac{1}{2}rP.$$

As the number of sides of the polygon increases, the perimeter of the polygon approaches the circumference of the circle and the area of the polygon approaches the area of the circle. Therefore, you obtain:

$$\text{area} = \frac{1}{2}rC = \frac{1}{2}r(2\pi r) = \pi r^2$$

The area A of a circle with radius r is given by the formula
$$A = \pi r^2.$$

A *sector* of a circle is a part of the interior of the circle bounded by two radii and an arc. In the figure, sector AOB is the shaded portion of the interior of the circle. The area of a sector is the fractional part of the area of the circle determined by the measure of the arc that borders the sector. Thus, if $m \stackrel{\frown}{AB} = 150$, then

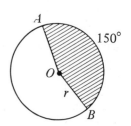

$$\text{area of sector } AOB = \frac{150}{360} \cdot \pi r^2, \text{ or } \frac{5}{12}\pi r^2.$$

The area A of a sector with an arc of measure n in a circle with radius r is given by the formula

$$A = \frac{n}{360} \cdot \pi r^2.$$

EXAMPLE In $\odot O$, the radius is 6 and $m\angle POQ = 120$. Find the area of the shaded portion.

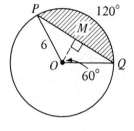

SOLUTION First find the area of sector POQ:

$$\text{area of sector } POQ = \frac{120}{360} \cdot \pi(6^2) = 12\pi$$

Next find the area of $\triangle POQ$: $\triangle QOM$ is a 30-60-90 triangle. Since $OQ = 6$, $OM = 3$ and $MQ = 3\sqrt{3}$. Therefore:

$$\text{Area of } \triangle POQ = 2 \cdot \text{Area of } \triangle QOM$$
$$= 2 \cdot \frac{1}{2}(3)(3\sqrt{3})$$
$$= 9\sqrt{3}$$

Then if A is the area of the shaded portion:

$$A = \text{area of sector } POQ - \text{area of } \triangle POQ$$
$$= 12\pi - 9\sqrt{3}$$

ORAL EXERCISES

Find the exact circumference and area of the circle with the given radius.

1. 5   2. 7   3. 8   4. 20   5. $\frac{1}{2}$ 6. $2\frac{1}{3}$

If $\overparen{AXB}$ has the given measure, express **(a)** the length of $\overparen{AXB}$ and **(b)** the area of the shaded sector in terms of the radius r.

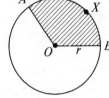

7. 90   8. 50   9. 135

10. 100   11. 300   12. 225

13. The circumference of a circle is 20π. Find the diameter of the circle.

14. The area of a semicircle is 32π. Find the radius of the semicircle.

15. The length of an arc is 4π. If the degree measure of the arc is 60, find the diameter of the circle.

16. The area of a sector of a circle is 18π. If the measure of the central angle of the sector is 80, find the radius of the circle.

WRITTEN EXERCISES

Find the exact circumference and area of a circle with the given radius.

A   **1.** 6   **2.** 13   **3.** $\sqrt{11}$ **4.** 0.3   **5.** 3.1   **6.** $4\sqrt{2}$

Find, to the nearest tenth, the circumference and area of the circle determined by the given information. Use $\pi \approx 3.14$.

   7. radius = 9   **8.** diameter = 7.4   **9.** diameter = 3.2   **10.** radius = 4.3

Use the given information to find **(a)** the length of $\overset{\frown}{PAQ}$ and **(b)** the area of the shaded sector.

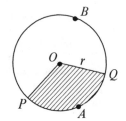

11. $r = 6,\ m\overset{\frown}{PAQ} = 45$

12. $r = 12,\ m\angle POQ = 130$

13. $r = 3,\ m\overset{\frown}{PAQ} = 110$

14. $r = 2.5,\ m\overset{\frown}{PBQ} = 270$

Find the radius of a circle with the given circumference.

15. 6π **16.** 8.2π **17.** $12\sqrt{2}\,\pi$ **18.** 17π

Find the diameter of a circle with the given area.

19. 16π **20.** π **21.** 20π **22.** $\dfrac{25\pi}{4}$

23. Find the circumference of a circle whose area is 121π.

24. Find the area of a circle whose circumference is 5π.

25. Find the degree measure of an arc whose length is 3π and which is part of a circle of radius 12.

26. The area of a sector of a circle is 15π. If the central angle of the sector has measure 150, find the radius of the circle.

B **27.** A square with side of length 10 is circumscribed about a circle. Find the area of the circle.

28. A square with perimeter 48 is inscribed in a circle. Find the area of the circle.

29. The side of a square is 8 cm long. Find the circumferences of both the inscribed and circumscribed circles.

30. The circumference of a circle and the perimeter of a square are each 40 cm Which has greater area, the circle or the square?

31. Two circles have radii of 3 and 4. Find the radius of a circle whose area equals the sum of the areas of the other two circles.

32. Two concentric circles have radii 4 and 6. Central $\angle COD$ intercepts $\overset{\frown}{AB}$ and $\overset{\frown}{CD}$ as shown. If the length of $\overset{\frown}{AB}$ is $\dfrac{5\pi}{3}$, find the length of $\overset{\frown}{CD}$.

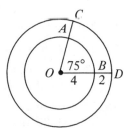

Find the area of the shaded portion of each figure.

33.

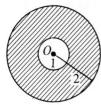

34.

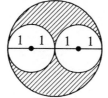

35.

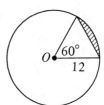

36.

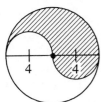

37.

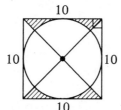

38.

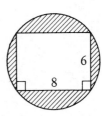

C 39. Find the area of the shaded portion in terms of x.

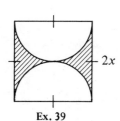

Ex. 39   Ex. 40

40. Find the area of the shaded portion to the nearest tenth. Use $\pi \approx 3.14$.

Find **(a)** the area and **(b)** the perimeter of the shaded portion.

41.

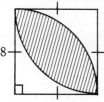

42.

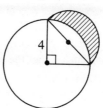

43. Find a formula for the area of a circle in terms of the circumference.

44. The diameter of the circle at the right is 6. Find the areas of region A, region B, and region C.

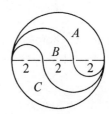

45. A goat is tied at one corner of a 10 m by 20 m barn. If the rope is 25 m long, find the area of the region in which the goat can graze. Leave your answer in terms of π.

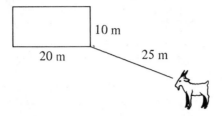

Section 6-8 CONSTRUCTIONS RELATED TO THE CIRCLE

In Chapter 5, you reviewed some basic straightedge-and-compass constructions. In this section you will study some constructions involving circles. Specifically, you will learn how to construct:
• the circumscribed circle of a given triangle
• the inscribed circle of a given triangle
• a tangent to a given circle at a given point on the circle
• a tangent to a given circle from a given point outside the circle

You may remember the first of these constructions from *Book 2*.

Construction   To construct the circumscribed circle of a given triangle.

GIVEN: $\triangle ABC$
CONSTRUCT: The circumscribed circle of $\triangle ABC$

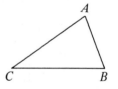

Procedure:
1. Construct the perpendicular bisectors of any two sides of $\triangle ABC$ ($\overline{AC}$ and $\overline{BC}$ in the diagram). Label the point of intersection of the perpendicular bisectors as O.
2. Draw a circle with center O and radius OA (or OB or OC).

The circle with center O and radius OA is the circumscribed circle of $\triangle ABC$.

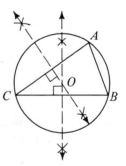

Justification: The perpendicular bisector of a chord of a circle contains the center of the circle. Since the perpendicular bisectors of $\overline{AC}$ and $\overline{BC}$ intersect at O, O must be the center of a circle of which $\overline{AC}$ and $\overline{BC}$ are chords. Thus A, B, and C lie on the circle, and the circle is the circumscribed circle of $\triangle ABC$.

To inscribe a circle in a given triangle, we must construct a circle that is tangent to all three sides of the triangle.

Construction   To construct the inscribed circle of a given triangle.

GIVEN: △*ABC*
CONSTRUCT: The inscribed circle of △*ABC*

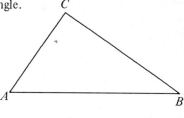

Procedure:
1. Construct the bisectors of ∠*A* and ∠*B* (or any other pair of angles of △*ABC*). Label the point of intersection of the angle bisectors as *O*.
2. Construct a perpendicular from *O* to $\overline{AB}$ (or $\overline{AC}$ or $\overline{BC}$), intersecting $\overline{AB}$ at *P*.
3. Draw a circle with *O* as center and radius *OP*.

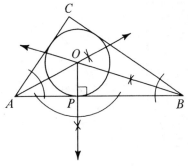

The circle with *O* as center and radius *OP* is the inscribed circle of △*ABC*.

Justification: Draw $\overline{OQ} \perp \overline{AC}$ and $\overline{OR} \perp \overline{BC}$. Since $\overline{OB} \cong \overline{OB}$, ∠*ORB* ≅ ∠*OPB*, and ∠*OBR* ≅ ∠*OBP*, △*ORB* ≅ △*OPB* (AAS Theorem). Likewise, △*OQA* ≅ △*OPA*. Thus $\overline{OR} \cong \overline{OP}$ and $\overline{OQ} \cong \overline{OP}$ (corr. parts of ≅ ⧌ are ≅). Therefore, you can draw a circle with center *O* that passes through *P*, *Q*, and *R*. Since $\overline{AB}$, $\overline{AC}$, and $\overline{BC}$ are perpendicular to radii of ⊙*O*, you know that $\overline{AB}$, $\overline{AC}$, and $\overline{BC}$ are tangent to ⊙*O*. Therefore, ⊙*O* is the inscribed circle of △*ABC*.

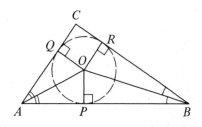

In both of the next two constructions, a tangent is constructed to a given circle.

Construction   To construct a tangent to a given circle at a given point on the circle.

GIVEN: Point *P* on ⊙*O*
CONSTRUCT: The line tangent to ⊙*O* at *P*

Procedure:
1. Draw $\overrightarrow{OP}$.
2. Construct $\overleftrightarrow{XY}$ perpendicular to $\overrightarrow{OP}$ at *P*.

$\overleftrightarrow{XY}$ is tangent to ⊙*O* at *P*.

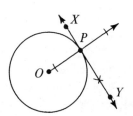

Justification: The justification is left as Exercise 9.

Construction   To construct a tangent to a given circle from a given point outside the circle.

GIVEN: Point P not on $\odot O$

CONSTRUCT: A ray with endpoint P tangent to $\odot O$

Procedure:

1. Draw $\overline{OP}$.
2. Construct the perpendicular bisector of $\overline{OP}$, intersecting $\overline{OP}$ at Q.
3. With Q as center and radius QO (or QP), construct a circle that intersects $\odot O$ at A and B.
4. Draw $\overrightarrow{PA}$ (or $\overrightarrow{PB}$).

$\overrightarrow{PA}$ is tangent to $\odot O$.

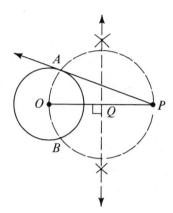

Justification: The justification is left as Oral Exercise 7.

ORAL EXERCISES

1. Describe how you would construct a circle that passes through three non-collinear points.

2. Describe how you would locate the center of a given circle by construction.

3. If $\overset{\frown}{AB}$ is an arc of $\odot O$, describe how you would locate by construction the point that divides $\overset{\frown}{AB}$ into two congruent arcs.

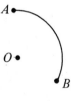

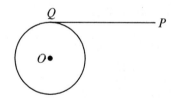

Ex. 3   Ex. 4

4. PQ is tangent to $\odot O$. Describe a very simple method of constructing the *other* tangent from P to $\odot O$.

5. Can a circle be circumscribed about any
   a. rectangle? **b.** square? **c.** parallelogram? **d.** rhombus? **e.** quadrilateral?
   Explain your answers.

6. Can a circle be inscribed in any
   a. rectangle? **b.** square? **c.** parallelogram? **d.** rhombus? **e.** quadrilateral?
   Explain your answers.

7. $\overrightarrow{PA}$ has been constructed tangent to $\odot O$ from external point
P as in the construction on page 264, and $\overline{OA}$ has been
drawn. Supply the reason for each statement in the following
justification of the construction.

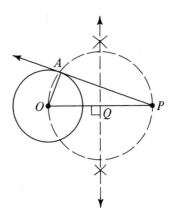

a. Q is the midpoint of $\overline{OP}$.
b. $\overline{OP}$ is a diameter of $\odot Q$.
c. $\overset{\frown}{OAP}$ is a semicircle.
d. $\angle OAP$ is a rt. $\angle$.
e. $\overline{OA} \perp \overrightarrow{PA}$
f. $\overline{OA}$ is a radius of $\odot O$.
g. $\overrightarrow{PA}$ is tangent to $\odot O$.

WRITTEN EXERCISES

A 1. Draw an acute $\triangle ABC$ and circumscribe a circle about it.

2. Draw an acute $\triangle PQR$ and inscribe a circle in it.

3. Draw a circle and a point D on the circle. Construct a tangent to the circle
at D.

4. Draw a circle and a point P outside the circle. Construct a tangent from P to
the circle.

5. Draw a circle and points X and Y on the circle. Construct M, the point that
divides $\overset{\frown}{XY}$ into two congruent arcs.

6. Draw a circle and a point H on the circle. Construct an inscribed isosceles right
triangle with a vertex at H. (*Hint*: See Corollary 2 to Theorem 6-1 on page
229.)

In Exercises 7 and 8 draw a diagram larger than the one shown. Then construct
the required line.

7. Line l is tangent to $\odot O$ at A. Construct a line m such that $m \parallel l$ and m is
tangent to $\odot O$.

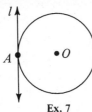

Ex. 7

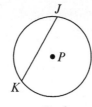

Ex. 8

8. Construct a line m such that $m \parallel \overline{JK}$ and m is tangent to $\odot P$.

B 9. Give a justification for the construction on page 263 of a tangent to a given
circle at a given point on the circle.

10. Construct a rectangle whose length is twice its width and circumscribe a circle
about it.

In each of Exercises 11-14 draw a large circle and label the center as *O*. Choose any point *A* on the circle, and with radius *OA*, mark off five points as shown in the diagram.

11. Draw $\overline{AB}$, $\overline{BC}$, $\overline{CD}$, $\overline{DE}$, $\overline{EF}$, and $\overline{FA}$. Explain why *ABCDEF* is an inscribed regular hexagon.

12. Construct an inscribed equilateral triangle.

13. Use the construction for dividing an arc into two congruent arcs to construct an inscribed regular dodecagon (12-sided polygon).

14. Construct a circumscribed equilateral triangle.

Exs. 11-14

In each of Exercises 15-17, begin by drawing a circle. Then do the indicated construction.

15. Construct an inscribed square.

16. Construct an inscribed regular octagon.

17. Construct a circumscribed square.

SELF-TEST 3

Find the exact circumference and area of a circle with the given radius.

1. 2.1

2. $\sqrt{5}$

Section 6-7

Complete.

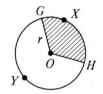

3. $r = 10$, $m\,\overset{\frown}{GXH} = 90$, area of shaded sector = ___?___

4. $r = 7$, length of $\overset{\frown}{GXH} = \dfrac{7\pi}{3}$, $m\angle GOH =$ ___?___

5. $r = 12$, $m\,\overset{\frown}{GYH} = 144$, length of $\overset{\frown}{GXH} =$ ___?___

In each of Exercises 6-8, draw a diagram larger than the one shown. Then do the required construction.

6. Locate the midpoint of $\overset{\frown}{AB}$ by construction.

Section 6-8

7. Construct a tangent to $\odot O$ at point *A*.

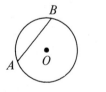

Exs. 6, 7

Ex. 8

8. Construct a tangent to $\odot P$ from point *Q*.

Computer Exercises

There is no way to calculate the exact value of π as a decimal. It is possible, however, to approximate its value as accurately as we like. One method for doing this was used by Archimedes as outlined in the beginning of this chapter. Another method, ideally suited for the computer, was developed in the seventeenth and eighteenth centuries. It involves infinite series formulas. One of the simplest of these, first published by the German mathematician Leibnitz in 1674, is:

$$\frac{\pi}{4} = 1 - \frac{1}{3} + \frac{1}{5} - \frac{1}{7} + \frac{1}{9} - \cdots$$

Using this series, the value of $\frac{\pi}{4}$ can be calculated to any desired degree of accuracy by taking enough of the terms on the right of the equals sign. The more terms taken, the more accurate the approximation to $\frac{\pi}{4}$. The final answer obtained, of course, must be multiplied by 4 to give an approximation of π.

The following program uses Leibnitz's formula to calculate approximations of π.

```
10    PRINT "APPROXIMATING PI"
20    PRINT
30    PRINT "HOW MANY TERMS";
40    INPUT T
50    LET P = 0
60    LET S = 1
70    REM***P = SUM OF TERMS
80    REM***S = 1 IF ADD, −1 IF SUBTRACT
90    FOR N = 1 TO T
100   LET P = P + S * (1 / (2 * N − 1))
110   REM***2 * N − 1 = 1,3,5,7, . . .
120   LET S = −S
130   REM***ALTERNATE + AND −
140   NEXT N
150   PRINT "APPROXIMATE VALUE OF PI"
160   PRINT "AFTER    "; T;"    TERMS:    ";4 * P
170   END
```

1. Type in the program. RUN the program to find an approximate value of π. Use the following numbers of terms.

   a. 5   b. 10   c. 100   d. 1000

2. How do the values you found in Exercise 1 compare with the actual value of π?

The formula

$$\frac{\pi^2}{6} = \frac{1}{1^2} + \frac{1}{2^2} + \frac{1}{3^2} + \frac{1}{4^2} + \cdots$$

is attributed to the Swiss mathematician Leonhard Euler. This formula can also be used to calculate the value of π.

3. After finding the sum on the right of the equals sign, what further calculations are needed to produce an approximate value of π?

4. Modify the program above to calculate approximations of π using Euler's formula. Note that S is no longer needed.

5. RUN the new program, using the same numbers of terms as in Exercise 1. Record the approximations for π.

CHAPTER REVIEW

State the term that best describes each set of points with respect to $\odot O$.

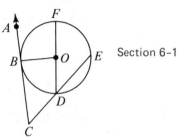

1. $\overrightarrow{CA}$
2. $\overparen{BF}$
3. $\overline{DE}$
4. $\overline{OB}$
5. $\overparen{FBE}$
6. $\overparen{DBF}$
7. A
8. $\overline{CE}$
9. $\overline{DF}$

Section 6-1

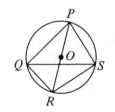

10. Find $m\angle PQR$.
11. Name an angle that is congruent to $\angle RSQ$.
12. If $m\angle QPS = 79$, find $m\angle QRS$.

Section 6-2

13. $\overline{QR}$ is tangent to $\odot P$, $m\angle QPR = 45$, and $QR = 6$. Find PR and SR.

14. $\overleftrightarrow{MN}$ is tangent to the circle. If $m\,\overparen{TA}:m\,\overparen{AB}:m\,\overparen{BT} = 5:6:7$, find $m\angle MTB$.

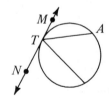

Section 6-3

Complete.

15. $m\,\overparen{AB} = 84$, $m\,\overparen{BC} = 32$, $m\angle APB = \underline{\ ?\ }$
16. $m\,\overparen{AE} = 126$, $m\angle APE = 38$, $m\,\overparen{CD} = \underline{\ ?\ }$
17. $m\,\overparen{AB} = 61$, $m\,\overparen{CDE} = 95$, $m\angle AQE = \underline{\ ?\ }$

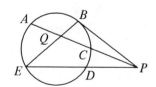

Section 6-4

Solve for *x*. (Point *O* is the center of the circle.)

18.

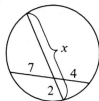

19.

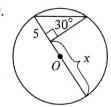

20.

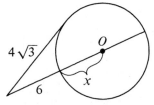

21.

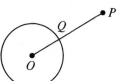

22. Find the diameter of a circle whose area is 24π.

23. An arc of a circle has measure 135. If the radius of the circle is 40, find the exact length of the arc.

In each of Exercises 24 and 25, draw a diagram larger than the one shown. Then do the required construction.

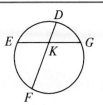

24. Construct a tangent to $\odot O$ at Q.

25. Construct a tangent from P to $\odot O$.

CHAPTER TEST

1. A chord is 8 cm from the center of a circle of radius 12 cm. Find the length of the chord.

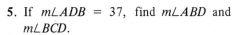

Complete.

2. $m\,\widehat{DG} = 50$, $m\angle DKG = 77$, $m\,\widehat{EF} = \underline{\;?\;}$

3. $DK = 3$, $KF = 12$, $GK = KE$, $GE = \underline{\;?\;}$

Exs. 2, 3

In Exercises 4 and 5, point *O* is the center of the circle.

4. If $m\,\widehat{QR} = m\,\widehat{RS} = m\,\widehat{ST}$ and $m\,\widehat{QXT} = 240$, find $m\angle ROT$.

5. If $m\angle ADB = 37$, find $m\angle ABD$ and $m\angle BCD$.

THE GEOMETRY OF THE CIRCLE **269**

Complete.

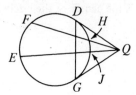

6. $m \overgroup{DEG} = 248$, $m\angle DQG = $ ___?___

7. $m\angle EQF = 27$, $m \overgroup{EF} = 68$, $m \overgroup{JH} = $ ___?___

8. $m\angle QDG = 52$, $m \overgroup{DJ} = 48$, $m \overgroup{JG} = $ ___?___

9. $QH = 5$, $HF = 11$, $QJ = 4$, $JE = $ ___?___

10. $DQ = 8$, $EJ = 12$, $JQ = $ ___?___

Exs. 6-10

11. Find the area of the shaded portion of the square.

12. Draw a large acute $\triangle XYZ$. Construct the inscribed circle of the triangle.

Careers — Urban Planner

Cities are often in conflict with their environments. Urban pollution is one serious concern. Today pollution is monitored by scientific instruments that allow pollutants to be measured to the parts per billion. Cities are spreading in all directions, but they often have inner cores that are wastelands of boarded-up windows and burnt-out buildings. These problems increase the challenge facing urban planners. It is their job to plan new urban growth, to find ways of rejuvenating older areas, and to estimate long-term urban needs.

Planners are involved in all aspects of change within urban, suburban, and rural communities. As a resource for decision makers, they must be aware of any legal issues related to development or redevelopment of an area. They must know building codes, and they must prepare for a changing demand on health care and on transportation systems.

Making estimations of long-range urban needs and providing a number of alternative solutions to those needs are important parts of a planner's job. The first step is to analyze current development, including the location of streets, water and sewer lines, libraries, schools, and parks. This information is then studied in light of the trends in the community, for example, recent employment and economic changes. Planners' recommendations for growth usually include estimations of costs.

Most urban planners work for city, county, or regional planning agencies. State and federal governments also use planners to solve housing, transportation, and environmental issues. Consulting and teaching are other options.

A master's degree in urban or regional planning is required for many entry-level jobs in this field. Possible undergraduate majors include architecture, landscape architecture, and engineering. As a planner, you will spend considerable time explaining and defending your ideas, which means you will need well-developed communications skills. Candidates for positions in government agencies must also pass a civil service examination.

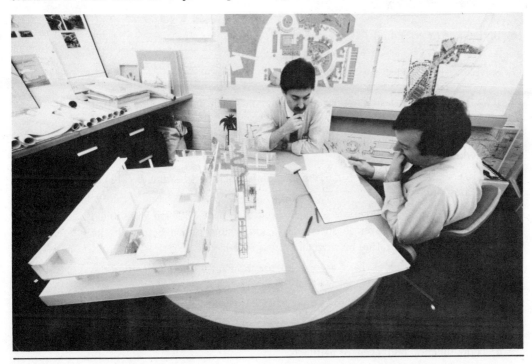

Be sure that you understand the meaning of these terms:

circle, p. 222

radius, p. 222

chord, p. 222

diameter, p. 222

secant, p. 222

tangent, p. 222

central angle, p. 223

inscribed angle, p. 223

inscribed polygon, p. 223

circumscribed polygon, p. 223

semicircle, p. 223

minor arc, p. 223

major arc, p. 223

arc of a chord, p. 245

circumference, p. 257

sector of a circle, p. 258

MIXED REVIEW

Simplify.

1. $(x^{-2} + y^{-2})^{-1}$

2. $\sqrt{-32} + \sqrt{-200} - \dfrac{1}{\sqrt{-2}}$

3. $\dfrac{15}{2 - i}$

4. Sketch a figure that has exactly two lines of symmetry, point symmetry, and no other rotational symmetry.

5. Chords $\overline{AB}$ and $\overline{CD}$ of $\odot O$ intersect at X. If $AX = 12$, $BX = 11.5$, and $CD = 29$, then $CX = \underline{\ ?\ }$ or $CX = \underline{\ ?\ }$.

6. If $f(x) = \dfrac{1}{3}(x - 2)$, find f^{-1}. Show that $f^{-1}(f(x)) = f(f^{-1}(x)) = x$.

7. Solve: a. $|5x - 1| \leqslant 6$ b. $3(2 - 3y) > -3$ or $\dfrac{5}{4}y + \dfrac{2}{3} \geqslant 4$

8. If $9x^2 + kx + 121$ has one real double root, find each possible value for that root.

9. A chord that is 10 cm long is 12 cm from the center of a circle. Find the circumference of the circle.

10. If $f(10) = 0.17$ and $f(15) = 0.26$, use linear interpolation to estimate $f(12)$ to the nearest hundredth.

11. Jesse drove 126 km at a certain average speed. The next 58.5 km were under construction, and his average speed was 6 km/h slower than before. If the entire trip took 2.25 h, find his original average speed.

12. If -5 is a root of $3x^3 + 14x^2 = 9x + 20$, use the Factor Theorem to find the other roots.

13. a. Graph the relation $y = 2\sqrt{4 - x^2}$.
    b. Explain why the relation is a function.
    c. Give the domain and range.
    d. Is the function odd, even, or neither?

State the coordinates of the image of $P(3, -6)$ under each transformation.

14. $D_{\frac{2}{3}}$ **15.** $T_{-3, 0}$ **16.** $r_{y\text{-axis}}$

17. R_{-270} **18.** $R_{180} \circ D_{P, 2}$ **19.** $r_{x\text{-axis}} \circ r_{x\text{-axis}}$

20. $r_k \circ r_j$ where j has equation $y = -x$ and k has equation $x = 2$

Solve for x. (Point O is the center of the circle.)

21. 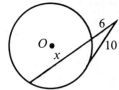   **22.** 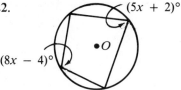   **23.**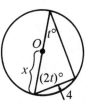

24. Regina has nickels, dimes, and quarters in the ratio $5:3:2$. If she has \$7.35 in all, how many dimes does she have?

25. Find and graph the solution set: **a.** $x^2 + 9 > 6x$ **b.** $|y + 3| \geqslant 1$

26. Express $0.0\overline{3}$ as a quotient of integers in lowest terms and give its multiplicative inverse.

Find a quadratic equation in standard form with integral coefficients and with the given numbers as roots.

27. $\dfrac{3}{4}, \dfrac{5}{4}$ **28.** $-1 + \sqrt{3}, -1 - \sqrt{3}$ **29.** $2 + 3i, 2 - 3i$

30. Construct a right triangle, $\triangle ABC$. Circumscribe a circle about $\triangle ABC$. Where is the center of this circle located?

31. If $f(x) = x^4 - 7$ and $g(x) = \sqrt{x}$, find **(a)** $[g \circ g](2)$, **(b)** $[g \circ f](2)$, **(c)** $[f \circ g](x)$, and **(d)** $[g \circ f](x)$.

Solve over the set of complex numbers.

32. $x^2 - 4x + 6 = 0$ **33.** $\sqrt{11 - 5j} = 1 - j$ **34.** $9v^2 = 6v + 1$

35. If $\angle AOB$ is a central angle of $\odot O$, $m\,\widehat{AB} = 60$, and $OA = 4$, find the area of the region inside $\odot O$ and outside $\triangle AOB$.

Is the given transformation always an isometry? a direct isometry?

36. a translation   **37.** a dilation   **38.** a line reflection

In trigonometry the concept of *angle* includes the idea of rotation of a ray about a point. The movement of the blades of a windmill suggests this type of rotation. In applications of trigonometry to the physical sciences, trigonometric functions are used to describe situations involving angular rotation.

Introduction to Trigonometry

7

As is true of many other fields of mathematics, *trigonometry* first developed as a response to the demands of astronomy, one of the earliest sciences. Babylonian and Greek astronomers developed tables of chords of circles showing the relationship between the length of a chord of a given circle and the central angle that intercepts the chord. Using such tables, astronomers could estimate celestial distances they could not measure directly. These tables are distant ancestors of modern tables of trigonometric ratios.

With the development of *calculus*, trigonometry evolved from tables of numbers into functions of the real numbers and is now studied from the point of view of function theory. In this chapter and Chapters 8, 10, and 11, you will learn many of the properties and some of the applications of the trigonometric functions.

Section 7-1 ANGLES

In geometry you consider only angles greater than $0°$ and less than or equal to $180°$. In trigonometry you will work with angles of all degree measures. In addition to expanding your concept of an angle, in this section you will learn about:
- angles in standard position
- quadrantal angles
- coterminal angles

Consider two rays that have the same endpoint and are in the same position. One ray is fixed while the other ray is allowed to rotate about the endpoint. The result is an *angle*. The endpoint of the rays is the *vertex* of the angle. The fixed ray is the *initial side* of the angle, and the rotated ray is the *terminal side*.

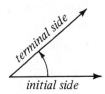

If the terminal side remains stationary, a $0°$ angle is formed. If the terminal side is rotated counterclockwise (as the curved arrow indicates) until it coincides with the initial side, a $360°$ angle is formed. Allowing the terminal side to rotate about its endpoint for more than one complete rotation will produce an angle greater than $360°$.

If the rotation is counterclockwise, the measure of the angle is positive. If the rotation is clockwise, the measure is negative.

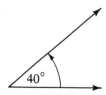 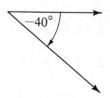

An angle is in *standard position* when the vertex of the angle is at the origin of a coordinate system and the initial side of the angle coincides with the positive *x*-axis. Depending on whether the terminal side falls in Quadrant I, II, III, or IV, we say that the angle lies in the first, second, third, or fourth quadrant. If the terminal side of an angle coincides with a coordinate axis, the angle is referred to as a *quadrantal angle*. Each of the angles shown at the right is in standard position and lies in the third quadrant.

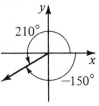

Angles sharing the same initial and terminal sides are called *coterminal angles*. The figure shows two coterminal angles, one of $210°$ and the other of $-150°$. Notice that there are an infinite number of angles coterminal with a $210°$ angle.

EXAMPLE State the measures of three angles coterminal with a $210°$ angle.

SOLUTION

$$360° + 210° = 570° \qquad 2(360°) + 210° = 930° \qquad -360° + (-210°) = -510°$$

ORAL EXERCISES

State the measure of the indicated angle.

1. 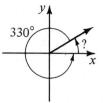 2. 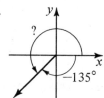 3.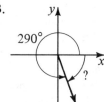

An angle with the given measure is in standard position. Name the quadrant in which the angle lies.

4. $210°$ 5. $154°$ 6. $-18°$ 7. $-200°$ 8. $-120°$

9. $300°$ 10. $400°$ 11. $-385°$ 12. $820°$ 13. $-600°$

Determine whether the following pairs of angles in standard position are coterminal.

14. $40°$ and $400°$

15. $-120°$ and $120°$

16. $180°$ and $-180°$

17. $270°$ and $-270°$

18. $-400°$ and $40°$

19. $90°$ and $-270°$

WRITTEN EXERCISES

In Exercises 1-10:

a. Use a protractor to sketch an angle in standard position with the given measure. Indicate the number of rotations and the direction of rotation with a curved arrow.

b. Name the quadrant in which the angle lies. If the angle is a quadrantal angle, so state.

A　**1.** $100°$　　**2.** $360°$　　**3.** $90°$　　**4.** $-100°$　　**5.** $-300°$

　　6. $270°$　　**7.** $-260°$　　**8.** $-25°$　　**9.** $-800°$　　**10.** $1140°$

An angle A is drawn in standard position. If $0° \leqslant m\angle A < 360°$ and the terminal side of $\angle A$ contains the given point, find the measure of $\angle A$.

11. $(1, 0)$　　**12.** $(-1, 0)$　　**13.** $(0, 1)$　　**14.** $(0, -1)$

15. $(1, 1)$　　**16.** $(-1, -1)$　　**17.** $(1, -1)$　　**18.** $(-1, 1)$

$\overrightarrow{OA}$ and $\overrightarrow{OB}$ coincide. Then $\overrightarrow{OB}$ is rotated in the manner described. Find the measure of $\angle AOB$.

EXAMPLE　　$\frac{1}{3}$ of a clockwise rotation

SOLUTION　　$\frac{1}{3}(-360°) = -120°$

B　**19.** 2 counterclockwise rotations

20. $\frac{1}{2}$ of a counterclockwise rotation

21. $\frac{3}{4}$ of a clockwise rotation

22. $3\frac{1}{2}$ clockwise rotations

23. $1\frac{1}{6}$ counterclockwise rotations

24. $2\frac{2}{5}$ clockwise rotations

Name the least possible positive measure and the greatest possible negative measure of an angle that is coterminal with the given angle.

25. $70°$　　**26.** $110°$　　**27.** $270°$　　**28.** $-180°$

29. $-60°$　　**30.** $225°$　　**31.** $-315°$　　**32.** $-930°$

C **33.** The figure shows two concentric circles. The radius of the larger circle is k times the radius of the smaller circle.

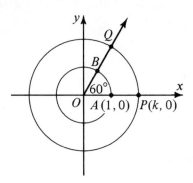

  a. Find the length of $\overset{\frown}{AB}$.

  b. Find the length of $\overset{\frown}{PQ}$ in terms of k.

  c. Find the ratio of the length of $\overset{\frown}{AB}$ to the radius of the circle that contains $\overset{\frown}{AB}$.

  d. Find the ratio of the length of $\overset{\frown}{PQ}$ to the radius of the circle that contains $\overset{\frown}{PQ}$.

  e. What is the relationship between the ratios you found in parts (c) and (d)?

Section 7-2 RADIAN MEASURE

The *degree* is not the only unit used for measuring angles. Another unit, called the *radian*, is more commonly used in advanced mathematics. An angle of 1 *radian* (measured counterclockwise from its initial side) is a central angle that intercepts an arc equal in length to the radius of the circle.

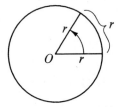

1 radian

An angle of 2 radians intercepts an arc twice as long as the radius of the circle, and so on. In general, an angle of θ radians will intercept an arc θ times as long as the radius.

> If θ is the measure in radians of a central angle of a circle, s is the length of the intercepted arc, and r is the radius of the circle, then:
>
> $$s = |\theta|r \quad \text{or} \quad |\theta| = \frac{s}{r}$$

To convert from degree measure to radian measure, and vice versa, we must first find a relationship between degrees and radians. Since a circle of radius 1 has a circumference of 2π, we can substitute 1 for r and 2π for s in the formula $|\theta| = \frac{s}{r}$, to get $|\theta| = \frac{2\pi}{1} = 2\pi$ radians. Thus, an angle of $360°$ is equivalent to an angle of 2π radians, and conversely.

$$360° = 2\pi \text{ radians}$$
$$180° = \pi \text{ radians}$$

> $$1° = \frac{\pi}{180} \text{ radians and } 1 \text{ radian} = \left(\frac{180}{\pi}\right)° \approx 57.3°$$

An angle that has a negative degree measure will also have a negative radian measure.

EXAMPLE   **a.** Express $-135°$ in radians.   **b.** Express $\dfrac{5\pi}{3}$ radians in degrees.

SOLUTION   **a.** $1° = \dfrac{\pi}{180}$ radians; $\;-135° = -135 \cdot \dfrac{\pi}{180}$ radians $= -\dfrac{3\pi}{4}$ radians

           b. 1 radian $= \left(\dfrac{180}{\pi}\right)°$; $\;\dfrac{5\pi}{3}$ radians $= \dfrac{5\pi}{3} \cdot \left(\dfrac{180}{\pi}\right)° = 300°$

Since the ratio $\dfrac{s}{r}$ is a constant for any given value of θ, the radian measure of a given central angle remains the same regardless of the radius of the circle containing the intercepted arc.

EXAMPLE   Find the positive radian measure of a central angle that intercepts an arc of 10 cm on a circle with radius 15 cm.

SOLUTION $\theta = \dfrac{s}{r}$

           $\theta = \dfrac{10}{15}$

           $\theta = \dfrac{2}{3}$ radians

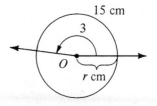

EXAMPLE   In a circle, a central angle of 3 radians intercepts an arc of 15 cm. Find the radius of the circle.

SOLUTION $s = \theta r$

           $15 = 3r$

           $5 = r$

     The radius is 5 cm.

Some texts use $m(\theta)$ to indicate the measure of angle θ, reserving the symbol θ for the name of an angle. We will use θ and $m(\theta)$ interchangeably when the meaning is clear from the context. If no units of angle measure are given, the units are assumed to be radians. For example, $\theta = 3$ is read "the measure of angle θ is 3 radians," but $\theta = 3°$ means "the measure of angle θ is $3°$."

ORAL EXERCISES

State the radian measure of the positive central angle described.

1. It intercepts an arc of length 1 on a circle of radius 1.

2. It intercepts an arc of length 3 on a circle of radius 3.

3. It intercepts an arc of length 4 on a circle of radius 2.

4. It intercepts an arc of length 1 on a circle of radius 3.

Express each degree measure in radians. (You may leave your answer in terms of π.)

  5. $90°$ **6.** $-30°$ **7.** $60°$

Express each radian measure in degrees.

  8. 2π **9.** $\dfrac{\pi}{4}$ **10.** $-\dfrac{5\pi}{6}$

WRITTEN EXERCISES

Express each degree measure in radians.

A **1.** $6°$ **2.** $110°$ **3.** $225°$ **4.** $300°$

  5. $-270°$ **6.** $-15°$ **7.** $-72°$ **8.** $-315°$

  9. $420°$ **10.** $570°$ **11.** $750°$ **12.** $495°$

Express each radian measure in degrees.

13. $\dfrac{\pi}{6}$ **14.** $\dfrac{\pi}{3}$ **15.** $\dfrac{2\pi}{3}$ **16.** $\dfrac{3\pi}{2}$

17. $-\dfrac{11\pi}{12}$ **18.** $-\dfrac{7\pi}{5}$ **19.** -3π **20.** $-\dfrac{9\pi}{10}$

21. $\dfrac{\pi}{8}$ **22.** $\dfrac{5\pi}{8}$ **23.** $\dfrac{\pi}{12}$ **24.** $-\dfrac{7\pi}{12}$

25. 1 **26.** -2 **27.** -8 **28.** 6

B **29.** Find the length of the radius of a circle in which a central angle of 2.5 radians intercepts an arc of 1.5 cm.

30. Find the measure of a positive central angle that intercepts an arc of 14 cm on a circle of radius 5 cm.

31. The pendulum of a clock swings through an angle of 0.9 radians as its tip travels 18 cm. Find the length of the pendulum.

32. Find the length of the arc intercepted by a central angle of 3.5 radians on a circle of radius 6 m.

33. a. Through how many degrees does the minute hand of a clock turn in 45 min?
  b. Through how many radians does the minute hand of a clock turn in 45 min?
  c. If the minute hand of a clock is 5 cm long, how far does its tip travel in 45 min?

34. A wheel of radius 18 cm is rotating at a rate of 90 revolutions per minute.
  a. How many radians per minute is this?
  b. How many radians per second is this?
  c. How far does a point on the rim of the wheel travel in one second?
  d. Find the speed of a point on the rim of the wheel in centimeters per second.

280   *CHAPTER 7*

C 35. Find **(a)** the degree measure and **(b)** the radian measure of the angle formed by the hands of a clock at 1:20.

36. **a.** In a circle of radius 1, find the area of a sector determined by an arc of length $\frac{\pi}{4}$ units.

   b. In a circle of radius 1, find the area of a sector determined by an arc of length k units.

   c. In a circle of radius 1, how long is the arc that determines a sector whose area is 1 square unit?

Section 7-3 THE SINE AND COSINE FUNCTIONS

The first trigonometric functions we will consider are the *sine* function and the *cosine* function. We will define these functions in terms of the *unit circle*, a circle with center at the origin and radius 1. Its equation is

$$x^2 + y^2 = 1.$$

In the figure at the right, angle θ is in standard position. Point P represents the intersection of the unit circle and the terminal side of angle θ in standard position. We define the functions *sine* and *cosine* as follows:

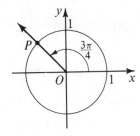

   The *sine* of θ is the *y*-coordinate of P.
   The *cosine* of θ is the *x*-coordinate of P.

We abbreviate sine θ by sin θ and cosine θ by cos θ. Thus,

$$\sin \theta = y \text{ and } \cos \theta = x,$$

where θ represents the measure, in either degrees or radians, of an angle in standard position.

Notice that the signs of these functions depend on the quadrant in which angle θ lies.

EXAMPLE Determine whether sin θ and cos θ are positive or negative if $\theta = \frac{3\pi}{4}$.

SOLUTION Sketch θ in standard position. You can see that θ is in the second quadrant. In Quadrant II, $x < 0$ and $y > 0$, so $\cos \frac{3\pi}{4} < 0$ and $\sin \frac{3\pi}{4} > 0$.

We will agree to follow custom and write $\sin^2 \theta$ for $(\sin \theta)^2$ and $\cos^2 \theta$ for $(\cos \theta)^2$. Then the following equation, which you will be asked to prove in Exercise 29, can be derived from the definitions of the sine and cosine functions.

$$\sin^2 \theta + \cos^2 \theta = 1$$

If you know the value of either $\sin \theta$ or $\cos \theta$ and the quadrant that angle θ is in, then this equation can be used to evaluate the other function.

EXAMPLE   If θ is in the third quadrant, and $\sin \theta = -\dfrac{3}{4}$, find $\cos \theta$.

SOLUTION $\sin^2 \theta + \cos^2 \theta = 1$

$$\left(-\frac{3}{4}\right)^2 + \cos^2 \theta = 1$$

$$\frac{9}{16} + \cos^2 \theta = 1$$

$$\cos^2 \theta = 1 - \frac{9}{16} = \frac{7}{16}$$

In the third quadrant, $x < 0$, so $\cos \theta < 0$.

Therefore: $\cos \theta = -\sqrt{\dfrac{7}{16}} = -\dfrac{\sqrt{7}}{4}$

Now consider the values of θ for which θ is a quadrantal angle. You can use the unit circle at the right to evaluate $\sin \theta$ and $\cos \theta$ for $\theta \in \left\{0, \dfrac{\pi}{2}, \pi, \dfrac{3\pi}{2}, 2\pi, \ldots\right\}$.

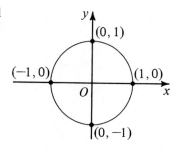

EXAMPLE   Find **(a)** $\sin \dfrac{\pi}{2}$ and **(b)** $\cos \pi$.

SOLUTION   **(a)** For $\theta = \dfrac{\pi}{2}$, $y = 1$, so $\sin \dfrac{\pi}{2} = 1$.

(b) For $\theta = \pi$, $x = -1$, so $\cos \pi = -1$.

In Exercises 30–37 you will learn how to find the values of $\sin \theta$ and $\cos \theta$ when you are given the coordinates of a point on the terminal side of θ (in standard position) but not on the unit circle.

ORAL EXERCISES

Complete with $>$ or $<$ to make a true statement.

1. In Quadrant I, $\sin \theta \underline{\ \ ?\ \ } 0$ and $\cos \theta \underline{\ \ ?\ \ } 0$.

2. In Quadrant II, $\sin \theta \underline{\ \ ?\ \ } 0$ and $\cos \theta \underline{\ \ ?\ \ } 0$.

3. In Quadrant III, $\sin \theta \underline{\ \ ?\ \ } 0$ and $\cos \theta \underline{\ \ ?\ \ } 0$.

4. In Quadrant IV, $\sin \theta \underline{\ \ ?\ \ } 0$ and $\cos \theta \underline{\ \ ?\ \ } 0$

5. What is the range of the sine function? of the cosine function?

6. What is the domain of the sine function? of the cosine function?

For the given angle, determine:

a. The quadrant in which θ lies

b. Whether $\sin \theta$ and $\cos \theta$ are positive or negative

7. $45°$ **8.** $210°$ **9.** $-15°$ **10.** $-120°$

11. $\dfrac{5\pi}{6}$ **12.** $\dfrac{9\pi}{4}$ **13.** $-\dfrac{7\pi}{8}$ **14.** $-\dfrac{\pi}{6}$

WRITTEN EXERCISES

Find the sine and cosine of the given angle.

A   1. $90°$ **2.** $180°$ **3.** $-\dfrac{\pi}{2}$ **4.** 2π

5. $-\pi$ **6.** $\dfrac{3\pi}{2}$ **7.** $-90°$ **8.** $0°$

In Exercises 9–12, the coordinates of a point on the unit circle are given. If the terminal side of angle θ in standard position passes through the given point, find $\sin \theta$ and $\cos \theta$.

9. $\left(\dfrac{\sqrt{2}}{2}, \dfrac{\sqrt{2}}{2} \right)$ **10.** $\left(\dfrac{1}{2}, -\dfrac{\sqrt{3}}{2} \right)$ **11.** $\left(-\dfrac{1}{3}, \dfrac{2\sqrt{2}}{3} \right)$ **12.** $\left(-\dfrac{\sqrt{2}}{3}, -\dfrac{\sqrt{7}}{3} \right)$

Given the values of $\sin \theta$ and $\cos \theta$, determine the quadrant in which θ lies.

13. $\sin \theta = -\dfrac{1}{4}$, $\cos \theta = -\dfrac{\sqrt{15}}{4}$ **14.** $\sin \theta = \dfrac{2}{3}$, $\cos \theta = -\dfrac{\sqrt{5}}{3}$

15. $\sin \theta = \dfrac{3}{4}$, $\cos \theta = \dfrac{\sqrt{7}}{4}$ **16.** $\sin \theta = -\dfrac{\sqrt{5}}{5}$, $\cos \theta = \dfrac{2\sqrt{5}}{5}$

Given the value of $\sin \theta$ or $\cos \theta$ and the quadrant in which θ lies, find the value of the other function.

17. $\sin \theta = \dfrac{\sqrt{2}}{2}$, Quadrant I   **18.** $\sin \theta = -\dfrac{1}{2}$, Quadrant IV

19. $\cos \theta = \dfrac{1}{4}$, Quadrant IV   **20.** $\cos \theta = -\dfrac{4}{5}$, Quadrant II

21. $\sin \theta = -\dfrac{5}{13}$, Quadrant III   **22.** $\cos \theta = \dfrac{24}{25}$, Quadrant I

Evaluate.

23. $\sin \pi \cdot \cos \dfrac{\pi}{2}$ **24.** $\sin \pi + \cos \pi$ **25.** $\cos \dfrac{3\pi}{2} - \sin \dfrac{\pi}{2}$

26. $\sin^2 \dfrac{3\pi}{2}$ **27.** $\cos^2 \dfrac{\pi}{2} + \cos^2 \left(-\dfrac{\pi}{2} \right)$ **28.** $\sin \left(-\dfrac{\pi}{2} \right) \cdot \cos 2\pi$

B 29. Prove that $\sin^2 \theta + \cos^2 \theta = 1$ for all $\theta \in \mathcal{R}$. (*Hint*: Use the equation of the unit circle.)

The figure shows concentric circles with radii 1 and r. The terminal side of angle θ intersects the unit circle at $A(\cos\theta, \sin\theta)$ and the other circle at $B(x, y)$. By the properties of similar triangles,

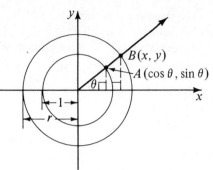

$$\frac{\sin\theta}{1} = \frac{y}{r} \quad \text{and} \quad \frac{\cos\theta}{1} = \frac{x}{r}$$

or

$$\sin\theta = \frac{y}{r} \quad \text{and} \quad \cos\theta = \frac{x}{r}.$$

EXAMPLE If the terminal side of θ passes through $(2, -1)$, find $\sin\theta$ and $\cos\theta$.

SOLUTION $x^2 + y^2 = r^2$
$2^2 + (-1)^2 = r^2$
$r = \sqrt{5}$

$$\sin\theta = \frac{y}{r} = -\frac{1}{\sqrt{5}} = -\frac{\sqrt{5}}{5}$$

$$\cos\theta = \frac{x}{r} = \frac{2}{\sqrt{5}} = \frac{2\sqrt{5}}{5}$$

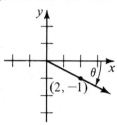

Find $\sin\theta$ and $\cos\theta$ if the terminal side of θ passes through the given point.

30. $(3, 4)$ **31.** $(-3, 4)$ **32.** $(8, -6)$ **33.** $(-\sqrt{2}, -\sqrt{2})$

34. $(-5, 12)$ **35.** $(1, \sqrt{15})$ **36.** $(-2\sqrt{3}, -2)$ **37.** $(3, -5)$

Find an angle θ between $0°$ and $90°$ that makes the statement true.

EXAMPLE $\sin\theta = \sin 150°$

SOLUTION Two points with the same y-coordinates lie on a horizontal line. Thus, $\sin\theta = \sin 150°$ and $\theta = 30°$.

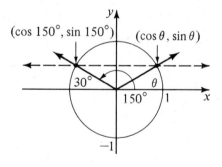

C 38. $\sin\theta = \sin 405°$ **39.** $\sin\theta = -\sin 240°$

40. $\sin\theta = -\sin 330°$ **41.** $\cos\theta = \cos(-45°)$

42. $\cos\theta = -\cos 120°$ **43.** $\cos\theta = -\cos 225°$

SELF-TEST 1

If θ is in standard position and has the given measure, name the quadrant θ lies in.

1. $-40°$ **2.** $160°$ **3.** $280°$ Section 7-1

Angle θ between $0°$ and $360°$ is in standard position. Its terminal side contains the given point. Find the degree measure of the angle.

4. $(-2, 0)$ **5.** $(-2, -2)$ **6.** $(0, -2)$

7. Express 60° in radians.

8. Express $\dfrac{3\pi}{4}$ radians in degrees.

9. In a circle, a central angle of 3 radians intercepts an arc 18 cm long. Find the radius of the circle.

10. Complete: If $\cos \theta = \dfrac{1}{2}$ and $\sin \theta < 0$, then angle θ lies in Quadrant $\underline{\ ?\ }$.

11. If $\sin \theta = \dfrac{3}{4}$ and $\cos \theta > 0$, find the value of $\cos \theta$.

12. Evaluate:

    a. $\sin 0$ **b.** $\cos \pi$ **c.** $\left(\sin \dfrac{\pi}{2} \right)\left(\cos \dfrac{\pi}{2} \right)$

Section 7-4 REFERENCE ANGLES AND SPECIAL ANGLES

Given an angle θ in standard position, the *reference angle* of θ is the acute positive angle formed by the terminal side of θ and the positive or negative portion of the *x*-axis. In each of the following figures, angle α is the reference angle of angle θ.

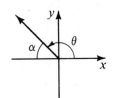 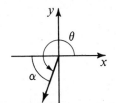 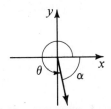

EXAMPLE   Sketch the reference angle α for each of the following angles: $320°$, $-155°$, $\dfrac{3\pi}{4}$. State the measure of angle α.

SOLUTION   Sketch each angle and its reference angle.

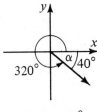 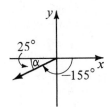 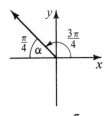

        $m(\alpha) = 40°$ $m(\alpha) = 25°$ $m(\alpha) = \dfrac{\pi}{4}$

    Reference angles enable you to express the sine or cosine of any angle in terms of the sine or cosine of a positive acute angle.

INTRODUCTION TO TRIGONOMETRY   **285**

EXAMPLE   Express cos 125° as a function of a positive acute angle.

SOLUTION   1. Sketch a 125° angle in standard position and its reference angle of 55°.

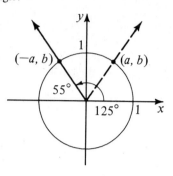

2. In the first quadrant, draw an angle in standard position congruent to the reference angle. (The terminal side is indicated by the dashed line in the figure.)

3. The terminal sides of the 125° angle and the first-quadrant 55° angle intersect the unit circle in points whose x-coordinates differ only in sign. Since $a = \cos 55°$ and $-a = \cos 125°$, you have:

$$\cos 125° = -\cos 55°$$

The diagrams below illustrate the relationship between the sine and cosine of an angle in each of the second, third, and fourth quadrants and the sine and cosine of its reference angle.

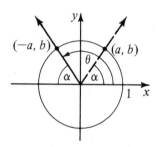

Quadrant II
$\cos \theta = -\cos \alpha$
$\sin \theta = \sin \alpha$

Quadrant III
$\cos \theta = -\cos \alpha$
$\sin \theta = -\sin \alpha$

Quadrant IV
$\cos \theta = \cos \alpha$
$\sin \theta = -\sin \alpha$

To find the sine or cosine of any angle, you simply find the sine or cosine of its reference angle and change the sign if needed in accordance with the quadrant of the angle.

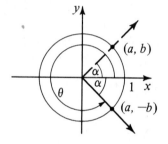

EXAMPLE   Express $\sin\left(-\dfrac{\pi}{6}\right)$ as a function of a positive acute angle.

SOLUTION The reference angle of $-\dfrac{\pi}{6}$ is $\dfrac{\pi}{6}$.

Since $\theta = -\dfrac{\pi}{6}$ is in the fourth quadrant, $\sin \theta < 0$.

Thus, $\sin\left(-\dfrac{\pi}{6}\right) = -\sin\dfrac{\pi}{6}$.

Some especially useful reference angles are related to the 45-45-90 triangle or the 30-60-90 triangle. You can use the properties of these triangles to find the sine and cosine of integral multiples of $30°$ $\left(\text{or } \dfrac{\pi}{6}\right)$ and $45°$ $\left(\text{or } \dfrac{\pi}{4}\right)$.

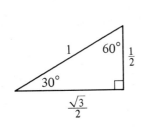
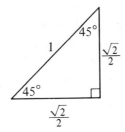

EXAMPLE Find **(a)** $\cos 30°$ and **(b)** $\sin 30°$.

SOLUTION Sketch a 30-60-90 triangle with hypotenuse 1 on the unit circle so that the $30°$ angle is in standard position. The terminal side of the $30°$ angle intersects the circle at $\left(\dfrac{\sqrt{3}}{2}, \dfrac{1}{2}\right)$. Thus,

(a) $\cos 30° = \dfrac{\sqrt{3}}{2}$ and **(b)** $\sin 30° = \dfrac{1}{2}$.

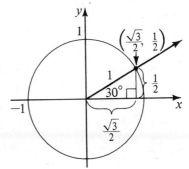

EXAMPLE Find **(a)** $\sin \dfrac{5\pi}{4}$ and **(b)** $\cos \dfrac{5\pi}{4}$.

SOLUTION $\theta = \dfrac{5\pi}{4}$ lies in the third quadrant. Therefore, the measure of its reference angle is $\dfrac{5\pi}{4} - \pi = \dfrac{\pi}{4}$, or $45°$. Since $\sin \theta < 0$ and $\cos \theta < 0$ in Quadrant III, we have:

(a) $\sin \dfrac{5\pi}{4} = -\sin \dfrac{\pi}{4} = -\dfrac{\sqrt{2}}{2}$

(b) $\cos \dfrac{5\pi}{4} = -\cos \dfrac{\pi}{4} = -\dfrac{\sqrt{2}}{2}$

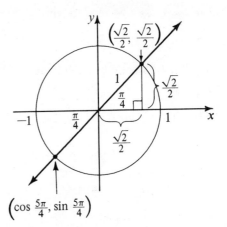

INTRODUCTION TO TRIGONOMETRY **287**

ORAL EXERCISES

In Exercises 1-9:
a. State the measure of the reference angle you would use to evaluate the following.
b. State whether the given function value is positive or negative.

1. $\sin 120°$
2. $\sin (-35°)$
3. $\cos 200°$
4. $\cos 350°$
5. $\sin 220°$
6. $\cos (-100°)$
7. $\sin \dfrac{3\pi}{5}$
8. $\cos \dfrac{3\pi}{4}$
9. $\cos \dfrac{7\pi}{6}$

WRITTEN EXERCISES

In Exercises 1-12:
a. Sketch the given angle in standard position, then sketch its reference angle. Label the reference angle as angle α.
b. State the measure of angle α.

A
1. $130°$
2. $245°$
3. $325°$
4. $95°$
5. $-40°$
6. $-120°$
7. $-325°$
8. $-465°$
9. $-\dfrac{5\pi}{3}$
10. $\dfrac{4\pi}{3}$
11. $\dfrac{5\pi}{6}$
12. $\dfrac{7\pi}{4}$

Express the stated value in terms of a function of a positive acute angle.

13. $\sin 138°$
14. $\cos 170°$
15. $\cos (-40°)$
16. $\sin (-120°)$
17. $\sin \dfrac{4\pi}{3}$
18. $\cos \dfrac{9\pi}{11}$
19. $\cos \left(-\dfrac{7\pi}{3}\right)$
20. $\sin \left(-\dfrac{2\pi}{3}\right)$
21. $\cos (-175°)$
22. $\sin 315°$
23. $\sin (-170°)$
24. $\cos (-230°)$

Evaluate (a) $\sin \theta$ and (b) $\cos \theta$ for the given angle θ.

25. $\dfrac{\pi}{4}$
26. $\dfrac{3\pi}{4}$
27. $\dfrac{\pi}{3}$
28. $-\dfrac{\pi}{3}$
29. $\dfrac{5\pi}{6}$
30. $\dfrac{7\pi}{6}$
31. $-\dfrac{7\pi}{4}$
32. $-\dfrac{2\pi}{3}$
33. $-330°$
34. $225°$
35. $315°$
36. $150°$

Find all values of θ between $0°$ and $360°$ that make the statement true.

EXAMPLE $\cos 75° = \cos \theta$

SOLUTION $\cos 75° = \cos 285°$
$\theta = 75°$ or $285°$

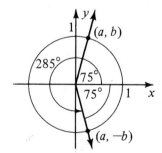

B **37.** $\cos 40° = \cos \theta$ **38.** $\cos 160° = \cos \theta$ **39.** $\sin 55° = \sin \theta$

40. $\sin 225° = \sin \theta$ **41.** $\sin 110° = \sin \theta$ **42.** $\cos 300° = \cos \theta$

Evaluate. Express your answer in simplified form.

43. $\sin 45° + \cos 45°$

44. $2 \sin 30° + 3 \cos 60°$

45. $3\left(\cos \dfrac{\pi}{6} - \sin \dfrac{\pi}{6}\right)$

46. $\sin \dfrac{3\pi}{2} + \cos \pi + \cos \dfrac{\pi}{4}$

47. $2 \cos 0° + 3 \sin 150°$

48. $3 \cos 120° \cdot \sin 210°$

49. $\cos \dfrac{\pi}{2} + 2 \sin \dfrac{\pi}{4}$

50. $4 \sin \dfrac{5\pi}{4} - 2 \cos \dfrac{7\pi}{6}$

51. $2 \sin^2 \dfrac{\pi}{3}$

52. $3 \cos^2 \dfrac{3\pi}{4}$

53. $8 \sin 30° \cos(-45°) \sin(-60°)$

54. $\sin 135°(\cos 225° - \sin 210°)$

Section 7-5 TRIGONOMETRIC TABLES

In Section 7-4 you used the properties of special triangles to find the values of the sine and cosine functions for angles that are integral multiples of 30° and of 45°. You can find the values of trigonometric functions of other angles by using Table 1 on pages 677–681. These values are approximations correct to four digits.

The first two columns give the measure of the angle. Column 1 is expressed in degrees and minutes, and Column 2 is expressed in radians. A degree is equivalent to 60 *minutes*, and 1 minute is equivalent to 60 *seconds*.

$$1° = 60' \quad \text{(minutes)}$$
$$1' = 60'' \quad \text{(seconds)}$$

Some texts use *decimal* degrees in place of minutes and seconds. For example:

$$27°30' = 27.5°$$

If you use a calculator frequently, you'll probably want to know how to convert from seconds and minutes to decimal degrees since the latter are often more convenient to use.

EXAMPLE   Convert $42°12'$ to decimal degrees.

SOLUTION $42°12' = \left(42 + \dfrac{12}{60}\right)^°$

$= (42 + 0.2)°$

$= 42.2°$

EXAMPLE   Express 27.035° in terms of degrees, minutes, and seconds.

SOLUTION   Let x = the number of minutes in 0.035°.

$$\frac{x}{60} = \frac{35}{1000}, \quad 1000x = 2100, \quad x = 2.1$$

Thus: $27.035° = 27°2.1'$

Let y = the number of seconds in 0.1'.

$$\frac{y}{60} = \frac{1}{10}, \quad 10y = 60, \quad y = 6$$

Thus: $27.035° = 27°2'6''$

If $0° \leqslant \theta \leqslant 45°$, you can read the value of sin θ or cos θ directly from the table. For example, sin 28°40' = 0.4797. If $45° \leqslant \theta \leqslant 90°$, you use the measures given in the far right-hand column along with the functions given at the bottom of the page. For example, cos 55°20' = 0.5688. (The column headings csc θ, tan θ, cot θ, and sec θ represent other trigonometric functions that we will consider in Chapter 8.)

$m(\alpha)$ Degrees	$m(\alpha)$ Radians	sin α	csc α	tan α	cot α	sec α	cos α		
27° 00′	.4712	.4540	2.203	.5095	1.963	1.122	.8910	1.0996	63° 00′
10′	.4741	.4566	2.190	.5132	1.949	1.124	.8897	1.0966	50′
20′	.4771	.4592	2.178	.5169	1.935	1.126	.8884	1.0937	40′
30′	.4800	.4617	2.166	.5206	1.921	1.127	.8870	1.0908	30′
40′	.4829	.4643	2.154	.5243	1.907	1.129	.8857	1.0879	20′
50′	.4858	.4669	2.142	.5280	1.894	1.131	.8843	1.0850	10′
28° 00′	.4887	.4695	2.130	.5317	1.881	1.133	.8829	1.0821	62° 00′
10′	.4916	.4720	2.118	.5354	1.868	1.134	.8816	1.0792	50′
20′	.4945	.4746	2.107	.5392	1.855	1.136	.8802	1.0763	40′
30′	.4974	.4772	2.096	.5430	1.842	1.138	.8788	1.0734	30′
40′	.5003	.4797	2.085	.5467	1.829	1.140	.8774	1.0705	20′
50′	.5032	.4823	2.074	.5505	1.816	1.142	.8760	1.0676	10′
29° 00′	.5061	.4848	2.063	.5543	1.804	1.143	.8746	1.0647	61° 00′
10′	.5091	.4874	2.052	.5581	1.792	1.145	.8732	1.0617	50′
50′	.5905	.5568	1.796	.6703	1.492	1.204	.8307	.9803	10′
34° 00′	.5934	.5592	1.788	.6745	1.483	1.206	.8290	.9774	56° 00′
10′	.5963	.5616	1.781	.6787	1.473	1.209	.8274	.9745	50′
20′	.5992	.5640	1.773	.6830	1.464	1.211	.8258	.9716	40′
30′	.6021	.5664	1.766	.6873	1.455	1.213	.8241	.9687	30′
40′	.6050	.5688	1.758	.6916	1.446	1.216	.8225	.9657	20′
50′	.6080	.5712	1.751	.6959	1.437	1.218	.8208	.9628	10′
35° 00′	.6109	.5736	1.743	.7002	1.428	1.221	.8192	.9599	55° 00′
10′	.6138	.5760	1.736	.7046	1.419	1.223	.8175	.9570	50′
20′	.6167	.5783	1.729	.7089	1.411	1.226	.8158	.9541	40′
30′	.6196	.5807	1.722	.7133	1.402	1.228	.8141	.9512	30′
40′	.6225	.5831	1.715	.7177	1.393	1.231	.8124	.9483	20′
50′	.6254	.5854	1.708	.7221	1.385	1.233	.8107	.9454	10′
36° 00′	.6283	.5878	1.701	.7265	1.376	1.236	.8090	.9425	54° 00′
		cos α	sec α	cot α	tan α	csc α	sin α	Radians	Degrees
								$m(\alpha)$	

If θ is not in the first quadrant, you use its reference angle to find the sine or cosine of θ. (It is not usually necessary to express the sine or cosine of an angle as a function of an acute angle when you're using a calculator. The calculator will accept any size angle as input, but be sure that you know whether your calculator accepts angles in degrees or radians. Check that you're using the right setting before you begin.)

EXAMPLE   Find the value of $\sin 234°40'$.

SOLUTION   The reference angle of $234°40'$ is $234°40' - 180° = 54°40'$.
Since sine is negative in Quadrant III, $\sin 234°40' = -\sin 54°40'$.

$$\sin 54°40' = 0.8158$$
$$\sin 234°40' = -0.8158$$

You can use linear interpolation, presented in Section 4-4, to find approximate values of trigonometric functions of angles not given in the table.

EXAMPLE   Find $\sin 32°15'$.

SOLUTION   Organize the data in a chart that includes the desired value $\sin 32°15'$.

$$10'\left[5'\left[\begin{array}{cc} \theta & \sin\theta \\ 32°10' & 0.5324 \\ 32°15' & \sin 32°15' \\ 32°20' & 0.5348 \end{array}\right]d\right]0.0024$$

$$\frac{5}{10} = \frac{d}{0.0024}$$
$$d = \frac{5}{10}(0.0024)$$
$$d = 0.0012$$
$$\sin 32°15' = \sin 32°10' + d$$
$$= 0.5324 + 0.0012$$
$$= 0.5336$$

EXAMPLE   Find $\cos 49°42'$.

SOLUTION

$$10'\left[2'\left[\begin{array}{cc} \theta & \cos\theta \\ 49°40' & 0.6472 \\ 49°42' & \cos 49°42' \\ 49°50' & 0.6450 \end{array}\right]d\right]-0.0022$$

$$\frac{2}{10} = \frac{d}{-0.0022}$$
$$d = \frac{2}{10}(-0.0022)$$
$$d = -0.0004 \text{ (rounded to four decimal places)}$$

(Note that in this case d is negative because cosine is decreasing between $49°40'$ and $49°50'$.)

$$\cos 49°42' = \cos 49°40' + d$$
$$= 0.6472 + (-0.0004) = 0.6468$$

You can also use interpolation to find to the nearest minute the measure of an angle whose sine or cosine is given.

EXAMPLE   Find θ to the nearest minute if θ is between $0°$ and $90°$ and $\sin \theta = 0.8940$.

SOLUTION   Since 0.8940 does not appear in the table, we look for the two entries that are closest to it, one less than 0.8940 and one greater than 0.8940.

$$10'\left[d\begin{bmatrix} \begin{array}{cc} \theta & \sin \theta \\ 63°20' & 0.8936 \\ \theta & 0.8940 \\ 63°30' & 0.8949 \end{array} \end{bmatrix}0.0004 \right]0.0013$$

$$\frac{d}{10'} = \frac{0.0004}{0.0013} = \frac{4}{13}$$

$$d = \frac{4}{13}(10') = 3' \text{ (rounded to the nearest minute)}$$

$$\theta = 63°20' + 3', \text{ or } 63°23'$$

ORAL EXERCISES

Use Table 1 on pages 677–681 to find each function value.

1. $\sin 26°40'$
2. $\cos 15°20'$
3. $\cos 72°30'$
4. $\sin 68°10'$
5. $\cos 53°$
6. $\sin 37°$

Use Table 1 to state the value of θ in degrees and minutes for which the given function has the given value.

7. $\sin \theta = 0.6428$
8. $\cos \theta = 0.7509$
9. $\cos \theta = 0.2979$
10. $\sin \theta = 0.8631$
11. $\sin \theta = 0.9397$
12. $\cos \theta = 0.4874$

WRITTEN EXERCISES

Use Table 1 to find a four-digit approximation of the given function value.

A   1. $\sin 42°15'$
2. $\cos 15°26'$
3. $\cos 36°3'$
4. $\sin 12°8'$
5. $\sin 70°18'$
6. $\cos 62°27'$
7. $\cos 100°$
8. $\sin 220°10'$
9. $\sin 275°40'$
10. $\cos (-325°)$
11. $\cos 814°$
12. $\sin 520°$

Express in decimal degrees to the nearest $0.01°$.

13. $18°15'$
14. $35°6'$
15. $47°36'$
16. $2°20'$
17. $54°12'20''$
18. $25°25'25''$

Express in degrees and minutes to the nearest minute.

19. $44.25°$ **20.** $72.17°$ **21.** $39.83°$

22. $63.2°$ **23.** $18.18°$ **24.** $51.44°$

Express in degrees, minutes, and seconds to the nearest second.

25. $27.48°$ **26.** $69.114°$ **27.** $12.923°$

28. $14.478°$ **29.** $25.842°$ **30.** $30.683°$

Find the value of θ to the nearest minute if θ is between $0°$ and $90°$.

31. $\cos \theta = 0.8425$ **32.** $\sin \theta = 0.2463$ **33.** $\sin \theta = 0.5530$

34. $\sin \theta = 0.9600$ **35.** $\cos \theta = 0.9908$ **36.** $\cos \theta = 0.4341$

Find the value of θ between $0°$ and $360°$ to the nearest $10'$.

EXAMPLE $\sin \theta = -0.3007$; $\cos \theta < 0$

SOLUTION   From Table 1, find θ so that $\sin \theta = 0.3007$. Since $\sin 17°30' = 0.3007$, the reference angle is $17°30'$.
Since both $\sin \theta$ and $\cos \theta$ are negative, θ is in the third quadrant.
$\theta = 180° + 17°30' = 197°30'$

B 37. $\sin \theta = 0.3256$; $\cos \theta < 0$ **38.** $\cos \theta = 0.8450$; $\sin \theta < 0$

39. $\cos \theta = -0.9757$; $\sin \theta < 0$ **40.** $\sin \theta = -0.8660$; $\cos \theta > 0$

41. $\cos \theta = -0.4488$; $\sin \theta > 0$ **42.** $\sin \theta = -0.2700$; $\cos \theta < 0$

Find the value of θ to the nearest $10'$ for the positive acute angle in standard position whose terminal side contains the given point.

EXAMPLE $(2, 4\sqrt{2})$

SOLUTION $x^2 + y^2 = r^2$ (See Exs. 30–37, p. 284.)
$2^2 + (4\sqrt{2})^2 = r^2$
$r^2 = 4 + 32 = 36$
$r = 6$

$\cos \theta = \dfrac{x}{r} = \dfrac{2}{6} = 0.3333$

$\theta = 70°30'$ (From Table 1)

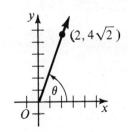

43. $(4, 3)$ **44.** $(3\sqrt{3}, 3)$ **45.** $(15, 8)$ **46.** $(5, 12)$

To the nearest $10'$ find the value of θ between $0°$ and $360°$ such that the terminal
side of θ in standard position contains the given point.

C 47. $(-3, 2\sqrt{10})$ **48.** $(-2\sqrt{21}, -4)$ **49.** $(\sqrt{7}, -3)$ **50.** $(2, -\sqrt{5})$

SELF-TEST 2

Evaluate.

1. $\sin \dfrac{\pi}{6}$ 2. $\cos \dfrac{\pi}{4}$ 3. $\sin \left(-\dfrac{2\pi}{3}\right)$ Section 7-4

Express as a function of a positive acute angle.

4. $\cos 195°$ 5. $\sin 110°$ 6. $\cos (-250°)$

7. Use Table 1 to find the value of $\sin 37°12'$ to four decimal places.   Section 7-5

8. Use Table 1 to find to the nearest minute the value of θ between $0°$ and $360°$ if $\cos \theta = 0.6230$.

9. Convert $83°24'$ to decimal degrees.

Section 7-6 THE REDUCTION FORMULAS

In Section 7-4 you learned how to sketch a reference angle and use it to express the sine or cosine of any angle as the sine or cosine of a first-quadrant angle. Another way to "reduce" a trigonometric function of any angle to a function of an acute angle is to use the *reduction formulas* that we will investigate in this section.

EXAMPLE   Show that $\sin (-\theta) = -\sin \theta$ and $\cos (-\theta) = \cos \theta$.

SOLUTION   Let's assume that θ is in the first quadrant.

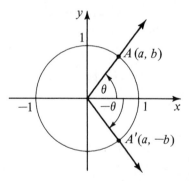

Recall from your study of transformations in Chapter 5 that a reflection over the x-axis maps the point $A(a, b)$ onto the point $A'(a, -b)$. Then, by the definitions of sine and cosine,

$$\sin \theta = y\text{-coordinate of } A = -(y\text{-coordinate of } A') = -\sin (-\theta)$$
$$\cos \theta = x\text{-coordinate of } A = x\text{-coordinate of } A' = \cos (-\theta)$$

Thus, $\sin (-\theta) = -\sin \theta$ and $\cos (-\theta) = \cos \theta$.

In Exercise 42, you will be asked to show that these formulas hold true when θ lies in the second, third, or fourth quadrant.

EXAMPLE   Show that $\sin (90^\circ - \theta) = \cos \theta$ and $\cos (90^\circ - \theta) = \sin \theta$.

SOLUTION   Again we assume that θ is in the first quadrant and draw a sketch.

As you learned in Chapter 5, a reflection over the line $y = x$ maps the point $A(a, b)$ onto the point $A'(b, a)$. Since $m\angle AOB = m\angle A'OB' = \theta$, and $m\angle B'OB = 90^\circ$, it follows that $m\angle A'OB = 90^\circ - \theta$.

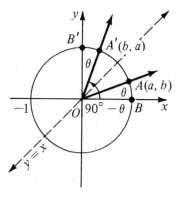

Thus, by the definitions of sine and cosine:

$$\sin \theta = y\text{-coordinate of } A$$
$$= x\text{-coordinate of } A'$$
$$= \cos (90^\circ - \theta)$$
$$\cos \theta = x\text{-coordinate of } A$$
$$= y\text{-coordinate of } A'$$
$$= \sin (90^\circ - \theta)$$

The most commonly used reduction formulas are listed below. We have already demonstrated the validity of Formulas 1 and 6. You will be asked to prove some of the others in Exercises 25, 33, 36, and 37.

The Reduction Formulas

1. a. $\sin (-\theta) = -\sin \theta$ b. $\cos (-\theta) = \cos \theta$
2. a. $\sin (180^\circ - \theta) = \sin \theta$ b. $\cos (180^\circ - \theta) = -\cos \theta$
3. a. $\sin (180^\circ + \theta) = -\sin \theta$ b. $\cos (180^\circ + \theta) = -\cos \theta$
4. a. $\sin (90^\circ + \theta) = \cos \theta$ b. $\cos (90^\circ + \theta) = -\sin \theta$
5. a. $\sin (360^\circ - \theta) = -\sin \theta$ b. $\cos (360^\circ - \theta) = \cos \theta$
6. a. $\sin (90^\circ - \theta) = \cos \theta$ b. $\cos (90^\circ - \theta) = \sin \theta$

Formulas 6a and 6b state that the sine of an angle is equal to the cosine of its complement. For this reason, sine and cosine are called *cofunctions*. This relationship is illustrated very clearly in Table 1, a portion of which is shown. Notice that $\sin 37^\circ 00' = \cos 53^\circ 00'$, for example.

$m(\alpha)$ Degrees	$m(\alpha)$ Radians	$\sin \alpha$	$\csc \alpha$	$\tan \alpha$	$\cot \alpha$	$\sec \alpha$	$\cos \alpha$		
36° 00′	.6283	.5878	1.701	.7265	1.376	1.236	.8090	.9425	54° 00′
10′	.6312	.5901	1.695	.7310	1.368	1.239	.8073	.9396	50′
20′	.6341	.5925	1.688	.7355	1.360	1.241	.8056	.9367	40′
30′	.6370	.5948	1.681	.7400	1.351	1.244	.8039	.9338	30′
40′	.6400	.5972	1.675	.7445	1.343	1.247	.8021	.9308	20′
50′	.6429	.5995	1.668	.7490	1.335	1.249	.8004	.9279	10′
37° 00′	.6458	.6018	1.662	.7536	1.327	1.252	.7986	.9250	53° 00′
10′	.6487	.6041	1.655	.7581	1.319	1.255	.7969	.9221	50′
20′	.6516	.6065	1.649	.7627	1.311	1.258	.7951	.9192	40′
30′	.6545	.6088	1.643	.7673	1.303	1.260	.7934	.9163	30′
40′	.6574	.6111	1.636	.7720	1.295	1.263	.7916	.9134	20′
50′	.6603	.6134	1.630	.7766	1.288	1.266	.7898	.9105	10′
		$\cos \alpha$	$\sec \alpha$	$\cot \alpha$	$\tan \alpha$	$\csc \alpha$	$\sin \alpha$	Radians	Degrees
								$m(\alpha)$	

EXAMPLE   Find the value of cos 164°20′.

SOLUTION

Method I   *Method II*

Use the reference angle of 164°20′.   Use a reduction formula.

The reference angle of 164°20′ is $164°20′ = 180° − 15°40′$
$180° − 164°20′$, or 15°40′. $\cos(164°20′) = \cos(180° − 15°40′)$
Since cosine is negative in Quadrant II, $= −\cos(15°40′)$
$\cos(164°20′) = −\cos(15°40′)$. $= −0.9628$ (By Table 1)

$\quad\quad \cos(15°40′) = 0.9628$ (By Table 1)
$\quad\quad \cos(164°20′) = −0.9628$

You should realize that corresponding formulas in terms of radians also hold true.

EXAMPLE   Find the value of $\sin \dfrac{7\pi}{4}$ without referring to Table 1.

SOLUTION $\dfrac{7\pi}{4} = 2\pi − \dfrac{\pi}{4}$

$$\sin \frac{7\pi}{4} = \sin\left(2\pi − \frac{\pi}{4}\right)$$

$$= −\sin \frac{\pi}{4}$$

$$= − \frac{\sqrt{2}}{2}$$

ORAL EXERCISES

1. Translate each of Formulas 2–6 on page 295 into a formula in radians.

Express each of the following in the form $90° + \theta$.

2. 120°　　　　　　　　　**3.** 135°　　　　　　　　　**4.** 164°

Express each of the following in the form $180° + \theta$.

5. 216°　　　　　　　　　**6.** 234°　　　　　　　　　**7.** 258°

Express each of the following in the form $180° − \theta$.

8. 95°　　　　　　　　　**9.** 130°　　　　　　　　　**10.** 117°

Express each of the following in the form $90° − \theta$.

11. 27°　　　　　　　　　**12.** 5°　　　　　　　　　**13.** 36°

Express each of the following in the form $2\pi − \theta$.

14. $\dfrac{11\pi}{6}$　　　　　　　　**15.** $\dfrac{5\pi}{3}$　　　　　　　　**16.** $\dfrac{5\pi}{4}$

Express each of the following in the form $\pi + \theta$.

17. $\dfrac{5\pi}{4}$

18. $\dfrac{7\pi}{6}$

19. $\dfrac{4\pi}{3}$

WRITTEN EXERCISES

Complete.

A 1. $118°0' = 90° +$ __?__

2. $242°40' = 180° +$ __?__

3. $117°20' = 180° -$ __?__

4. $57°40' = 90° -$ __?__

5. $315°10' = 360° -$ __?__

6. $147°50' = 180° -$ __?__

7. If $\sin \theta = \dfrac{1}{4}$, then $\cos (90° - \theta) =$ __?__.

8. If $\sin \theta = \dfrac{2}{5}$, then $\cos (90° + \theta) =$ __?__.

9. If $\cos \theta = -\dfrac{1}{3}$, then $\cos (180° + \theta) =$ __?__.

10. If $\cos \theta = \dfrac{5}{12}$, then $\sin (90° - \theta) =$ __?__.

11. If $\sin \theta = \dfrac{3}{4}$, then $\sin (-\theta) =$ __?__.

12. If $\cos \theta = -\dfrac{3}{5}$, then $\cos (-\theta) =$ __?__.

In Exercises 13–24:

a. Express each function value as a function of a positive acute angle.

b. Use Table 1 to find a four-digit approximation of the given function value.

13. $\cos 93°$

14. $\sin 114°$

15. $\sin (-25°)$

16. $\cos (-68°)$

17. $\cos 345°$

18. $\sin 308°$

19. $\sin 182°$

20. $\cos 105°$

21. $\cos (-27°30')$

22. $\sin (-78°10')$

23. $\sin (-100°)$

24. $\cos (-173°)$

B 25. Refer to the figure at the right.

a. Find the coordinates of A in terms of $\sin \theta$ and $\cos \theta$.

b. A' is a reflection of A over which axis?

c. Find the coordinates of A' in terms of a and b.

d. Find the coordinates of A' in terms of $\sin (180° - \theta)$ and $\cos (180° - \theta)$.

e. Write two equations that show the relationship between the coordinates you found in parts (a) and (d).

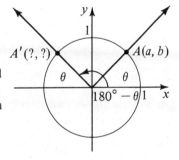

26. Refer to the figure at the right.

a. What is the relationship between $\overrightarrow{OB}$ and $\overrightarrow{OC}$?

b. What is the relationship between $\cos (90° - \theta)$ and $\cos (90° + \theta)$?

c. What is the relationship between $\sin (90° - \theta)$ and $\sin (90° + \theta)$?

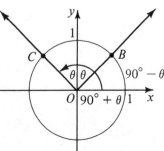

Find each function value without referring to Table 1.

27. $\sin \dfrac{11\pi}{6}$

28. $\cos \left(-\dfrac{2\pi}{3}\right)$

29. $\cos \left(-\dfrac{\pi}{4}\right)$

30. $\sin \left(-\dfrac{7\pi}{6}\right)$

31. $\sin \dfrac{5\pi}{4}$

32. $\cos \dfrac{3\pi}{4}$

33. Use the fact that a rotation of $180°$ about O maps the point (a, b) onto the point $(-a, -b)$ to show that $\sin (180° + \theta) = -\sin \theta$ and $\cos (180° + \theta) = -\cos \theta$.

34. In the formula $\cos (90° - \theta) = \sin \theta$, let $\theta = 90° - \alpha$ and show that $\cos \alpha = \sin (90° - \alpha)$.

35. In the formula $\sin (180° - \theta) = \sin \theta$, let $\theta = 90° - \alpha$ and show that $\sin (90° + \alpha) = \sin (90° - \alpha)$.

C 36. Prove that $\sin (90° + \theta) = \cos \theta$ by expressing $\sin (90° + \theta)$ as $\sin (180° - \alpha)$, where $\alpha = 90° - \theta$. Then use Formulas 2 and 6.

37. Prove that $\sin (360° - \theta) = -\sin \theta$ by expressing $\sin (360° - \theta)$ as $\sin (180° + \alpha)$, where $\alpha = 180° - \theta$. Then use Formulas 3 and 2.

38. Prove that $\cos (\theta - 90°) = \sin \theta$.

39. Prove that $\cos (\theta + 90°) = -\cos (\theta - 90°)$.

40. Prove that $\cos (270° + \theta) = \sin \theta$.

41. Prove that $\cos (270° - \theta) = -\sin \theta$.

42. Show that $\sin (-\theta) = -\sin \theta$ and $\cos (-\theta) = \cos \theta$ if (a) θ is in Quadrant II; (b) θ is in Quadrant III; (c) θ is in Quadrant IV.

Section 7-7 GRAPHING SINE AND COSINE

We will use the concepts developed in Sections 7-4 and 7-6 to graph the sine and cosine functions. In Section 7-4, you found values for $\sin \theta$ and $\cos \theta$ for the special angles $0, \dfrac{\pi}{6}, \dfrac{\pi}{4}, \dfrac{\pi}{3},$ and $\dfrac{\pi}{2}$. The values are summarized in the following table.

θ	0	$\dfrac{\pi}{6}$	$\dfrac{\pi}{4}$	$\dfrac{\pi}{3}$	$\dfrac{\pi}{2}$
$\sin \theta$	0	0.5	$\dfrac{\sqrt{2}}{2} \approx 0.71$	$\dfrac{\sqrt{3}}{2} \approx 0.87$	1
$\cos \theta$	1	$\dfrac{\sqrt{3}}{2} \approx 0.87$	$\dfrac{\sqrt{2}}{2} \approx 0.71$	0.5	0

The points plotted on the following graphs correspond to these special function values.

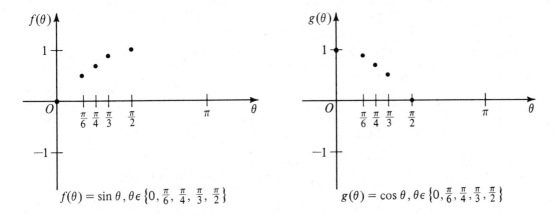

$$f(\theta) = \sin\theta, \theta \in \left\{0, \tfrac{\pi}{6}, \tfrac{\pi}{4}, \tfrac{\pi}{3}, \tfrac{\pi}{2}\right\}$$

$$g(\theta) = \cos\theta, \theta \in \left\{0, \tfrac{\pi}{6}, \tfrac{\pi}{4}, \tfrac{\pi}{3}, \tfrac{\pi}{2}\right\}$$

The same unit length is used on both axes. However, the coordinates of the points on the horizontal axis are given in multiples of π because the measure of angle θ is given in radians. Notice that the distance from 0 to 1 on the vertical axis is approximately the same as the distance from 0 to $\dfrac{\pi}{3}$ on the horizontal axis since $\dfrac{\pi}{3} \approx \dfrac{3.14}{3} \approx 1.05$. If you join the points with a smooth curve, you will obtain the graphs below.

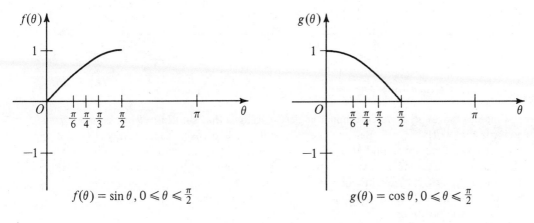

$$f(\theta) = \sin\theta, 0 \leqslant \theta \leqslant \tfrac{\pi}{2}$$

$$g(\theta) = \cos\theta, 0 \leqslant \theta \leqslant \tfrac{\pi}{2}$$

We can complete these graphs for the interval $\dfrac{\pi}{2} \leqslant \theta \leqslant \pi$ by observing that $\sin\left(\dfrac{\pi}{2} + \theta\right) = \cos\theta$ and $\cos\left(\dfrac{\pi}{2} + \theta\right) = -\sin\theta$. Thus we can obtain the graph of $f(\theta) = \sin\theta$ for $\dfrac{\pi}{2} \leqslant \theta \leqslant \pi$ by translating the graph of $g(\theta) = \cos\theta$ for $0 \leqslant \theta \leqslant \dfrac{\pi}{2}$ to the right $\dfrac{\pi}{2}$ units. (See the left-hand graph at the top of the following page.)

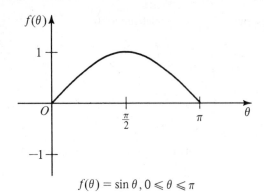

$f(\theta) = \sin \theta, 0 \leqslant \theta \leqslant \pi$

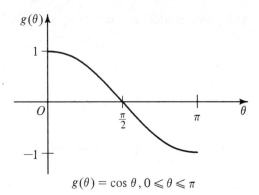

$g(\theta) = \cos \theta, 0 \leqslant \theta \leqslant \pi$

The graph of $g(\theta) = \cos \theta$ for $\dfrac{\pi}{2} \leqslant \theta \leqslant \pi$ is a reflection over the θ-axis of the graph of $f(\theta) = \sin \theta$, $0 \leqslant \theta \leqslant \dfrac{\pi}{2}$, followed by a translation to the right $\dfrac{\pi}{2}$ units. (See the diagram at the right above.)

From the equations

$$\sin (\pi + \theta) = -\sin \theta$$

and

$$\cos (\pi + \theta) = -\cos \theta$$

we can obtain the graphs of $\sin \theta$ and $\cos \theta$ for $\pi \leqslant \theta \leqslant 2\pi$ by reflecting the graphs of $\sin \theta$ and $\cos \theta$, $0 \leqslant \theta \leqslant \pi$, over the θ-axis, then translating to the right π units.

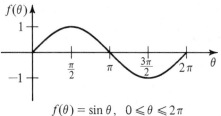

$f(\theta) = \sin \theta, \ 0 \leqslant \theta \leqslant 2\pi$

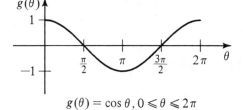

$g(\theta) = \cos \theta, 0 \leqslant \theta \leqslant 2\pi$

Since θ and $2\pi + \theta$ are coterminal angles, it follows that $\sin (2\pi + \theta) = \sin \theta$ and $\cos (2\pi + \theta) = \cos \theta$. Because the values of sine and cosine repeat every 2π radians, each function is said to have a *period* of 2π. The next two figures show the graphs of sine and cosine over the set of real numbers. Notice that in the interval $0 \leqslant \theta \leqslant 2\pi$, the sine and cosine functions both take on all values from -1 to 1 inclusive. Then the pattern repeats. Functions whose graphs repeat are called *periodic functions*.

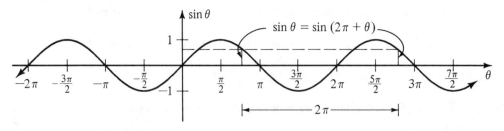

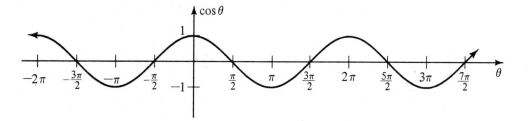

You may also notice that by translating the graph of sin θ to the left $\dfrac{\pi}{2}$ units, you obtain the graph of cos θ. This is a graphical illustration of the fact that $\sin\left(\dfrac{\pi}{2} + \theta\right) = \cos\theta$.

ORAL EXERCISES

Refer to the graphs of sin θ and cos θ.

1. State the maximum value of the range of sin θ. State the minimum value.

2. State the maximum value of the range of cos θ. State the minimum value.

Determine whether the function graphed is periodic and, if so, state its period. Assume that the pattern continues.

3.

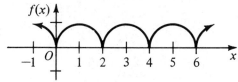

4.

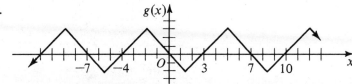

5.

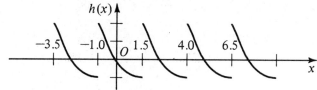

6.

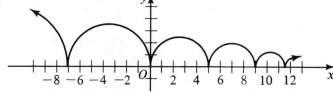

Copy and complete the following table.

A

		1.		2.		4.	5.	6.	7.
θ	0	$0<\theta<\dfrac{\pi}{2}$	$\dfrac{\pi}{2}$	$\dfrac{\pi}{2}<\theta<\pi$	π	$\pi<\theta<\dfrac{3\pi}{2}$	$\dfrac{3\pi}{2}$	$\dfrac{3\pi}{2}<\theta<2\pi$	2π
$\sin\theta$	0	increasing	?	?	?	?	?	?	?
$\cos\theta$	1	decreasing	?	?	?	?	?	?	?

Graph the two functions on the same set of axes for $-2\pi \leqslant \theta \leqslant 2\pi$. Then use your sketch to help you solve the given equation.

EXAMPLE $y = \sin\theta$, $y = 1$; $\sin\theta = 1$

SOLUTION

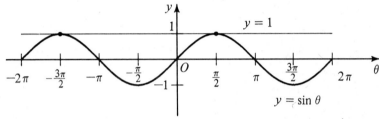

The solution set of $\sin\theta = 1$ over the domain $-2\pi \leqslant \theta \leqslant 2\pi$ is $\left\{-\dfrac{3\pi}{2}, \dfrac{\pi}{2}\right\}$.

8. $y = \cos\theta$, $y = 1$; $\cos\theta = 1$ **9.** $y = \cos\theta$, $y = 0$; $\cos\theta = 0$

10. $y = \sin\theta$, $y = -1$; $\sin\theta = -1$

11. $y = \cos\theta$, $y = \dfrac{\sqrt{2}}{2}$; $\cos\theta = \dfrac{\sqrt{2}}{2}$ $\left(\dfrac{\sqrt{2}}{2} \approx 0.7\right)$

12. On the same set of axes, graph $y = \cos\theta$ and $y = -\cos\theta$, $0 \leqslant \theta \leqslant 2\pi$. What transformation maps the graph of $y = \cos\theta$ onto the graph of $y = -\cos\theta$?

Draw a sketch of the image when the indicated translation is applied to the graph of the indicated function ($\sin\theta$ or $\cos\theta$). On the same set of axes, draw the graph of the remaining function ($\cos\theta$ or $\sin\theta$) and state the number of points of intersection of the graphs in the interval $0 \leqslant \theta \leqslant 2\pi$.

EXAMPLE $T_{\frac{\pi}{2},\,0}$; $\sin\theta$

SOLUTION   Applying $T_{\frac{\pi}{2},\,0}$ to $\sin\theta$ gives the graph indicated by the solid line. It intersects the graph of $\cos\theta$ in 2 points.

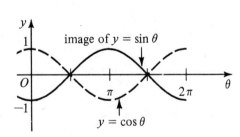

B 13. $T_{\frac{\pi}{2}, 0}$; $\cos \theta$

14. $T_{-\frac{\pi}{2}, 0}$; $\cos \theta$

15. $T_{\pi, 0}$; $\sin \theta$

16. $T_{2\pi, 0}$; $\sin \theta$

(*Note*: The translations in Exercises 17 and 18 are vertical.)

17. $T_{0,1}$; $\sin \theta$

18. $T_{0,1}$; $\cos \theta$

Graph $\cos \theta$ and $\sin \theta$ on the same set of axes for $0 \leqslant \theta \leqslant 2\pi$ and use your graph to solve the given equation or inequality.

19. $\cos \theta = \sin \theta$

20. $\cos \theta \geqslant \sin \theta$

21. $\sin \theta \geqslant \cos \theta$

22. $\cos \theta \geqslant 0$ and $\sin \theta \geqslant 0$

23. $\cos \theta \geqslant 0$ and $\sin \theta \leqslant 0$

24. $\cos \theta \leqslant 0$ and $\sin \theta \leqslant 0$

C 25. $\sin \theta + \cos \theta = 0$

26. $\sin \theta - \cos \theta = 0$

27. $\sin \theta \cdot \cos \theta > 0$

28. $\sin \theta \cdot \cos \theta < 0$

29. Sketch the graph of $y = |\sin \theta|$ for $-2\pi \leqslant \theta \leqslant 2\pi$.

30. Sketch the graph of $y = |\cos \theta|$ for $-\frac{\pi}{2} \leqslant \theta \leqslant \frac{5\pi}{2}$.

SELF-TEST 3

Complete with $\sin \theta$, $-\sin \theta$, or $\cos \theta$ to make a true statement.

1. $\sin(-\theta) =$ __?__

2. $\sin(90° - \theta) =$ __?__

3. $\sin(180° + \theta) =$ __?__

4. $\cos(90° - \theta) =$ __?__

Section 7-6

Evaluate without the use of Table 1.

5. $\cos 240°$

6. $\sin(-45°)$

7. $\cos 330°$

State whether $\cos \theta$ is increasing or decreasing in the given interval.

8. π to $\frac{3\pi}{2}$

9. 0 to $\frac{\pi}{2}$

Section 7-7

10. Complete with $y = \sin \theta$ or $y = \cos \theta$: The graph of __?__ is symmetric with respect to the line $\theta = \frac{\pi}{2}$.

11. Sketch the graph of $y = \sin \theta$ for $0 \leqslant \theta \leqslant 2\pi$.

INTRODUCTION TO TRIGONOMETRY   **303**

Computer Exercises

How does your calculator or computer find sine and cosine values? It uses formulas such as:

$$\sin x = x - \frac{x^3}{3 \cdot 2} + \frac{x^5}{5 \cdot 4 \cdot 3 \cdot 2} - \frac{x^7}{7 \cdot 6 \cdot 5 \cdot 4 \cdot 3 \cdot 2} + \ldots$$

The meaning of this equation is that for any x, $\sin x$ can be approximated by combining finitely many of the terms on the right side of the equation. The accuracy of the approximation depends on the number of terms—the more terms you use, the closer the approximate answer will be to the true value of $\sin x$. For example, taking two terms, you get this approximation to sin 1:

$$1 - \frac{1^3}{3 \cdot 2} = \frac{5}{6} \approx 0.833333$$

Taking four terms, you get: $1 - \frac{1}{6} + \frac{1}{120} - \frac{1}{5040} \approx 0.841468$. The actual value, correct to six decimal places, is 0.841471.

Here is a BASIC program that calculates, for any value of x, the value of $\sin x$ by using the built-in SIN function of BASIC and by using several terms of the formula above. (Of course, the built-in SIN function itself uses a formula equivalent to the one the program uses explicitly.)

```
10   PRINT "APPROXIMATING SIN X "
20   PRINT "X (IN RADIANS): ";
30   INPUT X
40   PRINT "NUMBER OF TERMS (>1): ";
50   INPUT N
60   PRINT
70   LET T = X
80   REM***T IS CURRENT TERM
90   LET S = 0
100  REM***S IS SUM OF TERMS
110  FOR C = 1 TO N
120  LET S = S + T
130  LET T = -T * (X * X) / ((2 * C + 1) * (2 * C))
140  REM***LINE 130 EVALUATES SUCCESSIVE TERMS:
142  REM***2*C+1 = 3, THEN 5, THEN 7, ETC.
150  NEXT C
160  PRINT N;" TERMS GIVE: "; TAB(26);S
170  PRINT "BUILT-IN FUNCTION GIVES: "; TAB(26);SIN (X)
180  END
```

1. Type in the program and RUN it several times, completing the following table as you go. (*Note:* You may encounter answers such as 3.042E−08. This is a form of scientific notation, and represents 3.042×10^{-8}, or 0.00000003042.)

x	$\sin x$	approximation		
		after 2 terms	after 5 terms	after 100 terms
0.2	?	?	?	?
-2	?	?	?	?
10	?	?	?	?
3.14159265	?	?	?	?

Do the approximations always get closer to the built-in value when more terms are used? How is the accuracy of the approximations affected by using relatively large values of x?

2. Alter the program to compute approximations of $\cos x$, using the formula:

$$\cos x = 1 - \frac{x^2}{2 \cdot 1} + \frac{x^4}{4 \cdot 3 \cdot 2 \cdot 1} - \frac{x^6}{6 \cdot 5 \cdot 4 \cdot 3 \cdot 2 \cdot 1} + \dots$$

Hint: For $\sin x$, you go from one term to the next by multiplying by $\frac{-x^2}{(2C+1)(2C)}$. For $\cos x$, you multiply instead by $\frac{-x^2}{(2C)(2C-1)}$.
Complete the chart.

x	$\cos x$	approximation	
		after 5 terms	after 20 terms
0	?	?	?
1	?	?	?
-1	?	?	?
6.2832	?	?	?

CHAPTER REVIEW _____

1. **a.** Sketch a $-110°$ angle in standard position. Section 7-1
   b. State the least possible positive measure of an angle coterminal with a $-110°$ angle.

2. State the measure of an angle formed by one-fourth of a clockwise rotation.

3. In a circle, a central angle of 4 radians intercepts an arc of 5 cm. Find the radius of the circle. Section 7-2

4. **a.** Express $240°$ in radians.

   b. Express $-\dfrac{2\pi}{3}$ radians in degrees.

5. Evaluate: $\cos 0° + \sin 270°$ Section 7-3

6. If $f(x) = \cos x \sin \dfrac{x}{2}$, find the numerical value of $f(\pi)$.

7. If $\sin \theta = -\dfrac{4}{5}$ and θ is in the fourth quadrant, find $\cos \theta$.

8. If $\sin \theta$ and $\cos \theta$ are both negative, name the quadrant θ lies in.

Express each of the following as a function of a positive acute angle.

9. $\sin 150°$ 10. $\cos 240°$ 11. $\sin(-110°)$ Section 7-4

Without the use of Table 1, evaluate the following.

12. $\sin 60°$ 13. $\cos \dfrac{2\pi}{3}$ 14. $\cos 225° + \sin 135°$

Use Table 1 to find a four-digit approximation of each of the following.

15. $\cos 38°20'$ 16. $\sin 82°18'$ Section 7-5

17. To the nearest minute, find the value of θ between $0°$ and $90°$ if $\cos \theta = 0.7159$.

True or false?

18. $\sin(-10°) = \cos 100°$ 19. $\sin 95° = \sin 85°$ Section 7-6

20. Complete with a number between 0 and 90 to make a true statement:
$$\cos 38° = \sin \underline{\ \ ?\ \ }°$$

21. Sketch the graph of $y = \sin \theta$ for $-\pi \leqslant \theta \leqslant \pi$.   Section 7-7

22. What transformation maps the graph of $y = \cos \theta$ onto the graph of $y = \sin \theta$?

CHAPTER TEST

1. Express each of the following angles in radians: **a.** $30°$;   **b.** $270°$

2. Express each of the following angles in degrees: **a.** $-\dfrac{7\pi}{6}$;   **b.** $\dfrac{3\pi}{4}$

3. Evaluate: $\sin 210° + \cos 300°$

4. Through how many radians does the minute hand of a clock turn in 48 min?

5. Express each of the following as a function of a positive acute angle:
   a. $\sin 115°$ **b.** $\cos(-39°)$

6. Without using Table 1, find: **a.** $\cos \dfrac{3\pi}{2}$;   **b.** $\sin 120°$

7. If $\cos \theta = -\dfrac{4}{5}$ and $\sin \theta$ is positive, name the quadrant θ lies in.

8. A central angle intercepts an arc whose length is equal to the diameter of the circle. What is the positive radian measure of the angle?

9. If $\sin \theta = \dfrac{3}{5}$, find $\cos (90° + \theta)$.

10. Simplify: $\sin (90° + \theta) + \cos (180° - \theta)$

11. If $\sin \theta = -\dfrac{5}{13}$ and θ is in the third quadrant, find $\cos \theta$.

12. Use Table 1 to find each value to four decimal places:
    a. $\sin 5°12'$ b. $\cos 127°40'$

13. To the nearest minute, find the value of θ between $0°$ and $90°$ if $\sin \theta = 0.4548$.

14. Evaluate: $\left(\sin \dfrac{\pi}{2}\right)(\cos 2\pi)$

15. State whether each of the following numbers may represent a value of $\sin \theta$.

    a. -1 b. $\sqrt{3}$ c. 0 d. $-\dfrac{\sqrt{2}}{2}$

16. Which graph, $y = \sin \theta$ or $y = \cos \theta$, has symmetry with respect to the y-axis?

CUMULATIVE REVIEW: CHAPTERS 1-7 _____

Indicate the best answer by writing the appropriate letter.

1. Express $108°$ in radian measure.
   a. $\dfrac{3\pi}{10}$ b. π c. $\dfrac{3}{10}$ d. $\dfrac{3\pi}{5}$

2. Which name has horizontal line symmetry?
   a. OTTO   b. AVA   c. FIFI   d. BOB

3. Which function is odd?
   a. $f(x) = x^3 + x$ b. $f(x) = x^2$ c. $f(x) = x^2 + 1$ d. $f(x) = 1$

4. The terminal side of an angle in standard position contains the point $(-1, -1)$. Which of the following could *not* be the measure of the angle?
   a. $225°$ b. $-135°$ c. $-585°$ d. $585°$

5. Simplify: $(3x + y)(3x - y)$
   a. $9x^2 - y^2$ b. $3x^2 - y^2$ c. $9x^2 - 6xy - y^2$ d. $9x^2 + y^2$

6. The complex number $i^2(2 - i) + i(3 + i)$ is equivalent to __?__.
   a. $-3 + 2i$ b. $3 + 2i$ c. $3 + 4i$ d. $-3 + 4i$

7. Express in degree measure an angle of $\dfrac{8\pi}{3}$ radians.
   a. $240°$ b. $480°$ c. $420°$ d. $300°$

8. Point O is the center of the circle. Find $m\stackrel{\frown}{BC}$.
   a. 130   b. 80   c. 50   d. 100

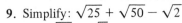

9. Simplify: $\sqrt{25} + \sqrt{50} - \sqrt{2}$
   a. $3\sqrt{25} - \sqrt{2}$
   c. $5 + 6\sqrt{2}$
   b. $5 + 2\sqrt{5} - \sqrt{2}$
   d. $5 + 4\sqrt{2}$

10. Find the pre-image of $(2, -4)$ under the rotation R_{-90}.
    a. $(-4, -2)$ b. $(2, 4)$ c. $(4, 2)$ d. $(-2, -4)$

11. Which kinds of symmetry does a parallelogram have?
    a. line and point
    c. point, line, and rotational
    b. point and rotational
    d. rotational only

12. Which expression is equivalent to $\sqrt{-343}$?
    a. $49i\sqrt{7}$ b. $-7i\sqrt{7}$ c. $-7\sqrt{7}$ d. $7i\sqrt{7}$

13. Which property is not preserved under a line reflection?
    a. betweenness   b. distance   c. orientation   d. perpendicularity

14. A translation maps $A(3, -1)$ onto $A'(-2, 3)$. Find the coordinates of the image of $B(-3, -3)$ under the same translation.
    a. $(2, -7)$ b. $(2, 1)$ c. $(-8, 1)$ d. $(-8, -7)$

15. For the graph of which function is the y-axis a line of symmetry?
    a. $y = x$ b. $y = \sin x$ c. $y = \cos x$ d. $y = -x$

16. In $\odot O$ with radius 8, $m\stackrel{\frown}{AB} = m\stackrel{\frown}{BC} = m\stackrel{\frown}{CD} = m\stackrel{\frown}{DA}$. Find the area of sector DOC.
    a. 16   b. 4π c. 16π d. 32π

17. If r_k is the line reflection in the line $y = x$ and A has coordinates $(8, -4)$, find the coordinates of $r_{x\text{-axis}} \circ r_k (A)$.
    a. $(4, 8)$ b. $(-4, -8)$ c. $(-4, 8)$ d. $(4, -8)$

18. Express $\cos 165°$ as a function of a positive acute angle.
    a. $\cos 15°$ b. $\cos 75°$ c. $-\cos 15°$ d. $\sin 15°$

19. Find the multiplicative inverse of 0.045.
    a. $\dfrac{1}{45}$ b. $-\dfrac{9}{200}$ c. $\dfrac{20}{9}$ d. $\dfrac{200}{9}$

20. Evaluate $\sin \dfrac{\pi}{3} \cos \pi$.
    a. $-\dfrac{\sqrt{3}}{2}$ b. $-\dfrac{1}{2}$ c. 0   d. $\dfrac{1}{2}$

21. State the sum and the product of the roots of $216x^2 + 36x + 12 = 0$.
    a. sum $-\dfrac{1}{18}$, product $\dfrac{1}{6}$
    b. sum $\dfrac{1}{18}$, product $-\dfrac{1}{6}$
    c. sum $-\dfrac{1}{6}$, product $\dfrac{1}{18}$
    d. sum $\dfrac{1}{6}$, product $-\dfrac{1}{18}$

22. If line k has the equation $y = -x$ and A has coordinates $(-6, 2)$, find $r_k(A)$.
    a. $(2, -6)$ b. $(6, -2)$ c. $(-6, -2)$ d. $(-2, 6)$

23. Evaluate $\cos\left(-\dfrac{11\pi}{6}\right)$.

a. $\dfrac{1}{2}$ b. $-\dfrac{1}{2}$ c. $\dfrac{\sqrt{3}}{2}$ d. $-\dfrac{\sqrt{3}}{2}$

24. For the transformations $S\colon (x,\ y) \longrightarrow (y,\ -x)$ and $T\colon (x,\ y) \longrightarrow \left(\dfrac{x}{3},\ 2y\right)$, find the image of $(-6,\ 9)$ under $S \circ T$.

a. $(3,\ 12)$ b. $(18,\ 2)$ c. $(-2,\ -18)$ d. $(3,\ -12)$

25. The vertices of an inscribed triangle divide a circle into three arcs whose measures are in the ratio $4:5:6$. Find the measure of the largest angle of the triangle.

a. 144   b. 72   c. 36   d. 90

26. If lines s and t are parallel, then $r_s \circ r_t$ is equivalent to a __?__ .

a. rotation   b. reflection   c. translation   d. dilation

27. A shopper spent $7.59 for 27 apples and oranges. If the apples sell at three for 99¢ and the oranges sell at four for 88¢, how many apples were purchased?

a. 5   b. 12   c. 15   d. 3

28. Factor: $m^3 - 216$

a. $(m + 6)(m^2 - 6m + 36)$ b. $(m - 6)(m^2 - 6m + 36)$

c. $m^3 - 216$ is prime.   d. $(m - 6)(m^2 + 6m + 36)$

29. In $\odot O$, $m\,\widehat{AB} = 75$ and $m\,\widehat{BC} = 85$. Find $m\angle E$.

a. 20   b. $27\dfrac{1}{2}$ c. $37\dfrac{1}{2}$ d. $47\dfrac{1}{2}$

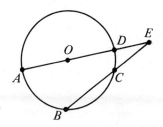

30. If $\sin \theta = 0.8852$ and $0° \leqslant \theta \leqslant 90°$, find the value of θ to the nearest minute.

a. $62°14'$ b. $27°43'$ c. $62°16'$ d. $27°47'$

31. In a circle, a central angle of 1.5 radians intercepts an arc of 18 cm. What is the length of the radius?

a. 6 cm   b. 27 cm   c. 24 cm   d. 12 cm

32. If θ is in Quadrant III and $\cos \theta = -\dfrac{1}{3}$, find $\sin \theta$.

a. $-\dfrac{2\sqrt{2}}{3}$ b. $\dfrac{2\sqrt{2}}{3}$ c. $-\dfrac{2}{3}$ d. $\dfrac{\sqrt{2}}{3}$

33. Which translation, when applied to the graph of $y = \cos x$, gives a result that coincides with the graph of $y = \sin x$?

a. $T_{2\pi,\ 0}$ b. $T_{-\frac{\pi}{2},\ 0}$ c. $T_{-\frac{3\pi}{2},\ 0}$ d. $T_{0,\ -\frac{\pi}{2}}$

34. Which of the following is the graph of the solution set of the inequality:

$$4 > 3x + 1 \text{ and } 5 - 4x \geqslant 13$$

a.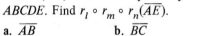

b.

c.

d.

35. Lines l, m, and n are symmetry lines for the regular pentagon $ABCDE$. Find $r_l \circ r_m \circ r_n(\overline{AE})$.

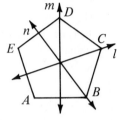

a. $\overline{AB}$ b. $\overline{BC}$ c. $\overline{CD}$ d. $\overline{DE}$

36. A line w with slope $\dfrac{1}{3}$ is reflected in the line k, where k has the equation $y = x$. What is the slope of the image of w?

a. $-\dfrac{1}{3}$ b. $\dfrac{1}{3}$ c. -3 d. 3

37. If $A = (-2, 3)$, find $r_{y\text{-axis}} \circ D_3(A)$.

a. $(-6, -9)$ b. $(5, 6)$ c. $(9, -6)$ d. $(6, 9)$

38. In $\odot O$, diameter $\overline{AB} \perp \overline{CD}$. If $CD = 8$ and $EB = 2$, find AB.

a. 4 b. 8 c. 10 d. 16

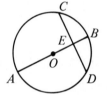

39. Points B, C, D, and F divide $\odot O$ into four arcs such that $m \, \widehat{BC} : m \, \widehat{CD} : m \, \widehat{DF} : m \, \widehat{FB} = 5:2:4:4$. $\overleftrightarrow{AE}$ is tangent to $\odot O$ at F. Find $m\angle E$.

a. 48 b. 60 c. 72 d. 96

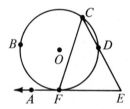

40. In the diagram, $\overline{MC}$ and $\overline{NC}$ are tangents to $\odot O$, $AO = 15$, and $MC = 20$. Find BC.

a. 10 b. 15 c. 20 d. 25

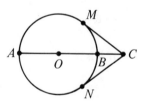

Careers — Aerospace Scientist

Aerospace engineers got their start with Wilbur and Orville Wright's invention of a powered aircraft. The aeronautical branch of the field has expanded from that flimsy, long-winged experiment into commercial, business, and military airplanes as well as helicopters. The term *aerospace* is used to refer to spacecraft, space probes, and satellites.

Space engineers design, develop, test, and help produce these aircraft. The technology is so complex that these engineers may specialize in areas such as structural design, navigational guidance and control, instrumentation and communication, or production methods. Space shuttles and other long-term experiments in space continue to present new areas for specialization. The advances the engineers achieve in design and efficiency are vital for the development of commercial aviation and space exploration.

The testing facilities for these craft, especially the spacecraft, require advanced knowledge in engineering, physics, and computers. Engineers must simulate the effects of flying and of space on both the craft itself and on astronauts or passengers. Everything from intense sunlight, meteorite showers, and no gravitation to heavy fog over airports and wind resistance must be taken into account. Engineers use facilities such as wind tunnels, acoustics laboratories, fatigue test machines, and vacuum chambers to test their calculations.

If flight intrigues you, you should take basic courses in physics, engineering, mathematics, and computer science. Further specialization in astrophysics and other specialties is available at the college and graduate levels. Most space engineers work for the aircraft and parts industry or for federal agencies such as the National Aeronautics and Space Administration.

Be sure that you understand the meaning of these terms:

standard position of an angle, p. 276
quadrantal angle, p. 276
coterminal angles, p. 276
radian, p. 278
unit circle, p. 281
sine, p. 281

cosine, p. 281
reference angle, p. 285
decimal degrees, p. 289
cofunctions, p. 295
periodic function, p. 300

MIXED REVIEW _____

1. Find the standard form of the multiplicative inverse of $3 - i$. Check by multiplying.

2. A square with perimeter 8 is inscribed in a circle. Find the area of the region inside the circle and outside the square.

3. If $f(x) = \dfrac{2}{|x|}$, (a) give the domain and range of f, (b) state if f is one-to-one, (c) graph f, (d) tell whether f is odd, even, or neither.

4. The lengths of two sides of a triangle are 5 and 7. If the length of the third side is an integer, give every possible value for this length.

5. Find the sum and the product of the roots of $6x^2 - 3x + 2 = 0$. Find the value of the discriminant of the equation and determine the nature of the roots.

6. Evaluate: a. $\sin 225° + \cos 225°$ b. $\sin^2 \dfrac{4\pi}{3} + \cos^2 \dfrac{4\pi}{3}$

7. Describe all the types of symmetry that a regular decagon has.

8. The sum of the squares of three consecutive integers is 194. Find the integers.

9. Find the inverse, g^{-1}, of $g(x) = \dfrac{1}{3}x + 2$. Sketch the graphs of g and g^{-1} on the same axes.

10. If θ is an angle in standard position and the terminal side of θ contains the given point, find $\sin \theta$ and $\cos \theta$. Then approximate θ to the nearest $10'$.

    a. $(-4, -4)$ b. $(-3, 0)$ c. $-\dfrac{1}{7}, \dfrac{4\sqrt{3}}{7}$ d. $(12, 5)$

11. If $\overset{\frown}{ABC}$ is a semicircle of $\odot O$ and $m \overset{\frown}{AB} : m \overset{\frown}{BC} = 7:3$, find $m\angle AOB$, $m\angle ABC$, and $m\angle ACB$.

Solve over the set of complex numbers.

12. $4x^2 + 5 = -4x$ 13. $\sqrt{x} - \sqrt{x-5} = 1$ 14. $x^4 = 16$

15. If $m \overset{\frown}{BC} = 48$ and $m \overset{\frown}{AB} = m \overset{\frown}{CD} = m \overset{\frown}{AD} + 12$, find $m\angle 1$, $m\angle 1$, $m\angle 2$, $m\angle 3$, and $m\angle 4$.

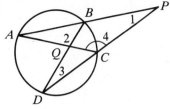

16. If $AQ = 12$, $QC = 6$, and $QD = 12.5$, find QB.

17. Solve: **a.** $|y + 3| - 2 = 0$ **b.** $a^4 + 2a^2 - 15 = 0$

18. Use linear interpolation to approximate $\sin 58°36'$.

Exs. 15, 16

Simplify.

19. $\dfrac{2\sqrt{3}}{\sqrt{3} - 1}$

20. $\dfrac{x - 1 + x^{-1}}{x^2 + x^{-1}}$

21. $\dfrac{6}{9y^2 - 1} + \dfrac{1}{3y + 1}$

22. Find the image of $(-5, 10)$ under the given transformation.
   a. $T_{4, -5}$ **b.** $D_{\frac{2}{5}}$ **c.** r_k, where k is the line $y = x$

23. A chord is 30 cm long in a circle of circumference 34π. How far is the chord from the center of the circle?

24. Solve: **a.** $z^3 + z^2 - 6z \leqslant 0$ **b.** $|5x - 3| \geqslant 8$

25. If $f(x) = 2x + 3$ and $g(x) = x^2 - 5$, find **(a)** $g(f(-4))$, **(b)** $f(g(-4))$, **(c)** $g(f(x))$, and **(d)** $f(g(x))$.

26. Under what conditions is a dilation an isometry?

27. Must a line that intersects a circle in exactly one point be a tangent? Explain.

28. Find the length of an arc of measure $200°$ in a circle with radius 18.

29. Draw two points, A and B. Then construct line t so that $r_t : A \longrightarrow B$.

30. If $\cos \theta = -\dfrac{3}{4}$ and θ is in Quadrant III, find $\sin \theta$.

Express as a function of a positive acute angle.

31. $\cos \left(-\dfrac{2\pi}{9}\right)$

32. $\cos 174°10'$

33. $\sin \dfrac{19\pi}{12}$

34. $\sin (-190°40')$

35. Divide $4s^3 - 31s + 10$ by $2s - 5$.

36. If j and k are intersecting lines, then $r_k \circ r_j$ is equivalent to what single transformation? Is $r_j \circ r_k$ a direct or a nondirect isometry?

37. **a.** Sketch the graph of $y = \cos \theta$ for $-2\pi \leqslant \theta \leqslant 2\pi$.
   b. Suppose the translation $T_{k, 0}$ is applied to this graph, and the graph of $y = \sin \theta$ is obtained. Give two possible values for k, one positive and one negative.

Trigonometric functions can be used to describe periodic motion, such as the apparent rising and falling of the sun caused by Earth's rotation. As described on the facing page, the Egyptians studied the relationship between the time of day and the length of the shadow cast by a vertical pole.

Trigonometric Functions, Identities, and Equations 8

The Egyptians were the first to record the relationship between the time of day and the length of the shadow cast by a vertical stick, as found in a sundial. From dawn till noon the shadow grew shorter, then from noon till sundown the shadow increased in length. When sundials later were built on vertical walls, the tables recording the relationship between the time of day and the length of the shadow cast by a horizontal stick showed the *inverse* relation. The shadow lengthened as noon approached and then decreased as the day wore on. These relationships between shadow lengths and the hours of the day were compiled in tables as early as 1200 B.C. The correspondence between the higher elevation of the sun and a shorter shadow is essentially the same as the *cotangent function* that you will study in this chapter. The inverse relationship, in which higher elevations of the sun correspond to longer shadows, is the basis of the *tangent function*, another trigonometric function you will encounter in Chapter 8.

Section 8-1 MORE TRIGONOMETRIC FUNCTIONS

In this section you will study four more trigonometric functions:
- tangent
- cotangent
- secant
- cosecant

In Section 7–3 we defined the cosine and sine of an angle θ as the x- and y-coordinates, respectively, of the point of intersection of the unit circle and the terminal side of angle θ in standard position. Now we will use these functions to define four new trigonometric functions: *tangent, cotangent, secant,* and *cosecant.* These are abbreviated tan, cot, sec, and csc, respectively.

$$\tan \theta = \frac{\sin \theta}{\cos \theta} = \frac{y}{x}, \ x \neq 0 \qquad \cot \theta = \frac{\cos \theta}{\sin \theta} = \frac{x}{y}, \ y \neq 0$$

$$\sec \theta = \frac{1}{\cos \theta} = \frac{1}{x}, \ x \neq 0 \qquad \csc \theta = \frac{1}{\sin \theta} = \frac{1}{y}, \ y \neq 0$$

$(\cos \theta, \sin \theta)$

Notice that the six trigonometric functions, sin, cos, tan, cot, sec, and csc, are divided into three pairs of *reciprocal functions*:

$$\cot \theta = \frac{1}{\tan \theta} \qquad \csc \theta = \frac{1}{\sin \theta} \qquad \sec \theta = \frac{1}{\cos \theta}$$

The signs of these functions in the four quadrants are summarized in the following table:

	Quadrant			
Function	I	II	III	IV
sine and cosecant	+	+	−	−
cosine and secant	+	−	−	+
tangent and cotangent	+	−	+	−

You can use reference angles to find values of these new trigonometric functions.

EXAMPLE   Use Table 1 to evaluate:

     a. tan 145°　　　**b.** csc 212°　　　**c.** sec (−68°)

SOLUTION   **a.** The reference angle of 145° is 180° − 145°, or 35°.
            Since tangent is negative in Quadrant II, tan 145° = −tan 35°.

$$\tan 35° = 0.7002$$
$$\tan 145° = -0.7002$$

     b. The reference angle of 212° is 212° − 180°, or 32°.
            Since cosecant is negative in Quadrant III, csc 212° = −csc 32°.

$$\csc 32° = 1.887$$
$$\csc 212° = -1.887$$

     c. The reference angle of −68° is 68°.
            Since secant is positive in Quadrant IV, sec (−68°) = sec 68°.

$$\sec 68° = 2.669$$
$$\sec (-68°) = 2.669$$

EXAMPLE   Without using Table 1, evaluate:

     a. tan 225°　　　**b.** cot 120°　　　**c.** csc $\dfrac{7\pi}{6}$

SOLUTION   **a.** The reference angle of 225° is 225° − 180°, or 45°.
            Since tangent is positive in Quadrant III:

$$\tan 225° = \tan 45° = \frac{\sin 45°}{\cos 45°} = \frac{\frac{\sqrt{2}}{2}}{\frac{\sqrt{2}}{2}} = 1$$

b. The reference angle of $120°$ is $180° - 120°$, or $60°$.

Since cotangent is negative in Quadrant II:

$$\cot 120° = -\cot 60°$$

$$\cot 60° = \frac{\cos 60°}{\sin 60°} = \frac{\dfrac{1}{2}}{\dfrac{\sqrt{3}}{2}} = \frac{1}{\sqrt{3}} = \frac{\sqrt{3}}{3}$$

$$\cot 120° = -\frac{\sqrt{3}}{3}$$

c. The reference angle of $\dfrac{7\pi}{6}$ is $\dfrac{7\pi}{6} - \pi$, or $\dfrac{\pi}{6}$.

Since cosecant is negative in Quadrant III:

$$\csc \frac{7\pi}{6} = -\csc \frac{\pi}{6}$$

$$\csc \frac{\pi}{6} = \frac{1}{\sin \dfrac{\pi}{6}} = \frac{1}{\dfrac{1}{2}} = 2$$

$$\csc \frac{7\pi}{6} = -2$$

After sine and cosine, the most important trigonometric function is *tangent*. Let's examine the graph of the tangent function. To begin, we'll consider values of θ between $-\dfrac{\pi}{2}$ and $\dfrac{\pi}{2}$.

θ	$\sin \theta$	$\cos \theta$	$\tan \theta = \dfrac{\sin \theta}{\cos \theta}$
$-\dfrac{\pi}{2}$	-1	0	undefined
$-\dfrac{\pi}{4}$	$-\dfrac{\sqrt{2}}{2}$	$\dfrac{\sqrt{2}}{2}$	-1
0	0	1	0
$\dfrac{\pi}{4}$	$\dfrac{\sqrt{2}}{2}$	$\dfrac{\sqrt{2}}{2}$	1
$\dfrac{\pi}{2}$	1	0	undefined

As θ increases from 0 to $\frac{\pi}{2}$, sin θ increases and cos θ decreases.

Thus, the ratio tan $\theta = \frac{\sin \theta}{\cos \theta}$ increases, becoming very great as θ

gets closer to $\frac{\pi}{2}$. The graph of tan θ for $0 \leqslant \theta < \frac{\pi}{2}$ is shown at the

right. The dashed line, $\theta = \frac{\pi}{2}$, is a vertical *asymptote* of the graph.
The graph gets closer and closer to its asymptote, but never reaches
it. Since tan $\theta = \frac{\sin \theta}{\cos \theta}$, tan θ is undefined when cos $\theta = 0$. Thus the
domain of tan θ is the set of all real numbers that are not odd
integral multiples of $\frac{\pi}{2}$.

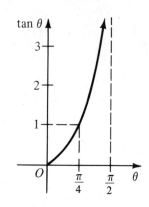

Because tan $(-\theta) = \dfrac{\sin(-\theta)}{\cos(-\theta)} = \dfrac{-\sin\theta}{\cos\theta} = -\tan\theta$, the graph of

tan θ for $-\frac{\pi}{2} < \theta \leqslant 0$ can be obtained by rotating the graph of

tan θ for $0 \leqslant \theta < \frac{\pi}{2}$ through an angle of 180° (or reflecting the

graph of tan θ, $0 \leqslant \theta < \frac{\pi}{2}$, through the point O). After examining
the graph at the right, you may be ready to guess that the period of
the tangent function is π units. You can verify that this is true by
showing that tan $(\theta + \pi) = \tan \theta$. (You will be asked to prove this
in Exercise 33.) Since the tangent function has a period of π,

repeating the graph that is shown for the interval $-\frac{\pi}{2} < \theta < \frac{\pi}{2}$

yields the graph of the tangent function. The graph of cot θ is similar
and is left to you to draw in Exercise 32.

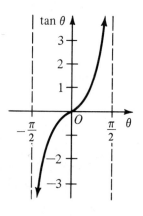

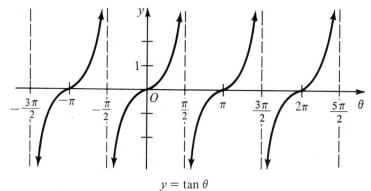

$y = \tan \theta$

We will use the relationship sec $\theta = \dfrac{1}{\cos \theta}$ and the facts we know about the
cosine function to prepare a table that analyzes the behavior of the secant function.

θ	0	$0 < \theta < \dfrac{\pi}{2}$	$\dfrac{\pi}{2}$	$\dfrac{\pi}{2} < \theta < \pi$	π	$\pi < \theta < \dfrac{3\pi}{2}$	$\dfrac{3\pi}{2}$	$\dfrac{3\pi}{2} < \theta < 2\pi$
$\cos\theta$	1	decreasing	0	decreasing	-1	increasing	0	increasing
$\dfrac{1}{\cos\theta}$	1	increasing	undef.	increasing	-1	decreasing	undef.	decreasing

Like $\cos\theta$, $\sec\theta$ has a period of 2π units. The graph of $y = \sec\theta$, $0 \leqslant \theta \leqslant 2\pi$, is shown below. You can use the relationship $\csc\theta = \dfrac{1}{\sin\theta}$ and a similar analysis to graph $y = \csc\theta$. (See Exercise 41.)

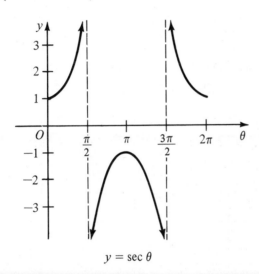

$y = \sec\theta$

ORAL EXERCISES

1. Complete.

   a. $\sec\theta = \dfrac{1}{?}$ b. $\csc\theta = \dfrac{1}{?}$ c. $\tan\theta = \dfrac{?}{?}$

2. For what values of θ (in radians) is the value of $\tan\theta$:

   a. undefined   b. 0

3. Given that $\tan 42° = 0.9004$, find:

   a. $\tan 222°$ b. $\tan 138°$ c. $\tan 318°$

4. Given that $\sec 14° = 1.031$, find:

   a. $\sec 166°$ b. $\sec 346°$ c. $\sec 194°$

Simplify. Express as a single trigonometric function of θ.

5. $\dfrac{1}{\cos \theta}$

6. $\dfrac{1}{\tan \theta}$

7. $\dfrac{1}{\csc \theta}$

8. $\dfrac{1}{\sin \theta}$

9. $\dfrac{1}{\cot \theta}$

10. $\dfrac{1}{\sec \theta}$

11. $\tan (-\theta)$

12. $\sec (-\theta)$

13. $\csc (-\theta)$

Determine the quadrant in which θ lies.

14. $\sin \theta < 0$, $\tan \theta > 0$

15. $\cos \theta > 0$, $\tan \theta < 0$

16. $\sec \theta > 0$, $\cot \theta > 0$

17. $\sec \theta < 0$, $\tan \theta < 0$

18. $\csc \theta > 0$, $\cos \theta > 0$

19. $\cos \theta > 0$, $\cot \theta < 0$

WRITTEN EXERCISES

A   1. Copy and complete without using Table 1.

θ (degrees)	θ (radians)	a. $\sin \theta$	b. $\cos \theta$	c. $\tan \theta$	d. $\cot \theta$	e. $\sec \theta$	f. $\csc \theta$
$0°$	0	?	?	?	?	?	?
$30°$	$\dfrac{\pi}{6}$	?	?	?	?	?	?
$45°$	$\dfrac{\pi}{4}$	?	?	?	?	?	?
$60°$	$\dfrac{\pi}{3}$	?	?	?	?	?	?
$90°$	$\dfrac{\pi}{2}$	?	?	?	?	?	?

Express as a function of a positive acute angle.

2. $\tan 230°$

3. $\cot 265°$

4. $\cot \left(-\dfrac{\pi}{9}\right)$

5. $\tan \left(-\dfrac{5\pi}{3}\right)$

6. $\sec 100°$

7. $\csc 220°$

8. $\csc \dfrac{7\pi}{12}$

9. $\sec \dfrac{4\pi}{3}$

Use Table 1 to evaluate.

10. $\tan 129°$

11. $\cot 215°$

12. $\cot 320°$

13. $\tan 91°$

14. $\sec (-17°)$

15. $\csc 108°$

16. $\csc 243°$

17. $\sec 269°$

18. $\cot 182°$

Evaluate without using Table 1.

19. a. $\tan 210°$ **b.** $\sec \dfrac{5\pi}{6}$ **c.** $\csc \dfrac{11\pi}{6}$

20. a. $\cot 135°$ **b.** $\csc 225°$ **c.** $\sec \dfrac{7\pi}{4}$

21. a. $\sec \dfrac{2\pi}{3}$ **b.** $\cot \dfrac{5\pi}{3}$ **c.** $\tan 240°$

22. $\sin 120° \tan 300°$ **23.** $\tan (-315°) \sec 240°$

24. $\dfrac{\sec 135°}{\cos 225°}$ **25.** $\sin \dfrac{7\pi}{6} - \tan \dfrac{3\pi}{4}$

26. $\sin \dfrac{11\pi}{6} \cos \dfrac{2\pi}{3} - \sec \dfrac{5\pi}{6} \tan \dfrac{2\pi}{3}$ **27.** $\cot \dfrac{2\pi}{3} \csc \dfrac{4\pi}{3} + \tan \dfrac{7\pi}{4} \cos \dfrac{4\pi}{3}$

Use the given information to find the values of the other five trigonometric functions.

EXAMPLE $\sin \theta = \dfrac{1}{2}$ and θ lies in Quadrant II

SOLUTION $\sin^2 \theta + \cos^2 \theta = 1$

$$\left(\dfrac{1}{2}\right)^2 + \cos^2 \theta = 1$$

$$\cos^2 \theta = 1 - \dfrac{1}{4} = \dfrac{3}{4}$$

$$\cos \theta = \pm \dfrac{\sqrt{3}}{2}$$

In Quadrant II, $\cos \theta < 0$, so $\cos \theta = -\dfrac{\sqrt{3}}{2}$.

$$\sec \theta = \dfrac{1}{\cos \theta} = \dfrac{1}{-\dfrac{\sqrt{3}}{2}} = -\dfrac{2\sqrt{3}}{3} \qquad \csc \theta = \dfrac{1}{\sin \theta} = \dfrac{1}{\dfrac{1}{2}} = 2$$

$$\tan \theta = \dfrac{\sin \theta}{\cos \theta} = \dfrac{\dfrac{1}{2}}{-\dfrac{\sqrt{3}}{2}} = -\dfrac{\sqrt{3}}{3} \qquad \cot \theta = \dfrac{\cos \theta}{\sin \theta} = \dfrac{-\dfrac{\sqrt{3}}{2}}{\dfrac{1}{2}} = -\sqrt{3}$$

28. a. $\cos \theta = \dfrac{\sqrt{2}}{2}$ and θ lies in Quadrant IV   **b.** $\sec \theta = \dfrac{5}{3}$ and θ lies in Quadrant I

29. a. $\csc \theta = -\dfrac{13}{5}$ and θ lies in Quadrant III   **b.** $\tan \theta = -1$ and θ lies in Quadrant II

30. a. $\tan \theta = \dfrac{8}{15}$ and $\cos \theta < 0$ **b.** $\csc \theta = \dfrac{41}{9}$ and $\cos \theta < 0$

31. a. $\sec \theta = -2$ and $\cot \theta > 0$ **b.** $\cot \theta = \dfrac{7}{24}$ and $\cos \theta > 0$

32. **a.** Sketch the graph of $y = \cot \theta$ for $-\pi < \theta < 2\pi$. You may wish to refer to the function values calculated in Exercise 1.
   b. What is the period of cotangent?
   c. For what values of θ (in radians) is cotangent undefined? equal to 0? equal to 1? equal to -1?
   d. State the domain and the range of the cotangent function.
   e. For what values of θ (in radians) does $\cot \theta = \tan \theta$?

B 33. Prove that $\tan (\theta + \pi) = \tan \theta$.

34. Prove that tangent and cotangent are *cofunctions*. That is, show that

$$\tan \left(\frac{\pi}{2} - \theta \right) = \cot \theta.$$

35. Prove that secant and cosecant are *cofunctions*. That is, show that

$$\sec \left(\frac{\pi}{2} - \theta \right) = \csc \theta.$$

Find the values of the six trigonometric functions if the terminal side of θ passes through the given point. (See Exercises 30–37, page 284.)

36. $(-1, 1)$ **37.** $(3, -4)$ **38.** $(12, 5)$ **39.** $(-3, -3)$

40. Determine the period of $\csc \theta$ and justify your answer.

41. On the same set of axes, graph $y = \sin \theta$ and $y = \csc \theta$ for $-\pi < \theta < 2\pi$.
   a. For what values of θ (in radians) is $\csc \theta$ undefined?
   b. State the domain and range of the cosecant function.

C 42. In the figure, $\overline{QB}$ is tangent to the unit circle at B, and $\overline{PA} \perp \overline{OB}$.
   a. Explain why $\triangle POA \sim \triangle QOB$.

   b. Use the results of part (a) to explain why $\dfrac{PA}{OA} = \dfrac{QB}{OB}$ and $\dfrac{OP}{OA} = \dfrac{OQ}{OB}$.

   c. Use the results of part (b) to explain why $\tan \theta = QB$ and $\sec \theta = OQ$. (Notice that you have found two line segments, namely a tangent segment and a segment of a secant of a circle, whose lengths represent the values of the tangent function and the secant function, respectively, of θ. This should help you see how the names *tangent* and *secant* were given to these functions.)

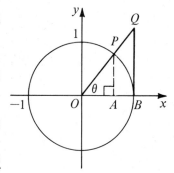

43. In the figure, $\overline{RS}$ is tangent to the unit circle at R, and $\overline{PA} \perp \overline{OA}$. Use reasoning similar to that of Exercise 42 to show that $\cot \theta = RS$ and $\csc \theta = OS$.

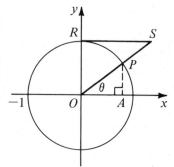

Section 8-2 TRIGONOMETRIC IDENTITIES

In this section you will learn how to use identities involving trigonometric functions to:
- express any trigonometric function in terms of another
- simplify trigonometric expressions

An *identity* is an equation that is true for all values of the variables for which the sides of the equation are defined. You are already familar with many algebraic identities, such as:

$$a^2 - b^2 = (a + b)(a - b) \quad \text{for all } a, b \in \mathbb{R}$$

$$\left(\frac{a}{b}\right)^2 = \frac{a^2}{b^2} \quad \text{for } a, b \in \mathbb{R}, b \neq 0$$

In fact, you have already seen a few *trigonometric identities*, although we didn't call them identities at the time. The reduction formulas listed on page 295 are identities. You should review them now. Another well-known trigonometric identity is the equation presented on page 281:

$$\sin^2 \theta + \cos^2 \theta = 1$$

This is the first of three identities called the *Pythagorean identities*.

The Pythagorean Identities

$$\sin^2 \theta + \cos^2 \theta = 1$$

$$\tan^2 \theta + 1 = \sec^2 \theta$$

$$\cot^2 \theta + 1 = \csc^2 \theta$$

You will be asked to prove the second and third Pythagorean identities in Exercises 17 and 18. (In Exercise 29, Section 7-3, you proved that $\sin^2 \theta + \cos^2 \theta = 1$.)

You are also familiar with the following identities.

$$\csc \theta = \frac{1}{\sin \theta}, \quad \sin \theta \neq 0 \qquad \qquad \sin \theta = \frac{1}{\csc \theta}, \quad \sin \theta \neq 0$$

$$\sec \theta = \frac{1}{\cos \theta}, \quad \cos \theta \neq 0 \qquad \qquad \cos \theta = \frac{1}{\sec \theta}, \quad \cos \theta \neq 0$$

$$\tan \theta = \frac{\sin \theta}{\cos \theta}, \quad \cos \theta \neq 0 \qquad \qquad \cot \theta = \frac{\cos \theta}{\sin \theta}, \quad \sin \theta \neq 0$$

$$\tan \theta = \frac{1}{\cot \theta}, \quad \sin \theta \neq 0, \cos \theta \neq 0 \qquad \qquad \cot \theta = \frac{1}{\tan \theta}, \quad \cos \theta \neq 0, \sin \theta \neq 0$$

EXAMPLE   Express cos α in terms of sin α.

SOLUTION   From the Pythagorean identity $\sin^2 \alpha + \cos^2 \alpha = 1$ we get:

$$\cos^2 \alpha = 1 - \sin^2 \alpha$$
$$\cos \alpha = \pm \sqrt{1 - \sin^2 \alpha}$$

(We can't tell which sign to use without more information, such as which quadrant α is in.)

From now on, unless otherwise specified, we will assume that *the domain of the variable includes only those values for which each expression is defined.*

EXAMPLE   Express in terms of a single function or constant:

$$\sin^2 \theta(\cot^2 \theta + 1)$$

SOLUTION   Since $\cot^2 \theta + 1 = \csc^2 \theta$, it follows that:

$$\sin^2 \theta(\cot^2 \theta + 1) = \sin^2 \theta \cdot \csc^2 \theta$$

But $\csc \theta = \dfrac{1}{\sin \theta}$, so:

$$\sin^2 \theta \cdot \csc^2 \theta = \sin^2 \theta \cdot \frac{1}{\sin^2 \theta} = 1$$

It follows that:

$$\sin^2 \theta(\cot^2 \theta + 1) = 1$$

If it is not immediately apparent how to simplify an expression, it may help to begin by expressing each function in terms of sine and/or cosine.

EXAMPLE   Express in terms of a single function or constant:

$$(\csc \alpha - \cot \alpha)(1 + \cos \alpha)$$

SOLUTION $\csc \alpha = \dfrac{1}{\sin \alpha}$ $\cot \alpha = \dfrac{\cos \alpha}{\sin \alpha}$

$$(\csc \alpha - \cot \alpha)(1 + \cos \alpha) = \left(\frac{1}{\sin \alpha} - \frac{\cos \alpha}{\sin \alpha}\right)(1 + \cos \alpha)$$
$$= \left(\frac{1 - \cos \alpha}{\sin \alpha}\right)(1 + \cos \alpha)$$
$$= \frac{1 - \cos^2 \alpha}{\sin \alpha}$$
$$= \frac{\sin^2 \alpha}{\sin \alpha}$$
$$= \sin \alpha$$

Since the original expression is defined if and only if $\sin \alpha \neq 0$, we have:

$$(\csc \alpha - \cot \alpha)(1 + \cos \alpha) = \sin \alpha$$

ORAL EXERCISES

1. Given that $\sin^2 \theta + \cos^2 \theta = 1$, complete:
   a. $1 - \cos^2 \theta = \underline{\quad?\quad}$
   b. $\sin^2 \theta - 1 = \underline{\quad?\quad}$
   c. $\sin^2 \theta = \underline{\quad?\quad}$

2. Given that $\tan^2 \theta + 1 = \sec^2 \theta$, complete:
   a. $\sec^2 \theta - 1 = \underline{\quad?\quad}$
   b. $\tan^2 \theta - \sec^2 \theta = \underline{\quad?\quad}$
   c. $\sec^2 \theta - \tan^2 \theta = \underline{\quad?\quad}$

State an equivalent expression in terms of $\sin \theta$ only.

3. $\csc \theta$ 4. $\tan \theta \cos \theta$ 5. $\cos \left(\theta + \dfrac{\pi}{2} \right)$

State an equivalent expression in terms of $\cos \theta$ only.

6. $\sec \theta$ 7. $\cos (-\theta)$ 8. $\sin \theta \cos \theta \csc \theta$

9. Explain why each of the identities in the last row in the second box on page 323 has *two* restrictions.

WRITTEN EXERCISES

Express in terms of a constant or a single function of θ.

A
1. $\cot^2 \theta + 1$
2. $1 - \sec^2 \theta$
3. $1 - \sin^2 \theta$
4. $1 - \csc^2 \theta$
5. $\csc \theta \sin \theta \cot \theta$
6. $\tan \theta \sec \theta \cos \theta$
7. $\csc \theta \tan \theta \cos \theta$
8. $\sin \theta \sec \theta \cot \theta$
9. $\cos^2 \theta \sec \theta \csc \theta$
10. $\sin^2 \theta \sec \theta \csc \theta$
11. $(\tan \theta + 1)^2 + (\tan \theta - 1)^2$
12. $2 \cos \theta \sec \theta - \tan \theta \cot \theta$

Express in terms of a constant or a single function.

EXAMPLE $\cos 2\theta \csc 2\theta$

SOLUTION $\cos 2\theta \csc 2\theta = \cos 2\theta \left(\dfrac{1}{\sin 2\theta} \right) = \dfrac{\cos 2\theta}{\sin 2\theta} = \tan 2\theta$

13. $\sin 2\theta \csc 2\theta$
14. $\sin 2\theta \sec 2\theta$
15. $\cos 3\alpha \tan 3\alpha$
16. $\cot 4\theta \sin 4\theta$
17. $\tan 2\alpha \csc 2\alpha$
18. $\sec 5\alpha \cos 5\alpha$

Express the first function in terms of the second function.

19. $\sin \theta$; $\cos \theta$
20. $\tan \theta$; $\sec \theta$
21. $\sec \alpha$; $\sin \alpha$
22. $\cot \alpha \sec \alpha$; $\cos \alpha$

23. Prove that $\tan^2 \theta + 1 = \sec^2 \theta$. (*Hint*: Substitute $\dfrac{\sin \theta}{\cos \theta}$ for $\tan \theta$ in $\tan^2 \theta + 1$ and simplify the result.)

24. Prove that $\cot^2 \theta + 1 = \csc^2 \theta$. (*Hint*: Substitute $\dfrac{\cos \theta}{\sin \theta}$ for $\cot \theta$ in $\cot^2 \theta + 1$ and simplify the result.)

Express in terms of a constant or a single function.

EXAMPLE $\sin (\pi + \theta) \sec (-\theta)$

SOLUTION $\sin (\pi + \theta) = -\sin \theta$ and $\sec (-\theta) = \dfrac{1}{\cos (-\theta)} = \dfrac{1}{\cos \theta}$

By substituting, you obtain:

$$\sin (\pi + \theta) \sec (-\theta) = -\sin \theta \cdot \frac{1}{\cos \theta} = -\left(\frac{\sin \theta}{\cos \theta} \right) = -\tan \theta$$

25. $\sin (\pi + \theta) + \sin (\pi - \theta)$ 26. $\cos (-\theta) \tan (\pi - \theta)$

27. $\sec (90° + \theta) \sin (180° - \theta)$ 28. $\cos (90° - \theta) \sin \theta + \sin (90° + \theta) \cos \theta$

B 29. $\tan (\theta + 90°) + \cot (180° - \theta)$ 30. $\cot (\pi + \theta) \cos \left(\dfrac{\pi}{2} - \theta \right)$

31. $\dfrac{\cot (-\theta)}{\tan \left(\dfrac{\pi}{2} + \theta \right)}$

32. $\cot (180° + \theta) + \tan (\theta - 270°)$
   (*Hint*: Express $\theta - 270°$ as $90° - (360° - \theta)$).

EXAMPLE $\dfrac{\sec \theta - \cos \theta}{\tan \theta}$

SOLUTION $\dfrac{\sec \theta - \cos \theta}{\tan \theta} = \dfrac{\dfrac{1}{\cos \theta} - \cos \theta}{\dfrac{\sin \theta}{\cos \theta}}$

To simplify a complex fraction, it may be necessary to multiply the numerator and the denominator of the complex fraction by a common denominator of its secondary fractions. In this problem, a common denominator is $\cos \theta$.

$$\frac{\dfrac{1}{\cos \theta} - \cos \theta}{\dfrac{\sin \theta}{\cos \theta}} \cdot \frac{\cos \theta}{\cos \theta} = \frac{\left(\dfrac{1}{\cos \theta} - \cos \theta \right) \cos \theta}{\left(\dfrac{\sin \theta}{\cos \theta} \right) \cos \theta}$$

$$= \frac{1 - \cos^2 \theta}{\sin \theta} = \frac{\sin^2 \theta}{\sin \theta} = \sin \theta$$

Therefore, $\dfrac{\sec \theta - \cos \theta}{\tan \theta} = \sin \theta$.

33. $\dfrac{\tan \theta}{\sec \theta}$ 34. $\dfrac{\csc \theta}{\cot \theta}$ 35. $\dfrac{\sin \theta \sec \theta}{\tan \theta}$

36. $\dfrac{\cot^2 \theta - \cos^2 \theta}{\cos^2 \theta}$ 37. $\dfrac{\tan \theta + 1}{\cot \theta + 1}$ 38. $\dfrac{\tan \theta \cos \theta}{\sin \theta \sec \theta}$

39. $\dfrac{\sin \alpha - \sec \alpha}{\csc \alpha - \cos \alpha}$ 40. $\dfrac{\cos \alpha + \cot \alpha}{1 + \sin \alpha}$ 41. $\dfrac{\sin \theta + \tan \theta}{1 + \sec \theta}$

42. $\dfrac{1 + \cot^2 \theta}{1 + \tan^2 \theta}$ 43. $\dfrac{\tan \alpha \csc^2 \alpha}{1 + \tan^2 \alpha}$ 44. $\dfrac{\cos \alpha + \sin \alpha \tan \alpha}{\sin \alpha \sec \alpha}$

Express in terms of a constant or a single function.

45. $\dfrac{2 \sin \theta \cos \theta}{\sin^2 \theta - \cos^2 \theta + 1}$

46. $\dfrac{(\sin \alpha + \cos \alpha)^2 - 1}{\sin \alpha \cos \alpha}$

C 47. $\sin^3 \beta + \sin \beta \cos^2 \beta$

48. $(1 - \sin \theta)(\csc \theta + 1) \csc \theta$

49. $\dfrac{\cot^2 \theta + 2 \cot \theta + 1}{\cot \theta \tan \theta + \cot \theta + \tan \theta + 1}$

50. $\dfrac{\cos^4 \alpha - \sin^4 \alpha}{\cos^2 \alpha - \sin^2 \alpha}$

51. $\sin (180° + \theta) \sec (-\theta) \cot (180° + \theta)$

52. $\sin \left(\theta - \dfrac{\pi}{2}\right) \sec (\pi - \theta) \tan \left(\dfrac{\pi}{2} + \theta\right)$

Section 8-3 PROVING IDENTITIES

To prove that an equation is an identity, you must show that it is true for all values of the variable for which each side of the equation is defined. You can use any of the following to help you verify an identity:

1. known trigonometric identities
2. algebraic identities
3. the properties of real numbers listed on page 6
4. the Distributive Property
5. the Substitution Property

The following examples illustrate one method of verifying an identity, that is, by manipulating *one* side of the equation until it is identical to the other side.

EXAMPLE Prove that $\dfrac{1}{\sin^2 \theta} + \dfrac{1}{\cos^2 \theta} = \dfrac{1}{\sin^2 \theta \cos^2 \theta}$.

SOLUTION
$$\dfrac{1}{\sin^2 \theta} + \dfrac{1}{\cos^2 \theta} = \dfrac{1}{\sin^2 \theta} \cdot \dfrac{\cos^2 \theta}{\cos^2 \theta} + \dfrac{1}{\cos^2 \theta} \cdot \dfrac{\sin^2 \theta}{\sin^2 \theta}$$

$$= \dfrac{\cos^2 \theta}{\sin^2 \theta \cos^2 \theta} + \dfrac{\sin^2 \theta}{\sin^2 \theta \cos^2 \theta}$$

$$= \dfrac{\cos^2 \theta + \sin^2 \theta}{\sin^2 \theta \cos^2 \theta}$$

$$= \dfrac{1}{\sin^2 \theta \cos^2 \theta}$$

Thus, $\dfrac{1}{\sin^2 \theta} + \dfrac{1}{\cos^2 \theta} = \dfrac{1}{\sin^2 \theta \cos^2 \theta}$ is an identity.

EXAMPLE Prove that $\sin^4 \theta - \cos^4 \theta = \sin^2 \theta - \cos^2 \theta$.

SOLUTION Begin by factoring the left-hand side. Then simplify.
$$\sin^4 \theta - \cos^4 \theta = (\sin^2 \theta - \cos^2 \theta)(\sin^2 \theta + \cos^2 \theta)$$
$$= (\sin^2 \theta - \cos^2 \theta)1$$
$$= \sin^2 \theta - \cos^2 \theta.$$
Thus, $\sin^4 \theta - \cos^4 \theta = \sin^2 \theta - \cos^2 \theta$ is an identity.

At other times, it is easier to simplify *each* side of the equation independently until the two sides look alike.

EXAMPLE Prove that $\tan \theta + \cot \theta = \csc \theta \sec \theta$.

SOLUTION First simplify the left-hand side.

$$\tan \theta + \cot \theta = \frac{\sin \theta}{\cos \theta} + \frac{\cos \theta}{\sin \theta}$$

$$= \frac{\sin \theta}{\cos \theta} \cdot \frac{\sin \theta}{\sin \theta} + \frac{\cos \theta}{\sin \theta} \cdot \frac{\cos \theta}{\cos \theta}$$

$$= \frac{\sin^2 \theta + \cos^2 \theta}{\sin \theta \cos \theta}$$

$$= \frac{1}{\sin \theta \cos \theta}$$

Now simplify the right-hand side.

$$\csc \theta \sec \theta = \frac{1}{\sin \theta} \cdot \frac{1}{\cos \theta} = \frac{1}{\sin \theta \cos \theta}$$

Thus, $\tan \theta + \cot \theta = \csc \theta \sec \theta$ is an identity.

In summary, here are some guidelines for verifying identities.
1. Try to simplify the more complicated side of the equation first.
2. Look for algebraic identities that you can apply.
3. Sometimes rewriting an expression in terms of sine or cosine may help to simplify it.
4. After simplifying one side as much as you can, work on the other side until the two sides look alike.

ORAL EXERCISES

Verify that the identity is valid for the given value of θ.

1. $\sin^2 \theta + \cos^2 \theta = 1$; $\theta = 45°$
2. $\sin^2 \theta + \cos^2 \theta = 1$; $\theta = 90°$
3. $\cot^2 \theta + 1 = \csc^2 \theta$; $\theta = 30°$
4. $1 + \tan^2 \theta = \sec^2 \theta$; $\theta = 30°$

WRITTEN EXERCISES

Prove that each equation is an identity.

A 1. $\sin \theta \cot \theta = \cos \theta$
2. $\sec \theta \sin \theta = \tan \theta$
3. $\cos \alpha \csc \alpha = \cot \alpha$
4. $\tan \theta \cos \theta = \sin \theta$
5. $\dfrac{\csc \alpha}{\sec \alpha} = \cot \alpha$
6. $\dfrac{\cot x}{\cos x} = \csc x$

7. $\cot \theta = \cot^2 \theta \tan \theta$

8. $\sin \theta \csc^2 \theta = \csc \theta$

9. $\dfrac{1}{\cos^2 x} - \dfrac{1}{\cot^2 x} = 1$

10. $\dfrac{1}{\sec^2 \theta} = 1 - \dfrac{1}{\csc^2 \theta}$

11. $\sec \theta (\sin \theta + \cos \theta) = \tan \theta + 1$

12. $\cot \alpha (1 - \sin \alpha) = \cot \alpha - \cos \alpha$

13. $(\cos \theta - \sin \theta)^2 = 1 - 2 \sin \theta \cos \theta$

14. $\cot^2 x = (\csc x - 1)(\csc x + 1)$

15. $\cos^2 \alpha (\cot^2 \alpha + 1) = \cot^2 \alpha$

16. $\dfrac{\sin \theta - 1}{\cos \theta} = \tan \theta - \sec \theta$

17. $\tan x (\cot x + \tan x) = \sec^2 x$

18. $\csc \alpha - \sin \alpha = \cot \alpha \cos \alpha$

19. $\sec \alpha (\sec \alpha - \cos \alpha) = \tan^2 \alpha$

20. $\sec^2 \theta + \tan^2 \theta \sec^2 \theta = \sec^4 \theta$

21. $1 - 2 \sin^2 \alpha = 2 \cos^2 \alpha - 1$

22. $\dfrac{\cos \alpha}{\csc \alpha} = \cos^2 \alpha \tan \alpha$

23. $\dfrac{\cot \theta}{\tan \theta} = \dfrac{1 - \sin^2 \theta}{1 - \cos^2 \theta}$

24. $\dfrac{1 + \tan \alpha}{\sin \alpha} = \csc \alpha + \sec \alpha$

25. $2 \cos^2 \theta - 1 = \cos^2 \theta - \sin^2 \theta$

26. $\dfrac{1 + \csc \theta}{1 - \csc \theta} = \dfrac{1 + \sin \theta}{\sin \theta - 1}$

B 27. $(\cos \theta - \sec \theta)^2 = \tan^2 \theta - \sin^2 \theta$

28. $\tan^2 \theta - \sin^2 \theta = \sin^2 \theta \tan^2 \theta$

29. $\tan^4 \theta - \sec^4 \theta = 1 - 2 \sec^2 \theta$

30. $\csc^2 \alpha + \cot^2 \alpha = \dfrac{\cos^2 \alpha + 1}{(\cos \alpha + 1)(1 - \cos \alpha)}$

31. $\sec \alpha - 1 = \dfrac{\tan^2 \alpha}{\sec \alpha + 1}$ (*Hint*: Multiply the numerator and denominator of the right-hand side by $\sec \alpha - 1$.)

32. $\dfrac{\sin \alpha}{1 + \cos \alpha} = \csc \alpha - \cot \alpha$ (*Hint*: Multiply the numerator and denominator of the left-hand side by $1 - \cos \alpha$.)

33. $\dfrac{1}{1 + \sin \theta} + \dfrac{1}{1 - \sin \theta} = 2 \sec^2 \theta$

34. $\dfrac{\sin^2 \theta}{1 - \cos \theta} = 1 + \cos \theta$

35. $\dfrac{\cot \theta}{\sec \theta - 1} = \dfrac{\cos^3 \theta + \cos^2 \theta}{\sin^3 \theta}$

36. $\dfrac{\csc \alpha}{1 + \sec \alpha} = \dfrac{\cot \alpha}{1 + \cos \alpha}$

37. $\sec \theta + \tan \theta = \dfrac{\cos \theta}{1 - \sin \theta}$

38. $\dfrac{\sin \theta + 1}{\sin \theta - 1} = 1 - 2 \sec^2 \theta - 2 \sec \theta \tan \theta$

Determine which of the following are identities.

C 39. $\dfrac{1 - \sin \theta}{\cos \theta} = \dfrac{\cos \theta}{1 - \cos \theta}$

40. $\dfrac{(\sec \theta - \tan \theta)^2 + 1}{\csc \theta (\sec \theta - \tan \theta)} = 2 \tan \theta$

41. $\sin \alpha - \cos \alpha = \dfrac{3 + \cot \alpha - 2 \csc^2 \alpha}{2 \cot \alpha \csc \alpha + \csc \alpha}$

SELF-TEST 1

Evaluate without using Table 1.

1. a. $\tan 225°$ **b.** $\cot 300°$ **c.** $\sec 150°$ Section 8-1

2. a. $\csc \left(-\dfrac{\pi}{4}\right)$ **b.** $\cot \dfrac{3\pi}{2}$ **c.** $\tan \dfrac{\pi}{3}$

3. $\dfrac{\tan 45°}{\cot 270° + \sec 180°}$

4. If $\sin \theta = -\dfrac{4}{5}$ and θ lies in Quadrant III, find:

   a. $\cos \theta$ **b.** $\tan \theta$ **c.** $\sec \theta$

5. a. Graph $y = -\tan \theta$ for $-\dfrac{\pi}{2} < \theta < \dfrac{3\pi}{2}$.

   b. State the period of the function.

Simplify.

6. $\cos^2 \theta (\tan^2 \theta + 1)$ **7.** $\dfrac{\cot^2 \theta}{\cos^2 \theta} - \dfrac{1}{\tan^2 \theta}$ Section 8-2

8. Express in terms of a single function: $\sin (\pi + \theta) \sec (-\theta)$

9. Express $\cot \theta$ in terms of $\csc \theta$.

Verify that each equation is an identity.

10. $\dfrac{1}{\cot \theta} + \dfrac{1}{\tan \theta} = \dfrac{1}{\cos \theta \sin \theta}$ Section 8-3

11. $\sin \theta \tan \theta = \sec \theta - \cos \theta$

12. $(\tan \theta + \sec \theta)^2 = \dfrac{1 + \sin \theta}{1 - \sin \theta}$

Section 8-4 TRIGONOMETRIC EQUATIONS

As you know, trigonometric identities are trigonometric equations that are true for *all* values of the variable for which each side of the equation is defined. In this section, you will study trigonometric equations that are true for only *some* replacements of the variable. For example, the solution of

$$\sin \theta = 0, \text{ where } \theta \in \mathcal{R}$$

is

$$\theta = n\pi, \text{ where } n \in Z.$$

This equation has an infinite number of solutions, which are called the *general solution* of the equation.

   To simplify matters, trigonometric equations are frequently solved over a particular interval, say $0 \leqslant \theta < 2\pi$.

EXAMPLE   Solve $2 \sin \theta + 5 = 4 \sin \theta + 6$ when $0° \leqslant \theta < 360°$.

SOLUTION $2 \sin \theta + 5 = 4 \sin \theta + 6$

$-2 \sin \theta = 1$

$$\sin \theta = -\frac{1}{2}$$

Since $\sin 30° = \frac{1}{2}$, the reference angle is $30°$.

$\sin \theta = -\frac{1}{2}$ when θ is in the third or fourth quadrant.

Thus, $\theta = 180° + 30° = 210°$ or $\theta = 360° - 30° = 330°$.

Check $2 \sin 210° + 5 \overset{?}{=} 4 \sin 210° + 6$

$$2\left(-\frac{1}{2}\right) + 5 \overset{?}{=} 4\left(-\frac{1}{2}\right) + 6$$

$-1 + 5 \overset{?}{=} -2 + 6$

$4 = 4$

You should check that $330°$ is also a solution.

EXAMPLE   For $4 \cos \theta + 3 = 4$, find:
    a. the solution to the nearest $10'$ for $0° \leqslant \theta < 360°$
    b. the general solution

SOLUTION   a. $4 \cos \theta + 3 = 4$

$4 \cos \theta = 1$

$\cos \theta = 0.25$

From Table 1, the reference angle is $75°30'$.
Since $\cos \theta > 0$, θ is in the first or fourth quadrant.
Thus, $\theta = 75°30'$
or $\theta = 360° - 75°30' = 284°30'$.

    b. Add $n \cdot 360°$, $n \in Z$, to each solution to account for the periodicity of the function. Thus the general solution is:
$\theta = 75°30' + n \cdot 360°$ or $\theta = 284°30' + n \cdot 360°$, $n \in Z$

You may need to use factoring and the Zero-Product Rule to solve a trigonometric equation.

EXAMPLE   Solve $2 \sin^2 \theta + \sin \theta - 1 = 0$, $0 \leqslant \theta < 2\pi$.

SOLUTION $2 \sin^2 \theta + \sin \theta - 1 = 0$

$(2 \sin \theta - 1)(\sin \theta + 1) = 0$

$2 \sin \theta - 1 = 0$ or $\sin \theta + 1 = 0$

$\sin \theta = \frac{1}{2}$ or $\sin \theta = -1$

$\theta = \frac{\pi}{6}$ or $\theta = \frac{5\pi}{6}$ $\bigg|$ $\theta = \frac{3\pi}{2}$

The solution is $\theta = \frac{\pi}{6}, \frac{5\pi}{6}, \frac{3\pi}{2}$.

EXAMPLE Solve $\tan^2 \theta = \tan \theta$, $0 \leqslant \theta < 2\pi$.

SOLUTION It is tempting to divide both sides of this equation by $\tan \theta$, but if we did we would lose the roots of $\tan \theta = 0$.

$$\tan^2 \theta = \tan \theta$$
$$\tan^2 \theta - \tan \theta = 0$$
$$\tan \theta(\tan \theta - 1) = 0$$

$\tan \theta = 0$ or $\tan \theta - 1 = 0$
$\tan \theta = 0$ | $\tan \theta = 1$

$\theta = 0$ or $\theta = \pi$ | $\theta = \dfrac{\pi}{4}$ or $\theta = \dfrac{5\pi}{4}$

$$\theta = 0, \frac{\pi}{4}, \pi, \frac{5\pi}{4}$$

EXAMPLE Solve $2 \sin 2\theta = \sqrt{3}$, $0 \leqslant \theta < 2\pi$.

SOLUTION $2 \sin 2\theta = \sqrt{3}$

$$\sin 2\theta = \frac{\sqrt{3}}{2}$$

Since $0 \leqslant \theta < 2\pi$, you know that $0 \leqslant 2\theta < 4\pi$.

Since $\sin 2\theta = \dfrac{\sqrt{3}}{2}$, you have: $2\theta = \dfrac{\pi}{3}, \dfrac{2\pi}{3}, \dfrac{7\pi}{3}, \dfrac{8\pi}{3}$

$$\theta = \frac{\pi}{6}, \frac{\pi}{3}, \frac{7\pi}{6}, \frac{4\pi}{3}$$

ORAL EXERCISES

Refer to the graph to solve for $0 \leqslant \theta < 2\pi$.

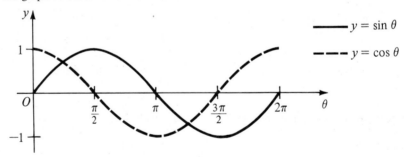

1. $\sin \theta = 1$

2. $\cos \theta = 1$

3. $\cos \theta = 0$

4. $\sin \theta = -1$

5. $\cos^2 \theta = 1$

6. $\sin \theta = \cos \theta$

How many values of θ in the given interval satisfy the equation?

7. $0° \leqslant \theta < 90°$; $\sin \theta = 0.7$

8. $0° \leqslant \theta < 180°$; $\sin \theta = 0.7$

9. $0 \leqslant \theta < \pi$; $\cos^2 \theta = \dfrac{1}{4}$

10. $0 \leqslant \theta < 2\pi$; $\cos^2 \theta = \dfrac{1}{4}$

11. $0 \leqslant \theta < 2\pi$; $\sin \theta + 1 = 3$

12. $0 \leqslant \theta < 2\pi$; $\cos \theta(\cos \theta + 1) = 0$

WRITTEN EXERCISES

Solve for $0° \leqslant \theta < 360°$

A 1. $\tan \theta = \sqrt{3}$ 2. $\cot \theta = 0$ 3. $3 \sec \theta = -2\sqrt{3}$

4. $\sqrt{2} \sin \theta - 1 = 0$ 5. $\sqrt{2} \cos \theta = -1$ 6. $\sin \theta + 3 = 3$

7. $3 \cos \theta + 1 = \cos \theta + 2$ 8. $2 \csc \theta + 5 = 4 \csc \theta + 6$ 9. $2 \sin \theta - \sqrt{3} = 0$

10. $\cos \theta + 2 = 3 \cos \theta$ 11. $\tan^2 \theta - 1 = 0$ 12. $\cos^2 \theta - 4 = 0$

13. $4 \sin^2 \theta = 3$ 14. $(2 \cos \theta)^2 = 3$ 15. $3 \cot^2 \theta = 1$

16. $\cos^2 \theta - \cos \theta = 0$ 17. $2 \sin^2 \theta - \sin \theta = 0$ 18. $\sin^2 \theta - 2 \sin \theta = 0$

19. $\sin^2 \theta + 2 \sin \theta - 3 = 0$ 20. $\cos^2 \theta - 3 \cos \theta - 4 = 0$ 21. $4 \sin^2 \theta - 4 \sin \theta + 1 = 0$

22. $4 \cos^2 \theta + 4 \cos \theta = 3$ 23. $\cos^2 \theta - 6 \cos \theta = -9$ 24. $(1 + \tan \theta)^2 = 2 \tan \theta + 2$

Find the general solution for α in radians.

25. $\tan \alpha - 1 = 0$ 26. $\cot \alpha - \sqrt{3} = 0$ 27. $\cos^2 \alpha - 2 \cos \alpha = 0$

28. $\sin^2 \alpha = \sin \alpha$ 29. $\sec^2 \alpha - 4 = 0$ 30. $\csc^2 \alpha - \sqrt{2} \csc \alpha = 0$

Solve for $0° \leqslant \theta < 360°$ to the nearest 10'. Use Table 1 as necessary.

31. $\cot^2 \theta + 4 \cot \theta + 3 = 0$ 32. $\tan^2 \theta + \tan \theta - 6 = 0$ 33. $5 \cos^2 \theta - 6 \cos \theta + 1 = 0$

34. $5 \sin^2 \theta - \sin \theta = 4$ 35. $6 \sin^2 \theta - 1 = \sin \theta$ 36. $3 \cos^2 \theta - 5 \cos \theta = 2$

Solve for $0 \leqslant \alpha < 2\pi$.

B 37. $\sin 2\alpha = 1$ 38. $\cos 2\alpha = 1$ 39. $\cot 3\alpha = -1$

40. $\sin 3\alpha = -\dfrac{\sqrt{3}}{2}$ 41. $\cos \dfrac{\alpha}{2} = \dfrac{1}{2}$ 42. $\sin \dfrac{\alpha}{2} - 1 = 0$

43. $\sec^2 \dfrac{\alpha}{2} = \dfrac{4}{3}$ 44. $\sin^2 2\alpha + \sin 2\alpha = 0$ 45. $(\cos 2\alpha + 1)(2 \cos 2\alpha + \sqrt{3}) = 0$

EXAMPLE Find the smallest positive value of θ that satisfies $2 \sin \left(\theta + \dfrac{\pi}{6} \right) - 1 = 0$.

SOLUTION Let $\alpha = \theta + \dfrac{\pi}{6}$ and solve for $\sin \alpha$. Then compare several values of α to find the one that gives the *smallest positive* value of θ: $2 \sin \alpha - 1 = 0$

$$\sin \alpha = \dfrac{1}{2}$$

$$\alpha = \dfrac{\pi}{6} \text{ or } \dfrac{5\pi}{6}$$

Substitute $\theta + \dfrac{\pi}{6}$ for α. $\theta + \dfrac{\pi}{6} = \dfrac{\pi}{6}$ or $\theta + \dfrac{\pi}{6} = \dfrac{5\pi}{6}$

$$\theta = 0 \qquad\qquad \theta = \dfrac{4\pi}{6} = \dfrac{2\pi}{3}$$

Which is the smaller *positive* value of θ? $\theta = \dfrac{2\pi}{3}$

Find the smallest positive value of θ that satisfies the equation. (See the example on the preceding page.)

46. $\cos\left(\theta + \dfrac{\pi}{3}\right) = 1$ **47.** $\tan\left(\theta - \dfrac{\pi}{4}\right) = -1$ **48.** $2\sin\left(\dfrac{\pi}{2} - \theta\right) = \sqrt{3}$

49. $\sec\left(\theta + \dfrac{\pi}{6}\right) = -2$ **50.** $3\cot\left(\theta - \dfrac{\pi}{2}\right) = \sqrt{3}$ **51.** $2\cos\left(\dfrac{\pi}{6} - \theta\right) = \sqrt{2}$

C **52.** $\tan(2\theta - \pi) = \sqrt{3}$ **53.** $\cot\left(\dfrac{\pi}{2} - 2\theta\right) = -\sqrt{3}$ **54.** $2\csc^2\left(\theta + \dfrac{\pi}{4}\right) = 3\csc\left(\theta + \dfrac{\pi}{4}\right) + 2$

Solve for $0° \leqslant \alpha < 360°$ to the nearest $10'$. Use Table 1 and the following values as necessary: $\sqrt{2} = 1.414$, $\sqrt{3} = 1.732$, $\sqrt{7} = 2.646$

55. $\sin^2\alpha - 4\sin\alpha + 1 = 0$ (*Hint:* Use the quadratic formula to solve for $\sin\alpha$.)

56. $2\cos^2\alpha + 6\cos\alpha + 1 = 0$ **57.** $2\tan^2\alpha + 4\tan\alpha + 1 = 0$

Section 8-5 EQUATIONS INVOLVING TWO TRIGONOMETRIC FUNCTIONS

The equations in the preceding section were expressed in terms of only one trigonometric function. In this section, you will consider trigonometric equations that contain more than one trigonometric function. Before we begin discussing the techniques used to solve such equations, you should review the identities on page 323.

When an equation contains more than one trigonometric function, you should try to transform it into an equivalent equation in terms of a single function. Then you can use the techniques presented in Section 8-4 to solve it.

In some cases, a transformation may not result in an equation equivalent to the original equation. For this reason, it is important to note the restrictions on the variable *and* to check the solution(s).

EXAMPLE   Solve $\sin\theta = -\cos\theta$, $0 \leqslant \theta < 2\pi$.

SOLUTION   If $\cos\theta \neq 0$, then you can divide both sides of the equation by $\cos\theta$.

$$\frac{\sin\theta}{\cos\theta} = \frac{-\cos\theta}{\cos\theta}$$

$$\tan\theta = -1$$

$$\theta = \frac{3\pi}{4}, \frac{7\pi}{4}$$

Notice that the equation $\tan\theta = -1$ is not necessarily equivalent to the original equation because if $\cos\theta = 0$, then $\tan\theta$ is undefined. On the other hand, both sides of the original equation are defined for all values of θ. The last step is checking that no roots were lost when both sides of the equation were divided by $\cos\theta$. To check, ask yourself if any of the values of θ that make $\cos\theta$ equal to 0 could be roots of $\sin\theta = \cos\theta$. You should convince yourself that the answer is "No," so the solution is $\theta = \dfrac{3\pi}{4}$ or $\dfrac{7\pi}{4}$.

$$\sin \frac{3\pi}{4} \overset{?}{=} -\cos \frac{3\pi}{4} \qquad\qquad \sin \frac{7\pi}{4} \overset{?}{=} -\cos \frac{7\pi}{4}$$

$$\frac{\sqrt{2}}{2} = -\left(\frac{-\sqrt{2}}{2}\right) \qquad\qquad -\frac{\sqrt{2}}{2} = -\frac{\sqrt{2}}{2}$$

EXAMPLE Solve $\sin^2 \theta + \cos \theta + 1 = 0$, $0 \le \theta < 2\pi$.

SOLUTION The equation is defined for all values of θ.
We can substitute $1 - \cos^2 \theta$ for $\sin^2 \theta$ to obtain:

$$(1 - \cos^2 \theta) + \cos \theta + 1 = 0$$
$$-\cos^2 \theta + \cos \theta + 2 = 0$$
$$\cos^2 \theta - \cos \theta - 2 = 0$$
$$(\cos \theta - 2)(\cos \theta + 1) = 0$$

$$\cos \theta - 2 = 0 \quad \text{or} \quad \cos \theta + 1 = 0$$
$$\cos \theta = 2 \qquad\qquad \cos \theta = -1$$
$$\text{no solution} \qquad\qquad \theta = \pi$$

The solution is $\theta = \pi$.

Check $\qquad \sin^2 \pi + \cos \pi + 1 = 0^2 + (-1) + 1 = 0$

EXAMPLE Solve $\tan \theta = \cot \theta$, $0° \le \theta < 360°$.

SOLUTION The expressions involved are defined if and only if $\cos \theta \ne 0$ and $\sin \theta \ne 0$. Therefore, $\theta \ne 0°, 90°, 180°, 270°$.

We can substitute $\dfrac{1}{\tan \theta}$ for $\cot \theta$ to obtain:

$$\tan \theta = \frac{1}{\tan \theta}$$
$$\tan^2 \theta = 1$$

Now we will solve this equation using the methods presented in Section 8-4.

$$\tan \theta = 1 \qquad \text{or} \qquad \tan \theta = -1$$
$$\theta = 45° \text{ or } 225° \qquad \theta = 135° \text{ or } 315°$$

Since none of the above values are on the restricted list, the solution is:

$$\theta = 45°, 135°, 225°, 315°$$

The check is left to you.

EXAMPLE Solve $\dfrac{\cos \theta + 1}{\sin \theta} = 1$, $0 \le \theta < 2\pi$.

SOLUTION The equation is defined if and only if $\theta \ne 0, \pi$.
Multiplying both sides by $\sin \theta$, we have:

$$\cos \theta + 1 = \sin \theta$$

If we square both sides of this equation, then we can use a form of the Pythagorean identity $\sin^2 \theta + \cos^2 \theta = 1$ to rewrite the resulting equation in terms of $\sin \theta$ or $\cos \theta$ only.

(The solution is continued on the following page.)

$$(\cos \theta + 1)^2 = \sin^2 \theta$$
$$\cos^2 \theta + 2 \cos \theta + 1 = \sin^2 \theta$$

But $\sin^2 \theta = 1 - \cos^2 \theta$, so:

$$\cos^2 \theta + 2 \cos \theta + 1 = 1 - \cos^2 \theta$$
$$2 \cos^2 \theta + 2 \cos \theta = 0$$
$$2 \cos \theta (\cos \theta + 1) = 0$$

$$\cos \theta = 0 \qquad \text{or} \qquad \cos \theta = -1$$

$$\theta = \frac{\pi}{2} \text{ or } \frac{3\pi}{2} \qquad \Bigg| \qquad \theta = \pi$$

Check We must reject the value $\theta = \pi$ because we have already noted that $\theta \neq 0$ and $\theta \neq \pi$. Checking the other values in the original equation, we have:

$$\frac{\cos \dfrac{\pi}{2} + 1}{\sin \dfrac{\pi}{2}} = \frac{0 + 1}{1} = 1 \qquad\qquad \frac{\cos \dfrac{3\pi}{2} + 1}{\sin \dfrac{3\pi}{2}} = \frac{0 + 1}{-1} = -1$$

We must reject the value $\theta = \dfrac{3\pi}{2}$. (We introduced an extra root when we squared both sides of the equation.) Thus the solution is $\theta = \dfrac{\pi}{2}$.

ORAL EXERCISES

State any necessary restrictions on θ, $0° \leqslant \theta < 360°$.

1. $\sin \theta = \cos \theta$
2. $\sin \theta + \csc \theta = 2$
3. $2 \tan \theta = \sec \theta$
4. $4 \cot \theta = \cos \theta$
5. $\tan \theta - 2 = \cot \theta$
6. $\sec^2 \theta - 3 \sec \theta - 4 = 0$

WRITTEN EXERCISES

Solve for $0 \leqslant \theta < 2\pi$.

A
1. $3 \sin \theta = \sqrt{3} \cos \theta$
2. $\sec \theta = \csc \theta$
3. $\sin^2 \theta = 3 \cos^2 \theta$
4. $4 \sin \theta = \csc \theta$
5. $\cos \theta \csc \theta = -1$
6. $\sin \theta = \sqrt{3} \cos \theta$
7. $2 \sin \theta = \csc \theta$
8. $\cot \theta - 3 \tan \theta = 0$
9. $\sin \theta + \csc \theta = 2$
10. $2 \sin \theta + 2 \csc \theta = 5$
11. $\csc \theta = 2 \cos \theta \csc \theta$
12. $\cos \theta = \sin \theta \cos \theta$
13. $\sqrt{2} \tan \theta = \sec \theta$
14. $2 - \sin^2 \theta = 2 \cos^2 \theta$
15. $3 \sin^2 \theta - \cos^2 \theta = 1$
16. $2 \csc^2 \theta = 3 \cot^2 \theta - 1$
17. $\csc \theta = \cot^2 \theta - 1$
18. $3 \sec^2 \theta = 4 \tan^2 \theta$
19. $2 \cos^2 \theta + \sqrt{3} \sin \theta = 2$
20. $\cos^2 \theta = 3 + 3 \sin \theta$
21. $2 + \sin \theta = 2 \cos^2 \theta$
22. $4 \cos^2 \theta + 8 \sin \theta - 7 = 0$
23. $2 \sin^2 \theta - 5 \cos \theta = 5$
24. $2 \cot^2 \theta + 3 = 3 \csc \theta$

25. $2 \sin \theta \cos \theta = 0$
26. $2 \tan^2 \theta = -3 \sec \theta$
27. $\sin^2 \theta + 2 = 3 \cos \theta \tan \theta$
28. $\tan \theta \cos \theta + \cos^2 \theta = 2 \sin \theta - 1$
29. $\tan \theta + \cot \theta = \sec \theta \csc \theta$
30. $\sin \theta + \cos \theta \cot \theta = \csc \theta$

B 31. $\tan \theta = 2 \sin \theta$ **32.** $\cot \theta = \cos \theta$ **33.** $2 \sin \theta \cos \theta = \tan \theta$

34. $1 - \sin \theta = \cos \theta$ **35.** $\sin^2 \theta - \tan \theta \cos^2 \theta = 0$ **36.** $2 \sin^3 \theta = \sin \theta - \cos^2 \theta + 1$

37. $2 \sec^3 \theta - 4 \sec \theta = 2 \tan^2 \theta + 2$ **38.** $\sec \theta + \cos \theta = \tan \theta \sin \theta - 1$

39. $\cos \left(\theta + \dfrac{\pi}{4}\right) = \sin \left(\theta + \dfrac{\pi}{4}\right)$ **40.** $2 \sin \left(\theta - \dfrac{\pi}{3}\right) = \csc \left(\theta - \dfrac{\pi}{3}\right)$

Solve for $0° \leqslant \theta < 90°$.

EXAMPLE $\sec (\theta + 10°) = \csc \theta$

SOLUTION   Since secant and cosecant are cofunctions, you can rewrite the equation in terms of one function, using the formula $\csc \theta = \sec (90° - \theta)$.

$$\sec (\theta + 10°) = \sec (90° - \theta)$$
$$\sec (\theta + 10°) = 90° - \theta + n \cdot 360° \text{ (The period of secant is 360°.)}$$
$$2\theta = 80° + n \cdot 360°$$
$$\theta = 40° + n \cdot 180°$$
$$\theta = 40°$$

41. $\sin (\theta - 32°) = \cos \theta$ **42.** $\cos (\theta + 28°) = \sin \theta$

43. $\cos (\theta + 30°) = \sin (\theta - 20°)$ **44.** $\tan (\theta + 24°) = \cot (\theta - 50°)$

45. $\tan (2\theta + 12°) = \cot (\theta - 21°)$ **46.** $\sec (2\theta - 27°) = \csc (\theta + 15°)$

47. $\csc 2\theta = \sec (60° - \theta)$ **48.** $\sin (2\theta - 18°) = \cos (\theta + 18°)$

49. $\cos (26° - 2\theta) = \sin (79° + \theta)$ **50.** $\sin (3\theta - 5°) = \cos (\theta + 15°)$

C 51. $\cot (\theta + 26°) = \tan (3\theta + 60°)$ (*Hint*: There are *two* solutions.)

52. $\tan (5\theta - 4°) = \cot (4\theta + 13°)$ (*Hint*: There are *five* solutions.)

Solve for $0 \leqslant \alpha < 2\pi$.

53. $\sec \alpha + \cos \alpha = \tan \alpha \sin \alpha - 1$ **54.** $\tan \alpha - \sec \alpha = \sqrt{3}$

55. $2 \sin \alpha \cos \alpha + 1 = -\cos \alpha - 2 \sin \alpha$ **56.** $2 \sin^4 \alpha - 2 \cos^4 \alpha = 1$

57. $\sec^4 \alpha - \tan^2 \alpha + 2 \tan \alpha - 1 = 0$ (*Hint*: The left-hand side can be written as the difference of two squares.)

SELF-TEST 2

Find the general solution in radians for θ.

1. $\sin \theta = -1$ **2.** $\cot \theta - \sqrt{3} = 0$ Section 8-4

Solve for $0° \leqslant \theta < 360°$.

3. $2 \cos^2 \theta = 3 \cos \theta - 1$ **4.** $\csc \theta + \csc^2 \theta = 2$

5. $2 \sin^2 \theta + 5 \sin \theta = 3$ **6.** $\sin 2\theta = \dfrac{\sqrt{3}}{2}$

7. $2 \tan^2 \theta + 3 \sec \theta = 0$ **8.** $\cos \theta - 3 \sec \theta = 2$ Section 8-5

9. $\cos \theta = \sin \theta \cos \theta$ **10.** $\sec \theta = 1 + \tan \theta$

Computer Exercises

This chapter introduces methods for solving many types of trigonometric equations. There are many other trigonometric equations, however, that cannot be solved by these methods. For example, the equation

$$3 \sin x = x$$

is satisfied by $x = 0$. Carefully drawn graphs of $y = 3 \sin x$ and $y = x$, using integral values of x on the x-axis, show that there are two other solutions (the x-coordinates of the intersections of the two graphs). What are these values? From the graphs you see that one solution is between 2 and 3. A computer program can give the approximate solutions.

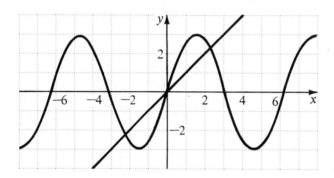

The problem is simpler to deal with if the equation is written

$$3 \sin x - x = 0.$$

The following program calculates $3*SIN(X) - X$ for $X = 2, 2.1, 2.2, \ldots, 2.9, 3.0$.

```
10   PRINT "SOLVE 3*SIN(X) — X = 0"
20   PRINT
30   PRINT "X", "3*SIN(X) — X"
40   FOR X = 2.0 TO 3.0 STEP .1
50   PRINT X, 3*SIN(X) — X
60   NEXT X
70   END
```

1. Type in and RUN the program above. You should find that the expression $3 \sin x - x$ is positive when $x = 2.2$ and negative when $x = 2.3$. Therefore, $3 \sin x - x$ must be zero for some value of x between 2.2 and 2.3.

2. Change line 40 to read:

```
40   FOR X = 2.20 TO 2.30 STEP .01
```

RUN the new program to find a better approximation to the positive solution of the equation.

3. Change line 40 to evaluate $3 \sin x - x$ by STEPs of 0.001 in the interval found in Exercise 2.

4. To the nearest hundredth, what is the positive solution of the equation?

5. Use the graphs to find the third solution of the equation.

6. Graph the equations $y = \cos x$ and $y = x^2$. How many solutions are there of the equation

$$x^2 - \cos x = 0?$$

7. Find the solutions of $x^2 - \cos x = 0$ to the nearest hundredth.

Computer solution of equations can be made much more efficient than the procedure just followed. One method involves a *binary search*. Suppose that we wish to solve an equation of the form $f(x) = 0$, where f is a *continuous* function (its graph has no skips or jumps). The user of the program supplies real numbers a and b such that $a < b$ and $f(a)$ and $f(b)$ have opposite signs. A solution must occur between a and b. The program computes $f\left(\dfrac{a+b}{2}\right)$, the value of the function at the point halfway between a and b. If $f(a)$ is of opposite sign from $f\left(\dfrac{a+b}{2}\right)$, then the root lies between a and $\dfrac{a+b}{2}$, and a new b is defined; b is given the value $\dfrac{a+b}{2}$. On the other hand, if $f(b)$ is of opposite sign from $f\left(\dfrac{a+b}{2}\right)$, then a is assigned the new value $\dfrac{a+b}{2}$. In either case, the root lies between the new values of a and b, and the new values are half as far apart as the old values were. This process of halving the interval in which the root must lie is repeated until a and b are very close together, say $|b - a| < 0.000001$.

8. Write a program to solve the equation $3 \sin x - x = 0$, using a binary search as outlined above. (You may find it convenient to use the BASIC function SGN(Y), where SGN(Y) = 1 if Y > 0, SGN(Y) = −1 if Y < 0, and SGN(Y) = 0 if Y = 0.)

CHAPTER REVIEW

Evaluate without using Table 1.

1. a. $\tan 150°$ **b.** $\cot \dfrac{2\pi}{3}$ **c.** $\csc\left(-\dfrac{\pi}{2}\right)$ Section 8-1

2. $\sin 120° \tan(-135°)$ **3.** $\sec 315° + \cot(-45°)$

4. If $\sec \theta = -2$ and $\cot \theta < 0$, find:
    a. $\tan \theta$ **b.** $\cos \theta$ **c.** $\sin \theta$

5. Simplify: **a.** $\cot \theta \sec \theta$ **b.** $(1 - \cos^2 \theta)(1 + \cot^2 \theta)$ Section 8-2

6. Express $\cos \theta$ in terms of $\sin \theta$.

Simplify. Express as a single function of θ or as a constant.

7. $\tan\left(\dfrac{\pi}{2} + \theta\right)$ **8.** $\sec(-\theta) \csc\left(\dfrac{\pi}{2} + \theta\right)$

Verify that each equation is an identity.

9. $\sin \theta + 1 = \dfrac{-\cos^2 \theta}{\sin \theta - 1}$

10. $\dfrac{\sin^2 \theta}{1 - \sin^2 \theta} = \dfrac{\tan \theta}{\cot \theta}$

Section 8-3

11. $\dfrac{\sec \theta + 1}{\sec \theta - 1} = \dfrac{\cos \theta + 1}{1 - \cos \theta}$

Solve for $0° \leqslant \theta < 360°$ to the nearest 10′. You may refer to Table 1 to solve Exercise 15.

12. $2 \sin \theta = 1$

13. $\cot^2 \theta - \sqrt{3} \cot \theta = 0$

Section 8-4

14. $(\sqrt{2} + 2 \sin \theta)(3 - \sin \theta) = 0$

15. $6 \cos^2 \theta - 7 \cos \theta + 2 = 0$

Solve for $0 \leqslant \theta < 2\pi$.

16. $3 \cot \theta = \tan \theta$

17. $\sin^2 \theta - \tan \theta \cos^2 \theta = 0$

Section 8-5

18. $2 \sin^2 \theta + 3 \cos \theta = 0$

19. $\sin^2 \theta + 2 = 3 \cos \theta \tan \theta$

CHAPTER TEST

Solve for $0° \leqslant \theta < 360°$.

1. $(2 \cos \theta - \sqrt{2})(\tan \theta + 1) = 0$

2. $\sin \theta = \sqrt{3} \cos \theta$

3. $\sin 2\theta = -1$

4. $2 \sin^2 \theta - 3 \sin \theta = -1$

5. $\cot^2 \theta = 1 + \csc \theta$

6. $\sec \theta - 4 \cos \theta = 0$

Express as a single function or constant.

7. $\tan \theta \csc \theta$

8. $\sec \theta \cos \theta$

9. $\dfrac{\sec \theta - \cos \theta}{\tan \theta}$

Complete.

10. If $\tan \theta > 0$ and $\sin \theta < 0$, then $\cos \theta \underline{\quad ? \quad} 0$.

11. If $\sec \theta < 0$ and $\tan \theta < 0$, then $\sin \theta \underline{\quad ? \quad} 0$.

12. If $\sin \theta = \dfrac{2}{3}$ and $\tan \theta < 0$, then $\cos \theta = \underline{\quad ? \quad}$.

13. If $\sec \theta = -\dfrac{4}{3}$ and $\tan \theta > 0$, then $\cot \theta = \underline{\quad ? \quad}$.

Verify that each equation is an identity.

14. $\tan^2 \theta \cos^2 \theta = 1 - \cos^2 \theta$

15. $\cot \theta + \tan \theta = \tan \theta \csc^2 \theta$

16. $(\sec \theta + 1)(1 - \cos \theta) = \dfrac{\sin^2 \theta}{\cos \theta}$

17. $\dfrac{\tan^2 \theta + 2}{\sec^2 \theta} = 1 + \cos^2 \theta$

18. a. Graph $y = \tan \theta$ and $y = \cot \theta$ on the same set of axes for $-\dfrac{\pi}{2} < \theta < \dfrac{3\pi}{2}$.

   b. Use your graph to determine what values of θ between $-\dfrac{\pi}{2}$ and $\dfrac{3\pi}{2}$ satisfy the equation $\cot \theta = \tan \theta$.

Biographical Note

Maria Gaetana Agnesi

Maria Agnesi's most important work, entitled *Analytical Institutions*, contained a discussion of the *versiera* curve shown below.

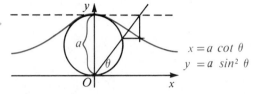

$$x = a \cot \theta$$
$$y = a \sin^2 \theta$$

The curve can be generated by rotating a line through a fixed point. "Versiera" describes this turning motion. Unfortunately, when a mathematician who published his English translation of Agnesi's Italian masterpiece in 1801 named the curve in her honor, he translated "versiera" incorrectly, and the curve became known as the "Witch of Agnesi."

A mathematician, linguist, philosopher, and philanthropist, Maria Gaetana Agnesi (1718-1799) was born in Milan, Italy. She was a child prodigy who could speak seven languages by age thirteen. While still a teenager, she presented theses in Latin, then the language of scholars, to the intellectuals that her father invited to their home. Afterward, she would discuss abstract mathematical and philosophical questions with the guests in their own languages.

When she was about twenty years old, Agnesi began to write a monumental mathematical work. For a decade she devoted herself to working on *Analytical Institutions*. When it was published in 1748, this two-volume text on algebra, analysis, and calculus created a sensation. Agnesi was universally acclaimed for her clear and comprehensive presentation of such complex mathematical material, which had to be gathered from numerous and diverse sources written in a number of languages. Agnesi also contributed a significant amount of original material to this work.

After completing *Analytical Institutions*, Agnesi devoted the remainder of her life to serving the sick, the aged, and the poor. For the last twenty-eight years of her life she was director of a home for the ill and aged.

Be sure that you understand the meaning of these terms:

tangent, p. 315
cotangent, p. 315
secant, p. 315
cosecant, p. 315
reciprocal function, p. 316

asymptote, p. 318
trigonometric identity, p. 323
Pythagorean identities, p. 323
general solution of an equation, p. 330

MIXED REVIEW

Evaluate.

1. $\dfrac{\sin 120°}{\cos 150°}$

2. $\cot 225° \cdot \csc 225°$

3. $\sin(-\theta) + \cos(90° - \theta)$

4. Given $\tan 72° = 3.078$, $\tan 72°10' = 3.108$, and $\tan \theta = 3.100$, use linear interpolation to find θ to the nearest minute.

5. Find the rational roots of $8x^3 + 14x^2 = 7x + 6$.

6. Find the images of $A(0, -3)$ and $B(-2, 5)$ under the given transformation.
   a. $D_{A, 2}$ b. $r_{y\text{-axis}}$ c. R_{270} d. $T_{-3, 0}$

7. Chords $\overline{AB}$ and $\overline{CD}$ of $\odot O$ intersect at a point, M, inside the circle. If $AM = 3x$, $MB = 4x$, $CM = 3x - 2$, and $MD = 5x - 3$, find the numerical value of CD.

8. Find the inverse, g, of $f(x) = \dfrac{1}{x - 1}$. Then show that $f(g(3)) = g(f(3))$ and $f(g(-2)) = g(f(-2))$.

9. Prove that $2 \csc^2 \theta = \dfrac{1}{1 - \cos \theta} + \dfrac{1}{1 + \cos \theta}$ is an identity.

10. If quadrilateral $ABCD$ is inscribed in $\odot P$ and $m\angle A : m\angle B : m\angle C = 3:4:6$, find the numerical measures of $\angle D$ and $\overset{\frown}{ADC}$.

Solve.

11. $|3a - 2| > 0$

12. $x^3 \geqslant 9x$

13. $v^2 - 8v + 11 = 0$

14. $2 + \sqrt{x - 2} = \sqrt{2x + 3}$

15. $\dfrac{1}{m} + \dfrac{m}{m - 1} = \dfrac{1}{6}$

16. $2(5t - 3) = -0.08$

Simplify.

17. $3\sqrt{-50} + \dfrac{4}{\sqrt{-32}}$

18. $\dfrac{i^8}{5 - 2i\sqrt{3}}$

19. $\dfrac{3}{2} \sqrt[3]{12} \cdot 4\sqrt[3]{-45}$

20. A 30-60-90 triangle is inscribed in a circle, and the shorter leg has length a. Find the circumference and the area of the circle in terms of a.

21. Which trigonometric functions are not defined for an angle θ in standard position whose terminal side passes through $(0, -4)$? Find the values of the other trigonometric functions.

22. Describe all types of symmetry that a regular pentagon has.

23. Draw a large acute triangle. Construct the inscribed circle.

24. Sketch the graph of $y = \cot \theta$ for $-\pi \leqslant \theta \leqslant 2\pi$. State the period, domain, and range of the function. Is $\cot (-\theta)$ equal to $\cot \theta$, $-\cot \theta$, or neither? Is $\cot \theta$ an even function, an odd function, or neither?

25. If line k has equation $y = -x$, $r_{x\text{-axis}} \circ r_k : (x, y) \longrightarrow \underline{\ ?\ }$ and $r_k \circ r_{x\text{-axis}} : (x, y) \longrightarrow \underline{\ ?\ }$.

26. Coffee worth $8/kg is blended with coffee worth $6/kg to produce 10 kg of a blend worth $6.70/kg. How many kilograms of each type are needed?

Simplify.

27. $\left(\dfrac{4t - \dfrac{9}{t}}{2t + 3} \right)^{-1}$

28. $\dfrac{100b^3 - 20b^2 + b}{10b^2 - 101b^3 + 10b^4}$

29. $\dfrac{3 - i}{3 + 4i}$

Solve for $0 \leqslant \alpha < 2\pi$.

30. $2 \sin^2 \alpha + 5 \sin \alpha = 3$

31. $\sec^2 \alpha = 1 - \tan \alpha$

32. $\dfrac{\cos \alpha + \sec \alpha}{\cos \alpha + \tan \alpha} = \dfrac{7}{5}$

33. Solve over the set of complex numbers: $z^2 + 8 = 4z$

34. Find the value of x in the diagram at right.

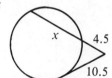

x 4.5   10.5

35. If $\csc \theta = -\dfrac{17}{15}$ and $\cos \theta < 0$, find the values of the other five trigonometric functions.

36. Evalute $a^b + b^a$ when $a = 2$ and $b = -4$.

37. Is $x^2 + y^2 = 1$ a function? Explain your answer.

38. Use Table 1 to find $\sin 204°20'$ and $\cot 297°50'$.

39. Through how many degrees and how many radians does the minute hand of a clock turn in 35 min?

40. Solve and graph the solution set: $5 - 4x \geqslant 11$ or $2 - 0.03x < 1.88$

41. Express $\dfrac{\cos \theta}{\sin \theta \tan \theta} + \sin \theta \csc \theta$ in terms of a single function.

For convenience, very small numbers and very large numbers, such as those occurring in astronomy, are often expressed in scientific notation. The relationship between scientific notation and common logarithms is discussed in this chapter. The photograph shows the spiral galaxy M83.

Exponents and Logarithms

9

Calculation has always been of great importance to scientists. Measurement yields numerical data, and these numbers demand accurate processing to yield useful information. Late in the sixteenth century this processing problem had become acute. In 1543 the theory of the great Polish astronomer Copernicus that the sun instead of Earth is the center of our planetary system was published. Much astronomical activity followed. Soon the data accumulated more rapidly than they could be processed by the arithmetic techniques available. These computations were becoming increasingly complex, involving not only addition, subtraction, multiplication, and division, but also powers, roots, and trigonometric functions. Some calculations were so complicated that they took weeks to complete!

Several mathematicians responded by developing a better computational tool, the *logarithm*. John Napier, a Scot, Henry Briggs, an Englishman, and Joost Bürgi, a Swiss, all contributed to this development, which not only simplified calculation but also answered questions long left open for lack of data-handling capacity. The work of these mathematicians set the stage for great theoreticians, such as Sir Isaac Newton, who unfolded many of the mysteries of the universe. Newton credited these and other predecessors when he said, "If I have seen far, it is because I have stood on the shoulders of giants."

Today you live at a time of a second major change in computation: the development of electronic calculators and computers. While this new calculation power has reduced the value of the logarithm as a computing tool, it has at the same time increased its value as a mathematical function. All modern scientific calculators and computers utilize the logarithm in their data processing.

Section 9-1 RATIONAL EXPONENTS

This entire chapter is about exponents. In this section you will return to the study of the properties of exponents begun in Chapter 2. You will learn:
- the meaning of rational exponents
- how to compute with rational exponents

In order to extend the properties of exponents, you should first recall what you already know. Here is a brief summary.

If a and b are real numbers, m and n are integers, and no denominator is 0, then:

Property	Example
1. When $n > 0$, $a^n = \underbrace{a \cdot a \cdot a \cdot \cdots \cdot a}_{n \text{ factors}}$	$5^3 = 5 \cdot 5 \cdot 5 = 125$
2. For $a \neq 0$, $a^0 = 1$	$\pi^0 = 1$
3. $a^{-n} = \dfrac{1}{a^n}$	$3^{-4} = \dfrac{1}{3^4} = \dfrac{1}{81}$
4. $a^m \cdot a^n = a^{m+n}$	$4^3 \cdot 4^{-2} = 4^1 = 4$
5. $\dfrac{a^m}{a^n} = a^{m-n}$	$\dfrac{4^3}{4^{-2}} = 4^5 = 1024$
6. $(a^m)^n = a^{mn}$	$(4^3)^{-2} = 4^{-6} = \dfrac{1}{4096}$
7. $a^m \cdot b^m = (ab)^m$	$2^3 \cdot 5^3 = 10^3 = 1000$
8. $\dfrac{a^m}{b^m} = \left(\dfrac{a}{b}\right)^m$	$\left(\dfrac{2}{3}\right)^4 = \dfrac{2^4}{3^4} = \dfrac{16}{81}$

When mathematicians extend rules to apply to new situations, they are careful to retain just as much as possible of what has already been developed. For example, a definition of rational exponents, such as $5^{\frac{1}{2}}$, should be such that properties 1 to 8 hold.

How then should we define $5^{\frac{1}{2}}$? If property 6 is to remain valid, it must be true that:

$$\left(5^{\frac{1}{2}}\right)^2 = 5^{\frac{1}{2} \cdot 2} = 5^1 = 5$$

This suggests that $5^{\frac{1}{2}}$ must equal $\sqrt{5}$.

With this example in mind, we define $a^{\frac{1}{n}}$: For any positive real number a and positive integer n,

$$a^{\frac{1}{n}} = \sqrt[n]{a}.$$

EXAMPLE Evaluate: **a.** $256^{\frac{1}{2}}$ **b.** $8^{\frac{1}{3}}$ **c.** $\left(\dfrac{27}{64}\right)^{\frac{1}{3}}$

SOLUTION **a.** $256^{\frac{1}{2}} = \sqrt{256} = 16$ **b.** $8^{\frac{1}{3}} = \sqrt[3]{8} = 2$

c. $\left(\dfrac{27}{64}\right)^{\frac{1}{3}} = \sqrt[3]{\dfrac{27}{64}} = \dfrac{3}{4}$

Now consider the expression $a^{\frac{p}{q}}$. Since $\frac{p}{q} = p \cdot \frac{1}{q} = \frac{1}{q} \cdot p$, we have:

$$a^{\frac{p}{q}} = a^{p \cdot \frac{1}{q}} = (a^p)^{\frac{1}{q}} = \sqrt[q]{a^p}$$

and

$$a^{\frac{p}{q}} = a^{\frac{1}{q} \cdot p} = \left(a^{\frac{1}{q}}\right)^p = (\sqrt[q]{a})^p$$

We define $a^{\frac{p}{q}}$: For any positive real number a and integers p and q, $q > 0$,

$$a^{\frac{p}{q}} = \sqrt[q]{a^p} = (\sqrt[q]{a})^p$$

To recall this definition, remember: $a^{\frac{p}{q}}$ $p \leftarrow$ **power** $q \leftarrow$ **root**

With this definition, we have now extended the concept of exponents to include all rational numbers. The laws of exponents, which were originally stated for integral exponents, apply to rational exponents as well.

EXAMPLE   Evaluate: **a.** $8^{\frac{2}{3}}$ **b.** $32^{-\frac{2}{5}}$

SOLUTION   **a.** $8^{\frac{2}{3}} = (\sqrt[3]{8})^2 = 2^2 = 4$

           b. $32^{-\frac{2}{5}} = 32^{\frac{-2}{5}} = (\sqrt[5]{32})^{-2} = 2^{-2} = \frac{1}{4}$

EXAMPLE   Simplify: $6^{\frac{3}{2}}$

SOLUTION $6^{\frac{3}{2}} = \sqrt{6^3} = \sqrt{6^2}\sqrt{6} = 6\sqrt{6}$

Sometimes equations involve variables in exponents. Use the fact that for $a > 0$ and $a \neq 1, a^m = a^n$ if and only if $m = n$.

EXAMPLE   Solve: $81^x = 9^{x+1}$

SOLUTION   Substitute 9^2 for 81 in order to make the bases the same.

$$81^x = 9^{x+1}$$
$$(9^2)^x = 9^{x+1}$$
$$9^{2x} = 9^{x+1}$$
$$2x = x + 1$$
$$x = 1$$

Check: $81^1 \overset{?}{=} 9^{1+1}$

         $81 \overset{?}{=} 9^2$

         $81 = 81$

ORAL EXERCISES

Express each of the following as a power of x.

1. $x^{\frac{1}{2}} \cdot x^{\frac{1}{2}}$

2. $x \cdot x^{\frac{1}{2}}$

3. $\dfrac{x}{x^{\frac{1}{2}}}$

4. $\left(x^{\frac{1}{3}}\right)^6$

Evaluate.

5. $27^{\frac{1}{3}}$

6. $-\left(27^{\frac{1}{3}}\right)$

7. $27^{-\frac{1}{3}}$

8. $-\left(27^{-\frac{1}{3}}\right)$

9. $4^{\frac{1}{2}}$

10. $-\left(4^{\frac{1}{2}}\right)$

11. $4^{-\frac{1}{2}}$

12. $-\left(4^{-\frac{1}{2}}\right)$

13. $25^{\frac{3}{2}}$

14. $1000^{\frac{2}{3}}$

15. $16^{\frac{5}{4}}$

16. $16^{\frac{3}{2}}$

WRITTEN EXERCISES

Simplify. Express answers that are irrational in simplest radical form.

A 1. $9^{\frac{1}{2}}$

2. $64^{\frac{2}{3}}$

3. $3^{\frac{1}{2}}$

4. $27^{\frac{4}{3}}$

5. $81^{\frac{3}{4}}$

6. $\left(\dfrac{9}{16}\right)^{\frac{3}{2}}$

7. $\left(\dfrac{9}{16}\right)^{-\frac{3}{2}}$

8. $81^{-\frac{3}{4}}$

9. $5^{\frac{5}{2}}$

10. $\left(3^{\frac{2}{3}}\right)^0$

11. $\left(\dfrac{1}{25}\right)^{-\frac{1}{2}}$

12. $\left(\dfrac{1}{16}\right)^{-\frac{1}{2}}$

13. $\left(\dfrac{1}{25}\right)^{-2}$

14. $\left(\dfrac{1}{16}\right)^{-2}$

15. $\dfrac{12^0}{9^{-\frac{3}{2}}}$

16. $8^{\frac{5}{3}}$

Evaluate $x^{\frac{1}{2}}$, $x^{\frac{3}{2}}$, and $x^{\frac{5}{2}}$ for the given value of x.

17. $x = 4$

18. $x = 25$

19. $x = \dfrac{1}{16}$

20. $x = 0.01$

Rewrite each of the following using fractional exponents.

21. $5\sqrt{x}$

22. $\sqrt[3]{5x^2}$

23. $\sqrt[5]{(x-y)^2}$

24. $\sqrt[5]{x^4 y^3}$

Write in simplest radical form.

25. $\dfrac{5^3}{5^{\frac{1}{2}}}$

26. $2^{\frac{1}{2}} + 2^{\frac{1}{2}}$

27. $12^{\frac{3}{4}} \cdot 12^{\frac{3}{4}}$

Solve.

28. $3^{2x} = 3^{x+5}$

29. $4^{x+5} = 64$

30. $5^{2x-1} = 125$

B 31. $8^x = 2^{2x+1}$

32. $27^x = 9^{x-1}$

33. $2^{x^2-5x} = 2^6$

Let $f(x) = x^{\frac{3}{2}}$, $g(x) = x^{-\frac{2}{3}}$, and $h(x) = 4^x$. Evaluate.

34. $f(9)$

35. $g(125)$

36. $h(0)$

37. $h\left(-\frac{3}{2}\right)$

38. $f\left(\frac{1}{4}\right)$

39. $f^{-1}(8)$

40. $g(0.001)$

41. $h^{-1}(16)$

42. $h^{-1}\left(\frac{1}{2}\right)$

43. $[f \circ h](2)$

44. $[g \circ f](4)$

45. $[g \circ h]\left(\frac{3}{2}\right)$

Is the given statement true for all positive values of x and y?

46. $\sqrt[3]{x^4}\,\sqrt[3]{y^5} = \sqrt[3]{x^4 y^5}$

47. $3\sqrt{x} = \sqrt{9x}$

48. $\sqrt{x} + \sqrt{x} = x$

49. $\sqrt{\sqrt{x}} = \sqrt[4]{x}$

50. $\sqrt[3]{\sqrt{y}} = \sqrt[5]{y}$

51. $y^2\sqrt{y} = \sqrt{y^5}$

52. $\dfrac{\sqrt{x}}{\sqrt[6]{x}} = \sqrt[4]{x}$

53. $\sqrt{x^{-2}} = \dfrac{1}{x}$

54. $x^{-3}\sqrt{x} = \dfrac{1}{\sqrt{x^5}}$

55. $\sqrt[6]{x^2} = \sqrt[3]{x}$

Write in simplest radical form.

56. $\sqrt[3]{b^8}$

57. $\sqrt{5^{-3}}$

58. $\sqrt[4]{9^9}$

EXAMPLE Write $\sqrt{2}\,\sqrt[4]{3}$ as a single radical.

SOLUTION $\sqrt{2}\,\sqrt[4]{3} = 2^{\frac{1}{2}} \cdot 3^{\frac{1}{4}}$

$= 2^{\frac{2}{4}} \cdot 3^{\frac{1}{4}}$

$= (2^2)^{\frac{1}{4}} \cdot 3^{\frac{1}{4}}$

$= 4^{\frac{1}{4}} \cdot 3^{\frac{1}{4}}$

$= (4 \cdot 3)^{\frac{1}{4}}$

$= \sqrt[4]{12}$

Write as a single radical.

C 59. $\sqrt{3}\,\sqrt[3]{2}$

60. $\sqrt{2}\,\sqrt[3]{3}$

61. $\sqrt[3]{2}\,\sqrt[4]{5}$

Complete with $>$, $<$, or $=$ to make the statement true.

62. For $x > 1$, $y > 1$, x^y __?__ x.

63. For $0 < x < 1$, $y > 1$, x^y __?__ x.

64. For $0 < x < 1$, $0 < y < 1$, x^y __?__ x.

65. For $x > 1$, $0 < y < 1$, x^y __?__ x.

Section 9-2 EXPONENTIAL FUNCTIONS

In Section 9-1 your understanding of exponents was extended from integers to rational numbers. In this section you will use your knowledge of exponents to:
• graph exponential functions
• further extend the idea of exponents to include the real numbers

A function of the form

$$f(x) = a^x \quad (a > 0, \ a \neq 1)$$

is called an exponential function with base a.

The functions $f(x) = 2^x$, $g(x) = 10^x$, and $h(x) = \left(\frac{1}{2}\right)^x$ are examples of exponential functions. Several values of $f(x) = 2^x$ are shown in the table, and the corresponding points are shown in the graph. A little thought should convince you that if some additional points of the function are plotted, then those to the left ($x = -4, -5, \ldots$) will get closer and closer to the x-axis and those to the right ($x = 4, 5, \ldots$) will climb higher very rapidly.

x	2^x
-3	$\frac{1}{8}$
-2	$\frac{1}{4}$
-1	$\frac{1}{2}$
0	1
1	2
2	4
3	8

But what happens between those points already plotted? As you might guess, the graph of $f(x) = 2^x$ is a smooth curve through the points already plotted, and f is an increasing function. Using $\sqrt{2} \approx 1.4$, you can verify this by calculating more values and plotting the corresponding points.

x	2^x	
$\frac{1}{2}$	$2^{\frac{1}{2}} \approx 1.4$	$\left(2^{\frac{1}{2}} = \sqrt{2}\right)$
$1\frac{1}{2}$	$2^{1\frac{1}{2}} \approx 2.8$	$\left(2^{1\frac{1}{2}} = 2^1 \cdot 2^{\frac{1}{2}}\right)$
$2\frac{1}{2}$	$2^{2\frac{1}{2}} \approx 5.7$	
$-\frac{1}{2}$	$2^{-\frac{1}{2}} \approx 0.71$	$\left(2^{-\frac{1}{2}} = \frac{1}{\sqrt{2}}\right)$
$-1\frac{1}{2}$	$2^{-1\frac{1}{2}} \approx 0.35$	
$-2\frac{1}{2}$	$2^{-2\frac{1}{2}} \approx 0.18$	

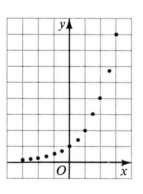
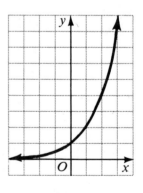

The assumption we have made in filling in the intermediate points with a smooth curve corresponds to the assumption that 2^x has a value for any real number x. This means that not only are there values of 2^x for rational values of x, like $2^{\frac{2}{3}}$ and $2^{0.37}$, which we could think of as $(\sqrt[3]{2})^2$ and $(\sqrt[100]{2})^{37}$, but also values like $2^{\sqrt{3}}$ and even 2^π. Although you will calculate in most exercises with rational powers, the rules you have learned apply to all real exponents as well. Thus, for example:

$$\pi^\pi \cdot \pi^{\sqrt{2}} = \pi^{\pi + \sqrt{2}}$$

The graph of any exponential function whose base is greater than 1 has the same general form as the graph of $f(x) = 2^x$. As shown on the left below, for different values of the base, a, the steepness of the graph of $f(x) = a^x$ will be different from that of $f(x) = 2^x$.

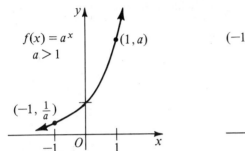
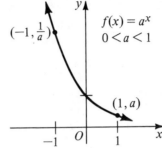

A representative graph of $f(x) = a^x$, for $0 < a < 1$, is shown on the right above. Notice that this is a decreasing function. This is consistent with your knowledge that if $0 < a < 1$ and $m < n$, then $a^m > a^n$. For example,

$$\left(\frac{1}{2}\right)^2 > \left(\frac{1}{2}\right)^3$$

Since a is positive in our definition of an exponential function, a^x is always positive. For any exponential function $f(x) = a^x$ ($a > 0$, $a \neq 1$), the domain is the set of real numbers and the range is the set of positive real numbers.

ORAL EXERCISES

Use the graph of $f(x) = 2^x$ on page 350 to estimate each value to the nearest whole number.

1. $f(2.3)$ 2. $f(0.8)$ 3. $f(1.6)$ 4. $f(0.1)$

5. $f(2.6)$ 6. $f(1.9)$ 7. $f(-0.2)$ 8. $f(-2.8)$

Use the graph of $f(x) = 2^x$ on page 350 to estimate the value of x to the nearest tenth.

9. $f(x) = 6.5$ 10. $2^x = 5$ 11. $f(x) = 3.2$ 12. $2^x = 0.8$

For each of the following functions, (a) tell whether the function is increasing or decreasing, and (b) indicate in which quadrants its graph lies.

13. $f(x) = 2^x$ 14. $f(x) = \left(\frac{1}{2}\right)^x$ 15. $f(x) = (0.1)^x$ 16. $f(x) = -(3^x)$

WRITTEN EXERCISES

A **1. a.** Graph the functions $f(x) = 2^x$ and $g(x) = x^2$ on the same set of axes.
  b. Use the graphs to estimate the solutions of the equation $2^x = x^2$ to the nearest tenth.
  c. Which graph is steeper for $1 < x < 3$?

2. a. Graph the functions $f(x) = 2^x$ and $g(x) = 3^x$ on the same set of axes.
  b. Find the y-intercept of each graph.
  c. Which graph is steeper for $x > 0$?
  d. Which graph is above the other for $x > 0$? for $x < 0$?

3. a. Graph the functions $f(x) = 3^x$ and $g(x) = \left(\dfrac{1}{3}\right)^x$ on the same set of axes.
  b. Find the y-intercept of each graph.
  c. How are the two graphs related to each other?

4. a. Graph the functions $f(x) = \left(\dfrac{1}{2}\right)^x$ and $g(x) = \left(\dfrac{1}{3}\right)^x$ on the same set of axes.
  b. Find the y-intercept of each graph.
  c. Which graph is above the other for $x > 0$? for $x < 0$?
  d. Which graph is steeper for $x < 0$?

Name the function whose graph is above the other in Quadrant I.

5. $f(x) = 3^x$; $g(x) = 5^x$

6. $f(x) = \left(\dfrac{1}{2}\right)^x$; $g(x) = \left(\dfrac{1}{5}\right)^x$

7. $f(x) = \left(\dfrac{1}{3}\right)^x$; $g(x) = 3^x$

8. $f(x) = x$; $g(x) = 2^x$

9. $f(x) = 4^x$; $g(x) = 2^x$

10. $f(x) = \left(\dfrac{1}{3}\right)^x$; $g(x) = \left(\dfrac{1}{5}\right)^x$

11. $f(x) = \left(\dfrac{1}{2}\right)^x$; $g(x) = 2^x$

12. $f(x) = \left(\dfrac{1}{3}\right)^x$; $g(x) = 2^x$

If $f(x) = 2^x$, use $\sqrt{2} \approx 1.4$ to evaluate each of the following to the nearest tenth.

B **13.** $f\left(4\dfrac{1}{2}\right)$

14. $f(-3.5)$

Let $2^{\frac{1}{3}} = m$. Express each of the following in terms of m.

EXAMPLE $\quad 2^{2\frac{1}{3}}$ $\qquad$ **SOLUTION** $\quad 2^{2\frac{1}{3}} = 2^{\left(2 + \frac{1}{3}\right)} = 2^2 \cdot 2^{\frac{1}{3}} = 4m$

15. $2^{1\frac{1}{3}}$ $\qquad$ **16.** $2^{-\frac{1}{3}}$ $\qquad$ **17.** $2^{\frac{2}{3}}$ $\qquad$ **18.** $\dfrac{1}{4}$

Graph each function.

19. $y = 2^x + 1$ $\qquad$ **20.** $f: x \longrightarrow 2^{x+1}$

C **21.** $g(x) = 3^{x-2}$ **22.** $y = 2^{|x|}$

23. Graph the function $y = 2^{-x}$. How does this graph compare with the graph of $y = 2^x$?

24. Graph the function $x = 2^y$. How does this graph compare with the graph of $y = 2^x$?

25. State a reason for not defining $a^{\frac{p}{q}}$ for $a < 0$.

Section 9-3 LOGARITHMS

Your earlier work with exponents and exponential functions has prepared you to study a new kind of function called a logarithmic function. In this section you will learn:
- the relationship between the exponential function $f(x) = b^x$ and the logarithmic function $g(x) = \log_b x$
- to evaluate some logarithms
- how to graph a logarithmic function

Here is a table of values for the exponential function $f(x) = 10^x$.

x	-3	-2	-1	0	1	2	3
$f(x)$	0.001	0.01	0.1	1	10	100	1000

Since f is a one-to-one function, it has an inverse, f^{-1}. By using the table of values for f, we can find some values of f^{-1}. For example,

$$f^{-1}(0.001) = -3 \quad \text{because} \quad f(-3) = 0.001.$$

A table of values of f^{-1} is shown below.

x	0.001	0.01	0.1	1	10	100	1000
$f^{-1}(x)$	-3	-2	-1	0	1	2	3

For convenience, the notation $\log_{10} x$, read "the logarithm of x to the base 10," has been adopted for this function. Thus we can write

$$f^{-1}(x) = \log_{10} x, \quad \text{or} \quad y = \log_{10} x,$$

for this function. This function is called the *logarithmic function to the base 10*. The domain is the set of positive real numbers and the range is the set of real numbers.

Using the table above, we have, for example,

$$\log_{10} 0.01 = -2, \quad \log_{10} 1 = 0, \quad \text{and} \quad \log_{10} 1000 = 3.$$

Since f and f^{-1} are inverses, you know that $[f \circ f^{-1}](x) = x$ and $[f^{-1} \circ f](x) = x$. In particular you have:

$$[f \circ f^{-1}](x) = f(f^{-1}(x)) = f(\log_{10} x) = 10^{\log_{10} x} = x \quad (x > 0)$$
$$[f^{-1} \circ f](x) = f^{-1}(f(x)) = f^{-1}(10^x) = \log_{10} 10^x = x$$

To summarize, the exponential and logarithmic functions to the base 10 are related as follows:

$$\log_{10} 10^x = x \qquad\qquad 10^{\log_{10} x} = x \quad (x > 0)$$

Suppose we are given that

$$\log_{10} c = d.$$

Then

$$10^{\log_{10} c} = 10^d$$
$$c = 10^d$$

The equations $\log_{10} c = d$ and $c = 10^d$ are equivalent. The logarithm may be thought of as an exponent.

EXAMPLE   Evaluate: $\log_{10} 1{,}000{,}000$

SOLUTION   Let $\log_{10} 1{,}000{,}000 = u$. Then $1{,}000{,}000 = 10^u$, so that $u = 6$.
$\log_{10} 1{,}000{,}000 = 6$

As you will see in Section 9-5, base 10 logarithms are of special interest because they simplify computation. The concept of logarithm applies, however, to any positive base except 1.

For any exponential function

$$f(x) = b^x \quad (b > 0,\ b \neq 1)$$

there is an inverse function. The inverse function, called a logarithmic function, is denoted

$$f^{-1}(x) = \log_b x \quad (b > 0,\ b \neq 1)$$

where $\log_b x$ is read "the logarithm of x to the base b."

Since the logarithmic function is the inverse of the exponential function with the same base, there are relationships similar to those developed earlier for base 10 logarithms:

$$\log_b b^x = x \qquad\qquad b^{\log_b x} = x, \quad x > 0$$

Also, we find that if

$$\log_b c = d, \quad \text{then} \quad b^{\log_b c} = b^d, \text{ or } c = b^d.$$

The equations $\log_b c = d$ and $c = b^d$ are equivalent.

EXAMPLE   Evaluate: $\log_2 8$

SOLUTION   Let $\log_2 8 = u$.
Then $8 = 2^u$, so that $u = 3$.
$\log_2 8 = 3$

EXAMPLE   Evaluate: $\log_9 3$

SOLUTION 1   Let $\log_9 3 = u$.
Then $3 = 9^u$.

We know that $3 = \sqrt{9} = 9^{\frac{1}{2}}$

By substitution:

$9^{\frac{1}{2}} = 9^u$, and $u = \dfrac{1}{2}$

$\log_9 3 = \dfrac{1}{2}$

SOLUTION 2 $3 = 9^u$

$3 = (3^2)^u$

$3^1 = 3^{2u}$

$1 = 2u$

$u = \dfrac{1}{2}$

$\log_9 3 = \dfrac{1}{2}$

You have already found that a logarithmic function is closely related to an exponential function. To see this geometrically, the graphs of a logarithmic function and the corresponding exponential function can be plotted together. For the sake of illustration we use the functions $y = 2^x$ and $y = \log_2 x$. Tables of values for these functions are shown below.

x		-3	-2	-1	0	1	2	3
$y = 2^x$		$\dfrac{1}{8}$	$\dfrac{1}{4}$	$\dfrac{1}{2}$	1	2	4	8

x		$\dfrac{1}{8}$	$\dfrac{1}{4}$	$\dfrac{1}{2}$	1	2	4	8
$y = \log_2 x$		-3	-2	-1	0	1	2	3

Note that, by drawing the graphs as smooth curves, we have assumed that the logarithm is a function of values of x other than powers of 2. In fact, it is a function whose domain is the set of all positive real numbers.

Placed together, the graphs display an attractive symmetry. In fact, each graph is the reflection of the other over the line $y = x$. The graphs emphasize the fact that the exponential and logarithmic functions with the same base are inverse functions.

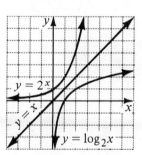

ORAL EXERCISES

Use the equivalence of the equations

$$\log_b c = d \quad \text{and} \quad c = b^d$$

to state an equivalent equation.

1. $1000 = 10^3$

2. $0.01 = 10^{-2}$

3. $16 = 2^4$

4. $\log_{10} 100 = 2$

5. $\log_{10} 10{,}000 = 4$

6. $3^{-2} = \dfrac{1}{9}$

7. $\log_2 8 = 3$

8. $5^3 = 125$

9. $\log_3 1 = 0$

10. $3^4 = 81$

11. $\log_9 27 = 1\dfrac{1}{2}$

12. $\left(\dfrac{1}{4}\right)^{-\frac{1}{2}} = 2$

EXPONENTS AND LOGARITHMS   **355**

Evaluate.

13. $\log_{10} 100,000$ **14.** $\log_2 4$ **15.** $\log_2 \dfrac{1}{8}$

16. $\log_{10} 0.001$ **17.** $\log_{10} 1$ **18.** $\log_2 32$

19. $\log_{10} 10$ **20.** $\log_2 \sqrt{2}$ **21.** $\log_2 0.25$

22. $\log_2 2\sqrt{2}$ **23.** $\log_{10} \sqrt[3]{10}$ **24.** $\log_{10} \sqrt[4]{1000}$

25. For $b > 1$, is $f(x) = \log_b x$ an increasing or a decreasing function?

26. In what quadrants does the graph of $y = \log_2 x$ lie?

27. In what quadrants does the graph of $y = \log_{10} x$ lie?

28. Are there any values of x for which $\log_2 x = 2^x$? (*Hint*: See the graphs on page 355.)

WRITTEN EXERCISES

Evaluate.

A **1.** $\log_3 9$ **2.** $\log_4 64$ **3.** $\log_4 2$

4. $\log_2 64$ **5.** $\log_5 1$ **6.** $\log_3 81$

7. $\log_6 \dfrac{1}{36}$ **8.** $\log_4 \dfrac{1}{2}$ **9.** $\log_{\frac{1}{2}} \dfrac{1}{4}$

10. $\log_9 \dfrac{1}{3}$ **11.** $\log_3 \dfrac{1}{9}$ **12.** $\log_5 0.04$

13. $\log_{16} 64$ **14.** $\log_9 243$ **15.** $\log_4 \dfrac{1}{8}$

Solve.

16. $\log_5 x = 4$ **17.** $\log_x 32 = 5$ **18.** $\log_6 x = 2$

19. $\log_x 5 = -1$ **20.** $\log_x \dfrac{1}{8} = 3$ **21.** $\log_x \dfrac{1}{8} = -1$

22. $\log_x \dfrac{1}{8} = -3$ **23.** $\log_4 x = 2.5$ **24.** $\log_8 x = 2\dfrac{1}{3}$

B **25.** $\log_x 3 = 2$ **26.** $\log_{25} x = \dfrac{1}{4}$ **27.** $\log_x \dfrac{2}{3} = -\dfrac{1}{2}$

28. $\log_x 0.125 = -1.5$ **29.** $\log_x 4 = -\dfrac{2}{3}$ **30.** $\log_x 2 = 3$

Evaluate.

31. **a.** $\log_3 27$ **b.** $\log_3 9$ **c.** $\log_3 (27 \cdot 9)$ **d.** $\log_3 \dfrac{27}{9}$

32. **a.** $\log_2 8$ **b.** $\log_2 (8^2)$ **c.** $\log_2 \sqrt[3]{8}$

33. a. $\log_3 81$ **b.** $\log_3 \dfrac{1}{9}$ **c.** $\log_3 \left(81 \cdot \dfrac{1}{9}\right)$ **d.** $\log_3 \sqrt{81}$

Graph the two functions on the same set of axes.

C 34. $y = 3^x$; $y = \log_3 x$ **35.** $y = \log_2 x$; $y = \log_3 x$

36. $y = \log_2 x$; $y = \log_{\frac{1}{2}} x$ **37.** $y = \log_{\frac{1}{2}} x$; $y = \log_{\frac{1}{3}} x$

38. For what values of x is $\log_2 x < \log_3 x$?   **39.** For what values of x is $\log_2 x > \log_3 x$?

SELF-TEST 1

Simplify.

1. $27^{\frac{2}{3}}$ **2.** $\left(\dfrac{2}{3}\right)^{-2}$ **3.** $100^{\frac{5}{2}}$ **4.** $\left(\dfrac{4}{25}\right)^{-\frac{3}{2}}$ Section 9-1

Solve.

5. $2^{x+3} = 32$ **6.** $3^{2x-1} = 27$ **7.** $5^{3-2x} = 25$

Name the function whose graph is steeper.

8. $f(x) = 3^x$; $g(x) = 4^x$ for $x > 0$ **9.** $f(x) = \left(\dfrac{1}{3}\right)^x$; $g(x) = \left(\dfrac{1}{4}\right)^x$ for $x < 0$ Section 9-2

10. Graph the functions $f(x) = 2^x$ and $g(x) = \left(\dfrac{1}{2}\right)^x$ on the same set of axes.

Evaluate.

11. $\log_4 16$ **12.** $\log_9 3$ **13.** $\log_2 \dfrac{1}{8}$ **14.** $\log_8 \dfrac{1}{4}$ Section 9-3

Solve.

15. $\log_x 64 = 3$ **16.** $\log_5 x = -3$ **17.** $\log_x 16 = -4$

Section 9-4 PROPERTIES OF LOGARITHMS

Since a logarithm is an exponent, the properties of logarithms you will study in this section are closely related to the properties of exponents you learned about in earlier sections.

Logarithms have the following basic properties. (Recall that the definition of $\log_b x$ requires that $b > 0$ and $b \neq 1$.)

1. $\log_b (xy) = \log_b x + \log_b y$

2. $\log_b \left(\dfrac{x}{y}\right) = \log_b x - \log_b y$

3. $\log_b x^n = n \log_b x$

EXAMPLE   Express as a sum: $\log_5 (2 \cdot 7)$

SOLUTION   Use property 1.

$$\log_5 (2 \cdot 7) = \log_5 2 + \log_5 7$$

Note that we use the properties even when we do not know a numerical value for $\log_5 2$ or $\log_5 7$.

EXAMPLE   Simplify: $\log_3 24 - \log_3 6$

SOLUTION   Use property 2.

$$\log_3 24 - \log_3 6 = \log_3 \left(\frac{24}{6} \right)$$
$$= \log_3 4$$

EXAMPLE   Express $\log_7 32$ as a multiple of $\log_7 2$.

SOLUTION   Use property 3.

$$\log_7 32 = \log_7 2^5$$
$$= 5 \log_7 2$$

These properties can be proved by using properties of exponents and the inverse function relationship developed earlier, that is,

$$b^{\log_b x} = x.$$

Now consider a proof of the property $\log_b(xy) = \log_b x + \log_b y$. Statements 1, 2, and 3 are all applications of the relationship $b^{\log_b x} = x$.

1. $xy = b^{\log_b (xy)}$

2. $x = b^{\log_b x}$

3. $y = b^{\log_b y}$

4. $xy = b^{\log_b x} \cdot b^{\log_b y}$ Multiplication Property of Equality, steps 2 and 3.

5. $xy = b^{\log_b x + \log_b y}$ $b^m \cdot b^n = b^{m + n}$

6. $b^{\log_b (xy)} = b^{\log_b x + \log_b y}$ Substitution from step 1.

7. $\log_b(xy) = \log_b x + \log_b y$ If $a^m = a^n$, then $m = n$.

Notice that once the expressions involved are written with exponents, the properties of exponents studied earlier can be used. Proofs of the other two logarithm properties are similar and are left as Exercises 40 and 41.

A fourth logarithm property is often stated:

$$\log_b \sqrt[r]{x} = \frac{1}{r} \log_b x$$

This is, however, simply a special case of the property $\log_b x^n = n \log_b x$.

$$\log_b \sqrt[r]{x} = \log_b x^{\frac{1}{r}} = \frac{1}{r} \log_b x$$

It is important that you become adept at using these basic properties to transform logarithmic expressions.

EXAMPLE   Express as a single logarithm: $3 \log_5 4 - \frac{4}{3} \log_5 8$

SOLUTION $3 \log_5 4 - \frac{4}{3} \log_5 8 = \log_5 4^3 - \log_5 8^{\frac{4}{3}}$

$$= \log_5 64 - \log_5 16$$

$$= \log_5 \frac{64}{16}$$

$$= \log_5 4$$

EXAMPLE   Write an expression equivalent to $\log_2 \dfrac{\sqrt[5]{6}}{15}$ in which the only logarithms are those of prime numbers.

SOLUTION $\log_2 \dfrac{\sqrt[5]{6}}{15} = \log_2 \sqrt[5]{6} - \log_2 15$

$$= \frac{1}{5} \log_2 6 - \log_2 15$$

$$= \frac{1}{5}(\log_2 2 + \log_2 3) - (\log_2 3 + \log_2 5)$$

$$= \frac{1}{5}(1 + \log_2 3) - (\log_2 3 + \log_2 5)$$

$$= \frac{1}{5} - \frac{4}{5} \log_2 3 - \log_2 5$$

Two warnings are in order.

1. No general property applies to $\log_b(x + y)$ or $\log_b(x - y)$.

2. No general property applies to $\dfrac{\log_b x}{\log_b y}$. Do not confuse this with $\log_b\left(\dfrac{x}{y}\right)$

ORAL EXERCISES

Use one of the basic properties of logarithms to replace each of the following with an equivalent expression.

1. $\log_{10}(3 \cdot 2)$ **2.** $\log_5 \dfrac{2}{3}$ **3.** $\log_2 3^2$ **4.** $3 \log_5 2$

5. $\log_{10} 56 - \log_{10} 7$ **6.** $\log_5 8 + \log_5 6$ **7.** $\log_3 \sqrt{5}$ **8.** $\dfrac{1}{3} \log_5 8$

Classify as true or false and give a reason for your answer.

9. $\log_{10} 2 + \log_{10} 3 = \log_{10} 5$

10. $\log_{10} 7 + \log_{10} 3 = \log_{10} 21$

11. $\log_5 8 - \log_5 2 = \log_5 4$

12. $\log_8 125 = 5 \log_8 3$

13. $\log_5 \dfrac{1}{3} = -\log_5 3$

14. $\log_7 12 = \log_7 3 + \log_7 4$

Solve for x.

15. $\log_5 x = \log_5 2 + \log_5 3$

16. $\log_3 x = \log_3 48 - \log_3 4$

17. $\log_2 x = 4 \log_2 3$

18. $\log_{10} x = \dfrac{1}{2} \log_{10} 49$

WRITTEN EXERCISES

Replace each expression with one involving only logarithms of prime numbers.

A 1. $\log_{10} 6$ 2. $\log_5 9$ 3. $\log_3 \dfrac{2}{5}$ 4. $\log_5 12$ 5. $\log_{10} 18$ 6. $\log_5 \dfrac{4}{3}$

7. $\log_5 \dfrac{3}{7}$ 8. $\log_6 21$ 9. $\log_4 \dfrac{1}{5}$ 10. $\log_3 \dfrac{1}{4}$ 11. $\log_6 \sqrt{7}$ 12. $\log_5 \sqrt[3]{13}$

Simplify.

13. $\log_6 9 + \log_6 4$

14. $\log_4 12 - \log_4 3$

15. $\log_4 7 + \log_4 \dfrac{1}{7}$

16. $\log_{10} 5 + \log_{10} 2$

17. $\log_{10} 300 - \log_{10} 3$

18. $\log_5 \dfrac{2}{3} + \log_5 \dfrac{75}{2}$

Replace each expression with an expression involving only $\log_m a$, $\log_m b$, $\log_m c$, and numerical coefficients. If this cannot be done, so state.

19. $\log_m ab$

20. $\log_m \dfrac{b}{c}$

21. $\log_m a^3$

22. $\log_m \sqrt[5]{b}$

B 23. $\dfrac{\log_m a}{\log_m c}$

24. $\log_m (a - b)$

25. $\log_m a^2 b$

26. $\log_m \dfrac{ab}{c}$

27. $\log_m a\sqrt{b}$

28. $\log_m \sqrt{ab}$

29. $\log_m b^2 \sqrt{c}$

30. $\log_m (ab)^3$

If $\log_m x = a$, $\log_m y = b$, and $\log_m z = c$, express each of the following in terms of a, b, and c.

31. $\log_m x^3$

32. $\log_m \dfrac{x}{y}$

33. $\log_m xyz$

34. $\log_m \dfrac{x^2 y}{z}$

35. $\log_m \sqrt{y}$

36. $\log_m x^2 \sqrt[3]{z}$

37. $\log_m \dfrac{x}{\sqrt{y}}$

38. $\log_m \sqrt[3]{\dfrac{x}{y}}$

39. $\log_m \sqrt{(xyz)^3}$

Prove each of the following properties. In each case, x, y, a, and b are positive real numbers.

C **40.** $\log_b \dfrac{x}{y} = \log_b x - \log_b y$ **41.** $\log_b x^n = n \log_b x$

42. $\log_b \dfrac{1}{x} = -\log_b x$ **43.** $\log_b ab^n = n + \log_b a$

Section 9-5 SCIENTIFIC NOTATION AND LOGARITHMS

Scientific notation is a method of writing numbers that is especially useful for extremely large and extremely small numbers. It is considered here because it is also useful in the study of logarithms. In this section you will learn:

- how to represent decimal numbers in scientific notation
- how to convert numbers expressed in scientific notation to standard decimal form
- how scientific notation is related to logarithms

The mass of Earth is about 5,980,000,000,000,000,000,000 metric tons. The average radius of an atom of silver is less than 0.00000003 cm. Unless you especially enjoy writing zeros, writing these numbers is a chore; calculating with them is even worse. For these reasons scientists use a system of notation called scientific notation to write numbers.

In scientific notation a number is expressed as the product of two factors:

1. A first factor n, with $1 \leqslant n < 10$
2. A second factor that is a power of 10

In scientific notation, the mass of Earth is about 5.98×10^{21} metric tons and the radius of an atom of silver is less than 3×10^{-8} cm.

The basis for scientific notation is the role of ten in decimal numeration. You should recall from arithmetic the ease of multiplying and dividing by powers of ten.

$$32 \times 100 = 3200 \qquad 52.46 \times 0.01 = 52.46 \div 100 = 0.5246$$
$$6.7 \div 1000 = 0.0067 \qquad 0.003 \times 10{,}000 = 30$$

All of these computations can be done by moving the decimal point in one of the factors. In fact, when the power of ten is written in exponential form, the number of places the decimal point is moved is the same as the absolute value of the exponent.

$32 \times 100 = 32 \times 10^2 = 3200$ 32.00

$6.7 \div 1000 = 6.7 \div 10^3 = 6.7 \times 10^{-3} = 0.0067$ 0.006.7

$52.46 \times 0.01 = 52.46 \times 10^{-2} = 0.5246$ 0.52.46

$0.003 \times 10{,}000 = 0.003 \times 10^4 = 30$ 0.0030.

Notice how extra zeros are annexed as needed.

These relationships lead to the following rules.

To change a number from decimal form to scientific notation:

1. Place the decimal point to give a number between 1 and 10.
2. Multiply this number by a power of 10. The exponent is determined by the number of places the decimal point must be moved to return to its original position. If the decimal point must be moved to the right, the exponent is positive. If the decimal point must be moved to the left, the exponent is negative.

EXAMPLE   Write in scientific notation: **a.** 57,600   **b.** 0.034

SOLUTION   **a.** Place the decimal point: 5.7600
To return to its original position, the decimal point must be moved 4 places to the right: 5.7600.

$$57,600 = 5.76 \times 10^4$$

b. Place the decimal point: 3.4
To return to its original position, the decimal point must be moved 2 places to the left: 0.03.4

$$0.034 = 3.4 \times 10^{-2}$$

To change a number from scientific notation to decimal form, use the properties of exponents.

EXAMPLE   Write in decimal form: **a.** 2.8×10^3 **b.** 9.06×10^{-4}

SOLUTION   **a.** $2.8 \times 10^3 = 2.8 \times 1000$
$= 2800$

b. $9.06 \times 10^{-4} = 9.06 \times \dfrac{1}{10^4}$
$= 9.06 \times 0.0001$
$= 0.000906$

If you use common sense and recall the meaning of powers of ten, you will not have to memorize these procedures. Just remember that numbers greater than 1 have powers of 10 with positive exponents, while numbers less than 1 have powers of 10 with negative exponents.

Most of the work in the remainder of this chapter will focus on base 10, or "common," logarithms. With this understanding, we now drop the subscript 10 in logarithmic expressions. That is, we now write $\log x$ rather than $\log_{10} x$. Also, you will notice that the word "logarithm" is sometimes replaced by the shorter term "log."

The relationship between scientific notation and common logs is both close and important.

EXAMPLE $\log (8.65 \times 10^5) = \log 8.65 + \log 10^5$
$= \log 8.65 + 5$

EXAMPLE   Given that $\log 3.52 = m$, express $\log 35,200$ in terms of m.

SOLUTION $\log 35{,}200 = \log (3.52 \times 10^4)$
$$= \log 3.52 + \log 10^4$$
$$= m + 4$$

EXAMPLE   Given that $\log 8.02 = 0.9042$, find $\log 0.00802$.

SOLUTION $\log 0.00802 = \log (8.02 \times 10^{-3})$
$$= \log 8.02 + \log 10^{-3}$$
$$= 0.9042 - 3$$

It is more useful to leave the log in this form, rather than proceeding with the subtraction. You will see why this is true in a later section.

Notice in these examples that the logarithm of a number has two parts.

$$\log (x \cdot 10^n) = \log x + n,$$

where $1 \leqslant x < 10$ and n is an integer. In the next section, when you learn how to locate the logarithms of numbers between 1 and 10 in tables, you will be able to use this result to find the logarithm of any positive number.

Finding a number when its logarithm is given is slightly more complicated.

EXAMPLE   Given that $\log 1.2 = 0.0792$ and $\log x = 1.0792$, find x.

SOLUTION   If $\log 1.2 = 0.0792$, then $10^{0.0792} = 1.2$.
Also, if $\log x = 1.0792$, then:
$$x = 10^{1.0792}$$
$$= 10^1 \times 10^{0.0792}$$
$$= 10 \times 1.2$$
$$= 12$$

EXAMPLE   Write as the logarithm of a single number: $\log 3.76 - 3$.

SOLUTION $\log 3.76 - 3 = \log 3.76 - \log 10^3$
$$= \log \frac{3.76}{10^3}$$
$$= \log 0.00376$$

ORAL EXERCISES

Convert to scientific notation.

1. 5280	**2.** 12,000,000	**3.** 0.056	**4.** 0.324
5. 37	**6.** 2.98	**7.** 10,000	**8.** 0.0003
9. 0.0303	**10.** 2 billion	**11.** 5.7 million	**12.** 230 million

Convert to decimal form.

13. 3.76×10^3	**14.** 5.48×10^1	**15.** 9.87×10^{-2}
16. 1.03×10^{-1}	**17.** 1.64×10^4	**18.** 8×10^{-2}
19. 6×10^5	**20.** 1×10^{-4}	**21.** 4.54×10^9

WRITTEN EXERCISES

Given that log 2 = m and log 3 = n, express the given log in terms of m and n.

A 1. log 200

2. log 0.002

3. log 20

4. log 2 million

5. log 0.003

6. log 3000

7. log 0.00003

8. log 0.3

9. log 6

Write as the sum (or difference) of an integer and the logarithm of a number between 1 and 10.

10. log 372

11. log 0.31

12. log 203

13. log 180,400

14. log 0.0037

15. log 90.8

16. log 7640

17. log 0.6

18. log 0.000573

Write as the logarithm of a single number.

19. log 7.62 + 2

20. log 4.81 + 5

21. log 9.89 − 3

22. log 4.7 − 4

23. log 8.3 + 4

24. 3 − log 2.5

Scientific notation is sometimes written in other ways. For example, the letter E is used on computers to show the exponent of 10; thus 3.65×10^5 would be written as 3.65E + 5.

Write the following using the E-notation.

25. 37,000

26. 0.0025

27. 0.000638

28. 58.7 million

Given that log 3 = a and log 4 = b, express each log in terms of a and b.

B 29. log 12

30. log 9

31. log 16

32. log 27

33. $\log \dfrac{10}{3}$

34. log 0.25

35. log 2

36. $\log \dfrac{3}{4}$

37. log 36

38. log 48

39. log 0.5

40. log 900

41. $\log \dfrac{3}{40}$

42. log 0.009

43. log 6

Use the given information to solve for x.

44. log 6.7 = 0.8261, log x = 3.8261

45. log 2.9 = 0.4624, log x = 5.4624

46. log 9.1 = 0.9590, log x = 0.9590 − 2

47. log 4.4 = 0.6435, log x = 0.6435 − 4

Multiplication and division of numbers in scientific notation are straightforward.

EXAMPLE   Multiply: $(3.7 \times 10^8)(2.1 \times 10^{-5})$

SOLUTION $(3.7 \times 10^8)(2.1 \times 10^{-5}) = (3.7 \times 2.1) \times (10^8 \times 10^{-5})$
$$= 7.77 \times 10^3$$

EXAMPLE Divide: $(1.4 \times 10^{-3}) \div (5.6 \times 10^4)$

SOLUTION $\dfrac{1.4 \times 10^{-3}}{5.6 \times 10^4} = \dfrac{1.4}{5.6} \times \dfrac{10^{-3}}{10^4}$

$= 0.25 \times 10^{-7}$
$= 2.5 \times 10^{-1} \times 10^{-7}$
$= 2.5 \times 10^{-8}$

Express the product or quotient in scientific notation.

48. $(2 \times 10^5)(3 \times 10^7)$

49. $(5 \times 10^{-4})(1.2 \times 10^{-7})$

50. $(5 \times 10^2)(3 \times 10^{-6})$

51. $(7 \times 10^{-4})(8 \times 10^7)$

52. $(1.8 \times 10^7) \div (9.0 \times 10^{-2})$

53. $(8.4 \times 10^{-2}) \div (4 \times 10^3)$

Addition and subtraction of numbers in scientific notation require conversion of the numbers so that they have the same power of ten.

EXAMPLE Add: $(3.7 \times 10^5) + (2.6 \times 10^4)$

SOLUTION $3.7 \times 10^5 + 2.6 \times 10^4 = 3.7 \times 10^5 + 0.26 \times 10^5$
$= 3.96 \times 10^5$

Express the sum or difference in scientific notation.

C 54. $(9.1 \times 10^6) + (8.3 \times 10^5)$

55. $(9.1 \times 10^6) - (8.3 \times 10^5)$

56. $(8.3 \times 10^{-5}) + (9.1 \times 10^{-6})$

57. $(8.3 \times 10^{-5}) - (9.1 \times 10^{-6})$

When you record a distance such as 5600 m, it is not possible to tell whether the distance was measured to the nearest 100 m, 10 m, or 1 m. That is, the precision of the measurement is not apparent. In scientific notation, only digits that correspond to the place value of the precision of the measurement are shown.

EXAMPLE Express 5600 m to the nearest 10 m, using scientific notation.

SOLUTION Since the measurement was to the nearest 10 m, only the underscored digits are significant:

$$5\underline{6}\underline{0}0 \text{ m}$$

In scientific notation, this is written:

$$5.60 \times 10^3 \text{ m}$$

It would be incorrect to write this measurement as 5.6×10^3 m, since this would indicate measurement to the nearest 100 m.

Express each of the following in scientific notation.

58. 2000 cm measured to the nearest 10 cm

59. 586 km measured to the nearest km

60. 380 mL measured to the nearest 0.1 mL

61. 0.6 L measured to the nearest 0.01 L

Section 9-6 USING LOGARITHM TABLES

In Section 9-5 you learned that the common logarithm of any positive number can be expressed in terms of the common log of a number between one and ten. Now you will learn to use a table to find logs of numbers between one and ten. This will make it possible to find the log of any positive number. Specifically, you will learn:

- how to use a log table to find the logarithm of a number
- how to use a log table to find a number, given its logarithm
- the meanings of the terms characteristic and mantissa
- how to use linear interpolation to find logs
- how to express a number to a given number of significant digits

Table 2 gives the common logs, correct to four decimal places, of numbers from 1.00 to 9.99. Using this table to find the logarithm of a number between 1.00 and 9.99 is straightforward except for one problem. In log tables the decimal points are usually omitted in both the entry value, N, and the logarithm. You will see in the example how this is handled.

EXAMPLE   Find log 1.26.

SOLUTION   Part of the log table is shown.

x	0	1	2	3	4	5	6	7	8	9
10	0000	0043	0086	0128	0170	0212	0253	0294	0334	0374
11	0414	0453	0492	0531	0569	0607	0645	0682	0719	0755
12	0792	0828	0864	0899	0934	0969	1004	1038	1072	1106
13	1139	1173	1206	1239	1271	1303	1335	1367	1399	1430

To find log 1.26, move down the column under N to 12. Then move across this row to the column headed 6, where you find 1004. Since the log of any number between 1 and 10 is a number between 0 and 1, it is understood that a decimal point preceding each log has been omitted. Therefore:

$$\log 1.26 = 0.1004$$

Although the value found in the preceding example is an approximation, it is customary to write = rather than ≈.

EXAMPLE   Solve for x: $10^x = 8.9$

SOLUTION $10^x = 8.9$ is equivalent to $\log 8.9 = x$. From Table 2:

$$x = \log 8.9 = 0.9494$$

The table may also be used to find a number, given its logarithm.

EXAMPLE   If $\log x = 0.1206$, find x.

SOLUTION   Locate 1206 in the body of the table. Since it is in the row labeled 13 and the column labeled 2:

$$x = 1.32$$

EXAMPLE   Evaluate $10^{0.8041}$

SOLUTION   Let $x = 10^{0.8041}$ Then $\log x = 0.8041$. Use Table 2; 8041 is in the row labeled "63" and the column labeled "7."

$$x = 6.37$$

To find the log of a number that is not between 1 and 10, first write the number in scientific notation. Then use log properties and Table 2.

EXAMPLE   Find log 376.

SOLUTION
$$\begin{aligned}
\log 376 &= \log (3.76 \times 10^2) \\
&= \log 3.76 + \log 10^2 \\
&= 0.5752 + 2
\end{aligned}$$

EXAMPLE   Find log 0.00376.

SOLUTION
$$\begin{aligned}
\log 0.00376 &= \log (3.76 \times 10^{-3}) \\
&= \log 3.76 - 3 \\
&= 0.5752 - 3
\end{aligned}$$

As you can see, the logarithm of a number has two parts: a decimal part, called the *mantissa*, which is a positive number found in the table, and an integer part, called the *characteristic*, which is the exponent of ten when the number is written in scientific notation. We usually do not combine the two parts into a single numeral. Although a calculator may write $\log 0.00367$ as -2.4248, in this text we will write $\log 0.00376$ as $0.5752 - 3$.

EXAMPLE   If $\log x = 2.9547$, find x.

SOLUTION $\log x = 2.9547 = 0.9547 + 2$

Locate the mantissa, 0.9547, in the table. The corresponding value of N is 9.01. Since the characteristic is 2:

$$x = 9.01 \times 10^2, \text{ or } 901$$

EXAMPLE   If $\log x = 0.7803 - 3$, find x.

SOLUTION   The mantissa, 0.7803, corresponds to a value of 6.03 for N. The characteristic is -3.

$$x = 6.03 \times 10^{-3}, \text{ or } 0.00603$$

In Chapter 4 you learned how to interpolate to find intermediate values in tables. The following examples use this process.

EXAMPLE   Find log 372.4.

SOLUTION
$$\begin{aligned}
\log 372.4 &= \log(3.724 \times 10^2) \\
&= \log 3.724 + 2
\end{aligned}$$

(Solution continued on the next page)

Find the values of N nearest to 3.724 in the table.

$$0.01 \left[0.004 \left[\begin{array}{cc} N & \log N \\ \hline 3.72 & 0.5705 \\ 3.724 & \log 3.724 \\ 3.73 & 0.5717 \end{array} \right] d \right] 0.0012$$

$$\frac{d}{0.0012} = \frac{0.004}{0.01}$$

$$\frac{d}{0.0012} = \frac{4}{10} = 0.4$$

$d = 0.0012\,(0.4) = 0.0005$, rounded to four decimal places because the mantissas in Table 2 are correct to only four decimal places.

$$\log 3.724 = 0.5705 + d = 0.5710$$

Thus, $\log 372.4 = \log 3.724 + 2$

$$= 0.5710 + 2$$

A significant digit of a decimal numeral is any nonzero digit or any zero whose purpose is not just to place the decimal point. For example consider the quotient $\frac{1.259}{256.8}$. The quotient is written as:

0.0049,   correct to two significant digits
0.00490,   correct to three significant digits
0.004903, correct to four significant digits

Notice that the zeros to the left of the 4 are not significant, while those to the right of the 4 are significant.

In some cases you cannot tell whether or not zeros in a numeral are significant. If the length of an object is reported to be 340 cm, it is possible that the length was measured to the nearest centimeter, and the zero is significant. It is also possible, however, that the length was measured only to the nearest ten centimeters, and the zero is not significant.

EXAMPLE   If $\log x = 0.8776 - 3$, find x correct to four significant digits.

SOLUTION   Locate the mantissas nearest to 0.8776 in the table.

$$0.01 \left[d \left[\begin{array}{cc} N & \log N \\ \hline 7.54 & 0.8774 \\ 7.54 + d & 0.8776 \\ 7.55 & 0.8779 \end{array} \right] 0.0002 \right] 0.0005$$

$$\frac{d}{0.01} = \frac{0.0002}{0.0005}$$

$$\frac{d}{0.01} = \frac{2}{5} = 0.4$$

$$d = 0.01\,(0.4) = 0.004$$

$$\log(7.54 + d) = 0.8776$$
$$\log 7.544 = 0.8776$$
$$\text{Since } \log x = 0.8776 - 3,$$
$$x = 7.544 \times 10^{-3}, \text{ or } 0.007544.$$

ORAL EXERCISES

State the characteristic of the logarithm of each number.

1. 8.07×10^4 **2.** 3.65×10^{-3} **3.** 325   **4.** 0.075

5. 621,000   **6.** 0.0003   **7.** 93.4   **8.** 4.83

9. 0.8659   **10.** 7653   **11.** 0.0308   **12.** 93 million

Use the fact that $\log 2 = 0.3010$ to evaluate the logarithm.

13. $\log 20$ **14.** $\log 200$ **15.** $\log 0.002$

16. $\log 0.00002$ **17.** $\log (2 \times 10^7)$ **18.** $\log (2 \times 10^{-5})$

WRITTEN EXERCISES

Evaluate each of the following.

A   **1.** $\log 5$ **2.** $\log 8.7$ **3.** $\log 2.3$

    4. $\log 1.09$ **5.** $\log 3.91$ **6.** $\log 9.95$

    7. $\log 6.81$ **8.** $\log 68.1$ **9.** $\log 0.00681$

    10. $\log 4.57$ **11.** $\log 4570$ **12.** $\log 0.0457$

13. x, if $\log x = 0.6561$ **14.** y, if $\log y = 0.4065$

15. z, if $\log z = 0.8432$ **16.** w, if $\log w = 0.4200$

17. u, if $\log u = 0.4065 + 2$ **18.** v, if $\log v = 0.8432 + 3$

19. s, if $\log s = 0.4065 - 3$ **20.** t, if $\log t = 0.8432 - 1$

Interpolate to find each of the following.

B   **21.** $\log 5.055$ **22.** $\log 9.992$ **23.** $\log 7.207$

    24. $\log 3.008$ **25.** $\log 63.31$ **26.** $\log 22.22$

    27. $\log 0.004567$ **28.** $\log 23,480,000$ **29.** $\log 1776$

Find each of the following correct to four significant digits.

30. x, if $\log x = 0.9316$ **31.** y, if $\log y = 0.6359$

32. z, if $\log z = 0.4070$ **33.** w, if $\log w = 0.9775$

34. a, if $\log a = 0.7740 + 2$ **35.** b, if $\log b = 0.8760 + 1$

36. c, if $\log c = 0.2390 - 3$ **37.** d, if $\log d = 0.3000 - 2$

Evaluate. Give answers correct to three significant digits.

38. $10^{0.9576}$ **39.** $10^{5.6571}$ **40.** $10^{0.6212-3}$

41. $10^{-0.3958}$ (*Hint:* $-0.3958 = 0.6042 - 1.$)

Evaluate. Give answers correct to four significant digits.

C   **42.** $10^{-0.5}$ **43.** $\sqrt[5]{10}$ **44.** $\dfrac{1}{\sqrt[4]{10}}$

SELF-TEST 2

Simplify.

1. $\log_5 10 - \log_5 2$ **2.** $\log_{12} 9 + \log_{12} 16$ **3.** $2\log_4 6 - 2\log_4 3$ Section 9-4

Given that $\log 3 = m$, express the given log in terms of m.

4. $\log 300$ **5.** $\log 0.0003$ **6.** $\log 30{,}000$ Section 9-5

Write as the logarithm of a single number.

7. $\log 6.08 + 4$ **8.** $\log 3.2 - 3$ **9.** $\log 8.986 + 2$

Evaluate each of the following. Use Table 2.

10. $\log 9$ **11.** $\log 7560$ **12.** $\log 0.00382$ Section 9-6

13. x, if $\log x = 0.6191 + 3$ **14.** y, if $\log y = 0.7443 - 2$

Section 9-7 COMPUTING WITH LOGARITHMS

You have now learned the basic properties of logarithms. You have also learned how to use tables of common logs. In this section you will apply these skills and concepts to computation problems. You will use common logs to:

- multiply and divide numbers
- find powers and roots of numbers
- combine these operations to make complex calculations

The basic properties of logarithms are listed below. All work in this section involves common, or base 10, logarithms.

$$\log xy = \log x + \log y$$

$$\log \frac{x}{y} = \log x - \log y$$

$$\log x^n = n \log x$$

$$\log \sqrt[n]{x} = \frac{1}{n} \log x$$

EXAMPLE   Multiply: $37{,}400 \times 863$. Find the product correct to three significant digits.

SOLUTION   Let $x = 37{,}400 \times 863$.

Then $\log x = \log 37{,}400 + \log 863$.

Use Table 2. $\log 37{,}400 = \log 3.74 \times 10^4$

$$= 0.5729 + 4$$

$$\log 863 = \log 8.63 \times 10^2$$

$$= 0.9360 + 2$$

$$\log x = (0.5729 + 4) + (0.9360 + 2)$$

$$= 1.5089 + 6$$

$$= 0.5089 + 7$$

Since you need only 3 significant digits, find the log in Table 2 nearest to 0.5089.

$$0.5089 = \log 3.23, \text{ correct to 3 significant digits.}$$

Thus, $x = 3.23 \times 10^7$, or $32{,}300{,}000$.

Notice that the answer to the preceding example is only an approximation of the actual product, which is $32{,}276{,}200$.

The next example would be much more difficult without logarithms.

EXAMPLE   Calculate $\sqrt[3]{0.03785}$ correct to four significant digits.

SOLUTION   Let $x = \sqrt[3]{0.03785}$.

Then $\log x = \dfrac{1}{3} \log 0.03785$.

Use the table and interpolate.

$$\log 0.03785 = \log 3.785 \times 10^{-2}$$

$$= 0.5781 - 2$$

$$\log x = \frac{1}{3}(0.5781 - 2)$$

In order to keep the characteristic an integer after dividing by 3, rewrite $0.5781 - 2$ as $1.5781 - 3$.

$$\log x = \frac{1}{3}(0.5781 - 2)$$

$$= \frac{1}{3}(1.5781 - 3)$$

$$= 0.5260 - 1$$

Notice that 0.5260 was rounded to four decimal places, since Table 2 is correct to four decimal places.

Using the table and interpolating again, you find that

$$0.5260 = \log 3.358.$$

Thus, $x = 3.358 \times 10^{-1}$, or 0.3358, correct to 4 significant digits.

In the preceding example $0.5781 - 2$ was rewritten as $1.5781 - 3$. Of course, it could also be written in other ways; for example, $4.5781 - 6$, $13.5781 - 15$, or $28.5781 - 30$.

EXAMPLE   Divide: $428 \div 0.000681$. Find the quotient correct to three significant digits.

SOLUTION   Let $x = 428 \div 0.000681$.

Then $\log x = \log 428 - \log 0.000681$.

$\log 428 = \log 4.28 \times 10^2$ $\log 0.000681 = \log 6.81 \times 10^{-4}$
$\qquad\quad = 0.6314 + 2$ $\qquad\qquad\qquad = 0.8331 - 4$

$$\log x = (0.6314 + 2) - (0.8331 - 4)$$

We can subtract the characteristics and mantissas separately. To avoid a negative mantissa in the result, rewrite $0.6314 + 2$ as $1.6314 + 1$.

$$\log x = (0.6314 + 2) - (0.8331 - 4)$$
$$= (1.6314 + 1) - (0.8331 - 4)$$
$$= 0.7983 + 5$$

Using the table, you find, without interpolation, that

$$0.7983 = \log 6.28, \text{ correct to 3 significant digits.}$$

Thus, $x = 6.28 \times 10^5$, or $628{,}000$.

EXAMPLE   Calculate $\dfrac{0.0743\sqrt[5]{5280}}{(3.14)^3}$ correct to three significant digits.

SOLUTION   Let $x = \dfrac{0.0743\sqrt[5]{5280}}{(3.14)^3}$.

Then $\log x = \log 0.0743 + \dfrac{1}{5}\log 5280 - 3\log 3.14$

$$= (0.8710 - 2) + \frac{1}{5}(0.7226 + 3) - 3(0.4969)$$

$$= (0.8710 - 2) + \frac{1}{5}(3.7226) - 1.4907$$

$$= 0.8710 - 2 + 0.7445 - 1.4907$$
$$= 0.8710 + 0.7445 - 1.4907 - 2$$
$$= 1.6155 - 1.4907 - 2$$
$$= 0.1248 - 2$$

Since $0.1248 = \log 1.33$ to three significant digits,

$$x = 1.33 \times 10^{-2}, \text{ or } 0.0133.$$

ORAL EXERCISES

Use logarithm properties to give an expression for $\log x$.

1. $x = 7840 \times 538{,}000$

2. $x = \dfrac{0.00159}{0.234}$

3. $x = (0.00621)^2$

4. $x = \sqrt[3]{0.0371}$

5. $x = (4870)^5$

6. $x = \dfrac{0.000273}{84{,}500}$

7. $x = 452(368)^3$

8. $x = \sqrt[4]{37.1}$

9. $x = 289\sqrt{0.0623}$

10. $x = \left(\dfrac{0.736}{9890}\right)^4$

11. $x = \dfrac{\sqrt[5]{88.9}}{(0.0263)^3}$

12. $x = (1760)^2(6.85)^3$

Suppose only the values of log 2 and log 3 were known. Describe how you could use these logs to find:

13. log 4 **14.** log 1.5 **15.** log 8 **16.** log 36

WRITTEN EXERCISES

A 1-12. In Oral Exercises 1-12, use logs to find the value of x correct to three significant digits.

Use logs to calculate the following correct to three significant digits.

13. $\sqrt{38} \sqrt[3]{101{,}000}$

14. $\dfrac{461}{\sqrt[3]{0.0579}}$

15. $\sqrt[3]{\dfrac{708}{1.27}}$

16. $\sqrt[5]{(29.1)^4}$

Use logs to calculate the following correct to four significant digits.

B 17. $(37.42)(643.5)$

18. $\dfrac{765.4}{390.7}$

19. $\sqrt[5]{289{,}500}$

20. $(2.715)^4$

21. $\dfrac{(919.7)^2}{6456}$

22. $(37.19)^2 \sqrt{64.38}$

23. If a principal of P dollars is invested at 12% annual interest, then the investment will grow to an amount A, in dollars, after t years, where
$$A = P(1.12)^t.$$
What is the value, to the nearest dollar, of an original investment of $1000 after 20 yr?

C 24. The formula $t = 2\pi \sqrt{\dfrac{l}{g}}$ gives the period t, in seconds, for a pendulum l centimeters long. Find t, correct to three significant digits, if $l = 25.4$ and $g = 980$. Use 0.4971 for log π.

25. You know that 2^{10} and 10^3 are approximately the same.
   a. Write an equation to express this fact.
   b. Find an approximation of log 2 by solving the equation in part (a) for log 2.
   c. How does the approximate value of log 2 in part (b) compare with the value in the table?

26. You know that 3^4 and 80 are approximately the same.
   a. Write an equation to express this fact, and solve it for log 3. Use the value of log 2 found in Exercise 25(b).
   b. How does the approximate value of log 3 in part (a) compare with the value in the table?

Section 9-8 EXPONENTIAL AND LOGARITHMIC EQUATIONS

You have already learned many properties of exponents and logarithms. You have also learned to use tables of common logarithms and to use common logs in complex calculations. You will now use these skills with logarithms to solve equations and problems that would be difficult or, in some cases, impossible without the theoretical basis provided by logarithms. In this section you will:

- solve exponential equations
- solve logarithmic equations
- learn how to change a logarithm from one base to another

Consider the exponential equation

$$x^y = z, \quad x > 0, x \neq 1, z > 0.$$

Given any two of the three values x, y, and z, it is now possible to solve for the third. (You have already dealt with some special cases of these equations.)

EXAMPLE Solve for x correct to three significant digits: $x = (3.1)^{2.3}$

SOLUTION $\log x = 2.3 \log 3.1$
$$= 2.3(0.4914)$$
$$= 1.1302, \text{ to 4 decimal places}$$
$$= 0.1302 + 1$$
$$x = 13.5$$

EXAMPLE Solve for x correct to four significant digits: $x^5 = 30$

SOLUTION $5 \log x = \log 30$

$$\log x = \frac{1}{5} \log 30$$

$$= \frac{1}{5}(0.4771 + 1)$$

$$= \frac{1}{5}(1.4771)$$

$$= 0.2954, \text{ to 4 decimal places}$$
$$x = 1.974$$

EXAMPLE Solve for x correct to three significant digits: $5^x = 30$

SOLUTION $x \log 5 = \log 30$
$$x(0.6990) = 0.4771 + 1$$
$$x(0.6990) = 1.4771$$
$$x = \frac{1.4771}{0.6990} = 2.11$$

Note that in the third example, unlike the first and second, it was not necessary to return to the table in the last step of the problem.

Now consider the logarithmic equation

$$\log_x z = y, \quad x > 0, \ x \neq 1, \ z > 0.$$

This equation is equivalent to the equation

$$x^y = z.$$

Thus any logarithmic equation can be expressed as an equivalent exponential equation, and can be solved using the methods for exponential equations.

EXAMPLE Solve for x correct to four significant digits: $\log_5 x = 3.2$

SOLUTION
$$5^{3.2} = x$$
$$3.2 \log 5 = \log x$$
$$\log x = 3.2(0.6990)$$
$$= 2.2368$$
$$= 0.2368 + 2$$
$$x = 172.5$$

EXAMPLE Solve for x correct to four significant digits: $\log_x 8 = 2.6$

SOLUTION
$$x^{2.6} = 8$$
$$2.6 \log x = \log 8$$
$$\log x = \frac{\log 8}{2.6}$$
$$= \frac{0.9031}{2.6}$$
$$= 0.3473$$
$$x = 2.225$$

EXAMPLE Evaluate $\log_4 87$ correct to three significant digits.

SOLUTION
$$\text{Let } x = \log_4 87.$$
$$4^x = 87$$
$$x \log 4 = \log 87$$
$$x = \frac{\log 87}{\log 4}$$
$$= \frac{0.9395 + 1}{0.6021}$$
$$= \frac{1.9395}{0.6021}$$
$$= 3.22$$
$$\log_4 87 = 3.22$$

Note that these examples were solved using base 10 logs even though the problems were stated in terms of logs with other bases. The third example leads directly to a formula for changing from one log base to another:

Change of Base Formula

$$\log_b n = \frac{\log_c n}{\log_c b}$$

A proof of the Change of Base Formula is not difficult.

Let $x = \log_b n$.
Then $b^x = n$
$$x \log_c b = \log_c n$$
$$x = \frac{\log_c n}{\log_c b}$$
$$\log_b n = \frac{\log_c n}{\log_c b} \quad \text{(by substitution)}$$

If we take $c = 10$, the formula is:
$$\log_b n = \frac{\log n}{\log b}$$

This version of the Change of Base Formula enables us to calculate logs in any base by using common logs.

EXAMPLE Find $\log_2 18$, correct to four significant digits.

SOLUTION $\log_2 18 = \dfrac{\log 18}{\log 2}$

$$= \frac{0.2553 + 1}{0.3010}$$

$$= \frac{1.2553}{0.3010}$$

$$= 4.170$$

An important base for logarithms is the irrational number e ($e \approx 2.718$), which has many applications in more advanced mathematics. The Change of Base Formula can be used to find the relationship between $\log_e x$ and common logs:

$$\log_e x = \frac{\log x}{\log e}$$

The abbreviation $\ln x$, read "the natural logarithm of x," is often used in place of $\log_e x$. Thus the above equation can be written:

$$\ln x = \frac{\log x}{\log e}$$

ORAL EXERCISES

Use logarithms to state an equivalent equation.

1. $x = (3.75)^{1.8}$

2. $3.75^x = 1.8$

3. $x^{1.8} = 3.75$

4. $2^x = \sqrt{3}$

5. $x^{\frac{2}{3}} = 5^{\frac{1}{2}}$

6. $4^{x+1} = 7^x$

State an equivalent exponential equation.

7. $\log_3 7.2 = x$ **8.** $\log_3 x = 7.2$ **9.** $\log_x 7.2 = 3$

10. $x = \log 3.7$ **11.** $\log x = 3.7$ **12.** $\log x^2 = 4.2$

Express the given logarithm in terms of common logs.

13. $\log_3 5$ **14.** $\log_{12} 10$ **15.** $\log_4 1065$

WRITTEN EXERCISES

Solve for x correct to three significant digits.

A **1.** $x^5 = 300$ **2.** $x^{\frac{5}{2}} = 100$ **3.** $(3.09)^x = 1000$

   4. $(63.1)^x = 216$ **5.** $x = (2.5)^{0.4}$ **6.** $x = (203)^{0.2}$

   7. $\log_2 x = 5.3$ **8.** $\log_3 x = 2.4$ **9.** $\log_x 5 = 3$

   10. $\log_x 3 = 5$ **11.** $x = \log_2 100$ **12.** $x = \log_{3.71} 1.07$

B **13.** $3^{2x} = 5$ **14.** $5^{2x} = 3$ **15.** $86.4 = (5.62)^{3x}$

   16. $\log_7 5 = 3x$ **17.** $\log_4 3x = 1.5$ **18.** $\log_6 x^2 = 3$

Solve the following equations for x, leaving solutions in terms of common logs.

EXAMPLE $(3.7)^{x+2} = 7.5$

SOLUTION $(x + 2) \log 3.7 = \log 7.5$

$$x + 2 = \frac{\log 7.5}{\log 3.7}$$

$$x = \frac{\log 7.5}{\log 3.7} - 2$$

19. $(5.4)^{x+1} = 106$ **20.** $(3.75)^{x-2} = 14.3$ **21.** $(7.04)^{x-1} = (4.19)^x$

Calculate, correct to four significant digits.

22. $\log_2 7$ **23.** $\log_7 2$ **24.** $\log_{100} 10$

25. $\ln 10$ **26.** $\ln 2$ **27.** $\ln 5$

Solve for x correct to three significant digits.

C 28. $(x + 2)^3 = 2000$ **29.** $(x + 3)^2 = 150$ **30.** $16^{3x+1} = 38.5$

For some special engineering applications, log log tables are available. These are tables that represent the log of the log of a number.

EXAMPLE   Find log log 200.

SOLUTION $\log \log 200 = \log (2.3010) = 0.3619$

Evaluate correct to four significant digits.

31. log log 100   **32.** log log 10   **33.** log log 63.1

Prove each property.

34. $\log_b a = \dfrac{1}{\log_a b}$ **35.** $\log_a b \, \log_b c = \log_a c$

36. For $x > 0$, $x \neq 1$, the ratio $\dfrac{\ln x}{\log x}$ is a constant. Find the value of this constant correct to four significant digits.

Section 9-9 APPLICATIONS

It may seem to you that the exponential and logarithmic functions we have studied are only abstract ideas. It has been found, however, that exponential equations are the essential mathematical model for a wide range of mathematical applications in such diverse fields as biology, finance, and the social sciences. In many of these applications, logarithms provide the only technique for solution.

Exponential equations arise in many situations where the rate of change of a quantity is proportional to the amount of the quantity. For example:

1. The increase in a population is proportional to the size of the population.
2. Interest on a bank account is proportional to the amount invested.
3. The rate at which an open container of water just removed from the stove returns to room temperature is proportional to the difference between the water temperature and the room temperature.

In the case of bank interest at an interest rate of r (per unit time) or population growth with constant growth rate r (per unit time), the original amount A_0 increases to an amount A_n according to the following pattern:

$$\text{after 1 unit of time,} \quad A_1 = A_0 + rA_0 = A_0(1 + r)$$
$$\text{after 2 units of time,} \quad A_2 = A_1 + rA_1$$
$$= A_1(1 + r) = A_0(1 + r)^2$$
$$\text{after 3 units of time,} \quad A_3 = A_2 + rA_2$$
$$= A_2(1 + r) = A_0(1 + r)^3$$
$$\text{after } n \text{ units of time,} \quad A = A_0(1 + r)^n$$

The formula $A_n = A_0(1 + r)^n$ is sometimes called the *growth model*.

EXAMPLE   The 1980 population of the United States was approximately 227,000,000. Suppose this population were to increase at the rate of 2% per year. Predict the 1990 population to the nearest million.

SOLUTION $A_n = A_0(1 + r)^n$, $A_0 = 227,000,000$, $r = 2\% = 0.02$, $n = 10$
$$A_n = 227,000,000(1 + 0.02)^{10}$$
$$= (2.27 \times 10^8)(1.02)^{10}$$

$$\log A_n = \log 2.27 + 8 + 10 \log 1.02$$
$$= 0.3560 + 8 + 10(0.0086)$$
$$= 0.4420 + 8$$
$$A_n = 277{,}000{,}000$$

The 1990 population would be about 277,000,000.

EXAMPLE If $1000 is invested at 12% annual interest, what is the value, to the nearest dollar, of the investment after 8 yr?

SOLUTION
$$A_n = A_0(1 + r)^n, \ A_0 = 1000, \ r = 0.12, \ n = 8$$
$$A_n = 1000(1.12)^8$$
$$\log A_n = \log 1000 + 8 \log 1.12$$
$$\log A_n = 3 + 8(0.0492)$$
$$\log A_n = 0.3936 + 3$$
$$A_n = 2475$$

The investment would be worth about $2475.

ORAL EXERCISES

Use logarithms to state an equivalent equation.

1. $P = p \cdot 2^t$

2. $A = P(1.01)^t$

3. $t = 2\pi \sqrt{\dfrac{L}{g}}$

4. $W = \dfrac{w(4000)^2}{(4000 + d)^2}$

5. $P = p\left(\dfrac{5}{4}\right)^t$

6. $A = \sqrt{s(s-a)(s-b)(s-c)}$

7. $A = ae^{-\frac{t}{12}}$

8. $A = \dfrac{s^2}{4}\sqrt{3}$

9. $H = \dfrac{nLW}{33{,}000}$

10. $E = \dfrac{pv^2}{2g}$

11. $A = P(1 + r)^t$

12. $r = \sqrt{\dfrac{(s-a)(s-b)(s-c)}{s}}$

WRITTEN EXERCISES

The amount of an investment, the annual interest rate, and the time period are given. Find the value of the investment, to the nearest dollar, at the end of the given time period.

A 1. $1000, 15%, 5 yr

2. $350, 10%, 3 yr

The population of the United States was about 227,000,000 in 1980. Use the given annual growth rate to predict the population, to the nearest million, in the year 2000.

5. 2%

6. 1%

7. 3%

8. 5%

A bacteria culture is found to double in number every 10 h. Under these conditions the population, P, of the culture is found by the formula $P = p(2)^{\frac{t}{10}}$ in which p is the initial number of bacteria and t is the number of hours of growth. Using this formula, calculate P correct to three significant digits.

9. $p = 1$, $t = 30$

10. $p = 1$, $t = 365$

11. $p = 1200$, $t = 14$

12. $p = 250$, $t = 5$

Doubling time is the length of time required for an original amount to double. Find the doubling time, to the nearest tenth of a year, for the given annual growth rate, r.

EXAMPLE $r = 5\%$

SOLUTION   Since the final amount is to be twice the original amount, let $A_n = 2A_0$. Also, $r = 5\% = 0.05$.

$$A_n = A_0(1 + r)^n$$
$$2A_0 = A_0(1 + r)^n$$
$$2 = (1 + r)^n$$
$$2 = (1.05)^n$$
$$\log 2 = n \log 1.05$$
$$n = \frac{\log 2}{\log 1.05} \approx 14.2$$

It will take about 14.2 yr for an amount to double at a 5% growth rate.

B 13. $r = 2\%$ 14. $r = 1\%$ 15. $r = 10\%$ 16. $r = 15\%$

Radioactive elements decay over time, changing into other elements. The half-life of an element is the time needed for half of the original amount of the element to change into another element. For an element with a half-life of 80 days, the formula

$$Q = q\left(\frac{1}{2}\right)^{\frac{t}{80}}$$

gives the amount Q remaining unchanged after t days, beginning with an original amount q. Use this formula to solve to the nearest gram.

17. How much of an original amount of 1000 g of the element remains unchanged after 160 d?

18. 350 g of the element is unchanged after 20 d. How much of the element was there to begin with?

19. How much of an original amount of 1000 g of the element remains unchanged after 30 d?

C 20. How long does it take, to the nearest day, for a sample of the element to decay so that one third of the original amount remains unchanged?

21. How long would it take, to the nearest day, for 1000 g of the element to decay so that 100 g remains unchanged?

22. Use the formula $A_n = A_0(1 + r)^n$ to derive a formula for the doubling time n in terms of the growth rate r.

23. At what annual interest rate will an investment double in value in 5 yr? Solve to the nearest tenth of a percent.

SELF-TEST 3

Use logs to calculate the following correct to three significant digits.

1. $(8270)^4$ 2. $\sqrt[3]{0.0336}$ 3. $\dfrac{0.00594}{95,600}$ Section 9-7

Solve for x correct to three significant digits.

4. $x = \log_5 22$ 5. $\log_x 4 = 2.4$ 6. $6^x = 45$ Section 9-8

Use the growth model, $A_n = A_0(1 + r)^n$, to answer the question.

7. What is the value, after 10 yr, of an investment of $800 at 14% annual interest?   Section 9-9
Find the value to the nearest dollar.

8. The population of Canada was about 24,100,000 in 1981. Use a growth rate of 2% per year to predict the population, correct to three significant digits, in 2025.

Computer Exercises

In the exercises that follow, you will be asked to write a computer program to find doubling times. In BASIC, the function LOG(X) gives $\log_e x$. Therefore, in deriving the doubling time formula we will use base e logs.

The *doubling time* for an investment is the time period required for the original amount to double. The growth model can be used to derive a formula for the doubling time in terms of the annual interest rate on the investment. Since the investment is to double, set $A_n = 2A_0$ in the equation of the growth model.

$$A_n = A_0(1 + r)^n$$
$$2A_0 = A_0(1 + r)^n$$
$$2 = (1 + r)^n$$
$$\log_e 2 = n \log_e (1 + r)$$
$$n = \frac{\log_e 2}{\log_e (1 + r)}$$

This formula gives the doubling time n, in years, for a given annual interest rate r. Since the formula is expressed in terms of base e logs, we can use the BASIC logarithm function.

1. Write a program to find the doubling time for an investment at interest rates of 2%, 4%, 6%, ..., 20%. Use N for the doubling time in years. Include the following line in your program:

$$N1 = INT (10*N + .5)/10$$

N1 will give the value of N rounded to the nearest tenth. Have the computer print each interesf rate and the corresponding doubling time to the nearest tenth of a year.

2. RUN your program and record the results.

3. People who are involved in financial activities often use a rule of thumb known as "the rule of 72." This is a simple way to find the approximate doubling time for an investment at a given interest rate. Examine the output of your program and explain the rule of 72.

CHAPTER REVIEW

Simplify.

1. $64^{\frac{4}{3}}$ 2. 2^{-2} 3. $\left(\frac{1}{8}\right)^{-\frac{2}{3}}$ 4. $32^{\frac{2}{5}}$ Section 9-1

Let $f(x) = x^{\frac{2}{3}}$ and $g(x) = 3^x$. Evaluate.

5. $f(27)$ 6. $g(-2)$ 7. $f(0.001)$ 8. $[g \circ f](8)$

9. Graph the functions $f(x) = 2^x$ and $g(x) = 2^x - 3$ on the same set of axes.   Section 9-2

Let $3^{\frac{1}{2}} = m$. Express each of the following in terms of m.

10. 3 11. $3^{-\frac{1}{2}}$ 12. $3^{1.5}$ 13. $\frac{1}{9}$

Evaluate.

14. $\log_9 27$ 15. $\log_2 \frac{1}{16}$ 16. $\log_4 \sqrt{2}$ 17. $\log_{16} \frac{1}{8}$ Section 9-3

Solve.

18. $\log_x 9 = -2$ 19. $\log_x 125 = -\frac{3}{2}$ 20. $\log_{27} x = \frac{1}{6}$

Replace each expression with one involving only logarithms of prime numbers.

21. $\log_4 15$ 22. $\log_3 20$ 23. $\log_5 24$ 24. $\log_6 \frac{5}{9}$ Section 9-4

If $\log_b x = m$ and $\log_b y = n$, express each of the following in terms of m and n.

25. $\log_b x^3 y$ **26.** $\log_b \dfrac{y}{x}$ **27.** $\log_b \sqrt[3]{y}$ **28.** $\log_b \sqrt{xy}$

Write as the sum of an integer and the logarithm of a number between 1 and 10.

29. $\log 0.043$ **30.** $\log 8890$ **31.** $\log 62.7$ **32.** $\log 0.00029$ Section 9-5

Use the given information to solve for x.

33. $\log 5.28 = 0.7226$, $\log x = 4.7226$

34. $\log 1.06 = 0.0253$, $\log x = 0.0253 - 3$

Use Table 2 to evaluate each of the following logs.

35. $\log 0.0384$ **36.** $\log 73,580$ **37.** $\log 0.005131$ Section 9-6

Solve for x correct to four significant digits.

38. $\log x = 0.9063 + 4$ **39.** $\log x = 0.5493 - 3$ **40.** $\log x = 0.6565 + 2$

Use logs to calculate, correct to three significant digits.

41. $\sqrt[5]{0.00227}$ **42.** $(497)^4$ **43.** $\dfrac{0.00726}{5840}$ Section 9-7

Solve for x correct to three significant digits.

44. $\log_2 x = 4.7$ **45.** $4^{3x} = 25$ **46.** $\log_5 8 = 3x$ Section 9-8

Calculate correct to four significant digits.

47. $\log_8 3$ **48.** $\log_2 9$ **49.** $\log_5 100$

The amount of an investment, the annual interest rate, and the time period are given. Find the value of the investment, to the nearest dollar, at the end of the given time period.

50. \$1000, 16%, 8 yr   **51.** \$1, 15%, 25 yr   Section 9-9

52. How long does it take, to the nearest tenth of a year, for a population to double at a growth rate of 3% per year? Use the growth model.

CHAPTER TEST_____

1. Graph the functions $f(x) = 2^x$ and $g(x) = \left(\dfrac{1}{3}\right)^x$ on the same set of axes.

Evaluate.

2. $8^{\frac{5}{3}}$ **3.** $\left(\dfrac{1}{4}\right)^{-3}$ **4.** $4^{-\frac{3}{2}}$

5. $\log_5 125$ **6.** $\log_5 \dfrac{1}{25}$ **7.** $\log_9 \dfrac{1}{27}$

EXPONENTS AND LOGARITHMS   **383**

Evaluate.

  8. log 281   **9.** log 7625   **10.** log 0.004536

Find each of the following correct to four significant digits.

  11. x, if log $x = 0.5599 + 2$ **12.** y, if log $y = 0.9114 - 5$

Given that log $5 = a$ and log $9 = b$, express each log in terms of a and b.

  13. log 45   **14.** log 1.8   **15.** log 0.04   **16.** log $\dfrac{1}{27}$

Solve.

  17. $9^{2x-3} = 81$ **18.** $16^x = 8^{2x-2}$ **19.** $\log_9 x = 2.5$ **20.** $\log_x 5 = 2$

Solve for x correct to three significant digits.

  21. $\log_3 x = 4.3$ **22.** $x = \log_4 35$

Use logs to calculate the following, correct to four significant digits.

  23. $\sqrt[4]{0.07168}$ **24.** $\dfrac{3285}{0.06474}$

In Questions 25 and 26, use the formula $A_n = A_0(1 + r)^n$.

25. Find the value, after 8 yr, of an investment of $500 at an annual interest rate of 15%. Find the value to the nearest dollar.

26. The population of the United States was about 76,000,000 in 1900. At a growth rate of 2% per year, what would the population have been in 1980, to the nearest million?

27. A radioactive element decays according to the formula

$$Q = q\left(\frac{1}{2}\right)^{\frac{t}{50}}$$

where q is the original amount and Q is the amount of the element remaining unchanged after t years. How much of an original sample of 500 g of the element remains unchanged after 80 yr? Solve to the nearest gram.

Application — Logarithmic Scales

The following diagram represents a base-10 logarithmic scale.

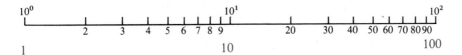

Notice that the distances between consecutive integer coordinates on the scale vary but that the distance between 1 and 10 is the same as the distance between 10 and 100. On logarithmic scales, the distances between coordinates that are consecutive integer powers of any positive base (other than 1) are equal. For example, on a base-10 logarithmic scale, the coordinates 10^0, 10^1, 10^2, 10^3, and so on, divide the scale into equal intervals. Notice on the logarithmic scale shown above that the consecutive integer powers of 2: 2^0, 2^1, 2^2, 2^3, and so on, are also equally spaced.

People in scientific or business professions often use logarithmic scales to graph data because a large range of values can be represented using a relatively small interval. Business forecasters, economists, urban planners, scientists, and others who work with data that are frequently exponential, graph data using a logarithmic scale on one axis because such a graph can reveal a pattern of the data that may not have been apparent before. Look at the graph below.

Notice that the vertical scale is logarithmic and that the horizontal scale is divided into equally spaced intervals. Graph paper ruled in this way is called *semilogarithmic* graph paper. Notice also that when the exponential curve represented by the equation $y = 2^x$, which we graphed in the usual way on page 350, is graphed on semilogarithmic paper, its graph is a straight line. Whenever exponential data is plotted on semilogarithmic graph paper, the resulting graph is a straight line. If a business forecaster, for example, graphed a straight line by plotting actual data on semilogarithmic paper, the forecaster would know that the business trend was exponential. (See Application on business forecasting on page 627.)

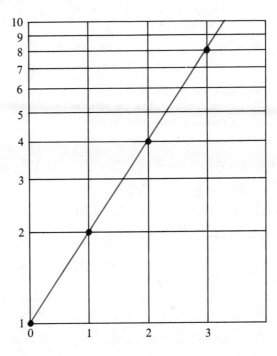

VOCABULARY REVIEW

Be sure that you understand the meaning of these terms:

exponential function, p. 350
logarithmic function, p. 353
scientific notation, p. 361
mantissa, p. 367

characteristic, p. 367
significant digit, p. 368
growth model, p. 378

MIXED REVIEW

1. Prove the identity $\tan \alpha + \cot \alpha = \sec \alpha \csc \alpha$.

2. Graph the image of the line with equation $y = -2$ under the dilation $D_{\frac{1}{2}}$.

Evaluate.

3. $125^{-\frac{4}{3}}$

4. $\log_3 81$

5. $\log_6 \dfrac{1}{216}$

6. $\log_{25} 125$

7. Given that -4 is a root of $2x^3 + 24x = 16 - 15x^2$, find the complete solution set.

8. If $\angle AOB$ is a central angle of $\odot O$, $m \overset{\frown}{AB} = 90$, and $OA = 6$, find (a) the length of $\overset{\frown}{AB}$, (b) the area of sector AOB, and (c) the area of the region inside $\odot O$ and outside $\triangle AOB$.

9. If $f(x) = \log_3 x$, write an equation for $f^{-1}(x)$.

10. Use Table 2 to estimate $\sqrt[3]{34.15}$ to four significant digits.

11. Quadrilateral $ABCD$ is circumscribed about $\odot O$. If $m\angle A = 82$, $m\angle B = 90$, and $m\angle C = 100$, find the measures of the four non-overlapping arcs formed by the points of tangency.

12. Find the pre-image of $(5, -2)$ under (a) $T_{-5,\, 2}$, (b) $r_{x\text{-axis}} \circ r_{y\text{-axis}}$, (c) R_{270}, (d) $T\!:\!(x, y) \longrightarrow \left(\frac{1}{2}y, 2x - 1\right)$, and (e) D_2, and (f) tell which of the transformations in (a)–(e) are isometries.

13. Find the standard form of the multiplicative inverse of $\sqrt{2} + i\sqrt{6}$.

Find and graph the solution set.

14. $|2x + 8| > 0$

15. $y^2 + 2y \leqslant 8$

16. $4(z - 1) \geqslant 7.2z$ or $5z - \dfrac{1}{4} > \dfrac{7}{2}$

17. Express $\dfrac{\csc^2 \theta}{\sin^2 \theta + \cos^2 \theta + \tan^2 \theta}$ in terms of a single function of θ.

18. In $\triangle ABC$, $AB = x + 3$ and $BC = x + 9$. Complete: $\underline{\ ?\ } < AC < \underline{\ ?\ }$

19. The width of a rectangle is 6 cm less than the length. If the area is 18 cm², find the length of the rectangle.

386   *CHAPTER 9*

20. If $f(x) = 3x^2 - 6$ and $g(x) = -2x + 1$, find (a) $[f \circ g](-2)$, (b) $[g \circ f](-2)$, (c) $[f \circ g](x)$, and (d) $[g \circ f](x)$ and (e) classify $g \circ f$ and $f \circ g$ as odd, even, or neither.

Simplify.

21. $\dfrac{2z^{-3} + z^{-2}}{8z^{-3} + 1}$

22. $\dfrac{6}{\sqrt{3} + 1}$

23. $\dfrac{4}{3} \sqrt[3]{-864}$

24. If $\sin \theta = \dfrac{24}{25}$ and θ lies in Quadrant II, find $\cos \theta$.

Solve.

25. $\log_{16} x = -\dfrac{5}{8}$

26. $\dfrac{1}{r-1} + \dfrac{r}{r+1} = \dfrac{5}{4}$

27. $\sqrt{4j + 1} = \sqrt{5j} - 1$

28. $81^{4y-9} = 27^{y+1}$

29. $4z^3 + 9z^2 = 9z$

30. $g^2 - 45 = 0$

31. If the terminal side of an angle θ in standard position contains $(-6, -8)$, find the values of the six trigonometric functions of θ.

32. Show that $4 - i$ is a root of $s^2 = 8s - 17$. Find the other root.

33. Solve for $0° \leqslant \theta < 360°$: **a.** $3 \tan \theta = \cot \theta$ **b.** $2 \sin^2 \theta - 7 \sin \theta = 4$

34. Simplify: $\sin (\pi + \theta) + \cos \left(\dfrac{\pi}{2} + \theta \right)$

35. How much water must be evaporated from 10 L of a 40% acid solution to make a 50% solution?

36. Name a geometric figure that has point symmetry but does not have line symmetry.

37. How long does it take, to the nearest tenth of a year, for an investment to double at an annual interest rate of 9%? Use the growth model.

38. Evaluate: **a.** $\csc \left(-\dfrac{2\pi}{3} \right)$ **b.** $\cot 210°$ **c.** $\cos (-45°)$

39. Draw a $\odot O$. Then construct two lines that are tangent to $\odot O$ and parallel to each other.

40. Use Table 1 to solve $\csc^2 \theta = 9$ to the nearest minute if $0° \leqslant \theta < 360°$.

41. State the domain, the range, and the period of the sine function.

42. What is the y-intercept of any exponential function?

43. Solve correct to three significant digits: **a.** $\log_x 1.3 = 7$ **b.** $x = \log_4 45$

44. Find all values of θ between $0°$ and $360°$ that make the statement $\sin 100° = \sin \theta$ true.

45. Find x correct to four significant digits if $\log x = 0.5580$.

46. Find the general solution for α in radians: $4(\sin \alpha + 1) = 3 \csc \alpha$

Vectors (page 416) are used to describe quantities, such as the force of the wind, that have both magnitude (size) and direction. The strength and direction of the wind are important factors to sailors.

Triangle Trigonometry 10

Until the last hundred years, the most frequent use of trigonometry has been to determine sides and angles of triangles. Originally, trigonometry was developed in response to a need for a mathematical model that could accurately predict the paths and positions of heavenly bodies.

Aristarchus of Samos (310–230 B.C.) tried to calculate the distances of the sun and moon from Earth. He observed that when the moon is half full, $\triangle EMS$ is a right triangle with a right angle at M. He measured $\angle MES$, determined it to be 87°, and then, using the mathematics of his time, calculated that the distance from Earth to the sun is 18 to 20 times the distance from Earth to the moon. The correct ratio is closer to 400. Aristarchus' mathematics was correct; his error lay in judging when the moon was exactly half full. In actuality, the measure of $\angle MES$ is 89°52′, to the nearest minute.

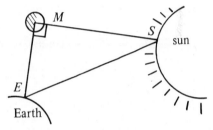

About one hundred thirty years later, another Greek astronomer, Hipparchus of Nicea, made the first systematic table of values of trigonometric functions, essentially a table of sines. Finally, about A.D. 160, Ptolemy of Alexandria made up tables, suggested by those of Hipparchus, that gave essentially the sines of angles in $\frac{1}{4}^{\circ}$ increments between 0° and 90°. Throughout the western world his tables remained the basis of trigonometric calculations for the next 1400 years.

Section 10-1 RIGHT-TRIANGLE TRIGONOMETRY

In Section 7-3 you learned the definitions of the sine and cosine functions based on the coordinates of points on the unit circle. As you will see, it is often convenient to think of the trigonometric functions in terms of the lengths of the sides of a right triangle. In this section you will:
- relate these definitions to ratios of the lengths of sides of right triangles
- use these ratios to find the measures of angles and lengths of sides of right triangles

In Section 7-3 you learned that in terms of the unit circle, with equation $x^2 + y^2 = 1$,

$$\sin \theta = y \quad \text{and} \quad \cos \theta = x.$$

Consider another right triangle with acute angle θ. By the AA Similarity Theorem, these triangles are similar. Thus we observe that the sine and the cosine of an acute angle can be described in terms of the lengths of the sides of a right triangle as follows:

$$\sin \theta = \frac{\sin \theta}{1} = \frac{\text{length of leg opposite } \theta}{\text{length of hypotenuse}}$$

$$\cos \theta = \frac{\cos \theta}{1} = \frac{\text{length of leg adjacent to } \theta}{\text{length of hypotenuse}}$$

Also, since $\tan \theta = \dfrac{\sin \theta}{\cos \theta}$:

$$\tan \theta = \frac{\text{length of leg opposite } \theta}{\text{length of leg adjacent to } \theta}$$

By the reciprocal relationships:

$$\sec \theta = \frac{1}{\cos \theta} = \frac{\text{length of hypotenuse}}{\text{length of leg adjacent to } \theta}$$

$$\csc \theta = \frac{1}{\sin \theta} = \frac{\text{length of hypotenuse}}{\text{length of leg opposite } \theta}$$

$$\cot \theta = \frac{1}{\tan \theta} = \frac{\text{length of leg adjacent to } \theta}{\text{length of leg opposite } \theta}$$

To *solve a triangle,* you find the lengths of all the sides not known and the measures of all the angles not given. We agree to label triangles so that a represents the length of the side opposite $\angle A$, and so on. In working with triangles, we will replace θ with the letter that names the vertex of the angle. Thus, we would write $\sin A$ to denote the sine of the angle with vertex A.

EXAMPLE Given $\triangle ABC$ in which $\angle C = 90°$, $c = 41$, and $a = 9$. Find b to the nearest integer. Then find, to the nearest $10'$, the measures of $\angle A$ and $\angle B$.

SOLUTION Draw and label a diagram.
By the Pythagorean Theorem:
$$9^2 + b^2 = 41^2$$
$$81 + b^2 = 1681$$
$$b^2 = 1600$$
$$b = 40$$

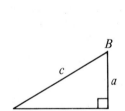

By definition:

$$\sin A = \frac{9}{41} \approx 0.2195$$

From Table 1:

$$\angle A = 12°40' \text{ (to the nearest } 10')$$

Therefore:

$$\angle B = 90° - \angle A$$
$$\angle B = 90° - 12°40' = 77°20' \text{ (to the nearest } 10')$$

EXAMPLE   Given $\triangle ABC$ in which $\angle C = 90°$, $a = 44$, and $\angle B = 62°$.
Find $\angle A$. Then find, to the nearest integer, b and c.

SOLUTION   From the diagram:

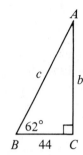

$$\angle A = 90° - \angle B \qquad \frac{b}{44} = \tan 62°$$
$$= 90° - 62° \qquad \qquad b = 44(\tan 62°)$$
$$= 28° \qquad \qquad \qquad = 44(1.881)$$
$$\qquad \qquad \qquad \qquad = 83 \text{ (to the nearest integer)}$$

To find c, you can use $\sec B = \dfrac{c}{a}$ or $\cos B = \dfrac{a}{c}$.

If you do not have a calculator available, but you do have a table of values of the secant function, the first equation is more convenient to solve, since solving involves multiplication rather than division.

$$\sec 62° = \frac{c}{44}$$
$$c = 44(\sec 62°)$$
$$c = 44(2.130)$$
$$c = 94 \text{ (to the nearest integer)}$$

Thus, $\angle A = 28°$, $b = 83$, and $c = 94$.

Our final example shows how you can use a triangle and a given trigonometric function value to evaluate other trigonometric functions of an acute angle by a method different from the one you learned in Chapter 8.

EXAMPLE   If $\tan \theta = \dfrac{3}{4}$, find $\cos \theta$ and $\sin \theta$.

SOLUTION   We need a right triangle with legs whose lengths are in the ratio $3:4$. It is convenient to assume that the lengths of the legs *are* 3 and 4. Then, by the Pythagorean Theorem, the length, x, of the hypotenuse is 5. Since

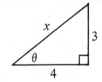

$$\tan \theta = \frac{\text{length of leg opposite } \theta}{\text{length of leg adjacent to } \theta},$$

we place θ opposite the leg of length 3.

Therefore:

$$\cos \theta = \frac{4}{5} \quad \text{and} \quad \sin \theta = \frac{3}{5}$$

ORAL EXERCISES

State each value in terms of r, s, and t.

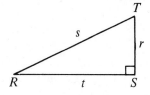

1. $\cos T$
2. $\tan R$
3. $\sec R$
4. $\sin T$
5. $\tan T$
6. $\sin R$
7. $\csc R$
8. $\cot T$
9. $\sec T$
10. $\cos R$

State a trigonometric equation that you could use to find the value of x. You need not solve the equation.

11.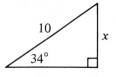

12.

13.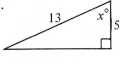

14.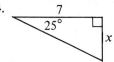

15.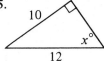

16.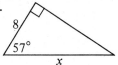

17. Justify the identities

$$\cos \theta = \sin (90° - \theta)$$
$$\sin \theta = \cos (90° - \theta)$$

in terms of the right-triangle definitions of the sine and cosine functions.

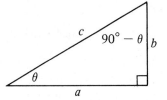

WRITTEN EXERCISES

Find the length of the third side. Then find the values of the six trigonometric functions of the indicated angle θ.

A 1.

2.

3.

4.

In the following exercises, if you are asked to find a length, find the length to the nearest integer, and if you are asked to find the measure of an angle, find the measure to the nearest $10'$.

Given $\triangle JKL$ in which $\angle L$ is a right angle, complete.

5. $KL = 12$, $\angle J = 38°40'$, $JL = $ ___?___

6. $JK = 32$, $\angle K = 41°$, $JL = $ ___?___

7. $JK = 185$, $\angle K = 35°50'$, $KL = \underline{\ ?\ }$

8. $JL = 45$, $\angle J = 73°40'$, $JK = \underline{\ ?\ }$

9. $JL = 66$, $\angle K = 59°$, $JK = \underline{\ ?\ }$

10. $JL = 125$, $\angle J = 36°20'$, $KL = \underline{\ ?\ }$

11. $JL = 420$, $KL - 500$, $\angle J = \underline{\ ?\ }$

12. $JK = 75$, $KL = 54$, $\angle K - \underline{\ ?\ }$

13. $JK = 90$, $JL = 39$, $\angle K = \underline{\ ?\ }$

14. $JL = 26$, $KL = 40$, $\angle J = \underline{\ ?\ }$

Refer to the triangle at the right. Solve, using the given information.

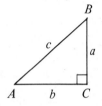

15. $c = 130$, $a = 50$

16. $b = 7$, $a = 24$

17. $c = 9$, $b = 4$

18. $\angle A = 48°$, $a = 53$

19. $\angle B = 70°$, $a = 75$

20. $\angle A = 37°$, $c = 30$

Use the given function value to find the values of the other five trigonometric functions.

21. $\sin \theta = \dfrac{15}{17}$

22. $\cot \theta = \dfrac{35}{12}$

23. $\tan \theta = \dfrac{56}{33}$

24. $\cos \theta = \dfrac{63}{65}$

25. $\sec \theta = \dfrac{25}{24}$

26. $\csc \theta = \dfrac{29}{21}$

B 27. Find the length of the altitude to the base of an isosceles triangle whose base has length 56 and each of whose base angles is $63°$.

28. Find the length of the base of an isosceles triangle if the altitude to the base has length 130 and if each base angle is $61°$.

29. Find the measures of the angles of an isosceles triangle whose sides have lengths 10, 13, and 13.

30. Find the measures of the angles of an isosceles triangle whose sides have lengths 17, 17, and 30.

31. Find the length of a rectangle whose width is 78 and each of whose diagonals makes an angle of $26°$ with the longer side.

32. Find the length of a diagonal of a rectangle of length 18 if each diagonal makes an angle of $51°$ with the shorter side of the rectangle.

33. Find the measure of the acute angle between the diagonals of a rectangle of width 16 and length 30.

34. The diagonals of a rectangle form an angle of $48°20'$. Find the length of the rectangle if the width is 140.

35. In quadrilateral $ABCD$, $\overline{AD} \parallel \overline{BC}$ and $\overline{CD} \perp \overline{AD}$. If $\angle CBD = 40°$, $\angle BAD = 65°$, and $CD = 20$, find:
   a. BC
   b. AD

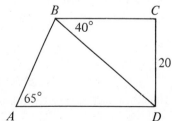

C 36. A regular octagon whose sides each have length 49 is inscribed in a circle. Find the radius of the circle.

37. A regular decagon (10-sided polygon) is inscribed in a circle of radius 68. Find the length of a side of the decagon.

38. Find the area of a parallelogram whose sides are 10 cm and 12 cm long and one of whose angles is 37°.

39. The length of the longer base of an isosceles trapezoid is 30. The length of each leg is 20, and the included angle is 53°. Find the area of the trapezoid.

40. Find the measure of the angle formed by a diagonal of a cube and a diagonal of a face of the cube from a common vertex.

Exercises 41–44 refer to the diagram at the right, in which $\overline{BD}$ is the altitude from B.

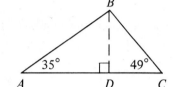

41. If $AB = 75$, find BC.

42. If $BC = 114$, find AB.

43. If $AC = 193$, find AD. (*Hint:* Let $AD = x$, $BD = y$, and set up two equations in x and y.)

44. If $AC = 177$, find DC.

Section 10-2 APPLYING RIGHT-TRIANGLE TRIGONOMETRY

In Section 10-1 you learned how to solve a right triangle when you are given the lengths of two sides of the triangle or the length of one side and the measure of one acute angle. In this section you will apply these techniques to solve problems dealing with physical situations.

First make an accurate sketch of the situation. In particular, draw a right triangle containing the acute angle whose measure is either given or desired.

EXAMPLE   Each ramp of a parking garage forms an angle of 7° with the horizontal. Each level of the garage is 3.5 m above the next lower level. To the nearest meter, how long is each ramp?

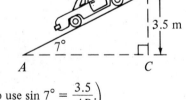

SOLUTION   Draw a sketch of the situation.
$AB =$ length of the ramp in meters.
Now write an equation that states a relation-ship between the given quantities and AB.

$$\csc 7° = \frac{AB}{3.5} \quad \left(\text{You could also use } \sin 7° = \frac{3.5}{AB}.\right)$$
$$AB = 3.5(\csc 7°)$$
$$= 3.5(8.206)$$
$$= 29 \text{ (to the nearest meter)}$$

Therefore, each ramp is 29 m long.

In describing physical situations, the terms *angle of elevation* and *angle of depression* are often used.

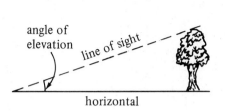

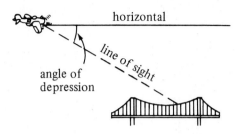

EXAMPLE   An observer whose eye level is 1.5 m above ground sights the top of the vertical wall of the El Capitan cliff at an angle of elevation of 79°. If the observer is 211 m from the base of the wall, find the height of El Capitan, to the nearest tenth of a meter.

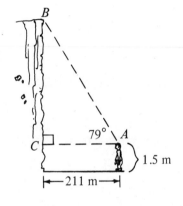

SOLUTION   The height of El Capitan $= BC + 1.5$

$$\tan 79° = \frac{BC}{211}$$

$$BC = 211(\tan 79°)$$
$$= 211(5.145) = 1085.6 \text{ m (to the nearest tenth of a meter)}$$

Thus, the height of El Capitan is $(1085.6 + 1.5)$ m, or 1087.1 m.

WRITTEN EXERCISES

In Exercises 1–10, find lengths to the nearest integer and angle measures to the nearest 10′.

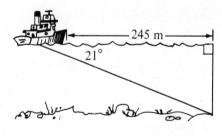

A 1. The angle of depression from a prospecting ship to a mineral deposit on the ocean floor is 21°. After sailing 245 m, the ship is directly above the mineral deposit. Find the depth of the ocean at that point.

2. The angle of elevation to the top of a tree from the base of a boulder 54 m distant is 23°30′. How tall is the tree?

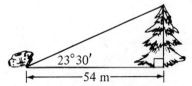

Find lengths to the nearest integer and angle measures to the nearest 10′.

3. A support wire runs from the top of a utility pole 12.2 m tall and makes an angle of 70° with the ground. Find the length of the wire.

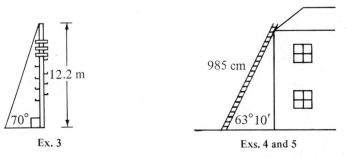

Ex. 3   Exs. 4 and 5

A ladder 985 cm long leans against the side of a building and makes an angle of 63°10′ with the ground.

4. How high above the ground is the top of the ladder?

5. How far is the foot of the ladder from the base of the building?

6. An engineer wants to grade a bridge ramp so that it rises 6.7 m vertically while traversing 72 m horizontally. What should be the measure of the angle the ramp forms with the ground?

7. In the figure at the right, a ship is 250 m from the base of the cliff. Find the angle of depression from the top of the lighthouse to the top of the ship.

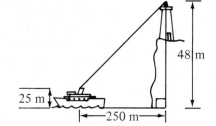

8. From an observation tower, a forest ranger whose eye level is 34 m above ground level sights a fire at ground level and at an angle of depression of 2°40′. How far is the fire from the base of the tower?

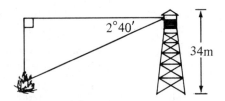

9. From the top of a control tower 70 m high, an air traffic controller sights an incoming plane at an angle of elevation of 16°. At that moment the plane is 500 m above the ground. How far is the plane from the top of the tower?

10. From the roof of one building an observer 2 m tall sights the top of a building 42 m tall at an angle of depression of 14°20′. If the bases of the two buildings are 94 m apart, how tall is the building on which the observer is standing?

11. In about 270 B.C., Greek astronomer Aristarchus of Samos tried to calculate the *relative* distances of the sun and the moon from Earth. He reasoned that when the moon is a half-moon, the lines connecting the moon to the sun and the moon to himself are perpendicular. If θ is $89°50'$ and the moon is 386,000 km from Earth, how far (to the nearest million kilometers) is the sun from Earth?

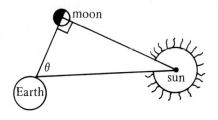

12. Observers at points A and B on Earth's equator observe the moon. To the person at A, the moon appears to be on the horizon. At the same time, the moon appears to be directly overhead to the person at B. If θ (the difference in longitude between A and B) is $89°$ and the radius, OA, of Earth is 6400 km, find the distance (to the nearest thousand kilometers) to the moon. (*Note:* This answer need not be 386,000 km because the distance varies!)

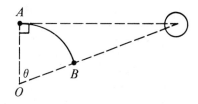

B 13. A boat at point A sights the top of a cliff at an angle of elevation of $31°$. After sailing 9.6 m closer to the cliff, the boat sights the top from B at an angle of elevation of $38°$.

a. How high is the cliff? (*Hint:* Let $x = CD$, $y = BC$. Set up two equations involving x and y.)

b. At the time of the first sighting, how far was the boat from the base of the cliff?

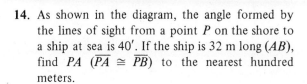

14. As shown in the diagram, the angle formed by the lines of sight from a point P on the shore to a ship at sea is $40'$. If the ship is 32 m long (AB), find PA ($\overline{PA} \cong \overline{PB}$) to the nearest hundred meters.

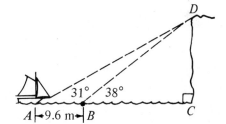

C 15. In the figure, two telephone poles of equal height h are a distance c apart. From a point P on the line connecting the bases of the poles, the angles of elevation to the tops of the poles are α and β. Show that

$$h = c\left(\frac{\tan \alpha \tan \beta}{\tan \beta - \tan \alpha}\right)$$

(*Hint:* Express x in terms of h, c, and $\tan \alpha$ or $\tan \beta$.)

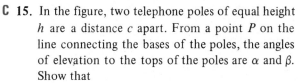
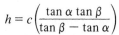
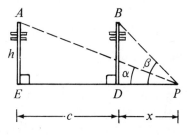

16. A plane is sighted from points D and E at angles of elevation of α and β as shown. If $DE = g$, show that the height h of the plane is:

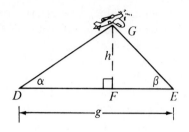

$$h = g\left(\frac{\tan \alpha \tan \beta}{\tan \alpha + \tan \beta}\right)$$

(*Hint:* Let $DF = x$. Express FE in terms of g and x. Set up two equations involving x and h, and then substitute to eliminate x.)

Section 10-3 THE LAW OF SINES

In the first two sections of this chapter you used the Pythagorean Theorem and the definitions of the trigonometric functions to solve a right triangle. In this section you will learn how to use a formula called the *Law of Sines* to solve *any* triangle if you are given the length of a side and the measures of two angles.

We will develop the Law of Sines for acute triangles. In the Oral Exercises you will be asked to prove that it is also true for obtuse and right triangles.

In acute $\triangle ABC$, let $\overline{CD}$ be the altitude from C.
In $\triangle ADC$:

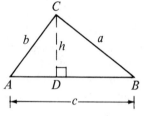

$$\sin A = \frac{h}{b}, \quad \text{or} \quad b \sin A = h$$

In $\triangle BDC$:

$$\sin B = \frac{h}{a}, \quad \text{or} \quad a \sin B = h$$

Thus:

$$b \sin A = a \sin B$$

Dividing both sides by ab, we obtain:

$$\frac{\sin A}{a} = \frac{\sin B}{b}$$

By drawing the altitude from A, we can also show that:

$$\frac{\sin B}{b} = \frac{\sin C}{c}$$

Combining the last two equations gives us the Law of Sines.

Law of Sines

In any triangle, the sine of an angle is proportional to the length of the side opposite the angle. In $\triangle ABC$:

$$\frac{\sin A}{a} = \frac{\sin B}{b} = \frac{\sin C}{c}$$

EXAMPLE In $\triangle ABC$, $\angle A = 72°$, $\angle C = 43°$, and $a = 25$. Find b and c to the nearest integer.

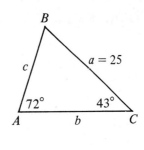

SOLUTION $\angle B = 180° - (72° + 43°) = 65°$

Use the Law of Sines to find b.

$$\frac{\sin A}{a} = \frac{\sin B}{b}$$

$$\frac{\sin 72°}{25} = \frac{\sin 65°}{b}$$

$$b = \frac{\sin 65° \cdot 25}{\sin 72°}$$

$$= \frac{(0.9063)25}{0.9511} \quad \text{(from Table 1 or a calculator)}$$

$$= 24 \quad \text{(to the nearest integer)}$$

Similarly,

$$\frac{\sin C}{c} = \frac{\sin A}{a}$$

$$\frac{\sin 43°}{c} = \frac{\sin 72°}{25}$$

$$c = \frac{\sin 43° \cdot 25}{\sin 72°}$$

$$= \frac{(0.6820)25}{0.9511}$$

$$= 18 \quad \text{(to the nearest integer)}$$

EXAMPLE In the figure, two observers at points A and C, 8 km apart, sight a boat at the same instant. How far (to the nearest kilometer) is the boat from the farther observer?

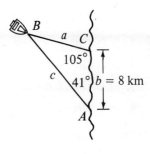

SOLUTION $\angle B = 180° - (105° + 41°) = 34°$

We want to find the value of c. (In a triangle, the longest side is opposite the largest angle.)

$$\frac{\sin B}{b} = \frac{\sin C}{c}$$

$$\frac{\sin 34°}{8} = \frac{\sin 105°}{c}$$

$$c = \frac{8 \cdot \sin 105°}{\sin 34°}$$

$$= \frac{(0.9659)8}{0.5592}$$

$$= 14 \text{ km} \quad \text{(to the nearest kilometer)}$$

The boat is 14 km from the farther observer.

ORAL EXERCISES

Exercises 1-6 demonstrate that the Law of Sines is true for obtuse $\triangle ABC$. $\overline{CD}$ is the altitude from C, and B refers to $\angle CBA$.

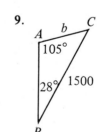

1. State an equation involving $\sin A$, h, and b.
2. State an equation involving $\sin (180° - B)$, h, and a.
3. Explain why $\sin (180° - B) = \sin B$.
4. Substitute to express $\sin B$ in terms of h and a.
5. Solve the equations obtained in Exercises 1 and 4 for h.
6. Refer to Exercise 5. What two quantities are equal?

Exercises 7-9 demonstrate that the Law of Sines is true for right $\triangle ABC$ with right $\angle C$. Complete.

7. $\dfrac{\sin A}{a} = \dfrac{\frac{a}{c}}{a} = \underline{\quad?\quad}$
8. $\dfrac{\sin B}{b} = \dfrac{\frac{b}{c}}{b} = \underline{\quad?\quad}$
9. $\dfrac{\sin C}{c} = \dfrac{\sin 90°}{c} = \underline{\quad?\quad}$

Thus, $\dfrac{\sin A}{a} = \dfrac{\sin B}{b} = \dfrac{\sin C}{c}$.

WRITTEN EXERCISES

A 1. In $\triangle ABC$, $a = 15$, $\sin A = \dfrac{1}{2}$, and $\sin B = \dfrac{1}{3}$. Find b.

2. In $\triangle ABC$, $b = 4$, $\sin B = \dfrac{1}{2}$, and $\sin C = \dfrac{3}{4}$. Find c.

3. In $\triangle ABC$, $a = 24$, $\sin A = 0.4$, and $\sin B = 0.5$. Find b.

4. In $\triangle ABC$, $a = 9$, $c = 18$, and $\sin C = 0.6$. Find $\sin A$.

5. In $\triangle ABC$, $\angle A = 30°$, $a = 8$, and $b = 6$. Find $\sin B$.

6. In $\triangle ABC$, $\angle B = 45°$, $a = 8$, and $b = 10$. Find $\sin A$.

Find the length of the indicated side to the nearest integer.

7.

8.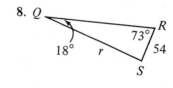

9.

10.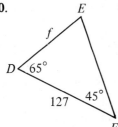

11.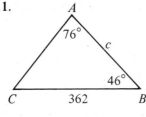

12.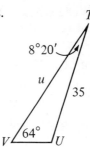

Find the length of the indicated side of $\triangle DEF$ to the nearest integer.

13. $f = 66$, $\angle D = 32°30'$, $\angle F = 111°40'$, $d =$ __?__

14. $e = 224$, $\angle D = 21°50'$, $\angle F = 33°40'$, $d =$ __?__

Find the indicated length in $\triangle ABC$. Leave your answer in simplified radical form.

15. $\angle A = 60°$, $\angle C = 45°$, $c = 20$, $a =$ __?__   **16.** $\angle B = 45°$, $\angle C = 30°$, $b = 16$, $c =$ __?__

17. $\angle A = 30°$, $\angle B = 105°$, $a = 8\sqrt{2}$, $c =$ __?__   **18.** $\angle B = 45°$, $\angle C = 75°$, $a = 10\sqrt{6}$, $b =$ __?__

Exercises 19–22 refer to the figure at the right. Find the indicated length to the nearest integer. (Surveyors use a similar procedure.)

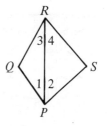

B 19. $PQ = 71$, $\angle Q = 74°$, $\angle 3 = 41°$, $\angle 2 = 69°$, $\angle S = 42°$, $RS =$ __?__

20. $PS = 82$, $\angle S = 38°$, $\angle 4 = 63°$, $\angle 1 = 46°$, $\angle Q = 79°$, $QR =$ __?__

21. $QR = 99$, $\angle 3 = 23°$, $\angle Q = 80°$, $\angle 4 = 65°$, $\angle S = 40°$, $PS =$ __?__

22. $RS = 120$, $\angle 2 = 62°$, $\angle S = 35°$, $\angle 1 = 46°$, $\angle 3 = 28°$, $PQ =$ __?__

23. In this exercise you will prove the Law of Sines by showing that
$$\frac{a}{\sin A} = \frac{b}{\sin B} = \frac{c}{\sin C} = d,$$ where d is the diameter of the circle circumscribed about $\triangle ABC$.

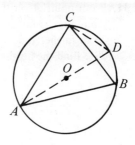

Given: Circle O is circumscribed about $\triangle ABC$;
$\overline{AD}$ is the diameter through A.

a. Explain why $\angle D = \angle B$.

b. Explain why $\angle ACD = 90°$ and show that $\sin D = \dfrac{AC}{AD}$.

c. Show that $d = \dfrac{b}{\sin B}$.

d. Draw $\overline{BD}$ and show that $d = \dfrac{c}{\sin C}$.

e. Show that $d = \dfrac{a}{\sin A}$.

Use the results of Exercise 23 to complete Exercises 24-27. Give all lengths to the nearest unit and all angles to the nearest 10′.

24. A chord, $\overline{AB}$, of a circle circumscribed about △ABC is 9 cm long. If the measure of ∠C is 30°, find the radius of the circle.

25. Find the diameter of a circle circumscribed about △ABC if $BC = 43$ and ∠$A = 23°$.

26. A circle of diameter 240 is circumscribed about △DEF. If ∠$D = 46°20′$, find EF.

27. A circle of radius 18 is circumscribed about △DEF. If $DF = 15$, find the measure of ∠E.

28. Two angles of a triangle are 30° and 50°, and the longest side of the triangle is 36 cm long. Find the length of the shortest side to the nearest centimeter.

29. Two angles of a triangle are 37° and 68°, and the shortest side is 143 cm long. Find the length of the longest side to the nearest centimeter.

30. To find the distance JM across the river, Doris found that the length of $\overline{KL}$ is 100 m, ∠$JLK = 38°20′$, and ∠$JKM = 41°40′$. What is the width (to the nearest meter) of the river?

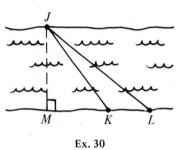

Ex. 30

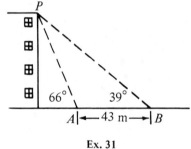

Ex. 31

31. From point A on the ground, the angle of elevation to P, a point at the top of a building, is 66°. Point B is in line with A and the base of the building and is 43 m farther than A from the building. The angle of elevation from B to P is 39°. Find the height of the building to the nearest meter.

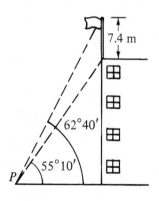

32. From point P at ground level, the angles of elevation to the top and bottom of a roof-top flagpole 7.4 m tall are 62°40′ and 55°10′, respectively. Find the height of the building to the nearest meter.

33. From the top of a cliff, the angles of depression to the top and bottom of a tower 30 m high are 75° and 80°, respectively. If the base of the tower is at the foot of the cliff, find the height of the cliff to the nearest meter.

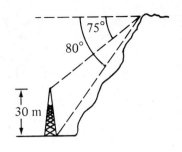

C 34. In $\triangle ABC$, $\cos A = \dfrac{3}{5}$, $\tan B = \dfrac{8}{15}$, and $AB = 42$. Without referring to Table 1, find **(a)** AC, **(b)** BC, and **(c)** $\sin C$.

Section 10-4 THE AMBIGUOUS CASE

When two sides and a nonincluded angle of a triangle (SSA) are given, the triangle may not be uniquely determined. For this reason, SSA is called the *ambiguous case*.

There are several possibilities to consider if you are given two sides, a and b, and an angle, $\angle A$. As the figures show, either 0, 1, or 2 triangles may be formed.

Case I $A < 90°$

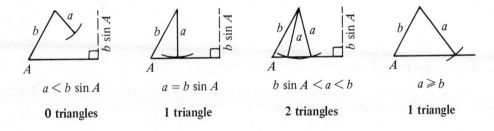

$a < b \sin A$	$a = b \sin A$	$b \sin A < a < b$	$a \geqslant b$
0 triangles	**1 triangle**	**2 triangles**	**1 triangle**

Case II $A \geqslant 90°$

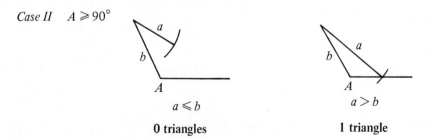

$a \leqslant b$	$a > b$
0 triangles	**1 triangle**

You can use the Law of Sines to solve a triangle if you are given SSA. First draw a sketch and determine the number of solutions.

EXAMPLE In $\triangle ABC$, $A = 30°$, $b = 10$, and $a = 2$. Find B to the nearest $10'$. If no solution exists, so state. If two solutions exist, state both.

SOLUTION A sketch suggests that no such triangle exists. Let's see what happens when we apply the Law of Sines.

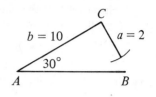

$$\frac{\sin A}{a} = \frac{\sin B}{b}, \quad \text{or} \quad \sin B = \frac{b \sin A}{a}$$

$$\sin B = \frac{10 \cdot 0.5}{2} = 2.5$$

Since $-1 \leqslant \sin \theta \leqslant 1$ for every angle θ, this equation has no solution.

EXAMPLE In $\triangle ABC$, $\angle A = 30°$, $b = 6$, and $a = 4$. Find $\angle B$ to the nearest $10'$. If no solution exists, so state. If two solutions exist, state them both.

SOLUTION A sketch suggests that there are two solutions. You can verify this by applying the Law of Sines.

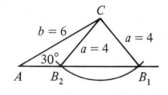

$$\frac{\sin A}{a} = \frac{\sin B}{b}, \quad \text{or} \quad \sin B = \frac{b \sin A}{a}$$

$$\sin B = \frac{6 \cdot \sin 30°}{4} = \frac{6 \cdot 0.5}{4} = 0.75$$

From Table 1, $\quad \angle AB_1C = 48°40'$, $\quad \angle AB_2C = 180° - (48°40') = 131°20'$.

EXAMPLE In $\triangle ABC$, $\angle A = 40°$, $b = 7$, and $a = 10$. What kind of triangle is $\triangle ABC$?

SOLUTION A sketch suggests that $\triangle ABC$ is obtuse. To check this, use the Law of Sines to find $\angle C$.

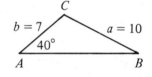

$$\frac{\sin A}{a} = \frac{\sin B}{b}, \quad \text{or} \quad \sin B = \frac{b \sin A}{a}$$

$$\sin B = \frac{7 \cdot \sin 40°}{10} = \frac{7 \cdot 0.6428}{10} = 0.4500$$

$\angle B = 26°40'$, $\quad \angle C = 180° - (40° + 26°40') = 113°20'$

Therefore, $\triangle ABC$ is obtuse.

Note: $\sin(180° - 26°40')$, or $\sin 153°20'$, also equals 0.4500.
Can $\angle B$ equal $153°20'$? If $\angle B = 153°20'$, then
$\angle C = 180° - (40° + 153°20') = 180° - 193°20' < 0°$.
So $\angle B \neq 153°20'$.

ORAL EXERCISES

1. If two sides and the included angle of one triangle are congruent to two sides and the included angle of another triangle, must the remaining three pairs of parts of the two triangles also be congruent? State a theorem from geometry that supports your answer.

2. Use the diagram to explain why the answer to Exercise 1 would be "No" if the words "a nonincluded angle" were substituted for the words "the included angle" everywhere.

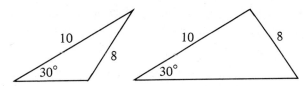

In Exercises 3–6, $\sin A$ and b are given for $\triangle ABC$. What value of a will make $\triangle ABC$ a right triangle with right $\angle B$?

3. $\sin A = 0.5$, $b = 14$

4. $\sin A = 0.25$, $b = 8$

5. $\sin A = 0.64$, $b = 5$

6. $\sin A = 0.83$, $b = 10$

7. Explain why any values of a and b will produce at most one value for $\angle B$ in any $\triangle ABC$ with $\angle A \geqslant 90°$.

WRITTEN EXERCISES

State whether $\triangle ABC$ is acute, obtuse, or right.

A 1. $\angle C = 30°$, $b = 12$, $c = 6$

2. $\angle B = 30°$, $b = 12$, $c = 6$

3. $\angle A = 60°$, $a = 15$, $b = 15$

4. $\angle A = 45°$, $a = 5\sqrt{2}$, $c = 10$

Find the number of triangles that satisfy the given conditions. You need not solve any triangle.

5. $\angle A = 120°$, $a = 2\sqrt{3}$, $b = 6$

6. $\angle A = 30°$, $a = 9$, $b = 18$

7. $\angle A = 98°$, $a = 10$, $b = 6$

8. $\angle A = 101°$, $a = 7$, $b = 7$

9. $\angle B = 45°$, $b = 7\sqrt{2}$, $c = 12$

10. $\angle B = 150°$, $b = 8$, $c = 9$

11. $\angle B = 56°$, $a = 20$, $b = 18$

12. $\angle B = 63°$, $a = 15$, $b = 14$

13. $\angle C = 45°$, $b = 32\sqrt{2}$, $c = 32$

14. $\angle A = 60°$, $a = 10\sqrt{3}$, $b = 9\sqrt{3}$

Use the given information to find two possible measures (to the nearest $10'$) of $\angle Q$ and $\angle R$ in $\triangle PQR$.

15. $\angle P = 48°$, $p = 65$, $q = 75$

16. $\angle P = 35°50'$, $p = 50$, $r = 80$

17. $\angle P = 21°$, $p = 220$, $r = 575$

18. $\angle P = 26°$, $p = 45$, $q = 92$

Solve $\triangle ABC$. Give lengths to the nearest unit and angles to the nearest degree. If there are two solutions, give both. If no triangle exists, so state.

19. $\angle A = 72°$, $a = 45$, $b = 26$

20. $\angle C = 51°$, $b = 92$, $c = 72$

21. $\angle B = 115°$, $a = 12$, $b = 22$

22. $\angle A = 46°$, $a = 72$, $b = 50$

23. $\angle A = 61°$, $a = 75$, $b = 120$

24. $\angle B = 117°$, $b = 16$, $c = 18$

B 25. $\angle B = 23°$, $b = 125$, $c = 150$

26. $\angle C = 39°$, $a = 112$, $c = 80$

27. $\angle B = 19°$, $a = 440$, $b = 350$

28. $\angle A = 59°$, $a = 16$, $c = 18$

Exercises 29 and 30 refer to ☐ABCD shown at the right.

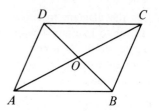

29. If $AC = 32$, $AB = 26$, and $\angle AOB = 124°$, find BD to the nearest integer.

30. If $AC = 74$, $BD = 48$, and $\angle ABD = 29°$, find AB to the nearest integer.

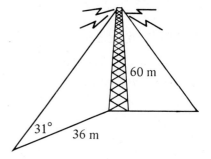

31. A radio transmission tower 60 m tall is situated at the top of a hill whose foot is 36 m from the base of the tower. A support wire that runs from the foot of the hill to the top of the tower makes an angle of $31°$ with the side of the hill. How long (to the nearest meter) is the wire?

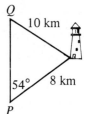

32. A ship at point P sights a lighthouse 8 km distant and at an angle of $54°$ from the direction in which the ship is sailing. After sailing another hour to point Q, the ship sights the same lighthouse, this time at a distance of 10 km. What is the ship's speed to the nearest kilometer per hour?

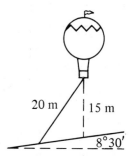

C 33. A hot-air balloon is launched from a hillside that forms an $8°30'$ angle with a horizontal plane. In the figure, a restraining rope 20 m long is pulled taut when the balloon has ascended 15 m. How far (to the nearest meter) from the point where the rope is anchored to the ground is the launch site of the balloon?

SELF-TEST 1

1. Given $\triangle PQR$ in which $\angle R$ is the right angle, complete. Give lengths to the nearest integer and angles to the nearest $10'$. Section 10-1
   a. $p = 72$, $\angle P = 34°$, $q = $ __?__
   b. $r = 45$, $\angle Q = 29°10'$, $p = $ __?__
   c. $p = 15$, $r = 30$, $\angle P = $ __?__

2. Find the measures of the angles (to the nearest degree) of an isosceles triangle Section 10-2
whose sides have lengths 14, 10, and 10.

3. A boat is 173 m from the source of light in a lighthouse. The angle of elevation from the boat to this source is 16°50'.

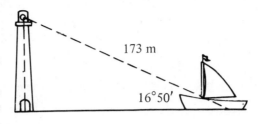

173 m

16°50'

    a. How tall (to the nearest meter) is the lighthouse?

    b. What is the distance (to the nearest meter) from the boat to the base of the lighthouse?

In $\triangle ABC$, use the Law of Sines to find c to the nearest integer.

4. $a = 52$, $\angle A = 37°$, $\angle C = 42°$ Section 10-3

5. $b = 100$, $\angle A = 55°$, $\angle C = 19°$

6. Find the number of triangles ABC that satisfy the given conditions. You need Section 10-4 not solve any triangle.

    a. $\angle A = 30°$, $a = 5$, $b = 10$
    b. $\angle A = 107°$, $a = 141$, $b = 92$
    c. $\angle A = 44°$, $a = 8$, $b = 15$
    d. $\angle A = 32°$, $a = 17$, $b = 20$

7. State whether $\triangle ABC$ is acute, obtuse, or right.

    a. $\angle B = 60°$, $b = 7\sqrt{3}$, $c = 14$
    b. $\angle A = 60°$, $b = 18$, $a = 21$
    c. $\angle A = 30°$, $b = 10$, $a = 12$

Section 10-5 THE LAW OF COSINES

In this section you will learn about the *Law of Cosines*, which can be used to solve a triangle determined by Side-Angle-Side (SAS) or Side-Side-Side (SSS).

    Place the coordinate axes so that vertex A of $\triangle ABC$ is at the origin and $\overline{AB}$ lies on the positive x-axis. Let the coordinates of C be (x, y). In the exercises on page 284, we showed that $\cos \theta = \dfrac{x}{b}$ and $\sin \theta = \dfrac{y}{b}$. Thus, $x = b \cos \theta$ and $y = b \sin \theta$.

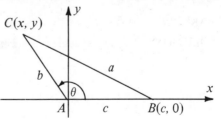

    According to the Distance Formula:

$$a^2 = (x - c)^2 + (y - 0)^2$$
$$= (b \cos \theta - c)^2 + (b \sin \theta)^2$$
$$= b^2 \cos^2 \theta - 2\,bc \cos \theta + c^2 + b^2 \sin^2 \theta$$
$$= b^2(\cos^2 \theta + \sin^2 \theta) + c^2 - 2bc \cos \theta$$

But $\cos^2 \theta + \sin^2 \theta = 1$, so $a^2 = b^2(\cos^2 \theta + \sin^2 \theta) + c^2 - 2bc \cos \theta$ simplifies to:

$$a^2 = b^2 + c^2 - 2bc \cos \theta$$

Replacing θ with A, we have:

$$a^2 = b^2 + c^2 - 2bc \cos A$$

By similar argument, two other forms of the Law of Cosines can be verified.

Law of Cosines

In any triangle, the square of the length of one side is equal to the sum of the squares of the lengths of the other two sides minus twice the product of the lengths of these sides and the cosine of the included angle. In $\triangle ABC$:

$a^2 = b^2 + c^2 - 2bc \cos A$ or $\cos A = \dfrac{b^2 + c^2 - a^2}{2bc}$

$b^2 = a^2 + c^2 - 2ac \cos B$ or $\cos B = \dfrac{a^2 + c^2 - b^2}{2ac}$

$c^2 = a^2 + b^2 - 2ab \cos C$ or $\cos C = \dfrac{a^2 + b^2 - c^2}{2ab}$

Although we have verified that the Law of Cosines is true for any obtuse triangle, it can easily be shown that the law is valid for any triangle. (See Oral Exercises 1–7 and 16.)

Now we will show you how the Law of Cosines can be used in solving triangles.

EXAMPLE   In $\triangle ABC$, $a = 10$, $b = 13$, and $\angle C = 61°20'$. Find c to the nearest integer.

SOLUTION   Since $\angle C$ is the given angle, use the Law of Cosines as follows:

$$c^2 = a^2 + b^2 - 2ab \cos C$$
$$c^2 = 10^2 + 13^2 - 2 \cdot 10 \cdot 13 \cdot \cos 61°20'$$
$$c^2 = 100 + 169 - 260(0.4797)$$
$$c^2 = 144.3$$
$$c = 12 \text{ (to the nearest integer)}$$

EXAMPLE   In $\triangle ABC$, $a = 8$, $b = 19$, and $c = 13$. Find the measure of the largest angle.

SOLUTION   The largest angle is opposite the longest side, so $\angle B$ is the largest angle.

$$\cos B = \frac{a^2 + c^2 - b^2}{2ac}$$

$$\cos B = \frac{8^2 + 13^2 - 19^2}{2 \cdot 8 \cdot 13}$$

$$\cos B \approx -0.6154$$

Since $\cos B$ is negative, $90° < \angle B < 180°$.
From Table 1, $0.6154 = \cos 52°$, so $\angle B = 180° - 52° = 128°$.
Therefore, the largest angle is $128°$.

ORAL EXERCISES

Justify each step in this proof of the Law of Cosines (for acute triangles). In the diagram, $\triangle ABC$ is an acute triangle and $\overline{CD}$ is the altitude from C.

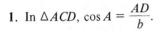

1. In $\triangle ACD$, $\cos A = \dfrac{AD}{b}$.

2. $b \cos A = AD$

3. $b^2 = (CD)^2 + (AD)^2$

4. In $\triangle BDC$, $a^2 = (CD)^2 + (DB)^2$

5. $a^2 = (CD)^2 + (c - AD)^2$

6. $a^2 = (CD)^2 + (AD)^2 + c^2 - 2c(AD)$

7. $a^2 = b^2 + c^2 - 2bc \cos A$

State an equation you could use to find the value of x. You need not solve the equation.

8.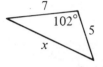

9.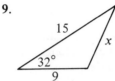

10.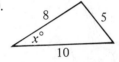

11.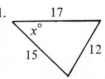

Does the information always yield a unique triangle? Explain.

12. SAS   13. SSA   14. AAA   15. SSS

16. **a.** What is the value of $\cos A$ when $\angle A$ is a right angle?
    b. Substitute the value for $\cos A$ you obtained in part (a) to simplify the Law of Cosines, $a^2 = b^2 + c^2 - 2bc \cos A$, in the case where $\triangle ABC$ is a right triangle with right $\angle A$. (The Pythagorean Theorem is a special case of the Law of Cosines.)

WRITTEN EXERCISES

Complete for $\triangle ABC$.

A   1. $a = 10$, $b = 4$, $c = 8$, $\cos B = \underline{\ ?\ }$ 2. $a = 8$, $b = 7$, $c = 5$, $\cos A = \underline{\ ?\ }$

    3. $a = 4$, $b = 6$, $c = 8$, $\cos C = \underline{\ ?\ }$ 4. $a = 5$, $b = 9$, $c = 5$, $\cos B = \underline{\ ?\ }$

Complete for △ABC. Find all lengths to the nearest integer and all angle measures to the nearest 10'.

5. $a = 3$, $c = 8$, $\angle B = 60°$, $b =$ __?__

6. $b = 4$, $c = 3$, $\angle A = 120°$, $a =$ __?__

7. $a = 33$, $b = 7$, $\angle C = 120°$, $c =$ __?__

8. $c = 5$, $a = 21$, $\angle B = 60°$, $b =$ __?__

9. $a = 16$, $b = 27$, $\angle C = 51°$, $c =$ __?__

10. $b = 12$, $c = 19$, $\angle A = 14°50'$, $a =$ __?__

11. $a = 23$, $c = 15$, $\angle B = 92°30'$, $b =$ __?__

12. $b = 14$, $c = 32$, $\angle A = 121°$, $a =$ __?__

13. $a = 5$, $b = 16$, $c = 19$, $\angle C =$ __?__

14. $a = 7$, $b = 37$, $c = 40$, $\angle B =$ __?__

15. $a = 9$, $b = 11$, $c = 6$, $\angle C =$ __?__

16. $a = 34$, $b = 12$, $c = 25$, $\angle A =$ __?__

State whether a △ABC exists that satisfies the given conditions. If so, state how many such triangles exist. You need not solve any triangle.

17. $a = 6$, $b = 8$, $c = 15$

18. $a = 25$, $b = 18$, $\angle C = 150°$

19. $\angle A = 30°$, $\angle B = 45°$, $a = 6$

20. $\angle B = 51°$, $\angle C = 143°$, $a = 12$

21. $\angle A = 50°$, $a = 18$, $b = 20$

22. $a = 10$, $b = 6$, $c = 11$

23. The top tube ($\overline{PQ}$) of a bicycle is 56 cm long and the seat tube ($\overline{QR}$) is 58 cm long. If $PR = 67$ cm, what is the angle between the seat tube and the top tube, to the nearest 10'?

24. Two sides of a parallelogram are 10 cm long and 15 cm long. The length of a diagonal of the parallelogram is 20 cm. Find the measure (to the nearest 10') of an obtuse angle of the parallelogram.

25. In a parallelogram, two sides that are 20 cm and 12 cm long include an angle of 40°. Find the length (to the nearest centimeter) of a shorter diagonal of the parallelogram.

26. The diagonals of a parallelogram are 18 cm long and 24 cm long, and they intersect in an angle of 120°. Find the length (to the nearest centimeter) of each side of the parallelogram.

27. The sides of a triangle are 4 cm, 5 cm, and 6 cm long. Find the measure (to the nearest 10') of the smallest angle of the triangle.

28. The sides of a triangle are 6 cm, 7 cm, and 9 cm long. Find the measure (to the nearest 10') of the largest angle of the triangle.

B 29. The hour and minute hands of a clock have lengths 6 cm and 10 cm, respectively. How far apart are the tips of the hands at four o'clock?

30. An air traffic controller sights two airplanes in the same vertical plane as the control tower and at angles of elevation of $32°$ and $28°$ as shown. If the first plane is 1000 m from the tower and the second is 3200 m from the tower, how far apart are the two planes?

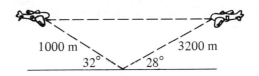

1000 m   3200 m

$32°$ $28°$

31. Use the Law of Cosines to find two possible (exact) values of c in $\triangle ABC$ if $\angle A = 60°$, $a = 7$, and $b = 8$.

32. Use the Law of Cosines to find two possible (exact) values of c in $\triangle ABC$ if $\angle B = 60°$, $b = 9$, and $a = 10$.

33. Find the length (to the nearest tenth) of a side of a regular pentagon inscribed in a circle of radius 4.

34. Find the length (to the nearest integer) of a diagonal of a regular pentagon inscribed in a circle of radius 11.

Exercises 35–38 refer to the figure at the right.
Find CD.

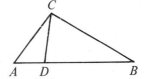

EXAMPLE $AD = 2$, $DB = 6$, $AC = 4$, $BC = 8$

SOLUTION   In $\triangle ABC$: $\cos A = \dfrac{(AB)^2 + (AC)^2 - (BC)^2}{2(AB)(AC)}$

$$\cos A = \frac{8^2 + 4^2 - 8^2}{2(8)(4)} = \frac{16}{64} = \frac{1}{4}$$

In $\triangle ADC$: $(CD)^2 = (AC)^2 + (AD)^2 - 2(AC)(AD) \cos A$

$$= 4^2 + 2^2 - 2(4)(2) \cdot \frac{1}{4}$$

$$= 16$$

$$CD = 4$$

35. $AD = 14$, $DB = 11$, $AC = 15$, $BC = 20$ **36.** $AD = 4$, $DB = 7$, $AC = 13$, $BC = 20$

37. $AD = 11$, $DB = 14$, $AC = 25$, $BC = 40$ **38.** $AD = 36$, $DB = 33$, $AC = 29$, $BC = 52$

39. In $\triangle PQR$, $PQ = 56$, $PR = 25$, and $QR = 39$. Find the length (to the nearest integer) of the median to $\overline{PQ}$. (*Hint*: Use a method like the one you used in Exercises 35–38.)

40. In $\triangle DEF$, $DE = DF = 62$ and $EF = 16$. Find the length (to the nearest integer) of the median to $\overline{DE}$.

C 41. In $\triangle ABC$, find $\cos A$ when $a:b:c = 2:2:1$.

42. The lengths of the sides of a triangle are in the ratio $5:7:9$. Find the ratio of the cosines of the smallest and largest angles of the triangle.

43. In $\triangle ABC$, $AB = AC$ and $BC = 8$. The median to $\overline{AB}$ has length 9. Find AB.

44. In $\triangle RST$, $RS = RT$ and $ST = 12$. The median to $\overline{RS}$ has length 19. Find RS.

Section 10-6 THE AREA OF A TRIANGLE

If you are given the length, b, of one side of a triangle and the length, h, of the altitude to that side, you can use the formula

$$A = \frac{1}{2}bh$$

to find the area of the triangle. In this section you will develop formulas to find the area of a triangle if you are given:
- SAS (two sides and an included angle)
- AAS or ASA (a side and any two angles)
- SSS (three sides)

Begin with the SAS case. In $\triangle ABC$, assume that a, b, and $\angle C$ are given. Draw $\overline{BD}$, the altitude from B, and let $h = BD$.

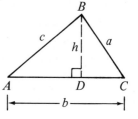

In $\triangle BCD$, $\sin C = \dfrac{h}{a}$, or:

$$h = a \sin C$$

Substitute in: Area $= \dfrac{1}{2}$(base)(height)

to get: Area $= \dfrac{1}{2}b(a \sin C)$, or

$$\text{Area} = \frac{1}{2}ab \sin C$$

Similarly, you can show that:

$$\text{Area} = \frac{1}{2}bc \sin A$$

$$\text{Area} = \frac{1}{2}ac \sin B$$

In other words:

The area of a triangle is equal to half the product of the lengths of two sides and the sine of the included angle.

EXAMPLE   Find the area of $\triangle DEF$ in which $e = 16$, $f = 12$, and $\angle D = 30°$.

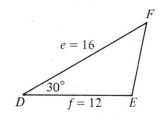

SOLUTION   Area $= \dfrac{1}{2}ef \sin D$

$$= \frac{1}{2}(16)(12)\sin 30° = \frac{1}{2}(192)\frac{1}{2}$$

$$= 48$$

Now we will derive formulas for the area of a triangle given any two angles and a side.

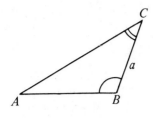

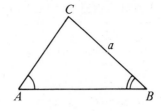

Case I (ASA)	Case II (AAS)

$\angle B$, $\angle C$, and a are given.
Thus we can find
$$\angle A = 180° - (\angle B + \angle C).$$

$\angle A$, $\angle B$, and a are given.
Thus we can find
$$\angle C = 180° - (\angle A + \angle B).$$

Since in both Case I and Case II we know $\angle A$, $\angle B$, $\angle C$, and a, the proofs are the same.

Applying the Law of Sines yields:
$$\frac{\sin A}{a} = \frac{\sin B}{b}$$

$$b = \frac{a \sin B}{\sin A}$$

Substitute into the formula
$$\text{Area} = \frac{1}{2}ab \sin C$$

to obtain:
$$\text{Area} = \frac{a^2 \sin B \sin C}{2 \sin A}$$

Similarly, you can show that:
$$\text{Area} = \frac{b^2 \sin A \sin C}{2 \sin B}$$

$$\text{Area} = \frac{c^2 \sin A \sin B}{2 \sin C}$$

EXAMPLE Find the area (to the nearest integer) of $\triangle ABC$ in which $a = 14$, $\angle B = 53°10'$, and $\angle C = 67°20'$.

SOLUTION $\angle A = 180° - (\angle B + \angle C) = 180° - 120°30'$
$\angle A = 59°30'$

$$\text{Area} = \frac{a^2 \sin B \sin C}{2 \sin A}$$

$$= \frac{(14)^2(0.8004)(0.9228)}{2(0.8616)} \quad \text{(from Table 1)}$$

$$= 84 \text{ (to the nearest integer)}$$

If you are given three sides of a triangle (SSS), you can use *Hero's Formula* (which you will prove in Exercises 37–40) to find its area. This formula expresses the area of $\triangle ABC$ in terms of s, its *semiperimeter*. The semiperimeter of a triangle is half the perimeter.

Hero's Formula

$$\text{Area} = \sqrt{s(s-a)(s-b)(s-c)} \quad \text{where } s = \frac{a+b+c}{2}$$

EXAMPLE Find the area (to the nearest cm²) of a triangle whose sides are 5 cm, 7 cm, and 10 cm long.

SOLUTION $s = \dfrac{5+7+10}{2} = 11$

$\text{Area} = \sqrt{(11)(6)(4)(1)}$

$\qquad = \sqrt{264}$

$\qquad = 16 \text{ cm}^2$ (to the nearest square centimeter)

ORAL EXERCISES

State a formula you could use to find the area of $\triangle ABC$. You need not solve.

1. $\angle A = 70°$, $\angle B = 49°$, $c = 12$
2. $a = 10$, $b = 9$, $c = 16$
3. $a = 14$, $b = 23$, $\angle C = 29°$
4. $c = 12$, $a = 35$, $\angle B = 107°$
5. $a = 25$, $\angle B = 18°$, $\angle C = 83°$
6. $a = b = 210$, $c = 75$

7. Simplify the formula Area $= \dfrac{1}{2}ab \sin C$ in the case where $\angle C = 90°$.

8. Two rods are hinged together at one end, and a string is connected to the other two ends to form a triangle. What should the measure of angle θ be in order to make the area of this triangle a maximum? Explain your answer on the basis of one of the formulas in this section.

9. Explain how you would find the area of a triangle if you were given two sides and a nonincluded angle.

WRITTEN EXERCISES

Find the area of $\triangle ABC$ to the nearest integer.

A
1. $\angle A = 30°$, $b = 12$, $c = 16$
2. $\angle B = 150°$, $a = 24$, $c = 17$
3. $a = 13$, $b = 4$, $c = 15$
4. $a = 17$, $b = 28$, $c = 25$
5. $\angle B = 40°$, $\angle C = 30°$, $a = 10$
6. $\angle A = 53°10'$, $\angle B = 67°20'$, $c = 14$
7. $a = 11$, $b = 20$, $c = 13$
8. $a = 25$, $b = 30$, $c = 11$
9. $\angle B = 14°$, $\angle C = 16°$, $b = 12$
10. $\angle A = 12°40'$, $\angle C = 36°50'$, $a = 25$
11. $\angle C = 13°$, $a = 10$, $b = 8$
12. $\angle A = 15°50'$, $b = 11$, $c = 40$

13. If the area of $\triangle ABC$ is 60, with $a = 25$ and $\angle B = 30°$, find c.

14. If the area of $\triangle ABC$ is 120, with $\angle A = 150°$ and $c = 18$, find b.

15. The area of a triangle is 45 and the lengths of two of its sides are 18 and 10. Find two possible values for the measure of the included angle.

16. The area of a triangle is $30\sqrt{3}$ and the lengths of two of its sides are 16 and 7.5. Find two possible values for the measure of the included angle.

17. Two sides of a parallelogram are 2 cm and 5 cm long. The length of a diagonal is 4 cm. Find the area of the parallelogram.

18. In a parallelogram, two sides 30 cm and 50 cm long include an angle of $63°$. Find the area of the parallelogram.

19. Two sides of a parallelogram are 12 cm and 18 cm long. The area of the parallelogram is 108 cm². Find the angles of the parallelogram.

20. In rhombus $ABCD$, $\angle ABC = 120°$ and the length of each side is 12. Find the exact area of the rhombus.

21. In rhombus $ABCD$, $\angle ABC = 50°$ and the length of each side is 8. Find the area (to the nearest integer) of the rhombus.

22. In the figure, $AB = AD$, $BC = DC$, and $AC = 36$. If $\angle DAB = 100°$ and $\angle BCD = 60°$, find the area of $ABCD$ to the nearest integer.

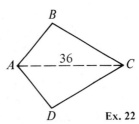

Ex. 22

Find two possible values for the measure of $\angle C$ in $\triangle ABC$. Illustrate each possibility with a sketch.

23. Area = 63, $a = 18$, $b = 14$

24. Area = 50, $a = 8$, $b = 25$

25. Area = $60\sqrt{3}$, $a = 24$, $b = 10$

26. Area = 72, $a = 12$, $b = 8\sqrt{3}$

B 27. Find the area of $\triangle ABC$ (to the nearest integer) in which $\angle A = 40°$, $a = 10$, and $c = 8$.

28. Find the area of $\triangle DEF$ in which $\angle D = 50°$, $d = 15$, and $f = 18$. (*Hint*: There are two possible answers.)

29. Find the exact area of a regular octagon inscribed in a circle of radius 10. Leave your answer in radical form.

30. Find the exact area of a regular pentagon inscribed in a circle of radius 12. Leave your answer in terms of a trigonometric function.

31. Find the area (to the nearest square centimeter) of an isosceles triangle whose base angles are each $75°$ and whose congruent sides are each 10 cm long.

32. An isosceles triangle has a base 8 cm long. Its base angles are each $70°$. Find its area to the nearest square centimeter.

33. In $\triangle ABC$, $\angle A = 60°$, $a = 6\sqrt{3}$, and $c = 6\sqrt{2}$. Find the area of $\triangle ABC$.

34. In $\triangle ABC$, $\angle A = 45°$, $a = 5\sqrt{6}$, and $b = 15$. Find the area of $\triangle ABC$.

C 35. In $\triangle DEF$, $\overline{FG}$ is the altitude from F.
Show that $\dfrac{FG}{DE} = \dfrac{\sin D \sin E}{\sin F}$.
(*Hint*: Find two expressions for the area of $\triangle DEF$.)

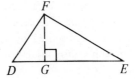

36. $\triangle ABC$ is an isosceles triangle with $AB = BC$. Show that the area

of $\triangle ABC$ is $\dfrac{b^2 \tan \theta}{4}$.

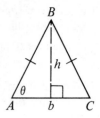

Exercises 37–40 suggest a proof of Hero's Formula.

37. Since $\sin^2 A = 1 - \cos^2 A$, use a form of the Law of Cosines to show that in $\triangle ABC$, it follows that:

$$\sin^2 A = 1 - \left(\frac{b^2 + c^2 - a^2}{2bc}\right)^2$$

38. Show that the expression in Exercise 37 simplifies to:

$$\sin^2 A = \left(\frac{1}{2bc}\right)^2 (b^2 + 2bc + c^2 - a^2)(a^2 - b^2 + 2bc - c^2)$$

$$= \left(\frac{1}{2bc}\right)^2 [(b + c)^2 - a^2] [a^2 - (b - c)^2]$$

39. Use the equation in Exercise 38 to show that:

$$\text{Area of } \triangle ABC = \sqrt{\frac{(b + c - a)(b + c + a)(a + b - c)(a - b + c)}{16}}.$$

40. Show how the equation in Exercise 39 is related to Hero's Formula.

Section 10-7 VECTORS

It is often important to describe a quantity such as a force or a velocity by both its magnitude (size) *and* its direction. For example, in reading a weather map a meteorologist needs to be able to distinguish between a wind of 10 km/h from the north and a wind of 10 km/h from the northwest. Such a quantity is called a *vector*. A vector has both magnitude and direction, and is represented by an arrow of a certain length pointing in a specified direction.

We name a vector by a special arrow over two letters, like $\overrightarrow{AB}$, which refers to the vector whose *tail* is at A and whose *head* is at B, as shown in the first figure at the right. We can also name a vector by an arrow over a letter, like $\vec{u}$ or $\vec{v}$. The second diagram at the right shows three vectors, $\vec{u}$, $\vec{v}$, and $\vec{w}$, that represent winds of 10 km/h from the northwest, 10 km/h from the north, and 20 km/h from the north, respectively.

The magnitude, or *norm*, of a vector $\vec{w}$ is denoted by $|\vec{w}|$. Since in this figure $\vec{w}$ represents a force twice as strong as the one represented by $\vec{v}$, $|\vec{w}| = 2|\vec{v}|$. The direction of each vector represents the direction of the wind.

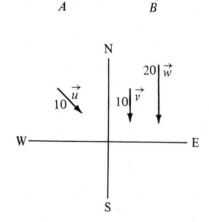

Two vectors are *equivalent* if they have the same magnitude and direction. Thus any of the vectors in the figure at the right could represent a wind of 10 km/h from the northwest since they are all equivalent.

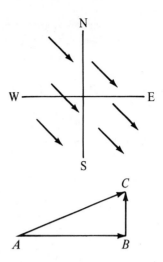

Suppose an airplane is flying due east and it encounters a wind from the south. If we represent the velocity of the airplane by $\overrightarrow{AB}$ and the velocity of the wind by $\overrightarrow{BC}$, then the resulting velocity of the airplane is given by $\overrightarrow{AC}$, the vector connecting the tail of $\overrightarrow{AB}$ with the head of $\overrightarrow{BC}$. We say that $\overrightarrow{AC} = \overrightarrow{AB} + \overrightarrow{BC}$. The next example shows two ways to find the sum of two vectors graphically.

EXAMPLE Draw a sketch to find $\vec{u} + \vec{v}$:

SOLUTION

The Triangle Method

Sketch a vector that is equivalent to $\vec{v}$ and whose tail coincides with the head of $\vec{u}$.

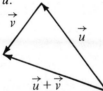

The vector joining the tail of $\vec{u}$ to the head of $\vec{v}$ represents $(\vec{u} + \vec{v})$.

The Parallelogram Method

Sketch a vector that is equivalent to $\vec{v}$ and whose tail coincides with the tail of $\vec{u}$.

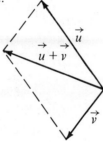

The diagonal of the parallelogram determined by $\vec{u}$ and $\vec{v}$ represents $(\vec{u} + \vec{v})$.

The parallelogram method is awkward to use to find the sum of more than two vectors. Instead we use the *polygon method*, a generalization of the triangle method. All the vectors to be added are joined head to tail. The last side of the polygon is formed by the vector that represents the sum. Its tail and head coincide with the tail of the first vector added and the head of the final vector added.

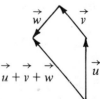

When two forces are acting on an object, their combined effect is known as the *resultant*. If each separate force is represented by a vector, the resultant is represented by the sum of the vectors.

EXAMPLE   At the same time a person is rowing north at 8 km/h directly across a river, a current of 3.2 km/h is pulling the boat eastward. Find the actual speed (to the nearest tenth of a kilometer) of the boat.

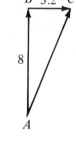

SOLUTION   In the figure, $\overrightarrow{AC}$ represents the resultant course of the boat.
$$\overrightarrow{AC} = \overrightarrow{AB} + \overrightarrow{BC}$$

By the Pythagorean Theorem:
$$|\overrightarrow{AC}|^2 = |\overrightarrow{AB}|^2 + |\overrightarrow{BC}|^2$$
$$|\overrightarrow{AC}|^2 = 8^2 + (3.2)^2 = 74.24$$
$$|\overrightarrow{AC}| = 8.6 \text{ (to the nearest tenth)}$$
The actual speed of the boat is 8.6 km/h.

To measure force, physicists use the metric unit *Newton* (N). A force of 1 N is required to support a mass of approximately 100 g against the gravitational pull of Earth.

EXAMPLE   Two forces of 25 N and 10 N act at an angle of 70° to each other. Find the magnitude (to the nearest Newton) and the direction (to the nearest degree) of the resultant.

SOLUTION   Draw a sketch. *ABCD* is a parallelogram, and $\overrightarrow{AC} = \overrightarrow{AB} + \overrightarrow{AD}$.

To find the magnitude of $\overrightarrow{AC}$, apply the Law of Cosines to $\triangle ABC$. Since $\overrightarrow{BC} \parallel \overrightarrow{AD}$, $\angle B = 180° - 70° = 110°$.
$$|\overrightarrow{AC}|^2 = |\overrightarrow{AB}|^2 + |\overrightarrow{BC}|^2 - 2|\overrightarrow{AB}| \, |\overrightarrow{BC}| \cos B$$
$$|\overrightarrow{AC}|^2 = 25^2 + 10^2 - 2(25)(10) \cos 110°$$
$$= 625 + 100 - 500(-0.3420)$$
$$= 896$$
$$|\overrightarrow{AC}| = 30 \text{ (to the nearest Newton)}$$
To find the direction of $\overrightarrow{AC}$, apply the Law of Sines to $\triangle ABC$.
$$\frac{\sin \angle BAC}{BC} = \frac{\sin B}{AC}$$
$$\sin \angle BAC = \frac{BC \cdot \sin B}{AC}$$
$$= \frac{10(0.9397)}{30}$$
$$= 0.3132$$
$$\angle BAC = 18° \text{ (to the nearest degree)}$$
The resultant force has a magnitude of 30 N and acts at an angle of 18° to the force of 25 N.

ORAL EXERCISES

Refer to the diagram at the right. Express the sum in terms of one vector.

1. $\vec{AB} + \vec{BC}$

2. $\vec{AC} + \vec{CD}$

3. $\vec{CD} + \vec{AC}$

4. $(\vec{AB} + \vec{BC}) + \vec{CD}$

5. $\vec{AB} + (\vec{BC} + \vec{CD})$

6. What property of vector addition is illustrated by your answers to Exercises 2 and 3?

7. What property of vector addition is illustrated by your answers to Exercises 4 and 5?

8. Is the following statement true or false?

$$|\vec{u} + \vec{v}| \leqslant |\vec{u}| + |\vec{v}|$$

Justify your answer.

WRITTEN EXERCISES

A 1. Copy the vectors on your paper. Make a sketch to find $\vec{u} + \vec{v}$.

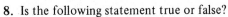

a.   b.   c.

2. Copy the vectors on your paper. Make a sketch to find $\vec{u} + \vec{v} + \vec{w}$.

a.   b.

  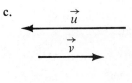

In the figure, $ABCD$ is a parallelogram. Name a single vector that is equivalent to the indicated vector or sum of vectors.

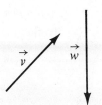

3. $\vec{AB}$

4. $\vec{BC}$

5. $\vec{EC}$

6. $\vec{DE}$

7. $\vec{AB} + \vec{AD}$

8. $\vec{BA} + \vec{AD}$

9. $\vec{CD} + \vec{BC}$

10. $\vec{CD} + \vec{CB}$

11. $\vec{AB} + \vec{BC} + \vec{CD}$

12. $\vec{BA} + \vec{BC} + \vec{DE}$

Find the magnitude and direction of the resultant of the given forces.

13. Two forces each of 4 N acting at a $90°$ angle to each other

14. Two forces of $60\sqrt{3}$ N and 60 N acting at a $90°$ angle to each other

15. Two forces each of 16 N acting at a $120°$ angle to each other

16. Two forces each of 5 N act at a 60° angle to each other. Find the magnitude and direction of the resultant of these forces.

17. Two forces of 30 N and 40 N act on an object. The resultant forms a 59° angle with the force of 30 N. Find the angle (to the nearest degree) between the two given forces.

18. Two forces of 25 N and 50 N act on an object. The resultant forms a 38°10′ angle with the force of 25 N. Find the angle (to the nearest degree) between the two given forces.

19. A 12 N force and another force act at an angle of 57°30′ to each other. The resultant forms a 35° angle with the 12 N force. Find the magnitude (to the nearest Newton) of the other force.

20. A 60 N force and another force act at an angle of 93°10′ to each other. The resultant forms a 38° angle with the 60 N force. Find the magnitude (to the nearest Newton) of the other force.

In Exercises 21-26 you are given the coordinates of points A and B, the heads of $\overrightarrow{OA}$ and $\overrightarrow{OB}$. If $O = (0, 0)$ and $\overrightarrow{OC} = \overrightarrow{OA} + \overrightarrow{OB}$, then:

a. Find $|\overrightarrow{OC}|$ to the nearest integer.

b. Find the direction of $\overrightarrow{OC}$ (to the nearest degree) with respect to the positive x-axis.

EXAMPLE $A(0, 4)$, $B(3, 0)$

SOLUTION The coordinates of C are $(3, 4)$.

By the Distance Formula:
$$|\overrightarrow{OC}|^2 = (3 - 0)^2 + (4 - 0)^2 = 9 + 16 = 25$$
$$|\overrightarrow{OC}| = 5$$
To find the direction of $\overrightarrow{OC}$, let $m\angle COB = \theta$.
$$\tan \theta = \frac{BC}{OB} = \frac{4}{3}$$
$$\tan \theta = 1.333$$
$$\theta = 53° \text{ (to the nearest degree)}$$
$\overrightarrow{OC}$ has magnitude 5 at an angle of 53° with the positive x-axis.

21. $A(5, 0)$, $B(0, 12)$ 　　　22. $A(0, -6)$, $B(-8, 0)$ 　　　23. $A(-8, 0)$, $B(0, 15)$

24. $A(0, 7)$, $B(-24, 0)$ 　　　25. $A(0, -4)$, $B(8, 0)$ 　　　26. $A(-12, 0)$, $B(0, -4)$

In Exercises 27-33, $\overrightarrow{OC} = \overrightarrow{OA} + \overrightarrow{OB}$, α and β are the directions of $\overrightarrow{OA}$ and $\overrightarrow{OB}$, respectively, with respect to the positive x-axis.

a. Find $|\overrightarrow{OC}|$ to the nearest integer.

b. Find the direction of $\overrightarrow{OC}$ to the nearest degree.

EXAMPLE $|\overrightarrow{OA}| = 10$, $\alpha = 30°$; $|\overrightarrow{OB}| = 18$, $\beta = 108°$

SOLUTION   a. In the figure, $|\overrightarrow{OA}| = 10$ and $|\overrightarrow{OB}| = 18$.

$\angle CAO = 180° - \angle BOA$
$\angle CAO = 180° - (108° - 30°)$
$\angle CAO = 102°$

Apply the Law of Cosines to $\triangle CAO$.
$|\overrightarrow{OC}|^2 = 18^2 + 10^2 - 2 \cdot 18 \cdot 10 \cdot \cos 102° = 499$
$|\overrightarrow{OC}| = 22$ (to the nearest integer)

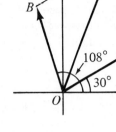

b. Let θ = the direction of $\overrightarrow{OC}$ with respect to the positive x-axis.
Then $\theta = 30° + \angle COA$. Apply the Law of Sines to find $\angle COA$.

$$\frac{22}{\sin 102°} = \frac{18}{\sin \angle COA}, \qquad \sin \angle COA = \frac{18 \cdot \sin 102°}{22} = 0.8003$$

$\angle COA = 53°$ (to the nearest degree)
$\theta = 30° + 53° = 83°$

B 27. $|\overrightarrow{OA}| = 9$, $\alpha = -40°$; $|\overrightarrow{OB}| = 11$, $\beta = 67°$

28. $|\overrightarrow{OA}| = 15$, $\alpha = 10°$; $|\overrightarrow{OB}| = 8$, $\beta = 130°$

29. $|\overrightarrow{OA}| = 17$, $\alpha = -20°$; $|\overrightarrow{OB}| = 10$, $\beta = 40°$

30. $|\overrightarrow{OA}| = 5$, $\alpha = 25°$; $|\overrightarrow{OB}| = 9$, $\beta = 90°$

31. $|\overrightarrow{OA}| = 7$, $\alpha = 15°$; $|\overrightarrow{OB}| = 9$, $\beta = 120°$

32. $|\overrightarrow{OA}| = 15$, $\alpha = 40°$; $|\overrightarrow{OB}| = 20$, $\beta = 135°$

33. $|\overrightarrow{OA}| = 17$, $\alpha = 110°$; $|\overrightarrow{OB}| = 15$, $\beta = 168°$

You will need to understand some new concepts to complete Exercises 34–37.

wind speed: the speed of the wind
air speed: the speed of a plane in still air
ground speed: the speed of a plane relative to the ground (A plane's ground speed is the length of the resultant of its air velocity and the wind velocity.)
heading: direction of the plane in still air
course: actual direction of the plane

In navigation, it is customary to regard North as $0°$, East as $90°$, and so on.

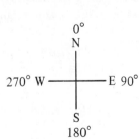

34. A plane with an air speed of 450 km/h is steering a heading of $45°$. The wind is 80 km/h from $0°$. Find the ground speed (to the nearest kilometer per hour) and the course (to the nearest degree) of the plane.

35. A plane with an air speed of 520 km/h is steering a heading of $120°$. The wind is 60 km/h from $180°$. Find the ground speed (to the nearest kilometer per hour) and the course (to the nearest degree) of the plane.

36. A plane with an air speed of 408 km/h is steering a heading of 90°. The wind is from 225° at 17 km/h. Find the ground speed (to the nearest kilometer per hour) and the course (to the nearest degree) of the plane.

C 37. The wind speed is 80 km/h from 45°. What heading should a pilot steer and at what air speed should the pilot fly if the plane's course is to be 150° with a ground speed of 600 km/h?

SELF-TEST 2

Complete for $\triangle PQR$. Find lengths to the nearest integer, angles to the nearest $10'$.

1. $p = 18$, $q = 12$, $\angle R = 81°$, $r =$ __?__   Section 10-5

2. $p = 8$, $q = 11$, $r = 15$, $\angle P =$ __?__

3. The lengths of the sides of a triangle are 6, 10, and 11. Find the measure (to the nearest $10'$) of the largest angle of the triangle.

Find the area of $\triangle HJK$ to the nearest integer.

4. $h = 50$, $j = 34$, $\angle K = 87°$ Section 10-6

5. $\angle H = 30°$, $\angle J = 103°$, $h = 17$

6. $h = 21$, $j = 10$, $k = 15$

7. The area of $\triangle ABC$ is 42. If $\angle A = 45°$ and $b = 7\sqrt{2}$, find c.

8. Copy the vectors on your paper. Make a sketch to find $\vec{u} + \vec{v}$.   Section 10-7

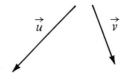

9. Find the magnitude and direction (to the nearest $10'$) of the resultant of a 6 N force and an 8 N force acting at a 90° angle to each other.

CHAPTER REVIEW

1. In $\triangle DEF$, $\angle D$ is a right angle, $d = 17$, and $e = 8$. Complete: $\sin E =$ __?__, Section 10-1 $\cos E =$ __?__, $\cot F =$ __?__

2. In $\triangle ABC$, $\angle B$ is a right angle, $a = 8$, and $b = 20$. Find the measure of $\angle A$ to the nearest $10'$.

3. If a person 2 m tall casts a shadow 3 m long, what is the angle of elevation, θ (to the nearest $10'$)?   Section 10-2

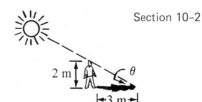

4. A support wire 21 m long runs from the top of a utility pole to a point on the ground 17 m from the base of the pole. Find the measure (to the nearest $10'$) of the angle formed by the pole and the wire.

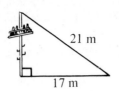

21 m

17 m

5. In $\triangle FGH$, $f = 16$, $g = 24$, and $\sin F = \frac{1}{3}$. Find $\sin G$.   Section 10-3

6. In $\triangle DEF$, $\angle E = 45°$, $f = 28$, and $\angle F = 30°$. Find e. Leave your answer in simplified radical form.

7. In $\triangle DEF$, $d = 100$, $\angle E = 51°10'$, and $\angle D = 31°20'$. Find e to the nearest integer.

8. Find the number of triangles that satisfy the given conditions.   Section 10-4
   a. $\angle A = 30°$, $a = 28$, $b = 56$
   b. $\angle A = 112°$, $a = 15$, $b = 16$
   c. $\angle A = 72°$, $a = 26$, $b = 30$

9. In $\triangle ABC$, $\angle A = 22°$, $a = 10$, and $b = 15$. Find two possible measures (to the nearest $10'$) for $\angle B$.

10. Find the length (to the nearest integer) of the indicated side of $\triangle PQR$.   Section 10-5
    a. $\angle P = 60°$, $q = 5$, $r = 18$, $p = $ _?_
    b. $\angle R = 103°$, $p = 13$, $q = 26$, $r = $ _?_

11. The lengths of the sides of a parallelogram are 7 cm and 8 cm. If the length of a diagonal is 13 cm, find the measure of an obtuse angle of the parallelogram.

12. Find the area of $\triangle ABC$. Leave your answer in simplified radical form.   Section 10-6
    a. $\angle B = 45°$, $a = 15$, $c = 10\sqrt{2}$
    b. $\angle B = 120°$, $\angle A = 30°$, $c = 8$

13. In $\square ABCD$, two sides whose lengths are 8 and 10 include an angle of $104°$. Find the area of the parallelogram to the nearest integer.

14. Quadrilateral $DEFG$ is a parallelogram. Name a vector that is equivalent to the given vector or the given sum of vectors.   Section 10-7
    a. $\overrightarrow{CG}$ b. $\overrightarrow{DC} + \overrightarrow{CE}$

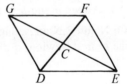

15. In the figure, a ship sails 300 km north, then changes its direction by $80°$ as shown, and travels another 200 km. How far (to the nearest ten kilometers) is the ship from its starting point?

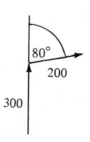

1. In $\triangle ABC$, $a = 9$, $b = 15$, and $\sin A = \dfrac{1}{3}$. Find $\sin B$.

2. In $\triangle CDE$, $\angle D$ is a right angle, $e = 4$, and $d = 12$. Find the measure of $\angle C$ to the nearest $10'$.

3. In the figure, $\angle Q = 35°$, $\angle S = 35°$, and $r = 93$. Find the perimeter (to the nearest integer) of $\triangle QRS$.

4. In $\triangle ABC$, $a = 12$, $b = 10$, and $\angle C = 30°$. Find c to the nearest integer.

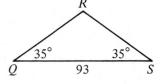

5. In $\triangle DEF$, $d = 15$, $e = 20$, and $\angle F = 75°$.
   a. Find f to the nearest integer.
   b. Find the area of $\triangle DEF$ to the nearest integer.

6. Determine whether $\triangle ABC$ is acute, right, or obtuse.
   a. $a = 4$, $b = 8$, $\angle A = 30°$
   b. $a = 12$, $b = 10$, $\angle A = 45°$
   c. $a = 7$, $b = 8.6$, $\angle A = 45°$

7. A surveyor uses an instrument known to be 1.2 m above ground level to sight the top of a tree at an angle of elevation $22°50'$. If the instrument is 50 m from the base of the tree, how tall (to the nearest tenth of a meter) is the tree?

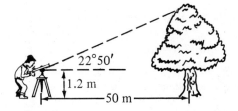

8. If $\angle A = 60°$, $a = 16$, and $c = 17$, then what is the total number of noncongruent triangles that can be constructed?

9. The sides of a triangle are 5 cm, 7 cm, and 9 cm long.
   a. Find the measure of the largest angle to the nearest $10'$.
   b. Find the area to the nearest square centimeter.

10. If $|\vec{u}| = 30$, $|\vec{v}| = 16$, and $|\vec{u} + \vec{v}| = 40$, find the measure of the angle (to the nearest $10'$) between $\vec{u}$ and $\vec{u} + \vec{v}$.

11. Forces of 6 N and 3 N are acting at a $60°$ angle to each other. Find the magnitude (to the nearest Newton) of the resultant.

Biographical Note

The hubbub that followed the publication of Isaac Newton's paper on light and colors caused him to say, "I was so persecuted . . . that I blamed my own imprudence for parting with so substantial a blessing as my quiet to run after a shadow." Newton (1642–1727), one of the most important scientists in history, made his discoveries in gravitation, universal motion, and calculus years before he published them.

Born in rural England, Newton received a sketchy education in Lincolnshire schools and then attended King's School in Grantham. He entered Cambridge University in 1661 and received a bachelor's degree in 1665. In that year, an outbreak of the plague forced the university to close for a time. Newton returned home, and in the next two years of independent study and reflection laid the groundwork for all his subsequent discoveries. He later returned to Cambridge and became a professor of mathematics at Trinity College.

Newton's early interest was in optics and theories of light. The reflecting telescope was one of the products of this interest.

The discovery of universal gravitation was Newton's most famous contribution to science. He believed that the same force—and therefore the same mathematical formula—controls both the sun's action on the planets and Earth's action on objects near it. Through a study of the motion of the moon, he worked out the mathematical formula for gravitation and defined laws of motion that describe the motions of objects on Earth. He published his findings in the great work generally known as *Principia Mathematica*.

Newton entered public life in 1689 as a member of Parliament. He later became Master of the Mint and successfully reformed the British system of coinage. He was knighted by Queen Anne in 1705.

At about this time, Newton's penchant for delaying publication led to a bitter battle between him and the German mathematician G. W. Leibnitz over which of them discovered the calculus. It now seems likely that the two men made the discovery independently.

Be sure that you understand the meaning of these terms:

solving a triangle, p. 390
angle of elevation, p. 395
angle of depression, p. 395
vector, p. 416

norm of a vector, p. 416
equivalent vectors, p. 417
resultant, p. 418

MIXED REVIEW

1. Given that $\log 5 = k$, express in terms of k: **a.** $\log 125$ **b.** $\log 5000$

2. Use Table 1 to find the value of θ to the nearest minute if $270° < \theta < 360°$ and $\cos \theta = 0.9$.

3. Show that $f(x) = \dfrac{4}{x-2}$ and $g(x) = \dfrac{2x+4}{x}$ are inverses.

4. Find the sum and the product of $-2 + 5i$ and $3 - 7i$.

5. Find two consecutive integers such that the sum of the squares of the integers is 43 more than their product.

6. Find the coordinates of the image of $(3, 7)$ under each transformation.
   a. $D_1 \circ D_2$
   $D_{\frac{1}{2}}$
   b. $T_{-3,0} \circ R_{180}$
   c. $r_{x\text{-axis}} \circ R_{-90}$

   d. reflection over the line with equation $y = x$

7. If $\triangle ABC$ is inscribed in $\odot O$, $m\angle A = 53$, and $m\angle C = 46$, find $m \overparen{ACB}$.

Simplify.

8. $\dfrac{\cos (180° + \theta)}{\sin (90° - \theta)}$

9. $\sin \theta + \cot \theta \cos \theta$

10. $\sqrt{-528}$

11. $\dfrac{i^{10}}{1 + i\sqrt{2}}$

12. $\dfrac{\sqrt{3} - 1}{\sqrt{3} - 2}$

13. $\log_{27} \sqrt{3}$

14. Draw a line segment $\overline{XY}$. Construct the image of Y under $D_{X, 3}$.

Solve.

15. $|9 - 2c| = 5$

16. $3y^2 + 3 = 8y$

17. $\dfrac{1}{x} + \dfrac{x}{1-x} = \dfrac{2x-1}{x^2-x}$

18. $\sqrt{5r - 1} = 7$

19. $\left(\dfrac{1}{25}\right)^z = 125^{z-5}$

20. $\log_x 4 = -\dfrac{2}{3}$

21. In $\triangle RST$, $m\angle R = 120$, $m\angle S = 45$, and $r = 12$. Find the exact value of s.

22. Solve over the set of complex numbers: $2x^2 + 6x + 5 = 0$

23. Find the doubling time, to the nearest tenth of a year, for an annual growth rate of 6%.

24. If $ABCD$ is a parallelogram, $m\angle B = 40$, $AB = 10$, and $BC = 8$, find **(a)** the lengths of $\overline{AC}$ and $\overline{BD}$ to the nearest tenth and **(b)** the area of $ABCD$ to the nearest integer.

25. Use logs to calculate **(a)** $12.9^{4.5}$ and **(b)** $\dfrac{36,700}{0.0298}$ to three significant digits.

26. If $f(x) = \sqrt{x^2 - 1}$, $g(x) = 3 - 2x$, and $h(x) = \dfrac{1}{x}$, find **(a)** $f(g(h(2)))$, **(b)** $h(f(g(-2)))$, **(c)** $f(g(x))$, and **(d)** $h(g(x))$.

27. If $\overline{XJ}$ is tangent to the circle, $m\,\widehat{JK} = 4x + 15$, $m\,\widehat{KL} = 9x + 5$, $m\,\widehat{LM} = 4x$, and $m\,\widehat{JM} = 6x - 5$, find the numerical measures of the angles of quadrilateral $JKLX$.

28. If $\overline{XJ}$ is tangent to the circle, $XJ = 5\sqrt{6}$, and $XM = ML$, find XL.

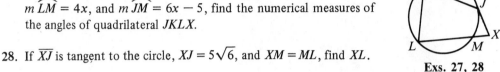

Exs. 27, 28

Solve for $0° \leqslant \theta < 360°$ and use Table 1 as needed.

29. $-\sqrt{3}\ \csc\theta = \sec\theta$ 30. $2\cos 2\theta = 1$ 31. $2\sin^2\theta = (\cos\theta + 1)^2$

32. Two forces of 70 N and 50 N act at an angle of $100°$ to each other. Find the magnitude to the nearest Newton and the direction to the nearest degree of the resultant.

33. Graph $y = \cos\theta$, $-2\pi \leqslant \theta \leqslant 2\pi$. Is the cosine function a one-to-one function? Explain.

34. Is it possible for a triangle to have line symmetry? point symmetry? rotational symmetry?

35. Find the circumference of a circle with area $\dfrac{5\pi}{4}$ cm^2.

36. If θ is in Quadrant III and $\tan\theta = 1$, find a value for θ and find the values of the other five trigonometric functions for θ.

Graph the solution set.

37. $|t - 2| > 3$

38. $-\dfrac{3}{2}z < 6$ and $4(1 - z) \geqslant z - 6$

Simplify:

39. $\log_2 2^{-5}$ 40. $\left(\dfrac{16}{25}\right)^{-\frac{3}{2}}$ 41. $\log_{4.5} 1$

Solve $\triangle RST$. Give lengths to the nearest integer and angle measures to the nearest $10'$. If no such triangle exists, so state.

42. $\overline{RS} \perp \overline{ST}$, $RT = 25$, and $RS = 24$ 43. $m\angle R = 60°$, $RS = 25$, and $ST = 20$

Sine and cosine functions, and the concepts of period and amplitude, can be used to write equations describing periodic phenomena, such as the rise and fall of the tides. (See page 471.)

Trigonometric Formulas and Inverse Functions 11

Until the beginning of the nineteenth century, imaginary and complex numbers were not well understood. They had been known since at least 1545, when Girolamo Cardano discovered that the solution of the problem "What are two numbers whose sum is 10 and whose product is 40?" was the pair of numbers $5 + \sqrt{-15}$ and $5 - \sqrt{-15}$. However, mathematicians of Cardano's time were not at all comfortable with these new numbers.

Around 1800 several mathematicians, including the Norwegian Caspar Wessel, the Swiss Jean Robert Argand, and the German Carl Friedrich Gauss, contributed to a major development that helped to bring complex numbers into the mainstream of mathematical thinking. These mathematicians were all involved in devising a geometric representation of complex numbers. Diagrams using a point or vector to represent a complex number in a coordinate plane came to be known as *Argand diagrams*.

With the ability to represent complex numbers geometrically, a theorem established by Abraham De Moivre in 1730 acquired a new significance. Now the rather intimidating problem of finding, for example, the five fifth roots of $1 - i\sqrt{3}$ was reduced to finding the coordinates of five particular points equally spaced around a particular circle centered at the origin.

These advances in the understanding of complex numbers were dependent on trigonometric identities called the *Angle-Sum Formulas* and on a system that uses *polar coordinates* to locate points in a plane.

Section 11-1 GRAPHING $y = A \sin x$ AND $y = \sin Bx$

In this section you will learn more about the graphs of the sine and cosine functions and some of their characteristics, namely:
- period
- cycle
- amplitude

You probably recall that because the function values of the sine function recur regularly every 2π units, the sine function is a periodic function. More generally, a function f has a *period* of p if there is some nonzero constant p such that:

$$f(x + p) = f(x) \quad \text{for all } x \text{ in the domain of } f$$

If p is the smallest positive constant for which f is periodic, then p is the *fundamental period* of f. A portion of the curve with endpoints $(x, f(x))$ and $(x + p, f(x + p))$ is called a *cycle* of the curve.

The graph of $y = \sin x$ has another distinctive characteristic, called *amplitude*. If a periodic function has a maximum value M and a minimum value m, its *amplitude* is $\frac{1}{2}(M - m)$. Therefore, the amplitude of the function $y = \sin x$ is $\frac{1}{2}(1 - (-1)) = 1$.

EXAMPLE Find the amplitude of $y = 3 \sin x$ and sketch its graph.

SOLUTION Since $\sin x$ varies between -1 and 1, $3 \sin x$ varies between 3 and -3. It follows that $M = 3$ and $m = -3$ for $y = 3 \sin x$. Thus the amplitude is $\frac{1}{2}(3 - (-3)) = 3$.

Since $y = \sin x$ has a fundamental period of 2π, $y = 3 \sin x$ also has a fundamental period of 2π. Therefore $y = 3 \sin x$ will complete one cycle as x goes from 0 to 2π. To aid in sketching the graph, find the coordinates of the points where the graph crosses the x-axis and where it reaches its maximum and minimum values. The x-coordinates of these points are the values that divide the interval from 0 to 2π into four equal parts.

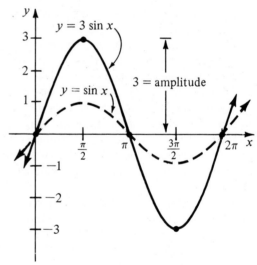

x	0	$\dfrac{\pi}{2}$	π	$\dfrac{3\pi}{2}$	2π
$y = 3 \sin x$	0	3	0	-3	0

Plot these points, join them with a smooth curve, and you will have sketched one cycle of the graph of $y = 3 \sin x$. Since the function is periodic, you can continue to sketch as much of the graph as you want by repeating the cycle to the right or left as desired.

This example suggests a fact you may have already observed: If $f(x) = A \sin x$, then the amplitude of f is $|A|$.

EXAMPLE Find the fundamental period of $y = \sin 2x$ and sketch the graph.

SOLUTION $y = \sin 2x$ will complete one cycle as $2x$ varies from 0 to 2π. Solve the following inequality for x to find the fundamental period of $y = \sin 2x$:

$$0 \leqslant 2x \leqslant 2\pi$$
$$0 \leqslant x \leqslant \pi$$

In other words, as x varies from 0 to π, $2x$ varies from 0 to 2π, and $y = \sin 2x$ completes 1 cycle. Thus, the period of $y = \sin 2x$ is the difference $\pi - 0 = \pi$.

Next use the values that divide the interval from 0 to π into four equal parts to help you plot the five key points in a cycle of $y = \sin 2x$.

x	0	$\dfrac{\pi}{4}$	$\dfrac{\pi}{2}$	$\dfrac{3\pi}{4}$	π
$y = \sin 2x$	0	1	0	-1	0

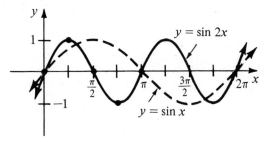

The graph is shown at the right. Notice that the graph of $y = \sin 2x$ completes two cycles in the interval over which the graph of $y = \sin x$ completes one cycle.

In general, if $f(x) = \sin Bx$, then the graph of f completes one cycle as Bx varies from 0 to 2π. Thus, solving the inequality

$$0 \leqslant Bx \leqslant 2\pi$$

gives us: $0 \leqslant x \leqslant \dfrac{2\pi}{B}$ if $B \geqslant 0$ and $0 \geqslant x \geqslant \dfrac{2\pi}{B}$ if $B < 0$

This shows us that if $f(x) = \sin Bx$, then f has a fundamental period of $\dfrac{2\pi}{|B|}$.

Since the graph of $y = \cos x$ is merely a horizontal translation of the graph of $y = \sin x$, all the facts you just learned about the graph of a sine function apply equally well to the graph of a cosine function.

EXAMPLE   State the amplitude and the fundamental period of $f(x) = -2 \cos 3x$. Sketch the graph.

SOLUTION   1. Find the period. Solve for x: $0 \leqslant 3x \leqslant 2\pi$

$$0 \leqslant x \leqslant \dfrac{2\pi}{3}$$

The period is $\dfrac{2\pi}{3}$.

2. The amplitude is $|-2|$, or 2.

3. Plot the points whose x-coordinates divide the interval $0 \leqslant x \leqslant \dfrac{2\pi}{3}$ into four equal parts.

x	0	$\dfrac{\pi}{6}$	$\dfrac{\pi}{3}$	$\dfrac{\pi}{2}$	$\dfrac{2\pi}{3}$
$\cos 3x$	1	0	-1	0	1
$-2 \cos 3x$	-2	0	2	0	-2

(The final step is on the following page.)

4. Sketch the graph.

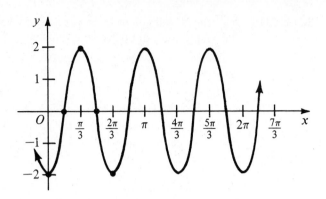

ORAL EXERCISES

Exercises 1–8 refer to the functions graphed below.

a.

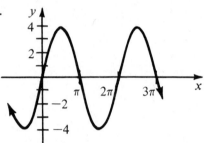

b.

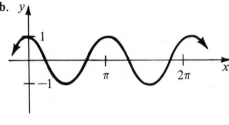

c.

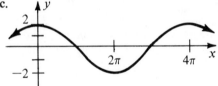

d.

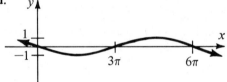

1. a–d. State the amplitude of each of the functions.

2. a–d. State the fundamental period of each of the functions.

State an equation of the function shown on the indicated graph.

3. Graph (a) **4.** Graph (b)

Use the relationship

$$\text{period} = \frac{2\pi}{|B|}$$

to find a value of B for the indicated graph.

5. Graph (c) **6.** Graph (d)

State an equation of the function shown on the indicated graph.

7. Graph (c) **8.** Graph (d)

State an equation of the form $y = A \sin Bx$ of a function with the indicated characteristics.

9. fundamental period $= 2\pi$, amplitude $= 1$

10. fundamental period $= 2\pi$, amplitude $= 6$

11. fundamental period $= 2\pi$, amplitude $= \dfrac{1}{2}$

12. fundamental period $= \pi$, amplitude $= 1$

13. fundamental period $= \dfrac{\pi}{2}$, amplitude $= 1$

14. fundamental period $= 4\pi$, amplitude $= 3$

WRITTEN EXERCISES

In Exercises 1-12:
a. Determine the amplitude of the function.
b. Determine the fundamental period of the function.
c. Graph at least two cycles of the function.

A　**1.** $y = 4 \sin x$

2. $y = -2 \sin x$

3. $y = \dfrac{3}{4} \cos x$

4. $y = \sin 6x$

5. $y = \cos 4x$

6. $y = 3 \cos 2x$

7. $y = -5 \cos x$

8. $y = -\cos \dfrac{x}{2}$

9. $y = \sin \dfrac{x}{3}$

10. $y = 4 \cos \dfrac{2}{3}x$

11. $y = -\dfrac{3}{2} \sin 2x$

12. $y = 3 \sin \dfrac{3}{2}x$

On the same set of axes, sketch the graphs of f and g in the interval $0 \leqslant x \leqslant 2\pi$. Then state the number of values of x in the interval $0 \leqslant x \leqslant 2\pi$ that satisfy the equation $f(x) = g(x)$.

B　**13.** $f(x) = \sin 2x$
$g(x) = \dfrac{1}{2} \cos x$

14. $f(x) = 2 \cos 3x$
$g(x) = \sin x$

15. $f(x) = \dfrac{1}{2} \sin x$
$g(x) = \cos 4x$

16. $f(x) = 2 \sin 2x$
$g(x) = \sin \dfrac{1}{2}x$

17. $f(x) = 2 \cos 2x$
$g(x) = \sin 3x$

18. $f(x) = 3 \cos x$
$g(x) = \sin \dfrac{3}{2}x$

19. a. Show that $\sin x \cos x = \sin (x + \pi) \cos (x + \pi)$.
　　b. State the fundamental period p of $f(x) = \sin x \cos x$.
　　c. Use the values of x that divide the interval $0 \leqslant x \leqslant p$ into four equal parts to find the maximum and minimum values of $f(x)$.
　　d. State the amplitude of $f(x)$.

20. a. Show that $\cos^2 x - \sin^2 x = \cos^2 (x + \pi) - \sin^2 (x + \pi)$.
　　b. State the fundamental period p of $g(x) = \cos^2 x - \sin^2 x$.
　　c. Use the values of x that divide the interval $0 \leqslant x \leqslant p$ into four equal parts to find the maximum and minimum values of $g(x)$.
　　d. State the amplitude of $g(x)$.

Find the fundamental period of each function and sketch one cycle of its graph.

EXAMPLE $f(x) = \sin\left(2x - \dfrac{\pi}{2}\right)$

SOLUTION One cycle of $y = \sin\left(2x - \dfrac{\pi}{2}\right)$ is completed as $\left(2x - \dfrac{\pi}{2}\right)$ varies from 0 to 2π.

$$0 \leqslant 2x - \frac{\pi}{2} \leqslant 2\pi$$

$$\frac{\pi}{4} \leqslant x \leqslant \frac{5\pi}{4}$$

Thus the period of f is $\dfrac{5\pi}{4} - \dfrac{\pi}{4} = \pi$.

If a cycle begins at $x = \dfrac{\pi}{4}$, then it

ends at $x = \dfrac{5\pi}{4}$. The crucial points

to graph are those where the graph
crosses the x-axis and those where
the function reaches its maximum

and minimum values: $\left(\dfrac{\pi}{4},\ 0\right)$,

$\left(\dfrac{\pi}{2},\ 1\right)$, $\left(\dfrac{3\pi}{4},\ 0\right)$, $(\pi,\ -1)$, and

$\left(\dfrac{5\pi}{4},\ 0\right)$.

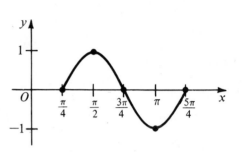

C 21. $f(x) = \sin\left(x + \dfrac{\pi}{4}\right)$

22. $g(x) = \cos\left(x - \dfrac{\pi}{6}\right)$

23. $g(x) = \cos(2x + \pi)$

24. $f(x) = \sin(4x - \pi)$

25. $f(x) = 2 \cos\left(\dfrac{x}{3} - \dfrac{\pi}{3}\right)$

26. $g(x) = 3 \sin\left(\dfrac{x}{2} + \dfrac{\pi}{2}\right)$

Section 11-2 SUM AND DIFFERENCE FORMULAS

Does $\cos(90° - 60°) = \cos 90° - \cos 60°$? We know that $\cos 90° = 0$, $\cos 60° = \dfrac{1}{2}$, and $\cos 30° = \dfrac{\sqrt{3}}{2}$. Substituting, we find that:

$$\cos(90° - 60°) = \cos 30° = \frac{\sqrt{3}}{2} \quad \text{and} \quad \cos 90° - \cos 60° = 0 - \frac{1}{2} = -\frac{1}{2}$$

Thus, we have shown that $\cos(90° - 60°) \neq \cos 90° - \cos 60°$.

Even though it is generally true that $\cos(\alpha - \beta) \neq \cos \alpha - \cos \beta$, you *can* find a general expression for $\cos(\alpha - \beta)$ in terms of trigonometric functions of α and β. In this section you will learn formulas for:

• the cosine, sine, and tangent of the difference of two angles
• the cosine, sine, and tangent of the sum of two angles

To derive the formula for cos (α − β), we will begin by drawing angles α and β in standard position on the unit circle as shown in the diagrams below.

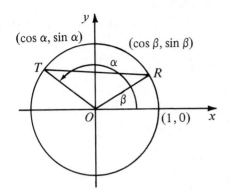

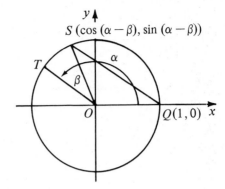

Since $\angle TOR = \alpha - \beta = \angle SOQ$, $\overset{\frown}{TR} \cong \overset{\frown}{SQ}$, and thus $TR = SQ$. Consequently, $(TR)^2 = (SQ)^2$.

We use the Distance Formula to write expressions for $(TR)^2$ and $(SQ)^2$.

$$(TR)^2 = (\cos \alpha - \cos \beta)^2 + (\sin \alpha - \sin \beta)^2$$
$$= \cos^2 \alpha - 2 \cos \alpha \cos \beta + \cos^2 \beta + \sin^2 \alpha - 2 \sin \alpha \sin \beta + \sin^2 \beta$$
$$= (\sin^2 \alpha + \cos^2 \alpha) + (\sin^2 \beta + \cos^2 \beta) - 2 \sin \alpha \sin \beta - 2 \cos \alpha \cos \beta$$
$$= 1 + 1 - 2 \sin \alpha \sin \beta - 2 \cos \alpha \cos \beta$$
$$= 2 - 2 \sin \alpha \sin \beta - 2 \cos \alpha \cos \beta$$

$$(SQ)^2 = [\cos (\alpha - \beta) - 1]^2 + [\sin (\alpha - \beta) - 0]^2$$
$$= \cos^2 (\alpha - \beta) - 2 \cos (\alpha - \beta) + 1 + \sin^2 (\alpha - \beta)$$
$$= [\sin^2 (\alpha - \beta) + \cos^2 (\alpha - \beta)] + 1 - 2 \cos (\alpha - \beta)$$
$$= 1 + 1 - 2 \cos (\alpha - \beta)$$
$$= 2 - 2 \cos (\alpha - \beta)$$

Since $(TR)^2 = (SQ)^2$, we can equate these expressions.

$$2 - 2 \sin \alpha \sin \beta - 2 \cos \alpha \cos \beta = 2 - 2 \cos (\alpha - \beta)$$
$$\sin \alpha \sin \beta + \cos \alpha \cos \beta = \cos (\alpha - \beta)$$

Hence we have:

$$\cos (\alpha - \beta) = \cos \alpha \cos \beta + \sin \alpha \sin \beta$$

Replacing β with −β, we obtain:

$$\cos (\alpha - (-\beta)) = \cos \alpha \cos (-\beta) + \sin \alpha \sin (-\beta),$$

Since cos (−β) = cos β and sin (−β) = −sin β, the equation above simplifies to:

$$\cos (\alpha + \beta) = \cos \alpha \cos \beta - \sin \alpha \sin \beta$$

If we replace α with $90° - \alpha$ in the preceding formula, we obtain:

$$\cos((90° - \alpha) + \beta) = \cos(90° - \alpha)\cos\beta - \sin(90° - \alpha)\sin\beta$$
$$\cos(90° - (\alpha - \beta)) = \cos(90° - \alpha)\cos\beta - \sin(90° - \alpha)\sin\beta$$

But $\cos(90° - \theta) = \sin\theta$ and $\sin(90° - \theta) = \cos\theta$ for all θ, so the last equation simplifies to:

$$\sin(\alpha - \beta) = \sin\alpha\cos\beta - \cos\alpha\sin\beta$$

Replacing β with $-\beta$ in the preceding formula, we obtain:

$$\sin(\alpha - (-\beta)) = \sin\alpha\cos(-\beta) - \cos\alpha\sin(-\beta)$$

This simplifies to:

$$\sin(\alpha + \beta) = \sin\alpha\cos\beta + \cos\alpha\sin\beta$$

We will call the boxed formulas the *Angle-Sum and Angle-Difference Formulas for the sine and the cosine.* These formulas apply to both degree and radian measure.

EXAMPLE   Find $\cos 15°$ without referring to Table 1.

SOLUTION   Let $\alpha = 45°$ and $\beta = 30°$. Then $\alpha - \beta = 15°$.

$$\cos(\alpha - \beta) = \cos\alpha\cos\beta + \sin\alpha\sin\beta$$
$$\cos(45° - 30°) = \cos 45° \cos 30° + \sin 45° \sin 30°$$
$$\cos 15° = \frac{\sqrt{2}}{2} \cdot \frac{\sqrt{3}}{2} + \frac{\sqrt{2}}{2} \cdot \frac{1}{2}$$
$$= \frac{\sqrt{6} + \sqrt{2}}{4}$$

EXAMPLE   Evaluate: $\sin 70° \cos 50° + \cos 70° \sin 50°$

SOLUTION   Let $\alpha = 70°$ and $\beta = 50°$.

$$\sin\alpha\cos\beta + \cos\alpha\sin\beta = \sin(\alpha + \beta)$$
$$\sin 70° \cos 50° + \cos 70° \sin 50° = \sin(70° + 50°)$$
$$= \sin 120°$$
$$= \frac{\sqrt{3}}{2}$$

In Exercises 35 and 36 you will be asked to derive the *Angle-Sum and Angle-Difference Formulas for the tangent function.*

$$\tan(\alpha + \beta) = \frac{\tan\alpha + \tan\beta}{1 - \tan\alpha\tan\beta} \qquad \cos\alpha, \cos\beta, \cos(\alpha + \beta) \neq 0$$

$$\tan(\alpha - \beta) = \frac{\tan\alpha - \tan\beta}{1 + \tan\alpha\tan\beta} \qquad \cos\alpha, \cos\beta, \cos(\alpha - \beta) \neq 0$$

ORAL EXERCISES

Express as the sine, cosine, or tangent of one angle.

1. $\cos 20° \cos 80° - \sin 20° \sin 80°$

2. $\sin 30° \cos 10° - \cos 30° \sin 10°$

3. $\sin 40° \cos 25° + \cos 40° \sin 25°$

4. $\cos \dfrac{\pi}{2} \cos \dfrac{\pi}{6} + \sin \dfrac{\pi}{2} \sin \dfrac{\pi}{6}$

5. $\dfrac{\tan 30° + \tan 15°}{1 - \tan 30° \tan 15°}$

6. $\dfrac{\tan 45° - \tan 30°}{1 + \tan 45° \tan 30°}$

Use an Angle-Sum or Angle-Difference Formula to expand each expression.

EXAMPLE $\sin (90° - 45°)$

SOLUTION $\sin (90° - 45°) = \sin 90° \cos 45° - \cos 90° \sin 45°$

7. $\cos (90° - 60°)$

8. $\cos (60° + 45°)$

9. $\sin (45° + 15°)$

10. $\sin (120° - 30°)$

11. $\cos (\alpha + \alpha)$

12. $\sin (\alpha + \alpha)$

13. $\tan \left(\dfrac{\pi}{3} - \dfrac{\pi}{4} \right)$

14. $\tan (30° + 15°)$

15. $\tan (\alpha + \alpha)$

WRITTEN EXERCISES

Evaluate using Angle-Sum and Angle-Difference Formulas.

A   **1.** $\sin 15°$

2. $\sin 75°$

3. $\cos 105°$

4. $\cos (-15°)$

5. $\cos 255°$

6. $\sin (-105°)$

7. $\sin 165°$

8. $\cos 75°$

9. $\cos \dfrac{11\pi}{12}$

10. $\cos \dfrac{13\pi}{12}$

11. $\sin \dfrac{5\pi}{12}$

12. $\sin \left(-\dfrac{\pi}{12} \right)$

13. $\tan 15°$

14. $\tan 75°$

15. $\tan 165°$

16. $\tan (-105°)$

Simplify and then find the exact value of the expression using Angle-Sum and Angle-Difference Formulas.

17. $\sin 110° \cos 20° - \cos 110° \sin 20°$

18. $\cos 35° \sin 155° - \sin 35° \cos 155°$

19. $\cos 40° \cos 10° + \sin 40° \sin 10°$

20. $\sin 20° \cos 25° + \cos 20° \sin 25°$

21. $\dfrac{\tan 70° - \tan 25°}{1 + \tan 70° \tan 25°}$

22. $\dfrac{\tan 5° + \tan 55°}{1 - \tan 5° \tan 55°}$

23. Use the Angle-Sum Formulas to show that:

a. $\sin (180° + \theta) = -\sin \theta$

b. $\cos \left(\dfrac{\pi}{2} + \theta \right) = -\sin \theta$

24. Use the Angle-Difference Formulas to show that:

a. $\sin (-\theta) = -\sin \theta$

b. $\cos (\pi - \theta) = -\cos \theta$

Use the given information to find sin $(\alpha + \beta)$ if α and β lie in the first quadrant.

EXAMPLE $\sin \alpha = \dfrac{1}{2}$, $\sin \beta = \dfrac{4}{5}$

SOLUTION First we must find $\cos \alpha$ and $\cos \beta$. Since α and β are acute angles, draw one right triangle with an angle α such that $\sin \alpha = \dfrac{1}{2}$. Draw another right triangle with an angle β such that $\sin \beta = \dfrac{4}{5}$.

The side adjacent to angle α is $\sqrt{3}$, and the side adjacent to angle β is 3. Thus $\cos \alpha = \dfrac{\sqrt{3}}{2}$ and $\cos \beta = \dfrac{3}{5}$.

$$\sin (\alpha + \beta) = \sin \alpha \cos \beta + \cos \alpha \sin \beta$$
$$= \frac{1}{2} \cdot \frac{3}{5} + \frac{\sqrt{3}}{2} \cdot \frac{4}{5} = \frac{3}{10} + \frac{4\sqrt{3}}{10}$$
$$= \frac{3 + 4\sqrt{3}}{10}$$

25. $\sin \alpha = \dfrac{3}{5}$, $\sin \beta = \dfrac{5}{13}$

26. $\cos \alpha = \dfrac{5}{13}$, $\sin \beta = \dfrac{12}{13}$

27. $\cos \alpha = \dfrac{7}{25}$, $\cos \beta = \dfrac{4}{5}$

28. $\tan \alpha = \dfrac{7}{24}$, $\tan \beta = \dfrac{4}{3}$

29. $\sin \alpha = \dfrac{56}{65}$, $\tan \beta = \dfrac{63}{16}$

30. $\cot \alpha = \dfrac{24}{7}$, $\sin \beta = \dfrac{8}{17}$

Prove each identity.

B **31.** $\cos (\alpha - \beta) + \cos (\alpha + \beta) = 2 \cos \alpha \cos \beta$

32. $\sin (\alpha + \beta) + \sin (\alpha - \beta) = 2 \sin \alpha \cos \beta$

33. $\sin (\alpha + \beta) - \sin (\alpha - \beta) = 2 \cos \alpha \sin \beta$

34. $\cos (\alpha - \beta) - \cos (\alpha + \beta) = 2 \sin \alpha \sin \beta$

35. Use the Angle-Sum Formulas for sine and cosine to prove that $\tan (\alpha + \beta) = \dfrac{\tan \alpha + \tan \beta}{1 - \tan \alpha \tan \beta}$ if $\cos \alpha \neq 0$, $\cos \beta \neq 0$, and $\cos (\alpha + \beta) \neq 0$.

36. Use the results of Exercise 35 and the fact that $\tan (-\theta) = -\tan \theta$ to prove that $\tan (\alpha - \beta) = \dfrac{\tan \alpha - \tan \beta}{1 + \tan \alpha \tan \beta}$ if $\cos \alpha \neq 0$, $\cos \beta \neq 0$, and $\cos (\alpha - \beta) \neq 0$.

37. If $\tan \alpha = \dfrac{1}{2}$ and $\tan \beta = \dfrac{1}{3}$, for α and β in the first quadrant, show that $(\alpha + \beta) = 45°$.

For each expression write an equivalent expression in terms of $\sin \theta$, $\cos \theta$, or both.

38. $\sin (45° + \theta) + \cos (45° + \theta)$

39. $\sin (30° + \theta) + \cos (60° + \theta)$

40. $\cos (60° - \theta) - \sin (30° - \theta)$

C **41.** Show that $\cos 3\alpha \cos \alpha + \sin 3\alpha \sin \alpha = 2 \cos^2 \alpha - 1$.

42. Show that $\sin (\alpha + \beta) \sin (\alpha - \beta) = \sin^2 \alpha - \sin^2 \beta$.

43. Show that $\cos (\alpha + \beta) \cos (\alpha - \beta) = \cos^2 \alpha - \sin^2 \beta$.

Section 11-3 DOUBLE-ANGLE FORMULAS

In this section you will use the formulas you learned in Section 11-2 to derive formulas that express the sine, cosine, and tangent of twice an angle in terms of functions of the given angle.

To derive the *Double-Angle Formula for the sine*, let $\beta = \alpha$ in the Angle-Sum Formula

$$\sin (\alpha + \beta) = \sin \alpha \cos \beta + \cos \alpha \sin \beta,$$

to obtain:

$$\sin (\alpha + \alpha) = \sin \alpha \cos \alpha + \cos \alpha \sin \alpha$$

That is:

$$\sin 2\alpha = 2 \sin \alpha \cos \alpha$$

You can derive the *Double-Angle Formula for the cosine* in a similar fashion:

$$\cos (\alpha + \beta) = \cos \alpha \cos \beta - \sin \alpha \sin \beta$$

Therefore:

$$\cos 2\alpha = \cos^2 \alpha - \sin^2 \alpha$$

Replacing $\sin^2 \alpha$ with $(1 - \cos^2 \alpha)$, we obtain:

$$\cos 2\alpha = \cos^2 \alpha - (1 - \cos^2 \alpha)$$

which simplifies to:

$$\cos 2\alpha = 2 \cos^2 \alpha - 1$$

If we had replaced $\cos^2 \alpha$ with $(1 - \sin^2 \alpha)$, we would have obtained:

$$\cos 2\alpha = (1 - \sin^2 \alpha) - \sin^2 \alpha$$

which simplifies to:

$$\cos 2\alpha = 1 - 2 \sin^2 \alpha$$

In Exercise 31 you will be asked to derive the *Double-Angle Formula for the tangent*.

$$\tan 2\alpha = \frac{2 \tan \alpha}{1 - \tan^2 \alpha} \quad (\cos \alpha, \ \cos 2\alpha \neq 0)$$

EXAMPLE   Find **(a)** $\cos 2\alpha$ and **(b)** $\cos 4\alpha$, if $\sin \alpha = \dfrac{2}{3}$.

SOLUTION   **a.** $\cos 2\alpha = 1 - 2 \sin^2 \alpha$ **b.** $\cos 4\alpha = \cos 2(2\alpha)$
$$= 1 - 2\left(\frac{2}{3}\right)^2 \qquad\qquad\qquad = 2 \cos^2 2\alpha - 1$$
$$= \frac{1}{9} \qquad\qquad\qquad\qquad\qquad = 2\left(\frac{1}{9}\right)^2 - 1$$
$$\qquad\qquad\qquad\qquad\qquad\qquad = -\frac{79}{81}$$

EXAMPLE   Find $\sin 2\alpha$ if $\sin \alpha = \dfrac{3}{5}$ and α lies in the first quadrant.

SOLUTION   To use the Double-Angle Formula, you need to know $\cos \alpha$.
$$\cos^2 \alpha = 1 - \sin^2 \alpha$$
$$= 1 - \left(\frac{3}{5}\right)^2$$
$$= \frac{16}{25}$$
$$\cos \alpha = \pm\frac{4}{5}$$

Since α is in the first quadrant, you know that $\cos \alpha = \dfrac{4}{5}$.
$$\sin 2\alpha = 2 \sin \alpha \cos \alpha$$
$$= 2\left(\frac{3}{5}\right)\left(\frac{4}{5}\right)$$
$$= \frac{24}{25}$$

EXAMPLE   Prove the identity $\dfrac{\cos 2\theta + 1}{\sin 2\theta} = \cot \theta$.

SOLUTION

$$\frac{\cos 2\theta + 1}{\sin 2\theta} = \frac{(2\cos^2 \theta - 1) + 1}{2\sin\theta\cos\theta}$$

$$= \frac{2\cos^2 \theta}{2\sin\theta\cos\theta}$$

$$= \frac{\cos\theta}{\sin\theta}$$

$$= \cot\theta$$

ORAL EXERCISES

In Exercises 1–5, use one of the Double-Angle Formulas to verify the equation.

1. Let $\alpha = 30°$ and show that $\sin 60° = \dfrac{\sqrt{3}}{2}$.

2. Let $\alpha = 30°$ and show that $\cos 60° = \dfrac{1}{2}$.

3. Let $\alpha = 60°$ and show that $\tan 120° = -\sqrt{3}$.

4. Show that $\sin 90° = 1$.   5. Show that $\cos 90° = 0$.

Simplify.

6. $2\sin 12° \cos 12°$ 7. $2\cos^2 10° - 1$

8. $\cos^2 \theta - \sin^2 \theta$ 9. $\dfrac{2\tan\beta}{1 - \tan^2 \beta}$

WRITTEN EXERCISES

Simplify and then find the exact value of the expression, using Double-Angle Formulas.

A 1. $2\cos^2 15° - 1$ 2. $2\sin 165° \cos 165°$

3. $2\sin \dfrac{\pi}{8} \cos \dfrac{\pi}{8}$ 4. $1 - 2\sin^2 \dfrac{\pi}{12}$

5. $\dfrac{2\tan 75°}{1 - \tan^2 75°}$ 6. $\dfrac{2\tan 165°}{1 - \tan^2 165°}$

7. $\cos^2 22°30' - \sin^2 22°30'$ 8. $2\cos^2 105° - 1$

Use the given information to find the exact value of $\cos 2\theta$.

9. $\cos\theta = \dfrac{1}{3}$ 10. $\sin\theta = \dfrac{3}{4}$ 11. $\sin\theta = -\dfrac{4}{5}$

12. $\cos\theta = -\dfrac{\sqrt{2}}{3}$ 13. $\sin\theta = \dfrac{\sqrt{5}}{3}$ 14. $\cos\theta = \dfrac{\sqrt{3}}{4}$

15. $\tan\theta = \dfrac{5}{12}$ 16. $\tan\theta = \dfrac{4}{3}$ 17. $\sec\theta = -\dfrac{3}{2}$

Use the given information to find the exact value of sin 2α.

18. $\sin \alpha = \dfrac{5}{13}, 0 < \alpha < \dfrac{\pi}{2}$

19. $\cos \alpha = \dfrac{8}{17}, 0 < \alpha < \dfrac{\pi}{2}$

20. $\cos \alpha = -\dfrac{\sqrt{5}}{3}, \pi < \alpha < \dfrac{3\pi}{2}$

21. $\sin \alpha = \dfrac{\sqrt{7}}{4}, \dfrac{\pi}{2} < \alpha < \pi$

22. $\cos \alpha = \dfrac{2\sqrt{2}}{3}, \dfrac{3\pi}{2} < \alpha < 2\pi$

23. $\sin \alpha = -\dfrac{\sqrt{15}}{4}, \pi < \alpha < \dfrac{3\pi}{2}$

24. $\tan \alpha = \dfrac{2}{3}, 0 < \alpha < \dfrac{\pi}{2}$

25. $\tan \alpha = -\dfrac{15}{8}, \dfrac{\pi}{2} < \alpha < \pi$

Use the given information to find the exact value of tan 2x.

26. $\tan x = 4$

27. $\tan x = -\dfrac{7}{24}$

28. $\cot x = \dfrac{12}{5}$

29. $\sin x = \dfrac{\sqrt{3}}{3}, 0 < x < \dfrac{\pi}{2}$

30. $\cos x = \dfrac{2}{3}, 0 < x < \dfrac{\pi}{2}$

Express as a function of sine, cosine, or tangent.

31. $2 \sin 9x \cos 9x$

32. $\cos^2 3\alpha - \sin^2 3\alpha$

33. $2 \cos^2 4x - 1$

34. $\dfrac{2 \tan 4\beta}{1 - \tan^2 4\beta}$

35. $\dfrac{2 \tan 5x}{\tan^2 5x - 1}$

36. $2 \cos 7\theta \sin 7\theta$

Prove each identity.

37. $\sin 2\theta \csc \theta = 2 \cos \theta$

38. $(\sin \alpha + \cos \alpha)^2 = 1 + \sin 2\alpha$

B **39.** Use the fact that $\tan 2\alpha = \dfrac{\sin 2\alpha}{\cos 2\alpha}$ to prove that $\tan 2\alpha = \dfrac{2 \tan \alpha}{1 - \tan^2 \alpha}$ if $\cos \alpha \neq 0$ and $\cos 2\alpha \neq 0$.

Prove each identity.

40. $\dfrac{1 - \cos 2\theta}{\sin 2\theta} = \tan \theta$

41. $\dfrac{2 \cos \theta}{1 + \cos 2\theta} = \sec \theta$

42. $\dfrac{\sin \theta}{\cos \theta + \sin \theta} + \dfrac{\sin \theta}{\cos \theta - \sin \theta} = \tan 2\theta$

43. $\cot \theta - \dfrac{1}{2} \sec \theta \csc \theta = \cot 2\theta$

44. $\dfrac{1}{2}(\cot \theta - \tan \theta) = \cot 2\theta$

45. $\sec \theta \csc \theta - 2 \tan \theta = 2 \cot 2\theta$

46. $\sin 4\theta = 4(\sin \theta \cos^3 \theta - \cos \theta \sin^3 \theta)$

47. $\cos 4\theta = 8 \cos^4 \theta - 8 \cos^2 \theta + 1$

C **48.** $\tan 4\theta = \dfrac{4 \tan \theta - 4 \tan^3 \theta}{1 - 6 \tan^2 \theta + \tan^4 \theta}$

49. $\cot 2\theta = \dfrac{\cos 3\theta \cos \theta + \sin 3\theta \sin \theta}{2 \sin \theta \cos \theta}$

50. $\dfrac{2 \cos \theta \cos 2\theta}{\cos 2\theta + \sin 2\theta + 1} = \cos \theta - \sin \theta$

51. $\cos 3\theta = 4 \cos^3 \theta - 3 \cos \theta$

52. $1 + \tan \alpha \tan 2\alpha = \sec 2\alpha$

53. $\tan^2 \left(\dfrac{\pi}{4} - \beta \right) = \dfrac{1 - \sin 2\beta}{1 + \sin 2\beta}$

Section 11-4 HALF-ANGLE FORMULAS

From the Double-Angle Formulas you can derive formulas for $\cos \frac{\alpha}{2}$ and $\sin \frac{\alpha}{2}$ in terms of $\cos \alpha$, which you can then use to derive a formula for $\tan \frac{\alpha}{2}$. These formulas are called the *Half-Angle Formulas*.

To derive the Half-Angle Formula for the cosine, replace α with $\frac{\alpha}{2}$ in the Double-Angle Formula.

$$\cos 2\alpha = 2 \cos^2 \alpha - 1$$
$$\cos 2\left(\frac{\alpha}{2}\right) = 2 \cos^2 \frac{\alpha}{2} - 1$$
$$\cos \alpha = 2 \cos^2 \frac{\alpha}{2} - 1$$

Solving this equation for $\cos \frac{\alpha}{2}$, you obtain:

$$\cos^2 \frac{\alpha}{2} = \frac{1 + \cos \alpha}{2}$$

or:

$$\cos \frac{\alpha}{2} = \pm \sqrt{\frac{1 + \cos \alpha}{2}}$$

If $\frac{\alpha}{2}$ is in Quadrant I or IV, then $\cos \frac{\alpha}{2}$ is positive. Otherwise, it is negative.

EXAMPLE Find the exact value of $\cos 15°$, using the Half-Angle Formula.

SOLUTION $\frac{\alpha}{2} = 15°$ is in Quadrant I. Therefore $\cos 15°$ is positive.

$$\cos 15° = \cos \frac{30°}{2}$$

$$\cos 15° = \sqrt{\frac{1 + \cos 30°}{2}}$$

$$= \sqrt{\frac{1 + \frac{\sqrt{3}}{2}}{2}}$$

$$= \sqrt{\frac{2 + \sqrt{3}}{4}}$$

$$= \frac{\sqrt{2 + \sqrt{3}}}{2}$$ (In Exercise 22, you will verify that this expression equals the value obtained for $\cos 15°$ on page 436.)

You can derive the Half-Angle Formula for the sine in the same way. In the Double-Angle Formula

$$\cos 2\alpha = 1 - 2 \sin^2 \alpha,$$

replace α with $\frac{\alpha}{2}$ to obtain:

$$\cos 2\left(\frac{\alpha}{2}\right) = 1 - 2 \sin^2 \frac{\alpha}{2}$$

$$\cos \alpha = 1 - 2 \sin^2 \frac{\alpha}{2}$$

This yields:

$$\sin^2 \frac{\alpha}{2} = \frac{1 - \cos \alpha}{2}$$

or:

$$\sin \frac{\alpha}{2} = \pm \sqrt{\frac{1 - \cos \alpha}{2}}$$

Choose the correct sign in the formula according to the quadrant $\frac{\alpha}{2}$ is in.

EXAMPLE Find $\sin \frac{\theta}{2}$ if $\sin \theta = \frac{24}{25}$ and $0 < \theta < \frac{\pi}{2}$.

SOLUTION Since θ is in Quadrant I, $\sin \theta$ and $\cos \theta$ are positive. To find the value of $\cos \theta$, use the identity:

$$\sin^2 \theta + \cos^2 \theta = 1$$
$$\left(\frac{24}{25}\right)^2 + \cos^2 \theta = 1$$
$$\cos^2 \theta = \frac{625}{625} - \frac{576}{625} = \frac{49}{625}$$
$$\cos \theta = \frac{7}{25}$$

Therefore:

$$\sin \frac{\theta}{2} = \sqrt{\frac{1 - \cos \theta}{2}} = \sqrt{\frac{1 - \frac{7}{25}}{2}} = \sqrt{\frac{\frac{18}{25}}{2}} = \sqrt{\frac{9}{25}} = \frac{3}{5}$$

Finally, you can derive the Half-Angle Formula for the tangent by using the fact that $\tan \alpha = \frac{\sin \alpha}{\cos \alpha}$. Thus:

$$\tan^2 \frac{\alpha}{2} = \frac{\sin^2 \frac{\alpha}{2}}{\cos^2 \frac{\alpha}{2}} = \frac{\frac{1 - \cos \alpha}{2}}{\frac{1 + \cos \alpha}{2}}$$

This equation is equivalent to:

$$\tan^2 \frac{\alpha}{2} = \frac{1 - \cos \alpha}{1 + \cos \alpha}, \quad \cos \alpha \neq -1$$

or:

$$\tan \frac{\alpha}{2} = \pm \sqrt{\frac{1 - \cos \alpha}{1 + \cos \alpha}} \quad \cos \alpha \neq -1$$

If $\frac{\alpha}{2}$ is in Quadrant I or III, $\tan \frac{\alpha}{2}$ is positive. Otherwise, it is negative.

EXAMPLE Find $\tan \frac{\theta}{2}$ if $\sin \theta = \frac{24}{25}$ and $0 < \theta < \frac{\pi}{2}$.

SOLUTION As in the preceding example, θ is in Quadrant I, so:

$$\cos \theta = \frac{7}{25}$$

$$\tan \frac{\theta}{2} = \sqrt{\frac{1 - \cos \theta}{1 + \cos \theta}}$$

$$= \sqrt{\frac{1 - \frac{7}{25}}{1 + \frac{7}{25}}} = \sqrt{\frac{\frac{18}{25}}{\frac{32}{25}}}$$

$$= \sqrt{\frac{9}{16}} = \frac{3}{4}$$

ORAL EXERCISES

Simplify.

1. $\pm \sqrt{\dfrac{1 - \cos \alpha}{2}}$

2. $\pm \sqrt{\dfrac{1 + \cos 2\beta}{2}}$

3. $\sqrt{\dfrac{1 + \cos 40°}{2}}$

4. $\sqrt{\dfrac{1 - \cos 12°}{1 + \cos 12°}}$

5. $\sqrt{\dfrac{1 + \cos 76°}{1 - \cos 76°}}$

6. $\sqrt{\dfrac{1 - \cos 128°}{2}}$

7. If θ lies in Quadrant II and $0° \leqslant \theta \leqslant 360°$, in what quadrant(s) can $\frac{\theta}{2}$ lie?

8. If θ lies in Quadrant III and $0° \leqslant \theta \leqslant 360°$, in what quadrant(s) can $\frac{\theta}{2}$ lie?

WRITTEN EXERCISES

Evaluate using Half-Angle Formulas.

A 1. $\sin 15°$ 2. $\cos 75°$ 3. $\cos 22\frac{1}{2}°$ 4. $\sin 292\frac{1}{2}°$

     5. $\tan 15°$ 6. $\tan 105°$ 7. $\sin \dfrac{17\pi}{12}$ 8. $\tan \dfrac{23\pi}{12}$

In Exercises 9 and 10 you will derive formulas for $\tan \dfrac{\theta}{2}$ that do not involve any ambiguity in sign. Thus they may be more convenient to use than the formula on page 445.

9. Use Double-Angle Formulas to show that $\tan \alpha = \dfrac{\sin 2\alpha}{1 + \cos 2\alpha}$. Then substitute $\dfrac{\theta}{2}$ for α and show that $\tan \dfrac{\theta}{2} = \dfrac{\sin \theta}{1 + \cos \theta}$, $\cos \theta \ne -1$.

10. Use Double-Angle Formulas to show that $\tan \alpha = \dfrac{1 - \cos 2\alpha}{\sin 2\alpha}$. Then substitute $\dfrac{\theta}{2}$ for α and show that $\tan \dfrac{\theta}{2} = \dfrac{1 - \cos \theta}{\sin \theta}$, $\sin \theta \ne 0$.

Use the given information to find $\sin \dfrac{\theta}{2}$, $\cos \dfrac{\theta}{2}$, and $\tan \dfrac{\theta}{2}$.

11. $\cos \theta = \dfrac{17}{25}, 0 < \theta < \dfrac{\pi}{2}$ 12. $\cos \theta = \dfrac{1}{8}, 0 < \theta < \dfrac{\pi}{2}$

13. $\sin \theta = \dfrac{12}{13}, 0 < \theta < \dfrac{\pi}{2}$ 14. $\sin \theta = \dfrac{15}{17}, \dfrac{\pi}{2} < \theta < \pi$

15. $\tan \theta = -\dfrac{12}{5}, \dfrac{\pi}{2} < \theta < \pi$ 16. $\cot \theta = -\dfrac{4}{3}, \dfrac{3\pi}{2} < \theta < 2\pi$

17. $\sec \theta = 2, \dfrac{3\pi}{2} < \theta < 2\pi$ 18. $\sec \theta = -1.5, \pi < \theta < \dfrac{3\pi}{2}$

B 19. If $\sin \theta = \dfrac{120}{169}$ and $\dfrac{\pi}{2} < \theta < \pi$, find $\sin \dfrac{\theta}{2}$ and $\sin \dfrac{\theta}{4}$.

20. If $\sin \theta = -\dfrac{21}{29}$ and $\dfrac{3\pi}{2} < \theta < 2\pi$, find $\tan \dfrac{\theta}{2}$ and $\tan \dfrac{\theta}{4}$.

21. If $\sin \theta = -\dfrac{24}{25}$ and $\dfrac{3\pi}{2} < \theta < 2\pi$, find $\cos \dfrac{\theta}{2}$ and $\cos \dfrac{\theta}{4}$.

22. In the examples on pages 436 and 443, we found two expressions for $\cos 15°$, namely $\dfrac{\sqrt{2 + \sqrt{3}}}{2}$ and $\dfrac{\sqrt{6} + \sqrt{2}}{4}$. Show that $\dfrac{\sqrt{2 + \sqrt{3}}}{2} = \dfrac{\sqrt{6} + \sqrt{2}}{4}$.
(*Hint:* Square both sides.)

Prove each identity.

C **23.** $\sec^2 \dfrac{\theta}{2} + \csc^2 \dfrac{\theta}{2} = 4 \csc^2 \theta$

24. $\cot^2 \dfrac{\theta}{2} - \tan^2 \dfrac{\theta}{2} = 4 \cot \theta \csc \theta$

25. $\tan^2 \dfrac{\theta}{2} - \sec^2 \dfrac{\theta}{2} + \csc^2 \dfrac{\theta}{2} = \left(\dfrac{1 + \cos \theta}{\sin \theta} \right)^2$

26. $\cot^2 \dfrac{\theta}{2} + \sec^2 \dfrac{\theta}{2} - \csc^2 \dfrac{\theta}{2} = (\csc \theta - \cot \theta)^2$

27. $\sin x \left(\cot \dfrac{x}{2} + \tan \dfrac{x}{2} \right) = 2$

28. $\tan x \left(\cot \dfrac{x}{2} - \tan \dfrac{x}{2} \right) = 2$

SELF-TEST 1

Determine the amplitude and fundamental period of the function and graph at least two cycles.

1. $y = \sin 3x$ **2.** $y = 4 \cos x$ Section 11–1

3. $y = \cos \dfrac{1}{4}x$ **4.** $y = -2 \sin 2x$

Evaluate, using the Angle-Sum and Angle-Difference Formulas.

5. $\sin \dfrac{11\pi}{12}$ **6.** $\tan (-15°)$ Section 11–2

7. $\cos 110° \cos 25° - \sin 110° \sin 25°$

8. $\sin 310° \cos 70° - \cos 310° \sin 70°$

Find the exact value of the given expression when $0 < \alpha < \dfrac{\pi}{2}$.

9. $\sin 2\alpha$ if $\sin \alpha = \dfrac{3}{5}$ **10.** $\cos 2\alpha$ if $\tan \alpha = \dfrac{12}{5}$ Section 11–3

11. $\tan 2\alpha$ if $\cos \alpha = \dfrac{\sqrt{5}}{3}$

Evaluate using Half-Angle Formulas.

12. $\sin 22\dfrac{1}{2}°$ **13.** $\cos 165°$ Section 11–4

14. $\tan \dfrac{\pi}{8}$

Section 11-5 TRIGONOMETRIC EQUATIONS

To solve a trigonometric equation containing functions of *more than one angle*, transform the equation into one in which only one angle is involved.

EXAMPLE   Solve $\sin 2\theta = \sin \theta$ for $0° \leqslant \theta < 360°$.

SOLUTION   This equation involves two different angles, θ and 2θ. Since $\sin 2\theta = 2 \sin \theta \cos \theta$, you can substitute to obtain:

$$2 \sin \theta \cos \theta = \sin \theta$$
$$2 \sin \theta \cos \theta - \sin \theta = 0$$
$$\sin \theta (2 \cos \theta - 1) = 0$$

$$\sin \theta = 0 \qquad \text{or} \qquad 2 \cos \theta - 1 = 0$$
$$\theta = 0°, 180° \qquad\qquad\qquad \cos \theta = \frac{1}{2}$$
$$\theta = 60°, 300°$$

The solutions are $\theta = 0°, 60°, 180°, 300°$.

EXAMPLE   Solve $\cos 2x = \cos x$ for $0 \leqslant x < 2\pi$.

SOLUTION   You can transform the given equation into one that involves only functions of x by means of any of the Double-Angle Formulas for the cosine. Choose $\cos 2x = 2 \cos^2 x - 1$, since that formula transforms the given equation into one that involves only the cosine function of x.

$$\cos 2x = \cos x$$
$$2 \cos^2 x - 1 = \cos x$$
$$(2 \cos x + 1)(\cos x - 1) = 0$$

$$2 \cos x + 1 = 0 \qquad \text{or} \qquad \cos x - 1 = 0$$
$$\cos x = -\frac{1}{2} \qquad\qquad\qquad \cos x = 1$$
$$x = \frac{2\pi}{3}, \frac{4\pi}{3} \qquad\qquad\qquad x = 0$$

The solutions are $x = 0, \dfrac{2\pi}{3}, \dfrac{4\pi}{3}$.

If an equation involves functions of only one angle, say 2θ, it may be best to solve directly without using any of the Double-Angle Formulas.

EXAMPLE   Solve $\sin 2\theta = 0.5$ for $0 \leqslant \theta < 2\pi$.

SOLUTION   You solved equations of this type in Section 8-4. Since $0 \leqslant \theta < 2\pi$, you must find all values of θ such that $0 \leqslant 2\theta < 4\pi$ and $\sin 2\theta = 0.5$.

Therefore, $2\theta = \dfrac{\pi}{6}, \dfrac{5\pi}{6}, \dfrac{13\pi}{6}, \dfrac{17\pi}{6}$.

Thus: $\theta = \dfrac{\pi}{12}, \dfrac{5\pi}{12}, \dfrac{13\pi}{12}, \dfrac{17\pi}{12}$

1. To solve $\cos^2 2x = 1$, would you use a Double-Angle Formula or solve for $\cos 2x$?

2. To solve $\cos 2x + \cos x = -1$, would you use a Double-Angle Formula or solve for $\cos 2x$?

Describe the method you would use to solve each equation.

3. $\sin^2 2\theta = \sin 2\theta$ 4. $\tan^2 2x = 1$ 5. $\sin 2\alpha + \cos \alpha = 0$ 6. $\sin 3\beta = \cos 3\beta$

7. To solve an equation involving an angle $3x$, what domain should you consider for $3x$ if you want $0° \leqslant x < 360°$?

WRITTEN EXERCISES

Solve for $0° \leqslant x < 360°$.

A 1. $2 \sin 2x = 1$ 2. $6 \cos 2x + 3 = 0$ 3. $4 \sin^2 2x = 3$

4. $\tan^2 2x = 1$ 5. $\cos 2x = \sin x$ 6. $\cos 2x + \cos x = 0$

7. $\sin 2x = \cos x$ 8. $\sin 2x + 3 \sin x = 0$ 9. $\cos 2x + \cos x + 1 = 0$

10. $\cos 2x - \sin x - 1 = 0$ 11. $\cos 2x - 3 \sin x + 1 = 0$ 12. $\cos 2x - \cos x - 2 = 0$

B 13. $\cos^2 2x = 2 \cos 2x$ 14. $\sin 2x = \cot x$ 15. $2 \cos^2 2x = 3 \sin 2x$

16. $\sin^2 3x = \cos^2 3x$ 17. $\tan 2x = 3 \tan x$ 18. $\tan 2x + \cot 2x = 2$

Solve for $0 \leqslant x < 2\pi$.

19. $3 \cos 2x = 2 \sin^2 2x$ 20. $\cos 2x = 1 - 4 \sin x$

C 21. $\sin x \cos x = 0.5$ 22. $\cos^2 2x + 5 \cos^2 x - 4 = 0$

23. $\sin^2 2x = 3 \cos^2 x$ 24. $\cos 2x + \cos^2 x = 5 \sin^2 x$

25. $\tan^2 2x + \sec 2x = 1$ 26. $\sec^2 2x + \tan 2x = 1$

Section 11-6 THE INVERSE TRIGONOMETRIC FUNCTIONS

As you learned in Section 4-6, only a one-to-one function has an inverse function. The function $f(x) = \sin x$, $x \in \mathcal{R}$, is not one-to-one, but we can restrict the domain of f to $-\dfrac{\pi}{2} \leqslant x \leqslant \dfrac{\pi}{2}$, thus creating a new function that *is* one-to-one. We will define a function Sin x as follows:

$$\text{Sin } x = \sin x, \quad -\frac{\pi}{2} \leqslant x \leqslant \frac{\pi}{2}$$

From the graph of $y = \text{Sin } x$, shown at the right, it is easy to see that $y = \text{Sin } x$ is one-to-one.

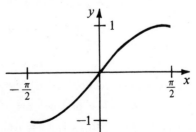

We will write the *inverse* of Sin x as

$$\text{Arcsin } x, \quad \text{or} \quad \text{Sin}^{-1} x,$$

which we read as "the Arcsine of x," or "The angle between $-\frac{\pi}{2}$ and $\frac{\pi}{2}$ whose sine is x." It is defined as follows:

$$\text{Arcsin } x = y, \quad \text{or} \quad \text{Sin}^{-1} x = y,$$

if and only if

$$\sin y = x \quad \text{and} \quad -\frac{\pi}{2} \leqslant y \leqslant \frac{\pi}{2}$$

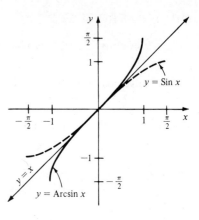

As shown at the right, the graph of $y = \text{Arcsin } x$ is the reflection in the line $y = x$ of the graph of $y = \text{Sin } x$.

EXAMPLE   Find the value of: **a.** $\text{Arcsin } \dfrac{\sqrt{3}}{2}$

b. $\text{Arcsin } 1$

c. $\text{Sin}^{-1}\left(-\dfrac{\sqrt{2}}{2}\right)$

SOLUTION   **a.** Let $\text{Arcsin } \dfrac{\sqrt{3}}{2} = A$.

Then $\sin A = \dfrac{\sqrt{3}}{2}$.

Since $\sin \dfrac{\pi}{3} = \dfrac{\sqrt{3}}{2}$ and $-\dfrac{\pi}{2} \leqslant \dfrac{\pi}{3} \leqslant \dfrac{\pi}{2}$, it follows that $A = \dfrac{\pi}{3}$.

Thus: $\text{Arcsin } \dfrac{\sqrt{3}}{2} = \dfrac{\pi}{3}$

b. Similarly, $\text{Arcsin } 1 = \dfrac{\pi}{2}$ since $\sin \dfrac{\pi}{2} = 1$.

c. $\text{Sin}^{-1}\left(-\dfrac{\sqrt{2}}{2}\right) = -\dfrac{\pi}{4}$ since $\sin\left(-\dfrac{\pi}{4}\right) = -\dfrac{\sqrt{2}}{2}$.

Like the sine function, the cosine function is not one-to-one. We can restrict the domain of the cosine function just as we did for the sine function so that the resulting function is one-to-one, but we cannot choose the same domain, $-\dfrac{\pi}{2} \leqslant x \leqslant \dfrac{\pi}{2}$, because the cosine function with this domain is *not* one-to-one. We will define the one-to-one function Cos x as:

$$\text{Cos } x = \cos x, \quad 0 \leqslant x \leqslant \pi$$

Then we can define $\text{Cos}^{-1} x$, or $\text{Arccos } x$, as:

$$\text{Arccos } x = y, \text{ or } \text{Cos}^{-1} x = y, \text{ if and only if } \cos y = x \text{ and } 0 \leqslant y \leqslant \pi$$

The graphs of $y = \text{Cos } x$ and $y = \text{Arccos } x$ are shown at the left on the next page.

450   *CHAPTER 11*

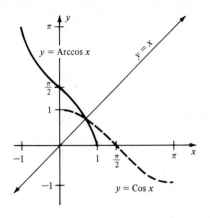

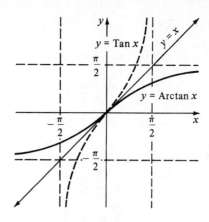

We will proceed in a similar fashion to define the inverse of the tangent function. We will define Tan x as:

$$\text{Tan } x = \tan x, \quad -\frac{\pi}{2} < x < \frac{\pi}{2}$$

Then we can define $\text{Tan}^{-1} x$, or Arctan x, as:

Arctan $x = y$, or $\text{Tan}^{-1} x = y$, if and only if $\tan y = x$ and $-\frac{\pi}{2} < y < \frac{\pi}{2}$

The graphs of $y = \text{Arctan } x$ and $y = \text{Tan } x$ are shown at the right above.

EXAMPLE Find $\cos\left(\text{Arctan } \frac{3}{4}\right)$.

SOLUTION Let $A = \text{Arctan } \frac{3}{4}$. Then $\tan A = \frac{3}{4}$.

Method 1: Use an identity.

$$\sec^2 A = 1 + \tan^2 A$$

$$\sec^2 A = 1 + \frac{9}{16} = \frac{25}{16}$$

$$\sec A = \pm\frac{5}{4}$$

Since $-\frac{\pi}{2} < \angle A < \frac{\pi}{2}$ and $\tan A$ is positive, $\angle A$ is in Quadrant I and sec A is positive. Therefore:

$$\sec A = \frac{5}{4}$$

$$\cos\left(\text{Arctan } \frac{3}{4}\right) = \cos A$$

$$= \frac{1}{\sec A}$$

$$= \frac{4}{5}$$

Method 2: Use a sketch.

Draw a right triangle with acute $\angle A$ such that $\tan A = \frac{3}{4}$.

The length of the hypotenuse is 5. So $\cos\left(\text{Arctan } \frac{3}{4}\right) = \cos A = \frac{4}{5}$.

ORAL EXERCISES

State each value. If the expression is undefined, so state.

1. Arccos 1

2. Arctan 1

3. Arcsin 2

4. $\mathrm{Sin}^{-1}\dfrac{1}{2}$

5. $\mathrm{Sin}^{-1}\left(-\dfrac{1}{2}\right)$

6. $\mathrm{Tan}^{-1} 0$

7. Arccos 0

8. $\mathrm{Cos}^{-1} (-3)$

Name an angle of $\triangle ABC$ whose measure equals the given value.

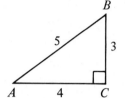

9. $\mathrm{Arcsin}\dfrac{3}{5}$

10. $\mathrm{Arccos}\dfrac{3}{5}$

11. $\mathrm{Arcsin}\dfrac{4}{5}$

12. $\mathrm{Tan}^{-1}\dfrac{4}{3}$

13. $\mathrm{Cos}^{-1}\dfrac{4}{5}$

14. $\mathrm{Tan}^{-1}\dfrac{3}{4}$

WRITTEN EXERCISES

Evaluate.

A 1. $\mathrm{Arcsin}\dfrac{\sqrt{2}}{2}$

2. $\mathrm{Arccos}\dfrac{\sqrt{3}}{2}$

3. $\mathrm{Arctan} (-1)$

4. $\mathrm{Cos}^{-1} (-1)$

5. $\mathrm{Tan}^{-1}\sqrt{3}$

6. $\mathrm{Cos}^{-1}\left(-\dfrac{\sqrt{3}}{2}\right)$

7. $\mathrm{Arcsin}\left(-\dfrac{\sqrt{3}}{2}\right)$

8. $\mathrm{Arcsin} (-1)$

9. $\mathrm{Arctan}\dfrac{\sqrt{3}}{3}$

10. $\mathrm{Tan}^{-1} (-\sqrt{3})$

11. $\mathrm{Cos}^{-1}\left(-\dfrac{\sqrt{2}}{2}\right)$

12. $\mathrm{Tan}^{-1}\left(-\dfrac{\sqrt{3}}{3}\right)$

Name an angle in the diagram whose measure equals the given value.

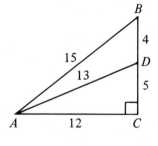

13. $\mathrm{Arcsin}\dfrac{5}{13}$

14. $\mathrm{Arctan}\dfrac{12}{5}$

15. $\mathrm{Arccos}\dfrac{4}{5}$

16. $\mathrm{Cos}^{-1}\dfrac{3}{5}$

17. $\mathrm{Tan}^{-1}\dfrac{4}{3}$

18. $\mathrm{Sin}^{-1}\dfrac{12}{13}$

Evaluate.

19. $\sin (\mathrm{Arccos}\ 0.5)$

20. $\cos (\mathrm{Arcsin}\ 0)$

21. $\cos (\mathrm{Arctan}\ 1)$

22. $\tan (\mathrm{Tan}^{-1}\ 3)$

23. $\sin (\mathrm{Sin}^{-1}\ 0.3)$

24. $\cos\left(\mathrm{Sin}^{-1}\dfrac{\sqrt{2}}{2}\right)$

25. $\tan (\mathrm{Arccos}\ 1)$

26. $\sin (\mathrm{Arctan}\ \sqrt{3})$

27. $\sin\left(\text{Arccos } \dfrac{5}{13}\right)$

28. $\cos\left(\text{Arcsin } \dfrac{15}{17}\right)$

B 29. $\tan(\text{Arcsin } 0.6)$

30. $\cos[\text{Arctan}(-2.5)]$

31. $\cos\left[\text{Sin}^{-1}\left(-\dfrac{24}{25}\right)\right]$

32. $\sin\left[\text{Cos}^{-1}\left(-\dfrac{8}{17}\right)\right]$

33. Explain why:

$$\text{Arcsin } x + \text{Arccos } x = \frac{\pi}{2} \text{ for } 0 < x < 1$$

(*Hint:* In the figure let $\angle A = \text{Arcsin } x$.)

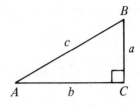

34. Explain why:

$$\text{Arctan } x + \text{Arctan } \frac{1}{x} = \frac{\pi}{2} \text{ for } x > 0$$

(*Hint:* In the figure let $\angle A = \text{Arctan } x$.)

Evaluate each expression.

EXAMPLE $\sin\left(\text{Arcsin } \dfrac{3}{5} + \text{Arcsin } \dfrac{5}{13}\right)$

SOLUTION Let $\alpha = \text{Arcsin } \dfrac{3}{5}$ and $\beta = \text{Arcsin } \dfrac{5}{13}$.

Thus, $\sin\left(\text{Arcsin } \dfrac{3}{5} + \text{Arcsin } \dfrac{5}{13}\right) = \sin(\alpha + \beta)$.

But $\sin \alpha = \dfrac{3}{5}$ and $\sin \beta = \dfrac{5}{13}$, and α and β are in Quadrant I.

You should verify that therefore $\cos \alpha = \dfrac{4}{5}$ and $\cos \beta = \dfrac{12}{13}$.

$$\sin(\alpha + \beta) = \sin \alpha \cos \beta + \cos \alpha \sin \beta$$
$$= \frac{3}{5} \cdot \frac{12}{13} + \frac{4}{5} \cdot \frac{5}{13} = \frac{56}{65}$$

Therefore, $\sin\left(\text{Arcsin } \dfrac{3}{5} + \text{Arcsin } \dfrac{5}{13}\right) = \dfrac{56}{65}$.

35. $\sin\left(\text{Arccos } \dfrac{4}{5} + \text{Arccos } \dfrac{15}{17}\right)$

36. $\cos\left(\text{Arccos } \dfrac{3}{5} - \text{Arcsin } \dfrac{12}{13}\right)$

37. $\tan\left(\text{Tan}^{-1} \dfrac{3}{4} - \text{Tan}^{-1} \dfrac{7}{24}\right)$

38. $\tan\left(\text{Tan}^{-1} \dfrac{2}{5} + \text{Tan}^{-1} \dfrac{1}{4}\right)$

39. $\sin\left(2 \text{ Arccos } \dfrac{4}{5}\right)$

40. $\cos\left(2 \text{ Sin}^{-1} \dfrac{5}{13}\right)$

C 41. Evaluate $\text{Arctan } \dfrac{1}{2} + \text{Arctan } \dfrac{1}{3}$. *Hint:* Find $\tan\left(\text{Arctan } \dfrac{1}{2} + \text{Arctan } \dfrac{1}{3}\right)$.

42. Show that $\text{Tan}^{-1} \dfrac{1}{2} = \text{Tan}^{-1} \dfrac{1}{3} + \text{Tan}^{-1} \dfrac{1}{7}$.

43. Evaluate $\text{Arctan }\dfrac{1}{5} + \text{Arctan }\dfrac{2}{3}$.

44. Values of the function Arctan x, for $-1 \leqslant x \leqslant 1$, can be found by means of the *infinite series*:

$$\text{Arctan } x = x - \frac{x^3}{3} + \frac{x^5}{5} - \frac{x^7}{7} + \cdots$$

(The "=" sign here means that by evaluating sufficiently many terms of the infinite formal sum on the right side, you can approximate Arctan x to any desired degree of accuracy.)

  a. Explain how you could use the infinite series above to find an approximation of the number π to any desired accuracy.

  b. Calculate π to three decimal places. (*Hint*: Use the results of Exercise 41.)

SELF-TEST 2

Solve for $0° \leqslant x < 360°$.

  1. $2 \cos 2x = 1$ **2.** $\sqrt{3} \cos x = \sin 2x$ Section 11–5

Evaluate.

  3. Arcsin 0   **4.** $\text{Cos}^{-1}\left(-\dfrac{\sqrt{2}}{2}\right)$ **5.** Arctan $\sqrt{3}$ Section 11–6

  6. $\sin\left(\text{Arccos }\dfrac{\sqrt{3}}{2}\right)$ **7.** $\tan\left[\text{Sin}^{-1}\left(-\dfrac{1}{2}\right)\right]$ **8.** $\cos\left(\text{Tan}^{-1} 3\right)$

Section 11-7 POLAR COORDINATES (Optional)

In a rectangular, or Cartesian, coordinate system a point is uniquely identified by an ordered pair of real numbers (x, y) that give the distances from the point to the y- and x-axes, respectively. Another way to uniquely determine the location of a point is by its *polar coordinates*.

In a polar coordinate system, a point O, called the *pole*, and a ray, called the *polar axis* and having its endpoint at O, are chosen. Usually the polar axis is thought of as a horizontal ray that points to the right. The location of a point P is described by giving its distance r from the pole O and the measure of an angle θ formed by ray OP and the polar axis. In the figure at the right, the polar coordinates of point P are (r, θ).

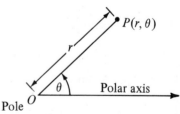

EXAMPLE Graph $Q(2, -150°)$.

SOLUTION 1. Draw an angle of $-150°$ in standard position.
2. On the terminal side of the angle plot the point Q that is 2 units from the pole O.

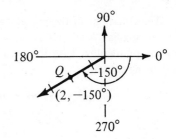

Note that although there is exactly one point determined by $(2, -150°)$, there is more than one pair of polar coordinates for the point Q in the preceding example. The location of Q can be given by any pair of polar coordinates of the form $(2, \theta)$, where θ is the measure of an angle coterminal with an angle of $-150°$. Other polar coordinates for Q are, for example, $(2, 210°)$ and $(2, 570°)$.

If we let r be negative, then there are even more ways to name Q. If $r < 0$, then the point (r, θ) is defined to be $|r|$ units from the origin on the ray *opposite* to the terminal side of θ. Thus, $(-2, 30°) = (2, -150°)$.

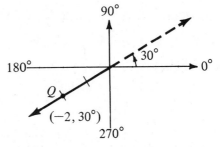

EXAMPLE For the point with polar coordinates $\left(1, \dfrac{\pi}{3}\right)$, find three other pairs of polar coordinates (r, θ) such that $-2\pi < \theta < 2\pi$.

SOLUTION Find three angles whose measures are between -2π and 2π and whose terminal sides coincide with the terminal side of $\dfrac{\pi}{3}$ or the ray opposite to this side. Thus, three other pairs of coordinates are $\left(1, -\dfrac{5\pi}{3}\right)$, $\left(-1, -\dfrac{2\pi}{3}\right)$, and $\left(-1, \dfrac{4\pi}{3}\right)$.

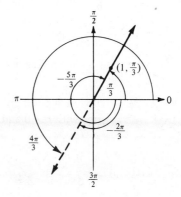

You can find a relationship between the polar coordinates of a point and its rectangular coordinates by letting the polar axis coincide with the positive x-axis and the pole coincide with the origin of a rectangular coordinate system. Since:

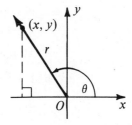

$$\cos\theta = \frac{x}{r} \text{ and } \sin\theta = \frac{y}{r}$$

you have:

$$x = r\cos\theta \quad \text{and} \quad y = r\sin\theta$$

The equations in the preceding box are used to convert from polar coordinates to rectangular coordinates. Similarly, if you are given the rectangular coordinates of any point other than the origin, you can find its polar coordinates by using the following equations.

$$r = \pm\sqrt{x^2 + y^2} \qquad \cos\theta = \frac{x}{r} \qquad \sin\theta = \frac{y}{r}$$

Notice that when $x = 0$ and $y = 0$, θ is not uniquely determined. Thus you can write the polar coordinates of the origin as $(0, \theta)$, where θ is any real number.

EXAMPLE   Find the rectangular coordinates of the point whose polar coordinates are:

a. $(4, 60°)$ **b.** $\left(2, \dfrac{7\pi}{4}\right)$

SOLUTION $x = r\cos\theta$ $y = r\sin\theta$

a. $x = 4\cos 60°$ $y = 4\sin 60°$

$\qquad x = 4(0.5) = 2$ $y = 4\left(\dfrac{\sqrt{3}}{2}\right) = 2\sqrt{3}$

The rectangular coordinates are $(2, 2\sqrt{3})$.

b. $x = 2\cos\dfrac{7\pi}{4}$ $y = 2\sin\dfrac{7\pi}{4}$

$\qquad x = 2\left(\dfrac{\sqrt{2}}{2}\right) = \sqrt{2}$ $y = 2\left(-\dfrac{\sqrt{2}}{2}\right) = -\sqrt{2}$

The rectangular coordinates are $(\sqrt{2}, -\sqrt{2})$.

EXAMPLE   For each point given in rectangular coordinates, find two pairs of polar coordinates, one with $r > 0$ and one with $r < 0$.

a. $(3, 3)$ **b.** $(-1, \sqrt{3})$

SOLUTION   **a.** If $r = \sqrt{x^2 + y^2}$, then $r = \sqrt{3^2 + 3^2} = \sqrt{18} = 3\sqrt{2}$.

Since $\cos\theta = \dfrac{3}{3\sqrt{2}} = \dfrac{\sqrt{2}}{2}$ and $\sin\theta = \dfrac{3}{3\sqrt{2}} = \dfrac{\sqrt{2}}{2}$, we can let $\theta = 45°$.

If $r = -\sqrt{x^2 + y^2}$, then $r = -3\sqrt{2}$, $\cos\theta = -\dfrac{\sqrt{2}}{2}$, $\sin\theta = -\dfrac{\sqrt{2}}{2}$, and $\theta = 225°$.

Thus, two pairs of polar coordinates are $(3\sqrt{2}, 45°)$ and $(-3\sqrt{2}, 225°)$.

b. If $r = \sqrt{x^2 + y^2}$, then $r = \sqrt{(-1)^2 + (\sqrt{3})^2} = \sqrt{1 + 3} = 2$.

Since $\cos\theta = -\dfrac{1}{2}$ and $\sin\theta = \dfrac{\sqrt{3}}{2}$, we can let $\theta = 120°$.

If $r = -\sqrt{x^2 + y^2}$, then $r = -2$, $\cos\theta = \dfrac{1}{2}$, $\sin\theta = -\dfrac{\sqrt{3}}{2}$, and $\theta = 300°$.

Thus, two pairs of polar coordinates are $(2, 120°)$ and $(-2, 300°)$.

ORAL EXERCISES

Convert the given rectangular coordinates to polar coordinates, $0° \leqslant \theta \leqslant 360°$.

1. $(0, 2)$ **2.** $(-3, 0)$ **3.** $(2, 2)$ **4.** $(\sqrt{3}, 1)$

Convert the given polar coordinates to rectangular coordinates.

5. $(4, 180°)$ **6.** $(6, 270°)$ **7.** $\left(5, \dfrac{\pi}{2}\right)$ **8.** $(0, 0°)$

State *two more* pairs of polar coordinates for the given point, $-180° \leqslant \theta \leqslant 180°$.

9. $(4, 350°)$ **10.** $(5, -270°)$ **11.** $(-3, 220°)$ **12.** $(-9, 330°)$

Classify each statement as true or false.

13. For any angle θ, (r, θ) and $(r, \theta + 2\pi)$ are polar coordinates of the same point.

14. For any angle θ, $(-r, \theta)$ and $(r, -\theta)$ are polar coordinates of the same point.

15. For any angle θ, (r, θ) and $(-r, \theta + \pi)$ are polar coordinates of the same point.

16. Two distinct points may have the same polar coordinates.

17. Two distinct pairs of polar coordinates may represent the same point.

WRITTEN EXERCISES

Plot the point whose polar coordinates are given and find its rectangular coordinates.

A   **1.** $(6, 135°)$ **2.** $(4, -60°)$ **3.** $\left(1, \dfrac{7\pi}{6}\right)$

    4. $\left(-2, \dfrac{5\pi}{6}\right)$ **5.** $\left(-3, -\dfrac{\pi}{4}\right)$ **6.** $(-3, -135°)$

Find the rectangular coordinates of the point whose polar coordinates are given.

    7. $(7\sqrt{2}, -45°)$ **8.** $\left(2\sqrt{6}, \dfrac{\pi}{6}\right)$ **9.** $\left(\sqrt{10}, -\dfrac{5\pi}{4}\right)$

    10. $(-4\sqrt{10}, 45°)$ **11.** $\left(8\sqrt{3}, -\dfrac{7\pi}{6}\right)$ **12.** $(-\sqrt{15}, 120°)$

For each point given in rectangular coordinates, find two pairs of polar coordinates, one with $r > 0$ and one with $r < 0$. (Give your answers in degrees.)

13. $(-5, 0)$ **14.** $(0, -1.5)$ **15.** $(6, -6)$

16. $(-2\sqrt{3}, 2)$ **17.** $(-4, -4\sqrt{3})$ **18.** $(8\sqrt{2}, -8\sqrt{2})$

19. $(-0.5, 0.5)$ **20.** $(-9\sqrt{3}, -9)$ **21.** $(\sqrt{2}, -\sqrt{6})$

22. $(-a, a)$, $a > 0$ **23.** $\left(b, \dfrac{b\sqrt{3}}{3}\right)$, $b > 0$ **24.** $(c\sqrt{3}, -c)$, $c > 0$

B 25. Show that the polar equation $r = 2 \cos \theta$ is equivalent to the Cartesian equation $(x - 1)^2 + y^2 = 1$. (*Hint*: Substitute $r \cos \theta$ for x and $r \sin \theta$ for y.)

26. Show that the Cartesian equation $x^2 + (y - 2)^2 = 4$ is equivalent to the polar equation $r = 4 \sin \theta$.

Sketch the graph of each equation.

EXAMPLE $r = 2 \sin \theta$

SOLUTION Make a table of values of pairs (r, θ) that satisfy the equation.

θ	0°	30°	45°	60°	90°	120°	135°	150°	180°
r	0	1	$\sqrt{2}$	$\sqrt{3}$	2	$\sqrt{3}$	$\sqrt{2}$	1	0

θ	210°	225°	240°	270°	300°	315°	330°	360°
r	-1	$-\sqrt{2}$	$-\sqrt{3}$	-2	$-\sqrt{3}$	$-\sqrt{2}$	-1	0

Plot the points in order, and connect them with a smooth curve.

The points indicated in the figure at the right are plotted twice; once for $0 \leqslant \theta \leqslant 180°$, and again for $180° \leqslant \theta \leqslant 360°$. It can be verified that the graph is a circle.

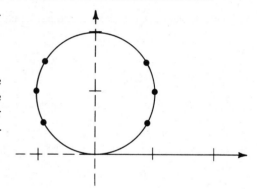

27. $r = 4$ 28. $\theta = 30°$ 29. $r \cos \theta = -1$

30. $r = -2$ 31. $\theta = 0°$ 32. $r \sin \theta = 3$

C 33. $r = \theta$ 34. $r = \cos 2\theta$ 35. $r = \sin 3\theta$

36. $r = 1 + \cos \theta$ 37. $r^2 = 4 \sin 2\theta$ 38. $r^2 = 4 \cos 2\theta$

39. Let R_θ be the rotation through θ. Follow the steps outlined below to show that

$$R_\alpha (x, y) = (x \cos \alpha - y \sin \alpha, x \sin \alpha + y \cos \alpha).$$

1. Let $x = r \cos \theta$ and $y = r \sin \theta$.
2. Express x' in terms of a function of $(\theta + \alpha)$.
3. Express y' in terms of a function of $(\theta + \alpha)$.
4. Show that $x' = x \cos \alpha - y \sin \alpha$ and $y' = x \sin \alpha + y \cos \alpha$.

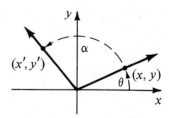

Section 11-8 THE ARGAND PLANE (Optional)

In this section you will learn how to represent a complex number as a point in the plane. You will also learn how to find:
- the absolute value of a complex number
- the polar form of a complex number

You know how to graph a real number as a point on a number line. In 1806, J. R. Argand showed how to graph a complex number as a point in a coordinate plane. His idea, called the *Argand plane*, associated the x-axis, or *real axis*, with the real numbers, and the y-axis, or *imaginary axis*, with the imaginary numbers. By representing the complex number $z = a + bi$ as the ordered pair (a, b), a one-to-one correspondence is established between the complex numbers and the points in the Argand plane. The graph of the complex number $z = a + bi$ is the point (a, b) or the vector from the origin to the point (a, b).

EXAMPLE   Graph each complex number.

a. $-3 + i$ b. $1 - 2i$ c. 5 d. $3i$

SOLUTION

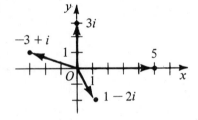

Note that:
$$5 = 5 + 0i = (5, 0)$$
$$3i = 0 + 3i = (0, 3)$$

Each complex number corresponds to a vector, and we can see that the sum of two complex numbers corresponds to the sum of two vectors.

EXAMPLE   If $z_1 = 3 + i$ and $z_2 = -1 + 4i$, find $z_1 + z_2$ and illustrate with a graph.

SOLUTION

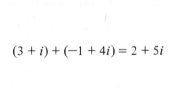

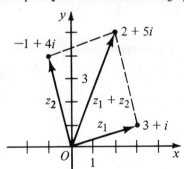

Just as the absolute value of a real number x is the distance from the origin to the point on the number line whose coordinate is x, the *absolute value*, or *modulus*, of a complex number z is the distance from the origin to the point in the Argand plane corresponding to z. If $z = a + bi$, so that the graph of z is the point (a, b), then the Distance Formula gives us:

$$|z| = \sqrt{a^2 + b^2}$$

In other words, the absolute value of a complex number z is equal to the norm of the vector corresponding to z.

EXAMPLE   If $z = 3 + 4i$, find $|z|$.

SOLUTION $|z| = \sqrt{3^2 + 4^2} = 5$

The complex number $a + bi$ also can be written in the *polar form*

$$r(\cos \theta + i \sin \theta),$$

where $r = \sqrt{a^2 + b^2}$, $\cos \theta = \dfrac{a}{r}$, and $\sin \theta = \dfrac{b}{r}$. This form of representation is sometimes more convenient to use, especially in finding products, powers, and roots of complex numbers.

EXAMPLE   Express $2\sqrt{3} + 2i$ in polar form.

SOLUTION $r = \sqrt{a^2 + b^2} = \sqrt{(2\sqrt{3})^2 + 2^2}$
$\qquad\qquad = \sqrt{12 + 4}$
$\qquad\qquad = 4$

$\qquad \cos \theta = \dfrac{a}{r} = \dfrac{2\sqrt{3}}{4} = \dfrac{\sqrt{3}}{2}, \quad \sin \theta = \dfrac{b}{r} = \dfrac{2}{4} = \dfrac{1}{2}$

Therefore, $\theta = 30°$.
Hence, $2\sqrt{3} + 2i = 4(\cos 30° + i \sin 30°)$.

In Exercise 35, you will prove the following formula for the *product of two complex numbers*.

If z_1 and z_2 are **complex numbers** with
$$z_1 = r_1(\cos \alpha + i \sin \alpha) \text{ and } z_2 = r_2(\cos \beta + i \sin \beta),$$
then $z_1 \cdot z_2 = r_1 r_2 [\cos (\alpha + \beta) + i \sin (\alpha + \beta)].$

EXAMPLE   If $z_1 = 3(\cos 30° + i \sin 30°)$ and $z_2 = 2(\cos 60° + i \sin 60°)$, find $z_1 \cdot z_2$.

SOLUTION $z_1 \cdot z_2 = 3 \cdot 2 [\cos (30° + 60°) + i \sin (30° + 60°)]$
$\qquad\qquad = 6(\cos 90° + i \sin 90°)$
$\qquad\qquad = 6(0 + i \cdot 1)$
$\qquad\qquad = 6i$

EXAMPLE   If $z_1 = 2 - 2i\sqrt{3}$ and $z_2 = 3i$, express $z_1 z_2$:
$\qquad\qquad$ **a.** in polar form $\qquad\qquad$ **b.** in the form $a + bi$

SOLUTION   For $z_1 = 2 - 2i\sqrt{3}$:

$$r_1 = \sqrt{2^2 + (-2\sqrt{3})^2} = 4$$

$$\cos \alpha = \frac{2}{4} = \frac{1}{2}$$

$$\sin \alpha = -\frac{2\sqrt{3}}{4} = -\frac{\sqrt{3}}{2}$$

$$\alpha = 300°$$

For $z_2 = 3i$

$$r_2 = \sqrt{3^2} = 3$$

$$\cos \beta = \frac{0}{3} = 0$$

$$\sin \beta = \frac{3}{3} = 1$$

$$\beta = 90°$$

Therefore,

$$z_1 = 4(\cos 300° + i \sin 300°) \text{ and } z_2 = 3(\cos 90° + i \sin 90°).$$

Using the formula for the product of two complex numbers, we have:

a. $z_1 \cdot z_2 = 12(\cos 390° + i \sin 390°)$

b. From part a: $z_1 \cdot z_2 = 12\left[\dfrac{\sqrt{3}}{2} + i\left(\dfrac{1}{2}\right)\right] = 6\sqrt{3} + 6i$

You get the same answer if you simplify the product $(2 - 2i\sqrt{3})(3i)$.

ORAL EXERCISES

Name the complex number corresponding to the given point in the diagram at the right.

1. A 2. B 3. C 4. D 5. E

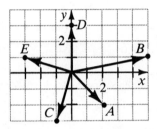

State the absolute value of each complex number.

6. i 7. -8 8. $-6i$

9. $-3 + 4i$ 10. $5 - 12i$

WRITTEN EXERCISES

Graph each complex number and express the number in polar form.

A   1. $-1 - i$ 2. $1 + i\sqrt{3}$ 3. $4i$ 4. -4

5. $-3\sqrt{3} + 3i$ 6. $-i$ 7. -3 8. $2 - 2i$

Express each number in the form $a + bi$.

9. $2(\cos 45° - i \sin 45°)$ 10. $3(\cos 90° + i \sin 90°)$ 11. $\cos \dfrac{\pi}{6} + i \sin \dfrac{\pi}{6}$

12. $\sqrt{2}\left(\cos \dfrac{7\pi}{4} + i \sin \dfrac{7\pi}{4}\right)$ 13. $2\sqrt{3}(\cos 150° + i \sin 150°)$ 14. $r(\cos \theta + i \sin \theta)$

On one set of axes graph z_1, z_2, and $z_1 + z_2$.

15. $z_1 = 4 - i$, $z_2 = 2 + 3i$ 16. $z_1 = -2 + 5i$, $z_2 = 5 + i$

17. $z_1 = 5i$, $z_2 = -3 - 6i$ 18. $z_1 = 7 - 2i$, $z_2 = -6$

19. $z_1 = -1 - 4i$, $z_2 = 3 + 4i$ 20. $z_1 = -4 + 2i$, $z_2 = 4 - 3i$

Find the absolute value of each complex number.

21. $-7 + i$ **22.** $4 + 6i$ **23.** $-5 - i\sqrt{11}$ **24.** $\sqrt{15} - i$

Express the product $z_1 z_2$:
a. in polar form   **b.** in the form $a + bi$

B 25. $z_1 = i, \; z_2 = 5\sqrt{3} + 5i$ **26.** $z_1 = 2\sqrt{2} + 2i\sqrt{2}, \; z_2 = -i$

27. $z_1 = 3\sqrt{2} - 3i\sqrt{2}, \; z_2 = -\sqrt{2} + i\sqrt{2}$ **28.** $z_1 = -\sqrt{3} - i, \; z_2 = 1 - i\sqrt{3}$

29. $z_1 = -2\sqrt{3} + 2i, \; z_2 = \sqrt{2} + i\sqrt{2}$ **30.** $z_1 = 3 - 3i, \; z_2 = -2 - 2i\sqrt{3}$

Express in the form $a + bi$.

31. $(4 \cos 13° + 4i \sin 13°)(3 \cos 32° + 3i \sin 32°)$

32. $(2 \cos 18° + 2i \sin 18°)(5 \cos 12° + 5i \sin 12°)$

C 33. Show that if $z = r(\cos \theta + i \sin \theta)$, then $z^2 = r^2(\cos 2\theta + i \sin 2\theta)$.

34. Show that if $z = r(\cos \theta + i \sin \theta)$, then $z^3 = r^3(\cos 3\theta + i \sin 3\theta)$.

35. Use the Angle-Sum Formulas for the sine and cosine to show that if $z_1 = r_1(\cos \alpha + i \sin \alpha)$ and $z_2 = r_2(\cos \beta + i \sin \beta)$, then
$$z_1 \cdot z_2 = r_1 r_2 [\cos (\alpha + \beta) + i \sin (\alpha + \beta)].$$

36. Show that if $z_1 = r_1(\cos \alpha + i \sin \alpha)$ and $z_2 = r_2(\cos \beta + i \sin \beta)$, $z_2 \neq 0$, then
$$\frac{z_1}{z_2} = \frac{r_1}{r_2} [\cos (\alpha - \beta) + i \sin (\alpha - \beta)]. \quad (\textit{Hint: Begin by multiplying the numera-}$$
tor and denominator of $\dfrac{z_1}{z_2}$ by $\cos \beta - i \sin \beta$.)

37. If $z = r(\cos \theta + i \sin \theta)$, $r \neq 0$, show that $z^{-1} = r^{-1}[\cos (-\theta) + i \sin (-\theta)]$. (*Hint*: Show that $z \cdot z^{-1} = 1$.)

38. Show that if $z_1 = r_1(\cos \theta_1 + i \sin \theta_1)$ and $z_2 = r_2(\cos \theta_2 + i \sin \theta_2)$ for $r_1 > 0$ and $r_2 > 0$, then $z_1 = z_2$ if and only if $r_1 = r_2$ and $\theta_1 = \theta_2 + 360° \cdot n$, $n \in Z$.

Section 11-9 DE MOIVRE'S THEOREM (Optional)

In Section 11-8 you learned that if:
$$z_1 = r_1(\cos \alpha + i \sin \alpha) \quad \text{and} \quad z_2 = r_2(\cos \beta + i \sin \beta),$$
then
$$z_1 \cdot z_2 = r_1 r_2 [\cos (\alpha + \beta) + i \sin (\alpha + \beta)]$$
Therefore (See Exercises 33 and 34, above), for $z = r(\cos \theta + i \sin \theta)$:
$$z^2 = z \cdot z = r \cdot r [\cos (\theta + \theta) + i \sin (\theta + \theta)]$$
$$= r^2(\cos 2\theta + i \sin 2\theta)$$
and:
$$z^3 = z \cdot z^2 = r \cdot r^2 [\cos (\theta + 2\theta) + i \sin (\theta + 2\theta)]$$
$$= r^3(\cos 3\theta + i \sin 3\theta)$$

These examples illustrate a very important theorem about complex numbers, *De Moivre's Theorem*. You will be asked to prove this theorem in Section 15-7, Mathematical Induction.

De Moivre's Theorem

If $z = r(\cos\theta + i\sin\theta)$ and n is a positive integer, then

$$z^n = r^n(\cos n\theta + i\sin n\theta).$$

EXAMPLE   Express $(2 + 2i)^6$ in the form $a + bi$.

SOLUTION   First express $2 + 2i$ in polar form.

$$r = \sqrt{2^2 + 2^2} = 2\sqrt{2}, \; \cos\theta = \frac{2}{2\sqrt{2}}, \text{ and } \sin\theta = \frac{2}{2\sqrt{2}}. \text{ Therefore, } \theta = 45°$$

Thus, $2 + 2i = 2\sqrt{2}(\cos 45° + i\sin 45°)$.

Using De Moivre's Theorem you have:

$$(2 + 2i)^6 = (2\sqrt{2})^6[\cos(6 \cdot 45°) + i\sin(6 \cdot 45°)]$$
$$= 512(\cos 270° + i\sin 270°)$$
$$= 512[0 + i(-1)] = -512i$$

You can also use De Moivre's Theorem to find roots of complex numbers.

EXAMPLE   Find the cube roots of 1.

SOLUTION $1 = 1(\cos 0° + i\sin 0°)$

Therefore, $r(\cos\theta + i\sin\theta)$ is a cube root of 1 if and only if

$$[r(\cos\theta + i\sin\theta)]^3 = 1(\cos 0° + i\sin 0°).$$

Applying De Moivre's Theorem, we have:

$$r^3(\cos 3\theta + i\sin 3\theta) = 1(\cos 0° + i\sin 0°)$$

In Exercise 38, page 462, you showed that:

$$r_1(\cos\theta_1 + i\sin\theta_1) = r_2(\cos\theta_2 + i\sin\theta_2)$$

if and only if

$$r_1 = r_2 \quad \text{and} \quad \theta_1 = \theta_2 + 360° \cdot n, \, n \in Z.$$

Therefore,

$$r^3 = 1 \text{ and } 3\theta = 0° + 360° \cdot n, \text{ or } r = 1 \quad \text{and} \quad \theta = 0° + 120° \cdot n, \, n \in Z.$$

Letting $n = 0$, 1, and 2, we find that the cube roots of 1 are:

$$1(\cos 0° + i\sin 0°) = 1(1 + i \cdot 0) = 1$$

$$1(\cos 120° + i\sin 120°) = 1\left(-\frac{1}{2} + i\frac{\sqrt{3}}{2}\right) = \frac{-1 + i\sqrt{3}}{2}$$

$$1(\cos 240° + i\sin 240°) = 1\left(-\frac{1}{2} - i\frac{\sqrt{3}}{2}\right) = \frac{-1 - i\sqrt{3}}{2}$$

In Exercise 27, you will be asked to verify the results of the preceding example.

ORAL EXERCISES

Simplify. Express in polar form.

1. $(\cos 30° + i \sin 30°)^2$

2. $(\cos 50° + i \sin 50°)^3$

3. $\left[2\left(\cos \dfrac{\pi}{2} + i \sin \dfrac{\pi}{2}\right)\right]^3$

4. $\left[3\left(\cos \dfrac{\pi}{3} + i \sin \dfrac{\pi}{3}\right)\right]^4$

Express in the form $a + bi$.

5. $(\cos 45° + i \sin 45°)^2$

6. $(\cos 225° + i \sin 225°)^2$

7. Complete to find the square roots of i.
   a. $[r(\cos \theta + i \sin \theta)]^2 = r^2(\cos \underline{} + i \sin \underline{})$
   b. In polar form, $i = 1(\cos \underline{} + i \sin \underline{})$
   c. If $[r(\cos \theta + i \sin \theta)]^2 = i$, then $r = \underline{}$ and $2\theta = \underline{} + 360° \cdot n, n \in Z$.
   d. If $n = 0$, $z_1 = \underline{}$.   If $n = 1$, $z_2 = \underline{}$.

WRITTEN EXERCISES

Express in the form $a + bi$.

A 1. $[2(\cos 15° + i \sin 15°)]^3$

2. $(\cos 12° + i \sin 12°)^5$

3. $(\cos 45° + i \sin 45°)^4$

4. $[3(\cos 35° + i \sin 35°)]^6$

5. $(-1 + i)^3$

6. $(\sqrt{3} + i)^5$

7. $(-\sqrt{2} - i\sqrt{2})^4$

8. $\left(-\dfrac{\sqrt{3}}{2} + \dfrac{i}{2}\right)^6$

9. $(\cos 15° + i \sin 15°)^6 [2(\cos 10° + i \sin 10°)]^3$

10. $\left(\dfrac{1 + i\sqrt{3}}{2}\right)^2$

Express the roots in polar form. Graph them in the Argand plane.

B 11. Cube roots of -1

12. Fourth roots of 1

13. Fourth roots of i

14. Cube roots of $-i$

15. Fifth roots of $1 - i\sqrt{3}$

16. Cube roots of $1 + i$

17. Verify that De Moivre's Theorem is true for $n = 0$.

C 18. Show that the graphs of the three cube roots of -1 (see Exercise 11) lie on a circle of radius 1 and that the measure of the angle between two consecutive roots is $120°$.

19. Show that the graphs of the five fifth roots of $1 - i\sqrt{3}$ (see Exercise 15) lie on a circle of radius $\sqrt[5]{2}$ and that the measure of the angle between two consecutive roots is $72°$.

Find all solutions of the equation. Express the roots in the form $a + bi$.

20. $x^2 = -4$

21. $x^3 = -27$

22. $x^2 = 2 - 2i\sqrt{3}$

23. $3x^2 = -6 - 6i\sqrt{3}$

24. $x^6 = 64$

25. $x^5 + x = 0$

26. Prove that De Moivre's Theorem is true for negative integers. (*Hint*: Use the results of Exercise 33, page 462.)

27. Refer to the example on page 463. Verify that the roots found are the cube roots of 1.

SELF-TEST 3

Find the rectangular coordinates of the point whose polar coordinates are given.

1. $(6, 135°)$ 　　　　　　　　　　**2.** $\left(10, -\dfrac{5\pi}{6}\right)$ 　　　　　　　　Section 11-7

For each point given below in rectangular coordinates, find two pairs of polar coordinates, one with $r > 0$ and one with $r < 0$.

3. $(4, -4\sqrt{3})$ 　　　　　　　　**4.** $(-1, 1)$

5. Express $\sqrt{3} + i$ in polar form and draw its graph in an Argand plane. 　　Section 11-8

6. If $z_1 = 4 + 2i$ and $z_2 = -2 - 5i$, graph z_1, z_2, and $z_1 + z_2$ on one set of axes.

Express the product $z_1 z_2$ in polar form.

7. $z_1 = -3 + 3i$, $z_2 = 2i$ 　　　　**8.** $z_1 = \sqrt{3} - i$, $z_2 = -2 + 2i\sqrt{3}$

Express in the form $a + bi$.

9. $[3(\cos 20° + i \sin 20°)]^3$ 　　　　**10.** $(-1 + i)^6$ 　　　　　　Section 11-9

11. Find the two square roots of $-i$ and graph them in an Argand plane.

Computer Exercises

Mathematicians have been interested in the problem of evaluating π since at least 1500 B.C. The program in this exercise uses some of the ideas that Archimedes used to calculate π in about 240 B.C.

Suppose a regular polygon of n sides is inscribed in a circle of radius 1. The more sides the polygon has, the more closely its area approximates the area of the circle, which is $\pi(1)^2$, or π.

Radii drawn to consecutive vertices of the polygon make an angle θ with each other. The area of the triangle formed is $\dfrac{1}{2} \cdot 1 \cdot 1 \cdot \sin \theta$, or $\dfrac{1}{2} \sin \theta$. Since the area of the polygon is equal to the area of n such triangles, the area of the polygon is $\dfrac{n}{2} \sin \theta$.

Begin with a regular polygon of 3 sides, that is, an equilateral triangle. Then $n = 3$ and $\theta = 120°$. Since $\sin 120° = \dfrac{\sqrt{3}}{2}$ and $\cos 120° = -\dfrac{1}{2}$, the area is easily calculated. For succeeding polygons, double the number of sides, which causes the new value of θ to be half the previous value. We then use Half-Angle Formulas and the old values of $\sin \theta$ and $\cos \theta$ to find the new $\sin \theta$ and $\cos \theta$. Following this procedure, we find areas of regular polgyons with 3, 6, 12, 24, ... sides.

Some lines have been left blank in the following program. You will be asked to complete these lines in Exercises 1-4.

```
10    LET N = 3
20    ?
30    ?
40    FOR K = 1 TO 8
50    ?
60    PRINT
70    PRINT "N = "; N, "A = "; A
80    ?
90    ?
100   ?
110   NEXT K
120   END
```

Notice that you will need to use the SQR function in Exercises 1 and 4 below.

1. In line 20, assign the value of $\sin 120°$ to S. In line 30, assign the value of $\cos 120°$ to C. These are the initial values of $\sin \theta$ and $\cos \theta$.

2. In line 50, compute the value of A, which is the area of the polygon.

3. In line 80, double the number of sides of the polygon. Make the new value of N twice the old value.

4. In lines 90 and 100, use Half-Angle Formulas to assign new values to S ($\sin \theta$) and C ($\cos \theta$) respectively.

5. RUN the completed program. What trend is apparent in the sequence of values of the areas of the polygons?

6. How does the final value of A, which is the area of a polygon with 384 sides, compare with the actual value of π?

CHAPTER REVIEW

Determine the amplitude and fundamental period of the function and graph at least two cycles.

1. $y = \cos \dfrac{x}{3}$
2. $y = -3 \sin 2x$
Section 11-1

Use Angle-Sum and Angle-Difference Formulas to evaluate the expression.

3. $\sin 345°$
4. $\tan 195°$
Section 11-2

5. Express as the sine or cosine of one angle:
$$\cos 175° \cos 55° + \sin 175° \sin 55°$$

6. Find $\tan 2x$ if $\sin x = \dfrac{\sqrt{5}}{3}$ and $\dfrac{\pi}{2} < x < \pi$. Section 11-3

7. Prove the identity: $\sin 2\theta + \cos 2\theta = 2 \cos \theta(\sin \theta + \cos \theta) - 1$

Use Half-Angle Formulas to evaluate the expression.

8. $\tan 165°$ **9.** $\sin 195°$ Section 11-4

10. $\cos \dfrac{\theta}{2}$, if $\cos \theta = \dfrac{3}{8}$ and $\dfrac{3\pi}{2} < \theta < 2\pi$

Solve for $0° \leqslant x < 360°$.

11. $2 \cos^2 x = \sin 2x$ **12.** $\cos 2x = \cos^2 x$ Section 11-5

Evaluate.

13. $\text{Arcsin } \dfrac{\sqrt{3}}{2}$ **14.** $\text{Tan}^{-1}(-1)$ Section 11-6

15. $\sin\left(\text{Arccos } \dfrac{3}{5}\right)$ **16.** $\cos(\text{Cos}^{-1} 0.7)$

For the point given in rectangular coordinates, find two pairs of polar coordinates, one with $r > 0$ and one with $r < 0$. Give answers in degrees.

17. $(0, -4)$ **18.** $(\sqrt{3}, -1)$ **19.** $(-3, -3)$ Section 11-7 (Optional)

Find the rectangular coordinates of the point whose polar coordinates are given.

20. $(-6, 60°)$ **21.** $\left(10, \dfrac{7\pi}{4}\right)$

Express the complex number in polar form.

22. $-4i$ **23.** -6 **24.** $-5 + 5i$ Section 11-8 (Optional)

Express in the form $a + bi$.

25. z^5, if $z = 2(\cos 72° + i \sin 72°)$ Section 11-9 (Optional)
26. $(-\sqrt{2} + i\sqrt{2})^6$

*CHAPTER TEST*_____

Determine the amplitude and fundamental period of the function and graph at least two cycles.

1. $y = -3 \sin \dfrac{x}{2}$ **2.** $y = \dfrac{1}{2} \cos 4x$

3. **a.** On the same set of axes, sketch the graphs of $y = \sin 2x$ and $y = 2\cos x$ for $0 \leqslant x \leqslant 2\pi$.

   b. How many values of x in the interval $0 \leqslant x \leqslant 2\pi$ satisfy the equation $2\cos x = \sin 2x$?

Evaluate. Do not use tables.

4. $\tan 105°$

5. $\cos \dfrac{5\pi}{12}$

6. $\sin\left(-112\dfrac{1}{2}^{\circ}\right)$

7. $\text{Arctan}\,(-\sqrt{3})$

8. $\sin\left(\text{Cos}^{-1}\dfrac{1}{2}\right)$

9. $\sin\left(\text{Arctan}\,\dfrac{3}{4}\right)$

10. $\cos 205° \cos 25° + \sin 25° \sin 205°$

11. If $\sin\theta = \dfrac{5}{13}$ and θ is a positive acute angle, find $\cos\dfrac{\theta}{2}$. Leave your answer in simplified radical form.

12. Express in terms of one trigonometric function only: $\sin 2\theta \csc \theta$

13. Solve: $\cos 2x + \sin 2x - 1 = 0$, $0° \leqslant x < 360°$

Questions 14–18 cover optional sections.

14. Find the rectangular coordinates of the point whose polar coordinates are $\left(-3, \dfrac{11\pi}{6}\right)$.

15. For the point whose polar coordinates are $(-5, 200°)$, find two more pairs of polar coordinates (r, θ), $-180° \leqslant \theta \leqslant 180°$.

16. Find a pair of polar coordinates with $r > 0$ for the point whose rectangular coordinates are $(3\sqrt{3}, -3)$.

17. For $z_1 = -3i$ and $z_2 = -4 + 4i$, express the product $z_1 z_2$ in polar form. .

18. Find the three cube roots of -8. Express the roots in the form $a + bi$.

CUMULATIVE REVIEW: CHAPTERS 8–11

Indicate the best answer by writing the appropriate letter.

1. Express $\csc(-200°)$ as a function of a positive acute angle.
   a. $\csc 200°$ **b.** $\csc 70°$ **c.** $\csc 20°$ **d.** $-\csc 20°$

2. What is the amplitude of the graph of $y = 3\cos 2x$?
   a. π **b.** 4π **c.** 2 **d.** 3

3. Find the value of $\tan \dfrac{7\pi}{4}$.

   a. 1 **b.** -1 **c.** $\dfrac{\sqrt{3}}{3}$ **d.** $-\dfrac{\sqrt{3}}{3}$

4. In $\triangle ABC$, $a = 18$, $\sin A = \dfrac{3}{4}$, and $\sin B = \dfrac{2}{3}$. Find b.

a. 9   b. 16   c. $20\dfrac{1}{4}$ d. 36

5. Find the y-intercept of the graph of $f(x) = \left(\dfrac{1}{4}\right)^x$.

a. 0   b. 4   c. $\dfrac{1}{4}$ d. 1

6. If $\log 2.06 = m$, then $\log 2060 = $ ___?___ .

a. $1000m$ b. $m + 3$ c. $m + 1000$ d. $3m$

7. A sonar device on a research vessel on the surface of the ocean detects an object at a depth of 300 m and at a distance of 575 m from the research vessel. What is the angle of depression, to the nearest degree, from the vessel to the object?

a. $62°$ b. $59°$ c. $28°$ d. $31°$

8. The expression $\sin(\pi - x)$ is equivalent to ___?___ .

a. $-\sin x$ b. $\sin x$ c. $-\cos x$ d. $\cos x$

9. If $f(x) = x^{-\frac{2}{3}}$, evaluate $f(64)$.

a. 512   b. $\dfrac{1}{16}$ c. 16   d. -16

10. Find $\sin \theta$ if $\sec \theta = -\dfrac{5}{3}$ and θ lies in Quadrant II.

a. $\dfrac{3}{5}$ b. $-\dfrac{3}{5}$ c. $\dfrac{4}{5}$ d. $-\dfrac{4}{5}$

11. In parallelogram $MNPQ$, $MN = 5$, $NP = 8$, and $m\angle QMN = 76°$. Find the area of $MNPQ$ to the nearest tenth.

a. 4.8   b. 9.7   c. 38.8   d. 40.0

12. Find the value of $\log_4 \dfrac{1}{8}$.

a. $-\dfrac{2}{3}$ b. $-\dfrac{3}{2}$ c. -2 d. $\dfrac{1}{2}$

13. Solve the equation $\sec \theta = \cos \theta$ for $0° \leqslant \theta \leqslant 360°$.

a. $\theta = 0°$ or $360°$ b. $\theta = 180°$ c. $\theta = 90°$ or $270°$ d. $\theta = 0°, 180°, 360°$

14. Find w correct to four significant digits if $\log w = 0.7336 - 3$.

a. 5415   b. 0.0054   c. 0.05415   d. 0.005415

15. The base angles of an isosceles triangle are each $71°$ and the length of the base is 43. Find the length of each of the congruent sides to the nearest integer.

a. 22   b. 66   c. 129   d. 44

16. If $\cos x = \dfrac{12}{13}$ and x is a positive acute angle, find $\cos 2x$.

a. $\dfrac{119}{169}$ b. $\dfrac{120}{169}$ c. $\dfrac{5}{13}$ d. $\dfrac{5\sqrt{26}}{26}$

17. The lengths of the sides of a triangle are 5, 8, and 10. Find the measure of the largest angle of the triangle to the nearest $10'$.
    a. $97°50'$ **b.** $82°10'$ **c.** $96°20'$ **d.** $94°0'$

18. Evaluate $\sqrt[5]{6.92}$ to the nearest hundredth.
    a. 1.38   **b.** 0.17   **c.** 1.47   **d.** 2.03

19. How many solutions of the equation $2 \cos x = \sin \dfrac{x}{2}$ are there in the interval $0 \leqslant x \leqslant 2\pi$?
    a. 0   **b.** 1   **c.** 2   **d.** 3

20. Solve: $3^{2x-1} = 27^x$
    a. $x = 1$ **b.** $x = \dfrac{1}{3}$ **c.** $x = -1$ **d.** $x = -\dfrac{1}{3}$

21. Which expression is equivalent to $\cos \theta \cot \theta \csc \theta$?
    a. $\cot \theta$ **b.** 1   **c.** $\tan \theta$ **d.** $\cot^2 \theta$

22. Solve for $0° \leqslant x \leqslant 360°$: $2 \sin x = \sec x$
    a. $x = 90°$ **b.** $x = 45°$ **c.** $x = 45°, 225°$ **d.** $x = 0°, 180°, 360°$

23. In $\triangle ABC$, $m\angle A = 63°$, $a = 11$, and $b = 12$. Find the number of triangles that satisfy these conditions.
    a. 0   **b.** 1   **c.** 2   **d.** 3

24. Two forces of 25 N and 35 N act on an object, forming an acute angle with each other. The resultant makes an angle of $28°40'$ with the force of 35 N. Find the angle, to the nearest $10'$, between the two given forces.
    a. $20°0'$ **b.** $42°10'$ **c.** $48°40'$ **d.** $70°50'$

25. Which expression is equivalent to $\tan^2 \theta - \sin^2 \theta$?
    a. 0   **b.** $\sec^2 \theta$ **c.** $\sin^2 \theta$ **d.** $\sin^2 \theta \tan^2 \theta$

26. In the diagram, $\overline{AB} \parallel \overline{DC}$, $\overline{AB} \perp \overline{AD}$, $AB = 38$, $m\angle ABC = 81$, and $m\angle ADB = 62$. Find BC to the nearest integer.
    a. 16   **b.** 20   **c.** 34   **d.** 71

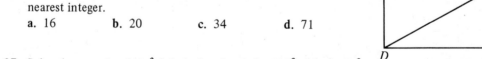

27. Solve the equation $2 \sin^2 \theta + \sin \theta - 1 = 0$ for $180° \leqslant \theta \leqslant 270°$.
    a. $\theta = 210°$ **b.** $\theta = 270°$ **c.** $\theta = 210°$ or $270°$ **d.** $\theta = 240°$ or $270°$

28. The population P of a bacteria culture is found by using the formula $P = p(2)^{\frac{t}{6}}$, where p is the initial number of bacteria and t is the number of hours of growth. Find P correct to three significant digits if $p = 1000$ and $t = 27$.
    a. 22,600   **b.** 4.35   **c.** 22.6   **d.** 16,000

Application — Periodic Phenomena

Many physical phenomena recur or move in cycles. Because the trigonometric functions are periodic, they can be used to represent changes repeated at relatively regular time intervals. For example, sine and cosine functions can be used to describe and predict the number of hours of daylight on a particular day, an Earth satellite's distance from the equator at a given time after blastoff, the voltage oscillating in an electrical circuit, and the height of tides at a given time.

The motion of the Earth, sun, and moon, and gravitational forces cause the regular ebb and flow of tides. At most coastal or island locations, high tides occur approximately every 12.4 h, with low tides occurring in between. Mean high water is the average height of tide at high tide when the water level is lowest. Mean low water is the average height of tide at low tide when the water level is lowest. The tidal range is the difference between the mean high water and mean low water.

The tidal range in the waters near Eastport, Maine, is about 5.6 m. If we let $y = 0$ represent mean low water, we can graph the height of tide t hours after high tide as follows:

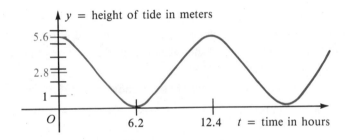

As you can see, this curve approximates the graph of a cosine function. The average height of the tide is found by averaging the mean high water and mean low water: $\dfrac{5.6 + 0}{2}$ = 2.8 m. The average height is the amplitude and represents a vertical translation. Thus, the equation graphed above is

$$y = 2.8 + 2.8 \cos \frac{2\pi}{12.4}t, \quad \text{or} \quad y = 2.8 + 2.8 \cos \frac{\pi}{6.2}t.$$

Translates cosine graph by 2.8 units vertically   Amplitude of 2.8   Period of 12.4

Using this equation, find the height of the tide near Eastport 4 h after high tide. Use the graph to check the reasonableness of your answer.

Be sure that you understand the meaning of these terms:

fundamental period of a function, p. 430
cycle, p. 430
amplitude, p. 430
$\text{Sin}^{-1} x$ (Arcsin x), p. 450
$\text{Cos}^{-1} x$ (Arccos x), p. 450
$\text{Tan}^{-1} x$ (Arctan x), p. 451
polar coordinates, p. 454

pole, p. 454
polar axis, p. 454
Argand plane, p. 459
absolute value (modulus) of a complex number, p. 459
polar form of a complex number, p. 460

MIXED REVIEW

1. Evaluate: **a.** $\tan\left(-\dfrac{5\pi}{12}\right)$ **b.** $\cos^2\dfrac{7\pi}{8} - \sin^2\dfrac{7\pi}{8}$ **c.** $\sin 157.5°$

2. If $r_k : (x, y) \longrightarrow (-y, -x)$, **(a)** find an equation for k, **(b)** find the pre-image of $(-3, 2)$, and **(c)** state whether r_k is a direct or a nondirect isometry.

3. Sketch the graph of $y = x^2 + 2x - 3$. State the x-intercepts and the coordinates of the vertex.

4. Davice jogs 1 km/h faster than her sister. If her sister needs 30 min more to jog 10 km than Davice does, how fast does each jog?

5. Find the value of k for which $kx^2 + 3x + 1$ has one real root.

6. On one set of axes, graph $f(x) = 4 - 2x$ and its inverse. f and f^{-1} are reflections of each other over what line?

7. If $\overline{AB}$ and $\overline{AC}$ are tangents to $\odot O$, $m\angle A = 60$, and $OA = 8$, find $m\,\overset{\frown}{BC}$, AB, and OB.

8. Use Table 1 to evaluate $\cos 129°20'$.

9. Solve: **a.** $\log_{64} x = -\dfrac{2}{3}$ **b.** $\left(\dfrac{1}{3}\right)^{y-1} = 27^{y-2}$

10. If $\cos\theta = \dfrac{4}{5}$ and $\dfrac{3\pi}{2} < \theta < 2\pi$, find **(a)** $\cot\theta$, **(b)** $\csc\theta$, **(c)** $\cos\dfrac{\theta}{2}$, **(d)** $\tan 2\theta$, and **(e)** $\sin\left(\dfrac{\pi}{6} + \theta\right)$.

Solve $\triangle ABC$, giving lengths to the nearest integer and angle measures to the nearest $10'$.

11. $\overline{AB} \perp \overline{BC}$, $AB = 60$, $AC = 61$

12. $AC = 8$, $m\angle A = 127°10'$, $AB = 6$

13. $m\angle B = 53°$, $a = 30$, $b = 25$

14–16. Find the area of $\triangle ABC$ in Exercises 11–13.

17. Find the linear function f such that $f(-3) = 7$ and $f(2) = 2$.

18. Brad's last two quiz grades were 72 and 65. What score must he achieve on the third quiz to maintain an average grade between 70 and 80?

19. Graph at least two cycles of $y = -3 \sin \frac{x}{2}$. Give the amplitude and the fundamental period.

20. Use logs to calculate $\frac{\sqrt[4]{0.0743}}{0.0051}$ to three significant digits.

21. Simplify: **a.** $(3 - \sqrt{-20})^2$ **b.** $\frac{3i}{1 - 2i}$ **c.** $\sqrt{\frac{3}{4}} + \sqrt{\frac{4}{3}}$

Solve.

22. $\sqrt{x + 9} = x - 3$ 23. $d^2 + 2d > -1$ 24. $\frac{s + 1}{s} - \frac{11}{2s + 4} = \frac{1}{3}$

25. Find the image of $(-8, -4)$, under **(a)** $r_{y\text{-axis}}$, **(b)** $D_{\frac{3}{2}}$, **(c)** R_{180}, **(d)** $T_{0,\,7}$, and **(e)** $R_{-180} \circ T_{4,\,8}$.

26. Prove: **a.** $\cos^2 \theta = \frac{\cot^2 \theta}{1 + \cot^2 \theta}$ **b.** $\tan \theta (\cos 2\theta + 1) = \sin 2\theta$

27. Given $O(0, 0)$, $A(-24, 0)$, and $B(0, 10)$, find the magnitude and the direction (with respect to the positive x-axis) of the resultant of $\overrightarrow{OA} + \overrightarrow{OB}$. Give the direction to the nearest $10'$.

28. Use Table 2 to find x such that $\log x = 0.9400 - 4$.

Simplify.

29. $\sin (\text{Arccos } 0)$ 30. $\cos (\text{Tan}^{-1} (-\sqrt{3}))$ 31. $\frac{\cot^2 \theta}{\csc \theta - \sin \theta}$

32. Solve to three significant digits: **a.** $\log_9 \sqrt{7} = x$ **b.** $\log_4 x = 7.04$

Solve for $0° < \theta \leqslant 360°$ to the nearest $10'$.

33. $4 \sin 2\theta = 2 \cot \theta$ 34. $\cos 3\theta = \frac{\sqrt{3}}{2}$ 35. $8 \tan \theta = \cot \theta$

36. Find the measures of two supplementary angles if the measures have the ratio $19:17$.

37. Divide $3x^3 + 4x^2 + 8$ by $x + 2$.

38. Name a transformation that is not an isometry.

39. Draw a large triangle and construct the inscribed circle.

40. A triangle has sides with lengths of $5, 6$, and 7. Find the measure to the nearest degree of the largest angle.

The concept of probability is often used in predicting outcomes of events in sports, such as a basketball game or a tennis match. (See Exercise 3, page 501.)

Probability 12

If 10 people are chosen at random, what is the *probability* that at least 2 of them share the same birthday? We assume that each of 365 days of the year is equally likely to be the birthday of a person within the group; we also ignore February 29 as a possibility.

First let's consider finding the probability of the *complementary event*: What is the probability that the 10 people all have different birthdays? The *sample space* for this experiment will consist of all the possible choices of birthdays. There are 365^{10} *outcomes* in the sample space since there are 10 people and each can have a birthday on any of 365 days. The *permutations* of 365 things taken 10 at a time, denoted as $_{365}P_{10}$, give the number of outcomes corresponding to 10 separate birthdays. Therefore:

$$P(\text{all 10 have different birthdays}) = \frac{_{365}P_{10}}{365^{10}}$$

$$P(\text{at least 2 people share the same birthday}) = 1 - \frac{_{365}P_{10}}{365^{10}}$$

$$\approx 1 - 0.883$$

$$\approx 0.117$$

In the computer exercises for this chapter you will verify the answer given above. You will also be asked to find the least number of people for which the probability of two sharing a birthday is greater than 0.5.

In this chapter you will learn about *conditional probability*, *Bernoulli experiments*, and the *binomial theorem*. First, however, you will review the basic ideas of probability that you have studied previously.

Section 12-1 BASIC CONCEPTS OF PROBABILITY

In this section you will review the terms:
- random experiment
- outcome
- sample space
- event
- simple event
- equally likely outcomes

- probability
- certain event
- impossible event
- mutually exclusive events
- complementary events
- intersecting events

A *random experiment* is an experiment in which you do not necessarily get the same *outcome* when you repeat the experiment under essentially the same conditions. The set of all the possible outcomes of an experiment is called the *sample space* of the experiment.

EXAMPLE   List the sample space for the following experiment: The wheel shown at the right is separated into 10 compartments by dividers placed around its outer edge. The wheel is spun, and the number and color (gray or white) corresponding to the compartment in which the ball lands are noted. (Each number identifies two compartments.)

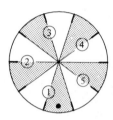

SOLUTION   If we denote the outcome shown in the diagram as (1, G), for example, then the sample space is {(1, W), (1, G), (2, W), (2, G), (3, W), (3, G), (4, W), (4, G), (5, W), (5, G)}.

An *event* is a subset of the sample space for a random experiment. When an event corresponds to a single outcome of the experiment, it is often called a *simple event*.

EXAMPLE   List the following events for the experiment described in the previous example:
    a. The number is 3, and the color is gray.
    b. The number is 3.
    c. The color is gray.
    d. The color is gray, or the color is white.
    e. The number is 7.

SOLUTION   a. {(3, G)}
    b. {(3, G), (3, W)}
    c. {(1, G), (2, G), (3, G), (4, G), (5, G)}
    d. {(1, W), (1, G), (2, W), (2, G), (3, W), (3, G), (4, W), (4, G), (5, W), (5, G)}
    e. ∅

Let us assume that the dividers on the wheel shown in the first example are spaced equally around its outer edge. Then the compartments will all have the same dimensions, and we can regard the elements of the sample space as *equally likely outcomes* of the experiment. When we toss a fair coin, heads and tails are the equally likely outcomes.

We can assign numbers, called *probabilities*, to events within sample spaces of random experiments. The probability of an event E is denoted by $P(E)$. For a random experiment with n equally likely outcomes $(n > 0)$:

1. The probability of any single outcome is $\frac{1}{n}$.

2. The probability of an event E consisting of k outcomes is given by the formula:

$$P(E) = \frac{k}{n}$$

Since $0 \leqslant k \leqslant n$, it follows that the probability of any event E is a number between 0 and 1, inclusive:

$$0 \leqslant P(E) \leqslant 1$$

EXAMPLE Find the probabilities of the following events in the sample space of the wheel experiment. These events were listed in the preceding example.

A: The number is 3, and the color is gray.
B: The number is 3.
C: The color is gray.
D: The color is gray, or the color is white.
E: The number is 7.

SOLUTION We showed earlier that the sample space for this experiment consists of 10 equally likely outcomes, or simple events. The last example shows that A consists of 1 simple event. Therefore:

$$P(A) = \frac{1}{10}$$

We can find the other probabilities similarly:

$$P(B) = \frac{2}{10} = \frac{1}{5} \qquad\qquad P(C) = \frac{5}{10} = \frac{1}{2}$$

$$P(D) = \frac{10}{10} = 1 \qquad\qquad P(E) = \frac{0}{10} = 0$$

An event that is sure to occur is called a *certain event*. The probability of a certain event is 1. An event that cannot occur is called an *impossible event*. The probability of an impossible event is 0. In the example above, D is a certain event, and E is an impossible event.

Two events that have no outcomes in common, such as those shown in the diagram at the right, are called *mutually exclusive*. For any two mutually exclusive events, the probability that an outcome will be in one event or the other is the sum of their individual probabilities.

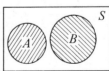

If A and B are mutually exclusive events:

$$P(A \text{ or } B) = P(A) + P(B)$$

EXAMPLE Two coins are tossed, and the number of heads and tails showing are observed. Find the probabilities of the following events:

A: Both coins show tails.
B: Both coins show heads.
C: Exactly one coin shows heads.
D: At least one coin shows heads.

SOLUTION Let (H, T) stand for the event "the first coin shows heads, and the second coin shows tails." (You might wish to think of the first coin as being a nickel and the second coin as being a dime.) The sample space for the experiment is:

$$\{(H, H), (H, T), (T, H), (T, T)\}$$

$$A = \{(T, T)\};\ P(A) = \frac{1}{4}$$

$$B = \{(H, H)\};\ P(B) = \frac{1}{4}$$

$$C = \{(H, T), (T, H)\};\ P(C) = \frac{2}{4} = \frac{1}{2}$$

The event D is equivalent to the event "B or C." Since B and C are mutually exclusive:

$$P(B \text{ or } C) = P(B) + P(C) = \frac{1}{4} + \frac{1}{2} = \frac{3}{4}$$

Therefore: $P(D) = \frac{3}{4}$. (You can confirm this result by observing that D consists of 3 outcomes.)

If A is an event within the sample space S of an experiment, then the *complement* of A, denoted A', consists of all the outcomes of S that are not in A. The following formula can be derived (Exercise 35) from the fact that A and A' are mutually exclusive:

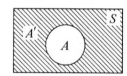

$$P(A') = 1 - P(A)$$

EXAMPLE In the two-coin experiment, the events A (two tails) and D (at least one head) are complementary events. Thus, we can calculate $P(D)$ as follows:

$$P(D) = 1 - P(D') = 1 - P(A) = 1 - \frac{1}{4} = \frac{3}{4}$$

Notice that the value agrees with the result found earlier.

When two events have some outcomes in common, as suggested in the diagram at the right, they are called *intersecting events*. An event is in $A \cap B$ if and only if both A and B have occurred. Thus, the event $A \cap B$ is the same event as "A and B." The following formula applies to intersecting events:

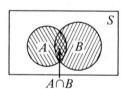

$A \cap B$

$$P(A \text{ or } B) = P(A) + P(B) - P(A \text{ and } B)$$

We subtract $P(A \text{ and } B)$ because the outcomes in "A and B" have been counted once as a part of A and once as a part of B, which is once too often.

Although the formula just given was developed for intersecting events, it also applies to mutually exclusive events. When events A and B are mutually exclusive, $P(A \text{ and } B) = 0$. Thus, the formula can be seen to be equivalent to the formula given earlier for mutually exclusive events.

> For any two events A and B:
>
> $$P(A \text{ or } B) = P(A) + P(B) - P(A \text{ and } B)$$

The next example refers to a standard bridge deck of 52 cards. The deck consists of four suits: spades and clubs, which are black, and hearts and diamonds, which are red. Each suit consists of 13 cards: an ace, 2, 3, 4, 5, 6, 7, 8, 9, 10, jack, queen, and king. Jacks, queens, and kings can be referred to as *face cards*. Sometimes we find it convenient to refer to a group of cards as a *hand*.

EXAMPLE   A card is drawn at random from a standard bridge deck. Find the probability that the card is a club or a 7.

SOLUTION $P(\text{club or } 7) = P(\text{club}) + P(7) - P(7 \text{ and a club})$

$$P(\text{club}) = \frac{13}{52}$$

$$P(7) = \frac{4}{52}$$

$$P(7 \text{ of clubs}) = \frac{1}{52}$$

Therefore: $P(\text{club or } 7) = \dfrac{13}{52} + \dfrac{4}{52} - \dfrac{1}{52} = \dfrac{16}{52} = \dfrac{4}{13}$

Notice in the preceding example that we assumed that any card in the deck is equally likely to be drawn. We assumed earlier that when a coin is tossed, it is equally likely to show heads or tails. You may make similar assumptions in the text and exercises in the rest of this book.

ORAL EXERCISES

The digits 0, 1, 2, 3, 4, 5, 6, 7, 8, and 9 are written on cards that are shuffled and placed face down in a stack. One card is selected at random.

1. State the sample space for the experiment.

2. Find the probability that the digit is even.

3. Find the probability that the digit is less than 3.

4. Find the probability that the digit is less than 10.

The keyboard of an electronic game is shown at the right. A key is pressed at random. Find the following probabilities.

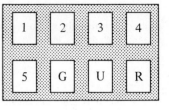

5. $P(2)$ 6. $P(R)$

7. P(odd number)   8. P(even number)

9. P(vowel)   10. P(odd number or consonant)

The needle on the spinner at the right is spun and the number or letter indicated is noted. (If the needle lands on a line, it is moved 1° clockwise.) Find the following probabilities.

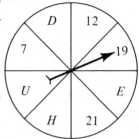

11. $P(7)$ 12. $P(E)$

13. P(a letter)   14. P(a number)

15. P(a number greater than 30)   16. P(a letter after B in the alphabet)

17. P(a number greater than 10)   18. P(a consonant)

WRITTEN EXERCISES

Exercises 1–6 refer to the following experiment: 3 coins are tossed and whether they show heads or tails is observed.

A   1. List the sample space for this experiment.

Find the following probabilities.

2. P(2 heads)   3. P(3 tails)

4. P(at least 2 tails)   5. P(at least 1 head)

6. P(all 3 coins show the same face)

Exercises 7–18 refer to the experiment of throwing two dice. In this experiment we are usually interested in the sum of the spots showing. For example, when one die shows 4 spots and the other shows 3 spots, we say that a 7 has been rolled.

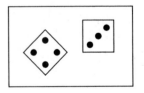

7. Specify the sample space for this experiment by copying and completing the diagram at the right. The entry (1, 2) corresponds to the outcome that the first die shows 1 spot and the second die shows 2 spots.

(1, 1), (1, 2), (1, 3), . . .
(2, 1), (2, 2), . . .
(3, 1), . . .
. . .

Find the following probabilities.

EXAMPLE $P(4)$

SOLUTION   There are 3 outcomes in this event: $\{(3, 1), (2, 2), (1, 3)\}$

Therefore: $P(4) = \dfrac{3}{36} = \dfrac{1}{12}$

8. $P(10)$ **9.** $P(12)$ **10.** $P(3)$

11. $P(6)$ **12.** P(even number)   **13.** P(odd number)

14. P(2 or 12)   **15.** P(doubles)   **16.** P(10 or more)

17. P(7 or less)   **18.** P(any number except 7 or 11)

Exercises 19–30 refer to the following experiment: A card is drawn from a standard deck. Find the following probabilities.

19. P(2 of diamonds)   **20.** P(4 of hearts)

21. $P(4)$ **22.** P(club)

23. P(jack or king)   **24.** P(spade or heart)

25. P(face card)   **26.** P(diamond or 4)

27. P(heart or king)   **28.** P(ace or face card)

29. P(face card or club)   **30.** P(jack or red card)

Exercises 31–34 refer to the following experiment: Four coins are tossed and whether they show heads or tails is observed. Find the following probabilities.

B   **31.** P(all heads)   **32.** P(2 heads and 2 tails)

     33. P(fewer than 2 heads)   **34.** P(3 heads or 3 tails)

     35. Derive the formula: $P(A') = 1 - P(A)$

C   **36.** Events A and B are in the sample space for a particular experiment; $P(A) = \dfrac{3}{5}$

       and $P(B) = \dfrac{3}{5}$.

       a. How do you know that A and B cannot be mutually exclusive?

       b. If C is equivalent to "A and B," show that $\dfrac{1}{5} \leqslant P(C) \leqslant \dfrac{3}{5}$.

Section 12-2 MULTISTAGE EVENTS

In this section you will review the use of *tree diagrams* to analyze experiments that can be regarded as consisting of two or more stages.

     Many probability experiments involve drawing two or more objects from a group of objects. When each object is replaced before the next is drawn, the drawing is said to be *with replacement*. Otherwise, the drawing is said to be *without replacement*. *In this book, you may assume that drawing is without replacement unless otherwise stated.*

EXAMPLE Two balls are drawn from an urn containing 3 black balls and 2 white balls. Find the probabilities of the following events:

a. 2 white balls are drawn.
b. 1 white ball and 1 black ball are drawn in that order.
c. 1 white ball and 1 black ball are drawn.
d. 2 black balls are drawn.

SOLUTION When we determine the probabilities at the second stage, we must think carefully about what happened in the first stage. For example, if 1 white ball is drawn at the first stage, then only 1 of the 4 balls remaining in the urn is white. The probabilities for each stage are shown in the *tree diagram* below.

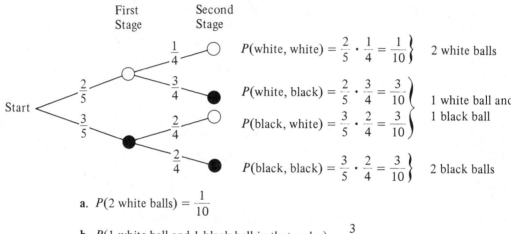

a. $P(\text{2 white balls}) = \dfrac{1}{10}$

b. $P(\text{1 white ball and 1 black ball in that order}) = \dfrac{3}{10}$

c. $P(\text{1 white ball and 1 black ball}) = \dfrac{3}{10} + \dfrac{3}{10} = \dfrac{3}{5}$

d. $P(\text{2 black balls}) = \dfrac{3}{10}$

The principle used in the previous solution is shown below. It enables us to find probabilities for certain experiments that are not easily analyzed using a sample space of equally likely outcomes.

The probability of any outcome in the sample space of a multistage experiment is the product of all probabilities along the path that represents that outcome on the tree diagram.

EXAMPLE Two cards are selected from the heart suit in a deck of cards. Find the probability of the following events. Give each answer as a fraction and as a decimal correct to the nearest thousandth.

a. Both cards are face cards.
b. Exactly 1 card is a face card.
c. Neither card is a face card.

SOLUTION

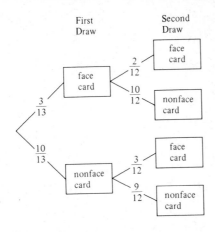

$$P(\text{face, face}) = \frac{3}{13} \cdot \frac{2}{12} = \frac{1}{26}$$

$$P(\text{face, nonface}) = \frac{3}{13} \cdot \frac{10}{12} = \frac{5}{26}$$

$$P(\text{nonface, face}) = \frac{10}{13} \cdot \frac{3}{12} = \frac{5}{26}$$

$$P(\text{nonface, nonface}) = \frac{10}{13} \cdot \frac{9}{12} = \frac{15}{26}$$

a. $P(\text{both cards are face cards}) = \dfrac{1}{26}$, or 0.038

b. $P(\text{exactly 1 card is a face card}) = \dfrac{5}{26} + \dfrac{5}{26} = \dfrac{5}{13}$, or 0.385

c. $P(\text{neither card is a face card}) = \dfrac{15}{26}$, or 0.577

Compare the probabilities of the events in the next example with those in the previous example. The next example differs from the previous one only in that the drawing is with replacement.

EXAMPLE   Two cards are selected with replacement from the heart suit in a deck of cards. Find the probability of the following events. Give each answer as a fraction and as a decimal correct to the nearest thousandth.
a. Both cards are face cards.
b. Exactly 1 card is a face card.
c. Neither card is a face card.

SOLUTION

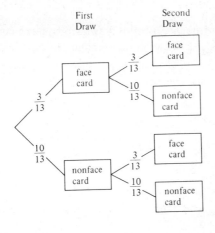

$$P(\text{face, face}) = \frac{3}{13} \cdot \frac{3}{13} = \frac{9}{169}$$

$$P(\text{face, nonface}) = \frac{3}{13} \cdot \frac{10}{13} = \frac{30}{169}$$

$$P(\text{nonface, face}) = \frac{10}{13} \cdot \frac{3}{13} = \frac{30}{169}$$

$$P(\text{nonface, nonface}) = \frac{10}{13} \cdot \frac{10}{13} = \frac{100}{169}$$

(Solution continued on the next page)

a. $P(\text{both cards are face cards}) = \dfrac{9}{169}$, or 0.053

b. $P(\text{exactly 1 card is a face card}) = \dfrac{30}{169} + \dfrac{30}{169} = \dfrac{60}{169}$, or 0.355

c. $P(\text{neither card is a face card}) = \dfrac{100}{169}$, or 0.592

Notice that the probability that both cards are face cards increases significantly when the drawing is with replacement.

ORAL EXERCISES

Exercises 1 and 2 refer to the following experiment: 2 balls are drawn from an urn containing 2 red balls and 2 green balls.

 1. Make a tree diagram for the experiment.

 2. Find the probabilities of the following events.
   a. 2 green balls are drawn.
   b. 1 red ball and 1 green ball are drawn in that order.
   c. 1 red ball and 1 green ball are drawn.
   d. 2 green balls are drawn.

 3–4. Repeat Exercises 1 and 2 under the assumption that the drawing is with replacement.

WRITTEN EXERCISES

A 1. The aces and kings are removed from a deck of cards and shuffled; 2 cards are drawn from them. Find the probabilities of the following events.
   a. 2 kings are drawn.   **b.** 1 ace and 1 king are drawn in that order.
   c. 1 ace and 1 king are drawn.   **d.** 2 aces are drawn.

 2. Repeat Exercise 1 under the assumption that the drawing is with replacement.

Exercises 3–12 refer to the following experiment: A ball is drawn from an urn containing 2 white and 5 red balls. Then a ball is drawn from a second urn containing 3 yellow, 2 red, and 6 white balls. Find the following probabilities.

 3. $P(\text{1 red ball and 1 yellow ball are drawn})$

 4. $P(\text{1 white ball and 1 yellow ball are drawn})$

 5. $P(\text{2 red balls are drawn})$

 6. $P(\text{2 white balls are drawn})$

 7. $P(\text{1 white ball and 1 red ball are drawn in that order})$

 8. $P(\text{1 red ball and 1 white ball are drawn in that order})$

 9. $P(\text{1 red ball and 1 white ball are drawn})$ 10. $P(\text{at least 1 red ball is drawn})$

 11. $P(\text{at least 1 white ball is drawn})$ 12. $P(\text{1 yellow ball is drawn})$

Exercises 13–20 refer to the following experiment: 2 balls are drawn from an urn containing 4 red balls, 3 white balls, and 1 yellow ball. Find the following probabilities.

13. P(2 red balls are drawn)

14. P(2 white balls are drawn)

15. P(2 yellow balls are drawn)

16. P(1 red ball and 1 white ball are drawn)

17. P(1 red ball and 1 yellow ball are drawn)

18. P(1 white ball and 1 yellow ball are drawn)

19. P(at least 1 red ball is drawn)

20. P(at least 1 yellow ball is drawn)

Exercises 21–24 refer to the following experiment: 2 balls are drawn with replacement from an urn containing 4 red balls, 3 white balls, and 1 yellow ball. Find the following probabilities.

21. P(2 red balls are drawn)

22. P(2 yellow balls are drawn)

23. P(1 white ball and 1 yellow ball are drawn)

24. P(at least one red ball is drawn)

Exercises 25–30 refer to the following experiment: 3 cards are drawn from a deck of cards. An ace, king, queen, or jack is considered to be a high card. Find the following probabilities. Give your answers: **(a)** as a fraction; **(b)** as a decimal correct to the nearest thousandth.

B 25. P(1 high card)

26. P(2 high cards)

27. P(3 high cards)

28. P(at least 2 high cards)

29. P(at least 1 high card)

30. P(no high cards)

A game is played as follows: A die is thrown. If the die shows 5 or 6, the player has lost the game. If the die shows a number less than 5, the player may toss a coin. The player wins if the coin shows heads. Otherwise, the player loses.

31. What is the probability of winning?

C 32. Suggest a way to change the game by adding another stage to make the probability of winning $\frac{1}{2}$. Justify your answer with a tree diagram.

33. One urn contains 2 red balls and 2 green balls; a second urn contains 1 red ball and 3 green balls. One ball is selected from each urn. Then the ball from the first urn is placed in the second urn, and the ball from the second urn is placed in the first urn. Find the probabilities of the following events. Give your answer as a fraction and as a decimal correct to the nearest thousandth.
a. One urn contains balls all of the same color.
b. The color composition of the balls in each urn remains the same.
c. The color composition of the balls in the urns is reversed.
(*Hint*: Consider this as a two-stage experiment with the first stage being the selection of the ball from the first urn.)

Section 12-3 INDEPENDENT AND DEPENDENT EVENTS

Suppose 2 balls are drawn without replacement from an urn containing 5 white balls and 2 red balls. We might wish to find

P(the second ball is red given the first ball is red).

Probabilities like the one just stated are called *conditional probabilities* because they refer to the probability of one event under the condition that another event has occurred. If A and B are events with positive probabilities, then $P(B \mid A)$, read "the probability of B given A," denotes the probability that B will occur under the condition that A has occurred.

We can state the following general rule for conditional probability:

If A and B are events in the sample space of an experiment:

$$P(A \text{ and } B) = P(A) \cdot P(B \mid A)$$

This relation is symmetric with respect to A and B:

$$P(A \text{ and } B) = P(B) \cdot P(A \mid B)$$

Next we apply the general rule for conditional probability to the experiment of drawing 2 balls from an urn containing 5 white balls and 2 red balls. We will refer to the following events.

A: the first ball is white.	C: the second ball is white.
B: the first ball is red.	D: the second ball is red.

We find the probability that both balls are red:

$$P(B \text{ and } D) = P(B) \cdot P(D \mid B) = \frac{2}{7} \cdot \frac{1}{6} = \frac{1}{21}$$

Finding this probability using a tree diagram gives the same result because the calculations made in a tree diagram are based on the general rule for conditional probability. Below we show the tree diagram for this experiment and the related cases of the general rule for conditional probability.

$$P(A \text{ and } C) = P(A) \cdot P(C \mid A) = \frac{5}{7} \cdot \frac{4}{6} = \frac{10}{21}$$

$$P(A \text{ and } D) = P(A) \cdot P(D \mid A) = \frac{5}{7} \cdot \frac{2}{6} = \frac{5}{21}$$

$$P(B \text{ and } C) = P(B) \cdot P(C \mid B) = \frac{2}{7} \cdot \frac{5}{6} = \frac{5}{21}$$

$$P(B \text{ and } D) = P(B) \cdot P(D \mid B) = \frac{2}{7} \cdot \frac{1}{6} = \frac{1}{21}$$

EXAMPLE   Two cards are drawn from a deck of cards. Events E and F are defined as follows:

E: The first card is a spade.

F: The second card is a spade.

1. Find the following probabilities if the drawing is without replacement.
   a. $P(E)$ b. $P(F \mid E)$ c. $P(E \text{ and } F)$ d. $P(F)$

2. Find the probabilities requested in part 1 if the drawing is with replacement.

SOLUTION   1. *Without replacement*:

a. $P(E) = \dfrac{13}{52} = \dfrac{1}{4}$

b. $P(F \mid E) = \dfrac{12}{51} = \dfrac{4}{17}$

c. $P(E \text{ and } F) = P(E) \cdot P(F \mid E)$

$$= \dfrac{1}{4} \cdot \dfrac{4}{17} = \dfrac{1}{17}$$

d. We can think of F as being made up of the two mutually exclusive events "E and F" and "E' and F." We found that $P(E \text{ and } F) = \dfrac{1}{17}$ in part (c).

$$P(E' \text{ and } F) = P(E') \cdot P(F \mid E')$$
$$= \dfrac{39}{52} \cdot \dfrac{13}{51}$$
$$= \dfrac{13}{68}$$

$$P(F) = P(E \text{ and } F) + P(E' \text{ and } F)$$
$$= \dfrac{1}{17} + \dfrac{13}{68}$$
$$= \dfrac{17}{68} = \dfrac{1}{4}$$

2. *With replacement*:

a. $P(E) = \dfrac{13}{52} = \dfrac{1}{4}$

b. $P(F \mid E) = \dfrac{13}{52} = \dfrac{1}{4}$

c. $P(E \text{ and } F) = P(E) \cdot P(F \mid E)$

$$= \dfrac{1}{4} \cdot \dfrac{1}{4} = \dfrac{1}{16}$$

d. $P(F) = \dfrac{13}{52} = \dfrac{1}{4}$

In the previous example notice that $P(F) = P(F \mid E)$ when the drawing was with replacement. Since the probability of F doesn't depend on whether or not E has occurred, we say that F is independent of E. In general, if A and B are events with positive probabilities and

$$P(A \mid B) = P(A),$$

we say that the event A is *independent of* the event B. Events that are not independent are called *dependent*. It can be shown that whenever event A is independent of an event B, event B is independent of event A (Exercise 30). For this reason we usually speak of pairs of independent events.

EXAMPLE   A red die and a green die are tossed. Events R, F, and T are defined as follows:

R: The red die shows an even number of spots.
F: The sum of the spots showing is 5.
T: The sum of the spots showing is 8.

a. Are events R and F independent?
b. Are events R and T independent?
c. Are events F and T independent?

SOLUTION   The diagram shows the sample space for the experiment and events R, F, and T. The point (3, 6), for example, represents the following outcome: a 3 on the red die and a 6 on the green die.

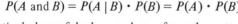

a. $P(F) = \dfrac{4}{36} = \dfrac{1}{9}$

To find $P(F \mid R)$, we observe that R consists of 18 equally likely outcomes, two of which are in F.

$$P(F \mid R) = \frac{2}{18} = \frac{1}{9}$$

Since $P(F) = P(F \mid R)$, events F and R are independent.

b. $P(T) = \dfrac{5}{36}$ and $P(T \mid R) = \dfrac{3}{18} = \dfrac{1}{6}$

Since $P(T) \neq P(T \mid R)$, events T and R are dependent events.

c. $P(T) = \dfrac{5}{36}$ and $P(T \mid F) = 0$

Since $P(T) \neq P(T \mid F)$, T and F are dependent events. In fact, the diagram shows that T and F are mutually exclusive events since they have no outcomes in common.

Part (c) of the example illustrates the fact that mutually exclusive events are always dependent events. Parts (a) and (b) of the example show, respectively, that intersecting events may be independent or dependent.

If A and B are independent events, we can use the following formula to find the probability of "A and B":

$$P(A \text{ and } B) = P(A \mid B) \cdot P(B) = P(A) \cdot P(B)$$

The formula is particularly useful when we know from the nature of the experiment that the two events are independent.

EXAMPLE One hat contains 3 slips of paper lettered A, B, and C, respectively. A second hat contains 4 slips of paper lettered B, C, D, and E, respectively. One slip of paper is drawn from each hat. Find the probabilities of the following events.

  a. Two B's are drawn.

  b. Two consonants are drawn.

SOLUTION It is apparent that the event of drawing a slip from one hat is independent of the event of drawing a slip from the other hat.

  a. $P(\text{two B's}) = P(\text{B from first hat}) \cdot P(\text{B from second hat})$

$$= \frac{1}{3} \cdot \frac{1}{4}$$

$$= \frac{1}{12}$$

  b. $P(\text{two consonants}) = P(\text{consonant from first hat}) \cdot P(\text{consonant from second hat})$

$$= \frac{2}{3} \cdot \frac{3}{4}$$

$$= \frac{1}{2}$$

ORAL EXERCISES

Use the given probabilities to determine whether or not events A and B are independent.

1. $P(A) = \frac{1}{3}$; $P(B) = \frac{1}{4}$; $P(A \text{ and } B) = \frac{7}{12}$

2. $P(A) = \frac{1}{5}$; $P(B) = \frac{2}{5}$; $P(A \text{ and } B) = \frac{2}{25}$

3. $P(A) = \frac{2}{3}$; $P(B) = \frac{3}{8}$; $P(A \text{ and } B) = \frac{1}{4}$

4. $P(A) = \frac{3}{5}$; $P(B) = \frac{1}{2}$; $P(A \text{ and } B) = \frac{1}{2}$

An urn contains 6 white balls and 3 green balls. Two balls are drawn without replacement. Consider these events.

  A: The first ball is white.
  B: The first ball is green.
  C: The second ball is white.
  D: The second ball is green.

Find the following probabilities.

  5. $P(A)$ **6.** $P(C \mid A)$ **7.** $P(D \mid A)$ **8.** $P(A \text{ and } D)$

  9. $P(B)$ **10.** $P(C \mid B)$ **11.** $P(D \mid B)$ **12.** $P(B \text{ and } C)$

  13. $P(A \text{ and } C)$ **14.** $P(A \text{ or } B)$ **15.** $P(B \text{ and } D)$ **16.** $P(C \text{ or } D)$

WRITTEN EXERCISES

Exercises 1–8 refer to the following experiment and events: Two balls are drawn from an urn containing 3 white, 5 yellow, and 2 red balls.

A: The first ball is white. D: The second ball is white.
B: The first ball is yellow. E: The second ball is yellow.
C: The first ball is red. F: The second ball is red.

A 1. Find the following probabilities.
   a. $P(D \mid A)$ **b.** $P(D \mid B)$ **c.** $P(D \mid C)$ **d.** $P(D)$

2. Find the following probabilities.
   a. $P(E \mid A)$ **b.** $P(E \mid B)$ **c.** $P(E \mid C)$ **d.** $P(E)$

3. Find $P(F)$.

4. Are events B and F independent? Justify your answer.

5. Are events C and E independent? Justify your answer.

6. Are events C and E mutually exclusive?

7. Are events E and F mutually exclusive?

8. Name a pair of mutually exclusive events that are not named in Exercises 6 or 7.

Exercises 9–14 refer to the following experiment and events: Two cards are drawn from a standard deck.

A: The first card is red. C: The first card is a 5.
B: The second card is red. D: The second card is a 5.

9. Find the following probabilities.
   a. $P(B \mid A)$ **b.** $P(B \mid A')$ **c.** $P(B)$

10. Find the following probabilities.
   a. $P(D \mid C)$ **b.** $P(D \mid C')$ **c.** $P(D)$

Find the following probabilities.

11. P(the second card is a spade | the first card is a club)

12. P(the second card is black | the first card is a club)

13. P(the first card is a club, and the second card is black)

14. P(the first card is a club, and the second card is red)

Two cards are drawn from a standard deck with replacement. For each pair of events E and F, state:
a. whether E and F are independent
b. whether E and F are mutually exclusive

15. E: The first card is a 7.
   F: The second card is a 7.

16. E: The first card is the ace of spades.
   F: The second card is the ace of spades.

17. E: Both cards are diamonds.
   F: Both cards are clubs.

18. E: Both cards are diamonds.
   F: The first card is the king of diamonds.

Exercises 19-23 refer to the following experiment: 8 slips lettered A, B, C, D, E, F, G, and H, respectively, are placed in a hat. Two slips are drawn, their letters are noted, and the slips are replaced; then two slips are drawn, and their letters are noted. Find the following probabilities.

B 19. P(two vowels are drawn; then two consonants are drawn)

20. P(four vowels are drawn)

21. P(the letter B is drawn)

22. P(the letter C is drawn twice)

23. P(the letter E is drawn no more than 1 time)

The formula $P(A \text{ and } B) = P(A) \cdot P(B|A)$ can be rewritten as follows when A is an event with positive probability.

$$P(B|A) = \frac{P(A \text{ and } B)}{P(A)}$$

Use this formula in Exercises 24-29.

24. A penny, nickel, and dime are tossed. Find:

   P(penny shows heads | exactly 2 coins show heads)

25. A red die and a green die are tossed. Find:

   P(red die shows an even number of spots | sum is 8)

26. Two dice are thrown. Find:

   P(at least one die shows exactly 1 spot | sum is 7)

27. Two dice are thrown. Find:

   P(doubles are thrown | sum is 8)

28. Two cards are drawn without replacement from a standard bridge deck. Find:

   P(the second card is a diamond | both cards are red)

29. Two cards are drawn without replacement from a standard bridge deck. Find:

   P(the first card is a king | both cards are face cards)

In Exercises 30-32 give a short justification of the result stated. In each exercise assume that A and B are events with positive probabilities.

C 30. If $P(A|B) = P(A)$, then $P(B|A) = P(B)$.

31. If A and B are independent events, then A' and B are independent events. (*Hint*: Express $P(A' \cap B)$ in terms of $P(A \cap B)$.)

32. If A and B are independent events, then A' and B' are independent events. (*Hint*: See Exercise 31.)

SELF-TEST 1

1. Find the probability that a card drawn from a standard deck is a 2, 4, or 6.   Section 12-1

2. Find the probability of rolling 9 or more on a throw of a pair of dice.

Questions 3 and 4 refer to an urn that contains 2 red balls and 6 green balls.

3. If 2 balls are drawn from the urn without replacement, what is the probability   Section 12-2
that both are red?

4. If 2 balls are drawn from the urn with replacement, what is the probability that
1 is red and the other is green?

Questions 5-8 refer to the following experiment and events: 2 cards are drawn
from a standard deck without replacement.

A: The first card is red. C: The first card is a 3.
B: The second card is red. D: The second card is a 3.

5. Find the following probabilities: Section 12-3
   a. $P(D \mid C)$ b. $P(D' \mid C)$ c. $P(D)$

6. Are C and D independent events?

7. Are A and B mutually exclusive events?

8. If the drawing is *with* replacement, are C and D independent events?

Section 12-4 PERMUTATIONS AND COMBINATIONS

Suppose the simple events in the sample space of an experiment are all equally
likely. If you know the number of events in the sample space and the number of
simple events in an event E, you can apply the definition of probability directly
to find $P(E)$. In certain probability problems, determining these numbers is the
most difficult aspect of the solution. For this reason, methods of counting are
important in the study of probability. You will review several types of counting
problems in this section. To solve them, we will use:
- factorial notation
- permutations
- combinations

Recall the following general counting principle.

If the first stage of a two-stage experiment can result in any of k outcomes
and if for each of these outcomes the second stage can result in any of n
outcomes, then the sample space for the two-stage experiment will consist of
kn outcomes.

This counting principle can be extended to multistage experiments with any number of stages.

492   *CHAPTER 12*

EXAMPLE License plates are to be made using three letters followed by three digits. How many different plates are possible?

SOLUTION We can regard this problem as a 6-stage experiment. Each of the first three stages consists of choosing a letter, and there are 26 ways to do so at each stage. Each of the last three stages consists of choosing a digit, and there are 10 ways to do so at each stage. Therefore it is possible to make $26 \cdot 26 \cdot 26 \cdot 10 \cdot 10 \cdot 10$, or 17,576,000, license plates.

EXAMPLE How many different arrangements are there of the letters in the word DRIVE?

SOLUTION We can regard this problem as a 5-stage experiment. The first stage is picking the first letter, the second stage is picking the second letter, and so on. There are 5 choices for the first letter, but there are only 4 choices for the second letter since the first letter cannot be used again. Continuing to reason in this fashion we see that there are 3 choices for the third letter, 2 choices for the fourth letter, and 1 choice for the fifth letter. Thus there are $5 \cdot 4 \cdot 3 \cdot 2 \cdot 1$, or 120, possible arrangements.

You may recall that the arrangements in the preceding example can be referred to as permutations and that $5 \cdot 4 \cdot 3 \cdot 2 \cdot 1$ can be referred to as five factorial. In general, distinguishable arrangements of a group of letters, numbers, or other objects are called *permutations*. There are $n!$ (read "*n factorial*") permutations of n distinguishable objects, where $n!$ is defined as follows. For each natural number n, where $n > 1$:

$$n! = n(n-1) \cdots (3)(2)(1)$$

We define 1! and 0! as follows:

$$1! = 1 \quad \text{and} \quad 0! = 1$$

EXAMPLE How many 6-digit numbers can be formed using the digits 4, 5, 6, 7, 8, and 9 without repetition?

SOLUTION $6! = 6 \cdot 5 \cdot 4 \cdot 3 \cdot 2 \cdot 1 = 720$
There are 720 numbers that can be formed using the digits 4, 5, 6, 7, 8, and 9.

You can use the following formula to find the number of permutations of n objects when some of the objects are not distinguishable.

If a collection of n objects has a objects of one kind, b objects of a second kind, c of a third kind, and so on, then the number of distinguishable permutations of those n objects is given by the expression:

$$\frac{n!}{a!\,b!\,c! \cdots}$$

EXAMPLE How many permutations are there of the letters in the word BANANA?

SOLUTION There are 6 letters; 2 of them are N's, 3 are A's, and the remaining letter is a B. Thus, we proceed as follows:

$$\frac{6!}{2!3!1!} = \frac{6 \cdot 5 \cdot 4 \cdot 3 \cdot 2 \cdot 1}{(2 \cdot 1)(3 \cdot 2 \cdot 1)(1)} = 60$$

There are 60 permutations of the letters in the word BANANA.

The number of permutations of n things taken r at a time, denoted $_nP_r$, can be found using either of the following equivalent formulas:

$$_nP_r = \frac{n!}{(n-r)!} \qquad\qquad _nP_r = n(n-1)\cdots(n-r+1)$$

EXAMPLE A club has 15 members. In how many ways can the president, secretary, and treasurer be selected for the club if all members are eligible for these offices?

SOLUTION $_{15}P_3 = \dfrac{15!}{(15-3)!} = 15 \cdot 14 \cdot 13 = 2730$

There are 2730 ways to fill these offices.

A *combination* is a set of objects. We use combinations in selection problems in which order is not important. The number of combinations of n things taken r at a time is denoted by $_nC_r$. We read $_nC_r$ as "n choose r." The formulas below can be used to find the number of combinations of n things taken r at a time.

$$_nC_r = \frac{n!}{r!\,(n-r)!} \qquad\qquad _nC_r = \frac{n(n-1)\cdots(n-r+1)}{r!}$$

EXAMPLE How many different 3-person committees can be selected from the 15-member club of the previous example?

SOLUTION $_{15}C_3 = \dfrac{15!}{3! \cdot (15-3)!} = \dfrac{15!}{3! \cdot 12!} = \dfrac{15 \cdot 14 \cdot 13}{3!} = 455$

There are 455 different 3-person committees that can be chosen.

We can verify the results of the last two examples by comparing them. Each 3-person committee could provide 3!, or 6, choices for the officers, depending on the assignments of individuals to the offices. Since $6 \cdot 455 = 2730$, the solutions agree.

The final examples of this section show how permutations and combinations are used in the solution of probability problems. We count permutations when order is significant. We count combinations when order is not significant.

In many probability problems finding the answer in terms of $_nP_r$ or $_nC_r$ is the most important step since it shows the reasoning used in the solution. It is also the step in which mistakes are most likely to occur. For this reason we will ask that answers be given in terms of $_nP_r$ or $_nC_r$, which we will refer to as being in *symbolic form*; we will also request that answers be given as decimals to a certain number of *significant digits*.

EXAMPLE   What is the probability that there are exactly 3 aces among 5 cards drawn from a deck? Give the answer: **(a)** in symbolic form; **(b)** as a decimal with 3 significant digits.

SOLUTION   There are $_{52}C_5$ possible hands. A hand with exactly 3 aces will contain 3 aces chosen from the 4 aces in the deck and 2 cards chosen from the 48 cards that are not aces. Thus there are $_4C_3 \cdot {}_{48}C_2$ hands with exactly 3 aces.

   a. $P(\text{exactly 3 aces}) = \dfrac{_4C_3 \cdot {}_{48}C_2}{_{52}C_5}$

   b. $_4C_3 = \dfrac{4 \cdot 3 \cdot 2}{3 \cdot 2 \cdot 1} = 4$ $_{48}C_2 = \dfrac{48 \cdot 47}{2 \cdot 1} = 1128$

   $_{52}C_5 = \dfrac{52 \cdot 51 \cdot 50 \cdot 49 \cdot 48}{5 \cdot 4 \cdot 3 \cdot 2 \cdot 1} = 2{,}598{,}960$

   Substituting these values in the symbolic form of the answer given in part (a):

   $P(\text{exactly 3 aces}) = \dfrac{4 \cdot 1128}{2{,}598{,}960} = \dfrac{4512}{2{,}598{,}960} \approx 0.00174$

EXAMPLE   Five books with different titles are placed side by side on a shelf in random order. What is the probability that the titles will be placed in alphabetical order reading left to right? Give the answer **(a)** in symbolic form; **(b)** as a decimal with 3 significant digits.

SOLUTION   **a.** There is only 1 way in which the titles can be placed in alphabetical order, reading left to right. There are $_5P_5$ ways of arranging the books on the shelf.

   $P(\text{alphabetical order}) = \dfrac{1}{_5P_5}$

   b. $P(\text{alphabetical order}) = \dfrac{1}{_5P_5} = \dfrac{1}{5 \cdot 4 \cdot 3 \cdot 2 \cdot 1} \approx 0.00833$

ORAL EXERCISES

In Exercises 1–4, express the indicated number: **(a)** in the form $_nP_r$; **(b)** as an integer.

1. The number of arrangements of the letters in the word MATH that use all the letters

2. The number of 3-letter arrangements you can create from 6 different letters

3. The number of 2-digit numbers that can be made by choosing digits from 7315

4. The number of arrangements of the letters in the word FLOWERS that use all the letters

In how many ways can you select a group of 3 people from a group of the size given? Express the answer:

a. in the form $_nC_r$ b. as an integer

5. 4 persons   **6.** 5 persons   **7.** 10 persons   **8.** 3 persons

WRITTEN EXERCISES

Evaluate.

A **1.** $_9P_7$ **2.** $_{10}P_{10}$ **3.** $_8P_4$ **4.** $_5P_4$

   5. $_9C_7$ **6.** $_6C_3$ **7.** $_{10}C_{10}$ **8.** $_7C_0$

9. An identification code for keys consists of a letter followed by a digit. How many such codes are there?

10. A license plate consists of 3 digits followed by 2 letters.
a. How many license plates are there?
b. How many license plates are there if the first letter cannot be O?

11. How many 2-letter permutations are there of the letters in the word SOAP?

12. A president, vice-president, secretary, and treasurer are to be selected from the 10 members of a club. How many different slates of officers are possible?

13. How many 3-digit numbers can be formed using the digits 1, 2, 3, 4, 5, and 6 with no repetition of digits?

14. How many 3-digit numbers can be formed using the digits 0, 1, 2, 3, 4, and 5 with no repetition of digits?

15. How many 3-digit numbers can be formed using the digits 1, 2, 3, 4, 5, and 6 if repetition of digits is allowed?

16. How many 3-letter arrangements are there of the letters in the word DRIVE?

17. How many 4-letter arrangements are there of the letters in the word BRAISE?

18. How many committees of 4 people can be formed from a club of 10 members?

19. A civics class of 30 students plans to send 4 students to visit the state legislature. In how many ways can a group of students be selected?

20. a. Each of the letters in the word CHEMISTRY is written on a separate card. A 3-card "hand" is drawn from the cards. How many such hands are possible?

b. How many different 3-letter "words" can be formed using the letters in the word CHEMISTRY?

Find the number of arrangements of the letters (using all the letters) for each word.

21. ARRANGE   **22.** PEPPER   **23.** SESSION

24. COMMITTEE   **25.** INTIMIDATE   **26.** RECESSES

27. A committee of 3 juniors and 3 seniors is to be formed from the members of a club having 18 juniors and 15 seniors. How many different committees are possible?

28. A college faculty consists of 42 professors from the College of Arts and Sciences and 37 professors from the College of Engineering.
   a. How many different 5-member committees can be formed from the faculty?
   b. How many different 5-member committees can be formed if the committee is to consist of 3 professors of arts and sciences and 2 professors of engineering?

Exercises 29–32 refer to the following experiment: 5 cards are drawn from a deck. Find the probability that the cards drawn include the cards listed. Give the answers: (a) in symbolic form; (b) as decimals with 3 significant digits.

B 29. 3 spades and 2 hearts

30. 5 spades

31. 2 kings and 3 queens

32. at least 3 fours

Exercises 33–38 refer to the following experiment: 6 cards are drawn from a deck and placed side by side, left to right, in the order in which they are drawn. Find the probability that the cards appear as shown below. Give the answers: (a) in symbolic form; (b) as decimals with 3 significant digits.

33. red card, red card, red card, red card, red card, red card

34. black card, black card, red card, red card, red card, red card

35. ace, ace, king, king, king, jack

36. ace, king, queen, jack, 10, 9

37. club, club, heart, diamond, diamond, diamond

38. 4, 4, 2, followed by any 3 cards that do not include a 4 or a 2

Exercises 39–42 refer to the following experiment: 3 balls are drawn from an urn containing 20 red balls, 15 green balls, and 10 white balls. Find the probability that the balls drawn are as described. Give the answers: (a) in symbolic form; (b) as decimals with 3 significant digits.

39. 3 green balls

40. 2 green balls and 1 white ball

41. 2 red balls and 1 white ball

42. at least 1 red ball

C 43. Show that there are $_nC_r$ arrangements of n objects if r of the objects are of one kind and the remaining objects are of another kind.

44. In the experiment for Exercises 29–32, find the probability that the cards drawn contain exactly 2 aces and no other matching cards.

Justify the following identities:

45. $_nC_r = {_nC_{n-r}}$

46. $_nC_r + {_nC_{r+1}} = {_{n+1}C_{r+1}}$

Exercises 47–51 refer to the following experiment: Each of the digits 1, 2, 3, 4, 5, 6, 7, 8, and 9 is written on a separate card, and the cards are shuffled. Three cards are drawn and placed side by side, left to right, in the order in which they were drawn to form a 3-digit integer. Find the following probabilities. Give the answers: **(a)** in symbolic form; **(b)** as decimals with 3 significant digits.

47. P(the number is less than 500)

48. P(the number is greater than 150)

49. P(the number is divisible by 5)

50. P(the number is even)

51. P(the number is greater than 500 | the number is divisible by 5)

Section 12-5 BERNOULLI EXPERIMENTS

In this section you will study certain random experiments that are named for the mathematician Jacob Bernoulli (1654–1705). You will learn to recognize these *Bernoulli experiments* and to use the formula that applies to them.

EXAMPLE If a coin is tossed 4 times, what is the probability that it shows heads only once?

SOLUTION First find the probability that the coin shows heads on the first toss and tails on the others. Each toss is independent, and for each toss $P(H) = P(T) = \frac{1}{2}$.

Therefore: $$P(\text{HTTT}) = \left(\frac{1}{2}\right)\left(\frac{1}{2}\right)\left(\frac{1}{2}\right)\left(\frac{1}{2}\right) = \left(\frac{1}{2}\right)^4$$

There are three other sequences of tosses that correspond to showing heads only once. The probability of each is $\left(\frac{1}{2}\right)^4$.

$$P(\text{THTT}) = \left(\frac{1}{2}\right)^4 \qquad P(\text{TTHT}) = \left(\frac{1}{2}\right)^4 \qquad P(\text{TTTH}) = \left(\frac{1}{2}\right)^4$$

Since the four sequences of tosses are mutually exclusive events:

$$P(\text{exactly one head}) = \left(\frac{1}{2}\right)^4 + \left(\frac{1}{2}\right)^4 + \left(\frac{1}{2}\right)^4 + \left(\frac{1}{2}\right)^4 = 4\left(\frac{1}{2}\right)^4 = \frac{1}{4}$$

EXAMPLE If a die is tossed 5 times, what is the probability that 6 is shown exactly twice?

SOLUTION Let "6" represent the event 6 is shown on a given toss, and let "X" represent the event that a number other than 6 is shown. Thus, "6XXX6" represents the event that 6 is shown on the first and fifth rolls, but not on the other rolls.

The event 6XXX6 is one sequence of rolls that corresponds to exactly two 6's being shown. Let us try to find the total number of such favorable sequences. We can regard this problem as finding the number of ways that two 6's and three X's can be arranged in 5 positions. Equivalently, we need to find the number of permutations of 5 symbols with 2 of one kind and 3 of another. Using the result of Exercise 43 in Section 12-4, we find that there are $_5C_2$ favorable sequences of tosses.

The probability of any particular favorable sequence will be $\left(\frac{1}{6}\right)^2 \left(\frac{5}{6}\right)^3$ for the following reason: $P(6) = \frac{1}{6}$ on any given toss, $P(X) = \frac{5}{6}$ on any given toss, and any favorable sequence includes two 6's and three X's. For example:

$$P(6XXX6) = \frac{1}{6} \cdot \frac{5}{6} \cdot \frac{5}{6} \cdot \frac{5}{6} \cdot \frac{1}{6} = \left(\frac{1}{6}\right)^2 \left(\frac{5}{6}\right)^3$$

Since there are $_5C_2$ favorable sequences, the sequences are mutually exclusive, and each has the probability just given:

$$P(\text{two 6's}) = {}_5C_2 \left(\frac{1}{6}\right)^2 \left(\frac{5}{6}\right)^3$$

We can calculate this result to three significant digits as follows:

$$P(\text{two 6's}) = {}_5C_2 \left(\frac{1}{6}\right)^2 \left(\frac{5}{6}\right)^3 = 10\left(\frac{1}{36}\right)\left(\frac{125}{216}\right) \approx 0.161$$

The previous examples have the following characteristics:
1. The experiment is a multistage experiment that can be regarded as a sequence of independent trials of a one-stage experiment.
2. In each trial we observe only whether or not one particular event has occurred.

A probability experiment that has the characteristics just listed can be referred to as a *Bernoulli experiment*. The following formula is useful in solving problems involving Bernoulli experiments:

Consider a multistage experiment that consists of n independent trials of a one-stage experiment where the event A can be observed to occur or not occur at each trial. If $P(A) = p$, then $P(A') = q$, where $q = 1 - p$, and the probability that A occurs exactly r times in the n trials is given by the following expression:

$$_nC_r \; p^r \; q^{n-r}$$

Often we speak of the occurrence of the event A as a *success*. Then the formula can be regarded as giving the probability of exactly r successes in n trials.

EXAMPLE   The probability that a certain machine breaks down during a day of operation is 0.1, regardless of whether or not the machine broke down on the previous day. What is the probability that the machine will break down on exactly 2 days during 10 days of operation?

SOLUTION   This is a Bernoulli experiment in which we are counting the number of days on which the machine breaks down.

$$p = 0.1 \qquad q = 1 - 0.1 = 0.9 \qquad n = 10 \qquad r = 2$$

$$P(\text{machine breaks down on exactly 2 days}) = {}_{10}C_2 (0.1)^2 (0.9)^{10-2}$$
$$\approx 45(0.01)(0.430)$$
$$\approx 0.194$$

EXAMPLE A student is given a multiple-choice test containing 6 questions. Each question has 4 choices for answers. Without reading the problems, the student chooses answers randomly. What is the probability that exactly 2 of the answers are correct? Give the answer: **(a)** in symbolic form; **(b)** as a decimal with 3 significant digits.

SOLUTION We can regard this problem as a Bernoulli experiment with 6 repetitions of the experiment of randomly answering a question. For each trial,

$$P(\text{correct answer}) = \frac{1}{4}.$$

Therefore, $p = \frac{1}{4}$ and $q = 1 - \frac{1}{4} = \frac{3}{4}$.

a. Apply the formula with $n = 6$ and $r = 2$.

$$P(2 \text{ correct answers}) = {}_6C_2 \left(\frac{1}{4}\right)^2 \left(\frac{3}{4}\right)^{6-2} = {}_6C_2 \left(\frac{1}{4}\right)^2 \left(\frac{3}{4}\right)^4$$

b. $P(2 \text{ correct answers}) = {}_6C_2 \left(\frac{1}{4}\right)^2 \left(\frac{3}{4}\right)^4 = 15 \left(\frac{1}{16}\right)\left(\frac{81}{256}\right) \approx 0.297$

EXAMPLE In the preceding example, what is the probability that the student answers at least 4 questions correctly? Give the answer: **(a)** in symbolic form; **(b)** as a decimal with 3 significant digits.

SOLUTION **a.** The first step in the solution is to decompose the event "at least 4 correct answers" into three mutually exclusive events.

$P(\text{at least 4 correct}) = P(4 \text{ correct or 5 correct or 6 correct})$
$= P(4 \text{ correct}) + P(5 \text{ correct}) + P(6 \text{ correct})$
$= {}_6C_4 \left(\frac{1}{4}\right)^4 \left(\frac{3}{4}\right)^2 + {}_6C_5 \left(\frac{1}{4}\right)^5 \left(\frac{3}{4}\right) + {}_6C_6 \left(\frac{1}{4}\right)^6 \left(\frac{3}{4}\right)^0$

b. ${}_6C_4 \left(\frac{1}{4}\right)^4 \left(\frac{3}{4}\right)^2 = 15\left(\frac{3^2}{4^6}\right) \approx 0.0330$

${}_6C_5 \left(\frac{1}{4}\right)^5 \left(\frac{3}{4}\right) = 6\left(\frac{3}{4^6}\right) \approx 0.00439$

${}_6C_6 \left(\frac{1}{4}\right)^6 \left(\frac{3}{4}\right)^0 = \frac{1}{4^6} \approx 0.000244$

$P(\text{at least 4 correct}) \approx 0.0330 + 0.00439 + 0.000244$
≈ 0.0376

ORAL EXERCISES

If the problem can be regarded as a Bernoulli experiment, state the values for n, p, q, and r, and give the answer in symbolic form. If the problem cannot be regarded as a Bernoulli experiment, explain why.

1. Four balls are drawn with replacement from an urn containing 4 red balls and 2 white balls. What is the probability of drawing exactly 2 red balls?

2. Four balls are drawn without replacement from an urn containing 4 red balls and 2 white balls. What is the probability of drawing exactly 2 red balls?

WRITTEN EXERCISES

In the following exercises give the answers in symbolic form and as decimals with 3 significant digits.

A **1.** A die is tossed three times. Find the probability of rolling:
  a. exactly one 5   **b.** exactly two 5's   **c.** no 5's   **d.** exactly three 5's

2. A student is given a quiz with 5 true-false questions. Without reading the questions, the student chooses answers randomly. Find the probability that the student answers:
  a. exactly 3 questions correctly
  b. exactly 1 question correctly
  c. all questions incorrectly
  d. no more than 1 question correctly
  e. exactly 4 questions correctly
  f. 4 or more questions correctly

3. Suppose that the probability Mary and her tennis partner will win a set of doubles against a certain team is $\frac{2}{3}$. If Mary and her partner play 6 sets of tennis playing against the other team, find the probabilities of the following events. (There are no ties.)
  a. Mary's team wins exactly 4 of the 6 sets.
  b. Mary's team loses exactly 4 of the 6 sets.
  c. Mary's team wins all 6 sets.
  d. Mary's team loses all 6 sets.

4. By examining a couple's family history, a geneticist states that the probability any child born to the couple will have blue eyes is $\frac{1}{4}$. Assuming that the couple will have 3 children, find the probabilities of the following events:
  a. All the children have blue eyes.
  b. None of the children has blue eyes.
  c. Only one of the children has blue eyes.
  d. At least one of the children has blue eyes.

5. A regular tetrahedron is a solid figure that has 4 congruent equilateral triangles as its faces. A regular tetrahedron is made into a die by marking its faces with the digits 1, 2, 3, and 4. When it is tossed, we note the number of the face upon which it lands. If this die is tossed 5 times, find the probability of obtaining:
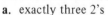
  a. exactly three 2's   **b.** exactly three 4's
  c. exactly four 2's   **d.** at least four 2's
  e. no 4's   **f.** all 4's

6. Experience has shown that $\frac{1}{6}$ of all fuses produced by a certain machine are defective. If a technician tests 8 fuses, what is the probability that
  a. exactly 1 fuse is defective?   **b.** half are defective?
  c. none is defective?   **d.** no more than 2 fuses are defective?

7. If the spinner shown at the right is spun 10 times, find the probability of the following events. Assume that the spinner does not land on a line.
   a. no 2's
   b. exactly four 2's
   c. exactly seven 2's
   d. fewer than three 2's

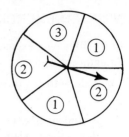

8. The keyboard of an electronic game is shown at the right. Each key is equally likely to be pressed.
   a. If 3 keys are pressed at random, what is the probability that exactly 2 even numbers are selected?
   b. If 4 keys are pressed at random, what is the probability that at least 2 letters are selected?

9. Suppose the probability of obtaining heads when a biased coin is tossed is $\frac{3}{5}$.

   a. Complete the following table showing the probabilities of obtaining various numbers of heads when the coin is tossed 5 times.

Number of Heads	Probability in Symbolic Form	to the Nearest Thousandth
0	$_5C_0 \left(\frac{3}{5}\right)^0 \left(\frac{2}{5}\right)^5$	0.010
1	?	?
2	?	?
3	?	?
4	?	?
5	?	?

   b. What is the sum of the expressions in the second column of the table?
   c. Add the numbers in the third column of the table to verify that they are correct.

10. During a baseball season the Willies play the Nillies 18 times. Before the season began, a mathematically inclined sports writer wrote, "In any game this season, the probability that the Willies will beat the Nillies is $\frac{2}{3}$." If the writer is correct, what is the probability that the Nillies will win exactly $\frac{1}{2}$ of the games they play with the Willies?

11. Suppose the probability that you will win a chess game played against a certain opponent is 40%. If you play that opponent 8 games of chess, what is the probability that you win more than 50% of the games?

12. The probability of obtaining a response to a certain questionnaire is 30%. If 10 such questionnaires are mailed, what is the probability that more than 25% of them will elicit responses?

Section 12-6 THE BINOMIAL THEOREM

In this section you will learn the *Binomial Theorem*, which provides a convenient way to express a binomial raised to a power as a polynomial in simplest form.

Study the following equations:

$$(p + q)^2 = (p + q)(p + q) \qquad (1)$$
$$= p(p + q) + q(p + q) \qquad (2)$$
$$= p^2 + pq + qp + q^2 \qquad (3)$$
$$= p^2 + 2pq + q^2 \qquad (4)$$
$$= {}_2C_0 p^2 + {}_2C_1 pq + {}_2C_2 q^2 \qquad (5)$$

Equation (5) follows from the fact that the coefficients in equation (4) represent the number of ways you can choose the appropriate number of q's (0, 1, or 2) from the two factors of the product $(p + q)(p + q)$. For example, the coefficient of pq in equation (4) is 2 because there are 2 terms, pq and qp, with exactly one q as a factor in equation (3). The first of these terms, pq, results from choosing the q from the second factor of $(p + q)(p + q)$. The second of these terms, qp, results from choosing the q from the first factor. Thus, ${}_2C_1$ in equation (5) represents the number of ways of choosing 1 q from 2 factors.

Similarly, each coefficient ${}_3C_n$ in the expansion of $(p + q)^3$ represents the number of ways you can choose exactly n q's from the three factors $(p + q)(p + q)(p + q)$:

$$(p + q)^3 = p^3 + 3p^2q + 3pq^2 + q^3 \qquad (6)$$
$$= {}_3C_0 p^3 + {}_3C_1 p^2 q + {}_3C_2 pq^2 + {}_3C_3 q^3 \qquad (7)$$

Equations (5) and (7) are particular examples of the Binomial Theorem:

The Binomial Theorem

$$(x + y)^n = {}_nC_0 x^n + {}_nC_1 x^{n-1} y + \cdots + {}_nC_{k-1} x^{n-(k-1)} y^{k-1} + \cdots + {}_nC_n y^n$$

EXAMPLE Expand $(a + b)^n$ for the following values of n: 0, 1, 2, 3, 4, 5

SOLUTION
$$(a + b)^0 = 1$$
$$(a + b)^1 = a + b$$
$$(a + b)^2 = a^2 + 2ab + b^2$$
$$(a + b)^3 = a^3 + 3a^2b + 3ab^2 + b^3$$
$$(a + b)^4 = a^4 + 4a^3b + 6a^2b^2 + 4ab^3 + b^4$$
$$(a + b)^5 = a^5 + 5a^4b + 10a^3b^2 + 10a^2b^3 + 5ab^4 + b^5$$

You can see several patterns in these expansions:

1. For any integer n, $(a + b)^n$ has $n + 1$ terms.

2. The powers of a in the expansion of $(a + b)^n$ decrease, starting with a^n, and ending with a^0. The powers of b increase, from b^0 to b^n.

3. The coefficients of the terms are symmetrical about the midpoint of the expansion. For example, in the expansion of $(a + b)^5$, which has six terms, the coefficients of the first and sixth terms are the same, the coefficients of the

second and fifth terms are the same, and the coefficients of the third and fourth terms are the same.

4. The coefficients of the first and last terms of $(a + b)^n$ are 1. The coefficients of the second term and the next-to-last term are n.

When one of the terms of the binomial has a negative coefficient, the terms of the expansion will alternate in sign.

EXAMPLE   Expand $(3x - y)^4$.

SOLUTION   Recall that $3x - y$ is a way of writing $3x + (-y)$.

Let us apply some of the observations listed previously. There are 5 terms in the expansion. The coefficients (before simplifying) of the first and last terms are 1. The coefficients of the second and next-to-last terms are 4. The coefficient of the third term can be found as follows:

$$_4C_{3-1} = {_4}C_2 = \frac{4 \cdot 3}{2 \cdot 1} = 6$$

$$(3x - y)^4 = (3x)^4 + 4(3x)^3(-y) + 6(3x)^2(-y)^2 + 4(3x)(-y)^3 + (-y)^4$$
$$= 81x^4 - 108x^3y + 54x^2y^2 - 12xy^3 + y^4$$

The coefficients $_nC_k$, where $k = 0, 1, \ldots, n$, are often written as $\binom{n}{k}$ and referred to as the *binomial coefficients*. For example, we write $_5C_3$ as $\binom{5}{3}$. We use this notation in the following alternative statement of the binomial theorem.

The expansion of $(x + y)^n$ is the sum of $n + 1$ terms where the kth term is given by:

$$\binom{n}{k-1} x^{n-(k-1)}y^{k-1}$$

EXAMPLE   **a.** Find the third term of $(2k + n)^5$.
                b. Find the first four terms of $(r - 2t)^{15}$.

SOLUTION   **a.** The coefficient of the third term can be found as follows:

$$\binom{5}{3-1} = \binom{5}{2} = \frac{5 \cdot 4}{2 \cdot 1} = 10$$

Therefore the third term is $10(2k)^{5-(3-1)}n^{3-1}$, or $80k^3n^2$.

b. First find the coefficients.

First term: $\binom{15}{0} = 1$ Second term: $\binom{15}{1} = 15$

Third term: $\binom{15}{3-1} = \binom{15}{2} = \frac{15 \cdot 14}{2 \cdot 1} = 105$

Fourth term: $\binom{15}{4-1} = \binom{15}{3} = \frac{15 \cdot 14 \cdot 13}{3 \cdot 2 \cdot 1} = 455$

We can write the first four terms as follows:

$$(r - 2t)^{15} = r^{15} + 15(r^{14})(-2t) + 105(r^{13})(-2t)^2 + 455(r^{12})(-2t)^3 + \cdots$$
$$= r^{15} - 30r^{14}t + 420r^{13}t^2 - 3640r^{12}t^3 + \cdots$$

Pascal's triangle, shown below, provides another method for finding binomial coefficients.

```
                              1
                          1       1
                      1       2       1
                  1       3       3       1
              1       4       6       4       1
          1       5      10      10       5       1
      1       6      15      20      15       6       1
  1       7      21      35      35      21       7       1
1     8      28      56      70      56      28       8      1
1   9    36      84     126     126      84      36     9      1
1  10   45     120     210     252     210     120     45    10    1
```

Pascal's triangle is constructed in the following way: The first and last entry in each row is 1. Each of the other entries in a row is the sum of the entries to its immediate left and right in the preceding row. For example, the sixth row is derived from the fifth row as follows:

```
    1     4     6     4     1
  1     5    10    10     5     1
```

The numbers in the $(n + 1)$st row of Pascal's triangle are the coefficients in the expansion of $(a + b)^n$.

EXAMPLE Expand $(3x + y)^6$.

SOLUTION The seventh row of Pascal's triangle gives the coefficients:

$$1 \quad 6 \quad 15 \quad 20 \quad 15 \quad 6 \quad 1$$

$$(3x + y)^6 = (3x)^6 + 6(3x)^5 y + 15(3x)^4 y^2 + 20(3x)^3 y^3 + 15(3x)^2 y^4 + 6(3x)y^5 + y^6$$
$$= 729x^6 + 1458x^5 y + 1215x^4 y^2 + 540x^3 y^3 + 135x^2 y^4 + 18xy^5 + y^6$$

EXAMPLE Find the value of $\binom{7}{4}$.

SOLUTION Since $\binom{7}{4}$ is the coefficient of the fifth term in the expansion of $(a + b)^7$, we need to find the fifth entry in the eighth row of Pascal's triangle, or 35. Therefore $\binom{7}{4} = 35$.

The following formula (derived in Exercise 52) shows the relationship between the coefficients of the $(k + 1)$st and kth terms of the expansion of $(x + y)^n$.

$$\binom{n}{k} = \frac{n - (k - 1)}{k} \cdot \binom{n}{k - 1}$$

EXAMPLE If the coefficient of the fourth term of $(x + y)^{11}$ is 165, find the fifth term.

SOLUTION The coefficients of the fifth term can be found as follows:

$$\frac{11 - (4 - 1)}{4} \cdot 165 = 330$$

The fifth term of the expansion is $330x^7y^4$.

ORAL EXERCISES

In Exercises 1–8, use Pascal's triangle as needed.

1. Find the twelfth line of Pascal's triangle.
2. Expand $(x + y)^5$.
3. Expand $(a - b)^4$.
4. Find the second term in the expansion of $(n - 5)^8$.
5. Find the fifth term in the expansion of $(2h + g)^5$.
6. Find the middle term in the expansion of $(2c + d)^4$.
7. Find the eighth term in the expansion of $(p + q)^7$.
8. Find the first term in the expansion of $(2m - n)^4$.

Use Pascal's triangle to find the following.

9. $\binom{5}{3}$ 10. $\binom{7}{2}$ 11. $\binom{8}{3}$

12. $\binom{6}{0}$ 13. $\binom{5}{5}$ 14. $\binom{8}{6}$

WRITTEN EXERCISES

Expand. Simplify terms when possible.

A 1. $(z + 5)^3$ 2. $(n + k)^4$ 3. $(r - s)^4$

4. $(z - 2)^5$ 5. $(4 + x)^4$ 6. $(y - 4)^3$

7. $(2z + k)^4$ 8. $(3c + d)^4$ 9. $(y - 2z)^5$

10. $(2w + 3z)^4$ 11. $(4q + 3x)^4$ 12. $(3n - 2m)^5$

13. $(f - q)^8$ 14. $(x + 2)^6$ 15. $(c - 3)^7$

Use Pascal's triangle to evaluate the following.

16. $\dbinom{5}{4}$ **17.** $\dbinom{7}{5}$ **18.** $\dbinom{7}{7}$ **19.** $\dbinom{9}{1}$

20. $\dbinom{5}{0}$ **21.** $\dbinom{8}{5}$ **22.** $\dbinom{10}{5}$ **23.** $\dbinom{10}{7}$

Find the requested term in the indicated expansion. Simplify when possible.

24. the last term; $(2m - p)^{25}$ **25.** the sixteenth term; $(12t + u)^{15}$

26. the tenth term; $(8w + z)^{10}$ **27.** the thirteenth term; $(2y - w)^{13}$

28. the third term; $(v - 2w)^5$ **29.** the fourth term; $(2x + 3y)^6$

30. the seventh term; $(3z + n)^9$ **31.** the eighth term; $(2x - y)^{10}$

32. the middle term; $(z - p)^4$ **33.** the middle term; $(2u - 3v)^8$

Give the first four terms of the indicated expansion.

34. $(3z - 4y)^{10}$ **35.** $(4x + 2y)^8$ **36.** $(x - 3k)^{15}$

Expand. Simplify terms when possible.

B **37.** $\left(4b + \dfrac{3}{4}c\right)^4$ **38.** $\left(2r - \dfrac{1}{4}t\right)^6$ **39.** $\left(xy + \dfrac{1}{y}\right)^5$

40. $\left(a^2b - \dfrac{c}{a}\right)^5$ **41.** $\left(3g - \dfrac{2}{g^2}\right)^4$ **42.** $\left(h^3t + \dfrac{z}{t}\right)^7$

EXAMPLE Find the term in the expansion of $(3x - 2y)^5$ that involves x^2y^3.

SOLUTION The kth term in this expansion is $\dbinom{5}{k-1}(3x)^{5-k}(-2y)^k$. When k is 3, the desired powers of the variables are produced.

$$\dbinom{5}{3-1}(3x)^{5-3}(-2y)^3 = (10)(9x^2)(-8y^3) = -720x^2y^3$$

43. Find the term in the expansion of $(2x - y)^4$ that involves xy^3.

44. Find the term in the expansion of $(a + 3b^2)^5$ that involves a^3b^4.

45. Find the term in the expansion of $\left(3t - \dfrac{2}{t}\right)^6$ that is a constant.

46. Find the term in the expansion of $\left(w^2 + \dfrac{2}{w}\right)^9$ that is a constant.

47. Find the sixth term of the expansion of $(a + b)^{11}$ given that the coefficient of the fifth term is 330.

48. Find the eighth term of the expansion of $(u - v)^{13}$ given that the coefficient of the seventh term is 1716.

49. Find the ninth term of the expansion of $(k - m)^{15}$ given that the coefficient of the eighth term is -6435.

Consider a Bernoulli experiment in which the probability of event A occurring is p and the probability of A not occurring is q, where $q = 1 - p$. The kth term of the expansion of $(q + p)^n$ will give the probability of exactly $k - 1$ successes in n trials of the experiment since the kth term of the expansion is

$$_nC_{k-1}q^{n-(k-1)}p^{k-1}, \text{ or } _nC_{k-1}p^{k-1}q^{n-(k-1)},$$

according to the Binomial Theorem. You may wish to use Pascal's triangle to solve the following problems concerning Bernoulli experiments. Give your answers in symbolic form and as decimals with 3 significant digits.

50. In a certain county, 20% of the registered voters are 30 years old or younger. If 10 voters are selected at random, find the probabilities of the events below. You may assume that

$$P(\text{a voter selected at random is 30 years old or younger}) = 0.2.$$

    a. Exactly 5 are older than 30.
    b. At least 5 are older than 30.
    c. Fewer than 5 are older than 30.

51. When a biased die is tossed, the probability of the die showing two spots is 0.25. If the die is tossed 9 times, find the probabilities of the following events.
    a. Two is thrown exactly 3 times.
    b. Two is thrown no more than 3 times.
    c. Two is thrown no more than 4 times.

C 52. Give a derivation of the following formula:
$$\binom{n}{k} = \frac{n - (k - 1)}{k} \cdot \binom{n}{k - 1}$$

53. If $-30jk^5$ is the sixth term in the expansion of a binomial difference with integral coefficients raised to the sixth power, what is the binomial?

54. If $40m^2n^6$ is the fourth term in the expansion of a binomial with positive integral coefficients raised to the fifth power, what is the binomial?

SELF-TEST 2

    1. How many permutations of the letters in each word are there? Section 12-4
        a. BLINK   **b.** CABBAGE

    2. How many 3-letter combinations are there of the letters in the word BLANCH?

    3. Four cards are drawn from a standard deck. What is the probability that exactly 3 of them are red?

Questions 4 and 5 refer to the following experiment: A coin is tossed 6 times. Find the probabilities of these events. Give the answers in symbolic form only.

  4. The coin shows heads exactly 4 times. Section 12-5

  5. The coin shows heads no more than 2 times.

In Questions 6-8 simplify terms when possible.

  6. Find the first 3 terms of the expansion of $(x - 2y)^6$. Section 12-6

  7. Find the fourth term of the expansion of $(3k + m)^7$.

  8. Expand $(2a - b)^4$.

Computer Exercises

What do you think is the probability that in a group of people, at least two have the same birthday? This question is closely related to other coincidences. For example, how likely is it that two people on the same bus will be reading the same magazine? Most people don't realize how high the probability is that coincidences will occur in their lives. The birthday question is a coincidence problem that is relatively easy to solve, and its answer is surprising to most people.

At the beginning of this chapter, there is a calculation of the probability that at least two out of ten randomly chosen people have a birthday in common. There is another way to look at this problem, which leads in a natural way to a computer program. Consider the probability that ten people chosen at random all have different birthdays. If we subtract this number from 1, we will get the probability of the complementary event, which is that at least two people have the same birthday. That is the probability we seek.

To make the problem simpler, let us calculate the probability that three people all have different birthdays. The probability that the second person has a different birthday from the first is $\frac{364}{365}$. If the first two have different birthdays, there are 363 days left for the third person. The probability that the third person's birthday is different from the other two, given that the birthdays of the first two are different, is $\frac{363}{365}$. Therefore, the probability that all three have different birthdays is $\frac{364}{365} \cdot \frac{363}{365}$. Continuing in this way, the probability that four people all have different birthdays is $\frac{364}{365} \cdot \frac{363}{365} \cdot \frac{362}{365}$, and so on.

On the next page there is a BASIC program that computes the probability that N people will all have different birthdays. By subtracting this number from 1, the program gives the probability that there will be at least one shared birthday.

```
10   PRINT "BIRTHDAY PROBABILITIES"
20   PRINT "HOW MANY PEOPLE (>1)";
30   INPUT N
40   LET P = 1
50   REM *** P IS PROBABILITY THAT ALL BIRTHDAYS ARE DIFFERENT
60   FOR C = 1 TO N − 1
70   REM *** THERE IS ONE LESS FACTOR THAN THERE ARE PEOPLE
80   LET P = P * (365 − C) / 365
90   NEXT C
100  PRINT "PROB. SHARED BIRTHDAY ="; 1 − P
110  END
```

1. Type in and RUN the program. Find the probability of a shared birthday among ten people.

2. Use the program to find the probability that at least two people among 30 have the same birthday. Surprised?

3. Find the smallest number of people for which the probability of a shared birthday is greater than:
   a. 0.5   **b.** 0.9   **c.** 0.99

CHAPTER REVIEW

1. Find the probability that a card drawn from a standard deck is a queen or jack.   Section 12–1

2. Find the probability of rolling 6 or less on a throw of a pair of dice.

3. If two cards are drawn from a standard deck (without replacement), what is   Section 12–2 the probability that both cards are clubs?

4. If two cards are drawn from a standard deck with replacement, what is the probability that both are jacks?

Questions 5–8 refer to the following experiment and events: Two balls are drawn (without replacement) from an urn containing 6 yellow balls and 9 green balls.
A: The first ball drawn is yellow.
B: The first ball drawn is green.
C: The second ball drawn is yellow.

5. Find the following probabilities.   Section 12–3
   a. $P(C \mid B)$ **b.** $P(C \mid B')$ **c.** $P(C)$

6. Are C and B independent events?

7. Are C and B mutually exclusive events?

8. If the drawing is done with replacement, are C and B then independent events?

9. How many different 4-digit numbers can be formed using the digits 5, 6, 7,   Section 12–4 and 8?

10. How many different 3-person committees can be chosen from a group of 10 people?

11. Five cards are drawn (without replacement) from a standard deck. What is the probability that exactly two of them are kings? Give the answer: **(a)** in symbolic form; **(b)** as a decimal with 3 significant digits.

Questions 12 and 13 refer to the following experiment: A die is tossed four times. Give the answers: **(a)** in symbolic form; **(b)** as a decimal with 3 significant digits.

12. What is the probability of rolling exactly two 6's? Section 12-5

13. What is the probability of rolling three or more 6's?

In Questions 14-16 simplify terms when possible.

14. Find the third term in the expansion of $(2y - z)^5$. Section 12-6

15. Find the first three terms in the expansion of $(2u + 5)^7$.

16. Expand $(x - 2a)^5$.

CHAPTER TEST

Questions 1-8 refer to the following experiment and events: Two dice are rolled.
A: The sum of the spots showing is an odd number.
B: The sum of the spots showing is an even number.
C: At least one die shows (exactly) one spot.
D: The sum of the spots showing is 6.
Find the following probabilities.

1. $P(A)$ 2. $P(B)$ 3. $P(C)$ 4. $P(C \text{ and } D)$

5. $P(C \text{ or } D)$ 6. $P(A \text{ or } B)$ 7. $P(B \text{ and } C)$ 8. $P(A \text{ and } B)$

Questions 9-11 refer to the following experiment and events: Two balls are drawn (without replacement) from an urn containing 2 red balls, 2 green balls, and 2 white balls.

F: The first ball drawn is green.
G: The second ball drawn is green.
H: The first ball drawn is white.
I: The second ball drawn is white.
J: Both balls drawn are the same color.

9. Find the following probabilities.
   a. $P(F)$ **b.** $P(G \mid F)$ **c.** $P(G)$ **d.** $P(F \text{ and } G)$

10. Find the following probabilities.
   a. $P(J)$ **b.** $P(J \mid F)$

11. State whether or not the events in each pair are independent.
   a. F and G **b.** H and I **c.** F and J **d.** H and J

12. How many 3-letter permutations are there of the letters in the word STAIR?

13. Find the number of arrangements of the letters in the word PEOPLE, using all the letters.

14. Three cards are drawn (without replacement) from a deck. Find the probability that all 3 cards are red. Give the answer: **(a)** in symbolic form; **(b)** as a decimal with 3 significant digits.

Exercises 15–17 refer to the following experiment: Ten light bulbs are chosen from a manufacturing lot and tested. If the probability of any bulb being defective is 0.1, find the probabilities of the following events. Give the answers: **(a)** in symbolic form; **(b)** as decimals with 3 significant digits.

15. Exactly 2 of the bulbs are defective.

16. No more than 3 of the bulbs are defective.

17. At least 9 of the bulbs are not defective.

In Questions 18–21 simplify terms when possible.

18. Expand $(n - 2b)^4$.

19. Give the first four terms in the expansion of $(v + 3w)^{10}$.

20. Find the third term of the expansion of $(2z - 3)^8$.

21. Find the term of the expansion of $(3b^2 - 2b)^7$ that involves b^{10}.

Application — Waiting in Line (Monte Carlo Method)

Managers must often make difficult decisions about proposals to improve business. Because computers can analyze large quantities of data quickly and proposed business changes can be simulated without the risks involved in actual experimentation, computer simulations are often used to help managers make business decisions. Monte Carlo methods, based on probability theory, are used extensively in computer simulations.

Suppose, for example, that a bank manager faced with customer complaints about long waits in line is considering a consultant's proposal for reducing the length of the customers' waiting periods by opening another window during certain peak periods of the day. The manager needs to know if the improvement in service would justify the cost.

A simulation model would have to be built to represent the situation: the customer arrives, the customer waits in line, the teller transacts the customer's business, and the customer leaves.

For the computer simulation to be meaningful, it must reflect reality. For example, it would be unwise to make a business decision based on a simulation that assumed a customer would require 20 minutes of service time to transact business if customer business never took longer than 13 minutes. It is therefore necessary to gather sample data on the time elapsing between the arrivals of successive customers, the time when customer service begins, and the time when customer service ends. Observing a small sample of customers could be misleading. Thus, it is important to gather data for a fairly large sample. If a five-minute wait occurs ten times more often than a ten-minute wait, then the simulation should reflect this.

The sample data gathered can be represented by frequency distributions of the times between successive customer arrivals and the lengths of service times. The computer program then simulates an actual day at the bank by using random numbers to assign arrival and service times to imaginary customers according to the distributions indicated by the sample data. This is the Monte Carlo method. To get a clear picture of what might actually happen, the user would run the simulation several times because different random numbers would be used each time.

The program could be designed so that variables such as the number of customers, the length of the period of observation, or the number of service windows available could be changed. For each "experiment" the computer could generate the average length of time a customer would have to wait before being served, the maximum length of time a customer would have to wait in line, how long tellers would be idle, or other information that might help the bank manager make a decision.

VOCABULARY REVIEW

Be sure that you understand the meaning of these terms:

MIXED REVIEW

Evaluate.

1. $\tan\left[\text{Arccos}\left(-\dfrac{12}{13}\right)\right]$

2. $\log_{100} 0.1$

3. $\cot \dfrac{5\pi}{4}$

4. $\left(\dfrac{1}{16}\right)^{-\frac{5}{4}}$

5. $\csc(-60°)$

6. $\log_5 1$

7. If $\sin\theta = \dfrac{1}{2}$ and $\dfrac{\pi}{2} < \theta < \pi$, find the values of the other five trigonometric functions.

8. If $m\,\overset{\frown}{AD} = 170$ and $m\,\overset{\frown}{BC} = 72$, find $m\angle AEB$.

9. If $AE = 8$, $EC = 6.6$, and $BE = 4.8$, find BD.

10. If $\overleftrightarrow{CF}$ is tangent to the circle and $m\,\overset{\frown}{AC} : m\,\overset{\frown}{ADC} = 1:2$, find $m\angle ACF$.

Exs. 8-10

11. Construct a 30–60–90 triangle.

Two balls are drawn without replacement from an urn containing 3 red balls, 6 black balls, and 9 white balls. Find the following probabilities.

12. P(2 white balls are drawn)

13. P(exactly 1 red ball is drawn)

14. P(both balls drawn are the same color)

Line j has equation $y = x - 1$, and points P and Q have coordinates $(-3, 6)$ and $(3, 0)$, respectively. Complete.

15. $T_{?,\,?} : P \longrightarrow Q$

16. $R_{90} : (\underline{\ ?\ }, \underline{\ ?\ }) \longrightarrow P$

17. $r_j \circ D_{Q,\,\frac{1}{2}} : P \longrightarrow (\underline{\ ?\ }, \underline{\ ?\ })$

18. State the domain, the range, and the fundamental period of the secant function.

19. Prove: $\sin 4x = 4\sin x \cos x(\cos x + \sin x)(\cos x - \sin x)$

20. How many four-digit numbers can be formed using the digits $1, 2, 3, 4, 5,$ and 6 if repetition of digits **(a)** is allowed and **(b)** is not allowed?

21. Solve over the set of complex numbers: $3x^2 + 2x + 5 = 0$. Find the sum and the product of the roots.

22. In $\triangle ABC$, $m\angle A = m\angle B = 50°10'$ and $AB = 27$. Find the perimeter and the area of $\triangle ABC$ to the nearest integer.

23. If $\sin \theta = \dfrac{\sqrt{5}}{3}$ and $\dfrac{\pi}{2} < \theta < \pi$, find **(a)** $\cos\left(\dfrac{\pi}{4} + \theta\right)$, **(b)** $\sin \dfrac{\theta}{2}$, **(c)** $\tan 2\theta$, and **(d)** $\csc\left(\dfrac{\pi}{2} - \theta\right)$.

24. If $f(x) = 2x - 5$, find $f^{-1}(x)$. Is f odd, even, or neither? Why?

Solve.

25. $\log_{25}\left(\dfrac{1}{125}\right) = x$

26. $\left(\dfrac{27}{48}\right)^{\frac{3}{4}} = y$

27. $\sqrt{t+1} = \sqrt{2t} - 1$

28. A die is tossed ten times. Write $P(\text{exactly two 5's})$ in symbolic form.

Solve for $0° \leqslant \theta < 360°$. If necessary, round θ to the nearest $10'$.

29. $\sin \dfrac{\theta}{2} = -\cos \dfrac{\theta}{2}$

30. $\csc^2 \theta = 2(2 \cot \theta - 1)$

31. The area of a sector of a circle is $\dfrac{15\pi}{2}$. If the measure of the central angle of the sector is 75, find the length of the arc of the sector.

32. Use Table 2 to calculate $\sqrt[4]{(0.527)^3}$ to three significant digits.

33. In $\triangle XYZ$, $XY = 9$, $m\angle Y = 150$, and $YZ = 6$. Find **(a)** XZ to the nearest integer, **(b)** $m\angle Z$ to the nearest degree, and **(c)** the exact area of $\triangle XYZ$.

34. Find the magnitude and direction (to the nearest $10'$) of the resultant of a 4 N force and a 6 N force acting at an angle of $90°$ to each other.

35. Two cards are drawn without replacement from a standard deck. Find $P(\text{second card is a 2/first card is a club})$. Are the events "second card is a 2" and "first card is a club" independent? mutually exclusive?

36. Graph the solution set: **a.** $2x^2 \geqslant x + 28$ **b.** $|5 - y| < 2$

37. Simplify: **a.** $\dfrac{1}{(2-i)^2}$ **b.** $-2\sqrt{3}\left(\dfrac{1}{2}\sqrt{6} + 4\sqrt{3}\right)$

38. If $f(x) = |2 - x|$ and $g(x) = x^2 + 2$, find **(a)** $f(g(-3))$, **(b)** $g(f(-3))$, **(c)** $f(g(x))$, and **(d)** $g(f(x))$.

39. What special kind of quadrilateral has one line of symmetry but no rotational symmetry?

Researchers trying to determine the opinion of a group of people on an issue usually can interview only a small sample from the group. Ideas from statistics help researchers select appropriate samples and know how much confidence to put in the responses from a particular sample.

Statistics 13

You have probably already studied at least one statistic, the *mean* (average). The mean, however, does not fully describe a set of data. The numbers 2, 5, 7, 8, 9, 11, 14 have a mean of 8; the numbers 7, 8, 8, 8, 8, 8, 9 also have a mean of 8. Obviously, the two sets of numbers are quite different. To describe sets like these more thoroughly, you will study other statistics, including the *variance* and *standard deviation*.

Many experiments or observations lead to sets of measurements that approximate a *normal distribution*. For example, the heights of all adults and the scores on national standardized tests approximate normal distributions. If the mean and standard deviation of a normal distribution are known, many questions about probabilities can be answered. For example, suppose you learn that the masses of the adults of a certain animal breed approximate a normal distribution, with a mean of 260 g and a standard deviation of 30 g. Using the techniques of this chapter, you will be able to conclude that about 68% of the animals are between 230 g and 290 g, about 95% are between 200 g and 320 g, and more than 99% are between 170 g and 350 g.

Section 13-1 THE RELATIONSHIP BETWEEN PROBABILITY AND STATISTICS

In Chapter 12 you learned that if you toss an unbiased coin, the probability that it shows heads is $\frac{1}{2}$. Does this mean that if you toss the coin 100 times, it will show heads 50 times? Probably not. In fact, you can try this yourself and see that you rarely have *exactly* $\frac{1}{2}$ of the tosses resulting in heads. In this section you will:

- use data to verify probabilities
- use data to find probabilities that are not already known

EXAMPLE   Toss a die 120 times, recording the number of times it shows 1, 2, 3, 4, 5, or 6.

SOLUTION   You can record your results in a table. One possible result of this experiment is shown. The number of times a given outcome happens is called the *frequency* of that outcome.

Outcome	Tallies	Frequency
1	~~HHH~~ ~~HHH~~ ~~HHH~~ |||	18
2	~~HHH~~ ~~HHH~~ ~~HHH~~ ||||	19
3	~~HHH~~ ~~HHH~~ ~~HHH~~ ~~HHH~~ ||||	24
4	~~HHH~~ ~~HHH~~ ~~HHH~~ ~~HHH~~	20
5	~~HHH~~ ~~HHH~~ ~~HHH~~ ||	17
6	~~HHH~~ ~~HHH~~ ~~HHH~~ ~~HHH~~ ||	22
	Total	120

You know that the probability of each outcome is $\frac{1}{6}$ for a fair die. In the preceding example, the ratio of the number of times each outcome occurred to the total number of tosses is about $\frac{1}{6}$.

Suppose, on the other hand, the experiment produced the following results.

Outcome	Tallies	Frequency
1	~~HHH~~ ~~HHH~~ ~~HHH~~		16
2	~~HHH~~ ~~HHH~~ ~~HHH~~ ~~HHH~~	20
3	~~HHH~~ ~~HHH~~ ~~HHH~~ ||||	19
4	~~HHH~~ ~~HHH~~ ~~HHH~~ ~~HHH~~	20
5	~~HHH~~ ~~HHH~~ ~~HHH~~ ~~HHH~~ ~~HHH~~ ~~HHH~~	30
6	~~HHH~~ ~~HHH~~ ~~HHH~~	15
	Total	120

You might be suspicious that the die is biased to favor landing on 5. Now you have the ratio

$$\frac{\text{number of fives}}{\text{total number of tosses}} = \frac{30}{120} = 0.25.$$

For a fair die, each outcome has a probability of $\frac{1}{6}$, or approximately 0.17. You might repeat the experiment to get more data. If after 1000 or more tosses the fraction

$$\frac{\text{number of fives}}{\text{number of tosses}}$$

is still closer to 0.25 than it is to 0.17, you could conclude that the die is probably biased. That is, the experimental evidence suggests that the statement "$P(5) = \frac{1}{6}$" is false.

Law of Large Numbers

When an experiment is performed a large number of times, and an outcome A has a probability of P, then

$$\frac{\text{number of times that } A \text{ occurs}}{\text{total number of trials}}$$

is approximately equal to P.

EXAMPLE   A political-survey company plans to call voters at random in a certain city. What is the probability that a voter selected at random is a registered Republican?

SOLUTION   In order to answer the question, you need some data. You would contact the voter-registration office to obtain the needed information. Suppose you receive the following information:

Democrats	7,548
Republicans	6,989
Others	616
Total	15,153

The probability that a voter selected at random is a registered Republican is:

$$\frac{6,989}{15,153}, \text{ or approximately } 0.46$$

Sometimes it is not possible to obtain all data needed to determine a probability. For example, suppose you want information about the average height of high school students in your state. It would be very difficult and expensive to measure the height of each student in the state. In this case, people who work with statistics find a *sample* of students. For example, you could measure all the students in 5 schools around the state. The information obtained might not give a completely accurate picture for all students, but a statistician learns ways to estimate how accurate the obtained estimate is.

You can see that some samples would not give a good estimate of the average height of high school students. For example, you would not use a sample composed of only the ninth graders in a school, since the average height of ninth graders would be less than the average height of high school students in general.

ORAL EXERCISES

In this experiment, each student tosses two coins. The outcomes of the experiment are two heads, two tails, or a tail and a head.

1. What is the probability of each of the three outcomes?

2. Perform the experiment 20 times and compile the information in a table.

Outcome	Tallies	Frequency
2 heads	?	?
2 tails	?	?
1 tail, 1 head	?	?
		Total 20

3. For each outcome A, compute the ratio of the number of times A occurs to the total number of trials (20).

4. Compare your ratios to the actual probabilities found in Oral Exercise 1.

WRITTEN EXERCISES

A 1. Toss a coin 20 times and record the number of heads and tails. What is the ratio of heads to total tosses?

2. Combine your information from Exercise 1 with that of another classmate and find the ratio of heads to total tosses. Is the ratio closer to $\frac{1}{2}$ than that of Exercise 1?

3. Check a pair of dice to see if they are unbiased by tossing each die separately 18 times. Record the number of times each side shows. What is the expected number of times each side will show? If any side shows more than 4 times or does not show at all, you may suspect that the die is biased. What do you conclude about your dice?

4. Choose a page at random from a telephone book. Record the number of times that each digit (0, 1, 2, 3, 4, 5, 6, 7, 8, or 9) appears as the *last* digit of a telephone number on that page. What do you expect? How do your expectations compare with the results?

Draw a card from a well-shuffled deck. After recording whether the card is red or black, replace it, shuffle, and draw again.

5. Repeat the experiment 5 times. Find the ratio $\frac{\text{red cards}}{5}$.

6. Repeat the experiment for another 5 draws. Combine the new results with the results from Exercise 5. Find the ratio $\frac{\text{red cards}}{10}$.

7. Repeat. Find the ratio $\dfrac{\text{red cards}}{15}$.

8. Repeat. Find the ratio $\dfrac{\text{red cards}}{20}$.

9. Combine your results with another classmate's results to find the ratio $\dfrac{\text{red cards}}{40}$.

10. Are the ratios getting closer to $\dfrac{1}{2}$?

In an opinion survey, subway riders were asked, "Is service better or worse than it was a year ago?" The results were:

Better, 5360 Worse, 3533 Neither, 1107

11. What is the probability that a rider chosen at random feels that service is better?

12. What is the probability that a rider chosen at random does not feel that service is better?

Toss two dice 30 times, recording the sums (2, 3, 4, 5, 6, 7, 8, 9, 10, 11, or 12).

B 13. Find the ratio $\dfrac{\text{number of 7's}}{30}$.

14. What is $P(7)$? Compare this with Exercise 13.

15. Find the ratio $\dfrac{\text{number of sums less than 6}}{30}$.

16. What is $P(\text{sum is less than 6})$? Compare with Exercise 15.

17. Combine your results with those of a classmate to get data for 60 tosses.
   a. Find the ratio $\dfrac{\text{number of 7's}}{60}$.
   b. Find the ratio $\dfrac{\text{number of sums less than 6}}{60}$.
   c. Are the new ratios closer to $P(7)$ and $P(\text{sum is less than 6})$, respectively, than the ratios obtained in Exercises 13 and 15?

18. Suppose you want to find out how students in your school feel about an issue, such as "Should computer programming be a required course for all high school students?" Devise a plan for selecting a sample of 100 students in your school so that your sample will show the opinion of the entire school as accurately as possible.

19. Suppose a government agency wishes to determine whether the public is in favor of an increase in the tax on gasoline. Explain why a sample of people leaving a subway station may not accurately show the opinion of the general public.

Carefully draw a grid with at least 8 rows and 8 columns and with squares the width of a penny.

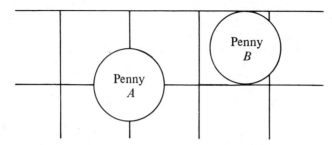

C **20.** Suppose you toss a penny so that it lands on the grid. What is the probability that the coin lands so that it covers a point where 2 lines cross? Express the probability in terms of π. (In the drawing above, penny A covers such a point; penny B does not.)

(*Hint:* The penny will cover a point where 2 lines cross if the center of the penny lands on the shaded area of a square as shown in the figure at the right.)

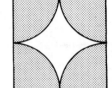

21. Toss a penny on your grid 20 times. Find the ratio of the number of times the coin covers a point of intersection of 2 lines to the total number of tosses.

22. Use Exercises 20 and 21 to find an experimental estimate for π.

Section 13-2 THE MEAN AND SUMMATION NOTATION

In this section you will:
- find the mean of a set of numbers
- learn to use summation notation
- use summation notation to write a formula for the mean

When a class takes a test, the scores are often averaged to give a statistic called the (arithmetic) *mean*. This number is found by adding all the scores and dividing the total by the number of people who took the exam. The mean gives some indication of the score that the typical student had on the exam. Another way to interpret the mean is that it gives a score that represents the entire class.

When doing calculations, we will give a mean correct to one more decimal place than the number of decimal places given in the data.

EXAMPLE   Find the mean of:

$$10, 15, 8, 12, 14, 16, 13, 12, 11, 9$$

SOLUTION   Since there are 10 numbers, the mean is:

$$\frac{10 + 15 + 8 + 12 + 14 + 16 + 13 + 12 + 11 + 9}{10} = \frac{120}{10} = 12.0$$

EXAMPLE Find the mean of: 2.3, 5.4, 8.7, 6.1, 4.0, 7.5, 1.9

SOLUTION There are 7 numbers, so the mean is:

$$\frac{2.3 + 5.4 + 8.7 + 6.1 + 4.0 + 7.5 + 1.9}{7} = \frac{35.9}{7}, \text{ or approximately } 5.13$$

Finding the mean is a process that involves finding a sum. Since there are so many statistical processes that use sums, it is helpful to have a symbol to indicate a sum. Suppose you have n numbers represented as $x_1, x_2, x_3, \ldots, x_n$. Their sum is:

$$x_1 + x_2 + x_3 + \cdots + x_n$$

In *summation notation* you write this sum as:

$$\sum_{i=1}^{n} x_i$$

The expression above, which is read "the sum of x_i for $i = 1$ to n," is just a short way of writing the sum. The symbol Σ is the Greek capital letter "sigma."

EXAMPLE Evaluate: $\displaystyle\sum_{i=1}^{5} 2i$

SOLUTION $\displaystyle\sum_{i=1}^{5} 2i = 2(1) + 2(2) + 2(3) + 2(4) + 2(5)$
$= 2 + 4 + 6 + 8 + 10$
$= 30$

Notice that i tells which term of the sum is being considered, and that i may be used in an expression showing how to compute the terms of the sum.

EXAMPLE Evaluate: $\displaystyle\sum_{i=1}^{8} i^2$

SOLUTION $\displaystyle\sum_{i=1}^{8} i^2 = 1^2 + 2^2 + 3^2 + 4^2 + 5^2 + 6^2 + 7^2 + 8^2$
$= 1 + 4 + 9 + 16 + 25 + 36 + 49 + 64$
$= 204$

In summation notation, i may begin with a value other than 1.

EXAMPLE Evaluate: $\displaystyle\sum_{i=5}^{7} (3i - 1)$

SOLUTION $\displaystyle\sum_{i=5}^{7} (3i - 1) = (3 \cdot 5 - 1) + (3 \cdot 6 - 1) + (3 \cdot 7 - 1)$
$= 14 + 17 + 20$
$= 51$

EXAMPLE   Evaluate: $\displaystyle\sum_{i=1}^{6} 10$

SOLUTION   For each value of i, the term is 10. Since there are 6 terms:

$$\sum_{i=1}^{6} 10 = 10 + 10 + 10 + 10 + 10 + 10 = 60$$

Examples like the one above lead to the following formula, where c is a constant.

$$\sum_{i=1}^{n} c = nc$$

The following formulas are useful in working with summations. Their proofs are left as exercises.

1. $\displaystyle\sum_{i=1}^{n} (x_i + y_i) = \sum_{i=1}^{n} x_i + \sum_{i=1}^{n} y_i$
    2. $\displaystyle\sum_{i=1}^{n} cx_i = c \sum_{i=1}^{n} x_i$, where c is any real number.

Another formula that can be helpful in simplifying summation problems gives the sum of the first n integers:

$$\sum_{i=1}^{n} i = \frac{n(n+1)}{2}$$

EXAMPLE   Evaluate:

   a. $\displaystyle\sum_{i=1}^{6} (i + 2)$ **b.** $\displaystyle\sum_{i=1}^{5} (3i + i^2)$

SOLUTION   **a.** $\displaystyle\sum_{i=1}^{6} (i + 2) = \sum_{i=1}^{6} i + \sum_{i=1}^{6} 2$ by formula 1

$$= \sum_{i=1}^{6} i + 2(6) \quad \text{by the formula } \sum_{i=1}^{n} c = nc$$

$$= \frac{6(7)}{2} + 12 = 33 \quad \text{by the formula for } \sum_{i=1}^{n} i$$

   b. $\displaystyle\sum_{i=1}^{5} (3i + i^2) = \sum_{i=1}^{5} 3i + \sum_{i=1}^{5} i^2$ by formula 1

$$= 3\sum_{i=1}^{5} i + \sum_{i=1}^{5} i^2 \quad \text{by formula 2}$$

$$= 3 \cdot \frac{5(6)}{2} + \sum_{i=1}^{5} i^2 \quad \text{by the formula for } \sum_{i=1}^{n} i$$

$$= 45 + (1 + 4 + 9 + 16 + 25)$$

$$= 45 + 55 = 100$$

Using summation notation, you can write a formula for the mean.

If $x_1, x_2, x_3, \ldots, x_n$ is a set of numbers, then the mean of the set, denoted by $\bar{x}$, is the number:

$$\bar{x} = \frac{1}{n} \sum_{i=1}^{n} x_i$$

ORAL EXERCISES

Evaluate the following.

1. $\displaystyle\sum_{i=1}^{5} i$

2. $\displaystyle\sum_{i=1}^{5} (i + 2)$

3. $\displaystyle\sum_{i=4}^{6} 3i$

4. $\displaystyle\sum_{i=4}^{8} 5i$

5. $\displaystyle\sum_{i=1}^{5} 10i$

6. $\displaystyle\sum_{i=5}^{8} (i - 3)$

Express the following using summation notation.

7. $1 + 2 + 3 + 4 + \cdots + 16$

8. $7 + 8 + 9 + 10 + \cdots + 30$

9. $1 + 4 + 9 + \cdots + 100$

10. $2 + 4 + 6 + 8 + \cdots + 50$

Find the mean of each set of numbers.

11. 5, 8, 9, 7, 10, 3

12. 12, 15, 8, 14, 11

13. 0.3, 1.6, 0.8, 1.3, 0.6

14. 3, 2, 2, 7, 8, 9, 8

15. 4, 5, 5, 6, 7, 7, 8

16. 1, 1, 3, 6, 9, 11, 11

WRITTEN EXERCISES

Evaluate.

A 1. $\displaystyle\sum_{i=1}^{10} 5i$

2. $\displaystyle\sum_{i=1}^{12} (i + 3)$

3. $\displaystyle\sum_{i=5}^{11} (i - 4)$

4. $\displaystyle\sum_{i=2}^{8} (2i - 1)$

5. $\displaystyle\sum_{i=5}^{15} i^2$

6. $\displaystyle\sum_{i=8}^{10} 3i^2$

7. $\displaystyle\sum_{i=10}^{15} i(i - 10)$

8. $\displaystyle\sum_{i=1}^{8} (i^2 - i)$

9. $\displaystyle\sum_{i=1}^{10} (2i - 4)$

10. $\displaystyle\sum_{i=1}^{11} (i - 6)$

Find the mean of each set of numbers.

11. 12, 18, 20, 13, 10, 17, 21, 15

12. 9, 30, 24, 18, 16, 21, 26, 28, 34, 14

13. 0.5, 1.9, 2.8, 1.3, 0.7, 1.6, 0.9, 1.2, 1.7

14. 13.1, 12.6, 14.5, 16.3, 18

15. 7, 8, 13, 9, 12, 14, 10, 11

16. 0.6, 0.4, 1.2, 0.7, 1.6, 1.9

17. Jose had test scores of 75, 80, and 81. What score must he get on the fourth test so that his average (mean) for the four tests is 82?

18. In the first four months of this year, the monthly amounts of rain were 5 cm, 3 cm, 6 cm, and 12 cm. How much rain is needed in May so that the mean monthly rainfall for January through May will be 6.5 cm?

Use summation notation to write each sum.

19. $50 + 51 + 52 + \cdots + 75$

20. $4 + 9 + 16 + 25 + 36 + 49 + 64 + 81$

21. $-3 - 2 - 1 + 0 + 1 + 2 + 3 + 4 + 5$

22. $2x_{10} + 2x_{11} + 2x_{12} + \cdots + 2x_{24}$

B 23. $1 + 3 + 5 + 7 + 9 + \cdots + 79$

24. $3 + 8 + 15 + 24 + 35 + 48 + 63 + 80$

25. If $\displaystyle\sum_{i=6}^{12} (i - 4) = \sum_{i=2}^{a} i$, find the value of a.

26. If $\displaystyle\sum_{i=6}^{12} (i - 4) = \sum_{i=4}^{10} (i + c)$, find the value of the constant c.

Use the formula $\displaystyle\sum_{i=1}^{n} i = \frac{n(n + 1)}{2}$ to evaluate each sum in Exercises 27–32.

27. $\displaystyle\sum_{i=1}^{10} i$

28. $\displaystyle\sum_{i=1}^{100} i$

29. $\displaystyle\sum_{i=1}^{50} (2i - 3)$

30. $\displaystyle\sum_{i=51}^{100} i$ (*Hint:* Write this as a difference of sums.)

C 31. $4 + 7 + 10 + 13 + 16 + \cdots + 121$

32. the sum of the even numbers between 999 and 2001

33. Show that $\displaystyle\sum_{i=1}^{n} (x_i + y_i) = \sum_{i=1}^{n} x_i + \sum_{i=1}^{n} y_i$.

34. Show that $\displaystyle\sum_{i=1}^{n} cx_i = c \sum_{i=1}^{n} x_i$, where c is a fixed real number.

35. Find a simple formula to express the sum of the first n odd numbers in terms of n. Use summation notation.

36. Simplify: $\displaystyle\sum_{i=1}^{n} \frac{i}{n}$

37. Simplify: $\displaystyle\sum_{i=1}^{n} \left(1 + \frac{2i}{n}\right)\frac{2}{n}$

Section 13-3 FREQUENCY TABLES

When you deal with large amounts of information, it is helpful to be able to organize the data in a compact, convenient form. In this section you will:
- use frequency tables to organize data
- calculate the mean from a frequency table

A *frequency table* is often used to organize data for easy reference. The word *frequency* is used to indicate how many times a given value occurs in the data.

EXAMPLE   A market research company conducted a telephone survey to find out how many cars a family had owned in the past 10 years. It listed the number of cars owned by each of the 30 families contacted in the survey. Then it prepared a frequency table.

$$3, 2, 5, 4, 3, 4, 2, 3, 5, 2, 4, 3, 2, 5, 5,$$
$$4, 3, 2, 5, 4, 3, 3, 2, 2, 5, 5, 3, 3, 4, 2$$

Frequency Table

Number of cars	Frequency
2	8
3	9
4	6
5	$\dfrac{7}{30}$

The information contained in the frequency table can be presented graphically in a *histogram*. A *histogram* is a bar graph in which the height of each bar represents the frequency of a particular value in the data.

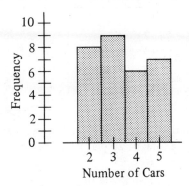

To find the mean number of cars the families in the preceding example had owned, you could add the 30 numbers in the original list and then divide by 30. However, once the frequency table has been made, you know that 2 occurs 8 times, 3 occurs 9 times, 4 occurs 6 times, and 5 occurs 7 times. So the mean, $\bar{x}$, is given by:

$$\bar{x} = \frac{2(8) + 3(9) + 4(6) + 5(7)}{30} = \frac{102}{30} = 3.4$$

In general, if there are n items altogether, having m distinct values, and f_i is the frequency of the value x_i, then

$$\bar{x} = \frac{\sum\limits_{i=1}^{m} x_i f_i}{\sum\limits_{i=1}^{m} f_i}$$

In the preceding example, $n = 30$ and $m = 4$. In the frequency table the values of x_i and f_i are listed in the first and second columns respectively.

Notice that $\sum\limits_{i=1}^{m} x_i f_i$ is the sum of all the items. Also, $\sum\limits_{i=1}^{m} f_i = n$; that is, the sum of the frequencies is the total number of items. This definition of $\bar{x}$, therefore, is equivalent to the one given in Section 13-2.

EXAMPLE The recreation director kept a record of the number of players using the Elm Street tennis court each day. The results are given in the frequency table at the right. Find the mean number of players per day.

Number of Players	Frequency
10	2
12	6
14	7
16	8
18	5

SOLUTION It is sometimes helpful to include a column that gives the product $x_i f_i$ for each value of the index i.

Index (i)	Number of Players (x_i)	Frequency (f_i)	$x_i f_i$
1	10	2	20
2	12	6	72
3	14	7	98
4	16	8	128
5	18	5	90
		28	408

As a matter of interpretation, notice that on the two days when there were 10 players each day there was a total of 20 players, and so on.

Since $\sum\limits_{i=1}^{5} f_i = 28$ and $\sum\limits_{i=1}^{5} x_i f_i = 408$, you find that $\bar{x} = \dfrac{408}{28} \approx 14.6$.

On the average, there were 14.6 players a day.

Sometimes a frequency table is compiled so that information is given for intervals. This is illustrated in the following example.

EXAMPLE The pulse rates of the members of a fitness program were recorded after an exercise session. The distribution of pulse rates is given in the frequency table shown.

Pulse Rate	Frequency
96–100	6
91–95	12
86–90	9
81–85	24
76–80	21
71–75	12
66–70	6

The mean of the data cannot be found exactly from the table, because you don't have the individual rate for each member. However, you can find an *approximate* value for $\bar{x}$ by supposing that all the rates in each interval are clustered at the middle of the interval, or, equivalently, that they are spread evenly throughout the interval. To do this, find the midpoint of each interval and use it for x_i. This value is called the *class mark* of the interval.

Index (i)	Pulse Rate	Class Mark (x_i)	Frequency (f_i)	$x_i f_i$
1	96–100	98	6	588
2	91–95	93	12	1116
3	86–90	88	9	792
4	81–85	83	24	1992
5	76–80	78	21	1638
6	71–75	73	12	876
7	66–70	68	6	408
			90	7410

$$\bar{x} = \frac{\sum_{i=1}^{7} x_i f_i}{\sum_{i=1}^{7} f_i} = \frac{7410}{90} \approx 82.3$$

An approximation of the mean pulse rate is 82.3. A histogram for the pulse rate data is shown below.

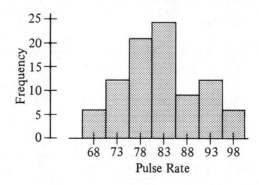

ORAL EXERCISES

1. A record was kept of the number of sick days each employee of a certain company took during one year:

$$7, 10, 0, 5, 4, 8, 2, 3, 6, 4,$$
$$10, 1, 3, 6, 5, 9, 8, 4, 5, 2,$$
$$7, 3, 4, 5, 3, 6, 10, 8, 4, 1$$

a. How many employees are there?

b. What were the greatest and least numbers of sick days any employee took?

c. Complete the frequency table.

Number of sick days	0	1	2	3	4	5	6	7	8	9	10
Frequency	?	?	?	?	?	?	?	?	?	?	?

d. How many employees took 6 or more sick days?

e. Did at least 50% of the employees take less than 6 sick days?

2. A survey was conducted to find the number of books read in the past year by a certain group of adults. The number of books read by each person was recorded:

3	14	9	17	1	22	12	8	9	15	16	8	13
20	12	4	15	24	18	10	6	11	18	15	25	

Complete the frequency table for these data.

Number of Books	Class Mark	Frequency
1–5	?	?
⋮	⋮	⋮
21–25	?	?

WRITTEN EXERCISES

A 1. The following scores were obtained on a 10-point auto safety checklist:

8	7	6	4	5	10	9	6	7	7
2	5	9	10	10	1	3	8	4	6
9	4	3	8	6	7	8	5	3	2
1	1	6	5	9	3	4	3	5	9

a. Complete the frequency table.

b. Use the table to find the mean score.

Score	1	2	3	4	5	6	7	8	9	10
Frequency	?	?	?	?	?	?	?	?	?	?

2. The number of computer terminals not being used was recorded each hour for 2 days at Data, Inc. The results were listed in a frequency table. Find the average (mean) number of unused terminals.

Number of Terminals	Frequency
0	5
1	17
2	12
3	6
4	8

3. The Midtown Meteors keep track of the distance each member runs per week. The distances, in kilometers, are listed for last week.

    48 62 55 38 46 40 53 63
    34 45 36 48 51 60 52 45
    33 47 55 42 39 57 49 56

a. Complete the table.

Distance	Class Mark	Frequency
31–35	?	?
⋮	⋮	⋮
61–65	?	?

b. Use the table to find an approximate value of the mean distance the members ran.

4. The mass of each apple picked from an experimental disease-resistant tree was recorded. The technician used tally marks as shown. Masses were measured to the nearest 10 g.

10–50 g ~~THL~~ ~~THL~~ |||
60–100 g ~~THL~~ ~~THL~~ ||
110–150 g ~~THL~~ ~~THL~~ ~~THL~~ ~~THL~~ |||

160–200 g ~~THL~~ ~~THL~~ ~~THL~~ ~~THL~~ ~~THL~~ ||
210–250 g ~~THL~~ ~~THL~~ ~~THL~~ |
260–300 g ~~THL~~ ~~THL~~ ||||

a. Complete the table.

Mass	Class Mark	Frequency
10–50 g	?	?
⋮	⋮	⋮
260–300 g	?	?

b. Use the table to find an approximate value of the mean mass of the apples.

Draw a histogram of the data in the frequency table of the indicated Written Exercise.

5. Exercise 1   6. Exercise 2   7. Exercise 3   8. Exercise 4

B 9. A forester measured the diameters of pine trees in a small area. The diameters, to the nearest centimeter, are given at the right.
  a. Organize the data in a frequency table with intervals 18-22, 23-27, and so on.
  b. Use the table to find an approximate value of the mean diameter.

35, 50, 42, 20, 32, 45, 61, 28, 43, 48, 52, 21, 37, 48, 53, 56, 22, 25, 38, 34, 37, 26, 18, 50, 45, 35, 32, 33, 41, 45, 35, 39, 34, 27, 23, 26, 37, 28, 24, 29, 36, 48, 51

10. Imagine that your computer has "crashed." You had a frequency table in memory, but all entries were destroyed except for those shown below. You also know that all data intervals are equal in width.
  a. Recreate the table by supplying all items that are missing.
  b. Use the table to find an approximate value of the mean.

Index (i)	Age	Class Mark (x_i)	Frequency (f_i)	$x_i f_i$
1	?	?	?	40
2	?	?	?	140
3	?	?	13	?
4	18-22	?	?	460
5	23-27	?	?	225

11. Make up an experiment in which you find out some information from each student in your class. For example, you could find out their heights, ages to the nearest month, or numbers of sisters and brothers. If your class is small, extend your sampling to obtain measurements from at least 20 students. Organize the data into a frequency table and find the mean.

C 12. Histograms for two sets of data are shown. What can you conclude about how the means of the two data sets compare with each other?

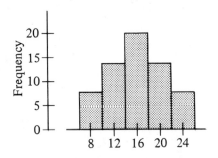 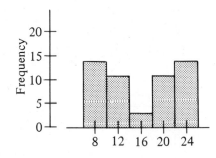

13. The histogram at the right shows the number of years of education beyond high school for a group of high-tech workers. Find the 40th percentile. Recall that this is the number of years of education at or below which the lowest 40% of the workers are found. Your answer should be one of the numbers 2, 3, 4, 5, or 6.

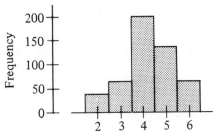

1. Construction permits were issued in Lake City as follows: Section 13-1
residential, 135   commercial, 42   industrial, 23
What is the probability that a permit chosen at random is for a commercial building?

Evaluate.

2. $\displaystyle\sum_{i=1}^{6} 4i$

3. $\displaystyle\sum_{i=2}^{8} (2i - 3)$

4. $\displaystyle\sum_{i=1}^{5} 2i^2$ Section 13-2

5. Find the mean of these test scores: 70, 62, 88, 95, 79, 84, and 82

6. The number of television sets per household was recorded in a certain neighbor-   Section 13-3
hood. Use the frequency table to find the mean number of television sets per household.

Number of TV's	0	1	2	3	4	5
Frequency	36	228	171	104	58	23

Section 13-4 MEASURES OF CENTRAL TENDENCY

As you saw in Section 13-2, the mean is often used in discussing data. The mean does not, however, give a complete picture of a set of data. Other widely used statistics are the median and the mode. The mean, median, and mode are *measures of central tendency*. A *measure of central tendency* is a single number, or statistic, that is considered representative of all the numbers in a set of data. In this section you will study:
• median
• mode

If a set of data is listed in numerical order, the *median* is the middle item. If there is an even number of data items, the *median* is the average of the two middle items. The median indicates the center, or middle, of the data set. Half, or 50%, of the data items are less than or equal to the median. Recall that the median could, therefore, be called the 50th percentile. The median of the list at the right is 5.

The *mode* is the number in a set of data that occurs most frequently. If all values in the set have the same frequency, there is no mode. Also, there may be more than one mode. The list at the right has two modes, 2 and 5.

```
2  2  3
4  5  5
6  7  8
```

EXAMPLE   The highway department kept a record of the number of accidents on a dangerous section of highway. The results are summarized in the table below. Find the median, mode, and mean of the number of accidents per month.

Jan	Feb	Mar	Apr	May	June	July	Aug	Sept	Oct	Nov	Dec
12	11	9	6	4	5	6	5	6	9	8	10

SOLUTION   Write the data in numerical order:

$$4, 5, 5, 6, 6, 6, 8, 9, 9, 10, 11, 12$$

Median: $\dfrac{6+8}{2} = 7$ Mode: 6

Mean: $\dfrac{4 + 5(2) + 6(3) + 8 + 9(2) + 10 + 11 + 12}{12} = \dfrac{91}{12}$, or approximately 7.6

EXAMPLE   A tire dealer analyzed sales of radial tires according to the number of tires sold to each customer in June. The data are shown in the frequency table. Find the median, mode, mean, and the 80th percentile of the number of tires per customer.

Number of Tires	Frequency
1	180
2	184
3	28
4	296
5	17

SOLUTION   Median: There were 705 sales. If the numbers of tires per sale were listed in numerical order, there would be 180 ones, 184 twos, and so on. The middle number would be the 353rd entry in this list. Since $180 + 184 = 364$, the 353rd item would be a 2.
Median = 2

Mode: The mode is simply the value with the greatest frequency.
Mode = 4

Mean: $\dfrac{1(180) + 2(184) + 3(28) + 4(296) + 5(17)}{180 + 184 + 28 + 296 + 17} = \dfrac{1901}{705}$.
The mean is approximately 2.7.

80th percentile: There were 705 sales, and 80% of 705 is 564. If the numbers of tires per sale were listed in increasing order, the first 564 sales would be for a number of tires that is less than or equal to the 80th percentile. The 564th and 565th sales were 4 tires each.
80th percentile = 4.

EXAMPLE   The quality-control engineer at Major Electric Company checks appliances for defects. For the appliances found defective, a record is kept of the number of defects. This information for a certain week was presented in the histogram shown at the top of the following page. Find the mode of the number of defects per appliance.

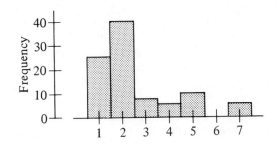

SOLUTION The mode is simply the value with the tallest bar in the histogram.

Mode = 2

ORAL EXERCISES

For inventory control, Valley Hardware kept a list of the number of wheelbarrows sold each day of their Spring Fling sale. Sales were: 12, 7, 6, 3, 4, 9, 13, 8, 5, 2, 6, 9, 7, 6, 3
For these sales figures, find the:

1. median   2. mode   3. mean   4. 80th percentile

Consider scores on a test on which the highest possible score is 100. What can you conclude if

5. the median is 90?   6. the median is 50?

7. the mode is 100?   8. the mode is 20?

9. the median is 75 and the mean is 85?

10. the 20th percentile is 80?

WRITTEN EXERCISES

A consumer testing agency rated 140 products. The rating scale had a total of 80 points. The agency's report included the following information:

The highest score was 76.
The median was 49.
The 90th percentile was 74.

A 1. How many products had scores of 49 or more?

2. How many products had a score of 49 or less?

3. Exactly 80% of the other products scored lower than Brand X. What do you know about Brand X's score?

4. At most how many products had scores of 75 or 76?

5. Federal Flavors, Inc., markets a 30 mL bottle of vanilla extract. To assure compliance with packaging standards, the contents of a sample of bottles were measured to the nearest 0.1 mL. The measured contents of the bottles were as shown below. Find the median and mode for these data.

     30.8   30.6   31.1   30.2   30.3   29.8   30.1   30.2
     29.9   30.4   30.1   30.0   30.1   30.2   29.9

In Exercises 6–8 find the median and mode for the data presented.

6. Each newborn baby is assigned an Apgar score to indicate its physical status at birth. The highest possible score is 10 points. The monthly report prepared by the director of Delta General Hospital included the following table, which shows the number of babies receiving each Apgar score.

Score	0	1	2	3	4	5	6	7	8	9	10
Frequency	0	0	3	2	5	7	6	17	21	16	22

7. The Director of City Planning conducted a survey to find the number of children in each family. The survey results were summarized in the frequency table below.

Number of Children	Frequency	Number of Children	Frequency
0	4852	6	287
1	8366	7	73
2	8971	8	18
3	4145	9	0
4	1383	10	2
5	692	11	3

8.

Note: The only data values are 5, 10, 15, ... These are not class marks for intervals.

9. The scores on a test were:

$$82 \quad 71 \quad 88 \quad 56 \quad 60 \quad 74 \quad 92 \quad 62 \quad 58 \quad 76$$
$$78 \quad 63 \quad 83 \quad 75 \quad 68 \quad 57 \quad 77 \quad 64 \quad 81 \quad 70$$

a. Find the median and mean of the scores.

b. The teacher decided to raise all test scores 5 points. Find the median and mean of the new test scores.

c. Compare the median and mean of the raised scores to the corresponding statistics for the original scores.

B 10. Find the mean number of children per family using the data in Exercise 7. Compare the mean to the median. Can you explain the difference?

The frequency table below shows the number of families at each income level in Wessex County. Incomes of $100,000 or more were excluded from the study. All incomes were rounded to the nearest thousand dollars.

Income	Frequency	Income	Frequency
0–$9,000	472	$50,000–$59,000	1126
$10,000–$19,000	1359	$60,000–$69,000	853
$20,000–$29,000	2864	$70,000–$79,000	504
$30,000–$39,000	2147	$80,000–$89,000	288
$40,000–$49,000	1481	$90,000–$99,000	239

11. In which income interval is the median income?

12. What is the modal interval (the interval with the greatest frequency)?

13. Use class marks for the intervals to find an approximate value of the mean income.

14. Construct a histogram to show the information in the frequency table.

Make a list of 10 different positive numbers having a:

15. Mean and median both 30

16. Mean of 40 and median 50

C 17. What can you conclude about the distribution of a set of data if the median is greater than the mean?

18. What can you conclude about the distribution of a set of data if the mean is greater than the median?

19. Could there be a set of numbers with the median the same as the greatest number in the set? Explain.

Section 13-5 MEASURES OF DISPERSION

In earlier sections you worked with the mean, median, and mode, which are measures of central tendency. These measures give an indication of where a set of data is "centered." It is quite possible, however, for two sets of data to have the same mean or median but to differ widely in other respects. In this section you will study statistics that measure how "concentrated" or how "scattered" data are. These statistics, which measure dispersion, are:
- range
- mean absolute deviation
- variance
- standard deviation

Consider the following sets of numbers.

I: 10, 24, 27, 29, 30, 31, 33, 36, 50

II: 10, 12, 16, 24, 30, 36, 44, 48, 50

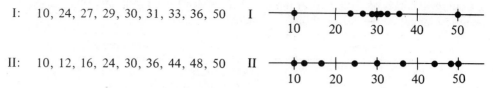

For each set, there are 9 numbers, and both the mean and median are 30. It is clear, though, that there is an important difference between the two sets. The numbers in set I are clustered, or concentrated, with most numbers near the mean. On the other hand, the numbers in set II are much more spread out; they are more widely scattered, or dispersed.

The mean gives a measure of the "center" of a data set. If this information is combined with a measure of the dispersion of the data, the result is a much more complete description of the data.

One very simple measure of dispersion is the *range*. The *range* of a set of data is the difference of the greatest and least values in the set. For sets I and II above, the range is $50 - 10$, or 40. Despite their great difference in scattering, both sets have the same range. Clearly, the range is not adequate for measuring dispersion, because it is based on only the two extreme values of the data.

Other measures of dispersion besides the range are needed. Consider, instead, how much each data value differs, or deviates, from the mean. In other words, compute $x_i - \overline{x}$ for each number in the data set. Using I and II above, you have the following results. Recall that $\overline{x}$ is 30.

	I		II
x_i	$x_i - \overline{x}$	x_i	$x_i - \overline{x}$
10	−20	10	−20
24	−6	12	−18
27	−3	16	−14
29	−1	24	−6
30	0	30	0
31	1	36	6
33	3	44	14
36	6	48	18
50	20	50	20
	0		0

The sum $\sum_{i=1}^{n} (x_i - \overline{x})$ is 0 in both cases and, indeed, for all sets. Therefore, for all sets of data, the average deviation from the mean is 0. This is not helpful. However, if you take the absolute value of each of these differences, this problem is eliminated. By taking the mean of these absolute values, you find a number that is the average amount by which each data item differs from the mean, disregarding whether the item is more than the mean or less than the mean. This provides a useful measure of dispersion called the *mean absolute deviation*.

For the numbers $x_1, x_2, \ldots, x_n$, the *mean absolute deviation* is

$$\frac{1}{n} \sum_{i=1}^{n} |x_i - \overline{x}|.$$

EXAMPLE Find the mean absolute deviation for sets I and II.

SOLUTION I. $\dfrac{1}{9} \displaystyle\sum_{i=1}^{9} |x_i - \overline{x}| = \frac{1}{9}(20 + 6 + 3 + 1 + 0 + 1 + 3 + 6 + 20) = \frac{60}{9} \approx 6.7$

II. $\dfrac{1}{9} \displaystyle\sum_{i=1}^{9} |x_i - \overline{x}| = \frac{1}{9}(20 + 18 + 14 + 6 + 0 + 6 + 14 + 18 + 20) = \frac{116}{9} \approx 12.9$

The results in the example are exactly what you would expect. Set II is more scattered than set I, and its mean absolute deviation is much greater than that of set I.

Another measure of dispersion is called the *variance*, denoted by the symbol s^2. For the numbers $x_1, x_2, \ldots, x_n$ the *variance* is

$$s^2 = \frac{1}{n} \sum_{i=1}^{n} (x_i - \overline{x})^2.$$

Thus, this statistic is the average value of the squares of the deviations from the mean.

The most widely used measure of dispersion is the *standard deviation*, denoted by s. For the numbers $x_1, x_2, \ldots, x_n$ the *standard deviation* is

$$s = \sqrt{\frac{1}{n} \sum_{i=1}^{n} (x_i - \overline{x})^2}.$$

Despite the complicated appearance of the formula defining the standard deviation, it should be apparent that it is simply the square root of the variance. The symbols s^2 and s for variance and standard deviation, respectively, were chosen to emphasize this relationship.

EXAMPLE Find the variance and standard deviation of sets I and II.

SOLUTION As noted earlier, $\overline{x} = 30$.

I. $s^2 = \dfrac{1}{9} \displaystyle\sum_{i=1}^{9} (x_i - \overline{x})^2$

$= \frac{1}{9}((-20)^2 + (-6)^2 + (-3)^2 + (-1)^2 + 0^2 + 1^2 + 3^2 + 6^2 + 20^2)$

$= \frac{1}{9}(400 + 36 + 9 + 1 + 0 + 1 + 9 + 36 + 400)$

$= \frac{1}{9}(892) \approx 99.1$, variance

$s = \sqrt{s^2} \approx \sqrt{99.1} \approx 10.0$, standard deviation   *(Solution continues.)*

II. $s^2 = \dfrac{1}{9} \displaystyle\sum_{i=1}^{9} (x_i - \bar{x})^2$

$\qquad = \dfrac{1}{9}((-20)^2 + (-18)^2 + (-14)^2 + (-6)^2 + 0^2 + 6^2 + 14^2 + 18^2 + 20^2)$

$\qquad = \dfrac{1}{9}(400 + 324 + 196 + 36 + 0 + 36 + 196 + 324 + 400)$

$\qquad = \dfrac{1}{9}(1912)$

$\qquad \approx 212.4$, variance

$s = \sqrt{s^2}$

$\qquad \approx \sqrt{212.4}$

$\qquad \approx 14.6$, standard deviation

Again, note that these results are consistent with what you would expect. Both the variance and standard deviation of set II, which is more scattered, are greater than those for set I.

The procedure for finding mean absolute deviation, variance, and standard deviation for data given in a frequency table is outlined in the next example.

EXAMPLE   A consumer panel performed a taste test on a new beverage. Each taster gave the beverage a rating on a scale from 1 to 5, with 5 being the best rating. The results of the test are shown in the first two columns of the table below. The remaining columns show calculations needed to find the mean absolute deviation, variance, and standard deviation of the test ratings. Results in the last column have been rounded to the nearest tenth.

Rating x_i	Frequency f_i	$x_i f_i$	$x_i - \bar{x}$	$|x_i - \bar{x}|f_i$	$(x_i - \bar{x})^2 f_i$
1	23	23	−1.3	29.9	38.9
2	35	70	−0.3	10.5	3.2
3	19	57	0.7	13.3	9.3
4	8	32	1.7	13.6	23.1
5	5	25	2.7	13.5	36.5
	90	207		80.8	111.0

$\bar{x} = \dfrac{207}{90} = 2.3$

mean absolute deviation: $\dfrac{80.8}{90} \approx 0.9$

variance: $\dfrac{111.0}{90} \approx 1.2$

standard deviation: $\sqrt{1.2} \approx 1.1$

ORAL EXERCISES

Two sets of numbers are given. For which set would you expect the standard deviation to be greater?

1. I: 2, 2, 3, 3, 3, 4, 4
   II: 1, 1, 2, 3, 5, 8, 10

2. I: 2, 3, 4, 6, 8, 9, 10
   II: 2, 4, 5, 6, 7, 8, 10

3. I: 1, 3, 5, 7, 9, 11
   II: 22, 23, 24, 25, 26, 27

4. I: 1, 3, 5, 7, 9
   II: 2, 4, 6, 8, 10

5-8. Find the range of each set of data in Oral Exercises 1-4.

9. Two sets of data are shown in the following histograms. Which data set has the smaller standard deviation?

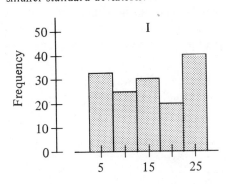
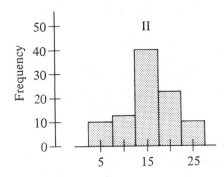

Find the standard deviation for the given data.

10. 2, 8   **11.** 1, 1, 1, 9, 9, 9   **12.** 2, 5, 8

WRITTEN EXERCISES

A **1.** Suppose all the data in a set are the same. What can you conclude about the
   a. range?   **b.** mean absolute deviation?
   c. variance?   **d.** standard deviation?

2. On a test, the mean was 70 and the standard deviation was 10.5. All scores within one standard deviation of the mean were assigned a grade of C. What scores will receive a C grade?

3. For set I, $\bar{x} = 500$ and $s = 100$. For set II, $\bar{x} = 500$ and $s = 200$. The two sets have the same number of data items. Which set would you expect to have the greater number of data items that are less than 200? Explain.

4. Sets I and II both have a mean of 80. In set I, 80% of the items are between 60 and 100. In set II, only 50% of the items are between 60 and 100. Which set would you expect to have the greater standard deviation? Explain.

5. The number of hours worked by each welder at Acme Metals is shown below. Find the range and the mean absolute deviation of the number of hours worked.

$$36, 40, 40, 32, 42, 37, 38, 40, 44, 38$$

6. The fire department responded to 12 calls Monday, 9 Tuesday, 13 Wednesday, 10 Thursday, and 16 Friday. Find the mean absolute deviation and the variance of the daily number of calls during this period.

7. Pearl received the following grades on her final exams: Math, 85; English, 76; History, 82; Biology, 94; French, 83. Find the variance and standard deviation of her exam grades.

8. In a cost-of-living survey, the leading grocery stores were found to be charging the following prices for a carton of milk: Spend & Save, 62¢; Sureway, 58¢; JHB, 66¢; Hi-Qual, 57¢; Right Buy, 61¢; Renaldo's, 62¢. Find the standard deviation of the milk prices.

B 9. The scores on a math test were all raised by 10 points.
   a. What is the relationship of the mean score after the raise to the mean before the raise?
   b. What is the relationship of the standard deviation of the scores after the raise to the standard deviation before the raise?

10. In a fatigue experiment, the time in minutes to complete a task was recorded for each person both before and after a long period of sleeplessness. The results are shown in the chart below.
   a. Find the standard deviation of each set of response times.
   b. Was there more variability in the response times before, or after, the loss of sleep?

	A	B	C	D	E
Before	24	30	22	27	31
After	30	35	25	31	32

11. The ages, to the nearest month, of a group of babies in an infant perception study are shown in the following frequency table. Find the variance and standard deviation of the ages.

Age	6	7	8	9
Frequency	4	11	16	5

12. The normal monthly temperature for two cities is shown in the table below.
   a. For each city, find the range of the temperatures.
   b. For each city, find the standard deviation of the temperatures.
   c. Which city has the more variable climate? Use the statistics calculated in parts (a) and (b) to explain your answer.

	Normal Temperature (in Celsius degrees)											
	Jan	Feb	Mar	Apr	May	Jun	Jul	Aug	Sep	Oct	Nov	Dec
Toronto	−4	−4	1	8	13	19	22	21	17	11	5	−2
Vancouver	2	4	6	9	12	15	17	17	14	10	6	4

13. Prove: $\sum_{i=1}^{n} x_i = n\overline{x}$

C 14. Prove: $s^2 = \frac{1}{n} \left(\sum_{i=1}^{n} (x_i)^2 \right) - (\overline{x})^2$

(*Hint*: $\overline{x}$ and $(\overline{x})^2$ are constants.)
This is sometimes called a "computing formula" for the variance.

15. A set of data consists only of k items with a value of $c + a$ each and k items with a value of $c - a$ each. Express the mean and standard deviation in terms of c and a.

16. A set of data consists of the numbers c, $c - a$, and $c + a$. Express the standard deviation in terms of a.

Section 13-6 NORMAL DISTRIBUTIONS

You learned how to compute the mean and standard deviation in earlier sections. Now you will learn how to use these statistics to find probabilities of experiments whose outcomes are, or approximate, normal distributions. In this section you will:
- learn the properties of a normal distribution
- use a table to find probabilities associated with a normal distribution
- learn certain reference points, expressed as percents, of a normal distribution.

The SAT examination that many high school students take is an example of a standardized test. Suppose that in a certain city the mean SAT score is 500 and the standard deviation is 100. Then a score of 400 is 100 points, or one standard deviation, lower than the mean score. A score of 750 is $\frac{250}{100}$, or 2.5, standard deviations higher than the mean score.

SAT scores approximate a *normal distribution*. The graph of a normal distribution, shown below, is sometimes called a "bell curve" because of its shape.

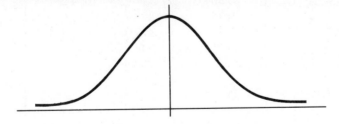

All normal distributions share certain common properties.

1. The total area under the curve and above the x-axis is 1.
2. The curve is bell-shaped.
3. The curve is symmetric about a vertical line through $\overline{x}$, the mean of the distribution.

4. The probability that a value of x will fall in the interval $a \leqslant x \leqslant b$ is equal to the area bounded by the curve, the x-axis, and the vertical lines $x = a$ and $x = b$. This probability is indicated as $P(a \leqslant x \leqslant b)$.

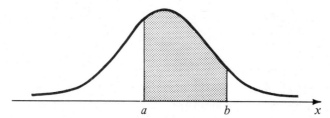

For all practical purposes, a normal distribution is defined by the graph and a table of values. Normal distributions are closely approximated by many experiments and observations, particularly those involving measurements of characteristics of large groups of individuals. In addition to test data, this includes such physical measurements as height and weight.

We now turn our attention to the use of the table in determining probabilities for normal distributions. Values in the table are expressed in terms of standard deviations from the mean. The table gives the probability that a given value of x will fall in the interval $0 \leqslant x \leqslant a$. This is the probability that x is between the mean and a value that is a standard deviations greater than the mean.

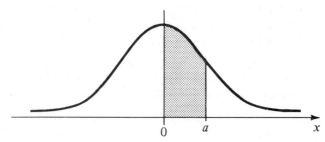

a	$P(0 \leqslant x \leqslant a)$	a	$P(0 \leqslant x \leqslant a)$	a	$P(0 \leqslant x \leqslant a)$
0.1	0.040	1.1	0.364	2.1	0.482
0.2	0.079	1.2	0.385	2.2	0.486
0.3	0.118	1.3	0.403	2.3	0.489
0.4	0.155	1.4	0.419	2.4	0.492
0.5	0.192	1.5	0.433	2.5	0.494
0.6	0.226	1.6	0.445	2.6	0.495
0.7	0.258	1.7	0.455	2.7	0.496
0.8	0.288	1.8	0.464	2.8	0.497
0.9	0.316	1.9	0.471	2.9	0.498
1.0	0.341	2.0	0.477	3.0	0.499

EXAMPLE   Use the table to find the probability.
  a. $P(0 \leqslant x \leqslant 1)$ b. $P(-1 \leqslant x \leqslant 0)$ c. $P(0 \leqslant x \leqslant 2)$
  d. $P(-2 \leqslant x \leqslant 0)$ e. $P(0 \leqslant x \leqslant 3)$ f. $P(-3 \leqslant x \leqslant 0)$

SOLUTION **a.** Find 1.0 in the a column. $P(0 \leqslant x \leqslant 1) = 0.341$.

b. Since the curve is symmetric, $P(-1 \leqslant x \leqslant 0) = P(0 \leqslant x \leqslant 1) = 0.341$.

c. $P(0 \leqslant x \leqslant 2) = 0.477$.

d. Use symmetry. $P(-2 \leqslant x \leqslant 0) = P(0 \leqslant x \leqslant 2) = 0.477$.

e. $P(0 \leqslant x \leqslant 3) = 0.499$.

f. $P(-3 \leqslant x \leqslant 0) = P(0 \leqslant x \leqslant 3) = 0.499$.

The results from the preceding example can be combined:

$$P(-1 \leqslant x \leqslant 1) = 0.682 \qquad P(-2 \leqslant x \leqslant 2) = 0.954$$
$$P(-3 \leqslant x \leqslant 3) = 0.998$$

This provides us with convenient reference points. For a normal distribution:

About 68% of the values lie within one standard deviation $(1s)$ of the mean.

About 95% of the values lie within $2s$ of the mean.

More than 99% of the values lie within $3s$ of the mean.

EXAMPLE Find the probability.

a. $P(x \geqslant 0)$	**b.** $P(x \geqslant 2)$
c. $P(x \leqslant 2.3)$	**d.** $P(x \leqslant -0.5)$
e. $P(0.4 \leqslant x \leqslant 1.3)$	**f.** $P(-0.5 \leqslant x \leqslant 1.5)$

SOLUTION **a.** By symmetry, $P(x \geqslant 0) = P(x \leqslant 0)$

Also, $P(x \geqslant 0) + P(x \leqslant 0) = 1$

Thus, $P(x \geqslant 0) = P(x \leqslant 0) = 0.500$

b. $P(x \geqslant 2) = P(x \geqslant 0) - P(0 \leqslant x \leqslant 2)$
$$= 0.500 - 0.477 = 0.023$$

c. $P(x \leqslant 2.3) = P(x \leqslant 0) + P(0 \leqslant x \leqslant 2.3)$
$$= 0.500 + 0.489 = 0.989$$

d. $P(x \leqslant -0.5) = P(x \geqslant 0.5)$
$$= P(x \geqslant 0) - P(0 \leqslant x \leqslant 0.5)$$
$$= 0.500 - 0.192 = 0.308$$

e. $P(0.4 \leqslant x \leqslant 1.3) = P(0 \leqslant x \leqslant 1.3) - P(0 \leqslant x \leqslant 0.4)$
$$= 0.403 - 0.155 = 0.248$$

f. $P(-0.5 \leqslant x \leqslant 1.5) = P(-0.5 \leqslant x \leqslant 0) + P(0 \leqslant x \leqslant 1.5)$
$$= P(0 \leqslant x \leqslant 0.5) + P(0 \leqslant x \leqslant 1.5)$$
$$= 0.192 + 0.433 = 0.625$$

We are now prepared to interpret data resulting from a normal distribution. Recall the SAT scores mentioned earlier, for which the mean $= 500$ and $s = 100$. We can state the following conclusions without reference to the table.

1. About 34% of those taking the exam scored between 500 and 600. This corresponds to $P(0 \leqslant x \leqslant 1)$, since 600 is $1s$ greater than the mean.

2. A score of 710 is above the 95th percentile. 710 is $2.1s$ higher than the mean. We know that about 95% of the scores lie within $2s$ of the mean.

3. Less than 20% of those taking the exam are expected to score 620 or higher.

We know that about 50% will score lower than 500, and about 34% will score between 500 and 600. This certainly leaves less than 20% of the scores above 600. To be more precise, we know that:

$$620 = 500 + 1.2(100) = 500 + 1.2s$$

This means that a score of 620 is $1.2s$ higher than the mean. Since

$$P(x \leqslant 0) = 0.500 \quad \text{and} \quad P(0 \leqslant x \leqslant 1.2) = 0.385,$$

we find that

$$P(x \leqslant 1.2) = 0.500 + 0.385 = 0.885.$$

If $P(x \leqslant 1.2) = 0.885$, then $P(x \geqslant 1.2) = 1 - 0.885 = 0.115$. Since we know that $P(x \geqslant 1.2) = 0.115$ or 11.5%, we conclude that 11.5% of those who take the exam are expected to score 620 or higher.

ORAL EXERCISES

Find the probability. Use the table on page 544 and symmetry, assuming a normal distribution.

1. $P(0 \leqslant x \leqslant 0.3)$
2. $P(0 \leqslant x \leqslant 1.4)$
3. $P(x \leqslant 0.3)$
4. $P(x \leqslant 1.4)$
5. $P(-0.3 \leqslant x \leqslant 0)$
6. $P(-1.4 \leqslant x \leqslant 0)$
7. $P(x \geqslant 0.3)$
8. $P(x \geqslant 1.4)$
9. $P(x \leqslant -0.3)$
10. $P(x \leqslant -1.4)$
11. $P(-0.3 \leqslant x \leqslant 0.3)$
12. $P(-1.4 \leqslant x \leqslant 1.4)$
13. $P(-0.3 \leqslant x \leqslant 1.4)$
14. $P(-1.4 \leqslant x \leqslant 0.3)$
15. $P(0.3 \leqslant x \leqslant 1.4)$
16. $P(-1.4 \leqslant x \leqslant -0.3)$

WRITTEN EXERCISES

Find the probability. Use the table on page 544, assuming a normal distribution.

A 1. $P(-1 \leqslant x \leqslant 2)$
2. $P(-2 \leqslant x \leqslant 3)$
3. $P(1.1 \leqslant x \leqslant 2.2)$
4. $P(0.8 \leqslant x \leqslant 2.8)$
5. $P(-0.6 \leqslant x \leqslant 1.4)$
6. $P(x \leqslant 1.8)$
7. $P(x \geqslant 0.9)$
8. $P(x \geqslant -0.7)$
9. $P(-1.3 \leqslant x \leqslant -0.7)$
10. $P(|x| \geqslant 0.4)$

The ages of first-year university students in a certain state approximate a normal distribution, with mean 19 and standard deviation 1. About what percent of the students are

11. not over 19?
12. 21 or older?
13. between 18 and 20, inclusive?
14. between 17 and 21, inclusive?

The lengths of the leaves of a certain variety of tree approximate a normal distribution, with mean length 12 cm and standard deviation 3 cm. If a leaf is chosen at random, what is the probability that the length is

15. not less than 15 cm?   **16.** not more than 18 cm?

17. at least 9 cm?   **18.** at most 6 cm?

The scores on a test approximate a normal distribution with a mean of 130 and a standard deviation of 20.

19. What is the probability that a person chosen at random from those who took the test has a score of 140 or more?

20. What percent of those who took the test had a score of 100 or less?

21. Does a score of 150 rank above the 80th percentile? the 90th percentile? Answer without using the table.

22. Does a score of 170 rank above the 95th percentile? (Do not use the table.)

B **23.** If the top 10% of the scores were assigned a grade of A, what score (to the nearest integer) was needed to get an A?

The number of defective items per day in an industrial process approximates a normal distribution, with mean 8.4 and standard deviation 1.5. On what percent of the days should we expect

24. 9 defects or less?   **25.** 6 or fewer defects?   **26.** between 9 and 12 defects, inclusive?

Gas consumption for new cars of a certain model approximates a normal distribution, with a mean of 14.50 km/L and a standard deviation of 1.25 km/L. What is the probability that a car chosen at random will get

27. between 13.25 and 15.75 km/L, inclusive?

28. between 12.00 and 17.00 km/L, inclusive?

29. between 14.0 and 15.0 km/L, inclusive?

30. 12.25 km/L or less?   **31.** 15.50 km/L or more?

32. A car gets 16.00 km/L. Does this rank above the 90th percentile?

33. A car gets 14.25 km/L. Does this rank above the 40th percentile?

Use the table on page 544, assuming a normal distribution. Solve for a.

34. $P(0 \leqslant x \leqslant a) = 0.364$ **35.** $P(x \leqslant a) = 0.816$

C **36.** $P(-1.0 \leqslant x \leqslant a) = 0.567$ **37.** $P(a \leqslant x \leqslant 1.5) = 0.241$

38. $P(|x| \leqslant a) = 0.806$ **39.** $P(|x| \geqslant a) = 0.090$

40. The average (mean) life of a certain motor is 5 years with a standard deviation of 2 years. Suppose the length of time the motor lasts is normally distributed. If a guaranteed motor is replaced when it fails, about how many months should the guarantee period be if the company wants to replace no more than 10% of the motors?

SELF-TEST 2

1. The scores on a test were:

Section 13-4

73 84 77 91 62 85 94 75 79 86
68 56 73 76 92 71 82 73 76 88

Find the median and mode of the scores.

The heights, in centimeters, of five people chosen at random were 175, 181, 172, 176, and 171.

2. Find the mean absolute deviation.

Section 13-5

3. Find the standard deviation.

The times required for a task approximate a normal distribution with a mean of 80.00 s and a standard deviation of 10.00 s. A person is chosen at random from those who performed the task.

4. What is the probability that the person had a time of 88.00 s or less?

Section 13-6

5. What is the probability that the person had a time between 70.00 s and 90.00 s, inclusive?

Computer Exercises

Polls are often conducted to predict the outcome of an election. Since a pollster can afford to ask only a small sample of voters which candidate they prefer, the conclusion of the poll may not be accurate. It is possible that a majority of the voters actually intend to vote for candidate A, but a majority of the people sampled in the poll may prefer candidate B. This can happen even in the most carefully designed polls, where the sample chosen is completely random.

A computer can simulate the polling process, using random numbers generated in BASIC. Suppose that in an election there are two candidates, and it is known that 55% of the voters will vote for candidate A. Clearly, candidate A will win the election. However, depending on the sample chosen, a poll might erroneously predict that B will win.

In the program that follows, a random number is chosen for each person in the sample used for the poll. Preferences for candidates have been assigned so that, for any given person in the sample, the probability is 55% that candidate A is preferred. (See lines 150–190 of the program.)

The purpose of the exercises is to investigate the possibility that a poll may give results that are not consistent with the preferences of the group from which the sample of the poll is taken.

548   *CHAPTER 13*

```
10     POKE 203, PEEK(78): POKE 204, PEEK(79)
20     REM***ON APPLE II, THIS GIVES A DIFFERENT SEQUENCE OF RAN-
       DOM NUMBERS EACH TIME THE COMPUTER IS TURNED ON. FOR
       OTHER MACHINES, CONSULT THE MANUAL.
30     PRINT "TYPE NUMBER IN SAMPLE:";
40     INPUT S
50     PRINT "TYPE NUMBER OF TIMES TO TAKE POLL:";
60     INPUT T
70     LET W = 0
80     REM***W = NUMBER OF TIMES A WON POLL
90     FOR J = 1 TO T
100    REM***SELECT T SAMPLES WITH S PEOPLE IN EACH
110    LET A = 0
120    REM***A = NUMBER IN CURRENT SAMPLE WHO PREFER CANDI-
       DATE A
130    FOR K = 1 TO S
140    REM***GO THROUGH S VOTERS
150    LET X = RND(1)
160    REM***THIS MAKES X A RANDOM NUMBER BETWEEN 0 AND 1 ON
       APPLE II. FOR THE TRS-80, CHANGE IT TO RND(0). FOR OTHER
       MACHINES, CONSULT YOUR MANUAL.
170    IF X > .55 THEN 200
180    LET A = A + 1
190    REM***VOTER PREFERS A IF RANDOM NUMBER IS LESS THAN .55,
       WHICH HAPPENS 55% OF THE TIME ON THE AVERAGE.
200    NEXT K
210    IF A < = S/2 THEN 240
220    LET W = W + 1
230    REM***IF MORE THAN HALF OF THE SAMPLE PREFERRED A, THEN
       A WINS THE POLL
240    NEXT J
250    PRINT
260    PRINT "A WON THE POLL   ";W;"   TIMES"
270    PRINT "OUT OF   ";T;"   TRIALS."
280    END
```

1. Type in and RUN the program. Take the poll 100 times, with 10 people in each sample.

   a. What percent of the time did the poll accurately reflect the voters' preference for candidate A?

   b. What percent of the time did the poll indicate that candidate A would not win the election?

   c. What is the probability, based on the results above, that a poll using a random sample of 10 people will not correctly predict the outcome of the election?

2. RUN the program again. Take the poll 10 times, with 1000 people in each sample. (This may take the computer several minutes.)
   a. What percent of the time did the poll accurately reflect the voter's preference for candidate A?
   b. How does a larger sample seem to affect the accuracy of the poll?

3. Suppose only 35% of the voters prefer candidate A. Change line 170 of the program and RUN it. Take the poll 100 times, with 10 people in each sample.
   a. What percent of the time did the poll indicate that candidate A would win the election?
   b. What is the probability, based on these results, that a poll using a random sample of 10 people will not correctly predict the outcome of the election?

4. RUN the program, as revised in Exercise 3, again. Take the poll 10 times, with 1000 people in each sample.
   a. What percent of the time did the poll indicate that candidate A would win the election?
   b. Refer to Exercise 3. Does increasing the size of the sample increase the accuracy of the poll?

CHAPTER REVIEW

Of the apples rated in a test of appearance and taste, 185 were rated excellent, 236 good, and 79 fair. What is the probability that an apple chosen at random is

1. excellent? 2. not excellent? Section 13-1

Evaluate.

3. $\displaystyle\sum_{i=2}^{7} 3i$ 4. $\displaystyle\sum_{i=1}^{6} (2i + 5)$ 5. $\displaystyle\sum_{i=1}^{5} (1 + i^2)$ Section 13-2

6. Find the mean of these weekly earnings:

$188.30, $241.80, $322.20, $211.50

7. The number of people per car was recorded at a toll booth during a certain time period. Find the mean number of people per car. Section 13-3

Number of people	1	2	3	4	5	6
Frequency	35	38	24	27	13	4

8. Use the frequency table to find an approximate value of the mean age of all students in Washington County.

Age	5-9	10-14	15-19	20-24
Frequency	391	658	516	327

The frequency table lists the number of projects having the given number of employees in a certain department.

Employees	3	4	5	6	7	8
Frequency	3	7	12	10	8	5

For the number of employees per project, find the:

9. median
10. mode
11. mean   Section 13-4

The ages of the heads of five leading companies are 48, 54, 39, 62, and 52. For these ages, find the:

12. range
13. mean absolute deviation   Section 13-5

14. variance
15. standard deviation

The fuel economy rates, in km/L, of a group of motorbikes approximate a normal distribution with mean 45.0 and standard deviation 4.0. What is the probability that a motorbike chosen at random has a fuel economy rate that is

16. between 41.0 and 49.0, inclusive?   Section 13-6

17. between 43.0 and 47.0, inclusive?

18. between 41.0 and 51.0, inclusive?

19. between 47.0 and 53.0, inclusive?

CHAPTER TEST

Evaluate.

1. $\sum_{i=3}^{8} 5i$
2. $\sum_{i=1}^{6} (2 - i^2)$
3. $\sum_{i=4}^{9} i(i + 3)$

4. Scores on a 10-point quiz were 8, 5, 7, 6, 7, 9, 8, 10, 6, 8, 5, 9, 7, 7, and 6. Find the mean, median, mode, and range of the scores.

5. A bird watcher recorded the number of days in April on which the given numbers of bird species were observed. Use the frequency table to find the mean and median of the number of species per day.

Number of species	6	7	8	9	10	11	12
Frequency	5	4	10	3	4	2	2

The scores on an exam approximate a normal distribution with mean 150 and standard deviation 30. If one of these scores is chosen at random, what is the probability that it is

6. 201 or less?
7. 132 or less?
8. between 90 and 210, inclusive?

9. Does a score of 175 rank above the 85th percentile?

10. The numbers of cyclists who completed a course in the given time intervals, in minutes, were recorded in a frequency table. Find an approximate value of the mean time.

Time	Frequency
16–20	7
21–25	21
26–30	29
31–35	13
36–40	10

The wingspans of a group of birds were measured to be 54 cm, 61 cm, 66 cm, 58 cm, and 56 cm. For these measurements, find the:

11. mean   12. mean absolute deviation

13. variance   14. standard deviation

A group of people were surveyed to find the number of days per week that each person exercises. The results are in the frequency table. Find the:

Days of exercise	0	1	2	3	4	5
Frequency	5	3	8	5	2	2

15. mean   16. variance

17. standard deviation

Careers — Marketing Researcher

Many industries have high entry barriers, which means that it costs a lot of money to get started in them. For example, if you wanted to sell your own brand of car, you would either have to build your own factory and hire workers for it, or you would have to buy a factory from someone else. Either option is very expensive and the first is also time-consuming. Considerations such as these make companies very careful when they are deciding whether or not to enter a market with a service or product. They use market researchers to test the waters first — in other words, to determine whether the service or product will generate enough profit to justify the expense. These researchers study company records, statistics, and personal opinion surveys. They also take into account the strength and number of competitors already in the industry in light of consumer demand for the product or service.

Marketing researchers are involved in many aspects of launching a new product. They may give advice on everything from choosing which geographical market to concentrate on to selecting the best name for the product. As computer analysis has made the gathering and evaluating of huge masses of consumer data easier, industries have begun doing market research on nearly every facet of a product's public image.

Companies also maintain a continuous flow of research on the markets in which they are already competing. Whenever a successful product or service begins to become less profitable, market researchers analyze the need it was fulfilling and why the need is no longer there. One of their primary duties is to examine what the competitors in the industry offer and how the company can best counter those offers or fill empty niches in the market.

Majors in economics or business administration are good preparation for this field. If you are interested in doing a particular type of market research, such as in engineering or advertising, then you should take courses in this applied field. Market research is good preparation for a number of other careers, including university teaching, statistics, and industrial research and development.

Be sure that you understand the meaning of these terms:

frequency, p. 518

sample, p. 519

mean, p. 519

summation notation, p. 523

frequency table, p. 527

histogram, p. 527

measure of central tendency, p. 533

median, p. 533

mode, p. 533

range, p. 538

mean absolute deviation, p. 539

variance, p. 539

standard deviation, p. 539

normal distribution, p. 543

MIXED REVIEW

1. How many different 11-letter arrangements can be formed from the word APPROPRIATE?

2. Find the number of triangles ABC such that **(a)** $c = 30$, $m\angle A = 120$, and $a = 25$, and **(b)** $c = 18$, $m\angle B = 41°20'$, and $b = 20$.

3. Use the table on page 544, assuming a normal distribution, to find $P(1.9 \leqslant x \leqslant 2.5)$.

4. If a chord 8 cm long is 6 cm from the center of a circle, find the diameter of the circle.

5. Draw a large $\triangle RST$. Then construct the image of $\triangle RST$ under reflection over $\overleftrightarrow{RS}$.

6. On one set of axes, sketch the graphs of $g(x) = \frac{1}{2}x^3$ and $g^{-1}(x)$.

7. If $\csc \theta = \dfrac{29}{20}$ and θ is in Quadrant I, find the values of the other five trigonometric functions.

8. A die is tossed six times. Find the probability of rolling exactly three 4's.

9. The Romeros' family car had the following weekly gasoline consumption averages: 10 km/L, 13 km/L, 13 km/L, and 12 km/L. Find the range, mean, median, mode, and variance for the data.

10. Find the area, to the nearest hundredth, of a triangle with sides of lengths 5, 6, and 9. Also, find the measure of the smallest angle to the nearest 10'.

11. Solve for x to three significant digits: **a.** $\log_x 126 = 2.5$ **b.** $x = (49.2)^{\frac{2}{3}}$

Evaluate.

12. $\displaystyle\sum_{i=1}^{200} 3i$

13. $\cos 157.5°$

14. $\tan\left[\text{Arcsin}\left(-\dfrac{\sqrt{3}}{2}\right)\right]$

Solve for $0 \leqslant \theta < 2\pi$.

15. $\csc^2 \theta = 2 \csc \theta$

16. $\cos 2\theta = \cos^2 \theta$

17. $\sin^2 \theta = 2 \sin \theta + 3$

18. $\overline{AE}$, $\overline{BF}$, $\overline{CG}$, and $\overline{DH}$ divide $\odot O$ into congruent sectors. Find the image of C under $R_{0,\,-135} \circ R_{0,\,315}$ and the image of 0 under translation T if $T:F \rightarrow O$.

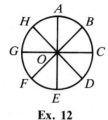

Ex. 12

Ex. 13

19. Find the values of x and y in the figure at the right above.

20. Use Angle-Sum and Angle-Difference Formulas to evaluate sec $105°$ and tan $\dfrac{13\pi}{12}$.

Solve.

21. $|m - 7| > 2$

22. $\dfrac{1}{d-2} - \dfrac{1}{d} = 2$

23. $\sqrt{5k - 1} = k - 3$

24. Show that $\dfrac{1}{2} - \dfrac{1}{2}i$ is a root of $2m^2 + 1 = 2m$.

25. Use Table 1 to find a four-digit approximation of sin $103°15'$.

26. Use the growth model to find the value after 6 yr of an investment of $200 at 10% annual interest. Give your answer to the nearest dollar.

27. In how many ways can three winning tickets be chosen randomly from among 1000 tickets?

28. Find the seventh term of $(3m - p)^{12}$.

29. If $O = (0, 0)$, $A = (5, 0)$, $B = (0, 3)$, and $\overrightarrow{OA} + \overrightarrow{OB} = \overrightarrow{OC}$, find $|\overrightarrow{OC}|$ to the nearest integer and the direction of $\overrightarrow{OC}$ (to the nearest degree) with respect to the positive x-axis.

30. A basketball player has point totals of 34, 21, 26, 35, 42, 18, and 23 for the last seven games. How many points must the player score in the next game to keep the average above 30?

31. Two cards are drawn from a standard deck. If A is the event that the first card is a heart and B is the event that the second card is red, find $P(B|A)$.

32. If $f(x) = 3x - 1$ and $g(x) = x^2 + 1$, find $f(g(2))$, $g(f(2))$, $f(g(x))$ and $g(f(x))$.

33. Prove: $\left(\sin \dfrac{1}{2}\theta + \cos \dfrac{1}{2}\theta \right)^2 = 1 + \sin \theta$

34. If SAT scores approximate a normal distribution with mean 500 and standard deviation 100, find the probability that a randomly chosen score is above 650.

Composite transformations are explored further in this chapter. One of the important results of the chapter is the Three-Line-Reflection Theorem, which states that
every isometry can be expressed as a composite of at most three line reflections.

Transformations and Geometry 14

The traditional high school course in geometry is developed from postulates much like those stated by Euclid in about 300 B.C. In Chapter 5 you were introduced to some geometric transformations, namely reflections, rotations, translations, and dilations. Now you will focus on the transformations that are related to two very important geometric concepts in Euclidean geometry, *congruence* and *similarity*.

In Euclidean geometry we examine the corresponding parts of figures such as triangles or quadrilaterals to determine whether the figures are congruent or similar. Can you use this method to determine whether the curves in Figure 1 are similar or whether the sets of points in Figure 2 are congruent?

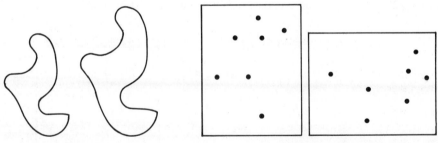

Figure 1   Figure 2

In this chapter you will study in more depth the properties preserved by various transformations and you will see how these properties can be applied to develop tests for congruence and similarity that will enable you to answer the questions posed about the figures above.

Section 14-1 MORE COMPOSITE TRANSFORMATIONS

In Chapter 5 you studied line reflections and the composite of two line reflections. In this section you will review these ideas and learn about:
- the composite of two translations
- the composite of two rotations with a common center
- the composite of two dilations with a common center

In general, if t_1 and t_2 are any two transformations such that $t_1\colon A \longrightarrow A'$ and $t_2\colon A' \longrightarrow A''$, then the composite transformation $t_2 \circ t_1$ maps A onto A''.

$$t_2 \circ t_1\colon A \longrightarrow A''$$
$$t_2 \circ t_1\,(A) = t_2\,(t_1\,(A))$$
$$= t_2\,(A')$$
$$= A''$$

As shown on the left below, if l and m are two parallel lines, then the composite reflection $r_m \circ r_l$ is a translation. If l and m intersect, as shown on the right below, $r_m \circ r_l$ is a rotation with center at the point of intersection. In either case, the composite of two line reflections is *not* a line reflection.

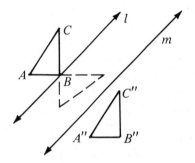 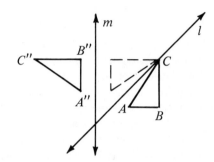

Now consider the composite of two translations. You learned in Section 5-6 that the translation that moves each point a units horizontally and b units vertically is denoted $T_{a,b}$.

$$T_{a,b}\colon (x, y) \longrightarrow (x + a, y + b)$$

EXAMPLE   Find the image of the triangle with vertices $A(3, -1)$, $B(3, 3)$, and $C(1, 0)$ under $T_{3,1} \circ T_{2,3}$.

SOLUTION $T_{3,1} \circ T_{2,3}\,(3, -1) = T_{3,1}\,(5, 2)$
$$= (8, 3)$$
$T_{3,1} \circ T_{2,3}\,(3, 3) = T_{3,1}\,(5, 6)$
$$= (8, 7)$$
$T_{3,1} \circ T_{2,3}\,(1, 0) = T_{3,1}\,(3, 3)$
$$= (6, 4)$$

Thus $T_{3,1} \circ T_{2,3}$ slides $\triangle ABC$ 5 units to the right and 4 units up.

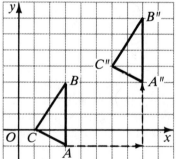

As the preceding example suggests, the composite of two translations is a translation. The following theorem, whose proof is left as Exercise 37, provides a simple formula for determining the coordinates of the image of a point under a composite of two translations.

Theorem 14-1   If $T_{a,\,b}$ and $T_{c,\,d}$ are two translations, then for each point (x, y) in the plane:

$$T_{a,\,b} \circ T_{c,\,d}\,(x, y) = T_{a+c,\,b+d}\,(x, y)$$

EXAMPLE   Use Theorem 14-1 to find the image of the point $(4, 3)$ under the translation $T_{-2,\,-7} \circ T_{1,\,4}$.

SOLUTION $T_{-2,\,-7} \circ T_{1,\,4}\,(4, 3) = T_{-1,\,-3}\,(4, 3)$
$= (3, 0)$

Since a rotation through $30°$ produces the same image as a rotation through $390°$ or through $-330°$, we will consider these rotations equivalent. In general, a rotation through $x°$ is equivalent to a rotation through $(x + 360n)°$, where $n \in Z$. As the next example suggests, the composite of two rotations with a common center is a rotation.

EXAMPLE   Under $R_{180} \circ R_{90}$ find the image of:
   a. $A(3, 0)$ b. $B(2, 4)$

SOLUTION   a. $R_{180} \circ R_{90}\,(3, 0) = R_{180}\,(0, 3)$ b. $R_{180} \circ R_{90}\,(2, 4) = R_{180}\,(-4, 2)$
$= (0, -3)$ $= (4, -2)$

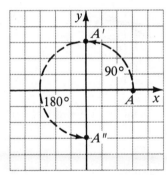
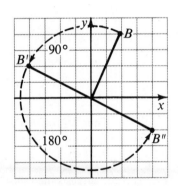

Thus $R_{180} \circ R_{90}$ rotates each point $270°$.

The preceding example suggests the following theorem.

Theorem 14-2   If $R_{P,\,\alpha}$ and $R_{P,\,\beta}$ are two rotations with a common center P, then for each point (x, y) in the plane:

$$R_{P,\,\alpha} \circ R_{P,\,\beta}\,(x, y) = R_{P,\,\alpha+\beta}\,(x, y)$$

EXAMPLE   Use Theorem 14-2 to find the image of the point $A(2, 0)$ under the rotation $R_{-20} \circ R_{110}$.

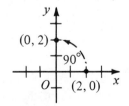

SOLUTION $R_{-20} \circ R_{110}\,(2, 0) = R_{90}\,(2, 0)$
$= (0, 2)$

Finally, we consider the composite of two dilations with a common center. Remember that if D_k is a dilation with center $(0, 0)$ and scale factor k, then $D_k(x, y) = (kx, ky)$.

The next example suggests that the composite of two dilations with a common center is a dilation with that center.

EXAMPLE Find the image of the triangle with vertices $A(2, 4)$, $B(-4, 1)$, and $C(3, 2)$ under $D_4 \circ D_{\frac{1}{2}}$.

SOLUTION $D_4 \circ D_{\frac{1}{2}} (2, 4) = D_4 (1, 2) = (4, 8)$

$D_4 \circ D_{\frac{1}{2}} (-4, 1) = D_4 \left(-2, \frac{1}{2}\right) = (-8, 2)$

$D_4 \circ D_{\frac{1}{2}} (3, 2) = D_4 \left(\frac{3}{2}, 1\right) = (6, 4)$

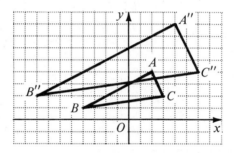

Thus $D_4 \circ D_{\frac{1}{2}}$ multiplies the x-coordinates and y-coordinates of points A, B, and C by 2.

This example suggests the following theorem.

Theorem 14-3 If D_{P, k_1} and D_{P, k_2} are two dilations, then for every point (x, y) in the plane:

$$D_{P, k_2} \circ D_{P, k_1} (x, y) = D_{P, k_2 k_1} (x, y)$$

In Exercise 38, you will prove that Theorem 14-3 is true when P is the origin.

EXAMPLE Use Theorem 14-3 to find the image of the point $(1, 2)$ under the dilation $D_{\frac{1}{3}} \circ D_6$.

SOLUTION $D_{\frac{1}{3}} \circ D_6 (1, 2) = D_2 (1, 2)$
$= (2, 4)$

Note that all the results we have shown to be true for rotations and dilations whose centers are at the origin are equally valid for rotations and dilations that have common centers not at the origin.

ORAL EXERCISES

Name a single transformation equivalent to the given composite.

1. $T_{1,\,4} \circ T_{0,\,0}$ 2. $T_{3,\,4} \circ T_{-3,\,-4}$ 3. $T_{1,\,2} \circ T_{4,\,-3}$ 4. $T_{0,\,-3} \circ T_{-3,\,1}$

5. $R_{360} \circ R_{45}$ 6. $R_{270} \circ R_{90}$ 7. $R_{120} \circ R_{180}$ 8. $R_{-300} \circ R_{45}$

9. $D_1 \circ D_3$ 10. $D_3 \circ D_{\frac{1}{3}}$ 11. $D_4 \circ D_2$ 12. $D_{\frac{1}{4}} \circ D_{\frac{1}{2}}$

13. What do the following transformations have in common: $T_{0,\,0}$, R_0, D_1?

14. Which of the following composites of transformations are the same as the identity mapping?

a. $D_{\frac{1}{3}} \circ D_3$ b. $T_{2,\,3} \circ T_{\frac{1}{2},\,\frac{1}{3}}$ c. $T_{2,\,3} \circ T_{0,\,0}$

d. $T_{1,\,3} \circ T_{-1,\,-3}$ e. $R_{-10} \circ R_{10}$ f. $D_{\frac{3}{4}} \circ D_{\frac{1}{4}}$

g. $R_{-100} \circ R_{-260}$ h. $R_{-10} \circ R_{-270}$ i. $D_{\frac{1}{2}} \circ D_{\frac{1}{2}}$

15. The inverse of the translation T is the translation T^{-1} such that $T \circ T^{-1} = I$, where $I = T_{0,\,0}$. State a rule for the inverse of $T_{a,\,b}$.

16. The inverse of the dilation D is the dilation D^{-1} such that $D \circ D^{-1} = I$, where $I = D_1$. State a rule for the inverse of D_k.

17. Name the inverse of R_θ, where $0° \leqslant \theta < 360°$, as R_α, where:
a. $0° \leqslant \alpha < 360°$ b. $-360° \leqslant \alpha < 0°$

WRITTEN EXERCISES

Graph the image of the triangle with vertices $A(1, 2)$, $B(3, 3)$, and $C(-2, 4)$ under the following composites.

A   1. $T_{3,\,2} \circ T_{1,\,0}$ 2. $T_{-2,\,4} \circ T_{6,\,-1}$ 3. $R_{60} \circ R_{120}$ 4. $R_{-45} \circ R_{135}$ 5. $D_1 \circ D_3$

6. $D_2 \circ D_{\frac{1}{4}}$ 7. $D_{A,\,6} \circ D_{A,\,\frac{1}{3}}$ 8. $D_{C,\,3} \circ D_{C,\,\frac{2}{3}}$ 9. $R_{A,\,225} \circ R_{A,\,-45}$ 10. $R_{B,\,70} \circ R_{B,\,20}$

Find the coordinates of the image of the point under the composite.

EXAMPLE $R_{60} \circ R_{75}\ (1, 0)$

SOLUTION $R_{60} \circ R_{75}\ (1, 0) = R_{135}\ (1, 0)$
$R_{135}\ (1, 0)$ lies on the unit circle. From the definition of sine and cosine we can conclude that:

$R_{135}\ (1, 0) = (\cos 135°,\ \sin 135°)$

$\qquad\qquad\quad = \left(-\dfrac{\sqrt{2}}{2},\ \dfrac{\sqrt{2}}{2}\right)$

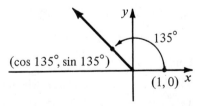

11. $R_{90} \circ R_{30}\ (0, 1)$ 12. $R_{60} \circ R_{90}\ (0, -1)$ 13. $R_{60} \circ R_{60}\ (-1, 0)$

14. $R_{-150} \circ R_{60}\ (0, 1)$ 15. $R_{270} \circ R_{45}\ (1, 0)$ 16. $R_{-30} \circ R_{-330}\ (2, 2)$

In Exercise 39, page 458, you showed that:
$$R_\theta(x, y) = (x \cos \theta - y \sin \theta, x \sin \theta + y \cos \theta)$$
Use this formula to find the coordinates of the image of the point under the given composite of rotations.

EXAMPLE $R_{50} \circ R_{70} (\sqrt{3}, 1)$

SOLUTION $R_{50} \circ R_{70} (\sqrt{3}, 1) = R_{120} (\sqrt{3}, 1)$

$$= (\sqrt{3} \cos 120° - \sin 120°, \sqrt{3} \sin 120° + \cos 120°)$$

$$= \left(\sqrt{3} \left(-\frac{1}{2}\right) - \frac{\sqrt{3}}{2}, \sqrt{3} \left(\frac{\sqrt{3}}{2}\right) + \left(-\frac{1}{2}\right)\right)$$

$$= \left(-\frac{2\sqrt{3}}{2}, \frac{3}{2} - \frac{1}{2}\right)$$

$$= (-\sqrt{3}, 1)$$

B 17. $R_{90} \circ R_{-30} \left(\frac{1}{2}, -\frac{\sqrt{3}}{2}\right)$ **18.** $R_{60} \circ R_{-90} (1, 1)$ **19.** $R_{100} \circ R_{35} (-\sqrt{2}, \sqrt{2})$

20. $R_{45} \circ R_{90} (2, 4)$ **21.** $R_{80} \circ R_{130} (\sqrt{3}, 4)$ **22.** $R_{200} \circ R_{25} (4, 1)$

Find the value of k.

23. $D_2 \circ D_k (-2, 4) = (-3, 6)$ **24.** $D_k \circ D_3 (1, -2) = (1, -2)$

Find the values of x and y.

EXAMPLE $T_{1, 4} \circ T_{-2, 3} (x, y) = (6, 4)$

SOLUTION $T_{1, 4} \circ T_{-2, 3} (x, y) = T_{-1, 7} (x, y) = (x - 1, y + 7)$
$(x - 1, y + 7) = (6, 4)$

Therefore: $x - 1 = 6$ and $y + 7 = 4$
$x = 7$ and $y = -3$

Check: $T_{1, 4} \circ T_{-2, 3} (7, -3) = T_{-1, 7} (7, -3) = (6, 4)$

25. $T_{2, -3} \circ T_{-5, 7} (x, y) = (1, -4)$ **26.** $T_{-1, -3} \circ T_{-3, 4} (x, y) = (0, -3)$

27. $D_6 \circ D_{\frac{1}{2}} (x, y) = (-6, -3)$ **28.** $D_{\frac{1}{2}} \circ D_4 (x, y) = (-4, 1)$

29. $R_{45} \circ R_{225} (x, y) = (3, -2)$ **30.** $R_{150} \circ R_{-60} (x, y) = (2, -1)$

31. $r_{x\text{-axis}} \circ r_{y\text{-axis}} (x, y) = (3, -4)$ **32.** $r_{x\text{-axis}} \circ r_{x\text{-axis}} (x, y) = (-1, 5)$

Find a rule for each isometry t.

33. $T_{-2, 4} \circ t(5, 2) = (5, 2)$, where t is a translation

34. $t \circ T_{1, -3} (0, -1) = (-2, 1)$, where t is a translation

35. $R_{120} \circ t(1, 5) = (1, 5)$, where t is a rotation with center $(0, 0)$

36. $R_{180} \circ t(-3, 4) = (4, 3)$, where t is a rotation with center $(0, 0)$

37. Prove Theorem 14-1.

Given: $T_{a,\,b}$ and $T_{c,\,d}$ are two translations.

Prove: $T_{a,\,b} \circ T_{c,\,d}\,(x,\,y) = T_{a+c,\,b+d}\,(x,\,y)$.

Hint: Use the definition of a composite transformation, $T_2 \circ T_1\,(A) = T_2\,(T_1\,(A))$.

38. Prove Theorem 14-3 for $P = (0,\,0)$.

Given: D_{k_1} and D_{k_2} are two dilations.

Prove: $D_{k_1} \circ D_{k_2}\,(x,\,y) = D_{k_1 k_2}\,(x,\,y)$.

(See the hint for Exercise 37.)

39. Graph the image of the triangle with vertices $A(3,\,1)$, $B(7,\,1)$, and $C(7,\,4)$ under the following composites.

a. $T_{2,\,-2} \circ r_k$ where k is the line with the equation $y = x$

b. $T_{4,\,-2} \circ R_{90}$

c. $R_{180} \circ R_{P,\,180}$ where P has coordinates $(3,\,0)$

d. $T_{-5,\,0} \circ r_{x\text{-axis}}$

e. Which of the composites above is a translation? a reflection? a rotation?

Section 14-2 GLIDE REFLECTIONS

In Section 14-1 you learned that the composite of two translations is a translation and the composite of two rotations is a rotation. In Exercise 39 of that section, you discovered that the composite of two isometries of different types may be a reflection, a rotation, a translation, or an isometry different from any of these. In this section you will investigate this new kind of isometry, called a *glide reflection*, which is the composite of a translation and a reflection that are related in a special way. You will learn how to:

• find the image of a figure under a glide reflection

• determine the reflecting line of a glide reflection G given two points and their images under G

Successive footprints are a familiar example of a glide reflection. If you reflect the left footprint over the dashed line and then "glide" the image in a direction parallel to the line, you will obtain the right footprint. A translation is sometimes called a *glide*, and this composite is called a *glide reflection*.

A *glide reflection* G is the composite of a line reflection r_l followed by a translation T (that is not the identity transformation) in a direction parallel to l.

$$G = T \circ r_l$$

In Chapter 5, you learned that composition of isometries is not commutative in general. However, in this case the composite transformation formed by r_l and T is the same regardless of the order in which the composition is performed. (See Exercise 22.) Thus we can extend the definition of a glide reflection G to:

$$G = T \circ r_l = r_l \circ T$$

Since a translation is a composite of two line reflections in which the lines of reflection are both perpendicular to the direction of the translation, it follows that a glide reflection can be written as a composite of three line reflections, where two lines of reflection are both perpendicular to the third line of reflection.

EXAMPLE   Let r_b be the reflection over the line with equation $x = 6$. Find the image of the triangle with vertices $A(-1, 1)$, $B(-2, 3)$, and $C(-5, 1)$ under $r_{x\text{-axis}} \circ r_b \circ r_{y\text{-axis}}$.

SOLUTION

$$
\begin{aligned}
r_{x\text{-axis}} \circ r_b \circ r_{y\text{-axis}} \, (-1, 1) &= r_{x\text{-axis}} \circ r_b \, (1, 1) \\
&= r_{x\text{-axis}} \, (11, 1) \\
&= (11, -1)
\end{aligned}
$$

$$
\begin{aligned}
r_{x\text{-axis}} \circ r_b \circ r_{y\text{-axis}} \, (-2, 3) &= r_{x\text{-axis}} \circ r_b \, (2, 3) \\
&= r_{x\text{-axis}} \, (10, 3) \\
&= (10, -3)
\end{aligned}
$$

$$
\begin{aligned}
r_{x\text{-axis}} \circ r_b \circ r_{y\text{-axis}} \, (-5, 1) &= r_{x\text{-axis}} \circ r_b \, (5, 1) \\
&= r_{x\text{-axis}} \, (7, 1) \\
&= (7, -1)
\end{aligned}
$$

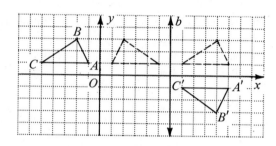

Since a glide reflection is a composite of three reflections, it is a nondirect isometry (Theorem 5-2), and thus reverses orientation of triangles. Glide reflections preserve distance, betweenness, angle measure, collinearity, perpendicularity, and parallelism.

In a glide reflection, the line of reflection has an interesting property, stated in the following theorem.

Theorem 14-4   If $G = T \circ r_l$ is a glide reflection and $G(A) = A''$, then l contains the midpoint of $\overline{AA''}$.

Proof: In the figure, $r_l(A) = A'$ and $T(A') = A''$. By the definition of a line reflection, l is the perpendicular bisector of $\overline{AA'}$ and thus contains the midpoint of $\overline{AA'}$. By the definition of a glide reflection, $\overline{A'A''} \parallel l$. In Book 2 you learned that the line that contains the midpoint of one side of a triangle and is parallel to another side bisects the remaining side. Thus l bisects $\overline{AA''}$.

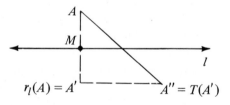

You can use Theorem 14-4 to find the reflecting line for a glide reflection, as demonstrated in the following example.

EXAMPLE   A glide reflection maps $\triangle ABC$ onto $\triangle A''B''C''$. Construct the reflecting line.

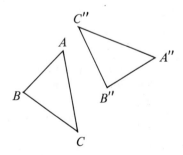

SOLUTION Theorem 14-4 states that the reflecting line contains the midpoints of $\overline{AA''}$, $\overline{BB''}$, and $\overline{CC''}$. You can connect two vertices of $\triangle ABC$ with their images and then locate the midpoints of the segments formed. The line joining these midpoints is the reflecting line.

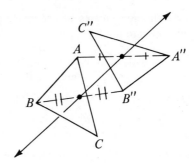

ORAL EXERCISES

In each exercise, a figure and its image under a transformation are shown. Can the transformation be a glide reflection? If not, explain why not.

1.

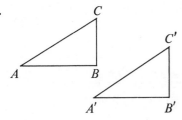

2.

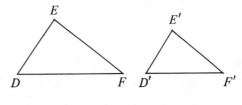

3.

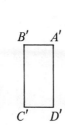

4.

5.

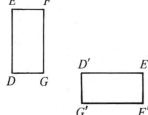

6.

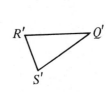

7. Is a reflection a glide reflection? Explain.

State the coordinates of the image of the given point under the given glide reflection.

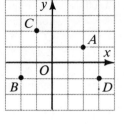

8. $A; T_{0,1} \circ r_{y\text{-axis}}$ 9. $B; r_{x\text{-axis}} \circ T_{3,0}$

10. $D; T_{0,4} \circ r_m$, where m is the line with equation $x = 2$.

11. $C; T_{1,1} \circ r_k$, where k is the line with equation $y = x$

12. $B; r_n \circ T_{-1,1}$, where n is the line with equation $y = -x$

13. $r_l \circ T_{0,1}$ is a glide reflection that maps A onto B. State an equation of line l.

14. $T_{2,0} \circ r_p$ is a glide reflection that maps B onto C. State an equation of line p.

15. $r_q \circ T_{0,3}$ is a glide reflection that maps C onto A. State an equation of line q.

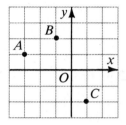

16. $T_{1,1} \circ r_m$ is a glide reflection that maps C onto B. State an equation of line m.

WRITTEN EXERCISES

Let k and n be the lines with equations $y = x$ and $y = -x$, respectively. Find the image of the triangle with vertices $A(-4, 5)$, $B(-2, 2)$, and $C(-6, 0)$ under the given glide reflection.

A 1. $T_{0,6} \circ r_{y\text{-axis}}$ 2. $T_{5,0} \circ r_{x\text{-axis}}$ 3. $r_{x\text{-axis}} \circ T_{3,0}$ 4. $r_{y\text{-axis}} \circ T_{0,-5}$

   5. $T_{1,1} \circ r_k$ 6. $T_{-1,1} \circ r_n$ 7. $r_n \circ T_{7,-7}$ 8. $r_k \circ T_{2,2}$

In Exercises 9 and 10, copy the diagram that shows $\triangle ABC$ and its image, $\triangle A''B''C''$, under a glide reflection, $T \circ r_m$.

a. Construct the reflecting line, m.   **b.** Construct $\triangle A'B'C'$, the image of $\triangle ABC$ under r_m.

9.   10.

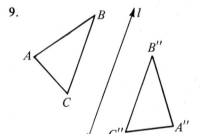   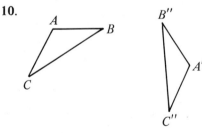

Copy the figure at the right. Sketch the image of $\triangle ABC$ under each composite.

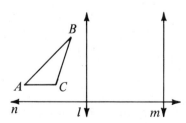

11. $r_m \circ r_n \circ r_l$ 12. $r_n \circ r_m \circ r_l$

13. $r_l \circ r_m \circ r_n$ 14. $r_l \circ r_n \circ r_m$

B **15.** $\triangle ABC$ has vertices $A(2, 1)$, $B(6, 2)$, and $C(7, 5)$. Find the coordinates of the vertices of:

    a. $\triangle A'B'C'$, the image of $\triangle ABC$ under $r_{y\text{-axis}}$.

    b. $\triangle A''B''C''$, the image of $\triangle A'B'C'$ under r_b, the reflection over the line with equation $x = -2$.

    c. $\triangle A'''B'''C'''$, the image of $\triangle A''B''C''$ under $r_{x\text{-axis}}$.

    d. Show that the composite $r_{x\text{-axis}} \circ r_b \circ r_{y\text{-axis}}$ is a glide reflection by finding a translation and a line reflection that form an equivalent composite.

In Exercises 16–19, a glide reflection $G = T_{a,\,b} \circ r_l$ maps $\overline{AB}$ onto $\overline{A''B''}$.

a. Find an equation of l, the line of reflection.

b. Sketch $\overline{A'B'}$, the reflection of $\overline{AB}$ over line l, and find the translation that maps $\overline{A'B'}$ onto $\overline{A''B''}$.

c. Find the image of $C(2, 1)$ under the glide reflection G.

EXAMPLE $G: A(2, 4) \longrightarrow A''(-2, -4)$
                  $G: B(-4, 2) \longrightarrow B''(0, 2)$

SOLUTION   **a.** We want to find an equation of the line through the midpoints of $\overline{AA''}$ and $\overline{BB''}$. The midpoint of the segment with endpoints $(x_1,\, y_1)$ and $(x_2,\, y_2)$ is $\left(\dfrac{x_1 + x_2}{2},\ \dfrac{y_1 + y_2}{2}\right)$. Thus the midpoint of $\overline{AA''}$ is

$$\left(\frac{2 + (-2)}{2},\ \frac{4 + (-4)}{2}\right) = (0, 0)$$

and the midpoint of $\overline{BB''}$ is

$$\left(\frac{-4 + 0}{2},\ \frac{2 + 2}{2}\right) = (-2, 2).$$

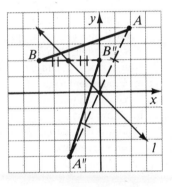

The slope of the line through these points is $\dfrac{2 - 0}{-2 - 0}$, or -1, and the y-intercept is 0. Thus an equation of l is $y = -x$.

b. In the figure, the reflecting line l is the dashed line; $r_l\,(\overline{AB}) = \overline{A'B'}$. From the graph we can see that $T_{2,\,-2}\,(\overline{A'B'}) = \overline{A''B''}$. Thus $T_{a,\,b} = T_{2,\,-2}$.

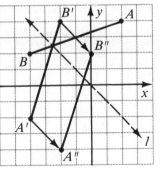

c. $T_{2,\,-2} \circ r_l\,(2, 1) = T_{2,\,-2}\,(-1, -2) = (1, -4)$

16. $G: A(4, 1) \longrightarrow A''(5, -1)$
     $G: B(3, 2) \longrightarrow B''(4, -2)$

17. $G: A(5, 1) \longrightarrow A''(-5, 4)$
     $G: B(3, 3) \longrightarrow B''(-3, 6)$

18. $G: A(3, 4) \longrightarrow A''(7, 6)$
     $G: B(0, 5) \longrightarrow B''(8, 3)$

19. $G: A(-1, 1) \longrightarrow A''(5, 3)$
     $G: B(1, -3) \longrightarrow B''(1, 5)$

In Exercises 20 and 21, follow the directions for parts (a) and (b) of Exercises 16-19.

C 20. $G: A(4, 2) \longrightarrow A''(-1, -3)$
$G: B(0, 0) \longrightarrow B''(-3, 1)$

21. $G: A(-2, 2) \longrightarrow A''(1, -2)$
$G: B(-1, -1) \longrightarrow B''(-2, -3)$

22. Follow the steps outlined below to show that
$$G = T \circ r_l = r_l \circ T$$
where T is a translation in a direction parallel to line l.
Given: $r_l(P) = P'$ and $T(P') = P''$;
$\qquad T(P) = P*$
Prove: $r_l(P*) = P''$

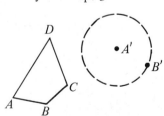

a. Show that $PP* = P'P''$ and $\overline{PP*} \parallel \overline{P'P''}$.
b. Show that quadrilateral $PP*P''P'$ is a $\square$ and thus $l \perp \overline{P* P''}$.
c. In *Book 2* you learned that if three parallel lines cut off congruent segments on one transversal, they cut off congruent segments on any transversal. Use this fact to show that l is the perpendicular bisector of $\overline{P* P''}$.
d. Why does it follow that $r_l(P*) = P''$?

23. The composite of three line reflections sometimes is a glide reflection even if two of the reflecting lines are not both perpendicular to the third line. In fact, the composite of three line reflections in which the lines of reflection are not all parallel and do not all pass through the same point is always a glide reflection. For example, let l be the line with equation $x = -1$, m be the line with equation $y = x + 2$, and n be the line with equation $y = x - 4$.
a. Find the image of the triangle with vertices $A(-4, 3)$, $B(-2, 3)$, and $C(-2, 7)$ under $r_n \circ r_m \circ r_l$.
b. Show that $r_n \circ r_m \circ r_l$ is a glide reflection by finding a line of reflection r_p and a translation $T_{a, b}$ such that $r_n \circ r_m \circ r_l = T_{a, b} \circ r_p$ and $T_{a, b}$ is in a direction parallel to line p.

Section 14-3 IDENTIFYING ISOMETRIES

You know that a translation or a rotation can be written as a composite of two line reflections. Since a glide reflection is the composite of a translation and a reflection, it can be written as a composite of three line reflections. In this section you will see that, in fact, *every* isometry can be written as a composite of *at most three* line reflections.

As you know, an isometry preserves distance and angle measure. We say that two figures $\mathcal{F}$ and $\mathcal{F}'$ are *congruent* if and only if there exists an isometry that maps $\mathcal{F}$ onto $\mathcal{F}'$. For this reason, isometries are sometimes called *congruence transformations*.

Let's investigate the images of B, C, and D under an isometry that maps vertex A of quadrilateral $ABCD$ onto point A'. The image B' of B under any isometry that maps A onto A' must be such that

$$A'B' = AB.$$

Thus B' must lie on a circle with center A' and radius AB. Choose any point B' on this circle and let t be an isometry that maps A onto A' and B onto B'. How many possible choices remain for the image of C under t? There are exactly two choices of C' such that

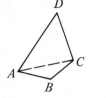

$$A'C' = AC \quad \text{and} \quad B'C' = BC.$$

One choice preserves orientation and the other does not. Once C' is chosen, how many possible images exist for D? Only one! This suggests the following theorem.

Theorem 14-5   An isometry is uniquely determined by three noncollinear points and their images.

Theorem 14-5 can help us prove an important theorem known as the *Three-Line Reflection Theorem*.

Theorem 14-6   Every isometry can be expressed as a composite of at most three line reflections. (Three-Line Reflection Theorem)

Proof: Let A, B, and C be three noncollinear points whose images are A', B', and C' under the isometry t. We will try to find a composite of line reflections that has the same effect on A, B, and C that the isometry t has.

1. If $A = A'$, $B = B'$, and $C = C'$, then t is the identity transformation. Since the identity transformation can be expressed as the composite of any line reflection with itself, we're done.

2. Suppose $A \neq A'$. Consider the perpendicular bisector l of $\overline{AA'}$. Then:

$$r_l(A) = A'$$

   If $r_l(B) = B'$ and $r_l(C) = C'$, then

$$t = r_l$$

   and we're done.

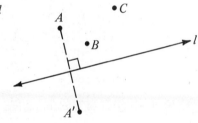

3. Suppose $r_l(A) = A'$ and $r_l(B) \neq B'$. Then let

$$r_l(B) = B_1.$$

   Consider the perpendicular bisector m of $\overline{B_1B'}$. In Exercise 21, you will prove that A' lies on m, so:

$$r_m(A') = A' \text{ and } r_m(B_1) = B'$$

   Thus:

$$r_m \circ r_l(A) = A' \text{ and } r_m \circ r_l(B) = B'$$

   If $r_m \circ r_l(C) = C'$, then

$$t = r_m \circ r_l$$

   and we're done.

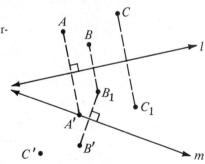

(The proof is continued on the next page.)

4. Suppose $r_m \circ r_l (A) = A'$, $r_m \circ r_l (B) = B'$, and $r_m \circ r_l (C) \neq C'$. Then let

$$r_l (C) = C_1 \text{ and } r_m (C_1) = C_2.$$

Consider the perpendicular bisector n of $\overline{C_2 C'}$. In Exercise 22 you will show that A' and B' lie on n. Thus:

$$r_n (A') = A', \ r_n (B') = B', \text{ and } r_n (C_2) = C'$$

Since three noncollinear points and their images uniquely determine an isometry (Theorem 14-5), it follows that the composite $r_n \circ r_m \circ r_l$ is the isometry t that maps A, B, and C onto A', B', and C'.

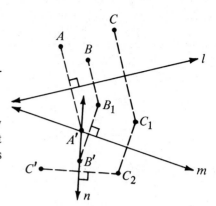

Recall Theorem 5-2: For any positive integer n, a composite of n line reflections is a direct isometry if n is even and a nondirect isometry if n is odd. This theorem along with Theorem 14-6 produces some very interesting results.

Corollary 1 Every direct isometry can be expressed as a composite of exactly two line reflections.

Corollary 2 Every nondirect isometry can be expressed as either a single line reflection or a composite of exactly three line reflections.

(Although it is beyond the scope of this book, it can be proved that the composite of three line reflections is either a reflection or a glide reflection.)

Theorem 14-7 Every isometry is either a line reflection, a translation, a rotation, or a glide reflection.

ORAL EXERCISES

1. Name all types of transformations that are direct isometries.

2. Name all types of transformations that are nondirect isometries.

In Exercises 3–8, pairs of congruent triangles are given.
a. State whether the isometry that maps one triangle onto the other is direct or nondirect.
b. State the type of isometry that seems to map one triangle onto the other.

3.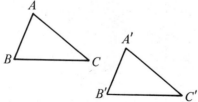

4.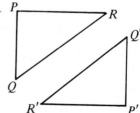

5.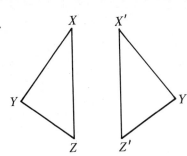

6.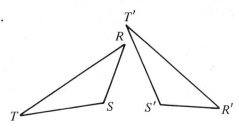

7.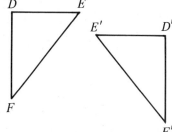

8.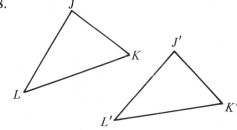

Determine whether each statement is *always*, *sometimes*, or *never* true.

9. The composite of two reflections is a reflection.

10. The composite of three reflections is a reflection.

11. The composite of two reflections is a glide reflection.

12. The composite of three reflections is a glide reflection.

13. The composite of two reflections is a rotation.

14. The composite of three reflections is a translation.

15. The composite of two reflections is an isometry.

16. The composite of three reflections is an isometry.

17. The composite of two reflections is a direct isometry.

18. The composite of three reflections is a direct isometry.

19. Name all types of transformations that can be expressed as composites of four reflections.

20. Name all types of transformations that can be expressed as composites of five reflections.

WRITTEN EXERCISES

In Exercises 1–6:

a. Name the type of isometry that maps $\triangle ABC$ onto $\triangle A'B'C'$.
b. If the isometry is a reflection or a glide reflection, construct the line of reflection.
c. If the isometry is a rotation, construct the center of the rotation.

A **1.**
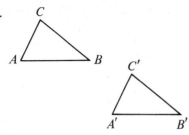

2.

3.
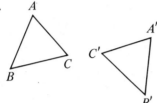

4.
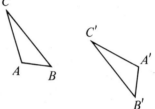

5.
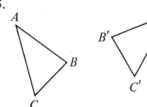

6.
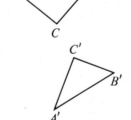

Copy the figure. Sketch the image of $\triangle ABC$ under $r_n \circ r_m \circ r_l$. Classify the resulting isometry as a reflection or a glide reflection.

7.
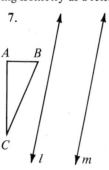

8.
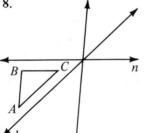

9.
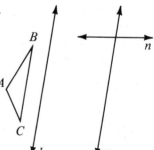

10. **a.** What is the result of the composition of two line reflections if the lines of reflection are parallel?

b. What is the result of the composition of three line reflections if the lines of reflection are parallel?

Copy the figure. Sketch a line p so that $r_l \circ r_m \circ r_n = r_p$.

11.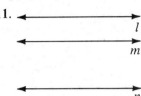

12.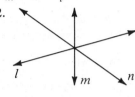

13. $\triangle ABC$ has vertices $A(-3, 0)$, $B(-1, 5)$, and $C(-4, 6)$. Find the coordinates of the vertices of:

   a. $\triangle A'B'C'$, where $r_l (\triangle ABC) = \triangle A'B'C'$ and l is the y-axis.

   b. $\triangle A''B''C''$, where $r_m (\triangle A'B'C') = \triangle A''B''C''$ and m is the line with equation $x = 4$.

   c. $\triangle A'''B'''C'''$, where $r_n (\triangle A''B''C'') = \triangle A'''B'''C'''$ and n is the line with equation $x = -1$.

   d. Show that the composite $r_n \circ r_m \circ r_l$ is a line reflection r_q by finding an equation of the reflecting line q for which $r_q (\triangle ABC) = \triangle A'''B'''C'''$.

14. $\triangle ABC$ has vertices $A(-4, 1)$, $B(0, 3)$, and $C(-1, 1)$. Find the coordinates of the vertices of:

   a. $\triangle A'B'C'$, where $r_m (\triangle ABC) = \triangle A'B'C'$ and m is the line with equation $y = -x$.

   b. $\triangle A''B''C''$, where $r_n (\triangle A'B'C') = \triangle A''B''C''$ and n is the y-axis.

   c. $\triangle A'''B'''C'''$, where $r_p (\triangle A''B''C'') = \triangle A'''B'''C'''$ and p is the line with equation $y = x$.

   d. Show that the composite $r_p \circ r_n \circ r_m$ is a line reflection r_q by finding an equation of the reflecting line q for which $r_q (\triangle ABC) = \triangle A'''B'''C'''$.

Classify the isometry as a line reflection, a glide reflection, a translation, or a rotation.

B 15. $r_{x\text{-axis}} \circ r_{y\text{-axis}}$

16. a reflection over the x-axis followed by a reflection over the line with equation $y = 10$

17. a translation that maps (x, y) onto $(x + 2, y + 1)$ followed by a reflection over the y-axis

18. a translation that maps (x, y) onto $(x + 1, y + 1)$ followed by a rotation of $90°$ about $(0, 0)$

19. a reflection over the x-axis followed by a rotation of $180°$ about $(0, 0)$

20. a rotation of $270°$ about $(0, 0)$ followed by a reflection over the y-axis

Complete the proof of Theorem 14-6 on pages 569–570.

21. Show that $A'B' = A'B_1$ so that A' is on m, the perpendicular bisector of $\overline{B'B_1}$. (*Hint*: Consider the images of $\overline{AB}$ under the isometries t and r_l.)

22. Show that A' and B' are on n, the perpendicular bisector of $\overline{C'C_2}$.

Show that the given isometries are equivalent by showing that $\triangle ABC$ with vertices $A(2, 2)$, $B(4, -2)$, and $C(6, 4)$ has the same image under each isometry.

EXAMPLE $r_{y\text{-axis}} \circ T_{-4, \, 0}$ and r_l, where l is the line with equation $x = 2$

SOLUTION $r_{y\text{-axis}} \circ T_{-4, \, 0} \, (2, 2) = r_{y\text{-axis}} \, (-2, 2) = (2, 2)$ $r_l \, (2, 2) = (2, 2)$
$r_{y\text{-axis}} \circ T_{-4, \, 0} \, (4, -2) = r_{y\text{-axis}} \, (0, -2) = (0, -2)$ $r_l \, (4, -2) = (0, -2)$
$r_{y\text{-axis}} \circ T_{-4, \, 0} \, (6, 4) = r_{y\text{-axis}} \, (2, 4) = (-2, 4)$ $r_l \, (6, 4) = (-2, 4)$

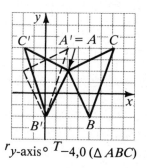

$r_{y\text{-axis}} \circ T_{-4,0} \, (\triangle ABC)$

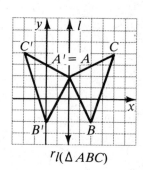

$r_l(\triangle ABC)$

By Theorem 14-5, $r_{y\text{-axis}} \circ T_{-4, \, 0}$ is equivalent to r_l.

23. $r_l \circ r_k$ and $r_p \circ r_q$, where l is the line with equation $x = 2$, k is the line with equation $y = x$, p is the line with equation $y = 2$, and q is the line with equation $y = -x + 4$.

24. $T_{2, \, -2} \circ r_k$ and r_a, where k is the line with equation $y = x$, and a is the line with equation $y = x - 2$.

25. $T_{0, \, -2} \circ r_n$ and $T_{1, \, -1} \circ r_b$, where n is the line with equation $y = -x$ and b is the line with equation $y = -x - 1$.

26. $T_{-4, \, -4} \circ r_l$ and $T_{-6, \, -2} \circ r_k$, where l is the line with equation $y = x + 2$ and k is the line with equation $y = x$.

Find the equations of at most three lines that determine line reflections whose composite maps $\triangle ABC$ onto $\triangle A'B'C'$, where the triangles have the given vertices.

C **27.** $A(-2, -4)$, $B(-4, -1)$, $C(-7, -4)$ **28.** $A(-4, 1)$, $B(-2, 1)$, $C(-2, 5)$
$A'(2, -4)$, $B'(4, -7)$, $C'(7, -4)$ $A'(1, -4)$, $B'(-1, -4)$, $C'(-1, -8)$

29. $A(8, 2)$, $B(2, 2)$, $C(5, 6)$ **30.** $A(2, -4)$, $B(5, -4)$, $C(6, 0)$
$A'(8, -2)$, $B'(14, -2)$, $C'(11, 2)$ $A'(-2, 0)$, $B'(-2, -3)$, $C'(-6, -4)$

Using the fact that two figures are congruent if and only if there exists an isometry that maps one figure onto the other provides us with another means of proving congruency. Using only definitions, the properties of line reflections and isometries, and the Perpendicular Bisector Theorem (page 231), you should be able to prove the following.

31. Given: $r_l: A \longrightarrow C$, $r_l: C \longrightarrow A$
    Prove: $\triangle ABC$ is isosceles.

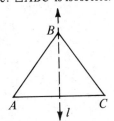

32. Given: $BA = BC$
    Prove: $\angle A \cong \angle C$
    (*Hint*: Show that there is a line reflection that maps A onto C, C onto A, and B onto itself.)

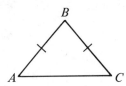

33. Given: Line l is a symmetry line of pentagon $ABCDE$.
    Prove: $\triangle AED \cong \triangle ABC$

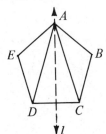

34. Given: $PQRS$ is a rhombus; l is $\overleftrightarrow{PR}$.
    Prove: $r_l(Q) = S$

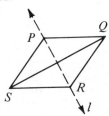

SELF-TEST 1

1. Name a single transformation that is equivalent to the given composite. Section 14-1
   a. $T_{-3,\,5} \circ T_{1,\,0}$
   b. $D_{\frac{1}{2}} \circ D_4$
   c. $R_{-30} \circ R_{110}$

2. Graph the image of the segment with endpoints $A(-2, 3)$ and $B(2, -1)$ under each composite.
   a. $T_{1,\,-1} \circ T_{-3,\,-2}$
   b. $D_{\frac{1}{3}} \circ D_{\frac{3}{2}}$
   c. $R_{30} \circ R_{60}$

3. Which of the following composites are equivalent?
   a. $D_4 \circ D_{\frac{1}{4}}$
   b. $R_{20} \circ R_{160}$
   c. $T_{5,\,5} \circ T_{-4,\,-4}$
   d. $R_{480} \circ R_{240}$

4. Graph the image of the triangle with vertices $A(-2, 1)$, $B(1, -1)$, and $C(2, 2)$ Section 14-2 under the composite $r_k \circ T_{2,\,2}$ where k is the line with equation $y = x$.

5. A glide reflection $T \circ r_l$ maps $\triangle ABC$ onto $\triangle A''B''C''$. Copy the diagram, then:
   a. Construct the line of reflection, l.
   b. Construct $\triangle A'B'C'$ such that $r_l(\triangle ABC) = \triangle A'B'C'$.

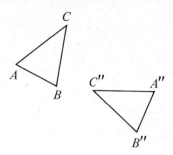

Identify the type of isometry that maps $\triangle ABC$ onto $\triangle A'B'C'$.

6.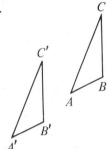

7.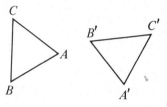

Section 14-3

Classify the isometry as a reflection, a glide reflection, a translation, or a rotation.

8. $r_{y\text{-axis}} \circ r_a$

9. $r_n \circ r_a$

10. $r_{x\text{-axis}} \circ r_a \circ r_{y\text{-axis}}$

11. $r_{x\text{-axis}} \circ r_k \circ r_n$

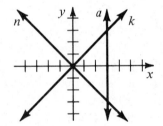

Section 14-4 SIMILARITY TRANSFORMATIONS

In Section 14-3 you learned a transformational definition of congruence: two figures $\mathcal{F}$ and $\mathcal{F}'$ are congruent if and only if there exists an isometry that maps $\mathcal{F}$ onto $\mathcal{F}'$. In this section you will see how *similarity* is related to the composition of an isometry and a dilation.

In the diagram, $\triangle CA''B''$ is the image of $\triangle CAB$ under the composite of the half-turn with center C and the dilation with center C and scale factor 2. Since the dilation and the half-turn have the same center, the order in which they are composed doesn't matter; that is:

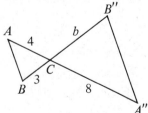

$$D_{C,\,2} \circ R_{C,\,180}(\triangle CAB) = R_{C,\,180} \circ D_{C,\,2}(\triangle CAB)$$

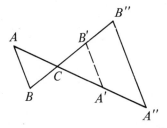

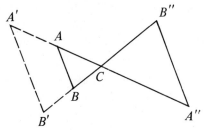

$$D_{C,2} \circ R_{C,180} (\triangle CAB) = \triangle CA''B''$$

$$R_{C,180} \circ D_{C,2} (\triangle CAB) = \triangle CA''B''$$

This transformation is an example of a type of transformation called a *similarity transformation*. A *similarity transformation* is any transformation that can be written as the composite of an isometry and a dilation. We say that two figures $\mathcal{J}$ and $\mathcal{J}'$ are *similar* if and only if there exists a similarity transformation that maps $\mathcal{J}$ onto $\mathcal{J}'$.

A similarity transformation preserves all the properties preserved by both its component transformations—the isometry and the dilation. Thus angle measure, betweenness, collinearity, perpendicularity, and parallelism are preserved by a similarity transformation. Distance is not.

As the next example suggests, a similarity transformation can usually be expressed in more than one way.

EXAMPLE Express the transformation that maps $\triangle ABC$ with vertices $A(-1, 6)$, $B(-3, 4)$, and $C(0, 4)$ onto $\triangle A''B''C''$ with vertices $A''(6, 6)$, $B''(2, 2)$, and $C''(8, 2)$ as a composite of:
a. an isometry following a dilation
b. a dilation following an isometry

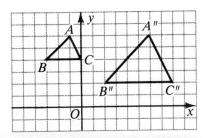

SOLUTION Choose a vertex of $\triangle ABC$; we have chosen point A.

a. The dilation $D_{A, 2}$ maps $\triangle ABC$ onto a $\triangle AB'C'$ that is congruent to $\triangle A''B''C''$. Then $T_{7, 0}$ is the isometry that maps $\triangle AB'C'$ onto $\triangle A''B''C''$. Thus:

$$T_{7, 0} \circ D_{A, 2} (\triangle ABC) = \triangle A''B''C''$$

b. The isometry $T_{7, 0}$ maps:
   A onto A''
   B onto the point B' on $\overline{A''B''}$ such that
   $$A''B' = AB$$
   C onto the point C' on $\overline{A''C''}$ such that
   $$A''C' = AC$$

The dilation $D_{A'', 2}$ maps $\triangle A''B'C'$ onto $\triangle A''B''C''$. Thus:

$$D_{A'', 2} \circ T_{7, 0} (\triangle ABC) = \triangle A''B''C''$$

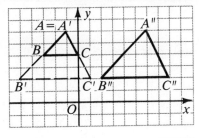

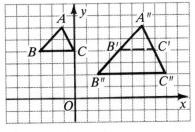

Just as an isometry is uniquely determined by three noncollinear points and their images, a similarity transformation is uniquely determined by three non-collinear points and their images. Thus the preceding example shows that

$$T_{7,\,0} \circ D_{A,\,2} \quad \text{and} \quad D_{A'',\,2} \circ T_{7,\,0}$$

are equivalent ways of expressing the same similarity transformation. In Exercise 27 you will explore some additional ways of expressing this similarity transformation as the composite of an isometry and a dilation.

Notice that $D_{A,\,2}$ and $D_{A'',\,2}$ are *different* dilations because they have different centers. However, they have the same scale factor, 2. No matter how a similarity transformation is expressed, the scale factor of its component dilation remains the same.

If one polygon is mapped onto another polygon by a similarity transformation whose component dilation has a scale factor of k, then the ratio of the lengths of corresponding sides of the two similar polygons is k. That is, if a similarity transformation maps A onto A'' and B onto B'' and the scale factor of its component dilation is k, then

$$A''B'' = k \cdot AB, \quad \text{or} \quad k = \frac{A''B''}{AB}.$$

The number k that is the ratio of the lengths of corresponding sides of similar polygons is called the *constant of proportionality* or *scale factor*.

EXAMPLE $r_{x\text{-axis}} \circ D_3$ maps $\triangle ABC$ onto $\triangle A''B''C''$. Find the lengths of the sides of $\triangle A''B''C''$ if $AB = 7$, $BC = 4$, and $AC = 5$.

SOLUTION The scale factor is 3, so:

$$\frac{A''B''}{AB} = \frac{B''C''}{BC} = \frac{A''C''}{AC} = 3$$

$$\frac{A''B''}{7} = 3 \qquad \frac{B''C''}{4} = 3 \qquad \frac{A''C''}{5} = 3$$

$$A''B'' = 21 \qquad B''C'' = 12 \qquad A''C'' = 15$$

ORAL EXERCISES

Explain why each statement is true.

1. Every dilation is a similarity transformation.

2. Every isometry is a similarity transformation.

State whether the statement is *always*, *sometimes*, or *never* true.

3. Congruent figures are similar.

4. Similar figures are congruent.

5. Two isosceles triangles are similar.

6. Two equilateral triangles are similar.

7. Two line segments are similar.

8. Two angles are similar.

9. Two circles are similar.

10. Dilations preserve orientation of points.

11. Similarity transformations preserve orientation of points.

A similarity transformation $t \circ D_{C,k}$ maps $\triangle ABC$ onto $\triangle A'B'C'$.
a. Name the scale factor of the dilation $D_{C,k}$.
b. Describe the *type* of the isometry t.

12.
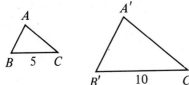

13.
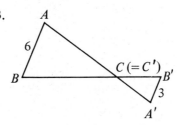

14.
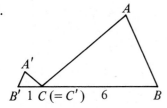

15.
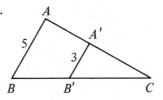

16.
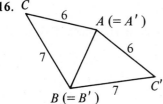

17.
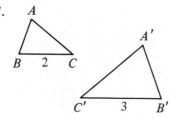

WRITTEN EXERCISES

$\triangle A'B'C'$ is the image of $\triangle ABC$ under the given similarity transformation.
a. If $BC = 4$, find $B'C'$.   **b.** If $A'B' = 30$, find AB.

A **1.** $r_{y\text{-axis}} \circ D_2$

2. $D_5 \circ T_{-1,\,4}$

3. $D_3 \circ R_{30}$

4. $R_{90} \circ D_{\frac{1}{2}}$

5. $D_{\frac{1}{3}} \circ r_{y\text{-axis}} \circ T_{2,\,2}$

6. $D_{\frac{3}{2}} \circ r_{y\text{-axis}} \circ T_{0,\,7}$

If $\triangle ABC$ has vertices $A(2,\,4)$, $B(4,\,2)$, and $C(8,\,4)$, find the coordinates of the vertices of its image under the given similarity transformation.

7. $r_{x\text{-axis}} \circ D_{\frac{1}{2}}$

8. $D_3 \circ r_{y\text{-axis}}$

9. $T_{1,\,3} \circ D_2$

10. $D_{\frac{1}{2}} \circ T_{-3,\,2}$

11. $D_2 \circ R_{180}$

12. $R_{90} \circ D_{\frac{1}{2}}$

13. $r_m \circ D_{B,\,2}$, where m has equation $y = 1$

14. $r_k \circ D_{A,\,\frac{1}{2}}$, where k has equation $y = x$

15. $D_{\frac{1}{2}} \circ T_{-2,\,2} \circ r_k$, where k has equation $y = x$

16. $r_{y\text{-axis}} \circ T_{0,\,-4} \circ D_{C,\,\frac{1}{2}}$

Copy the diagram and sketch the image of $\triangle ABC$ under each similarity transformation.

17. a. $r_l \circ D_{C,\,2}$ b. $D_{C,\,2} \circ r_l$

18. a. $R_{B,\,180} \circ D_{B,\,\frac{1}{2}}$ b. $R_{E,\,180} \circ D_{E,\,\frac{1}{2}}$

Express the similarity transformation that maps $\triangle ABC$ onto $\triangle A''B''C''$ as a composite of an isometry following a dilation with center A.

B 19. $A(0, 0)$, $B(-1, 1)$, $C(2, 1)$
  $A''(0, 0)$, $B''(4, 4)$, $C''(-8, 4)$

20. $A(0, 0)$, $B(3, 9)$, $C(3, 0)$
  $A''(0, 0)$, $B''(-3, -1)$, $C''(0, -1)$

21. $A(1, 2)$, $B(7, 2)$, $C(5, -2)$
  $A''(1, 2)$, $B''(-2, 2)$, $C''(-1, 4)$

22. $A(-1, -1)$, $B(-2, 0)$, $C(-4, -1)$
  $A''(-1, -1)$, $B''(2, 2)$, $C''(-1, 8)$

23. $A(-2, 0)$, $B(-1, -1)$, $C(-4, -2)$
  $A''(2, -1)$, $B''(4, -3)$, $C''(-2, -5)$

24. $A(2, -1)$, $B(6, 5)$, $C(6, -1)$
  $A''(-2, 1)$, $B''(-4, -2)$, $C''(-4, 1)$

25. $A(4, 0)$, $B(1, -1)$, $C(3, 1)$
  $A''(2, 0)$, $B''(-7, 3)$, $C''(-1, -3)$

26. $A(-1, -5)$, $B(-2, -5)$, $C(0, -3)$
  $A''(-3, 1)$, $B''(-3, -2)$, $C''(3, 4)$

C 27. On page 577 you saw that the similarity transformation that maps $\triangle ABC$ with vertices $A(-1, 6)$, $B(-3, 4)$, and $C(0, 4)$ onto $\triangle A''B''C''$ with vertices $A''(6, 6)$, $B''(2, 2)$, and $C''(8, 2)$ can be expressed as either $T_{7,\,0} \circ D_{A,\,2}$ or $D_{A'',\,2} \circ T_{7,\,0}$. Express this similarity transformation as:
  a. an isometry following a dilation with center B
  b. a dilation following an isometry that maps $\angle B$ onto $\angle B''$
  c. an isometry following a dilation with center C
  d. a dilation following an isometry that maps $\angle C$ onto $\angle C''$
  e. an isometry following a dilation with center at $O(0, 0)$
  f. a dilation with center at $O(0, 0)$ following an isometry
  g. the identity transformation followed by a dilation
  h. Pick any point E other than A, B, and C and show that the image of E is the same under each composite you found in parts (a)-(g).

28. $\triangle ABC$ has vertices $A(-1, 2)$, $B(-1, 5)$, and $C(-3, 6)$. $\triangle A''B''C''$ has vertices $A''(3, 0)$, $B''(3, -6)$, and $C''(7, -8)$. Find four composites of one isometry and one dilation (in any order) that map $\triangle ABC$ onto $\triangle A''B''C''$.

Section 14-5 TRANSFORMATION GROUPS

In *Book 2* you were introduced to the mathematical system known as a *group*. The *transformation groups* you will study in this section provide some of the clearest and simplest examples of groups.

In Chapter 5 you studied line symmetry, rotational symmetry (and point symmetry), and translational symmetry. A given figure has one of these types of symmetry when there is a line reflection, rotation, or translation (other than the identity) that maps the figure onto itself. An isometry that maps a figure onto itself is called a *symmetry-producing isometry*. In other words, for any figure $\mathcal{F}$, t is a symmetry-producing isometry for $\mathcal{F}$ if and only if $t(\mathcal{F}) = \mathcal{F}$.

EXAMPLES OF SYMMETRY-PRODUCING ISOMETRIES

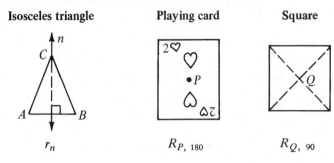

Isosceles triangle	Playing card	Square
r_n	$R_{P,\,180}$	$R_{Q,\,90}$

Notice that although a symmetry-producing symmetry maps a figure onto itself, the isometry does not necessarily map each point onto itself. For example, in the isosceles triangle shown above, r_n maps the triangle onto itself, but the image of A under r_n is B rather than A.

The set of *all* symmetry-producing isometries for a given figure is called its *symmetry set*. Every figure coincides with its image under the identity transformation I, so I is a symmetry-producing isometry for every figure. Thus every figure has a non-empty symmetry set.

Consider rectangle $WXYZ$ with lines of symmetry l and m that intersect at P.

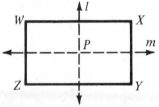

$r_l: W \longrightarrow X$

$r_l: X \longrightarrow W$

$r_l: Y \longrightarrow Z$ $\qquad r_l: WXYZ \longrightarrow XWZY$

$r_l: Z \longrightarrow Y$

Notice that we name the image and pre-image in such a way that corresponding letters denote points that are mapped onto each other. Similarly:

$$r_m: WXYZ \longrightarrow ZYXW$$

and $\qquad R_{P,\,180}: WXYZ \longrightarrow YZWX$

The symmetry set S of rectangle $WXYZ$ is:

$$S = \{I, r_l, r_m, R_{P,\,180}\}$$

Let us choose two elements of S, say r_l and r_m, and form their composite, $r_l \circ r_m$. Then:

$$r_l \circ r_m (WXYZ) = r_l (r_m (WXYZ)) = r_l (ZYXW) = YZWX$$

But $R_{P,\,180}(WXYZ) = YZWX$. Therefore

$$r_l \circ r_m = R_{P,\,180}$$

The *operation table* shown on the next page summarizes the results of composing all possible pairs of elements of S.

$\circ$	I	r_l	r_m	$R_{P,\,180}$
I	I	r_l	r_m	$R_{P,\,180}$
r_l	r_l	I	$R_{P,\,180}$	r_m
r_m	r_m	$R_{P,\,180}$	I	r_l
$R_{P,\,180}$	$R_{P,\,180}$	r_m	r_l	I

To find the result of $r_l \circ r_m$ in the table, find r_l in the left-hand column and read across until you come to the entry in the column headed by r_m, namely $R_{P,\,180}$. (Five entries of the table will be verified in Exercises 9–13.)

Since every entry in the operation table is an element of S, we say that S is *closed* under composition. This result can be generalized as follows:

Theorem 14-8   The symmetry set of any figure is closed under composition.

Proof: Let S be the symmetry set of a figure $\mathcal{F}$. If $t_1 \in S$ and $t_2 \in S$, then $t_1(\mathcal{F}) = \mathcal{F}$ and $t_2(\mathcal{F}) = \mathcal{F}$. Therefore:

$$t_1 \circ t_2(\mathcal{F}) = t_1(t_2(\mathcal{F})) = t_1(\mathcal{F}) = \mathcal{F}$$

EXAMPLE   Determine the symmetry set, S, for an equilateral triangle and construct an operation table for S under composition.

SOLUTION   Let l, m, and n be the lines of symmetry of equilateral $\triangle ABC$ and let P be the point where l, m, and n intersect. Then

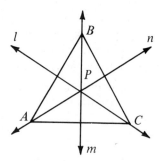

$$S = \{I, r_l, r_m, r_n, R_{P,\,120}, R_{P,\,240}\}.$$

To complete an operation table for S under composition, we must find the results of composing all possible pairs of elements of S. For example:

$$r_l \circ r_m (\triangle ABC) = r_l(r_m(\triangle ABC))$$
$$= r_l(\triangle CBA) = \triangle CAB$$

But $\triangle CAB = R_{P,\,120}(\triangle ABC)$. Therefore:

$$r_l \circ r_m = R_{P,\,120}$$

The operation table is shown below. You will verify some of the entries in Exercises 14–16.

$\circ$	I	r_l	r_m	r_n	$R_{P,\,120}$	$R_{P,\,240}$
I	I	r_l	r_m	r_n	$R_{P,\,120}$	$R_{P,\,240}$
r_l	r_l	I	$R_{P,\,120}$	$R_{P,\,240}$	r_m	r_n
r_m	r_m	$R_{P,\,240}$	I	$R_{P,\,120}$	r_n	r_l
r_n	r_n	$R_{P,\,120}$	$R_{P,\,240}$	I	r_l	r_m
$R_{P,\,120}$	$R_{P,\,120}$	r_n	r_l	r_m	$R_{P,\,240}$	I
$R_{P,\,240}$	$R_{P,\,240}$	r_m	r_n	r_l	I	$R_{P,\,120}$

Note that in the example, $r_l \circ r_m = R_{P,\,120}$ and $r_m \circ r_l = R_{P,\,240}$. Thus

$$r_l \circ r_m \ne r_m \circ r_l,$$

and the operation $\circ$ is not *commutative* on this symmetry set.

Recall from *Book 2* that a set G, together with an operation $\circ$, is a *group*, denoted $(G, \circ)$, if:

1. G is closed under $\circ$.
2. $\circ$ is associative on G.
3. G contains an identity element for $\circ$.
4. Every element of G has an inverse in G.

The symmetry set S of an equilateral triangle and the operation of composition form a group, called the *symmetry group* of an equilateral triangle, because:

1. S is closed under $\circ$. (Theorem 14-8)
2. $\circ$ is associative on S. (Composition of functions and hence transformations, is associative.)
3. S contains an identity element for $\circ$, namely I.
4. Every element of S has an inverse in S:

$$I^{-1} = I,\ r_l^{-1} = r_l,\ r_m^{-1} = r_m,\ r_n^{-1} = r_n,\ R_{P,\,120}^{-1} = R_{P,\,240},\ R_{P,\,240}^{-1} = R_{P,\,120}$$

This suggests the following theorem:

Theorem 14-9   The symmetry set S of any figure $\mathcal{J}$, together with the operation of composition, forms a group called the *symmetry group* of $\mathcal{J}$.

Proof: We must show that $(S, \circ)$ satisfies the four properties of a group.
1. S is closed under $\circ$. (Theorem 14-8).
2. Composition of functions is associative.
3. Every symmetry set contains the identity transformation.
4. Assume that $t \in S$. Since t is an isometry and every isometry has an inverse, t^{-1} exists such that:

$$t^{-1} \circ t(\mathcal{J}) = \mathcal{J}$$

But $t(\mathcal{J}) = \mathcal{J}$. Therefore:

$$t^{-1} \circ t(\mathcal{J}) = t^{-1}[t(\mathcal{J})] = t^{-1}(\mathcal{J})$$

Thus:

$$\mathcal{J} = t^{-1}(\mathcal{J})$$

Therefore $t^{-1} \in S$ by definition.

Note that the entries in the operation table for the symmetry set S of a rectangle are symmetric about the main diagonal. Thus, for a rectangle, $\circ$ is *commutative* on S, and S is called a *commutative*, or *abelian*, group.

If H is a set of transformations and $(H, \circ)$ is a group, then $(H, \circ)$ is called a *transformation group*.

EXAMPLE   Let $G = \{$all transformations$\}$. Show that $(G, \circ)$ is a group.

SOLUTION   1. The composite of two transformations is a transformation (page 172).
2. Composition of functions is associative.
3. The identity transformation is an identity for $(G, \circ)$.
4. Every transformation is one-to-one and so has an inverse.

Other examples of transformation groups are as follows:

$(C, \circ)$, where $C = \{$all isometries$\}$; $(C, \circ)$ is sometimes called the *congruence group.*

$(E, \circ)$, where $E = \{$all direct isometries$\}$

$(T, \circ)$, where $T = \{$all translations$\}$

$(Q, \circ)$, where $Q = \{$all similarity transformations$\}$; $(Q, \circ)$ is sometimes called the *similarity group.*

$(R_P, \circ)$, where $R_P = \{$all rotations with a given center $P\}$

$(D_C, \circ)$, where $D_C = \{$all dilations with a given center $C\}$

In Exercises 22–27, you will show that all the systems in the examples above are groups.

Although it may appear that every set of transformations is a group, such is not the case. For example, the set of line reflections is not a group under $\circ$. Nor is the set of glide reflections a group under $\circ$. The justification of these statements is left as Oral Exercise 8.

You may recall from *Book 2* that if $(G, \circ)$ is a group, and H is a subset of G such that $(H, \circ)$ is a group, then $(H, \circ)$ is a *subgroup* of $(G, \circ)$. Since each symmetry-producing transformation is an isometry, each symmetry group is a subgroup of the congruence group. Since every isometry is a similarity transformation (with scale factor 1), the congruence group is a subgroup of the similarity group.

ORAL EXERCISES

Classify as true or false.

1. The symmetry set for every figure is a group under composition.

2. The symmetry group of a non-isosceles triangle has one element.

3. The group $(G, \circ)$, where $G = \{$all transformations$\}$, is abelian.

4. A regular pentagon has a symmetry set consisting of 10 elements.

5. Let $N = \{$all nondirect isometries$\}$. $(N, \circ)$ is a group.

6. Describe the symmetry set of a circle with center O.

7. **a.** Determine the symmetry set, S, for $\overline{AB}$.
   b. Make an operation table for S.
   c. Show that $(S, \circ)$ is a group.

   $A \bullet\!\!\longrightarrow\!\!\bullet B$

8. Let $L = \{$all line reflections$\}$ and $G = \{$all glide reflections$\}$. What group properties are not satisfied by $(L, \circ)$ and $(G, \circ)$?

WRITTEN EXERCISES

Determine the symmetry set of the given figure.

A 1. isosceles triangle   2. rhombus   3. parallelogram   4. non-isosceles trapezoid

5. isosceles trapezoid   6. square   7. ellipse   8. parabola

Verify the given entry in the operation table for the symmetry group of a rectangle.

9. $r_m \circ R_{P,\ 180} = r_l$ 10. $R_{P,\ 180} \circ r_m = r_l$ 11. $R_{P,\ 180} \circ r_l = r_m$

12. $r_l \circ R_{P,\ 180} = r_m$ 13. $r_m \circ r_l = R_{P,\ 180}$

Verify the given entry in the operation table for the symmetry group of an equilateral triangle.

14. $r_l \circ r_n = R_{P,\ 240}$ 15. $r_m \circ R_{P,\ 240} = r_l$ 16. $R_{P,\ 120} \circ r_m = r_l$

Make an operation table for the symmetry group of the given figure. Is the symmetry group abelian?

B 17. isosceles triangle   18. rhombus   19. parallelogram   20. square

21. a. Use the operation table for the symmetry group of an equilateral triangle to show that
$$r_m \circ (R_{P,\ 120} \circ r_l) = (r_m \circ R_{P,\ 120}) \circ r_l.$$

b. What property of groups is illustrated by the equation in part (a)?

Show that the given set forms a group under composition.

22. $C = \{\text{all isometries}\}$ 23. $E = \{\text{all direct isometries}\}$

24. $T = \{\text{all translations}\}$ 25. $Q = \{\text{all similarity transformations}\}$

26. $R_P = \{\text{all rotations with a given center } P\}$

27. $D_C = \{\text{all dilations with a given center } C\}$

28. Why is the set of all nondirect isometries not a group under $\circ$?

29. Why is the set R of all rotations not a group under $\circ$?
(Hint: Consider $R_{P,\ 270} \circ R_{Q,\ 90}$, where P and Q are different points.)

30. In terms of n, how many elements are there in the symmetry set for a regular n-gon (n-sided polygon)?

Prove that the given system is a subgroup of the group of all translations $(T, \circ)$.

31. $(X, \circ)$, where X is the set of all translations of the form $T_{a,\ 0}$, with $a \in \mathcal{R}$.

32. $(Y, \circ)$, where Y is the set of all translations of the form $T_{a,\ a}$, with $a \in \mathcal{R}$.

Prove that if the first rotation listed is an element of the symmetry set of a given figure, then the second rotation is also an element of the symmetry set.

33. $R_{P,\ 18};\ R_{P,\ -18}$ 34. $R_{P,\ 20};\ R_{P,\ 60}$

List all subgroups of the symmetry group for the given figure.

C 35. rectangle   36. equilateral triangle   37. square

SELF-TEST 2

1. a. Copy the figure and sketch $\triangle A'B'C'$, the image of $\triangle ABC$ under the similarity transformation $r_m \circ D_{C,\frac{1}{2}}$.

Section 14-4

b. If $AB = 4.8$, find $A'B'$.

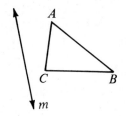

2. A similarity transformation $t \circ D_{A, k}$ maps $\triangle ABC$ onto $\triangle A'B'C'$.

a. Name the scale factor of the dilation $D_{A, k}$.

b. Classify the type of isometry t.

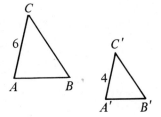

Quadrilateral $ABCD$ shown at the right is called a *kite*; $AB = CB$ and $AD = CD$.

Section 14-5

3. Determine the symmetry set, S, of the kite.

4. Make an operation table for S under $\circ$.

5. Determine the inverse of each element in S under $\circ$.

6. Without using Theorem 14-9, show that $(S, \circ)$ is a group.

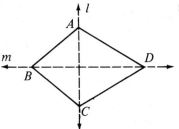

CHAPTER REVIEW

Lines l, m, and n are the perpendicular bisectors of the sides of equilateral $\triangle DEF$. Find the image of each vertex of $\triangle DEF$ under each composite.

1. $R_{P, 60} \circ R_{P, 60}$

Section 14-1

2. $R_{P, 300} \circ R_{P, -60}$

3. $R_{P, 180} \circ R_{P, 180}$

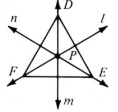

4. Complete: If D_{k_1} and D_{k_2} are dilations with the same center, then the scale factor of their composite $D_{k_1} \circ D_{k_2}$ is __?__.

5. a. Name a single transformation that is equivalent to $T_{-1, 4} \circ T_{3, 6}$.

b. Name a single transformation that is equivalent to the inverse of $T_{-1, 4} \circ T_{3, 6}$.

6. A glide reflection $T \circ r_k$ maps $\triangle ABC$ onto $\triangle A'B'C'$. Copy the figure and construct k, the line of reflection.

7. Which of the following properties are preserved under a glide reflection?
   a. perpendicularity
   b. orientation
   c. distance
   d. collinearity

Name the type of isometry that maps $\triangle DEF$ onto $\triangle D'E'F'$.

8. 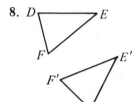   9.   10.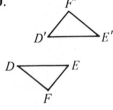

11. Classify as true or false: Any line segment can be mapped onto any other line segment by a similarity transformation.

12. A similarity transformation $D_{C,\,k} \circ t$ maps $\triangle ABC$ onto $\triangle A'B'C'$.
    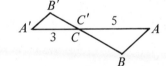
    a. Describe the type of isometry t.
    b. Determine the scale factor k.

13. If $\triangle ABC$ has vertices $A(2,\,2)$, $B(4,\,3)$, and $C(4,\,-1)$, find the coordinates of the vertices of its image under the similarity transformation $r_l \circ D_{A,\,2}$ where l has equation $y = x$.

14. Classify as true or false: The symmetry set of a non-isosceles triangle is the empty set.

15. $\triangle DEF$ is an equilateral triangle with symmetry set
    $$\{I, R_{P,\,120}, R_{P,\,240}, r_l, r_m, r_n\}.$$
    a. Find the inverse of $R_{P,\,240}$.
    b. Find the inverse of r_m.
    c. Determine $R_{P,\,120} \circ r_m \,(\triangle DEF)$, then name an element of the symmetry set that is equivalent to $R_{P,\,120} \circ r_m$.

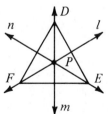

Determine whether the statement is *always*, *sometimes*, or *never* true.

1. The composite of two line reflections is a translation.

2. The composite of three line reflections is a rotation.

3. The composite of four line reflections is a line reflection.

4. A similarity transformation preserves orientation.

5. An isometry is a similarity transformation.

6. A symmetry group is commutative.

Find the image of the point with coordinates $(-4, -3)$ under each composite.

7. $T_{9,\,-8} \circ T_{-5,\,11}$　　　8. $D_{\frac{1}{5}} \circ D_{10}$　　　9. $R_{30} \circ R_{240}$

10. Rectangle $ABCD$ has symmetry set $S = \{I, r_l, r_m, R_{P,\,180}\}$.
Copy and complete the operation table for $(S, \circ)$.

$\circ$	I	r_l	r_m	$R_{P,\,180}$
I	I	r_l	r_m	$R_{P,\,180}$
r_l	r_l	?	?	?
r_m	r_m	?	I	?
$R_{P,\,180}$	$R_{P,\,180}$	?	?	I

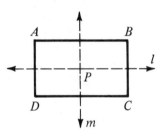

Exs. 10, 11

11. State the inverse of each element of S.

A glide reflection $G = T_{a,\,b} \circ r_l$ maps $\triangle ABC$ onto $\triangle A''B''C''$.

12. Find an equation of the reflecting line l of G.

13. Sketch $\triangle A'B'C'$, where $r_l (\triangle ABC) = \triangle A'B'C'$.

14. Find a rule for $T_{a,\,b}$ such that
$$T_{a,\,b} (\triangle A'B'C') = \triangle A''B''C''.$$

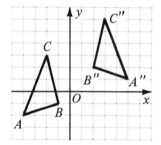

Exs. 12-14

15. Copy the figure, in which $l \parallel m \parallel n$. Sketch the image of $\triangle DEF$ under $r_n \circ r_m \circ r_l$. Classify the resulting isometry as a reflection, glide reflection, translation, or rotation.

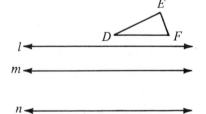

16. $\triangle A'B'C'$ is the image of $\triangle ABC$ under the composite $D_{B',\,\frac{1}{2}} \circ r_l$, where l has equation $y = x$. If $\triangle ABC$ has vertices $A(4, 0)$, $B(3, 2)$ and $C(6, 2)$, find the coordinates of the vertices of $\triangle A'B'C'$.

Careers — Retail Department Store Manager

Retail store managers sell everything from fish to designer clothes and oversee anywhere from several to hundreds of employees. The smaller the store, the more directly involved the manager is in all aspects of its operation. Whatever the store's size, however, all managers deal with the same types of issues.

A manager's responsibilities can be broken down into three areas: statistics, which is how profit is measured; leadership and communication, which is public relations and overseeing personnel; and merchandising, which is the choosing, advertising, and presentation of what the store sells.

Goal-setting and image-setting are important parts of a manager's job. In large department stores, managers discuss goals and policies almost daily with their assistants. These assistants, who are in charge of such areas as building security or personnel, then put these goals into action. In smaller operations, managers themselves see that the goals are met.

Every store has an image, which grows out of the store's location, its merchandise, its prices, and its salespeople. Managers are in charge of recognizing and maintaining that image in a way that satisfies customers. For instance, if a large department store is known as a good place to buy coats, it is up to the manager to be sure that the coat racks are kept filled with coats of the appropriate style, size, and price.

Managing a retail store involves working with many different people. Store personnel must be given the motivation and direction needed to keep the store profitable. Managers also need mathematical skills so they can analyze profit and loss statistics. They must be able to interpret trends and recognize what their customers want.

Store managers have many different backgrounds. Some start as salespersons, others as buyers, still others as assistant managers of departments. Small operations are less formal in their requirements than large department stores. You should get a college degree if you are interested in a management position in a large store.

Be sure that you understand the meaning of these terms:

glide reflection, p. 563

congruence transformations, p. 568

similarity transformation, p. 577

constant of proportionality (scale factor),
  p. 578

symmetry-producing isometry, p. 581

symmetry set, p. 581

operation table, p. 581

symmetry group, p. 583

commutative (abelian) group, p. 583

transformation group, p. 583

subgroup, p. 584

MIXED REVIEW

1. Find the probability of drawing two clubs and three diamonds when drawing five cards from a deck of cards.

2. The 1980 population of the United States was about 227,000,000. If the annual growth rate is 4%, predict the population, to the nearest million, in the year 2000.

Simplify.

3. $\tan\left(\dfrac{\pi}{2} + \theta\right) \cos\left(\dfrac{\pi}{2} - \theta\right)$

4. $(5 - 2i)^2$

5. $\dfrac{\cos\theta + 1}{\cot\theta + \csc\theta}$

6. $\dfrac{x^{-2} + x^{-1}}{x^{-1} + x}$

7. Graph $f(x) = \log_3 x$ and $f^{-1}(x)$ on the same set of axes. Write an equation for f^{-1}.

8. In $\square ABCD$, $AB = 8$, $BC = 6$, and $m\angle A = 42$. Find the lengths of the diagonals to the nearest integer and the area of $\square ABCD$ to the nearest integer.

9. A quality control inspector recorded the number of defective items produced in a factory per hour, as shown. Find the mean, median, mode, range, mean absolute deviation, and variance of the data.

No. of defective items	0	1	2	3	4
Frequency	2	5	8	9	6

10. The composite of three line reflections is equivalent to a __?__ or a __?__ .

11. Solve $\triangle JKL$ if $m\angle J = 110°20'$, $m\angle K = 37°10'$, and $KL = 12$. Give lengths to the nearest integer.

12. Find the image of $(0, -1)$ under the composition $R_{-180} \circ R_{315}$.

13. If $\cos\theta = 0.6$ and $\dfrac{3\pi}{2} < \theta < 2\pi$, find (a) $\sin 2\theta$, (b) $\sin(\pi - \theta)$, and (c) $\cos\dfrac{\theta}{2}$.

14. $G = T_{a,b} \circ r_l$ is a glide reflection such that $G:A(4, 3) \rightarrow A''(0, -3)$ and $G:B(-2, 3) \rightarrow B''(0, 3)$. Find an equation of l, the line of reflection.

15. Use the table on page 544, assuming a normal distribution, to find $P(-1 \leqslant x \leqslant 0.3)$.

16. Solve $\cos^2 \theta = (\sin \theta - 1)^2$ for $0° \leqslant \theta < 360°$.

17. How many triangles ABC can be drawn if $m\angle B = 46°50'$, $c = 36$, and $b = 26$?

Evaluate.

18. $\cos \left[\text{Sin}^{-1} \left(-\dfrac{\sqrt{2}}{2} \right) \right]$

19. $\tan \left(2 \arcsin \dfrac{3}{5} \right)$

20. $\log_{32} 4$

21. Give the first four terms of $(2a - 3b)^9$.

22. (a) What is the result of the composition of two line reflections if the lines of reflection intersect? (b) What is the result of the composition of three line reflections if the three lines of reflection intersect in one point?

23. Write a formula for the mean using summation notation.

24. Express $\log_9 2$ in terms of common logarithms.

25. Prove: $\dfrac{\cos x}{1 + \sin x} = \dfrac{\cot x}{1 + \csc x}$

26. How many 5-letter arrangements can be formed from the letters in the word PAINTER if repetition of letters (a) is allowed and (b) is not allowed?

27. A rectangle 21 cm long and 20 cm wide is inscribed in a circle. Find the area of the region inside the circle and outside the rectangle.

28. If $\triangle ABC$ has vertices $A(-4, 2)$, $B(2, 6)$, and $C(4, 0)$, find the coordinates of the vertices of its image under $D_{-2} \circ r_k$, where k is the line with equation $y = -x$.

29. If $f(x) = 3x + 2$ and $g(x) = \dfrac{1}{3}x - 2$, find $f(g(x))$ and $g(f(x))$.

30. Find the exact values of $\csc \dfrac{13\pi}{12}$ and $\tan \left(-\dfrac{9\pi}{4} \right)$.

31. Graph at least two cycles of $y = 3 \cos \dfrac{x}{2}$.

32. A normal distribution has mean 200 and standard deviation 20. What percent of the observations are expected to be less than 230?

33. Make an operation table for the symmetry group of an ellipse.

34. The contestants in a free-throw contest scored the following numbers of points: 24, 20, 16, 32, 36, 18, 26, and 12. Find the variance and standard deviation of the scores.

The line of tuba players in the marching band shown above suggests a *sequence*. Arithmetic and geometric sequences and series are discussed in this chapter.

Sequences and Series   15

When the great German mathematician Carl Friedrich Gauss was ten, he and his classmates were asked by their teacher to add all the integers from 1 to 100. The teacher, believing that he had assigned the students an exercise that would occupy them for a long time, was surprised when, a few moments later, Gauss handed in his slate with a single number written on it. When the slates were all handed in, the teacher checked them and was surprised to see that Gauss had found the correct answer.

Gauss had discovered a clever shortcut. His idea was to find twice the sum, using the following scheme:

$$\begin{array}{r} 1 + 2 + 3 + \cdots + 99 + 100 \\ 100 + 99 + 98 + \cdots + 2 + 1 \\ \hline 101 + 101 + 101 + \cdots + 101 + 101 \end{array}$$

Thus, twice the sum is 100(101), or 10,100. Gauss concluded that the sum was $10,100 \div 2$, or 5050.

Although Gauss was not the first to use this method, his independent discovery of it foreshadowed some of the remarkable mathematical achievements of his later life. In this chapter you will see how Gauss's method can be used to derive a formula for the sum of an *arithmetic series*.

Section 15-1 DEFINITION OF A SEQUENCE

Do you recognize the following *sequence* of numbers?

$$31, 29, 31, 30, 31, 30, 31, 31, 30, 31, 30, 31$$

The sequence gives the number of days in each successive month during a leap year. In this section you will study:

- finite sequences
- infinite sequences

In each of the following lists of numbers the order of the entries is important.

EXAMPLES   **1.** The value of a house in 3 successive years:
$$\$65,000, \ \$70,000, \ \$74,000$$

2. The temperature at noon on 4 successive days:
$$15°C, \ 16°C, \ 14°C, \ 16°C$$

3. The cubes of the first 5 natural numbers:
$$1, \ 8, \ 27, \ 64, \ 125$$

Each of the lists just presented is an example of a finite sequence. A *finite sequence* is defined to be a function whose domain is $\{1, 2, 3, \ldots, n\}$ for some natural number n, and whose range is a set of real numbers. (In this chapter the variables k and n will always represent natural numbers.)

Any list of real numbers consisting of n entries defines a finite sequence. For example, when we write

$$3, 7, 11, 15, 19, 23, 27, 31,$$

we are saying: "The *first* number is 3, the *second* number is 7, and so on." Thus, we have established the following correspondence between the set $\{1, 2, 3, 4, 5, 6, 7, 8\}$ and the set $\{3, 7, 11, 15, 19, 23, 27, 31\}$.

1	2	3	4	5	6	7	8
↓	↓	↓	↓	↓	↓	↓	↓
3	7	11	15	19	23	27	31

It is easy to see that the list defines a function whose domain is $\{1, 2, 3, 4, 5, 6, 7, 8\}$ and whose range is the set of real numbers $\{3, 7, 11, 15, 19, 23, 27, 31\}$.

An *infinite sequence* is a function whose domain is the entire set of natural numbers and whose range is a set of real numbers.

EXAMPLE   The sequence of squares of the natural numbers is an infinite sequence:
$$1, 4, 9, 16, 25, \ldots$$

We refer to members of the range of a sequence as the *terms* of the sequence. We use subscript notation rather than function notation when working with sequences. Thus, we write the value of the third term of the previous sequence as follows:

$$a_3 = 9$$

The kth term of the same sequence is given by the following equation:

$$a_k = k^2$$

In fact, the equation above can be used to give the following *explicit rule* for the sequence.

$$a_k = k^2, \quad k \in \{1, 2, 3, \ldots\}$$

EXAMPLE   Give an explicit rule for the sequence: 3, 8, 13, 18, 23, 28

SOLUTION   Note that: $a_2 = a_1 + 5$

$$a_3 = a_2 + 5 = (a_1 + 5) + 5 = a_1 + 2(5)$$
$$a_4 = a_3 + 5 = [a_1 + 2(5)] + 5 = a_1 + 3(5)$$

These equations suggest that:

$$a_k = a_1 + (k - 1)(5)$$
$$= 3 + 5k - 5$$
$$= 5k - 2$$

Thus, an explicit rule for this sequence is:

$$a_k = 5k - 2, \quad k \in \{1, 2, 3, \ldots, 6\}$$

EXAMPLE   Give an explicit rule for the sequence: $-1, 4, -9, 16, -25, 36, -49, \ldots$

SOLUTION   Except for the fact that the odd-numbered terms are negative, this sequence is the sequence of squares of the natural numbers. In order to make the odd-numbered terms of the sequence negative, the factor $(-1)^k$ is introduced.

$$t_k = (-1)^k \cdot k^2, \quad k \in \{1, 2, 3, \ldots\}$$

If you had wanted the even-numbered terms in the previous example to be negative, you could have used the factor $(-1)^{k+1}$.

Another way to give a rule for a sequence is to state the value for the first term and then give an equation for each successive term by relating it to the preceding term (or terms). Such a rule is called a *recursive* rule.

We will now find the recursive rule for the sequence 3, 8, 13, 18, 23, 28, which was presented in the example at the top of this page. We observed the following relationships between the terms:

$$a_2 = a_1 + 5$$
$$a_3 = a_2 + 5$$
$$a_4 = a_3 + 5$$

These equations suggest the following recursive rule for the sequence.

$$a_1 = 3$$
$$a_k = a_{k-1} + 5, \quad k \in \{2, 3, \ldots, 6\}$$

EXAMPLE   Find the first 4 terms of the sequence with the following recursive rule.

$$a_1 = \frac{2}{3}$$
$$a_k = 3a_{k-1}, \quad k \in \{2, 3, 4, \ldots\}$$

SOLUTION $a_1 = \dfrac{2}{3}$

$$a_2 = 3a_1 = 3 \cdot \frac{2}{3} = 2$$
$$a_3 = 3a_2 = 3 \cdot 2 = 6$$
$$a_4 = 3a_3 = 3 \cdot 6 = 18$$

The first 4 terms are $\dfrac{2}{3}$, 2, 6, and 18.

A sequence of particular mathematical interest is the *Fibonacci sequence,* named after the Italian mathematician of the thirteenth century who first studied it extensively. The Fibonacci sequence can be defined by the following recursive rule:

$$a_1 = 1$$
$$a_2 = 1$$
$$a_k = a_{k-1} + a_{k-2}, \quad k \in \{3, 4, 5, \ldots\}$$

The first 14 terms of this infinite sequence are:

F_1	F_2	F_3	F_4	F_5	F_6	F_7	F_8	F_9	F_{10}	F_{11}	F_{12}	F_{13}	F_{14}
1	1	2	3	5	8	13	21	34	55	89	144	233	377

You will investigate some of the mathematical properties of this sequence in the exercises for this section.

ORAL EXERCISES

State the first 4 terms of each sequence. In the rule for each sequence, $k \in \{1, 2, 3, \ldots\}$.

1. $a_k = k + 2$

2. $a_k = 3k - 1$

3. $a_k = 3^k$

4. $b_k = (-1)^k$

5. $c_k = 3 \cdot 2^k$

6. $t_k = k^2 + 1$

State the first 4 terms of each sequence. In the rule for each sequence, $k \in \{2, 3, 4, \ldots\}$.

7. $a_1 = 5, \ a_k = a_{k-1} + 2$

8. $a_1 = 16, \ a_k = \dfrac{1}{2} a_{k-1}$

9. $a_1 = 2, \ a_k = 2 - a_{k-1}$

10. $b_1 = 7, \ b_k = b_{k-1} - 5$

11. $c_1 = -3, \ c_k = -2c_{k-1}$

12. $t_1 = 2, \ t_k = \dfrac{1}{t_{k-1}}$

WRITTEN EXERCISES

Give an explicit rule for each sequence.

A **1.** 1, 8, 27, 64, 125

2. 0, 1, 4, 9, 16, 25

3. -2, 1, 4, 7, 10, 13, 16

4. 2, 4, 8, 16, 32, 64

5. $\dfrac{1}{2}$, 1, 2, 4, 8, $\ldots$

6. -3, 9, -27, 81, $\ldots$

Give a recursive rule for each sequence.

7. -3, 1, 5, 9, 13, 17, 21

8. $\dfrac{1}{2}, \dfrac{3}{2}, \dfrac{9}{2}, \dfrac{27}{2}, \dfrac{81}{2}, \dfrac{243}{2}$

9. $-\dfrac{3}{2}$, 6, -24, 96, $\ldots$

10. $\dfrac{5}{2}$, 1, $-\dfrac{1}{2}$, -2, $\ldots$

11. $3, \dfrac{1}{3}, 3, \dfrac{1}{3}, 3, \ldots$ **12.** $0, 1, 0, 1, 0, \ldots$

13. Make a list of the values of F_{15} through F_{20} in the Fibonacci sequence. Keep the list handy for reference in later exercises.

Give an explicit rule for each sequence. (*Hint*: Consider $(-1)^k$.)

B 14. $0, 2, 0, 2, 0, \ldots$ **15.** $1, 0, 1, 0, 1, \ldots$

16. Give an explicit rule for the sequence defined by the recursive rule:

$$a_1 = s$$
$$a_k = a_{k-1} + d, \quad k \in \{2, 3, 4, \ldots\}$$

17. Give an explicit rule for the sequence defined by the recursive rule:

$$a_1 = t$$
$$a_k = ra_{k-1}, \quad k \in \{2, 3, 4, \ldots\}$$

Exercises 18–23 refer to the Fibonacci sequence.

18. a. Find the value of each expression:

$$(F_1)^2 + (F_2)^2, \quad (F_2)^2 + (F_3)^2, \quad (F_3)^2 + (F_4)^2, \quad (F_4)^2 + (F_5)^2$$

   b. State as an equation the theorem that is suggested by these values.
   c. Verify the theorem you stated in part (b) for two more pairs of Fibonacci numbers.

19. a. Find the value of each expression:

$$(F_3)^2 - (F_1)^2, \quad (F_4)^2 - (F_2)^2, \quad (F_5)^2 - (F_3)^2, \quad (F_6)^2 - (F_4)^2$$

   b. State as an equation the theorem that is suggested by the values in part (a).
   c. Verify the theorem you stated in part (b) for two more pairs of Fibonacci numbers.

Follow the procedure used in Exercises 18 and 19 to state and verify for two additional cases a theorem that is suggested by evaluating the given expressions.

20. $F_4 F_3 - F_2 F_1, \quad F_5 F_4 - F_3 F_2, \quad F_6 F_5 - F_4 F_3$

21. $F_1 F_2 + F_2 F_3, \quad F_2 F_3 + F_3 F_4, \quad F_3 F_4 + F_4 F_5$

22. a. Which of the first 20 Fibonacci numbers are divisible by F_3? What can you say about the subscripts of these numbers?
   b. Which of the first 20 Fibonacci numbers are divisible by F_4? What can you say about the subscripts of these numbers?
   c. What can you say about the subscripts of the Fibonacci numbers that are divisible by F_5? by F_6?
   d. Use the observations you made in parts (a–c) to state a conjecture about the divisibility of Fibonacci numbers by F_k.

23. Consider a Fibonacci number that is also a prime number. What do the results of Exercise 22 suggest must be true of the subscript?

Section 15-2 ARITHMETIC SEQUENCES

A sequence $a_1, a_2, a_3, a_4, \ldots$ that satisfies the recursive equation

$$a_k = a_{k-1} + d,$$

for some real number d, is called an *arithmetic sequence* (or an *arithmetic progression*). The real number d is called the *common difference* of the sequence, and a_1 is called the *first term* of the sequence. To find the common difference of an arithmetic sequence, you can subtract from any term the immediately preceding term.

EXAMPLE   Determine whether or not the following sequence is arithmetic.

$$-4, -1, 2, 5, 8$$

SOLUTION   If the sequence is arithmetic, you can find the common difference as follows:

$$d = a_4 - a_3 = 5 - 2 = 3$$

You can verify that the terms of the sequence satisfy the resulting recursive equation:

$$a_k = a_{k-1} + 3$$

Therefore the sequence is arithmetic.

We can derive an explicit rule for an arithmetic sequence as follows:

$$a_1 = a_1 + (0)d$$
$$a_2 = a_1 + d = a_1 + (1)d$$
$$a_3 = a_2 + d = (a_1 + d) + d = a_1 + 2d$$
$$a_4 = a_3 + d = (a_1 + 2d) + d = a_1 + 3d$$
$$a_5 = a_4 + d = (a_1 + 3d) + d = a_1 + 4d$$

These equations suggest the following general result.

If $a_1, a_2, a_3, \ldots$ is an arithmetic sequence with common difference d, then

$$a_k = a_1 + (k-1)d.$$

The formula just given applies to both finite and infinite arithmetic sequences. It shows that you can find any term of an arithmetic sequence if you know the first term and the common difference.

EXAMPLE   Find the thirteenth term of the arithmetic sequence: $-7, 1, 9, 17, \ldots$

SOLUTION   In order to apply the formula, you must know the value of d.

$$d = a_2 - a_1 = 1 - (-7) = 8$$

Substitute -7 for a_1, 13 for k, and 8 for d in the formula:

$$a_k = a_1 + (k-1)d$$
$$a_{13} = -7 + (13-1)(8) = -7 + 12 \cdot 8 = 89$$

EXAMPLE   Find the third term of an arithmetic sequence whose first term is 5 and whose ninth term is -7.

SOLUTION   You know that $a_1 = 5$ and $a_9 = -7$.

Substitute these values in the formula and solve for d:

$$a_9 = a_1 + (9 - 1)d$$
$$-7 = 5 + 8d$$
$$-12 = 8d$$
$$d = -\frac{12}{8} = -\frac{3}{2}$$

Thus: $a_3 = a_1 + (3 - 1)d = 5 + 2\left(-\frac{3}{2}\right) = 2$

The concept of an arithmetic sequence provides a way to find a number or numbers that are equally spaced between two given numbers. We say that a number m is the *arithmetic mean* (or *average*) of two numbers a and b if the sequence

$$a, m, b$$

is arithmetic. You can see that the formula given for the mean in Section 13-2,

$$m = \frac{a + b}{2},$$

still applies. The sequence

$$a, \frac{a + b}{2}, b$$

is arithmetic with common difference $\dfrac{b - a}{2}$.

We say that $m_1, m_2, m_3, \ldots, m_n$ are the *n arithmetic means* between two numbers a and b if the sequence

$$a, m_1, m_2, m_3, \ldots, m_n, b$$

is arithmetic. When a is less than b, the n arithmetic means between a and b can be shown on the number line as follows.

EXAMPLE   Insert 5 arithmetic means between 2 and 68.

SOLUTION   You are asked to find an arithmetic sequence of 7 terms (the 2 given numbers and the 5 arithmetic means) such that

$$a_1 = 2 \quad \text{and} \quad a_7 = 68.$$

Substitute in the formula as follows:
$$a_7 = a_1 + (7 - 1)d$$
$$68 = 2 + 6d$$
$$66 = 6d$$
$$d = 11$$

The desired sequence is 2, 13, 24, 35, 46, 57, 68. Therefore the 5 arithmetic means between 2 and 68 are 13, 24, 35, 46, and 57.

ORAL EXERCISES

State the first 4 terms of an arithmetic sequence $a_1, a_2, a_3, \ldots$ satisfying the given conditions.

1. $a_1 = 5, d = -2$
2. $a_1 = 17\frac{1}{2}, d = 10$
3. $a_2 = 6, d = 8$
4. $a_2 = -14, d = 5$
5. $a_k = 3k + 7$
6. $a_k = 3 - k$
7. $a_k = -1 + (k-1)(2)$
8. $a_k = 3 + (k-1)(6)$

State whether or not each sequence is arithmetic. Give a reason for your answer.

9. $-2, 6, 14, 22, 30$
10. $3, 6, 9, 15, 21$
11. $5, 1, -3, -7, -11$
12. $-5, -7, -9, -11, -13$
13. $-10\frac{1}{4}, -9\frac{1}{2}, -8\frac{3}{4}, -8, -7\frac{1}{4}$
14. $-3, -5, -7, -11, -13$

State the common difference of each arithmetic sequence.

15. $3\sqrt{2}, 5\sqrt{2}, 7\sqrt{2}, \ldots$
16. $b - c, b, b + c, \ldots$
17. $a_k = 5 + 12(k-1)$
18. $a_k = 3 - 4(k-1)$
19. $\log 3, \log 6, \log 12, \ldots$
20. $\frac{1}{x}, \frac{1+x}{x}, \frac{1+2x}{x}, \ldots$

WRITTEN EXERCISES

Find the specified term of the arithmetic sequence satisfying the given conditions.

A

1. $a_1 = -12, d = 7; a_{21} = \underline{\quad?\quad}$
2. $a_1 = 40, d = -5; a_{32} = \underline{\quad?\quad}$
3. $a_1 = -3, d = -\frac{1}{2}; a_{17} = \underline{\quad?\quad}$
4. $a_1 = 18, d = -\frac{2}{3}; a_{28} = \underline{\quad?\quad}$
5. $a_1 = 3, a_2 = \frac{1}{2}; a_{41} = \underline{\quad?\quad}$
6. $a_1 = -25, a_2 = -23\frac{1}{2}; a_{33} = \underline{\quad?\quad}$
7. $a_2 = \frac{3}{5}, a_3 = 1; a_{26} = \underline{\quad?\quad}$
8. $a_2 = \frac{3}{2}, a_3 = 0; a_{18} = \underline{\quad?\quad}$
9. $a_{45} = 57, d = 2; a_1 = \underline{\quad?\quad}$
10. $a_{39} = -2, d = -3; a_1 = \underline{\quad?\quad}$
11. $a_{51} = 48, d = -\frac{3}{2}; a_1 = \underline{\quad?\quad}$
12. $a_{29} = -5, d = \frac{3}{4}; a_1 = \underline{\quad?\quad}$

Insert the given number of arithmetic means between the given numbers.

13. 1 between -5 and 15
14. 1 between -12 and -22
15. 4 between 7 and 72
16. 6 between -25 and 3
17. 8 between -13 and -1
18. 7 between $-\frac{1}{2}$ and $11\frac{1}{2}$

Find the first term a_1 and the common difference d of the arithmetic sequence having the given terms.

EXAMPLE $a_5 = 3$, $a_{12} = 45$

SOLUTION   Substitute in the formula to obtain the system of equations shown at the right below.

$$a_5 = a_1 + (5-1)d$$
$$a_{12} = a_1 + (12-1)d$$

$3 = a_1 + 4d$
$45 = a_1 + 11d$

Subtract the second equation from the first to eliminate a_1. Then solve for d.

$-42 = -7d$
$d = 6$

Substitute the value of d in the first equation and solve for a_1.

$3 = a_1 + 4d$
$3 = a_1 + 4(6)$
$a_1 = -21$

B 19. $a_7 = 15$, $a_{23} = -113$ 20. $a_3 = -2$, $a_{15} = 6$

21. $a_{12} = -25$, $a_{36} = 11$ 22. $a_9 = -7$, $a_{41} = -31$

23. Find the value of x if the sequence $2x - 8$, $x + 3$, $3x - 1$ is arithmetic.

24. Repeat Exercise 23 for the sequence $5x + 2$, $x - 7$, $3x + 2$.

25. Find all possible values of x if the sequence $-2x$, $x^2 - 3$, $3x^2 - 14$ is arithmetic.

26. Repeat Exercise 25 for the sequence $3x$, $3x^2 - 2$, $4x^2 - 2$.

27. Show that the sequence $\log a$, $\log ab$, $\log ab^2$, $\log ab^3$, ... is arithmetic for any positive real numbers a and b.

C 28. Suppose the sequence a_1, a_2, a_3, a_4, ... is arithmetic, with $a_1 = 1$ and a common difference of $\dfrac{1}{2}$.

a. Give a recursive rule for the sequence:

$$2^{a_1},\ 2^{a_2},\ 2^{a_3},\ 2^{a_4}, \ldots$$

b. Find the values of the first 5 terms of the sequence defined in part (a).

29. Repeat Exercise 28 if the common difference of the first sequence is 1 and $a_1 = \log_2 3$.

Section 15-3 ARITHMETIC SERIES

At the beginning of this chapter you read about the special method Gauss used to find the sum of the integers from 1 to 100. That sum can also be found by a direct application of one of the formulas you will learn in this section, which deals with a type of formal sum known as an *arithmetic series*.

A *series* is the indicated sum of a sequence. A *finite series* will be an expression of the form

$$a_1 + a_2 + a_3 + \cdots + a_n.$$

You can think of a series as a sequence in which + signs replace the commas. As in a sequence, the numbers a_1, a_2, a_3, . . . are called the *terms* of the series.

EXAMPLE   Sequence: 15, 8, 1, −6, −13
                Related series: $15 + 8 + 1 - 6 - 13$ (Notice that we write $+(-6)$ as -6.)

If the terms of a series form an arithmetic sequence, then the series is called an *arithmetic series*. To find the *sum* of an arithmetic series, $a_1 + a_2 + a_3 + \cdots + a_n$, you can proceed as follows. Let S_n represent the sum of the arithmetic series and write:

$$S_n = a_1 + a_2 + a_3 + \cdots + a_n$$
$$S_n = a_n + a_{n-1} + a_{n-2} + \cdots + a_1$$

Adding the two equations, you get:

$$2S_n = (a_1 + a_n) + (a_2 + a_{n-1}) + (a_3 + a_{n-2}) + \cdots + (a_n + a_1)$$

Next you can find a method for combining the expressions in parentheses. Note that

$$a_2 = a_1 + d \quad \text{and} \quad a_{n-1} = a_n - d,$$

where d is the common difference of the arithmetic sequence of terms. Thus:

$$a_2 + a_{n-1} = (a_1 + d) + (a_n - d) = a_1 + a_n$$

Similarly:

$$a_3 + a_{n-2} = (a_2 + d) + (a_{n-1} - d) = a_2 + a_{n-1} = a_1 + a_n$$

In fact, each expression within parentheses in the equation giving the value of $2S_n$ is equal to $(a_1 + a_n)$. Thus:

$$2S_n = \underbrace{(a_1 + a_n) + (a_1 + a_n) + (a_1 + a_n) + \cdots + (a_1 + a_n)}_{n \text{ times}}$$

$$2S_n = n(a_1 + a_n)$$

Dividing each side by 2, you obtain the formula below.

If S_n denotes the sum of the arithmetic series $a_1 + a_2 + a_3 + \cdots + a_n$, then

$$S_n = \frac{n(a_1 + a_n)}{2}.$$

EXAMPLE   Find the sum of the arithmetic series of 12 terms with first term 7 and twelfth term 91.

SOLUTION   In this series $n = 12$, $a_1 = 7$, and $a_n = a_{12} = 91$. Substitute these values in the formula:

$$S_n = \frac{n(a_1 + a_n)}{2}$$

$$S_{12} = \frac{12(7 + 91)}{2} = 6(98) = 588$$

EXAMPLE Find the sum of the positive *even* integers less than or equal to 100.

SOLUTION Since you know that $a_1 = 2$, $a_n = 100$, and $d = 2$, you can find n by substituting in the formula.

$$a_n = a_1 + (n - 1)d$$
$$100 = 2 + (n - 1)2$$
$$98 = 2(n - 1)$$
$$49 = n - 1$$
$$50 = n$$

Use the formula to find the sum.

$$S_n = \frac{n(a_1 + a_n)}{2}$$

$$S_{50} = \frac{50(2 + 100)}{2} = 25(102) = 2550$$

Since the terms of an arithmetic series form an arithmetic sequence, you can derive a formula that expresses the sum of an arithmetic series in terms of the first term and the common difference. Consider the arithmetic series $a_1 + a_2 + \cdots + a_n$ with common difference d. Since the terms form an arithmetic sequence:

$$a_n = a_1 + (n - 1)d$$

Substituting for a_n in the sum formula

$$S_n = \frac{n(a_1 + a_n)}{2}$$

you obtain:

$$S_n = \frac{n(a_1 + (a_1 + (n - 1)d))}{2}$$

Simplifying the expression on the right gives the following general result.

If S_n denotes the sum of the arithmetic series $a_1 + a_2 + a_3 + \cdots + a_n$, then

$$S_n = \frac{n}{2}(2a_1 + (n - 1)d).$$

EXAMPLE Find the sum of the arithmetic series of 21 terms beginning

$$-2 + 3 + 8 + \cdots.$$

SOLUTION In this series $a_1 = -2$ and $n = 21$. To find d, you can subtract any term from the term immediately following it. For example:

$$d = a_2 - a_1 = 3 - (-2) = 5$$

Substitute in the formula:

$$S_n = \frac{n}{2}(2a_1 + (n - 1)d)$$

$$S_{21} = \frac{21}{2}(2(-2) + (21 - 1)5) = \frac{21}{2}(-4 + 100) = 1008$$

SEQUENCES AND SERIES **603**

You have now studied two formulas that give the sum of an arithmetic series. If you know (or can find) n, a_1, and a_n, then use the formula involving the last term:

$$S_n = \frac{n(a_1 + a_n)}{2}$$

If you know (or can find) n, a_1, and d, use the formula involving the common difference:

$$S_n = \frac{n}{2}(2a_1 + (n-1)d)$$

Often you can use either formula.

ORAL EXERCISES

Give the values of a_1, n, and either d or a_n for the arithmetic series satisfying the given conditions. Tell how you would find the sum of the series.

EXAMPLE   The series of 10 terms beginning $-5 - 2 + 1 + 4 + \cdots$

SOLUTION $a_1 = -5$; $n = 10$; $d = 3$. Substitute these values in the sum formula involving the common difference.

1. The series whose first term is 5 and whose twelfth (and last) term is 126.

2. The series of 15 terms beginning $-8 - 2 + 4 + \cdots$

3. The series of 18 terms beginning $1 - 5 - 11 - \cdots$

4. The series consisting of all the positive multiples of 3 beginning with 3 and ending with 300

5. The series of 23 terms whose first term is $-\frac{1}{2}$ and whose terms can be defined recursively by the relationship $a_k = a_{k-1} + \frac{3}{2}$

6. The series of all integers greater than -25 and less than 52

7. State another arithmetic series with the same sum as the series defined in Exercise 6.

8. The sum of any arithmetic series of the form
$$1 + 2 + 3 + 4 + \cdots + n$$
is called a *triangular number*. For example, 10 is the fourth triangular number because $1 + 2 + 3 + 4 = 10$. The diagram shows why the name is appropriate.
   a. Find the first 8 triangular numbers.
   b. If you add any two consecutive triangular numbers, what kind of number do you get?

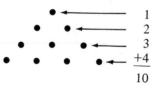

WRITTEN EXERCISES

Find the sum of the arithmetic series
$$a_1 + a_2 + a_3 + \cdots + a_n$$
with common difference d, using the given information.

A 1. $a_1 = 12$, $a_n = a_{21} = 212$ 2. $a_1 = -56$, $a_{13} = 72$, $n = 13$

3. $a_1 = 5$, $a_n = -133$, $n = 17$ 4. $a_1 = 12$, $d = 2$, $n = 10$

5. $a_1 = -3$, $n = 8$, $d = 3$ 6. $a_1 = -8$, $d = 4$, $n = 12$

7. The series of 25 terms beginning $-\dfrac{1}{2} + 1 + \dfrac{5}{2} + \cdots$

8. The series of 26 terms beginning $19 + 11 + 3 + \cdots$

9. The series whose terms are the first 21 positive multiples of 3

10. The series whose terms are the first 50 positive *odd* integers

11. The series of 29 terms whose first term is 15 and whose terms can be defined recursively by the equation $a_k = a_{k-1} - \dfrac{1}{2}$

12. The series of 20 terms defined explicitly by the equation $a_k = 7k - 4$

13. The series $\displaystyle\sum_{k=1}^{24} (5k - 2)$ 14. The series $\displaystyle\sum_{k=1}^{19} \left(\dfrac{2}{3}k + \dfrac{1}{3}\right)$

B 15. The series whose first 2 terms are $\dfrac{1}{2}$ and 4, and whose last term is 60

16. The series whose first term is 7.6 and whose last 2 terms are -5 and -5.2

17. The series of 16 terms whose last 2 terms are 8 and 14

18. The series of 21 terms such that $a_{20} = -3$ and $a_{21} = -7$

Use the information given about the arithmetic series to find the requested number.

19. $S_{12} = 126$, $a_{12} = 45$; $a_1 = $ __?__   20. $S_9 = 81$, $a_1 = -12$; $a_9 = $ __?__

21. $S_{16} = 104$, $a_1 = -16$; $d = $ __?__   22. $S_{21} = 126$, $a_1 = 36$; $d = $ __?__

23. $S_n = 32$, $a_1 = -3$, $d = 2$; $n = $ __?__   24. $S_n = -30$, $a_1 = 5$, $d = -4$; $n = $ __?__

C 25. For what value of n is the sum of the first n positive integers equal to 1275?

26. For what value of n is the sum of the first n positive *even* integers equal to 930?

27. a. Show that $1 + 3 + 5 + \cdots + (2k - 1) = k^2$.
   b. For what value of k does the diagram illustrate the result of part (a)?

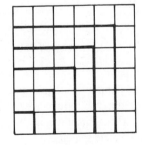

Ex. 27

28. a. Prove that if T_k represents the kth triangular number, as defined in Oral Exercise 8, then

$$T_k + T_{k+1} = (k+1)^2.$$

b. Use a 5-by-5 array of dots to illustrate the result of part (a) when k is 4.

SELF-TEST 1

Give a recursive rule for each sequence.

1. $\dfrac{1}{2}, \dfrac{2}{3}, \dfrac{5}{6}, 1, \ldots$ **2.** $1, -2, 4, -8, \ldots$ Section 15-1

Give an explicit rule for each sequence.

3. $5, 7, 9, 11, \ldots$ **4.** $2, 5, 10, 17, \ldots$

Find the specified term of the arithmetic sequence satisfying the given conditions.

5. $a_1 = 4$, $d = 3$; $a_{10} = \underline{\ ?\ }$ **6.** $a_{20} = 10$, $d = -\dfrac{1}{2}$; $a_1 = \underline{\ ?\ }$ Section 15-2

7. Insert 3 arithmetic means between 4 and 28.

Find the sum of the arithmetic series $a_1 + a_2 + a_3 + \cdots + a_n$, using the given information.

8. $a_1 = 5$, $a_n = 15$, $n = 30$ **9.** $a_1 = -10$, $d = \dfrac{1}{2}$, $n = 200$ Section 15-3

10. The sum of an arithmetic series having 10 terms is 15. If the common difference is 2, what is the first term in the series?

Section 15-4 GEOMETRIC SEQUENCES

You often hear that the price of a certain item has gone up by a certain percent each year. For example, suppose a particular make of car cost $5000 two years ago, and its cost has increased 10% per year. You can state:

$$\text{price at a given time} = (1.10)(\text{price a year earlier})$$

Therefore, the car cost $(1.10)(5000)$, or 5500, dollars one year ago, and the car costs $(1.10)(5500)$, or 6050, dollars this year. The sequence of prices,

$$\$5000, \$5500, \$6050,$$

is an example of a type of sequence called a *geometric sequence*. Successive terms of a geometric sequence are found by a recursive equation that involves multiplication rather than addition. In this section you will learn about:
- geometric sequences
- geometric means

In general a sequence that satisfies the recursive equation

$$a_k = a_{k-1}r,$$

for some real number r, is called a *geometric sequence* (or a *geometric progression*). The real number r is called the *common ratio* of the sequence. To find the common ratio of a sequence, you can divide any term by the immediately preceding (non-zero) term.

EXAMPLE Determine whether or not the following sequence is geometric:

$$3, 6, 12, 24, 48, 96$$

SOLUTION If the sequence is geometric, we can find the common ratio as follows:

$$r = \frac{a_2}{a_1} = \frac{6}{3} = 2$$

You can verify that the terms of the sequence satisfy the resulting recursive equation:

$$a_k = a_{k-1} \cdot 2$$

Therefore the sequence is geometric. (You can readily see that this sequence is not arithmetic because the differences of consecutive terms are not constant. For example, $6 - 3 \neq 12 - 6$.)

To find an explicit rule for any geometric sequence whose first term is a_1 and whose common ratio is the real number r, we may proceed as follows:

$$a_1 = a_1$$
$$a_2 = a_1 r = a_1 r^1$$
$$a_3 = a_2 r = (a_1 r)r = a_1 r^2$$
$$a_4 = a_3 r = (a_1 r^2)r = a_1 r^3$$

These equations suggest the following general result.

If the sequence $a_1, a_2, a_3, \ldots$ is geometric witn common ratio r, then for $k > 1$,

$$a_k = a_1 r^{k-1}.$$

EXAMPLE Find the eighth term of the geometric sequence:

$$\frac{5}{27}, \frac{5}{9}, \frac{5}{3}, 5, \ldots$$

SOLUTION $r = 5 \div \frac{5}{3} = 5 \cdot \frac{3}{5} = 3$

Substitute in the formula:

$$a_k = a_1 r^{k-1}$$
$$a_8 = a_1 r^7$$
$$= \frac{5}{27} \cdot 3^7 = \frac{5}{3^3} \cdot 3^7 = 5 \cdot 3^4 = 5 \cdot 81 = 405$$

The computation in the preceding example illustrates that it is often best to leave expressions that arise from geometric sequences in exponential form and simplify before multiplying. Of course, you can always multiply out the exponential expressions first and then simplify.

The *geometric mean*, or *mean proportional*, of two positive real numbers a and b is defined to be the unique *positive* real number m such that the sequence

$$a, m, b$$

is geometric. Notice that a geometric mean bears the same relationship to a geometric sequence that an arithmetic mean bears to an arithmetic sequence. When m is the geometric mean of a and b, both $\dfrac{m}{a}$ and $\dfrac{b}{m}$ must equal a common ratio r. Therefore:

$$\frac{b}{m} = \frac{m}{a}$$
$$m^2 = ab$$
$$m = \sqrt{ab}$$

EXAMPLE   Find the geometric mean of 2 and 32.

SOLUTION $m = \sqrt{2 \cdot 32} = \sqrt{64} = 8$.

The geometric mean of 2 and 32 is 8.

The positive numbers $m_1, m_2, m_3, \ldots, m_n$ are the *n geometric means* between two positive numbers a and b if the sequence

$$a, m_1, m_2, m_3, \ldots, m_n, b$$

is geometric.

EXAMPLE   Insert 3 geometric means between 2 and 162.

SOLUTION   You want a geometric sequence of 5 terms (the 2 given numbers and the 3 geometric means). In this sequence:

$$a_1 = 2 \quad \text{and} \quad a_5 = 162$$

Substitute in the formula:

$$a_k = a_1 r^{k-1}$$
$$a_5 = a_1 \cdot r^{5-1}$$

Substitute the values of a_1 and a_5.

$$162 = 2r^4$$
$$r^4 = 81$$
$$r = \pm\sqrt[4]{81} = \pm 3$$

Since the geometric means are defined to be positive numbers, we use the value 3 for r. Thus, you obtain the sequence of 5 terms:

$$2, 6, 18, 54, 162$$

The 3 geometric means between 2 and 162 are 6, 18, and 54.

ORAL EXERCISES

Classify each sequence as arithmetic, geometric, or neither. If the sequence is arithmetic, state the common difference. If the sequence is geometric, state the common ratio.

1. $\frac{1}{2}$, 1, 2, 4, ...

2. 1, 4, 9, 16, ...

3. -4, 2, 8, 14, ...

4. 2, $\frac{1}{2}$, -1, $-\frac{5}{2}$, ...

5. 18, 6, 2, $\frac{2}{3}$, ...

6. 1, 2, 4, 7, 11, ...

7. 2, -2, 2, -2, ...

8. 3, $3\sqrt{2}$, 6, $6\sqrt{2}$, ...

9. $a - b$, a, $a + b$, $a + 2b$, ...

10. a, ak^2, ak^4, ak^6, ...

11. 1234, 123.4, 12.34, 1.234, ...

12. 10^a, 10^{a+b}, 10^{a+2b}, 10^{a+3b}, ...

Find the third term of the given sequence if the sequence is: **(a)** arithmetic; **(b)** geometric.

13. 4, 12, ...

14. 4, -2, ...

15. $\frac{1}{2}$, $\frac{5}{2}$, ...

16. -7, 7, ...

WRITTEN EXERCISES

Find the specified term of the given geometric sequence.

A   1. a_7; $\frac{3}{2}$, 3, 6, ...

2. a_8; 40, 20, 10, ...

3. a_9; $\frac{1}{27}$, $\frac{1}{9}$, $\frac{1}{3}$, ...

4. a_9; 0.007, 0.07, 0.7, ...

5. a_6; 9, 6, 4, ...

6. a_7; $\frac{1}{27}$, $\frac{1}{18}$, $\frac{1}{12}$, ...

7. a_8; 5, -10, 20, ...

8. a_9; -96, 48, -24, ...

9. a_6; $333\frac{1}{3}$, $33\frac{1}{3}$, $3\frac{1}{3}$, ...

10. a_7; $1\frac{1}{9}$, $-11\frac{1}{9}$, $111\frac{1}{9}$, ...

11. a_7; 3, $3\sqrt{2}$, 6, ...

12. a_8; $4\sqrt{3}$, 4, $\frac{4}{3}\sqrt{3}$, ...

13. a_{10}; $\frac{P}{Q^2}$, $\frac{P}{Q}$, P, ...

14. a_{12}; xy^3, x^2y^2, x^3y, ...

Use the information given about the geometric sequence to find the requested number.

15. $a_6 = \frac{4}{81}$, $r = \frac{1}{3}$; $a_1 = $ ___?___

16. $a_5 = 666\frac{2}{3}$, $r = 10$; $a_1 = $ ___?___

17. $a_7 = 12$, $r = \frac{3}{2}$; $a_1 = $ ___?___

18. $a_8 = \frac{1}{125}$, $r = \frac{2}{5}$; $a_1 = $ ___?___

19. $a_n = \frac{3}{32}$, $r = \frac{1}{2}$, $a_1 = 3$; $n = $ ___?___

20. $a_n = -\frac{81}{4}$, $r = \frac{3}{2}$, $a_1 = -\frac{8}{3}$; $n = $ ___?___

Find r in the given geometric sequence. There may be more than one correct answer.

B 21. $a_1 = \dfrac{1}{2},\ a_5 = 5000$
22. $a_1 = \dfrac{16}{25},\ a_5 = 25$
23. $a_1 = -15,\ a_6 = \dfrac{5}{81}$

24. $a_1 = \dfrac{3}{4},\ a_8 = -96$
25. $a_1 = 3,\ a_7 = 24$
26. $a_1 = 5,\ a_9 = 405$

Insert the given number of geometric means between the given numbers.

27. 1 between $\dfrac{1}{2}$ and $\dfrac{1}{8}$
28. 1 between 5 and 10

29. 3 between 3 and 48
30. 3 between 2 and 1250

31. 3 between 16 and 81
32. 4 between $\dfrac{3}{16}$ and 192

33. If you received 1¢ on the first of January, 2¢ on the second, 4¢ on the third, 8¢ on the fourth, and so on, approximately how much would you receive on the thirty-first of the month? (Use the approximation $2^{10} \approx 1000$.)

34. The number of bacteria in a culture doubles every 3 days. After 40 days the dish containing the culture is one quarter full. How many days altogether would it take to fill the dish?

C 35. Prove that if a and b are two positive numbers, the arithmetic mean of a and b is greater than or equal to the geometric mean of a and b. (*Hint*: Consider the quantity $(\sqrt{a} - \sqrt{b})^2$.)

36. Show that if $a_1, a_2, a_3, \ldots$ is a geometric sequence, then the sequence $\log a_1$, $\log a_2, \log a_3, \ldots$ is arithmetic.

37. Suppose that the sequence of equilateral triangles whose first 3 elements are shown in the diagram meets the following condition. A side of the first triangle has length 1, a side of the second triangle in the sequence has length equal to the *height* of the first triangle, a side of the third triangle has length equal to the height of the second, and so on. Show that the sequence of lengths of sides of these triangles is geometric.

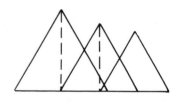

38. Show that the sequence of the *areas* of the triangles defined in Exercise 37 is also geometric.

Section 15-5 GEOMETRIC SERIES

When you replace the commas in a geometric sequence by + signs, you have an indicated sum called a *geometric series*. In this section you will learn two formulas for evaluating the sum of a geometric series.

A sum of the form

$$a_1 + a_2 + a_3 + \cdots + a_n,$$

where the sequence $a_1, a_2, a_3, \ldots, a_n$ is geometric, is called a *finite geometric series*. The numbers $a_1, a_2, a_3, \ldots, a_n$ are called the *terms* of the series, as in any series. Since the terms of a geometric series form a geometric sequence, you can find the value of any particular term if you know the first term a_1 and the common ratio r.

We can derive a formula for the sum of a geometric series as follows: Suppose $a_1 + a_2 + a_3 + \cdots + a_n$ is a geometric series with common ratio r such that $r \neq 1$. Let

$$S_n = a_1 + a_2 + a_3 + \cdots + a_n.$$

Then:

$$rS_n = ra_1 + ra_2 + ra_3 + \cdots + ra_n$$

By the recursive equation for a geometric sequence:

$$ra_1 = a_2, \quad ra_2 = a_3, \quad ra_3 = a_4, \quad \ldots, \quad ra_{n-1} = a_n$$

Substituting these values gives:

$$rS_n = a_2 + a_3 + \cdots + a_n + ra_n.$$

Let us subtract the equation just derived from the first equation.

$$\begin{aligned} S_n &= a_1 + a_2 + \cdots + a_{n-1} + a_n \\ rS_n &= a_2 + a_3 + \cdots \phantom{+ a_{n-1}} + a_n + ra_n \\ \hline S_n - rS_n &= a_1 - ra_n \end{aligned}$$

Factoring the left-hand side gives the following equation.

$$S_n(1 - r) = a_1 - ra_n$$

Dividing each side by $(1 - r)$ gives the following general result.

If S_n denotes the sum of the geometric series $a_1 + a_2 + a_3 + \cdots + a_n$ with common ratio r such that $r \neq 1$.

$$S_n = \frac{a_1 - ra_n}{1 - r}.$$

EXAMPLE   Find the sum of the geometric series:

$$3 + 6 + 12 + \cdots + 192$$

SOLUTION   In this series $a_1 = 3$, $a_n = 192$, and $r = \dfrac{6}{3} = 2$. Substitute in the formula:

$$\begin{aligned} S_n &= \frac{a_1 - ra_n}{1 - r} \\ &= \frac{3 - 2 \cdot 192}{1 - 2} = \frac{-381}{-1} = 381 \end{aligned}$$

You can use the common ratio and number of terms instead of the last term to find the sum of a geometric series. You know that for a series with common ratio r,

$$a_n = a_1 r^{n-1}.$$

Substituting $a_1 r^{n-1}$ for a_n in the previous formula for the sum, you get:

$$S_n = \frac{a_1 - r \cdot a_1 r^{n-1}}{1-r}$$

$$= \frac{a_1 - a_1 r^n}{1-r}$$

Factoring the numerator of the last expression gives the following general result.

If S_n denotes the sum of the geometric series $a_1 + a_2 + a_3 + \cdots + a_n$ with common ratio r such that $r \neq 1$,

$$S_n = \frac{a_1(1-r^n)}{1-r}.$$

EXAMPLE   Find the sum of the geometric series of 5 terms beginning:

$$54 + 18 + 6 + \cdots$$

SOLUTION   In this series $a_1 = 54$, $r = \frac{6}{18} = \frac{1}{3}$, and $n = 5$.

Substitute in the formula involving the nth power of the common ratio.

$$S_n = \frac{a_1(1-r^n)}{1-r}$$

$$S_5 = \frac{54\left(1 - \left(\frac{1}{3}\right)^5\right)}{1 - \frac{1}{3}}$$

$$= \frac{54\left(1 - \frac{1}{243}\right)}{\frac{2}{3}} = 54\left(\frac{242}{243}\right)\frac{3}{2} = \frac{242}{3} = 80\frac{2}{3}$$

ORAL EXERCISES

State the values of a_1, r, and either a_n or n for the geometric series. Tell how you would find the sum of the series.

EXAMPLE   The series $\frac{1}{8} + \frac{1}{4} + \frac{1}{2} + \cdots + 2$

SOLUTION $a_1 = \frac{1}{8}$; $r = 2$; $a_n = 8$. Substitute in the formula involving the last term.

1. The series of 7 terms beginning $\frac{3}{4} + \frac{3}{2} + 3 + \cdots$

2. The series $4 + 6 + \cdots + \frac{81}{4}$

3. The series $0.02 - 0.2 + \cdots - 2000$

4. The series $7 + 7\left(\frac{1}{10}\right) + \cdots + 7\left(\frac{1}{10}\right)^5$

5. The first 6 positive integral powers of 5: $5 + 5^2 + \cdots$

6. The series $a_1 + \cdots + a_8$ in which $a_1 = 4$ and $a_k = -\frac{5}{2}a_{k-1}$

7. The series of 6 terms beginning $x + xy^2 + xy^4 + \cdots$

8. The series $p - pq + pq^2 - \cdots + pq^8$

WRITTEN EXERCISES

Find the sum of the given geometric series.

A 1. $10 + 20 + \cdots + 2560$ 2. $625 + 125 + \cdots + 1$

3. $384 - 192 + \cdots - 3$ 4. $-2 + 6 - \cdots + 486$

5. $81 + 54 + \cdots + 16$ 6. $3 + 3\sqrt{2} + \cdots + 24\sqrt{2}$

Find the requested sum of the geometric series satisfying the given conditions.

7. $a_1 = 5,\ a_n = 160;\ r = 2;\ S_n = \underline{\ ?\ }$ 8. $a_1 = 1,\ a_n = 81,\ r = -3;\ S_n = \underline{\ ?\ }$

9. $a_1 = 24,\ r = \frac{1}{2};\ S_5 = \underline{\ ?\ }$ 10. $a_1 = 0.1,\ r = 2;\ S_6 = \underline{\ ?\ }$

11. $a_1 = \frac{1}{111},\ r = 10;\ S_6 = \underline{\ ?\ }$ 12. $a_1 = 64,\ r = -\frac{1}{2};\ S_7 = \underline{\ ?\ }$

13. $a_1 = 4,\ r = -\frac{1}{3};\ S_6 = \underline{\ ?\ }$ 14. $a_1 = \frac{3}{8},\ r = 4;\ S_5 = \underline{\ ?\ }$

15. $a_1 = 27,\ r = \frac{2}{3};\ S_5 = \underline{\ ?\ }$ 16. $a_1 = 8,\ r = -\frac{3}{2};\ S_6 = \underline{\ ?\ }$

17. Find the sum of the first 6 nonnegative integral powers of 2: $2^0 + 2^1 + \cdots$

18. Find the sum of the first 6 nonnegative integral powers of $\frac{1}{2}$.

B 19. Generalize the result of Exercise 17 by finding a formula for the sum of the first k nonnegative integral powers of 2.

20. Generalize the result of Exercise 18 by finding a formula for the sum of the first k nonnegative integral powers of $\frac{1}{2}$.

Use the information given about the geometric series to find the requested numbers.

EXAMPLE $S_n = 889$, $a_1 = 7$, $r = 2$; $a_n = \underline{\quad?\quad}$, $n = \underline{\quad?\quad}$

SOLUTION To find a_n, substitute in the formula: To find n, substitute in the formula:

$$S_n = \frac{a_1 - ra_n}{1 - r}$$

$$889 = \frac{7 - 2a_n}{1 - 2}$$

$$889 = -7 + 2a_n$$

$$448 = a_n$$

$$a_n = a_1 r^{n-1}$$

$$448 = 7(2)^{n-1}$$

$$64 = 2^{n-1}$$

$$2^6 = 2^{n-1}$$

$$6 = n - 1$$

$$7 = n$$

21. $S_n = 1820$, $a_1 = 5$, $r = 3$; $a_n = \underline{\quad?\quad}$, $n = \underline{\quad?\quad}$

22. $S_n = -63$, $r = -2$, $a_n = -96$; $a_1 = \underline{\quad?\quad}$, $n = \underline{\quad?\quad}$

23. $S_n = 105$, $a_1 = 160$, $a_n = -5$; $r = \underline{\quad?\quad}$, $n = \underline{\quad?\quad}$

24. $S_n = -4168$, $r = -5$, $a_1 = -8$; $a_n = \underline{\quad?\quad}$, $n = \underline{\quad?\quad}$

C 25. $S_6 = 8x - 1$, $r = 2$, $a_1 = x - 7$; $x = \underline{\quad?\quad}$, $a_6 = \underline{\quad?\quad}$

26. $S_5 = 10x - 8$, $r = -3$, $a_1 = x - 11$; $x = \underline{\quad?\quad}$, $a_5 = \underline{\quad?\quad}$

Section 15-6 INFINITE GEOMETRIC SERIES

Suppose you wanted to find the sum of the following *infinite geometric series*:

$$0.3 + 0.03 + 0.003 + \cdots$$

You could add several terms and observe that the sum of the series is equal to the repeating decimal $0.333 \ldots$. In your previous work with rational numbers, you learned that this decimal is equal to $\frac{1}{3}$. Thus, you could conclude that the sum of the infinite geometric series is $\frac{1}{3}$. In this section you will learn a formula for finding the sum of an infinite geometric series. You will also learn how this formula can be used to express repeating decimals as quotients of integers.

Recall the formula for the sum S_n of a geometric series of n terms whose first term is a_1 and whose common ratio is r:

$$S_n = \frac{a_1(1 - r^n)}{1 - r}$$

If $r = \frac{1}{4}$, for example, you have the equation at the top of the next page.

$$S_n = \frac{a_1\left(1 - \left(\frac{1}{4}\right)^n\right)}{1 - \frac{1}{4}}$$

If the series has a great many terms, n will be a large number. The larger n is, the closer $1 - \left(\frac{1}{4}\right)^n$ will be to 1. For example, when n is 15:

$$1 - \left(\frac{1}{4}\right)^{15} \approx 1 - 0.0000000009$$

$$\approx 0.9999999991$$

For very large values of n:

$$S_n \approx \frac{a_1(1)}{1 - \frac{1}{4}} = \frac{a_1}{1 - \frac{1}{4}}$$

A similar result will hold whenever $-1 < r < 1$, that is, whenever $|r| < 1$. The sum S of the *infinite geometric series* $a_1 + a_2 + a_3 + \cdots$ with common ratio r, such that $|r| < 1$, is given by

$$S = \frac{a_1}{1 - r}.$$

Note that the preceding result applies only to infinite series for which $|r| < 1$. If $|r| \geq 1$, that is, if $r \geq 1$ or $r \leq -1$, there is no sum S. We then say that the sum does not exist.

EXAMPLE   Find the sum of the infinite geometric series $6 - 4 + \frac{8}{3} - \cdots$.

SOLUTION   In this series $a_1 = 6$ and $r = \frac{-4}{6} = -\frac{2}{3}$. Substitute in the formula.

$$S = \frac{a_1}{1 - r} = \frac{6}{1 - \left(-\frac{2}{3}\right)} = \frac{6}{1 + \frac{2}{3}} = \frac{6}{\frac{5}{3}} = 6 \cdot \frac{3}{5} = \frac{18}{5}$$

You can use the formula for the sum of an infinite geometric series to express a repeating decimal as the quotient of two integers.

EXAMPLE   Express $0.\overline{27}$ as a quotient of integers in lowest terms.

SOLUTION   You can write:
$$0.\overline{27} = 0.272727\ldots = 0.27 + 0.0027 + 0.000027 + \cdots$$

The right-hand side of this equation is an infinite geometric series in which $a_1 = 0.27$ and $r = 0.01$. Substitute in the formula.

$$S = \frac{a_1}{1 - r} = \frac{0.27}{1 - 0.01} = \frac{0.27}{0.99} = \frac{3}{11}$$

Thus $0.\overline{27} = \frac{3}{11}$.

You can solve the preceding example using the method you learned earlier to compare the two methods.

ORAL EXERCISES

State whether or not the sum of each infinite geometric series exists.

1. $100 + 50 + 25 + \cdots$

2. $\dfrac{1}{1000} + \dfrac{1}{100} + \dfrac{1}{10} + \cdots$

3. $1 - 1 + 1 - 1 + \cdots$

4. $27 - 9 + 3 - 1 + \cdots$

State the first three terms and common ratio of an infinite geometric series whose sum is equal to the given repeating decimal.

5. $0.\overline{7}$
6. $0.\overline{23}$
7. $0.4\overline{81}$
8. $0.0\overline{56}$

State in terms of x the sum of the infinite geometric series. Assume that $|x| < \dfrac{1}{2}$.

9. $1 + x + x^2 + x^3 + x^4 + \cdots$

10. $1 + x^2 + x^4 + x^6 + \cdots$

11. $2 - 2x + 2x^2 - 2x^3 + \cdots$

12. $1 + 2x + 4x^2 + 8x^3 + \cdots$

WRITTEN EXERCISES

Find the sum of the infinite geometric series, if it exists. If the series has no sum, so state.

A
1. $12 + 6 + 3 + \cdots$

2. $36 + 12 + 4 + \cdots$

3. $2 + 3 + \dfrac{9}{2} + \cdots$

4. $3 + 2 + \dfrac{4}{3} + \cdots$

5. $100 - 20 + 4 - \cdots$

6. $8 - 20 + 50 - \cdots$

7. $\dfrac{25}{9} + \dfrac{5}{3} + 1 + \cdots$

8. $64 + 48 + 36 + \cdots$

9. $0.1 + 0.02 + 0.004 + \cdots$

10. $6 + 3\sqrt{2} + 3 + \cdots$

11. $9\sqrt{3} - 9 + 3\sqrt{3} - \cdots$

12. $2\sqrt{5} - 10 + 10\sqrt{5} - \cdots$

Express the repeating decimal as a quotient of integers in lowest terms.

13. $0.\overline{8}$
14. $0.0\overline{6}$
15. $0.\overline{36}$
16. $0.0\overline{72}$

17. $0.\overline{135}$
18. $0.\overline{540}$
19. $5.\overline{12}$
20. $3.4\overline{06}$

Find the common ratio of the infinite geometric series with the given first term and the given sum.

B
21. $a_1 = 12$, $S = 36$

22. $a_1 = 30$, $S = 42$

23. $a_1 = 28$, $S = 16$

24. $a_1 = 72$, $S = 45$

25. Find the value of x if the sum of the infinite geometric series $2x + 4x^2 + 8x^3 + \cdots$ is 5.

26. Find the value of x if the sum of the infinite geometric series $6x + 6x^3 + 6x^5 + \cdots$ is 4.

27. A ball is dropped to the floor from a height of 2 m. Assume that it bounces up and down infinitely many times, returning each time to a maximum height that is 0.6 of its maximum height on the preceding bounce. What is the total distance traveled by the ball?

C 28. A bicyclist starts from point P and travels east at 20 km/h. At the same moment a bee starts from point Q, 80 km east of P, and travels west at 60 km/h. After meeting the bicyclist, the bee instantaneously reverses direction and flies back to point Q.

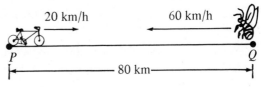

The bee continues flying back and forth between Q and the bicyclist at 60 km/h until the bicyclist arrives at Q. Express the total distance traveled by the bee as an infinite geometric series. Find the sum of the series. Is there a simpler way to find the total distance traveled by the bee?

Section 15-7 MATHEMATICAL INDUCTION

Let us try to prove the following theorem about the sum of the series whose kth term is $\dfrac{1}{k(k + 1)}$.

$$\frac{1}{1 \cdot 2} + \frac{1}{2 \cdot 3} + \frac{1}{3 \cdot 4} + \cdots + \frac{1}{n(n + 1)} = \frac{n}{n + 1}$$

Notice that the series is neither arithmetic nor geometric. Thus we cannot use the sum formulas given earlier in this chapter. We can prove the theorem for particular values, however.

When $n = 1$: $\dfrac{1}{1 \cdot 2} = \dfrac{1}{1 + 1}$

When $n = 2$: $\dfrac{1}{1 \cdot 2} + \dfrac{1}{2 \cdot 3} = \dfrac{3}{6} + \dfrac{1}{6} = \dfrac{4}{6} = \dfrac{2}{3} = \dfrac{2}{2 + 1}$

Recall that the replacement set for n is the set of natural numbers. Of course it would be impossible to prove the theorem by showing that it is true for each natural number n. Instead, we will prove the theorem by using the Principle of Mathematical Induction, which is stated on the following page.

Parts 1 and 2 of the proof of the theorem correspond to parts 1 and 2 of the Principle of Mathematical Induction.

1. We have already shown the theorem to be true when $n = 1$.

2. We now prove that if the theorem is true when $n = k$, then the theorem is true when $n = k + 1$.

GIVEN: $\dfrac{1}{1 \cdot 2} + \dfrac{1}{2 \cdot 3} + \cdots + \dfrac{1}{k(k + 1)} = \dfrac{k}{k + 1}$

PROVE: $\dfrac{1}{1 \cdot 2} + \dfrac{1}{2 \cdot 3} + \cdots + \dfrac{1}{k(k + 1)} + \dfrac{1}{(k + 1)[(k + 1) + 1]} = \dfrac{k + 1}{(k + 1) + 1}$

Proof: We are given: $\dfrac{1}{1 \cdot 2} + \dfrac{1}{2 \cdot 3} + \cdots + \dfrac{1}{k(k + 1)} = \dfrac{k}{k + 1}$

Add the $(k + 1)$st term to both sides and simplify the right side to obtain the desired expression.

$$\dfrac{1}{1 \cdot 2} + \dfrac{1}{2 \cdot 3} + \cdots + \dfrac{1}{k(k + 1)} + \dfrac{1}{(k + 1)[(k + 1) + 1]} = \dfrac{k}{k + 1} + \dfrac{1}{(k + 1)[(k + 1) + 1]}$$

$$= \dfrac{k}{k + 1} + \dfrac{1}{(k + 1)(k + 2)}$$

$$= \dfrac{k(k + 2)}{(k + 1)(k + 2)} + \dfrac{1}{(k + 1)(k + 2)}$$

$$= \dfrac{k^2 + 2k + 1}{(k + 1)(k + 2)}$$

$$= \dfrac{k + 1}{k + 2}$$

$$= \dfrac{k + 1}{(k + 1) + 1}$$

Therefore the theorem is proved by the Principle of Mathematical Induction.

WRITTEN EXERCISES

Prove by induction that each statement is true for any natural number n.

A 1. $1 + 3 + 5 + \cdots + (2n - 1) = n^2$

2. $1 + 2 + 3 + \cdots + n = \dfrac{n(n + 1)}{2}$

3. $\dfrac{1}{2} + \dfrac{1}{4} + \dfrac{1}{8} + \cdots + \dfrac{1}{2^n} = 1 - \dfrac{1}{2^n}$

4. $\dfrac{2}{3} + \dfrac{4}{9} + \cdots + \left(\dfrac{2}{3}\right)^n = 2 - \dfrac{2^{n+1}}{3^n}$

5. $1^2 + 2^2 + 3^2 + \cdots + n^2 = \dfrac{n(n+1)(2n+1)}{6}$

6. $1^2 + 3^2 + 5^2 + \cdots + (2n-1)^2 = \dfrac{n(2n-1)(2n+1)}{3}$

7. $1^3 + 2^3 + 3^3 + \cdots + n^3 = \dfrac{n^2(n+1)^2}{4}$

8. $1 - 1 + 1 - 1 + \cdots + (-1)^{n+1} = \dfrac{1+(-1)^{n+1}}{2}$

9. $\dfrac{1}{2^1} + \dfrac{2}{2^2} + \dfrac{3}{2^3} + \cdots + \dfrac{n}{2^n} = 2 - \dfrac{n+2}{2^n}$

10. $(F_1)^2 + (F_2)^2 + (F_3)^2 + \cdots + (F_n)^2 = F_n F_{n+1}$ where $F_1, F_2, \ldots$ are Fibonacci numbers.

B 11. $\dfrac{1}{1 \cdot 2} + \dfrac{2}{1 \cdot 2 \cdot 3} + \dfrac{3}{1 \cdot 2 \cdot 3 \cdot 4} + \cdots + \dfrac{n}{(n+1)!} = 1 - \dfrac{1}{(n+1)!}$

12. $\dfrac{3}{1^2 \cdot 2^2} + \dfrac{5}{2^2 \cdot 3^2} + \dfrac{7}{3^2 \cdot 4^2} + \cdots + \dfrac{2n+1}{n^2(n+1)^2} = 1 - \dfrac{1}{(n+1)^2}$

13. $(1+p)^n \geqslant 1 + np$, where p is any fixed positive number

14. If f is a function with the property that $f(a+b) = f(a) + f(b)$ for all real numbers a and b, then $f(n) = n \cdot f(1)$.

15. If g is a function with the property that $g(a+b) = g(a) \cdot g(b)$ for all real numbers a and b, then $g(n) = [g(1)]^n$.

C 16. The number of diagonals in any n-sided ($n \geqslant 3$) convex polygon is $\dfrac{n(n-3)}{2}$.

17. Prove De Moivre's Theorem: If $z = r(\cos\theta + i\sin\theta)$ and n is any positive integer, then $z^n = r^n(\cos n\theta + i\sin n\theta)$.

18. Explain the fallacy in the following "proof" by induction of the statement: In any room containing n people, all the people have the same color hair, for any natural number n.

  1. The statement is obviously true for $n = 1$.
  2. Suppose the statement is true for $n = k$, and consider $k+1$ people in a room. If they are lined up in some order, the first k of them have the same color hair, and the last k of them have the same color hair, since the statement is true for $n = k$. Since these two sets have some members in common, all $k+1$ people have the same color hair.

Therefore, by the Principle of Mathematical Induction, the statement is true for all natural numbers n.

SELF-TEST 2

Use the information given about the geometric sequence to find the requested term.

1. $a_1 = 3$, $r = 2$; $a_4 = \underline{\quad?\quad}$

2. $a_6 = 2$, $r = -\dfrac{1}{2}$; $a_1 = \underline{\quad?\quad}$

Section 15-4

3. Insert 2 geometric means between 4 and 500.

Find the requested sum of the geometric series satisfying the given conditions.

4. $a_1 = 5$, $a_n = 1215$, $r = 3$; $S_n = \underline{\quad?\quad}$

Section 15-5

5. $a_1 = 16$, $r = \dfrac{1}{2}$; $S_4 = \underline{\quad?\quad}$

Find the sum of the infinite geometric series.

6. $10 + 8 + 6.4 + \cdots$

7. $405 - 270 + 180 - 120 + \cdots$

Section 15-6

8. Express as a quotient of integers in lowest terms: $0.\overline{36}$

9. Prove by induction that the statement is true for any natural number n.

Section 15-7

$$3 + 7 + 11 + \cdots + (4n - 1) = n(2n + 1)$$

Computer Exercises

The Fibonacci sequence is defined recursively by the rule:

$$F_1 = 1, \quad F_2 = 1, \quad F_n = F_{n-1} + F_{n-2}$$

The following program uses this rule to generate the first 20 Fibonacci numbers.

```
10    REM***PRINT COLUMN HEADINGS
20    PRINT "N", "F(N)"
30    REM***FIRST TERM IS 1
40    LET A = 0
50    LET B = 1
60    REM***RECURSIVE RULE FOR SUCCESSIVE TERMS
70    FOR N = 1 TO 20
80    PRINT N, B
90    REM***COMPUTE NEW (N)TH TERM
100   REM***MOVE OLD (N)TH TERM TO (N − 1)TH TERM
110   LET C = A + B
120   LET A = B
130   LET B = C
140   NEXT N
150   END
```

1. Type in and RUN the program. Compare the results with the numbers in Exercise 13 on page 597. Keep a list of the first 20 Fibonacci numbers for use in a later exercise.

2. **a.** Modify the program so that, each time the nth Fibonacci number is printed, the sum of the first n Fibonacci numbers is also printed. Use the variable S for the sum, and give S an initial value of 0. Before printing B, the value of F_n, in line 80, add this value to S to find the new sum of the terms.

   b. RUN the modified program and examine your results. Write a formula that relates the sum, S, of the first n terms to one of the values of F_n.

3. It is possible to define the Fibonacci sequence explicitly rather than recursively. The nth Fibonacci number is given by the formula:

$$F_n = \frac{1}{\sqrt{5}}\left(\left(\frac{1+\sqrt{5}}{2}\right)^n - \left(\frac{1-\sqrt{5}}{2}\right)^n\right)$$

Using this formula, write a new program to print the first 20 Fibonacci numbers. RUN the program and compare the results with those you obtained in Exercise 1. You may notice some slight variations due to round-off error in the computer.

4. **a.** Modify the original program so that, beginning with the second term, the computer will print the values of n, F_n, and the ratio of the nth term to the preceding term $\left(\text{that is, } \dfrac{F_n}{F_{n-1}}\right)$. RUN the modified program.

   b. The number $\dfrac{1+\sqrt{5}}{2}$, known as the golden ratio, was of special interest to ancient Greek mathematicians. Use a single PRINT statement to evaluate the golden ratio.

   c. Describe the relationship between the results of part (a) and part (b).

CHAPTER REVIEW

Give an explicit rule for each sequence.

1. $1, 3, 9, 27, \ldots$ 2. $-2, 4, -8, 16, \ldots$ Section 15-1

Give a recursive rule for each sequence.

3. $6, -6, 6, -6, \ldots$ 4. $4, 2, 0, -2, \ldots$

Find the specified term of the arithmetic sequence satisfying the given conditions.

5. $a_1 = 6, d = 10; a_{20} = \underline{\ ?\ }$ 6. $a_1 = 100, a_{101} = 50; a_{10} = \underline{\ ?\ }$ Section 15-2

7. Insert 5 arithmetic means between -2 and 1.

Find the sum of the arithmetic sequence
$$a_1 + a_2 + \cdots + a_n$$
using the given information.

Section 15-3

8. $a_1 = 5$, $a_n = 95$, $n = 30$ 9. $a_1 = 50$, $a_2 = 48$, $n = 21$

Find the fifth term of the given geometric sequence.

10. $16, 8, 4, \ldots$ 11. $a_1 = 8$, $r = -\dfrac{3}{2}$

Section 15-4

12. Insert 2 geometric means between 9 and $\dfrac{8}{3}$.

Find the sum of the geometric series, using the given information.

13. $2 + 6 + 18 + \cdots + 13{,}122$ 14. $a_1 = 6$, $r = \dfrac{2}{3}$, $n = 5$

Section 15-5

Find the sum of the infinite geometric series.

15. $192 + 144 + 108 + \cdots$ 16. $250 - 150 + 90 - \cdots$

Section 15-6

Express each repeating decimal as a quotient of integers in lowest terms.

17. $0.\overline{63}$ 18. $0.\overline{72}$

19. Prove by induction that
$$4 + 12 + 36 + \cdots + 4 \cdot 3^{n-1} = 2 \cdot 3^n - 2$$
is true for any natural number n.

Section 15-7

CHAPTER TEST

State whether the given sequence is arithmetic, geometric, or neither.

1. $\dfrac{4}{3}, \dfrac{3}{4}, \dfrac{2}{5}, \dfrac{1}{6}, \ldots$ 2. $5, 3, 1, -1, \ldots$

3. $\dfrac{3}{8}, \dfrac{3}{4}, \dfrac{3}{2}, 3, \ldots$ 4. $\dfrac{5}{8}, \dfrac{3}{4}, \dfrac{7}{8}, 1, \ldots$

Write the one-hundredth term in the sequence satisfying the given conditions.

5. Arithmetic sequence: first term is 15; common difference is 10.

6. Arithmetic sequence: first term is 0; second term is $-\dfrac{1}{2}$.

7. Geometric sequence: first term is 2; common ratio is (-1).

8. Geometric sequence: first term is $\dfrac{1}{2^{96}}$; common ratio is 2.

Find the sum of each arithmetic or geometric series.

9. $5 + 8 + 11 + \cdots + 302$ (100 terms)

10. $40 + 20 + 10 + \cdots + \dfrac{5}{8}$ (7 terms)

11. $50 + 46 + 42 + \cdots + -14$

12. $243 + 81 + 27 + \cdots$ (infinite)

Express each repeating decimal as a quotient of integers in lowest terms.

13. $0.\overline{21}$

14. $0.2\overline{16}$

15. Insert 3 arithmetic means between 4 and 64.

16. Insert 3 geometric means between 4 and 64.

17. Prove by induction that $10 + 14 + 18 + \cdots + (4n + 6) = 2n(n + 4)$ for any natural number n.

CUMULATIVE REVIEW: CHAPTERS 1–15

Indicate the best answer by writing the appropriate letter.

Chapters 1–13

1. For which set of data are the median and mode the same?
   a. 18, 16, 13, 18, 15
   b. 56, 67, 51, 56, 62, 54
   c. 31, 19, 24, 28, 19
   d. 45, 38, 42, 38, 33, 46

2. Which property is not preserved under a dilation?
   a. orientation   **b.** angle measure   **c.** distance   **d.** collinearity

3. What is the domain of the function $f(x) = \dfrac{2}{\sqrt{x-3}}$?
   a. $\mathcal{R}$ **b.** $\{x: x \geqslant 3\}$ **c.** $\{x: x \geqslant 0\}$ **d.** $\{x: x > 3\}$

4. Find the value of x if $\log_2 16 = x$.
   a. $x = 8$ **b.** $x = -4$ **c.** $x = 4$ **d.** $x = \dfrac{1}{4}$

5. In the diagram, $ABCD$ is a parallelogram. Which vector is equivalent to $\overrightarrow{DA} + \overrightarrow{AB}$?
   a. $\overrightarrow{BD}$ **b.** $\overrightarrow{DB}$
   c. $\overrightarrow{AC}$ **d.** $\overrightarrow{CA}$

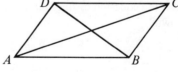

6. Express $2.0\overline{54}$ as a quotient of two integers in lowest terms.
   a. $\dfrac{37}{18}$ **b.** $\dfrac{113}{55}$ **c.** $\dfrac{226}{11}$ **d.** $\dfrac{1027}{500}$

7. If g is a linear function, $g(3) = -4$, and $g(0) = 1$, then $g(x) = \underline{\quad?\quad}$.
   a. $mx + b$ **b.** $x - \dfrac{5}{3}$ **c.** $-\dfrac{5}{3}x + 1$ **d.** $\dfrac{5}{3}x - 1$

8. Find the value of $\log 681.3$ correct to four decimal places.
   a. 0.8333   **b.** $0.8333 + 3$ **c.** $0.8333 + 2$ **d.** $0.8336 + 2$

9. Which equation is equivalent to $1 - \dfrac{6}{t^2} = \dfrac{1}{t}$?

    a. $(t-3)(t+2)=0$ b. $(2t+1)(3t-1)=0$

    c. $(2t-1)(3t+1)=0$ d. $(t-2)(t+3)=0$

10. Evaluate $\cos 38°12'$ correct to four decimal places.

    a. 0.7858   b. 0.7848   c. 0.7866   d. 0.6184

11. A reflection maps $P(5, -1)$ onto $P'(5, -5)$. Find the image of $A(-3, 3)$ under the same reflection.

    a. $(13, 3)$ b. $(-3, -1)$ c. $(3, 3)$ d. $(-3, -9)$

12. If the shoe sizes of adult women approximate a normal distribution, approximately what percent of women have a shoe size within two standard deviations of the mean?

    a. 68%   b. 95%   c. 99%   d. 47%

13. Which of the following is the graph of the solution set of $-15 \leqslant -3 - 4x < 5$?

    a. (number line, open circle at -2, filled circle at 3)

    b. (number line, no marks at -2 and 3)

    c. (number line, open circle at -2, filled circle at 3)

    d. (number line, filled circle at -2, open circle at 3)

14. How many solutions are there of the equation $\sin \theta = \cos \theta$, $0 \leqslant \theta \leqslant 2\pi$?

    a. 0   b. 1   c. 2   d. 3

15. If $x = 8^2 \sqrt[3]{5}$, which expression is equivalent to $\log x$?

    a. $2 \log 8 + 3 \log 5$ b. $2 \log 8 + \dfrac{1}{3} \log 5$

    c. $2\left(\log 8 + \dfrac{1}{3} \log 5\right)$ d. $(2 \log 8)\left(\dfrac{1}{3} \log 5\right)$

16. Four coins are tossed. What is the probability of getting at least 2 heads?

    a. $\dfrac{1}{4}$ b. $\dfrac{5}{16}$ c. $\dfrac{3}{8}$ d. $\dfrac{11}{16}$

17. Which expression is equivalent to $\csc 2\theta \tan 2\theta$?

    a. $\sec 2\theta$ b. $\sin 2\theta \sec^2 2\theta$ c. $\csc 2\theta$ d. $\cot 2\theta$

18. What is the equation of the function whose graph is shown?

    a. $y = 2 \sin \dfrac{x}{2}$ b. $y = 2 \sin 2x$

    c. $y = 2 \cos 2x$ d. $y = 2 \cos \dfrac{x}{2}$

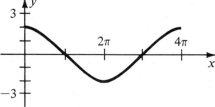

19. If $\angle A = 50°$, $a = 9$, and $b = 7$, what kind of triangle is $\triangle ABC$?

    a. obtuse   b. acute   c. right   d. isosceles

20. What is the mean of the test scores shown in the frequency table?

    a. 78   b. 80

    c. 82   d. 85

Score (x_i)	70	80	90	100
Frequency (f_i)	9	14	5	2

21. Solve the equation $\sin^2 \theta = \cos^2 \theta$ for $0° \leqslant \theta \leqslant 180°$.
    a. $\theta = 45°$ **b.** $\theta = 45°$ or $135°$ **c.** $\theta = 30°$ or $150°$ **d.** $\theta = 135°$

22. Which of the following is the graph of the solution set of $x^2 + 3x < 10$?

    a. (number line marked -2, 0, 2)   **b.** (number line marked -4, 0, 4, 8)

    c. (number line marked -6, -3, 0, 3, 6)   **d.** (number line marked -6, -3, 0, 3, 6)

23. Find the value(s) of k for which the equation $kx^2 + 4x + 8 = 0$ has one real double root.

    a. $\left\{ k: k < \dfrac{1}{2} \right\}$ **b.** $-\dfrac{1}{2}$ **c.** $\dfrac{1}{2}$ **d.** $\left\{ k: k > -\dfrac{1}{2} \right\}$

24. Evaluate Arctan (tan 225°).
    a. $225°$ **b.** 1 **c.** $-45°$ **d.** $45°$

25. How many different committees of 4 people can be chosen from a club with 9 members?
    a. 126   **b.** 24   **c.** 6561   **d.** 3024

26. Solve for x to the nearest tenth: $3^x = 10$
    a. 3.3   **b.** 0.5   **c.** 2.2   **d** 2.1

27. A team's probability of winning any given game in a 4-game series is 0.2. What is the probability that the team will win exactly 3 games in the series?
    a. $(0.2)^3$ **b.** $(0.2)^3(0.8)$ **c.** $12(0.2)^3(0.8)$ **d.** $4(0.2)^3(0.8)$

28. If x and y are acute angles, $\sin x = \dfrac{1}{2}$, and $\sin y = \dfrac{1}{3}$, then $\cos (x + y) = \underline{\quad ? \quad}$.

    a. $\dfrac{2\sqrt{6} - 1}{6}$ **b.** $\dfrac{1}{6}$ **c.** $\dfrac{2\sqrt{6} + 1}{6}$ **d.** $\dfrac{2\sqrt{2} + \sqrt{3}}{6}$

29. In $\triangle ABC$, $a = 8$, $b = 10$, and $c = 14$. Find the value of $\cos A$ to the nearest hundredth.
    a. 0.71   **b.** 0.57   **c.** -0.20 **d.** 0.83

30. The graph of $y = \log_5 x$ lies entirely in Quadrants $\underline{\quad ? \quad}$.
    a. I and II   **b.** I and III   **c.** II and III   **d.** I and IV

31. In $\odot O$, $m\angle BOC = 80$ and $m\angle ACO = 18$. Find $m\angle ABO$.
    a. 18   **b.** 49   **c.** 58   **d.** 80

32. Find the solution set of $x = 5 - \sqrt{x + 7}$.
    a. $\{-2, -9\}$ **b.** $\{2, 9\}$ **c.** $\{9\}$ **d.** $\{2\}$

33. Ratings given by a consumer panel approximate a normal distribution, with a mean of 150 and a standard deviation of 25. Find the probability that a rating chosen at random is between 135 and 170, inclusive.
    a. 0.452   **b.** 0.514   **c.** 0.576   **d.** 0.062

34. The point A is reflected in the origin, giving an image A'. A' is reflected in the point $(1, -3)$, giving an image A''. If the coordinates of A are $(-6, 2)$, find the coordinates of A''.
    a. $(-5, -4)$ **b.** $(-4, -4)$ **c.** $(-4, -8)$ **d.** $(-8, 8)$

35. Scores on a standardized test approximate a normal distribution, with a mean of 82 and a standard deviation of 6. Which range of scores is expected to occur less than 15% of the time?
   a. 90 or more   b. 88 or more   c. 85 or more   d. 84 or more

36. Find the fifth term in the expansion of $(3m + n)^5$.
   a. n^5 b. $5mn^4$ c. $15m^4n$ d. $15mn^4$

37. Six cards are drawn from a standard deck of cards without replacement. What is the probability of getting 4 hearts and 2 spades?
   a. $\dfrac{_{13}C_4 \cdot {}_{39}C_2}{_{52}C_6}$ b. $\dfrac{_{13}C_4 \cdot {}_{13}C_2}{52!}$ c. $\dfrac{_{13}C_4 \cdot {}_{13}C_2}{_{52}C_6}$ d. $\dfrac{_6C_4 \cdot {}_6C_2}{_{52}C_6}$

38. The numbers of pets per family for a certain group of people are given in the table. Find the standard deviation, to the nearest tenth, of the number of pets per family.

Number of pets (x_i)	0	1	2	3	4
Frequency (f_i)	1	4	1	2	2

   a. 1.0   b. 1.3   c. 1.4   d. 1.8

39. The heights of a group of people approximate a normal distribution, with a mean of 178 cm and a standard deviation of 12 cm. A person who is 192 cm tall would rank __?__.
   a. above the 98th percentile   b. above the 80th percentile
   c. between the 70th and 80th percentiles   d. between the 60th and 70th percentiles

Chapter 14

40. How many transformations are there in the symmetry set of a rhombus?
   a. 2   b. 3   c. 4   d. 5

41. Which of the given transformations is not a similarity transformation?
   a. $R_{180°} \circ D_5$ b. $r_{y\text{-axis}}$
   c. $T:(x, y) \longrightarrow (x + 2, y + 3)$ d. $T:(x, y) \longrightarrow (2x, 3y)$

42. Find the image of the point $(-2, 5)$ under the glide reflection $T_{2,\,2} \circ r_k$, where k has the equation $y = x$.
   a. $(7, 0)$ b. $(5, -2)$ c. $(-3, 4)$ d. $(0, 7)$

Chapter 15

43. In an arithmetic sequence, $a_4 = 9$ and $a_{16} = 25$. Find a_{25}.
   a. 41   b. 37   c. 36   d. $38\dfrac{1}{3}$

44. Find the sum of the infinite geometric series $0.8 - 0.2 + 0.05 - \cdots$.
   a. $\dfrac{16}{25}$ b. $\dfrac{16}{15}$ c. $\dfrac{3}{4}$ d. 1

45. Two geometric means are inserted between 32 and 500. The greater of the two means is __?__.
   a. 80   b. 200   c. 266   d. $40\sqrt{10}$

Application — Business Forecasting (Exponential Smoothing)

Businesses use short-term forecasts to plan for immediate needs. For example, short-term forecasts might be used to schedule work shifts in businesses that experience seasonal changes in demand for their product. Forecasts are also used to help management make long-range plans. For example, a company might decide to open an additional facility if long-term forecasts seemed to indicate that it would be advantageous to do so. Because the survival of a business can depend on the accuracy of its forecasts, forecasts must continually be revised in light of actual data.

Business forecasting starts with plotting actual data, such as the amount of sales, over time. An analyst studies the resulting graph to see if there is a pattern or trend. The graph below indicates a linear trend.

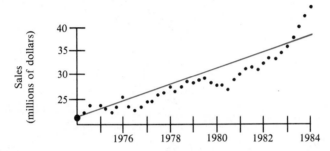

Exponential, parabolic, and S-shaped trend patterns also occur frequently.

The pattern of the graph and cost considerations are major factors in determining which forecasting technique will be used.

One well-known forecasting technique is *exponential smoothing*, an averaging technique that weights data for more recent periods more heavily than data for successively older periods. The weights, represented by expressions of the form $\alpha(1-\alpha)^0$, $\alpha(1-\alpha)^1$, $\alpha(1-\alpha)^2$, and so on, decrease exponentially, giving this technique its name.

The simplest exponential smoothing model forecasts a value for a variable, such as product sales, using the equation

Forecast for next period $= \alpha$(Most recent data) $+ (1-\alpha)$(Previous forecast).

The smoothing constant α $(0 < \alpha < 1)$ is chosen based on analysis of the data graph. Its appropriateness can be checked by comparing forecasts with actual data.

Each time data for the current period are complete, the forecast is updated. The forecast for the next period, F_n, can be represented in terms of the most recent data, D_{n-1}, and the next most recent data, D_{n-2}, and so on, as shown by the equation below:

$$F_n = \alpha(1-\alpha)^0 D_{n-1} + \alpha(1-\alpha)^1 D_{n-2} + \alpha(1-\alpha)^2 D_{n-3} + \cdots$$

Since $\alpha(1-\alpha)^0 > \alpha(1-\alpha)^1 > \alpha(1-\alpha)^2$, and so on, as new data are obtained, data from a previous period have a rapidly decreasing effect on current forecasts.

Be sure that you understand the meaning of these terms:

MIXED REVIEW

Find the sum of the indicated series.

1. $7 + 2 - 3 - \cdots - 103$ 　　2. $81 - 54 + 36 - \cdots + a_9$ 　　3. $0.1 + 0.07 + 0.049 + \cdots$

4. If you toss a coin eight times, what is the probability that you get no more than three tails? Give your answer in symbolic form.

5. In $\triangle ABC$, $m\angle C = 19°30'$, $a = 12$, and $c = 6$. Find $m\angle A$ to the nearest $10'$.

6. Use logs to calculate $\sqrt[8]{906}$ to three significant digits.

7. Solve for $0° \leqslant \theta < 360°$: $\sin 2\theta = \cos \theta$.

8. If $\cot \theta = -\dfrac{5}{12}$ and $\dfrac{\pi}{2} < \theta < \pi$, find (a) $\csc \theta$, (b) $\cos 2\theta$, (c) $\sin \dfrac{\theta}{2}$,

　(d) $\tan \left(\theta + \dfrac{\pi}{3}\right)$, and (e) $\cos \left(\theta - \dfrac{\pi}{2}\right)$.

9. A license plate number consists of two letters followed by four digits. How many different numbers are possible?

10. Determine the amplitude and the fundamental period of the function

$y = 4 \sin \dfrac{4}{3}x$. Graph at least two cycles.

11. Two tangents drawn to a circle from an external point divide the circle into arcs with measures in the ratio $1:4$. Find the measure of the angle formed by the tangents.

12. Given the data 19, 27, 12, and 14, find (a) the mean, (b) the median, (c) the mean absolute deviation, and (d) the standard deviation to the nearest integer.

13. If $\triangle XYZ$ has vertices $X(0, -3)$, $Y(6, 0)$, and $Z(3, 3)$, find the coordinates of the vertices of its image under $r_{x\text{-axis}} \circ D_{\frac{2}{3}}$.

14. Insert four geometric means between 3 and 96.

15. Prove: $\dfrac{\tan \theta + 1}{\tan \theta - 1} = \dfrac{1 + 2 \sin \theta \cos \theta}{\sin^2 \theta - \cos^2 \theta}$

16. Use the formula $\displaystyle\sum_{i=1}^{n} i = \frac{n(n+1)}{2}$ to evaluate $\displaystyle\sum_{i=1}^{25} (i+3)$.

17. An isosceles trapezoid has three sides of length 8 and a base angle of measure 60. Find the exact length of a diagonal.

18. Is the composite of two line reflections *always, sometimes,* or *never* a translation? Explain.

19. Prove by induction that the following is true for any natural number n:

$$1 \cdot 2 + 2 \cdot 3 + 3 \cdot 4 + \cdots + n(n+1) = \frac{n(n+1)(n+2)}{3}$$

20. Solve over the set of complex numbers: $9x^2 - 2x + 1 = 0$

21. Graph the solution set: $2w^3 + 5w^2 \leqslant 18w$

22. Simplify: a. $\dfrac{3\sqrt{3}}{2-\sqrt{3}}$ b. $\dfrac{1-2i}{3+i}$ c. $\sqrt[3]{45} \cdot \sqrt[3]{6}$

23. Use interpolation to find a four-digit approximation for $\tan 336°24'$.

24. If $f(x) = x^2 + 1$ and $g(x) = -x$, find $f(g(x))$ and $g(f(x))$. Classify each composite as odd, even, or neither.

25. Solve: $32^{x+1} = 4^{3x}$

26. Let k be the line with equation $y = x$. Find the image of the triangle with vertices $A(-6, -3)$, $B(6, -2)$, and $C(2, 5)$ under the glide reflection $r_k \circ T_{3, -4}$.

27. Find S_5 for the geometric series with $a_1 = 16$ and $r = -\dfrac{1}{2}$.

28. Find the image of $(12, -6)$ under the transformation $T_{-4, 3} \circ D_{\frac{5}{6}}$.

29. Classify the isometry $r_{x\text{-axis}} \circ R_{90}$ as a line reflection, a glide reflection, a translation, or a rotation.

30. Show that there is no $\triangle XYZ$ such that $XY = 8$, $m\angle X = 32$, and $YZ = 3$.

31. Find the area to the nearest integer of $\triangle ABC$ with $b = 8$, $a = 6$, and $c = 12$.

32. Find (a) $\tan\left(\text{Arcsin } \dfrac{1}{2}\right)$ and (b) $\sin\left[\text{Arccos}\left(-\dfrac{21}{29}\right)\right]$.

33. Find the probability of drawing two cards of the same suit when two cards are drawn without replacement from a deck of cards.

34. Find the arithmetic mean and the geometric mean between 3 and 12.

35. Find the sum of the series $\displaystyle\sum_{k=1}^{18} (3k+2)$ 36. Simplify: $\dfrac{\cot^2 x \sec^2 x - 1}{\sin x \cot^2 x \csc x}$

37. The scores on a test approximate a normal distribution with a mean of 82 and a standard deviation of 8. What percent of those who took the test had a score of 90 or less?

Extra Practice

A   **1.** Express as a decimal: **a.** $\dfrac{18}{125}$ **b.** $2\dfrac{1}{12}$

    2. Express as a quotient of two integers in lowest terms: **a.** 0.71 **b.** 0.90625

    3. Simplify: **a.** $-2^2 + 7 - 12 \div 6$ **b.** $\dfrac{4^3 - 2 \cdot 7}{7 + 6 \div 2}$

    4. Evaluate when $r = -9$, $s = 6$, and $t = -3$: $\dfrac{r^2 - st}{2r + s + t}$

    5. Find the additive inverse and the multiplicative inverse of $-1\dfrac{3}{5}$.

Solve and check.

    6. $14x + 12 = 3(4x + 3)$ **7.** $1.6y - 36 = 0.4y$ **8.** $\dfrac{7}{8}z + 10 = -4 - \dfrac{1}{8}z$

    9. Find three consecutive even integers with a sum of 72.

    10. Find the measure of an angle if the sum of the measures of its complement and its supplement is 118.

Find and graph the solution set of each inequality.

    11. $2(6 + x) \leqslant 3(4 + x)$ **12.** $4(2 - t) > -4t - 8$ **13.** $-9 \leqslant \dfrac{4}{5}m - 1$

    14. $7 - c \geqslant 11$ or $-3c \leqslant -6$ **15.** $-3 < 4x + 1 < 19$

    16. The Williams family traveled 480 km by car. How long did the trip take if the average speed was between 80 km/h and 90 km/h?

Solve and graph.

    17. $|y + 2| = 4$ **18.** $|2k| = 6$ **19.** $|2 - h| < 3$ **20.** $16 \leqslant |8x|$

B   **21.** Express as a quotient of integers in lowest terms: **a.** $0.\overline{24}$ **b.** $0.4\overline{6}$

Solve.

    22. $\dfrac{5x}{4} = \dfrac{7x}{6} + 4$ **23.** $6 - 2.5y = 31.5$ **24.** $\dfrac{8z}{9} > \dfrac{5}{3} + \dfrac{2z}{3}$

    25. $4(t - 1) > 2t - 6$ and $2t - 6 > 3(t + 1)$ **26.** $9a - 7 < 11$ or $\dfrac{1}{3}(a - 1) \geqslant 1$

    27. $|4m - 1| < 7$ **28.** $|5(j - 2)| \geqslant 0$ **29.** $|1 + 3(2 - w)| > 2$

    30. Peanuts worth \$6.50 per kilogram were mixed with almonds worth \$8.00 per kilogram to produce 20 kilograms of mixture worth \$7.10 per kilogram. How many kilograms of almonds were used?

Chapter 2

A   1. Simplify: **a.** $\left(\dfrac{24x^3y^2z}{45xyz^4}\right)^{-2}$ **b.** $(-2a^5b)^3\left(\dfrac{1}{2}a^{-5}b^0\right)$

2. Write as a single power of 2:   **a.** $\dfrac{1}{32}\cdot 4^2$ **b.** 8^4

3. Simplify: $(-9+5x^2-8x)-(3x+2x^2-6)$

4. Multiply: **a.** $(5t-3)^2$ **b.** $(2r^2-9rs+7s^2)(r-3s)$

5. Factor completely: **a.** $15j^2+j-6$ **b.** w^3+64 **c.** $4c^2-4$

6. Solve: **a.** $(y-1)(2y+3)=5y$ **b.** $18z^2+19z+5=0$

7. Divide $6y^3-y^2-6$ by $2y-3$ and express the result as an equation.

Simplify.

8. $\dfrac{4x^2y}{27z^3}\div\dfrac{20xy^2}{9z^5}$ 9. $\dfrac{3g^2-11g+10}{-10g+5g^2}$ 10. $\dfrac{c^3-1}{2c-2}\cdot\dfrac{c^2-1}{c^2+2c+1}$

11. $\dfrac{\dfrac{3}{2}+\dfrac{1}{3}}{\dfrac{5}{6}-\dfrac{3}{4}}$ 12. $\dfrac{x+2^{-1}}{2+x^{-1}}$ 13. $\dfrac{\dfrac{1}{y^2}-1}{\dfrac{1}{y}-1}$

14. Solve: **a.** $\dfrac{5}{6}-\dfrac{2}{r}=\dfrac{7}{10}$ **b.** $\dfrac{a}{7a-2}+\dfrac{4a+1}{4a}=1$

15. Find and graph the solution set: **a.** $k^2>4k$ **b.** $h^2+7h\leqslant h-8$

B   16. Simplify: **a.** $\left(\dfrac{2ab^{-3}c^0}{2^{-1}a^{-2}b}\right)^{-3}$ **b.** $\dfrac{x^2-3x-10}{3x^2+5x-2}\div\dfrac{x^2-7x+10}{9x^2-1}$

17. A triangle has base $4x+8$ and height $2x-3$.
   a. Express the area of the triangle as a polynomial in simplest form.
   b. If the area is 98 square units, find the value of x.

18. Factor completely: **a.** $4a^3b+6a^2b^2-4ab^3$ **b.** $4x^4+21x^2-25$

19. Solve $2y^2+2y=3$ by using the quadratic formula.

20. Find the rational roots of $2e^3+5e^2-32e-35=0$.

21. Simplify: **a.** $\dfrac{z}{z^2+6z+9}+\dfrac{2}{z^2+4z+3}$ **b.** $\dfrac{\dfrac{1}{x}+\dfrac{1}{x-3}}{2+\dfrac{x+3}{x^2-3x}}$

22. Diego can paint one room in 6 h. If Mel helps him, they can do the job in 3.3 h. How long would it take Mel, working alone, to do the job?

23. Find and graph the solution set of $2r^3-7r^2+5r>0$.

Simplify. Assume that all variables represent positive real numbers.

A 1. $\dfrac{\sqrt{98x^3y^4}}{\sqrt{50x^7y}}$

2. $\dfrac{3}{2}\sqrt{160} - \dfrac{2}{3}\sqrt{810}$

3. $\sqrt{45} + 2\sqrt{20} - \sqrt{\dfrac{5}{9}}$

4. $\dfrac{\sqrt{35r^5s^2}}{\sqrt{15s^3}}$

5. $(2\sqrt{3} - \sqrt{6})^2$

6. $\dfrac{6}{3 + \sqrt{7}}$

Solve and check each apparent solution.

7. $\sqrt{2x-5} - 4 = 5$

8. $\sqrt{x-2} = x-2$

9. $\sqrt{x+11} = 1-x$

Simplify.

10. $\dfrac{\sqrt{84}}{-\sqrt{-63}}$

11. $\dfrac{i^3\sqrt{7}}{i^6\sqrt{5}}$

12. $\sqrt{-8} \cdot \sqrt{-36}$

Find **(a)** the sum, **(b)** the difference (the first minus the second), and **(c)** the product of the numbers. Give answers in standard form.

13. $\sqrt{3} + 2i,\ -5\sqrt{3} - i$

14. $1 + 5i,\ 1 - 5i$

15. $\dfrac{3 - 4i}{5},\ \dfrac{2 - 7i}{5}$

Express in standard form.

16. $\dfrac{9}{4 + 2i\sqrt{5}}$

17. $\dfrac{1}{3 - 3i}$

18. $\dfrac{2\sqrt{7} + i}{2\sqrt{7} - i}$

Solve for x over the set of complex numbers.

19. $x^2 - 4x + 5 = 0$

20. $2x^2 = x + 2$

21. $x^2 + 2x + 6 = 0$

22. Find a quadratic equation with integral coefficients and $2 + i\sqrt{3}$ and $2 - i\sqrt{3}$ as roots.

Simplify. Assume that all variables represent positive real numbers.

B 23. $\sqrt[3]{48} - \sqrt[3]{-162}$

24. $\sqrt[4]{\dfrac{32}{3}} + \sqrt[4]{\dfrac{243}{2}}$

25. $\sqrt{5x^7} + 2\sqrt{20x^3}$

26. $\dfrac{x}{\sqrt{2x+y} - \sqrt{y}}$

27. $\sqrt[3]{4} \cdot \sqrt[3]{18} \cdot \sqrt[3]{-96}$

28. $\dfrac{\sqrt{11} + \sqrt{35}}{2\sqrt{11} - \sqrt{35}}$

29. Solve: **a.** $\sqrt{3x-2} - \sqrt{x-1} = 1$ **b.** $\sqrt{x+1} = \sqrt{4-x} + 1$

30. Show that $-\dfrac{1}{2}i$ is a root of $4x^3 - 12x^2 + x - 3 = 0$.

31. Express as a single complex number in standard form:

a. $\dfrac{1 + 2i}{1 - 2i} + \dfrac{1}{1 + 2i}$ **b.** $\dfrac{\sqrt{2} - i\sqrt{3}}{3\sqrt{2} + i\sqrt{3}}$

32. Sketch the graph of $y = 8 + 2x - x^2$. State the x-intercepts and the coordinates of the vertex.

33. If -3 is a root of $kx^2 + 10x + k = 0$, find the other root and the value of k.

Give the domain of each function. Find the image and pre-image(s) of 2.

A   **1.** $y = 2|x| - 4$

2. $y = \dfrac{4 + x}{x}$

3. $y = \dfrac{1}{\sqrt{x + 2}}$

Sketch the graph of the relation. State whether or not it is a function. If it is, state its domain and range.

4. $y = |x| - 3$

5. $x = y^2$

6. $y = -3$

Find $f(1)$, $f(3)$, $f(-3)$, and $f(-x)$. Is $f(x)$ odd, even, or neither?

7. $f(x) = 2x^6 + 3$

8. $f(x) = 2x^2 - 3x + 1$

9. $f(x) = \dfrac{1}{3}x$

10. Find a linear function, h, such that $h(3) = -4$ and $h(-1) = 0$.

11. Interpolate between $\sqrt{25}$ and $\sqrt{36}$ to approximate $\sqrt{30}$ to the nearest tenth.

12. If $f(5) = 1.6094$ and $f(6) = 1.7918$, use linear interpolation to find an approximation for $f(5.7)$. Round your answer to four decimal places.

In Exercises 13–15, let $f(x) = |x|$, $g(x) = x^2 - 1$, and $h(x) = \sqrt{x + 4}$.

13. Find $f(g(-1))$ and $g(f(-1))$.

14. Find $g(h(5))$ and $h(g(5))$.

15. Find a simplified formula for **(a)** $g \circ h$ and **(b)** $h \circ g$.

Find the inverse of the function.

16. $y = 3x + 2$

17. $y = 2\sqrt[3]{x}$

18. $f(x) = x^2 - 2$, $x \geqslant 0$

Find the value of k if the given function associates the two given numbers.

B   **19.** $y = \sqrt{x^2 - k}$; $3 \longrightarrow 4$

20. $y = \dfrac{3k}{\sqrt{kx + 1}}$; $2 \longrightarrow 4$

21. Give the domain: **a.** $y = \dfrac{1}{|4 - x^2|}$ **b.** $y = \dfrac{x}{\sqrt{3 - x}}$

22. Graph the relation $4x^2 + y^2 = 4$. State if it is a function.

23. Show that if a quadratic function $f(x) = ax^2 + bx + c$ is even, then $b = 0$.

24. If $f(7) = 1.2148$ and $f(8) = 1.2311$, use interpolation to approximate $f^{-1}(1.2182)$ to the nearest tenth.

Show that $[g \circ h](x) = x$ for all x in the domain of $g \circ h$ and that $[h \circ g](x) = x$ for all x in the domain of $h \circ g$.

25. $g(x) = \dfrac{3x - 2}{x}$; $h(x) = \dfrac{2}{3 - x}$

26. $g(x) = x^4 - 2$, $x \geqslant 0$; $h(x) = \sqrt[4]{x + 2}$

On one set of axes, sketch the graph of the given function and its inverse.

27. $y = -x + 4$

28. $y = \sqrt{25 - x^2}$, $0 \leqslant x \leqslant 5$

A 1. If $T:(x, y) \longrightarrow (-x, -y)$, classify T as a direct or nondirect isometry and find the coordinates of the image of $A(-3, 2)$ and the pre-image of $C'(7, -2)$ under T.

2. Find the coordinates of the image of $(4, -1)$ under **(a)** $r_{x\text{-axis}}$, **(b)** $r_{y\text{-axis}}$, and **(c)** r_k, where k is the line with equation $y = -x$.

3. Is it possible for a trapezoid to have no line of symmetry? one line of symmetry? two lines of symmetry?

4. If m and k are symmetry lines for $\triangle ABC$, find each of the following.
   a. $r_m(A)$
   b. $r_m(\overline{CB})$
   c. $r_k(\angle C)$
   d. $r_k \circ r_m(\angle B)$
   e. $r_m \circ r_k(\overline{BA})$
   f. $r_k \circ r_m(\angle A)$

In Exercises 5 and 6, $\triangle ABC$ has vertices $A(-3, 2)$, $B(0, 4)$, and $C(1, 0)$.

5. Let k be the line with equation $y = x$. Graph $\triangle ABC$ and its image, $\triangle A''B''C''$, under $r_{x\text{-axis}} \circ r_k$.

6. Graph the image of $\triangle ABC$ under the translation $T_{4, -2}$.

7. Trace the diagram. Then sketch the images of $\triangle XYZ$ under r_l and $r_m \circ r_l$.

8. Complete: $R_{-180}:(2, -3) \longrightarrow \underline{\quad?\quad}$

9. Describe the types of symmetry that a regular pentagon has.

10. Find the coordinates of the image of the origin under reflection in point $(-5, -4)$.

11. If $D_k:(15, 10) \longrightarrow (18, 12)$, find **(a)** the value of k and **(b)** $D_k(-25, -5)$.

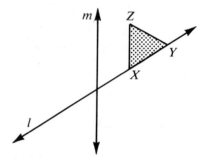

B 12. If $S:(x, y) \longrightarrow (3x, -y)$ and $T:(x, y) \longrightarrow (-y, -x)$, find a formula for $S \circ T$.

13. Find the coordinates of the images of $P(-2, -1)$, $Q(3, 5)$, and $R(3, 1)$ under reflection in the line $y = -x + 3$.

14. Sketch the graph of $y = |4 - 2x|$ and write the equation of the symmetry line.

15. If k is the line with equation $y = x$, find the image of $(-4, 3)$ under **(a)** $r_{x\text{-axis}} \circ r_k \circ r_{y\text{-axis}}$ and **(b)** $r_{y\text{-axis}} \circ r_{x\text{-axis}} \circ r_k$.

16. If $T:(-7, 2) \longrightarrow (-9, 5)$, then $T: \underline{\quad?\quad} \longrightarrow (0, -1)$.

17. Determine a translation $T_{a, b}$ that would map $f(x) = x^2$ to $g(x) = (x + 2)^2$.

18. Find the coordinates of the pre-image of $(3, 2)$ under R_{90}.

19. Graph the image of the line with equation $y = 4x - 2$ under $D_{\frac{1}{2}}$. State an equation of the image line.

Chapter 6

A　**1.** If $\overset{\frown}{ABD}$ is a semicircle of $\odot O$, find each of the following.

　　a. $m\,\overset{\frown}{CD}$　　**b.** $m\,\overset{\frown}{BC}$　　**c.** $m\angle AOC$　　**d.** $m\,\overset{\frown}{ACD}$

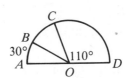

Find the value of each variable. P is the center of the circle.

2.

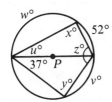

3.

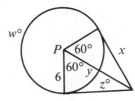

4.

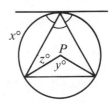

Find the value of x. O is the center of the circle.

5.

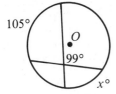

6.

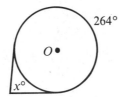

7.

8.

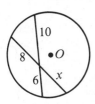

9.

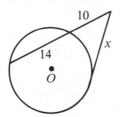

10.

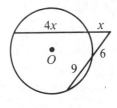

11. Find, to the nearest tenth, the circumference and area of a circle with diameter 0.6.

12. Draw a large obtuse $\triangle RST$ and inscribe a circle in it.

B　**13.** In $\odot O$, at the left below, $m\angle OAB = 56$. Find $m\,\overset{\frown}{AB}$ and $m\,\overset{\frown}{ACB}$.

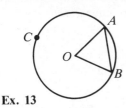

Ex. 13

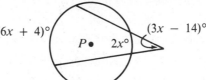

Ex. 14

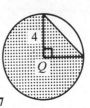

Ex. 17

14. Find the value of x for $\odot P$ in the diagram above.

15. If $\triangle XYZ$ is inscribed in a semicircle, $m\,\overset{\frown}{XY} = 2 \cdot m\,\overset{\frown}{YZ}$, and $XZ = 8$, find XY.

16. If a chord 30 cm long is 8 cm from the center of a circle, how far from the center is a chord 17 cm long?

17. Find the area of the shaded region of $\odot Q$ in the diagram at the right above.

A 1. An angle with measure $-470°$ is in standard position. Name the quadrant in which it lies.

2. The terminal side of an angle, $\angle 1$, in standard position, contains point $(-3, -3)$. Find $m\angle 1$ if $0° \leqslant m\angle 1 < 360°$.

3. Express in radians: **a.** $195°$ **b.** $312°$ **c.** $-90°$

4. Express in degrees: **a.** $\dfrac{3\pi}{4}$ **b.** 4 **c.** $-\dfrac{13\pi}{6}$

5. If $\cos \theta = \dfrac{15}{17}$ and θ is in Quadrant IV, find $\sin \theta$.

6. Evaluate: **a.** $\sin\left(-\dfrac{3\pi}{2}\right)$ **b.** $\cos 90°$ **c.** $\sin 2\pi - \cos 2\pi$

7. Express as a function of a positive acute angle.
   a. $\cos(-100°)$ **b.** $\sin 138°$ **c.** $\sin(-20°)$ **d.** $\cos 170°$

8. Evaluate: **a.** $\cos \dfrac{7\pi}{4}$ **b.** $\sin \dfrac{4\pi}{3}$ **c.** $\sin 270°$ **d.** $\cos 60°$

9. Express $15.42°$ in degrees, minutes, and seconds.

10. Find the value of θ to the nearest minute if $0° < \theta < 90°$ and $\cos \theta = 0.5100$. (Use Table 1.)

11. Use Table 1 to approximate: **a.** $\cos 290°20'$ **b.** $\sin 195°50'$

12. Complete: **a.** $\cos(180° - \theta) = \underline{\ ?\ }$ **b.** $\cos(90° + \theta) = \underline{\ ?\ }$

13. Graph $y = \sin \theta$ and $y = 0$ on the same set of axes for $-2\pi \leqslant \theta \leqslant 2\pi$. Use your sketch to help you solve $\sin \theta = 0$ over the domain $-2\pi \leqslant \theta \leqslant 2\pi$.

B 14. State the measures of three angles coterminal with a $130°$ angle.

15. In a circle of radius 12 cm, a central angle of 1.8 radians intercepts an arc. Find the length of that arc.

16. Through how many radians does the minute hand of a clock turn in 24 min?

17. Find $\sin \theta$ and $\cos \theta$ if θ is an angle in standard position and the terminal side of θ passes through: **a.** $(-1, 2\sqrt{2})$ **b.** $(-2, -4)$

18. Find all values of θ between $0°$ and $360°$ that make $\sin 15° = \sin \theta$ true.

19. If $\sin \theta = 0.1234$ and $\cos \theta < 0$, find the value of θ between $0°$ and $360°$ to the nearest $10'$.

20. Find the value of θ to the nearest $10'$ for the positive acute angle in standard position whose terminal side contains $(6, 8)$.

21. Graph $y = \cos \theta$ and $y = \sin \theta$ on the same set of axes for $0 \leqslant \theta \leqslant 2\pi$. Use your graph to find the values of θ for which both $\cos \theta \leqslant 0$ and $\sin \theta \leqslant 0$.

Chapter 8

A 1. For the function $y = \tan \theta$, **(a)** state the period of the function, **(b)** graph one period of the function, and **(c)** give the domain and the range.

2. Evaluate: **a.** $\csc \dfrac{7\pi}{6}$ **b.** $\sec (-45°)$ **c.** $\cot \dfrac{4\pi}{3}$ **d.** $\tan 480°$

3. If $\sin \theta = -\dfrac{21}{29}$ and $\cos \theta < 0$, find the values of the other five trigonometric functions.

Express in terms of a constant or a single function.

4. $(1 - \sec \theta)(1 + \sec \theta)$ 5. $\cot 2\alpha \cos 2\alpha$ 6. $\cos 3\theta \sec 3\theta$

7. $(1 - \sin^2 \theta)(\cot^2 \theta + 1)$ 8. $\sin (90° - \theta) \sec (-\theta)$ 9. $\dfrac{\sec (360° - \theta)}{\csc (360° - \iota)}$

Prove that each equation is an identity.

10. $\cos \theta(\csc \theta - \sec \theta) = \cot \theta - 1$ 11. $1 - \sin \alpha \cos \alpha \tan \alpha = \cos^2 \alpha$

Solve for $0° \leqslant \theta < 360°$ to the nearest 10'. Use Table 1 as necessary.

12. $2 \sin^2 \theta - 4 = 7 \sin \theta$ 13. $\cot^2 \theta + \cot \theta = 0$

14. $4 \cos^2 \theta - 3 = 0$ 15. $3 \csc^2 \theta + 10 \csc \theta = 8$

16. $\sin^2 \theta - \cos^2 \theta = 1$ 17. $\tan \theta = \sec^2 \theta - 1$

18. $\sin \theta + \cos \theta = 1$ 19. $\sin \theta \tan \theta + \cos \theta = \sec \theta$

B 20. Find the values of the six trigonometric functions if θ is an angle in standard position and the terminal side of θ passes through: **a.** $(4, -4)$ **b.** $(-4, -3)$

21. On the same set of axes, graph $y = \cos \theta$ and $y = \sec \theta$ for $-\pi < \theta < 2\pi$. For which values in this interval is $\cos \theta = \sec \theta$?

Express in terms of a constant or a single function.

22. $\dfrac{\tan^2 \alpha \csc^2 \alpha - 1}{\sin \alpha \tan^2 \alpha \csc \alpha}$ 23. $\dfrac{\sin \theta - \csc \theta}{\cot \theta}$ 24. $\dfrac{\sec \alpha + \csc \alpha}{1 + \tan \alpha}$

Prove that each equation is an identity.

25. $\dfrac{\cos \theta}{1 + \cos \theta} - \dfrac{1}{1 - \cos \theta} = -(2 \cot^2 \theta + 1)$ 26. $\dfrac{\cot^3 \alpha - 1}{\cot \alpha - 1} = \cot \alpha + \csc^2 \alpha$

Solve for $0 \leqslant \theta < 2\pi$.

27. $\csc^2 \dfrac{\theta}{2} = 4$ 28. $\sin^2 \theta + \sec^2 \theta = \cos^2 \theta$ 29. $\cos^2 2\theta = \cos 2\theta$

30. Find the smallest positive value of θ such that $\tan \left(\theta - \dfrac{\pi}{6}\right) = \sqrt{3}$.

31. Solve for $0° \leqslant \theta < 90°$: $\cos (2\theta - 11°) = \sin (\theta + 10°)$

Chapter 9

Simplify.

A 1. $27^{\frac{4}{3}}$ 2. $\left(\dfrac{100}{49}\right)^{-\frac{1}{2}}$ 3. $\dfrac{32^{-\frac{1}{4}}}{4^0}$ 4. $8^{\frac{1}{2}} - 2^{-\frac{1}{2}}$

5. Graph $f(x) = 0.5^x$ and $g(x) = 0.8^x$ on the same axes. Which graph is above the other when $x < 0$?

6. Evaluate: **a.** $\log_5 \dfrac{1}{125}$ **b.** $\log_3 243$ **c.** $\log_{64} 4$

Simplify.

7. $\log_2 \dfrac{100}{3} - \log_2 \dfrac{25}{3}$ 8. $\log_6 12 + \log_6 108$ 9. $\log_3 27^{\frac{1}{2}}$

10. Use Table 2 to evaluate: **a.** $\log 301$ **b.** x, if $\log x = 0.7612 - 2$

Use logs to calculate the following correct to three significant digits.

11. $\sqrt[4]{\dfrac{67.2}{5.69}}$ 12. $(94{,}200)^6$ 13. $\sqrt[3]{0.00385}$

Solve correct to three significant digits.

14. $\log_x 9 = 4$ 15. $x = \log_8 79$ 16. $\log_{4.1} x = 3.5$

17. If \$2000 is invested at 8% annual interest, find the value of the investment after 4 yr, correct to three significant digits.

18. Find the population, P, of a culture if $P = p(2)^{\frac{t}{10}}$, $p = 1$, and $t = 24$.

B 19. Solve: **a.** $2^{2x-1} = 8^{x-1}$ **b.** $\left(\dfrac{1}{9}\right)^{x-1} = \left(\dfrac{1}{3}\right)^{6x}$

20. If $3^{\frac{1}{4}} = y$, express in terms of y: **a.** $3^{\frac{7}{4}}$ **b.** $3^{-\frac{1}{2}}$

21. Solve: **a.** $\log_x 8 = -\dfrac{3}{4}$ **b.** $\log_x 3 = 5$

If $\log_m x = a$, $\log_m y = b$, and $\log_m z = c$, express in terms of a, b, and c.

22. $\log_m \dfrac{x^3}{yz}$ 23. $\log_m \sqrt{xy}$ 24. $\log_m \dfrac{\sqrt[3]{x}}{z^4}$

25. Interpolate to find: **a.** $\log 0.01234$ **b.** x if $\log x = 0.5116 + 2$

26. Use logs to calculate $\sqrt[3]{92.54}$ to four significant digits.

27. Solve: $\log_4 x^2 = 5$

28. Calculate $\ln 8$ to three significant digits.

29. Find the doubling time, to the nearest tenth of a year, when the annual growth rate is 6%.

638   *EXTRA PRACTICE*

In the following exercises, find lengths to the nearest integer and angle measures to the nearest 10' unless you are told otherwise.

A
1. In $\triangle RST$, $\overline{RS} \perp \overline{ST}$, $\angle T = 26°$, and $ST = 40$. Solve $\triangle RST$.

2. If θ is an acute angle and $\sec \theta = \dfrac{29}{21}$, find the values of the other five trigonometric functions.

3. A child is holding the end of a kite string 15 m long at eye level. If the altitude of the kite is 11 m above the child's eye level, find the angle of elevation of the kite.

4. In $\triangle ABC$, $\angle A = 18°50'$, $\angle B = 100°20'$, and $a = 36$. Find c.

5. In $\triangle PQR$, $\angle P = 135°$, $\angle Q = 30°$, and $q = 12$. Find p. Leave your answer in simplified radical form.

Find the number of triangles ABC that satisfy the given conditions.

6. $\angle A = 48°$, $a = 10$, $b = 12$
7. $\angle B = 72°$, $c = 16$, $b = 14$

8. In $\triangle ABC$, $\angle A = 58°$, $a = 54$, and $b = 62$. Find two possible measures (to the nearest 10') of $\angle B$ and $\angle C$.

9. The lengths of the sides of a triangle are 4, 6, and 7. Find the measure of the smallest angle of the triangle.

10. In $\triangle XYZ$, $\angle Z = 64°30'$, $x = 4$, and $y = 5$. Find z.

Find the area of $\triangle DEF$ to the nearest integer.

11. $\angle F = 42°$, $\angle E = 98°$, $d = 10$
12. $d = 5$, $e = 7$, $f = 8$

13. Find the magnitude and direction of the resultant of two 8 N forces acting at a 150° angle to each other.

B
14. In $\triangle JKL$, $JK = KL = 10$, and $JL = 14$. Find the measure of $\angle J$.

15. Find RS using the given diagram.

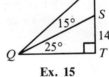

Ex. 15

16. Solve $\triangle ABC$ if $\angle B = 43°$, $b = 20$, and $a = 25$.
17. Solve $\triangle PQR$ if $\angle P = 28°$, $\angle Q = 110°$, and $r = 50$.
18. Solve $\triangle DEF$ if $DE = 8$, $EF = 7$, and $\angle E = 57°$.

19. Find the length, to the nearest tenth, of a side of a regular polygon with nine sides if the polygon is inscribed in a circle of radius 12.

20. Find an expression for the area of the polygon described in Exercise 19. Leave your answer in terms of a trigonometric function.

21. A plane with an air speed of 500 km/h is steering a heading of 60°. The wind is 50 km/h from 180°. Find the ground speed of the plane to the nearest kilometer per hour and its course to the nearest degree.

A 1. Determine the amplitude and the fundamental period of the function. Graph at least two cycles of the function.

    a. $y = -\dfrac{3}{2}\cos x$ **b.** $y = 3\sin 2x$ **c.** $y = 2\cos \dfrac{x}{3}$

2. Evaluate using Angle-Sum and Angle-Difference Formulas.

    a. $\tan \dfrac{17\pi}{12}$ **b.** $\sin(-105°)$ **c.** $\cos(-105°)$

3. If $\sin \alpha = \dfrac{21}{29}$, $\cot \beta = \dfrac{15}{8}$, and α and β lie in Quadrant I, find $\sin(\alpha + \beta)$ and $\cos(\alpha - \beta)$.

4. If $\sin \theta = -\dfrac{3}{5}$ and $\dfrac{3\pi}{2} < \theta < 2\pi$, find $\sin 2\theta$, $\cos 2\theta$, and $\tan 2\theta$.

5. Prove the identity $\cot \theta - \tan \theta = \dfrac{2}{\tan 2\theta}$.

6. Use Half-Angle Formulas to evaluate $\sin 67.5°$, $\cos 67.5°$, and $\tan 67.5°$.

7. If $\sin \theta = -\dfrac{\sqrt{3}}{2}$ and $\pi < \theta < \dfrac{3\pi}{2}$, find $\sin \dfrac{\theta}{2}$, $\cos \dfrac{\theta}{2}$, and $\tan \dfrac{\theta}{2}$.

8. Solve for $0° \le x < 360°$:   **a.** $\tan^2 \dfrac{x}{2} = \dfrac{1}{3}$ **b.** $\sin 2x = 4\sin x$

9. Evaluate: **a.** $\mathrm{Cos}^{-1}\left(-\dfrac{1}{2}\right)$ **b.** $\mathrm{Arctan}\, 1$ **c.** $\tan\left(\mathrm{Sin}^{-1} \dfrac{\sqrt{3}}{2}\right)$

10. (Optional) Plot $\left(-4, \dfrac{4\pi}{3}\right)$ and find its rectangular coordinates.

11. (Optional) Find two pairs of polar coordinates for $(-3, -3)$.

12. Express in the form $a + bi$:   **a.** $2\sqrt{6}(\cos 180° + i \sin 180°)$ **b.** $(2 - 2i)^5$

B 13. Use a graph to decide the number of values of x in the interval $0 \le x \le 2\pi$ that satisfy $f(x) = \cos 2x$ and $g(x) = \cos 3x$.

Prove each identity.

14. $\sin(135° - x) = \dfrac{\sqrt{2}}{2}(\sin x + \cos x)$ 15. $\dfrac{1 - \sin 2\theta}{\cos 2\theta} = \dfrac{1 - \tan \theta}{1 + \tan \theta}$

16. If $\sin \theta = -\dfrac{4\sqrt{2}}{9}$ and $\pi < \theta < \dfrac{3\pi}{2}$, find $\sin \dfrac{\theta}{2}$ and $\sin \dfrac{\theta}{4}$.

17. Solve for $0° \le x < 360°$: $\cos 2x = (\sin x + \cos x)^2$

18. Evaluate: **a.** $\sin\left(\mathrm{Arctan}\, 1 + \mathrm{Arccos}\, \dfrac{9}{41}\right)$ **b.** $\cos\left(2\,\mathrm{Sin}^{-1} \dfrac{8}{17}\right)$

19. (Optional) Find the polar form of the cube roots of $\sqrt{3} + i$.

Two dice are thrown. Find each probability.

A   **1.** $P(5)$ **2.** P(two different numbers)   **3.** P(multiple of three)

Find the probability that the two cards are chosen from a deck of cards if the cards are drawn **(a)** with replacement and **(b)** without replacement.

   4. P(two aces)   **5.** P(two red cards)   **6.** P(at least one king)

Exercises 7 and 8 refer to the following experiment and events: Two balls are drawn, with replacement, from a jar containing 4 green balls, 3 red balls, and 5 white balls.

A: The first ball is red. B: The second ball is red.

C: The second ball is not green.

   7. Are events A and B independent or dependent?

   8. Are events B and C independent or dependent?

   9. How many three-digit numbers can be formed using the digits 0 to 8 **(a)** if repetition of digits is allowed and **(b)** if repetition of digits is not allowed?

  10. How many permutations are there of the letters in the word DISTILL?

  11. In how many different ways can a biologist choose five samples of soil from twenty samples?

  12. A die is tossed eight times. Find **(a)** P(exactly three 2's), **(b)** P(no 2's), and **(c)** P(at least six 2's). Give answers in symbolic form and as decimals with three significant digits.

  13. Evaluate: **a.** $\dbinom{12}{0}$ **b.** $\dbinom{15}{1}$ **c.** $\dbinom{5}{3}$

  14. Give the first four terms of $(x - 3y)^{11}$.

B   **15.** Find P(all heads) when five coins are tossed.

In Exercises 16–18, four cards are drawn, without replacement, from a deck of cards.

  16. Find the probability of drawing at least one ace.

  17. Find the probability of drawing a jack, a queen, a king, and an ace.

  18. If the cards are placed side by side, left to right, in the order they are drawn, find the probability that the cards appear as follows: jack, queen, king, ace.

  19. If the probability of rain is 30% every day for a week, find the probability of fewer than three rainy days that week.

  20. Expand and simplify: $\left(2x^3 - \dfrac{y}{6x}\right)^6$

  21. Can two events be mutually exclusive and independent? Explain.

  22. Find the twelfth term of the expansion of $(a - b)^{16}$, given that the coefficient of the eleventh term is 8008.

A
1. In an opinion poll of 500 voters, 204 chose Candidate A, 185 chose Candidate B, and the rest were undecided. Of 8400 voters, how many can be expected to vote for Candidate B?

2. Evaluate: **a.** $\displaystyle\sum_{i=1}^{5} 2i^2$ **b.** $\displaystyle\sum_{i=6}^{10} (3i-2)$

3. Find the mean of the data: 1.5, 1.9, 1.1, 1.5, 1.7, 1.4, 1.2, 1.9

The number of gold medals won by sixteen countries in the Olympics one year is shown at the right.

No. of Gold Medals Won	Frequency
0	4
1	5
2	3
3	2
7	1
13	1

4. Find the mean number of gold medals won that year.

5. Draw a histogram of the data.

6. Find the median.

7. Find the mode.

8. During one week, the number of new cars sold each day at the Williams Motor Mart was 4, 4, 3, 5, 8, 6, and 5. Find **(a)** the mean absolute deviation, **(b)** the variance, and **(c)** the standard deviation, correct to two decimal places.

The scores on a test approximate a normal distribution with a mean of 75 and a standard deviation of 5. A person is chosen at random from those who took the test.

9. Find the probability that the person's score was between 80 and 90, inclusive.

10. Find the probability that the person's score was under 65.

B
11. Suppose you toss a penny, a nickel, and a dime 1000 times.
    a. How many times would you expect to get exactly two heads?
    b. If 120 tosses resulted in three heads, would you suspect that the coins were biased? 200 tosses?

12. Use summation notation to write $2 + 5 + 8 + 11 + \cdots + 179$. Then evaluate the sum.

Exercises 13–15 refer to the data in the table at the right.

Score	Frequency
1–15	2
16–30	3
31–45	12
46–60	15
61–75	8

13. Find an approximate value of the mean of the data.

14. In which interval does the median occur?

15. Construct a histogram for the information.

16. If all the data in a set are doubled, compare **(a)** the original mean and the new mean and **(b)** the original standard deviation and the new standard deviation.

17. Use the table on page 544 to find the value of a if $P(x \leqslant a) = 0.986$.

Find the coordinates of the image of $(0, -1)$ under the composite.

A   1. $T_{5, -2} \circ T_{-5, -3}$ 2. $R_{180} \circ R_{30}$ 3. $D_{\frac{2}{3}} \circ D_6$ 4. $R_{45} \circ R_{15}$

Let k be the line with equation $y = x$. State the image of $(-3, 5)$ under the given glide reflection.

5. $r_{x\text{-axis}} \circ T_{7, 0}^{\,(}$ 6. $T_{0, -1} \circ r_{y\text{-axis}}$ 7. $T_{4, 4} \circ r_k$ 8. $r_k \circ T_{-3, -3}$

Identify the type of isometry that maps $\triangle ABC$ onto $\triangle A'B'C'$.

9. 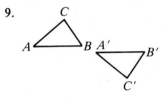   10. 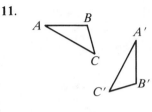   11.

If $\triangle RST$ has vertices $R(-3, 3)$, $S(6, 3)$, and $T(0, 9)$, find the coordinates of the vertices of its image under the given similarity transformation.

12. $r_{y\text{-axis}} \circ D_2$ 13. $D_{\frac{1}{3}} \circ R_{180}$ 14. $T_{1, -2} \circ D_{\frac{2}{3}}$ 15. $r_{x\text{-axis}} \circ D_{R, \frac{1}{3}}$

16. Determine the symmetry set of a regular hexagon.

17. Refer to the operation table for the symmetry group of an equilateral triangle on page 582. Verify the entry $R_{P, 240} \circ r_m = r_n$.

B   18. Find the values of x and y if $R_{145} \circ R_{-325} (x, y) = (-7, -5)$.

19. If $r_m \circ T_{-1, 1}$ is a glide reflection that maps $(-3, 0)$ to $(0, 5)$, find an equation of line m.

20. G is a glide reflection such that $G = T_{a, b} \circ r_k$, $G:(-1, 3) \longrightarrow (1, 1)$, and $G:(4, -2) \longrightarrow (-4, -4)$. Find (a) an equation for k, (b) the values of a and b, and (c) the image of $(3, 7)$ under G.

21. Given: $r_k \circ r_j \circ r_{x\text{-axis}}$ maps $\triangle ABC$ onto $\triangle A'B'C'$, line j has equation $y = -4$, and k has equation $y = 2$. Show that $r_k \circ r_j \circ r_{x\text{-axis}}$ is a line reflection, r_q, by finding an equation of the reflecting line, q, for which $r_q(\triangle ABC) = \triangle A'B'C'$.

Is the composite a line reflection, a glide reflection, a translation, or a rotation?

22. $r_{x\text{-axis}} \circ r_k$, where k has equation $y = x$

23. $r_{y\text{-axis}} \circ r_{x\text{-axis}} \circ r_m$, where m has equation $x = 3$

24. A transformation maps $\triangle ABC$ with vertices $A(0, 0)$, $B(3, 1)$, and $C(1, 4)$ onto $\triangle A''B''C''$ with vertices $A''(0, 0)$, $B''(-2, 6)$, and $C''(-8, 2)$. Express the transformation as a composite of an isometry following a dilation with center A.

A 1. Give an explicit rule for the sequence $0, \frac{1}{2}, 2, \frac{9}{2}, 8, \frac{25}{2}, 18$.

2. Give a recursive rule for $10, 7, 4, 1, -2, \ldots$.

3. Find the fiftieth term of the arithmetic sequence whose third and fourth terms are -1 and $1\frac{1}{2}$, respectively.

4. Insert six arithmetic means between -37 and -2.

Find the sum of the arithmetic series.

5. $a_1 = 50$, $a_n = -90$, $n = 41$ 　　　　　 6. $\displaystyle\sum_{k=1}^{24} (3k - 4)$

7. The series whose terms are the first 27 positive even integers

Find the specified term of the given geometric sequence.

8. a_7; $4, 8\sqrt{2}, 32, \ldots$ 　　　　　 9. a_1; $a_7 = 320$; $r = 4$

10. Find the sum of the geometric series $486 - 162 + \cdots + 6$.

11. Find S_6 for the geometric series with $a_1 = 32$ and $r = \frac{3}{2}$.

Find the sum of the infinite geometric series, if it exists.

12. $2 + 1 + 0.5 + \cdots$ 　　　 13. $1 - 2 + 4 - 8 + \cdots$ 　　　 14. $25 + 5\sqrt{5} + 5 + \cdots$

15. Prove by induction that $3 + 7 + 11 + \cdots + (4n - 1) = n(2n + 1)$ is true for any natural number n.

B 16. Give a recursive rule for the sequence $1, \frac{1}{2}, \frac{1}{6}, \frac{1}{24}, \ldots$.

17. Find the first term, a_1, and the common difference, d, of the arithmetic sequence with $a_9 = -57$ and $a_{15} = -105$.

18. Find the sum of the arithmetic series of 18 terms such that $a_{16} = 15$ and $a_{18} = 12$.

19. If $-13 - 9 - 5 - \cdots + a_n = 143$, find the value of n.

20. In a geometric sequence, $a_1 = 96$ and $a_4 = 40.5$. Find the value of r.

21. Insert three geometric means between 25 and $\frac{16}{25}$.

22. Find the common ratio of the infinite geometric series with first term 4 and with sum 32.

23. Find the value of x if the sum of the infinite geometric series $4x + 2x^2 + x^3 + \cdots$ is 2.

24. Prove by induction that $n^3 + 2n$ is a multiple of 3 for any natural number n.

Algebra Review Exercises

Simplify.

A 1. $\frac{1}{2}(2x + 1) - x$ 2. $\frac{2}{3}(3x + 6) + 4$ 3. $|2 - 7|$

Evaluate when $a = 3$, $b = -2$, and $c = -1$.

4. $\dfrac{a^2 - 2a + 4}{ab - 1}$ 5. $(a + c)(b - a)$ 6. $\dfrac{4b - 2ac}{ab^2}$

Solve and check.

7. $12t + 7 = 9$ 8. $\dfrac{2x}{3} + 1 = \dfrac{3}{2}x$ 9. $6.2x + 2.6 = 8.8$

10. $8 - (x - 3) = 12$ 11. $\dfrac{2}{3}r + \dfrac{3}{2}r = 1$ 12. $|x + 5| = 2$

13. $|2x + 1| = 17$ 14. $|3(3w + 1)| = 1$ 15. $|3 - 2t| = 8$

Solve.

16. Two positive numbers are in the ratio 6:5 and their sum is 77. Find the two numbers.

17. The perimeter of an isosceles triangle is 14. The sum of the lengths of the congruent sides is 10 more than the length of the base. Find the lengths of the sides of the triangle.

18. Two runners begin running in the same direction at the same time. At the end of 15 minutes, the faster runner is 1 km ahead of the slower runner. If the slower runner's rate is 12 km/h, find the faster runner's rate.

19. The lengths of two sides of a triangle are 15 and 8. Find the possible lengths of the third side.

Solve and graph the solution set.

20. $5x + 2 \leqslant 1$ 21. $3 - 2y > 1$ 22. $-7 < 2 - x \leqslant 10$

23. $-1 \leqslant 100 - x < 1$ 24. $|x| \geqslant 3$ 25. $|x + 1| < 5$

Solve each equation or inequality.

B 26. $3(2t - 1) + 2(4t - 3) = 3(1 - t)$ 27. $0.5z - 0.95 = 4.4$

28. $\dfrac{1}{2} + \dfrac{2}{3}x \leqslant \dfrac{3}{4}x$ 29. $\dfrac{r}{2} + \dfrac{r}{3} \leqslant \dfrac{4}{5}$

30. $3 - 5x \geqslant 2x - 11$ and $3x + 7 > 4$ 31. $5k - 9 < 2k \leqslant 3(k + 4)$

32. $\left|\dfrac{x+2}{3}\right| \leqslant 10$

33. $\left|\dfrac{2t+3}{10}\right| < 1$

34. $3 + x < 6 < x - 12$

35. $\dfrac{1}{2}(x-2) < \dfrac{1}{3}(x+2) < \dfrac{1}{2}(x+6)$

Solve.

36. Claudia needs to average at least $50 for each painting she sells. She has sold six paintings for $60, $28, $54, $35, $40, and $58. Find the minimum selling price of her next painting if she is to maintain her average.

37. Sailor Dan's charges a boat rental fee of $40 plus $5 per hour or fraction of an hour. Blue Wave charges $25 plus $8.50 per hour or fraction of an hour. Under what conditions does it cost less to rent from Blue Wave?

Chapter 2

Simplify.

A

1. $(3ab^2)^2 \cdot (2a^2b)^3$

2. $(3^7) \cdot \left(\dfrac{1}{9}\right)$

3. $\dfrac{(4kl)^2}{4kl^2}$

4. $\dfrac{6xy}{6x^{-1}y^2}$

5. $\left(\dfrac{2}{3x^2}\right)^{-3}$

6. $\left(\dfrac{x}{y^{-2}}\right)^{-2}$

7. $(3x^2 + y) + (x^2 - xy + y)$

8. $(3x^2 + 1) - (x^2 - 2)$

9. $yz(7y^2 - 2yz + z^4)$

10. $(2x + 3)(x - 2)$

11. $(4b - 3)(4b + 3)$

12. $(5x + 3y)^2$

13. $\dfrac{2w^2 - 8}{w} \cdot \dfrac{w^2}{2}$

14. $\left(\dfrac{1}{a} - \dfrac{1}{a+h}\right) \div ah$

15. $\dfrac{2}{a+b} - \dfrac{2a}{a^2 + b^2}$

16. $\dfrac{n^{-1} + 2^{-1}}{2n}$

17. $\dfrac{w}{w-1} + \dfrac{1}{1-w}$

18. $\dfrac{x}{x+1} - \dfrac{x+1}{x+2}$

Factor completely.

19. $x^2 - 3x - 10$

20. $2x^2 + 2x - 12$

21. $3m^2 - 75n^2$

22. $4x^2 + 20x + 25$

23. $5z^3 - 40$

24. $64y^3 + 1$

Solve.

25. $3t^2 - 8t + 5 = 0$

26. $z^2 - 9z + 18 = 0$

27. $w^2 + 3w = 28$

28. Divide $x^3 + 2x^2 + 3x + 6$ by $x + 2$.

29. Solve: $\dfrac{k}{2} + \dfrac{2}{k} = \dfrac{4k+1}{6}$

30. Find and graph the solution set: $n^2 \leqslant 2n + 15$

B

31. One number is 2 more than another and the sum of their reciprocals is $-\dfrac{4}{3}$. Find the two numbers.

32. Allison and Bentley leave on a bike trip at the same time. After 3 h, Allison

has ridden half again as far as Bentley. If Allison can ride 6 km/h faster than Bentley, how fast can each ride?

33. Simplify: $\left(\dfrac{3y^{-4}z^{-2}}{5y^{-8}w^2}\right)^3$

Solve using the quadratic formula.

34. $x^2 - 7x + 2 = 0$

35. $3x^2 + 5x - 1 = 0$

36. $2x^2 - x - 4 = 0$

37. If 2 is a root of $x^3 - 5x^2 + 12 = 0$, find the other roots.

38. Find the rational roots of the equation $6x^3 - 11x^2 + 6x - 1 = 0$.

39. The lengths of the altitude and the base of a triangle are two consecutive even integers. If the area of the triangle is 40 cm², find the lengths of the altitude and the base.

Solve.

40. $6x^3 - 13x^2 + 6x = 0$

41. $x^4 + 5x^2 - 6 = 0$

Simplify.

42. $\dfrac{(a+b)^{-1}}{a^{-1} + b^{-1}}$

43. $\dfrac{(x^{-1} + y^{-1})^2}{(x^{-2} + y^{-2})^{-1}}$

44. $\dfrac{1}{2 + \dfrac{3}{4 + \dfrac{5}{6}}}$

Chapter 3

Simplify.

A

1. $\sqrt{72}$

2. $\sqrt{\dfrac{7}{18}}$

3. $2\sqrt{128} + 15\sqrt{192}$

4. $\sqrt{3}(7\sqrt{2} - 5)$

5. $(4\sqrt{11} - 3)(4\sqrt{11} + 3)$

6. $(\sqrt{5} - \sqrt{6})^2$

7. $(5\sqrt{3} - \sqrt{8})(2\sqrt{8} - \sqrt{3})$

8. $\dfrac{3}{\sqrt{8} - 2}$

9. $\dfrac{\sqrt{3}}{\sqrt{2} - 1}$

Solve. Check each apparent solution.

10. $\sqrt{4 - x} = 3$

11. $2\sqrt{x + 3} + 6 = 2x$

12. $3x + \sqrt{2x + 3} = 7x + 6$

Simplify. Express the answer in standard form.

13. $\sqrt{-81}$

14. $\dfrac{-\sqrt{12}}{\sqrt{-4}}$

15. $(i\sqrt{2})(i\sqrt{6})$

16. i^{10}

17. i^{-3}

18. $(2 + 3i)^2$

19. $(1 - i)(2 + 2i)$

20. $\dfrac{2 - 3i}{1 + i}$

21. $\dfrac{2 - i\sqrt{5}}{2 + i\sqrt{5}}$

Solve over the set of complex numbers.

22. $x^2 + 3x + 4 = 0$

23. $x^2 + x + 5 = 0$

24. $2x^2 - x + 7 = 0$

25. Find the standard form of the multiplicative inverse of $3 + 4i$.

Find a quadratic equation in standard form with integral coefficients and having the given numbers as its roots.

26. $7, -7$ **27.** $2 + 3i, 2 - 3i$ **28.** $1 - \sqrt{2}, 1 + \sqrt{2}$

29. Show that $3 - i$ is a root of $x(x - 6) + 10 = 0$.

Simplify. Assume that all variables represent positive real numbers and express the answers in standard form.

B   **30.** $2\sqrt{\dfrac{4}{3}} + \sqrt{75}$ **31.** $\sqrt{\dfrac{3}{4}} + \sqrt{\dfrac{4}{3}}$ **32.** $\sqrt[3]{81} + \sqrt[3]{192}$

33. $3\sqrt{x} + 5\sqrt{x^5}$ **34.** $\dfrac{\sqrt{20} + \sqrt{12}}{\sqrt{5} - \sqrt{3}}$ **35.** $\sqrt{\dfrac{a}{b}} - \sqrt{\dfrac{b}{a}}$

36. $5\sqrt[3]{4} \cdot 6\sqrt[3]{2}$ **37.** $\dfrac{5\sqrt{3} - 7i\sqrt{2}}{\sqrt{3} + i\sqrt{2}}$ **38.** $\dfrac{-3(\sqrt{10} - 2i\sqrt{5})}{4\sqrt{10} + 3i\sqrt{5}}$

39. Express $\dfrac{3}{1 + 2i} + \dfrac{5}{1 - 2i}$ as a single complex number in standard form.

Solve. Check each apparent solution.

40. $x\sqrt{2} + x = 2$ **41.** $2m + m\sqrt{3} + m = 1$ **42.** $7 - \sqrt{x} = \sqrt{7 + x}$

43. $\sqrt{x} - \sqrt{x - 3} = 1$ **44.** $\sqrt{3x + 4} - \sqrt{x + 1} = 3$ **45.** $\sqrt{x^2 + 9} - 2 = \sqrt{x^2 - 7}$

46. Find the value(s) of m for which the equation $mx^2 + x - 4 = 0$ has:
     a. one real double root   **b.** two real roots   **c.** no real roots

Find a quadratic equation in standard form with integral coefficients and having the given numbers as roots.

47. $\dfrac{3 - \sqrt{2}}{4}, \dfrac{3 + \sqrt{2}}{4}$ **48.** $\dfrac{3 + 8i\sqrt{2}}{5}, \dfrac{3 - 8i\sqrt{2}}{5}$

Chapter 4

Give the domain and range of each function and state whether or not the function is one-to-one.

A   **1.** $y = 4x$ **2.** $y = |x|$ **3.** $y = \sqrt{x - 2}$

     4. $y = |x + 2|$ **5.** $y = \sqrt{x^2 - 1}$ **6.** $y = 1 - |x|$

Sketch the graph of the relation. State whether or not it is a function. If it is, state its domain and range.

     7. $\{(1, 0), (5, 2), (5, -2), (10, 3), (10, -3), (17, 4), (17, -4)\}$

     8. $x = 5$ **9.** $y = 5$ **10.** $y = |1 - x|$

Tell whether the given function is odd, even, or neither.

11. $y = x^3$ **12.** $y = \dfrac{|x|}{1+x}$ **13.** $y = \sqrt{x^2}$

14. Use linear interpolation, with $a = 5$ and $b = 6$, to find $f(5.6)$ if $f(x) = \dfrac{1}{1+x}$. Round your answer to the nearest hundredth.

For the given functions, find **(a)** $[g \circ h](4)$ and **(b)** $[h \circ g](4)$.

15. $g(x) = x^2 + 1$, $h(x) = |2x - 1|$ **16.** $g(x) = \dfrac{1}{x} + x$, $h(x) = \dfrac{1}{1+x}$

Find the inverse of each function.

17. $\{(2, 3), (-1, 8), (3, 2)\}$ **18.** $y = 4 - 2x$ **19.** $f(x) = x + 6$

In Exercises 20 and 21, answer *True* or *False*.

20. All one-to-one functions have inverses.

21. f and g are inverse functions if and only if $[f \circ g](x) = x$.

22. Find a linear function h such that $h(-5) = 5$ and $h(5) = 0$.

Find the value of k if the given function associates the two given numbers.

B   **23.** $y = kx^2 + 2$; $2 \longrightarrow -1$ **24.** $y = \dfrac{k-x}{k+x}$; $3 \longrightarrow -\dfrac{1}{2}$

25. Give the domain of the function $y = \dfrac{10}{\sqrt{2x^2 - 50}}$.

26. Sketch the part of the graph of the function $f(x) = 1 - x^2$ that corresponds to the values of x such that $x \geqslant 0$. Then use the oddness or evenness of the function to sketch the rest of the graph.

Exercises 27 and 28 refer to the table at the right, which relates values of a variable b to values of a variable a.

a	b
3	1.24
4	2.55
5	3.03
6	3.20

27. Use linear interpolation to find the approximate value of b when $a = 3.40$.

28. Use linear interpolation to find the approximate value of a when $b = 2.00$.

29. Let $g(x) = \dfrac{1}{x+1}$ and $h(x) = \dfrac{1}{x} - 1$. Show that $[g \circ h](x) = x$ for all x in the domain of $g \circ h$, and $[h \circ g](x) = x$ for all x in the domain of $h \circ g$.

Show that each function is its own inverse by showing that $f(f(x)) = x$ for all x in the domain of f.

30. $f(x) = 5 - x$ **31.** $f(x) = \dfrac{4}{x}$

32. Let $f(x) = |x + 2|$ for $x > -2$. On one set of axes sketch the graph of the function, f, and its inverse.

Simplify. Express answers that are irrational in simplest radical form.

A 1. $8^{\frac{2}{3}}$ 2. $4^{-\frac{3}{2}}$ 3. $243^{-\frac{1}{3}}$ 4. $\left(\dfrac{16}{81}\right)^{\frac{3}{4}}$

5. $\left(\dfrac{16}{81}\right)^{-\frac{3}{4}}$ 6. $\left(\dfrac{27}{8}\right)^{\frac{2}{3}}$ 7. $8^{\frac{3}{4}} \cdot 8^{\frac{3}{4}}$ 8. $8^{\frac{3}{4}} + 8^{\frac{3}{4}}$

9. If $f(x) = \left(\dfrac{1}{3}\right)^{x}$ and $g(x) = \left(\dfrac{1}{4}\right)^{x}$, name the function whose graph is above the other in Quadrant I.

Evaluate.

10. $\log_3 81$ 11. $\log_{16} \dfrac{1}{2}$ 12. $\log_2 \dfrac{1}{16}$

13. $\log_{10} 40 + \log_{10} \dfrac{5}{2}$ 14. $\log_2 10 - \log_2 5$ 15. $\log_5 300 - \log_5 12$

16. $\log_2 \sqrt{2}$ 17. $\log_5 \sqrt[3]{\dfrac{1}{5}}$ 18. $\log_3 \sqrt[4]{\dfrac{1}{3}}$

19. $\log 7$ 20. $\log 5.2$ 21. $\log 8.2$

22. $\log 4.31$ 23. $\log 43.1$ 24. $\log 0.0431$

25. y, if $\log y = 0.8075$ 26. t, if $\log t = 0.5717 - 3$

Solve for x. In Exercises 31–35, give your answers correct to three significant digits.

27. $\log_x 125 = 3$ 28. $\log_3 x = -3$ 29. $\log_7 343 = x$

30. $3^x = 81$ 31. $2^x = 6$ 32. $5^x = 8$

B 33. $\log_x 3 = 4$ 34. $\log_4 3 = x$ 35. $\log_5 2 = x$

Find each of the following correct to four significant digits. Use logs in Exercises 41 and 42.

36. $\log 3.204$ 37. $\log 81.07$ 38. $\log 4123$

39. x, if $\log x = 0.6215$ 40. y, if $\log y = 0.3565 + 2$

41. $\dfrac{(325.4)^3}{2135}$ 42. $\sqrt[6]{524,000}$

43. The population of a town has doubled every 12 yr. If the population is 23,000 now, use the formula $A_n = A_0(1 + r)^n$ to find the population 23 yr from now, to the nearest thousand.

44. The population of a town has been increasing at a rate of 2% per year. If the population is now 10,000, find the population 12 yr from now, to the nearest thousand.

Give an explicit rule for each sequence.

A 1. $1, 4, 7, 10, 13, \ldots$

2. $1, -\dfrac{1}{2}, \dfrac{1}{3}, -\dfrac{1}{4}, \dfrac{1}{5}, \ldots$

Give a recursive rule for each sequence.

3. $4, -4, 4, -4, 4, \ldots$

4. $2, 5, 8, 11, 14, \ldots$

Find the specified term of the arithmetic sequence satisfying the given conditions.

5. $a_1 = 3;\ d = 4;\ a_{22} = \underline{\ \ ?\ \ }$

6. $a_9 = 11;\ d = 2;\ a_1 = \underline{\ \ ?\ \ }$

Insert the given number of arithmetic means between the given numbers.

7. 1 between -8 and 42

8. 5 between 4 and 52

Find the sum of the arithmetic series.

9. the series of 25 terms beginning $15 + 11 + 7 + 3 + \cdots$

10. the series whose terms are the first 30 positive even integers

Find the specified term of the geometric sequence satisfying the given conditions.

11. $1, 3, 9, \ldots;\ a_{10} = \underline{\ \ ?\ \ }$

12. $a_8 = 625\sqrt{5};\ r = \sqrt{5};\ a_1 = \underline{\ \ ?\ \ }$

13. Find the sum of the geometric series of 25 terms beginning $1 + 2 + 4 + 8 + \cdots$.

14. Find S_6 for the geometric series with $a_1 = 128$ and $r = \dfrac{1}{2}$.

15. Find the sum of the infinite geometric series $2 + \dfrac{3}{2} + \dfrac{9}{8} + \cdots$.

B 16. Find the first term and the common difference of the arithmetic sequence with $a_{14} = 18$ and $a_{31} = 52$.

17. Find the sum of the arithmetic series whose first two terms are 1 and 3 and whose last term is 29.

Insert the given number of geometric means between the given numbers.

18. 1 between 8 and 18

19. 3 between $\dfrac{3}{4}$ and 192

20. Find a value of r for the geometric sequence with $a_1 = 8$ and $a_6 = \dfrac{1}{32}$.

21. Find the common ratio of the infinite geometric series with $a_1 = 40$ and $S = 64$.

Programming in BASIC

1. Introduction to Computers

A *computer* contains a *central processing unit* (CPU), which does the work, and a *memory*, in which information is stored. It must also have *input* and *output* devices.

COMPUTER

Computers are important because they can work with large amounts of data very fast. They work so rapidly that the directions for each project must be written out and stored ahead of time. Such a list of directions is called a *program*. Data and programs used with microcomputers (personal computers) are generally input by means of a *keyboard*. Everything that is typed in appears on the *monitor*, which is like a television screen. Sometimes a *printer* is also attached.

The actual instructions to the computer are given in *machine language*. Such a language may be written down by using 0's and 1's, where 0 and 1 may represent "off" and "on" switches, respectively. Numbers written with 0's and 1's are said to be written in the *binary system* in contrast to the decimal system, which we ordinarily use. In the decimal system, 10 means ten. In the binary system, 10 means two, 11 means three, 100 means four, and so on. Other systems that are sometimes used are the octal (base eight) and the hexadecimal (base sixteen).

Most programmers use one of the so-called "higher level" languages, such as BASIC, COBOL, FORTRAN, or Pascal. The computer contains a program, called a *compiler*, or *interpreter*, that translates such a program into machine language. Since some form of BASIC is available on each of the microcomputers, as well as on larger computers, that language has been chosen for use in this book.

2. BASIC symbols, FOR-NEXT, PRINT, END

BASIC uses many of the familiar signs and symbols of mathematics:

$+$ for addition	( ) grouping symbols
$-$ for subtraction	$>$ is greater than
$=$ equals	$<$ is less than

Other symbols are slightly different:

$*$ for multiplication	$>=$ for $\geq$
$/$ for division	$<=$ for $\leq$
$X \uparrow 3$ or $X \wedge 3$ for x^3	$<>$ for $\neq$

A computer program may be thought of as being made up of blocks like this:

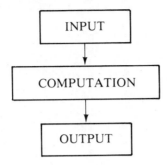

However, sometimes the blocks may overlap and sometimes one block may contain several processes.

A BASIC program consists of a list of numbered lines, or *statements*. It is customary to number the statements 10, 20, . . . , as shown below so that additional statements may be inserted when needed.

BASIC handles *variables* much as you do in mathematics. There are several ways of giving values to variables. When a fixed number of sequential values are to be given to a variable, a FOR-NEXT *loop* may be convenient, as shown below in lines 10 to 30.

```
10   FOR N=1 TO 10
20   PRINT N,N*N,N^3
30   NEXT N
40   END
```

(Some versions of BASIC do not require an END statement—line 40.) In this program, the value of the variable N is printed as 1, 2, . . . , 10. Thus, the input (line 10) and the computation and the output (line 20) are all contained in one block—the loop. Line 20 is a PRINT statement. It computes the values of N, N*N, and N^3 and then prints them. The *commas* in line 20 will cause the values to be printed on the same line but spaced apart. Type in this program and then type the *command* RUN. (A command has no line number because it is not part of a program.) The output will consist of ten lines and three columns.

You can use a PRINT statement with *quotation marks* and commas to print headings for the columns, as in line 5 below. Line 7 will "print" a blank line. Insert these lines:

```
5   PRINT "N", "N^2", "N^3"
7   PRINT
```

Type the command LIST to see the revised program, and then RUN it. The output should look something like that shown at the top of the following page.

N	N^2	N^3
1	1	1
2	4	8
3	9	27
4	16	64
5	25	125
6	36	216
7	49	343
8	64	512
9	81	729
10	100	1000

The program on page 37 contains several **FOR-NEXT** loops. The program can be blocked out as follows:

```
┌10    FOR N=0 TO 18
│ . . .
└60    NEXT N
  70    PRINT
┌80    FOR N=0 TO 18
│ . . .
└100   NEXT N
 110   PRINT
┌120   FOR X=−9 TO 9
│ . . .
└170   NEXT X
 180   PRINT
┌190   FOR X=−9 TO 9
│ . . .
└240   NEXT X
 250   PRINT
 260   END
```

Notice that each loop is followed by a simple **PRINT** statement. Since the **PRINT** statement within each loop ends with a *semicolon* (which causes the items to be printed close together), the simple **PRINT** statement is needed at the end of the loop to bring the carriage (or cursor) back to the left margin. (It does not print a blank line here.)

3. IF-THEN(-ELSE), REM, GOTO, INT, TAB, STEP, ABS, SQR

A very powerful tool of computer programming is the **IF-THEN(-ELSE)** construction. This is used on page 37 in the first, third, and fourth loops. Look at the first loop. The **IF-THEN(-ELSE)** construction provides two branches. If the statement in line 20 is true, the execution goes to line 40. Otherwise (ELSE) the program continues to line 30. To emphasize these branches, insert these lines:

```
25   REM***ELSE
35   REM***THEN
```

Such lines are called REM (remark) statements and can be used at any point in a program to add comments or explanations. They have no effect on the execution of the program.

Notice that in this program, the ELSE branch does nothing except skip over the other branch to the NEXT N by means of a GOTO statement (line 30). Where would you insert the corresponding REM statements in the third and fourth loops?

A special function is used in line 20. The *greatest integer function*, INT(X), will give the greatest integer less than or equal to X. Thus:

$$INT(4) = 4 \quad \text{and} \quad INT(4.9) = 4$$

Thus, "If N/3 = INT(N/3)" is equivalent to saying "If N is divisible by 3."

The TAB function is used in PRINT statements to allow spacing more varied than that allowed by commas and semicolons. See lines 40, 150, and 220 on page 37. Type and RUN this short program on your computer.

```
10   PRINT TAB(5);"A";TAB(10);"B"
20   END
```

Count the number of blank spaces before "A" to see how your PRINT TAB works.

Explain why the number 19 is used in lines 150 and 220.

You can see from the summary on page 36 that a FOR-NEXT loop can have a STEP value specified. Try this program:

```
10   FOR I=1 TO 18 STEP 3
20   PRINT TAB(I);I—9;
30   NEXT I
40   PRINT
50   END
```

The exercises at the bottom of page 37 will need another function, the *absolute value function*, where ABS(X) means $|X|$.

Still another function is the *square root function*, where SQR(X) means $\sqrt{X}$. This is used in line 70 of the program on page 126.

4. Subscripted variables, DIM, INPUT, LET

Subscripted variables are described in the summary on page 36. In general, a subscripted variable is convenient when a *list* (or *array*) of values is to be used as, for example, the coefficients of a polynomial, as shown on page 86. If a subscripted variable is to have more than 10 (or, in some cases, 11) values, a DIM (dimension) statement must be provided. For example, DIM C(20) would allow for up to 20 (or 21) values. Since the polynomials that you will be dealing with will have degrees less than 10, no DIM statement will be needed here.

Up to now, we have been using FOR-NEXT loops to give values to variables. Two other ways are mentioned on page 86. One is to use an INPUT statement. The statement

INPUT D

will cause the computer to print a question mark and wait for you to type in a value for D. (See also page 36.)

The other way is to use a LET statement. This will "let" a variable be given its value directly or by means of a formula. For example:

LET A = 5
LET A = L * W

On page 86, we also have the statement:

$$\text{LET } Y = Y * X + C(J)$$

Here it is helpful to read the "LET" statement:

"Take the value of Y, multiply it by X, add C(J), and give Y this new value."

If you needed to find values of the polynomial for several values of X without retyping the coefficients each time, you could arrange the program to INPUT the value of X *after* the coefficients and then add lines like these:

```
PRINT
PRINT "ANOTHER VALUE OF X?"
PRINT "TYPE 1 FOR YES, 0 FOR NO";
INPUT T
IF T = 1 THEN . . . (GOTO statement where value of X is INPUT)
```

5. Multiple IF-THEN statements, GOSUB, RETURN

A series of IF-THEN statements can be used to provide more than two branches. For example, the program on page 126 provides three branches:

$$D < 0$$
$$D = 0$$
$$D > 0$$

The program below will count test scores (0 to 100) into the categories listed. Notice that the three IF-THEN statements in lines 100 to 120 provide four branches. Notice also that line 90 provides an escape in case a larger number is entered by mistake. The LET statements in lines 140, 160, 180, and 200 provide the "counters." You may read line 140 as:

"Take the value of A, add 1 to it, and store the sum in A."

Notice that the four counters are given the initial values 0 in lines 10–40.

Line 60 illustrates a way of ending a loop when the number of entries is not known ahead of time. The ending number, in this case −1, must be outside the set of numbers being used.

At the end of the program, a small bar graph is printed by using a *subroutine*. A subroutine is a block of statements that may be inserted into a program with a GOSUB statement and ended with a RETURN statement. Subroutines are most convenient when the same block of statements is to be used in different places in a program. This subroutine appears in lines 380–420. The RETURN statement returns the execution of the program to the line following the GOSUB statement from which it started.

```
10    LET A=0                              230   PRINT
20    LET B=0                              240   PRINT "0 − 69:";TAB(10);
30    LET C=0                              250   LET M=A
40    LET D=0                              260   GOSUB 380
50    PRINT "INPUT TEST SCORE (0 TO 100)." 270   PRINT "70 − 79:";TAB(10);
60    PRINT "INPUT −1 TO END INPUT."       280   LET M=B
70    INPUT S                              290   GOSUB 380
80    IF S<0 THEN 230                      300   PRINT "80 − 89:";TAB(10);
90    IF S>100 THEN 50                     310   LET M=C
100   IF S>89 THEN 200                     320   GOSUB 380
110   IF S>79 THEN 180                     330   PRINT "90 − 100:";TAB(10);
120   IF S>69 THEN 160                     340   LET M=D
130   REM***0<=S<70                        350   GOSUB 380
140   LET A=A+1                            355   PRINT
150   GOTO 70                              360   END
160   LET B=B+1                            370   REM***SUBROUTINE
170   GOTO 70                              380   FOR I=1 TO M
180   LET C=C+1                            390   PRINT "*";
190   GOTO 70                              400   NEXT I
200   LET D=D+1                            410   PRINT
210   GOTO 70                              420   RETURN
220   REM***OUTPUT
```

RUN this program, using these scores:

100, 95, 93, 94, 88, 95, 85, 80, 78, 100, 87, 88, 68, 72, 86, 88, 65, 85, 60, 100, 77, 84, 96, 75

6. String variables, DIM, READ-DATA, RESTORE

The program on page 159 introduces string variables and READ and DATA statements in a very limited way.

In general, a *string* is a set of characters, usually enclosed in quotation marks. A *string variable* is a variable whose values are strings. It is denoted by using $, as in L$ in line 120 on page 159.

Variables may be given values by using **READ** and **DATA** statements. The **READ** statement will appear in the program where that value is needed. **DATA** statements may be placed anywhere in the program, but it is convenient to place them near the beginning or near the end.

In the program on page 159, the **DATA** are single-character strings and are listed in line 360. (On some computers, each would be enclosed in quotation marks.) The **READ** statements appear in lines 120 and 230, and the data are printed in lines 170 and 270, where they are used to represent the axes.

Another use of single-character strings is shown in lines 170–220 at the end of the program on page 213. Compare this with the use of 0 and 1 in the program at the end of section 4.

We can use **READ-DATA** statements to simulate reading data from a business file. The program below computes the weekly pay for each employee when the number of hours is **INPUT**. The "file" contains the employees' names and hourly rates.

In this program, N$ is the string variable for the names of the employees and R is the variable for the hourly rates. The number of employees is given in line 30.

The **DATA** must appear in the order in which it is to be **READ** (line 120 and later in line 190). A "pointer" moves through the **DATA** as it is **READ** in line 120, arriving at the end of the list. Before reading through the **DATA** again in line 190, the pointer must be brought back to the beginning by line 160 **RESTORE**.

```
10    PRINT "WEEKLY PAY REPORT"        120   READ N$,R
20    PRINT                            130   PRINT N$;":";
25    REM***N=NO. OF EMPLOYEES         140   INPUT W(I)
30    LET N=5                          150   NEXT I
40    DATA "JOHN SMITH",6              160   RESTORE
50    DATA "PAUL O'BRIEN",8            170   PRINT
60    DATA "JOSE LOPEZ",7              180   FOR I=1 TO N
70    DATA "MARY MCDONALD",8           190   READ N$,R
80    DATA "RUTH ANDERSON",7           200   PRINT N$; ": $";R*W(I)
100   PRINT "INPUT NO. OF HOURS FOR WEEK:"   210   NEXT I
110   FOR I=1 TO N                     220   END
```

READ and DATA statements can also be used to give initial values to variables. For example, instead of the lines 10–40 at the beginning of the program in the preceding section, we could have used:

```
10    DATA 0, 0, 0, 0
20    READ A, B, C, D
```

7. SIN, COS, TAN, ATN, scientific notation, rounding

BASIC provides built-in values for three trigonometric functions, SIN(X), COS(X), and TAN(X), and one inverse trigonometric function, the inverse tangent, ATN(X). (See Chapters 7, 8, and 11.) In BASIC, X must be in radians. To change degrees to radians, multipy by $\pi/180$, and to change radians to degrees, divide by $\pi/180$ (see page 279). From page 317, we see that

$$\tan \frac{\pi}{4} = 1,$$

and so

$$\frac{\pi}{4} = \text{ATN}(1) \quad \text{or} \quad \pi = 4 * \text{ATN}(1).$$

Therefore:

$$R = \pi/180 = 4 * \text{ATN}(1)/180$$

$$R = \text{ATN}(1)/45$$

Type in this program, RUN it, and compare the values with those given in the table at the back of the book.

```
10   LET R=ATN(1)/45
20   PRINT "ANGLE",
30   PRINT "SIN(A)"
40   FOR A=0 TO 45 STEP 5
50   LET A1=A*R
60   PRINT A,SIN(A1)
70   NEXT A
80   END
```

Change lines 30 and 60 and PRINT values of COS(A) and TAN(A).

The value of sin 5° may be given in BASIC's version of *scientific notation* (compare page 361). For example,

$$8.71559\text{E-}02$$

means

$$8.171559 \times 10^{-2}, \quad \text{or} \quad 0.0871559.$$

The function INT is used to *round off* numbers. To round off the values to ten-thousandths, change line 60 above to:

```
60   PRINT A, INT(10000*SIN(A1) + .5)/10000
```

RUN the revised version, and compare the results with those obtained earlier.

A general formula for rounding can be given as follows:

$$\text{INT}(P * X + .5)/P,$$

where $P = 100$ for hundredths and $P = 0.01$ for hundreds.

8. SGN, LOG, EXP, RND, ON N GOTO

BASIC has several more functions.

SGN(X) is defined and used on page 339.

LOG(X) means $\log_e x$. (See page 381.)

EXP(X) means e^x.

The properties of the *random function*, RND, vary from one version of BASIC to another. Type in and RUN the following program:

```
10   FOR I=1 TO 20
20   PRINT RND(1),
30   NEXT I
40   END
```

This program may print out 20 different numbers N such that N is between 0 and 1. Several RUNs should give different lists. If your computer fails to give either of these results, consult your manual and find out what adjustments must be made in the program. Make the corresponding adjustments in the remaining programs given here.

Change line 20 to   20   PRINT INT(2 * RND(1) + 1)

and write down the list of twenty numbers. Such a statement can be used in a program to simulate tossing a coin.

Change line 20 to   20   PRINT INT(6 * RND(1) + 1)

and write down the list of twenty numbers. Such a statement can be used in a program to simulate rolling a die.

The following program will generate five quadratic equations (line 10) with the three coefficients (line 30) selected at random such that $-6 \leqslant C \leqslant 6$, omitting 0 (see lines 50 and 60).

```
10    FOR I=1 TO 5
20    PRINT I;".";
30    FOR J=1 TO 3
40    LET C=INT(13*RND(1))
50    IF C=6 THEN 40
60    PRINT C−6;
70    ON J GOTO 80,100,120
80    PRINT "X^2 + (";
90    GOTO 130
100   PRINT ")X + (";
110   GOTO 130
120   PRINT ") = 0"
130   NEXT J
140   NEXT I
150   END
```

Notice that the J-loop is entirely within the I-loop. Such loops are called *nested loops*.

Write down the possible integers generated by line 40, and then write down C − 6 for each.

Line 70 contains a *conditional* GOTO statement. When J = 1, the program goes to line 80; when J = 2, it goes to line 100; when J = 3, it goes to line 120.

Type in this program, and then RUN it several times.

9. Solving Triangles

Since the only inverse trigonometric function available in BASIC is ATN (inverse tangent), it is necessary to find TAN(X) in order to find X. If SIN(X) = m, then COS(X) = $\sqrt{1 - m^2}$, TAN(X) = $m/\sqrt{1 - m^2}$, and

$$X = \text{ATN}(m/\sqrt{1 - m^2}).$$

When two sides and the included angle or three sides are given, formulas corresponding to the following are useful:

$$\tan \frac{C}{2} = \sqrt{\frac{(c + a - b)(c - a + b)}{(a + b + c)(a + b - c)}}$$

Such formulas are used in the following program. RUN it for the Examples on page 408.

```
10    REM***THE PROGRAM FIRST DRAWS A
20    REM*** DIAGRAM OF A TRIANGLE
30    PRINT TAB(7);"B"
40    PRINT TAB(7);"."
50    FOR I=1 TO 5
60    IF I<>3 THEN 80
70    PRINT TAB(2);"C1";
80    PRINT TAB(7-I);".";TAB(7+2*I);".";
90    IF I<>3 THEN 120
100   PRINT TAB(14);"A1"
110   GOTO 130
120   PRINT
130   NEXT I
140   PRINT "A";
150   FOR I=1 TO 19
160   PRINT ".";
170   NEXT I
180   PRINT "C"
190   PRINT TAB(8);"B1"
200   PRINT
210   LET R=ATN(1)/45
220   PRINT "TO SOLVE A TRIANGLE GIVEN:"
```

```
230   PRINT " (1) A1, B1, C   (2) A1, B1, C1"
240   PRINT "    (ANGLES IN DEGREES)"
250   PRINT
260   PRINT "TYPE NUMBER 1 OR 2";
270   INPUT N
280   PRINT "INPUT A1, B1:";
290   INPUT A1,B1
300   IF N=2 THEN 360
310   PRINT "INPUT C";
320   INPUT C
330   LET C1=SQR(A1*A1+B1*B1-2*A1*B1*COS(C*R))
340   PRINT "C1 =";INT(100*C1+.5)/100
350   GOTO 460
360   PRINT "INPUT C1";
370   INPUT C1
380   IF A1+B1 <= C1 THEN 540
390   IF B1+C1 <= A1 THEN 540
400   IF C1+A1 <= B1 THEN 540
410   LET N3=(C1+A1-B1)*(C1-A1+B1)
420   LET D3=(A1+B1+C1)*(A1+B1-C1)
430   LET T3=SQR(N3/D3)
440   LET C=2*ATN(T3)/R
450   PRINT "C =";INT(100*C+.5/100;" DEGREES"
460   LET N1=(A1+B1-C1)*(A1-B1+C1)
470   LET D1=(B1+C1+A1)*(B1+C1-A1)
480   LET T1=SQR(N1/D1)
490   LET A=2*ATN(T1)/R
500   PRINT "A =";INT(100*A+.5)/100;" DEGREES"
510   LET B=180-A-C
520   PRINT "B =";INT(100*B+.5)/100;" DEGREES"
530   GOTO 550
540   PRINT "NO TRIANGLE"
550   END
```

Preparing for Regents Examinations

The Regents examination for Sequential Math–Course III is a comprehensive achievement test of the course objectives outlined in the New York State syllabus. It is prepared by a committee of teachers and State Education Department specialists. The test is scheduled for January, June, and August each year.

The test is divided into two parts. Part I consists of 35 short-answer and multiple-choice questions. The student must answer 30 questions, each worth 2 points. Part II consists of 7 analytical problems related to major strands or topics of the course. The student must answer 4 questions, each worth 10 points. Included in each test booklet is a page of formulas designated by the testing committee. These consist of the major trigonometric relationships as well as the formula for determining the standard deviation for a statistical distribution. These are included to maintain the proper test philosophy (application rather than memorization), thereby maintaining the integrity of the examination. Also included are three reference tables to be used during the examination: Table of Mantissas for Common Logarithms, Table of Values for the four major trigonometric functions (sine, cosine, tangent, and cotangent), and Table of Logarithms of the four major trigonometric functions.

As mentioned above, the test is designed to measure a student's ability to apply what he or she has learned to a variety of different problem settings. The course philosophy of topic integration and concept unification is clearly displayed in questions requiring insights and skills from several different strands. Most noteworthy is the integration of algebra and geometry, especially in transformational geometry and its use in developing and displaying the skills and theories of trigonometry.

To prepare effectively for this examination, you should organize a list of the fundamental concepts, principles, and theorems. Then you should review and drill the various skills and procedures related to these topics. You should strive for both accuracy and the ability to apply these skills and strategies to solve problems.

To assist you in this preparation, go back to the Cumulative Reviews on pages 162–164, 307–310, 468–470, and 623–626. They provide ample practice for the short-answer and multiple-choice sections of the test and help you sharpen your test-taking skills such as eliminating choices that are clearly in error. A list of formulas for your use is given on the next page.

The following pages contain checklists of each topic as well as many sample questions. These questions are similar in form and style to those found on the Regents exam but are longer in order to provide comprehensive review of the concepts involved. While a typical Regents question is shorter and more selective in its scope, these problems will help you consider all aspects of topic applications. They are designed to help you to further organize course objectives in a manner consistent with Regents testing philosophy.

Formulas

Pythagorean and Quotient Identities

$$\sin^2 A + \cos^2 A = 1 \qquad \tan A = \frac{\sin A}{\cos A}$$
$$\tan^2 A + 1 = \sec^2 A$$
$$\cot^2 A + 1 = \csc^2 A \qquad \cot A = \frac{\cos A}{\sin A}$$

Functions of the Sum of Two Angles

$$\sin (A + B) = \sin A \cos B + \cos A \sin B$$
$$\cos (A + B) = \cos A \cos B - \sin A \sin B$$
$$\tan (A + B) = \frac{\tan A + \tan B}{1 - \tan A \tan B}$$

Functions of the Difference of Two Angles

$$\sin (A - B) = \sin A \cos B - \cos A \sin B$$
$$\cos (A - B) = \cos A \cos B + \sin A \sin B$$
$$\tan (A - B) = \frac{\tan A - \tan B}{1 + \tan A \tan B}$$

Functions of the Double Angle

$$\sin 2A = 2 \sin A \cos A$$
$$\cos 2A = \cos^2 A - \sin^2 A$$
$$\cos 2A = 2 \cos^2 A - 1$$
$$\cos 2A = 1 - 2 \sin^2 A$$
$$\tan 2A = \frac{2 \tan A}{1 - \tan^2 A}$$

Functions of the Half Angle

$$\sin \frac{1}{2}A = \pm \sqrt{\frac{1 - \cos A}{2}}$$

$$\cos \frac{1}{2}A = \pm \sqrt{\frac{1 + \cos A}{2}}$$

$$\tan \frac{1}{2}A = \pm \sqrt{\frac{1 - \cos A}{1 + \cos A}}$$

Law of Sines

$$\frac{a}{\sin A} = \frac{b}{\sin B} = \frac{c}{\sin C}$$

Law of Cosines

$$a^2 = b^2 + c^2 - 2bc \cos A$$

Area of Triangle

$$K = \frac{1}{2}ab \sin C$$

Standard Deviation

$$\text{S.D.} = \sqrt{\frac{1}{n} \sum_{i=1}^{n} (\bar{x} - x_i)^2}$$

Algebraic Skills—Checklist

Laws of exponents
  positive
  negative
  fractional
Polynomials
  simplifying
  operations with
  factoring
    greatest common monomial factor
    trinomials
    difference of squares
    sum and difference of cubes

Solving quadratic equations
  factoring
  completing the square
  quadratic formula
Factor Theorem
Remainder Theorem
Rational expressions
  simplifying
  operations with
  solving fractional equations
Complex fractions
Quadratic inequalities
  factoring
  sign graphs

Absolute values
  definition
  equations
  inequalities
Parabolas: analysis of
          discriminant
  graphs
  intercepts
  vertex (minimum or
          maximum)
  axis of symmetry

Algebraic Skills—Sample Problems

1. Determine the real values (if any) of x for which the expression is undefined.

a. $\dfrac{1}{2x+3}$ **b.** $\dfrac{x+3}{x^2+4x+3}$ **c.** $\dfrac{1}{x} \cdot -2$ **d.** $\dfrac{1}{x} - \dfrac{2x}{x-1}$

e. $\dfrac{4}{x^2-4}$ **f.** $\dfrac{1}{|x-3|}$ **g.** $\sqrt{x+4}$ **h.** $\dfrac{1}{\sqrt{x+4}}$

i. x^{-2} **j.** $(x-2)^{-2}$ **k.** $x^{\frac{1}{2}}$ **l.** $x^{-\frac{1}{2}}$

2. Perform the indicated operations.

a. $\left(\dfrac{x-y}{x}\right)\left(\dfrac{xy}{x^2-2xy+y^2}\right)$ **b.** $\dfrac{x^2+5x}{x^2+3x-10}$

c. $\dfrac{x-2}{3} - \dfrac{x+1}{6x}$ **d.** $\dfrac{3}{x^2-16} + \dfrac{4}{4-x}$

e. $(3x^2-5x+2)(x+3)$ **f.** $(4x^2+5x-6) \div (4x-3)$

g. $\dfrac{\dfrac{3}{x-1} - \dfrac{1}{x-2}}{\dfrac{5}{x^2-3x+2}}$ **h.** $\dfrac{x^2-9}{9x^2} \div \dfrac{x^2-x-12}{6x^3-24x^2}$ **i.** $\dfrac{\dfrac{1}{x}+1}{1-\dfrac{1}{x}}$

3. Factor completely.

a. $27x^3-3x$ **b.** $12x^3y-32x^2y-12xy$ **c.** $4x^2-9y^2$ **d.** x^4-y^6

e. x^3-a^2x **f.** x^3-8 **g.** x^3+1 **h.** x^4-81y^4

4. Solve for x. Check

a. $11x-7=3(2x-5)-7$ **b.** $\dfrac{3}{4}x + \dfrac{7}{8} = -1$

c. $\dfrac{x}{2} + \dfrac{x}{3} = 4$ **d.** $1.4x-7=5-0.6x$

e. $\dfrac{1}{2x} - \dfrac{3}{4} = \dfrac{1}{x}$ **f.** $\dfrac{x+3}{x+1} = \dfrac{x+2}{x-1}$

g. $\dfrac{4}{x^2-4} = \dfrac{-1}{x+2} + \dfrac{5}{x-2}$ **h.** $\dfrac{1}{a} + \dfrac{1}{b} = \dfrac{1}{x}$

i. $x^2+2x-8=0$ **j.** $x^2+6x+8<0$

k. $x^2-10x+16>0$ **l.** $6-5x-x^2<0$

m. $|4-2x|=6$ **n.** $|9-6x|>3$

o. $-4|x+2| \leqslant -8$

5. Determine where the graph of the equation intersects the x-axis and the y-axis, if either. Find the equation of the axis of symmetry. Determine the coordinates of the vertex. Does the parabola open upward or downward?

     a. $y=x^2+3x+2$ **b.** $y=2x^2+4x+1$ **c.** $y=-x^2+6x-9$

6. If 3 is a root of $x^3-x^2-14x+24=0$, find the complete solution set.

Radicals and Complex Numbers–Checklist

Radicals
  simplifying
  operations with
  conjugates
nth roots
Radical equations

The number i
  definition
  powers of
  pure imaginary numbers

Complex numbers
  form
  operations with
  conjugates
Complex roots of quadratic equations
Solving equations with complex
          coefficients

Radicals and Complex Numbers–Sample Problems

1. Simplify. Assume that x and y represent positive real numbers.

  a. $\sqrt{50}$
      b. $\sqrt{72x^2y}$
      c. $(5\sqrt{3})^2$

  d. $(6\sqrt{2})(3\sqrt{24})$
      e. $\sqrt{\dfrac{5}{8}} + \sqrt{40}$
      f. $(\sqrt{3} + 6)(\sqrt{3} + 1)$

  g. $\dfrac{\sqrt{6}}{3 - \sqrt{2}}$
      h. $\sqrt{-54}$
      i. $\dfrac{-\sqrt{-4}}{\sqrt{32}}$

  j. $\sqrt{-12} - \sqrt{-3}$
      k. $\sqrt{-49} - 2\sqrt{-16}$
      l. $(3 + 4i) + (7 - i)$

  m. $(-3i) - (6 + 2i)$
      n. i^{10}
      o. i^{39}

  p. $4i(3 + 4i)$
      q. $\dfrac{2 - 3i}{4 + 2i}$
      r. $(2 - 3i)^2$

2. Solve for x.

  a. $\sqrt{3x - 2} + 4 = 12$
      b. $\sqrt{2x + 7} = \sqrt{x} + 2$
      c. $\sqrt{x^2 + 16} - x = 2$

3. Solve for x and y.

  a. $x + 3yi = 4$
      b. $5x - yi = 2i$
      c. $3x + 4 - 2yi = -6 - 3i$

4. Find a quadratic equation in standard form with integral coefficients and having the given numbers as roots.

  a. $1 - i, 1 + i$
      b. $3 + 2i, 3 - 2i$
      c. $2 - i\sqrt{2}, 2 + i\sqrt{2}$

5. If $3 + 4i$ is one root of the given equation, find the other root(s).

  a. $x^2 - 6x + 25 = 0$
              b. $x^3 - 8x^2 + 37x - 50 = 0$
  c. $x^4 - 10x^3 + 54x^2 - 130x + 125 = 0$

Functions–Checklist

Definitions

domain   relation
range   function
image   one-to-one
pre-image inverse

Graphs of functions
  vertical line test
  horizontal line test
  inverses
Composition
  notation
  of two functions
  of a function and its inverse

Functions—Sample Problems

1. Determine if the relation is a function. If it is, give its domain and range and state whether it is one-to-one.
   - **a.** $\{(-3, 2), (0, 2), (3, 5)\}$
   - **b.** $\{(-5, 0), (0, 5), (5, -5)\}$
   - **c.** $\{(x, y): x = 3\}$
   - **d.** $\{(x, y): x + y = -2\}$
   - **e.** $\{(x, y): x = y^2\}$
   - **f.** $\{(x, y): y = \sin x\}$

2. Determine the domain.
   - **a.** $f(x) = |x^2 + x|$
   - **b.** $f(x) = 1 + \dfrac{1}{x}$
   - **c.** $f(x) = \dfrac{1}{\sqrt{4 - x^2}}$

3. Find $f(2)$ for the given function, f.
   - **a.** $f(x) = 2x - 3$
   - **b.** $f(x) = \sqrt{x^2 - 3x + 11}$
   - **c.** $f(x) = |5 - 3x|$

4. Find the inverse of the given function.
   - **a.** $\{(6, -3), (-2, 4), (-3, 6), (4, -2)\}$
   - **b.** $\{(x, y): 3x + 2y = 6\}$
   - **c.** $f(x) = x - 4$
   - **d.** $y = 5x - 3$
   - **e.** $\{(x, y): x - y = 4\}$

5. If $f(x) = 2x + 3$, $g(x) = x - 4$, and $h(x) = -x + 1$, find each of the following.
   - **a.** $(f \circ g)(x)$
   - **b.** $(g \circ f)(x)$
   - **c.** $(f \circ h)(x)$
   - **d.** $(g \circ h)(x)$
   - **e.** $(f \circ f^{-1})(x)$
   - **f.** $(h^{-1} \circ g^{-1})(x)$

Transformational Geometry—Checklist

Transformations
- definition
- images
- inverses
- properties
- isometries
  - direct
  - nondirect

Line reflections
- definition
- images
  - in coordinate axis
  - in line $y = x$
  - in horizontal lines
  - in lines of symmetry
- fixed points
- inverse
- properties

Composite reflections
- notation
- images
- properties
  - direct isometry
  - nondirect isometry

Translations
- definition
- images
- distance of translation
- properties
- composite translations

Rotations
- definition
- images
  - quadrantal angles of magnitude
  - general angle θ
- fixed point
- magnitude of rotation
- properties
- composite

Symmetry
- line
- rotational
- point
- translational

Dilations
- definition
- images
- scale factor (magnitude)
- properties
- composite

Glide reflection
- definition
- image
- properties

Isometries
- definition
- congruence
- Three-Line Reflection Theorem

Transformational Geometry—Sample Problems

1. Given points $A(0, 0)$, $B(2, 3)$, and $C(5, 2)$ and the line k with equation $y = x$, find the coordinates of the images of points A, B, and C under each of the following transformations.
   a. reflection over the y-axis
   b. reflection over k
   c. reflection over the line with equation $y = 2$
   d. $r_{x\text{-axis}} \circ r_k$
   e. $r_{y\text{-axis}} \circ r_k$
   f. $r_k \circ r_k$
   g. rotation of $90°$ centered at the origin
   h. dilation of magnitude 2, centered at the origin
   i. R_{-90} j. $T_{4, -2}$ k. $T_{0, -3}$ l. $D_{\frac{2}{3}}$ m. $D_3 \circ r_k$ n. $T_{0, 2} \circ r_k$

2. Complete.
   a. If $T_1(2, 4) = (-2, 4)$ and $T_1(0, 3) = (0, 3)$, then $T_1(1, 2) = $ __?__ .
   b. If $T_2(2, 3) = (4, 3)$ and $T_2(3, 0) = (3, 0)$, then $T_2(1, 2) = $ __?__ .

3. Determine all possible transformations that map the figure onto itself.
   a. isosceles triangle
   b. equilateral triangle
   c. square
   d. rectangle
   e. rhombus
   f. isosceles trapezoid
   g. regular pentagon
   h. regular octagon

4. Given regular hexagon $ABCDEF$ with symmetry lines k, $\overleftrightarrow{BE}$, and $\overleftrightarrow{CF}$, find:
   a. $r_k(A)$
   b. $r_k(\angle FED)$
   c. $r_{\overline{BE}}(A)$
   d. $r_{\overline{BE}}(E)$
   e. $r_{\overline{BE}}(\overline{ED})$
   f. $r_{\overline{CF}}(B)$
   g. $R_{P, 60}(C)$
   h. $R_{P, 180}(\overline{FE})$
   i. $R_{P, -120}(\angle FED)$
   j. $r_k \circ r_{\overline{BE}}(D)$
   k. $r_{\overline{BE}} \circ r_k(D)$
   l. $R_{P, 60} \circ r_k(\overline{BC})$

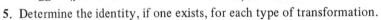

5. Determine the identity, if one exists, for each type of transformation.
   a. line reflection r_k
   b. rotation $R_{P, \theta}$
   c. translation $T_{a, b}$
   d. dilation $D_{P, k}$

6. Find the inverse of the transformation.
   a. r_x
   b. R_{60}
   c. $T_{4, -1}$
   d. $D_{\frac{3}{2}}$

Geometry of the Circle—Checklist

Definition of circle
Parts
  segments
  arcs

Angles
  central
  inscribed
  formed by:
    tangent and chord
    two chords
    two secants
    a secant and a tangent
    two tangents

Chords
  and arcs
  and perpendicular diameter
  distance from center
  intersecting

Tangents
  from a common external point
  and radius to point of tangency
Secants
Measurement
  circumference
  arc length
  area
  sector area

Constructions
  inscribed circles
  circumscribed circles

Geometry of the Circle—Sample Problems

1. $\overline{EC}$ and $\overline{CB}$ are tangent to the circle with center O (not labeled), the intersection of $\overline{EB}$ and $\overline{AD}$. Assume that $m\,\overset{\frown}{FG} = 20$ and $\triangle BCD$ is equilateral.

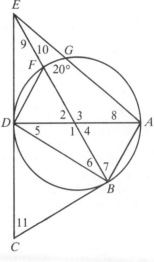

  a. Find:

    (1) $m\,\overset{\frown}{BD}$ (2) $m\angle 1$ (3) $m\angle 2$

    (4) $m\angle 3$ (5) $m\angle 4$ (6) $m\,\overset{\frown}{FD}$

    (7) $m\,\overset{\frown}{AB}$ (8) $m\,\overset{\frown}{GA}$ (9) $m\angle 5$

    (10) $m\angle 6$ (11) $m\angle 7$ (12) $m\angle 8$

    (13) $m\angle 9$ (14) $m\angle 10$ (15) $m\angle 11$

  b. Prove: $\overline{FD} \parallel \overline{AB}$

  c. Prove: $\triangle BCD \sim \triangle ODF$

  d. If $OD = 6$, find:

    (1) DB

    (2) the area of $\triangle ODF$

    (3) the area of $\triangle BCD$

    (4) the circumference of $\odot O$

    (5) the length of $\overline{FD}$

    (6) the area of $\odot O$

    (7) the area of sector OFD

2. In $\odot O$ diameter $\overline{AC}$ is perpendicular to $\overline{BD}$.

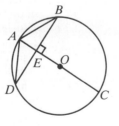

  a. Tell why $\triangle ADE \cong \triangle ABE$.

  b. Tell why $\triangle ABE \sim \triangle DCE$.

  c. If $AE = 4$ and $EC = 9$, find:

    (1) DB

    (2) the perimeter of $\triangle ABD$

    (3) the area of $\triangle ABD$

  d. If $m\angle ADB = 30$, find:

    (1) $m\,\overset{\frown}{AB}$ (2) $m\,\overset{\frown}{AD}$

    (3) $m\,\overset{\frown}{BC}$ (4) $m\,\overset{\frown}{DC}$

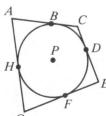

3. $\overline{AG}$, $\overline{AC}$, $\overline{CE}$, and $\overline{GE}$ are tangent to circle P. If $BC:AB = 1:2$, $GF:FE = 4:3$, $DE:CD = 3:2$, and the perimeter of $ACEG = 52$, find:

  a. AB **b.** BC

  c. DE **d.** FG

4. Given: Two concentric circles with common center Q, and square $ABCD$ that circum-scribes the inner circle and is inscribed in the outer circle.

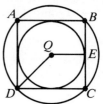

   a. If $QE = 3$, find:
- (1) the area of the inner circle
- (2) the area of square $ABCD$
- (3) the area of trapezoid $DQEC$
- (4) the area of the outer circle
- (5) the perimeter of $ABCD$

   b. If the area of $ABCD$ is 64, find:
- (1) the area of the inner circle
- (2) the circumference of the inner circle
- (3) the area of the outer circle
- (4) the circumference of the outer circle

Trigonometry—Checklist

Angles
  position
  measure
   radians
   degrees
  arc length
  reference angles
  coterminal angles
  quadrantal angles
  special angles

Functions
  definition
  conversions (reduction formulas)
  simplifying to a single function
  using tables (interpolation)
  graphs
   amplitude
   period
   symmetry
    reflection
    translation
   simultaneous graphs
  identities
   cofunctions
   reciprocal functions
   quotient relations
   Pythagorean identities
   formulas
    sum and difference
    double-angle
    half-angle
  Equations
  Inverse functions

Applications
  solving triangles
   Pythagorean Theorem
   Law of Sines
   Law of Cosines
  finding areas of triangles
  problems
   vectors
   angles of elevation
       (depression)
   miscellaneous

Trigonometry—Sample Problems

1. $\overline{DA}$ is a diameter of $\odot O$.
   a. Express $72°$ in radian measure.
   b. Express $m\angle AOD$ in radian measure.
   c. If $\overline{OE}$ is perpendicular to $\overline{DA}$, express the measure of $\angle 1$ in radians.
   d. If $m\angle DOE = \dfrac{\pi}{2}$, find the degree measure of $\angle DOE$.
   e. If $m\angle BOD = \dfrac{3\pi}{5}$, find the degree measure of $\angle BOD$.
   f. If $AD = 9$ and $m\angle AOC = 3$ radians, find the length of $\overset{\frown}{ABC}$.
   g. If $m\angle BOD = 2$ radians and $\overset{\frown}{BCD}$ has a length of 12 cm, find OD.
   h. The lengths of $\overset{\frown}{BC}$ and $\overline{OA}$ are 8 cm and 6 cm, respectively. Find the positive radian measure of $\angle BOC$.
   i. If $m\angle AOB$ is denoted by θ and $\sin \theta = \dfrac{4}{5}$, express the value of the other trigonometric functions of θ.
   j. Using your answers for part (i), express the value of the six trigonometric functions for $\angle BOD$.
   k. If $m\angle COD = \dfrac{\pi}{6}$, express the value of the six trigonometric functions for $\angle COD$.

2. Evaluate each of the following for (1) $\theta = \pi$ radians, (2) $\theta = \dfrac{7\pi}{6}$ radians, (3) $\theta = 135°$, and (4) $\theta = -60°$.
   a. $\sin \theta$
   b. $\cos \theta$
   c. $\tan \theta$
   d. $\sin 2\theta$
   e. $4 \cos \theta$
   f. $\cos 2\theta + 2 \sin \theta$
   g. $\cos \dfrac{\theta}{2}$
   h. $\sin (180° + \theta)$

3. Express each of the following as a function of a positive acute angle.
   a. $\sin (-150°)$
   b. $\cos 140°$
   c. $\tan 310°$
   d. $\cot (-140°)$
   e. $\sec \left(-\dfrac{9\pi}{5}\right)$
   f. $\csc \dfrac{3\pi}{4}$

4. Find the positive value of y in each of the following.
   a. $y = \cos \left(\text{Arcsin } \dfrac{1}{2}\right)$
   b. $y = \sin \left(\text{Arccos } \dfrac{\sqrt{3}}{2}\right)$
   c. $y = \sin (\text{Arctan } \sqrt{3})$
   d. $y = \tan \left(\text{Arcsin } \dfrac{4}{5}\right)$

5. Evaluate each of the following for acute angles A and B where $\sin A = \dfrac{4}{5}$ and $\cos B = \dfrac{12}{13}$.
   a. $\sin (180° - A)$
   b. $\tan (90° + A)$
   c. $\sin (A + B)$
   d. $\cos (A + B)$
   e. $\tan (A + B)$
   f. $\sin (A - B)$
   g. $\cos (A - B)$
   h. $\sin 2A$
   i. $\cos 2B$
   j. $\tan 2A$
   k. $\cos \dfrac{1}{2}A$
   l. $\tan \dfrac{1}{2}B$

6. Express each of the following in terms of a single trigonometric function.
   a. $(\cot \theta)(\sec \theta)$
   b. $(\tan \theta)(\cos \theta)$
   c. $(\tan^2 \theta + 1)(\cos \theta)$
   d. $(1 - \sin^2 \theta)(\tan^2 \theta)$
   e. $\dfrac{\csc \theta - \sin \theta}{\tan \theta}$
   f. $\dfrac{\sec \theta}{\cot \theta + \tan \theta}$

7. Prove the following identities.
   a. $\dfrac{\sec \theta}{\tan \theta} = \dfrac{\cot \theta}{\cos \theta}$
   b. $\cot^2 \theta + \cos^2 \theta = \csc^2 \theta - \sin^2 \theta$
   c. $1 + \tan \theta = \sin \theta(\csc \theta + \sec \theta)$
   d. $\dfrac{\csc \theta - 1}{\sec \theta} = \cot \theta - \cos \theta$
   e. $\dfrac{\sin \theta + \tan \theta}{\sin \theta \tan \theta} = \cot \theta + \csc \theta$
   f. $\dfrac{\cos 2\theta + 1}{2 \sin^2 \theta} = \cot^2 \theta$

8. Solve each of the following for θ, where $0° \leqslant \theta < 360°$.
   a. $2 \sin \theta + 3 = 4$
   b. $3 \cos^2 \theta + 4 = 7$
   c. $\sin^2 \theta = \sin \theta$
   d. $2 \cos^2 \theta + 3 \cos \theta + 1 = 0$
   e. $\sin \theta = \csc \theta$
   f. $\cos 2\theta = \sin \theta$
   g. $\cot \theta + \csc \theta = 1$
   h. $\sin^2 \theta = \sin \theta + 2$

9. On the same set of axes, sketch the graphs of $y = 2 \sin x$ and $y = 3 \cos \dfrac{1}{2}x$ for values of x in the interval $0° \leqslant x \leqslant 360°$.
   a. State the period of each function.
   b. State the amplitude of each function.
   c. For how many values of x in the interval $0° \leqslant x \leqslant 360°$ does $2 \sin x = 3 \cos \dfrac{1}{2}x$?

10. Given: $\triangle ABC$ with $a = BC$, $b = AC$, and $c = AB$
    a. If $a = 8$, $b = 6$, and $\angle A = 30°$, find $\sin B$.
    b. If $a = 4\sqrt{2}$, $\angle A = 45°$, and $\angle B = 30°$, find b.
    c. If $a = 8$, $b = 12$, and $\sin A = \dfrac{1}{3}$, find $\angle B$.
    d. If $a = 4$, $b = 5$, and $\sin A = \dfrac{1}{2}$, how many distinct triangles can be constructed?
    e. If $a = 2\sqrt{3}$, $b = 2$, and $\angle A = 60°$, find $\angle B$ and the area of $\triangle ABC$.
    f. If $a = 3$, $b = 2$, and $c = 4$, find $\cos C$.
    g. If $a = 5$, $b = 6$, and $c = 9$, find the measure of the largest angle to the nearest $10'$.

11. Given parallelogram $ABCD$ with $AD = 8$, $AB = 10$, and $\angle ADC = 50°$, find each of the following to the nearest integer.
    a. AC
    b. BD
    c. the area of $\triangle ADC$
    d. the area of $\square ABCD$

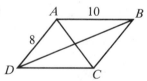

12. A television tower is supported by two cables as shown in the figure. The two cable stakes are 84 m apart. To the nearest meter,
    a. find the lengths of the cables.
    b. find the height of the tower.
    c. how far is each stake from the base of the tower?

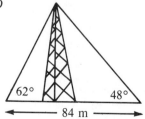

13. Two forces, each of 8 N, act at an angle of 40° to each other.

    a. Find the magnitude of the resultant force to the nearest Newton.

    b. Find, to the nearest degree, the direction of the resultant force.

Exponents and Logarithms—Checklist

Exponents
  laws
  simplifying rational exponents
  evaluating expressions
  solving equations
Exponential function
  definition
  graph of $y = a^x$
    for $a > 1$
    for $0 < a < 1$
  inverse

Logarithms
  definition
  relationship with exponents
  evaluating
  computing with common logarithms
  properties
  simplifying expressions
  solving equations
  changing from one base to another
Logarithmic function
  graph of
  inverse

Exponents and Logarithms—Sample Problems

1. Simplify.

  a. $27^{\frac{2}{3}}$ **b.** $3^{-\frac{3}{2}}$ **c.** $\left(\frac{1}{16}\right)^{\frac{1}{4}}$ **d.** $(25a^0)^{\frac{3}{2}}$ **e.** $\frac{1}{3^{-4}}$

2. Evaluate for $x = 2$.

  a. $f(x) = (3x)^{-2}$ **b.** $f(x) = 4^x$ **c.** $f(x) = \log_x 4$ **d.** $f(x) = 3 \log_x 4$

3. Express in logarithmic form.

  a. $y = 2^x$ **b.** $y = 3^{2x-1}$ **c.** $y = 5^{x^2}$ **d.** $y = \left(\frac{1}{4}\right)^{-x+1}$

4. Express in exponential form.

  a. $y = \log_3 x$ **b.** $y = \log_x 16$ **c.** $h = \log_5 x^2$ **d.** $y = \log_x \frac{1}{4}$

5. Evaluate the following.

  a. $\log_2 8$ **b.** $\log_7 1$ **c.** $\log_9 \frac{1}{3}$ **d.** $\log_5 0.008$

  e. $\log_9 27$ **f.** $\log_8 \frac{1}{4}$ **g.** $\log_2 64$

6. Solve for x.

  a. $2^{x-4} = 16$ **b.** $3^{x+2} = 9^{x-3}$ **c.** $5^{2x-4} = 25$

  d. $2^{x^2} = 512$ **e.** $\log_5 x = -3$ **f.** $\log_9 x = 1\frac{1}{2}$

  g. $\log_x 1000 = 3$ **h.** $\log_x \frac{4}{9} = -2$ **i.** $\log_x 0.125 = 3$

7. Solve for x correct to four significant digits.

    a. $x = 3480(604{,}000)$
    b. $x = \sqrt[3]{1280}$
    c. $x = (0.0627)^5$

    d. $x = 38\sqrt[4]{0.503}$
    e. $x = \dfrac{\sqrt[5]{29.3}}{(643)^2}$
    f. $x^4 = 6$

    g. $x = 1.6^{2.4}$
    h. $4^x = 6$
    i. $x = \log_7 2$

    j. $\log_4 x = 1.4$
    k. $\log_x 6 = 3.7$
    l. $\log_3 2 = \log_7 x$

8. Sketch the graph of each function and its inverse. State an equation of the inverse.

    a. $y = 2^x$
    b. $y = 5^x$
    c. $y = \log x$
    d. $y = \log_3 x$

Probability—Checklist

Sample space
  list
  tree diagram
  chart
Probabilities
  equally likely outcomes
  certain events
  impossible events
  mutually exclusive events
  complementary events
  intersecting events
  multistage events
    with replacement
    without replacement
  conditional probabilities
  independent events
  dependent events

Permutations
  distinguishable arrangements
    of distinguishable objects
    of non-distinguishable objects
  $_nP_n$
  $_nP_r$
  probabilities
Combinations
  $_nC_n$
  $_nC_r$
  probabilities
Bernoulli experiments
Binomial expansion
  finding kth term
    using formula
    using Pascal's triangle

Probability—Sample Problems

1. A fair coin is tossed four times. Find:

    a. $P(4\text{ heads})$
    b. $P(4\text{ tails})$
    c. $P(\text{exactly 3 heads})$
    d. $P(\text{exactly 2 heads})$
    e. $P(\text{the first toss is a head})$
    f. $P(\text{head on second toss} \mid \text{head on first})$
    g. $P(\text{at least 3 heads})$
    h. $P(\text{at most 2 heads})$

2. Repeat Problem 1 if the coin is unfair, with the probability of a head equal to three times the probability of a tail.

3. A multiple-choice test consists of ten questions, each with four possible answers, $A, B, C,$ and D. If a student guesses all answers randomly, find:

    a. $P(\text{answering a given question correctly})$
    b. $P(\text{answering exactly 7 questions correctly})$ in symbolic form
    c. $P(\text{answering at least 8 questions correctly})$ in symbolic form

4. An urn contains 4 black marbles and 3 white marbles. If 2 marbles are selected without replacement, find:
   a. P(2 black marbles)
   b. P(2 white marbles)
   c. P(black, then white)
   d. P(at least 1 black)
   e. P(white on second selection | white on first)

5. Repeat Problem 4 if selections are made with replacement.

6. A star basketball player can make 80% of the free throws attempted. Find:
   a. P(making 1 free throw in 1 attempt)
   b. P(missing 1 free throw in 1 attempt)
   c. P(making exactly 5 free throws in 6 attempts)
   d. P(making at least 4 free throws in 6 attempts)
   e. P(missing 5 free throws in a row in 5 attempts)
   f. P(making second free throw | missed first)

7. Given: the letters in the word MAMMAL
   a. Find the number of possible arrangements of the letters.
   b. If three letters are selected at random, without replacement, find:
      (1) P(exactly 3 M's)
      (2) P(at least 2 M's)
      (3) P(at least 1 A)
      (4) P(3 different letters)

8. Given: the polynomial $(2x + 3y)^n$
   a. Let $n = 3$.
      (1) Find the second term of the expansion.
      (2) Expand the polynomial.
   b. Let $n = 6$.
      (1) Find the third term of the expansion.
      (2) Find the fifth term of the expansion.
   c. Let $n = 8$ and $y = -2$.
      (1) Find the first 3 terms of the expansion.
      (2) Find the sixth term of the expansion.
   d. Let $n = 5$ and $x = \frac{1}{2}$.
      (1) Find the last 3 terms of the expansion.
      (2) Find the product of the second and fourth terms.
      (3) What is the coefficient of the y^3 term?

Statistics–Checklist

Law of Large Numbers
Distribution
  frequency charts and histograms
  measures of central tendency
    mean
    mode
    median

Distribution
  measures of dispersion
    range
    mean absolute deviation
    variance
    standard deviation

Summation notation
Normal distributions
  properties
  reference points for
    standard deviation

1. Evaluate.

   a. $\displaystyle\sum_{k=1}^{4} 2k + 1$

   b. $\displaystyle\sum_{k=1}^{3} k^2 - 4k + 4$

   c. $\displaystyle\sum_{k=3}^{5} (k-3)^2$

2. Ten golfers had the following scores for 9 holes of golf: 41, 38, 42, 46, 44, 36, 41, 42, 41, 49.

   a. Find the range of the scores.
   b. Make a frequency chart for the data.
   c. Make a frequency histogram for the data.
   d. Find the mean, the mode, and the median.
   e. Find the standard deviation to the nearest tenth.
   f. How many scores are within 1 standard deviation of the mean?
   g. How many scores are within 2 standard deviations of the mean?

3. The ages of the math teachers in one school are given in the table.

Index (i)	Age (x_i)	Frequency (f_i)
1	23	1
2	29	3
3	33	2
4	36	4

   a. Find the mean, the median, and the mode.
   b. Find the standard deviation to the nearest tenth.
   c. How many teachers' ages are within 1 standard deviation of the mean?

4. The scores on a certain test approximate a normal distribution as displayed in the graph.

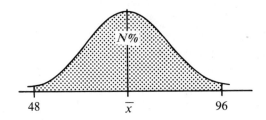

   a. Find the mean, $\overline{x}$.
   b. If $N = 68$, find the standard deviation.
   c. If $N = 95$, find:
      (1) the standard deviation
      (2) the score that is 1 standard deviation above the mean
   d. Let $N = 99$.
      (1) Find the standard deviation.
      (2) Find the score that is 2 standard deviations below the mean.
      (3) A score of 65 is within how many standard deviations of the mean?

Summary of Transformations

A *transformation* is a one-to-one mapping (or function) whose domain and range are the points of the plane (p. 170). The special transformation that maps each point onto itself is called the *identity* transformation, denoted I (p. 172). A *composite, $G \circ H$*, of two transformations, G following H, is the result of performing the transformations in succession (pp. 150, 172). Being one-to-one, every transformation has an *inverse* transformation associated with it (p. 153). If the inverse of T is denoted T^{-1}, then $T \circ T^{-1} = T^{-1} \circ T = I$ (p. 561). In general, the operation of composition is not commutative (p. 150).

ISOMETRIES

An *isometry* is a transformation that preserves distances (and therefore congruence of figures) (p. 172).

Line reflections

A *reflection over line l*, denoted r_l, is the transformation that maps:

1. any point A not on line l onto the point A' such that l is the perpendicular bisector of $\overline{AA'}$
2. any point B on line l onto itself (p. 175)

The reflection of $\triangle ABC$ over line l is illustrated in the figure at the left below. The reflection of the triangle with vertices $A(6, 5)$, $B(2, 0)$, and $C(-2, 3)$ over the x-axis is shown in the figure at the right below.

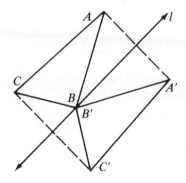 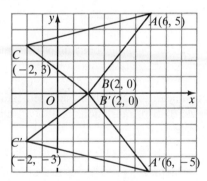

Reflection in the x-axis
$r_{x\text{-axis}}: (x, y) \rightarrow (x, -y)$
(P.176)

Besides preserving distances, line reflections also preserve angle measure, betweenness, collinearity, parallelism, and perpendicularity (p. 185). However, a line reflection reverses point orientation (p. 185).

Those isometries that preserve point orientation are *direct* isometries. Those that reverse point orientation are *nondirect* isometries (p. 173). A line reflection is a nondirect isometry (p. 185).

For any positive integer n, a composite of n line reflections is:

1. a direct isometry if n is even
2. a nondirect isometry if n is odd (p. 190)

Thus, a composite of *two* line reflections is *not* a line reflection (p. 558). Furthermore, a reflection is its own inverse, since for any point A,

$$\text{if } r_l(A) = A', \quad \text{then } r_l(A') = A. \quad \text{Thus } r_l \circ r_l = I.$$

Translations

A *translation* is the composite of two line reflections in which the lines of reflection are parallel (or identical, resulting in the identity transformation I) (pp. 192, 558). This is illustrated in the figure at the left below.

A translation, denoted $T_{a,b}$, "slides" each point in the plane a units horizontally and b units vertically onto its image:

$$T_{a,b} : (x, y) \longrightarrow (x + a, y + b)$$

The translation $T_{5,-4}$ is illustrated in the figure at the right below.

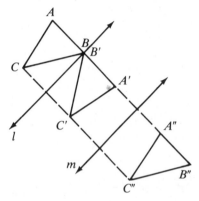

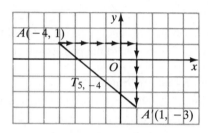

$$T_{5,-4} : (x, y) \rightarrow (x + 5, y - 4)$$

Note that a translation "slides" points onto their images a distance equal to *twice* the distance between the parallel lines of reflection (p. 192).

Moreover, a translation also is a direct isometry that preserves angle measure, betweenness, collinearity, parallelism, and perpendicularity (p. 193).

The composite of two translations is also a translation. As on pages 558 and 559, we may write:

$$T_{a,b} \circ T_{c,d} : (x, y) \longrightarrow (x + a + c, y + b + d)$$

The identity translation is $T_{0,0}$. The inverse of a translation $T_{a,b}$ is the translation $T_{-a,-b}$.

Rotations

A *rotation* is the composite of two line reflections in which the lines of reflection intersect at a point, called the *fixed,* or *center, point* of the rotation (pp. 197, 558). This fact is illustrated in the first of the two diagrams at the top of the next page.

A rotation, denoted $R_{P,\theta}$, "rotates" each point in the plane the same number of degrees θ about that one fixed center point P. Note that a rotation "rotates" points through an angle whose measure is *twice* the measure of the angle between the two intersecting lines of reflection (p. 197).

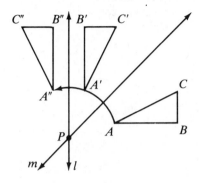

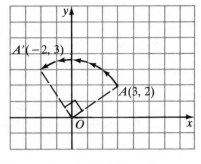

$$R_{90}: (x, y) \rightarrow (-y, x)$$

A rotation centered at the origin is denoted simply R_θ (p. 198). Rotations through angles of positive measure are oriented counterclockwise, while rotations through angles of negative measure are oriented clockwise (p. 198). The figure at the right above illustrates a rotation through 90° counterclockwise about the origin.

A rotation also is a direct isometry that preserves angle measure, betweenness, collinearity, parallelism, and perpendicularity (p. 199).

The composite of two rotations with a common center point is also a rotation (p. 559), and we may write:

$$R_\theta \circ R_\phi = R_{\theta+\phi}$$

The inverse of a rotation R_θ is the rotation $R_{-\theta}$.

Glide reflections

A *glide reflection* is a composite of a reflection over a line l, followed by a translation in a direction parallel to that of line l (p. 563). A glide reflection is actually a composite of three line reflections, where two of the lines of reflection are each perpendicular to the third line of reflection (p. 564). This is illustrated at the left below.

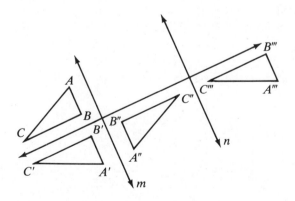

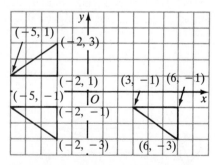

$$T_{8,0} \circ x\text{-axis}: (x, y) \rightarrow (x+8, -y)$$

A glide reflection is a nondirect isometry that also preserves angle measure, betweenness, collinearity, parallelism, and perpendicularity (p. 564).

Every isometry is uniquely defined by three noncollinear points and their respective images (p. 569). Furthermore, every isometry can be expressed as a composite of at most three line reflections (*The Three-Line Reflection Theorem*) (p. 569). Isometries are sometimes called *congruence transformations* (p. 568).

EXERCISES

Given: lines k: $y = x$, l: $y = -x$, m: $y = 3$, and n: $x = -2$, find the image of points $A(4, 0)$, $B(-3, 2)$, $C(-2, 1)$, and $D(0, -2)$ under each of the following:

1. $r_{y\text{-axis}}$

2. $r_{x\text{-axis}}$

3. r_k

4. r_l

5. r_m

6. r_n

7. $r_{x\text{-axis}} \circ r_k$

8. $r_l \circ r_{y\text{-axis}}$

9. $r_m \circ r_n$

10. $r_n \circ r_m$

11. $r_m \circ r_{x\text{-axis}}$

12. $r_{y\text{-axis}} \circ r_n$

13. $r_n \circ r_{y\text{-axis}} \circ r_{x\text{-axis}}$

14. $r_{x\text{-axis}} \circ r_m \circ r_{y\text{-axis}}$

15. $T_{-2, 3}$

16. $T_{1, -4}$

17. $T_{2, 4} \circ T_{-1, 3}$

18. R_{90}

19. R_{-90}

20. $R_{90} \circ R_{180}$

Identify the inverse for each of the following transformations:

21. $r_{y\text{-axis}}$

22. R_{60}

23. $T_{-1, 4}$

24. $T_{4, 1} \circ T_{-2, 3}$

25. $r_{x\text{-axis}} \circ r_{y\text{-axis}}$

26. $R_{120} \circ R_{120}$

Determine all isometries that map each figure onto itself.

27. square

28. rhombus

29. parallelogram

30. equilateral triangle

31. rectangle

32. regular octagon

SIMILARITY TRANSFORMATIONS

Dilations

A *dilation* with center C and scale factor k ($k > 0$), denoted $D_{C, k}$, is the transformation that maps C onto itself and any other point A onto A' along $\overrightarrow{CA}$, such that $CA' = k \cdot CA$. If $k > 1$, the dilation is called an *expansion*. If $0 < k < 1$, the dilation is called a *contraction*. If $k = 1$, the dilation is the *identity* (p. 208).

If C is the origin, then the dilation is denoted simply D_k, and it maps (x, y) onto (kx, ky). The figure at the right below illustrates the dilation $D_3: (x, y) \rightarrow (3x, 3y)$.

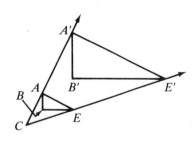

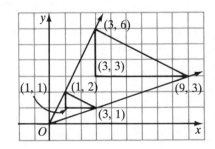

The composite of two dilations with a common center is the dilation with that same center, whose scale factor is the product of the respective scale factors.

The inverse of a dilation $D_{C,k}$ is a dilation with the same center, whose scale factor is the reciprocal of the given scale factor, namely $D_{C,\frac{1}{k}}$.

A *similarity transformation* is either a dilation or a transformation that can be written as a composite of a dilation and an isometry. While not preserving distances (except for the identity dilation), a similarity transformation does preserve all the other properties preserved by its component isometry (pp. 209, 577). In this way, such transformations preserve not the congruence, but the similarity, of figures, and hence their name: similarity transformations.

A similarity transformation is uniquely determined by three noncollinear points and their images (p. 578).

EXERCISES

Find the images of $A(2,0)$, $B(-2,4)$, and $C(0,0)$ under each of the following similarity transformations:

1. D_2 **2.** D_3 **3.** $D_{\frac{1}{2}}$

4. D_1 **5.** $r_{y\text{-axis}} \circ D_3$ **6.** $D_2 \circ r_{x\text{-axis}}$

Given: Square $ABCD$ below where P is the midpoint of $\overline{AC}$ and $\overline{DB}$, and where points E, F, G, and H are the midpoints of $\overline{AP}$, $\overline{BP}$, $\overline{CP}$, and $\overline{DP}$, respectively. Find:

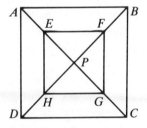

7. $D_{P,2}(F)$ **8.** $D_{P,2}(G)$

9. $D_{G,3}(P)$ **10.** $D_{F,\frac{1}{2}}(H)$

11. $D_{P,\frac{1}{2}}(B)$ **12.** $D_{H,\frac{1}{3}}(B)$

13. $R_{P,90} \circ D_{P,2}(G)$ **14.** $R_{P,-90} \circ D_{P,\frac{1}{2}}(D)$

15. the ratio of the perimeters of $ABCD$ and $EFGH$.

16. the ratio of the areas of $ABCD$ and $EFGH$.

Identify the inverse of each of the following similarity transformations:

17. D_3 **18.** D_4 **19.** $D_{\frac{1}{2}}$

20. $D_{\frac{3}{2}}$ **21.** $D_2 \circ D_3$ **22.** $D_4 \circ D_{\frac{1}{4}}$

23. Given: Triangle GHI is similar to triangle GKL such that $D_{G,4}(\triangle GHI) = \triangle GKL$.
    Find: (a) the ratio of perimeters of $\triangle GHI$ and $\triangle GKL$.
            (b) the ratio of areas of $\triangle GHI$ and $\triangle GKL$.

APPENDIX 1

USING A GRAPHING CALCULATOR

The features and capabilities of different graphing calculators vary widely. Be sure to read the manual provided with your calculator before you begin with any of these experiments. The keyboards of most graphing calculators have several levels. The first level is the set of symbols and functions on the keys themselves. The second level, obtained by pressing $\boxed{\text{SHIFT}}$ or $\boxed{\text{2nd}}$, is a set of symbols and special functions. The third level, obtained by pressing $\boxed{\text{ALPHA}}$, is a set of alphabetic and special characters.

The following is a list of keys you may use frequently.

- $\boxed{\text{EXE}}$ or $\boxed{\text{ENTER}}$

  Press this key to obtain a result or to move on to the next thing you want to do.
- $\boxed{\text{Cls}}$ or $\boxed{\text{CLEAR}}$

  Use this key when you want to clear the screen.
- $\boxed{\text{Graph}}$ Graph key

  Press this key before you enter the equation you want to graph.
- $\boxed{\text{TRACE}}$ Trace key

  If you press this key you can trace along a graph that is on the screen. The screen will also display the x- and/or y-coordinate of the point the cursor is on.
- $\boxed{\text{MODE}}$ Mode key

  Press this key to specify graphing options. For example, using the Mode key, you can specify angle measurements in degrees or radians.
- $\boxed{\text{RANGE}}$ Range key

  This key allows you to adjust the viewing range of the screen.

The range values shown at the right are appropriate for most graphing exercises. Xmin and Xmax determine the least and greatest values on the x-axis. Xscl determines the distance between successive tick marks along the x-axis. Likewise for Ymin, Ymax, and Yscl.

```
RANGE
  Xmin: –8.
   max: 8.
   scl: 1.
  Ymin: –5.
   max: 5.
   scl: 1.
```

The Inverse of a Function   Use with Section 4-6

Two functions f and g are inverse functions if and only if $[g \circ f](x) = x$ and $[f \circ g](x) = x$. In this experiment you will explore the graphs of inverse functions.

1. On the same set of axes graph $y = 3x + 2$, $y = \frac{x-2}{3}$, and $y = x$. The functions $f(x) = 3x + 2$ and $g(x) = \frac{x-2}{3}$ are inverses. Compare the graphs of f and g. What is their relationship to the line $y = x$?

2. On the same set of axes graph $y = x^3$ and $y = \sqrt[3]{x}$.

   a. What line do you think goes through the points of intersection of the two graphs?

   b. Use the $\boxed{\text{TRACE}}$ key to find the coordinates of the points where the graphs intersect. Then write an equation of the line that contains these points. Is this the same line as in part (a)?

3. On the same set of axes graph $y = x^2$, $y = \sqrt{x}$, $y = -\sqrt{x}$, and $y = x$. Why do you have to graph the inverse of $f(x) = x^2$ in two parts when you use a graphing calculator?

Before graphing any of the trigonometric functions, make sure your calculator is in radian mode, and then clear the graph screen. Change the range so that the x-axis scale is in multiples of $\frac{\pi}{2}$. Use **Xmin: −6.28, Xmax: 6.28, Xscl: 1.57**.

Graphing Sine and Cosine   Use with Sections 7-7, 11-1

1. On the same set of axes, graph $y = \sin x$ and $y = \cos x$.

   a. The *period* of a function can be thought of as the shortest distance along the x-axis over which the curve has one complete cycle. In terms of π, what is the period of the sine function? of the cosine function?

   b. The *maximum* value of a function is the y-coordinate of the highest points on the curve, while the *minimum* value is the y-coordinate of the lowest points. What are the maximum and minimum values of the sine function? the cosine function?

   c. The *amplitude* of a function is half the difference between the maximum and minimum values of the function. What is the amplitude of the sine function? the cosine function?

   d. As you can see from your answers to parts (a) – (c), the sine and cosine curves have many features in common. In fact, if all the points on the cosine curve were translated to the right some distance d, the translated cosine curve would coincide with the sine curve. In terms of π, what is the smallest possible value of d?

2. On the same set of axes, graph $y = \sin x$, $y = 4 \sin x$, and $y = \frac{1}{2} \sin x$.

Copy and complete the following table. State each period in terms of π.

	Equation	Period	Maximum	Minimum	Amplitude
a.	$y = \sin x$				
b.	$y = 4 \sin x$				
c.	$y = \frac{1}{2} \sin x$				

d. Describe the effect of a constant A, $A > 0$, on the graph of $y = A \sin x$.

e. Do you think a constant A would have the same effect on the graph of $y = A \cos x$? Confirm your answer by graphing $y = \cos x$ and $y = 4 \cos x$.

3. On the same set of axes, graph $y = \sin 4x$ and $y = \sin \frac{1}{2} x$.

Copy and complete the following table. State each period in terms of π.

	Equation	Period	Maximum	Minimum	Amplitude
a.	$y = \sin 4x$				
b.	$y = \sin \frac{1}{2} x$				

c. Describe the effect of a constant B, $B > 0$, on the graphs of $y = \sin Bx$ and $y = \cos Bx$.

4. On the same set of axes graph $y = 2 + \sin x$ and $y = -3 + \sin x$.
Copy and complete the following table. State each period in terms of π.

	Equation	Period	Maximum	Minimum	Amplitude
a.	$y = 2 + \sin x$				
b.	$y = -3 + \sin x$				

c. Describe the effect of a constant C on the graphs of $y = C + \sin x$ and $y = C + \cos x$.

Tangent, Cotangent, Secant, and Cosecant   Use with Section 8–1

1. Graph $y = \tan x$.

a. The graph has *vertical asymptotes*, lines that the graph approaches but does not cross. The vertical line $x = \frac{\pi}{2}$ is one such asymptote. Write the equations of at least three other vertical asymptotes of the graph.

b. State the period of the tangent function in terms of π.

684   *APPENDIX 1*

2. Graph $y = \cot x$.

    a. This graph also has vertical asymptotes. Write the equations of at least four vertical asymptotes of the graph.

    b. State the period of the cotangent function in terms of π.

3. On the same set of axes graph $y = \cos x$ and $y = \sec x$. Use the fact that $\sec x = \dfrac{1}{\cos x}$ and the graphs to answer the following questions.

    a. The period of the cosine function is 2π. What is the period of the secant function?

    b. The range of $y = \cos x$ is $[y: -1 \le y \le 1]$. What is the range of $y = \sec x$?

    c. How are the vertical asymptotes of the graph of $y = \sec x$ related to the graph of $y = \cos x$?

    d. For what values of x does $\cos x = \sec x$?

4. Graph $y = \sin x$.

    a. Use the fact that $\csc x = \dfrac{1}{\sin x}$ as well as the results of Exercise 3 to sketch the graph of $y = \csc x$.

    b. Use your graphing calculator to confirm your answer to part (a).

5. On the same set of axes graph $y = \tan x$, $y = -3 + \tan x$, and $y = 2 + \tan x$.

    a. Describe the effect of a constant C on the graph of $y = C + \tan x$.

    b. Use your answer to part (a) to sketch the graph of $y = -1 + \tan x$.

    c. Use your graphing calculator to confirm your sketch.

6. On the same set of axes graph $y = \tan x$, $y = \tan \dfrac{1}{2}x$, and $y = \tan \dfrac{1}{4}x$.

    a. Describe the effect of a positive constant B on the graph of $y = \tan Bx$.

    b. Use your answer to part (a) to predict the period of $y = \tan \dfrac{2}{3}x$.

    c. Use your graphing calculator to confirm your prediction.

Solving Trigonometric Equations   Use with Sections 8-4 and 8-5

You can use a graphing calculator to find approximate solutions to trigonometric equations. For the purposes of these exercises, work in the degree **MODE**. As your **RANGE**, use **Xmin:** 0, **Xmax:** 360, **Xscl:** 15. Adjust the range of the y-axis so that you can view the graphs completely.

EXAMPLE   Solve $2 \sin x + 5 = 4 \sin x + 6$, $0° \le x < 360°$.

SOLUTION 1   On the same set of axes graph $y = 2 \sin x + 5$ and $y = 4 \sin x + 6$. The x-coordinates of the points of intersection of the graphs give you the approximate solutions of the equation.

(continued)

SOLUTION 2 $2 \sin x + 5 = 4 \sin x + 6$
$2 \sin x + 1 = 0$
Graph $y = 2 \sin x + 1$. The x-intercepts of the graph give you the approximate solutions of the equation.

In both Solution 1 and Solution 2 you can use $\boxed{\text{TRACE}}$ and the cursor keys to determine the x-coordinates of all points that yield solutions to the equation. Some calculators have a ZOOM feature that allows you to magnify the graph in the vicinity of a point, thereby allowing you to find answers to greater accuracy.

The approximate solutions are $211°$ and $329°$. If you magnify the graphs by a factor of 4 in the vicinity of each solution, you will get $210°$ and $330°$.

Use a graphing calculator to find approximate solutions of the following equations for $0° \le x < 360°$. Round answers to the nearest degree.

1. $\cos 2x = \sin x$ **2.** $\sin^2 x = \cos^2 x$ **3.** $\sin 2x + \sin x = 0$

4. $\cos 2x = \dfrac{1}{2}$ **5.** $\tan (x - 20°) = \sqrt{3}$ **6.** $\tan x = \cos x$

Exponential Functions   Use with Section 9-2

You can use a graphing calculator to explore the graph of $y = b^x$, $b > 0$, for various values of b. As your RANGE use Xmin: –5, Xmax: 5, Xscl: 1, Ymin: 0, Ymax: 8, Yscl: 1.

1. On the same set of axes graph $y = 2^x$, $y = 3^x$, $y = 4^x$.

    a. Find the y-intercept for each graph.

    b. Which graph lies above the other two for $x > 0$?

    c. Which graph lies above the other two for $x < 0$?

2. On the same set of axes graph $y = \left(\dfrac{2}{3}\right)^x$ and $y = \left(\dfrac{3}{2}\right)^x$.

    a. Find the y-intercept for each graph.

    b. Which graph is increasing from left to right?

    c. Which graph is decreasing from left to right?

    d. How are the graphs related to each other?

3. a. Use your answer to Exercise 2 to predict whether the graph of $y = 1.2^x$ is increasing or decreasing.

    b. Use your answer to Exercise 2 to predict whether the graph of $y = 0.8^x$ is increasing or decreasing.

    c. Use a graphing calculator to confirm your answers to parts (a) and (b).

4. Generalize the results of Exercises 2 and 3.

    a. Under what conditions does the graph of $y = b^x$ increase left to right?

    b. Under what conditions does the graph of $y = b^x$ decrease left to right?

    c. For what value(s) of b would the graph of $y = b^x$ neither increase nor decrease?

TABLE 1   VALUES OF TRIGONOMETRIC FUNCTIONS

m(α) Degrees	m(α) Radians	sin α	csc α	tan α	cot α	sec α	cos α		
0° 00′	.0000	.0000	Undefined	.0000	Undefined	1.000	1.0000	1.5708	90° 00′
10′	.0029	.0029	343.8	.0029	343.8	1.000	1.0000	1.5679	50′
20′	.0058	.0058	171.9	.0058	171.9	1.000	1.0000	1.5650	40′
30′	.0087	.0087	114.6	.0087	114.6	1.000	1.0000	1.5621	30′
40′	.0116	.0116	85.95	.0116	85.94	1.000	.9999	1.5592	20′
50′	.0145	.0145	68.76	.0145	68.75	1.000	.9999	1.5563	10′
1° 00′	.0175	.0175	57.30	.0175	57.29	1.000	.9998	1.5533	89° 00′
10′	.0204	.0204	49.11	.0204	49.10	1.000	.9998	1.5504	50′
20′	.0233	.0233	42.98	.0233	42.96	1.000	.9997	1.5475	40′
30′	.0262	.0262	38.20	.0262	38.19	1.000	.9997	1.5446	30′
40′	.0291	.0291	34.38	.0291	34.37	1.000	.9996	1.5417	20′
50′	.0320	.0320	31.26	.0320	31.24	1.001	.9995	1.5388	10′
2° 00′	.0349	.0349	28.65	.0349	28.64	1.001	.9994	1.5359	88° 00′
10′	.0378	.0378	26.45	.0378	26.43	1.001	.9993	1.5330	50′
20′	.0407	.0407	24.56	.0407	24.54	1.001	.9992	1.5301	40′
30′	.0436	.0436	22.93	.0437	22.90	1.001	.9990	1.5272	30′
40′	.0465	.0465	21.49	.0466	21.47	1.001	.9989	1.5243	20′
50′	.0495	.0494	20.23	.0495	20.21	1.001	.9988	1.5213	10′
3° 00′	.0524	.0523	19.11	.0524	19.08	1.001	.9986	1.5184	87° 00′
10′	.0553	.0552	18.10	.0553	18.07	1.002	.9985	1.5155	50′
20′	.0582	.0581	17.20	.0582	17.17	1.002	.9983	1.5126	40′
30′	.0611	.0610	16.38	.0612	16.35	1.002	.9981	1.5097	30′
40′	.0640	.0640	15.64	.0641	15.60	1.002	.9980	1.5068	20′
50′	.0669	.0669	14.96	.0670	14.92	1.002	.9978	1.5039	10′
4° 00′	.0698	.0698	14.34	.0699	14.30	1.002	.9976	1.5010	86° 00′
10′	.0727	.0727	13.76	.0729	13.73	1.003	.9974	1.4981	50′
20′	.0756	.0756	13.23	.0758	13.20	1.003	.9971	1.4952	40′
30′	.0785	.0785	12.75	.0787	12.71	1.003	.9969	1.4923	30′
40′	.0814	.0814	12.29	.0816	12.25	1.003	.9967	1.4893	20′
50′	.0844	.0843	11.87	.0846	11.83	1.004	.9964	1.4864	10′
5° 00′	.0873	.0872	11.47	.0875	11.43	1.004	.9962	1.4835	85° 00′
10′	.0902	.0901	11.10	.0904	11.06	1.004	.9959	1.4806	50′
20′	.0931	.0929	10.76	.0934	10.71	1.004	.9957	1.4777	40′
30′	.0960	.0958	10.43	.0963	10.39	1.005	.9954	1.4748	30′
40′	.0989	.0987	10.13	.0992	10.08	1.005	.9951	1.4719	20′
50′	.1018	.1016	9.839	.1022	9.788	1.005	.9948	1.4690	10′
6° 00′	.1047	.1045	9.567	.1051	9.514	1.006	.9945	1.4661	84° 00′
10′	.1076	.1074	9.309	.1080	9.255	1.006	.9942	1.4632	50′
20′	.1105	.1103	9.065	.1110	9.010	1.006	.9939	1.4603	40′
30′	.1134	.1132	8.834	.1139	8.777	1.006	.9936	1.4573	30′
40′	.1164	.1161	8.614	.1169	8.556	1.007	.9932	1.4544	20′
50′	.1193	.1190	8.405	.1198	8.345	1.007	.9929	1.4515	10′
7° 00′	.1222	.1219	8.206	.1228	8.144	1.008	.9925	1.4486	83° 00′
10′	.1251	.1248	8.016	.1257	7.953	1.008	.9922	1.4457	50′
20′	.1280	.1276	7.834	.1287	7.770	1.008	.9918	1.4428	40′
30′	.1309	.1305	7.661	.1317	7.596	1.009	.9914	1.4399	30′
40′	.1338	.1334	7.496	.1346	7.429	1.009	.9911	1.4370	20′
50′	.1367	.1363	7.337	.1376	7.269	1.009	.9907	1.4341	10′
8° 00′	.1396	.1392	7.185	.1405	7.115	1.010	.9903	1.4312	82° 00′
10′	.1425	.1421	7.040	.1435	6.968	1.010	.9899	1.4283	50′
20′	.1454	.1449	6.900	.1465	6.827	1.011	.9894	1.4254	40′
30′	.1484	.1478	6.765	.1495	6.691	1.011	.9890	1.4224	30′
40′	.1513	.1507	6.636	.1524	6.561	1.012	.9886	1.4195	20′
50′	.1542	.1536	6.512	.1554	6.435	1.012	.9881	1.4166	10′
9° 00′	.1571	.1564	6.392	.1584	6.314	1.012	.9877	1.4137	81° 00′
		cos α	sec α	cot α	tan α	csc α	sin α	Radians	Degrees
								m(α)	

TABLE 1   VALUES OF TRIGONOMETRIC FUNCTIONS

m(α) Degrees	m(α) Radians	sin α	csc α	tan α	cot α	sec α	cos α		
9° 00'	.1571	.1564	6.392	.1584	6.314	1.012	.9877	1.4137	81° 00'
10'	.1600	.1593	6.277	.1614	6.197	1.013	.9872	1.4108	50'
20'	.1629	.1622	6.166	.1644	6.084	1.013	.9868	1.4079	40'
30'	.1658	.1650	6.059	.1673	5.976	1.014	.9863	1.4050	30'
40'	.1687	.1679	5.955	.1703	5.871	1.014	.9858	1.4021	20'
50'	.1716	.1708	5.855	.1733	5.769	1.015	.9853	1.3992	10'
10° 00'	.1745	.1736	5.759	.1763	5.671	1.015	.9848	1.3963	80° 00'
10'	.1774	.1765	5.665	.1793	5.576	1.016	.9843	1.3934	50'
20'	.1804	.1794	5.575	.1823	5.485	1.016	.9838	1.3904	40'
30'	.1833	.1822	5.487	.1853	5.396	1.017	.9833	1.3875	30'
40'	.1862	.1851	5.403	.1883	5.309	1.018	.9827	1.3846	20'
50'	.1891	.1880	5.320	.1914	5.226	1.018	.9822	1.3817	10'
11° 00'	.1920	.1908	5.241	.1944	5.145	1.019	.9816	1.3788	79° 00'
10'	.1949	.1937	5.164	.1974	5.066	1.019	.9811	1.3759	50'
20'	.1978	.1965	5.089	.2004	4.989	1.020	.9805	1.3730	40'
30'	.2007	.1994	5.016	.2035	4.915	1.020	.9799	1.3701	30'
40'	.2036	.2022	4.945	.2065	4.843	1.021	.9793	1.3672	20'
50'	.2065	.2051	4.876	.2095	4.773	1.022	.9787	1.3643	10'
12° 00'	.2094	.2079	4.810	.2126	4.705	1.022	.9781	1.3614	78° 00'
10'	.2123	.2108	4.745	.2156	4.638	1.023	.9775	1.3584	50'
20'	.2153	.2136	4.682	.2186	4.574	1.024	.9769	1.3555	40'
30'	.2182	.2164	4.620	.2217	4.511	1.024	.9763	1.3526	30'
40'	.2211	.2193	4.560	.2247	4.449	1.025	.9757	1.3497	20'
50'	.2240	.2221	4.502	.2278	4.390	1.026	.9750	1.3468	10'
13° 00'	.2269	.2250	4.445	.2309	4.331	1.026	.9744	1.3439	77° 00'
10'	.2298	.2278	4.390	.2339	4.275	1.027	.9737	1.3410	50'
20'	.2327	.2306	4.336	.2370	4.219	1.028	.9730	1.3381	40'
30'	.2356	.2334	4.284	.2401	4.165	1.028	.9724	1.3352	30'
40'	.2385	.2363	4.232	.2432	4.113	1.029	.9717	1.3323	20'
50'	.2414	.2391	4.182	.2462	4.061	1.030	.9710	1.3294	10'
14° 00'	.2443	.2419	4.134	.2493	4.011	1.031	.9703	1.3265	76° 00'
10'	.2473	.2447	4.086	.2524	3.962	1.031	.9696	1.3235	50'
20'	.2502	.2476	4.039	.2555	3.914	1.032	.9689	1.3206	40'
30'	.2531	.2504	3.994	.2586	3.867	1.033	.9681	1.3177	30'
40'	.2560	.2532	3.950	.2617	3.821	1.034	.9674	1.3148	20'
50'	.2589	.2560	3.906	.2648	3.776	1.034	.9667	1.3119	10'
15° 00'	.2618	.2588	3.864	.2679	3.732	1.035	.9659	1.3090	75° 00'
10'	.2647	.2616	3.822	.2711	3.689	1.036	.9652	1.3061	50'
20'	.2676	.2644	3.782	.2742	3.647	1.037	.9644	1.3032	40'
30'	.2705	.2672	3.742	.2773	3.606	1.038	.9636	1.3003	30'
40'	.2734	.2700	3.703	.2805	3.566	1.039	.9628	1.2974	20'
50'	.2763	.2728	3.665	.2836	3.526	1.039	.9621	1.2945	10'
16° 00'	.2793	.2756	3.628	.2867	3.487	1.040	.9613	1.2915	74° 00'
10'	.2822	.2784	3.592	.2899	3.450	1.041	.9605	1.2886	50'
20'	.2851	.2812	3.556	.2931	3.412	1.042	.9596	1.2857	40'
30'	.2880	.2840	3.521	.2962	3.376	1.043	.9588	1.2828	30'
40'	.2909	.2868	3.487	.2994	3.340	1.044	.9580	1.2799	20'
50'	.2938	.2896	3.453	.3026	3.305	1.045	.9572	1.2770	10'
17° 00'	.2967	.2924	3.420	.3057	3.271	1.046	.9563	1.2741	73° 00'
10'	.2996	.2952	3.388	.3089	3.237	1.047	.9555	1.2712	50'
20'	.3025	.2979	3.357	.3121	3.204	1.048	.9546	1.2683	40'
30'	.3054	.3007	3.326	.3153	3.172	1.049	.9537	1.2654	30'
40'	.3083	.3035	3.295	.3185	3.140	1.049	.9528	1.2625	20'
50'	.3113	.3062	3.265	.3217	3.108	1.050	.9520	1.2595	10'
18° 00'	.3142	.3090	3.236	.3249	3.078	1.051	.9511	1.2566	72° 00'
		cos α	sec α	cot α	tan α	csc α	sin α	Radians	Degrees
								m(α)	

TABLE 1   VALUES OF TRIGONOMETRIC FUNCTIONS

Degrees	Radians	sin α	csc α	tan α	cot α	sec α	cos α		
18° 00′	.3142	.3090	3.236	.3249	3.078	1.051	.9511	1.2566	72° 00′
10′	.3171	.3118	3.207	.3281	3.047	1.052	.9502	1.2537	50′
20′	.3200	.3145	3.179	.3314	3.018	1.053	.9492	1.2508	40′
30′	.3229	.3173	3.152	.3346	2.989	1.054	.9483	1.2479	30′
40′	.3258	.3201	3.124	.3378	2.960	1.056	.9474	1.2450	20′
50′	.3287	.3228	3.098	.3411	2.932	1.057	.9465	1.2421	10′
19° 00′	.3316	.3256	3.072	.3443	2.904	1.058	.9455	1.2392	71° 00′
10′	.3345	.3283	3.046	.3476	2.877	1.059	.9446	1.2363	50′
20′	.3374	.3311	3.021	.3508	2.850	1.060	.9436	1.2334	40′
30′	.3403	.3338	2.996	.3541	2.824	1.061	.9426	1.2305	30′
40′	.3432	.3365	2.971	.3574	2.798	1.062	.9417	1.2275	20′
50′	.3462	.3393	2.947	.3607	2.773	1.063	.9407	1.2246	10′
20° 00′	.3491	.3420	2.924	.3640	2.747	1.064	.9397	1.2217	70° 00′
10′	.3520	.3448	2.901	.3673	2.723	1.065	.9387	1.2188	50′
20′	.3549	.3475	2.878	.3706	2.699	1.066	.9377	1.2159	40′
30′	.3578	.3502	2.855	.3739	2.675	1.068	.9367	1.2130	30′
40′	.3607	.3529	2.833	.3772	2.651	1.069	.9356	1.2101	20′
50′	.3636	.3557	2.812	.3805	2.628	1.070	.9346	1.2072	10′
21° 00′	.3665	.3584	2.790	.3839	2.605	1.071	.9336	1.2043	69° 00′
10′	.3694	.3611	2.769	.3872	2.583	1.072	.9325	1.2014	50′
20′	.3723	.3638	2.749	.3906	2.560	1.074	.9315	1.1985	40′
30′	.3752	.3665	2.729	.3939	2.539	1.075	.9304	1.1956	30′
40′	.3782	.3692	2.709	.3973	2.517	1.076	.9293	1.1926	20′
50′	.3811	.3719	2.689	.4006	2.496	1.077	.9283	1.1897	10′
22° 00′	.3840	.3746	2.669	.4040	2.475	1.079	.9272	1.1868	68° 00′
10′	.3869	.3773	2.650	.4074	2.455	1.080	.9261	1.1839	50′
20′	.3898	.3800	2.632	.4108	2.434	1.081	.9250	1.1810	40′
30′	.3927	.3827	2.613	.4142	2.414	1.082	.9239	1.1781	30′
40′	.3956	.3854	2.595	.4176	2.394	1.084	.9228	1.1752	20′
50′	.3985	.3881	2.577	.4210	2.375	1.085	.9216	1.1723	10′
23° 00′	.4014	.3907	2.559	.4245	2.356	1.086	.9205	1.1694	67° 00′
10′	.4043	.3934	2.542	.4279	2.337	1.088	.9194	1.1665	50′
20′	.4072	.3961	2.525	.4314	2.318	1.089	.9182	1.1636	40′
30′	.4102	.3987	2.508	.4348	2.300	1.090	.9171	1.1606	30′
40′	.4131	.4014	2.491	.4383	2.282	1.092	.9159	1.1577	20′
50′	.4160	.4041	2.475	.4417	2.264	1.093	.9147	1.1548	10′
24° 00′	.4189	.4067	2.459	.4452	2.246	1.095	.9135	1.1519	66° 00′
10′	.4218	.4094	2.443	.4487	2.229	1.096	.9124	1.1490	50′
20′	.4247	.4120	2.427	.4522	2.211	1.097	.9112	1.1461	40′
30′	.4276	.4147	2.411	.4557	2.194	1.099	.9100	1.1432	30′
40′	.4305	.4173	2.396	.4592	2.177	1.100	.9088	1.1403	20′
50′	.4334	.4200	2.381	.4628	2.161	1.102	.9075	1.1374	10′
25° 00′	.4363	.4226	2.366	.4663	2.145	1.103	.9063	1.1345	65° 00′
10′	.4392	.4253	2.352	.4699	2.128	1.105	.9051	1.1316	50′
20′	.4422	.4279	2.337	.4734	2.112	1.106	.9038	1.1286	40′
30′	.4451	.4305	2.323	.4770	2.097	1.108	.9026	1.1257	30′
40′	.4480	.4331	2.309	.4806	2.081	1.109	.9013	1.1228	20′
50′	.4509	.4358	2.295	.4841	2.066	1.111	.9001	1.1199	10′
26° 00′	.4538	.4384	2.281	.4877	2.050	1.113	.8988	1.1170	64° 00′
10′	.4567	.4410	2.268	.4913	2.035	1.114	.8975	1.1141	50′
20′	.4596	.4436	2.254	.4950	2.020	1.116	.8962	1.1112	40′
30′	.4625	.4462	2.241	.4986	2.006	1.117	.8949	1.1083	30′
40′	.4654	.4488	2.228	.5022	1.991	1.119	.8936	1.1054	20′
50′	.4683	.4514	2.215	.5059	1.977	1.121	.8923	1.1025	10′
27° 00′	.4712	.4540	2.203	.5095	1.963	1.122	.8910	1.0996	63° 00′
		cos α	sec α	cot α	tan α	csc α	sin α	Radians	Degrees
								m(α)	

TABLE 1   VALUES OF TRIGONOMETRIC FUNCTIONS

m(α) Degrees	Radians	sin α	csc α	tan α	cot α	sec α	cos α		
27° 00′	.4712	.4540	2.203	.5095	1.963	1.122	.8910	1.0996	63° 00′
10′	.4741	.4566	2.190	.5132	1.949	1.124	.8897	1.0966	50′
20′	.4771	.4592	2.178	.5169	1.935	1.126	.8884	1.0937	40′
30′	.4800	.4617	2.166	.5206	1.921	1.127	.8870	1.0908	30′
40′	.4829	.4643	2.154	.5243	1.907	1.129	.8857	1.0879	20′
50′	.4858	.4669	2.142	.5280	1.894	1.131	.8843	1.0850	10′
28° 00′	.4887	.4695	2.130	.5317	1.881	1.133	.8829	1.0821	62° 00′
10′	.4916	.4720	2.118	.5354	1.868	1.134	.8816	1.0792	50′
20′	.4945	.4746	2.107	.5392	1.855	1.136	.8802	1.0763	40′
30′	.4974	.4772	2.096	.5430	1.842	1.138	.8788	1.0734	30′
40′	.5003	.4797	2.085	.5467	1.829	1.140	.8774	1.0705	20′
50′	.5032	.4823	2.074	.5505	1.816	1.142	.8760	1.0676	10′
29° 00′	.5061	.4848	2.063	.5543	1.804	1.143	.8746	1.0647	61° 00′
10′	.5091	.4874	2.052	.5581	1.792	1.145	.8732	1.0617	50′
20′	.5120	.4899	2.041	.5619	1.780	1.147	.8718	1.0588	40′
30′	.5149	.4924	2.031	.5658	1.767	1.149	.8704	1.0559	30′
40′	.5178	.4950	2.020	.5696	1.756	1.151	.8689	1.0530	20′
50′	.5207	.4975	2.010	.5735	1.744	1.153	.8675	1.0501	10′
30° 00′	.5236	.5000	2.000	.5774	1.732	1.155	.8660	1.0472	60° 00′
10′	.5265	.5025	1.990	.5812	1.720	1.157	.8646	1.0443	50′
20′	.5294	.5050	1.980	.5851	1.709	1.159	.8631	1.0414	40′
30′	.5323	.5075	1.970	.5890	1.698	1.161	.8616	1.0385	30′
40′	.5352	.5100	1.961	.5930	1.686	1.163	.8601	1.0356	20′
50′	.5381	.5125	1.951	.5969	1.675	1.165	.8587	1.0327	10′
31° 00′	.5411	.5150	1.942	.6009	1.664	1.167	.8572	1.0297	59° 00′
10′	.5440	.5175	1.932	.6048	1.653	1.169	.8557	1.0268	50′
20′	.5469	.5200	1.923	.6088	1.643	1.171	.8542	1.0239	40′
30′	.5498	.5225	1.914	.6128	1.632	1.173	.8526	1.0210	30′
40′	.5527	.5250	1.905	.6168	1.621	1.175	.8511	1.0181	20′
50′	.5556	.5275	1.896	.6208	1.611	1.177	.8496	1.0152	10′
32° 00′	.5585	.5299	1.887	.6249	1.600	1.179	.8480	1.0123	58° 00′
10′	.5614	.5324	1.878	.6289	1.590	1.181	.8465	1.0094	50′
20′	.5643	.5348	1.870	.6330	1.580	1.184	.8450	1.0065	40′
30′	.5672	.5373	1.861	.6371	1.570	1.186	.8434	1.0036	30′
40′	.5701	.5398	1.853	.6412	1.560	1.188	.8418	1.0007	20′
50′	.5730	.5422	1.844	.6453	1.550	1.190	.8403	.9977	10′
33° 00′	.5760	.5446	1.836	.6494	1.540	1.192	.8387	.9948	57° 00′
10′	.5789	.5471	1.828	.6536	1.530	1.195	.8371	.9919	50′
20′	.5818	.5495	1.820	.6577	1.520	1.197	.8355	.9890	40′
30′	.5847	.5519	1.812	.6619	1.511	1.199	.8339	.9861	30′
40′	.5876	.5544	1.804	.6661	1.501	1.202	.8323	.9832	20′
50′	.5905	.5568	1.796	.6703	1.492	1.204	.8307	.9803	10′
34° 00′	.5934	.5592	1.788	.6745	1.483	1.206	.8290	.9774	56° 00′
10′	.5963	.5616	1.781	.6787	1.473	1.209	.8274	.9745	50′
20′	.5992	.5640	1.773	.6830	1.464	1.211	.8258	.9716	40′
30′	.6021	.5664	1.766	.6873	1.455	1.213	.8241	.9687	30′
40′	.6050	.5688	1.758	.6916	1.446	1.216	.8225	.9657	20′
50′	.6080	.5712	1.751	.6959	1.437	1.218	.8208	.9628	10′
35° 00′	.6109	.5736	1.743	.7002	1.428	1.221	.8192	.9599	55° 00′
10′	.6138	.5760	1.736	.7046	1.419	1.223	.8175	.9570	50′
20′	.6167	.5783	1.729	.7089	1.411	1.226	.8158	.9541	40′
30′	.6196	.5807	1.722	.7133	1.402	1.228	.8141	.9512	30′
40′	.6225	.5831	1.715	.7177	1.393	1.231	.8124	.9483	20′
50′	.6254	.5854	1.708	.7221	1.385	1.233	.8107	.9454	10′
36° 00′	.6283	.5878	1.701	.7265	1.376	1.236	.8090	.9425	54° 00′
		cos α	sec α	cot α	tan α	csc α	sin α	Radians	Degrees
								m(α)	

TABLE 1   VALUES OF TRIGONOMETRIC FUNCTIONS

m(α) Degrees	m(α) Radians	sin α	csc α	tan α	cot α	sec α	cos α		
36° 00′	.6283	.5878	1.701	.7265	1.376	1.236	.8090	.9425	54° 00′
10′	.6312	.5901	1.695	.7310	1.368	1.239	.8073	.9396	50′
20′	.6341	.5925	1.688	.7355	1.360	1.241	.8056	.9367	40′
30′	.6370	.5948	1.681	.7400	1.351	1.244	.8039	.9338	30′
40′	.6400	.5972	1.675	.7445	1.343	1.247	.8021	.9308	20′
50′	.6429	.5995	1.668	.7490	1.335	1.249	.8004	.9279	10′
37° 00′	.6458	.6018	1.662	.7536	1.327	1.252	.7986	.9250	53° 00′
10′	.6487	.6041	1.655	.7581	1.319	1.255	.7969	.9221	50′
20′	.6516	.6065	1.649	.7627	1.311	1.258	.7951	.9192	40′
30′	.6545	.6088	1.643	.7673	1.303	1.260	.7934	.9163	30′
40′	.6574	.6111	1.636	.7720	1.295	1.263	.7916	.9134	20′
50′	.6603	.6134	1.630	.7766	1.288	1.266	.7898	.9105	10′
38° 00′	.6632	.6157	1.624	.7813	1.280	1.269	.7880	.9076	52° 00′
10′	.6661	.6180	1.618	.7860	1.272	1.272	.7862	.9047	50′
20′	.6690	.6202	1.612	.7907	1.265	1.275	.7844	.9018	40′
30′	.6720	.6225	1.606	.7954	1.257	1.278	.7826	.8988	30′
40′	.6749	.6248	1.601	.8002	1.250	1.281	.7808	.8959	20′
50′	.6778	.6271	1.595	.8050	1.242	1.284	.7790	.8930	10′
39° 00′	.6807	.6293	1.589	.8098	1.235	1.287	.7771	.8901	51° 00′
10′	.6836	.6316	1.583	.8146	1.228	1.290	.7753	.8872	50′
20′	.6865	.6338	1.578	.8195	1.220	1.293	.7735	.8843	40′
30′	.6894	.6361	1.572	.8243	1.213	1.296	.7716	.8814	30′
40′	.6923	.6383	1.567	.8292	1.206	1.299	.7698	.8785	20′
50′	.6952	.6406	1.561	.8342	1.199	1.302	.7679	.8756	10′
40° 00′	.6981	.6428	1.556	.8391	1.192	1.305	.7660	.8727	50° 00′
10′	.7010	.6450	1.550	.8441	1.185	1.309	.7642	.8698	50′
20′	.7039	.6472	1.545	.8491	1.178	1.312	.7623	.8668	40′
30′	.7069	.6494	1.540	.8541	1.171	1.315	.7604	.8639	30′
40′	.7098	.6517	1.535	.8591	1.164	1.318	.7585	.8610	20′
50′	.7127	.6539	1.529	.8642	1.157	1.322	.7566	.8581	10′
41° 00′	.7156	.6561	1.524	.8693	1.150	1.325	.7547	.8552	49° 00′
10′	.7185	.6583	1.519	.8744	1.144	1.328	.7528	.8523	50′
20′	.7214	.6604	1.514	.8796	1.137	1.332	.7509	.8494	40′
30′	.7243	.6626	1.509	.8847	1.130	1.335	.7490	.8465	30′
40′	.7272	.6648	1.504	.8899	1.124	1.339	.7470	.8436	20′
50′	.7301	.6670	1.499	.8952	1.117	1.342	.7451	.8407	10′
42° 00′	.7330	.6691	1.494	.9004	1.111	1.346	.7431	.8378	48° 00′
10′	.7359	.6713	1.490	.9057	1.104	1.349	.7412	.8348	50′
20′	.7389	.6734	1.485	.9110	1.098	1.353	.7392	.8319	40′
30′	.7418	.6756	1.480	.9163	1.091	1.356	.7373	.8290	30′
40′	.7447	.6777	1.476	.9217	1.085	1.360	.7353	.8261	20′
50′	.7476	.6799	1.471	.9271	1.079	1.364	.7333	.8232	10′
43° 00′	.7505	.6820	1.466	.9325	1.072	1.367	.7314	.8203	47° 00′
10′	.7534	.6841	1.462	.9380	1.066	1.371	.7294	.8174	50′
20′	.7563	.6862	1.457	.9435	1.060	1.375	.7274	.8145	40′
30′	.7592	.6884	1.453	.9490	1.054	1.379	.7254	.8116	30′
40′	.7621	.6905	1.448	.9545	1.048	1.382	.7234	.8087	20′
50′	.7650	.6926	1.444	.9601	1.042	1.386	.7214	.8058	10′
44° 00′	.7679	.6947	1.440	.9657	1.036	1.390	.7193	.8029	46° 00′
10′	.7709	.6967	1.435	.9713	1.030	1.394	.7173	.7999	50′
20′	.7738	.6988	1.431	.9770	1.024	1.398	.7153	.7970	40′
30′	.7767	.7009	1.427	.9827	1.018	1.402	.7133	.7941	30′
40′	.7796	.7030	1.423	.9884	1.012	1.406	.7112	.7912	20′
50′	.7825	.7050	1.418	.9942	1.006	1.410	.7092	.7883	10′
45° 00′	.7854	.7071	1.414	1.000	1.000	1.414	.7071	.7854	45° 00′
		cos α	sec α	cot α	tan α	csc α	sin α	Radians	Degrees
								m(α)	

TABLE 2   COMMON LOGARITHMS OF NUMBERS*

x	0	1	2	3	4	5	6	7	8	9
10	0000	0043	0086	0128	0170	0212	0253	0294	0334	0374
11	0414	0453	0492	0531	0569	0607	0645	0682	0719	0755
12	0792	0828	0864	0899	0934	0969	1004	1038	1072	1106
13	1139	1173	1206	1239	1271	1303	1335	1367	1399	1430
14	1461	1492	1523	1553	1584	1614	1644	1673	1703	1732
15	1761	1790	1818	1847	1875	1903	1931	1959	1987	2014
16	2041	2068	2095	2122	2148	2175	2201	2227	2253	2279
17	2304	2330	2355	2380	2405	2430	2455	2480	2504	2529
18	2553	2577	2601	2625	2648	2672	2695	2718	2742	2765
19	2788	2810	2833	2856	2878	2900	2923	2945	2967	2989
20	3010	3032	3054	3075	3096	3118	3139	3160	3181	3201
21	3222	3243	3263	3284	3304	3324	3345	3365	3385	3404
22	3424	3444	3464	3483	3502	3522	3541	3560	3579	3598
23	3617	3636	3655	3674	3692	3711	3729	3747	3766	3784
24	3802	3820	3838	3856	3874	3892	3909	3927	3945	3962
25	3979	3997	4014	4031	4048	4065	4082	4099	4116	4133
26	4150	4166	4183	4200	4216	4232	4249	4265	4281	4298
27	4314	4330	4346	4362	4378	4393	4409	4425	4440	4456
28	4472	4487	4502	4518	4533	4548	4564	4579	4594	4609
29	4624	4639	4654	4669	4683	4698	4713	4728	4742	4757
30	4771	4786	4800	4814	4829	4843	4857	4871	4886	4900
31	4914	4928	4942	4955	4969	4983	4997	5011	5024	5038
32	5051	5065	5079	5092	5105	5119	5132	5145	5159	5172
33	5185	5198	5211	5224	5237	5250	5263	5276	5289	5302
34	5315	5328	5340	5353	5366	5378	5391	5403	5416	5428
35	5441	5453	5465	5478	5490	5502	5514	5527	5539	5551
36	5563	5575	5587	5599	5611	5623	5635	5647	5658	5670
37	5682	5694	5705	5717	5729	5740	5752	5763	5775	5786
38	5798	5809	5821	5832	5843	5855	5866	5877	5888	5899
39	5911	5922	5933	5944	5955	5966	5977	5988	5999	6010
40	6021	6031	6042	6053	6064	6075	6085	6096	6107	6117
41	6128	6138	6149	6160	6170	6180	6191	6201	6212	6222
42	6232	6243	6253	6263	6274	6284	6294	6304	6314	6325
43	6335	6345	6355	6365	6375	6385	6395	6405	6415	6425
44	6435	6444	6454	6464	6474	6484	6493	6503	6513	6522
45	6532	6542	6551	6561	6571	6580	6590	6599	6609	6618
46	6628	6637	6646	6656	6665	6675	6684	6693	6702	6712
47	6721	6730	6739	6749	6758	6767	6776	6785	6794	6803
48	6812	6821	6830	6839	6848	6857	6866	6875	6884	6893
49	6902	6911	6920	6928	6937	6946	6955	6964	6972	6981
50	6990	6998	7007	7016	7024	7033	7042	7050	7059	7067
51	7076	7084	7093	7101	7110	7118	7126	7135	7143	7152
52	7160	7168	7177	7185	7193	7202	7210	7218	7226	7235
53	7243	7251	7259	7267	7275	7284	7292	7300	7308	7316
54	7324	7332	7340	7348	7356	7364	7372	7380	7388	7396

*Mantissas, decimal points omitted. Characteristics are found by inspection.

TABLE 2   COMMON LOGARITHMS OF NUMBERS

x	0	1	2	3	4	5	6	7	8	9
55	7404	7412	7419	7427	7435	7443	7451	7459	7466	7474
56	7482	7490	7497	7505	7513	7520	7528	7536	7543	7551
57	7559	7566	7574	7582	7589	7597	7604	7612	7619	7627
58	7634	7642	7649	7657	7664	7672	7679	7686	7694	7701
59	7709	7716	7723	7731	7738	7745	7752	7760	7767	7774
60	7782	7789	7796	7803	7810	7818	7825	7832	7839	7846
61	7853	7860	7868	7875	7882	7889	7896	7903	7910	7917
62	7924	7931	7938	7945	7952	7959	7966	7973	7980	7987
63	7993	8000	8007	8014	8021	8028	8035	8041	8048	8055
64	8062	8069	8075	8082	8089	8096	8102	8109	8116	8122
65	8129	8136	8142	8149	8156	8162	8169	8176	8182	8189
66	8195	8202	8209	8215	8222	8228	8235	8241	8248	8254
67	8261	8267	8274	8280	8287	8293	8299	8306	8312	8319
68	8325	8331	8338	8344	8351	8357	8363	8370	8376	8382
69	8388	8395	8401	8407	8414	8420	8426	8432	8439	8445
70	8451	8457	8463	8470	8476	8482	8488	8494	8500	8506
71	8513	8519	8525	8531	8537	8543	8549	8555	8561	8567
72	8573	8579	8585	8591	8597	8603	8609	8615	8621	8627
73	8633	8639	8645	8651	8657	8663	8669	8675	8681	8686
74	8692	8698	8704	8710	8716	8722	8727	8733	8739	8745
75	8751	8756	8762	8768	8774	8779	8785	8791	8797	8802
76	8808	8814	8820	8825	8831	8837	8842	8848	8854	8859
77	8865	8871	8876	8882	8887	8893	8899	8904	8910	8915
78	8921	8927	8932	8938	8943	8949	8954	8960	8965	8971
79	8976	8982	8987	8993	8998	9004	9009	9015	9020	9025
80	9031	9036	9042	9047	9053	9058	9063	9069	9074	9079
81	9085	9090	9096	9101	9106	9112	9117	9122	9128	9133
82	9138	9143	9149	9154	9159	9165	9170	9175	9180	9186
83	9191	9196	9201	9206	9212	9217	9222	9227	9232	9238
84	9243	9248	9253	9258	9263	9269	9274	9279	9284	9289
85	9294	9299	9304	9309	9315	9320	9325	9330	9335	9340
86	9345	9350	9355	9360	9365	9370	9375	9380	9385	9390
87	9395	9400	9405	9410	9415	9420	9425	9430	9435	9440
88	9445	9450	9455	9460	9465	9469	9474	9479	9484	9489
89	9494	9499	9504	9509	9513	9518	9523	9528	9533	9538
90	9542	9547	9552	9557	9562	9566	9571	9576	9581	9586
91	9590	9595	9600	9605	9609	9614	9619	9624	9628	9633
92	9638	9643	9647	9652	9657	9661	9666	9671	9675	9680
93	9685	9689	9694	9699	9703	9708	9713	9717	9722	9727
94	9731	9736	9741	9745	9750	9754	9759	9763	9768	9773
95	9777	9782	9786	9791	9795	9800	9805	9809	9814	9818
96	9823	9827	9832	9836	9841	9845	9850	9854	9859	9863
97	9868	9872	9877	9881	9886	9890	9894	9899	9903	9908
98	9912	9917	9921	9926	9930	9934	9939	9943	9948	9952
99	9956	9961	9965	9969	9974	9978	9983	9987	9991	9996

ANSWERS TO SELF-TESTS

CHAPTER 1

SELF-TEST 1, page 10
1. Any four of: $N = \{\text{natural numbers}\}$, $W = \{\text{whole numbers}\}$, $Z = \{\text{integers}\}$, $Q = \{\text{rational numbers}\}$, and $\{\text{irrational numbers}\}$. (Other answers are also possible.)   2. 0.375   3. −1.2
4. $-0.41\overline{6}$ 5. $1.\overline{09}$ 6. $-\dfrac{9}{50}$ 7. $\dfrac{15{,}021}{5000}$ 8. $\dfrac{7}{9}$ 9. $\dfrac{25}{12}$ 10. 18
11. 8   12. 4   13. −12   14. 7   15. $-\dfrac{4}{5}$ 16. $-8; \dfrac{1}{8}$ 17. $2\dfrac{1}{3}; -\dfrac{3}{7}$
18. 0.05 or $\dfrac{1}{20}$; 20

SELF-TEST 2, pages 24–25
1. $\emptyset$ 2. $\{6\}$ 3. $\{6\}$ 4. $\{3\}$ 5. $n + 1$ 6. $10n + 15$ cents   7. 11 A.M.
8. 40 kg   9. Frank, 11 years old; Bill, 33 years old
10. $\{y: y \geqslant -2\}$ 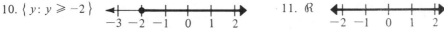   11. $\mathcal{R}$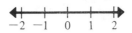

12. $\left\{w: w > \dfrac{13}{2}\right\}$ 13. $\{x: x \leqslant -2\}$

SELF-TEST 3, page 36
1. $\{a: 1 < a \leqslant 2\}$ 2. $\{z: -1 < z < 3\}$ 3. $\{w: w < -1 \text{ or } w \geqslant 3\}$

4. Dean is less than 17.   5. 15, 17, 19 or 17, 19, 21   6. $\{-10, 0\}$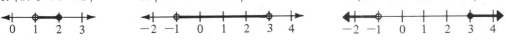

7. $\{-1, 5\}$ 8. $\{x: x \leqslant -4 \text{ or } x \geqslant 4\}$

9. $\{x: -2 < x < 1\}$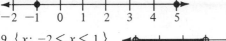

CHAPTER 2

SELF-TEST 1, page 63
1. $20x^3y^4$ 2. $\dfrac{z^2}{2w^3}$ 3. $\dfrac{27x^6}{y^3}$ 4. $8x^2 - 4x + 3$ 5. $3b^2 + 4b - 12$
6. $24n^2 - 34n - 10$ 7. $16a^2 - 9b^2$ 8. $(v - 5)(v - 4)$ 9. $(3x + 2)(2x - 5)$
10. $(7k - 2)^2$ 11. $3u(u + 2)(u - 2)$ 12. $\{8, 3\}$ 13. $\left\{3\dfrac{1}{2}, -1\dfrac{1}{3}\right\}$
14. $\left\{\dfrac{3}{4}, -1\dfrac{2}{5}\right\}$ 15. $\left\{\dfrac{5}{3}, -\dfrac{1}{2}\right\}$ 16. 3, 4, 5

SELF-TEST 2, page 75
1. $\dfrac{q^3 + q^2 - 2q + 14}{q + 3} = q^2 - 2q + 4 + \dfrac{2}{q + 3}$ 2. $\{-4, -3, 2\}$ 3. $\dfrac{t^2}{4}$
4. $\dfrac{(v - 5)(v - 2)}{v^2}$ 5. $\dfrac{r^2 + r - 3}{r(r - 3)}$ 6. $\dfrac{3}{z(z + 3)(z - 2)}$

SELF-TEST 3, page 85

1. $\dfrac{10x + 16}{4x + 3}$ 2. $\dfrac{a + b}{ab(a - b)}$ 3. $\{-6, 2\}$ 4. $\{\pm 3\}$

5. $\{x: -1 < x < 6\}$ 6. $\{y: y \leqslant -5 \text{ or } y \geqslant 2\}$

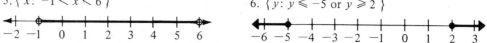

CHAPTER 3

SELF-TEST 1, page 105

1. $7x^3y\sqrt{y}$ 2. $2\sqrt{11}$ 3. $7\sqrt{2}$ 4. $24\sqrt{3} - 20\sqrt{2}$ 5. $4ab^4\sqrt{2a}$

6. $2 + 6\sqrt{6}$ 7. $8 - 4\sqrt{6} + 2\sqrt{2} - 2\sqrt{3}$ 8. $36 + 10\sqrt{11}$ 9. $\dfrac{\sqrt{30}}{5}$

10. $\dfrac{5\sqrt{6} - 10}{2}$ 11. $\{32\}$ 12. $\{1, 2\}$ 13. $\{4\}$

SELF-TEST 2, page 115

1. $8i$ 2. -6 3. $-2i$ 4. $-15\sqrt{2}$ 5. $-\dfrac{5}{3}i$ 6. i 7. $\{6i, -6i\}$

8. $4i$ 9. $-3 - 4i$ 10. $3 - 6i\sqrt{2}$ 11. $\dfrac{29}{2}$ 12. $x = -2, y = \dfrac{4\sqrt{3}}{3}$

13. $\dfrac{1}{5} + \dfrac{1}{10}i$ 14. $-\dfrac{1}{9} + \dfrac{4\sqrt{5}}{9}i$

SELF-TEST 3, page 125

1. -11; 2 imaginary conjugate roots   2. 0; 1 real double (rational) root   3. 64; 2 real

(rational) roots   4. $\left\{\dfrac{3 \pm i\sqrt{3}}{6}\right\}$

5.   a. $-2, 3$ 6. $x^2 + 4x - 12 = 0$ 7. $x^2 - 2x - 5 = 0$

b. $\left(\dfrac{1}{2}, -\dfrac{25}{4}\right)$ 8. $x^2 - 10x + 74 = 0$ 9. Methods may vary.

$-\dfrac{b}{a} = -\dfrac{-2}{1} = 2$ and $\dfrac{c}{a} = \dfrac{2}{1} = 2$; $(1 + i) + (1 - i) =$

c. $x = \dfrac{1}{2}$ $2 = -\dfrac{b}{a}$ and $(1 + i)(1 - i) = 1 + 1 = 2 = \dfrac{c}{a}$

10. other root, $-\dfrac{11}{2}$; $k = 7$

CHAPTER 4

SELF-TEST 1, page 146

1. $\mathcal{R}$; 2   2. $\{x: x \geqslant -6\}$; 2   3. $\{x: x \neq 3, x \neq -3\}$; $-\dfrac{1}{5}$

4. yes; $\{-2, 0, 1, 2, 3\}$;   5. yes; $\mathcal{R}$; $\mathcal{R}$ 6. no
   $\{-3, 2, 4, 5\}$

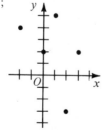   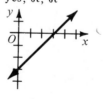   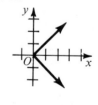

7. $7\frac{7}{8}$; $-7\frac{7}{8}$; $-x^3 + \dfrac{1}{x^3}$; odd

8. 32; 32; $|x^5|$; even

9. $g(x) = -\dfrac{3}{5}x + \dfrac{1}{5}$

10.

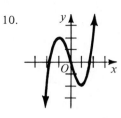

SELF-TEST 2, page 158

1. 6.3   2. 8.44   3. a. -2 b. -6 c. $4 - 3x$ d. $-3x$ 4. a. 15   b. 49

c. $4x^2 - 1$ d. $(4x - 1)^2$, or $16x^2 - 8x + 1$ 5. $f^{-1}(x) = 2 - \dfrac{5}{x} = \dfrac{2x - 5}{x}$

6. $g^{-1}(x) = x^3 - 4$ 7. $f(f(x)) = f(\sqrt{1 - x^2}) = \sqrt{1 - (\sqrt{1 - x^2})^2} = \sqrt{1 - (1 - x^2)} = \sqrt{x^2} = x$

CHAPTER 5

SELF-TEST 1, page 188

1. $A'(3, -1)$, $B'(-1, 1)$, $C'(-2, -2)$ 2. $A'(-2, 0)$, $B'(2, 6)$, $C'(3, -3)$
3. $A'(-1, -1)$, $B'(3, 5)$, $C'(4, -4)$ 4. $D'(3, -2)$, $E'(-1, 4)$ 5. $D'(-3, 2)$, $E'(1, -4)$
6. $D'(2, 3)$, $E'(-4, -1)$ 7. $D'(-2, -3)$, $E'(4, 1)$ 8. 3   9. 0   10. 4
11.

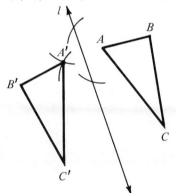

Note: In the diagram for Exercise 11, the construction arcs are shown only for point A'. Points B' and C' are constructed similarly.
12. a. yes   b. yes   c. yes   d. yes   e. no   f. yes

SELF-TEST 2, page 202

1. A 2. $\overline{EF}$ 3. E 4. $(-3, 4)$ 5. $(6, 4)$ 6. $(-9, 11)$ 7. $(1, 2)$
8. $(2, -4)$ 9. E

SELF-TEST 3, pages 212–213

1. $R_{P,\ 90}$, $R_{P,\ 180}$, $R_{P,\ 270}$
2. H, I
3. $(-2, 5)$
4. $(8, -4)$
5. $(-2, -4)$
6. See figure at right.
   $R'(-2, 2)$, $S'(2, 2)$, $T'(2, 0)$, $W'(-2, 0)$

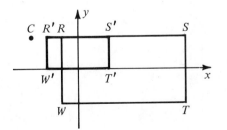

CHAPTER 6

SELF-TEST 1, page 238
1. true   2. false   3. false   4. true   5. $x = 50$, $y = 25$ 6. $x = 60$, $y = 110$
7. $x = 78$, $y = 110$ 8. $x = y = 62$ 9. $x = 54$, $y = 117$ 10. $x = 5$, $y = 5\sqrt{3}$,
$z = 5$

SELF-TEST 2, page 256
1. $x = 77$, $y = 108$ 2. $x = 23$, $y = 59$ 3. 248 and 112   4. $x = 4.5$
5. $x = 4\sqrt{2}$, $y = 2\sqrt{2}$ 6. $x = \sqrt{13}$ 7. 10 cm   8. 10   9. $\sqrt{14}$ 10. 5

SELF-TEST 3, page 266
1. $C = 4.2\pi$, $A = 4.41\pi$ 2. $C = 2\pi\sqrt{5}$, $A = 5\pi$ 3. 25π 4. 60   5. $\dfrac{72\pi}{5}$
6. Construct the $\perp$ bis. of $\overline{AB}$, intersecting $\overset{\frown}{AB}$ at its midpoint. (Or, construct the $\perp$ from O
to $\overline{AB}$.)   7. Use the construction at the bottom of p. 263.   8. Use the construction
on p. 264.

CHAPTER 7

SELF-TEST 1, pages 284–285
1. fourth   2. second   3. fourth   4. $180°$ 5. $225°$ 6. $270°$
7. $\dfrac{\pi}{3}$ radians   8. $135°$ 9. 6 cm   10. IV   11. $\dfrac{\sqrt{7}}{4}$ 12. a. 0   b. -1
c. 0

SELF-TEST 2, page 294
1. $\dfrac{1}{2}$ 2. $\dfrac{\sqrt{2}}{2}$ 3. $-\dfrac{\sqrt{3}}{2}$ 4. $-\cos 15°$ 5. $\sin 70°$ 6. $-\cos 70°$
7. 0.6046   8. $51°28'$ 9. $83.4°$

SELF-TEST 3, page 303
1. $-\sin\theta$ 2. $\cos\theta$ 3. $-\sin\theta$ 4. $\sin\theta$ 5. $-\dfrac{1}{2}$
6. $-\dfrac{\sqrt{2}}{2}$ 7. $\dfrac{\sqrt{3}}{2}$ 8. increasing   9. decreasing
10. $y = \sin\theta$ 11. See graph at right.

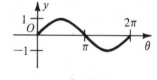

Ex. 11

CHAPTER 8

SELF-TEST 1, page 330
1. a. 1   b. $-\dfrac{\sqrt{3}}{3}$ c. $-\dfrac{2\sqrt{3}}{3}$ 2. a. $-\sqrt{2}$ b. 0   c. $\sqrt{3}$ 3. -1 4. a. $-\dfrac{3}{5}$
b. $\dfrac{4}{3}$ c. $-\dfrac{5}{3}$
5. a.

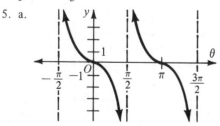

5. b. π units   6. 1   7. 1
8. $-\tan\theta$ 9. $\cot\theta = \pm\sqrt{\csc^2\theta - 1}$
10. $\dfrac{1}{\cot\theta} + \dfrac{1}{\tan\theta} = \tan\theta + \cot\theta =$
$\dfrac{\sin\theta}{\cos\theta} + \dfrac{\cos\theta}{\sin\theta} = \dfrac{\sin^2\theta + \cos^2\theta}{\sin\theta\cos\theta} =$
$\dfrac{1}{\sin\theta\cos\theta}$

11. $\sin \theta \tan \theta = \sin \theta \cdot \dfrac{\sin \theta}{\cos \theta} = \dfrac{1 - \cos^2 \theta}{\cos \theta} = \dfrac{1}{\cos \theta} - \cos \theta = \sec \theta - \cos \theta$

12. $(\tan \theta + \sec \theta)^2 = \left(\dfrac{\sin \theta}{\cos \theta} + \dfrac{1}{\cos \theta} \right)^2 = \dfrac{\sin^2 \theta}{\cos^2 \theta} + \dfrac{2 \sin \theta}{\cos^2 \theta} + \dfrac{1}{\cos^2 \theta} = \dfrac{1 + 2 \sin \theta + \sin^2 \theta}{\cos^2 \theta} =$
$\dfrac{(1 + \sin \theta)^2}{1 - \sin^2 \theta} = \dfrac{(1 + \sin \theta)^2}{(1 + \sin \theta)(1 - \sin \theta)} = \dfrac{1 + \sin \theta}{1 - \sin \theta}$

SELF-TEST 2, page 337

1. $\theta = \dfrac{3\pi}{2} + 2n\pi$, $n \in Z$ 2. $\theta = \dfrac{\pi}{6} + n\pi$, $n \in Z$ 3. $\theta = 0°, 60°, 300°$ 4. $\theta = 90°$,
$210°, 330°$ 5. $\theta = 30°, 150°$ 6. $\theta = 30°, 60°, 210°, 240°$ 7. $\theta = 120°, 240°$
8. $\theta = 180°$ 9. $\theta = 90°, 270°$ 10. $\theta = 0°$

CHAPTER 9

SELF-TEST 1, page 357

1. 9   2. $\dfrac{9}{4}$ 3. 100,000   4. $\dfrac{125}{8}$ 5. $x = 2$ 6. $x = 2$ 7. $x = \dfrac{1}{2}$

8. g 9. g

10.

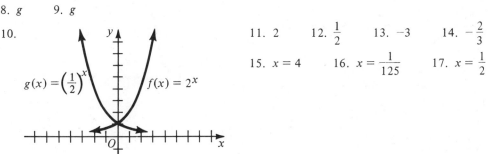

11. 2   12. $\dfrac{1}{2}$ 13. -3 14. $-\dfrac{2}{3}$

15. $x = 4$ 16. $x = \dfrac{1}{125}$ 17. $x = \dfrac{1}{2}$

SELF-TEST 2, page 370

1. 1   2. 2   3. 1   4. $m + 2$ 5. $m - 4$ 6. $m + 4$ 7. log 60,800
8. log 0.0032   9. log 898.6   10. 0.9542   11. $0.8785 + 3$ 12. $0.5821 - 3$
13. 4160   14. 0.0555

SELF-TEST 3, page 381

1. 4,680,000,000,000,000   2. 0.323   3. 0.0000000621   4. $x = 1.92$
5. $x = 1.78$ 6. $x = 2.12$ 7. $2966   8. 57,600,000

CHAPTER 10

SELF-TEST 1, pages 406–407

1. a. 107   b. 39   c. 30°   2. 46°, 46°, 88°   3. a. 50 m   b. 166 m
4. 58   5. 34   6. a. 1   b. 1   c. 0   d. 2   7. a. right   b. acute   c. obtuse

SELF-TEST 2, page 422

1. 20   2. 31°20′   3. 82°50′   4. 849   5. 206   6. 69
7. 12   8. See figure at right.   9. magnitude: 10 N; direction: 36°50′
to the 8 N force, 53°10′ to the 6 N force

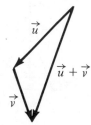

Ex. 8

CHAPTER 11

SELF-TEST 1, page 447

1. amplitude: 1; fundamental period: $\frac{2\pi}{3}$

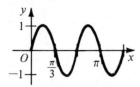

2. amplitude: 4; fundamental period: 2π

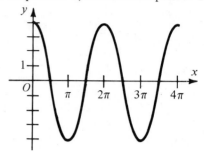

3. amplitude: 1; fundamental period: 8π

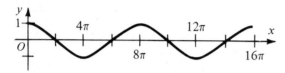

4. amplitude: 2; fundamental period: π

5. $\dfrac{\sqrt{6} - \sqrt{2}}{4}$ 6. $\sqrt{3} - 2$ 7. $-\dfrac{\sqrt{2}}{2}$ 8. $-\dfrac{\sqrt{3}}{2}$ 9. $\dfrac{24}{25}$ 10. $-\dfrac{119}{169}$

11. $4\sqrt{5}$ 12. $\dfrac{\sqrt{2 - \sqrt{2}}}{2}$ 13. $-\dfrac{\sqrt{2 + \sqrt{3}}}{2}$ 14. $\sqrt{2} - 1$

SELF-TEST 2, page 454

1. $x = 30°, 150°, 210°, 330°$ 2. $x = 60°, 90°, 120°, 270°$ 3. 0 4. $\dfrac{3\pi}{4}$

5. $\dfrac{\pi}{3}$ 6. $\dfrac{1}{2}$ 7. $-\dfrac{\sqrt{3}}{3}$ 8. $\dfrac{\sqrt{10}}{10}$

SELF-TEST 3, page 465

1. $(-3\sqrt{2}, 3\sqrt{2})$ 2. $(-5\sqrt{3}, -5)$ 3. Answers may vary.
For example, $(8, 300°)$ and $(-8, 120°)$.   4. Answers may vary.
For example, $(\sqrt{2}, 135°)$ and $(-\sqrt{2}, -45°)$.   5. $2(\cos 30° + i \sin 30°)$;
see figure at right.

6.

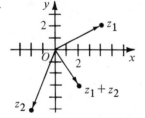

7. $6\sqrt{2}(\cos 225° + i \sin 225°)$

8. $24(\cos 15° + i \sin 15°)$

9. $\dfrac{27}{2} + \dfrac{27\sqrt{3}}{2} i$ 10. $8i$

11. $\dfrac{\sqrt{2}}{2} - \dfrac{\sqrt{2}}{2} i$ $-\dfrac{\sqrt{2}}{2} + \dfrac{\sqrt{2}}{2} i$

and

$-\dfrac{\sqrt{2}}{2} + \dfrac{\sqrt{2}}{2} i$

Ex. 5

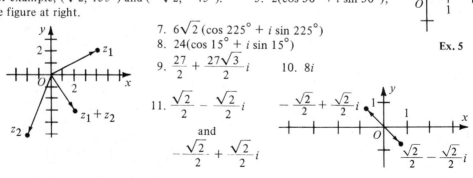

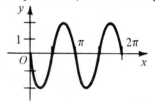

CHAPTER 12

SELF-TEST 1, page 492

1. $\dfrac{3}{13}$ 2. $\dfrac{5}{18}$ 3. $\dfrac{1}{28}$ 4. $\dfrac{3}{8}$ 5. a. $\dfrac{1}{17}$ b. $\dfrac{16}{17}$ c. $\dfrac{1}{13}$ 6. no   7. no

8. yes

SELF-TEST 2, pages 508–509

1. a. 120   b. 1260   2. 20   3. 0.250   4. $_6C_4\left(\dfrac{1}{2}\right)^4\left(\dfrac{1}{2}\right)^2$ 5. $_6C_0\left(\dfrac{1}{2}\right)^0\left(\dfrac{1}{2}\right)^6 +$

$_6C_1\left(\dfrac{1}{2}\right)^1\left(\dfrac{1}{2}\right)^5 + {}_6C_2\left(\dfrac{1}{2}\right)^2\left(\dfrac{1}{2}\right)^4$ 6. $x^6 - 12x^5y + 60x^4y^2$ 7. $2835k^4m^3$

8. $16a^4 - 32a^3b + 24a^2b^2 - 8ab^3 + b^4$

CHAPTER 13

SELF-TEST 1, page 533

1. 0.21   2. 84   3. 49   4. 110   5. 80   6. 2.0

SELF-TEST 2, page 548

1. median: 76.5; mode: 73   2. 2.8   3. 3.5   4. 0.788   5. 0.682

CHAPTER 14

SELF-TEST 1, pages 575–576

1. a. $T_{-2,\,5}$ b. D_2 c. R_{80}

2. a.

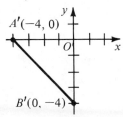

b.

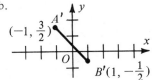

c.

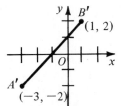

3. a and d are the same.   4.

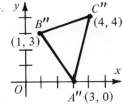

5.

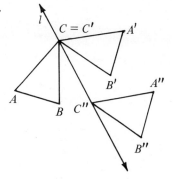

6. translation   7. rotation   8. translation   9. rotation   10. glide reflection
11. reflection

SELF-TEST 2, page 586

1. a.

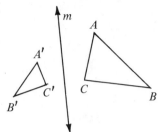

1. b. 2.4   2. a. $\dfrac{2}{3}$ b. Translation

3. $S = \{I, r_m\}$

4.

$\circ$	I	r_m
I	I	r_m
r_m	r_m	I

5. $I^{-1} = I$, $r_m{}^{-1} = r_m$ 6. (1) S is closed under $\circ$. (Theorem 4–8)   (2) Composition of transformations is associative.   (3) $I \in S$.   (4) Each element in S has an inverse in S. (See Question 5.) Therefore, $(S, \circ)$ is a group.

CHAPTER 15

SELF-TEST 1, page 606

1. $a_1 = \dfrac{1}{2}$; $a_k = a_{k-1} + \dfrac{1}{6}$, $k \in \{2, 3, 4, \ldots\}$ 2. $a_1 = 1$; $a_k = -2a_{k-1}$,
$k \in \{2, 3, 4, \ldots\}$ 3. $a_k = 2k + 3$, $k \in \{1, 2, 3, \ldots\}$ 4. $a_k = k^2 + 1$, $k \in \{1, 2, 3, \ldots\}$
5. 31   6. $\dfrac{39}{2}$ 7. 10, 16, 22   8. 300   9. 7950   10. $-\dfrac{15}{2}$

SELF-TEST 2, page 620

1. 24   2. -64 3. 20; 100   4. 1,820   5. 30   6. 50   7. 243
8. $\dfrac{4}{11}$ 9. If $n = 1$, the statement is $4 \cdot 1 - 1 = 1(2 \cdot 1 + 1)$, which is true. Assume the
statement is true for $n = k$, so $3 + 7 + 11 + \cdots + (4k - 1) = k(2k + 1)$. Then
$3 + 7 + 11 + \cdots + (4k - 1) + (4(k + 1) - 1) = k(2k + 1) + (4(k + 1) - 1) = 2k^2 + 5k + 3 =$
$(k + 1)(2k \cdot + 3) = (k + 1)(2(k + 1) + 1)$.

INDEX

Polynomial(s), 50
  addition of, 51
  degree of, 51
  division of, 64–65
  factoring, 54
  least common multiple of, 72
  multiplication of, 51
  prime, 55
  quadratic, 55
  simplest form of, 50
  subtraction of, 51
  terms of, 50
Postulates, 6
  review list, 227
Power of a number, 46
Pre-image, 135, 170
Probability
  basic concepts of, 476–479
  conditional, 486
  for normal distributions, 544–545
  and statistics, 517–519
Problem solving, 15
  checking solutions in, 18
  mixtures, 16
  using linear equations, 15
  using linear inequalities, 28–30
  uniform motion, 17
  work, 81
Programming in BASIC, 652–662
Progression
  arithmetic, 598
  geometric, 607
Proof
  indirect, 232
  by mathematical induction, 617–618
Properties of the real numbers
  addition, 6
  distributive, 7
  equality, 11
  inequality, 22
  multiplication, 6
  multiplicative, of 0, 7
  multiplicative, of −1, 7
  order, 22
  substitution, 11
  zero-product, 58
Proportion, 79
PTOLEMY, 389

Quadratic equation(s), 45, 58
  with complex roots, 115
  discriminant of, 116
  double root of, 116
  nature of roots of, 116
  number of roots of, 116
  solution by factoring, 58–59, 116
  solution by formula, 59
  standard form of, 58
  sum and product of roots of, 121
Quadratic formula, 59
  and complex numbers, 115

Quadratic inequalities, 82
  solution by factoring, 82
  solution using sign graph, 83

Radian(s), 278
  converting to degrees, 278
Radical, 94
Radical equations, 102
Radical expressions
  division of, 98, 99
  multiplication of, 98, 99
  simplified form, 95, 96
Radicand, 94
  negative, 106, 115
Radius, 222
Range, 538
Rational expressions, 68
  addition of, 72–73
  division of, 69–70
  least common denominator of, 73
  multiplication of, 69
  simplified, 68
  subtraction of, 72–73
Rational Root Theorem, 67
Real number system, 1–5
  properties of, 6–7
Reciprocal, 2, 6
Reduction formulas, 294–295
Reflections, 156
  composition of line, 189–190, 678, 680
  glide, 563–568, 679–680
  line, 174–177, 184–185, 677–678
Relation, 138–139
Remainder Theorem, 65
Repetend, 3
Replacement in probability, 481
Resultant, 418
Reviews
  algebra, 645–651
  chapter, 38–39, 87–88, 127, 160–161, 214–215,
    268–269, 305–306, 339–340, 382–383,
    422–423, 466–467, 510–511, 550–551,
    586–587, 621–622
  cumulative, 162, 307, 468, 623
  mixed, 42–43, 90–91, 130–131, 166–167, 218–219,
    272–273, 312–313, 342–343, 386–387,
    426–427, 472–473, 514–515, 554–555,
    590–591, 628–629
  for Regents examinations, 663–676
  vocabulary, 42, 90, 130, 166, 218, 272, 312, 342,
    386, 426, 472, 514, 554, 590, 628
Root(s) of an equation, 11, 116
  double, 116
  extra, 336
  imaginary, 116
  loss of, 382
  product of, 121
  real, 94
  relation to coefficients, 121
  sum of, 121

SELECTED ANSWERS

PAGE 5 1–8. Answers may vary. 1. $\dfrac{10}{2}$ 3. $\dfrac{0}{1}$ 5. $\dfrac{9}{4}$ 7. $\dfrac{3}{10}$ 9. 0.7

11. -0.4 13. 0.6 15. -0.875 17. 1.18 19. -1.2 21. $0.8\overline{3}$

23. $-0.\overline{8}$ 25. $\dfrac{2}{5}$ 27. $-\dfrac{257}{100}$ 29. $\dfrac{239}{200}$ 31. $\dfrac{1}{16}$ 33. $\dfrac{1}{3}$ 35. $\dfrac{2}{11}$

37. $\dfrac{104}{333}$ 39. $\dfrac{559}{99}$ 41. $\dfrac{1}{6}$ 43. $\dfrac{49}{15}$ 45. $\dfrac{3}{110}$ 47. $\dfrac{76}{55}$ 49. a. every

rational number except 0 b. 1, −1, 3, −3 51. a. every rational number except −1

b. every rational number $x = \dfrac{n}{5-n}$ where n is an integer other than 5 53. Let $x = 0.\overline{9}$;

$10x = 9.\overline{9}$; $10x - x = 9.\overline{9} - 0.\overline{9}$; $9x = 9$; $x = 1$ 55. $\dfrac{11}{12} = 1 - \dfrac{1}{12} = 0.99\overline{9} - 0.08\overline{3} = 0.91\overline{6}$

PAGES 8–9 1. 35 3. −13 5. 28 7. −4.5 9. 3 11. 39 13. 24

15. 84 17. $\dfrac{9}{5}$ 19. 29 21. 25 23. 5 25. a. −2 b. $\dfrac{1}{2}$ 27. a. 3

b. $-\dfrac{1}{3}$ 29. a. $-\dfrac{7}{8}$ b. $\dfrac{8}{7}$ 31. a. $2\dfrac{1}{4}$ b. $-\dfrac{4}{9}$ 33. a. $-\dfrac{7}{5}$ b. $\dfrac{5}{7}$ 35. a. $\dfrac{5}{8}$

b. $-\dfrac{8}{5}$ 37. a. $-\dfrac{2}{3}$ b. $\dfrac{3}{2}$ 39. a. $\dfrac{104}{333}$ b. $-\dfrac{333}{104}$ 41. Assoc. prop. of add.;

inverse prop. of add.; identity prop. of add. 47. $\dfrac{1}{x+3}$, −3 49. $\dfrac{x-1}{x+1}$, 1 and −1

51. $\dfrac{6}{x}$, 0 53. $(8 + 7 \cdot 6) \div (3 + 2)^2 = 2$ 55. $(8 + 7) \cdot 6 \div 3 + 2^2 = 34$

57. $6 + 4 \cdot 3 \div (2^3 - 2) \cdot 3 = 12$ or $6 + 4 \cdot 3 \div (2^3 - 2 \cdot 3) = 12$
59. $6 + (4 \cdot 3 \div 2)^3 - 2 \cdot 3 = 216$

PAGES 13–15 1. $\left\{-\dfrac{1}{6}\right\}$ 3. $\{6\}$ 5. $\{-18\}$ 7. $\{-50\}$ 9. $\{0.05\}$

11. $\{70\}$ 13. $\{-5\}$ 15. $\{35\}$ 17. $\{-3.1\}$ 19. $\{7\}$ 21. $\{-6\}$
23. $\{-18\}$ 25. $\{4\}$ 27. $\{1\}$ 29. $\{-3\}$ 31. $\varnothing$ 33. $\{42\}$ 35. $\{16\}$
37. $\{-9\}$ 39. $\{-70\}$ 41. $\{10\}$ 43. $\{-12\}$ 45. $\Re$ 47. $\{8.5\}$ 49. $\{10\}$
51. $\{75\}$ 53. $\{1\}$ 55. $\{1\}$ 57. $t = \dfrac{d}{r}$ 59. $n = \dfrac{l + d - a}{d}$ 61. $a = \dfrac{2s}{t^2}$

PAGES 19–21 1. 11 3. 4 and 12 5. −14, −13, and −12 7. 91 and 52

9. 25 and 65 11. 20 cm long and 6 cm wide 13. 24 cm² 15. $14\dfrac{1}{2}$ and $5\dfrac{1}{2}$ are

not integers. 17. 7, 9, and 11 are not even integers. 19. In a 30–60–90 triangle, the
measure of the third angle, 90, is 3 times that of the *smaller* of the complementary angles.
21. The local train reaches its destination at 5:20 P.M., 10 min before the express.
23. 50 cm 25. 80 dimes 27. 9 kg of cocoa worth $7.50/kg, 3 kg of cocoa worth
$9.50/kg 29. $8000 at 10%, $5000 at 12% 31. Joe, 12 years old; father, 42 years old
33. 54 km/h, 69 km/h

PAGES 23–24
1. $\{x: x > 3\}$

3. $\{y: y \geqslant -1\}$

5. $\{y: y < -\dfrac{1}{2}\}$

7. $\{c: c \leqslant -6\}$

9. $\{z: z \leqslant 15\}$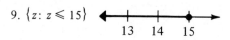

11. $\{x: x \leqslant 11\}$

13. $\{x: x \geqslant 2\}$

15. $\{x: x > 1\}$

17. $\{x: x \leqslant 1\}$

19. $\emptyset$ 21. $\{x: x > 6\}$ 23. $\{x: x < -3\}$ 25. $\{c: c < 15\}$ 27. $\{x: x > 5\}$

29. $\{n: n \geqslant 2\}$ 31. $\{x: x < -\frac{2}{3}\}$ 33. $\{x: x > -10\}$ 35. $\{r: r < 2\}$ 37. $\mathcal{R}$

39. $\{x: x \geqslant -2\}$ 41. $\{y: y \geqslant -15\}$ 43. $\{y: y \geqslant 1\}$ 45. $\{k: k \geqslant -40\}$

47. $\{x: x < \frac{9}{8}\}$ 49. $\{c: c < 1\}$ 51. $\{k: k \geqslant 17\}$ 53. $\{x: x \leqslant 1\}$

PAGE 28

1. $\{x: -8 \leqslant x < -4\}$

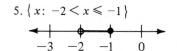

3. $\{x: 9 \leqslant x < 11\}$

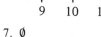

5. $\{x: -2 < x \leqslant -1\}$

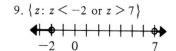

7. $\emptyset$

9. $\{z: z < -2 \text{ or } z > 7\}$

11. $\{c: c \leqslant -2 \text{ or } c \geqslant 1\}$

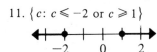

13. $\{r: -2 < r < 1\}$

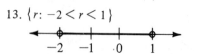

15. $\{x: 0 < x \leqslant 4\}$

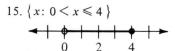

17. $\{z: 4 \leqslant z < 6\}$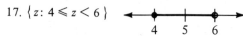

19. $\{d: -1 < d < -\frac{2}{5}\}$ 21. $\{w: -2 \leqslant w < 1\}$ 23. $\{d: d < \frac{3}{2}\}$

25. $\{x: x < -2 \text{ or } x > -1\}$ 27. $\{x: -3 < x < -1\}$ 29. $\mathcal{R}$ 31. $\{z: z \leqslant -7 \text{ or } z > 2\}$

33. $\{w: -1 < w < 2\}$ 35. $\{v: -3 < v \leqslant 2\}$

PAGES 30–32   1. $3 \leqslant w \leqslant 3.6$ 3. 7, 8, and 9   5. 8, 13, and 15   7. at most

7 transistors   9. His next test score must be at least 83.   11. $m\angle B < 27$ 13. 10 min

15. a. $\{-3, -6, -12\}, \{-2, -4, -8\}, \{-1, -2, -4\}$ b. $-21 \leqslant l + \frac{l}{2} + \frac{l}{4} < 0$, or

$-12 \leqslant l < 0$ c. The greatest number is at least -3 and less than 0 ($-3 \leqslant x < 0$).

17. more than 137 min   19. if you plan to drive more than 790 km   21. at most 44 L

23. fewer than 600 km

PAGE 35   1. 5   3. 1   5. 3   7. 2   9. $\{3, -7\}$ 11. $\{-3, -5\}$

13. $\emptyset$ 15. $\{4, -9\}$ 17. $\{2, -\frac{11}{2}\}$ 19. $\{\frac{3}{2}\}$ 21. $\{1, -5\}$ 23. $\{-5, 13\}$

25. $\{9, -\frac{29}{3}\}$

27. $\{x: -3 < x < 3\}$

（number line: open circles at −3 and 3, marks −4 −2 0 2 4）

29. $\varnothing$

31. $\{y: y \leqslant -8 \text{ or } y \geqslant 8\}$

（number line: closed circles at −8 and 8, marks −8 −4 0 4 8）

33. $\{y: y < -3 \text{ or } y > 3\}$

（number line: open circles at −3 and 3, marks −4 −2 0 2 4）

35. $\varnothing$

37. $\{w: w \leqslant -2 \text{ or } w \geqslant 2\}$

（number line: closed circles at −2 and 2, marks −4 −2 0 2 4）

39. $\{z: -3 \leqslant z \leqslant 3\}$

（number line: closed circles at −3 and 3, marks −4 −2 0 2 4）

41. $\{z: -7 < z < 3\}$

（number line: open circles at −7 and 3, marks −8 −6 −4 −2 0 2 4）

43. $\{z: z < -8 \text{ or } z > -6\}$

（number line: open circles at −8 and −6, marks −9 −8 −7 −6 −5）

45. $\{z: z < -2 \text{ or } z > 8\}$

（number line: open circles at −2 and 8, marks −4 0 4 8 12）

47. $\{w: -5 < w < 12\}$ 49. $\{x: x < -6 \text{ or } x > \frac{7}{2}\}$ 51. $\{z: -1 < z < 5\}$

53. $\{x: x \leqslant -\frac{1}{7} \text{ or } x \geqslant \frac{13}{7}\}$ 55. $\{z: -12 < z < 6\}$ 57. $\{x: x \leqslant 0 \text{ or } x \geqslant \frac{2}{3}\}$

59. $\{y: -\frac{13}{2} < y < \frac{11}{2}\}$ 61. $\{x: x \leqslant 0 \text{ or } x \geqslant 4\}$ 63. $\{y: y < -2 \text{ or } y > 6\}$

65. $-|a| \leqslant a \leqslant |a|$ and $-|b| \leqslant b \leqslant |b|$; $-(|a| + |b|) \leqslant a + b \leqslant |a| + |b|$; if $-t \leqslant x \leqslant t$, then $|x| \leqslant t$, so $|a + b| \leqslant |a| + |b|$.

PAGES 38-39 · CHAPTER REVIEW   1. 1.875   2. $-0.4\overline{6}$ 3. $-\frac{753}{125}$ 4. $\frac{19}{99}$

5. 4   6. 8   7. 25   8. 31   9. a. 5   b. $-\frac{1}{5}$ 10. a. $-1\frac{1}{4}$ b. $\frac{4}{5}$

11. $\{3\}$ 12. $\{-1\}$ 13. $\{10\}$ 14. $\{10\}$ 15. 40, 60, 80   16. 20 nickels, 25 dimes

17. $\{k: k < 5\}$

（number line: open circle at 5, marks 2 3 4 5 6）

18. $\{x: x \geqslant -2\}$

（number line: closed circle at −2, marks −3 −2 −1 0 1）

19. $\{z: z \leqslant 11\}$

20. $\{w: w > -6\}$

21. $\{x: -7 \leqslant x < -3\}$

（number line: closed circle at −7, open circle at −3, marks −7 −6 −5 −4 −3）

22. $\{x: -9 < x < 9\}$

（number line: open circles at −9 and 9, marks −9 0 9）

23. $\{y: y < -1\}$

（number line: open circle at −1, marks −4 −3 −2 −1 0）

24. $\{k: -2 < k < 1\}$

（number line: open circles at −2 and 1, marks −2 −1 0 1 2）

25. $14{,}400 \leqslant e \leqslant 18{,}000$ 26. It is between 10 and 22.   27. $\{-3, \frac{3}{2}\}$

28. $\{-\frac{3}{2}, \frac{27}{10}\}$

29. $\{x: x < 1 \text{ or } x > 5\}$

（number line: open circles at 1 and 5, marks 0 1 2 3 4 5 6）

30. $\{x: -9 \leqslant x \leqslant 3\}$

（number line: closed circles at −9 and 3, marks −9 −6 −3 0 3）

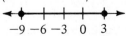

1. 9, 10, 11, 12   3. $\{x: -8 \leqslant x \leqslant 3\}$

5. $\dfrac{1000}{1}$ 7. $\dfrac{70}{9}$ 9. $\{r: r < -7 \text{ or } r > 7\}$

11. $\{2, 3\}$ 13. $\{m: -3 < m < 7\}$

15. a. Identity prop. of mult.   b. Distributive prop.   c. Inverse prop. of add.   d. Mult. prop. of 0   17. $\{g: -4 \leqslant g \leqslant -1\}$ 19. 12   21. -216 23. always   25. 126, 54

27. $\{t: t \geqslant -125\}$ 29. a. $5\dfrac{3}{4}$ b. $-\dfrac{4}{23}$ 31. a. $-0.\overline{3}$ b. 3

33. $\{v: 1 < v < 7\}$ 35. 16   37. $\dfrac{2}{5}$ 39. 0.984

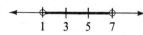

1. $6k^6m^4$ 3. $-3a^6x^2$ 5. $16a^8x^4$ 7. $\dfrac{8t^3u^3}{27}$ 9. $\dfrac{256}{625n^{12}}$

11. $\dfrac{4}{3xy^5}$ 13. $\dfrac{1}{9m^2}$ 15. $14x^5y^2$ 17. $\dfrac{125y^6}{64x^{12}}$ 19. 3^4 21. 3^0 23. 3^8

25. 3^3 27. xy^{-3} 29. $3hz^{-2}$ 31. -3^4n^5k, or $-81n^5k$ 33. n^2k^{-2}

35. $\dfrac{x^9y^2}{z^3}$ 37. $\dfrac{2w^4z^8}{x^3}$ 39. $\dfrac{2}{3b^2c^4}$

1. $17x - 2y$ 3. $18a^2 - a$ 5. $4x^2y - 6x^2 - 13xy^2$
7. $-2a + b - 3c$ 9. $7p - 16q - 4r$ 11. $-5x^2 + 26xy - y^2$ 13. $k^2 - 2km - 3m^2$
15. $c^2 - 16cd + 64d^2$ 17. $3w^2 - 19wz + 28z^2$ 19. $24a^2 + 17ab - 20b^2$
21. $16z^2 - 121$ 23. $9z^2 + 78z + 169$ 25. $12m^3 - 24m^2 + 21m$
27. $42b^4d - 56b^3d^2 + 28b^2d^3$ 29. $8x^3 - 19x^2 + 11x - 10$ 31. $9a^3 - 7a + 2$
33. $12x^3 - 7x^2y + 16x + xy^2 - 4y$ 35. $-11w - 16u$ 37. $s^4 + s^3 - 5s^2 - s - 12$
39. $2x^4 - 13x^3y + 20x^2y^2 + 2xy^3 - 5y^4$ 41. 0   43. $-11c - 45$ 45. $-15m - 109$
47. $21x^2 + 10x - 16$ 49. $8x^2 + 13x + 12$ 51. $x = 2$ 53. $x = 2$

1. $3p(4q^2 - p)$ 3. $4b^3(8b^2 - 3b + 12)$ 5. $(x + 3)(x + 2)$
7. $(c - 6)(c + 2)$ 9. $(h - 2k)(h + k)$ 11. $(3y - 1)(2y + 1)$ 13. $(4x - 1)(2x - 3)$
15. $(4v - 7)(3v + 5)$ 17. $(4z + 1)(7z - 3)$ 19. $(4y + 3z)(4y - z)$ 21. $(p - 9)^2$
23. $(2y + 5)^2$ 25. $(k + 8)(k - 8)$ 27. prime   29. $(y - 3)(y^2 + 3y + 9)$
31. $(3v + 5)(9v^2 - 15v + 25)$ 33. $(4n^2 + 1)(2n + 1)(2n - 1)$ 35. $4x(x + 8)(x - 2)$
37. $(n + 1)^2(n - 1)^2$ 39. $2b(8b^2 + 31b - 36)$ 41. $2(2z - 5)(4z^2 + 10z + 25)$
43. $5(x^2 + 36)$ 45. $-3x(9x - 4)^2$ 47. $(4a - 3)(3a - b)$ 49. $(9h + k)(7h + 4)$
51. $(d - 1 - 7df)(d + 1)$ 53. $(a^3 + 12)(a - 2)(a^2 + 2a + 4)$
55. $2x^kw^4(x^2 - 5)(x^2 + 1)$ 57. $(2a^m + b^k)(a^m - b^k)$

1. $\{-4, 2\}$ 3. $\{13, 3\}$ 5. $\{\pm 9\}$ 7. $\{0, -\dfrac{3}{4}\}$ 9. $\{\pm \dfrac{5}{4}\}$

11. $\{-\dfrac{2}{7}, -\dfrac{2}{5}\}$ 13. $\{-1, \dfrac{32}{15}\}$ 15. $\{-\dfrac{4}{3}, \dfrac{1}{2}\}$ 17. $\{\dfrac{5}{6}, -\dfrac{1}{2}\}$ 19. $\{0, 15\}$

21. $\{12, -4\}$ 23. $\{15, 4\}$ 25. $\{\dfrac{2}{3}, -8\}$ 27. $\{7, 8\}$ 29. $\{-\dfrac{5}{6}, -2\}$

31. $\{\dfrac{3 \pm \sqrt{5}}{2}\}$ 33. $\{\dfrac{-3 \pm \sqrt{37}}{2}\}$ 35. $\{\dfrac{9 \pm \sqrt{53}}{14}\}$ 37. 11   39. 9, 11

41. a. $x = 3$ b. altitude, 6 units; base, 8 units

43.

45. $\left\{ 0, \dfrac{1}{2}, -3 \right\}$ 47. $\left\{ 0, -2\dfrac{1}{2}, \dfrac{1}{7} \right\}$ 49. 5 s   51. 3 s

53. $\{ \pm 3, \pm 2 \}$ 55. $\{ \pm 5, \pm 2 \}$ 57. $\left\{ \pm 2, \pm \dfrac{3}{2} \right\}$

59. $\left\{ \pm \dfrac{2}{5}, \pm \dfrac{1}{3} \right\}$

PAGES 67-68   1. $7a^2 - 2ab^2 + 3b - 7a$ 3. $4mk - 2k - \dfrac{7}{5m} + \dfrac{2}{5k}$

5. $\dfrac{p^3 + p^2 - p - 1}{p - 1} = p^2 + 2p + 1$ 7. $\dfrac{q^3 - 7q^2 + 10q + 8}{q - 4} = q^2 - 3q - 2$

9. $\dfrac{b^3 + b^2 - 6b + 24}{b + 4} = b^2 - 3b + 6$ 11. $\dfrac{4z^3 + 6z^2 - 4}{z + 2} = 4z^2 - 2z + 4 - \dfrac{12}{z + 2}$

13. $\dfrac{4m^3 - m + 16}{2m + 3} = 2m^2 - 3m + 4 + \dfrac{4}{2m + 3}$ 15. $\dfrac{6c^3 - 9c^2d - 4cd^2 + d^3}{2c + d} =$

$3c^2 - 6cd + d^2$ 17. $\{ -1, 2, 3 \}$ 19. $\left\{ -2, \dfrac{1}{3}, 2 \right\}$ 21. $\left\{ -4, \dfrac{1}{4}, 1 \right\}$

23. $\left\{ -3, -\dfrac{1}{4}, \dfrac{2}{3} \right\}$ 25. $\{ 1, 2, 3 \}$ 27. $\left\{ -\dfrac{1}{2}, \dfrac{1}{2}, 2 \right\}$ 29. $\left\{ -\dfrac{1}{4}, \dfrac{1}{3}, \dfrac{1}{2} \right\}$

PAGES 70-71   1. $\dfrac{a}{b^2}$ 3. $\dfrac{4h}{h - 1}$ 5. $\dfrac{x}{4}$ 7. $\dfrac{1}{2a}$ 9. $-\dfrac{k + 2}{5k}$ 11. $\dfrac{r - 3}{r + 2}$

13. $\dfrac{4h - k}{4hk}$ 15. $\dfrac{3}{4}$ 17. $\dfrac{u - 2}{u + 3}$ 19. $\dfrac{e + f}{e^2 + 2ef}$ 21. $-\dfrac{k}{8k + 24}$ 23. $\dfrac{t + 4}{t + 3}$

25. $\dfrac{2c}{a}$ 27. $\dfrac{3p - 3q}{2pq + 2q^2}$ 29. $\dfrac{2}{3x}$ 31. $\dfrac{15k^2 + 17k + 4}{12k^2 + 7k - 10}$ 33. $\dfrac{6a - b}{3a + 2b}$

35. $\dfrac{q - 5r}{q - r}$ 37. $\dfrac{4y + 3}{3y - 5}$ 39. $\dfrac{x^2 + x - 12}{x - 5}$ 41. $y + 1$

PAGES 74-75   1. $\dfrac{2}{5z}$ 3. $\dfrac{2}{7z}$ 5. $\dfrac{7x - 2}{2x^2}$ 7. $\dfrac{x^2 - 2x - 6}{x(x + 3)}$ 9. $\dfrac{2n - 11}{n - 4}$

11. $\dfrac{3y^2 + 32y + 112}{4y(y + 4)}$ 13. $\dfrac{-x + 20}{(x - 2)(x + 4)}$ 15. $\dfrac{6a^2 - 13a}{(2a - 1)(a - 3)}$ 17. $\dfrac{5z - 2}{2z(z + 2)}$

19. $\dfrac{x + 4}{x - 4}$ 21. $\dfrac{-4r + 11}{2r(r - 3)}$ 23. $\dfrac{8v^2 + 3v - 15}{4v(v - 5)(v + 3)}$ 25. $\dfrac{5u - 2}{(u + 2)^2(u - 2)}$

27. $\dfrac{1}{(y - 3)(y - 4)}$ 29. $\dfrac{3m^2 + m + 24}{(3m - 8)^2(3m + 8)}$ 31. $\dfrac{2z^2 - 4z - 3}{(2z + 1)(2z - 1)(z - 5)}$

33. $\dfrac{1}{a + b}$ 35. $\dfrac{2x^2 - 5xy - 5y^2}{(x + y)(x - y)(x + 2y)}$ 37. $\dfrac{44x^2 + 199x - 58}{(3x + 1)(2x - 1)(x + 2)}$

PAGE 77   1. 6   3. $\dfrac{1}{3}$ 5. $\dfrac{4(3r + 2s)}{3(2r - s)}$ 7. $\dfrac{x - 2}{6x}$ 9. $\dfrac{7w + 3}{6 - w}$ 11. $\dfrac{x + 1}{2}$

13. $\dfrac{3(4z - w)}{2(9z - w)}$ 15. $\dfrac{2x + 1}{x(x + 1)}$ 17. $\dfrac{k + z}{z(z^2 + 1)}$ 19. $2a + 1$ 21. $\dfrac{xy}{x + y}$

23. $\dfrac{w - 2}{w^2 - 2w - 8}$ 25. $\dfrac{t + 1}{4t + 3}$ 27. $\dfrac{27}{35}$

PAGES 80-82   1. $\left\{ 5\dfrac{1}{4} \right\}$ 3. $\left\{ 4\dfrac{1}{3} \right\}$ 5. $\left\{ 1\dfrac{3}{7} \right\}$ 7. $\{ 1 \}$ 9. $\left\{ -\dfrac{8}{3} \right\}$ 11. $\{ 8 \}$

13. $\left\{ 4, -\dfrac{4}{9} \right\}$ 15. $\left\{ \dfrac{1}{3} \right\}$ 17. $\{ -4 \}$ 19. $\{ 1, 8 \}$ 21. $\{ -8, 3 \}$ 23. $\left\{ \dfrac{2}{3}, -3 \right\}$

25. $\{9, -3\}$ 27. $\{-\frac{1}{2}, 1\}$ 29. $\{-\frac{1}{2}\}$ 31. 4   33. $AC = 4.8$; $ED = 3$; $CB = 3.6$

35. 50 km/h, then 90 km/h   37. 3 h   39. 3 h   41. $\frac{7}{6}$

PAGE 85

1. $\{x: 2 < x < 6\}$

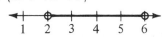

3. $\{h: h \leq 1 \text{ or } h \geq 8\}$

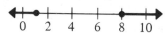

5. $\{m: m < -2 \text{ or } m > 2\}$

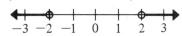

7. $\{c: c \leq -2 \text{ or } c \geq 3\}$

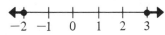

9. $\{d: d < -4 \text{ or } d > 0\}$

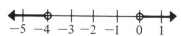

11. $\{s: s < 1 \text{ or } s > 9\}$

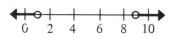

13. $\{y: 2 \leq y \leq 10\}$

15. $\{w: -2 < w < \frac{1}{2}\}$

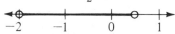

17. $\{u: u \leq -1 \text{ or } u \geq \frac{5}{2}\}$

19. $\{z: z \leq -2 \text{ or } 0 \leq z \leq 1\}$

21. $\{v: v \leq -4 \text{ or } 0 \leq v \leq 5\}$

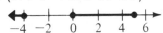

23. $\{x: x > 1\}$

25. $\{z: z < 3 \text{ or } z > 5\}$

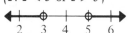

27. $\{k: -6 < k < 0\}$

29. $\{h: 0 < h < 5 \text{ or } h > 10\}$

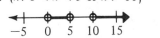

31. $\{b: b \neq 2\}$

33. $\{b: b < -5 \text{ or } -5 < b < -3\}$

PAGES 87-88 · CHAPTER REVIEW   1. $\frac{7x^2y^4}{2}$ 2. $\frac{k^3}{8n^6}$ 3. $\frac{x^2}{16}$ 4. $75a^2b$

5. $7x^2 + 2x + 2$ 6. $5a + 5$ 7. $12z^2 + 26z - 16$ 8. $16x^2 - 40xy + 25y^2$

9. $(2x + 7)(x + 5)$ 10. $(5y + 6)(4y - 3)$ 11. $2(v + 5)(v - 5)$ 12. $(3k + 4)^2$

13. $\{-\frac{3}{2}\}$ 14. $\{\frac{5}{6}, \frac{2}{3}\}$ 15. $\frac{y^3 - 2y - 12}{y - 3} = y^2 + 3y + 7 + \frac{9}{y - 3}$

16. $\{-1, -\frac{1}{2}, 3\}$ 17. $\frac{3(u - 4)}{2u^2}$ 18. $\frac{3(x - 2)}{(x + 2)(x + 4)}$ 19. $\frac{x^2 + 2x + 8}{(x - 2)(x + 2)}$

20. $\frac{-5}{v(v + 5)}$ 21. $\frac{4v + 1}{u(1 - 5v)}$ 22. $\frac{2n + 1}{n(n + 1)}$ 23. $\{-5, 3\}$ 24. $\{6, 4\}$

714   *SELECTED ANSWERS*

25. $\{y: -4 < y < 3\}$

26. $\{n: n \leqslant 1 \text{ or } n \geqslant 4\}$

PAGES 90–91 · MIXED REVIEW   1. $\dfrac{3x + 4}{3x - 4}$ 3. $-\dfrac{4}{3}$ 5. $\{-6\}$ 7. $\{7\}$

9. $\{-3, 2\}$ 11.   13.   15. $0.\overline{5742}$

17. 1.21875 19. Identity prop. of mult.   21. Mult. prop. of -1 23. $\dfrac{25}{3}$

25. $x \geqslant 18$ 27. $-0.75;\ \dfrac{4}{3}$, or $1.\overline{3}$ 29. 6 31. $\dfrac{(s + 1)^2}{2s}$ 33. $\dfrac{3}{16}$

35. $9a^3 - 11ab^2 + \dfrac{15b^7}{a^2}$ 37. $(6a - 5)(a + 4)$ 39. There is no x such that $x > 2$ and

$x \leqslant -1$.   41. $\{x: x < 0 \text{ or } x > 4\}$

43. $\{y: y \leqslant -3 \text{ or } y \geqslant -1\}$

PAGE 97   1. $3\sqrt{2}$ 3. $6\sqrt{5}$ 5. $6\sqrt{11}$ 7. $-18\sqrt{6}$ 9. $6x^2 y$

11. $2a^2 y^3 \sqrt{6a}$ 13. $-4km^4\sqrt{7km}$ 15. 4 17. $\dfrac{11}{7}\sqrt{2}$ 19. $\dfrac{3}{2}x^2 y^4 \sqrt{y}$

21. $\dfrac{c}{b}$ 23. $5\sqrt{3}$ 25. $-3\sqrt{6}$ 27. $3\sqrt{10}$ 29. $36\sqrt{10} - 18\sqrt{3}$

31. $4\sqrt{2}$ 33. $\dfrac{\sqrt{3}}{4}$ 35. $\dfrac{5}{2}\sqrt{5} - \dfrac{4}{3}\sqrt{3}$ 37. $3\sqrt[3]{5}$ 39. $-29\sqrt[3]{2}$

41. $7\sqrt[4]{2}$ 43. $(x^2 + 3x)\sqrt{2x}$ 45. $\dfrac{(-2x^2 + 3x + 25)\sqrt{3x}}{15}$

47. $\dfrac{(5n^2 k + 2 - 4kn)\sqrt{7n}}{2k^2}$ 49. a. 2 b. $-x$

PAGES 100–101   1. $18\sqrt{10}$ 3. 99 5. $30\sqrt{2}$ 7. $-60\sqrt{10}$ 9. $x^2 y\sqrt{y}$

11. $-70n^4\sqrt{6}$ 13. $\dfrac{\sqrt{6}}{2}$ 15. $2\sqrt{15}$ 17. $\dfrac{5\sqrt{15}}{3}$ 19. $\dfrac{\sqrt{xy}}{x^2}$

21. $-\sqrt{15} - \sqrt{21}$ 23. $60 - 30\sqrt{3}$ 25. $-3 + 2\sqrt{5}$ 27. -1

29. $47 + 4\sqrt{70}$ 31. -23 33. $323 - 16\sqrt{15}$ 35. -18 37. $16 + 8\sqrt{5}$

39. $2\sqrt{11} - 6$ 41. $18 - 12\sqrt{2}$ 43. $\dfrac{29 + 12\sqrt{5}}{11}$ 45. $-6 - 5\sqrt{2}$

47. $\sqrt{6a} - \sqrt{3a}$ 49. $-d + \sqrt{d(d + e)}$ 51. $\dfrac{2a - b + 2\sqrt{a(a - b)}}{b}$

53. $\dfrac{\sqrt{3}}{3} - \dfrac{\sqrt{2}}{4}$ 55. $\dfrac{4\sqrt{5}}{5} - \dfrac{\sqrt{15}}{12}$ 57. $\dfrac{(ab + bc + ac)\sqrt{abc}}{abc}$ 59. $24\sqrt[3]{3}$

61. $10 - 2\sqrt[3]{50}$ 63. $5\sqrt[4]{5} + 5$ 65. $\dfrac{\sqrt[3]{28}}{6}$ 67. $x + 2\sqrt{xy} + y - z$

69. $x = \dfrac{5\sqrt{3}}{3}$ 71. $x = 4 + 2\sqrt{6}$ 73. $x = \dfrac{3 + \sqrt{2}}{7}$ 75. $\dfrac{1 - \sqrt[3]{7} + \sqrt[3]{49}}{8}$

77. $(p - q)(3 + \sqrt{p + q})$ 79. $\sqrt{a} - \sqrt{b}$

PAGE 104   1. $\{4\}$ 3. $\{47\}$ 5. $\{-1\}$ 7. $\{0, -1\}$ 9. $\{-4\}$ 11. $\{8, 2\}$

13. $\{4\}$ 15. $\{3, 7\}$ 17. $\{-3\}$ 19. $\{0\}$ 21. $\{4\}$ 23. $\{0, 3\}$

25. $\{2, -1\}$ 27. $\{8\}$ 29. $\{-1\}$ 31. $\{0, -1\}$ 33. $\emptyset$ 35. $\{29\}$

37. $\{-2\}$ 39. $\{\frac{1}{4}, 1\}$ 41. $\{11\}$

PAGES 107–108   1. $5i$ 3. $-3i\sqrt{2}$ 5. $5i\sqrt{7}$ 7. $10i\sqrt{3}$ 9. $-5i\sqrt{6}$

11. $13\sqrt{5}$ 13. $\sqrt{2}$ 15. $-\dfrac{5i\sqrt{10}}{4}$ 17. $-2i\sqrt{2}$ 19. $\dfrac{2i\sqrt{3}}{3}$ 21. $-12\sqrt{7}$

23. $-\dfrac{\sqrt{2}}{2}$ 25. $-\dfrac{8i\sqrt{5}}{25}$ 27. $-i$ 29. $-i$ 31. $-i$ 33. 0

35. $\{5i, -5i\}$ 37. $\{2\sqrt{3}, -2\sqrt{3}\}$ 39. $\{3i\sqrt{2}, -3i\sqrt{2}\}$

41. $(2i)^3 - 3(2i)^2 + 4(2i) - 12 = 8i^3 - 12i^2 + 8i - 12 = 8(-i) - 12(-1) + 8i - 12 = 0$

43. $(-2i)^4 - (-2i)^3 + 7(-2i)^2 - 4(-2i) + 12 = 16i^4 + 8i^3 + 28i^2 + 8i + 12 =$

$16(1) + 8(-i) + 28(-1) + 8i + 12 = 0$ 45. $-i$ 47. i 49. If n is a positive integer,

then $i^{a+4n} = i^a \cdot i^{4n} = i^a \cdot (i^4)^n = i^a \cdot 1^n = i^a \cdot 1 = i^a$.

PAGES 111–112   1. $5i$ 3. $-i$ 5. $26i\sqrt{3}$ 7. a. $6 - 3i$ b. $6 + 7i$

c. $10 - 30i$ 9. a. $-3 + 4i$ b. $-7 + 2i$ c. $-13 + i$ 11. a. $\dfrac{9}{2} - \dfrac{17}{2}i$

b. $-\dfrac{7}{2} + \dfrac{23}{2}i$ c. $17 + i$ 13. a. 16 b. $2i\sqrt{5}$ c. 69 15. a. $1 - i\sqrt{6}$

b. $7 + 3i\sqrt{6}$ c. $-11i\sqrt{6}$ 17. a. $\sqrt{3} - 3i\sqrt{2}$ b. $-3\sqrt{3} - i\sqrt{2}$ c. $-10 - 3i\sqrt{6}$

19. a. $\dfrac{11}{2}$ b. $\dfrac{3}{2} - 2i\sqrt{3}$ c. $10 + \dfrac{3i\sqrt{3}}{2}$ 21. $x = 5, y = -1$ 23. $x = \dfrac{1}{2}, y = 4$

25. $(2 + 3i)^2 - 4(2 + 3i) + 13 = (-5 + 12i) - 8 - 12i + 13 = 0$ 27. $(-5 - 2i)^2 +$

$10(-5 - 2i) + 29 = (21 + 20i) - 50 - 20i + 29 = 0$ 29. $(2 + i)\left(\dfrac{2}{5} - \dfrac{1}{5}i\right) =$

$\dfrac{4}{5} - \dfrac{2}{5}i + \dfrac{2}{5}i - \dfrac{1}{5}i^2 = \dfrac{4}{5} - \dfrac{1}{5}(-1) = 1$ 37. $(a + bi)(3 + 4i) = (3a - 4b) + (4a + 3b)i = 1$;

$3a - 4b = 1$ and $4a + 3b = 0$; $a = \dfrac{3}{25}$ and $b = -\dfrac{4}{25}$

PAGE 114   1. $\dfrac{1}{10} - \dfrac{1}{5}i$ 3. $\dfrac{\sqrt{3}}{4} - \dfrac{1}{4}i$ 5. $2 - i$ 7. $-2 - 2i\sqrt{3}$

9. $\dfrac{\sqrt{2}}{6} - \dfrac{1}{6}i$ 11. $\dfrac{3}{2} - \dfrac{1}{2}i$ 13. $2 + i$ 15. $-\dfrac{1}{2} - \dfrac{7\sqrt{3}}{6}i$ 17. $-\dfrac{1}{5} + \dfrac{2\sqrt{6}}{5}i$

19. $\dfrac{40}{29} - \dfrac{7\sqrt{7}}{29}i$ 21. $-1 - i\sqrt{15}$ 23. $\dfrac{40}{19} - \dfrac{25\sqrt{21}}{19}i$ 25. $\dfrac{7}{10} + \dfrac{9}{10}i$

27. $\dfrac{\sqrt{5}}{30} - \dfrac{11}{6}i$ 29. $(a + bi)(a - bi)$ 31. $(2x + 9i)(2x - 9i)$

33. $(x + i)(x - i)(x + 1)(x - 1)$ 35. $(y + 2i)^2(y - 2i)^2(y + 2)^2(y - 2)^2$

37. $(a + bi)(u + vi) = (au - bv) + (av + bu)i$ and $av + bu = 0$; $bu = -av$; $\dfrac{u}{v} = -\dfrac{a}{b}$

PAGES 119–120   1. -16; 2 imaginary conjugate roots   3. 81; 2 real (rational) roots

5. -20; 2 imaginary conjugate roots   7. 0; 1 real double (rational) root   9. -7;

2 imaginary conjugate roots   11. 0; 1 real double (irrational) root   13. $\{1 \pm 2i\}$

15. $\{-3 \pm i\sqrt{3}\}$ 17. $\left\{\dfrac{3 \pm 3i}{2}\right\}$ 19. $\left\{\dfrac{-3 \pm 2i\sqrt{3}}{3}\right\}$ 21. $\left\{\dfrac{3 \pm i\sqrt{3}}{6}\right\}$

23. $\left\{\dfrac{7 \pm 3i}{2}\right\}$ 25. a. $-1, 1$ b. $(0, -1)$ c. $x = 0$ 27. a. 2 b. $(2, 0)$ c. $x = 2$

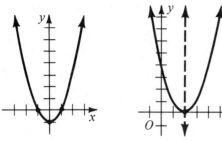
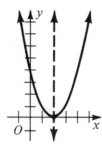
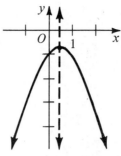
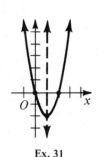

Ex. 25   Ex. 27   Ex. 29   Ex. 31

29. a. none   b. $\left(\dfrac{1}{2}, -\dfrac{3}{4}\right)$ c. $x = \dfrac{1}{2}$ 31. a. $0, 2$ b. $(1, -2)$ c. $x = 1$

33. a. $k = \dfrac{9}{2}$ b. $x = \dfrac{3}{2}$ 35. a. $k = 12$ b. $x = -2$ 37. a. $k = \pm 12$ b. If $k = 12$,

$x = 3$; if $k = -12$, $x = -3$.   39. a. $k = \dfrac{1}{2}$ or $k = -\dfrac{9}{2}$ b. If $k = \dfrac{1}{2}$, $x = 3$; if $k = -\dfrac{9}{2}$,

$x = -\dfrac{1}{3}$.   41. $k < \dfrac{9}{2}$ 43. $k < 12$ 45. $k > \dfrac{9}{2}$ 47. $k > 12$ 49. $\{3i, -i\}$

51. $\{i \pm 1\}$ 53. $\left\{\dfrac{3i \pm \sqrt{11}}{2}\right\}$ 55. $(2 - 5i)^2 - (2 - 5i) - 4 = (-21 - 20i) - 2 + 5i - 4 =$

$-27 - 15i$; $(2 + 5i)^2 - (2 + 5i) - 4 = (-21 + 20i) - 2 - 5i - 4 = -27 + 15i$

57. $(-1 + i\sqrt{3})^2 = -2 - 2i\sqrt{3}$; $(-1 + i\sqrt{3})^3 - 7 = (-1 + i\sqrt{3})(-2 - 2i\sqrt{3}) - 7 = 8 - 7 = 1$;

$(-1 - i\sqrt{3})^2 = -2 + 2i\sqrt{3}$; $(-1 - i\sqrt{3})^3 - 7 = (-1 - i\sqrt{3})(-2 + 2i\sqrt{3}) - 7 = 8 - 7 = 1$

PAGES 124–125   1. $x^2 + 2x - 35 = 0$ 3. $x^2 + 12x + 36 = 0$ 5. $6x^2 + x - 2 = 0$
7. $x^2 - 3 = 0$ 9. $x^2 + 12x + 23 = 0$ 11. $x^2 - 6x - 19 = 0$ 13. $x^2 - 6x + 25 = 0$
15. $x^2 + 2x + 3 = 0$ 17. $x^2 - 10x + 49 = 0$ 19–21. Methods may vary.

19. $-\dfrac{b}{a} = -\dfrac{-6}{1} = 6$ and $\dfrac{c}{a} = \dfrac{58}{1} = 58$; $(3 + 7i) + (3 - 7i) = 6 = -\dfrac{b}{a}$ and $(3 + 7i)(3 - 7i) =$

$9 + 49 = 58 = \dfrac{c}{a}$ 21. $-\dfrac{b}{a} = -\dfrac{2}{1} = -2$ and $\dfrac{c}{a} = \dfrac{4}{1} = 4$; $(-1 + i\sqrt{3}) + (-1 - i\sqrt{3}) =$

$-2 = -\dfrac{b}{a}$ and $(-1 + i\sqrt{3})(-1 - i\sqrt{3}) = 1 + 3 = 4 = \dfrac{c}{a}$ 23. $9x^2 + 30x + 23 = 0$

25. $8x^2 - 28x + 47 = 0$ 27. $r_2 = -12$; $k = 8$ 29. $r_2 = \dfrac{5}{2}$; $k = -3$

31. $r_2 = \dfrac{5}{2}$; $k = 15$ 33. $r_2 = -\dfrac{1}{2}$; $k = 4$ 35. $r_2 = -2$; $k = 6$ 37. $k = 6$ or $k = -6$

39. $r_1 + r_2 = \dfrac{-b + \sqrt{b^2 - 4ac}}{2a} + \dfrac{-b - \sqrt{b^2 - 4ac}}{2a} = \dfrac{-2b}{2a} = -\dfrac{b}{a}$;

$r_1 r_2 = \dfrac{-b + \sqrt{b^2 - 4ac}}{2a} \cdot \dfrac{-b - \sqrt{b^2 - 4ac}}{2a} = \dfrac{b^2 - (b^2 - 4ac)}{4a^2} = \dfrac{4ac}{4a^2} = \dfrac{c}{a}$

PAGE 127 · CHAPTER REVIEW   1. $3\sqrt{7}$ 2. $2a^2 b^3 \sqrt{5a}$ 3. $\dfrac{2}{xy}$ 4. $9\sqrt{6}$

5. $14 - 42\sqrt{2}$ 6. $12 + 10\sqrt{3}$ 7. $61 - 28\sqrt{3}$ 8. $\dfrac{2 + 5\sqrt{2}}{23}$ 9. $\{14\}$

10. $\{1\}$ 11. $3i\sqrt{11}$ 12. $-8i\sqrt{14}$ 13. $\dfrac{2i\sqrt{2}}{3}$ 14. $60\sqrt{2}$ 15. $-\dfrac{5i\sqrt{6}}{6}$

16. 1   17. $\{\pm 2i\sqrt{13}\}$ 18. $23i\sqrt{7}$ 19. $8 + i\sqrt{7}$ 20. $x = 0,\ y = -\dfrac{1}{2}$

21. $\dfrac{1}{5} + \dfrac{\sqrt{6}}{15}i$ 22. $-\dfrac{2}{5} - \dfrac{19}{5}i$ 23. 0; 1 real double (rational) root   24. 48; 2 real (irrational) roots   25. -139; 2 imaginary conjugate roots   26. $\{1 \pm i\sqrt{7}\}$

27. $k = \dfrac{25}{4}$ 28. $x^2 + 49 = 0$ 29. $x^2 - 6x - 11 = 0$ 30. Methods may vary.

$(3 - 5i) + (3 + 5i) = 6 = -\dfrac{b}{a}$ and $(3 - 5i)(3 + 5i) = 9 + 25 = 34 = \dfrac{c}{a}$

PAGES 130–131 · MIXED REVIEW

1. 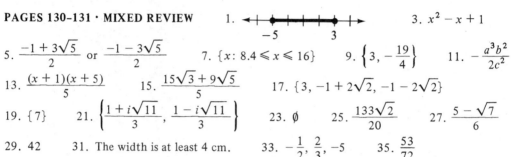   3. $x^2 - x + 1$

5. $\dfrac{-1 + 3\sqrt{5}}{2}$ or $\dfrac{-1 - 3\sqrt{5}}{2}$ 7. $\{x: 8.4 \leqslant x \leqslant 16\}$ 9. $\left\{3, -\dfrac{19}{4}\right\}$ 11. $-\dfrac{a^3 b^2}{2c^2}$

13. $\dfrac{(x + 1)(x + 5)}{5}$ 15. $\dfrac{15\sqrt{3} + 9\sqrt{5}}{5}$ 17. $\{3, -1 + 2\sqrt{2}, -1 - 2\sqrt{2}\}$

19. $\{7\}$ 21. $\left\{\dfrac{1 + i\sqrt{11}}{3}, \dfrac{1 - i\sqrt{11}}{3}\right\}$ 23. $\varnothing$ 25. $\dfrac{133\sqrt{2}}{20}$ 27. $\dfrac{5 - \sqrt{7}}{6}$

29. 42   31. The width is at least 4 cm.   33. $-\dfrac{1}{2}, \dfrac{2}{3}, -5$ 35. $\dfrac{53}{72}$

37. 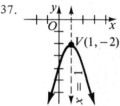   Since $b^2 - 4ac = -16 < 0$, there are no x-intercepts.

39.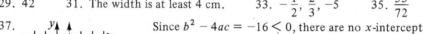

41. $\dfrac{30y^2 - 11y + 5xy^2}{5}$ 43. $\{\pm 10i\}$ 45. $1 - 10i$

47. $-17 + 34i$ 49. $-\dfrac{5}{2};\ k = 4$ 51. 2 km/h

PAGES 137–138

1. $\{x: x \geqslant 7\}$; 3   3. $\{x: x \neq 0\}$; $\dfrac{1}{4}$ 5. $\{$real numbers$\}$; $\sqrt{257}$

7. $\{$real numbers$\}$; 0   9. For any nonzero value of x, there are two values for y; for example, when $x = -5$, $y = \pm 5$.   11. For every value of x, there are two values for y, $\sqrt{x^2 + 9}$ and $-\sqrt{x^2 + 9}$.   13. a. 4   b. 0   c. 2   d. $\dfrac{5}{2}$ 15. a. not defined   b. $-\dfrac{1}{4}$ c. $-\dfrac{1}{2}$

d. $-\dfrac{2}{3}$ 17. a. 11   b. -5 c. -1 d. 2   19. $\dfrac{3}{4}$ 21. 2   23. 72

25. $\{x: x \neq 0\}$ 27. $\{a: 0 \leqslant a < 4$ or $a > 4\}$ 29. $\{$real numbers$\}$ 31. $\{$real numbers$\}$

33. a. $(-3, 1)$ b. $(-6, 3)$ c. $(-1, 5)$ 35. a. $(2, 0)$ b. $(-4, 4)$ c. $(6, 8)$

PAGE 141

1. yes; $\{0, 1, 2, 3, 4\}$; $\{-1, 2, 3\}$

3. no

5. no

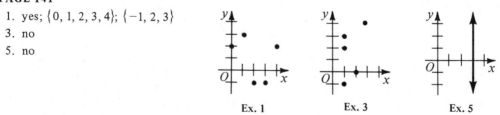

Ex. 1   Ex. 3   Ex. 5

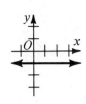

Ex. 7

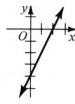

Ex. 9

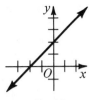

Ex. 11

7. yes; $\mathfrak{R}$; $\langle-1\rangle$ 9. yes; $\mathfrak{R}$; $\mathfrak{R}$ 11. yes; $\mathfrak{R}$; $\mathfrak{R}$

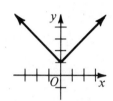

Ex. 13

Ex. 15

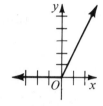

Ex. 17

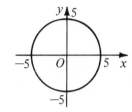

Ex. 19

13. yes; $\mathfrak{R}$; $\langle y: y \geqslant 1\rangle$ 15. no   17. yes; $\mathfrak{R}$; $\langle y: y \geqslant 0\rangle$ 19. no   21. yes;
$\langle x: -4 \leqslant x \leqslant 4\rangle$; $\langle y: 0 \leqslant y \leqslant 4\rangle$ 23. no   25. yes; $\mathfrak{R}$; $\langle$the integers$\rangle$

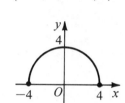

Ex. 21

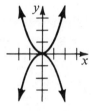

Ex. 23

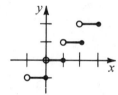

Ex. 25

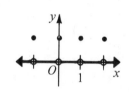

Ex. 27

27. yes; $\mathfrak{R}$; $\langle 0, 1\rangle$

29. See figure at right; $\langle x: x \geqslant 0\rangle$; $\langle y: y = 20 + 17k$
   where k is a nonnegative integer$\rangle$

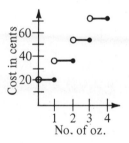

PAGES 144–145   1. 0; 0; -6; $-x - |x|$; neither   3. 1; 267;
-267; $-x^5 - x^3 + x$; odd   5. 2; $9\frac{1}{9}$; $9\frac{1}{9}$; $x^2 + \frac{1}{x^2}$; even

7. 0; 2; 4; $|-x - 1|$; neither   9. 1; 27; 27; $|x^3|$; even
11. $\sqrt{2}$; $3\sqrt{2}$; $3\sqrt{2}$; $\sqrt{2x^2}$; even   13. $f(x) = 2x - 3$

15. $h(x) = \frac{3}{2}x - 1$ 17. $f(x) = \frac{5}{9}x - \frac{160}{9}$ 19. See figure.

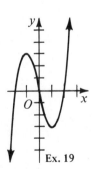

Ex. 19

21. See figure.   23. $f(-x) = -f(x)$; $m(-x) + b = -(mx + b)$;
$-mx + b = -mx - b$; $b = -b$; $2b = 0$; $b = 0$ 25. $g(0 + 0) =$
$g(0) + g(0)$; $g(0) = g(0) + g(0)$; $0 = g(0)$ 27. $g\!\left(\dfrac{1}{2} + \dfrac{1}{2}\right) =$

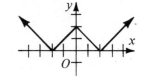

$g\!\left(\dfrac{1}{2}\right) + g\!\left(\dfrac{1}{2}\right)$; $g(1) = 2 \cdot g\!\left(\dfrac{1}{2}\right)$; $g\!\left(\dfrac{1}{2}\right) = \dfrac{1}{2}g(1)$ 29. a. $g(0) =$
$-1 = -g(2)$ b. $g(-1) = -8 = -g(3)$ c. $g(-2) = -27 = -g(4)$
d. The graph is symmetric with respect to the point $(1, 0)$.

Ex. 21

31. $f(2 - k) = \dfrac{1}{[(2 - k) - 2]^2} = \dfrac{1}{(-k)^2} = \dfrac{1}{k^2}$; $f(2 + k) =$

$\dfrac{1}{[(2 + k) - 2]^2} = \dfrac{1}{k^2} = f(2 - k)$; the graph is symmetric with respect to the line $x = 2$.

PAGES 149–150   1. $1\dfrac{2}{3}$, or 1.7   3. $4\dfrac{5}{9}$, or 4.6   5–8. Approximations may vary.

5. 34.4   7. 3.8   9. $\dfrac{d}{(7m + k) - (4m + k)} = \dfrac{5 - 4}{7 - 4}$; $\dfrac{d}{3m} = \dfrac{1}{3}$; $d = \dfrac{3m}{3} = m$ and
$f(5) = (4m + k) + m = 5m + k = f(5)$ 11. 0.8603   13. 0.8680   15. 7.13
17. 7.84   19. 7.67   21. 7.47   23. Larger; the line through $(2, 4)$ and $(4, 16)$ is
much steeper than the more gradual curve of the graph of $y = x^2$.   25. $\triangle PST \sim \triangle PQR$;
$\dfrac{ST}{QR} = \dfrac{PT}{PR}$; $\dfrac{f(b) - f(a)}{y_c - f(a)} = \dfrac{b - a}{c - a}$ 27. $\sqrt{10} = \sqrt{4} + \dfrac{6}{5}(1) = 3.2$

PAGE 152   1. 5   3. 4   5. 5   7. 4   9. $x - 2$ 11. $\sqrt{x - 2}$
13. $x\sqrt{x} + 8$ 15. $\dfrac{1}{x^3 + 8}$ 17. $g(h(x)) = g\!\left(\dfrac{1}{2}(x - 3)\right) = 2\!\left[\dfrac{1}{2}(x - 3)\right] + 3 =$
$x - 3 + 3 = x$; $h(g(x)) = h(2x + 3) = \dfrac{1}{2}((2x + 3) - 3) = \dfrac{1}{2}(2x) = x$ 19. $g(h(x)) =$
$g\!\left(\dfrac{1}{x} + 2\right) = \dfrac{1}{\left(\dfrac{1}{x} + 2\right) - 2} = \dfrac{1}{\dfrac{1}{x}} = x$; $h(g(x)) = h\!\left(\dfrac{1}{x - 2}\right) = \dfrac{1}{\left(\dfrac{1}{x - 2}\right)} + 2 = x - 2 + 2 = x$
21. $g(h(x)) = g(\sqrt{x - 4}) = (\sqrt{x - 4})^2 + 4 = x - 4 + 4 = x$; $h(g(x)) = h(x^2 + 4) =$
$\sqrt{(x^2 + 4) - 4} = \sqrt{x^2} = x$ when $x \geqslant 0$ 23. $h(x) = \dfrac{x + 3}{4}$; $[g \circ h](x) = g\!\left(\dfrac{x + 3}{4}\right) =$
$4\!\left(\dfrac{x + 3}{4}\right) - 3 = x + 3 - 3 = x$ 25. $h(x) = 3 - \dfrac{2}{x}$; $[g \circ h](x) = g\!\left(3 - \dfrac{2}{x}\right) =$
$\dfrac{2}{3 - \left(3 - \dfrac{2}{x}\right)} = \dfrac{2}{\dfrac{2}{x}} = 2 \cdot \dfrac{x}{2} = x$ 27. a. $\{x : x \neq 0\}$ b. $\{x : x \neq -3\}$
29. a. $\{x : x \geqslant 4\}$ b. $\{x : x \geqslant 0\}$

PAGES 157–158   1. $f^{-1}(x) = -\dfrac{1}{5}x$ 3. $h^{-1}(x) = \dfrac{x + 7}{5}$ 5. $y = \dfrac{x + 1}{4x}$

7. $y = \sqrt[3]{\dfrac{x - 9}{2}} = \dfrac{1}{2}\sqrt[3]{4x - 36}$ 9. $f^{-1}(x) = x^3 + 2$ 11. $f^{-1}(x) = \sqrt[4]{x - 1}$
13. $f(f(x)) = f(-x) = -(-x) = x$ 15. $f(f(x)) = f(\sqrt[3]{1 - x^3}) = \sqrt[3]{1 - (\sqrt[3]{1 - x^3})^3} =$
$\sqrt[3]{1 - (1 - x^3)} = \sqrt[3]{x^3} = x$ 17. $g^{-1}(x) = 2\sqrt{x^2 - 4}$, $x \geqslant 2$

720   SELECTED ANSWERS

19.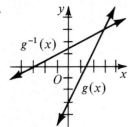

21.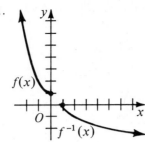

23.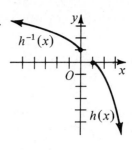

27. If $f(x_1) = f(x_2)$, then $mx_1 + b = mx_2 + b$, $mx_1 = mx_2$, and $x_1 = x_2$. By definition, f is a one-to-one function.

25.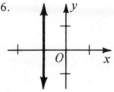

29.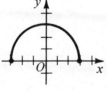

$f^{-1}(x) = 2 + \sqrt{x+1}$, $x \geqslant -1$; $f(f^{-1}(x)) = f(2 + \sqrt{x+1}) = (2 + \sqrt{x+1})^2 - 4(2 + \sqrt{x+1}) + 3 = 4 + x + 1 - 8 + 3 = x$; $f^{-1}(f(x)) = f^{-1}(x^2 - 4x + 3) = 2 + \sqrt{x^2 - 4x + 3 + 1} = 2 + \sqrt{(x-2)^2} = 2 + x - 2 = x$

PAGES 160–161 · CHAPTER REVIEW   1. $\{x: x \neq 1\}$; $-\frac{1}{3}$; $\frac{1}{2}$ 2. $\mathcal{R}$; -2; -3

3. $\{x: x \geqslant 2 \text{ or } x \leqslant -2\}$; 0; $\sqrt{5}$ 4. $k = -3$

5.   6.   7.

yes; $\{-2, 0, 1, 2, 3\}$;   no   yes; $\{x: -3 \leqslant x \leqslant 3\}$;
$\{-1, 1, 2, 4\}$ $\{y: 0 \leqslant y \leqslant 3\}$

8. $1\frac{1}{3}$; $\frac{2}{3}$; $1 - \frac{1}{x}$; neither   9. 30; 30; $|x^3 + x|$; even

10. $g(x) = -\frac{4}{3}x + \frac{2}{3}$ 11. 7.3 12. 5.08

13. a. $\sqrt{26}$ b. $3\sqrt{3} - 1$ c. $\sqrt{x^3 - 1}$ d. $x\sqrt{x} - 1$

14. a. 11 b. 25 c. $2 + x^2$ d. $(2 + x)^2 = 4 + 4x + x^2$

15. $\{(2, 1), (4, 3), (5, -1)\}$ 16. $y = \dfrac{x + 5}{4}$

17. $h^{-1}(x) = \sqrt[3]{4x - 2}$ 18. See figure.

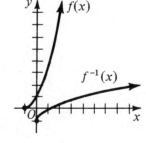

1. a   2. c   3. b
4. b   5. b   6. a   7. c   8. d   9. b   10. a   11. c   12. b
13. d   14. a   15. c   16. d   17. a   18. b   19. b   20. d
21. a   22. c   23. b   24. b   25. a   26. d   27. a   28. b
29. a   30. d   31. c   32. b   33. a

PAGES 166–167 · MIXED REVIEW   1. 3.3   3. $\left\{\dfrac{3 \pm 2\sqrt{3}}{3}\right\}$ 5. $\{\pm 5i\}$

7. a. -3 b. $\sqrt{3}$ c. $f(g(x)) = -2 - x$ 9. $\{-4\}$ 11. a. yes   b. no   c. $\mathbb{R}$
d. $\{y : y \geqslant 0\}$ e. See figure at right.   f. 3   13. $-i$

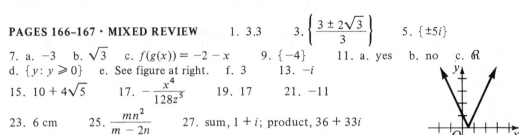

15. $10 + 4\sqrt{5}$ 17. $-\dfrac{x^4}{128z^5}$ 19. 17   21. -11

23. 6 cm   25. $\dfrac{mn^2}{m - 2n}$ 27. sum, $1 + i$; product, $36 + 33i$

29. $g^{-1}(x) = \dfrac{1 + 3x}{x}$; $[g \circ g^{-1}](x) = g(g^{-1}(x)) = \dfrac{1}{\dfrac{1 + 3x}{x} - 3} = \dfrac{x}{1 + 3x - 3x} = x$;

$[g^{-1} \circ g](x) = g^{-1}(g(x)) = \dfrac{1 + 3\left(\dfrac{1}{x - 3}\right)}{\dfrac{1}{x - 3}} = \dfrac{(x - 3) + 3}{1} = x$ 31. $\varnothing$ 33. 45 and 60

35. Methods may vary. $(-2 - i\sqrt{3})^2 + 4(-2 - i\sqrt{3}) + 7 = 0$; $4 + 4i\sqrt{3} + i^2(3) - 8 - 4i\sqrt{3} + 7 = 0$; $4 + 4i\sqrt{3} - 3 - 1 - 4i\sqrt{3} = 0$; $0 = 0$; $-2 + i\sqrt{3}$

37. Infinitely many vertical lines intersect the graph twice, so the relation is not a function.

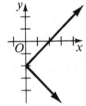

PAGES 173–174   1. $A'(6, 0)$, $B'(-2, -4)$, $C'(-2, 4)$ 3. $A'(0, 18)$, $B'(-12, -6)$, $C'(12, -6)$ 5. $A'(-2, 8)$, $B'(-6, 0)$, $C'(2, 0)$ 7. $A'(0, 12)$, $B'(4, -4)$, $C'(-4, -4)$
9. $A'(0, 6)$, $B'(-64, -2)$, $C'(64, -2)$ 11. $(1, -3)$ 13. $\left(-1, \dfrac{1}{3}\right)$ 15. $(-1, -1)$
17. $\left(3, \dfrac{1}{2}\right)$ 19. $(\sqrt[3]{-3}, 1)$ 21. a. $(-2, 4)$ b. $S \circ T : (x, y) \longrightarrow (y + 2, x - 2)$
23. a. $(6, -4)$ b. $S \circ T : (x, y) \longrightarrow (x, y)$ 25. a. $(-65, 217)$
b. $S \circ T : (x, y) \longrightarrow (y^3 - 1, x^3 + 1)$ 31. $A'(-2, -1)$, $B'(-4, 5)$; slopes are opposites.
33. $A'(4, -2)$, $B'(8, 10)$; slopes are equal.   35. T_1 is an isometry.   37. T_3 is not an isometry.

PAGES 178–179   1. Use the construction on p. 175 to construct collinear points U', V', and X'; $W = W'$.   3. a. $(0, 7)$ b. $(0, -7)$ 5. a. $(4, -3)$ b. $(-4, 3)$
7. a. $(-6, 1)$ b. $(6, -1)$ 9. $(0, -2)$ 11. $(-4, 3)$ 13. $(0, 2)$ 15. $(4, -3)$
17. $(-y, -x)$ 19. $A'(2, 1)$; $B'(4, 8)$; $C'(-2, 9)$; $D'(0, 3)$ 21. $A'(-6, 5)$;
$B'(-8, -2)$; $C'(-2, -3)$; $D'(-4, 3)$

23. $A'(3, 4)$; $B'(-4, 6)$; $C'(-5, 0)$; $D'(1, 2)$

25. $A'(-3, 0)$, $B'(4, -2)$, $C'(5, 4)$, $D'(-1, 2)$

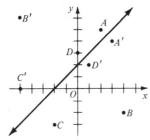

Ex. 23

Ex. 25

27. $(x, 6 - y)$ 29. $(-4 - x, y)$ 31. $x = 4$ 33. $y = x$ 35. $y = 0$

37. $y = x + 1$ 39. $AB' = 10$ 41. 100 m from the shorter tower.

PAGES 183–184

1.    3.   5.   11.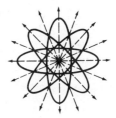

7. None   9. None   13. an isosceles triangle that is not equilateral   15. a square

17. an isosceles trapezoid   19. an isosceles triangle   21. an isosceles triangle

23. B, C, D, E, H, I, K, O, X   25. F, G, J, L, N, P, Q, R, S, Z

27. $x = 0$ 29. $y = 0$ 31. $x = -3$ 33. $y = -6$

 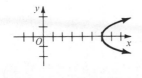 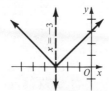

35. $y = 0$ 37. $x = \dfrac{3}{2}$ 39. $x = \dfrac{3}{2}$ 41. $y = 2$

 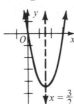 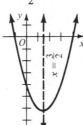

PAGES 186–188   9. 30   11. 60   13. 62   15. B 17. C 19. $\overline{BA}$

21. $\angle BCD$ 23. $\overleftrightarrow{AC}$ 25. V 27. Y 29. X 31. $\overline{VZ}$ 33. $\overline{ZY}$

35. $\overline{YX}$ 37. $\angle WVZ$ 39. $\angle Z$ 41. $\angle W$ 43. $(3, -4)$ 45. $(3, 1)$

47. $m' = 2$ 49. $m' = \frac{1}{2}$ 51. $m' = -2$ 53. $m' = -\frac{1}{2}$

  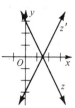 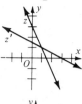

55. The slopes are opposites.   57. The slopes are reciprocals.

59. $y = -4x - 1$ 61. $y = \frac{1}{3}x - \frac{2}{3}$ 63. $y = x - 2$

65. a. $x = 3y + 2$ b. $x = y + 2$ c. inverse   d. See figure at right.

PAGES 191-192

1. $r_m \circ r_n: A \longrightarrow A_1''$
   $r_n \circ r_m: A \longrightarrow A_2''$

3. $r_m \circ r_n: C \longrightarrow C_1''$
   $r_n \circ r_m: C \longrightarrow C_2''$

5. Ex. 2

7.

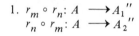

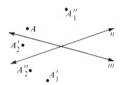 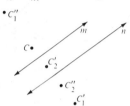 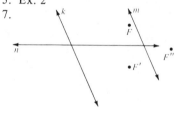

9.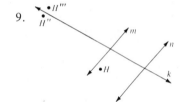

11. Y 13. X 15. $\overline{WV}$ 17. $\angle WXY$
19. W 21. Y 23. W 25. $A''(0, -1)$,
$B''(-4, -4)$, $C''(-5, 0)$ 27. $A''(1, 0)$, $B''(4, -4)$,
$C''(0, -5)$ 29. $A''(1, 0)$, $B''(4, -4)$, $C''(0, -5)$
31. $D''(1, 7)$, $E''(4, 6)$, $F''(4, 2)$, $G''(-2, 3)$
33. $D''(-1, -7)$, $E''(-4, -6)$, $F''(-4, -2)$, $G''(2, -3)$
35. $D''(9, 3)$, $E''(12, 2)$, $F''(12, -2)$, $G''(6, -1)$
37. $D''(-3, -7)$, $E''(-2, -4)$, $F''(2, -4)$, $G''(1, -10)$
39. $A'''(-1, 0)$, $B'''(-4, -4)$, $C'''(0, -5)$ 41. $A'''(1, 0)$, $B'''(4, 4)$, $C'''(0, 5)$ 43. $A'''(-1, 0)$,
$B'''(-4, -4)$, $C'''(0, -5)$ 45. $D'''(-5, 1)$, $E'''(-6, 4)$, $F'''(-10, 4)$, $G'''(-9, -2)$
47. $D'''(-7, -3)$, $E'''(-4, -2)$, $F'''(-4, 2)$, $G'''(-10, 1)$ 49. $D'''(9, -7)$, $E'''(12, -6)$,
$F'''(12, -2)$, $G'''(6, -3)$ 51. $D'''(7, -1)$, $E'''(4, -2)$, $F'''(4, -6)$, $G'''(10, -5)$
53. $D'''(9, -7)$, $E'''(12, -6)$, $F'''(12, -2)$, $G'''(6, -3)$ 55. $D'''(3, -11)$, $E'''(2, -8)$,
$F'''(-2, -8)$, $G'''(-1, -14)$

PAGES 195-196

1. 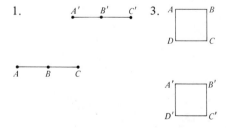   3. 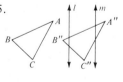   5. 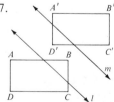   7.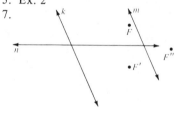

9. $A'(1, 7)$, $B'(5, 5)$, $C'(1, 5)$ 11. $A'(-1, 5)$, $B'(3, 3)$, $C'(-1, 3)$ 13. $A'(4, 4)$,
$B'(8, 2)$, $C'(4, 2)$ 15. $A'(-5, 8)$, $B'(-1, 6)$, $C'(-5, 6)$ 17. $T_{0, 2}$ 19. $T_{3, -2}$
21. $T_{-8, 3}$ 23. $(5, 3)$ 25. $(4, 0)$ 27. $(-2, -4)$ 29. $(-5, 9)$ 31. $(-6, 0)$
33. $(1, -5)$ 35. $(2, -6)$ 37. $(1, 2)$
39. $T_{0, 3}$ 41. $T_{0, -2}$

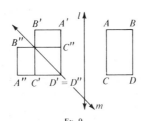

43. a. $E''(5, 2)$, $F''(8, 5)$, $G''(10, 3)$ b. $E''(5, 2)$,
$F''(8, 5)$, $G''(10, 3)$ c. $E''(5, 2)$, $F''(8, 5)$, $G''(10, 3)$
d. $E''(-3, 2)$, $F''(0, 5)$, $G''(2, 3)$ e. $E''(-3, 2)$, $F''(0, 5)$,
$G''(2, 3)$ f. $E''(-3, 2)$, $F''(0, 5)$, $G''(2, 3)$
g. parts (a)–(c): $T_{4, 0}$; parts (d)–(f): $T_{-4, 0}$
45. a. $y = -\dfrac{5}{2}$ b. $y = \dfrac{5}{2}$ 47. $A''(-1, 2)$, $B''(1, -1)$,
$C''(-3, -3)$

PAGES 200–202   1. $(-2, 3)$ 3. $(-6, -5)$ 5. $(-4, -5)$ 7, 9. See diagrams
below.   11. T 13. L 15. D 17. $15, -345$ 19. $90, -270$ 21. 240,
-120 23. J 25. D 27. N 29. $\overline{IJ}$ 31. $\overline{QM}$ 33. $\angle UPV$

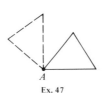

Ex. 7   Ex. 9   Ex. 47   Ex. 49

35. Square $ZFLT$ 37. D 39. C 41. D   43. a. $(0, 4)$ b. $(4, 0)$ c. $(0, -4)$
45. a. $(4, -2)$ b. $(-2, -4)$ c. $(-4, 2)$ 47, 49. See diagrams above.
53. *Hint*: Let $A' = r_m(A)$. Since line m is the perpendicular bisector of $\overline{AA'}$, $\angle ACB \cong \angle BCA'$
(corr. parts of $\triangle$ that are $\cong$ by SAS).

PAGES 206–207   1. line symm. about the $\perp$ bis. of the base   3. pt. symm. $(180°$ rotational symmetry) about the intersection of the diagonals   5. 5 lines of symm. formed by
joining opposite vertices, 5 lines of symm. formed by joining the midpts. of opposite sides, pt.
symm. about the intersection of the lines of symm., and rotational symmetries about the same pt.
of $36°$, $72°$, $108°$, $144°$, $180°$, $216°$, $252°$, $288°$, and $324°$.   7. line symm. about each
diameter, pt. symm. about the center, rotational symm. (through any angle) about the center
9. $(3, 4)$ 11. $(-2, -1)$ 13. $(-5, -2)$ 15. $(4, 2)$ 17. $(4, 6)$ 19. $(1, 8)$
21.

23. $A \longrightarrow D$, $B \longrightarrow C$, $C \longrightarrow B$, $D \longrightarrow A$ 25. $A \longrightarrow C$,
$B \longrightarrow D$, $C \longrightarrow A$, $D \longrightarrow B$ 27. $R_{P, 180}$ 29. r_m 30. r_m
31. a. $(2, -2)$ b. $x = 2$, $y = -2$, $y = -x$, $x - y = 4$
33. $A \longrightarrow B$, $B \longrightarrow A$, $C \longrightarrow C$ 35. $A \longrightarrow A$, $B \longrightarrow C$,
$C \longrightarrow B$ 37. $A \longrightarrow B$, $B \longrightarrow C$, $C \longrightarrow A$ 39. $R_{P, 120}$
41. r_n 43. r_m 45. $R_{P, 360}$ 49. $A'''(6, 4)$, $B'''(5, 1)$,
$C'''(1, 7)$

PAGES 210–212   1. $(8, 12)$ 3. $(-4, 2)$ 5. 2   7. 22   9. 3   11. $\dfrac{1}{3}$

13. 2   15. D_4 17. D_3 19. $D_{\frac{1}{2}}$ 21. $(4, 2)$ 23. $(-3, 2)$

25. 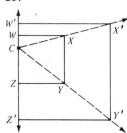 27. 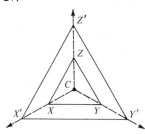 29. 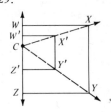 31.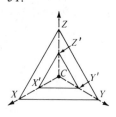

33. $A'(3, 3)$, $B'(12, -3)$, $C'(15, 3)$ 35. $E'(-5, 9)$, $F'(3, 1)$, $G'(-5, -5)$ 37. $(5, 1)$; 4
39. On $\overrightarrow{A'A}$ construct point C so that $A'C = 2 \cdot A'A$
(thus $CA' = 2 \cdot CA$). On $\overrightarrow{CB}$ construct point B' so that
$CB' = 2 \cdot CB$.   43. $y = 2x$ 45. $y = 1$
47. $y = 2x - 6$ 49. a. $y = mx$ b. $y = kc$ c. $x = kd$
51. $A''(1, 0)$, $B''(-1, -2)$, $C''(-3, -1)$
53. $A'''(-6, 6)$, $B'''(-4, 0)$, $C'''(0, 2)$

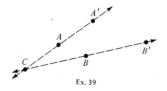

Ex. 39

55. a. 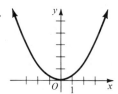   b.   c. $y = \frac{1}{3}x^2$, $y = -2x^2$

d. $y = \dfrac{ax^2}{k}$

PAGES 214–215 · CHAPTER REVIEW   1. $A'(2, 2)$, $B'(-3, 8)$, $C'(-5, -4)$ 2. $A''(3, 1)$,
$B''(9, -4)$, $C''(-3, -6)$ 3. $(-3, -1)$ 4. $(3, 1)$ 5. $(1, -3)$ 6. $(-1, 3)$
7. a. E, H, I, O   b. A, H, I, O   8. E 9. $\angle C$ 10. D 11. B 12. $(5, 2)$
13. $T_{7, -3}$ 14. $(4, 2)$ 15. $(7, -1)$ 16. $(4, 3)$ 17. $(-3, 2)$ 18. R_{-90} and
R_{270} are equivalent.   19. line symm. about the $\perp$ bisectors of the sides, point symm. about
the intersection, X, of the diagonals, and rotational symm., $R_{X, 180}$ 20. $(4, 0)$
21. $(-6, 12)$ 22. $A'(-3, 4)$, $B'(5, 6)$, $C'(1, -2)$ 23. preservation of distances

PAGES 218–219 · MIXED REVIEW   1. a. $\dfrac{1}{15}$ b. $\dfrac{1}{162}$ c. $\dfrac{1}{x^2 - 1}$ d. $\dfrac{1}{2(2x - 1)^2}$
3. 4 lines of symm. formed by joining opposite vertices, 4 lines of symm. formed by joining the
midpts. of opposite sides, and rotational symmetries about O of $45°, 90°, 135°, 180°$ (pt. symm.),
$225°, 270°,$ and $315°$ 5. $5\sqrt[4]{3}$ 7. $21 + 6\sqrt{6}$ 9. C 11. D 13. O

15. yes, about point O 17. $\{2\}$ 19. $-2, \dfrac{5}{6},$ and $\dfrac{1}{3}$

21. a. $\{x: -2 \leqslant x \leqslant 2\}$; $\{y: -2 \leqslant y \leqslant 2\}$ b. See figure at right.
c. There are infinitely many vertical lines that intersect the graph
in two points, so the relation is not a function.   23. $\left\{ \pm \dfrac{3}{5}i \right\}$

25. $(-4, -2)$ 27. $(-4, 2)$ 29. $(12, -6)$

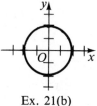

Ex. 21(b)

31. See figure at right.　　　33. 8.2　　　35. $\{0, 2\}$

37. $f(f(x)) = x$; $f^{-1}(x) = f(x)$　　　39. $\dfrac{2}{m}$　　　41. a. S is neither;

T is a direct isometry.　　b. $(-9, 5)$; $(5, 13)$　　　43. -30
45. $x = -3$, $y = -8$

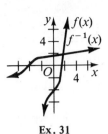

Ex. 31

PAGES 225–226　　　1. radius　　　3. chord　　　5. tangent　　　7. central angle
9. semicircle　　　11. major arc　　　13. $m\,\overset{\frown}{BC} = m\,\overset{\frown}{AD} = 105$; $m\,\overset{\frown}{AC} = m\,\overset{\frown}{BD} = 75$
15. a. 20　b. 60　c. 180　d. 60　e. 120　f. 100　g. 200　h. 300　i. 260
17. $x = 40$, $y = z = 140$　　　19. $x = 33$, $y = z = 66$　　　21. $x = 75$, $y = 15$, $z = 90$
23. $x = 90$, $y = z = 45$　　　25. $m\angle AOE = 72$, $m\angle EOB = 108$　　　27. $m\angle XOZ = 72$,

$m\angle Y = 36$, $m\,\overset{\frown}{XZ} = 72$; $m\angle Y = \dfrac{1}{2}\,m\,\overset{\frown}{XZ}$

PAGES 230–232　　　1. 30　　　3. 22.5　　　5. $2x$　　　7. 32　　　9. 172　　　11. $8x$
13. $x = 35$, $y = 90$, $z = 55$　　　15. $x = 50$, $y = 20$, $z = 140$　　　17. $x = y = 27$
19. $w = 77$, $x = 63$, $y = 103$, $z = 117$　　　21. $x = 56$, $y = 28$, $z = 55$　　　23. $m\angle B = 36$,
$m\angle D = 144$　　　25. 1:2　　　27. $w = 120$, $x = 64$, $y = 128$, $z = 105$　　　29. $v = w = 29$,
$x = 58$, $y = z = 61$　　　31. (1) Draw the diameter, BD, through B. (Two points determine

a line.);　　(2) $m\angle ABD = \dfrac{1}{2}\,m\,\overset{\frown}{AD}$; $m\angle DBC = \dfrac{1}{2}\,m\,\overset{\frown}{DC}$ (Case 1 of Thm. 6–1);　　(3) $m\angle ABD +$

$m\angle DBC = \dfrac{1}{2}\,m\,\overset{\frown}{AD} + \dfrac{1}{2}\,m\,\overset{\frown}{DC}$ (Add. Prop. of Eq.);　　(4) $m\angle ABD + m\angle DBC = m\angle ABC$

(Angle Add. Post.);　　(5) $m\angle ABC = \dfrac{1}{2}\,m\,\overset{\frown}{AD} + \dfrac{1}{2}\,m\,\overset{\frown}{DC}$ (Subst. Prop.);　　(6) $m\angle ABC =$

$\dfrac{1}{2}(m\,\overset{\frown}{AD} + m\,\overset{\frown}{DC})$ (Distrib. Prop.);　　(7) $m\,\overset{\frown}{AD} + m\,\overset{\frown}{DC} = m\,\overset{\frown}{AC}$ (Arc Add. Post.);

(8) $m\angle ABC = \dfrac{1}{2}\,m\,\overset{\frown}{AC}$ (Subst. Prop.)　　　33. $m\angle A = m\angle B = 55$, $m\angle C = m\angle D = 125$

35. Given: quadrilateral $ABCD$ inscribed in $\odot O$.　　Prove: $\angle A$ and $\angle C$ are supp.;　　$\angle B$ and $\angle D$
are supp.　　(1) $m\angle A = \dfrac{1}{2}\,m\,\overset{\frown}{BCD}$; $m\angle B = \dfrac{1}{2}\,m\,\overset{\frown}{CDA}$; $m\angle C = \dfrac{1}{2}\,m\,\overset{\frown}{BAD}$; $m\angle D = \dfrac{1}{2}\,m\,\overset{\frown}{ABC}$

(The measure of an inscribed $\angle$ is $\dfrac{1}{2}$ the measure of its intercepted arc.)　　(2) $m\angle A + m\angle C =$

$\dfrac{1}{2}\,m\,\overset{\frown}{BCD} + \dfrac{1}{2}\,m\,\overset{\frown}{BAD} = \dfrac{1}{2}(m\,\overset{\frown}{BCD} + m\,\overset{\frown}{BAD})$; $m\angle B + m\angle D = \dfrac{1}{2}\,m\,\overset{\frown}{CDA} + \dfrac{1}{2}\,m\,\overset{\frown}{ABC} =$

$\dfrac{1}{2}(m\,\overset{\frown}{CDA} + m\,\overset{\frown}{ABC})$ (Add. Prop. of Eq. and Distrib. Prop.);　　(3) $m\,\overset{\frown}{BCD} + m\,\overset{\frown}{BAD} = 360$;

$m\,\overset{\frown}{CDA} + m\,\overset{\frown}{ABC} = 360$ (The measure of an entire circle is 360.);　　(4) $m\angle A + m\angle C =$

$\dfrac{1}{2}(360) = 180$; $m\angle B + m\angle D = \dfrac{1}{2}(360) = 180$ (Subst. Prop.);　　(5) $\angle A$ and $\angle C$ are supp.;

$\angle B$ and $\angle D$ are supp. (Def. of supp. $\angle$s)　　　37. $m\angle DOE = m\,\overset{\frown}{DAE} = 360 - 2y$

PAGES 235–238　　　1. $x = 120$　　　3. $x = 85$, $y = 40$, $z = 55$　　　5. $x = 70$, $y = 70$,
$z = 70$　　　7. $x = y = 45$, $z = 90$　　　9. $x = 30$, $y = 60$, $z = 60$　　　11. $x = y = z = 60$
13. 13　　　15. 20　　　17. 98, 262　　　19. 30　　　21. 80　　　23. 43　　　25. 3
27. 86　　　29. $m\,\overset{\frown}{AB} = 106$, $m\,\overset{\frown}{BC} = 66$, $m\,\overset{\frown}{CD} = 76$, $m\,\overset{\frown}{DA} = 112$; thus, in quad. $ABCD$,
$m\angle A = 71$, $m\angle B = 94$, $m\angle C = 109$, $m\angle D = 86$.　　　31. (1) $\overline{NQ} \perp \overline{PQ}$ (Given);

(2) $\angle NQP$ is a rt. $\angle$. (Def. of $\perp$ lines and def. of rt. $\angle$);   (3) $\angle NPM$ is a rt. $\angle$. (An $\angle$ inscribed in a semicircle is a rt. $\angle$.);   (4) $\angle NQP \cong \angle NPM$ (All rt. $\angle$s are $\cong$.);   (5) $\overleftrightarrow{PQ}$ is tangent at P. (Given);   (6) $m\angle QPN = \frac{1}{2} m \overarc{PN}$ (The measure of an $\angle$ formed by a tangent and a chord is $\frac{1}{2}$ the measure of the intercepted arc.);   (7) $m\angle PMN = \frac{1}{2} m \overarc{PN}$ (The measure of an inscribed $\angle$ is $\frac{1}{2}$ the measure of its intercepted arc.);   (8) $m\angle QPN = m\angle PMN$; $\angle QPN \cong \angle PMN$ (Subst. Prop.);   (9) $\angle QNP \cong \angle PNM$ (If 2 $\angle$s of a $\triangle$ are $\cong$ to 2 $\angle$s of another $\triangle$, then the third $\angle$s are $\cong$.); (10) $\overleftrightarrow{PN}$ bisects $\angle MNQ$. (Def. of $\angle$ bisector)   33. 12

PAGES 242–243   1. $m\angle 1 = 20$ 3. $m\angle 3 = 50$ 5. $m\angle 5 = 40$ 7. $m\angle 7 = 90$
9. $m\angle 9 = 55$ 11. $x = 125$ 13. $x = 52$ 15. $x = 60$ 17. $x = 30$
19. $x = 223$ 21. 270 and 90   23. 80   25. $m\angle A = 120$, $m\angle B = 150$, $m\angle C = 60$,
$m\angle D = 30$ 27. a. 54   b. 36   c. 90   d. 98   29. $x = 17$ 31. 82 or 198
33. a. $m\angle K = 180 - x$ b. The measures are supplementary.   35. Given: $\overleftrightarrow{PC}$ is tangent to the circle at C; $\overleftrightarrow{PA}$ is a secant.   Prove: $m\angle P = \frac{1}{2} (m \overarc{AC} - m \overarc{BC})$.   (1) Draw $\overline{BC}$. (Two pts. determine a line.);   (2) $m\angle P + m\angle C = m\angle ABC$ (The measure of an ext. $\angle$ of a $\triangle$ is equal to the sum of the measures of the 2 remote int. $\angle$s of the $\triangle$.);   (3) $m\angle P = m\angle ABC - m\angle C$ (Subt. Prop. of Eq.);   (4) $m\angle ABC = \frac{1}{2} m \overarc{AC}$ (The measure of an inscribed $\angle$ is $\frac{1}{2}$ the measure of the intercepted arc.);   (5) $\overleftrightarrow{PC}$ is tangent at C. (Given);   (6) $m\angle C = \frac{1}{2} m \overarc{BC}$ (The measure of an $\angle$ formed by a tangent and a chord is $\frac{1}{2}$ the measure of the intercepted arc.);   (7) $m\angle P = \frac{1}{2} m \overarc{AC} - \frac{1}{2} m \overarc{BC}$ (Subst. Prop.);   (8) $m\angle P = \frac{1}{2} (m \overarc{AC} - m \overarc{BC})$ (Distrib. Prop.)   37. $y = 360 - 2x$

PAGES 248–250   1. $x = 16.5$ 3. $x = 4$, $y = 8$ 5. $x = 71$, $y = z = 109$ 7. 4
9. 2   11. 30   13. $\sqrt{58}$ 15. 5   17. 12   19. $3\sqrt{5}$ cm   21. $2\sqrt{33}$ cm
23. $x = 3$ or $x = -2$ 25. $x = 8$ 27. $PQ = 14$ and $RS = 11$, or $PQ = 15$ and $RS = 13$
29. (1) Draw $\overline{OR}$ and $\overline{OS}$. (Two pts. determine a line.);   (2) E is the midpt. of $\overline{RS}$. (Given);
(3) $\overline{RE} \cong \overline{SE}$ (Def. of midpt.);   (4) $\overline{OR} \cong \overline{OS}$ (All radii of a $\odot$ are $\cong$.);   (5) $\overline{OE} \cong \overline{OE}$ (Refl. Prop. of $\cong$);   (6) $\triangle OER \cong \triangle OES$ (SSS Post.);   (7) $\angle OER \cong \angle OES$ (Corr. parts of $\cong$ $\triangle$ are $\cong$.);   (8) $\overline{PQ} \perp \overline{RS}$ (If 2 lines form $\cong$ adj. $\angle$s, the lines are $\perp$.)   31. $4\sqrt{3}$ 33. Let $\overline{OP}$ and $\overline{AB}$ intersect at X. (1) $\overline{OA} \cong \overline{OB}$; $\overline{PA} \cong \overline{PB}$ (All radii of a $\odot$ are $\cong$.);   (2) $\overline{OP} \cong \overline{OP}$ (Refl. Prop. of $\cong$);   (3) $\triangle OAP \cong \triangle OBP$ (SSS Post.);   (4) $\angle AOP \cong \angle BOP$ (Corr. parts of $\cong$ $\triangle$ are $\cong$.);   (5) $\overline{OX} \cong \overline{OX}$ (Refl. Prop. of $\cong$);   (6) $\triangle AOX \cong \triangle BOX$ (SAS Post.);
(7) $\overline{AX} \cong \overline{BX}$; $\angle OXA \cong \angle OXB$ (Corr. parts of $\cong$ $\triangle$ are $\cong$.);   (8) $\overline{OP}$ bisects $\overline{AB}$. (Def. of midpt. and of bisects);   (9) $\overline{OP} \perp \overline{AB}$ (If 2 lines form $\cong$ adj. $\angle$s, the lines are $\perp$.);   (10) $\overline{OP}$ is the $\perp$ bis. of $\overline{AB}$. (Def. of $\perp$ bis.)   35. $12\sqrt{3}$ 37. $12(2 + \sqrt{3})$

PAGES 253–255   1. $x = 13$ 3. $x = 4\sqrt{3}$ 5. $x = 16$ 7. $x = 5$ 9. $x = 7$
11. 12   13. 2.5   15. 2.8   17. $4\sqrt{5}$ cm   19. $AF = 2$, $FE = 6$, $PA = 2\sqrt{15}$,
$PD = 4$, $DE = 11$ 21. (1) Draw $\overline{AD}$ and $\overline{AC}$. (Two pts. determine a line.);   (2) $\angle P \cong \angle P$ (Refl. Prop. of $\cong$);   (3) $m\angle D = \frac{1}{2} m \overarc{AC}$ (The measure of an inscribed $\angle$ is equal to $\frac{1}{2}$ the measure of its intercepted arc.);   (4) $\overleftrightarrow{PA}$ is a tangent. (Given);   (5) $m\angle PAC = \frac{1}{2} m \overarc{AC}$ (The measure of an $\angle$ formed by a tangent and a chord is $\frac{1}{2}$ the measure of the intercepted arc.);

(6) $\angle D \cong \angle PAC$ (Subst. Prop. and def. of $\cong \angle s$);   (7) $\triangle PAD \sim \triangle PCA$ (AA $\sim$ Thm.);
(8) $\dfrac{PA}{PC} = \dfrac{PD}{PA}$ (Lengths of corr. sides of $\sim \triangle$ are proportional.);   (9) $(PA)^2 = PC \cdot PD$ (A prop.
of proportions)   23. (1) $\overline{QS}$ and $\overline{QT}$ are tangents. (Given);   (2) $(QS)^2 = QX \cdot QY$;
$(QT)^2 = QX \cdot QY$ (If a tangent and a secant are drawn to a $\odot$ from an ext. pt., the tangent is the
geom. mean between the secant and the external segment of the secant);   (3) $(QS)^2 = (QT)^2$
(Subst. Prop.);   (4) $QS = QT$ (If $a \geqslant 0$, $b \geqslant 0$, and $a^2 = b^2$, then $a = b$.)   25. $AR = 5$,
$RB = BS = 2$, $SC = CT = 6$, $TA = 5$

PAGES 260–262   1. $C = 12\pi$; $A = 36\pi$ 3. $C = 2\pi\sqrt{11}$; $A = 11\pi$ 5. $C = 6.2\pi$;
$A = 9.61\pi$ 7. $C = 57$; $A = 254$ 9. $C = 10$; $A = 8$ 11. a. $\dfrac{3}{2}\pi$ b. $\dfrac{9}{2}\pi$

13. a. $\dfrac{11}{6}\pi$ b. $\dfrac{11}{4}\pi$ 15. 3   17. $6\sqrt{2}$ 19. 8   21. $4\sqrt{5}$ 23. 22π

25. 45   27. 25π 29. inscribed $\odot = 8\pi$; circumscribed $\odot = 8\pi\sqrt{2}$ 31. 5

33. 8π 35. $24\pi - 36\sqrt{3}$ 37. $50 - \dfrac{25}{2}\pi$ 39. $(4 - \pi)x^2$ 41. a. $32\pi - 64$

b. 8π 43. $A = \dfrac{C^2}{4\pi}$ 45. Grazing area: $\dfrac{3}{4}\pi(25)^2 + \dfrac{1}{4}\pi(15)^2 + \dfrac{1}{4}\pi(5)^2 = \dfrac{2125\pi}{4}$ m^2

PAGES 265–266   1. Use the construction on p. 262.   3. Use the construction at the
bottom of p. 263.   5. Construct the $\perp$ bisector of $\overline{XY}$, which intersects $\overparen{XY}$ at its midpoint, M.
7. Draw $\overrightarrow{AO}$ intersecting $\odot O$ at pt. B. Use the construction at the bottom of p. 263 to construct
the tangent, line m, to $\odot O$ at B. (In a plane, 2 lines $\perp$ to the same line are $\parallel$.)   9. By defini-
tion, $\overline{OP}$ is a radius of $\odot O$. By construction, $\overleftrightarrow{XY} \perp \overline{OP}$ at P. A line that lies in the plane of a $\odot$
and is $\perp$ to a radius at a pt. of the $\odot$ is tangent to the circle, so $\overleftrightarrow{XY}$ is tangent to $\odot O$ at P.
11. By construction, the radii and chords that form $\triangle s$ AOB, BOC, COD, DOE, EOF, and FOA
are $\cong$. Hence, each $\triangle$ is equilateral and the hexagon is equilateral. Also, each interior angle of
the hexagon is an inscribed angle that intercepts an arc of measure 240, so the $\angle s$ are $\cong$ and have
measure 120. By def., $ABCDEF$ is regular.
13. Choose a point A on circle O and construct point B as shown in the diagram. Use the
method of Oral Ex. 3 or Written Ex. 5 to locate M, such that $\overparen{AM} \cong \overparen{MB}$. With radius AM, locate
10 additional pts. on $\odot O$ to divide $\odot O$ into 12 $\cong$ arcs. Draw segments joining consecutive arc
endpts. to form an inscribed regular dodecagon.   15. Draw a $\odot$ with center O and any
diameter $\overline{XY}$. Construct diameter $\overline{AB}$ so that $\overline{AB} \perp \overline{XY}$. Then $\overparen{XA}$, $\overparen{AY}$, $\overparen{YB}$, and $\overparen{BX}$ are $\cong$.
Draw $\overline{XA}$, $\overline{AY}$, $\overline{YB}$, and $\overline{BX}$, the sides of square $XAYB$. (Each $\angle$ intercepts a semicircle, so each $\angle$
is a rt. $\angle$. Also, $\cong$ arcs have $\cong$ chords, so the sides are $\cong$.)   17. Divide a $\odot O$ into 4 $\cong$ arcs as
in Ex. 15. Use the construction at the bottom of p. 263 to construct tangents to $\odot O$ at X, A, Y,
and B. The 4 tangents intersect to form a circumscribed square. (The 4 small quadrilaterals are $\cong$
squares, so the large quadrilateral is also a square.)

PAGES 268–269 · CHAPTER REVIEW   1. tangent   2. minor arc   3. chord
4. radius   5. major arc   6. semicircle   7. external point   8. secant
9. diameter   10. 90   11. $\angle RPQ$ 12. 101   13. $PR = 6\sqrt{2}$, $SR = 6\sqrt{2} - 6$
14. 110   15. 26   16. 50   17. 102   18. $x = 16$ 19. $x = 15$
20. $x = 1$ 21. $x = 1$ 22. $4\sqrt{6}$ 23. 30π 24. Use the construction at the
bottom of p. 263.   25. Use the construction on p. 264.

PAGES 272-273 · MIXED REVIEW   1. $\dfrac{x^2y^2}{x^2+y^2}$ 3. $6+3i$ 5. 23 or 6

7. a. $\left\{x: -1 \leqslant x \leqslant \dfrac{7}{5}\right\}$ b. $\left\{y: y < 1 \text{ or } y \geq \dfrac{8}{3}\right\}$ 9. 26π cm   11. 84 km/h

13. a. 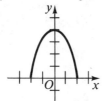   b. For every value of x in the domain, there is exactly one value of y in the range.   c. $\{x: -2 \leqslant x \leqslant 2\}$; $\{y: 0 \leqslant y \leqslant 4\}$
d. even   15. $(0, -6)$ 17. $(6, 3)$ 19. $(3, -6)$

21. $\dfrac{32}{3}$ 23. 4

25. a. $\{x: x < 3 \text{ or } x > 3\}$ b. $\{y: y \leqslant -4 \text{ or } y \geqslant -2\}$ 27. $16x^2 - 32x + 15 = 0$

29. $x^2 - 4x + 13 = 0$ 31. a. $\sqrt[4]{2}$ b. 3   c. $x^2 - 7$ d. $\sqrt{x^4 - 7}$ 33. $\{-5\}$
35. $16\pi - 4\sqrt{3}$ 37. no; no

PAGES 277-278

1. a. 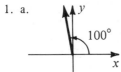   3. a. 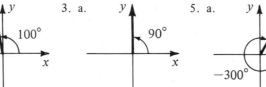   5. a. 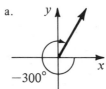   7. a.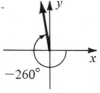

9. a. 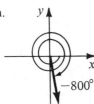   1. b. second   3. b. quadrantal   5. b. first
7. b. second   9. b. fourth

11. $0°$ 13. $90°$ 15. $45°$ 17. $315°$ 19. $720°$ 21. $-270°$ 23. $420°$
25. $430°, -290°$ 27. $630°, -90°$ 29. $300°, -420°$ 31. $45°, -675°$
33. a. $\dfrac{\pi}{3}$ b. $\dfrac{k\pi}{3}$ c. $\dfrac{\pi}{3}$ or $\pi : 3$ d. $\pi : 3$ e. They are equal.

PAGES 280-281   1. $\dfrac{\pi}{30}$ radians   3. $\dfrac{5\pi}{4}$ radians   5. $-\dfrac{3\pi}{2}$ radians   7. $-\dfrac{2\pi}{5}$ radians

9. $\dfrac{7\pi}{3}$ radians   11. $\dfrac{25\pi}{6}$ radians   13. $30°$ 15. $120°$ 17. $-165°$ 19. $-540°$

21. $22\dfrac{1}{2}°$ 23. $15°$ 25. $\left(\dfrac{180}{\pi}\right)°$ 27. $\left(\dfrac{-1440}{\pi}\right)°$ 29. 0.6 cm   31. 20 cm

33. a. $270°$ b. $\dfrac{3\pi}{2}$ radians   c. $\dfrac{15\pi}{2}$ cm   35. a. $80°$ b. $\dfrac{4\pi}{9}$ radians

PAGES 283-284   1. $1; 0$ 3. $-1; 0$ 5. $0; -1$ 7. $-1; 0$ 9. $\dfrac{\sqrt{2}}{2}; \dfrac{\sqrt{2}}{2}$

11. $\dfrac{2\sqrt{2}}{3}$; $-\dfrac{1}{3}$ 13. III   15. I   17. $\cos\theta = \dfrac{\sqrt{2}}{2}$ 19. $\sin\theta = -\dfrac{\sqrt{15}}{4}$

21. $\cos\theta = -\dfrac{12}{13}$ 23. 0   25. -1 27. 0   29. For any point $P(x, y)$ on the
unit circle, $x^2 + y^2 = 1$; $x = \cos\theta$ and $y = \sin\theta$, so $(\cos\theta)^2 + (\sin\theta)^2 = 1$; $\sin^2\theta + \cos^2\theta = 1$

31. $\dfrac{4}{5}$; $-\dfrac{3}{5}$ 33. $-\dfrac{\sqrt{2}}{2}$; $-\dfrac{\sqrt{2}}{2}$ 35. $\dfrac{\sqrt{15}}{4}$; $\dfrac{1}{4}$ 37. $-\dfrac{5\sqrt{34}}{34}$; $\dfrac{3\sqrt{34}}{34}$ 39. 60°

41. 45°   43. 45°

PAGES 288–289

1. a. 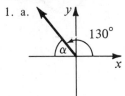   3. a.   5. a. 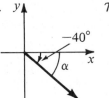   7. a.

9. a.   11. a.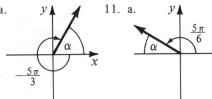

1. b. $m(\alpha) = 50°$ 3. b. $m(\alpha) = 35°$
5. b. $m(\alpha) = 40°$ 7. b. $m(\alpha) = 35°$
9. b. $m(\alpha) = \dfrac{\pi}{3}$ 11. b. $m(\alpha) = \dfrac{\pi}{6}$

13. $\sin 42°$ 15. $\cos 40°$ 17. $-\sin\dfrac{\pi}{3}$ 19. $\cos\dfrac{\pi}{3}$ 21. $-\cos 5°$

23. $-\sin 10°$ 25. a. $\dfrac{\sqrt{2}}{2}$ b. $\dfrac{\sqrt{2}}{2}$ 27. a. $\dfrac{\sqrt{3}}{2}$ b. $\dfrac{1}{2}$ 29. a. $\dfrac{1}{2}$ b. $-\dfrac{\sqrt{3}}{2}$

31. a. $\dfrac{\sqrt{2}}{2}$ b. $\dfrac{\sqrt{2}}{2}$ 33. a. $\dfrac{1}{2}$ b. $\dfrac{\sqrt{3}}{2}$ 35. a. $-\dfrac{\sqrt{2}}{2}$ b. $\dfrac{\sqrt{2}}{2}$ 37. 40° or

320°   39. 55° or 125°   41. 110° or 70°   43. $\sqrt{2}$ 45. $\dfrac{3\sqrt{3}-3}{2}$ 47. $\dfrac{7}{2}$

49. $\sqrt{2}$ 51. $\dfrac{3}{2}$ 53. $-\sqrt{6}$

PAGES 292–293   1. 0.6724   3. 0.8085   5. 0.9415   7. -0.1736
9. -0.9951 11. -0.0698 13. 18.25°   15. 47.6°   17. 54.21°
19. 44°15′   21. 39°50′   23. 18°11′   25. 27°28′48″   27. 12°55′23″
29. 25°50′31″   31. 32°36′   33. 33°34′   35. 7°47′   37. 161°
39. 192°40′   41. 116°40′   43. 36°50′   45. 28°   47. 115°20′
49. 311°20′

PAGES 297–298   1. 28°0′   3. 62°40′   5. 44°50′   7. $\dfrac{1}{4}$ 9. $\dfrac{1}{3}$ 11. $-\dfrac{3}{4}$

13. a. $-\cos 87°$ b. -0.0523 15. a. $-\sin 25°$ b. -0.4226 17. a. $\cos 15°$
b. 0.9659   19. a. $-\sin 2°$ b. -0.0349 21. a. $\cos 27°30′$ b. 0.8870
23. a. $-\sin 80°$ b. -0.9848 25. a. $A(a, b) = (\cos\theta, \sin\theta)$ b. y-axis   c. $A'(-a, b)$
d. $(-a, b) = (\cos(180° - \theta), \sin(180° - \theta))$ e. $\cos\theta = -\cos(180° - \theta)$, so $\cos(180° - \theta) =$
$-\cos\theta$ and $\sin(180° - \theta) = \sin\theta$ 27. $-\dfrac{1}{2}$ 29. $\dfrac{\sqrt{2}}{2}$ 31. $-\dfrac{\sqrt{2}}{2}$

35. $\sin(180° - \theta) = \sin\theta$; if $\theta = 90° - \alpha$, $\sin(180° - (90° - \alpha)) = \sin(90° - \alpha)$; $\sin(90° + \alpha) =$
$\sin(90° - \alpha)$ 37. If $\theta = 180° - \alpha$, $\sin(360° - \theta) = \sin(360° - (180° - \alpha)) =$
$\sin(180° + \alpha) = -\sin\alpha$ (by Formula 3a) $= -\sin(180° - \theta) = -\sin\theta$ (by Formula 2a).
39. $\cos(\theta + 90°) = \cos(90° + \theta) = -\sin\theta$ (by Formula 4b) $= -\cos(\theta - 90°)$ (by Ex. 38)
41. If $\theta = 90° - \alpha$, $\cos(270° - \theta) = \cos(270° - (90° - \alpha)) = \cos(180° + \alpha) = -\cos\alpha$
(by Formula 3b) $= -\cos(90° - \theta) = -\sin\theta$ (by Formula 6b).

PAGES 302–303   1. $\sin\theta = 1$; $\cos\theta = 0$ 3. $\sin\theta = 0$; $\cos\theta = -1$ 5. $\sin\theta = -1$;
$\cos\theta = 0$ 7. $\sin\theta = 0$; $\cos\theta = 1$
9. The graph of $y = \cos\theta$ intersects the θ-axis at

$-\dfrac{3\pi}{2}, \ -\dfrac{\pi}{2}, \ \dfrac{\pi}{2},$ and $\dfrac{3\pi}{2}$; $\left\{-\dfrac{3\pi}{2}, \ -\dfrac{\pi}{2}, \ \dfrac{\pi}{2}, \ \dfrac{3\pi}{2}\right\}$

11. The graph of the horizontal line $y = \dfrac{\sqrt{2}}{2}$ inter-

sects the graph of $y = \cos\theta$ at $\theta = -\dfrac{7\pi}{4}, \ -\dfrac{\pi}{4}, \ \dfrac{\pi}{4}, \ \dfrac{7\pi}{4}$; $\left\{-\dfrac{7\pi}{4}, \ -\dfrac{\pi}{4}, \ \dfrac{\pi}{4}, \ \dfrac{7\pi}{4}\right\}$

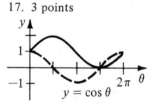
Exs. 9-11

13. The graphs coincide;   15. 2 points   17. 3 points
   infinitely many points

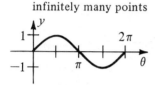

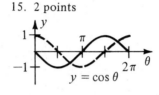

19. The graphs intersect when $\theta = \dfrac{\pi}{4}, \ \dfrac{5\pi}{4}$; $\left\{\dfrac{\pi}{4}, \ \dfrac{5\pi}{4}\right\}$

21. $\left\{\theta: \dfrac{\pi}{4} \leq \theta \leq \dfrac{5\pi}{4}\right\}$ 23. $\left\{\theta: \dfrac{3\pi}{2} \leq \theta \leq 2\pi\right\}$

25. $\sin\theta = -\cos\theta$ when $\theta = \dfrac{3\pi}{4}, \ \dfrac{7\pi}{4}$; $\left\{\dfrac{3\pi}{4}, \ \dfrac{7\pi}{4}\right\}$

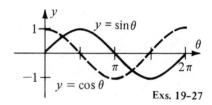
Exs. 19-27

27. $\sin\theta$ and $\cos\theta$ are both positive or both negative

for $\left\{\theta: 0 < \theta < \dfrac{\pi}{2} \text{ or } \pi < \theta < \dfrac{3\pi}{2}\right\}$.   29.

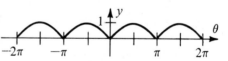

PAGES 305–306 · CHAPTER REVIEW   1. a. See figure at right.
b. $250°$ 2. $-90°$ 3. 1.25 cm   4. a. $\dfrac{4\pi}{3}$ b. $-120°$

5. $1 + (-1) = 0$ 6. $\cos\pi \cdot \sin\dfrac{\pi}{2} = -1 \cdot 1 = -1$ 7. $\dfrac{3}{5}$

8. Quadrant III   9. $\sin 30°$ 10. $-\cos 60°$ 11. $-\sin 70°$

12. $\dfrac{\sqrt{3}}{2}$ 13. $-\dfrac{1}{2}$ 14. $-\dfrac{\sqrt{2}}{2} + \dfrac{\sqrt{2}}{2} = 0$ 15. 0.7844

16. 0.9910 17. $44°17'$ 18. true   19. true   20. 52
21.   22. $T_{\frac{\pi}{2}, \ 0}$, or translating the graph to the right $\dfrac{\pi}{2}$ units.

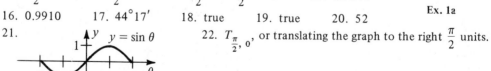

Ex. 1a

PAGES 307-310 · CUMULATIVE REVIEW: CHAPTERS 1-7   1. d   2. d   3. a
4. c   5. a   6. d   7. b   8. d   9. d   10. c   11. b   12. d
13. c   14. c   15. c   16. c   17. b   18. c   19. d   20. a   21. c
22. d   23. c   24. b   25. b   26. c   27. c   28. d   29. b   30. c
31. d   32. a   33. c   34. c   35. a   36. d   37. d   38. c   39. b
40. a

PAGES 312-313 · MIXED REVIEW   1. $\dfrac{3}{10} + \dfrac{1}{10}i$; $(3 - i)\left(\dfrac{3 + i}{10}\right) = \dfrac{10}{10} = 1$

3. a. $\{x: x \neq 0\}$; $\{y: y > 0\}$ b. no   c. See figure at right.

d. even   5. sum, $\dfrac{1}{2}$; product, $\dfrac{1}{3}$; $b^2 - 4ac = -39$;

2 complex conjugate roots   7. 5 lines of symm. formed
by joining opposite vertices; 5 lines of symm. formed by
joining midpts. of opposite sides; rotational symmetries
about the pt. of intersection of the lines of symm. of 36°,
72°, 108°, 144°, 180° (pt. symm.), 216°, 252°, 288°,
and 324°

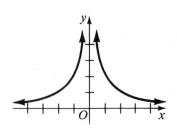

9. $g^{-1}(x) = 3x - 6$

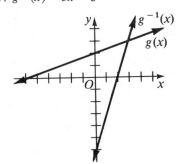

11. $m\angle AOB = 126$; $m\angle ABC = 90$; $m\angle ACB = 63$.
13. $\{9\}$ 15. $m\angle 1 = 24$, $m\angle 2 = 108$,
$m\angle 3 = 24$, $m\angle 4 = 132$ 17. a. $\{-5, -1\}$
b. $\{\pm\sqrt{3}, \pm i\sqrt{5}\}$ 19. $3 + \sqrt{3}$
21. $\dfrac{3y + 5}{(3y + 1)(3y - 1)}$ 23. 8 cm   25. a. 20
b. 25   c. $4x^2 + 12x + 4$ d. $2x^2 - 7$
27. no; If the line and the circle are not coplanar,
then the line is not a tangent.   29. Use Construction 3 on p. 177 to construct line t, the $\perp$ bis.
of $\overline{AB}$.

31. $\cos\dfrac{2\pi}{9}$ 33. $-\sin\dfrac{5\pi}{12}$ 35. $2s^2 + 5s - 3 - \dfrac{5}{2s - 5}$

37. a.   b. For example, $k = \dfrac{\pi}{2}$ or $k = -\dfrac{3\pi}{2}$.

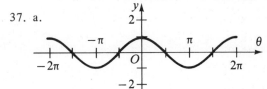

PAGES 320-322   1. a. 0; $\dfrac{1}{2}$; $\dfrac{\sqrt{2}}{2}$; $\dfrac{\sqrt{3}}{2}$; 1 b. 1; $\dfrac{\sqrt{3}}{2}$; $\dfrac{\sqrt{2}}{2}$; $\dfrac{1}{2}$; 0 c. 0; $\dfrac{\sqrt{3}}{3}$; 1; $\sqrt{3}$;

undefined d. undefined; $\sqrt{3}$; 1; $\dfrac{\sqrt{3}}{3}$; 0 e. 1; $\dfrac{2\sqrt{3}}{3}$; $\sqrt{2}$; 2; undefined f. undefined;

2; $\sqrt{2}$; $\dfrac{2\sqrt{3}}{3}$; 1   3. $\cot 85°$ 5. $\tan\dfrac{\pi}{3}$ 7. $-\csc 40°$ 9. $-\sec\dfrac{\pi}{3}$

11. 1.428   13. -57.29 15. 1.051   17. -57.30 19. a. $\dfrac{\sqrt{3}}{3}$ b. $-\dfrac{2\sqrt{3}}{3}$

c. -2 21. a. -2 b. $-\dfrac{\sqrt{3}}{3}$ c. $\sqrt{3}$ 23. -2 25. $\dfrac{1}{2}$ 27. $\dfrac{7}{6}$

29. a. $\sin \theta = -\dfrac{5}{13}$; $\cos \theta = -\dfrac{12}{13}$; $\sec \theta = -\dfrac{13}{12}$; $\tan \theta = \dfrac{5}{12}$; $\cot \theta = \dfrac{12}{5}$ b. $\sin \theta = \dfrac{\sqrt{2}}{2}$;

$\cos \theta = -\dfrac{\sqrt{2}}{2}$; $\csc \theta = \sqrt{2}$; $\sec \theta = -\sqrt{2}$; $\cot \theta = -1$ 31. a. $\cos \theta = -\dfrac{1}{2}$; $\sin \theta = -\dfrac{\sqrt{3}}{2}$;

$\csc \theta = -\dfrac{2\sqrt{3}}{3}$; $\tan \theta = \sqrt{3}$; $\cot \theta = \dfrac{\sqrt{3}}{3}$ b. $\tan \theta = \dfrac{24}{7}$; $\sin \theta = \dfrac{24}{25}$; $\cos \theta = \dfrac{7}{25}$;

$\csc \theta = \dfrac{25}{24}$; $\sec \theta = \dfrac{25}{7}$ 33. $\tan(\theta + \pi) = \dfrac{\sin(\theta + \pi)}{\cos(\theta + \pi)} = \dfrac{-\sin \theta}{-\cos \theta} = \dfrac{\sin \theta}{\cos \theta} = \tan \theta$

35. $\sec\left(\dfrac{\pi}{2} - \theta\right) = \dfrac{1}{\cos\left(\dfrac{\pi}{2} - \theta\right)} = \dfrac{1}{\sin \theta} = \csc \theta$ 37. $\sin \theta = -\dfrac{4}{5}$; $\cos \theta = \dfrac{3}{5}$;

$\csc \theta = -\dfrac{5}{4}$; $\sec \theta = \dfrac{5}{3}$; $\tan \theta = -\dfrac{4}{3}$; $\cot \theta = -\dfrac{3}{4}$ 39. $\sin \theta = -\dfrac{\sqrt{2}}{2}$; $\cos \theta = -\dfrac{\sqrt{2}}{2}$;

$\csc \theta = -\sqrt{2}$; $\sec \theta = -\sqrt{2}$; $\tan \theta = 1$; $\cot \theta = 1$

41.

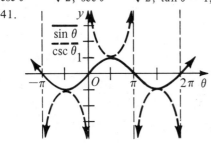

a. integral multiples of π b. the set of real numbers that are not integral multiples of π; the set of real numbers greater than or equal to 1 or less than or equal to -1

43. $\overline{RS}$ is tangent to the circle, so $\overline{RS} \perp \overline{OR}$ and $\overline{RS} \parallel \overline{OA}$; thus, $\angle ORS \cong \angle PAO$ and

$\angle OSR \cong \angle LPOA$ (alt. int. $\angle$s);   by the AA Similarity Thm., $\triangle ORS \sim \triangle PAO$; $\dfrac{RS}{AO} = \dfrac{RO}{AP}$ and

$\dfrac{OS}{PO} = \dfrac{RO}{AP}$; $\dfrac{RS}{RO} = \dfrac{AO}{AP}$ and $\dfrac{OS}{RO} = \dfrac{PO}{AP}$; $\dfrac{RS}{1} = \dfrac{\cos \theta}{\sin \theta}$ and $\dfrac{OS}{1} = \dfrac{1}{\sin \theta}$; $RS = \cot \theta$ and

$OS = \csc \theta$.

PAGES 325–327   1. $\csc^2 \theta$ 3. $\cos^2 \theta$ 5. $\cot \theta$ 7. 1   9. $\cot \theta$

11. $2 \sec^2 \theta$ 13. 1   15. $\sin 3\alpha$ 17. $\dfrac{1}{\cos 2\alpha}$, or $\sec 2\alpha$

19. $\sin \theta = \pm\sqrt{1 - \cos^2 \theta}$ 21. $\sec \alpha = \dfrac{\pm\sqrt{1 - \sin^2 \alpha}}{1 - \sin^2 \alpha}$ 23. $\tan^2 \theta + 1 = \left(\dfrac{\sin \theta}{\cos \theta}\right)^2 + 1 =$

$\dfrac{\sin^2 \theta + \cos^2 \theta}{\cos^2 \theta} = \dfrac{1}{\cos^2 \theta} = \sec^2 \theta$ 25. 0   27. -1 29. $-2 \cot \theta$ 31. 1

33. $\sin \theta$ 35. 1   37. $\tan \theta$ 39. $-\tan \alpha$ 41. $\sin \theta$ 43. $\cot \alpha$

45. $\cot \theta$ 47. $\sin \beta$ 49. $\cot \theta$ 51. $-\sin \theta \cdot \dfrac{1}{\cos \theta} \cdot \dfrac{-\cos \theta}{-\sin \theta} = -1$

PAGES 328–329   1. $\sin \theta \cot \theta = \sin \theta \cdot \dfrac{\cos \theta}{\sin \theta} = \cos \theta$ 5. $\dfrac{\csc \alpha}{\sec \alpha} = \dfrac{1}{\sec \alpha} \cdot \dfrac{1}{\sin \alpha} \cdot \cos \alpha =$

$\dfrac{\cos \alpha}{\sin \alpha} = \cot \alpha$ 9. $\dfrac{1}{\cos^2 x} - \dfrac{1}{\cot^2 x} = \sec^2 x - \tan^2 x = 1$ 13. $(\cos \theta - \sin \theta)^2 =$

$\cos^2 \theta - 2 \cos \theta \sin \theta + \sin^2 \theta = 1 - 2 \sin \theta \cos \theta$ 15. $\cos^2 \alpha (\cot^2 \alpha + 1) = \cos^2 \alpha \csc^2 \alpha =$

$\cos^2 \alpha \cdot \dfrac{1}{\sin^2 \alpha} = \dfrac{\cos^2 \alpha}{\sin^2 \alpha} = \cot^2 \alpha$

21. $1 - 2\sin^2\alpha = 1 - 2(1 - \cos^2\alpha) = 1 - 2 + 2\cos^2\alpha = 2\cos^2\alpha - 1$

23. $\dfrac{\cot\theta}{\tan\theta} = \dfrac{\dfrac{\cos\theta}{\sin\theta}}{\dfrac{\sin\theta}{\cos\theta}} = \dfrac{\cos^2\theta}{\sin^2\theta} = \dfrac{1 - \sin^2\theta}{1 - \cos^2\theta}$

27. $(\cos\theta - \sec\theta)^2 = \cos^2\theta - 2\cos\theta\sec\theta + \sec^2\theta = \cos^2\theta - 2\cos\theta \cdot \dfrac{1}{\cos} + \sec^2\theta =$

$\cos^2\theta - 2 + \sec^2\theta = (\cos^2\theta - 1) + \sec^2\theta - 1 = -\sin^2\theta + \tan^2\theta = \tan^2\theta - \sin^2\theta$

39. not an identity   41. an identity

PAGE 333   1. $\theta = 60°, 240°$ 3. $\theta = 150°, 210°$ 5. $\theta = 135°, 225°$
7. $\theta = 60°, 300°$ 9. $\theta = 60°, 120°$ 11. $\theta = 45°, 135°, 225°, 315°$ 13. $\theta = 60°,$
$120°, 240°, 300°$ 15. $\theta = 60°, 120°, 240°, 300°$ 17. $\theta = 0°, 30°, 150°, 180°$

19. $\theta = 90°$ 21. $\theta = 30°, 150°$ 23. no solution   25. $\alpha = \dfrac{\pi}{4} + n\pi,\ n \in Z$

27. $\alpha = \dfrac{\pi}{2} + n\pi,\ n \in Z$ 29. $\alpha = \dfrac{\pi}{3} + n\pi$ or $\alpha = \dfrac{2\pi}{3} + n\pi,\ n \in Z$ 31. $\theta = 135°, 315°,$

$161°30', 341°30'$ 33. $\theta = 0°, 78°30', 281°30'$ 35. $\theta = 30°, 150°, 199°30', 340°30'$

37. $\alpha = \dfrac{\pi}{4}, \dfrac{5\pi}{4}$ 39. $\alpha = \dfrac{\pi}{4}, \dfrac{7\pi}{12}, \dfrac{11\pi}{12}, \dfrac{5\pi}{4}, \dfrac{19\pi}{12}, \dfrac{23\pi}{12}$ 41. $\alpha = \dfrac{2\pi}{3}$ 43. $\alpha = \dfrac{\pi}{3}, \dfrac{5\pi}{3}$

45. $\alpha = \dfrac{5\pi}{12}, \dfrac{\pi}{2}, \dfrac{7\pi}{12}, \dfrac{17\pi}{12}, \dfrac{3\pi}{2}, \dfrac{19\pi}{12}$ 47. $\theta = \pi$ 49. $\theta = \dfrac{\pi}{2}$ 51. $\theta = \dfrac{5\pi}{12}$

53. $\theta = \dfrac{\pi}{3}$ 55. $\alpha = 15°30', 164°30'$ 57. $\alpha = 120°20', 163°40', 300°20', 343°40'$

PAGES 336–337   1. $\theta = \dfrac{\pi}{6}, \dfrac{7\pi}{6}$ 3. $\theta = \dfrac{\pi}{3}, \dfrac{2\pi}{3}, \dfrac{4\pi}{3}, \dfrac{5\pi}{3}$ 5. $\theta = \dfrac{3\pi}{4}, \dfrac{7\pi}{4}$

7. $\theta = \dfrac{\pi}{4}, \dfrac{3\pi}{4}, \dfrac{5\pi}{4}, \dfrac{7\pi}{4}$ 9. $\theta = \dfrac{\pi}{2}$ 11. $\theta = \dfrac{\pi}{3}, \dfrac{5\pi}{3}$ 13. $\theta = \dfrac{\pi}{4}, \dfrac{3\pi}{4}$

15. $\theta = \dfrac{\pi}{4}, \dfrac{3\pi}{4}, \dfrac{5\pi}{4}, \dfrac{7\pi}{4}$ 17. $\theta = \dfrac{\pi}{6}, \dfrac{5\pi}{6}, \dfrac{3\pi}{2}$ 19. $\theta = 0, \dfrac{\pi}{3}, \dfrac{2\pi}{3}, \pi$

21. $\theta = 0, \pi, \dfrac{7\pi}{6}, \dfrac{11\pi}{6}$ 23. $\theta = \pi$ 25. $\theta = 0, \dfrac{\pi}{2}, \pi, \dfrac{3\pi}{2}$ 27. no solution

29. $0 < \theta < 2\pi$ and $\theta \neq \dfrac{\pi}{2}, \pi, \dfrac{3\pi}{2}$ 31. $\theta = 0, \dfrac{\pi}{3}, \pi, \dfrac{5\pi}{3}$ 33. $\theta = 0, \dfrac{\pi}{4}, \dfrac{3\pi}{4}, \pi, \dfrac{5\pi}{4}, \dfrac{7\pi}{4}$

35. $\theta = 0, \dfrac{\pi}{4}, \pi, \dfrac{5\pi}{4}$ 37. $\theta = \dfrac{\pi}{3}, \pi, \dfrac{5\pi}{3}$ 39. $\theta = 0, \pi$ 41. $\theta = 61°$

43. $\theta = 40°$ 45. $\theta = 33°$ 47. $\theta = 30°$ 49. $\theta = 15°$ 51. $\theta = 1°, 46°$

53. $\alpha = \dfrac{2\pi}{3}, \dfrac{4\pi}{3}$ 55. $\theta = \pi, \dfrac{7\pi}{6}, \dfrac{11\pi}{6}$ 57. $\theta = 0, \dfrac{3\pi}{4}, \pi, \dfrac{7\pi}{4}$

PAGES 339–340 · CHAPTER REVIEW   1. a. $-\dfrac{\sqrt{3}}{3}$ b. $-\dfrac{\sqrt{3}}{3}$ c. -1 2. $\dfrac{\sqrt{3}}{2} \cdot 1 =$

$\dfrac{\sqrt{3}}{2}$ 3. $\sqrt{2} - 1$ 4. a. $-\sqrt{3}$ b. $-\dfrac{1}{2}$ c. $\dfrac{\sqrt{3}}{2}$ 5. a. $\csc\theta$ b. 1

6. $\cos\theta = \pm\sqrt{1 - \sin^2\theta}$ 7. $\dfrac{\cos\theta}{-\sin\theta} = -\cot\theta$ 8. $\dfrac{1}{\cos\theta} \cdot \dfrac{1}{\cos\theta} = \dfrac{1}{\cos^2\theta}$, or $\sec^2\theta$

9. $\dfrac{-\cos^2\theta}{\sin\theta - 1} = \dfrac{-(1 - \sin^2\theta)}{\sin\theta - 1} = \dfrac{\sin^2\theta - 1}{\sin\theta - 1} = \dfrac{(\sin\theta + 1)(\sin\theta - 1)}{\sin\theta - 1} = \sin\theta + 1$

10. $\dfrac{\tan\theta}{\cot\theta} = \dfrac{\sin\theta}{\cos\theta} \div \dfrac{\cos\theta}{\sin\theta} = \dfrac{\sin\theta}{\cos\theta} \cdot \dfrac{\sin\theta}{\cos\theta} = \dfrac{\sin^2\theta}{\cos^2\theta} = \dfrac{\sin^2\theta}{1 - \sin^2\theta}$ 11. $\dfrac{\sec\theta + 1}{\sec\theta - 1} =$

$$\frac{\frac{1}{\cos\theta}+1}{\frac{1}{\cos\theta}-1}\cdot\frac{\cos\theta}{\cos\theta}=\frac{1+\cos\theta}{1-\cos\theta}=\frac{\cos\theta+1}{1-\cos\theta}$$ 12. $\emptyset$ 13. $\theta=30°,\ 90°,\ 210°,\ 270°$

14. $\theta=225°,\ 315°$ 15. $\theta=48°10',\ 60°,\ 300°,\ 311°50'$ 16. $\theta=\dfrac{\pi}{3},\ \dfrac{2\pi}{3},\ \dfrac{4\pi}{3},\ \dfrac{5\pi}{3}$

17. $\theta=0,\ \dfrac{\pi}{4},\ \pi,\ \dfrac{5\pi}{4}$ 18. $\theta=\dfrac{2\pi}{3},\ \dfrac{4\pi}{3}$ 19. $\theta=\dfrac{\pi}{2}$

PAGES 342–343 · MIXED REVIEW   1. -1 3. 0 5. $-\dfrac{1}{2},\ \dfrac{3}{4}$, and -2 7. 43

9. $\dfrac{1}{1-\cos\theta}+\dfrac{1}{1+\cos\theta}=\dfrac{(1+\cos\theta)+(1-\cos\theta)}{(1+\cos\theta)(1-\cos\theta)}=\dfrac{2}{1-\cos^2\theta}=\dfrac{2}{\sin^2\theta}=2\csc^2\theta$

11. $\left\{a:a<\dfrac{2}{3}\text{ or }a>\dfrac{2}{3}\right\}$ 13. $\{4\pm\sqrt{5}\}$ 15. $\left\{\dfrac{3}{5},-2\right\}$ 17. $\dfrac{29i\sqrt{2}}{2}$

19. $-18\sqrt[3]{20}$ 21. $\tan\theta$ and $\sec\theta$ are not defined; $\sin\theta=\csc\theta=-1$; $\cos\theta=\cot\theta=0$

23. Use the construction at the top of p. 263.   25. $(-y,x);\ (y,-x)$ 27. $\dfrac{t}{2t-3}$

29. $\dfrac{1-3i}{5}$ 31. $\left\{0,\ \dfrac{3\pi}{4},\ \pi,\ \dfrac{7\pi}{4}\right\}$ 33. $\{2\pm 2i\}$ 35. $\sin\theta=-\dfrac{15}{17},\ \cos\theta=-\dfrac{8}{17},$

$\tan\theta=\dfrac{15}{8},\ \sec\theta=-\dfrac{17}{8},\ \cot\theta=\dfrac{8}{15}$ 37. no; For any real number x between -1 and 1

there are two values of y; for example, if $x=0$, $y=1$ or $y=-1$.   39. $210°;\ \dfrac{7\pi}{6}$

41. $\csc^2\theta$

PAGES 348–349   1. 3 3. $\sqrt{3}$ 5. 27 7. $\dfrac{64}{27}$ 9. $25\sqrt{5}$ 11. 5

13. 625 15. 27 17. $x^{\frac{1}{2}}=2;\ x^{\frac{3}{2}}=8;\ x^{\frac{5}{2}}=32$ 19. $x^{\frac{1}{2}}=\dfrac{1}{4};\ x^{\frac{3}{2}}=\dfrac{1}{64};$

$x^{\frac{5}{2}}=\dfrac{1}{1024}$ 21. $5x^{\frac{1}{2}}$ 23. $(x-y)^{\frac{2}{5}}$ 25. $25\sqrt{5}$ 27. $24\sqrt{3}$ 29. $x=-2$

31. $x=1$ 33. $\{-1,6\}$ 35. $\dfrac{1}{25}$ 37. $\dfrac{1}{8}$ 39. 4 41. 2 43. 64

45. $\dfrac{1}{4}$ 47. True   49. True   51. True   53. True   55. True   57. $\dfrac{\sqrt{5}}{25}$

59. $\sqrt[6]{108}$ 61. $\sqrt[12]{2000}$ 63. $<$ 65. $<$

PAGES 352–353

1. a.

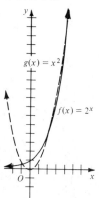

1. b. 2, 4, and approximately -0.8
   c. $g(x)=x^2$

3. a.

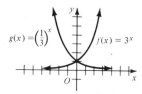

b. 1 is the y-intercept for each.
c. The graphs are reflections of one another over the y-axis.

5. g 7. g 9. f 11. g 13. 22.4   15. $2m$ 17. m^2

19.    21.   23.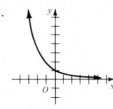

23. See figure above. $y = 2^{-x}$ is the reflection of $y = 2^x$ over the y-axis.

PAGES 356–357   1. 2   3. $\dfrac{1}{2}$ 5. 0   7. -2 9. 2   11. -2 13. $\dfrac{3}{2}$

15. $-\dfrac{3}{2}$ 17. $x = 2$ 19. $x = \dfrac{1}{5}$ 21. $x = 8$ 23. $x = 32$ 25. $x = \sqrt{3}$

27. $x = \dfrac{9}{4}$ 29. $x = \dfrac{1}{8}$ 31. a. 3   b. 2   c. 5   d. 1   33. a. 4   b. -2 c. 2
d. 2

35. 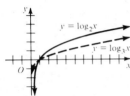   37. 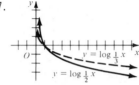   39. $\{x: x > 1\}$

PAGES 360–361   1. $\log_{10} 3 + \log_{10} 2$ 3. $\log_3 2 - \log_3 5$ 5. $\log_{10} 2 + 2 \log_{10} 3$

7. $\log_5 3 - \log_5 7$ 9. $-\log_4 5$ 11. $\dfrac{1}{2} \log_6 7$ 13. 2   15. 0   17. 2

19. $\log_m a + \log_m b$ 21. $3 \log_m a$ 23. cannot be restated   25. $2 \log_m a + \log_m b$

27. $\log_m a + \dfrac{1}{2} \log_m b$ 29. $2 \log_m b + \dfrac{1}{2} \log_m c$ 31. $3a$ 33. $a + b + c$

35. $\dfrac{1}{2} b$ 37. $a - \dfrac{1}{2} b$ 39. $\dfrac{3(a + b + c)}{2}$

PAGES 364–365   1. $m + 2$ 3. $m + 1$ 5. $n - 3$ 7. $n - 5$ 9. $m + n$
11. $\log 3.1 - 1$ 13. $\log 1.804 + 5$ 15. $\log 9.08 + 1$ 17. $\log 6 - 1$
19. $\log 762$ 21. $\log 0.00989$ 23. $\log 83,000$ 25. $3.7E + 4$ 27. $6.38E - 4$

29. $a + b$ 31. $2b$ 33. $1 - a$ 35. $\dfrac{b}{2}$ 37. $2a + b$ 39. $-\dfrac{b}{2}$

41. $a - b - 1$ 43. $a + \dfrac{b}{2}$ 45. $x = 290,000$ 47. $x = 0.00044$ 49. 6×10^{-11}

51. 5.6×10^4 53. 2.1×10^{-5} 55. 8.27×10^6 57. 7.39×10^{-5}
59. 5.86×10^2 km   61. 6.0×10^{-1} L

PAGES 369–370   1. 0.6990   3. 0.3617   5. 0.5922   7. 0.8331
9. $0.8331 - 3$ 11. $0.6599 + 3$ 13. 4.53   15. 6.97   17. 255   19. 0.00255
21. 0.7038   23. 0.8577   25. $0.8015 + 1$ 27. $0.6596 - 3$ 29. $0.2494 + 3$
31. 4.324   33. 9.495   35. 75.17   37. 0.01995   39. 454,000   41. 0.402
43. 1.585

PAGE 373   1. 4,220,000,000   3. 0.0000386   5. 2,740,000,000,000,000,000
7. 22,500,000,000   9. 72.1   11. 134,000   13. 287   15. 8.23   17. 24,080

19. 12.37   21. 131.0   23. $9,638   25. a. $2^{10} \approx 10^3$ b. $\log 2 \approx 0.3$
c. $\log 2 = 0.3010$ in the table. The two values differ by approximately 0.001.

PAGES 377-378   1. $x = 3.13$ 3. $x = 6.12$ 5. $x = 1.44$ 7. $x = 39.4$
9. $x = 1.71$ 11. $x = 6.64$ 13. $x = 0.733$ 15. $x = 0.861$ 17. $x = 2.67$
19. $x = \dfrac{\log 106}{\log 5.4} - 1$ 21. $x = \dfrac{\log 7.04}{\log 7.04 - \log 4.19}$ 23. 0.3562   25. 2.303
27. 1.609   29. 9.25 or -15.2 31. 0.3010   33. 0.2553

PAGES 379-381   1. $2011   3. $1553   5. 337,000,000   7. 410,000,000
9. 8.00   11. 3170   13. 35.0 yr   15. 7.3 yr   17. 250 g   19. 771 g
21. 266 d   23. 14.9%

PAGES 382-383 · CHAPTER REVIEW   1. 256   2. $\dfrac{1}{4}$ 3. 4   4. 4   5. 9

6. $\dfrac{1}{9}$ 7. 0.01   8. 81

9.   10. m^2 11. m^{-1} 12. m^3 13. m^{-4} 14. $\dfrac{3}{2}$

15. -4 16. $\dfrac{1}{4}$ 17. $-\dfrac{3}{4}$ 18. $x = \dfrac{1}{3}$

19. $x = \dfrac{1}{25}$ 20. $x = \sqrt{3}$ 21. $\log_4 3 + \log_4 5$

22. $\log_3 5 + 2\log_3 2$ 23. $\log_5 3 + 3\log_5 2$

24. $\log_6 5 - 2\log_6 3$ 25. $3m + n$ 26. $n - m$

27. $\dfrac{1}{3}n$ 28. $\dfrac{1}{2}m + \dfrac{1}{2}n$ 29. $\log 4.3 - 2$

30. $\log 8.89 + 3$ 31. $\log 6.27 + 1$ 32. $\log 2.9 - 4$ 33. $x = 52,800$
34. $x = 0.00106$ 35. $0.5843 - 2$ 36. $0.8668 + 4$ 37. $0.7102 - 3$
38. $x = 453.4$ 39. $x = 0.003543$ 40. $x = 80,600$ 41. 0.296
42. 61,000,000,000   43. 0.00000124   44. $x = 26.0$ 45. $x = 0.774$
46. $x = 0.431$ 47. 0.5283   48. 3.170   49. 2.861   50. $3278   51. $33
52. 23.5 yr

PAGES 386-387 · MIXED REVIEW   1. $\tan \alpha + \cot \alpha = \dfrac{\sin \alpha}{\cos \alpha} + \dfrac{\cos \alpha}{\sin \alpha} = \dfrac{\sin^2 \alpha + \cos^2 \alpha}{\cos \alpha \sin \alpha} =$

$\dfrac{1}{\cos \alpha \sin \alpha} = \dfrac{1}{\cos \alpha} \cdot \dfrac{1}{\sin \alpha} = \sec \alpha \csc \alpha$ 3. $\dfrac{1}{625}$ 5. -3 7. $\left\{ -4, \dfrac{1}{2} \right\}$

9. $f^{-1}(x) = 3^x$ 11. 98, 90, 80, and 92   13. $\dfrac{\sqrt{2}}{8} - \dfrac{i\sqrt{6}}{8}$

15. $\{y : -4 \leqslant y \leqslant 2\}$

17. $\cot^2 \theta$ 19. $3 + 3\sqrt{3}$ cm

21. $\dfrac{1}{z^2 - 2z + 4}$ 23. $-8\sqrt[3]{4}$ 25. $\left\{ \dfrac{\sqrt{2}}{8} \right\}$

27. $\{20\}$ 29. $\left\{ 0, \dfrac{3}{4}, -3 \right\}$ 31. $\sin \theta = -\dfrac{4}{5}$, $\cos \theta = -\dfrac{3}{5}$, $\tan \theta = \dfrac{4}{3}$, $\csc \theta = -\dfrac{5}{4}$,

$\sec \theta = -\dfrac{5}{3}$, $\cot \theta = \dfrac{3}{4}$ 33. a. $\{30°, 150°, 210°, 330°\}$ b. $\{210°, 330°\}$ 35. 2 L

37. 8.0 yr   39. Use the construction at the bottom of p. 263 to construct a tangent to $\odot O$
at pt. P. Draw diameter QP, and use the construction again to construct the line tangent to $\odot O$ at
pt. Q. (In a plane, 2 lines $\perp$ to the same line are $\parallel$.)   41. $\mathcal{R}$; $\{y : -1 \leqslant y \leqslant 1\}$; 2π
43. a. 1.04   b. 2.75   45. 3.614

PAGES 392–394 1. 10; $\sin \theta = \frac{3}{5}$, $\csc \theta = \frac{5}{3}$, $\cos \theta = \frac{4}{5}$, $\sec \theta = \frac{5}{4}$, $\tan \theta = \frac{3}{4}$, $\cot \theta = \frac{4}{3}$

3. 3. 4; $\sin \theta = \cos \theta = \frac{\sqrt{2}}{2}$, $\csc \theta = \sec \theta = \sqrt{2}$, $\tan \theta = \cot \theta = 1$ 5. 15 7. 150

9. 77 11. $50°$ 13. $25°40'$ 15. $b = 120$, $\angle A = 22°40'$, $\angle B = 67°20'$

17. $a = 8$, $\angle A = 63°40'$, $\angle B = 26°20'$ 19. $\angle A = 20°$, $b = 206$, $c = 219$ 21. $\csc \theta = \frac{17}{15}$,

$\cos \theta = \frac{8}{17}$, $\sec \theta = \frac{17}{8}$, $\tan \theta = \frac{15}{8}$, $\cot \theta = \frac{8}{15}$ 23. $\cot \theta = \frac{33}{56}$, $\sin \theta = \frac{56}{65}$, $\csc \theta = \frac{65}{56}$,

$\cos \theta = \frac{33}{65}$, $\sec \theta = \frac{65}{33}$ 25. $\cos \theta = \frac{24}{25}$, $\sin \theta = \frac{7}{25}$, $\csc \theta = \frac{25}{7}$, $\tan \theta = \frac{7}{24}$, $\cot \theta = \frac{24}{7}$

27. 55 29. $67°20'$, $67°20'$, $45°20'$ 31. 160 33. $56°10'$ 35. a. 24 b. 33

37. 42 39. 288 square units   41. 57 43. 120

PAGES 395–398   1. 94 m   3. 13 m   5. 445 cm   7. $5°20'$ 9. 1500 m

11. $133{,}000{,}000$ km   13. a. 25 m   b. 42 m   15. Let $x = DP$, $\tan \alpha = \dfrac{h}{c + x}$, and

$\tan \beta = \dfrac{h}{x}$; $x = \dfrac{h - c \tan \alpha}{\tan \alpha}$ and $x = \dfrac{h}{\tan \beta}$; $\dfrac{h - c \tan \alpha}{\tan \alpha} = \dfrac{h}{\tan \beta}$; $h \tan \beta - c \tan \alpha \tan \beta =$

$h \tan \alpha$; $h(\tan \beta - \tan \alpha) = c \tan \alpha \tan \beta$; $h = c \left(\dfrac{\tan \alpha \tan \beta}{\tan \beta - \tan \alpha} \right)$.

PAGES 400–403   1. 10 3. 30 5. 0.375 7. 180 9. 729 11. 316

13. 38 15. $10\sqrt{6}$ 17. 16 19. 145 21. 141 25. 110 27. $24°40'$

29. 230 cm   31. 54 m   33. 88 m

PAGES 405–406   1. right   3. acute   5. 0 7. 1 9. 2 11. 2

13. 1 15. $\angle Q = 59°$ and $\angle R = 73°$, or $\angle Q = 121°$ and $\angle R = 11°$ 17. $\angle R = 69°30'$

and $\angle Q = 89°30'$, or $\angle R = 110°30'$ and $\angle Q = 48°30'$ 19. $\angle B = 33°$, $\angle C = 75°$, $c = 46$

21. $\angle A = 30°$, $\angle C = 35°$, $c = 14$ 23. No triangle exists.   25. $\angle C = 28°$, $\angle A = 129°$,

$a = 248$ or $\angle C = 152°$, $\angle A = 5°$, $a = 28$ 27. $\angle A = 24°$, $\angle C = 137°$, $c = 735$ or

$\angle A = 156°$, $\angle C = 5°$, $c = 97$ 29. 27 31. 88 m   33. 11 m

PAGES 409–411   1. 0.925 3. -0.25 5. 7 7. 37 9. 21 11. 28

13. $120°$ 15. $33°$ 17. no triangle   19. one triangle   21. two triangles

23. $72°$ 25. 13 cm   27. $41°20'$ 29. 14 cm   31. 3 or 5 33. 4.7

35. 13 37. 30 39. 17 41. 0.25 43. 14

PAGES 414–416   1. 48 3. 24 5. 17 7. 66 9. 41 11. 9

13. 9.6 15. $30°, 150°$ 17. 8 cm^2 19. $30°; 150°$ 21. 49 23. $30°, 150°$

25. $60°, 120°$ 27. 38 29. $200\sqrt{2}$ 31. 25 cm^2 33. 43 35. Area $=$

$\frac{1}{2}(DE)(FG)$ and area $= \dfrac{(DE)^2 \sin D \sin E}{2 \sin F}$; $\dfrac{(DE)(FG)}{2} = \dfrac{(DE)^2 \sin D \sin E}{2 \sin F}$;

$FG = \dfrac{DE \cdot \sin D \sin E}{\sin F}$; $\dfrac{FG}{DF} = \dfrac{\sin D \sin E}{\sin F}$ 37. $\cos A = \dfrac{b^2 + c^2 - a^2}{2bc}$ and

$\sin^2 A + \cos^2 A = 1$; $\sin A = \sqrt{1 - \cos^2 A}$; by substitution $\sin A = \sqrt{1 - \left[\dfrac{b^2 + c^2 - a^2}{2bc} \right]^2}$;

$\sin^2 A = 1 - \left(\dfrac{b^2 + c^2 - a^2}{2bc} \right)^2$ 39. Multiplying both sides of $\sin A =$

$\dfrac{1}{2bc} \sqrt{[(b + c)^2 - a^2][a^2 - (b - c)^2]}$ by $\frac{1}{2}bc$, we get $\frac{1}{2}bc \sin A =$

$\frac{1}{4}\sqrt{[(b+c)^2 - a^2][a^2 - (b-c)^2]}$. So Area of $\triangle ABC = \sqrt{\dfrac{[(b+c)^2 - a^2][a^2 - (b-c)^2]}{16}}$

or Area of $\triangle ABC = \sqrt{\dfrac{(b+c-a)(b+c+a)(a-b+c)(a+b-c)}{16}}$

PAGES 419–422   1. a. 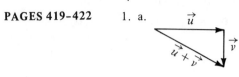   b.   c.

3. $\overrightarrow{DC}$ 5. $\overrightarrow{AE}$ 7. $\overrightarrow{AC}$ 9. $\overrightarrow{BD}$ 11. $\overrightarrow{AD}$ 13. $4\sqrt{2}$ N at a $45°$ angle to each force   15. 16 N at an angle of $60°$ with each force   17. $99°$ 19. 18 N 21. a. 13   b. $67°$ 23. a. 17   b. $118°$ 25. a. $4\sqrt{5}$ b. $333°$ 27. a. 12 b. $21°$ 29. a. 24   b. $1°$ 31. a. 10   b. $77°$ 33. a. 28   b. $137°$ 35. 493 km/h at a course of $114°$ 37. 584 km/h at a heading of $142°$

PAGES 422–423 · CHAPTER REVIEW   1. $\sin E = \dfrac{8}{17}$, $\cos E = \dfrac{15}{17}$, $\cot F = \dfrac{8}{15}$

2. $23°30'$ 3. $33°40'$ 4. $54°$ 5. $\dfrac{1}{2}$ 6. $28\sqrt{2}$ 7. 150   8. a. one b. none   c. none   9. $34°10'$, $145°50'$ 10. a. 16   b. 32   11. $120°$ 12. a. 75   b. $16\sqrt{3}$ 13. 78   14. a. $\overrightarrow{EC}$ b. $\overrightarrow{DE}$ 15. 390 km

PAGES 426–427 · MIXED REVIEW   1. a. $3k$ b. $k+3$ 3. $f(g(x)) = \dfrac{4}{\dfrac{2x+4}{x} - 2} =$

$\dfrac{4x}{2x+4-2x} = x$ and $g(f(x)) = \dfrac{2\left(\dfrac{4}{x-2}\right) + 4}{\dfrac{4}{x-2}} = \dfrac{8 + 4(x-2)}{4} = \dfrac{4x}{4} = x$ 5. -7 and -6

or 6 and 7   7. 268   9. $\csc\theta$ 11. $-\dfrac{1}{3} + \dfrac{i\sqrt{2}}{3}$ 13. $\dfrac{1}{6}$ 15. $\{2,7\}$ 17. $\{-1\}$ 19. $\{3\}$ 21. $4\sqrt{6}$ 23. 11.9 yr   25. a. 99,500   b. 1,230,000 27. $m\angle J = 142.5$, $m\angle K = 72.5$, $m\angle L = 80$, $m\angle X = 65$ 29. $\{120°, 300°\}$ 31. $\{70°30', 180°, 289°30'\}$

33.

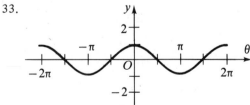

Each element in the range of $y = \cos\theta$ has many pre-images, so the function is not one-to-one. 35. $\pi\sqrt{5}$ cm   37. ◄─┼─┼─○─┼─┼─┼─┼─┼─○─┼─┼─►   39. -5 41. 0
               -1 5
43. No triangle exists.

PAGES 433–434   1. a. 4   b. 2π c. See below.   3. a. $\dfrac{3}{4}$ b. 2π c. See below.

5. a. 1   b. $\dfrac{\pi}{2}$ 7. a. 5   b. 2π 9. a. 1   b. 6π 11. a. $\dfrac{3}{2}$ b. π

c. See below.   13. 4 values   15. 8 values

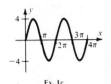

Ex. 1c

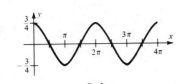

Ex. 3c

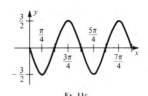

Ex. 11c

17.

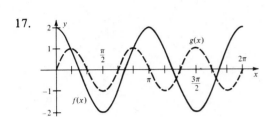

17. 4 values

19. b. π c. $\dfrac{1}{2}$, $-\dfrac{1}{2}$ d. $\dfrac{1}{2}$

21. 2π 23. π

25. 6π

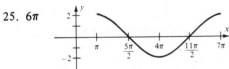

PAGES 437–439   1. $\dfrac{\sqrt{6} - \sqrt{2}}{4}$ 3. $\dfrac{\sqrt{2} - \sqrt{6}}{4}$ 5. $\dfrac{\sqrt{2} - \sqrt{6}}{4}$ 7. $\dfrac{\sqrt{6} - \sqrt{2}}{4}$

9. $\dfrac{-\sqrt{2} - \sqrt{6}}{4}$ 11. $\dfrac{\sqrt{6} + \sqrt{2}}{4}$ 13. $2 - \sqrt{3}$ 15. $\sqrt{3} - 2$ 17. $\sin 90°$; 1

19. $\cos 30°$; $\dfrac{\sqrt{3}}{2}$ 21. $\tan 45°$; 1   25. $\dfrac{56}{65}$ 27. $\dfrac{117}{125}$ 29. $\dfrac{119}{169}$ 39. $\cos \theta$

PAGES 441–442   1. $\cos 30° = \dfrac{\sqrt{3}}{2}$ 3. $\sin \dfrac{\pi}{4} = \dfrac{\sqrt{2}}{2}$ 5. $\tan 150° = -\dfrac{\sqrt{3}}{3}$

7. $\cos 45° = \dfrac{\sqrt{2}}{2}$ 9. $-\dfrac{7}{9}$ 11. $-\dfrac{7}{25}$ 13. $-\dfrac{1}{9}$ 15. $\dfrac{119}{169}$ 17. $-\dfrac{1}{9}$

19. $\dfrac{240}{289}$ 21. $-\dfrac{3\sqrt{7}}{8}$ 23. $\dfrac{\sqrt{15}}{8}$ 25. $-\dfrac{240}{289}$ 27. $-\dfrac{336}{527}$ 29. $2\sqrt{2}$

31. $\sin 18x$ 33. $\cos 8x$ 35. $-\tan 10x$ 37. $\sin 2\theta \csc \theta = 2 \sin \theta \cos \theta \left(\dfrac{1}{\sin \theta}\right) =$

$2 \cos \theta$ 41. $\dfrac{2 \cos \theta}{1 + \cos 2\theta} = \dfrac{2 \cos \theta}{1 + 2 \cos^2 \theta - 1} = \dfrac{2 \cos \theta}{2 \cos^2 \theta} = \dfrac{1}{\cos \theta} = \sec \theta$

49. *Hint:* $\cot 2\theta = \dfrac{\cos 2\theta}{\sin 2\theta}$, but $\cos 2\theta = \cos (3\theta - \theta)$.   51. *Hint:* Let $\cos 3\theta = \cos(2\theta + \theta) =$

$\cos 2\theta \cos \theta - \sin 2\theta \sin \theta$.

PAGES 446–447   1. $\dfrac{\sqrt{2 - \sqrt{3}}}{2}$ 3. $\dfrac{\sqrt{2 + \sqrt{2}}}{2}$ 5. $2 - \sqrt{3}$ $\left(\text{or } \sqrt{7 - 4\sqrt{3}}\right)$

7. $-\dfrac{\sqrt{2 + \sqrt{3}}}{2}$ 11. $\dfrac{2}{5}$, $\dfrac{\sqrt{21}}{5}$, $\dfrac{2\sqrt{21}}{21}$ 13. $\dfrac{2\sqrt{13}}{13}$, $\dfrac{3\sqrt{13}}{13}$, $\dfrac{2}{3}$ 15. $\dfrac{3\sqrt{13}}{13}$,

$\dfrac{2\sqrt{13}}{13}, \dfrac{3}{2}$ 17. $\dfrac{1}{2}, -\dfrac{\sqrt{3}}{2}, -\dfrac{\sqrt{3}}{3}$ 19. $\dfrac{12}{13}, \dfrac{2\sqrt{13}}{13}$ 21. $-\dfrac{4}{5}, \dfrac{\sqrt{10}}{10}$

PAGE 449   1. $15°, 75°, 195°, 255°$ 3. $30°, 60°, 120°, 150°, 210°, 240°, 300°,$
$330°$ 5. $30°, 150°, 270°$ 7. $30°, 90°, 150°, 270°$ 9. $90°, 120°, 240°, 270°$
11. $30°, 150°$ 13. $45°, 135°, 225°, 315°$ 15. $15°, 75°, 195°, 255°$

17. $0°, 30°, 150°, 180°, 210°, 330°$ 19. $\dfrac{\pi}{6}, \dfrac{5\pi}{6}, \dfrac{7\pi}{6}, \dfrac{11\pi}{6}$ 21. $\dfrac{\pi}{4}, \dfrac{5\pi}{4}$

23. $\dfrac{\pi}{3}, \dfrac{\pi}{2}, \dfrac{2\pi}{3}, \dfrac{4\pi}{3}, \dfrac{3\pi}{2}, \dfrac{5\pi}{3}$ 25. $0, \dfrac{\pi}{3}, \dfrac{2\pi}{3}, \pi, \dfrac{4\pi}{3}, \dfrac{5\pi}{3}$

PAGES 452–454   1. $\dfrac{\pi}{4}$ 3. $-\dfrac{\pi}{4}$ 5. $\dfrac{\pi}{3}$ 7. $-\dfrac{\pi}{3}$ 9. $\dfrac{\pi}{6}$ 11. $\dfrac{3\pi}{4}$

13. $\angle DAC$ 15. $\angle BAC$ 17. $\angle B$ 19. $\dfrac{\sqrt{3}}{2}$ 21. $\dfrac{\sqrt{2}}{2}$ 23. 0.3 25. 0

27. $\dfrac{12}{13}$ 29. $\dfrac{3}{4}$ 31. $\dfrac{7}{25}$ 35. $\dfrac{77}{85}$ 37. $\dfrac{44}{117}$ 39. $\dfrac{24}{25}$ 41. $\dfrac{\pi}{4}$ 43. $\dfrac{\pi}{4}$

PAGES 457–458

1. 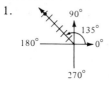   3. 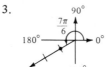   5.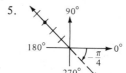

$(-3\sqrt{2}, 3\sqrt{2})$ $\left(-\dfrac{\sqrt{3}}{2}, -\dfrac{1}{2}\right)$ $\left(-\dfrac{3\sqrt{2}}{2}, \dfrac{3\sqrt{2}}{2}\right)$

7. $(7, -7)$ 9. $(-\sqrt{5}, \sqrt{5})$ 11. $(-12, 4\sqrt{3})$ 13–23. Answers may vary.
13. $(5, 180°), (-5, 0°)$ 15. $(6\sqrt{2}, -45°), (-6\sqrt{2}, 135°)$ 17. $(8, 240°), (-8, 60°)$
19. $\left(\dfrac{\sqrt{2}}{2}, 135°\right), \left(-\dfrac{\sqrt{2}}{2}, 315°\right)$ 21. $(2\sqrt{2}, 300°), (-2\sqrt{2}, 120°)$
23. $\left(\dfrac{2b\sqrt{3}}{3}, 30°\right), \left(-\dfrac{2b\sqrt{3}}{3}, 210°\right)$ 25. $(x - 1)^2 + y^2 = 1$ becomes $(r \cos \theta - 1)^2 +$
$(r \sin \theta)^2 = 1$; $r^2 \cos^2 \theta - 2r \cos \theta + 1 + r^2 \sin^2 \theta - 1 = 0$; $r^2(\cos^2 \theta + \sin^2 \theta) - 2r \cos \theta = 0$;
$r^2 - 2r \cos \theta = 0$; $r^2 = 2r \cos \theta$; $r = 2 \cos \theta$

27.   29.   33.   35.

PAGES 461–462   1–7. Answers may vary.   1. $\sqrt{2}(\cos 225° + i \sin 225°)$
(See figure at right.)   3. $4(\cos 90° + i \sin 90°)$
5. $6(\cos 150° + i \sin 150°)$ 7. $-3(\cos 0° + i \sin 0°)$

9. $\sqrt{2} - i\sqrt{2}$ 11. $\dfrac{\sqrt{3}}{2} + \dfrac{1}{2}i$ 13. $-3 + i\sqrt{3}$

15.

21. $5\sqrt{2}$ 23. 6   25–29. Answers may vary for part (a).   25. a. $10(\cos 120° + i \sin 120°)$
b. $-5 + 5i\sqrt{3}$ 27. a. $12(\cos 450° + i \sin 450°)$
b. $12i$ 29. a. $8(\cos 195° + i \sin 195°)$
b. $(-2\sqrt{6} - 2\sqrt{2}) + (2\sqrt{2} - 2\sqrt{6})i$
31. $6\sqrt{2} + 6i\sqrt{2}$

PAGES 464–465   1. $4\sqrt{2} + 4i\sqrt{2}$ 3. -1 5. $2 + 2i$ 7. -16
9. $-4 + 4i\sqrt{3}$ 11–15. Answers may vary.   11. $\cos 60° + i \sin 60°, \cos 180° + i \sin 180°, \cos 300° + i \sin 300°$ (See graph below.)

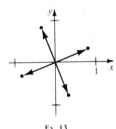
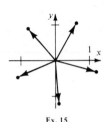

Ex. 11   Ex. 13   Ex. 15

13. $\cos 22.5° + i \sin 22.5°, \cos 112.5° + i \sin 112.5°, \cos 202.5° + i \sin 202.5°,$
$\cos 292.5° + i \sin 292.5°$ (See graph above.)   15. $\sqrt[5]{2}\,(\cos 60° + i \sin 60°),$
$\sqrt[5]{2}\,(\cos 132° + i \sin 132°),\ \sqrt[5]{2}\,(\cos 204° + i \sin 204°),\ \sqrt[5]{2}\,(\cos 276° + i \sin 276°),$
$\sqrt[5]{2}\,(\cos 348° + i \sin 348°)$ (See graph above.)   21. $\dfrac{3}{2} + \dfrac{3\sqrt{3}}{2}i, -3, \dfrac{3}{2} - \dfrac{3\sqrt{3}}{2}i$

23. $-1 + i\sqrt{3}, 1 - i\sqrt{3}$ 25. $0, \dfrac{\sqrt{2}}{2} + i\dfrac{\sqrt{2}}{2}, -\dfrac{\sqrt{2}}{2} + i\dfrac{\sqrt{2}}{2}, -\dfrac{\sqrt{2}}{2} - i\dfrac{\sqrt{2}}{2},$
$\dfrac{\sqrt{2}}{2} - i\dfrac{\sqrt{2}}{2}$

PAGES 466–467 · CHAPTER REVIEW

1. amp. $= 1$, period $= 6\pi$ 2. amp. $= 3$, period $= \pi$

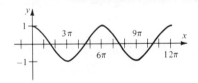
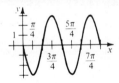

3. $\dfrac{-\sqrt{6} + \sqrt{2}}{4}$ 4. $2 - \sqrt{3}$ 5. $\cos 120°$ 6. $-4\sqrt{5}$ 7. $\sin 2\theta + \cos 2\theta =$
$2 \sin \theta \cos \theta + 2 \cos^2 \theta - 1 = 2 \cos \theta(\sin \theta + \cos \theta) - 1$ 8. $\sqrt{3} - 2 \left(\text{or} -\sqrt{7 - 4\sqrt{3}}\right)$

9. $-\dfrac{\sqrt{2 - \sqrt{3}}}{2}$ 10. $-\dfrac{\sqrt{11}}{4}$ 11. $45°, 90°, 225°, 270°$ 12. $0°, 180°$

13. $\dfrac{\pi}{3}$ 14. $-\dfrac{\pi}{4}$ 15. $\dfrac{4}{5}$ 16. 0.7   17–19. Answers may vary.
17. $(4, 270°), (-4, 90°)$ 18. $(2, 330°), (-2, 150°)$ 19. $(3\sqrt{2}, 225°), (-3\sqrt{2}, 45°)$
20. $(-3, -3\sqrt{3})$ 21. $(5\sqrt{2}, -5\sqrt{2})$ 22–24. Answers may vary.
22. $4(\cos 270° + i \sin 270°)$ 23. $6(\cos 180° + i \sin 180°)$
24. $5\sqrt{2}(\cos 135° + i \sin 135°)$ 25. 32   26. $64i$

1. c   2. d   3. b
4. b   5. d   6. b   7. d   8. b   9. b   10. c   11. c   12. b
13. d   14. d   15. b   16. a   17. a   18. c   19. c   20. c   21. d
22. c   23. c   24. d   25. d   26. b   27. b   28. a

PAGES 472–473 · MIXED REVIEW   1. a. $-2 - \sqrt{3}$ (or $-\sqrt{7 + 4\sqrt{3}}$)   b. $\dfrac{\sqrt{2}}{2}$

c. $\dfrac{1}{2}\sqrt{2 - \sqrt{2}}$

3.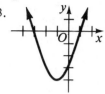

1 and -3; $(-1, -4)$

5. $k = \dfrac{9}{4}$ 7. $m\,\widehat{BC} = 120$; $AB = 4\sqrt{3}$; $OB = 4$

9. a. $\left\{\dfrac{1}{16}\right\}$ b. $\left\{\dfrac{7}{4}\right\}$ 11. $BC = 11$, $m\angle A = 10°20'$, $m\angle B = 90°$,
$m\angle C = 79°40'$ 13. $m\angle A = 73°20'$, $m\angle C = 53°40'$, $c = 25$ or
$m\angle A = 106°40'$, $m\angle C = 20°20'$, $c = 11$ 15. $A \approx 19$ square
units   17. $f(x) = -x + 4$

19.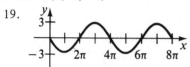

amp. $= 3$, period $= 4\pi$

21. a. $-11 - 12i\sqrt{5}$ b. $-\dfrac{6}{5} + \dfrac{3}{5}i$

c. $\dfrac{7\sqrt{3}}{6}$ 23. $\{d : d \neq -1\}$ 25. a. $(8, -4)$

b. $(-12, -6)$ c. $(8, 4)$ d. $(-8, 3)$
e. $(4, -4)$ 27. magnitude, 26; direction,
$157°20'$ 29. 1   31. $\csc\theta$

33. $\{30°, 90°, 150°, 210°, 270°, 330°\}$ 35. $\{19°30', 160°30', 199°30', 340°30'\}$
37. $3x^2 - 2x + 4$ 39. Use the construction at the top of p. 263.

PAGES 480–481   1. $\{(H, H, H), (H, H, T), (H, T, H), (T, H, H), (H, T, T), (T, H, T),$
$(T, T, H), (T, T, T)\}$ 3. $\dfrac{1}{8}$ 5. $\dfrac{7}{8}$ 7. See array below.   9. $\dfrac{1}{36}$ 11. $\dfrac{5}{36}$

7. $(1, 1), (1, 2), (1, 3), (1, 4), (1, 5), (1, 6)$
$(2, 1), (2, 2), (2, 3), (2, 4), (2, 5), (2, 6)$
$(3, 1), (3, 2), (3, 3), (3, 4), (3, 5), (3, 6)$
$(4, 1), (4, 2), (4, 3), (4, 4), (4, 5), (4, 6)$
$(5, 1), (5, 2), (5, 3), (5, 4), (5, 5), (5, 6)$
$(6, 1), (6, 2), (6, 3), (6, 4), (6, 5), (6, 6)$

13. $\dfrac{1}{2}$ 15. $\dfrac{1}{6}$ 17. $\dfrac{7}{12}$ 19. $\dfrac{1}{52}$
21. $\dfrac{1}{13}$ 23. $\dfrac{2}{13}$ 25. $\dfrac{3}{13}$ 27. $\dfrac{4}{13}$
29. $\dfrac{11}{26}$ 31. $\dfrac{1}{16}$ 33. $\dfrac{5}{16}$

PAGES 484–485   1. a. $\dfrac{3}{14}$ b. $\dfrac{2}{7}$ c. $\dfrac{4}{7}$ d. $\dfrac{3}{14}$ 3. $\dfrac{15}{77}$ 5. $\dfrac{10}{77}$ 7. $\dfrac{4}{77}$

9. $\dfrac{34}{77}$ 11. $\dfrac{52}{77}$ 13. $\dfrac{3}{14}$ 15. 0   17. $\dfrac{1}{7}$ 19. $\dfrac{11}{14}$ 21. $\dfrac{1}{4}$ 23. $\dfrac{3}{32}$

25. a. $\dfrac{504}{1105}$ b. 0.456   27. a. $\dfrac{28}{1105}$ b. 0.025   29. a. $\dfrac{44}{65}$ b. 0.677   31. $\dfrac{1}{3}$

33. a. $\dfrac{1}{8} = 0.125$ b. $\dfrac{1}{2} = 0.5$ c. $\dfrac{3}{8} = 0.375$

PAGES 490–491   1. a. $\dfrac{2}{9}$ b. $\dfrac{1}{3}$ c. $\dfrac{1}{3}$ d. $\dfrac{3}{10}$ 3. $\dfrac{1}{5}$ 5. no; $P(E) = \dfrac{1}{2}$ and

$P(E \mid C) = \dfrac{5}{9}$ 7. yes   9. a. $\dfrac{25}{51}$ b. $\dfrac{26}{51}$ c. $\dfrac{1}{2}$ 11. $\dfrac{13}{51}$ 13. $\dfrac{25}{204}$ 15. a. yes

b. no   17. a. no   b. yes   19. $\dfrac{15}{784}$ 21. $\dfrac{7}{16}$ 23. $\dfrac{15}{16}$ 25. $\dfrac{3}{5}$ 27. $\dfrac{1}{5}$ 29. $\dfrac{1}{3}$

PAGES 496–498   1. 181,400   3. 1680   5. 36   7. 1   9. 260   11. 12
13. 120   15. 216   17. 360   19. 27,405   21. 1260   23. 840

25. 302,400   27. 371,280   29. a. $\dfrac{_{13}C_3 \cdot {}_{13}C_2}{_{52}C_5}$ b. 0.00858   31. a. $\dfrac{_4C_2 \cdot {}_4C_3}{_{52}C_5}$

b. 0.00000923   33. a. $\dfrac{_{26}P_6}{_{52}P_6}$ b. 0.0113   35. a. $\dfrac{_4P_2}{_{52}P_2} \cdot \dfrac{_4P_3}{_{50}P_3} \cdot \dfrac{_4P_1}{_{47}P_1}$

b. 0.0000000786   37. a. $\dfrac{_{13}P_2}{_{52}P_2} \cdot \dfrac{_{13}P_1}{_{50}P_1} \cdot \dfrac{_{13}P_3}{_{49}P_3}$ b. 0.000237   39. a. $\dfrac{_{15}C_3}{_{45}C_3}$

b. 0.0321   41. a. $\dfrac{_{20}C_2 \cdot {}_{10}C_1}{_{45}C_3}$ b. 0.134   47. a. $\dfrac{_4P_1}{_9P_1} \cdot \dfrac{_8P_2}{_8P_2}$ b. 0.444

49. $\dfrac{_8P_2}{_9P_2} \cdot \dfrac{_1P_1}{_7P_1}$ b. 0.111   51. a. $\dfrac{_4P_1}{_8P_1} \cdot \dfrac{_7P_1}{_7P_1}$ b. 0.5

PAGES 501–502   1. a. $_3C_1\left(\dfrac{1}{6}\right)\left(\dfrac{5}{6}\right)^2 \approx 0.347$ b. $_3C_2\left(\dfrac{1}{6}\right)^2\left(\dfrac{5}{6}\right) \approx 0.0694$

c. $_3C_0\left(\dfrac{1}{6}\right)^0\left(\dfrac{5}{6}\right)^3 \approx 0.579$ d. $_3C_3\left(\dfrac{1}{6}\right)^3\left(\dfrac{5}{6}\right)^0 \approx 0.00463$ 3. a. $_6C_4\left(\dfrac{2}{3}\right)^4\left(\dfrac{1}{3}\right)^2 \approx 0.329$

b. $_6C_2\left(\dfrac{2}{3}\right)^2\left(\dfrac{1}{3}\right)^4 \approx 0.0823$ c. $_6C_6\left(\dfrac{2}{3}\right)^6\left(\dfrac{1}{3}\right)^0 \approx 0.0878$ d. $_6C_0\left(\dfrac{2}{3}\right)^0\left(\dfrac{1}{3}\right)^6 \approx 0.00137$

5. a. $_5C_3\left(\dfrac{1}{4}\right)^3\left(\dfrac{3}{4}\right)^2 \approx 0.0879$ b. $_5C_3\left(\dfrac{1}{4}\right)^3\left(\dfrac{3}{4}\right)^2 \approx 0.0879$ c. $_5C_4\left(\dfrac{1}{4}\right)^4\left(\dfrac{3}{4}\right)^1 \approx 0.0146$

d. $_5C_4\left(\dfrac{1}{4}\right)^4\left(\dfrac{3}{4}\right)^1 + {}_5C_5\left(\dfrac{1}{4}\right)^5\left(\dfrac{3}{4}\right)^0 \approx 0.0156$ e. $_5C_0\left(\dfrac{1}{4}\right)^0\left(\dfrac{3}{4}\right)^5 \approx 0.237$

f. $_5C_5\left(\dfrac{1}{4}\right)^5\left(\dfrac{3}{4}\right)^0 \approx 0.000977$ 7. a. $_{10}C_0\left(\dfrac{2}{5}\right)^0\left(\dfrac{3}{5}\right)^{10} \approx 0.00605$ b. $_{10}C_4\left(\dfrac{2}{5}\right)^4\left(\dfrac{3}{5}\right)^6 \approx 0.251$

c. $_{10}C_7\left(\dfrac{2}{5}\right)^7\left(\dfrac{3}{5}\right)^3 \approx 0.0425$ d. $_{10}C_0\left(\dfrac{2}{5}\right)^0\left(\dfrac{3}{5}\right)^{10} + {}_{10}C_1\left(\dfrac{2}{5}\right)^1\left(\dfrac{3}{5}\right)^9 + {}_{10}C_2\left(\dfrac{2}{5}\right)^2\left(\dfrac{3}{5}\right)^8 \approx 0.167$

9. a. 1 head: $_5C_1\left(\dfrac{3}{5}\right)^1\left(\dfrac{2}{5}\right)^4 \approx 0.077$;   2 heads: $_5C_2\left(\dfrac{3}{5}\right)^2\left(\dfrac{2}{5}\right)^3 \approx 0.230$;

3 heads: $_5C_3\left(\dfrac{3}{5}\right)^3\left(\dfrac{2}{5}\right)^2 \approx 0.346$;   4 heads: $_5C_4\left(\dfrac{3}{5}\right)^4\left(\dfrac{2}{5}\right)^1 \approx 0.259$;

5 heads: $_5C_5\left(\dfrac{3}{5}\right)^5\left(\dfrac{2}{5}\right)^0 \approx 0.078$ b. 1   c. 1   11. $_8C_5(0.4)^5(0.6)^3 + {}_8C_6(0.4)^6(0.6)^2 +$
$_8C_7(0.4)^7(0.6) + {}_8C_8(0.4)^8 \approx 0.167$

PAGES 506–508   1. $z^3 + 15z^2 + 75z + 125$ 3. $r^4 - 4r^3s + 6r^2s^2 - 4rs^3 + s^4$
5. $256 + 256x + 96x^2 + 16x^3 + x^4$ 7. $16z^4 + 32z^3k + 24z^2k^2 + 8zk^3 + k^4$
9. $y^5 - 10y^4z + 40y^3z^2 - 80y^2z^3 + 80yz^4 - 32z^5$ 11. $256q^4 + 768q^3x + 864q^2x^2 +$
$432qx^3 + 81x^4$ 13. $f^8 - 8f^7q + 28f^6q^2 - 56f^5q^3 + 70f^4q^4 - 56f^3q^5 + 28f^2q^6 -$
$8fq^7 + q^8$ 15. $c^7 - 21c^6 + 189c^5 - 945c^4 + 2835c^3 - 5103c^2 + 5103c - 2187$
17. 21   19. 9   21. 56   23. 120   25. u^{15} 27. $26w^{12}y$ 29. $4320x^3y^3$
31. $-960x^3y^7$ 33. $90,720u^4v^4$ 35. $65,536x^8 + 262,144x^7y + 458,752x^6y^2 +$
$458,752x^5y^3$ 37. $256b^4 + 192b^3c + 54b^2c^2 + \dfrac{27}{4}bc^3 + \dfrac{81}{256}c^4$ 39. $x^5y^5 + 5x^4y^3 +$

$10x^3y + \dfrac{10x^2}{y} + \dfrac{5x}{y^3} + \dfrac{1}{y^5}$ 41. $81g^4 - 216g + \dfrac{216}{g^2} - \dfrac{96}{g^5} + \dfrac{16}{g^8}$ 43. $-8xy^3$

45. -4320 47. $462a^6b^5$ 49. $6435k^7m^8$ 51. a. $_9C_3(0.25)^3(0.75)^6 \approx 0.056$
b. $_9C_0(0.25)^0(0.75)^9 + {}_9C_1(0.25)^1(0.75)^8 + {}_9C_2(0.25)^2(0.75)^7 + {}_9C_3(0.25)^3(0.75)^6 \approx 0.834$
c. $_9C_0(0.25)^0(0.75)^9 + {}_9C_1(0.25)^1(0.75)^8 + {}_9C_2(0.25)^2(0.75)^7 + {}_9C_3(0.25)^3(0.75)^6 +$
$_9C_4(0.25)^4(0.75)^5 \approx 0.951$ 53. $(5j - k)^6$

PAGES 510-511 · CHAPTER REVIEW   1. $\dfrac{2}{13}$ 2. $\dfrac{5}{12}$ 3. $\dfrac{1}{17}$ 4. $\dfrac{1}{169}$

5. a. $\dfrac{3}{7}$ b. $\dfrac{5}{14}$ c. $\dfrac{2}{5}$ 6. no   7. no   8. yes   9. 24   10. $_{10}C_3 = 120$

11. a. $\dfrac{_4C_2 \cdot {}_{48}C_3}{_{52}C_5}$ b. 0.0399   12. a. $_4C_2\left(\dfrac{1}{6}\right)^2\left(\dfrac{5}{6}\right)^2$ b. 0.116   13. a. $_4C_3\left(\dfrac{1}{6}\right)^3\left(\dfrac{5}{6}\right) +$

$_4C_4\left(\dfrac{1}{6}\right)^4\left(\dfrac{5}{6}\right)^0$ b. 0.0162   14. $80y^3z^2$ 15. $128u^7 + 2240u^6 + 16800u^5$

16. $x^5 - 10x^4a + 40x^3a^2 - 80x^2a^3 + 80xa^4 - 32a^5$

PAGES 514-515 · MIXED REVIEW   1. $-\dfrac{5}{12}$ 3. 1   5. $-\dfrac{2\sqrt{3}}{3}$ 7. $\cos\theta =$

$-\dfrac{\sqrt{3}}{2}$, $\tan\theta = -\dfrac{\sqrt{3}}{3}$, $\csc\theta = 2$, $\sec\theta = -\dfrac{2\sqrt{3}}{3}$, $\cot\theta = -\sqrt{3}$ 9. 15.8

11. Constructions may vary. One solution is given at the right.

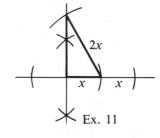

Ex. 11

13. $\dfrac{5}{17}$ 15. $T_{6,\,-6}$ 17. $(4, -1)$ 19. $\sin 4x =$
$2\sin 2x \cos 2x = 2 \cdot 2 \sin x \cos x (\cos^2 x - \sin^2 x) =$
$4\sin x \cos x (\cos x + \sin x)(\cos x - \sin x)$

21. $\left(\dfrac{-1 \pm i\sqrt{14}}{3}\right)$; sum, $-\dfrac{2}{3}$; product, $\dfrac{5}{3}$

23. a. $-\dfrac{2\sqrt{2} + \sqrt{10}}{6}$ b. $\dfrac{\sqrt{30}}{6}$ c. $4\sqrt{5}$ d. $-\dfrac{3}{2}$

25. $\left\{-\dfrac{3}{2}\right\}$ 27. $\{8\}$ 29. $\{270°\}$ 31. $\dfrac{5\pi}{2}$ 33. a. 15   b. 18°

c. 13.5 square units   35. $\dfrac{7}{51}$; no; no   37. a. $\dfrac{3}{25} + \dfrac{4}{25}i$ b. $-24 - 3\sqrt{2}$

39. an isosceles trapezoid (other answers possible)

PAGES 520-522   1-10. Answers will vary.   11. 0.536

PAGES 525-526   1. 275   3. 28   5. 1210   7. 205   9. 70   11. 15.8

13. 1.4   15. 10.5   17. 92   19. $\displaystyle\sum_{i=50}^{75} i$; answers may vary.   21. $\displaystyle\sum_{i=1}^{9} (i - 4)$;

answers may vary.   23. $\displaystyle\sum_{i=0}^{39} (2i + 1)$; answers may vary.   25. 8   27. 55

29. 2400   31. 2500   35. $\displaystyle\sum_{i=1}^{n} (2i - 1) = n^2$ 37. $\dfrac{2(2n + 1)}{n}$

PAGES 530-532   1. a. $1:3$; $2:2$; $3:5$; $4:4$; $5:5$; $6:5$; $7:4$; $8:4$; $9:5$; $10:3$
b. 5.7

3. a.

Distance	Class Mark	Freq.
31–35	33	2
36–40	38	4
41–45	43	3
46–50	48	5
51–55	53	5
56–60	58	3
61–65	63	2

3. b. 48 km

5.

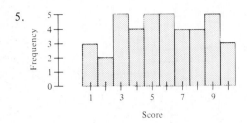

7.

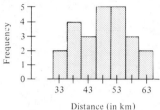

Distance (in km)

9. a.

Diameter (in cm)	Class Mark	Freq.
18–22	20	4
23–27	25	6
28–32	30	5
33–37	35	10
38–42	40	4
43–47	45	4
48–52	50	7
53–57	55	2
58–62	60	1

9. b. 37.0 cm
13. 4

PAGES 535–537   1. at least 70   3. Score was at least 49 but less than 74.
5. median: 30.2; modes: 30.1 and 30.2   7. median: 2; mode: 2   9. a. median: 72.5;
mean: 71.8   b. median: 77.5; mean: 76.8   c. Each is 5 higher than the original statistic.
11. $30,000–$39,000   13. $38,200   15. Answers will vary; example: 10, 15, 20,
25, 28, 32, 35, 40, 45, 50.   17. The numbers less than the median vary from the median to
a greater degree than the numbers greater than the median.   19. Yes. For example; 9, 9, 9

PAGES 541–543   1. a. It is 0.   b. It is 0.   c. It is 0.   d. It is 0.   3. II; the fact that
s is larger (200 compared to 100) indicates that the data are spread farther from the mean.
5. Range: 12; mean absolute deviation: 2.5   7. $s^2 = 34$; $s \approx 5.8$ 9. a. It is 10 points
higher   b. It is the same.   11. $s^2 \approx 0.74$; $s \approx 0.86$ 15. $\overline{x} = c$; $s = |a|$

PAGES 546–547   1. 0.818   3. 0.122   5. 0.645   7. 0.184   9. 0.145
11. 50%   13. 68.2%   15. 0.159   17. 0.841   19. 0.308   21. a. Yes
b. No   23. 156   25. 5.5%   27. 0.682   29. 0.31   31. 0.212   33. Yes
35. 0.9   37. $a = 0.5$ 39. $a = 1.7$

PAGES 550–551 · CHAPTER REVIEW   1. $\dfrac{37}{100}$ 2. $\dfrac{63}{100}$ 3. 81   4. 72

5. 60   6. $240.95   7. 2.7   8. 14.1   9. 6   10. 5   11. 5.6   12. 23
13. 6   14. 56.8   15. 7.5   16. 0.682   17. 0.384   18. 0.774
19. 0.285

PAGES 554–555 · MIXED REVIEW   1. 1,663,200 arrangements   3. 0.023
5. Use the construction on p. 175 to construct pt. T'; $R = R'$; $S = S'$.   7. $\sin \theta = \dfrac{20}{29}$,

$\cos \theta = \dfrac{21}{29}$, $\tan \theta = \dfrac{20}{21}$, $\sec \theta = \dfrac{29}{21}$, $\cot \theta = \dfrac{21}{20}$ 9. range, 3; mean, 12; median, 12.5;

mode, 13; variance, 1.5   11. a. $\{6.92\}$ b. $\{13.4\}$ 13. $-\dfrac{\sqrt{2+\sqrt{2}}}{2}$ 15. $\left\{\dfrac{\pi}{6}, \dfrac{5\pi}{6}\right\}$

17. $\left\{\dfrac{3\pi}{2}\right\}$ 19. $x = 144$; $y = 36$ 21. $\{m: m < 5 \text{ or } m > 9\}$ 23. $\{10\}$

25. 0.9734   27. 997,002,000   29. 6; 31°   31. $\dfrac{25}{51}$ 33. $\left(\sin \dfrac{1}{2}\theta + \cos \dfrac{1}{2}\theta\right)^2 =$

$\sin^2 \dfrac{1}{2}\theta + 2 \sin \dfrac{1}{2}\theta \cos \dfrac{1}{2}\theta + \cos^2 \dfrac{1}{2}\theta = 1 + 2 \sin \dfrac{1}{2}\theta \cos \dfrac{1}{2}\theta = 1 + \sin\left(2 \cdot \dfrac{1}{2}\theta\right) = 1 + \sin \theta$

PAGES 561–563   1. $A''(5, 4)$, $B''(7, 5)$, $C''(2, 6)$ 3. $A''(-1, -2)$, $B''(-3, -3)$,
$C''(2, -4)$ 5. $A''(3, 6)$, $B''(9, 9)$, $C''(-6, 12)$ 7. $A''(1, 2)$, $B''(5, 4)$, $C''(-5, 6)$
9. $A''(1, 2)$, $B''(-1, 1)$, $C''(4, 0)$ 11. $\left(-\dfrac{\sqrt{3}}{2}, -\dfrac{1}{2}\right)$ 13. $\left(\dfrac{1}{2}, -\dfrac{\sqrt{3}}{2}\right)$
15. $\left(\dfrac{\sqrt{2}}{2}, -\dfrac{\sqrt{2}}{2}\right)$ 17. $(1, 0)$ 19. $(0, -2)$ 21. $\left(\dfrac{1}{2}, -\dfrac{5\sqrt{3}}{2}\right)$ 23. $\dfrac{3}{4}$
25. $x = 4$, $y = -8$ 27. $x = -2$, $y = -1$ 29. $x = 2$, $y = 3$ 31. $x = -3$, $y = 4$
33. $t = T_{2, -4}$ 35. Answers may vary. For example, R_{240} 39. a. $A''(3, 1)$, $B''(3, 5)$,
$C''(6, 5)$ b. $A''(3, 1)$, $B''(3, 5)$, $C''(0, 5)$ c. $A''(-3, 1)$, $B''(1, 1)$, $C''(1, 4)$
d. $A''(-2, -1)$, $B''(2, -1)$, $C''(2, -4)$ e. translation: c; reflection: a; rotation: b

PAGES 566–568   1. $A''(4, 11)$, $B''(2, 8)$, $C''(6, 6)$ 3. $A''(-1, -5)$, $B''(1, -2)$,
$C''(-3, 0)$ 5. $A''(6, -3)$, $B''(3, -1)$, $C''(1, -5)$ 7. $A''(2, -3)$, $B''(5, -5)$, $C''(7, -1)$
9. Draw any two of $\overline{AA''}$, $\overline{BB''}$, and $\overline{CC''}$, say $\overline{AA''}$ and $\overline{BB''}$. Then construct $\perp$ bisectors to find
the midpts., P and Q, of $\overline{AA''}$ and $\overline{BB''}$, respectively. Draw $\overleftrightarrow{PQ}$. $m = \overleftrightarrow{PQ}$
11, 13.

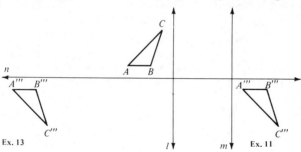

15. a. $A'(-2, 1)$, $B'(-6, 2)$, $C'(-7, 5)$ b. $A''(-2, 1)$, $B''(2, 2)$, $C''(3, 5)$
c. $A'''(-2, -1)$, $B'''(2, -2)$, $C'''(3, -5)$ d. $r_{x\text{-axis}} \circ r_b \circ r_{y\text{-axis}} = r_{x\text{-axis}} \circ T_{-4, 0}$
17. a. $x = 0$ b. $T_{a, b} = T_{0, 3}$ c. $(-2, 4)$ 19. a. $y = x$ b. $T_{a, b} = T_{4, 4}$ c. $(5, 6)$
21. a. $y = 2x + 1$ b. $T_{a, b} = T_{-1, -2}$ 23. a. $A'''(8, -3)$, $B'''(6, -3)$, $C'''(6, 1)$
b. p is the line $x = 2$; $T_{a, b} = T_{0, -6}$

PAGES 572–575   1. a. translation   3. a. reflection   5. a. glide reflection
7. reflection   9. glide reflection   13. a. $A'(3, 0)$, $B'(1, 5)$, $C'(4, 6)$ b. $A''(5, 0)$,
$B''(7, 5)$, $C''(4, 6)$ c. $A'''(-7, 0)$, $B'''(-9, 5)$, $C'''(-6, 6)$ d. q is the line $x = -5$

15. rotation   17. glide reflection   19. reflection   21. $AB = A'B_1$ because r_l is an isometry. $AB = A'B'$ because t is an isometry. By substitution, $A'B_1 = A'B'$.
23. $r_l \circ r_k(2, 2) = r_p \circ r_q(2, 2) = (2, 2)$; $r_l \circ r_k(4, -2) = r_p \circ r_q(4, -2) = (6, 4)$; $r_l \circ r_k(6, 4) = r_p \circ r_q(6, 4) = (0, 6)$.   25. $T_{0, -2} \circ r_n(2, 2) = T_{1, -1} \circ r_b(2, 2) = (-2, -4)$;. $T_{0, -2} \circ r_n(4, -2) = T_{1, -1} \circ r_b(4, -2) = (2, -6)$; $T_{0, -2} \circ r_n(6, 4) = T_{1, -1} \circ r_b(6, 4) = (-4, -8)$.   27. Answers may vary. For example, $x = 0$, $y = -4$.   29. Answers may vary. For example, $y = 0$, $x = 8$, $y = -2$.

PAGES 579–580   1. a. 8   b. 15   3. a. 12   b. 10   5. a. $\frac{4}{3}$ b. 90
7. $A''(1, -2)$, $B''(2, -1)$, $C''(4, -2)$ 9. $A''(5, 11)$, $B''(9, 7)$, $C''(17, 11)$
11. $A''(-4, -8)$, $B''(-8, -4)$, $C''(-16, -8)$ 13. $A''(0, -4)$, $B''(4, 0)$, $C''(12, -4)$
15. $A'''(1, 2)$, $B'''(0, 3)$, $C'''(1, 5)$

17. a.   b.

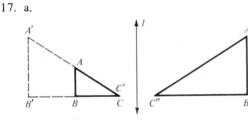 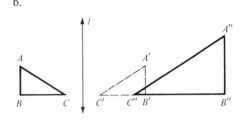

19. $r_{y\text{-axis}} \circ D_4$ 21. $R_{A, 180} \circ D_{A, \frac{1}{2}}$ 23. $T_{4, -1} \circ D_{A, 2}$ 25. $(T_{-2, 0} \circ r_{x\text{-axis}}) \circ D_{A, 3}$
27. a. $T_{5, -2} \circ D_{B, 2}$ b. $D_{B'', 2} \circ T_{5, -2}$ c. $T_{8, -2} \circ D_{C, 2}$ d. $D_{C'', 2} \circ T_{8, -2}$
e. $T_{8, -6} \circ D_2$ f. $D_2 \circ T_{4, -3}$ g. $D_{P, 2} \circ I$, where $P = (-8, 6)$ h. Answers will vary.

PAGE 585   1. $\{I, r_l\}$, where l is the $\perp$ bis. of base   3. $\{I, R_{P, 180}\}$, where P is pt. of intersection of diagonals   5. $\{I, r_l\}$, where l contains the midpts. of both bases.
7. $\{I, r_l, r_m, R_{P, 180}\}$, where l and m are the major and minor axes and P is their pt. of intersection   9. $r_m \circ R_{P, 180}(WXYZ) = r_m(R_{P, 180}(WXYZ)) = r_m(YZWX) = XWZY = r_l(WXYZ)$. Therefore, $r_m \circ R_{P, 180} = r_l$.   11. $R_{P, 180} \circ r_l(WXYZ) = R_{P, 180}(r_l(WXYZ)) = R_{P, 180}(XWZY) = ZYXW = r_m(WXYZ)$. Therefore, $R_{P, 180} \circ r_l = r_m$.
13. $r_m \circ r_l(WXYZ) = r_m(r_l(WXYZ)) = r_m(XWZY) = YZWX = R_{P, 180}(WXYZ)$. Therefore, $r_m \circ r_l = R_{P, 180}$.   15. $r_m \circ R_{P, 240}(\triangle ABC) = r_m(R_{P, 240}(\triangle ABC)) = r_m(\triangle BCA) = \triangle BAC = r_l(\triangle ABC)$. Therefore, $r_m \circ R_{P, 240} = r_l$.
17. Let l be the line of symmetry.

$\circ$	I	r_l
I	I	r_l
r_l	r_l	I

The symmetry group is abelian.

19. Let P be the point of intersection of the diagonals.

$\circ$	I	$R_{P, 180}$
I	I	$R_{P, 180}$
$R_{P, 180}$	$R_{P, 180}$	I

The symmetry group is abelian.

21. a. $r_m \circ (R_{P, 120} \circ r_l) = r_m \circ r_n = R_{P, 120}$; $(r_m \circ R_{P, 120}) \circ r_l = r_n \circ r_l = R_{P, 120}$; therefore, $r_m \circ (R_{P, 120} \circ r_l) = (r_m \circ R_{P, 120}) \circ r_l$.   b. The Assoc. Prop.   23. (1) By Corollary 1 to Thm. 14–6 and Thm. 5–2, the composite of two direct isometries is a direct isometry. (2) Comp. of transformations is assoc.   (3) I is a direct isometry, so $I \in D$.   (4) Every direct isometry has an inverse under $\circ$ that is a direct isometry. Therefore D is a group under $\circ$.

29. R is not closed under $\circ$.   35. Let l and m be the $\perp$ bis. of the sides of the rectangle and P be their point of intersection. Subgroups: $(\langle I\rangle, \circ)$, $(\langle I, r_l\rangle, \circ)$, $(\langle I, r_m\rangle, \circ)$, $(\langle I, R_{P,\,180}\rangle, \circ)$, $(\langle I, r_l, r_m, R_{P,\,180}\rangle, \circ)$

PAGES 586-587 · CHAPTER REVIEW   1. $D \longrightarrow F$, $E \longrightarrow D$, $F \longrightarrow E$
2. $D \longrightarrow E$, $E \longrightarrow F$, $F \longrightarrow D$ 3. $D \longrightarrow D$, $E \longrightarrow E$, $F \longrightarrow F$ 4. $k_1 \cdot k_2$
5. a. $T_{2,\,10}$ b. $T_{-2,\,-10}$
6.
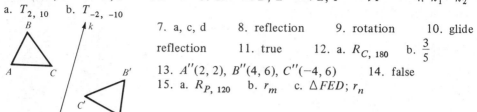
7. a, c, d   8. reflection   9. rotation   10. glide reflection   11. true   12. a. $R_{C,\,180}$ b. $\dfrac{3}{5}$
13. $A''(2, 2)$, $B''(4, 6)$, $C''(-4, 6)$ 14. false
15. a. $R_{P,\,120}$ b. r_m c. $\triangle FED$; r_n

PAGES 590-591 · MIXED REVIEW   1. $\dfrac{143}{16,660} \approx 0.00858$

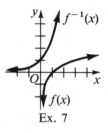
Ex. 7

3. $-\cos\theta$ 5. $\sin\theta$ 7. See graphs at right; $f^{-1}(x) = 3^x$
9. mean, 2.4; median, 2.5; mode, 3; range, 4; mean absolute deviation, 1; variance, $\dfrac{41.2}{30} \approx 1.37$ 11. $m\angle L = 32°30'$, $JK = 7$, $JL = 8$

13. a. -0.96 b. -0.8 c. $-\dfrac{2\sqrt{5}}{5}$ 15. 0.459

17. none   19. $\dfrac{24}{7}$ 21. $512a^9$, $-6912a^8b$, $41{,}472a^7b^2$, and $-145{,}152a^6b^3$

23. $\bar{x} = \dfrac{1}{n}\sum_{i=1}^{n} x_i$ 25. $\dfrac{\cot x}{1 + \csc x} = \dfrac{\dfrac{\cos x}{\sin x}}{1 + \dfrac{1}{\sin x}} \cdot \dfrac{\sin x}{\sin x} = \dfrac{\cos x}{\sin x + 1} = \dfrac{\cos x}{1 + \sin x}$

27. $\dfrac{841\pi}{4} - 420$ cm^2 29. $f(g(x)) = x - 4$; $g(f(x)) = x - \dfrac{4}{3}$

31.
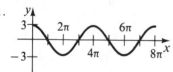

33. Let l and m be the two lines of symmetry, and let P be their point of intersection.

$\circ$	I	r_l	r_m	$R_{P,\,180}$
I	I	r_l	r_m	$R_{P,\,180}$
r_l	r_l	I	$R_{P,\,180}$	r_m
r_m	r_m	$R_{P,\,180}$	I	r_l
$R_{P,\,180}$	$R_{P,\,180}$	r_m	r_l	I

PAGES 596-597   1. $a_k = k^3$, $k \in \{1, 2, 3, 4, 5\}$ 3. $a_k = 3k - 5$, $k \in \{1, 2, 3, 4, 5, 6, 7\}$
5. $a_k = 2^{k-2}$, $k \in \{1, 2, 3, \ldots\}$ 7. $a_1 = -3$; $a_k = a_{k-1} + 4$, $k \in \{2, 3, 4, 5, 6, 7\}$
9. $a_1 = -\dfrac{3}{2}$; $a_k = (-4)a_{k-1}$, $k \in \{2, 3, 4, \ldots\}$ 11. $a_1 = 3$; $a_k = (a_{k-1})^{-1}$,
$k \in \{2, 3, 4, 5, \ldots\}$ 13. $F_{15} = 610$, $F_{16} = 987$, $F_{17} = 1597$, $F_{18} = 2584$, $F_{19} = 4181$,
$F_{20} = 6765$ 15. $a_k = \dfrac{1 - (-1)^k}{2}$, $k \in \{1, 2, 3, \ldots\}$ 17. $a_k = tr^{k-1}$, $k \in \{1, 2, 3, \ldots\}$

PAGES 600-601   1. 128   3. −11   5. −97   7. $\frac{51}{5}$ 9. −31   11. 123

13. 5   15. 20, 33, 46, 59   17. $-\frac{35}{3}$, $-\frac{31}{3}$, −9, $-\frac{23}{3}$, $-\frac{19}{3}$, −5, $-\frac{11}{3}$, $-\frac{7}{3}$

19. $a_1 = 63$; $d = -8$ 21. $a_1 = -\frac{83}{2}$; $d = \frac{3}{2}$ 23. 5   25. 4, −2

27. The common difference is $\log b$, and using the formula $a_k = a_1 + (k-1)d$ we get $a_k = \log a + (k-1)\log b$ or $a_k = \log a + \log b^{k-1} = \log ab^{k-1}$, $k \in \{1, 2, \ldots\}$.

29. a. Let $b_k = 2^{a_k}$; $b_1 = 3$, $b_k = 2b_{k-1}$, $k \in \{2, 3, 4, \ldots\}$ b. 3, 6, 12, 24, 48

PAGE 605   1. 2352   3. −1088   5. 60   7. $\frac{875}{2}$ 9. 693   11. 232

13. 1452   15. $\frac{1089}{2}$ 17. −496   19. −24   21. 3   23. 8   25. 50

27. a. $S_k = \frac{k(1 + (2k-1))}{2} = \frac{k(2k)}{2} = \frac{2k^2}{2} = k^2$ b. 6

PAGES 609-610   1. 96   3. 243   5. $\frac{32}{27}$ 7. −640   9. $\frac{1}{300}$ 11. 24

13. PQ^8 15. 12   17. $\frac{256}{243}$ 19. 6   21. ±10   23. $-\frac{1}{3}$ 25. $\pm\sqrt{2}$

27. $\frac{1}{4}$ 29. 6, 12, 24   31. 24, 36, 54   33. 1,000,000,000 cents, or $10,000,000

PAGES 613-614   1. 5110   3. 255   5. 211   7. 315   9. $\frac{93}{2}$ 11. 1001

13. $\frac{728}{243}$ 15. $\frac{211}{3}$ 17. 63   19. $2^k - 1$ 21. $n = 6$; $a_n = 1215$

23. $r = -\frac{1}{2}$; $n = 6$ 25. $x = 8$; $a_6 = 32$

PAGES 616-617   1. 24   3. no sum   5. $\frac{250}{3}$ 7. $\frac{125}{18}$ 9. $\frac{1}{8}$

11. $\frac{27\sqrt{3} + 27}{2}$ 13. $\frac{8}{9}$ 15. $\frac{4}{11}$ 17. $\frac{5}{37}$ 19. $5\frac{4}{33}$ 21. $\frac{2}{3}$ 23. $-\frac{3}{4}$

25. $\frac{5}{12}$ 27. 8 m

PAGES 621-622 · CHAPTER REVIEW   1. $a_k = 3^{k-1}$, $k \in \{1, 2, 3, \ldots\}$ 2. $a_k = (-2)^k$, $k \in \{1, 2, 3, \ldots\}$ 3. $a_1 = 6$; $a_k = -a_{k-1}$, $k \in \{2, 3, 4, \ldots\}$ 4. $a_1 = 4$; $a_k = a_{k-1} - 2$, $k \in \{2, 3, 4, \ldots\}$ 5. 196   6. $\frac{191}{2}$ 7. $-\frac{3}{2}$, −1, $-\frac{1}{2}$, 0, $\frac{1}{2}$ 8. 1500

9. 630   10. 1   11. $\frac{81}{2}$ 12. 6, 4   13. 19,682   14. $\frac{422}{27}$ 15. 768

16. $\frac{625}{4}$ 17. $\frac{7}{11}$ 18. $\frac{8}{11}$ 19. When $n = 1$; $4 \cdot 3^{1-1} = 2 \cdot 3^1 - 2$, or $4 = 4$.

Assume the statement is true when $n = k$ and prove it is true when $n = k + 1$.
GIVEN: $4 + 12 + 36 + \cdots + 4 \cdot 3^{k-1} = 2 \cdot 3^k - 2$. PROVE: $4 + 12 + 36 + \cdots + 4 \cdot 3^k = 2 \cdot 3^{k+1} - 2$. *Proof:* $4 + 12 + 36 + \cdots + 4 \cdot 3^{k-1} = 2 \cdot 3^k - 2$; $4 + 12 + 36 + \cdots + 4 \cdot 3^{k-1} + 4 \cdot 3^k = 2 \cdot 3^k - 2 + 4 \cdot 3^k = 2 \cdot 3^k - 2 + 2(2 \cdot 3^k) = 2 \cdot 3^k[1 + 2] - 2 = 2 \cdot 3^k \cdot 3 - 2 = 2 \cdot 3^{k+1} - 2$

1. b   2. c   3. d   4. c
5. b   6. b   7. c   8. c   9. a   10. a   11. d   12. b   13. a
14. c   15. b   16. d   17. a   18. d   19. a   20. b   21. b
22. c   23. c   24. d   25. a   26. d   27. d   28. a   29. d
30. d   31. c   32. d   33. b   34. b   35. a   36. d   37. c
38. b   39. b   40. c   41. d   42. a   43. b   44. a   45. b

PAGES 628–629 · MIXED REVIEW   1. -1104 3. $\frac{1}{3}$ 5. $41°50'$ or $138°10'$

7. $\{30°, 90°, 150°, 270°\}$ 9. 6,760,000 numbers   11. 108   13. $X'(0, 2)$, $Y'(4, 0)$,

$Z'(2, -2)$ 15. $\dfrac{\tan\theta + 1}{\tan\theta - 1} = \dfrac{\frac{\sin\theta}{\cos\theta} + 1}{\frac{\sin\theta}{\cos\theta} - 1} \cdot \dfrac{\cos\theta}{\cos\theta} = \dfrac{\sin\theta + \cos\theta}{\sin\theta - \cos\theta} \cdot \dfrac{\sin\theta + \cos\theta}{\sin\theta + \cos\theta} =$

$\dfrac{\sin^2\theta + \cos^2\theta + 2\sin\theta\cos\theta}{\sin^2\theta - \cos^2\theta} = \dfrac{1 + 2\sin\theta\cos\theta}{\sin^2\theta - \cos^2\theta}$ 17. $8\sqrt{3}$ 19. When $n = 1$; $1 \cdot 2 =$

$\dfrac{1 \cdot 2 \cdot 3}{3}$, or $2 = 2$. Assume the statement is true when $n = k$ and prove it is true when $n = k + 1$.

GIVEN: $1 \cdot 2 + 2 \cdot 3 + 3 \cdot 4 + \cdots + k(k + 1) = \dfrac{k(k + 1)(k + 2)}{3}$.   PROVE: $1 \cdot 2 + 2 \cdot 3 +$

$3 \cdot 4 + \cdots + (k + 1)(k + 2) = \dfrac{(k + 1)(k + 2)(k + 3)}{3}$.   *Proof:* $1 \cdot 2 + 2 \cdot 3 + \cdots + k(k + 1) +$

$(k + 1)(k + 2) = \dfrac{k(k + 1)(k + 2)}{3} + (k + 1)(k + 2) = (k + 1)(k + 2)\left[\dfrac{k}{3} + 1\right] =$

$(k + 1)(k + 2)\left(\dfrac{k + 3}{3}\right) = \dfrac{(k + 1)(k + 2)(k + 3)}{3}$

21.   23. -0.4369 25. $\{5\}$

27. 11   29. line reflection   31. 21 square units   33. $\dfrac{4}{17}$ 35. 549

37. 84.1%

EXTRA PRACTICE

PAGE 630 · CHAPTER 1   1. a. 0.144   b. $2.08\overline{3}$ 3. a. 1   b. 5   5. $1\frac{3}{5}$; $-\frac{5}{8}$

7. $\{30\}$ 9. 22, 24, 26   11. $\{x\colon x \geqslant 0\}$ 13. $\{m\colon m \geqslant -10\}$

15. $\left\{x\colon -1 < x < \dfrac{9}{2}\right\}$ 17. $\{2, -6\}$

19. $\{h\colon -1 < h < 5\}$ 21. a. $\dfrac{8}{33}$ b. $\dfrac{7}{15}$ 23. $\{-10.2\}$ 25. $\varnothing$

27. $\left\{m\colon -\dfrac{3}{2} < m < 2\right\}$ 29. $\left\{w\colon w < \dfrac{5}{3} \text{ or } w > 3\right\}$

PAGE 631 · CHAPTER 2   1. a. $\dfrac{225z^6}{64x^4y^2}$ b. $-4a^{10}b^3$ 3. $3x^2 - 11x - 3$

5. a. $(5j - 3)(3j + 2)$ b. $(w + 4)(w^2 - 4w + 16)$ c. $4(c + 1)(c - 1)$

7. $\dfrac{6y^3 - y^2 - 6}{2y - 3} = 3y^2 + 4y + 6 + \dfrac{12}{2y - 3}$ 9. $\dfrac{3g - 5}{5g}$ 11. 22   13. $\dfrac{1 + y}{y}$

15. a. $\{k: k < 0 \text{ or } k > 4\}$ b. $\{h: -4 \leqslant h \leqslant -2\}$ 17. a. $4x^2 + 2x - 12$ b. 5

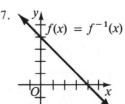

-1 0 1 2 3 4 5   -4 -2

19. $\left\{\dfrac{-1 \pm \sqrt{7}}{2}\right\}$ 21. a. $\dfrac{z^2 + 3z + 6}{(z + 3)^2(z + 1)}$ b. $\dfrac{1}{x - 1}$

23. $\left\{r: 0 < r < 1 \text{ or } r > \dfrac{5}{2}\right\}$

-1 0 1 2 3 4

PAGE 632 · CHAPTER 3   1. $\dfrac{7y\sqrt{y}}{5x^2}$ 3. $\dfrac{20\sqrt{5}}{3}$ 5. $18 - 12\sqrt{2}$ 7. $\{43\}$

9. $\{-2\}$ 11. $\dfrac{i\sqrt{35}}{5}$ 13. a. $-4\sqrt{3} + i$ b. $6\sqrt{3} + 3i$ c. $-13 - 11i\sqrt{3}$

15. a. $1 - \dfrac{11}{5}i$ b. $\dfrac{1}{5} + \dfrac{3}{5}i$ c. $-\dfrac{22}{25} - \dfrac{29}{25}i$ 17. $\dfrac{1}{6} + \dfrac{1}{6}i$ 19. $\{2 \pm i\}$

21. $\{-1 \pm i\sqrt{5}\}$ 23. $5\sqrt[3]{6}$ 25. $(x^3 + 4x)\sqrt{5x}$ 27. $-12\sqrt[3]{4}$ 29. a. $\{1, 2\}$

b. $\{3\}$ 31. a. $-\dfrac{2}{5} + \dfrac{2}{5}i$ b. $\dfrac{3}{21} - \dfrac{4i\sqrt{6}}{21}$ 33. $-\dfrac{1}{3}$; $k = 3$

PAGE 633 · CHAPTER 4   1. $\{$real numbers$\}$; the image of 2 is 0; the pre-images of 2 are 3 and -3.   3. $\{x: x > -2\}$; the image of 2 is $\dfrac{1}{2}$; the pre-image of 2 is $-\dfrac{7}{4}$.

5. See figure at right; not a function
7. $f(1) = 5$; $f(3) = f(-3) = 1461$; $f(-x) = 2x^6 + 3$; even
9. $f(1) = \dfrac{1}{3}$; $f(3) = 1$; $f(-3) = -1$; $f(-x) = -\dfrac{1}{3}x$; odd
11. 5.5   13. $f(g(-1)) = g(f(-1)) = 0$
15. a. $x + 3$ b. $\sqrt{x^2 + 3}$ 17. $y = \dfrac{1}{8}x^3$ 19. -7
21. a. $\{x: x \neq \pm 2\}$ b. $\{x: x < 3\}$ 23. If $f(x)$ is even, then
$f(x) = f(-x)$; $ax^2 + bx + c = a(-x)^2 + b(-x) + c$; $ax^2 + bx + c = ax^2 - bx + c$; $2bx = 0$; since

$x \neq 0$, $b = 0$.   25. $g(h(x)) = \dfrac{3\left(\dfrac{2}{3 - x}\right) - 2}{\left(\dfrac{2}{3 - x}\right)} = \dfrac{6 - 2(3 - x)}{2} = \dfrac{2x}{2} = x$;

$h(g(x)) = \dfrac{2}{3 - \left(\dfrac{3x - 2}{x}\right)} = \dfrac{2x}{3x - (3x - 2)} = \dfrac{2x}{2} = x$ 27.

$f(x) = f^{-1}(x)$

PAGE 634 · CHAPTER 5   1. direct; $(3, -2)$; $(-7, 2)$ 3. yes; yes; no

5. 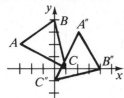   7.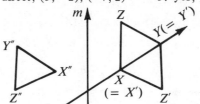

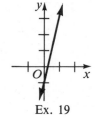

9. 5 lines of symm., each the perpendicular bisector of a side; the pentagon has rotational symmetries about their point of intersection of $72°$, $144°$, $216°$, and $288°$.   11. a. $\dfrac{6}{5}$ b. $(-30, -6)$ 13. $P'(4, 5)$, $Q'(-2, 0)$, $R'(2, 0)$ 15. a. $(3, -4)$ b. $(-3, 4)$ 17. $T_{-2, 0}$
19. See figure; $y = 4x - 1$

Ex. 19

PAGE 635 · CHAPTER 6   1. a. 110   b. 40   c. 70   d. 180   3. $w = 240$, $x = 6\sqrt{3}$, $y = 12$, $z = 30$ 5. 57   7. 5   9. $4\sqrt{15}$ 11. $C = 1.9$; $A = 0.3$
13. $m\,\widehat{AB} = 68$; $m\,\widehat{ACB} = 292$ 15. $4\sqrt{3}$ 17. $8 + 12\pi$

PAGE 636 · CHAPTER 7   1. third   3. a. $\dfrac{13\pi}{12}$ b. $\dfrac{26\pi}{15}$ c. $-\dfrac{\pi}{2}$ 5. $-\dfrac{8}{17}$
7. a. $-\cos 80°$ b. $\sin 42°$ c. $-\sin 20°$ d. $-\cos 10°$ 9. $15°25'12''$ 11. a. 0.3475
b. -0.2728 13. See figure; $\{-2\pi, -\pi, 0, \pi, 2\pi\}$

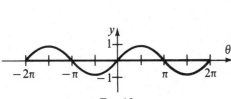

Ex. 13

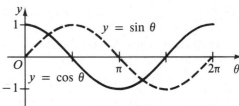

Ex. 21

15. 21.6 cm   17. a. $\sin \theta = \dfrac{2\sqrt{2}}{3}$, $\cos \theta = -\dfrac{1}{3}$ b. $\sin \theta = -\dfrac{2\sqrt{5}}{5}$, $\cos \theta = -\dfrac{\sqrt{5}}{5}$

19. $172°50'$ 21. See figure; $\pi \leqslant \theta \leqslant \dfrac{3\pi}{2}$

PAGE 637 · CHAPTER 8   1. a. π b. Graphs may vary.
See figure at right.   c. $\{$real numbers that are not odd integral
multiples of $\dfrac{\pi}{2}\}$; $\{$real numbers$\}$ 3. $\cos \theta = -\dfrac{20}{29}$, $\tan \theta = \dfrac{21}{20}$,
$\cot \theta = \dfrac{20}{21}$, $\sec \theta = -\dfrac{29}{20}$, $\csc \theta = -\dfrac{29}{21}$ 5. $\dfrac{1 - \sin^2 2\alpha}{\sin 2\alpha}$
7. $\cot^2 \theta$ 9. $-\tan \theta$ 11. $1 - \sin \alpha \cos \alpha \tan \alpha =$
$1 - \sin \alpha \cos \alpha \cdot \dfrac{\sin \alpha}{\cos \alpha} = 1 - \sin^2 \alpha = \cos^2 \alpha$

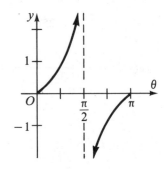

13. $\theta = 90°, 135°, 270°, 315°$ 15. $\theta = 194°30', 345°30'$ 17. $\theta = 0°, 45°, 180°, 225°$
19. $0° \leqslant \theta < 90°$ or $90° < \theta < 270°$ or $270° < \theta < 360°$

21. 0 and π

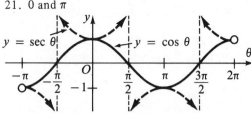

23. $-\cos\theta$ 25. $\dfrac{\cos\theta}{1+\cos\theta} - \dfrac{1}{1-\cos\theta} =$

$\dfrac{(\cos\theta - \cos^2\theta) - (1 + \cos\theta)}{(1+\cos\theta)(1-\cos\theta)} = \dfrac{-\cos^2\theta - 1}{1 - \cos^2\theta} =$

$\dfrac{-\cos^2\theta - (\cos^2\theta + \sin^2\theta)}{\sin^2\theta} = \dfrac{-2\cos^2\theta}{\sin^2\theta} -$

$\dfrac{\sin^2\theta}{\sin^2\theta} = -2\cot^2\theta - 1 = -(2\cot^2\theta + 1)$

27. $\theta = \dfrac{\pi}{3}, \dfrac{5\pi}{3}$ 29. $\theta = 0, \dfrac{\pi}{4}, \dfrac{3\pi}{4}, \pi, \dfrac{5\pi}{4}, \dfrac{7\pi}{4}$ 31. $\dfrac{91°}{3}$

PAGE 638 · CHAPTER 9   1. 81   3. $\dfrac{\sqrt[4]{8}}{4}$

5. See figure at right; the graph of $f(x)$ is above that of $g(x)$
when $x < 0$.   7. 2   9. $\dfrac{3}{2}$ 11. 1.85

13. 0.157   15. 2.10   17. \$2720   19. a. 2

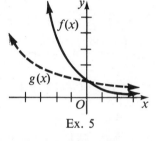

Ex. 5

b. $-\dfrac{1}{2}$ 21. a. $\dfrac{1}{16}$ b. $\sqrt[5]{3}$ 23. $\dfrac{1}{2}(a+b)$
25. a. $0.0913 - 2$ b. 324.8   27. $\{\pm 32\}$ 29. 11.9 yr

PAGE 639 · CHAPTER 10   1. $m\angle S = 90$, $m\angle R = 64$, $RS = 20$, $RT = 45$ 3. $47°10'$
5. $12\sqrt{2}$ 7. 0   9. $34°50'$ 11. 52   13. 4 N at a $75°$ angle to each force
15. 11   17. $\angle R = 42°$, $p = 35$, $q = 70$ 19. 8.2   21. 527 km/h at a heading of $55°$

PAGE 640 · CHAPTER 11   1. a. $\dfrac{3}{2}; 2\pi$ b. $3; \pi$ c. $2; 6\pi$

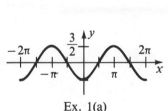

Ex. 1(a)

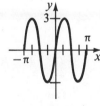

Ex. 1(b)

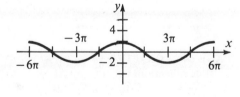

Ex. 1(c)

3. $\dfrac{475}{493}; \dfrac{468}{493}$ 5. $\dfrac{2}{\tan 2\theta} = \dfrac{2}{\dfrac{2\tan\theta}{1-\tan^2\theta}} = \dfrac{2(1-\tan^2\theta)}{2\tan\theta} = \dfrac{1-\tan^2\theta}{\tan\theta} = \dfrac{1}{\tan\theta} - \dfrac{\tan^2\theta}{\tan\theta} =$

$\cot\theta - \tan\theta$ 7. $\dfrac{\sqrt{3}}{2}; -\dfrac{1}{2}; -\sqrt{3}$

9. a. $\dfrac{2\pi}{3}$ b. $\dfrac{\pi}{4}$ c. $\sqrt{3}$ 11. for
example, $(3\sqrt{2}, 225°)$ and $(-3\sqrt{2}, 45°)$
13. See figure at right; six

15. $\dfrac{1 - \sin 2\theta}{\cos 2\theta} = \dfrac{1 - 2 \sin \theta \cos \theta}{\cos^2 \theta - \sin^2 \theta} = \dfrac{(\sin^2 \theta + \cos^2 \theta) - 2 \sin \theta \cos \theta}{\cos^2 \theta - \sin^2 \theta} =$

$\dfrac{(\sin \theta - \cos \theta)(\sin \theta - \cos \theta)}{(\cos \theta - \sin \theta)(\cos \theta + \sin \theta)} = \dfrac{-(\sin \theta - \cos \theta)}{\cos \theta + \sin \theta} = \dfrac{\cos \theta - \sin \theta}{\cos \theta + \sin \theta} \cdot \dfrac{\frac{1}{\cos \theta}}{\frac{1}{\cos \theta}} = \dfrac{1 - \tan \theta}{1 + \tan \theta}$

17. $\{0°, 135°, 180°, 315°\}$ 19. $\sqrt[3]{2}\,(\cos 10° + i \sin 10°)$, $\sqrt[3]{2}\,(\cos 130° + i \sin 130°)$, $\sqrt[3]{2}\,(\cos 250° + i \sin 250°)$

PAGE 641 · CHAPTER 12   1. $\dfrac{1}{9}$ 3. $\dfrac{1}{3}$ 5. a. $\dfrac{1}{4}$ b. $\dfrac{25}{102}$ 7. independent

9. a. 648   b. 448   11. 15,504   13. a. 1   b. 15   c. 10   15. $\dfrac{1}{32}$

17. $\dfrac{256}{270,725}$ 19. $_7C_0(0.7)^2(0.3)^0 + _7C_1(0.7)^6(0.3) + _7C_2(0.7)^5(0.3)^2 \approx 0.647$

21. no; suppose events A and B are mutually exclusive, $P(A) \neq 0$, and $P(B) \neq 0$. Then $P(A \text{ and } B) = 0 = P(A|B)$; since $P(A|B) \neq P(A)$, A and B are dependent.

PAGE 642 · CHAPTER 13   1. 3108 voters   3. 1.525   5. See below.   7. 1
9. 0.158   11. a. 375 times   b. no; yes   13. 47   15. See below.   17. 2.2

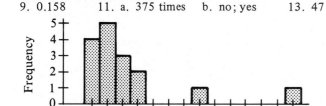

Number of Gold Medals
Ex. 5

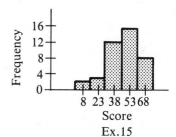

Score
Ex.15

PAGE 643 · CHAPTER 14   1. $(0, -6)$ 3. $(0, -4)$ 5. $(4, -5)$ 7. $(9, 1)$
9. glide reflection   11. rotation   13. $R'(1, -1)$, $S'(-2, -1)$, $T'(0, -3)$
15. $R'(-3, -3)$, $S'(0, -3)$, $T'(-2, -5)$ 17. $R_{P, 240} \circ r_m(\triangle ABC) = R_{P, 240}(r_m(\triangle ABC)) = R_{P, 240}(\triangle CBA) = \triangle ACB = r_n(\triangle ABC)$ 19. $y = -x + 1$ 21. $y = 6$ 23. glide
reflection

PAGE 644 · CHAPTER 15   1. $a_k = \dfrac{1}{2}(k - 1)^2$, $k \in \{1, 2, 3, \ldots, 7\}$ 3. $116\dfrac{1}{2}$

5. -820 7. 756   9. $\dfrac{5}{64}$ 11. 665   13. no sum   15. When $n = 1$;

$3 = 1(2 \cdot 1 + 1)$, or $3 = 3$. Assume the statement is true when $n = k$ and prove it is true when $n = k + 1$. GIVEN: $3 + 7 + 11 + \cdots + (4k - 1) = k(2k + 1)$. PROVE: $3 + 7 + 11 + \cdots + 4k + 3 = (k + 1)(2k + 3)$. *Proof:* $3 + 7 + 11 + \cdots + (4k - 1) = k(2k + 1)$; $3 + 7 + 11 + \cdots + (4k - 1) + (4k + 3) = k(2k + 1) + (4k + 3) = 2k^2 + k + 4k + 3 = 2k^2 + 5k + 3 = (k + 1)(2k + 3)$

17. $a_1 = 7$, $d = -8$ 19. 13   21. $10, 4, \dfrac{8}{5}$ or $-10, 4, -\dfrac{8}{5}$ 23. $\dfrac{2}{5}$

ALGEBRA REVIEW EXERCISES

PAGES 645–646 · CHAPTER 1 1. $\frac{1}{2}$ 3. 5 5. -10 7. $\left\{\frac{1}{6}\right\}$ 9. $\{1\}$

11. $\left\{\frac{6}{13}\right\}$ 13. $\{8, -9\}$ 15. $\left\{-\frac{5}{2}, \frac{11}{2}\right\}$ 17. 6, 6, 2 19. The length must be between 7 and 23. 21. $\{y: y < 1\}$

23. $\{x: 99 < x \leqslant 101\}$ 25. $\{x: -6 < x < 4\}$

27. $\{10.7\}$ 29. $\left\{r: r \leqslant \frac{24}{25}\right\}$ 31. $\{k: -12 \leqslant k < 3\}$ 33. $\left\{t: -\frac{13}{2} < t < \frac{7}{2}\right\}$

35. $\{x: -14 < x < 10\}$ 37. when one rents a boat for 4 hours or less

PAGES 646–647 · CHAPTER 2 1. $72a^8b^7$ 3. $4k$ 5. $\frac{27x^6}{8}$ 7. $4x^2 - xy + 2y$

9. $7y^3z - 2y^2z^2 + yz^5$ 11. $16b^2 - 9$ 13. $w(w + 2)(w - 2)$ 15. $\frac{2b(b - a)}{(a + b)(a^2 + b^2)}$

17. 1 19. $(x - 5)(x + 2)$ 21. $3(m + 5n)(m - 5n)$ 23. $5(z - 2)(z^2 + 2z + 4)$

25. $\left\{\frac{5}{3}, 1\right\}$ 27. $\{-7, 4\}$ 29. $\{-4, 3\}$ 31. -3 and -1 or $-\frac{1}{2}$ and $\frac{3}{2}$

33. $\frac{27y^{12}}{125z^6w^6}$ 35. $\left\{\frac{-5 \pm \sqrt{37}}{6}\right\}$ 37. $\frac{3 + \sqrt{33}}{2}$ and $\frac{3 - \sqrt{33}}{2}$ 39. 8 cm and 10 cm

41. $\{1, -1\}$ 43. $\frac{(x + y)^2(x^2 + y^2)}{x^4y^4}$

PAGES 647–648 · CHAPTER 3 1. $6\sqrt{2}$ 3. $16\sqrt{2} + 120\sqrt{3}$ 5. 167

7. $22\sqrt{6} - 31$ 9. $\sqrt{6} + \sqrt{3}$ 11. $\{6\}$ 13. $9i$ 15. $-2\sqrt{3}$ 17. i

19. 4 21. $-\frac{1}{9} - \frac{4\sqrt{5}}{9}i$ 23. $\left\{\frac{-1 \pm i\sqrt{19}}{2}\right\}$ 25. $\frac{3}{25} - \frac{4}{25}i$

27. $x^2 - 4x + 13 = 0$ 29. $(3 - i)[(3 - i) - 6] + 10 = (3 - i)(-3 - i) + 10 =$

$-9 + i^2 + 10 = -1 + 1 = 0$ 31. $\frac{7\sqrt{3}}{6}$ 33. $(3 + 5x^2)\sqrt{x}$ 35. $\left(\frac{a - b}{ab}\right)\sqrt{ab}$

37. $\frac{1}{5} - \frac{12\sqrt{6}}{5}i$ 39. $\frac{8}{5} + \frac{4}{5}i$ 41. $\left\{\frac{3 - \sqrt{3}}{6}\right\}$ 43. $\{4\}$ 45. $\{4, -4\}$

47. $16x^2 - 24x + 7 = 0$

PAGES 648–649 · CHAPTER 4

1. $\mathcal{R}$; $\mathcal{R}$; one-to-one
3. $\{x: x \geqslant 2\}$; $\{y: y \geqslant 0\}$; one-to-one
5. $\{x: x \leqslant -1 \text{ or } x \geqslant 1\}$; $\{y: y \geqslant 0\}$; not one-to-one   7. no
9. yes; $\mathcal{R}$; $\{5\}$ 11. odd
13. even   15. a. 50   b. 33

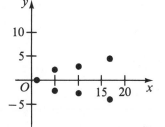
Ex. 7

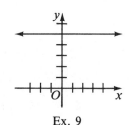
Ex. 9

17. $\{(3, 2), (8, -1), (2, 3)\}$ 19. $f^{-1}(x) = x - 6$ 21. false   23. $-\dfrac{3}{4}$

25. $\{x: x < -5 \text{ or } x > 5\}$ 27. 1.76   29. $g(h(x)) = \dfrac{1}{\left(\dfrac{1}{x} - 1\right) + 1} = \dfrac{1}{\dfrac{1}{x}} = x$;

$h(g(x)) = \dfrac{1}{\left(\dfrac{1}{x + 1}\right)} - 1 = x + 1 - 1 = x$ 31. $f(f(x)) = f\left(\dfrac{4}{x}\right) = \dfrac{4}{\dfrac{4}{x}} = \dfrac{4x}{4} = x$

PAGE 650 · CHAPTER 9   1. 4   3. $\dfrac{\sqrt[3]{3}}{9}$ 5. $\dfrac{27}{8}$ 7. $16\sqrt{2}$ 9. The graph of

$f(x)$ is above the graph of $g(x)$.   11. $-\dfrac{1}{4}$ 13. 2   15. 2   17. $-\dfrac{1}{3}$

19. 0.8451   21. 0.9138   23. 0.6345 + 1   25. 6.42   27. $\{5\}$ 29. $\{3\}$
31. $\{2.58\}$ 33. $\{1.32\}$ 35. $\{0.431\}$ 37. 0.9089 + 1   39. 4.183
41. 16,140   43. 87,000

PAGE 651 · CHAPTER 15   1. $a_k = 3k - 2, k \in \{1, 2, 3, \ldots\}$ 3. $a_1 = 4, a_k = -a_{k-1},$
$k \in \{2, 3, 4, \ldots\}$ 5. 87   7. 17   9. −825   11. 19,683   13. $2^{25} - 1 =$

33,554,431   15. 8   17. 225   19. 3, 12, 48   21. $\dfrac{3}{8}$

PREPARING FOR REGENTS EXAMINATIONS

PAGE 665 · ALGEBRA   1. a. $-\dfrac{3}{2}$ b. −3, −1   c. 0   d. 0, 1   e. ±2   f. 3

g. $x < -4$ h. $x \leqslant -4$ i. 0   j. 2   k. $x < 0$ l. $x \leqslant 0$ 3. a. $3x(3x + 1)(3x - 1)$
b. $4xy(3x + 1)(x - 3)$ c. $(2x + 3y)(2x - 3y)$ d. $(x^2 + y^3)(x^2 - y^3)$ e. $x(x + a)(x - a)$
f. $(x - 2)(x^2 + 2x + 4)$ g. $(x + 1)(x^2 - x + 1)$ h. $(x^2 + 9y^2)(x + 3y)(x - 3y)$

5. a. x-intercepts: −2 and −1; y-intercept: 2; $x = -\dfrac{3}{2}$; $V\left(-\dfrac{3}{2}, -\dfrac{1}{4}\right)$; upward

b. x-intercepts: $\dfrac{-2 \pm \sqrt{2}}{2}$; y-intercept: 1; $x = -1$; $V(-1, -1)$; upward   c. x-intercept: 3;
y-intercept: −9; $x = 3$; $V(3, 0)$; downward

PAGE 666 · RADICALS AND COMPLEX NUMBERS   1. a. $5\sqrt{2}$ b. $6x\sqrt{2y}$ c. 75
d. $72\sqrt{3}$ e. $\dfrac{9\sqrt{10}}{4}$ f. $9 + 7\sqrt{3}$ g. $\dfrac{3\sqrt{6} + 2\sqrt{3}}{7}$ h. $3i\sqrt{6}$ i. $-\dfrac{i\sqrt{2}}{4}$ j. $i\sqrt{3}$

k. $-i$ l. $10 + 3i$ m. $-6 - 5i$ n. −1   o. $-i$ p. $-16 + 12i$ q. $\dfrac{1}{10} - \dfrac{4}{5}i$ r. $-5 - 12i$

3. a. $x = 4; y = 0$ b. $x = 0; y = -2$ c. $x = -\dfrac{10}{3}; y = \dfrac{3}{2}$ 5. a. $3 - 4i$
b. $2; 3 - 4i$ c. $3 - 4i; 2 \pm i$

PAGE 667 · FUNCTIONS   1. a. yes; $\{-3, 0, 3\}$; $\{2, 5\}$; not one-to-one   b. yes;
$\{-5, 0, 5\}$; $\{-5, 0, 5\}$; one-to-one   c. no   d. yes; $\mathfrak{R}$; $\mathfrak{R}$; one-to-one   e. no   f. yes; $\mathfrak{R}$;
$\{y: -1 \leqslant y \leqslant 1\}$; not one-to-one   3. a. 1   b. 3   c. 1   5. a. $2x - 5$ b. $2x - 1$
c. $-2x + 5$ d. $-x - 3$ e. x f. $-x - 3$

PAGE 668 · TRANSFORMATIONAL GEOMETRY   1. a. $A'(0,0)$, $B'(-2,3)$, $C'(-5,2)$
b. $A'(0,0)$, $B'(3,2)$, $C'(2,5)$ c. $A'(0,4)$, $B'(2,1)$, $C'(5,2)$ d. $A''(0,0)$, $B''(3,-2)$, $C''(2,-5)$
e. $A''(0,0)$, $B''(-3,2)$, $C''(-2,5)$ f. $A''(0,0)$, $B''(2,3)$, $C''(5,2)$ g. $A'(0,0)$, $B'(-3,2)$,
$C'(-2,5)$ h. $A'(0,0)$, $B'(4,6)$, $C'(10,4)$ i. $A'(0,0)$, $B'(3,-2)$, $C'(2,-5)$ j. $A'(4,-2)$,
$B'(6,1)$, $C'(9,0)$ k. $A'(0,-3)$, $B'(2,0)$, $C'(5,-1)$ l. $A'(0,0)$, $B'\left(\frac{4}{3},2\right)$, $C'\left(\frac{10}{3},\frac{4}{3}\right)$

m. $A''(0,0)$, $B''(9,6)$, $C''(6,15)$ n. $A''(0,2)$, $B''(3,4)$, $C''(2,7)$ 3. a. I; r_k, where k is the
perpendicular bisector of the base   b. I; r_j, r_k, and r_n, where j, k, and n are the perpendicular
bisectors of the sides; $R_{P,120}$ and $R_{P,240}$, where P is the intersection of j, k, and n
c. I; r_j and r_k, where j and k are the lines containing the diagonals; r_l and r_m, where l and m each
bisect two opposite sides of the square; $R_{P,90}$, $R_{P,180}$, and $R_{P,270}$, where P is the intersection of
j and k d. I; r_j and r_k, where j and k each bisect two opposite sides of the rectangle; $R_{P,180}$,
where P is the intersection of j and k e. I; r_j and r_k, where j and k are the lines containing the
diagonals; $R_{P,180}$, where P is the intersection of j and k f. I; r_m, where m is the line through
the midpoints of the bases   g. I; reflections over the perpendicular bisectors of the 5 sides;
$R_{P,72}$, $R_{P,144}$, $R_{P,216}$, and $R_{P,288}$, where P is the intersection of the lines of reflection
h. I; 4 reflections over the perpendicular bisectors of the sides; $R_{P,45}$, $R_{P,90}$, $R_{P,135}$, $R_{P,180}$,
$R_{P,225}$, $R_{P,270}$, and $R_{P,315}$, where P is the intersection of the perpendicular bisectors of the sides;
4 reflections over the lines joining the opposite vertices   5. a. none   b. $R_{P,0}$ c. $T_{0,0}$
d. $D_{P,1}$

PAGES 669–670 · GEOMETRY OF THE CIRCLE   1. a. (1) 120   (2) 120   (3) 60
(4) 120   (5) 60   (6) 60   (7) 60   (8) 100   (9) 30   (10) 30   (11) 60   (12) 40
(13) 30   (14) 20   (15) 60   b. (1) $\overline{EC}$ and $\overline{CB}$ are tangent to $\odot O$; $m\,\overset{\frown}{FG} = 20$; $\triangle BCD$ is
equilateral (Given);   (2) $m\,\overset{\frown}{BD} = 120$ (Ex. 1 (a), above);   (3) $m\angle DFB = \frac{1}{2} m\,\overset{\frown}{BD} = 60$

(The measure of an inscribed $\angle$ is $\frac{1}{2}$ the measure of its intercepted arc.);   (4) $m\angle 7 = 60$

(Ex. 1 (a), above);   (5) $\overline{FD} \parallel \overline{AB}$ (If 2 lines are cut by a trans. so that alt. int. $\angle$s are $\cong$, then the
lines are $\parallel$.)   c. (1) $\overline{EC}$ and $\overline{CB}$ are tangent to $\odot O$; $m\,\overset{\frown}{FG} = 20$; $\triangle BCD$ is equilateral. (Given);
(2) $m\angle 2 = 60$ (Ex. 1 (a), above);   (3) $m\angle DFB = 60$ (Ex. 1 (b), above);   (4) $m\angle DBC =$
$m\angle CDB = 60$ (The measure of each $\angle$ of an equilateral $\triangle$ is 60.);   (5) $\triangle BCD \sim \triangle ODF$
(AA $\sim$ Thm.)   d. (1) $6\sqrt{3}$ (2) $9\sqrt{3}$ (3) $27\sqrt{3}$ (4) 12π (5) 6   (6) 36π
(7) 6π 3. a. 8   b. 4   c. 6   d. 8

PAGES 671–673 · TRIGONOMETRY   1. a. $\frac{2\pi}{5}$ b. π c. $\frac{3\pi}{2}$ d. 90   e. 108   f. 13.5

g. 6 cm   h. $\frac{4}{3}$ i. $\cos\theta = \frac{3}{5}$; $\tan\theta = \frac{4}{3}$; $\csc\theta = \frac{5}{4}$; $\sec\theta = \frac{5}{3}$; $\cot\theta = \frac{3}{4}$ j. $\sin\angle BOD = \frac{4}{5}$;

$\cos\angle BOD = -\frac{3}{5}$; $\tan\angle BOD = -\frac{4}{3}$; $\csc\angle BOD = \frac{5}{4}$; $\sec\angle BOD = -\frac{5}{3}$; $\cot\angle BOD = -\frac{3}{4}$

k. $\sin\angle COD = \frac{1}{2}$; $\cos\angle COD = \frac{\sqrt{3}}{2}$; $\tan\angle COD = \frac{\sqrt{3}}{3}$; $\csc\angle COD = 2$; $\sec\angle COD = \frac{2\sqrt{3}}{3}$;

$\cot\angle COD = \sqrt{3}$ 3. a. $-\sin 30°$ b. $-\cos 40°$ c. $-\tan 50°$ d. $\cot 40°$ e. $\sec\frac{\pi}{5}$

f. $\csc\frac{\pi}{4}$ 5. a. $\frac{4}{5}$ b. $-\frac{3}{4}$ c. $\frac{63}{65}$ d. $\frac{16}{65}$ e. $\frac{63}{16}$ f. $\frac{33}{65}$ g. $\frac{56}{65}$ h. $\frac{24}{25}$ i. $\frac{119}{169}$

j. $-\dfrac{24}{7}$ k. $\dfrac{2\sqrt{5}}{5}$ l. $\dfrac{1}{5}$ 7. a. $\dfrac{\sec\theta}{\tan\theta} = \dfrac{\dfrac{1}{\cos\theta}}{\dfrac{\sin\theta}{\cos\theta}} = \dfrac{1}{\cos\theta}\cdot\dfrac{\cos\theta}{\sin\theta} = \dfrac{1}{\sin\theta}\cdot\dfrac{\cot\theta}{\cot\theta} =$

$\dfrac{\cot\theta}{\sin\theta\cdot\dfrac{\cos\theta}{\sin\theta}} = \dfrac{\cot\theta}{\cos\theta}$ b. $\cot^2\theta + \cos^2\theta = \dfrac{\cos^2\theta}{\sin^2\theta} + \cos^2\theta\cdot\dfrac{\sin^2\theta}{\sin^2\theta} = \dfrac{\cos^2\theta(1+\sin^2\theta)}{\sin^2\theta} =$

$\dfrac{(1-\sin^2\theta)(1+\sin^2\theta)}{\sin^2\theta} = \dfrac{1-\sin^4\theta}{\sin^2\theta} = \dfrac{1}{\sin^2\theta} - \dfrac{\sin^4\theta}{\sin^2\theta} = \csc^2\theta - \sin^2\theta$

c. $\sin\theta\,(\csc\theta + \sec\theta) = \sin\theta\left(\dfrac{1}{\sin\theta} + \dfrac{1}{\cos\theta}\right) = 1 + \dfrac{\sin\theta}{\cos\theta} = 1 + \tan\theta$

d. $\dfrac{\csc\theta - 1}{\sec\theta} = \dfrac{\dfrac{1}{\sin\theta} - 1}{\dfrac{1}{\cos\theta}}\cdot\dfrac{\sin\theta\,\cos\theta}{\sin\theta\,\cos\theta} = \dfrac{\cos\theta - \sin\theta\,\cos\theta}{\sin\theta} = \dfrac{\cos\theta}{\sin\theta} - \cos\theta = \cot\theta - \cos\theta$

e. $\dfrac{\sin\theta + \tan\theta}{\sin\theta\,\tan\theta} = \dfrac{\sin\theta + \dfrac{\sin\theta}{\cos\theta}}{\sin\theta\cdot\dfrac{\sin\theta}{\cos\theta}} = \dfrac{1 + \dfrac{1}{\cos\theta}}{\dfrac{\sin\theta}{\cos\theta}}\cdot\dfrac{\cos\theta}{\cos\theta} = \dfrac{\cos\theta + 1}{\sin\theta} = \dfrac{\cos\theta}{\sin\theta} + \dfrac{1}{\sin\theta} =$

$\cot\theta + \csc\theta$ f. $\dfrac{\cos 2\theta + 1}{2\sin^2\theta} = \dfrac{(2\cos^2\theta - 1) + 1}{2\sin^2\theta} = \dfrac{2\cos^2\theta}{2\sin^2\theta} = \left(\dfrac{\cos\theta}{\sin\theta}\right)^2 = \cot^2\theta$

9. a. $y = 2\sin x,\ 2\pi;\ y = 3\cos\dfrac{1}{2}x,\ 4\pi$ b. $y = 2\sin x,\ 2;\ \ y = 3\cos\dfrac{1}{2}x,\ 3$ c. 3

11. a. 8   b. 16   c. 31   d. 61   13. a. 15 N   b. $20°$ to each force

PAGES 673–674 · EXPONENTS AND LOGARITHMS   1. a. 9   b. $\dfrac{\sqrt{3}}{9}$ c. $\dfrac{1}{2}$ d. 125

e. 81   3. a. $\log_2 y = x$ b. $\log_3 y = 2x - 1$ c. $\log_5 y = x^2$ d. $\log_{\frac{1}{4}} y = -x + 1$

5. a. 3   b. 0   c. $-\dfrac{1}{2}$ d. -3 e. $\dfrac{3}{2}$ f. $-\dfrac{2}{3}$ g. 6   7. (Answers based on Table 2;
answers found using a calculator may differ slightly.)   a. 2,102,000,000   b. 10.86
c. 0.0000009694   d. 32.01   e. 0.000004753   f. ± 1.565 g. 3.089   h. 1.292
i. 0.3562   j. 6.965   k. 1.623   l. 3.413

PAGES 674–675 · PROBABILITY   1. a. $\dfrac{1}{16}$ b. $\dfrac{1}{16}$ c. $\dfrac{1}{4}$ d. $\dfrac{3}{8}$ e. $\dfrac{1}{2}$ f. $\dfrac{1}{2}$

g. $\dfrac{5}{16}$ h. $\dfrac{11}{16}$ 3. a. $\dfrac{1}{4}$ b. $_{10}C_7\left(\dfrac{1}{4}\right)^7\left(\dfrac{3}{4}\right)^3$ c. $_{10}C_8\left(\dfrac{1}{4}\right)^8\left(\dfrac{3}{4}\right)^2 + {}_{10}C_9\left(\dfrac{1}{4}\right)^9\left(\dfrac{3}{4}\right)^1 +$

$_{10}C_{10}\left(\dfrac{1}{4}\right)^{10}\left(\dfrac{3}{4}\right)^0$ 5. a. $\dfrac{16}{49}$ b. $\dfrac{9}{49}$ c. $\dfrac{12}{49}$ d. $\dfrac{40}{49}$ e. $\dfrac{3}{7}$ 7. a. 60   b. (1) $\dfrac{1}{20}$

(2) $\dfrac{1}{2}$ (3) $\dfrac{4}{5}$ (4) $\dfrac{3}{10}$

PAGE 676 • STATISTICS   1. a. 24   b. 2   c. 5   3. a. mean: 32; median: 33;
mode: 36   b. 4.2   c. 9

APPENDIX 1

PAGE 683 • THE INVERSE OF A FUNCTION
1. The graphs are symmetric with respect to the line $y = x$.   3. The calculator only graphs functions.

PAGES 683–684 • GRAPHING SINE AND COSINE

1. a. 2π ; 2π b. 1, –1; 1, –1   c. 1; 1   d. $\dfrac{\pi}{2}$ 3. a. $\dfrac{\pi}{2}$, 1, –1, 1   b. 4π , 1, –1, 1   c. determines
the period of the function.

PAGES 684–685 • TANGENT, COTANGENT, SECANT, AND COSECANT

1. a. $x = -\dfrac{\pi}{2}$, $x = \dfrac{3\pi}{2}$, $x = -\dfrac{3\pi}{2}$ b. π 3. a. 2π b. $y \geq 1$ or $y \leq -1$ c. asymptotes through points
where $\cos x = 0$ d. $-\pi$, 0, π , 2π 5. a. translates the graph up or down

PAGE 686 • SOLVING TRIGONOMETRIC EQUATIONS
1. 30°, 150°, 270°   3. 0°, 120°, 180°, 240°   5. 80°, 260°

PAGE 686 • EXPONENTIAL FUNCTIONS
1. a. 1   b. $y = 4^x$ c. $y = 2^x$ 3. a. increasing   b. decreasing

ANSWERS TO COMPUTER EXERCISES

Pages 36–38   1. {−1, 0, 1, . . . , 4, 5, 6}   2. {−9, −8, −7, . . . , −4, −3, −2}
3. {−3}   4. ∅   5. {−2, −1}   6. {−5, −4, −3, . . . , 2, 3, 4}   7. {−1, 0, 1}
8. {−3, −2, −1, 0, 1, 2, 3}
Make the following changes:
```
260   FOR X = −9 TO 9
270   IF . . . THEN 290
280   GOTO 310
290   PRINT TAB(19 + 2 * X); "X";
300   REM *** TAB (20 + 2 * X) FOR APPLE
310   NEXT X
320   PRINT
330   END
```

9. {3, 4, 5}   10. {−3, −2, 2, 3}

Pages 86–87
```
1.  10   PRINT "DEGREE"
    20   INPUT D
    30   PRINT "VALUE OF X";
    40   INPUT X
    50   PRINT "GIVE COEFFICIENTS, STARTING WITH"
    60   PRINT "HIGHEST DEGREE TERM"
    70   FOR J = 1 TO D + 1
    80   INPUT C(J)
    90   NEXT J
   100   LET Y = C(1)
   110   FOR J = 2 TO D + 1
   120   LET Y = Y * X + C(J)
   130   NEXT J
   140   PRINT "VALUE OF POLYNOMIAL: "; Y
   150   END
```

2. a. 2   b. 18   c. 0   d. 11   e. 71   3. a. Yes   b. No   c. Yes

Page 126
```
1.  30   LET D = B * B − 4 * A * C
    90   PRINT "TWO IRRATIONAL ROOTS"
   130   PRINT "DOUBLE RATIONAL ROOT"
   150   PRINT "NO REAL ROOTS"
```

2. a. 1, double, rational   b. no real roots   c. 2, rational   d. 2, irrational   e. 2, irrational
f. no real roots   3. 160   IF B < > 0 THEN 180   4. e

Pages 159–160

1.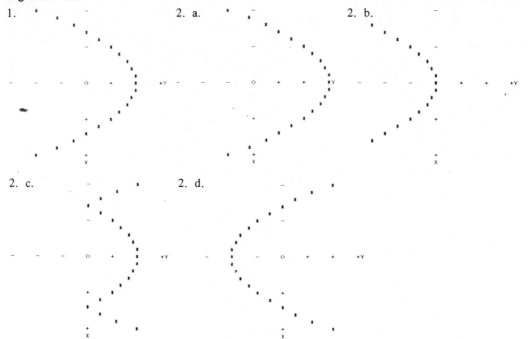

2. a.

2. b.

2. c.

2. d.

3. Answers will vary.

4. a. The graph of f is shifted upward 1 unit.   b. The graph of f is shifted downward 2 units.
c. The graph of f is reflected in the x-axis.   d. The part of the graph of f that is below the
x-axis is reflected in the x-axis; the part of the graph of f that is above the x-axis stays the same.

Pages 213–214   2. $(-0.8, 0.4)$, $(2, 5)$, $(7.4, 2.8)$,
$(1.68, 7.26)$ 3. a. $(4.8, -2.4)$, $(6.8, 2.6)$, $(1.8, 5.6)$,
$(8.8, 3.7)$ b. $u = 4.8$, $v = -2.4$ 4. a. $(3.6, 4.8)$,
$(-1, 2)$, $(1.2, -3.4)$, $(-3.26, 2.32)$ b. See figure at
right; $\theta \approx 165°$

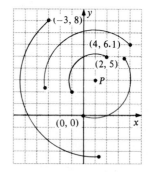

Pages 267–268   1. a. 3.33968   b. 3.04184
c. 3.13159   d. 3.14059   2. Successive values get
closer and closer to π. The value in (d) agrees with π to two
decimal places.   3. Multiply the sum by 6, then find
the square root of the result.

4. Delete lines 60, 80, 110, 120, and 130. Change lines 100 and 160 as follows:

```
100    LET P = P + (1/(N * N))
160    PRINT "AFTER  "; T; "  TERMS:  "; SQR(6 * P)
```

5. a. 2.96339   b. 3.04936   c. 3.13208   d. 3.14064

1.

x	sin x	approximation		
		after 2 terms	after 5 terms	after 100 terms
0.2	0.198669	0.198667	0.198669	0.198669
−2	−0 909298	−0.666667	−0.909348	−0.909298
10	−0.544021	−156.667	1448.27	0.544059
3.14159265	0	−2.02612	6.92527E-03	−3.82747E-09

Approximations get closer to the actual value of sin x as more terms are used. For large values of x, approximations are less accurate.

2. The essential changes are:

```
70    LET T = 1
130   LET T = −T * (X * X)/((2 * C) * (2 * C − 1))
180   PRINT "BUILT-IN FUNCTION GIVES:   "; TAB(26); COS(X)
```

x	cos x	approximation	
		after 5 terms	after 20 terms
0	1	1	1
1	0.540302	0.540303	0.540302
−1	0.540302	0.540303	0.540302
6.2832	1	20.9885	1

2. $2.27 < x < 2.28$
3. $2.278 < x < 2.279$ 4. 2.28
5. −2.28   6. See figure at right; 2 solutions
7. 0.82, −0.82

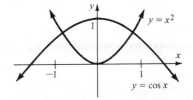

8.
```
10    PRINT "SOLVE 3 * SIN(X) − X = 0"
20    PRINT "INPUT A AND B (A < B) SUCH THAT"
30    PRINT "3 * SIN(A) − A AND 3 * SIN(B) − B"
40    PRINT "HAVE OPPOSITE SIGNS"
50    PRINT "A =   ";
60    INPUT A
70    PRINT "B =   ";
80    INPUT B
90    LET M = (A + B)/2
100   LET Y1 = 3 * SIN(A) − A
110   LET Y2 = 3 * SIN(M) − M
120   IF SGN(Y1) * SGN(Y2) = −1 THEN 150
130   LET A = M
140   GOTO 160
150   LET B = M
160   IF ABS(A − B) > = .000001 THEN 90
170   PRINT "APPROXIMATE SOLUTION IS   "; A
180   END
```

To 5 decimal places, solution is 2.27886.

Pages 381–382

1. 10   REM ∗∗∗ COLUMN HEADINGS
  20   PRINT "RATE", "DOUBLING TIME"
  30   REM ∗∗∗ R IS INTEREST RATE AS PERCENT
  40   FOR R = 2 TO 20 STEP 2
  50   REM ∗∗∗ CONVERT R TO DECIMAL
  60   LET R1 = R/100
  70   LET N = LOG(2)/LOG(1 + R1)
  80   REM ∗∗∗ ROUND N TO NEAREST TENTH
  90   LET N1 = INT(10 ∗ N + .5)/10
  100   PRINT
  110   PRINT R; "%", N1; "YEARS"
  120   NEXT R
  130   END

2. 2%, 35 yr; 4%, 17.7 yr; 6%, 11.9 yr; 8%, 9 yr; 10%, 7.3 yr; 12%, 6.1 yr; 14%, 5.3 yr; 16%, 4.7 yr; 18%, 4.2 yr; 20%, 3.8 yr   3. Dividing 72 by the interest rate (2, 4, 6, and so on) gives the approximate doubling time.

Pages 465–466   1. 20   LET S = SQR(3)/2   30   LET C = −.5
2. 50   LET A = (N/2) ∗ S   3. 80   LET N = 2 ∗ N   4. 90   LET S = SQR((1 − C)/2)
100   LET C = SQR((1 + C)/2)   5. The areas of the polygons increase as N increases, approaching π.   6. The computed value of A agrees with the actual value of π to at least the second decimal place.

Pages 509–510   1. 0.116948   2. 0.706316   3. a. 23 b. 41 c. 57

Pages 548–550   Answers will vary. Typical results are given. 1. a. 53% b. 47% c. 47%, or 0.47   2. a. 100% b. With a larger sample the poll is more accurate.
3. Change line 170 to: 170   IF X > .35 THEN 200   a. 10% b. 10%, or 0.10
4. a. 0% b. Yes

Pages 620–621

2. a. Make the following changes:
        20   PRINT "N", "F(N)", "SUM"
        55   LET S = 0
        75   LET S = S + B
        80   PRINT N, B, S
  b. $S_n = F_{n+2} - 1$
3. 10   REM ∗∗∗ PRINT COLUMN HEADINGS
  20   PRINT "N", "F(N)"
  30   FOR N = 1 TO 20
  40   LET F = (((1 + SQR(5))/2) ↑ N − ((1 − SQR(5))/2) ↑ N)/SQR(5)
  50   PRINT N, F
  60   NEXT N
  70   END
The results are the same except for minor variations in the 5th decimal place or beyond.
4. a. Make the following changes:
        20   PRINT "N"; TAB(5); "F(N)", "F(N)/F(N − 1)"
        75   IF N < 2 THEN 110
        80   PRINT N; TAB(5); B, B/A
b. Golden ratio is approximately 1.61803.   c. The ratios in (a) approximate the golden ratio more and more closely as n increases.